The American Revolution, 1775–1783

Military History of the United States
(Vol. 1)

Garland Reference Library of the Humanities
(Vol. 933)

The
AMERICAN REVOLUTION
1775–1783

An Encyclopedia

VOLUME II: M–Z

RICHARD L. BLANCO • *Editor*

PAUL J. SANBORN • *Contributing Editor*

GARLAND PUBLISHING, INC.

New York & London • 1993

© 1993 Richard L. Blanco

Library of Congress Cataloging-in-Publication Data

The American Revolution, 1775–1783: an encyclopedia / Richard L.
    Blanco, editor ; Paul J. Sanborn, contributing editor.
        p. cm. — (Garland reference library of the humanities ; vol.
    933. Military history of the United States ; v. 1)
        Includes index.
        ISBN 0-8240-5623-X
        1. United States—History—Revolution, 1775–1783—Encyclopedias.
    I. Blanco, Richard L. II. Sanborn, Paul J. III. Series: Garland
    reference library of the humanities ; vol. 933. IV. Series: Garland
    reference library of the humanities. Military history of the United
    States ; v. 1.
    E208.A433 1993
    973.3'03—dc20   92-42541

    CIP

In memory of my wife Renée

Table of Contents

List of Maps

List of Maps

M

Macaulay, Catharine
(1731–1791) ·

English historian. Catharine Sawbridge Macaulay, known as "the historian in petticoats," was England's first major female historian. Born on March 23, 1731, at Olantigh in Kent, the ancestral home of her Whig family, Catharine had prominent family ties. Her grandfather had served as a director of the South Sea Bubble and was an advocate of Robert Walpole; her mother, who died when Catharine was a child, was an heiress of a London banking family. Her father, a country squire, rarely attended personally to his daughter and permitted her to pursue her own interests. As a result of her unsupervised childhood, Catharine educated herself: she explored intellectual topics and expressed political views uncommon to most eighteenth-century women.

She quickly became a controversial figure in England. Married shortly before he thirtieth birthday to Scottish physician Dr. George Macaulay, who was 15 years her senior, Catharine soon published the first volume of *The History of England from the Accession of James I to that of the Brunswick Line* in 1763. This eight-volume trea-

tise represented Macaulay's pro-democratic views—influenced by her love of reading Roman and Greek history—that corrupt royal power had usurped representative privileges of the English people and criticized such enlightenment figures as Hobbes and Burke, who she also attacked in the 1767 *Loose Remarks on Certain Positions to be Found in Mr. Hobbes's Philosophical Rudiments of Government and Society.*

She also penned pamphlets, including *Short Sketch of a Democratic form of Government addressed to Paoli* (1767) and *A Modest Plea for Property of Copyright* (1774). Influential political and intellectual figures, including Walpole and Dr. Johnson, criticized—both positively and negatively—Macaulay's work. Macaulay and her husband resided in London, where Catharine gave birth to a daughter. When her elderly husband died six years into their marriage, Macaulay wrote prolifically while grieving and copying with the stress of her recent widowhood.

In the colonies, Macaulay's works were widely acclaimed. John Adams identified with her commentary that English liberty had been corrupted by royal power, comparing it to the political-economic situation in the colonies. Adams lauded Macaulay as "one of the brightest ornaments not only of her Sex but of her Age and Country."

Catharine enjoyed studying despots and crusading for improvements for the lower classes. With support from her brother John Sawbridge, who was Lord Mayor of London and a member of Parliament, Catharine campaigned for such unpopular causes as ending the peerage, equality for women and men, prison improvement, limits on the wealth accumulated by aristocrats, and rights and freedom of the individual. As a result of her liberal views, Catharine attracted enemies in England eager to attack her ideas and works.

Especially disliking the monarch George III, Macaulay entered into correspondence with Mercy Otis Warren and Abigail Adams, two colonial women who greatly admired her, and they informed her of events and opinions from the colonial viewpoint. Macaulay became a popular figure in the colonies. Both European and colonial newspapers enjoyed printing the latest gossip or news concerning Catharine. The November 1772 *New-York Gazette* described Macaulay as "so much admired for her great Learning, Writing and amiable Character."

In 1775 Catharine published *An Address to the People of England, Scotland and Ireland on the Present Important Crisis of Affairs*, in which she warned of the harm that could debilitate England in a war with the colonists. She suggested that people in England would suffer enslavement in their own country and that England would be weakened globally. She stated, "If a civil war commences between Great Britain and her Colonies, either the Mother Country, by one great exertion, may ruin both herself and America, or the Americans, by a lingering contest, will gain an independency."

Ill, she traveled to Bath, England, in 1775 for therapeutic treatment and soon initiated a scandal when she moved into the home of the Reverend Dr. Thomas Wilson, the rector of London's St. Stephen's Church. The elderly Wilson, an infatuated but platonic admirer, was enamored of Catharine and erected a life-size statue of her in his church, symbolizing her as the muse of history. His offended parishioners complained, and Wilson reluctantly removed the statue.

Catharine, meanwhile, traveled to France and corresponded with Benjamin Franklin in Paris, although she feared she might be accused of fraternizing with the enemy. In her correspondence she stated that France would seize an opportunity to hurt England and would participate in a colonial war as an American ally, but remained staunch in her belief that a colonial war would have negative repercussions for England. In England, cruel criticism of Catharine circulated, targeting her elaborate dress and makeup, plain looks, and crude manners by noting her tendency to paint her face heavily with rouge and to spice her rhetoric with profanity. Journalist John Wilkes sardonically described Catharine as "Painted up to the eyes," and "looking rotten as an old Catherine Pear."

Catharine became an intimate acquaintance of the wax sculptress Patience Wright, a spy who designed a statue of Catharine that became the focus of a 1777 war joke. According to storytellers, the trio of Wright, Macaulay, and Wilson raised this statue on the Saratoga battlefield to commemorate the victory.

Macaulay's relationship with Wilson soon ended when, in 1778, she married William Graham, a 21-year-old Edinburgh surgeon's mate who was the brother of a medical quack despised by many influential leaders. Catharine's peers in England, unlike the majority of her colonial associates, considered this marriage a social *faux pas* and shunned her. (Walpole pithily remarked, "Dame Thucydides has made an uncouth match.") As a result, Catharine's book sales declined. British feminist Hannah More complained that Macaulay's actions might damage the emerging women's movement. A disappointed and disillusioned More said of Macaulay, "I knew her to be absurd, vain, and affected; . . . She was not feminine either in her writings or her manners. She was only a clever man."

Macaulay received additional threats from Wilson, who stated he would publish letters she had written to him and damage her reputation. Her repute as a historian was also criticized. For example, Isaac Disraeli, the father of future prime minister Benjamin, claimed that while researching at the British Museum, Catharine destroyed papers that countered her opinions, and, that in her writings she distorted facts.

Catharine and her husband traveled to the United States in 1784, visiting George Washington at Mount Vernon and discussing the democratic foundations of the new nation. Still unpopular with many Americans, Macaulay suffered criticism. Sarah Vaughan cattily commented to a friend about Macaulay's appearance, "I heard in company that her teeth are false, has plumpers in her cheeks to hide the hollowness toothlessness gives, and that she paints." Despite negative rumors and unkind barbs, Macaulay still had followers who read her books and complimented her abilities as an analytical thinker.

In 1790 Catharine published *Letters on Education; with Observations on Religious and Metaphysical Subjects*; in the following year she printed *Observations on the Reflections of . . . Edmund Burke*. She died on June 22, 1791, leaving a legacy of inspiration to other women writers such as Mercy Warren, who, following Macaulay's example, penned a political pamphlet and history of the American Revolution. Mary Wollstonecraft in her 1792 *Vindication of the Rights of Women* eulogized Macaulay as "the woman of the greatest abilities, undoubtedly, that this country has ever produced."

Elizabeth D. Schafer

REFERENCES

Mildred Chaffee Beckwith, "Catharine Macaulay: Eighteenth Century Rebel," Ph.D. Dissertation, Ohio State University (1953); Sally Smith Booth, *The Women of '76* (1973); Lyman H. Butterfield, ed., *Adams Family Correspondence* (1963); Lucy Martin Donnelly, "The Celebrated Mrs. Macaulay," *William and Mary Quarterly*, ser. 3 (1949):173–207; Manfred S. Guttmacher, "Catharine Macaulay and Patience Wright—Patronesses of the American Revolution," *The Johns Hopkins Alumni Magazine*, 24 (1936); Charles Coleman Sellers, *Patience Wright: American Artist and Spy in George III's London* (1976).

McCall, Hugh (1767–1824)

Georgia historian. Georgia's first true historian was a South Carolinian writing on the American Revolution, a war in which he participated as a boy soldier. Hugh McCall was the son of James and Elizabeth McCall. James had been active in the North Carolina Regulator rebellion before the American Revolution. During the Revolution he was a colonel in the South Carolina militia, dying of wounds and disease before the war ended.

Hugh was born in North Carolina on February 17, 1767. He steadily rose in rank in the regular United States Army until, at the end of the War of 1812, he retired as a breveted major.

Aside from being jailer in Savannah, Georgia, from 1806 until 1823, no real reason is known why Hugh McCall decided to write a history of Georgia. Some efforts by others to write such an account, particularly in response to the omissions of Georgia in the histories of the Revolution by David Ramsay, had been attempted, but none was ever published. McCall published Volume One of his *The History of Georgia Containing Brief Sketches of the Most Remarkable Events up to the Present Day* (1811). It was hardly more than a revision of Alexander Hewat's *Historical Account of the Colonies of South Carolina and Georgia* (1799). This lack of originality is not surprising, for McCall was by that time an invalid, confined largely to a crude wheelchair and without access to the colonial records of Georgia.

However, for Volume Two, dealing exclusively with the American Revolution, McCall composed what was largely an original work, based upon authentic documents such as his father's now lost diary, correspondence with such veterans as General Andrew Pickens, and his own memories. He openly solicited information on the war from the public. No doubt McCall benefited from his long association with Georgia Revolutionary War hero Elijah Clarke. The resulting work was one of the first truly extensive histories of the Revolution on the state level. It is so detailed that it might also be called a pioneer work in local historiography. McCall's prejudices for the American cause are plainly evident in his writings, and some mistakes crept into the memories of the old soldiers he interviewed. However, the resulting volume remains an indispensable source for all histories of Revolutionary War Georgia and was the major influence for several of Georgia's histories that followed. Despite the title of his two-volume history, McCall did not bring the history from 1783 to his own time.

Hugh McCall as Savannah jailer was frequently charged with various offenses, including carelessness in keeping the prisoners' property, but generally with incompetence. During the War of 1812 he was suspended as jailer in 1814 for conversing with a British prisoner of war about Savannah's defenses. The city council later reinstated him by a vote of only five to four. Historian Gordon B. Smith believes that the popularity of McCall's history probably saved

McCall's job. Hugh McCall died June 10, 1824, and is buried in Savannah's old Colonel Cemetery.

Robert Scott Davis, Jr.

REFERENCES

E. Merton Coulter, *Joseph Vallence Bevan: Georgia's First Official Historian* (1964); Hugh McCall, *The History of Georgia* (1811–1816), rpr. 1909.

McCauley, Mary Ludwig Hays ("Molly Pitcher") (1744/54–1832)

American heroine. Commonly referred to as "Molly Pitcher," Mary (Molly) Ludwig Hays was a camp follower who first carried water to the soldiers heatedly fighting at Monmouth and then stepped out of that more domestic role to man an artillery piece. Years after the war, the Pennsylvania legislature recognized her services to the country by awarding her an annuity. From that time on, the story of Mary Ludwig Hays or Molly Pitcher grew from a local into a national legend.

Mary Ludwig was born in 1744 or 1754; the year varies in the many accounts about her life. However, it appears the later date is the more likely one, for her father, John George Ludwig, immigrated to the colonies from the German Palatinate in 1749 and settled in Mercer County, New Jersey, and that is where supposedly (it is undocumented) his daughter was born and raised.

In 1769, Mary Ludwig was a domestic servant in Doctor William Irvine's household in Carlisle, Pennsylvania. There she met John Casper Hays, a barber. After a short courtship, they were married on July 24, 1769. The union produced a son, John Ludwig Hays, who later served as a sergeant in the War of 1812.

John Casper Hays enlisted as a gunner in Colonel Thomas Proctor's First Pennsylvania Artillery on December 1, 1775. In January 1777 he reenlisted in the army as a private in the Seventh Pennsylvania Regiment that was nominally commanded by Colonel William Irvine (Mary Hays's employer was on parole after his capture at Trois Rivieres and could not officially take command until after his exchange in May 1778). Initially, when John left Carlisle with his unit, Mary remained behind and continued to work for the Irvines, but sometime in the next year, she joined her husband with the army.

On June 28, 1778, a very hot day, the American and British armies clashed at Monmouth, New Jersey. To relieve the suffering soldiers, Mary Hays hauled buckets, pails, or "pitchers" of water up to the lines. On one of her many trips, Hays found her husband lying wounded by the cannon that he had been operating (although officially an infantryman, John Hays's experiences as a gunner in Proctor's artillery led him to be detailed to an attached artillery battery). Hays stood in for her husband and helped load the cannon through the rest of the battle. According to various reports, her actions resulted in her receiving one or more of the following titles: Molly Pitcher, Sergeant Molly, Captain Molly, or Major Molly.

Mary and John Hays eventually returned to Carlisle, where John died in the late 1780s (one account recorded that Mary's husband "William" died in 1787). A few years later, around 1792, Mary Ludwig Hays married John McCauley, also a veteran of the war. Her life was not improved by her marriage to McCauley: Molly McCauley, as she was then called, continued to work, generally as a cleaning woman.

On February 21, 1822, the Pennsylvania legislature voted to reward the widow McCauley with a $40 annuity in recognition of her services during the Revolution. The award itself supported her story, for it was offered in honor of her actions during the war, not because of the military service of either of her husbands. Mary Ludwig Hays McCauley received the annuity until her death at Carlisle in 1832. *See also*: Camp Followers (American and British)

Holly A. Mayer

REFERENCES

Elizabeth Cometti, *Notable American Women 1600–1950: A Biographical Dictionary*, 2 (1971); John B. Landis, "Investigation into American Tradition of Woman Known as 'Molly Pitcher,'" *Journal of American History*, 5 (1911):82–95; William Davison Perrine, *Molly Pitcher of Monmouth County, New Jersey and Captain Molly of Fort Washington, New York, 1778–1937* (1937); J.A. Murray, "Molly McCauley," *American Volunteer*, Carlisle, Pa., September 12, 1883 (copy of this newspaper article in Molly Pitcher papers at U.S. Army Military History Institute, Carlisle, Pa.).

McCrea, Jane, Massacre of (July 1777)

This may be one of the most complex events to piece together in the entire War of Revolution. At this point, it is impossible to relate exactly what happened the day Jane McCrea died. There is a lack of agreement on almost every key point by anyone who has written on the event. There is even a strong debate over its significance to the war.

According to Arthur Reid (who took this information from the research of David Wilson and published a monograph on Jane McCrea in 1859), Benson J. Lossing, and others, it appears that Jane McCrea was born sometime in the 1750s (with 1757 being mentioned) to a Presbyterian minister from Scotland. She seems to have been the only daughter in a family with five sons. Three of these remained loyal to the United States in the war and two seem to have joined the British, including one who served with or knew General John Burgoyne.

The family settled in New Jersey. Jane's mother died when she was very young, and when she was 16, her father either died or remarried, depending on which source one consults. In any event, she left New Jersey and went north to live with John McCrea, a brother who was farming along the Hudson River south of Fort Edward. There she enjoyed the pleasure of reading and expanding her intellect while helping out on her brother's farm.

By accident or design, the Jones family of New Jersey followed Jane to New York and settled in the same area where Jane's brother was living. Acquainted from childhood, Jane and David Jones soon renewed their friendship and fell in love. When the war broke out, Jane's brother, John served in the militia and became a colonel of New York troops. David Jones, however, decided to remain loyal to the Crown and served with the British. Because of his ability, David was soon appointed a lieutenant in Peter's Provincial Rangers and served in General Simon Fraser's advanced corps, leading Burgoyne's army south toward Fort Edward in July 1777.

Burgoyne was attempting to seize control of the Champlain-Hudson waterway, splitting the colonies, and capturing that vital transportation network. David Jones was in the van of this 7,500-man force as it slowly moved south toward Albany. Jane's family decided it would be safer to move into Albany rather than stay on the farm.

The danger from Indians and Tories was great, especially after July 17.

That was the day that 400 Ottawa and Indians from other tribes were led into Burgoyne's camp by the Chevalier St. Luc de Le Corne and Charles de Langlade. The 65-year-old Le Corne was a ruthless leader who is said to have planned and executed the ambush that destroyed Braddock's force in 1755. These Indians were cautioned by Burgoyne to restrain themselves and not to engage in wanton murder and destruction in front of the British march. Led by Le Corne and Langlade, the Indians had other ideas.

As Americans of all persuasions fled with the advance of the enemy, David Jones decided it was a good time to be married to Jane McCrea. He sent her word to wait for the army to get closer to where she was living, and he would send direction for her to follow. Jane had moved in with Mrs. McNeil, an elderly Scots widow who also happened to be the cousin of Fraser of the British army. Word soon arrived, and Jane was dressed in her wedding dress on Saturday, July 26 as she left Mrs. McNeil's to join Lieutenant Jones.

For a barrel of rum, Jones had hired an Indian chief named Duluth to protect Jane as she walked into the British camp from Mrs. McNeil's. The Indians were to hide in the woods, to give a signal, and then Jane would be walking. The Indians would stay hidden but would move along with her to afford her protection for the four-mile trip. Jones waited for her with a chaplain in camp.

On this same day, a band of Huron Indians under a chief known as Le Loup, the wolf, had massacred the Allen family of nine people. The Allens happened to be Loyalists who thought they were to be protected. Leaving the Allen cabins, the Indians then attacked an American picket south of Fort Edward and chased them into Jane McCrea's path. Jane ran back to Mrs. McNeil's house along with the American picket that kept retreating past the house.

Le Loup and his band pursued her into the house and seized both women. They put Jane on a horse and forced Mrs. McNeil, who was grossly fat, to walk, after stripping off most of her clothing. At a stream on the way back to British lines, just off Route 4 in the village of Fort Edward today, Duluth and his Indians appeared and claimed Jane as his responsibility. Le

Loup claimed her as a captive. The two argued. Neither would yield on the issue.

At this point as the argument intensified between the two chiefs, the American picket rallied itself and pursued the Indians, perhaps to save the two women. Duluth seized the horse's reins and began to lead Jane away. In a rage, Le Loup threw his axe, hitting Jane in the side and knocking her off the horse and killing her. Le Loup then scalped her. The American soldiers never caught up with the Indians.

When the Indians returned to the British camp, Jones recognized his loved one's hair/scalp and went into a deep and seemingly never ending mourning for her. He requested to be discharged from the army, but his request was denied. He deserted the next day, went to Canada, and lived a solitary and secluded life.

Colonel John McCrea was also heartbroken over the death of his sister and could not speak of her without crying, even years later. Mrs. McNeil, a first-class termagant, protested to her cousin, General Fraser. Fraser explained to her that these things happened in war.

The scalps of the Allen family, father, mother, three children, another adult male, and three black slaves, were brought into camp along with that of Jane McCrea. An old Indian, according to legend, looked on the scalps of the women and children and uttered a prophesy: "that army can not prosper, that tolerates taking the scalps of women and little children." Whatever the effects of such words, Burgoyne and his army did find truth in them some three months later. Le Loup vanished into history, never to be heard from again.

Jane was described as medium sized, well formed with long, full hair that reached to the floor when untied. She was beautiful and prepossessing. Graceful in manners, she was a favorite of all who knew her. She was also said to have short hair, blond, while others said the hair came in lovely, dark tresses. Major James Wilkinson, an officer attached to the American general Gates as an aide, did not feel she was any great beauty but just a typical country girl. She may have been 23 years old, 17 years old, or anywhere in the middle. One person even claimed she was 26 at the time of her death. She may have died on July 25, 26, or 27, 1777.

British lieutenant Thomas Anburey explained the story as a dispute that arose over conducting Jane to Jones, between two Indians sent to fetch her, within a mile of the British camp. Fearful of losing the reward, one Indian killed her with his tomahawk. This act was a direct violation of Burgoyne's orders against shedding blood unless attacked. British lieutenant William Digby felt that cruelties committed by the Indians were too shocking to relate. He believed that she was 18 years old, of a Loyalist family, with a pleasing personality and engaged to be married to a provincial officer. British sergeant Roger Lamb felt her death was not premeditated barbarity but an act of passion over fear of losing the reward of bringing her in.

There were, however, two eyewitnesses to the event. Mrs. McNeil, whose physical characteristics and personality everyone agreed to, claimed the American pickets shot Jane on the horse by aiming high and missing the Indians. She condemned the British army, the Indians, and the war—right to her cousin's face when she reached his camp. Her story was passed down in the family to her granddaughter who told it to Benson J. Lossing almost 70 years after the event.

The second witness was Samuel Standish. A member of the American picket, he had been captured by the Indians and was present at the spring of water on the hill when the Indians brought Mrs. McNeil and Jane from McNeil's house. The two women walked willingly with the Indians. Neither woman was naked. No mention was made of a horse. They all stopped at the spring.

Soon an argument broke out among the Indians who began hitting each other with their muskets. Evidently there were two parties of Indians together, and Standish says one group was Ottawa and the other Caughnawaga. In the middle of this heated debate, one of the chiefs shot McCrea in the chest with his musket and she died instantly. The chief scalped her where she lay. She had long, flowing hair. At this, the quarrel ceased and the whole party, Samuel included, moved off to the British camp. Standish always suspected that some of the Caughnawaga Indians may have been Tories dressed in Indian garb. Standish was sent to Fort Ticonderoga after being interviewed by Fraser and escaped two months later. He told his story to Jared Sparks, the American historian, in 1830.

The significance of Jane McCrea's death is also difficult to authenticate. Christopher Ward felt she became "a martyred saint in the patriotic hierarchy," John R. Elting felt her murder did nothing to bring out the American militia to defeat Burgoyne. They were already on their way to assembly before word of this murder leaked out, and it could not have influenced their decision to fight Burgoyne. The militia that were coming out were already out. It can be argued that Jane McCrea's death, as a symbol, may have brought out more militia, especially in October when Burgoyne's army was fleeing north along the Hudson and found itself surrounded by militia forces on all sides.

General Horatio Gates replaced General Philip Schuyler in command of the American army and used the McCrea murder to his advantage in his letter to Burgoyne on September 2. Gates berated Burgoyne for hiring Indians and then described McCrea as a lovely young lady who was murdered, scalped, and mangled in a most shocking manner. The miserable fate of Miss McCrea was particularly aggravating because she was dressed in her wedding dress at the time. Gates accused the Indians of killing over 100 men, women, and children and accused Burgoyne of paying for the scalps. He promised retaliation.

Burgoyne replied on September 6 that he did not pay for scalps but that he gave the Indians compensation for prisoners turned over alive. He argued that McCrea's fate was not a premeditated act but a sad and horrible accident. He went on to relate the story of the two chiefs given above.

When Burgoyne learned of Miss McCrea's death, he immediately went to the Indian camp and demanded the murderer. But he was advised not to harm him since the Indians would not look kindly on such action. So the Indian, whoever he was, was released and not punished. It did Burgoyne little good. Soon after this event, the Indians left him and returned to their homes. Burgoyne's army was left in the woods without Indian allies who had provided scouting services until the moment when the British and American armies joined in final battles of Saratoga. It was then that Burgoyne needed them most.

The newspapers of the time did not make much over Miss McCrea's death. But her name was the battle cry at Bennington just over two weeks after her death. The British were counting on the help of Loyalists flocking into the service for the Crown, bringing with them their food, animals, and weapons to help put down the rebellion. The Germans put fear into Ameri-

can hearts. The hired Indians sealed the British fate at winning the hearts and minds of the once loyal colonists. Whatever their original faction was, the Indians and Germans deflected any potential support for Burgoyne. This lack of local aid directly led to the defeat of Burgoyne in October 1777. McCrea's death was a signal flare that all could point to as a prime example of the king's policy toward his colonies. It was a convincing argument. For that reason Jane McCrea did not die in vain.

McCrea's body was buried by some Loyalists. It was later reburied in the Union Cemetery on Route 4 north of the village of Fort Edward. Her body was examined at that time, and the skull was found to be intact. There was some evidence of bullet wounds to the body itself. The mystery continues.

Paul J. Sanborn

REFERENCES

John R. Elting, *The Battle of Saratoga* (1977); Gerald Howson, *Burgoyne of Saratoga* (1973); R. Lamb, *Journal of Occurrences* (rpr. 1968); Benson J. Lossing, *The Pictorial Field Book of the American Revolution*, 2 vols. (1851–52), rpr. 1972; James Lunt, *John Burgoyne* (1975).

MacDonald, Flora (1722–1790)

Scot heroine, Loyalist heroine. Born in 1722 at her family's farm named Milton on South Uist in the Hebrides, Flora MacDonald was the daughter of Ranald MacDonald, a gentleman farmer who rented out land, and Marion, the daughter of a minister. Chronicled most prominently for her role in helping Jacobite Prince Charles Edward Stuart escape his English pursuers in the summer of 1746, Flora disguised Charles as her maidservant, Betty Burke, and guided him to safety. Considered a Scottish heroine, Flora was arrested by English officers and incarcerated first on prison ships then in London, being released in July 1747.

She married Allan MacDonald, with whom she had several children, and lived on the island of Skye. The famous Dr. Samuel Johnson and James Boswell, eager to meet Flora, visited the MacDonalds. Boswell described Flora as being small and having a "mild and genteel appearance, mighty soft and well bred." Johnson noted her "middle stature, soft features, gentle manners and elegant presence." He also sensed their economic despair: "She and her husband are poor, and are going to try their fortune in America."

At this time many Highlanders were immigrating to the colonies, and the MacDonalds, faced with poverty, chose to migrate also; Flora—skeptical of the move and not wanting to leave her home on the island of Skye—lamented "we cannot promise ourselves but poverty and oppression, haveing [*sic*] last Spring and this time two years lost almost our whole Stock of Cattle and horses." She later acknowledged that she was ready to "begin the world again, anewe, in anothere [*sic*] Corner of it." With rents too expensive for their meager budget and encouragement from friends who had already moved to America several years before, Flora, her husband, and children began their trek across the Atlantic Ocean.

They settled in Anson County, North Carolina, in the spring of 1775, moving onto a plantation. Soon, the MacDonald family was involved in Revolutionary activities. Supporting the British cause in colonial disputes, Allan agreed to represent Loyalists by traveling to the governor and informing him of their support as well as raising military troops. At muster meetings, Flora, revered by Scottish emigrants, gave inspirational speeches, supporting Loyalist actions. Tories held her in high esteem, respecting the modest, quiet woman.

While the Loyalists prepared to support the Crown, Whigs planned to counter them. At the Battle of Moore's Creek in February 1776, the Whigs decimated Loyalist troops led by Allan in three minutes. This confidence-building victory encouraged the rebels to continue their quest for independence and resulted in the imprisonment of many Loyalist leaders. Victorious Whig soldiers roamed the countryside, supposedly threatening and damaging Loyalists' property.

Influenced by these rumors, Flora wrote to Sir John MacPherson that she had "contracted a severe fever, and was dayly oppressed with stragling partys of plunderers from their Army, and night robbers who more than once threatened her life, wanting a confession where her husbands money was." She also complained that her servants were insolent and disloyal.

In May 1776 the North Carolina Provisional Congress appointed commissioners to investigate prisoners' wives and families and insure that they had enough food and supplies. Instead of being charitable inspectors, many of the commissioners proved to be marauders who enjoyed stealing Loyalist property and committing acts of violence against the women and children. The victims blamed Allan and the MacDonalds for their torment.

Riding her horse to visit prisoners' wives, Flora fell and broke her arm. She also was stripped of her plantation when she refused to take an oath of allegiance to the rebels in 1777. She moved in with her daughter and relatives. Flora resisted rebel inspectors, and a Loyalist legend insists that Flora's daughters were raped by rebels in the fall of 1777, who thrust "their swords into their bosoms, split down their silk dresses and, taking them out into the yard, stripped them of all their outer clothing."

Meanwhile, Allan, in a July 18, 1777, letter to Congress, pleaded that "My wife in North Carolina 700 miles from me [is] in a very sickly tender state of health, with a younger Son, a Daughter, & four Grand Children." Allan asked to be exchanged for an American prisoner and was released in August, locating in New York. Flora traveled to New York to be with him in 1778 and, despite ill health, she followed him in Canadian engagements. Homesick for Skye, Flora departed for home in October 1779. At Skye she reminisced about her aid to Prince Charles in the Forty-Five and her activity as a Loyalist, commenting that she and Allan "both have suffered in our person, family and interest, as much as if not more than any two going under the name of Refugees or Loyalists, without the Smallest recompence."

Flora MacDonald died on March 4, 1790, and her mourners attended a large, festive funeral near Kilmuir—replete with mirthful pipers and savory whiskey—celebrating the Scottish heroine. Pilgrims chipped off slivers of her marble memorial which had to be replaced twice. Dr. Samuel Johnson composed an eloquent epitaph for the third monument erected to commemorate Flora: "Her name will be mentioned in history, and if courage and fidelity be virtues, mentioned with honour."

Elizabeth D. Schafer

REFERENCES

Catherine S. Crary, ed., *The Price of Loyalty: Tory Writings from the Revolutionary Era* (1973); Robert DeMond, *The Loyalists in North Carolina During the Revolution* (1960); Linda K. Kerber, *Women of* the Republic: Intellect and Ideology in Revolutionary America* (1980); Allan Reginald MacDonald, *The Truth about Flora MacDonald* (1938); Elizabeth Gray Vining, *Flora MacDonald in the Highlands and America* (1967).

McDougall, Alexander (1732–1786)

Continental Army officer. A New York merchant and politician, Major General Alexander McDougall served much of the war in command of American forces guarding West Point and the Hudson Highlands.

Alexander McDougall was born in the parish of Kildalton on Islay, one of the Inner Helrides Islands, off the western coast of Scotland in July or August 1732. The actual birth date is unknown. His parents, Ronald and Elizabeth McDougall, left Scotland in 1738 for New York with Alexander and two other children. They joined a group of Highland Scots who had intended to purchase land near Fort Edward, New York. There the Scots would find cheap land and would serve as a buffer between the English and French.

The transaction fell through, and the McDougall family remained in the New York City area. Ronald McDougall became a dairy farmer and milk dealer. While living in New York, the McDougalls would eventually add two more children to the family. Alexander grew up as one of New York City's milk boys, delivering his family's product to customers in the city. Due to his early experiences in the dairy business, Alexander grew up showing more interest in trade and commerce than in farming.

By his late teens, Alexander had left his father's dairy farm and worked aboard vessels operated by the Walton family, one of New York City's leading mercantile firms. In 1751 the 19-year-old Alexander completed a voyage to Great Britain, at which time a stop was made at the Island of Islay. After a very short courtship, Alexander married Nancy McDougall, a distant relative, and brought her back to New York on the return trip.

Alexander McDougall was a muscular, heavyset man, rather rugged in appearance. He spoke with a heavy, stuttering brogue. This speaking impediment made it difficult for him to address large crowds. He usually left that chore to others. However, in small groups, McDougall was often accused of talking too much.

Generally self-educated, McDougall was a principled man with a methodical, active mind. He wrote well and was adept at dealing and negotiating with others. He impressed George Washington and others as being a pious, intelligent, and enterprising businessman, and a solid, reliable general officer.

In the early 1750s, McDougall became master of several small sloops, which he used to exchange cargoes with traders in the Carolinas, Florida, and the West Indies. During the French and Indian War, McDougall became one of several successful privateers operating out of New York harbor under letters of marque. In 1757 he commanded the *Tyger*, a six-gun vessel with a crew of 50. Two years later, McDougall had elevated his command to the *Barrington*, a nine-ton sloop with 12 guns and a crew of 80.

On February 21, 1763, McDougall's wife, Nancy, died, leaving behind two sons, John Henry and Ronald Stephen, and one daughter, Elizabeth. Shortly after his wife's death, McDougall suffered another tragedy with the death of his father. McDougall found himself caring for his aged mother and three children of his own. The two boys were sent off to the Presbyterian School in the Jerseys that would later be called Princeton.

After the war, McDougall became a fairly wealthy New York City merchant. He owned his own vessel, *The Schuyler*, and served as an agent for various planters. He also was an investor and a factor, loaning money and financial support to friends and associates on selected business ventures.

In 1767 McDougall married Hannah Bostwick, the daughter of his landlady, and moved to Chapel Street in New York City. A Presbyterian of plain tastes and modest wealth, McDougall was perceived by many upper-class New Yorkers as a social climber who preferred to drink rum rather than wine and play the role of the "Tar" rather than that of the "Gentleman."

When the British enacted the stamp tax, the resulting uproar encouraged McDougall to become involved in public affairs, especially those related to American liberty. McDougall joined the Livingston faction in opposition to the De Lanceys in a struggle for control of New York. Using his contacts along the waterfront, McDougall was able to become an influential leader of the New York Sons of Liberty by 1769.

In December 1769, the De Lancey faction and the lieutenant governor worked out a complicated deal involving a paper currency bill, the Quartering Act and funding of the salary of the governor of New York. In reply to this suspicious agreement, McDougall wrote directly to the people in an anonymously published broadside called "To the betrayed inhabitants of the city and colony of New York." McDougall accused the De Lanceys and Lieutenant Governor Cadwallader Colden of conceding to Parliament and surrendering American liberty. The New York Assembly was charged with betraying the people's trust.

The De Lanceys counterattacked by offering 100 pounds sterling as a reward for information leading to the conviction of the author of the broadside, which was characterized as a "False, seditious and infamous libel." The assembly and the lieutenant governor became more unpopular as the people read the broadside. Riots broke out between the people and the British 16th Regiment in New York. The soldiers cut down a liberty pole, and the Sons of Liberty promptly erected a new one on February 6, 1770. Tensions ran high.

Two days later, on February 8, 1770, McDougall was arrested. Bail was set at 2,000 pounds. McDougall refused to plead guilty nor would he pay bail. He spent the next 80 days in the new jail that would later be a debtor's prison. McDougall was betrayed by the printer, Parker. Parker had an Irish journeyman named Cummins, who had been discharged for improper conduct. In revenge, Cummins went to the authorities and informed on his former master. The authorities questioned Parker, and he admitted McDougall's involvement with the broadside.

McDougall became famous overnight. He was compared to John Wilkes in England when Wilkes had been arrested for criticizing the king's speech in Parliament on the colonies in 1763. An account of Wilkes's arrest had appeared in the Number 45 issue of the North Briton. The number "45" became a symbol for McDougall's cause.

It was carried to such lengths that McDougall was visited by 45 virgins in jail, where he entertained them appropriately. On February 14, 1770, the forty-fifth day of his imprisonment, McDougall ate with 45 men in the jail, eating 45 pounds of steak from a steer 45 months old.

On the anniversary of the repeal of the Stamp Act, 300 Whigs toasted to his health and sent a delegation to dine with him in jail. In time, so many visitors came to meet with him that McDougall had to establish visiting hours to control his fans. In the streets, people sang songs lionizing him as "The Wilkes of America."

On April 17, the jury was called. It was composed of 15 De Lancey men and three Livingston men. McDougall had no chance. The vote was 15 to 3 that McDougall was guilty. The McDougall case was handed over to the Supreme Court for trial, and bail was set at 1,000 pounds. This time McDougall posted it.

Although a leader of the Sons of Liberty and a popular symbol of the American cause, McDougall experienced some hard times after his release from jail. The New York merchants refused to continue the nonimportation policy against British goods. The De Lanceys controlled the assembly. But there was one favorable development. The courts had to drop the case against McDougall when its chief witnesss, the printer Parker, died before the case could be heard.

The De Lancey faction did not give up. The assembly called McDougall to testify before them. When McDougall refused to admit his authorship of the seditious broadside or other printed items that circulated about New York, the assembly placed McDougall back in jail for another 82 days. Once again McDougall's popularity climbed. On March 4, 1771, when the new governor, Lord Dunmore, prorogued the assembly, McDougall was released from his confinement. It was the custom then to release all political prisoners when a new royal governor assumed office.

McDougall had indeed performed a significant service for the American cause. McDougall, an advocate of republican government and the guardian of individual rights of all Englishmen, home or abroad, had written a vital document that challenged the idea of allowing a small oligarchy to dominate the government.

McDougall went directly to the crowd to warn them that their liberty was at stake if they permitted others to rule without the direct participation of the people. In time, McDougall became a proponent of popular sovereignty. He believed the populace had the power to make political decisions that affected the common good. If McDougall's belief was correct, the assembly could not afford to ignore his charges.

There was a brief period of calm before the great tea crisis of 1773. McDougall then reentered the fight for American liberty by preventing tea from being landed in the port of New York. The tea ship *Nancy* arrived, and its captain agreed to ship the tea back to England. Another tea ship, the *London*, however, attempted to land its cargo.

McDougall, well versed in the ways of the waterfront, helped organize a group of "Mohawks" who dumped the cargo of tea into the East River. This was the first major instance of McDougall's leadership with the Sons of Liberty. The event was carried out without violence.

McDougall then presided over an assembly of the people called "The Great Meeting in the Fields" on July 6, 1774, at which time a nonimportation resolution, drafted by McDougall, was passed, along with other related measures. At this meeting, Alexander Hamilton made his first appearance as a public speaker on behalf of American liberty.

McDougall served as a member of the Committee of 51, a group of New York Whigs formed to respond to the crisis caused by Parliament's passage of the Coercive Acts. McDougall was one of the Patriot leaders who actively worked for the calling of a Continental Congress.

When the First Continental Congress met in the fall of 1774 to form a collective reply to Parliament's actions, McDougall was present in Philadelphia to observe the proceedings. Then he returned to New York to help enforce the congressionally agreed upon nonimportation acts with the local merchants.

McDougall served in the New York Provincial Congress, and he was chosen on May 5, 1775, to be a member of the Committee of 100, appointed to develop a working government for the new state of New York. On April 30, 1775, New York's army was organized. It consisted of four regiments. McDougall was appointed colonel of the 1st New York Regiment. McDougall's two sons also joined their father's unit as junior officers and assisted in recruiting soldiers.

When his regiment was sent north in the summer of 1775 to participate in the Canadian campaign under General Richard Montgomery, McDougall remained in New York City. Lieutenant Colonel Rudophus Ritzema took field command of the troops. McDougall remained behind with General Philip Schuyler's permission to bolster New York's commitment to the American cause. He had to counter personally the very real Tory influence in the city.

McDougall's regiment suffered greatly in the months of campaigning leading up to the failed assault on Quebec and the subsequent retreat from Canada. On November 15, his oldest son, John, died of the bilious fever at La Prairie, Canada, and was buried there in the church graveyard. McDougall came under some criticism for not leading personally his regiment through its trials. Due to the death of his son, McDougall now took an active role in the military.

On March 8, 1776, mainly due to his substantial political contributions to the American cause, Congress appointed McDougall colonel of the New York 1st Continentals. As the focus of the war shifted from Boston to New York, McDougall worked closely with General Charles Lee to develop an overall defensive plan for New York City. It was a slow process with many obstacles to overcome. McDougall's political connections were quite helpful to Lee in completing the task.

During the summer of 1776, McDougall's men, with their colonel at their side, labored on digging entrenchments and building the defenses of New York. On August 9, at General George Washington's request, Congress promoted McDougall to brigadier general.

When the British attacked the Americans on Long Island, McDougall's brigade of two regiments formed part of the reserve. They were positioned on Manhattan Island and crossed over to Long Island on August 28, just after the battle was over. During the evacuation of Long Island on the night of August 29–30, McDougall was responsible for calling the various units down to the beach to be ferried across the East River by Colonel John Glover's brigade of Marblehead fisherman. McDougall was one of the last to cross as dawn broke. Washington was in the last boat.

General William Smallwood's Marylanders were added to McDougall's brigade at this time. McDougall's men followed in Washington's retreat to White Plains as a part of General Charles Lee's division. Lee had recently returned to Washington's army on October 4 from a successful defense of Charleston, South Carolina, against an attack by General Henry Clinton.

On October 28, 1776, McDougall's brigade fought the Hessians and British line on Chatterton's Hill at White Plains. McDougall's regulars performed well and were finally forced to withdraw only after the Hessians had successfully routed the militia on the American right, thus exposing McDougall's flank.

MacDougall's men crossed the Hudson in early December to march across the Jerseys, still a part of Lee's division. Washington had ordered Lee to bring his troops to join him in Pennsylvania. Lee was slow in following orders and was captured by the British along the way. McDougall came down with a severe case of rheumatism at Haverstraw, New Jersey, and was forced to send his men on with General John Sullivan. McDougall himself wound up in bed for a month.

In early January, Washington ordered McDougall to the vital Hudson Highlands and to take charge of military stores in that sector. McDougall arrived at Peekskill shortly after to assume his command. Once again, McDougall had to overcome immense obstacles to achieve his goal. For example, during a British raid of March 1777, McDougall could muster but 300 men and several guns to protect his supplies, yet he still managed to save the military stores from enemy hands.

Major General Israel Putnam arrived to take over command of the Hudson Highlands in 1777. McDougall remained during the summer months to help Putnam complete Forts Montgomery and Clinton. Then Washington ordered McDougall south to join the main army with his brigade.

When McDougall reached Washington on September 27 at Pennypacker's Mill, Pennsylvania, there were fewer than 1,000 men in his brigade. On October 4, 1777, Washington attacked the British army camped outside Philadelphia at Germantown. McDougall's brigade marched at the head of General Nathanael Greene's wing, which numbered two-thirds of Washington's strength.

Greene's wing moved down the Limekiln Pike and over Church Lane in the fog and amidst much confusion to hit the British in the rear. McDougall and General John Peter Muhlenberg managed to get their men to Market Square in Germantown, where they hit James Grant's and Edward Mathew's British brigades before being forced to fall back in retreat. McDougall's men provided cover for the withdrawal of Greene's troops.

After the Battle of Germantown, McDougall was appointed to serve on the board of inquiry into General Anthony Wayne's conduct at Paoli, General John Sullivan's conduct at Staten Island, and General Adam Stephen's conduct at Germantown. The first two were found blameless, while Stephen was removed from command. On October 20, 1777, Congress promoted McDougall major general, and he was given command of the brigades of James Varnum and Jedediah Huntington.

In late November, McDougall's division joined that of Greene in fighting with Lord Cornwallis's British force in the Jerseys for control of Fort Mercer. The fort fell, and the American attempts to save it failed. McDougall's men returned to Washington's army. The effects of active service in the field and the poor weather combined to break McDougall's health once more. He retired to Morristown to spend the next seven weeks in bed enervated from the effects of a "nervous fever."

When McDougall had recovered in the spring, Washington sent him to the Hudson Highlands to investigate charges against Putnam for his loss of the Highland forts in the campaign of 1777. McDougall served with General Jedediah Huntington and Colonel Edward Wigglesworth on this board. Huntington returned to Washington with the findings of the board, and McDougall remained to take command of the Highlands with his headquarters at Fishkill. McDougall was very concerned about West Point and worked hard to improve American defenses at that post.

Washington did not leave McDougall in the Highlands long. It late July 1778, McDougall rejoined Washington's army for several months during a time of general inactivity. General Horatio Gates replaced McDougall in command in the Highlands. McDougall commanded a division of three brigades that was shifted back and forth across Connecticut in response to British maneuvers. Finally, on November 24, 1778, Washington ordered McDougall back to the Hudson Highlands once more.

McDougall again concentrated on perfecting West Point in spite of the many obstacles hindering his work. Captain Thomas Machin of the artillery succeeded with McDougall's support in getting an effective chain placed across the Hudson to block possible British passage to the northern reaches of the Hudson River. Fortifications were built and artillery emplaced. West Point grew stronger as time went on.

After General Henry Clinton had come north in 1779 to capture the American works at Stony Point and Verplanck's Point, McDougall remained in command at West Point while Washington had General Anthony Wayne and the light infantry retake Stony Point and destroy it. Washington had great confidence in McDougall and kept him in command in the Highlands for most of the remaining years of the war. For example, McDougall commanded West Point July 19 through December 6, 1779, from June 20 to July 4 and September 25 through October 5, 1780, and June 20, 1781, to January 18, 1782.

During the winter of 1779–1780, McDougall was at Fishkill suffering from the effects of "the stone." He was also an active member of the general officers who negotiated with Congress that winter asking for increased benefits immediately and pensions for officers once their army service had ended. The petition, or memorial, sent by the officers was ignored by Congress.

When General Wilhelm von Knyphausen raided the Jerseys in June 1780 and Clinton returned shortly thereafter from his successful siege of Charleston to threaten the Highlands once more, McDougall was sent to aid General Robert Howe in command of five brigades to block any British move north. When the threat ended, McDougall was sent by his fellow general officers to Congress in Philadelphia to present a second memorial, asking for financial relief. As a politician himself, McDougall was the perfect choice for such a delicate mission.

McDougall arrived in the capital on August 1, 1780. In spite of his vigorous efforts, Congress was slow to react. McDougall was stuck in Philadelphia for seven weeks, and even then, he came away with nothing. Congress had no money and did not wish to create an officer class in society. The officers would have to make do with what they had.

McDougall returned just as General Benedict Arnold defected to the British. He immediately took command of West Point until relieved a short time later by General Arthur St. Clair. McDougall was then elected to the Continental Congress by New York. He served a total of 37 days. His plan was to work to assist his fellow officers, aid the cause of American liberty, help New York, and help himself by remaining a general on the army rolls, subject to call if Washington needed him. Congress was not happy with the conflict of interest of having an army general mixed in with politics. McDougall was offered a position in the ministry of marine and was forced to make a choice.

Financially unable to give up his military salary, as small as it was, McDougall resigned from Congress and returned to the army. His term of service ran from January 17 to March 2, 1781. By the end of May, he was back in the Hudson Highlands.

During the Yorktown campaign, reasons of health kept McDougall from service in the field. He remained the commander at West Point while Washington and the French forced General Lord Cornwallis to surrender. During this time, he entered into a feud with General William Heath, who commanded the entire Highlands sector, over various military issues. The acrimonious relations resulted in Washington removing McDougall from command at West Point in January 1782.

At his court-martial, McDougall was charged by Heath with seven counts of insubordination. Washington appointed General Lord Stirling as president of the board. McDougall objected, making an enemy of Stirling in the process. General Robert Howe was sent by Washington as a replacement. The court found McDougall innocent of six of the seven charges and recommended a reprimand be placed in the general orders.

By this time in the war, McDougall's finances were in dire straits. He and his wife were living from the garden produce of the Beverly Robinson house, where McDougall had his quarters. General Henry Knox was now in command at West Point, which angered McDougall all the more. Washington offered McDougall command of a division with the army, but his health would not permit service in the field. He was again quite sick.

The year 1782 was also a very bad one for the army and for the entire country. Finances were horrible. Conditions were bad. The people were restive. And the army was dissatisfied with their lot. Congress had no funds, little power, and lacked ability to deal with a war that continued but seemed to be winding down. It was a demoralizing period for most Americans.

By August, the officers of the army were meeting once more in Newburgh to protest their treatment at the hands of Congress. They were concerned with their pay, their allowances for expenses, and their financial reward or pensions for services rendered during the course of the war. For a second time, McDougall, along with Colonel John Brooks of Massachusetts and Colonel Matthias Ogden of New Jersey, was sent to Congress in Philadelphia.

The officers arrived in Philadelphia on December 29, 1782. The men presented their case to a congressional committee on January 13, 1783, but Congress had no funds and no means of raising any from the states without state permission. Then events at Newburgh added force to McDougall's arguments. Washington's report of a conspiracy persuaded Congress on March 22 to grant commutation of half-pay for life into five years full pay for officers of the state lines who as a group chose it. McDougall remained in Philadelphia until mid-May 1783 and then returned to New Windsor.

McDougall joined Knox as a founder of the Society of Cincinnati and was elected the first president of the New York chapter. McDougall entered New York City along with Washington when the British under General Guy Carleton evacuated it at the end of 1783.

McDougall spent the remaining years of his life working to improve the condition of southern New York. On January 5, 1784, he was elected to the state senate and served in that office until his death. McDougall also served another brief term in the Continental Congress (1784–1785) and was the first president of the Bank of New York.

After suffering through ten weeks of a fever, General Alexander McDougall died at home on the night of June 8, 1786. That same year, his second son, Ronald, also died. McDougall was buried in the family vault at the First Presbyterian Church in New York City. Washington characterized General McDougall as "a brave soldier and a distinguished patriot." *See also:* Newburgh Conspiracy

Paul J. Sanborn

REFERENCES

Roger J. Champagne, *Alexander McDougall and the American Revolution* (1975); Lincoln Diamant, *The Claiming of the Hudson* (1989); *DAB*; T.W. Egly, Jr., *The History of the First New York Regiment* (1981); Leopold S. Launitz-Schuker, Jr., *Loyal Whigs and Revolutionaries* (1980); *National Cyclopedia of American Biography* (1967); Thomas J. Wirtenbaker, *Father Knickerbocker Rebels* (1969).

McGillivray, Alexander
(c. 1759–1793)

Creek Indian leader. Alexander McGillivray was the most prominent Creek headman of the Revolutionary and Early National periods. He was the son of Lachlan McGillivray, a prominent Indian trader to the Upper Creek Indians, and Sehoy Marchand, a Creek woman of mixed blood. His early life was spent at his father's trading store in the Creek country. As a young man, he was sent to Charleston, South Carolina, where he studied history, Latin, and commerce at his uncle Farquar McGillivray's business establishment. Alexander was in South Carolina when the Revolution began.

His father, Lachlan, remained loyal to the British government and returned to his native Scotland. The Patriot government of Georgia confiscated the McGillivray property within the state, and Alexander returned to his home town of Little Tallahassee during the early part of 1777. McGillivray returned home at a tense time for Creek headmen. The British government had already made the decision to enlist Indian warriors in their attempts to put down the colonial rebellion. At the same time, the American Indian agents in the South were urging the tribes to remain neutral. Following the devastating reprisals by Patriot armies against the Cherokees in 1776–1777, sentiment for the American/neutralist position reached a peak under the able orchestration of George Galphin, the American Indian Superintendent. Neutralist Lower Creek headmen learned that British agents David Taitt, Alexander Cameron, and William McIntosh were raising warriors and gathering ammunition for attacks on the American frontier. The Creek leaders determined that the agents and their leading supporter, Emisteseguo of the Little Tallahassee, should be killed before they could take action that might bring an invasion of the Creek towns by American forces. It was during this time, during the fall of 1777, that Alexander McGillivray apparently accepted a position as assistant commissary for the British Indian Department. When the neutralist faction attempted to kill the British agents, McGillivray prevented the action and was instrumental in averting civil war.

McGillivray's education, natural ability, and position as spokesman for the Wind Clan enabled him to become the most powerful force in the Upper Creek Towns during the American

Revolution. His influence in the Lower Towns was limited. In early 1779, McGillivray led Creek warriors in raids around Augusta, Georgia. McGillivray personally gathered 600 Creek warriors for the defense of Pensacola in early 1780, and he was responsible for the presence of over 1,000 others. By the time Pensacola was actually attacked in the spring of 1781, Creek numbers had dwindled due to poor planning by the commander at Pensacola.

After the war, McGillivray's primary concerns were securing adequate trade goods and ammunition for his people and protecting Creek lands from American encroachment. With these things in mind, he headed the Creek delegation that negotiated the Treaty of Pensacola with Spain in 1784. Under the terms of the treaty, McGillivray secured trade relations with Spanish Florida, thereby freeing Creek towns from dependence on American supplies. The Spanish promised to respect Creek lands in Florida and provided the Creeks with an ally in their negotiations with Georgia and the new United States government. McGillivray was also made Spanish commissary to the Creeks. Earlier, McGillivray had aligned himself with the Loyalist trading firm Patnon, Leslie and Company. His partnership with the firm was mutually beneficial: the company was awarded the right to conduct trade through Spanish Florida, and McGillivray's access to trade goods bolstered his position in Creek councils. In the years following the war, McGillivray became the best known and most powerful Creek headman, and he attempted to institute a wide range of reforms in Creek government. In 1790, McGillivray headed the highly successful Creek delegation that negotiated the Treaty of New York with the Washington administration. He died in 1793.

Kathryn Braund

REFERENCES

John W. Caughey, *McGillivray of the Creeks* (1938); David H. Corkran, *The Creek Frontier* (1967); Michael D. Green, "Alexander McGillivray," in *American Indian Leaders: Studies in Diversity*, ed. By R. David Edmunds (1980); James H. O'Donnell, III, "Alexander McGillivray: Training for Leadership, 1777–1783," *Georgia Historical Quarterly*, 49 (1965):172–186; J. Leitch Wright, Jr., *Creeks and Seminoles* (1986).

McGirth, Daniel (?–1804)

Loyalist. Separating the real from the mythical Daniel McGirth has been almost impossible from the American Revolution to the present. The real McGirth was an in-law to the famous Patriot Kershaw family of Camden, South Carolina. The McGirth of legend was also a Patriot until he was arrested, beaten, and imprisoned by an officer in Georgia merely as a pretense to steal McGirth's horse. Whatever his reasons, Daniel McGirth, the real and imagined, became a terror to supporters of the American cause.

The real Daniel McGirth early in the American Revolution arrived in British East Florida, where he became a Loyalist raider. With small bands of men, McGirth stole cattle from neighboring Georgia that were necessary for the survival of the soldiers and civilians in East Florida. His "gang" rustled cattle, horses, and slaves, becoming the very epitome of what respectable southerners feared most, an armed band of "Indians, with Negro and White savages disguised like them, and Back settlers of North and South Carolina." In East Florida, McGirth learned the importance of mixing politics with banditry, achieving at least some cooperation from the military and political officials.

When the British invaded Georgia in 1778, McGirth moved his base of operations there. Often he used the Loyalist community at Buckhead Creek as a haven. While there on one of his raids on August 24, 1779, McGirth's band was surprised by a continent of Georgia militia under Colonel John Twiggs and some Continentals under a Major Jamison. McGirth escaped the fight at Widow Lockhart's plantation, but he was so badly wounded that his trail of blood led to false report that he had died. Patriot fear of McGirth was so strong that the Loyalist partisan was credited as present in almost every battle and skirmish in Georgia.

When all of Georgia was returned to royal rule in 1780, Daniel McGirth still continued his banditry unabated, taking his loot to British East Florida and reportedly boasting that he had stolen enough to buy his weight in gold. However, British General Augustin Prevost considered creating a special cavalry corps under McGirth to stop rebel raids on Loyalist property. Georgia's restored royal governor, Sir James Wright, knew of McGirth's robberies, but when Augusta was besieged by American forces in June 1781,

McGirth alone volunteered to organize a relief force for the Loyalists trapped there. Wright granted McGirth a commission as colonel of the militia. However, the Loyalist bandit did not march to Augusta but used his commission instead as official sanction for his robberies. Attempts to stop him by legal means failed when he had witnesses threatened and false testimony sworn on his behalf.

When the American Revolution was over and East Florida was returned to Spain, the outgoing British officials and the new Spanish colonial government worked together to stop McGirth. The bandit was captured and held at the Castillio de San Marcos in St. Augustine in 1784. His confinement was no more than a few months—not the five years claimed in the legends—before he escaped and was back at Buckhead Creek in Georgia.

In May 1788, McGirth was captured in Effingham County, Georgia, by Georgia militia under Captain William Cone. Because he was cited in Georgia's Act of Banishment, the Loyalist bandit could have been hanged. However, for reasons that escaped the official records, McGirth departed confinement. In 1795, he was again captured, this time on the Georgia-Florida border. He was brought before Camden County, Georgia, authorities, but again nothing is known of the outcome, except that he was again free.

Contrary to the stories, Daniel McGirth did not return to South Carolina, where he died broken and penniless. Research by Gordon B. Smith and John H. Christian reveals that McGirth actually continued to live in Camden County, and the town of St. Mary's, on Georgia's southernmost seaside border, remained a center for organized crime for decades after McGirth's death.

The American Revolution was the major turning point in America's political, social, and economic history. Daniel McGirth typified one of the darker aspects of this change—the beginnings of crime not only as individual actions but as large-scale activities that functioned with political support and defeated the existing judicial system.

Robert Scott Davis, Jr.

REFERENCES

Robert Scott Davis, Jr., *Georgia Citizens and Soldiers of the American Revolution* (1979); ———, *Georgians in the American Revolution* (1979); Edward J. Cashin and Heard Robertson, *Augusta in the Revolution:* *Events in the Georgia Back Country* (1986); Wilbur Henry Siebert, *Loyalists in East Florida* (1972).

McIntosh, John (1755–1826)

Continental Army officer. John McIntosh, a nephew of General Lachlan McIntosh, was born in McIntosh County, Georgia. He was appointed a captain in the Continental Army in January 1776; he commanded a company of the Georgia battalion. In November 1778, his unit, the 3rd Georgia, successfully defended Ft. Morris (Sunbury, Georgia), a bastion that was a key to the control of the state. When the British commander in the assault, Colonel L.V. Fuser, demanded surrender of the fort, McIntosh defiantly replied: "Come and take it." This action made him Georgia's first war hero. At the Battle of Briar Creek (March 3, 1779), McIntosh's unit fought gallantly, but he was captured. He was later exchanged in the autumn of 1780 for John Harris Cruger. McIntosh served until the end of the war.

John Turner

REFERENCES

Henry B. Carrington, *Battles of the American Revolution* (1988); Henry Steele Commager and Richard B. Morris, eds., *The Spirit of 'Seventy-Six* (1983); Charles C. Jones, *The History of Georgia*, vol. 2 (1883); Ronald G. Killion and Charles T. Waller, *Georgia and the Revolution* (1975).

McIntosh, Lachlan (1725–1806)

Continental Army officer. In the summer of 1778, various Indian tribes of the Upper Ohio Valley were making serious incursions on the frontier of western Pennsylvania. Those warriors were incited by British officials who were headquartered on the Great Lakes at Fort Detroit. To end these forays Congress directed Washington to take action. Accordingly, Washington ordered Brigadier General Lachlan McIntosh to draw up plans to mount a major punitive campaign beyond the forks of the Ohio River.

Prior to 1778, Lachlan McIntosh had experienced a controversial career in both the military and political spheres. He was born in Badenod, Scotland, in 1725, the son of John McIntosh, the titular chieftain of Clan McIntosh. Most of that clan, including Lachlan's immediate family, were ardent Jacobites; therefore, in the 1730s they immigrated to North America to escape political persecution. John McIntosh established a plantation at the mouth of the Altamaha River near the town of Darien, Georgia. In 1745 the elder McIntosh was killed while on a border raid into Spanish Florida.

Not wishing to be a planter, Lachlan moved to Charleston, South Carolina, in 1747 to work as a mercantile trader. Although he soon tired of this career, Lachlan, in these years, gained a valuable friend in the prominent South Carolinian Henry Laurens. By the mid-1750s McIntosh had returned to the family plantation. He also became active in Georgia politics as a member of the colonial legislature representing St. Andrew Parish. Correspondingly, he was commissioned a colonel in the Georgia militia.

Unlike many Scottish expatriates, McIntosh supported actively the American independence cause. On September 16, 1776, he was granted a congressional commission to the rank of brigadier general in the Continental Army; moreover, Lachlan was assigned to command the American coastal defenses around Savannah. He performed his duties ably, but his long years in politics had earned him personal enemies, including Button Gwinnett, a signer of the Declaration of Independence. In early 1777, Gwinnett blocked a field promotion, and an angry McIntosh issued a duel challenge. At the contest McIntosh mortally wounded his longtime rival.

The family of Gwinnett unsuccessfully attempted to have Lachlan arrested for murder, but nothing came of the effort. McIntosh's effectiveness in Georgia, however, was finished. Through the intercession of friends, McIntosh in November 1777 was transferred to Washington's command at Valley Forge. While serving as a senior staff officer, he cultivated an enduring friendship with Washington. On May 2, 1778, Washington selected Lachlan to replace Colonel Edward Hand as commandant of Fort Pitt; furthermore, he was designated officially as the commander of the Western Military Department of the United States.

His primary task was to neutralize the Anglo-Indian attacks along the frontier, an endeavor at which Hand had been singularly inept in accomplishing. But before he could frame any concrete plans, McIntosh was ordered eastward with units of the 13th Virginia Regiment to guard Congress, which had reconvened in Lancaster, Pennsylvania, after fleeing Philadelphia ahead of the British invaders.

While on that duty, news arrived that a Tory-Indian force under Colonel John Butler had "massacred" Pennsylvania militiamen in the Wyoming Valley on July 3, 1778. McIntosh promptly led his command into that locale to bolster the American defense. After observing the bloody results of Butler's incursion, Lachlan made a personal vow that he would forestall similar raids in his jurisdiction.

McIntosh proposed to mount a campaign in late summer to capture distant Fort Detroit. He was well aware that a small mobile company of Virginians under Major George Rogers Clark was already in the Illinois Territory pursuing a similar objective. In contrast, McIntosh intended to take a substantial army and build a military road in the process. He also wanted to construct a series of frontier bastions along the march. Clearly he wished to follow the example of General William Forbes in his successful campaign to capture Fort Duquesne two decades earlier.

To accomplish his goals, McIntosh on September 16, 1778, concluded a military pact with Chief White Eyes of the Delawares; consequently, Delaware warriors were to serve the Americans as scouts. Unfortunately, the Indian braves perpetually brawled with McIntosh's troopers during the march.

Various logistical problems forced McIntosh to delay the expedition until late September. Accordingly, he was denounced by Colonel Daniel Brodhead, the commander of the 8th Pennsylvania Regiment, and Lachlan's second in command. On October 1, a force of 1,300 troops (including 500 regulars) started down the Ohio river from Fort Pitt. They stopped initially at the mouth of the Beaver River to build Fort McIntosh. Brodhead and his friends complained loudly when construction took nearly a month. It was not until October 25 that the army recommenced the march. Brodhead remained at Fort McIntosh to command the garrison.

Heavy rains stalled the marchers in central Ohio, where a very disastrous event occurred. During a violent free-for-all on November 1, a drunken Pennsylvania militiaman fatally shot Chief White Eyes. Inevitably, all the Delaware scouts deserted the Americans. Some of these warriors promptly joined the Shawnee war parties, out of Fort Detroit, who were regularly skirmishing with the invaders.

Meanwhile, McIntosh had again halted to build a second outpost on the Tuscarawas River (near modern Bolivar, Ohio) which he named Fort Laurens after his old friend, Henry Laurens. Colonel John Gibson and 150 soldiers of the 13th Virginia were to serve at this remote post that was to be the operational base for the final advance on Fort Detroit. But McIntosh had already decided to postpone the campaign until the spring of 1779.

Upon returning to Fort Pitt, Lachlan had to confront the problem of supplying the two isolated garrisons. Indian attackers, led by the notorious Simon Girty, frequently cut the supply road. No provision wagons had reached Fort Laurens in weeks by the time an Anglo-Indian force had surrounded the stockade in February 1779. This siege was broken only on March 23 when McIntosh arrived with a relief column.

Eventually, Lachlan's critics convinced key congressmen that he had to be recalled as commander of the Western Department. On February 20, Washington bowed to intense legislative pressure and replaced him with Brodhead. An angry McIntosh subsequently returned to Philadelphia to confront his various detractors.

Although he had repeatedly denounced McIntosh's deliberate approach, Brodhead displayed little inclination to resume the frontier campaign. After great temporizing, Brodhead and his staff decided to abrogate the effort permanently. Moreover, by October 1779 both of the new American forts had been abandoned. Throughout the remainder of the war, therefore, Fort Detroit continued as a staging ground for new Indian raiding ventures.

Washington used his influence to have McIntosh command two Continental regiments in South Carolina. On May 18, 1780, he was taken prisoner by the British after the fall of Charleston. During his two years of detention some of his indicative enemies in Congress had him suspended from active duty for supposedly cooperating with British occupation authorities. Through the good offices of congressional friends, including James Monroe of Virginia, McIntosh was later restored to duty with full pay.

Following the American Revolution, McIntosh, now a major general, returned with his family to Savannah. He professed a desire to spend his mature years as a "gentleman planter," but he was drawn inevitably into politics. In 1784 he was elected to serve a term in Congress. During the next two decades the former general held a series of appointive offices in Georgia. He headed a delegation that escorted President Washington to Savannah in 1791. Lachlan McIntosh died in Savannah on February 20, 1806, after a long illness.

Miles S. Richards

REFERENCES

Solon J. Buck, *The Planting of Civilization in Western Pennsylvania* (1939); Edgar W. Hassler, *Old Westmoreland: A History of Western Pennsylvania during the Revolution* (1900); C.C. Jones, *A History of Georgia*, 2 vols. (1883); Francis C. Philbrick, *The Rise of the West* (1965); C. Hale Sipe, *The Indian Wars of Pennsylvania* (1931); George Swetnam, *The Pittssylvania Country* (1959).

McKee, Alexander (1720–1799)

British Indian agent. Born in Ireland, McKee immigrated to Pennsylvania about 1740 and was an Indian trader on the Ohio before the Revolution. In 1771 he became justice of the peace for Bedford County and later for Westmoreland County, Pennsylvania. In 1771 he succeeded George Croghan as deputy agent in the British Indian department at Fort Pitt, and in 1774 he played an important role in preventing Dunmore's War from spreading into a general Indian war.

After the outbreak of the Revolution, McKee was suspected of Loyalist sympathies, and he was confined to Fort Pitt for a time in 1777. In March 1778, together with Matthew Elliott and Simon Girty, he fled to Detroit, where he offered his services to the British. He was made a captain in the British Indian Department and then deputy agent. McKee had a Shawnee wife and his influential connections among that tribe, combined with his experience as an Indian agent and trader, made him an important figure in Indian country during the Revolution. He functioned as a vital intermediary between the western tribes and their British allies and led several expeditions against the American frontier.

Following the Revolution he became a colonel and continued to organize Indian resistance in the Old Northwest. From 1794 to 1799 he served as deputy superintendent of Indian affairs. The Battle of Fallen Timbers in 1794, which ended Indian resistance to American expansion in Ohio, was fought near his home and store on the Maumee River. In 1796, McKee moved to Malden, Ontario, and died at his home on the Thames River in 1799.

Colin G. Calloway

REFERENCES

Colin G. Calloway, *Crown and Calumet: British-Indian Relations, 1783–1815* (1987); Randolph C. Downes, *Council Fires on the Upper Ohio* (1940); Reginald Horseman, *Matthew Elliott, British Indian Agent* (1964).

McLane, Allen (1748–1829)

Continental Army officer. Born in Philadelphia, McLane married in 1771 and settled in Kent County, Delaware. His first combat was at Great Bridge, Virginia. On September 11, McLane joined the Delaware regiment as a captain and horseman.

At the Battle of Long Island, he demonstrated a cavalry tactic that made him famous. He pounced upon a British patrol, captured some prisoners, and then quickly withdrew. McLane fought at White Plains, Trenton, and Princeton. By late 1777, McLane was regarded as one of Washington's best sources of military intelligence. It was McLane who received information from Lydia Darragh in Philadelphia about General William Howe's proposed attack on Whitemarsh. In the spring of 1778 McLane raced to warn Lafayette about the exposed American encampment at Barren Hill. At Valley Forge, Washington ordered McLane to spy and to scout. With a force that varied from 100 to 200 men, McLane raided isolated British detachments and invariably he surprised them. His exploits became legends. In one account McLane was captured by two British dragoons, but he killed both of them, hid in a pond at night, and escaped his pursuers. After the British evacuated Philadelphia, McLane was the first American soldier in the city, and he seized 30 British prisoners.

After participating in the Battle of Monmouth, McLane then feuded with General Benedict Arnold, the commandant of Philadelphia, and with James Mease, the clothier general, both of whom McLane accused of profiteering. But when McLane presented the charges to Washington he was rebuffed. For reasons that are not clear, McLane never again held an independent command. Although he performed capably at Stony Point and at Paulus Hook, McLane was upstaged by Light-Horse Harry Lee, the commander of the Second Partisan Corps. Hurt by the lack of recognition, McLane was not promoted to major until 1780. His last army services were under General Friedrich von Steuben in Virginia, on a privateer off Charleston, and at the siege of Yorktown.

After the war, McLane operated a business, and he became collector of the port of Wilmington, Delaware. A fearless Patriot, McLane may have been too resentful about his lack of honors, yet he became a romantic hero in the nation's history.

Richard L. Blanco

REFERENCES

Appleton's Cyclopaedia of American Biography, 6 vols. (1886–1889), *1*; Thomas Boyd, *Light-Horse Harry Lee* (1939); Fred J. Cook, *What Matter of Men* (1959); Alexander Garden, *Anecdotes of the American Revolution*, 3 vols. (1865); Noel B. Gerson, *Light-Horse Harry* (1966); Henry P. Johnson, *The Storming of Stony Point on the Hudson* (1971).

MacLean, Allen (1725–1798)

British army officer. MacLean had an adventurous manhood. He served in the Jacobite army at Culloden, Scotland (1745). After the collapse of the Pretender's cause MacLean fled to the Netherlands, where he joined the Scots Brigade (1746). After George III granted an amnesty to Scot rebels in 1750, MacLean returned home. In 1756 he was a lieutenant in the Royal Americans (the 62nd and later the 60th Foot) that served in North America. During the French and Indian War he was wounded at Fort Carillon (1758) and at Fort Niagara (1759). MacLean was at the capture of Quebec in 1761. Returning to Scotland, MacLean raised his own regiment, the 114th Foot (MacLean's Highlanders), which was soon posted to North America but which soon after was disbanded. For his services MacLean received a land grant on St. John Island (Prince Edward Island), but apparently he did not reside there.

In 1775 General Thomas Gage authorized Lieutenant Colonel MacLean to raise a provincial corps—the Royal Highland Emigrants. The two regiments of the corps were recruited from Scots living in New York, Nova Scotia, Quebec, St. John, and the Carolinas. During the American invasion of Canada in late 1775, MacLean gathered 200 Highlanders, some British regulars, and assorted volunteers from the Maritimes and eastern Canada and hurried to Quebec before the enemy forces under Colonel Benedict Arnold arrived there. Under the direction of General Sir Guy Carleton, MacLean repulsed Arnold's attack upon the city (December 31, 1775). The siege continued until May 1776, when British reinforcements that had departed from Cork, Ireland, under General John Burgoyne sailed up the St. Lawrence and forced the Americans to retreat. In the decisive British victory of Trois Rivieres (June 8, 1776), MacLean played an important role.

In June 1777 MacLean was appointed brigadier general and military governor of Montreal. In October 1777, after the recapture of Fort Ticonderoga during the disastrous invasion of New York by Burgoyne, MacLean had to withdraw his defenses in order to concentrate on protecting posts along the Richelieu River.

MacLean returned to Britain in 1783, retired, and died in London. Though he saw little action in the Revolution after 1776, MacLean is enshrined as one of Canada's heroes, and his name is symbolic of the widespread influence of Scots in the Maritime Provinces. *See also:* Loyalists in Canada

Richard L. Blanco

REFERENCES

Robert S. Allen, ed., *The Loyal Americans* (1983); *CDB*; Mary B. Fryer, *King's Men* (1980); Alexander McDonald, "Letter-Book of Captain Alexander McDonald of the Royal Highland Emigrants, 1775–1779," *Collection of the New York Historical Society for the Year 1882* (1883):203–498; J.P. McLean, *An Historical Account of the Settlement of Scottish Highlanders in America Prior to the Peace of 1783* (1900), rpt. 1968; G.F.B. Stanley, *Canada Invaded, 1775–1776* (1973).

Madison, James (1751–1836)

Fourth president of the United States. Born March 16, 1751, the eldest son of the wealthiest landholder in Orange County, Virginia, James Madison was destined for a life of privilege and responsibility. The triad of land, slaves, and tobacco supported him throughout his long life, allowing him to concentrate on politics and the intellectual pursuits he loved. Though poor health dogged him from the start, Madison quickly found his real interest lay in books. From 11 to 16 he boarded at a school kept by Donald Robertson in King and Queen County, an inspiring teacher of whom Madison would later say "all that I have been in life I owe largely to that man." Robertson whetted the intellectual appetite of the young man and instilled a love of learning that never deserted him. In 1769, after two years with private tutor Thomas Martin in Montpelier, Madison matriculated at the College of New Jersey at Princeton, shunning William and Mary, the traditional college of choice. There he came under the influence of John Witherspoon, who introduced him to the thinkers of the Scottish Enlightenment—Frances Hutcheson, David Hume, and Adam Smith, among others. Madison proved voracious, consuming four years of course work in two, and graduating in 1771. Yet, after spending another year at Princeton in further study, Madison returned home, at once stimulated, exhausted, and uncertain about his vocation in life. Isolated in the Virginia Piedmont and discontented with the idea of spending his life as a gentleman farmer, Madison toyed with becoming a minister, dipped into law books, but decided nothing. His sole passion seemed to be in defending the local Baptists against persecution by the Anglican majority, a mission in which, he wrote a friend, "I have squabbled and scolded abused and ridiculed so long about it to so little purpose that I am without common patience." The intolerance of the Virginia Piedmont stood in sharp contrast to Princeton and Philadelphia and only exacerbated the young man's depression.

Madison's apparent disinterest in the growing dispute between the colonies and Great Britain was dispelled during a visit to Philadelphia in April 1774. Word had just arrived of the passage by Parliament of the Coercive Acts, and Madison's letters from that time on reflected strong Whiggish sentiments. Although he was appointed to the Orange County Committee of Safety in December 1774 and commissioned a colonel of the county militia in October 1775, he was overshadowed by his father, who chaired the one and commanded the other. It was not until the next spring that Madison really plunged into the political ferment of the Revolution. With his election to the Virginia Convention of 1776, he emerged as a man of potential in his own right. It was there he made his first contribution to American constitutional law—by his defense of the free exercise of religion as a right and not a privilege—and where he found a vocation: politics.

In October 1776 Madison participated in the newly created Virginia House of Delegates. There he continued his apprenticeship in the ways of governance and, more importantly, made the acquaintance of Thomas Jefferson. The political friendship of these two brilliant men lasted until Jefferson's death and would remain unmatched in American history for its intellectual depth and its consequences for the Republic.

Madison lost his election for the 1777 session of the House of Delegates, purportedly because he refused to provide liquor for the voters, a tradition affectionately referred to as "swilling the planters with bumbo." His good offices in the legislature were not forgotten, however, and he was elected to a seat on the eight-member Council of State. The council was designed as the governor's advisory body without real power of its own, but because it sat year-round, more and more tasks were delegated to it. Madison's two years of regular attendance provided him with practical experience in government, as the council went about the mundane work of collecting taxes, raising men and supplies, and supporting the war. His efforts were rewarded when in December 1779 he was elected a delegate to the Continental Congress, sitting in Philadelphia.

Madison served in Congress from March 1780, when the war had reached its nadir, to December 1783, soon after its triumphant conclusion. He was a conscientious legislator who was admired for his committee work as well as his forcefully argued and closely reasoned speeches. The revealing notes he took on the debates while a member are evidence of his immersion in congressional politics, as well as an invaluable supplement to the official congressional journal. He was a determined advocate in Congress of Virginia's position on its western lands while at the same time encouraging his state to cede those lands to ensure the ratification of the Articles of Confederation, an event that finally took place in February 1781. In general, he supported enhanced powers for the Confederation government at the expense of the states, but he was unwilling to push beyond constitutional limits to achieve them. He engineered compromises in the spring of 1783 on taxation and import duties—including the famous three-fifths ratio, in which, for purposes of representation, five slaves would be equivalent to three free persons—only to watch the Confederation continue to lose power and prestige in the wake of the war's end. In spite of his disappointments, he left Congress that fall a Continental figure of stature.

Madison was elected to the Virginia House of Delegates in 1784 and for the two subsequent years. There he fought doggedly to strengthen the political union of the states but was unsuccessful in his attempts to open Virginia courts to British debt suits or to garner acceptance of congressional power over interstate trade. He was only slightly more successful in working for the passage of Jeffersons' revised law code, gaining the enactment of 36 of the 118 bills proposed. His major triumph was blocking the reestablishment of a state church, and no one worked harder than Madison for passage of the Act for Establishing Religious Freedom in 1785, the success of which, Madison assured Jefferson, "extinguished for ever the ambitious hope of making laws for the human mind."

While Madison had focused on Virginia matters since leaving Congress, his commitment to national concerns had not wavered. Every year he had traveled north to Philadelphia and New York, touching base with friends and colleagues in other states and keeping an eye on political developments. At the fall session of the House of Delegates in 1785, Madison was appointed a delegate to a convention on interstate trade to be held in Annapolis in September 1786. Attendance at the meeting was scanty, but those who came were influential. Their report called for a general convention to meet the following summer in Philadelphia to revise the Articles of Confederation in such a way as to make "the Federal Government adequate to the exigencies of the Union." In the fall session of the Virginia legislature, Madison helped secure the acceptance of the report and the selection of a delegation of distinguished Virginians, himself among them, to attend the convention.

In the meantime, Madison took up his duties as a Virginia delegate to Congress, arriving in New York in February 1787. That spring, when committee work and congressional sessions allowed, Madison pored over the history of ancient republics and confederations, seeking in the past answers to present problems. In letters to friends and in a memorandum entitled "Vices of the Political System of the U.S.," he investigated the reasons the republican experiment was failing so miserably. And in putting his ideas to paper, Madison prepared no less than a theory of government that he, along with the rest of the Virginia delegation, would present to that summer's convention in Philadelphia. Uppermost in Madison's mind was the necessity to restrain the states from unwise and unjust legislation and to strengthen the national government without destroying state sovereignty.

Madison was first on the ground when the Constitutional Convention convened in May 1787, and he seized the initiative by proposing a plan of government that scrapped the Articles of Confederation and substituted a national government that operated directly on individual citizens rather than the states. He not only took a leading role in shaping the Constitution that emerged, he also kept notes of the proceedings that are the most complete record of the debates. Though disappointed in the outcome— the convention had not accepted two of Madison's strongly held beliefs: a federal veto on state laws, and proportional representation in both houses of the legislature—he resolved to back the new government as the only practical alternative to the moribund Confederation.

Madison's efforts on behalf of ratification took place on a number of levels. The first took place the week after the convention adjourned, when he worked successfully in Congress to secure action sending the Constitution to the states with no amendments or prior judgments. That accomplished, Madison began, along with Alexander Hamilton and John Jay, to write a series of essays for the newspapers exploring the benefits of the new Constitution and defending some of its more controversial provisions. Of the hundreds of pro- and anti-constitutional pieces published, these 85 essays, of which Madison wrote some 29, stand out for their calmly reasoned and persuasive insights into the nature of government in general and the Constitution in particular. Written with an eye toward the New York ratification battle, and later collected and published in 1788 as *The Federalist Papers*, they undoubtedly had less effect there than they have had as glosses on the conduct of republican government ever since.

In March 1788, Madison returned home for election to the Virginia ratifying convention, where he ably defended the Philadelphia convention's handiwork against the wily and impassioned oratory of Patrick Henry. Madison spoke long, often, and successfully, as Virginia became the tenth state to ratify the Constitution. Henry's voice had not been without effect, however. Virginia demanded the Constitution be amended to include a bill of rights, amendments Madison felt to be not only inappropriate but dangerous. He reasoned that since all power not expressly given to the federal or state governments remained with the people, any list of enumerated rights was unnecessary and might be incomplete. Overwhelming public support for them, however, obliged Madison to change his mind in the course of his close but successful race against James Monroe for a seat in the U.S. House of Representatives.

The work of the First Federal Congress was of great importance. If the Constitution laid the foundation and frame of the new government, then Congress made the house habitable by its passage of laws creating a revenue, executive departments, and the federal court system. And by its decisions in matter of protocol, it set precedents for subsequent administrations to this day. In all this activity, Madison took the lead. George Washington, in particular, relied on him for advice on how to conduct a Republican presidency. In addition, Madison composed a number of the president's early speeches, including Washington's first inaugural address. He then went on to write the House of Representatives' reply to the president's address, as well as Washington's answer to both the House and the Senate. Of greater consequence to the Republic's future, however, Madison fulfilled his pledge to sponsor a series of amendments that would safeguard individual rights. More than 200 such amendments had been proposed by the states; Madison distilled this mass into 19 articles, which were further reduced in debate to 12. Congress approved these amendments and sent them to the states, where ten were subsequently ratified and became the Bill of Rights.

Madison quickly found himself at odds with the powerfully influential secretary of the treasury, Alexander Hamilton, over the latter's financial plans for the new Republic. The two parted company over trade issues, in which Madison favored a policy of preferential and reciprocal treatment toward other nations; the assumption of state debts by the federal government, which Madison opposed; and finally, on fully reimbursing holders of U.S. financial paper at par, a cornerstone of Hamilton's policy. Madison lost on all three counts, gaining in return only a decision to build a new national capital along the Potomac River.

The breach between the two men only widened in the Second Congress—and the two subsequent ones as well. From disputes over matters of policy, they soon became arguments over differences of principle. The rift that began over differing interpretations of the Constitution soon created two factions and laid the basis for the emergence of the first party system, the division of the mass of the people into two distinct and antagonistic parties: Federalists and Republicans. Madison in the House, and Secretary of State Jefferson in the Cabinet, were led, issue by issue, into opposition to the government. At the heart of the dispute was Hamilton's financial system. The two Virginians believed that Hamilton was aping the corrupt policy of Great Britain, with its national bank, gigantic public debt, and hordes of speculators. In recreating that system in the U.S., they believed, Hamilton was betraying the ideals of the American Revolution. Madison further felt that Hamilton was breaching the limits of power of the federal government as designed in the Constitutional Convention. In Hamilton's hands, certain phrases like "necessary and proper" were capable of great elasticity. Hamilton's willingness to subvert the intent of the framers was for Madison the crux of the issue.

To complicate matters, the revolutionary republican government in France had declared war on Great Britain in January 1793, thereby plunging the U.S. into a quandary. The U.S. was formally allied with the French; yet no American wished to be drawn into the maelstrom of a European war. Both sides wished for neutrality, yet Anglophiles like Hamilton wished to abrogate the Franco-American Treaty of 1778 altogether, and pursue a policy of neutrality heavily tilted in favor of Great Britain. Hamilton's *Pacificus* essays ably advanced this position. Madison countered with a series of essays signed *Helvidius*, taking the stance that the Neutrality Proclamation signed by Washington in 1793 was unconstitutional. As Federalists sided with Great Britain and Republicans with France, domestic questions became embroiled with foreign policy issues, introducing into the simplest difference of opinion a heavy dose of ideological fervor.

British outrages against American shipping in December 1793—over 250 ships were captured without warning in the West Indies

alone—precipitated a new crisis. Chief Justice John Jay was dispatched to Great Britain to attempt to negotiate an end to difficulties and to avoid a war. The treaty he brought back, which was ratified by the Senate in June 1795 and signed by the president two months later, accomplished that end but at the price of significant concessions to British power. Madison and his Republican band were incensed at what they viewed as an abrogation of American independence, a confirmation of American economic dependence on Great Britain, and they vowed to defeat the treaty by blocking appropriations for its implementation. When their effort was set back in a close House vote, Madison took the defeat very hard. His years in opposition had taken their toll. Madison resolved to retire from Congress when his term ended in early 1797. Part of his decision was no doubt prompted by his 1794 marriage to the young Philadelphia widow Dolley Payne Madison and a desire to enjoy the sweets of domesticity far from the scenes of factional discord. And part of his decision to retire also was due to the death of his brother, Ambrose, and the increasing responsibilities entailed in caring for his aging parents. Thus when the time came, he quietly relinquished his party leadership and returned to Virginia.

At Montpelier, Madison undertook the life of a gentleman farmer, turning his energies to agriculture and the management of a large plantation. He expanded the house, ensuring a measure of privacy for himself, his wife, and her son, Payne Todd, and his parents, and room for the many Madison relations. But European events, the actions of the Adams administration, and the urgings of such Republican friends as Jefferson, John Dawson, James Monroe, and John Taylor of Caroline, soon led him to take a more active, if behind-the-scenes, role in the politics of the late 1790s.

The spring of 1797 brought heightened tensions between the U.S. and France as word reached Philadelphia that France had refused to accept Charles Cotesworth Pinckney as U.S. minister. President Adams called a special session of Congress to deal with the crisis, and he appointed a trio of commissioners to negotiate an end to differences with France. But the three envoys who arrived in Paris met with obstructions and humiliating demands for money, which when known in the U.S. caused public uproar and cries for reprisals against France. To this

XYZ Affair, as it came to be known, the Adams administration responded by greatly expanding the army and navy, levying new taxes to support war preparations, and passing the Alien and Sedition Acts. Madison's initial reaction to the draft Alien bill was that it was "a monster that must for ever disgrace its parents," and he maintained throughout his life the opinion that the federal government had greatly overstepped its bounds and that the two acts were unconstitutional. In December 1798, at Jefferson's urging, he drafted a document of protest that was submitted to the Virginia House of Delegates with his authorship concealed. The Virginia Resolutions called on the states to protest the infringement of their rights and liberties by the passage of the Alien and Sedition Acts and generally criticized the enlargement of federal powers that had taken place in the past five years. Coupled with Jefferson's more dramatic and extreme Kentucky Resolutions, the statement provided a rallying point for Republicans, but it was not well received by the other state legislatures. In their avowal of the compact theory of government and their call for the states to resist encroachments on their rights by the federal government, the Virginia and Kentucky Resolutions were later used—as the intellectual foundations of nullification and secession—in ways that Madison had never foreseen nor could ever condone.

Reactions from other states to the resolutions were so censorious that Madison was persuaded to stand for election to the Virginia Assembly in 1799 in order to defend them. He was elected and undertook their defense by producing the *Report of 1800*, a comprehensive attack on the unconstitutionality of the two acts as well as a ringing statement of the inviolability of the right of free speech. It is for the latter element that the *Report* is read today, as a critically important document for the interpretation of the First Amendment.

The measures of the Adams administration provoked a backlash that captured the presidency for the Republicans. Madison was elected a presidential elector for Virginia on the Republican ticket and cast his vote for Jefferson and Aaron Burr. But he played no role in the dramatic election in the House of Representatives that resulted from a tie in the electoral voting between the Republican presidential and vice-presidential candidates. With Jefferson securely seated in the presidential chair, Republicans began to

dismantle the Federalist machinery of government in what the president termed, "the Revolution of 1800," eliminating internal taxes and judicial positions, and reducing the military to a bare necessity. In this new order, Madison took on the responsibility of the State Department and remained as Jefferson's right-hand man and heir-apparent through the eight years of his fellow Virginian's two-term presidency.

As secretary of state, Madison was charged with a host of duties besides the conduct of American foreign policy. He was responsible for the Patent Office, for publishing and distributing the public laws, and for issuing federal commissions. He was the keeper of the great seal and acted as liaison between the federal government and the governors of the states and territories. In the realm of foreign policy, he handled correspondence from five ministers and over fifty consuls.

Besides this flow of business, three great issues stand out for the period of Madison's tenure in the department. The greatest achievement of the Jefferson administration was the purchase of the Louisiana Territory from France. In addition, a great deal of unsuccessful diplomatic effort was undertaken to gain the Floridas—especially West Florida—from Spain. But the thorniest and most frustrating problem of all was the attempt to maintain the rights of a neutral nation in the face of the provocations and aggressions of France and Great Britain. No amount of argument about free trade or the injustice of impressment could stop the depredations enacted on American commerce and seamen. Madison's painstaking study, *An Examination of the British Doctrine, Which Subjects to Capture a Neutral Trade, Not Open in Time of Peace* (1806), which demonstrated that British maritime practices were not in accordance with international law, had no practical effect on either Great Britain or France, as each grappled for a stranglehold on the other's economy. Great Britain's Orders in Council in 1807 prohibited the common American practice of trading between European ports and later required all ships trading with the Continent to obtain a license in Britain. Napoleon's Milan Decree retaliated by making any ship complying with the British regulation subject to confiscation. Caught in this intractable bind, Madison and Jefferson turned to economic coercion as an alternative to war. The embargo that was enacted in 1807 solved the problem of foreign depredations on American commerce, but only by destroying for a time American commerce altogether. The weapon that was intended to cripple the British economy brought instead a wave of popular revulsion and widespread lawbreaking. It was not Madison's—or Jefferson's—finest hour.

Not only did the embargo spur public outrage, but it also exacerbated the widening divisions in the Republican party. With the demise of the Federalists, the Republicans had begun to split hairs over the true course of Republicanism, and Madison nearly fell its first victim. As Jefferson's hand-picked successor, Madison won the 1808 presidential election handily, despite a challenge from his estranged friend, James Monroe. But Madison failed to unite the party behind his efforts to find a diplomatic substitute for the embargo, which had lapsed with Jefferson's retreat to Monticello in March 1809. In spite of its failure, Madison's faith remained in economic coercion, and he floated a number of alternative measures in the next two years designed to bring Great Britain and France to respect neutral commerce. None of these measures proved effective, and pressure grew on Madison to lead the country into war. This he finally did in June 1812 by asking Congress to declare war on Great Britain.

Elected president for a second time in 1812, Madison launched a series of invasion strikes at Canada as the most vulnerable British target. The war effort was hampered, however, not only by the poor condition of the armed forces (a legacy of three Republican administrations), poor leadership in the army, in the states, and in the cabinet, and New England opposition to the war, but also by his own style of leadership. Madison believed the president should limit himself to carrying out the laws and defending the Constitution. It was not his brief to be a party leader, to submit programs and whip together support for their passage in Congress, or to veto obnoxious but constitutional legislation. Coupled with factional fighting among Republicans and the intransigent opposition of a small but hardly Federalist contingent, the administration found the prosecution of the war to be heavy slogging.

If the war effort lacked direction at the top, it lacked as well a measure of energy down through the chain of command. With the exception of Albert Gallatin, Madison was surrounded by a number of jealous, quarreling, incompetent cabi-

net secretaries. Only the navy provided a bright spot, and that was almost entirely due to the Federalist frigate-building program of the Adams administration and the experience gained by U.S. naval officers in the Barbary wars. With the Canadian campaigns of 1812 and 1813 in shambles, his own capital burned by British invaders in 1814, and the prospect of Wellington's veterans available to carry on the war against him, Madison was happy to accept a peace on the basis of the prewar relationship with Great Britain in 1815. The nearly miraculous victory at New Orleans in January 1815 put a happy coda on what was for the most part a disastrous experience. And as important, the immediate causes of the war—commercial restrictions and impressment—had vanished with the demise of Napoleon and the end of the European conflict.

Madison's final years in office allowed him, for the first time in 15 years, to turn his attention to domestic affairs. Ironically, he proposed several measures that he had earlier strongly opposed—the recharter of a national bank, a limited protective tariff, and a constitutional amendment to allow the federal government to undertake internal improvements. The Second Bank of the United States was established by Madison's signature in 1816, but a Bonus Bill that provided for federal support of roads and canals was vetoed by the president as unconstitutional in one of his last official acts. He retired to Montpelier for the second, and last, time in March 1817.

It was to be a long and active retirement. Of necessity Madison threw himself into the management of his large plantation, interesting himself in scientific farming as a means to counter the increasing unprofitability of Virginia agriculture. Beginning in 1816 he sat on the Board of Visitors, planning the creation of the University of Virginia, and when Jefferson died in 1826, he became its second rector. He also found time to renew his correspondence, finding in it an opportunity to interpret for the present generation the legacy of the Revolutionary past. Part of the responsibility Madison shouldered was the preservation of his personal papers, especially his notes taken at the Constitutional Convention in 1787. These he prepared for posthumous publication. His last public political appearance came in 1829 at the Virginia convention to draw up a new state constitution, where he spoke against the overrepresentation of the Tidewater region in the House of Delegates. He died at his home on June 28, 1836.

David B. Mattern

REFERENCES

William T. Hutchinson, et al., eds., *The Papers of James Madison*, 1st ser., vols. 1–10 (1962–77); vols. 11–, (1977–); Irving Brant, *James Madison*, 6 vols. (1941–61); Ralph Ketcham, *James Madison: A Biography* (1971); Jack N. Rakove, *James Madison and the Creation of the American Republic* (1990); J.C.A. Stagg, *Mr. Madison's War: Politics, Diplomacy, and Warfare in the Early American Republic, 1783–1830* (1983).

Madjeckewiss (Matchekewis) (c. 1735–c. 1805)

Chippewa Indian chief. Born into a Chippewa band living in northern Michigan, Madjeckewiss grew to be a tall, well-built young man. In 1763 during Pontiac's uprising, Madjeckewiss was instrumental in capturing the British force at Fort Michilimackinac (Mackinaw City, Michigan) by a well-planned stratagem. Staging a lacrosse game outside the fort, the warriors suddenly rushed the gate as unsuspecting British soldiers watched in horror. Later Madjeckewiss made his peace with the British and became a firm ally. During the American Revolution he assisted in John Burgoyne's invasion of New York as well as attacks into the Illinois country. In 1780 he led the Indian forces in the unsuccessful British attack on St. Louis.

Even after the Revolution ended, Madjeckewiss continued as an ally of the British until the Indian forces were defeated by General Anthony Wayne at Fallen Timbers in 1794. During the next year the chief, now using the name of Bad Bird, signed the Treaty of Greenville surrendering much of Ohio to the Americans. The old chief died sometime around 1805.

David A. Armour

REFERENCES

DCB; David Arthur Armour and Keith R. Widder, *At the Crossroads: Michilimackinac during the American Revolution* (1978); L.C. Draper, "Notice of Match-e-ke-wis, the Captor of Mackinaw, 1763," *Wisconsin State Historical Society Collection*, *VII* (1876): 188–194.

Margaretta Affair (June 12, 1775)

The *Margaretta* was a Royal Navy schooner that Americans seized in the Machias River off the town of Machias in the eastern district of Massachusetts (present-day Maine). She was taken on June 12, 1775, in what has been called the "naval Lexington."

Machias had undergone a difficult winter and was short of provisions. The British army at Boston was short of wood, and Ichabod Jones, a Loyalist merchant, proposed to General Thomas Gage that he ship supplies to the settlement in exchange for lumber. Gage agreed but, as a precaution, sent the 100-ton schooner *Margaretta*, armed with four 3-pounders and 14 swivels, to convoy two timber sloops, the *Unity* and *Polly*, to Machias. Midshipman James Moore commanded the *Margaretta*.

The three vessels arrived off Machias on the evening of June 2, 1775. Jones went ashore the next day and insisted that the townspeople sign a contract guaranteeing protection. He assured them that the lumber was for firewood, but many suspected that it would be used for building fortifications.

Dissatisfied with the number of signatures he was able to secure, Jones demanded a town meeting, which was held on June 6. The Reverend James Lyon, chairman of the town Committee of Public Safety, later reported to the Massachusetts Provincial Congress that "the people . . . seemed so averse to the measures proposed" that Jones secretly asked Midshipman Moore to bring the *Margaretta* closer so "that her Guns would reach the Houses." The vote was in favor of the contract, but Lyon reported the townspeople considered themselves "nearly as prisoners of war, in the hands of the common enemy."

Jones then ordered the two timber sloops to the wharf and began unloading the provisions, but he distributed them only to those who had voted favorably at the town meeting. This angered the others, and they plotted with people from nearby settlements to seize Jones when he attended Sunday services ashore on June 11. This was thwarted when Jones, Moore, and his second in command all jumped through a window. Jones escaped to the woods while the two officers ran for the wharf and the schooner's boat. Once he was safely back on the *Margaretta*, Moore sent a message to the townspeople threatening to burn the town if any harm came to Jones or they tried to stop his vessels.

The insurgents quickly seized the *Unity* and the *Polly*. That evening Moore moved the schooner near one of the sloops with the intention of retaking her. A considerable number of the insurgents then set out for the *Margaretta*'s anchorage in canoes and boats. They demanded Moore "surrender to America." He replied "fire and be damn'd," and they immediately opened fire. This exchange, limited to small arms, lasted about an hour and a half before the *Margaretta* withdrew farther downstream and was lashed to a small sloop for the night.

At dawn the next day, Moore ordered all sail made, but in a "smart breeze, in jibbing," the *Margaretta* lost her boom and gaff. Moore used the schooner's boat to get to a nearby timber sloop and refitted the schooner with her boom and gaff. The British also took the sloop's master, Captain Robert Avery, to serve as pilot.

The schooner then weighted anchor and stood for the sea. She was pursued by a group of about 40 men under command of Jeremiah O'Brien in the *Unity*, armed with "guns, swords, axes & pick forks." Another 20, under command of Benjamin Foster, were in a small schooner. The *Margaretta* cut her boats from the stern and made all sail. Unfortunately for the British, she was a "dull sailor." The *Polly* came up quickly, and the British opened fire on her with stern swivels and small arms. When the *Unity* was within hailing distance of the *Margaretta*, O'Brien demanded the British surrender, promising to treat the men well if they did so but to put them to death if they did not. Seeing no possibility of escaping, Moore brought the schooner about and fired a broadside, along with swivels and small arms, cutting up the sails and rigging of the *Unity* in the process. Moore also threw some hand grenades. The two American vessels were soon on either side of the *Margaretta*, and Moore was mortally wounded by two shots. The Americans then boarded the *Margaretta* and captured her. Moore was carried to his cabin, where he was asked why he had not surrendered. He said that he "preferred Death before yielding to such a sett of Vilains." He died ashore the next day. Also killed was the unfortunate Avery. Four other British were wounded, while one American died during the battle and five were wounded—one mortally.

The *Margaretta* was the first Royal Navy vessel to strike the rebellious Americans. Her captors transferred the schooner's guns to the *Unity*, subsequently renamed the *Machias Liberty*. Under O'Brien's command, she was the first armed cruiser of the American Revolution. She soon took two unsuspecting prizes, the armed schooner *Diligent* and the tender *Tattamagouche*. In order to prevent O'Brien and his crew from being treated as pirates if captured, the Massachusetts Assembly voted to commission both the *Machias Liberty* and the *Diligent*.

Spencer Tucker

REFERENCES

Nathan Miller, *Sea of Glory. The Continental Navy Fights for Independence 1775–1783* (1974); Eyewitness accounts by pilot Nathaniel Gregory and James Lyons in U.S., Navy Department, *Naval Documents of the American Revolution, Vol. I* (1964).

Marine Committee

During the Revolution the Continental Congress created four successive agencies to administer the navy. They were the Naval Committee (1775–1776), the Marine Committee (1775–1779), the Board of Admiralty (1779–1781), and the Agent of Marine (1791–1784). By far, the most important of these was the Marine Committee. Established by congressional action on December 14, 1775, the committee was composed of 13 members, one from each state. Charged with bringing "into execution the resolutions of Congress for fitting out armed vessels," the committee moved forward to its task.

Its chief business was to oversee the completion of 13 frigates authorized by Congress. It was not an easy chore, and for the next three years this Committee tried to steer the Continental Navy through waters littered with obstacles. Like all committees of the Continental Congress, the Marine Committee suffered from an alarming rate of turnover. It has been estimated that during its three years of existence more than 60 different members of Congress served on the Committee. Adding to the woes of the Committee was the fact that its members were required to serve on so many other committees at the same time. Congress was committee-driven, and the heavy burdens placed on the members of the Marine Committee created a strong centrifugal force that kept them always out on the periphery of problems, never leaving them with sufficient time or energy to come to grips with the issues.

In their efforts to manage the construction, fitting out, manning, and operations of the navy, the Committee depended heavily upon their agents in the various ports, as well as on two official naval boards. One in Philadelphia was in close touch and acted directly under the supervision of the Committee. In Boston, matters were different, and the board in that town sometimes acted in a quasi-independent capacity. The Marine Committee had virtually no control over operations of the Continental Navy in European waters.

Unhappy with committee government in general, and with the Marine Committee in particular, in the fall of 1779 Congress took steps to tighten administration. They voted to establish a Board of Admiralty composed of five members, three to be appointed from outside the Congress and two from the membership of that body.

William M. Fowler, Jr.

REFERENCES

Edmund C. Burnett, *The Continental Congress* (1941); William M. Fowler, Jr., *William Ellery. A Rhode Island Politico and Lord of Admiralty* (1973); Frank C. Mevers, *Congress and the Navy* (1972); C.O. Paullin, *The Navy of the American Revolution* (1906); Stephen T. Powers, *The Decline and Extinction of American Naval Power, 1781–1787* (1965).

Marines in the American Revolution

The genesis of the United States Marine Corps can be found in the American Revolution. While the Marine Corps itself was not officially inaugurated until 1798, when it became an individual service (although under the aegis of the navy), formations of American marines served as far back as 1740 (War of Jenkin's Ear), as well as the French and Indian War (1754–1763). However, it was during the American Revolution that American marines played their most important pre-1798 role, especially in enforcing discipline upon often unruly and motley ship crews.

Marines originally seem to have been developed by the Royal Navy to protect officers from their "pressed" crews, but as time went on, marines evolved into special troops that acted as seaborne infantry for landing operations, as well as shipborne assault troops to enhance a warship's fighting capabilities. The usual ratio of marines per ship worked out to about one marine per gun.

American marine formations of the Revolution began early, with Congress authorizing in November 1775 the creation of two marine battalions, with the specific mission of an expedition to Nova Scotia. However, this mission soon fell by the wayside, and it was decided to raise five companies, with the first marine officer—Samuel Nicholas—being appointed at the end of November. Nicholas, the owner of Conestoga Wagon Inn in Philadelphia, was commissioned as a captain in the Continental Marines, and was to remain the senior marine officer through the course of the Revolution. Nicholas traditionally also has been looked upon as the first marine commandant.

Recruiting proceeded at a fairly rapid pace (aided by the abilities of Robert Mullan, who was subsequently appointed a captain), with the ranks filled out by late December (to serve one-year enlistments). As part of the formation of the Continental Navy, regulations were drawn up for the marines as well. While weapons were obtained after a bit of scrambling, uniforms proved to be a problem not resolved until later in 1776.

The first major action for the newly formed Continental Marines came in the raid on the Bahamas by an expedition of the Continental Navy led by Commodore Esek Hopkins. The rebels had received intelligence that the British were stockpiling large quantities of powder at New Providence Island in the archipelago. The Americans were desperately short of powder and thus proceeded with what was possibly the only planned major operation of the Continental Navy in the war.

Nicholas led the marine contingent (220 marines accompanied by 50 seamen), which captured Fort Montague on March 3–4, 1776. The capture of the fort, as well as Fort Nassau, was uncontested as the locals proved reluctant to fight. The occupation of Nassau itself was also uncontested. The Americans captured over 100 cannon and mortars, although not as much powder as hoped for as the bulk had been sneaked out by two British ships. The expedition reembarked on March 16.

Upon the return home of the expedition, the squadron engaged in the first unit action of the war, with the American frigates *Cabot* and *Alfred* squaring off against the British frigate *Glasgow*. The action was inconclusive as the *Glasgow* managed to escape; however, the marines suffered seven losses, including John Fitzpatrick, the first marine officer to be killed in the war.

The rest of the year the Continental Marines participated in a number of sea actions. One notable collision was the defense of the Delaware River (which gave access to Philadelphia) against two British frigates leading a small expedition to clear the river of obstructions. The rebels beat off the British and the action represented the first time that the Continental Marines had cooperated with state naval and marine forces.

It should be mentioned at this point that other American marine units had also been forming up, although largely on an informational basis, to meet critical needs. The makeshift fleet that Benedict Arnold raised to defend Lake Champlain in mid-1776 included soldiers detached from other units (supposedly on the basis of previous sea experience but usually not the case) and designated as marines. The only real differentiation from other regulars was their being equipped with brass blunderbusses.

Washington's New England navy also included marine detachments that were largely improvised by the ship captains themselves. While both fleets provided a training ground for a number of Continental Marines, the improvised formations were not successful, primarily because the army, not experienced naval personnel, controlled their use. Adding to this limitation was Washington's own dislike of marines, who he felt did not do anything that the regular soldier could not do.

As 1776 progressed, the Marine Committee of the fledgling country focused on the construction and manning of the 13 frigates authorized by Congress in the waning days of 1775 for the nascent Continental Navy. While the Marine Committee had hoped that at least some of the new frigates would be put to sea before the end of 1776, this did not come to pass, primarily because enlisting and retaining seamen and marines proved so troublesome. The incentives for gain in privateer service were too great.

The Continental Marines closed out 1776 by participating in the Trenton/Princeton cam-

paign. Four new companies had been formed up in mid-1776 to man the four new frigates that were being built in or near Philadelphia. Three of these were called out to help Washington, although not all of these actually went to Washington since some men were detached for service on board the frigate *Delaware*. The rest of the men (130 in all ranks) were put under the command of Colonel John Cadwalader and located on the west bank of the Delaware (Pennsylvania) as part of the thin rebel defenses. The ensuing actions marked the first time that Continental Marines had engaged in joint operations with the regular army. The marines served both as infantry and artillery support troops.

The marines did not take part in the initial attack on Trenton, since Cadwalader's troops were unable to cross the ice-choked Delaware with all their elements. Due to a failure in communications, Cadwalader's troops crossed the next day, even though Washington was already back on the west bank of the Delaware. When Washington heard the news, he decided to bring forward his already scheduled recrossing.

The next major event in this campaign came on January 2, 1777, when a retaliatory force of 8,000 British troops under Lord Cornwallis forced an engagement at Assunpink Bridge (also known as the Second Battle of Trenton). With Nicholas commanding, the marines supported Cadwalader's light troops in coming to the aid of Washington at a critical juncture, leading to a standoff.

On January 3, after slipping through the British lines at night using the old trick of false campfires, the marines (in three sections commanded by Nicholas, Captain William Shippen, and Captain William Brown, respectively) supported Washington's attack on a new lightly defended Princeton, which was captured after a brisk engagement. From Princeton, Major Nicholas's troops followed Washington into winter encampment at Morristown, New Jersey.

The year 1776, the first full year of marine operations, saw the number of marines grow from 234 men in January, to over 600 men by the end of 1776. The later months of 1776 also saw the selection of green and white as the basic colors for the marine uniform. However, by the end of the winter of 1776–1777, the marines suffered a very serious setback. In December 1775, the marines were established as an independent "corps." By the spring of 1777, the marines were incorporated into the regular army, no longer an independent corps, and Nicholas was relegated to being a high-ranking commander without assignment. Now marine companies were to be raised independently of the original battalion structure that had been instituted in 1775. Nicholas's men were incorporated into the army as artillerymen or returned to naval duty.

In 1777 marine shipboard activity was introduced into European waters. However, American naval success was limited, with French reluctance to allow American ships to linger in French ports a significant constraint. In this time period, more often than not, American ships lost the engagements that they were involved in.

By the beginning of 1778, the prospects brightened for American operations in European waters. The arrival in France in December 1777 of the American captain John Paul Jones (carrying news of the British defeat at Saratoga) changed the outlook of the French to one of alliance with the Americans. Jones was a firm supporter of using marines, whom he considered to be very valuable in the naval fighting role, and he brought a larger number of marines on board his sloop *Ranger*. The marines soon saw action in various ship engagements and in two raids on British soil (Whitehaven and St. Mary's Isle) in April, shortly followed by a brisk action against and defeat of the British sloop *Drake*.

Back in America, marines participated in a second expedition in late January 1778 against New Providence, again in search of naval stores, but this time using only one ship, the sloop *Providence*. Even though much smaller than the one mounted earlier, this expedition still proved to be quite successful. A total of 28 marines (including Captain John Trevett, who participated in the earlier expedition) were able to capture Fort Nassau and Fort Montagu. The forts were manned by only two guards, but 500 men could be quickly dispatched from nearby at the sound of a signal gun. Trevett managed to hoodwink the locals into thinking that his forces were actually ten times as large. The marines went on to capture the 16-gun ship *Mary* and to recapture four American ships. The expedition was able to return with very badly needed war stores.

However, the months of March, April, and May 1778 proved to be calamitous for the Continental Navy and marines in American waters, with more misfortunes being handed the Americans than in any similar period during the entire war. The marines saw a significant shrinkage in their ranks as the result of the heavy losses of American warships.

While sea operations in 1778 did not often end well for the marines, a land expedition of marines led by James Willing (bestowed rank of navy captain) that raided by river from Pittsburgh down to New Orleans gave the marines something to cheer about. The expedition, manned by about 34 marines who had volunteered to get away from the boredom of garrison duty (apparently most were actually from Continental Army ranks), sailed from Pittsburgh on the night of January 10, 1778, on board the armed boat *Rattletrap*. The expedition proceeded down the Ohio River and then the Mississippi River, instilling fear in Loyalist hearts as their property was plundered, especially south of Natchez on the Mississippi. From this point a ruthless campaign was waged against British planters, including the destruction of their crops, homes, and livestock. When the British sent the sloop *Rebecca* up the river to counter the expedition, an advance party of marines seized the vessel. This resulted in the loss of British control of the waterway for some time. With local assistance, a British brig loaded with lumber was also captured.

The arrival of Willing in New Orleans in late February resulted in an anomalous situation since the Spanish governor Bernardo de Galvez allowed both the British and Americans freedom of the city. However, considerable friction arose when the Spanish allowed the Americans to sell their plunder here. Many British planters had taken refuge with the Spanish, and they fiercely resented the welcome extended to the Americans. British protests resulted in de Galvez requiring that certain of the booty be returned.

By this time the British began to challenge American control of the river, and the net result was that Willing's communications up the river with Fort Pitt were cut off, or intermittent at best. Also, by now Willing had worn out his welcome due to his prickly personality and all concerned wanted him on his way. Much of the marine contingent was granted permission by the Spanish to join George Rogers Clark at Kaskaskia (present-day Illinois), whom they reached by June 1779. Willing himself went by sea to Philadelphia but had the misfortune to be captured before he arrived.

Meanwhile, one of Willing's officers, Lieutenant Daniel Longstreet, remained behind and ended up commanding a Marine detachment on board the armed sloop *West Florida* (recently captured from the British). This sloop took part in Spanish operations (now an ally) against the British in Mobile and Pensacola in the latter part of 1779.

In 1779 the most significant event that involved the marines was the expedition to seize a British fort established at Penobscot in Maine. By this time American privateer action had become particularly nettlesome in the area between New York and Nova Scotia, and the British wanted a protected anchorage from which to mount aggressive sea patrols. The British established their base in June 1779, and the Americans quickly responded to this obvious threat, with Massachusetts being particularly instrumental in the organization of the biggest American naval expedition of the war.

The American fleet included seven Continental Navy and state warships and some 22 transports carrying about 2,500 men, although estimates vary considerably as to the quantity of men. No figure is available as to the total number of marines involved, but apparently both state and Continental Marines were involved, with one source putting the total of Continental Marines at about 300, apparently commanded by Captain John Welsh of the frigate *Warren*.

The outcome of the expedition was an almost total fiasco for the Americans, although the marines performed admirably. The campaign, which stretched from late July to August 1779, started out well, with the marines executing two successful assault landings. The first landing, on July 26, involved the capture of Banks Island, a move not contested by the small force of Royal Marines present on the island, who had retired just before the landing.

The second landing was much more difficult, coming as it did at the foot of a steep bluff. The right wing, which consisted of 227 marines under Captain Welsh, encountered the heaviest opposition. The heights were gained after stiff fighting, with Welsh killed almost immediately, and a total of 33 marines killed or wounded before the British withdrew to their fort. Sad to say, the American forces squandered their hard-earned gains by not immediately following up

with an assault on the fort. The commanding British general stood ready to lower the flag in the face of numerically superior forces, but the Americans, lacking a forceful commander, fell into confusion as to how to proceed, settling finally into a defensive position.

The subsequent arrival of a British relief fleet panicked the disorganized American forces. The American fleet was captured or fired by the Americans themselves, and the American troops were forced to return to Boston by land, marching back some 180 miles. The failure of the Penobscot expedition raised great controversy, and courts-martial were held for many of the top commanders, although the marines themselves did not come under fire because of their admirable conduct. However, it should be noted that the marines did not attempt another sizable amphibious landing until the Mexican War in the 1840s.

Back in European waters, John Paul Jones was finding it very difficult to recruit the right officers to command the motley collection of marines on board his flagship, the *Bonhomme Richard*. Jones ended up going to the Infanterie Irlandaise, Regiment de Walsh-Serrant, of the French Army. Jones recruited three lieutenants who subsequently were issued Continental Marine commissions. Appointing a captain for his marines proved to be even more problematical. An American, Alexander Dick, withdrew from the appointment. Thus, Jones ended up selecting two French lieutenant colonels who, however, were not granted Continental Marine commissions. Jones's officers, as volunteers approved by him, were personally loyal to Jones, but the marine rank and file were another matter, and fights between marines and the other crew members of Jones's ships were to cause significant problems.

In mid-August Jones's small squadron sailed from France to cruise the British coast, going west to east by way of Scotland. A month later on September 24, 1779, came the famous Battle of Flamborough Head in Yorkshire, where the *Bonhomme Richard* dueled with the HMS *Serapis*, a new 50-gun frigate that both outmanned and outgunned the American ship. The marines on board the *Bonhomme Richard* played a very significant part in the battle by laying down a withering fire on the *Serapis* from the tops and rigging of the American ship. Jones was aware that his only advantage against the superior British frigate was the marksmanship of his marines and seamen, who were able to clear the tops of the *Serapis*, fire with impunity on the decks (clearing the weather deck), and even firing down the hatches. The capper was a grenade thrown from the tops by an American seaman that went down a hatch of the *Serapis* and set off a big explosion. Finally, the *Serapis* surrendered.

The next significant battle to involve the marines came during May 1780 in the unsuccessful American defense of Charleston, South Carolina. Here, marines from the squadron commanded by Commodore Abraham Whipple assisted the local forces under General Benjamin Lincoln. One of the first duties was the blowing up of navigational aids such as the beacon and lighthouse, as well as Fort Johnson. When Whipple's squadron was forced to retreat up the Cooper River, the marines on board the ships were landed to bolster shore artillery units. It was all for naught, however, as superior British strength forced an American surrender on May 10.

With the surrender of Charleston, only five marine detachments remained afloat on board four frigates and a sloop-of-war. By April 1781, one of the frigates, the *Confederacy*, and the sloop-of-war, the *Saratoga*, had been lost to the Continental Navy. Later that year, the frigate *Trumbull* was also captured. Thus, by the end of 1781 the marines were down to their lowest force level of the war, with the detachments on board the frigates *Alliance* and *Deane* being the sole survivors. Over the previous two years 200 marines had been lost (on board seven warships).

The last real duty that Nicholas performed as a Continental Marine officer came in October and November 1781. He commanded a special detachment that escorted more than 2.5 million crowns (money loaned by France) from Boston to Philadelphia. While bills of exchange had been purchased, over a million crowns in hard money remained to be transported, requiring special containers. The convoy arrived safely in Philadelphia on November 6.

The remaining months of the war saw some action for what was left of the marines, namely those on board the two frigates. The *Alliance*, commanded by John Barry, was the more active of the two and participated in a number of brisk ship-to-ship actions all the way into March 1783, just before word was received of the final peace settlement. Marines on board the *Hague* (for-

merly the *Deane*) assisted in the capture of the British ship *Baille* in the West Indies in January, 1783.

The discharge of marine lieutenant Thomas Elwood in September 1783 marked the end of the Continental Marines, although June 3, 1785, is also used as a milestone, since this was when the last Continental Navy ship, the *Alliance*, was authorized by Congress to be sold.

While the focus has been on the Continental Marines, significant numbers of marines served with the various state navies and privateers. All of the 13 original states (except apparently Delaware and New Jersey) fielded one or more armed vessels. The main mission for these state forces was the defense of seaports, coastlines, and trade routes. For these purposes small craft were the norm. Offensive operations were secondary in importance and mostly consisted of the destruction of British commerce. Thus state marine formations were local forces, with local concerns in mind, and their military role tended to reflect local imperatives.

In regards to privateers, all important private vessels carried marines, although they were often referred to by other terms such as "gentlemen sailors." It is thought that the numbers of marines that served aboard privateers numbered in the thousands, but little information is available on them. Privateer service siphoned off some of the best men, leaving the regular navy with a continual inability to recruit as fully as it wanted to. The pay in the privateer service, as well as the chance for prizes, proved to be a stronger inducement than patriotism in all too many cases, even drawing men who had already signed up for Continental service. Interestingly, marines who served aboard privateers subsequently received pensions from the U.S. Government.

In summing up the role of the Continental Marines during the American Revolution, it must be admitted that their numbers were not large, with about 131 officers having held Continental Marine commissions, and the number of noncommissioned officers and enlisted men probably never exceeding 2,000. However, the marines did much to enforce discipline on often undisciplined crews, as well as providing much needed support in ship-to-ship actions. While amphibious operations, the hallmark of the present-day Marine Corps, were few, the marines displayed a mettle that would be characteristic of their descendants. The role of the state and privateer marines is more difficult to determine because it is less documented, but their contribution cannot be denied.

Tom Baranauskas

REFERENCES

Louis S. Fagan, "Samuel Nicholas, First Office of American Marines," *Marine Corps Gazette*, 18 (1933):5–15; Major Edwin N. McClellan, *History of the United States Marine Corps* (1925–31) unpublished but available at the MC Headquarters and some libraries; Charles R. Smith, *Marines in the Revolution* (1975).

Marion, Francis ("the Swamp Fox") (1732–1795)

South Carolina partisan. In the wake of the stunning disasters suffered by regular Patriot forces in the Southern Department during the Revolutionary War, it was Francis Marion and like-minded Patriot guerrilla leaders who would keep alive the cause of independence until final victory.

After the Battle of Monmouth, New Jersey (June 28, 1778), the war in the northern states remained stalemated until the end of hostilities. In that year, General Sir Henry Clinton, commander of British forces in North America, turned southward, attracted by reports by royal governors of large numbers of Loyalists, yearning to turn on their Whig tormentors.

Savannah fell to the British in December 1778, and Charleston in May 1780. A force of Virginia Continentals was soon after massacred at the Waxhaws on the North Carolina border, and on August 16 the Battle of Camden destroyed the last regular American army of any size in the Southern Department.

But this string of Patriot disasters threw up a military genius who would mercilessly harass Crown forces, and play a major role in driving the British from the Carolinas, into Virginia and surrender at Yorktown.

Of Huguenot descent, Francis Marion had already been blooded in two Cherokee wars (1759 and 1761), he had played a notable role in the repulse of the British before Charleston in 1776, and he was involved in a desperate but unsuccessful assault on British-occupied Savannah in 1779. Marion, lean and wiry, had developed into a superb horseman, but in some ways he was an unlikely frontier guerrilla leader. In the hard-drinking backcountry he stood out as a teetotaler (who supposedly had injured himself in jumping from a second-story window to escape a regimental drinking party). And in a land of frequent barbecues and pig pickings, Marion ate sparingly. In fact, his abstemious ways probably kept him fit for grueling campaigns in the Carolina swamps and backwoods. Although a cavalryman, Marion rarely engaged in the saberplay favored by that arm, and, in fact, on a rare occasion when he tried to draw his short infantryman's sword, he found it rusted into the scabbard. Finally, Marion was somewhat deformed in his knees and ankles, and was well into middle age when dispatched by exiled South Carolina governor John Rutledge to take command and organize resistance to the Crown in the Santee–Pee Dee districts of South Carolina. But Marion's troops quickly overcame their initial reserve toward their commander, inspired by his obvious courage, innate sense of leadership, knowledge of the countryside, and moral character.

From the start, Marion went on the offensive, ambushing and punishing small enemy detachments. Soon the Loyalist elements in the Pee Dee district were cowed and quiescent.

In December 1780 Washington appointed Major General Nathanael Greene, commander of the Southern Department, replacing the discredited General Horatio Gates. Lacking much of a regular force, Greene realized the value of guerrilla warfare, and dispatched Lieutenant Colonel Henry ("Light-Horse Harry") Lee with his legion of Continental cavalry to fight alongside Marion. The backwoods Marion and the aristocratic Lee campaigned together effectively, the strengths of each supplemented the weaknesses of the other.

Skirmishing continued through 1781, with Marion soon earning the grudging admiration of his opponents and the name that stuck to him until death, "the Swamp Fox." British colonel Banastre Tarleton confessed in disgust that the "devil himself could not catch" Marion. And it was at this time that Marion's exploits began to enter the realms of myth and folklore; an unauthenticated but persistent legend has a British officer under flag of truce at Marion's headquarters so taken with the humble fare of campfire-roasted sweet potatoes, even for the officers, that he vows upon returning to his base never more to fight against a people so dedicated.

Other British offices were not so gallant. Major John Wemyss, acting on direct orders from General Lord Cornwallis, British southern commander, plundered plantations, and hanged outright anyone deemed to have broken his parole. Wemyss also made a point of burning Presbyterian churches, declaring them "sedition shops." But Wemyss's terroristic campaign had little effect, save to drive into the arms of the rebels many who had previously given their paroles or who had attempted to stay out of the war. Wemyss's actions were not isolated atrocities; Loyalist major Thomas Browne had 13 Patriot prisoners hanged in his presence, and turned others over to the Cherokees to be tortured to death. (Ironically, both Wemyss and Browne were captured, and both given honorable treatment, at some hazard from outraged Patriots who had suffered much at their hands.) Marion, by contrast, often intervened to prevent the hanging of captured Tory ruffians. In fact, he was able to work out a cease-fire with one prominent Loyalist leader and his troops well before Yorktown.

The forces of the Crown were unable to keep the Carolina backcountry in subjection. In the classic pattern of guerrilla warfare, regular forces controlled the towns and could patrol the countryside by day; at night the country was guerrilla territory, and distinctly inhospitable to Loyalists.

Marion was well aware of his troops' need to return home from time to time to tend their crops and thus preserve the economy as well as their livelihoods. He also forbade pillage, in contrast to "Sumter's Law" by which his fellow partisan leader, Thomas Sumter, attracted and compensated his troops.

It was the small-unit, unconventional, savage backcountry engagements of southern partisans such as Francis Marion, who lost about as many engagements as they won, that frustrated British strategy for the Carolinas and Georgia, and led to Yorktown.

Oddly, Marion was beaten by Crown forces in his last three engagements, fought after Yorktown. But in each case he extricated his men and retired in good order. On December 14, 1782, the last British soldier left Charleston, and Marion, his militia disbanded, headed home.

But that home, Pond Bluff, lay in ruins, plundered promiscuously by Patriot, Tory, and British alike, a microcosm of what had happened throughout the Southern Department. Marion somehow rebuilt his plantation, and served as South Carolina state senator, again revealing his magnanimity by sponsoring bills easing former Tories back into community life, and objecting to any exemption from the legal consequences of "Sumter's Law."

Marion's financial straits were eased when the 54-year-old bachelor married a prosperous spinster, Mary Esther Videau, from his own parish, but no heir emerged from this late union.

Marion, a mild Federalist in the postwar years, seems to have been devoid of political ambition, devoting his political activities to education, militia affairs, and serving as a delegate to South Carolina's new constitutional convention in 1790.

Francis Marion, perhaps the greatest guerrilla leader in American military history, died at Pond Bluff on February 27, 1795, but is buried at his brother's plantation, Belle Isle, South Carolina.

Stanley Sandler

REFERENCES

Robert T. Bass, *Swamp Fox: The Life and Campaigns of General Francis Marion* (1959); James William Dolbein, *A Sketch of the Life of Brigadier General Francis Marion and a History of His Brigade* (1821); Brigadier General Horry and M.L. ("Parson") Weems, *The Life of General Francis Marion. Philadelphia, 1847.* An exercise in hagiography by one of Marion's chief lieutenants, and the man responsible for "George Washington and the Cherry tree"; Henry Lee, *The Campaigns of 1781, in the Carolinas: With Remarks Historical and Critical on Johnson's Life of Greene with Appendix of Original Documents Relating to the History of the Revolution,* rpr. (1875); Terry W. Lipscomb, "South Carolina Battles," *Names in South Carolina,* pts. i–vii (1973–1979); David Ramsey, *The History of the Revolution of [sic] South Carolina,* 2 vols. (1785); Hugh F. Rankin, *Francis Marion: The Swamp Fox* (1973); William Gilmore Simms, *The Life of Francis Marion* (1854); Russell F. Weigley, *The Partisan War. The South Carolina Campaigns of 1780–1782,* South Carolina Tricentennial Booklet #3 (1970).

Marksmanship

The ability of the soldier to hit his opponent under combat conditions, using the small arms with which he has been issued, has never borne any relationship to the tested accuracy of the weapon itself, and seldom reflects the degree of training given the soldier with these arms. The psychological factors activated by a combat situation, where the target is able to inflict death or permanent injury, are the chief reason for this inability of the line infantryman to achieve the results that the inherent design of the weapon and the degree of his training should make possible. Beginning with this basic situation, any lack of precision in the design and construction of the weapon, or weaknesses in the training program, or the absence or infrequency of training, subtract further from the perceived theoretical potential of combat marksmanship. The initial evidence obtained through target practice or regulated trials, that a given weapon, at a certain distance, can strike a target of a certain size with consistency and a demonstrated level of precision, has little to do with the results when this same evidence is applied in combat conditions where the target is responding in kind, or may do so. The historical evidence shows that soldiers were frequently unaware that they had fired their weapons, even though in training the weapon might have a reputation for noise and recoil. The noise of artillery, screams of the wounded and dying, surrounding and opposing musketry created by hundreds or thousands of men, the need to listen for commands, and to maintain one's place in the line, and often the inability to see the target because of clouds of dirty white smoke, created conditions that generally reduced all but instinctive actions to a bare minimum. Because these conditions were recognized by the planners of infantry training in all armies, great emphasis was given to training the men to react without thinking to the various commands for moving them about the battlefield and for shooting at the enemy. If this discipline was inadequately instilled, cohesion in the face of the enemy was almost invariably lost. It was recognized that about three ordered volleys could be fired before control was lost and firing became general and individual. Accuracy declined progressively from about the fifth shot as fouling in the barrels built up and loading became more difficult. Since priming was done first, varying amounts of powder finally entered the barrel as the main charge, which altered velocity and point of impact.

In the purely technical sense, under calm ideal conditions a clean cool musket properly and carefully loaded will strike the figure of a man consistently at 100 yards; a dirty hot musket loaded and fired hurriedly but still under otherwise ideal conditions will do so about seven out of ten shots. Rifles, using a patched ball, carefully loaded and fired from some form of rest under calm ideal conditions, will reliably strike the figure of a man at 200 yards. These results would be obtained by a man well acquainted with the use of the arms in question, and represent an average optimum achievement. Highly skilled men could probably improve slightly on these results, but combat conditions would subtract from them significantly.

British Army

The peacetime allowance for ball practice per man was four rounds per year, the idea being to accustom the new recruit to the recoil of a full service charge, but not to frighten him too much with the recoil. This allowance was service-wide, and from this point it was, as with so much else in the British army, up to regimental officers. The majority of line regiments contented themselves with blank firing volley and platoon-fire training. The Guards' regiments received a semi-annual allowance of powder and ball for firing at butts in Hyde Park, and they normally overdrew this allowance and got more. But the surviving evidence (there are no organized regimental records for the eighteenth century) indicates that "firing at marks" was common in line regiments at times, particularly with regiments in the field, and especially during the Seven Years' War and the American Revolution.

The older habit of holding the head straight and high and taking no deliberate aim was done away with, at least in theory (and the evidence indicates also in practice) by the instructions promulgated by order of the Duke of Cumberland in 1754–1755, which include "the whole [body of men] taking good aim by leaning their Heads to the right and looking along the Barrels." Marksmanship training in the 8th Foot in 1759 gives an example of what could be done, and what was considered good shooting:

> I [the commanding officer] have fired them man by man the whole winter, and only a few rounds by Platoons to accustom them to fire over and be fired over. A Company of about sixty will in five rounds hit a target of about 2¹/₂ feet in diameter at 300 yards eight or ten times and throw forty or fifty ball close enough about it to do execution if a Platoon was before them . . . at two hundred and one hundred and fifty yards they would thin an enemy considerably.

Light infantry, which became a formal part of every line regiment from 1771, was trained to load and fire individually at individual targets, and as might be expected from troops acting in open order and able to find cover when necessary, their accuracy was considerably better than that of the volley-firing line infantrymen, simply because the psychological factors were somewhat watered down.

American Army

Demographic studies have clearly shown that the rebel army was composed largely of urban-based men and that the militias had a somewhat higher proportion from the rural areas. The vast majority of these men had no more experience of firearms than the average British recruit, and the idea that the rebel forces were composed of people bred to the use of arms is clearly untrue. Even familiarity with the use of a fowling piece or pocket pistol does not contribute vitally toward the military use of a musket and bayonet: loading with cartridge by a fixed system, sound, and recoil were very different. Veterans of the "old French war" would have gained this experience, but these men were a very small percentage of the rebel armies. Until at least 1779 there was a great shortage of powder and lead, and target practice must therefore have been at a minimum. The frontiersmen who made up the several rifle corps and some of the militias, especially in the South, were certainly familiar with their arms, but the same psychological factors discussed above applied to them when in combat conditions, even those men who had previously experienced actual combat when fighting Indians, which was quite a different type of combat than confronting clearly visible massed ranks of targets shooting back.

German, French, and Spanish Troops

Marksmanship in these armies was similar to that in the British army, but no information has come to light to indicate that individual aim was encouraged, or that "firing at marks" was much practiced when regiments were in the field. The emphasis was on rapid volley firing, although in the French army of the *ancien regime* this was not of a high standard.

Our ability to accurately assess marksmanship during the war is critically affected by the absence of sufficient reliable casualty figures and

medical evidence on the means by which wounds were inflicted (whether by artillery, small arms, bayonet, or sword).

De Witt Bailey

REFERENCES

John A. Holdings, *"Fit for Service": The Training of the British Army, 1715–1795* (1981).

Martha's Vineyard

See Grey, Charles, 1st Earl Grey; Massachusetts in the American Revolution.

Martinique, West Indies, Battles of (April–May 1780)

The three battles fought off Martinique in April 1780 were strategically indecisive but were pregnant with changes in naval combat that would see their reward for the British at the Battle of the Isles de Saintes in 1782. It was the first of three actions until May 19 that would see the 62-year-old Admiral George Brydges Rodney attempt to fall with his entire force on the rear line of the French line. These actions were indecisive largely due to the era's poor signaling, a rigid and inflexible tactical system, and uninspiring leadership. It was important, though, to see tactical innovation beginning to come to the forefront.

The 67-year-old Vice Admiral Luc Urbain Guichen arrived first at Martinique in the West Indies with his concentrated fleet, which numbered 22 ships of the line. His orders were to attack the British-held island and to destroy what he could not take, except in the case of St. Lucia, which he was to keep if captured. Guichen was also to "keep the seas as much as the English forces maintained in the Windward Islands might allow him, without too much compromising his own forces."

Rodney cruised off of Martinique, but Guichen declined battle. Therefore, Rodney left a squadron of five coppered ships of the line and two frigates off the port while he retired to Gros Islet Bay, St. Lucia. On April 13, Guichen headed to sea with 22 ships of the line and 3,000 troops, trying to attack Barbados. But Rodney chased him with 20 ships of the line and one 50-gun ship to fight the First Battle of Martinique on April 17. Below is a listing of the ships involved on either side, given in order from van to rear that they fought in:

French Fleet	Guns	
Destin	74	Van
Vengeur	64	
Saint-Michel	60	
Pluton	74	
Triomphant	80	
Souverain	74	
Solitaire	64	
Citoyen	74	Center
Caton	64	
Victoire	74	
Fendant	74	
Couronne	80	Flagship
Palmier	74	
Indien	64	
Actionnaire	64	
Intrepide	74	Rear
Triton	64	
Magnifique	74	
Robuste	74	
Sphinx	64	
Artesien	64	
Hercule	74	
	1,546	

Five frigates and one corvette were also present. The *Dauphin Royal* (70 guns) joined after April 17.

British Fleet	Guns	
Stirling Castle	64	Van
Ajax	74	
Elizabeth	74	
Princess Royal	90	
Albion	74	
Terrible	74	
Trident	64	
Grafton	74	Center
Yarmouth	64	
Cornwall	74	
Sandwich	90	Flagship
Suffolk	74	
Boyne	70	
Vigilant	64	
Vengeance	74	Rear
Medway	60	
Montagu	74	
Conqueror	74	
Intrepid	64	
Magnificent	74	
Centurion	50	(to assist rear if needed)
	1,494	

Five frigates were also present. The Triumph (74 guns) joined before the action of St. Lucia Channel.

Rodney had informed his captains over the previous two days that he intended to have his entire fleet fall upon the rear and center of the French line, thus bringing his 20 ships of the line against 15 or 16 of the French line. He had the windward on April 17 as he approached the French line. Guichen ordered his line to war just as Rodney began to fall upon the French line. By wearing, or having his entire line turn 180 degrees about, Guichen had made his rear the van and thwarted Rodney's attempt by sheer accident, for Guichen, at the time he ordered his fleet to war, did not realize what Rodney was attempting. Rodney then tried to signal his intention to fall upon the new French rear. Unfortunately, the lead ship, the *Stirling Castle*, misunderstood Rodney's orders and, instead, sailed down against his opposite number, with all other ships following this lead. As a result, each ship in line fought against its opposite number. The result was a typical line-to-line action that was tactically indecisive.

Each flagship roughly handled enemy ships opposite them, and eventually the French flagship *Couronne* directly engaged the *Sandwich*, causing much damage to her. Rodney was forced to shift his flag to the *Montagu*. The *Sandwich* might have been lost except for the French doctrine of keeping a line intact; thus the French would not break their line to capture her. Losses were 222 French dead and 537 wounded, while the British had 120 dead and 354 wounded. The *Sandwich* alone fired 3,288 rounds off, or an average of 73 for each gun on the engaged broadside. The British suffered more damage to their spars and sails, while the French had more hits to their hulls. This was quite typical as the French tended to fire high to disable the enemies' movement, while the British fired low. Additionally, this was a quite common occurrence due to the windward fleet having its broadside facing the enemy being pushed downward, while the leeward fleet would have that broadside pushed up from the wind.

Rodney was unhappy with the conduct of his two subordinate commanders, Rear Admiral Hyde "Vinegar" Parker and Rear Admiral Joshua Rowley, both of whom were to leave his command shortly thereafter. Guichen lost his son in this action, which hurt him.

Guichen followed up the action, and without running the risk of battle, with an attempt against St. Lucia. Rodney, with 21 ships of the line fac-

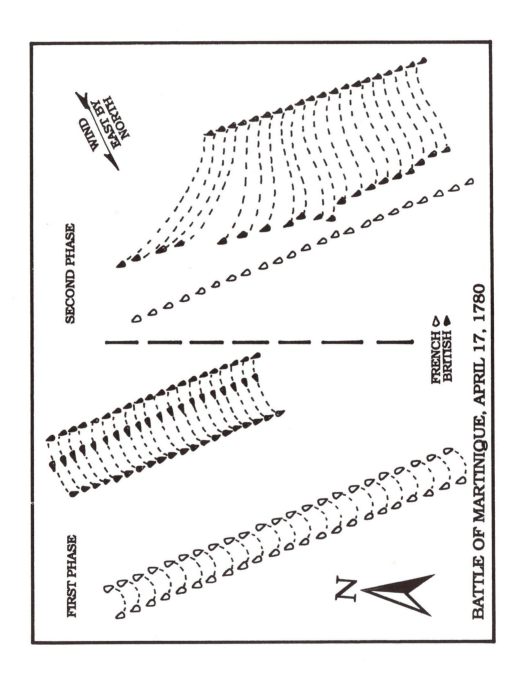

SECOND PHASE

FIRST PHASE

WIND EAST BY NORTH

FRENCH ◊
BRITISH ●

BATTLE OF MARTINIQUE, APRIL 17, 1780

ing Guichen's 23 ships of the line, kept him from success and, after some smart maneuvering, caught Guichen on May 15, 1780. The Battle of St. Lucia Channel followed and was equally indecisive.

The action was prefixed with maneuvering for five days with Rodney moving onto the frigate *Venusso* in order to issue orders more clearly. This was a tactic developed by Rear Admiral Samuel Hood earlier in the war, but it was not entirely successful, though even the French tried it later in the war. The French had the windward most of the time and in the afternoons would bear down on the British, but no action ensued. On May 15, action was desultory, in part due to the changing wind giving first the British and then the French the wind gauge. The result was that each fleet passed each other in opposite directions and at such an angle that the British van and the French rear were the only parts of the fleets that engaged in any sort of heated combat. Casualties were 26 killed for the French and 52 wounded, while the British lost 21 killed and 100 wounded. The British had one ship, the *Albion*, badly damaged.

These fleets cruised about until May 19, when yet a third action was fought. In this three-hour action, the Second Battle of Martinique, the British van engaged the French rear in a distant battle. The British were roughly handled and eventually the *Cornwall* sank from damage. The British lost 47 killed and 113 wounded, while the French suffered about 45 killed and 95 wounded.

Both fleets were now in need of repair and replenishment and so retired to their respective home ports in Martinique and Barbados. The result of these three battles was indecisive for either side, and the French never captured Barbados in the course of the war. *See also:* Copper Sheathing

Jack Greene

REFERENCES

William Laird Clowes, et al., *The Royal Navy: A History,* 7 vols. (1898), 3; John Creswell, *British Admirals of the Eighteenth Century, Tactics in Battle* (1972); W.M. James, *The British Navy in Adversity* (1933); Charles Lee Lewis, *Admiral De Grasse and American Independence* (1945); Piers Mackesy, *The War for America 1775–1783* (1965).

Massachusetts in the American Revolution

The American Revolution is the most important event in the long history of the commonwealth of Massachusetts. The period 1775–1783 saw the onset of political crisis, the outbreak of war, effects of the war upon the circumstances of government and society, and then the return to peace. Since Massachusetts was the center and focus of the events that led to the American Revolution, the early battles of the War of Revolution were fought there. Finally, during the Revolutionary years Massachusetts laid the groundwork for its important social and economic development in the nineteenth century.

No doubt the deepest causes of all these events in Massachusetts are to be sought in the Puritan mentality and early history of the commonwealth. English Puritan immigrants planted Massachusetts, and their stormy temper and their distrust of English and European institutions insured political novelty in the early years of colonization. Massachusetts evolved then a habit of political independence and later a tradition of personal liberty. The Puritan tradition was always deeply radical from the English and, in many ways, a further stage of Puritanism. We shall briefly return to Puritanism at the end of this article. It must be a first and a last concern in any history of the Revolution in Massachusetts.

The more immediate or proximate cause of the American Revolution was political crisis. Were Whigs and Tories in Massachusetts and in Britain alike bewildered by events far beyond the scope of original expectation? Or was there premeditated political determination on any side? Each accused the other of premeditated determination, and each exculpated itself in this regard.

Elbridge Gerry, long prominent in Massachusetts politics and an early advocate of independence during the Revolutionary period, said that clearly there could have been no premeditation among his colleagues in the provincial congress, for the British had by their actions denied to Massachusetts the advantages of general government and therefore had made impossible the very concerted action of which they complained. It is a good point, but the king's circle saw things differently.

For his part, King George III told Parliament at its convocation in 1775 that there existed "a premeditated and general revolt" in Massachusetts. The king believed that many loyal subjects remained nonetheless, and that he had a duty to protect them.

When he gave that speech to parliament, the king had months before he signed the Intolerable Acts that closed the port of Boston and suspended the Massachusetts province charter, dated from 1691. Regular British troops occupied Boston. General Thomas Gage (1721–1787), commander of the Boston garrison, had been made governor of the province in place of Thomas Hutchinson (1711–1780).

King George III and his servants in London decided upon these measures because they felt deeply challenged by the failure of the province government to maintain order. A chief grievance was the loss of East India Company tea thrown into the harbor on December 10, 1773, during the famous Boston Tea Party.

There was some English legal precedent for the severe measures upon which the King and his servants resolved, and the measures were also popular outside Parliament, and perhaps even proper from a narrow English point of view. But the king's policies were unusual if not illegal in America, and they were to the greatest degree foolish in terms of Massachusetts politics. The king, after all, was, or became mad.

Many Whigs thought that the king had acted not like a madman but like a tyrant. The denounced British occupation of Boston and disdained British pretensions to administer the province. Whigs in Massachusetts resolved to resist, and not a few Whigs in England shared their dismay and applauded their resolve. War broke out, and the Massachusetts militia formed into an army. Troops from other New England colonies joined them, and then officers were appointed by the Continental Congress called into being by the crisis. British troops were expelled from Boston, allegiance to the Crown was abandoned, and then the province constructed a form of popular government that somewhat resembled the former charter of 1629.

Could either Whig or Tory have foreseen the course of events? American Whigs accused the king and his ministers of a design or plot long matured and now thwarted only just in time. Thomas Jefferson in the Declaration of Independence the next year spoke of a long train of abuses and usurpations by which the king had designed to place Americans under an "absolute tyranny."

Massachusetts Loyalists ridiculed Jefferson's charges. Thomas Hutchinson, the former governor, and Peter Oliver (1713–1791), who had been a distinguished jurist in the province before the Revolution, separately wrote from London to refute Jefferson. Neither believed in a royal design to reduce Massachusetts under absolute government, and both men accused the ministry in London instead of indifference and neglect of American affairs. Both Hutchinson and Oliver said that earlier notice should have been taken in London of disorder in Massachusetts government.

Hutchinson and Oliver may be taken to summarize the Loyalist apologia. The London authorities had shown restraint, but also inattention and shifting or divided counsels. A timely show of firm resolve might have averted much harm. It came too late. There had been no premeditation, still, on the British side, Hutchinson and Oliver agreed. There had been a duty to hold to the law, and that duty had been tardily done.

Hutchinson and Oliver summarized also the list of Loyalist grievances against the Revolution and its Whig proponents. Hutchinson professed himself numbed by the violence of the hatred that had erupted toward himself and toward the British government. There had, he felt, been a long train of abuses and usurpations, but they had been on the American side. Peter Oliver agreed, and in his *Origins and Progress of the American Rebellion* he laid out a list of the particular injuries just as John Foxe had done in his famous *Book of Martyrs* (1563), an account of the sufferings of Protestants in Queen Mary's reign of 1553–1558. The modern reader should balance this list of complaints against the list of wrongs in the Declaration of Independence.

Loyalists differed on the causes of the disorder. Oliver dated it from the time James Otis (1725–1783) was refused a place on the judicial bench of the province. Perhaps Oliver mistook the American Revolution for the Wilkesite cause in England: the malcontent John Wilkes was much as Oliver makes James Otis out to be. Thwarted ambition, Oliver believed, made Otis so bitter that he became convinced sincerely that his personal rejection was due to a systematic fault in the government of the province. His bitterness in turn inflamed other malcontents and raised against innocent servants of the Crown a party of enemies whose personal ambition was clothed in the dress of popular liberty.

Oliver thought that a quarrelsome temper proceeded from the early religious history of Massachusetts. Hutchinson made the same point in his *History of Massachusetts Bay*. Hutchinson's *History* is well worthy of attention, as is his pamphlet, *Strictures upon the Declaration of the Congress at Philadelphia*, in which he analyzed Jefferson's arguments in the Declaration of Independence. A small group of men, Hutchinson said, had inflamed the colony against the Parliament. In consequence people clung to foolish rights that were of doubtful legality. The people were too much attached, Hutchinson believed, to the charter of 1629, and they had never reconciled themselves to King William and Queen Mary's charter of 1691 by which the province had been governed in his day, and well governed. Learned in the law, he thought there was insufficient understanding in the province of the powers and the duties of offices of the Crown under that new charter. The present king and his ministers had been scrupulous in their adherence to that charter and to the common law, so Hutchinson felt, as he had been himself.

Hutchinson's point about the law is most important. The charter of 1629 gave to Massachusetts a degree of self-government that was lacking in the so-called provincial period from 1691 onward. Massachusetts claimed in 1775 rights and liberties that had long been extinguished in English law.

Let us turn to a narrative of events. In 1774, Gage, who succeeded Hutchinson as governor that year, had called into session the Provincial Legislature or Assembly. In Massachusetts this body was called the General Court, a remembrance that Parliament itself is a high court. Gage had become governor, said Hutchinson, because it was thought in London convenient that the commander of the army in Boston also should be governor of the province.

Gage did not make things convenient for the General Court when he summoned them to meet at Salem, then remote from Boston. Much was made of this: the Declaration of Independence mentioned it. Gage could not at Salem or elsewhere obtain from the General Court such measures as he wished. Upon their disagreement with the governor, the lower house of the General

Court constituted themselves a Provincial Congress and named John Hancock (1737–1793) to head a committee of public safety. Rich, and perhaps a little vain, Hancock had suffered much, for the closure of the Boston port greatly injured Hancock's fortunes in trade. He was to become governor after the Revolution. The Committee of Public Safety was in fact a quasi-Revolutionary body, and their activities harked back to American resistance to the hated Stamp Act. Some violence had attended those efforts, and violence now was nearly inevitable should Gage make an effort to control the colony with his troops.

The constitutional and legal situation in Massachusetts was by 1774 ambiguous. As Thomas Hutchinson pointed out in his pamphlet, every step taken by the authorities in London followed the letter of the English law. The appointment of Gage as governor and even his subsequent declaration of martial law were legal. The question in Massachusetts still was whether law in the province followed the dictates of the provincial congress or whether law flowed from acts of the Parliament at St. Stephen's, Westminster.

British authority in Massachusetts came to the point of crisis in early 1775. While Hancock and his colleagues prepared their resistance, Whigs in England attempted to persuade the king and his ministers of the need for reconciliation. The ailing elder William Pitt, perhaps the most distinguished British statesman of that age, brought in Parliament a bill to effect a compromise in Massachusetts. Majority opinion in Parliament had shifted to the side of the king. Pitt's plan was defeated, and Lord North, acting in the king's behalf, brought forth another proposal by which Parliament would forbear to tax any American colony that through its own legislature voted money for the maintenance of the king's troops and of his civil officers. Few Massachusetts Whigs would countenance such a plan, and the opportunity for compromise was lost, and with it British rule in America.

A Second Provincial Congress met at Cambridge in February 1775. Hancock and Joseph Warren were the leaders. They anticipated the need to prepare the province for war with Britain, and they undertook for that purpose to obtain the support of other colonies. All New England took alarm at events in Massachusetts.

So did many in old England. The Duke of Grafton (1735–1811), at whose orders troops had been stationed in Boston at the time of the Boston Massacre, now opposed the king's policies there. Grafton came down to London for an audience with George III, but nothing would move the king from his course. Grafton resigned from his post as Lord Privy Seal.

Many others would do the king's imprudent bidding. The Earl of Dartmouth (1731–1801), who advocated the use of force in America, was given Grafton's office. In March, Parliament passed the New England Restraining Act by which trade from those colonies was restricted to Britain itself and to the British colonies in the West Indies. While Gage claimed authority throughout the province, the Provincial Congress controlled Massachusetts outside the capital. The troops in Boston were in effect under siege. General Gage was ordered to use such force as he thought necessary to constrain Massachusetts to comply with acts of Parliament.

The king and his servants were foolish to proclaim in Massachusetts political goals that force was necessary to support. This folly arose from two miscalculations. First, they overestimated the capacity of their arms. They did this despite repeated warnings from British officials in Massachusetts. Hutchinson long ago had warned that British troops in Boston were not an adequate political solution. Gage also had said that his troops were not equal to the tasks set them by London. Second, the king and his servants greatly underestimated the capability of the American with whom they now quarreled.

While there was some military maneuver before, war began in earnest at Lexington and at Concord just outside Boston. The city of Boston of course was then very different from what it is now. Boston then was a small town on a peninsula with, to the south, a narrow neck of land that connected it to the main. Boston lacked bridges to connect it with Charlestown and with Cambridge. Large portions of the bay have since been filled in, but were then still water. The king's great ships of war were unopposed there.

In June occurred two more decisive events. First, the Continental Congress met at Philadelphia, in clear evidence that Massachusetts would not stand isolated in defense of its liberties. Congress chose George Washington to command a Continental Army. Two days after that, on June 17, 1775, long before Washington could reach Massachusetts, occurred the Battle of Bunker Hill.

British officers held the militia in contempt. Lord Percy (1742–1817), Gage's second in command, called the militia rabble. Gage issued a proclamation, written by General John Burgoyne, that spoke with scorn of the militia and that especially reviled by name Samuel Adams and John Hancock. This arrogance was a great mistake. Hancock, Adams, and the militia lacked powder, ships, and guns. They did not lack courage or skill.

Washington's arrival at the headquarters in Cambridge marked the beginning of organization for the Continental Army. The militia at Lexington, Concord, and Bunker Hill had proved not only their courage but also their want of central control or command. Despite the leadership of General Artemas Ward at the Battle of Bunker Hill, Colonel William Prescott and other officers had acted almost independently. Washington established order and, as far as possible, discipline. The task was difficult. Washington had never encountered the spirit of New England soldiers, but he set to work.

Washington complained of his shortages and of the ample stocks of the enemy. Munitions were the difficulty: powder and artillery were especially short. Washington had a few light fieldpieces, but they were old. Further, there was often a mismatch between the types of shot and a few light cannon available. His nearest available supply of heavy artillery was at Fort Ticonderoga in upstate New York. A motley force under Ethan Allen and Benedict Arnold had taken Ticonderoga from a tiny British garrison. Colonel Henry Knox set his men to the task of transporting the captured guns to Boston. The difficulties were formidable, but Knox and his men overcame them.

The British troops had the materials of war, but they lacked food and fuel for the winter. There was much sickness in Boston, and the situation there was not an easy one.

The Continental Congress had been timid and hesitant previously, but after 1775 they voted to authorize Washington to attempt the expulsion from Boston of the British army, now commanded by General William Howe. John Hancock, now the president of the Continental Congress, warmly commended the scheme to Washington.

Just as Knox arrived with the cannon from New York, fresh troops reached Washington at his Cambridge headquarters. These additions greatly strengthened both his position and his determination to remove the British garrison.

Lechemere and Dorchester were the crucial points in his plan. The ground was still frozen hard in the March chill, but American troops dispatched by Washington took position on the Dorchester Heights to the consternation of General Howe and of the British Admiral Thomas Graves, who commanded the Royal Navy in the bay and who thought it unwise to keep the king's ships under the American guns.

Washington expected an attack to dislodge his troops, but just then a storm made difficult the movement of British ships and men. The British hesitated and lost their chance. They resolved to withdraw from Boston.

Howe ordered the destruction of Castle William, the fortification on an island to the east of the city. Peter Oliver records in his *Origins and Progress* that he himself was on a British ship while this was done, and the spectacle was very fine, although his feelings were most melancholy. Howe also ordered all military stores to be carried away or destroyed, but that was not fully done. Howe offered to spare the town itself, if Washington would allow the safe evacuation of British forces. One hundred forty sail, or thereabouts, carried the British away from Boston.

Washington anticipated that Howe would attempt to remove his troops to New York City, and sent General Charles Lee (1731–1782) with a portion of the Continental Army toward New York in anticipation of that purpose. Washington himself remained for a time in Boston to prevent any recapture of that city.

Washington's triumph was very great—his greatest personal triumph in the whole course of the war—and yet the condition of the city and of the province was one of misery. The city was filled with disease and destruction. The province had undergone its most severe disruption at least since King Philip's War of 1675–1676, and perhaps the most severe in all its history. Trade had dwindled cruelly. There was now no settled government.

Let us take survey of the situation that then prevailed in Boston and in the province of Massachusetts as a whole. Boston first. The occupation of Boston by the British force and the encirclement and siege of the city by the militia do not seem such grisly events by comparison with the scale of twentieth-century wars. Bostonians in 1775 lacked such sense of diminutive scale in the events through which they passed. Andrew Eliot (1718–1778), a congregational clergyman, spoke for many when he said that the siege of Boston was the most trying happening of his life. Eliot's case may be typical in other ways. He was bewildered by the Revolution. Eliot was not a Loyalist, though he was a friend of Thomas Hutchinson. Eliot simply sought his duty in circumstances that he did not understand.

There were of course many Loyalists in Boston at the time of the British occupation. The occupation itself made the city a refuge for them. They also were bewildered by the Revolution, but they also sought to do their duty. Many of them held property outside the town and sought British protection for it, vainly, because the Provincial Congress seized the property of Loyalist exiles to finance the war.

As Loyalists fled to Boston, so Whigs fled from Boston to the area just outside the town. Sympathy for the Whig cause was especially common in there. Gage gave great offense by the methods of his occupation, and many who fled the city told stories of mistreatment by British soldiers. Whigs said property was wrongly taken when Gage broke his word over arrangements that allowed them to flee the city.

So much for Boston and its surrounding area. Western Massachusetts was far from these events. It had developed into a distinctive region long before the Revolution. Hampshire County, which comprised much of the Connecticut River valley and the western portion of the state, knew itself to be somewhat different from Boston. The Connecticut River valley proved a most fertile region for agriculture. There, more than anywhere else in the province, it was possible to practice English agriculture with the least need for adaptation. There, more than in the seacoast towns, grew up habits of deference, and there, great landowners, called "River Gods," exercised a political power that lacked a real counterpart in Boston. This regional difference expressed itself in political tension. When Boston was Whig before the Revolution, Hampshire County was Tory. After the Revolution, the west joined the Whig cause but continued to express a political independence. The hardships of the Revolution increased complaints about the local western courts, and of such unrest Shays's Rebellion (August 31, 1786–February 4, 1787) is a later example.

Economic complaints may have caused Shays's Rebellion, but we should divest ourselves of any belief that heavy British taxation or other economic oppression caused the American Revolution. Political crisis caused the American Revolution, not economic crisis. The question in Massachusetts before the Revolution was not the size of the tax burden but the method by which taxes might be legally imposed.

The Revolution, nonetheless, had the most dramatic effects upon the economy and social structure of Massachusetts. The Revolution accelerated the process of economic and social change that was already underway. This process may be called, in a word, modernization. The American Revolution freed New England to participate fully with Britain and with other parts of the Atlantic world in the growth of an industrial economy in the nineteenth century.

Massachusetts was already by 1775 a most prosperous place. People then in Massachusetts had the longest expectation of life, and one of the highest material standards of life, in the Western world in the eighteenth century.

It had not always been thus. Massachusetts developed, as Cotton Mather (1663–1728) said, from humble beginnings. The early years of the colony were hard ones because English immigrants did not bring with them the skills to thrive in the New World. These skills had to be gotten, in part borrowed, from the Indians and in part invented.

During Charles I's personal rule in the 1630s many English Puritans despaired of the condition of England, and perhaps 30,000 of them immigrated to Massachusetts. Their quarrel with the king raised even higher in their eyes the importance of their little group of "pilgrims" in New England.

The English Civil War of 1640–1660 coincided with a maturation of Massachusetts. Economic adversity and political controversy continued to inspire emigration from England throughout the seventeenth century. Massachusetts became a stable community with a growing population and a secure adaptation to the material circumstances of the New World. Fishing had originally brought the English to Massachusetts Bay, and fisheries continued to be a source of prosperity. Abundant wood allowed the construction of ships and the export of timber.

Massachusetts seldom complained before the Peace of Paris of 1763, which ended the French and Indian War, about the economic regulations that comprised the British mercantile system. The purpose of mercantile regulation was, as the acts of Parliament said, to encourage trade and navigation, and there was striking success. Britain and the American colonies profited equally from their mutual involvement. Massachusetts obtained protected markets for its timber, naval stores of many kinds, finished ships, rum, salted fish, and other items. Britain sold manufactured goods in Massachusetts. Trade flourished.

Massachusetts had of course some specific objections. The most severe complaints concerned the rules that forbade cutting, even on private land, the great trees thought by Parliament to be essential for the Royal Navy.

Under the traditional Navigation Act system, Massachusetts obtained the convenience of protected markets with the sure and certain hope that many other restrictions on trade could be evaded. Enforcement of the duties on imports was lax.

There could be a new customs system, for Parliament claimed the right to add rules at will. The Crown appointed commissioners to compel compliance with regulations enacted by the Parliament.

What if the Crown regularized or modernized enforcement? Since the very word "economics" referred before 1776 only to the management of a private household, many Massachusetts lawyers and politicians understood trade regulation and enforcement to be a political rather than economic question. Was Parliament competent to pass regulations for Massachusetts over the objections of the General Court? Was the Crown competent to enforce them there over the objections of the General Court?

The most severe and reasoned economic objections to new regulations came, oddly, not from an American but from a Scot writer, Adam Smith (1723–1790). Smith's *Wealth of Nations*, published in 1776, is the first book of scientific economics in the English-speaking world. He explained the word "economics" in its modern sense. Smith contrasted the flourishing condition of the British Empire with the decay of imperial Spain. He believed the cause of Britain's success to lie exactly in the laxity with which it enforced trade regulations. Light as the burden of British regulation was, it was still too great, thought Smith.

Freer trade would result in still greater efficiency in production and in trade, in a still greater prosperity, and in a still closer interdependence of Britain and America.

Smith was right. The American Revolution eased the full participation of Massachusetts and of New England in the Industrial Revolution. This result was unforeseen and unintended by the Provincial Congress of Massachusetts at the time of the American Revolution.

The Revolution maintained or restored to Massachusetts its tradition of popular government. Local government is the most obvious example. After Gage's administration lost control of the province outside Boston, the town governments reconstituted themselves into altered but still traditional forms. The towns always provided local government: they were a firm foundation even while the superstructure of province government tottered and fell.

Given the break with Britain, what should be the new form of provincial government? The period 1774–1780 saw that question debated. The towns supplied the framework for the debate, and also much of the answer, for people insisted upon a return to the tradition of popularity sovereignty. The new constitution of 1780 was also a powerful expression of the old Puritan idea of compact government.

The intervention of Great Britain and the resulting Revolution had killed the charter of 1691. The constitution of 1780 bore much resemblance to the ideas in the colony during the early seventeenth century. To understand that, we must review a bit of the political history of Massachusetts and its charters of 1629 and 1691.

There is an irony in the story of these charters. The absolutism of the Stuart kings was a shield by which Puritan Massachusetts claimed its liberties. The problem was that the autonomy of Massachusetts rested, in English law, upon the power of the Crown to issue its charter. The Glorious Revolution in England made the king's prerogative power there clearly subordinate to the authority of statute made by Parliament. When the prerogative power of the Crown was not absolute, then the charter of 1692, made by the Crown, became subject to the supervision of Parliament.

The charter of 1629 is very famous in the history of colonial Massachusetts, and important in the history of old England as well. Charles I issued the charter as a sop to his Puritan opponents during his quarrel with Parliament in that year. Charles wished to rule without a Parliament, and he did not call another Parliament until the momentous year 1640, the beginning of the English Civil War. The liberties that he gave to Massachusetts in 1629 must be placed among English events before the war. The Petition of Right of 1628 is useful in this regard.

The charter of 1629 came to embody the claims of Massachusetts to autonomy. The charter granted such extensive rights of election and of self-government that John Winthrop (1588–1649), whom Cotton Mather named the Moses of New England, found them almost too radical. Since nothing in the charter required them to keep it in England, Winthrop and others of the company carried it overseas into New England. There it underwent a sea change into something rich and rare, a self-governing commonwealth.

Self-government under the charter came to hold much the same place in Massachusetts that Magna Carta occupied in England, according to Puritan lawyers like Sir Edward Coke (1552–1634). Coke thought Magna Carta had restored to England an ancient Saxon constitution lost at the Norman conquest in 1066. Many in Massachusetts came to regard self-government as an ancient right, native to the place, which subsequent British action had abrogated by force.

The English Civil War greatly strengthened the autonomy of Massachusetts. When King Charles I was defeated and in 1649 executed in England by Puritan revolutionaries there, the new government, under the Lord Protector Oliver Cromwell (1599–1658), had little inclination to interfere with the affairs of Puritan Massachusetts. Also this period of benevolent neglect coincided with a maturation of the colony. English immigrants in Massachusetts became a stable community with a growing population and a secure adaptation to the material conditions of life in the New World.

The monarchy was restored in England in 1660 in the person of King Charles II, son of the executed king. Massachusetts received this news with misgiving. Further exiles from the Puritan party fled to New England. The liberties of Massachusetts and the charter of 1629 became all the more precious, because of the loss of the Puritan cause, the good old cause, in England.

Charles II did not share esteem for charters. He called in or revised charters for many royal foundations in England, and he wished to do the same for Massachusetts. Cautious, as his father's example taught him to be in dealing with Puritans, Charles II obtained from Edward Randolph (1632–1703), an agent for this purpose, intelligence on revision of the charter. Randolph had a long talk with Governor John Leverett (1616–1679), an old Cromwellian. The governor told him that the laws of England did not apply in Massachusetts. The charter protected the colony from further legislation. Charles II died in 1685 before the charter could be revised. His brother James became king.

James II had plans for reform of government in New England, but Massachusetts fell into turmoil when James was deposed by the Glorious Revolution of 1688. King William III and Queen Mary, Protestant daughter of James II, succeeded.

They effected in New England the reform of the charter planned by the Crown in the two previous reigns. They issued a new charter for Massachusetts in 1691, and by it the province was governed until just before the American Revolution.

The English legal position after the Glorious Revolution was well stated by the great English authority Sir William Blackstone (1723–1780). The government of chartered colonies, Blackstone said in his *Commentaries on the Laws of England* (1765–1769), was established by authority of the Crown and therefore had powers inferior to statute. Acts of the Parliament at Westminster because statutes with the royal assent. Thus colonial legislative bodies, created by charter and therefore by Crown prerogative, had a purview similar to that of royal proclamations. They could carry out, they could point and enforce, but they could not set aside, statute law.

The supremacy of statute, said Blackstone, was all the more clear in conquered countries like Massachusetts, since by right of conquest local laws and customs could be set aside. The country was inhabited by Indians in whose hands the previous sovereign power had been. That power passed from them to Westminster, and local colonists were nothing in the matter. They brought no sovereign power into that country, for it was certain that Great Britain had carried sovereign power out of it by conquest. Recall that Governor Thomas Hutchinson made much of the legality of his actions under the charter of 1691. Learned in the law, he assumed Black-

stone's point that the sovereign power lay at Westminster.

Apologists for the royal power seized upon the weak point in Whig argument. Claims to exemption from the law had to rest, in law, upon the royal power. Since, went the loyal argument, the king of England could not be a tyrant, Parliament supervised the execution of the royal power. Further, there could be only one source of sovereign power in a state, and all subjects of the British Empire had an equal duty to recognize the sovereign power of the imperial Parliament, though not all sent representatives to Westminster.

Oliver and Hutchinson were well aware that Loyalist argument turned upon the supremacy of Parliament, not the royal prerogative. Oliver also claimed the support of the social contract theory of John Locke (1632–1704), for, he said, no careful reader could conclude that the actions of government in Massachusetts had met Locke's test for general revolt.

If they were to counter that argument, Whigs in Massachusetts had to find a way to vest power in the province. Several attempts were made in Massachusetts to find a new basis for the old claims to popular power there under English laws. James Otis (1725–1783) argued that, since the English law did not apply in Massachusetts, the power of Parliament there was also nil. Peter Oliver and Thomas Hutchinson knew they were closer to the position of many English Whigs than was James Otis. So were many others in Massachusetts who upheld the royal authority there.

Other Whig lawyers in Massachusetts remembered the old claims that under the charter of 1629 the English law did not apply in Massachusetts. These arguments begged the question posed by the main point of English Whiggery, the supremacy of Parliament. How did one apply in Massachusetts the doctrine of the supremacy of Parliament over the royal prerogative?

Otis made a weak case, and he deliberately misquoted Blackstone. John Adams took up the challenge. He made a much stronger, clearer case than had Otis. Adams thought that the common law was beside the point. The laws about colonies were obsolete and inadequate. The great engine of state, he said, required a new wheel, and he suggested that Massachusetts acknowledge the power of the Crown but not that of

Parliament—shades of Stuart absolutism. It was only too true, said Adams, that in the past the General Court had paid homage to the supervising power of Parliament. They were misguided. "We owe allegience," said Adams, "to the person of His Majesty, King George III, whom God preserve." George should assume the separate title King of Massachusetts and should rule in Massachusetts through the General Court. It would have there the powers that the Westminster Parliament had in Britain.

Adams challenged deeply held assumptions about the nature of sovereign power. Howe should the Empire survive if there were no clear sovereign power at the center? The common law provided no answer to that puzzle, and the idea of popular sovereignty filled the gap.

In 1776 Massachusetts was without a proper constitution. The town of Pittsfield challenged the General Court's authority to govern the province. Society, they said, required a contract, and the contract had been dissolved by the king and must be reconstituted. Only the people could do so, and not the General Court. The General Court proposed to draft a constitution, nonetheless, and proceeded to do so. In February 1778, they submitted it to the people for ratification. It was rejected.

Opponents issued a document known as the "Essex Result" in which they listed their objections. They regretted the lack of a bill of rights, and they echoed the great Montesquieu (1689–1755) in their call for a clear separation of the branches of government. Radicals in their turn dissented from the "Essex Result" in matters of property protection, but both groups agreed on the need for a formal bill of rights. The "Essex Result" foreshadowed conservative politics in Massachusetts when the Federalists came to dominance later.

The General Court acceded to the will of the towns and permitted a convention to meet and decide the constitutional question. All adult freemen were allowed to vote for the convention, and 293 delegates met as a constitutional convention at Cambridge after the summer of 1779. John Adams emerged as the person most qualified to draft a new constitution.

He did so, and the constitution was ratified and accepted, though not without demur. The towns objected to particulars of the Declaration of Rights. An especial difficulty was the consti-

tutional position of the established Congregational church.

The new constitution is a vindication of Adams's comments before the Revolution. The principles of social contract theory and of popular sovereignty had become the basis of government in Massachusetts. But the controversy over adoption of the constitution presaged confrontations later.

Many eighteenth-century observers remarked on the continuity between political radicalism in Massachusetts in their time and the Puritan tradition of the previous century. The English Whig Edmund Burke (1729–1797) said of American radicals that "they smelt tyranny on every tainted breeze, that they embodied the dissidence of dissent and the protest of the protestant religion." Thomas Hutchinson and Peter Oliver also found the root of Boston radicalism in the previous Puritan opposition to royal authority. Many Boston preachers recalled in sermons the history of New England, how their fathers, who had come into the New World at God's command and on God's errand, had always been the enemies of kings and tyrants. The Congregational minister of Concord said much the same thing when he addressed the militia on the day of the battle there.

Of course Puritanism did not originate in Massachusetts. The word, originally a term of abuse, was coined in Queen Elizabeth's day to identify English followers of John Calvin. The word came to signify a wide range of persons who sought to reform the established Church of England or at least to rid it of the remnants of Roman Catholic practice and belief. The Puritan movement had its source in exiles who fled England at the time of the persecutions of Protestants in Queen Mary's reign of 1553–1558. John Foxe's *Book of Martyrs* told their tale.

It is well to distinguish clearly between Calvin himself and English Calvinism or Puritanism. Puritanism was very diverse, a bundle of different sects. Church of England issues, still, did give Puritans some distinctive English national character and even at times the appearance of united action.

They sought to reform the established national church according to the model that they found in *The Book of the Acts of the Apostles*. They were opposed to the use of bishops in the government of the English church, and over this issue they fought the civil war in England. They opposed distinctive clerical vestments and *The Book of Common Prayer* that Thomas Cranmer (1489–1556) had compiled in 1548 during King Edward VI's reign.

The Church of England, established by the law in England and in many parts of British America, never gained more than sufferance in Massachusetts, and neither did the hierarchy and social deference characteristic of English society and of the established church. Famous writers such as Cotton Mather and Jonathan Edwards (1703–1758) kept the Puritan spirit alive and well in eighteenth-century Massachusetts. By that time England was monarchist and Church of England, but Massachusetts had still central to it a version of the radicalism that had caused the turmoil of the seventeenth century.

Gage's arrival in arms in Massachusetts had something of the aspect of a coup d'etat. By ordering these measures, George III and his servants provoked a reaction that spread radical doctrines of popular sovereignty throughout the other American colonies.

Radical doctrines had long distinguished Massachusetts. If the spirit of Massachusetts is the spirit of America, or at least of the American Revolution, then the spirit of Puritanism is the spirit of Massachusetts. Massachusetts was from its foundation a society constructed upon the basis of Puritan ideas. Puritanism in one form or another was characteristic of Massachusetts at every stage in the Colonial period. By the eighteenth century's close, Massachusetts had evolved Puritanism into a secular political ideology. The American Revolution gave to all Americans the radical secularized political ideology of Puritan Massachusetts.

John A. Taylor

REFERENCES

Bernard Bailyn, *Faces of Revolution, Personalities and Themes in the Struggle for American Independence* (1990); John Stetson Barry, *The History of Massachusetts*, 3 vols. (1857); Sacvan Bercovitch, *The Puritan Origins of the American Self* (1975); Richard D. Brown, *Modernization, the Transformation of American Life 1600–1865* (1976); Richard L. Bushman, *King and People in Provincial Massachusetts* (1985); James Deetz, *In Small Things Forgotten, The Archeology of Early American Life* (1977); Robert A. Gross, *The Minutemen and Their World* (1976); Dirk Hoerder, *Crown Action in Revolutionary Massachusetts 1765–1780* (1977); Thomas Hutchinson, *The History of the Colony and Province of Massachusetts Bay*, 3 vols. (1936); ———, *Strictures upon the Declaration of the Congress at Philadelphia; a Letter to a Noble Lord*, ed. by Malcolm Freiberg (1958); David S. Lovejoy, *The Glorious Revolution in America* (1972); Samuel Eliot Morison, *Sources and Documents Illustrating the American Revolution 1764–1788 and the Formation of the Federal Constitution* (1979); Peter Oliver, *Peter Oliver's Origin and Progress of the American Rebellion, A Tory View*, ed. by Douglas Adair and John A. Schultz (1961); Richard L. Perry and John C. Cooper, *Sources of Our Liberties, The Documentary Origins of Individual Liberties in the United States Constitution and Bill of Rights* (1978) Robert J. Taylor, *Western Massachusetts in the Revolution* (1967).

Massey, Eyre (1719–1804)

British army officer. Eyre Massey had seen extensive service by the time of his arrival at Halifax in 1776. He was born May 24, 1719, in County Limerick, Ireland. Two dates have been given for his entry into the British army. Massey claimed to have purchased an ensigncy in the 27th Regiment of Foot in 1739 and thus to have served in Admiral Edward Vernon's expedition against the Spanish in the Caribbean, returning to the British Isles in 1740. Official sources, however, give the date of his commission as January 25, 1741. Service in Europe during the next decade, including action in Scotland in 1745–1746, saw Massey steadily promoted. He was appointed captain lieutenant and captain in 1747, captain on May 24, 1751, and major on December 10, 1755.

Eyre Massey began his duty in North American in June 1756, when the 27th Regiment arrived at New York. He served in the debacle at Ticonderoga in 1758, and on July 16 he was commissioned lieutenant colonel of the 46th Regiment of Foot, which had suffered badly in that battle. Massey's most notable service occurred during Brigadier John Prideaux's 1759 campaign against Fort Niagara. The British began a siege on July 6, but Prideaux and his second in command, Colonel John Johnston of the New York Regiment, were both killed in the sap on July 20. The question of command was resolved during a council of war. The choice was between Massey and Sir William Johnson, who had accompanied the expedition at the head of a large body of Iroquois. Massey claimed to have deferred to Johnson to ensure the continued support of the Indians. On July 23, Sir William learned of the approach of a French relief force and sent a detachment to block the route they would necessarily follow. Early in the morning on July 24, Johnson dispatched Massey with most of his 46th Regiment to reinforce the position. Soon afterward Lieutenant Colonel Massey, whose force numbered only 454 white troops, fought a determined action at the Battle of La Belle Famille and routed an enemy estimated variously at between 80 and 1,500 French and Indians. Fort Niagara surrendered the next day.

Despite his role at La Belle Famille, Massey received little mention in official dispatches from Niagara. Johnson garnered the credit not only for capturing Niagara, but for defeating the relief force as well. Massey was most resentful of this slight. He continued an active role for the rest of the war, leading the grenadiers in General Jeffery Amherst's advance on Montreal in 1760. Massey returned to the 27th Regiment as lieutenant colonel on March 2, 1761, and led it at Martinique in 1761 and the siege of Havana in 1762. The 27th returned to New York in 1763, and then moved to Canada for garrison duty in the St. Lawrence Valley.

When the 27th Regiment returned to Ireland in 1767 Massey had spent 11 years in America. He was promoted to colonel in the army on May 25, 1772, and colonel in the 27th Regiment on February 19, 1773. The 27th was sent to Boston in October 1775, and evacuated to Halifax in March 1776. The regiment went with Howe to New York in 1776 and Massey took command of the important post of Halifax. He was promoted major general on August 29, 1777. Massey returned to Ireland in 1780 to command the garrison of Cork and achieved the grade of lieutenant general on November 20, 1782.

Eyre Massey then appears to have been unemployed for some time, although in 1794, at an advanced age, he once again obtained command of the garrison of Cork. There he dealt with difficulties in the regiments under his command, including a near mutiny. He commanded Cork until his promotion to full general in 1796. On December 27, 1800, General Massey was raised to the Irish peerage as Baron Clarina of Elm Park, County Limerick. He died May 17, 1804, still colonel of the 27th Regiment of Foot, marshal of the army in Ireland, and governor of Limerick. He had married Catherine Clements by whom he had four children.

Brian Leigh Dunnigan

REFERENCES

British Army Lists, London: 1750–1796; *DAB*, Brian Leigh Dunnigan, *Siege—1759: The Campaign Against Niagara* (1986); Charles H. Stewart, *The Services of British Regiments in Canada and North America* (1964).

Maxwell, William (c. 1733–1796)

Continental Army officer. "Scotch Willie" Maxwell was a gentlemen of refinement and an officer of high character. Tall, ruddy with a florid complexion, his one vice seems to have been liquor. A stalwart man, he was the commander of the New Jersey Continental Line until 1780.

Little is known about both his early life or even his later personal life. He was born to Scot-Irish parents in Newtown Stewart, County Tyrone, Ireland, around 1733. He spoke with a Scottish burr the rest of his life. He was the eldest of four children. His parents came to America when Maxwell was very young and settled in Jersey's Sussex (now Warren) County as farmers, at least by 1747. Maxwell received a typical rural education and became a farmer in the family tradition.

At 21 years of age, he joined the provincial forces of the British army and was present at Edward Braddock's defeat in 1755. He soon became an ensign in John Johnston's New Jersey regiment and later a lieutenant in the New Jersey regiment of Colonel Peter Schuyler. He was in James Abercromby's disastrous attack on Ticonderoga and some accounts place him with James Wolfe at the battle of Quebec in 1759.

After the war he remained in the British service and was a commissary officer at Mackinac until 1774 when he returned to New Jersey, a 20-year veteran of the British army. It may very well have been the boredom of the endless years of garrison duty on the frontier that first propelled him into the drinking he practiced so frequently.

When the War of Revolution began, Maxwell did not hesitate to cast his fate with the American cause. He was active in political affairs in Jersey and became the colonel of the 2nd New Jersey Regiment on November 8, 1775. The following year, he and his men accompanied General John Sullivan on the march to support the American invasion of Canada. Maxwell served with General William Thompson in the defeat at Trois Rivieres and was one of the field officers who protested the surrender of Crown Point without a fight by General Philip Schuyler. Washington sided with Schuyler in this matter to maintain proper order, but privately he agreed with the field officers.

Primarily because of his bravery at Trois Rivieres, Maxwell was promoted to brigadier general on October 23, 1776, and returned to his state in time to help in its defense as the British pursued Washington in his retreat across Jersey. Stationed in Morristown, Maxwell harassed the flank of the Jersey posts that the British established at the end of the 1776 campaign. He was not engaged at Trenton or Princeton. He later was posted at Elizabethtown to guard the Jersey coast against British invasion.

The next year brought the Pennsylvania campaign. Maxwell was selected to command the first formally raised light infantry corps of approximately 110 officers and men from each brigade in the army. This unit would perform the duties of the rangers/light infantry since Daniel Morgan and his riflemen had been dispatched north to assist Schuyler against Burgoyne. Maxwell's light infantry fought a skirmish at Cooches Bridge on September 3, 1777, against General William Howe's advanced guard. This was the first action of the American light infantry and also may have been the first time the American Stars and Stripes flag was flown in battle.

Maxwell continued to serve at Brandywine and later at Germantown. When the campaign stalled, charges were brought against Maxwell for his inactivity in the face of the enemy as light corps commander, and his excessive drinking. Time permitted a trial, which resulted in a compromise. Maxwell was permitted to retain his command, since the charges were not substantiated, but he was not able to demonstrate his innocence either. During the winter at Valley Forge, Maxwell commanded the New Jersey brigade of the 1st, 2nd, 3rd, and 4th New Jersey regiments. The light corps had been disbanded for the winter.

As the British left Philadelphia to return to New York, Maxwell led his brigade in the complicated maneuvering that resulted in the Battle of Monmouth. He and his men were battling for their homes and knew well the ground over which they were fighting. He was a witness for the commander-in-chief at General Charles Lee's court-martial following Lee's conduct and removal from command at the Battle of Monmouth.

In 1779, Maxwell performed well in Sullivan's march into the Iroquois confederation to destroy the Indians' towns and crops. This extended raid came in retribution for the Cherry Valley Massacre and other related instances of frontier terror committed by England's Indian allies. Sullivan had specifically requested the services of the Jersey Line for this expedition. When General Sullivan became ill in August on the march, Maxwell assumed temporary overall command of the column and effectively substituted for Sullivan until his recovery.

Upon completion of the Sullivan march, the Jersey Line returned to the main army. In 1780, Maxwell was instrumental in organizing militia and regular line forces to repel Wilhelm von Knyphausen's attacks at Springfield and Connecticut farms in June. Maxwell was not a brilliant leader. But he was a faithful subordinate officer, and he was steady and calm in battle.

Discontented with his rank and treatment in the army, Maxwell made the fatal mistake of turning in his resignation to Congress, assuming they valued his service enough to refuse it and satisfy his demands. He used the excuse of poor health. This was always a risk, and in this case, Maxwell lost. He evidently realized this too late, for he tried to retrieve his letter of resignation, showing signs of a quick recovery in health. However, his resignation was accepted. As of July 25, 1780, General William Maxwell was once again a civilian. Colonel Elias Dayton replaced Maxwell in command of the Jersey Line.

Maxwell continued his political activities in New Jersey but did not distinguish himself to any degree. In 1783, he served a term in the Jersey State Legislature. He never married and had no family. An old soldier of many years' service, he died visiting a friend in Lansdowne, New Jersey, on November 4, 1796.

At the time of his resignation from the army, "Scotch Willie" was characterized by Washington as "an honest man, a warm friend to this country, and firmly attached to her interests." Perhaps because of his provincial background, and in spite of his 20 years in the British army, Maxwell never lost his respect for his fellow Americans as soldiers.

Paul J. Sanborn

REFERENCES

DAB; Mark E. Lender, *The New Jersey Soldier* (1975); Benson J. Lossing, *The Pictorial Field Book of the American Revolution*, 2 vols. (1851–1852), rpr. 1972; Christopher Ward, *The War of Revolution*, 2 vols. (1952).

Mecklenburg Declaration (Resolves) (May 1775)

On May 31, 1775, a committee of delegates of each of the militia districts of Mecklenburg County, North Carolina, passed a series of resolves that fell just short of declaring permanent independence from Great Britain. The Resolves called for all acts, commissions, and charters of the king and Parliament to be suspended and that each colony be governed by its respective provincial congress. Colonel Thomas Polk, who had called and led the meeting, read the Mecklenburg Resolves from the courthouse steps to a crowd remembered as having half of the county's population. The Resolves were published in several American newspapers of the time, the most complete version appearing in the *South Carolina Gazette and Country Journal*, Charleston, June 13, 1775.

The Resolves can be considered as the first real declaration of independence in the revolting colonies. Captain James Jack took a copy of the Resolves to Philadelphia for the North Carolina delegates to the Continental Congress and along the way allowed them to be read in open court in Salisbury, North Carolina. Royal governors Josiah Martin of North Carolina and James Wright of Georgia separately sent newspaper copies to Lord Dartmouth, British Secretary of the Colonies, as an example of the deteriorating situation in America.

However, at that moment the Continental Congress was still striving for reconciliation with the British government and had not yet advised any colony to assume control of its own affairs. The Mecklenburg Resolves would have been detrimental to Congress' claims of being opposed to independence except as a last resort. The Resolves were not formally presented to Congress or even published in the Philadelphia newspapers (although it could have been copied from the newspapers of the other colonies).

The importance of the events in Charlotte, Mecklenburg County, North Carolina, unfortunately, are obscured by misguided efforts at their commemoration. In 1819, a national debate was raging about the birthplace of American independence. Dr. Joseph McKnitt Alexander helped to put forth a claim for Mecklenburg County but, not having a copy of the Resolves, instead published what is almost certainly a fictional Mecklenburg Declaration of Independence dated May 20, 1775, that suggested that Thomas Jefferson's Declaration of Independence plagiarized the earlier Mecklenburg Declaration. Jefferson and John Adams disclaimed any knowledge of the Mecklenburg Declaration and cast serious doubt on its authenticity. The debate still rages and was heightened by the publication of a fraudulent copy of the *Cape Fear Mercury* in *Collier's* magazine of July 1, 1905, that contained the Mecklenburg Declaration. It was quickly discredited by both pro and con Mecklenburg Declaration partisans. *See also:* North Carolina in the American Revolution

Robert Scott Davis, Jr.

REFERENCES

William Henry Hoyt, *The Mecklenburg Declaration of Independence* (1907).

Medicine, Military

When the American Revolution began in 1775, it has been estimated that there were 3,500 medical practitioners in colonial America, some 1,400 served in the Continental Army and approximately 10 percent of these had a formal medical degree. Most of the men who became the military physicians of the American Revolution received their medical education through the apprenticeship system. In return for an annual fee the student received room and board and a closely personal education from an established, reputable doctor. Upon completion the student received a certificate, usually as a letter from the doctor attesting to the student's apprenticeship and ability to practice medicine. As the colonies grew and prospered, more and more students traveled abroad to the medical schools of Britain and the Continent to further their medical education. The Medical School at the University of Philadelphia was established in 1765 and by 1775 had graduated 41 students.

Colonial American physicians occupied prominent positions within the community. Physicians often held public office, both on the local and colonial levels. They were well represented in the Continental Congress, and five doctors were among the signers of the Declaration of Independence. The leaders of the colonial medical profession served with distinction in the Army Hospital Department and the Continental Army; a few served as line officers, took command, and rose to become general officers.

The European military medical knowledge that influenced the practice of American medical men came from the writings and teachings of such men as John Pringle, Richard Brockelsby, and Gerhard van Sweiten, who were known and available to the leaders of the American Continental Army. Based upon European military experience, the published works of Pringle in *Observations on Diseases of the Army* (1752), of van Sweiten in *The Diseases Incident to Armies with the Method of Cure* (1758), and of Brocklesby in his *Oeconomical and Medical Observations* (1764) set forth the rules of preventive medicine for an army in the field. These included personal hygiene, proper clothing, diet and exercise, the need for adequate ventilation in barracks and hospitals, the construction and maintenance of latrines, the selection and policing of campsites, and the supervision and control of rations and drinking water. These writings were all addressed to commanders and officers and emphasized that the preservation of the health of the troops was a responsibility of command.

Pringle's book influenced Dr. John Jones, a professor of surgery at King's College Medical School in New York City, to write the first medical book published in North America in 1775. The book, *Plain Concise Practical Remarks on the Treatment of Wounds and Fractures*, was essentially a compendium from the European authors and was of great use to young military surgeons of the Continental Army for whom it was "principally designed."

An important contribution by medical officers of the Continental Army was the publication of the first American pharmacopoeia. It was a small 32-page booklet known as the "Lititz Pharmacopoeia" and was compiled by army medical officers at the time of the winter camp at Valley Forge. A second edition was published in Philadelphia in 1781 with authorship ascribed to Dr. William Brown, who was surgeon general of the Hospital of the Middle Department at Lititz, Pennsylvania, in 1777–1778.

What did American medical staff actually do? Colonial American medical practice was in keeping with eighteenth-century European medical theories that explained disease in terms of chemical and physical qualities, such as acidity and alkalinity, or tension and relaxation. Dr. William Cullen, an influential teacher at the University of Edinburgh who taught many of the future leaders of the Hospital Department, believed that nervous tension was the cause of all disease, and that nervous irritation altered body fluids and caused illness. Too much nervous tension resulted in fever, to be treated by a depleting regimen of bleeding, purging, and rest with a restricted diet. A lack of nervous tension or too much relaxation, on the other hand, resulted in a cold or chill requiring restorative measures. Cullen was so influential that the American edition of his work "was read with peculiar attention by the physicians and surgeons of our Army, and in a few years regulated in many things the practice in our hospitals." A healthy soldier was thought to have a proper balance between nerve stimuli and the excitability of his body tissues. Once his nerves were irritated by stimuli such as bad air, spoiled food or drink, exposure to the cold or wounds, then spasms of the blood vessels and muscles would occur. The patient would develop a fever, rapid pulse, and tightened muscles would begin to ache. The Continental Army physician would set out to relieve the pain and remove the excessive excitability.

The modern specific therapy for specific diseases was unknown in the eighteenth century, and certain treatments were used for almost all febrile disease conditions, among them bleeding, blistering, purging, and sweating. To restore the body's balance and return the soldier to health, the doctor's bag contained a lancet for bloodletting to remove excesses of the blood and restore balance of the humors. The amount of bleeding (as much as eight to twenty ounces) and frequency of bloodletting varied with the individual physician. In addition to bleeding, a soldier with a severe case of pneumonia, often called pleurisy, might be treated with blisters and plasters, that is, caustics and skin irritants applied to the skin that would act as a counterirritant to tissue elsewhere and encourage pus to drain. To relieve pain, swelling, or the discharge of pus, a poultice of hot, moist paste was applied to the skin and covered with flannel. Cleansing the digestive tract was another general treatment for excessive intestinal irritation; the laxatives and purges included rhubarb, jalap, calomel, and castor oil. Mercury was used against venereal disease and as a purgative, but it was also widely used in the form of calomel to treat many other diseases. After 1750 it was increasingly prescribed for inflammatory diseases and was eventually also used for typhus, yellow fever, dysentery, smallpox, tuberculosis, dropsy, and diseases of the liver. Although it was widely praised and given in massive doses, it did have unpleasant side effects, such as diarrhea, nosebleeds, bleeding gums, and loosing of the teeth. Despite these side effects calomel continued in its popularity until the Civil War when the surgeon general forbade its use.

To further cleanse the body after the intestinal symptoms were controlled, doctors would prescribe sudorifics or diaphoretics to sweat the poisons out of the system. These included camphor, Dover's Powder (opium and ipecac), and rhubarb. When nervous stimulation exhausted the body's tissues a "general debility" would result. To restore nervous energy, doctors would prescribe cathartics to scour the intestines, rubefacients to irritate and redden the skin, and stimulants such as pepper, cinnamon, cloves, horseradish, and spearmint, among others. A low diet of thin, diluted drinks and nourishing broths was recommended. Soothing, warm-water baths were also used.

The most widely used pain relief medication was opium; often in the form of laudanum, composed of opium and saffron extracted with canary wine, it was administered orally to lessen pain, relax the patient, and produce sleep. Cinchona bark of the Peruvian Cinchona tree, from which quinine was first derived in 1820, was a popular antifebrile medication used for the ague, fevers, and malaria along with laxatives, clysters (enemas), cold baths, and vomits. Cinchona was one of the few effective medications available if the patient had malaria, but the pulverized bark was difficult to administer and often in low supply during the war.

Smallpox was the only disease for which effective preventive measures were available, in the form of inoculation. The method most commonly used at the time of the American Revolution was the Dimsdale method. The treatment required a lengthy preparation period during which the patient was kept on a light diet, dosed with mercury, bled, and purged. The procedure itself involved introducing the serum from a pox vesicle of a smallpox victim into a cut made on the arm or leg of the healthy patient. Those inoculated were kept isolated so as to prevent the spread of the disease while on a "cooling regimen" of exposure to cold air, drinking cold water, and with a further dose of mercurial purgatives. It was a tolerable prophylactic measure, and only about 1 in 1,000 died from the procedure. It was used until the early nineteenth century when it was replaced by Dr. Edward Jenner's safer cowpox vaccination.

Following the Battles at Lexington and Concord on April 19, 1775, the colonial militias of Massachusetts, Connecticut, New Hampshire, and Rhode Island established camps in the Massachusetts Bay area and began a siege of the British forces in Boston. Through its Committees of Safety and of Supplies, the Massachusetts Provincial Congress took early steps to provide of the medical support of the rebel forces. The challenges they faced included securing a supply of medicine, of physicians, and the establishment of an organized system of medical care.

The medical service for the siege of Boston was haphazard at best. There was no organized corps of stretcher bearers, no medical corps, nor director of hospitals or chief physician, and the medical men were never organized into a distinct branch with its own command and control. There were two basic kinds of medical establishment—small regimental hospitals under the care of regimental surgeons who were appointed by regimental commanders and the larger general hospitals staffed by hospital physicians and surgeons. Regimental surgeons operated independently without any particular medical oversight, and there was little coordination between them and those in the general hospitals. The most serious medical supply problem during the siege of Boston, and throughout the war, was that of supplying belligerent and independent-minded regimental surgeons. In June the Massachusetts Provincial Congress directed its Committee of Supplies to provide one medical chest each for two of the Massachusetts regiments, and all other regimental surgeons were to draw their supplies from these two chests, which was indicative of the supply shortage. In May and June the Provincial Congress designated examination committees to review the qualifications of the regimental surgeons. In June and July the committee examined candidates to be appointed as regimental surgeons and mates and assigned others to the general hospitals. The medical organization of the force besieging Boston was confused and disorganized. Patients were scattered in homes and churches in the bay area, and there was virtually no field sanitation in the camps. Bickering between regimental and hospital surgeons over supplies and patients became serious. The situation clearly called for the creation of an organized system of medical care within the new Continental Army.

On May 10, 1775, the Second Continental Congress adopted the soldiers who had besieged Boston as the Continental Army and appointed George Washington as the "commander of all the Continental Forces." On June 17 at the Battle of Breed's Hill (Bunker Hill) the British forces in Boston assaulted the fortified and entrenched American positions. Although a British victory, the casualty rate was high. The British suffered 1,040 casualties, or approximately 42 percent of their forces; the Americans had 453 casualties, or approximately 32 percent of their forces. The British general Sir Henry Clinton said, "A few more such victories would have shortly put an end to British dominion in America." During the battle Dr. Joseph Warren, president of the Massachusetts Provincial Congress, who fought as a major general with the volunteer militia, was killed. Thus, the first American general officer killed in action was a doctor.

General Washington arrived at Cambridge, Massachusetts, and took command of the Continental Army on July 3, 1775. It was obvious that the medical system was inadequate, and soon after he wrote to Congress, "I have made inquiry with respect to the establishment of the Hospital, and find it in a very unsettled condition. There is no principal Director, nor any subordination among the surgeons; of consequence disputes and contentions have arisen and must continue until it is reduced to some system."

On July 27, 1775, the Congress passed the Hospital Bill. It established the Hospital Department of the Continental Army, or what is now called the Army Medical Department. By this resolution Congress created positions for the officers of the Hospital Department, briefly described their duties, and established their pay as follows: the director general and chief physician, $4.00 per day; four surgeons and one apothecary, $1.66 per day; one clerk, 66¢ per day; two storekeepers, $4.00 per month; and nurses, the lowest paid members, $2.00 per month. For an army of 20,000 this legislation authorized the hiring of only 29 persons plus occasional laborers and 1 nurse for every 10 patients. The duties of the director general were to "furnish Medicines, Bedding and all other necessities, to pay for the same, superintend the whole, and make his report to and receive orders from the commander in chief." This legislation was a major source of confusion: it did not describe the relationship of the new department and its director to the existing system of regimental surgeons and hospitals, to the regimental commanders, to the various colonial militias and governments or to the Congress. When the army and its medical service moved beyond Massachusetts it did not define the relationship between the director general and the directors of hospitals in other theaters of the war. The Hospital Department was repeatedly reorganized and modified during the war through the efforts of a Congressional Medical Committee established in September 1775 "to devise ways and means for supplying the Continental Army with Medicines" and by resolutions of the Congress, which continued to involve itself in the operations of the Hospital Department.

Dr. Benjamin Church was "unanimously elected" by Congress to be the first Director General and Chief Physician of the Hospital Department trained in London, practiced in Boston, and served in Massachusetts as a member of both the Provincial Congress and the Boston Committee of Correspondence. Church continued the policy begun by the Massachusetts Provincial Congress of examining candidates for appointment in the Hospital Department, a practice that was continued throughout the war. Dr. James Thatcher, in his *Military Journal of the American Revolution* (1823), described the examinations as so rigorous that when one candidate was asked how he would promote sweating in a rheumatic patient he responded, "I would have him examined by a medical committee."

Director General Church moved to consolidate the many hospitals in the Boston area by ordering the regimental surgeons to send their patients to the general hospitals. The Massachusetts surgeons cooperated, but the regiments from the other colonies generally did not. General John Sullivan commented that half of the patients ordered by Church to go to the general hospitals refused to go, "Declaring they would rather die where they were and under the care of those physicians they were aquainted with." The controversy over the hospitals and medical support had a negative affect upon morale and enlistments and would continue to do so throughout the war. Sullivan commented, "I greatly fear that if it does not ruin the present Army it will prevent another being raised in America." Washington ordered an investigation of the problems of the Hospital Department, but before it could be completed Church was found to be in "criminal correspondence with the enemy," the British commander in Boston, General Thomas Gage. Church was court-martialed, jailed, and dismissed from the army, but allowed to sail for the West Indies (his ship was lost at sea and he was never heard from again). The Army Medical Department was not off to a very good start.

What were the medical and surgical problems faced by the American medical staff? The chief cause of death during the war was disease. The ratio of Americans who died due to disease was ten to one over those who were killed in action or died of their wounds. The medical problems faced by Washington's army were epidemic and endemic diseases—smallpox, dysentery, typhus, typhoid, malaria, pneumonia, and influenza. The chief preventive measures used to combat epidemic diseases were quarantine and isolation. Medical treatment in general during early colonial American times was largely centered around the heroic practices of purging, sweating, bleeding, and blistering.

The major British weapon was the Brown Bess musket with a socket bayonet. It used a 0.71 caliber lead ball, and was fired in massed volleys at 50 yards, followed by a bayonet charge. Artillery used case and cannister shot as antipersonnel rounds, but was not a major wounding agent. In his surgical practice the colonial doctor faced serious difficulties; the only major operations undertaken were amputation of extremities and trephination for skull fractures. Amputations were used to treat compound fractures and wounds of the major joints. Without antiseptic methods, gunshot wounds and amputations almost always led to severe or fatal infection. Without effective anesthesia, a surgeon's most prized assets were his strength, speed, and knowledge of human anatomy. Although colonial doctors had a reasonable understanding of anatomy, sur-

gery of the head, chest, and abdomen was avoided because of uniformly fatal outcomes.

In June 1775 Congress ordered an invasion of Canada, thinking that the British forces there easily could be defeated and that the French would come to the American side; and thus the "Fourteenth Colony" would be established. Major General Philip Schuyler, Commander of the Northern Department, moved north from Ticonderoga to capture Montreal and other parts of Quebec, with Dr. Samuel Stringer as medical director of his command.

On October 17 Dr. John Morgan was selected by Congress as the new Director General of the Hospital Department. Morgan was a prominent colonial physician, European trained, and co-founder of the Philadelphia Medical School. The conflict between the Hospital Department and the regimental hospital system continued under Morgan and was intensified by the lack of medicines and hospital supplies. Congress failed to define the relationship between Morgan and Stringer in the newly created Northern Department, and this led to a heated controversy between the two doctors. Congress only made matters worse by adding to the confusion in June 1776 when it created the Southern Department in Virginia and appointed Dr. William Rickman as Physician and Director General. It was not until August 1776 that Congress decided that Morgan had authority over all the regional hospitals.

Schuyler moved up Lake Champlain in September 1775, and a second invading column commanded by Colonel Benedict Arnold marched from Boston across the wilderness of Maine to attack the city of Quebec. The attack on Quebec City failed, enlistments were expiring, adequate food and clothing of the harsh winter environment were lacking, and the Americans were crippled by a smallpox epidemic (brought on partly by self-inoculation). The Americans fled from Quebec city in full retreat and ended the most disastrous American campaign of the Revolutionary War, losses from battle, disease, and desertion in this campaign amounted to more than 5,000 men.

This episode illustrates the effect that contagious disease can have on a military campaign. After visiting the sick at Crown Point, John Adams wrote, "Our misfortune in Canada is enough to melt a heart of stone. The smallpox is ten times more terrible than the British, Canadians, and Indians together. The smallpox, the smallpox, what shall we do with it!" The hero of the Canadian invasion was Dr. Johnathan Potts, who served as Stringer's second in command as Physician and Surgeon of the Canada Department. In August 1776, soon after arriving at Fort George, he wrote to Samuel Adams,

> The distressing situation of the sick here is not to be described. . . . To attend this large number we have four surgeons and four mates, exclusive of myself, and our little shop doth not afford a grain of jalap, ipecac, bark, salts, opium, and sundry other capitol articles, and nothing of the kind is to be had in this quarter.

At Fort George, at what was to become the largest military hospital of the Revolution, Dr. Potts treated approximately 1,500 soldiers from the failed Canadian invasion. He went on to serve with Washington at Trenton, Princeton, and Valley Forge, and with Horatio Gates at Saratoga. After the American victory at Saratoga, Dr. Potts and his fellow doctors received high praise from the medical profession and line commanders alike. On November 6, 1777, Congress resolved

> That the unremitting attention showed by Dr. Potts and the officers of the General Hospital in the Northern Department . . . to the sick and wounded soldiers under their care, is a proof not only of their humanity, but of their zeal, so deeply interested in the preservation of the health and lives of the gallant assertors of their country's cause; and therfore that Congress cannot but entertain a high sense of the services which they have rendered during this Campaign by a diligent discharge of their respective functions.

This congressional praise was the only such testimony to the service of army doctors during the Revolutionary War.

During the American Revolution, as in earlier colonial times, there was no real distinction between physicians and surgeons, they were one and the same. Because the caliber of the regimental surgeons varied widely, in July 1776 Director General Morgan issued *A Copy of the Order and Instructions Given to the Regimental Surgeons, in case of Action.* In these *Instructions* Morgan advised regimental surgeons of their duties to provide emergency medical care for the wounded—stop the bleeding, remove foreign bodies from the wound, reduce fractures, apply

dressings, and evacuate the patients to the hospitals. Regimental surgeons were to provide only emergency care; "capital operations" were to be avoided. Since there was no organized corps of stretcher bearers, Morgan advised surgeons to check with regimental officers before battle for men and wagons to evacuate the wounded. Few regimental surgeons brought their own instruments and medicines, believing they would be supplied by the army. In his *Instructions* Morgan included a recommended list for the contents of regimental medical chests. Later when he called for a "Return" of the surgical equipment and supplies in the regimental medical chests it was shown that there was a fearful shortage of everything, including amputating sets, crooked and straight needles, scalpels, forceps, bandages, ligatures, tourniquets, linen, and lint. The general hospitals of Morgan's own Hospital Department fared little better.

The need for independence was crystallized during the first half of 1776 as King George and Parliament continued to scorn Congress' appeals for redress of grievances, and the tempo of the war increased. After the British evacuated Boston in March 1776, Washington, believing that the enemy would attack New York in the summer, shifted his command to the lower Hudson River, divided his forces and prepared to defend Manhattan and Long Island. In anticipation of the medical requirements, Morgan's Hospital Department established general hospitals on Manhattan, had large stocks of drugs sent to the city from New England, recruited staff and examined candidates, and initiated procedures for weekly reports. Morgan had great difficulty with the regimental surgeons, with whom he quarreled frequently. Many of them kept seriously ill patients in their regimental hospitals while they complained bitterly to Congress about Morgan's refusal to distribute badly needed medicines and hospital supplies. Morgan had not received any instructions concerning his responsibilities to support regimental surgeons and complained to Washington that they all thought they had "a right to insist upon my furnishing every regiment . . . with whatever articles they are pleased to demand." Later in July 1776 Morgan wrote to the Medical Committee of Congress, "They all look to me, for supplies of everything they want: I have no authority for that purpose . . . I call for orders, but leave me without orders," he pleaded. Morgan characterized them as "unlettered, ignorant, crude to a degree scarcely to be imagined. . . . Some of them were never educated to the profession of physick, nor had ever seen an operation of surgery." Washington was annoyed with the regimental surgeons' constant bickering and neglect of patients. In a letter to John Hancock he wrote that "many [regimental surgeons] are great rascals, countenancing the men to sham complaints to exempt them from duty . . . receiving bribes to certify indisposition." The regimental surgeons were supported by their regimental commanders, who frequently wrote to Congress with criticisms of the Hospital Department, which undermined Morgan's already faltering position.

Further undermining Morgan's authority, on July 15, 1776, Congress appointed Dr. William Shippen, Jr., as chief physician of the Flying Camp in New Jersey, commanded by Brigadier General (Dr.) Hugh Mercer. Dr. Shippen was co-founder of the Philadelphia Medical School and had become a bitter rival of Morgan. Congress had authorized the Flying Camp and called for 10,000 militia from New Jersey, Pennsylvania, and Maryland to defend against British invasion and provide reinforcements in the defense of New York. Congress did not define Shippen's position as chief physician of the "Flying Hospital," and he soon began to encroach upon Morgan's authority. After much correspondence on the issue between Washington, Shippen and Mercer, Congress resolved that Shippen was responsible for all of the sick in New Jersey hospitals, and Morgan, "for the Army posted on the east side of Hudson's river."

In response to the critical medical supply shortage and partly in response to requests from Morgan that regimental surgeons be "placed in some subordination," on July 17, 1776, Congress passed legislation that addressed medical supply and other issues, but did not firmly clarify the relationship between the two medical systems. Congress resolved that "no regimental surgeons be allowed to draw upon the hospital of his department, for any stores except medicines and instruments." The regiments were required to send their patients to the general hospital if they needed any other supplies. Further, the regimental hospitals were to make weekly reports of their sick and account for their use of medicines and supplies to the Hospital Department. The regimental surgeons resented these restrictions. This legislation failed to alleviate the conflict

between the two systems, and complaints against the general hospital continued.

On August 27 the British outflanked and defeated the Americans who were guarding Brooklyn Heights at the Battle of Long Island. Washington retreated into Pennsylvania on December 6, and New Jersey was abandoned to the enemy. The defense of New York was a disaster; the Americans had 600 combat casualties, 4,500 were taken prisoner, thousands of desertions, and several thousand deaths from disease.

During the retreat Morgan organized the evacuation of patients from Long Island to Manhattan and then again to New Jersey. His command and control of the Hospital Department disintegrated as the army scattered. Surgeons, nurses and orderlies deserted. The flow of sick and wounded exceeded the capacity of the temporary field hospitals. When these were threatened by the British offense the patients had to be dispersed to distant location in New York, Connecticut, and New Jersey. The patients were transported in open wagons in the winter cold without blankets over miles of rutted roads; all of them suffered, and more than a few died as a result of these transport conditions.

In such confusion the Hospital Department was blamed for the defects in the handling of the casualties. General Nathanael Greene complained that surgeons were not provided with drugs and equipment, that much bitterness prevailed in the ranks about the hospital conditions, and that such feeling would prove "an unsurmountable obstacle to recruiting the new Army." Greene declared, "It is wholly immaterial, in my opinion, whether a man dies in a general hospital or a regimental hospital."

Determined to end the campaign year on a high note, on Christmas night 1776 Washington led his men across the Delaware River in a surprise attack and after capturing Trenton and Princeton withdrew to Morristown, New Jersey, for the winter.

Dissatisfied with Morgan's performance, Congress dismissed him on January 9, 1777. Morgan was very upset with the way he was dismissed and waged a personal two-year campaign with Congress before he was finally exonerated. In March the Congress appointed a special committee to study the problems of the Hospital Department and on April 7–8 passed legislation for an elaborate and detailed reorganization. This legislation provided for a hierarchy of deputy and assistant deputy director generals, each responsible for a regional department: the Northern, Eastern, Middle, and if the military situation required, a Southern department. In addition to his other duties, the director general was to be responsible for the supervision of the Middle Department. To supervise the practice of medicine and surgery a physician general and a surgeon general were appointed for each geographical region subordinate to their respective deputy director general. In addition, a physician and surgeon general were assigned for each separate army "to superintend the regimental surgeons and their mates, and to see that they do their duty." On April 11, after choosing the other high-ranking members, Congress elected Dr. Shippen as the third Director General of the Hospital Department.

From this point on, the Hospital Department had clear and legitimate authority over the independent regimental surgeons. The regimental surgeons, however, though technically under the supervision of the Hospital Department, continued in their loyalty to their regimental commanders, who were still reluctant to allow hospital surgeons to tell them how to run their hospitals. Further, Congress once again contributed to the confusion by announcing in August that the reforms were not to be applied to the hospital operating in Virginia.

While at his winter headquarters at Morristown, Washington made one of his wisest medical decisions of the war. On January 6, 1777, he wrote to Dr. Shippen,

> Finding the small pox to be spreading much and fearing that no precaution can prevent it from running thro' the whole of our Army, I have determined that the troops shall be inoculated. This Expedient may be attended with some inconveniences and some disadvantages, but yet I trust in its consequences will have the most happy effects . . . [S]hould the disorder infect the Army . . . we should have more to dread from it, than the Sword of the enemy . . . [W]ithout delay inoculate all the Continental Troops that are in Philadelphia and those that shall come in, as fast as they arrive.

Smallpox inoculation had been Dr. Morgan's idea while he was director general. In April 1776 he wrote and recommended it "to surgeons of the hospital, and those in the Army under my direction." The results of inoculation were good.

At the time the mortality from naturally acquired smallpox was about 160 per 1,000 in the army. Inoculation reduced this to 3 per 1,000. After the introduction of smallpox inoculation the army was not entirely free of the disease, but it would no longer cause losses like those during the first two years of the war. Smallpox inoculation contributed substantially to the American cause for independence. This was the first immunization program by command order in military operations in Europe or America.

The British strategy for the campaign of 1777 sent General John Burgoyne south from Canada to divide the colonies and isolate New England. Poorly planned and coordinated, surrounded in the New York wilderness and with no hope of reinforcements, Burgoyne surrendered to General Horatio Gates after his defeat at Saratoga on October 17. It was an important victory for the Americans because it brought France and later Spain and Holland into the war on the American side. Dr. James Thacher provides a vivid account of the hospital conditions during the Saratoga campaign in his *Military Journal*:

> Not less than one thousand wounded and sick are now in this city [Saratoga]; the Dutch church and several private houses are occupied as hospitals. We have about thirty surgeons and mates; and all are constantly employed. I am obliged to devote the whole of my time, from eight o'clock in the morning to a late hour in the evening, to the care of our patients. Here is a fine field for professional improvement. Amputating limbs, trepanning fractured skulls, and dressing the most formidable wounds, have familiarized my mind to scenes of woe.

Meanwhile, in August General Howe left New York and sailed up Chesapeake Bay, where his army crossed north overland to Philadelphia. Washington's failed attempts to defend Philadelphia resulted in defeats at Brandywine, Paoli, and Germantown. Howe's army occupied Philadelphia, and Washington's army spent that famous, terrible winter of 1777–1778 at Valley Forge. The army was hard pressed to provide food, clothing, and shelter for the 12,000 men at Valley Forge, as it was throughout much of the war, partly because of poor roads, scarcity of resources, the inflation of the Continental currency, and faltering support from Congress. Dr. Albigence Waldo, surgeon of the 1st Connecticut Regiment, left the following vivid description of the soldiers that winter at Valley Forge in his journal:

> There comes a soldier—His bare feet are seen through his wornout shoes—his legs nearly naked from the tattered remains of an only pair of stockings—his breeches not sufficient to cover his Nakedness—his shirt hangs in strings—his hair dishevelled—his face meagre—his whole appearance pictures a person forsaken and discouraged. This poor fellow comes to the doctor and cries with an air of wretchedness and despair.

The medical system of the Middle Department was also hard pressed to provide support for the battle casualties and camp fevers, especially dysentery and typhus, and for another round of winter smallpox inoculation. Patients were crowded into numerous hospitals and convalescent centers that sprang up all over New Jersey and eastern Pennsylvania in houses, barns, churches, and courthouses, wherever the Hospital Department could find space. In a January 1778 report to Congress, in which Washington gave an assessment of his nine army departments, his harshest comments were for the Hospital Department:

> There has been and, I fear will continue, difficulties and imperfections in this department . . . One powerful reason, no doubt . . . is the extreme scarcity of proper supplies . . . But one thing, which has had a very pernicious influence, is the continual jealousies and altercations, subsisting between the hospital and regimental surgeons.

The sick rate for the Continental Army reached its peak of 35 percent while at Valley Forge in February 1778.

That same month Baron Friedrich von Steuben reported to Washington at Valley Forge. Washington obtained for him the rank of major general and appointed him inspector general of the Continental Army. Dr. James Tilton wrote that "When Baron Steuben was appointed inspector general, besides the muster of clothing, he introduced a number of salutary regulations, which contributed more to the health and comfort of the troops, than did the utmost efforts of all the medical staff." During that winter von Steuben produced his *Regulations for the Order and Discipline of the Troops of the United States* (1779), which were approved by Washington and later adopted by Congress. These regulations formalized the principles of hygiene and pre-

ventive medicine that had long been preached by British and Continental physicians. The *Regulations* were addressed to commanders and line officers, emphasizing that the preservation of the health of the troops was a responsibility of command. Congress ordered that the regulations "be observed by all troops of the United States, and that all General and other officers cause the same to be executed with all possible exactness." These were the first regulations of the army and the Hospital Department. Von Steuben's "Instructions for the Commandant of a Regiment" implicitly stated that the preservation of the health of the troops was a responsibility of command: "The preservation of the soldiers health should be his first and greatest care; and as that depends in great measure on their cleanliness and manner of living, he must have a watchful eye over the officers of companies, that they pay the necessary attention to their men in those respects."

Chapter XXIII, "Of the Treatment of the Sick," in the *Regulations* explained the duties of the officers:

> There is nothing which gains an officer the love of his soldiers more than his care of them under the distress of sickness; it is then he has the power of exerting his humanity and making their situation as agreeable as possible. Two or three tents should be set apart in every regiment for the reception of such sick as cannot be sent to the general hospital, or whose cases may not require it.

> The sergeants and corporals shall every morning at roll-call give a return of the sick of their respective squads to the first sergeant, who must make out one for the company, and lose no time in delivering it to the surgeon, who will immediately visit them. . . .

> When a soldier has been sick he must not be put on duty till he has recovered sufficient strength, of which the surgeon should be judge.

The enforcement of these regulations greatly improved discipline for the benefit of both the fighting power and health of the soldiers.

In a similar attempt to improve conditions, in 1777 Dr. Benjamin Rush had published his *Directions for Preserving the Health of Soldiers*. Rush was a highly influential physician, a signer of the Declaration of Independence, and a one-time Physician General of the Hospital in the Middle Department. He addressed his *Directions* to the officers of the army and strongly emphasized that the health of the troops was the responsibility of command. He wrote,

> The skill of physicians and surgeons will avail but little in preventing mortality from sickness among our soldiers without the concurrence of the officers of the Army. Your authority gentleman is absolutely necessary to enforce the most salutory plans and precepts for preserving the health of the soldiers.

In this statement, Rush emphasized the basic principle of operational preventive medicine that is as sound today as it was then.

The experience at Valley Forge was a decisive point in the American Revolution. The army that survived the ordeal at Valley Forge was a healthier, better disciplined and trained, more confident force and would remain so for the remainder of the war, as evidenced by the partial success at the Battle of Monmouth. At Monmouth on June 28, Washington regrouped faltering troops and repelled repeated British attacks. The British slipped away to the safety of New York and the British navy. Although the Battle of Monmouth was not a victory for the Americans, it showed that the Continental Army was eager and able to fight. After this battle the war in the northern states became a stalemate. The war would be decided in the South.

Before the end of the war Washington's army would endure another severe winter encamped at Morristown. It was near Morristown as Basking Ridge during the winter of 1779–1780 that Dr. James Tilton "contrived" his hospital hut "upon the plan of an Indian hut" designed to "avoid infection." Tilton had studied the hospital system and was shocked by the unsanitary conditions. In rhetorical overstatement he wrote in his *Economical Observations on Military Hospitals* (1813) that "it would be shocking . . . to relate the history of our General Hospital in the years 1777 and 1778 when it swallowed up at least one half of our army owing to a fatal tendency in the system to throw all of the sick of the army into the general hospital." Tilton's hospital hut was a single-story log cabin structure with a large central section and two smaller wards on the ends at right angles to the central room. It provided for a small, well-ventilated hospital in which up to 28 patients could be isolated from cross infection. Tilton's design was apparently used only once during that winter as an experimental hospital. He said that it was used with success, and Dr. Benjamin Rush wrote that Tilton's log hospitals "were found to be very conducive to recovery of soldiers with hospital fever." It was an important early effort to apply preventive medicine principles by the construction of isolation wards against cross infection in field hospitals.

As a result of his efforts to improve the hospital system, Tilton was influential in the Congressional Act of 1780 that brought about yet another reform of the Hospital Department and the appointment of its fourth director general. Benjamin Rush had resigned from the Hospital Department and joined with Morgan in making allegations of misconduct against Director General Shippen, who was later tried by a military court-martial. Although Shippen was acquitted of all charges on June 27, 1780, it was noted that he had engaged in the speculation of hospital supplies and that this was "highly improper and justly reprehensible."

In the reform of the Hospital Department that followed on September 30, Congress officially created the Officer of Purveyor, thereby taking the supply functions out of the hands of the director general, and forbidding any employees or members of the Department from participating in trade of hospital stores. Congress reduced the size of the Department by eliminating the separate staff of the geographical regions and replaced them with three chief hospital physicians and surgeons and 15 senior hospital physicians and surgeons responsible for the general hospital system. Congress reaffirmed the subordination of the regimental surgeons it had established by its law of April 1777 by directing the chief physician and surgeons for the separate armies to supervise regimental surgeons and mates. Congress addressed the medical supply problem by elevating the apothecary's position and appointed Dr. Andrew Craigie as Apothecary General of the Continental Army. Craigie had served as an apothecary for the army of the Northern Department during the failed Canada invasion and later as apothecary for the Middle Department. In the election of officers for the newly reorganized Department on October 6–7, Congress appointed Dr. John Cochran to the number two post as Chief Physician and Surgeon General of the Continental Army. Although Shippen was reelected as director general, on January 3, 1781, he resigned, claiming he did so because Congress had decided that his part-time duties as Philadelphia professor of anatomy and that of director general were incompatible.

Of our first three surgeon generals one was dismissed as a traitor, one was relieved due to complaints from regimental surgeons, and one was tried by court-martial, acquitted, and then he resigned.

On January 17, 1781, Dr. Cochran was appointed director general. He was the first director general to be entirely apprentice-trained, but he did have considerable experience. He had served as a surgeon's mate in the French and Indian War, and in the Continental Army as Surgeon General of the Middle Department and as Chief Physician and Surgeon of the Continental Army. He was able to remain as director general through the end of the war.

During the last three years of the war Congress made various changes to the organization and policies of the Hospital Department. The last wartime change of the command structure of the Department occurred in March 1781, when the Southern Department was finally brought under the control of the director general. The spring brought with it a major administrative change for the Department on May 28, 1781, when Congress abolished its Medical Committee and transferred its powers and duties to a Board of War, whose powers were in turn transferred to Secretary of War Benjamin Lincoln when he was appointed on September 30, 1781.

The war in the South began with American defeat at Camden and Charleston, South Carolina, followed by victories at Cowpens and Guilford Court House, North Carolina, and ended with the final American victory at Yorktown. The French fleet commanded by Admiral de Grasse drove off the British fleet at Chesapeake Bay and prevented the escape of General Lord Cornwallis. The combined armies of Washington and Frenchman Marquis de Lafayette surrounded and besieged Cornwallis at Yorktown. On October 19, 1781, Cornwallis surrendered, and his men marched out to the victorious American army. The war was essentially over. The British signed the Paris Peace Treaty in 1783, and the Americans had officially won their independence.

It is almost impossible to determine the exact number of Americans who were sick, wounded, or died during the Revolution. The variety of enlistment terms among regular and militia soldiers makes it difficult to determine how many served during the war. There are no means of determining how many soldiers deserted or were taken prisoner. During the war thousands of soldiers were furloughed home because of illness or injury, and the number of these who subsequently died will never be known. Incomplete hospital records add to the difficulty of determining exact figures. It is possible, however, to determine casualty rates based upon the estimates of those who participated in the war.

Dr. Tilton, the Delaware physician who later became Surgeon General of the United States Army during the War of 1812, saw active service throughout the war and recognized the high mortality caused by disease. In his *Economical Observations*, which was based on his Revolutionary War experiences, he wrote,

> I have no hesitation in declaring it is my opinion that we lost not less than from ten to twenty of camp diseases for one by weapons of the enemy. . . . [I]nfection is more dangerous in military life, than the weapons of war. . . . [U]se all possible care and diligence in warding off that greatest of all evils, the plague of infection.

Dr. Thacher, one of this country's first military historians, who also saw action during the entire war, estimated in his *Military Journal* that the total deaths during the war were 70,000. Military historian Louis C. Duncan believes that Thacher's estimate is the best made by a contemporary writer, but he cautions that this figure does not include the thousands who were furloughed home and did not return, were killed in lesser known small engagements, or died as prisoners of war. By using many sources, Duncan estimated that 1,000 soldiers were killed or died of battle wounds each year, for a total of 7,000 battle deaths during the seven years of the war. He concluded that "ten men died of disease to every one whose life was taken by the enemy is a safe estimate. Where bullets killed one, disease killed at least ten."

The British forces fared better than the Continental Army in both battle and disease casualties for several reasons. The British army was a well-organized and disciplined force, well equipped and clothed, with a more efficient medical department. For the most part they were professional soldiers; older, seasoned veterans who had survived the deprivations of army life and developed some immunity to the infectious diseases of that age. This was in contrast to the American colonists, who were generally from isolated rural farming communities. They were susceptible to infectious diseases, and when they were brought together in defense of their country they were exposed to typhus, smallpox, dysentery, and measles, both in the field and especially in the crowded hospitals. Throughout much of the war the British were quartered in the cities, such as New York, Philadelphia, and Charleston, where they were comfortably housed and well provided for.

With the disbanding of the army the task of the medical staff may have been said to have ended. Many, however, continued their service to the new country in public life. Three Revolutionary War doctors later became Surgeon General of the United States Army—Dr. Richard Allison, Dr. James Craik, and Dr. James Tilton, Three who had been education as physicians and had served as line officers later went on to command the army—Dr. James Wilkinson, Dr. Henry Dearborn, and Dr. Arthur St. Clair. Still others rose to become Secretary of War—Dr. William Eustis, Dr. Henry Dearborn, and Dr. James McHenry. Many other physicians later became state governors, United States congressmen, and ambassadors to foreign nations. It is doubtful that in the history of any nation the men of the medical profession played a more important role than those of the American Revolution.

Military medicine during the American Revolution was characterized by quarrels and a lack of cooperation between the regimental and general hospital system. No one reason can be attributed for the failures of the Hospital Department. Before the war the army and the Hospital Department were nonexistent and had to be created; as such they had some growing to do. Although Congress made several reforms and modification to the organization of the Hospital Department, it is probably safe to say that the Congress' primary concern was to establish and maintain the fighting army. The reputation of the Hospital Department and the medical care provided to soldiers were not aided by the personal bickering between Morgan, Shippen, and Rush, nor the manner in which the first three directors were dismissed from the army. The two greatest contributions to military medicine, the health of the troops, and the ultimate victory of the American army were smallpox inoculation and von Steuben's *Regulations*. The principle that the health of the troops is a responsibility of command was repeatedly stressed by line offices and physicians alike. It is a lesson that is still taught today.

Allison P. Clark, III

REFERENCES

Stanhope Bayne-Jones, *The Evolution of Preventive Medicine in the United States Army, 1607–1939* (1968); Richard L. Blanco, *Physician of the American Revolution: Jonathan Potts* (1979); Philip Cash, *Medical Men at the Siege of Boston* (1973); John Duffy, *The Healers: A History of American Medicine* (1976); Louis C. Duncan, *Medical Men in the American Revolution, 1775–1783* (1931); Fielding H. Garrison, *Notes on the History of Military Medicine* (1922); James E. Gibson, *Dr. Bodo Otto and the Medical Background of the American Revolution* (1937); Mary C. Gillett, *The Army Medical Department, 1775–1818* (1981); Don Higgenbotham, *The War of American Independence* (1977); John Jones, *Plain Concise Practical Remarks, On the Treatment of Wounds and Fractures; To Which Is Added, An Appendix, On Camp and Military Hospitals; Principally Designed, for the Use of Young Military and Naval Surgeons; in North-America* (1775); Keith C. Wilbur, *Revolutionary Medicine 1700–1800* (1980).

Meigs, Return Jonathan (1740–1823)

Continental Army officer. As a lieutenant in the Connecticut militia, Meigs fought at the siege of Boston. He then marched with Benedict Arnold through Maine to invade Canada. During the expedition he was promoted to captain and then major. During the attempted storming of Quebec (December 31, 1775) he was captured. Meigs was exchanged in July 1776 and soon after became a colonel.

Meigs became famous for his raid on Sag Harbor, New York (May 23, 1777). After a British force under Governor William Tryon of New York had ravaged the American supply depot at Danbury, Connecticut, on April 27, 1777, General Samuel Parsons sought revenge. He knew that Sag Harbor held large quantities of provisions for the enemy. Parsons selected Meigs for the operation.

On May 23, Meigs left Guilford, Connecticut, with 3 sloops, 13 whaleboats, and 120 men. At Southold, Long Island, the Americans grounded their boats in the darkness and pulled and tugged the boats ashore. Meigs led the attack on Sag Harbor. Some British were killed, a few escaped, but about 83 were captured. The Americans destroyed 12 brigs and sloops, 100 tons of pressed hay, and large quantities of rum, grain, and stores. Meigs returned with his prisoners and a captured schooner without losing a man. To some degree Tryon's raid on Danbury was avenged. Congress awarded Meigs a special sword.

Meigs later fought under General Anthony Wayne at Stony Point (June 16, 1779), and he helped to quell a mutiny of the Connecticut Line (May 25, 1780). He retired from service June 1781 as a brigadier general.

After the war Meigs became a surveyor with the Ohio Company, and in 1788 he led settlers to the Muskingum River (Ohio). By 1801 he was a federal agent to the Cherokee Indians. In 1808 he assisted in a treaty between the Cherokee and the state of Tennessee.

Richard L. Blanco

REFERENCES

Charles I. Bushnell, *Crumbs for Antiquarians*, 2 vols. (1864–65), *1*; Henry P. Johnson, "Return Jonathan Meigs," *Magazine of History*, *4* (1880):282–292; Kenneth L. Roberts, ed., *March to Quebec: Journals of the Members of Arnold's Expedition* (1940).

Mennonites in the American Revolution

The years of the American Revolution from 1775 through 1783 proved to be a time of severe trial for the Amish and Mennonites, Quakers, Schwenkfelders, and Tunkers (Church of the Brethren) as the historic peace churches. The more ambiguous peace witness of the Moravian Church brought legal penalties on its members. Their experience led the pacifists to reassess their role in the state and to become by choice "the quiet in the land." The newly independent United States also had to reassess its understanding of religious liberty in response to the firm stand taken by Mennonites, Quakers, and others during the war.

The leaders of the American Revolution put more and more emphasis on military service as an essential element in the definition of a good citizen. Christians who believed the nonresistance and peace were integral parts of the Gospel found themselves in a dilemma. They had always been faithful subjects, paying their taxes and obeying the laws, but they could not acknowledge any obligation "of Testifying our Loyalty defending him with Sword in hand." King George III and his colonial governors had never asked that of them.

Mennonites in Virginia explained their situation in a petition to their state legislature shortly after the close of the Revolutionary War:

> They have wished at all times to be faithful to the Laws that have given them protection, and ever wish so to be, when consistent with the dictates of their religious Profession. There forefathers and Predecessors came from a far Country to America to Seek Religious Liberty; this they have enjoyed except by the Infliction of penalties for not bearing Arms which for some time lay heavy on them.

Political leaders in the legislatures also faced a dilemma. Was religious liberty to be construed as broadly as in William Penn's 1701 Charter of Privileges, so that no one could be obliged "to do or to suffer anything contrary to their religious persuasion," or was religious liberty to be defined more narrowly as freedom of worship? Was the right of conscientious objection absolute or were these religious pacifists merely indulged in their claims at the convenience of the state? With the nation in danger, should they forego their liberty of conscience in defense of American liberties?

Should conscientious objection be contingent on the performance of some equivalent duty or the payment of an equivalent tax? The British colonies in North America had never followed this policy, but it was similar to the practice in the Palatinate and other German states where Mennonites paid a special tax in return for military exemption.

In the context of the American Revolution, the historic peace churches moved away from asserting natural rights to religious liberty and invoked a more European understanding of religious liberty as *privilegium*. The men who framed American state constitutions also moved in this direction. They linked exemption for those conscientiously scrupling to bear arms to payment of an equivalent for such service. When Congress debated the amendments to the United States Constitution known as the Bill of Rights, the lawmakers deleted James Madison's words providing that "no one religiously scrupulous of bearing arms shall be compelled to render military service." In voting to eliminate this provision they agreed with Egbert Benson of New York who argued that conscientious objection "may be a religious persuasion, but it is no natural right, and therefore ought to be left to the discretion of the government."

Christian pacifists were relatively few in the British colonies, perhaps no more than 36,000 in a population of 1.3 million. Two-thirds of them were concentrated in Pennsylvania and the rest scattered through the other colonies primarily from New Jersey to South Carolina. The 18,000 to 20,000 members of the Society of Friends (Quakers) were the largest group, with 12,000 to 15,000 Mennonites and Amish, some 3,000 Tunkers, and a few hundred Schwenkfelders. The Friends, mainly of British ancestry, used English, but German was the common language of the other peace churches. They all had prospered in the colonies. Contemporary observers often spoke of "the rich Mennonites and Quakers." They were generally successful farmers, millers, and artisans of many kinds. None of these groups, except the Amish, lived in isolation. Their members voted, held public office at the local and county levels and occasionally in the Colonial Assembly.

Quaker-dominated Pennsylvania imposed no military obligation on anyone, since the colony had no militia laws and depended wholly on volunteers. In Maryland and Virginia, Mennonites and Quakers enjoyed exemption from military duty. Colonial law permitted affirmation by anyone with scruples about taking an oath. Religious freedom in the colonies meant that Mennonites and others could enter any profession, testify in court, inherit property, buy and sell land, vote or hold office without any restriction. They had reason to remember King George III in their prayers.

The gathering storm of the American Revolution caused some strain within the peace churches. When the First Continental Congress met in September 1774 and imposed a boycott on British goods through a non-importation agreement, they also required committees in every county and every township to enforce this regulation. Several Mennonites voluntarily served on these committees, more than a dozen on the Lancaster County Committee alone. Like their Quaker neighbors, Mennonites participated in the general feeling that Parliament should alter its policy toward the American colonies, but they drew back from any step in the direction of violence or disloyalty to the Crown.

The historic peace churches drew together in this crisis. Mennonites looked to the leadership of the Quakers, who had long played a major role in the affairs of Pennsylvania. In January 1775 a delegation of Mennonite leaders met with the Quakers at Gwynned Meeting House. The Quaker leaders provided a German edition of a statement emphasizing the peace testimony and counseling patience and nonviolence, which the Mennonites circulated.

The pacifists already anticipated the next problem. Late in January a provincial congress met in Philadelphia. Since the Pennsylvania Assembly had done nothing about passing a militia law, the Congress was under some pressure to create a militia. The peace churches saw such an action, in the words of Berks County leader Christopher Schultz, "at this time of professing and petitioning for peace . . . would be a very foremost step towards War, before the other Colonies." But the Congress also adjourned without adopting a militia law.

The county committees seized the initiative in May by ordering every able-bodied male over the age of 15 to sign a voluntary association and assemble "to learn the art of war" in companies of associators. They imposed this obligation primarily as a political move. The entire population would be in arms against Parliament, and any man who failed to sign the association, for whatever reason, would declare himself an enemy to American liberty.

Members of the peace churches could not "provide themselves with Arms and Ammunition, and learn Military discipline" with their neighbors. They received rough treatment here and there. Church leaders proposed to the committees an alternative—a voluntary assessment for the poor, especially refugees from British-held Boston. This alternative was well rooted in peace church tradition. During the French and Indian War (1754–1763) Mennonites, Moravians, and Schwenkfelders had provided relief for refugees from Indian raids and ransomed other settlers taken prisoner by the Indians. Mennonites and Quakers independently proposed something of the same sort. Local authorities accepted a voluntary assessment, equal to each man's annual taxes, but they could not promise the money would only be used for non-military purposes.

For many who drilled with associators, this seemed too little. A company of associators forced the Lancaster Committee to resign, and other companies all over Pennsylvania petitioned the assembly to take harsher measures with non-associators. Matters had reached a crisis by November 1775 when the Mennonites and Tunkers sent their "Short and Sincere Declaration" to the assembly. Benjamin Hershey, a Lancaster Mennonite, wrote the text.

They expressed gratitude to the assembly for prior benefits and urged the assembly "to grant Liberty of Conscience to all Inhabitants" as William Penn had done. They were willing to pay taxes and to render to Caesar the things that are Caesar's and to be subject to the higher powers, but they informed the assembly "that we are not at Liberty in Conscience to take up Arms to conquer our Enemies, but rather to pray to God for us and them." They explained further:

> The Advice to those who do not find Freedom of conscience to take up arms, that they should be helpful to those who are in Need and distressed Circumstances, we receive with Cheerfulness towards all Men of what Station they may be—it being our Principle to feed the Hungry and give the Thirsty Drink; we have dedicated ourselves to serve all Men in everything that can be helpful to the Preservation of Men's Lives; but we find no Freedom in giving, or doing, or assisting in any Thing by which Men's Lives are destroyed or hurt.

In spite of eloquent petitions from the pacifist sects, the Pennsylvania Assembly laid a special tax on all non-associators. Many more petitions reached the assembly from associators who wanted the penalties increased. This was the beginning of a series of additional taxes imposed on religious pacifists because they failed to perform some patriotic duty. Here was the crux of their problem. They had heretofore paid all their taxes and obeyed all the laws to the letter and, having demonstrated their loyalty in this way, they appealed for exemption from the one duty that they could not undertake. The Revolutionary authorities had now made this duty the sole test of loyalty and no payment of taxes, as penalty or otherwise, nor observance of the civil law could remove the suspicion of disloyalty that clung to all pacifists.

Mennonites compounded that suspicion by supporting conservatives and moderates in two elections held in 1776. They joined a majority of Pennsylvania voters who returned members of the assembly favorable to compromise between Britain and the colonies in the May election. The vote did not fairly represent opinion in the province since election rules and the apportionment of seats favored conservative eastern counties over the newer western counties. After the election, radicals maneuvered to call for a constitutional convention to establish a government they thought would be more responsive to the popular will and more committed to the cause of American independence. They wanted to set aside Penn's venerable Charter of Privileges and to write a new constitution for a newly independent state.

Mennonites expressed fear "that our liberty might be endangered" and attended township meetings in substantial numbers. Christian Funk, a Mennonite bishop, attended the meeting in Franconia Township in what was then Philadelphia County; Mennonites formed about two-thirds of the meeting and evidently agreed with Bishop Funk that as "a defenseless people" they could not be involved "in tearing ourselves from the king" nor "institute or destroy any government." Such neutrality must have sounded like a pledge of support to the Crown. Mennonites everywhere took this stand.

Neutrality did not prevent them from voting in record numbers against the new constitution. When the first elections under the new government were held in November, Mennonites again went to the polls. One Patriot lamented that "a very great Number of the German Menonists" voted in Lancaster County and he feared the results: "I am ready to pronounce our Convention are Blown up."

The Constitution of 1776 guaranteed the right of conscientious objection, but made explicit the link between exemption and some equivalent in lieu of personal service. The newly elected assembly proceeded to enact a militia law embodying these features. Military service was a common obligation, and every able-bodied man would be enrolled in a militia company. Anyone scrupulous of bearing arms could serve by substitute, hiring another man to take his place if his company should be drafted into actual service. Otherwise he would be carried on the muster roll and be fined for missing drills. Since the peace churches objected as much to hiring a substitute as to serving in person, the militia authorities had the right to seize property of whatever value they believed necessary to pay a substitute. Virginia levied the cost of the substitute on the Mennonite or Quaker community as a whole. Other states adopted plans similar to Pennsylvania's.

The peace churches found themselves reluctant participants in the war effort. Occasional militia excesses, arresting and parading pacifists through the streets, reminded them that their conscientious objection was merely tolerated at best. The special tax on non-associators remained in force and other taxes and militia fines mounted up. By the war's end Mennonites and Quakers were paying 20 times their normal taxes in wartime fines. They also contributed wagons and teams, cattle, horses, grain, and whatever the army needed, sometimes willingly and sometimes by distraint.

The definition of a loyal citizen was given further refinement in 1777. Pennsylvania, Maryland, and Virginia and nearly every other state passed a Test Act that year in an effort to smoke out covert Loyalists. The Pennsylvania legislators provided a loyalty oath that could be offered to suspicious characters, and heavy penalties for any who refused to take it. After several opportunities to subscribe his abjuration of King George and his government, his readiness to fight for American liberty, and his unswerving loyalty to the new regime, the Tory recusant would face banishment and seizure of all his property.

Local Patriots in Northampton County, Pennsylvania, seized on this new law in a way unintended by its framers. They offered the Test Oath to every Mennonite in the county and, when they refused to pledge to defend their country by force of arms, began legal proceedings against them. All their property, "not a Morsel of Bread left them for their Children," was sold at auction and a sentence of banishment pronounced on the adult males. Protests that they had always been loyal and inoffensive, paid their taxes, provided wagons and teams and food for the army, and even served in nonmilitary capacities were to no avail.

A storm of protest blew up over this incident. Pennsylvania authorities overturned the action of the Northampton justices and instructed them on the real meaning of the act passed the previous session. But they did not respond favorably to suggestions that Mennonites and other religious pacifists be exempted from the Test Act or the oath modified so that they could take it. In

December 1778 the Pennsylvania Assembly repealed the harsher provisions of the Test Act, but substituted a new section on juries and continued the provision for double taxation of nonjurors.

George Bryan had explained his government's intentions in framing the original Test Act. It was intended solely to entrap "persons whose character & conduct shall threaten active mischief against the State" and only such Tories should be compelled to take the oath or brought before a justice. But the act had another purpose. Bryan wrote that it was not by accident that those who did not voluntarily take the Test Oath would be excluded from voting or being elected to office. There were probably "no Moravian, Schwenkfelder, or Menonists" in the first category, Bryan acknowledged, but "if many of these people should be found to qualify themselves for enjoying all privileges, they might by appearing at elections disturb the plans layed for the defense of the State."

Pennsylvania used the Test Act to deprive Mennonites and other religious pacifists of their civil rights to keep them from voting. The assembly modified the law in December 1778 to allow the sectarians to pursue their professions, conduct their schools, preserve their property, and wait upon the outcome of the war without prejudice. In 1779 the assembly voted a new Test Act which required that all citizens take the prescribed oath by the end of December 1779 or be forever barred from political participation in the state.

Maryland and Virginia maintained harsher provisions in their laws, closing certain professions, including preaching and teaching school, to nonjurors, but they repealed these laws after the war. Pennsylvania's law remained in effect after the adoption of the United States Constitution in 1789. Periodic efforts to have the Pennsylvania law repealed cited the loss to the state by disfranchising these good citizens. An editorial in the *Pennsylvania Gazette* commented:

> There are many thousands of good foederalists who will never vote at our elections while that weak and unnecessary law is in force. Virginia, and the governor of Canada, have already taken advantage of our folly; . . . It is said, that thirty families of the people called Menonists are about to emigrate from Lancaster county to Niagara, on purpose to avoid the disagreeable consequences of our ridiculous and tyrannical test law.

The sympathies of many Amish, Mennonites, Quakers, and Tunkers were undoubtedly with the old order exemplified in Penn's Charter of Privileges. They hesitated to do anything that would further the war effort. A meeting of some Lancaster County Mennonites in 1780 even questioned whether planting and harvesting crops did not serve some military purpose. As the war dragged on, they found it difficult to draw the line. Millers were grinding grain "for the public service," and most peacetime occupations had acquired some indirect link with supporting the men in the army. An Amish farmer went to jail, charged with treason, for refusing to give a horse "to such blood-spilling people." Many others handed over their livestock, flour, or other property to the commissary officers on demand.

The payment of taxes, once the mark of loyalty, became an issue. Some had no trouble in rendering to the Congress what belonged to the Congress. Many others scrupled at paying taxes that were intended as a direct equivalent for military service. Quakers and Mennonites both had problems with the payment of "war taxes," but the Mennonite concern was especially with the non-associator tax from its identification as a substitute for personal service. In the end, there was little they could do except compel the authorities to take their goods by distraint.

The peace church tradition of feeding the hungry and giving drink to the thirsty took on political implications. Mennonites, Quakers, and Tunkers were sometimes arrested for sheltering escaped British prisoners as well as American soldiers wandering the roads. In some cases the authorities decoyed pacifists with men who pretended to be deserters or fleeing prisoners of war. Kindness to men of the other side was no excuse.

Some Mennonites and Quakers took an active part on the British side, just as other Quakers and Mennonites willingly served the Patriot cause. In both cases the church excommunicated members who took up arms.

The official Mennonite position was one of waiting the outcome. They believed that government was established by God and that they must be "subject to the higher powers," as St. Paul had instructed his own converts in the Roman Empire. They were obliged "to be true to the State," but in a revolutionary situation "it is so uncertain upon what side God almighty will bestow the victory" that they could "not know whether God has rejected the king and chosen the Congress." This was a point of view appropriate to a withdrawn sect, but seemed questionable for people who voted and held public office.

By depriving the pacifist sects of those rights, through the Test Acts, the Pennsylvania Assembly helped them in the process of withdrawal from the larger society. Indeed the events of the American Revolution encouraged them step by step to withdraw from political life and to concentrate on strengthening their own religious communities.

As the Mennonites retreated to an outlook familiar to them in the Palatinate and other European states that tolerated their presence, American law withdrew from that broad understanding of freedom of conscience enunciated in Penn's Charter. Militia laws in each of the United States provided exemption for those with conscientious scruples against war at the price of providing substitutes or paying fines. The religious pacifist labored under the difficulty that these alternatives also required him to do his part in providing for the common defense. The authorities knew this. Roger Sherman of Connecticut observed in a speech in Congress in 1789:

> It is well known that those who are religiously scrupulous of bearing arms, are equally scrupulous of getting substitutes or paying an equivalent. Many of them would rather die than to do either one or the other.

The question of conscientious objection naturally rose during the debates on the United States Constitution. Ratifying conventions held in Pennsylvania, Virginia, North Carolina, and Rhode Island proposed amendments guaranteeing this right. It was difficult to find an appropriate formula that would not somehow weaken the link between military service and the good citizen forged during the Revolution. In the last analysis no such formula could be found. Congress rejected James Madison's provision for conscientious objection as part of the Bill of Rights, agreeing with Egbert Benson that this "religious persuasion" was "no natural right" and ought to be "left to the discretion of the government." A constitutional guarantee, Benson argued, would wreak havoc with state militia laws that rested on the assumption that personal military service was the duty of every citizen.

Some Mennonites and Quakers migrated to Upper Canada at the war's end, where the authorities welcomed them and gave them the same exemptions from militia duty they had enjoyed in Pennsylvania. A steady stream of "Late Loyalists" followed through the 1790s, but they represented a very small fraction of the peace churches. Most chose internal exile.

In 1795 William Duke, a Methodist preacher, offered some insight into the way Americans looked at Mennonites as the eighteenth century neared its end. In his *Observations on the Present State of Religion in Maryland*, Duke noted that Mennonites had "a scheme of discipline" that was divisive to the social order and clashed with "the common methods of government and civil society." But it was obvious that they were "remarkably peaceable and passive" and did not "intend any disturbance or innovation," so they were "readily tolerated and excused."

The quiet in the land had found a place within American denominationalism. Americans could tolerate these hard-working and successful farmers, craftsmen, and small-scale businessmen since they confined their potentially disruptive ideas of pacifism and religion within the walls of their meetinghouses. Eighteenth-century American pluralism could make room for them on these terms, which were essentially its own terms. *See also:* Quakers in the American Revolution

Richard K. McMaster

REFERENCES

Peter Brock, *Pacifism in the United States from the Colonial Era to the First World War* (1968); Donald F. Durnbagh, *The Brethren in Colonial America* (1967); Richard K. McMaster, *Conscience in Crisis: Mennonites and Other Peace Churches in America 1739–1789* (1979); ———, *Land, Piety, Peoplehood: The Establishment of Mennonite Communities in America 1683–1790* (1985); Arthur J. Mckeel, *The Relation of the Quakers to the American Revolution* (1979); Richard A. Overfield, "A Patriot Dilemma: Passive Loyalists and Neutrals in Revolutionary Maryland," *Maryland Historical Magazine*, 67 (1973):140–159.

Mercenaries

For years it has been fashionable to refer to Britain's German troops in the Revolution as "mercenaries," while the foreign troops in the American service are called "volunteers." In truth, these German soldiers were no more mercenaries than were the American troops who went to Vietnam almost 200 years later. In both cases they were merely soldiers sent where their legally constituted governments ordered them. The fact that the various German princes sold their armies for what amounted to "blood money" should in no way reflect on the soldiers themselves.

Upon closer examination, the term mercenary would better fit the volunteers on the American side. Von Steuben, de Kalb, Pulaski, Kosciuszko, and a host of lesser lights were individuals whose own governments had no part in the conflict. And yet they signed on the American side for a variety of reasons—some fairly noble, others not. Even Lafayette joined the American cause as an individual before France formally allied itself with the Americans. And even after France joined in, French officers clamored over each other to join the American army, rather than participate in a French expeditionary force, because of the better possibilities for higher rank and prestige. Most of the major German commanders—von Riedesel, von Heister, von Knyphausen—were already seasoned professionals with no need to build reputations for themselves. *See also:* German Auxiliaries

David T. Zabecki

REFERENCES

Rodney Atwood, *Mercenaries from Hesse-Kessel in the American Revolution* (1980); Aram Bakshian, "Foreign Adventurers in the American Revolution," *History Today*, 21 (1971):187–197; Thomas Balch, *The French Army in America during the War of Independence of the United States, 1775–1783*, 2 vols. (1891–95); Stephen Bonsal, *When the French Were Here* (1945); Baron Ludwig von Closen, *Revolutionary Journal, 1780–1783*, trans. and ed. by Evelyn M. Acomb (1958); Max von Elking, *The German Allied Troops in the North American War of Independence, 1776–1783*, trans. by J. G. Rosengarten (1893), rpr. 1969; Johann Ewald, *Diary of the American War: A Hessian Journal*, trans. and ed. by Joseph P. Tustin (1979); Stephen Gradisch, "The German Mercenaries in North America during the American Revolution: A Case Study," *Canadian Journal of History*, 4 (1969):23–46; Lee Kennett, *The French Forces in America, 1780–1783* (1977); Ernst Kipping, *The Hessian View of America, 1776–1783* (1973).

Mercer, Hugh (1725–1777)

Continental Army officer. Hugh Mercer was born in Scotland, the son of a Presbyterian minister. The exact date of his birth has been lost. He was, however, 19 years old when he graduated from the University of Aberdeen in 1744. His training was in the field of medicine. Mercer was a large man with broad shoulders and a short neck, characteristics that gave one the distinct impression of a strong, powerful man. Mercer was a fiery Scot with red hair and intense passions that he learned to master as he matured.

A year after his graduation from the university, "the Pretender," Bonnie Prince Charlie, the last of the house of the Stuarts, returned from France to Scotland to reclaim his rightful throne from the Hanoverian kings, and in particular, George II. Sympathetic to the cause, though his grandfather served in the English army and died fighting in battle against the Scots, Hugh Mercer joined the Prince's army as an assistant surgeon in the surgeon's corps.

Mercer was present at the Battle of Culloden Moor on April 16, 1746. Prince Charles's highland army was defeated by the English, and Mercer gained a great deal of experience in handling military wounds, especially bayonet wounds inflicted by the English. The English were brutal in putting the rebellion down and arrested even physicians who had served as noncombatants in the highland army, since they had aided the rebellion. Mercer hid with relatives for several months and then decided his future rested in the colonies of North America.

Mercer arrived in Philadelphia in May 1747 and soon moved west along the Lancaster Highway into the beautiful Cumberland Valley. Along with other Scots and Scots-Irish settlers, he cleared land and farmed between today's towns of Greencastle and Mercersburg, Pennsylvania. His medical talents were needed on the frontier and brought him the respect of his neighbors.

Mercer was on the frontier when the French and Indian War broke out. He did not take part in Braddock's march to Fort Duquesne, but he did go to Fort Cumberland to volunteer his medical services to Dr. James Craik, surgeon in the Virginia militia, to treat the wounded survivors of Braddock's defeat. (A side note: Braddock was an officer in the British army that defeated the Scots at Culloden Moor, and Fort Cumberland was named after King George II's son, the Duke of Cumberland, who had commanded the British army at Culloden.)

Once the Pennsylvania Assembly assumed its responsibility and began organizing for the defense of the frontier settlements in western Pennsylvania, Mercer's military star began to climb. His accomplishments in the French and Indian War were many. He commanded several key forts protecting the frontier as a captain of a company in the Pennsylvania regiment.

The Pennsylvania regiment was the military unit established by the assembly to protect the frontier. It varied in strength and organization but generally it had two battalions with sixteen companies in each battalion. Later, for a short time, it consisted of three battalions. Colonel John Armstrong commanded the force. Armstrong's son would later serve as an aide to Mercer in the War of Revolution.

Mercer played a key role in the destruction of Captain Jacobs' town, Kittaning, on September 8, 1756, where Jacobs was killed and Mercer had his right arm broken by a ball. His adventurous escape while wounded and his return to the settlements only enhanced Mercer's reputation as a hardy, brave, and fierce fighting officer.

He rose to the rank of major in 1757 and then to colonel in May 1758. He took part in the Forbes expedition to take Fort Duquesne as the commander of the 3rd Battalion of the Pennsylvania regiment. On September 15, 1758, he met Washington, a Virginia militia commander, for the first time at Raystown. Washington was there for a conference with Forbes on the proper approach to be taken to capture Fort Duquesne. The friendship that developed between these two men would affect the career of both.

When the French evacuated Fort Duquesne, it was Mercer who was placed in command and saw to the rebuilding of the fort, which the British named Fort Pitt to honor the current prime minister. As the war died down, the Pennsylvania Assembly disbanded the regiment in the west, and Mercer was mustered out of the service on January 15, 1761.

During the war, Mercer had learned firsthand the benefits of careful planning in military campaigns. He had seen the need for discipline and organization. He had learned the skills of leadership under the most trying conditions of controlling frontier militia. Through his command positions, Mercer became skilled in logistics, communications, and cooperation so that others could claim the victory but the common goal was accomplished. He was "a team player."

He had demonstrated his personal courage any number of times and was a proven cool and calculating officer in battle. Perhaps most importantly of all, he came to believe that the essence of winning a war was to seize the offensive whenever possible so that the enemy continually felt the pressure of responding rather than maneuvering to surprise.

Within a month of discharge, Hugh Mercer was in Fredericksburg, Virginia, where he was to make his home until the War of Revolution. In talking with Washington and other Virginia officers during their service together, Mercer felt that Fredericksburg was a place better suited to his personal needs. A town of some 3,000 people, it was a river port with a thriving economy. Virginia was also a colony that still fielded a militia, and Mercer could remain involved in military matters, such as providing medical services to the soldiers. He opened an apothecary shop, first with Dr. Ewen Clements, and later with Dr. John Julian, as his partners. He practiced medicine and became friends with many of the Virginians who inhabited Fredericksburg, including Washington, who grew up on the Ferry farm, just across the Rappahannock River from town.

Mercer joined Washington's Masonic Lodge at Fredericksburg and expanded his medical practice. His apothecary shop did well. The Mercer family lived a comfortable life in Fredericksburg. In 1772, Mercer purchased the Ferry farm from Washington, who had just built a home for his mother in town and moved her off the farm. A political moderate, Mercer walked a delicate line during the years of unrest from 1763 until 1775. He was on the American side but hoped to avoid a war with the British. He distanced himself from the more radical thinkers of the time.

When Lord Dunmore, the governor of Virginia, seized the gunpowder at Williamsburg and placed it aboard a British ship, many Virginians, including Mercer, became upset and saw this as a threat to their liberty and safety. On September 12, 1775, Mercer was appointed colonel of the local militia of Spotsylvania, Caroline, Stafford, and King George counties. On February 13, 1776, he was appointed colonel of the 3rd Virginia Regiment and mustered them into service at Williamsburg. There he developed them into a disciplined and orderly military unit

that would later serve with honor during the New York, Trenton, and Princeton campaigns.

When Congress established the concept of the flying camp in the spring of 1776, Washington requested that his old friend, Mercer, be given command of the unit. Congress promoted Mercer to brigadier general of the Continental Line on June 5 and assigned him to command the flying camp. Mercer left his regiment, which George Weedon later commanded, and returned to Fredericksburg to visit with his family one last time before he went off to war. His wife was pregnant at the time with what would be their last child, Hugh, Jr. Saying his farewells, Mercer set out to join Washington in New York.

Reporting to headquarters on July 3, 1776, Mercer assumed command of the flying camp and did his best to support Washington during the difficult campaign that followed in the defense of New York City. The flying camp seemed suitable in theory, but it lacked the support of the states. It was too difficult to organize with militia coming and going almost at will, and finally it dissolved itself in Late November 1776. Mercer was then given command of a new brigade created by Washington and composed of troops from the Cumberland Valley of Pennsylvania and Mercer's old 3rd Virginia, among others.

With this brigade, Mercer provided his greatest service to the American cause during the time that would later be known as the "ten crucial days." His insights, his coolness under pressure, and his tactical skills of leading men in battle served Washington well in a period when the war itself and American fortunes hung in the balance. Mercer's men swept the streets and houses of Trenton clear of Rall's Hessians during the American attack of December 26, forcing them into open fields to the east of town, where the three regiments of Rall's brigade surrendered. Then, a few days later, Mercer provided Washington with support and advice as the flaking march around Cornwallis from Trenton to Princeton was executed with professional precision.

Unfortunately at Princeton, leading his men against the British 17th Regiment of Foot, just outside of town in the orchard of William Clark, Mercer had his horse shot from under him. On foot, and refusing to yield to the British infantry who quickly surrounded him, Mercer was bayoneted seven times, including once under his sword arm. It was Culloden all over again, 30 years later. Left on the field of battle for dead, Mercer was later taken to the Thomas Clark house where Dr. Benjamin Rush and other physicians, including Cornwallis's personal doctor, administered to him as well as they could. The British surgeon examined him and at first thought Mercer might survive. Mercer asked an aide to lift his arm. There, under the sword arm, was a relatively small wound made by a bayonet. Mercer told those around his bed that this would be the fellow that would kill him.

Under the care of the Clark family, Mercer survived from January 3 until January 12, 1777, when he finally died of his wounds. His body was taken to Philadelphia in a hearse that rode right across the ice on the Delaware River. He was buried in Christ Church Burial Ground at first, and then, years later, his body was moved to Laurel Hill Cemetery, still in Philadelphia but west out along the Schuylkill River. There he rests today.

Washington missed his friend dearly. Here was a man who supported Washington, had solid insights into both military strategy and tactics, was daring, courageous, and able. Mercer understood the principles of logistics and support. He was an excellent organizer and always held the respect of his men. He did not threaten Washington professionally as did Horatio Gates and Charles Lee but helped him, especially during the New York campaign and the ten crucial days. It is quite unfortunate for the American cause that such a man died when he did. He would have been a great help to the American army in the campaigns that followed.

Paul J. Sanborn

REFERENCES

Frederick English, *General Hugh Mercer, The Forgotten Hero of the American Revolution* (1975); John T. Goolrich, *The Life of General Hugh Mercer* (1906); Richard M. Ketchum, *The Winter Soldiers* (1973); Joseph M. Waterman, *With Sword and Lancet* (1941).

Meschianza (Philadelphia, Pennsylvania) (May 18, 1778)

General Sir William Howe had turned in his resignation to the king and was given permission to return home to England to defend his actions in the North American war to Parliament. Howe's upcoming departure prompted a series of parties and celebrations in Philadelphia, for rarely was a commanding general as loved and idolized by his troops as was Sir William.

The Meschianza was but one of a series of these tributes to the departing general. But it was surely the greatest and most spectacular of the lot. Approximately 22 British officers subscribed £140 each in cash to help defray the expenses and proceeded to help organize the event. While Captain John André was not the leader of the affair, it was his direction that guided the development of all that would unfold in Howe's honor.

The event itself was actually a series of activities, a mixture of entertainments and hence the term "Meschianza," which derived from the Italian for mixing and mingling. There was a procession of decorated watercraft carrying the participants down the Delaware River to the Wharton Mansion, where the action would be. There was a jousting tournament of knights in the tradition of Don Quixote, followed by gambling and dancing with light refreshments and fireworks. Then a large banquet was held with more fireworks and dancing from late evening into the next morning.

André seems to have designed and produced the setting, costumes, and banquet hall decor. Research was conducted. Furniture and items were borrowed from all over the city of Philadelphia. The site chosen was the Wharton Mansion, Walnut Grove, headquarters of one of the organizing officers. The Wharton family at that point was being held under arrest in Winchester, Virginia, by the rebels for being Quaker sympathizers to the king's forces. The 600 yards from the house to the river bank were set up for the joust with two arches erected, one honoring Sir William and the other, his brother, Sir Richard, commander of the British fleet in North America.

The day before the event, specially engraved invitations went out to invited guests, with the Howe family crest prominently displayed on the front cover. Over 400 people were invited to honor Howe. Over 500 people showed up for the affair.

Finally the great day arrived, dawning dark and cloudy but turning fair and breezy later. While Washington and his army watched from their camp at Valley Forge, the British officer corps and the ladies of Philadelphia, along with several influential civilians, boarded their barges and floated down the Delaware River. Beginning at 3:30 P.M. a water pageant of gayly decked-out boats proceeded downstream with bands accompanying the participants, playing martial and patriotic songs. The regatta was saluted as it passed the various ships in harbor with 17 guns and more music.

Reaching Walnut Grove, the officers and their guests left the "fleet" and walked up the lawn through one of the arches to the scene of the tournament. This ceremony of the carousel involved a joust between eight Knights of the Blended Rose and eight Knights of the Burning Mountain. Dressed in white satins with the motto "We droop when separated," these Rose Knights broke lances, fired pistols, and fought with swords against their counterparts, dressed in black satins with the motto "I burn forever." At the end, the knights stepped back to allow the lead knights for each side to conduct an individual combat for the honor of the ladies championed by each side. Neither side could prevail, and the marshall of the joust had to determine that the honor of both groups of ladies had been upheld and the joust was at an end.

The ladies championed by the knights were dressed in turbans, veils, feathers, tassels, and all types of rich cloth such as satins and silks. The only damper on the festivity was that Mr. Shippen had refused to give permission to his daughter to participate in wearing such clothing. His teenaged daughter Peggy threw a terrible tantrum, but she could not change her father's mind. Within a few months, she would meet a man twice her age, a general in the American army, and to everyone's surprise, marry him. His name was General Benedict Arnold.

Peggy Chew was championed by Captain Andrew and also served as the "Queen of the Tilt." She led the party into the mansion through the second arch from the lawn for light refreshments and dancing. A faro table with a bank of 2,000 guineas was set up for the pleasure of the officers. At 11 P.M. fireworks were ignited to the delight of all present and this was followed by the main banquet which began at midnight. There were 1,030 dishes served by 24 housemen dressed in rich style. While the people ate, 108 oboists played favorite musical selections. Four hundred eighty people were seated, with the overflow standing about the room. People ate, toasted the health of General and Admiral Howe

and the king, and numerous cheers and salutes were given. All of this was illuminated by the light of 1,200 of the highest grade candles. Later, those that could went back to gambling and dancing until the sun appeared on the horizon.

The total cost of the affair was about 4,000 guineas, a sum difficult to translate into today's money. To André, it was the greatest tribute ever given by an army to its general. To a Quaker woman in Philadelphia, Elizabeth Drinker, it was a day remembered by many for its scenes of folly and vanity. To Abigail Adams, who heard of the events from friends, she felt it to be an outrage on all decency.

That same night, during the Meschianza, 7 officers and 49 enlisted men escaped the British prisons in town by using a carefully dug tunnel. Captain Allen McLane attacked the British outposts with loaded kettles of gunpowder, which the Americans exploded, causing an alert of the guards. But all this uproar did not deter the celebration at Walnut Grove at all. The party members thought the noise all a part of the overall plan.

The next day, May 19, General Howe received word that General Lafayette had moved several thousand American troops to an exposed position at Barren Hill, very close to the British lines in Germantown. The general ordered the appropriate moves to try to catch "that boy" and his men. The war resumed.

Six days later, General Sir William Howe boarded one of his brother's ships and began his trip back home to England. He had won battles, such as at Long Island, Brandywine, Fort Washington, and Germantown. He had captured the rebel capital at Philadelphia. He had failed, though, to end the rebellion. He had failed to destroy Washington's army. Another general would come to take his place. The war would continue for another five years. But no one there would ever forget that May evening of the Meschianza in Philadelphia.

And Peggy Chew, André's chosen lady of the Meschianza? What ever became of her? She would later marry a rebel, John Edgar Howard of Maryland, but she always would remember that night and the poem left behind by her champion:

> If at the close of war and strife,
> my destiny once more
> should in the varied paths of life
> conduct me to this shore:

Should British banners guard the land,
and factions be restrained,
and Clivedon's mansion peaceful stand,
no more with blood be stained,

Say! Wilt thou then receive again
and welcome to thy sight,
the youth who bids with stifled pain
his sad farewell tonight?

Peggy treasured it all her life. They never saw each other again.

Paul J. Sanborn

REFERENCES

James T. Flexner, *The Traitor and the Spy* (1953); Robert M. Hatch, *Major John André* (1986); John W. Jackson, *With the British Army in Philadelphia* (1979); Ernst Kipping and Samuel Stella Smith, eds., *At General Howe's Side 1776–78* (1974).

Michilimackinac

Michilimackinac is the Indian name for the area where Lakes Michigan and Huron come together in a narrow strait about four miles wide. The name, meaning "big turtle," is derived from the shape of Michilimackinac Island (the present-day Mackinac Island, Michigan), which resembles a large turtle rising from the lake. Sacred to the Chippewa Indians, its 350-foot height was a landmark to paddling French voyagers who first penetrated the region in the 1630s.

The French, drawn to the area in search of furs, found that Michilimackinac was the crossroads of the Upper Great Lakes. Settling first on the north shore, the French traders and military followed the Indians to the south shore about 1715. A palisaded village of approximately 40 houses became the home of a few French families and a small military contingent. During the summer hundreds of voyagers and Great Lakes Indians rendezvoused here to trade for furs.

When the British forces captured Canada in 1760 the community passed under British control, though most of the French inhabitants remained. During Pontiac's uprising in 1763 the local Chippewa captured the post, but in the following year it was reoccupied by British redcoats.

In 1774 the fort was garrisoned by two companies of the king's 8th Regiment under the command of Captain Arent Schuyler DePeyster, whose primary goal was to maintain friendship with the local Indians and to settle disputes between warring tribes. Indian relations became increasingly important in 1775 when the Revolution erupted in Massachusetts. There defiant colonists battled redcoat troops, some of whom were from the 10th Regiment of Foot, which had recently garrisoned Michilimackinac.

The traders at Michilimackinac were particularly concerned by the rebellion when the American forces in November 1775 captured Montreal and cut the trade lifeline that led upcountry to Michilimackinac. The British recapture of Montreal reopened the trade that flourished throughout the war. In 1778, 128 canoes brought over 2,100 kegs of rum and brandy, 1,500 muskets, 28 tons of gunpowder, 35 tons of shot and ball, and hundreds of bales of trade goods to be exchanged for furs.

When George Rogers Clark's rebel forces successfully captured Vincennes, Kaskaskia, and Cahokia in the Illinois country, Michilimackinac was gravely threatened. As a result of Clark's capture of Henry Hamilton, commandant of Detroit, DePeyster was transferred to that post. The threat of a naval attack against Michilimackinac led to plans to move the fort and town to the more defensible cliffs of Mackinac Island. When Lieutenant Governor Patrick Sinclair arrived in 1779 the move was begun. During the next two years, with tremendous effort the entire community moved to Mackinac Island, where a strong limestone fort was erected overlooking the harbor.

Indian allies recruited at Michilimackinac were led by British officers to fight in distant battlefields. Sioux, Menominee, Winnebago, Sac, Fox, Ottawa, and Chippewa warriors went in 1776 to Montreal to defend Canada, in 1777 to assist General John Burgoyne's assault on New York, in 1778 to defend Canada, in 1779 to St. Joseph (Niles, Michigan) to resist an anticipated rebel advance against Detroit, in 1780 to attack unsuccessfully the Spanish post at St. Louis, and in 1782 to Kentucky to help defeat Daniel Boone at Blue Licks.

While British soldiers were laboring to complete the new fort on the island they received word in 1783 of the Peace of Paris, which ended the war. To their chagrin they also learned that the treaty included Michilimackinac in the new United States of America. Reluctant to leave and abandon the lucrative fur trade, the British stayed on for 13 years. Not until 1796, as a result of Jay's Treaty, did the Stars and Stripes replace the Union Jack on the flag pole of Michili-mackinac.

David A. Armour

REFERENCES

David A. Armour and Keith R. Widden, *At the Crossroads: Michilimackinac During the American Revolution* (1778); ———, *Michilimackinac: A Handbook to the Site* (1980); Lyk M. Stone, *Fort Michilimackinac 1715–1781: An Archaeological Perspective on the Revolutionary Frontier* (1974).

Middleton, Charles (Lord Barham) (1726–?)

Royal Navy administrator. Born in Dundee to a family on the fringes of the Scottish academic and legal establishments, Charles Middleton's grandfather had been principal of King's College, Aberdeen, and his mother was a cousin of Henry Dundas, later Lord Advocate of Scotland and confidant of the Younger Pitt. His father was a collector of customs, a class of men who despised sea officers as smugglers in the king's pay but sent their sons into the navy in great numbers. Charles first went to sea as a captain's servant at the age of 12. In 1745 he passed the lieutenant's examination and in 1758, at the height of the Seven Years' War, was made a post captain. Commanding a series of small frigates he cruised the West Indies, preying on French merchantmen and enriching himself with prize money. Coming ashore in 1763, he settled down as a gentleman farmer in Kent, close enough to London and the Chatham dockyard to keep in touch with naval affairs.

His return to active service in early 1775 was apparently unrelated to the troubles in North America. French support for the American rebels and the threat of Spanish Intervention, however, soon created a naval crisis. In August 1778 Middleton's reputation as a man with a head for business as well as his connection with the Earl of Sandwich, the First Lord of the Admiralty, thrust him into the controllership of the navy. As the de facto chairman of the Navy Board, the controller headed the shore establishment, a domain encompassing everything that went into building, repairing, and manning ships and keeping them at sea. The nearly 10,000 Navy Office and dockyard workers under his authority, the vast expanses of property and stores in his charge, made Middleton the manager of the largest industrial enterprise in Britain.

Frigates and a handful of ships of the line had been enough to protect the Atlantic supply line and support military operations in North America. Countering the fleets of France and Spain and defending the home islands from invasion, if it came to that, required dozens of heavy ships. Every ship of the line that would float was being withdrawn from Ordinary (a kind of mothball fleet) and hurried to sea when Middleton took office. These strenuous exertions, however, fell far short of putting the navy on an equal footing with the combined French and Spanish fleet. Middleton championed a radical means of compensating for Britain's numerical advantage. The war emergency, he insisted, required coppering the entire fleet. In the two decades preceding the outbreak of the American rebellion, the navy had experimented with copper sheathing as an antidote to the ravages of the shipworm. Sea trials with a handful of small ships revealed that copper deterred the worm, but it also promoted the corrosion of the iron fastenings holding wooden hulls together. Claiming to have found a method of preventing corrosion, Middleton cajoled the Admiralty into giving priority to ships of the line, whose coppered bottoms, he argued, would make them nimbler and faster than their counterparts in the enemy fleet. Requiring relatively little maintenance, copper sheathing would save the Navy Office money and yield the dockyards time, space, and labor for urgent repairs.

In less than two years, the yards coppered nearly 200 vessels, from first rates down to cutters. In the short run, this was a remarkable technical and administrative achievement. Nevertheless, Middleton's confidence in his watertight seal was misplaced, for routine inspections of coppered vessels turned up badly corroded iron fastenings even before the American war ended. All such fastenings had to be replaced, at enormous expense, with copper-alloy bolts. The vast coppering project exemplified Middleton's strengths and weaknesses as a wartime administrator. Tireless advocacy, headlong enthusiasm, and relentless badgering enabled the navy controller to get what he wanted from superiors and subordinates alike. His overweening self-confidence, however, sometimes made him deaf to the well-founded advice of shipwrights and sea officers.

The dockyards managed to put only a handful of coppered ships of the line at sea in time to meet the greatest naval threat Britain had faced since the Armada of 1588. For in mid-summer 1779 the Franco-Spanish fleet gave the Western Squadron the slip and momentarily gained control of the Channel, the first step required of any plan for invading England. The French scheme—which aimed to win the American war by setting off a financial panic in London—was far from well conceived, and the British fleet managed to regain its up-Channel advantage over the enemy. Middleton and his colleagues paid no heed to the invasion scare sweeping England. They understood that the real threat was not the French and Spanish expeditionary force but the combined fleet, without whose help in defeating or barring the way of the British squadron, no troops could be put ashore. The appropriate operational response to the seaborne threat lay wholly outside Middleton's official purview. This did not keep the navy controller from showering the First Lord with advice, however, or from corresponding directly with commanders at sea, and he proved as circumspect a tactician as he was an audacious administrator. By withdrawing up the Channel, he argued, the outnumbered and outgunned British squadron could snatch an opportunity from necessity. Enticed into waters unfamiliar to its navigators, the combined fleet would find its once formidable advantages steadily diminishing. Other voices called for bolder action, but they failed to receive a hearing before the combined fleet, ravaged by sickness and hunger, sailed home.

Everyone in the naval establishment expected the Franco-Spanish armada to reappear in the spring of 1780. Since outgunning the enemy was out of the question, Middleton proposed narrowing the disparity in firepower between the two fleets by means of the carronade—a squat, comparatively light naval gun capable of hurling a large shot with great force over a short distance. Middleton urged on his colleagues the many advantages of this new and untried weapon over the long cannon: lighter by several thousand pounds, it fired more rapidly and could be served by a much smaller crew. As an auxiliary weapon it would disproportionately increase any ship's firepower, and Middleton went so far as to advocate arming several ships of the line entirely with carronades. The Ordnance Department, jealous of its prerogative of testing and supplying the navy's guns, looked askance at the carronade. But Middleton, making the most of

the Admiralty's resentment of interfering artillery officers and of testimonials from the handful of captains who had used the carronade in action, surmounted Ordnance objections and ignored the reservations other sea officers expressed. By the close of 1781—too late to figure significantly in action against the combined fleet—more than 150 vessels had been fitted out with carronades. During the wars of the French Revolution and Napoleon the carronade became a mainstay of naval armament, and from the outset of that grueling struggle the navy drew on the stockpile Middleton had created during the American war.

The combined fleet's appearance in the Channel succeeded in distracting the British government from the American rebellion, but sustaining the forces in North America over a 3,000-mile supply line posed a far greater threat to continued British rule. For the rebels had made the eastern seaboard so inhospitable to the redcoats that virtually every bean, musketball, and tent peg they consumed had to be brought by sea from England. Shipping delays occasioned by wind and weather were compounded by managerial incompetence and outright graft, so that by the end of 1778, British storehouses in New York held less than a week's rations and starving seemed a likely prospect. Shortly after taking office, Middleton moved to assume control of the transport service from the Treasury, which was eager to be relieved of a task for which it had no expertise.

The navy controller drove a hard bargain with his Treasury colleagues. Over Lord George Germain's objections he insisted on putting the transports under naval convoy rather than allowing each to sail on its own (no armed merchantman, he believed, stood a chance against a frigate). A sense of duty, he also emphasized, would not sufficiently compensate him and his colleagues for the burdens they were about to assume; they would require more pay. Finally, taking his customarily imperial view of his own administrative prerogatives, Middleton demanded the authority to name his own transport managers. For once, the navy controller got nearly everything he asked for, and under the Navy Board's aegis, supplying the British forces in America slowly improved. Agents directly answerable to an extremely inquisitive Middleton received provisions from contractors, inspected them, and released them for delivery in America on hired ships. By eliminating competition among government agencies for the same pool of ships, Middleton drove down the cost of chartering merchantmen. Not everything went smoothly—for a time the convoy system created worse delays than ever, as Germain feared it would—but storehouses never fell to the level of the early winter of 1779. Indeed, in the summer of 1782 a Hessian officer at New York wrote in his journal that "Our store of provisions has never been so plentiful as it now is."

By then, of course, General Washington, not hunger, had defeated the British; sustaining the expeditionary force in North America had given way to the problem of extricating it. In keeping with the inadvertence that characterized his government's conduct of the war, Middleton learned of the decision to evacuate America from reading the newspaper. No one, he complained, had thought to consult the man chiefly responsible for providing the shipping this vast enterprise would require. For at issue was withdrawing not only the troops, their baggage and equipment, but also several thousand forlorn Loyalists and their belongings. Evacuating all these soldiers and civilians required more shipping than the Navy Office had on hand; most of the ships already engaged in the transport service were scattered from Halifax to Jamaica. It required all Middleton's ingenuity to scare up enough merchantmen to remove the remnants of British rule in North America, but in November 1783 the last redcoat walked up the gangplank of a troopship waiting in New York harbor, and a long episode in the history of the Empire came to a close.

Losing the American war had a far more salutary effect on the British navy than winning it might have done. Middleton was determined to eliminate the confusion verging on panic (at least as he remembered it) he had found at every level of the shore establishment in 1778. The navy had not been prepared to meet France at sea, let alone in the company of a formidable ally. So as soon as he had arranged the laying up of the fleet, he turned to improving its state of readiness. With a view to vastly reducing the time required to prepare warships for sea, he ordered stores for each rate to be set aside at the principal dockyards: for every 74-gun ship of the line, for instance, storekeepers established a reserve of masts, spars, sails, rigging, cordage, blocks, anchors, stoves, and so on. So when an order to

commission a 74 arrived, nearly everything needed to ready that ship for sea—save guns, gunpowder, and crew—lay at hand. This was a far cry from the circumstances of 1778, when mobilizing against the French had been catch-as-catch-can. Thanks in large part to the new system, when the navy mobilized against France in 1792, the dockyards put dozens of ships of the line at sea in a matter of weeks.

Frustrated by the poor state of communications between the Navy Board and its far-flung dependencies, Middleton was determined to make the periphery more responsive to the center's instruction. In the Standing Orders of the Navy Board, he found the instrument for expressing his will. Covering everything from how to build a 74-gun ship of the line to the duties of the dockyard gatekeeper, the Standing Orders had fallen into disuse. On his own time (as he never tired of pointing out), Middleton extracted them from the scattered volumes in which they had lain dormant, eliminated those that no longer served a purpose, and returned the rest to a useful life. It is hard to gauge the impact of Middleton's housekeeping on communications between London and the dockyards, but at the very least dockyard officers could no longer claim to be ignorant of what the Navy Board wanted; they could be sure the navy controller had them under surveillance.

The prewar Navy Office had not made it easy for a navy controller to keep his eye on anything. Bureaucratic procedures that Samuel Pepys, Middleton's great seventeenth-century predecessor, had already condemned as grossly unsatisfactory, simply collapsed under wartime pressures. The navy controller, not shy about asserting that only the force of his own personality had held things together during the war, doggedly pushed for a sweeping reorganization of the Navy Board's responsibilities. The prospects for Middleton's scheme seemed to be enlarged when the Younger Pitt included it in his program of economical reform. These hopes were dashed in 1787, however, when the king's illness triggered a constitutional crisis. Frustrated by the looming failure of what he had expected to be his crowning achievement as navy controller, in March 1790 Middleton resigned, turning his still formidable energies to agricultural innovation.

Far from withdrawing from naval affairs, he remained an informal advisor to Pitt and in 1795, at the height of the war with revolutionary France, achieved his long-thwarted ambition of membership on the Admiralty Board. He had not reckoned with the young Earl Spencer's determination to be his own First Lord, however, and before the year was out Middleton resigned in a clash over naval appointments. Short of neither years nor enemies, he could only have expected his public career to be at an end. In 1805, however, a financial scandal drove Dundas (now Lord Melville) from office as First Lord of the Admiralty, and Middleton took his place, extracting as his price the title of Lord Barham. Approaching his eightieth year, he was nevertheless, as the naval historian Sir Julian Corbett once remarked, "the man who, for ripe experience in the direction of naval war in all its breadth and detail, had not a rival in the service or in Europe." Thus Barham found himself the chief strategist of the campaign that culminated in Horatio Nelson's annihilating victory at Trafalgar.

Middleton's greatness as a naval administrator lay not in presiding over a triumph but in fending off disaster. True, the American war ended in a British defeat, but without the navy controller's exertions at the Navy Office, things could have been worse. He was in some respects the ideal man for an emergency: taking risks, casting precedents aside, abiding by his own counsel, he pushed through, at the height of a great war, technical innovations scarcely imaginable in peacetime. By unsnarling the supply line to the expeditionary force, he succeeded in keeping starvation at bay; once "the world turned upside down," he assured the evacuation of America in a reasonably orderly fashion. In peacetime he turned with scarcely a pause to making the most of the harrowing lessons of a lost war. The British navy's performance in the wars of the French Revolution and Napoleon suggests how well these lessons were learned. *See also:* Copper Sheathing; Royal Dockyards; Sandwich, John Montagu, 4th Earl of

J.E. Talbott

REFERENCES

Julian S. Corbett, *The Campaign of Trafalgar*, 2 vols. (1919); John Knox Laughton, ed., *Letters and Papers of Charles Lord Barham*, 3 vols. (1906–1911); Piers Mackesay, *The War for America* (1964); Bernard Pool, "Lord Barham: A Great Naval Administrator," *History Today*, 15 (1965):347–354; J.E.

Talbott, "The Rise and Fall of the Carronade," *History Today*, 29 (1989):24–30.

Middleton, Peter (?–1781)

Loyalist. Peter Middleton, whose date and place of birth in Scotland are unknown, studied medicine under Dr. Thomas Simson at the University of St. Andrews in Edinburgh. After receiving his degree from that university in 1752, he went to New York City and entered into the practice of medicine with Dr. John Bard. Middleton became one of the most prominent physicians in New York, performing with Bard the first recorded dissection of a human body for the purpose of anatomical instruction in Colonial America. As suggested by his medical ledger, Middleton developed an extensive and a lucrative practice, treating the illnesses of such eminent New York families as the DeLancey's, the Livingstons, the Schuylers, the Franks, the Hays, and the Myers. Moreover, during the French and Indian War, he was appointed as surgeon general of provincial armies and rendered medical services during the Crown Point expedition.

During the 1760s and early 1770s, Middleton played a central role in fostering medical education in New York. With Dr. Samuel Bard and four other physicians, he established in 1767 the medical school of King's College (now Columbia University)—the first institution of its kind in New York City. Middleton assiduously worked to promote the activities of this school; he served during the early 1770s as a faculty member in the department of materia medica, of pathology, and of physiology. He was named in 1773 as a governor of King's College, was intimately involved the next year with the establishment of the New York Hospital, and became one of the first physicians appointed to its staff. Middleton was a major contributor to colonial medical historiography, publishing in 1769 *A Medical Discourse* and in it explaining how the discoveries of ancient Egyptian, Jewish, Greek, and Roman physicians were important to the knowledge of Enlightenment medicine.

In other ways, Middleton promoted civic and sociocultural activities in New York before the American Revolution. He actively participated in the New York Society Library Club—an organization that resembled Franklin's Library Company and an Enlightenment learned society sponsored lectures given by the city's leading gentlemen scholars. Middleton also was one of the founders of the St. Andrew's Society of New York and served as its president from 1767 to 1770. Freemasonry, too, was important to Middleton, for he served as Deputy Grand Master of the Modern Grand Lodge of New York prior to 1776.

Despite his civic and Enlightenment activities, Middleton in 1776 refused to support the cause of the Patriots. For "prudential motives," he left New York in April of that year and went to Bermuda. When the British occupied New York, he decided to return and died there on January 9, 1781. The wife of this eminent New York Tory physician had died ten years before him, and their daughter Susannah, who was an only child, would inherit her father's large estate.

William Weisberger

REFERENCES

Thomas Bender, *New York Intellect* (1983); *DAB*; Leo Hershkowitz, "Powdered Tin and Rose Petals: Myer Myers, Goldsmith and Peter Middleton, Physician," *American Jewish History*, 10(1981):482–467; Ossian Lang, *History of Freemasonry in the State of New York* (1922); W.B. McDaniel, "The Beginnings of American Medical Historiography," *Bulletin of the History of Medicine, 26* (1952):46–50.

Mifflin, Thomas (1744–1800)

American statesman. Mifflin was born on January 10, 1744, into a wealthy Quaker merchant family in Philadelphia. He entered the College of Philadelphia at a young age, graduating from the school in 1760. During the 1760s he openly opposed the Stamp Act and the Townsend Acts. He supported the various nonimportation movements, and he was regarded as a moderate Whig.

Beginning with his election to the Pennsylvania Assembly in 1772 he started drifting toward the radical end of the political spectrum. After the Boston Port Bill he organized support for that city from Philadelphia, and he became a member of the Philadelphia Committee of Correspondence. He favored the idea of calling a congress to deal with the problems affecting America and organized support for such a body in Philadelphia. He eventually became Philadelphia's representative in the First Continental Congress.

Mifflin, who was reelected to the assembly in 1774, sat on many committees, one of which established the American Association, a group committed to the enforcement of the boycott on British imports. In Philadelphia he served on the committee that enforced the Association. By this time he was a radical Whig.

By April 1775 Mifflin became increasingly involved in military affairs. He actively recruited troops and became a major of one company. For these efforts he was ejected from the Society of Friends. At this time he became a member of the Second Continental Congress.

After Washington became the commander-in-chief he selected Mifflin as one of his aides-de-camp (July 4, 1775), and on August 14 Mifflin became the quartermaster general (Q.M.G.). Mifflin quickly rose in rank, as he was a colonel on December 22, 1775, and a major general on February 19, 1777. Mifflin proved to be a fine and honest administrator, which won him the respect and admiration of Washington.

However, Mifflin longed for the glory of battle. Shortly after arriving in New York City, where he was to assist in the preparation of its defenses, he resigned as Q.M.G. and was placed in command of two Pennsylvania regiments and Fort Washington.

Mifflin's replacement as Q.M.G., Stephen Moylan, proved to be incompetent, and Mifflin once again became Q.M.G. Mifflin kept the army well supplied during the retreat to White Plains. However, Mifflin was hampered in the performance of his duties by a serious lack of funds, which kept him from obtaining needed supplies.

Before the British moved against Philadelphia in August 1777, Mifflin urged Washington to defend the city. When it was captured by the British, Mifflin believed that Washington had not done enough to defend the American capital. On October 8, 1777, Mifflin tendered his resignation stating that he was resigning for reasons of health, but in reality he no longer wished to serve under Washington and he hoped to obtain a better position.

The quartermaster corp was crippled as a result of Mifflin's resignation. A replacement was not found until March 2, 1778. During the time that the quartermaster corp was without a head, the army's suffering was increased while it was in winter quarters at Valley Forge. As a result, Mifflin fell into great disfavor with Washington.

On November 7, 1777, the day that Congress accepted Mifflin's resignation, Mifflin, who remained a major general, was appointed to the newly formed Board of War, which was to oversee the affairs of the army. After this appointment charges surfaced of improprieties in the quartermaster corps, and rumors abounded that he wanted to oust Washington.

This was the infamous Conway Cabal. General Thomas Conway and other army officers were supposedly conspiring to replace Washington with General Horatio Gates, the victor of Saratoga. Mifflin and Gates were good friends, and Mifflin was thus implicated in the plan. Mifflin, believing that he could no long carry out his duties at the Board of War, left that post and joined Washington's army, where he was given a command on May 21, 1778.

However, Mifflin's stay with the army was short-lived, for on June 15, 1778, Congress decided to investigate Mifflin's activities as Q.M.G. Mifflin had to take a leave of absence from the army to prepare his defense. By mid-August neither the army nor Congress had done anything, so on August 17, 1778, Mifflin decided to resign his commission and "take his case to the people." In September 1778, Congress provided Mifflin with funds so that he could settle his public accounts. Then on January 13, 1779, Congress decided that Mifflin should be court-martialed by Washington. Washington refused to do so since Mifflin was no longer a member of the army. Congress let the matter drop and accepted Mifflin's resignation on February 25, 1779.

In 1782 Mifflin was elected to Congress, where he would serve for the next three years. On November 3, 1783, he became president of Congress. While he held that position his most memorable action was to accept Washington's resignation from the army. During his tenure as governor of Pennsylvania he personally commanded Pennsylvania's troops during the Whiskey Rebellion. After his term in the governor's office came to an end he retired from politics. On January 20, 1800, he died. *See also:* Supplying the Continental Army

Anthony P. Inguanzo

REFERENCES

Charles W. Heathcate, "General Thomas Mifflin—Colleague of Washington and Pennsylvania Leader," *Picket Post*, 62 (1958):7–12; Joel T. Hendley, *Washington and His Generals* (1847);

William Rawle, "Sketch of the Life of Thomas Mifflin," *Pennsylvania Historical Society*, Memoirs, 2 (1830):105–126; Kenneth R. Rossman, "Thomas Mifflin–Revolutionary Patriot," *Pennsylvania History*, 15 (1948):9–23; ———, *Thomas Mifflin and the Politics of the American Revolution* (1952).

Military Strategy in the American Revolution

American Military Strategy

Historians and military analysts have rarely given serious consideration to the strategic aspects of the American Revolution. Falling as it did, between the wars of Frederick the Great and those of Napoleon, the Revolution has been overshadowed by these two great sets of conflicts. American strategy in the war traditionally has been seen as simply a matter of holding out while the British blundered their way to self-defeat. This deterministic and far too simplistic view suggests that in the long run there was nothing the British could have done to win. But had American strategy been different, the outcome of the war may well have been entirely different. The British might have won, or the war could have ended with them holding much more than Canada in North America.

Washington, as the Continental Army's commander-in-chief for the entire war, was the principal architect of American strategy. Besides Washington, only General Nathanael Greene played any real role in shaping or executing strategy. By the end of 1778, the focus of military operations had shifted to the South. After Gates's defeat at Camden in August 1780, Washington sent Greene to the South to run the war there, an operation that he conducted right up until the Battle of Yorktown. Any analysis of American strategy, then, must also be an analysis of the generalships of Washington and Greene. In both of these generals we can see strong elements of the strategic concepts that would be formalized in the writings of Mao Tse-tung over 150 years later.

For most of the twentieth century the fashionable view of Washington has painted him as the American Fabius. (Fabius was the Roman general [275–203 B.C.] who advocated avoiding direct battle with Hannibal, letting time, frustration, and attrition defeat the Carthaginians.) Russell Weigley, in his historical study of U.S. Strategy, *The American Way of War*, holds to the traditional view of Washington as a Fabian strategist; but he does credit Washington with more foresight and skill than many previous authors. According to Weigley, "American Revolutionary armies were never able to meet British armies of approximately equal size on equal terms on the battlefield"—even after Valley Forge. American strategy, therefore, had to be "a strategy founded on weakness."

Weigley credits Washington with realizing that the survival of the American army was the key to the survival of the Revolutionary cause. Washington's primary objective, then, was one of not losing, rather than one of winning—the two objectives are not necessarily synonymous. From the very start Washington knew he would have to fight on the strategic defensive, but he initially tried to combine that posture with the tactical offensive. After the American defeat at New York City, however, Washington realized that he would have to avoid fighting the British main army whenever possible. Washington then turned to what Weigley has termed a "strategy of erosion," with the goal of wearing away the "resolution of the British by gradual, persistent action against the periphery of their armies."

The only time after the New York campaign that Washington fought a full-scale action with his own main army against the British main force was at Brandywine. With British troops threatening the American capital of Philadelphia, Washington had little choice but to attempt a full-scale effort. He lost. At Trenton, Princeton, Germantown, and Monmouth, the American army fought against only parts of the British army. Even at Yorktown, Washington attacked an already weakened and isolated portion of Britain's southern army; and even then the Americans had heavy support from the French army and especially the French fleet.

General Dave R. Palmer, in his book *The Way of the Fox*, presents a somewhat different view of Washington and his strategy. According to General Palmer, the war from the American standpoint can be divided into four distinct phases; and Washington deftly matched American strategy to the unique conditions and goals of each of those phases.

Palmer's first phase, which he calls "toward independence," started with the opening of hostilities at Lexington and ended 14 months later in July 1776. When the first phase began, the colonists' main objective was the redress of grievances with the Mother Country. By the time the phase ended, the Americans had declared their independence and had seized military and political control of all 13 colonies. During this phase the insurgents had nothing to lose and everything to gain. The British military establishment in America was weak. It was to the Americans' advantage to strike before the king could send reinforcements. The situation called for boldness, and Washington struck at the enemy every way he could within his limited means. He even sent an invasion force up the Kennebec River into Canada at the same time his main army was besieging Boston.

The Declaration of Independence drastically altered the strategic situation. Once American Independence became an established fact, the primary goal became defending that independence, and the war entered a new phase. The only two times Britain sent major expeditionary forces to America (1776 and 1777) came during this phase, and the enemy quickly gained a position of overwhelming strength. It was not possible for the Americans to win at that point, but it was possible for them to lose. Not losing had to be the primary goal of the American army.

While the first phase had called for aggressiveness, the second phase required caution; and Washington turned cautious. Writing to the Congress on September 8, 1776, Washington outlined his key strategic concepts: ". . . on our side the war should be defensive. . . . It has even been called a war of posts . . . we should on all occasions avoid a general action . . . we should protract the war if possible." As Palmer points out, Washington's strategic plan reads like something that Mao Tse-tung could have written.

Washington made only one major strategic blunder during the second phase—that was trying to defend New York City (which was a trap) with his whole army. Lack of aggressiveness by the Howe brothers prevented a complete disaster for the Americans, and Washington never made the same mistake again. Washington made many tactical blunders; but he was not a school-trained soldier, and he did learn from his mistakes. He never lost sight of his strategic objectives and he did manage to score some impressive tactical victories along the way. British historian George Trevlelyan has noted: "From Trenton onward, Washington was recognized as a farsighted and able general all Europe over."

With the entry of France into the war in early 1778, the strategic situation shifted again, and the war entered its third phase. From the American standpoint, the French fleet was the most significant new factor. So long as the British controlled the sea and could project power at will anywhere along the American coast, Washington was forced to remain on the strategic defensive. The support of the French fleet would allow Washington to move to the offensive.

The results of General Friedrich von Steuben's training at Valley Forge were another significant difference in this third phase. Disagreeing with Weigley, Palmer maintains that "for the first time, George Washington led an army . . . the equal or better of its foe in many respects. Battles henceforth would be fought between British regulars and American regulars." Citing the American performance at Monmouth, Palmer notes that "it was a landmark in the war, for Continentals that day performed in open battle as well or better than the Europeans."

During the almost four years between Valley Forge and Yorktown, Washington repeatedly tried to engineer a decisive victory over the British, and Palmer criticizes most historians for failing to recognize this. His efforts took so long to come to fruition because of the depressed social, political, and economic situation in America, combined with the inherent problems of coordinating operations with a foreign army and fleet so far from their home base. Washington sought a decisive victory—any decisive victory. Although he ultimately attacked at Yorktown, his first choice had been New York City—which was where Clinton had his main force. But Washington kept his options open while he maneuvered toward New York. When he learned that de Grasse would bring the French fleet to Chesapeake Bay in early September, Washington decided to try for Yorktown. Although Washington was a self-taught soldier whose experience had been all on land, he understood sea power would be the decisive factor in this campaign.

Yorktown spelled the end of Britain's attempt to subdue its 13 rebellious colonies. The war dragged on for two more years, but the main fighting shifted to other theaters of the world, particularly the negotiating arena. During this fourth phase, Washington faced what might well have been his most difficult challenge of the war. Although the fighting in America seemed to be virtually over, Washington understood the need to maintain a strategically offensive stance to give the new nation the advantage of bargaining from a position of strength. "There is nothing," Washington wrote, "which will so soon produce a speedy and honorable peace as a state of preparation for war, and we must either do this, or lay our account for a patched up inglorious peace after all the toil, blood, and treasure we have spent." For most of its history, America has never quite been able to understand or apply the wisdom of Washington's words.

During that final phase of the Revolution, Washington maintained a strategically offensive posture, but he tempered it with caution. He realized all America's hard-won gains could still be lost. Washington planned a number of offensive operations, but he never had a chance to execute them because the British remained entrenched in New York City and Charleston, and refused to come out and fight. Washington also lost a great deal of his potential for offensive action when the Royal Navy destroyed Admiral Comte de Grasse's fleet off Saints Passage in April 1782. For most of the remainder of the war Washington kept the main force of his army perched above New York City, waiting for the British to give him an opening to pounce.

In the South, meanwhile, Greene held the American strategic reins during the critical period between Camden and Yorktown. Weigley and Palmer regard Greene quite differently. Weigley sees him as a strategic innovator, a "strategist far subtler than General Washington." Palmer, on the other hand, sees Greene primarily as a practitioner of the strategic approach he learned from Washington: "He had closely observed Washington's astute manipulation of the reins in 1776 and 1777. Now, with some modifications to adapt that strategy to conditions peculiar to the South, he demonstrated that he had learned well from watching the Virginian." Palmer and Weigley both agree, however, Greene's southern campaign was one of the most brilliant in American history.

One of Greene's great accomplishments was his ability to coordinate the operations of his army with those of the partisan groups operating in the South. The partisan opposition, particularly in South Carolina, resulted in large part from Clinton's heavy-handed occupation policies. These policies included an ingrained suspicion of most of the region's Scotch-Irish inhabitants and hostility toward the Presbyterian

Church. Right after he took command, Greene made the unorthodox move of splitting his force into three groups. Retaining control of the center, he sent one group under Daniel Morgan to operate in the west. He sent the other detachment, under Henry Lee, to operate along the coast, in conjunction with partisans under Francis Marion, "the Swamp Fox."

Weigley maintains Greene's intentional violation of the principle of concentration was something Washington never would have attempted. In doing so, Greene tempted Cornwallis to do the same thing. But Cornwallis was operating in a hostile environment, and by splitting his own forces he would make himself even more vulnerable to partisan action. Cornwallis eventually did take the bait and sent Banastre Tarleton after Morgan, while the main British element tried to pin Greene down. Heavily augmented by partisans and local militia, Morgan won a stunning victory over Tarleton at the Cowpens.

Cornwallis went right after Morgan, figuring the Americans would sit tight and regroup after their victory. But Morgan immediately moved out to rejoin with Greene. When Cornwallis discovered his error, he immediately turned after Greene and Morgan, ordering his troops to destroy all extra supplies they could not carry in their haversacks. Cornwallis did not want anything to impede his swift march. When Greene learned that Cornwallis destroyed his supplies, he is supposed to have said, "Then, he is ours!" During the ensuing race to the Dan River, partisan groups continually harassed the British column and prevented them from drawing any sustenance from the countryside. By the time Cornwallis's exhausted and hungry troops reached the Dan, the Americans were already out of reach on the far side. Along the way, Cornwallis had lost 500 of his original 2,500-man force.

After building up his forces in Virginia with Continental recruits, Greene came back across the Dan about a month later and offered the British battle at Guilford Court House. Cornwallis won the battle, but he lost his army in the process. He suffered another 500 casualties, and when it was over he was still surrounded by hostile partisans and had no supplies. Cornwallis withdrew into Virginia and eventually landed in Yorktown. The month following Guilford Court House, Greene did the same thing at Hobkirk's Hill to another British force under Lord Rawdon. Again, the British won the battle, but they were left with an army so depleted they had to evacuate Camden. The following September saw a repeat of the same scenario at Eutaw Springs. The British, under Stewart, won the field, but both sides suffered about 25 percent casualties. The Americans could build back up, the British could not. After Eutaw Springs the British hold on the South was reduced to Wilmington, Charleston, and Savannah.

Ironically, Greene lost all three of the major battles in his campaign. But each time the British won the field, they lost an army in the process. Unable to rebuild their lost forces, the British lost their grip on the South. Strategically, Greene won the campaign by reversing what had been Britain's single greatest success of the war. Weigley rates it the war's most impressive campaign. Greene himself said: "I have been obliged to practice that by finesse which I dare not attempt by force. There are few generals that has run oftener, or more lustily than I have done. But I have taken care not to run too far, and commonly have run as fast forward as backward to convince our enemy that we were like a crab that could run either way." Many years later Mao Tse-tung would write, "the ability to run away is the characteristic of the guerrilla."

British Military Strategy

The American Revolution was a two-phase war from the British perspective. In fact, it was almost two different wars for them. During the colonial phase, Britain's primary objective was simply subduing the rebellion in her colonies and restoring the status quo. Britain never had any intention of annihilating the rebels or destroying their countryside. During the war's international phase, Britain's primary objective quickly became one of survival. The entry of first France, and then Spain and the Netherlands, turned the war into a worldwide conflict that threatened the very security of the British home island itself. Once that happened, North America became a secondary theater for military operations.

Britain faced a number of strategic disadvantages that hampered her ability throughout the course of the war to conduct successful military operations in North America. Two of the most significant were geographic; the size of the country and the width of the Atlantic. America was too big to occupy. It was sparsely populated, and it had not yet developed a tightly knit economic infrastructure. Hence there were few key cities and no city was so important that its loss would bring the collapse of the rebellion. Yet the British continually went for the big cities, and wound up merely holding real estate. The Atlantic, on the other hand, presented an even greater problem—a 3,000-mile line of communications. Supplies, replacements, and even simple messages took almost two months to get from England to America.

The condition of the Royal Navy further complicated the maritime problem. As a cost-cutting measure, Britain had allowed the fleet to slip into a sad state of readiness, following her global triumph during the Seven Years' War. As long as Britain only had to deal with her rebellious colonies, that was not a great difficulty. But France and Spain together had 140 capital ships to Britain's 123. When the war became a global one, Britain, for one of the few times in her history, lost the absolute mastery of both the Atlantic and the English Channel.

Britain also suffered from a self-inflicted handicap, a muddled military command structure. Although the army came under the Secretary of State for War, the Colonial Office, headed by Lord George Germain, actually controlled the military operations in North America. Germain was a former general who had been court-martialed out of the army for his ineptness during the Battle of Minden in 1759. Politically adept, however, Germain managed to work himself back into a position of power when George III came to the throne. The field commanders in North America then found themselves in the awkward and distasteful position of taking orders from a publicly disgraced former officer.

To make matters worse, Britain had no overall military commander in North America to coordinate operation. General Guy Carleton commanded in Canada, and Thomas Gage, William Howe, and finally Henry Clinton commanded in turn in the 13 colonies. Each answered directly to Germain, who further violated the principle of unity of command by issuing direct orders to subordinate commanders, such as Cornwallis. The British only established a unified command after Yorktown, when Carleton became the overall commander. By that time,

however, London had already written off the 13 colonies.

Britain also faced a number of social problems that only compounded her geographical and organizational difficulties. The war against the colonies was not popular in England. The landed gentry, who had traditionally borne the costs of Britain's wars, were generally against this one. In opposition to the war, Sir Jeffery Amherst refused to accept the appointment as the army's commander-in-chief, and that office went vacant for several years. He finally accepted the job when France entered the war; but during the colonial phase, the army had no military chief who might have brought order to Germain's confused organization.

On the other side of the Atlantic, Britain never managed to mobilize the Loyalist element in America. London continually assumed that the rebels were a minority and most of the colonists would rush to support the restoration of British authority. And while perhaps up to one-third of the American population opposed the Revolution, Britain managed to recruit, organize, and field only a very few effective Loyalist units. Tarleton's British Legion and the Queen's Rangers were among the exceptions, but they were not enough to make any real difference. This meant the British army in North America, at the end of its 3,000-mile supply line, became a nonreplaceable asset itself.

Britain had five basic strategic options. At one point or another in the war she tried them all. Sometimes she even tried to execute more than one at a time. Some of these options had promise, but Britain never managed to make any of them work.

The naval strategy would have been the most likely option for a traditionally maritime power, and it was one of the first Britain considered. But a naval blockade and economic strangulation would have been slow. With the war unpopular, the British government sought a quicker victory. The economic effects of a blockade would have cut both ways, as well. England, still deeply in debt from the Seven Years' War, could not afford to suspend trade, even for a short period. The weakened posture of the Royal Navy also argued against this option. Most of the admirals did not think they had the resources to seal off the entire American coast. Many ships were in a poor state of repair and were undermanned. The Revolution even made the Royal

Navy's manpower problem worse by cutting off the colonies as a major source of recruits. Britain finally did go over to the naval strategy after Yorktown; but by then the war was well into its international phase, and the retention of the 13 colonies was no longer the primary objective.

The second strategic option was the direct elimination of the rebel army. Washington recognized this as his own weak point, and only once after the New York campaign (at Brandywine) did he risk his own main army in a direct confrontation with the British main force. The problem with this approach for the British was that the thin red line was already spread about as thin as it could get. In 1775 the entire British army amounted to only something like 27,000 infantry and cavalry. By 1782 that number had grown to 150,000, with an additional 29,000 German auxiliaries; but it was also a global war by that point.

After the New York campaign, Howe had a golden opportunity to eliminate Washington's army. The New Jersey campaign started out that way; but Howe also tried to pursue a policy of conciliation with the rebels. The New Jersey campaign eventually degenerated into a traditional eighteenth-century exercise in occupying places. Howe also believed that his army was an irreplaceable national asset he must avoid squandering at all costs. There was a certain amount of validity to this point of view, as Cornwallis later learned when he beat Greene at Guilford Court House, only to lose a quarter of his army in the process.

The Hudson line strategy might have worked for the British, too. New England was the heart of the rebellion. By gaining control of the Hudson–Lake Champlain line into Canada, the British could box New England in from two sides on the land and two sides from the sea. It would also provide an interior line to the British power base in Canada. Burgoyne tried to execute this strategy when he started moving south out of Canada in June 1777. Although he made more than his share of mistakes on the ground, the muddled command structure did him in more than any other single factor. Burgoyne expected Howe to come up the river to meet him roughly half way. Howe went to Philadelphia instead. There was no overall commander in North America to coordinate the movements of the two armies, and Germain did not resolve this matter.

Many historians doubt that the British control of the Hudson line would have been fatal to the Revolutionary cause. Washington thought otherwise. He built West Point as the key American strong point on the river to prevent the British from doing just that. He called it "the key to America." Benedict Arnold was so sure of the line's decisive nature that he gambled his reputation and his future on its control.

The British achieved some of their greatest tactical successes of the war with their southern strategy. After Burgoyne surrendered his army and Clinton withdrew from Philadelphia back to New York, the war in the North ground to a stalemate. Clinton, looking for a way to get it moving again, shifted operations to the South in late 1779. As a region, the South was the least enthusiastic about the Revolution, and the British still sought that wellspring of Loyalist support they were sure must be somewhere. Clinton's inept occupation policies, however, alienated the large Scotch-Irish element of the population, and the British soon faced a level of partisan resistance they never encountered in the North.

A major attraction of the southern strategy was the closer proximity of British naval power operating out of the Caribbean bases. This gave the British undisputed control of the southern coastal cities. When the French fleet entered the picture, however, the British lost absolute control over the American coastal waters, and their troops in the South were always in danger of being isolated by a superior French naval force.

At first, the southern campaign seemed to work beautifully. General Benjamin Lincoln lost one American army at Charleston, and Horatio Gates lost another at Camden. Then Greene arrived on the scene and started chipping away at the one resource the British could not replace—the troops. In the course of six months, three different British commanders (Cornwallis, Rawdon, and Alexander Stewart) beat Greene on the battlefield, but each emerged from the fighting with a decimated army.

The middle colonies strategy probably had the least chance of success. The idea was to separate New England and New York from the South, by controlling the large section of the country in the center. Howe tried it with his Philadelphia campaign in 1777. Arnold tried it again when he moved into Virginia in December 1780. After Guilford Court House, Cornwallis moved into Virginia and he assumed command of the combined forces and the campaign. Because of its disastrous ending at Yorktown, this campaign is usually considered a blunder from start to finish. It was not, however, quite that simple.

Ironically, Cornwallis was probably the best senior British commander of the war. He certainly was the most aggressive; and like Washington, he learned from his mistakes. After his experiences in the South, he realized he could never eliminate Greene by attacking him directly; but he could neutralize him by going after his supply base. Greene's supply base was the state of Virginia, with its rich tobacco-based economy. Virginia was also one of the key reasons the American economy held together. By taking Virginia out of the war, Cornwallis could strangle Greene's army, and he could seriously damage the entire rebel economy. Virginia was especially vulnerable at that point. Most of the Virginia Continental Line had been captured at Charleston, leaving the local militia as the state's first line of defense.

For the next several months, Cornwallis waged the closest thing to total war that the Revolution ever saw. It was a sharp reversal of all previous tactics. The British attacked property and economic targets, burned crops, slaughtered livestock, and most terrifying of all to plantation owners, freed Black slaves. Cornwallis also seized thousands of Virginia's fine horses to give his dragoons an unlimited supply of remounts. He put an additional 700 of his infantry on horseback, and for the first time in the war, a British force had superior mobility. Washington sent Lafayette and Wayne to Virginia with 2,600 Continental troops, but they were helpless against Cornwallis's superior and more mobile force.

Yorktown was not Cornwallis's idea. In the summer of 1781, Clinton ordered him to retire to the coast, establish a naval base, and send 2,000 troops back to New York. Clinton and Cornwallis had usually disagreed in the past, and it is possible that Clinton felt threatened by Cornwallis's successes in Virginia, while he sat immobile in New York. The British lost Yorktown before the first shot ever was fired on land. De Grasse's narrow victory off the Capes gave the French temporary naval superiority in Chesapeake Bay and Cornwallis was doomed.

The North ministry fell after Yorktown. The new government in London decided to write off the American colonies, and Britain shifted over to a naval strategy in her worldwide struggle. During the course of the next two years Britain managed to hold on to the rest of her empire, and she emerged from the war in better shape than France.

Could Britain have won in America? Perhaps. With a unified command structure, more capable and aggressive generals, a more skillful handling of American Loyalists, and a better overall sense of objective, Britain just might have overcome its geographical handicaps. The Americans could have had a much tougher time than they did, and the war might have ended with Britain still holding on to some of the colonies. On the other hand, it is quite possible that an old and sick William Pitt was thinking of his country's self-inflicted handicaps when he stood up in the House of Lords and said, "You cannot, I venture to say, you cannot conquer America!"

French Military Strategy

In 1775 France could have been the most dominant country in the world. With 25 million people, her population was three times as large as Britain's and 10 times as large as that of the 13 colonies. During the Seven Years' War, however, France had lost much of her world power to the British. Although France still retained her Caribbean islands and certain fishing rights off Newfoundland, she had lost Canada, most of her power in India, and had been forced to give up all claims to land east of the Mississippi. The Seven Years' War resulted in a role reversal of the two countries, and from that point on, Britain's diplomats took precedence over France's in the court ceremonies of Europe.

When the French decided to help the Americans, they were not motivated by any love of democratic principles. For the most part, France saw the American Revolution as an opportunity to extract some revenge and deflate Britain's position in the world. Although the French did go through the motions of mounting an invasion of the British Isles, they never had any serious intention of trying to completely conquer and destroy England. Nor did France ever try to regain Canada, although she did not necessarily want to see it fall into American hands either. As early as May 1776, France had decided on a policy of covert aid to the Revolutionaries. After

Saratoga, the Comte de Vergennes started open negotiations with the Americans. It was not so much that he felt the Americans had a chance to win, rather he was afraid that a stunned government in London would try to offer the colonists terms and bring the hostilities to an end. Vergennes wanted to drag out the British agony for as long as possible.

On the political front, Vergennes deftly orchestrated the isolation of Britain. France first entered into the Treaty of Amity and Commerce and the Treaty of Conditional and Defensive Alliance with the Americans. Then she secretly signed the Convention of Aranjuez with the Spanish. Finally, France maneuvered the Baltic powers into forming the League of Armed Neutrality, which was, in fact, more anti-British than it was neutral. The involvement of Spain did make the equation more complex for France. While Spain's primary goal was Gibraltar, she also had claims on lands west of the Mississippi— the same territory coveted by many Americans. But France needed Spain. Although the British had allowed their navy to deteriorate after the Seven Years' War, it could still hold its own against the French fleet. The combined Spanish and French fleets, however, had 140 capital ships to Britain's 123.

On the military side, Vergennes pursued a primarily naval strategy. His goal was to draw the bulk of the Royal Navy into defensive operations in the Channel, while he sent a separate French squadron overseas for what he hoped would be a decisive operation. Geography favored the French in this plan. With key naval bases at both Toulon and Brest, they could slip in and out of the Atlantic almost at will. The ends of the French power base were spread too far apart for the British navy to blockade.

The ill-fated French overseas strike force sailed from Toulon in April 1778. Under its commander, Admiral Comte d'Estaing, the French squadron passed up an opportunity to attack the British fleet in New York harbor that July, failed against Newport the following month, planned and then abandoned an amphibious assault against Halifax, and finally ended with the Franco-American fiasco at Savannah in October 1779. D'Estaing's fleet limped back into French waters in December 1779, having accomplished nothing.

While d'Estaing was wasting his time and French resources on the western side of the Atlantic, the rest of the French fleet fumbled around trying to stage an invasion of England from the Channel. In 1778 the British had only about 10,000 trained troops in their home islands. By the spring of 1779, the French had assembled an invasion force of 50,000, and had the ability to put overwhelming naval superiority into the Channel. For some reason, however, they never pulled it off. The original plan had the invasion scheduled for May 1779. But the combined French-Spanish fleet of 66 ships of the line (under the command of Admiral d'Orvillers) did not enter the Channel until that August. Then they remained for another six weeks trying to get organized. The French and Spanish navies had much difficulty operating together. The invasion was finally called off in mid-September, at the approach of the bad weather season in the Channel.

Aside from the operational incompetence of the aborted invasion, the whole enterprise was a poor idea from the start. An invasion of the main British island would have been a measure far out of proportion with Vergennes's limited goal of reducing British power, as opposed to completely destroying Britain. A more realistic, and achievable, military objective would have been the occupation of the Isle of Wight. The control of this strategic piece of land would have bottled up Portsmith, Britain's principal dockyard. Closing Portsmith would have strangled the Royal Navy, which was still, despite its depleted condition, Britain's major strategic force.

With the failure of both the 1779 invasion and d'Estaing's mission, French military efforts became erratic and struck out in several different directions. Up to that point, French aid to the ground fighting efforts in America had been limited to money and supplies. Although d'Estaing had a large body of troops with his squadron, they were an amphibious strike force, never intended for sustained operations on land. Now France sent a full-fledged expeditionary corps to America, with Comte de Rochambeau, supported by eight ships of the line, landing 6,000 troops in Rhode Island in July 1780. At the same time France stepped up joint naval operations with the Spanish against the British targets in the Mediterranean, Gibraltar, and Minorca. In March 1781 France struck out in a third direction, sending Admiral de Grasse with 24 ships of the line and 3,000 troops to the West Indies. In the summer of 1781 the French and Spanish made another attempt to mount an invasion of England, with the same results they experienced two years earlier. Finally, in late 1781, the French launched off in yet a fifth tangent, sending a squadron under Vice Admiral Pierre-Andre de Suffren to the Indian Ocean.

Only once did the French manage to bring together their fragmented military power on the western side of the Atlantic. Fortunately for the American cause, it was the right place at the right time. Fortunately, too, Rochambeau shared Washington's appreciation for the decisive nature of French naval power in the Yorktown operation. De Grasse moved his squadron north to the Chesapeake, while the Comte de Barras moved his small squadron south from Newport, and Washington and Rochambeau moved south over land to link up with Lafayette. The jaws of this three-pronged pincer slammed shut on Cornwallis when Admiral Thomas Graves failed to beat de Grasse off the Capes on September 5, 1781. The battle itself was a tactical draw, but a strategic defeat for the British. A few days later de Barras linked up with de Grasse, and Graves found 36 French ships facing his 19. Graves withdrew to New York, leaving Cornwallis to his fate.

Immediately following Cornwallis's surrender, the French forces split again, and de Grasse headed back for the West Indies. The British abandoned military operations in North America, and shifted all of their efforts to the war at sea. With the British back in their traditional element, the war turned against France and their Spanish and Dutch allies. Starting with their victory at Dogger Bank on August 5, 1781, the British ran up a string of naval successes that was only partially offset by the loss of Minorca in February 1792. On December 12, 1781, the Royal Navy won a battle in the Atlantic at Ushant; and on April 12, 1782, they soundly defeated de Grasse at the Saints in the West Indies. Finally, in September 1782, Admiral Lord Richard Howe lifted the siege of Gibraltar with 34 Royal navy ships of the line.

The American Revolution was the last war of the ancien regime. Although France's military strategy had been as inept as her political strategy was sound, the French support was crucial to the American success. French financial and material assistance, and French naval power were by far the most important contributions. The direct involvement of French troops mattered only once, at Yorktown; but even in that battle French sea power was the decisive factor.

French support had helped America win her Revolution, and yet paradoxically, France was probably the big loser of the war. Although France did succeed in deflating part of Britain's Empire, France, in the end, was even more drained than Britain—and had little to show for it. The subsidies and loans to the Americans, in addition to the direct costs of the mostly ineffective French military operations, wrecked the already shaky finances of the French monarchy and drove it into bankruptcy. After that, Louis XVI had little choice but to summon the Estates-General. And with the American's success as an example, the Third Estate was ready for an opportunity to assert its rights.

David T. Zabecki

REFERENCES

American Military Strategy

Dave R. Palmer, *The War of the Fox: American Strategy in the War for America* (1975); Russel F. Weigley, *The American Way of War* (1973);

British Military Strategy

George A. Billias, ed., *George Washington's Opponents* (1989); Dave R. Palmer, *The War of the Fox: American Strategy in the War for America* (1975); Gregory J.W. Urwin, "Cornwallis in Virginia: A Reappraisal," *Military Collector and Historian*, 37 (1985):111–126; Russel F. Weigley, *The American Way of War* (1973);

French Military Strategy

Ernest R. Dupuy, Gay Hammerman, and Grace P. Hayes, *The American Revolution: A Global War* (1977); Lee B. Kennett, *The French Forces in America, 1780–1783* (1977); James B. Perkins, *France in the American Revolution* (1911).

Militia

Militia units had been in existence for many years before the outbreak of fighting at Lexington and Concord in Massachusetts on April 19, 1775. In America the militia dates back to approximately the founding of each colony. In the seventeenth century the militia was in many cases a colony's only defense against Indians and the only means available of preserving law and order. In the eighteenth century the responsibilities of the militia were enlarged. During the French and Indian War, militia units were assigned to the protection of supply lines, to garrison duty in forts and cities, and to guard prisoners. In the South the militia's primary duty was the prevention or suppression of slave uprisings. Thus, former or present slaves, indentured servants, and others of the lower classes like poor whites were barred from serving in the militia. Only those whites between the age of 16 and 60 who possessed property, and therefore a stake in seeing the established order maintained, and who could provide themselves with a weapon, were allowed to enroll in the militia.

The militia, therefore, was the preserve of the middle class. While the militia often selected their own officers, they often picked what may be described as their social betters—men who had more wealth, prestige, or years in the town or county than the average man. Militia units were never intended to serve far away from home. Their duty was to defend their homes and communities. Rarely were they sent off to distance places or involved in long campaigns.

The militia was not only the protector of the societal order but also of the liberties of the people. A defense based on militia was the ideal state of military preparedness because the citizen-soldiers of the militia had a stake in the political and social system of the nation, and they would not be threat to the liberties of the people. A standing army was a threat, however. It owed its allegiance to its sovereign, and it could be used to destroy the liberties of the people. Late in the eighteenth century and into the early nineteenth the Jeffersonian Republicans opposed the efforts of the Federalists to establish even a small standing army. The militia of the citizen-soldier was adequate they believed for the defense of a republic.

Thus, when the fighting began there were many Patriot leaders who had high hopes for the militia. Charles Lee believed that, in some instances, militiamen could be more valuable than regulars. He also pointed out that America could produce more militiamen than Britain could produce regulars. Some Patriot leaders even asserted that the militia would be more dedicated in zeal than regulars, but events that took place during the Revolution shattered such high opinions of the militia. Washington, in particular, after only a year in command came to distrust the militia. Particularly influential in changing his mind was the desertion of over 6,000 militiamen from the army after the Battle of Long Island. Washington wanted to create a regular standing army to fight the war, but this desire was not supported in Congress because of the traditional fear of standing armies.

Other American commanders had unfortunate experiences with the militia. Generals Horatio Gates and John Stark must have cursed the militiamen who arrived on the morning of October 7, 1777, the day of the second Battle of Saratoga, but who left before midday. The militiamen claimed their enlistments were up. This determination to leave camp was a very common occurrence during the war. Another problem that American commanders experienced was that when militiamen came under fire, they would often break and run. Daniel Morgan came up with a way to prevent such fiascoes. At the Battle of Cowpens (January 17, 1781) he positioned his troops, which included many militiamen, so that their backs would be to the Broad River. Hence he gave them no choice but to fight. Morgan explained why he did this: "When men are forced to fight they will sell their lives dearly. . . . Had I cross the river, one half of the militia would immediately have abandoned me." At other times American commanders had to be particularly harsh, warning that soldiers who deserted in the face of the enemy would be executed.

Despite all their shortcomings sometimes the militia performed like regulars. At Cowpens, the militia assisted the Continental regulars in defeating the British. It was militia who made the British retreat from Lexington and Concord on April 19, 1775, into a living nightmare. A little over two months later it was the militia who repulsed two British attacks against their positions during the Battle of Bunker Hill.

The performance of the militia was erratic, but this did produce one benefit for the American cause—doubt. British commanders never knew if the militia would turn out in large numbers to the Continental Army or would turn to guerrilla warfare and harass British lines of communication and supply. This was one reason why in 1777 General William Howe decided to sail to the Chesapeake Bay and then make a short march to Philadelphia rather than make a more dangerous march through New Jersey.

Scholars have estimated that during the War of the American Revolution that approximately 250,000 to 375,000 men served in various militia units throughout the 13 colonies. Most of these men were never engaged in combat, but they were used to guard supply depots, to guard prisoners, to act as scouts, and so on. Some were never used, since they were called up in anticipation of attacks that never took place. Nevertheless, the militia did make a valuable contribution to winning the war.

The Loyalists had militia units as well. Several Loyalist militia units that were organized in the vicinity of New York City served in that city's garrison, guarded American prisoners of war, built fortifications, and conducted raids into territory surrounding the city. Generally, the Tory militiaman was better armed and supplied than the Patriot militiaman. The Loyalists were also organized into units that were in nature and quality like regular army units. These units of the "Provincial Line," as the British called them, had a definite length of enlistment and could have been sent to any theater of war in North America. The contributions of the Loyalist militia to the British cause was not as great as those made by their rebel counterparts to the American cause, but this was not due to any defects in their performance. Some British officers angered supporters because of their contempt for all colonials.

Anthony P. Inguanzo

REFERENCES

Lawrence Cress, "Radical Whiggery on the Role of the Militia: Ideological Roots of the American Militia," *Journal of the History of Ideas*, 40(1979):43–60; William Walker Edwards, "Morgan and His Rifleman," *William and Mary Quarterly*, 23 (1914):73–108; Edward Leach, *Arms for Empire: A Military History of the British Colonies in North America, 1607–1763* (1973); Louis Morton, "The Origins of American Military Policy," *Military Affairs*, 22 (1958):75–82; John W. Shy, *A People Numerous and Armed: Reflections on the Military Struggle for Independence* (1976).

Militia of the Middle States

The American Revolutionary War began in Massachusetts in April 1775, and quickly spread throughout the North American colonies. Within days, the conflict reached New York City and the Hudson River valley, a place of particular importance to both sides. Immediately the Loyalists, who kept their allegiance to the British government, and the Whigs, who supported the rebellion, clashed over control of this vital region. Meanwhile, in neighboring Connecticut and New Jersey, Whigs began to wrest control

of the governments and local militia units from any remaining British control. For the next eight years, local Whig militiamen fought against Loyalists and British soldiers in an effort to maintain control of this critical area surrounding New York City.

The militia units of these three states (Connecticut, New York, New Jersey) had several duties to perform throughout the war. Their two principal responsibilities to their own states were suppressing Loyalist activities that threatened Whig control of the state governments or that undermined the support of the people for the rebellion, and defending the coasts and lines near the British forces against British and Loyalist raids. In addition, militiamen often provided reinforcements to Washington's Continental Army, scouted and sent information to the state and Continental officers in the area, and coordinated with the regular army to harass isolated enemy units and to support Continental soldiers hovering near the enemy's army.

The contest for control of New York City began as soon as news of the fighting at Lexington and Concord arrived. The inhabitants of the city seized 600 arms from the royal arsenal, distributed them to loyal Whigs, and placed control of the city government into the hands of a Whig committee. The struggle continued through the winter and even into the early spring of 1776, as Connecticut and New Jersey militia units marched into New York to help suppress Loyalist sentiment. Whig militiamen disarmed the Loyalists, punishing or imprisoning anyone who spoke against the Whig governments or who raised or joined a unit to serve with the British forces.

Meanwhile, New Jersey and Connecticut also prepared for war. Jonathan Trumbull, Connecticut's royal governor who sided with the rebels, joined his legislative assembly to organize their militia and station units along the coast to guard against the expected raids from British warships in the Long Island Sound. New Jersey's leading Whigs ousted their royal governor, while the local militia units assembled and prepared to defend the state's coast.

Until the spring and summer of 1776, the militia units of these three states were mostly on their own. Then, after the British evacuation of Boston in March 1776, Washington shifted his army to New York City and Long Island, and the militia had to learn how to cooperate and coordinate with the larger regular army. The Continental Congress expect the state militia to be a source of reinforcement for the army, and though Washington did not have much faith in the quality of the militia soldiers, the weakness of his army forced him to depend upon the militia.

The campaign of 1776 opened with the British attack on Long Island on August 27, and ended after Washington's counterattacks in December 1776 and January 1777. Throughout this campaign, the militia saw action at all levels of the war. New Jersey militia defended the coast across from British-held Staten Island, while militia from all three states suppressed uprisings and other efforts by the Loyalists to assist the British forces fighting in New York and New Jersey.

During this campaign Washington, the Congress, and the state governments learned which roles militiamen performed best, and which they executed less effectively. The militia was effective at hunting, capturing, and killing Loyalists. Local militia units would quickly assemble and chase any band of Loyalists reported to be organizing to join the British or to disrupt American supplies. At the height of the crisis in New Jersey in November 1776, as Washington and his dwindling army retreated toward the Delaware River and Washington needed every man he could get, he still detached a New Jersey militia regiment from the army to return to its home county in order to stop a local insurrection by Loyalists.

The militia proved less useful when serving in place of regular soldiers. The Continental Congress ordered the establishment of an army of militiamen to be stationed in New Jersey with the hope that this army would be available to join Washington if the fighting shifted to New Jersey. When Washington retreated into New Jersey in November after the loss of New York City, the militia army disintegrated and proved useless to Washington. He then tried to rally the New Jersey militia to his small army, but the local militia refused to assemble despite the efforts of the newly elected governor, William Livingston. Washington retreated south of the Delaware River with less than 3,000 men left in his army. The militia had proven to be a failure as a reinforcement for the regular Army.

On the other hand, the militia proved to be a source of local strength to check the British army.

When Washington entered New Jersey, he left part of his army behind to defend north of New York City in the vital Highlands area along the Hudson River. New York and Connecticut militiamen rallied to this army detachment to bolster the strength of the forts along the river. In addition, Connecticut militia guarded along the Connecticut–New York border northeast of New York City.

Washington has learned that attempts to collect several thousand militiamen together at once were fruitless, so in December 1776, he initiated a series of counterattacks using smaller militia forces supported by a few Continental soldiers. In this way he took advantage of the local availability of the militia without trying to assemble a charge force. Continentals and New York militiamen attacked along the western side of the Hudson into northeast New Jersey, while a small Continental detachment joined a New Jersey militia regiment to harass the British garrisons near the coast across from Staten Island. Washington then recrossed the Delaware and joined some Pennsylvania and local New Jersey militiamen to attack and defeat German and British troops at Trenton and Princeton, New Jersey. Finally, Washington ordered an attack on New York City itself by a larger force of militia. Although the assault on New York City failed, this series of attacks had the desired effect, as the British abandoned most of their posts in New Jersey and retreated to the coast.

The lessons of the 1776 campaign remained with Washington and the state militia units throughout the rest of the war. Militiamen served better as partisans, fighting in small detachments of a hit-and-run strategy. They were not effective in long-term operations and in pitched battled against British regulars, but they were good at harassing British movements and sniping at isolated British units. In 1777, the British army marched out of its New Jersey base of New Brunswick and moved inland toward Washington's army. The New Jersey militia rallied to the scene and hovered around the British line of march, fighting a running battle with the British flank and rear units while Washington kept his army safely out of the British reach. Washington and the militia had learned the proper mode of coordinating the army and the militia.

During the winter and spring months of 1777, the militia adapted to its other main role in coordination with the army. Militia units of Connecticut, New York, and New Jersey helped man the lines between the British and American armies, cooperating with Continental units to watch for British moves and to prevent the British from collecting supplies or information from the people in the countryside. In effect, Washington used the local militia and small detachments of the army to form a blockade around the British army in New Jersey and New York.

This effort sparked numerous clashes between militia and British units. In late January 1777, New Jersey militia general Philemon Dickinson and 400 militiamen plunged through a deep river, attacked an equal number of enemy soldiers who were collecting goods near Somerset Courthouse, and defeated the foragers, capturing 9 prisoners, 40 wagons, and about 100 horses. In February, 250 New Jersey militiamen joined 50 Pennsylvania militia, attacking and capturing one-half of a Loyalist regiment south of New Brunswick. Such skirmishes occurred frequently throughout the three states, and as spring came, the numbers engaged increased on both sides.

The Connecticut militia, meanwhile, engaged in a series of raids onto Long Island. Loyalists who fled Connecticut set up bases on the island and then raided across the Sound along Connecticut's coast. The Connecticut militia returned the favor and raided British and Loyalist posts, capturing men and supplies. Washington and Governor Jonathan Trumbull even considered larger raids of several thousand men, but the presence of British ships in the Sound prevented any such expedition.

In the summer of 1777, the British army based in New York City shifted to the head of the Chesapeake Bay and marched on Philadelphia. Washington moved his army into Pennsylvania to meet the British, and the militia of New Jersey, New York, and Connecticut were given the responsibility of guarding the area around New York City. They did not do well when General Sir Henry Clinton, the British commander left in New York City, ordered an expedition up the Hudson River in an attempt to support another British thrust in northern New York under General John Burgoyne.

Clinton and his force sailed up the Hudson and attacked the militia garrisons in the forts along the river. George Clinton, the recently elected governor of New York, and his brother James, were in personal command at one fort that held out for an entire day before the British

swept over the defenses with the bayonet. The governor and his brother escaped at the last minute, and many of the militiamen dove into the Hudson, swimming to safety. Clinton continued upriver, capturing or destroying all of the forts, until he heard of Burgoyne's surrender in mid-October to the American army commanded by Horatio Gates. Throughout the British advance and subsequent retreat along the lower Hudson, New York, New Jersey, and Connecticut militia units followed along the shores to prevent a British penetration inland.

After a winter of duty along the lines, the militia once again had to rally to Washington's army in the summer of 1778. The British army, which had taken Philadelphia in late 1777, marched across New Jersey to return to its base in New York City. Washington again employed the militia as he had in 1777, using them in small detachments to hover around the British line of march. When the British finally turned and fought Washington's army at Monmouth courthouse on June 28, 1778, Washington concentrated his regular soldiers and kept the militia units out of the main battle. He understood that militia soldiers did not fare so well in a field battle against battle-hardened British veterans.

For the next four years, the war in the Middle States settled into what could be called a loose siege of New York City by Washington's army and the state militia units. Militiamen and Continental soldiers took post along the line in a continuing effort to keep supplies and information away from the British. When the British sent part of their army into the field, as they did in June 1780, Washington repeated the tactics of 1777, pushing militia and Continental detachments out toward the British while keeping the main army just out of reach.

Meanwhile, the raids between Whig and Loyalist militia units increased. Connecticut militia units continuously raided Long Island, as New York militiamen skirmished with the bands of Loyalist horsemen that plundered and burned the New York and Connecticut towns near the border of those two states northeast of New York City. New Jersey militiamen, at times supported by Continental soldiers, ran expeditions onto Staten Island. These different raids helped maintain pressure against the Loyalist bases while allowing the Americans occasionally to take the offensive.

Every summer and fall during 1778 through 1780, Washington heard encouraging news that the French, who allied with the United States in 1778, were sending a fleet and army to link with Washington and to assault New York City. Therefore, each spring and summer, despite the lessons of the earlier years, Washington tried to collect large numbers of militia to bolster his under-strength army in anticipation of the desired attack. Each year, however, the results were disappointing. He and the French were unable to join, and the militia never mustered in the strength Washington wanted. These failures further demonstrated that the local militia was not an effective source of reinforcements for regular field operations.

By this period of the war, the state governments were experiencing great difficulty getting their militiamen to serve. Money was in short supply, and the people were exhausted after manning the lines and defending the coasts for so many years. The Connecticut government had trouble maintaining a few hundred men along its southwestern border despite its efforts to raise several thousand for the job. New Jersey and New York had similar problems trying to defend along the rivers and coasts. One reason for this predicament was that none of the three states resorted to any form of compulsion to force men to serve. Local units could try to persuade men to join their units when it was their turn, but the stiffest penalty a man faced for refusing to serve was a monetary fine. As war-weariness set in, financial punishments were not enough to get men into the field.

In 1781, Washington and the army again left the area, leaving the defense of the Middle States to the militia. Unlike the situation in 1777, the British did not sally forth from their defenses, and duty along the line continued to be one of skirmishing with British foraging parties and Loyalist raiders. The need to suppress Loyalists within the states had mostly ended by this time, as almost all Loyalists who wanted to fight for the British cause had already fled the states and had joined one of the many Loyalist bands operating from within the safety of the British army. Thus, the principal duty for the Whig militiamen now was to prevent the Loyalist raiders from gathering supplies and discouraging the people.

The war would last only two more years after the surrender of the British army at Yorktown, Virginia, in October 1781. Washington and the state governments, however, did not yet know they had won. During the final two years, the states tried to maintain militia units along the coasts and near the British lines, but had increasing difficulty getting the men to serve. Washington, on the other hand, refrained from calling the militia to the army, waiting to see if the British were going to make any further efforts at winning the war in the Middle States. He planned to call on the local soldiers if he could convince the French to try another joint operation, but he doubted such an effort would be made. He was right, and the war ended without additional field operations.

The militia, however, helped the state governments make the transition from war to peace. Militia units were the only armed force at the disposal of the state governments, and therefore the governments turned to the militiamen to continue the war against the Loyalists, and to guard public supplies and defensive works from American citizens who wanted to destroy or vandalize such public property. Thus, as the war ended, the militia made the shift from wartime state soldiers to peacetime state police forces.

Throughout the war, the state militia forces had remained under the direct control of the state governments and governors. Washington and the other Continental generals carefully respected the authority of the state governments, working through the governors and legislatures to get more state troops or to move militia units. The Continental generals did command militia units when they coordinated with the regular army in the field. The militiamen were, however, first and foremost state military forces. In this way, the Revolutionary War was fought as much by local and state forces as it was by national armies.

The governors had a great impact on the use of their state militia soldiers. Trumbull was a strong executive, retaining his position as governor of Connecticut throughout the war and working with the legislature to organize and use the militia. He remained in constant communication with Washington, other Continental generals, and the neighboring states. William Livingston took the office of New Jersey governor in 1776, and then proceeded to wage a seven-year struggle with the legislature to organize the state's militia more efficiently. He was an advocate of stronger measures to compel men to serve when called. He did not, however, take a direct role in commanding his state's militia forces, leaving the mustering and commanding of them to his militia generals.

George Clinton, on the other hand, was more of a warrior-governor. He was a militia general before being elected governor of New York, and even after taking his office, he often took the field to command in person the men of his state. Washington and the Continental Congress entrusted him with several key commands, particularly of the critical forts along the Hudson River in the Highlands region. Clinton remained the governor until after the war ended.

The American Revolutionary War, therefore, was more than a traditional eighteenth-century conflict, and more than a backwoods war between American partisans and British regulars. It was a combination of both, a revolutionary or people's war, where regular armies and citizen-soldiers all fought for control of the people, governments, cities, and resources of the area. Nowhere in North America was the conflict more a combination of regular and partisan warfare than in the three states surrounding the main British stronghold of New York City. The local state forces fought on their own and in conjunction with the regular army to frustrate and finally defeat the British army and their Loyalist supporters.

Mark V. Kwasny

REFERENCES

Richard Buel, Jr., *Dear Liberty: Connecticut's Mobilization for the Revolutionary War* (1980); Douglas Southall Freeman, *George Washington: A Biography*, 7 vols. (1948–1957); Don Higginbotham, *The War of American Independence: Military Attitudes, Policies, and Practice, 1763–1789* (1983); Leonard Lundin, *Cockpit of the Revolution: The War for Independence in New Jersey* (1940); Howard H. Peckham, ed., *The Toll of Independence: Engagements and Battle Casualties of the American Revolution* (1974).

Minisink, New York, Raid on (July 19, 1779)

By March 1779 the Continental Army was preparing for an expedition into the heartland of New York. The expedition of over 5,000 men was hard to conceal. Their intent was quickly discovered by Colonel John Butler, a Loyalist leader, and Joseph Brant, a Mohawk chief. They were responsible for the British, Tory, and In-

dian forces occupying the interior of New York State. They attempted to divert Major General John Sullivan and Brigadier General James Clinton, who headed the American expedition, from accomplishing their mission. One such attempt was the raid on Minisink in Orange County, New York. On July 8, 1779, the combined British, Tory, and Indian forces departed from Chemung, New York. Its purpose was to divert Clinton as he was moving southward to join with Sullivan's forces. On July 19, 1779, they attacked the settlement at Minisink, killing four settlers and burning most of the structures.

When the news of the raid reached Lieutenant Colonel Benjamin Tusten he called upon his regiment of militia to pursue the enemy. This force was later joined by Colonel John Hawthorn and a few men. Hawthorn then took command of the force. A small scouting party soon fell into an ambush, but the main body continued. Hawthorn split his forces, sending about 50 men to pursue Brant toward the Delaware River. This force could not find the enemy, and they began to return when they were sighted by the enemy. Hawthorn's small force formed a square on top of a rock hill and engaged the Indians with musket fire for about four hours. At one point Brant and his men charged one corner of the square, pouring deadly fire into the militia. The militia square soon crumbled, and Brant pursued, killing all of the Patriots. Tusten had gathered about 17 of the wounded together and began to tend to their injuries. However, the Indians discovered Tusten's party and massacred all 18. The militia lost a total of 45 men killed in this raid.

The Battle at Minisink was a blow to the Continentals, but it did not achieve the results that Butler and Brant expected. The Sullivan-Clinton expedition continued as planned and conducted a very successful campaign in New York.

John M. Keefe

REFERENCES

Frederick W. Bogert, "Marauders in the Minisink," *New Jersey Historical Society Proceedings*, 82 (1964):271–282; Donald F. Clark, "Joseph Brant and the Battle of the Minisink," *Daughters of the American Revolution Magazine*, 113 (1979):785–795; Isabel Thompson Kelsay, *Joseph Brant, 1743–1807: Man of Two Worlds* (1984); Donald R. McAdams, "The Sullivan Expedition: Success or Failure," *New York Historical Society Quarterly*, 54

(1970):53–81; New York Division of Archives, *The Sullivan-Clinton Campaign in 1777: Chronology and Selected Documents* (1929).

Minutemen

An essential part of a militia tradition that dated back to the very beginnings of Massachusetts Bay colony, a Minuteman was generally defined as a citizen, over 16 years of age, usually in the prime of life, who was a member of a unit drawn mostly from the rolls of the regular militia. This individual was specially equipped with weapons and was experienced in the military arts. Most importantly, the Minuteman was to have been prepared at all times to assemble in short order with his fellow Minutemen to meet a threat to the colony.

In 1645 the Massachusetts Council ordered the commanders of every military company to have 30 percent of their men armed, drilled, and supplied to move within a half-hour's notice at the Order of Council. The concept of the Minuteman was again used by Massachusetts to protect its settlements during King Philip's War of 1675.

Minutemen surfaced once more between 1700 and 1743 in the form of the "Snow Shoe Men." In order to guard its frontiers from the French and the Indians, Massachusetts supported a loosely organized group of men, constantly available, who worked in shifts to provide early warning and protection from the raids of the enemy along the outermost reaches of the colony. In 1755, during the French and Indian War, the "Picket Guards" were formed in Massachusetts to serve in a similar "Minuteman" fashion.

While other colonies may have developed the concept and implemented it during the American Revolutionary (prewar) period, the Minuteman is most closely associated with Massachusetts. As tensions mounted in Massachusetts after Parliament had passed the Coercive Acts and after the Port of Boston was closed down, the Whig (radical) leaders decided that the province needed an organized military defense against possible British offensive moves.

The Whig leadership of Worcester County took the initiative and reorganized their militia in September 1774. It was considered necessary to do this to eliminate known Loyalists, particularly officers, from positions of responsibility. All men aged 16 to 60 were registered and formed into companies. They elected company officers of the correct political persuasion. These officers in turn elected the field officers.

In all, seven militia regiments were organized in Worcester County. It was then decided that one-third of each regiment would form into Minutemen companies and hold themselves ready to assemble under arms on a minute's notice. From the very beginning these units enjoyed a high *esprit*, since being asked to join one was considered a great honor.

On October 26, 1774, the First Massachusetts Provincial Congress, meeting in Cambridge, passed resolutions requiring all towns and districts in Massachusetts to reorganize their militia on the same lines as the regiments from Worcester. Each militia regiment commander was to specify 25 percent of his men to form into companies of 50 men and be prepared at a moment's notice to move at the direction of the newly appointed Committee of Safety, an 11-member executive board headed by Dr. Joseph Warren.

Each Minuteman company was to have a captain and two lieutenants. These officers in turn were to elect field officers to command the nine-company Minutemen battalions. The towns and districts also were ordered to provide arms and ammunition for their units. The Minutemen themselves were ordered to exercise their arms at least three times a week, and more if possible. While this process of reforming the militia into a functional military force was incomplete at the time that the fighting broke out, much was accomplished in the six months before Lexington. Fortunately for the militia, the winter of 1774–1775 was one of the mildest on record, allowing for frequent outside drill and military exercises.

The towns and districts of Massachusetts generally classified their able-bodied men into three categories. There were the regular militia rolls, which listed the men considered to be in their prime and able to fight. The Minutemen were selected from this group, since they were usually the best fighters or most experienced men in town. Men who had the liberty to be available at a moment's notice were also included as Minutemen if they could fight. The third group of men were those on the alarm lists. These were the young boys and old men who would be used only in dire emergencies, or to protect the town when the regular militia was absent.

Traditionally the first public use of the word "Minutemen" is credited to Colonel William

Henshaw of Leicester, Worcester County. On November 24, 1774, he petitioned the Provincial Congress to allow his "Minutemen" to use the Norfolk Drill instead of the 1764 manual of arms used at the time by the British regulars. Since the term was used without further elaboration, it is apparent that "Minutemen" was the word already in common usage by the time Colonel Henshaw wrote his petition.

The first official notice containing "Minutemen" came on December 10, 1774, from the Massachusetts Provincial Congress in their address to the people called "to the freeholders and other inhabitants of the towns and districts of Massachusetts Bay." Copied and published throughout the colony, it stated that

> the improvement of the militia in general in the art military has been therefore thought necessary & strongly recommended by this congress. We now think that particular care should be taken by the towns and districts in this colony, that each of the Minute Men not already provided therewith, should be immediately equipped with an effective firearm, bayonet, pouch, knapsack, thirty rounds of cartridges and ball, and that they be disciplined three times a week and oftener as opportunity may offer.

The Provincial Congress, trying to balance itself between the radicals and those who were more conservative in their protest against the king's government, wished to provide some type of defense for the colony. A standing army was greatly feared by the people and would be interpreted by the British as provocative, if not treasonous. The age-old militia, organized into approximately 40 to 50 regiments in Massachusetts, was considered much too cumbersome to bring to the defense of the colony in an emergency.

It was to the Minutemen that the Provincial Congress turned in 1774 to provide the colony with a force of well-trained, lightly armed infantry that could respond to any call from the Committee of Safety. Formed that fall and drilled through the winter, the Minutemen were ready when General Thomas Gage began sending expeditions into the country to disarm the people. The Minutemen had already responded well at Charlestown, Salem, Cambridge, and other sites before that fateful day, April 19, 1775.

When Lieutenant Colonel William Smith led his force of light infantry and grenadiers toward Concord to seize provincial military stores on the morning of April 19, it was the Minutemen who responded at Lexington and later at Concord to contest the British advance. As the British began their retreat back to Boston that afternoon, it was the Minutemen units from towns and districts near and far who streamed in to fight a 20-mile running battle with His Majesty's shocked regulars.

These trained, already organized, rapid-deployment troops, many led by veteran officers, proved to be the match of Gage's British soldiers, who, by their actions that day, showed themselves to be relatively unprepared and inexperienced in the conduct of a tactical withdrawal. In the British defense, it can be argued that they encountered a large force. But this was war, and the question still to be answered is why the British, with all their spies, intelligence, and previous expeditions, were surprised by the reception they received.

Concord and the retreat back to Boston was the hour of greatest glory and fame for the Minutemen. They were soon absorbed into a more formal, regular army that surrounded the British in Boston. The idea was not forgotten, however. The Continental Congress encouraged the other colonies (states) to follow Massachusetts' example and to form similar units. Minutemen from Maryland, North Carolina, New Hampshire, and Connecticut, along with those from Massachusetts, are known to have served with distinction throughout the war. Their chief function was to cover those geographic regions that the regular forces under General George Washington were unable to protect from British raids.

Paul J. Sanborn

REFERENCES

Fred Anderson Berg, *Encyclopedia of Continental Army Units* (1972); Norman Castle, ed., *The Minute Men* (1977); Allen French, *The Day of Concord and Lexington* (1925); John R. Galvin, *The Minute Men* (1967); John Harris, *American Rebels* (1976); James Kirby Martin and Mark Edward Lender, *A Respectable Army* (1982); Arthur R. Tourtellot, *Lexington and Concord* (1963); Christopher Ward, *The War of Revolution*, 2 vols. (1952), *1*.

Miralles, Juan de (1738–1780)

Spanish statesman. A native of Havana, Juan de Miralles was a successful merchant who descended from a line of wealthy traders that had specialized in commerce with British possessions along the Atlantic coast and throughout the Caribbean. During the Seven Years' War, he had used his fluency in English and his widespread mercantile contacts to provide intelligence information for the captain general of Cuba. In 1777 this official picked Miralles to be part of an espionage operation that would monitor the events of the American Revolution. At the specific approval of colonial minister José de Galvez, Miralles was chosen to travel to Philadelphia, take up residence there under the guise of being a merchant engaged in the flour trade, and thereafter provide secret information to Spain regarding events at the Continental Congress. Miralles arrived in Philadelphia in 1778, where he established strong friendships among the American leadership, including especially Henry Laurens, Charles Willson Peale, John Jay, and George Washington. The Spaniard began immediately to send copious amounts of news and information about the revolt back to Cuba and Spain by means of the flour trading vessels, which provided the cover for his espionage activities.

The Americans quickly suspected that Miralles was some sort of "quasi-official" agent of the Spanish government and accorded him the respect normally given an accredited diplomatic envoy. They styled him Spain's "Observer" in the United States. Indeed, he was treated on a basis of diplomatic equality with the French ambassador. Miralles proved to be very sympathetic to the American cause, and this sympathy was clearly reflected in his numerous reports to Havana and Madrid. By late 1779, Miralles had become involved in matters of a diplomatic nature. He was the first person, for example, to articulate the Spanish position regarding the boundary between Florida and the United States, to note his government's desire to keep Americans from enjoying full and free navigation of the Mississippi River, and to deny them a "right of deposit" at New Orleans. These discussions were cut short by his sudden death in early 1780 while he was visiting George Washington's encampment at Morristown, New Jersey. His replacement as observer, Francisco Rendon, remained in Philadelphia until the arrival of Diego de Gardoqui in 1785. Rendon, however, failed to enjoy the successes achieved by Miralles in advocating the American cause and serving as a source of information for the Spanish about events in North America.

Light Townsend Cummins

REFERENCES

Manuel Conrotte, *La intervencion de Espana en la independencia de los Estados Unidos de la America del Norte* (192); Light T. Cummins, "Spanish Espionage in the South During the American Revolution," *Southern Studies*, 29 (1980):39–49; Miguel Gomez Campillo, ed., *Relaciones diplomaticas entre Espana y los Estados Unidos segun los documentos del archivo historico nacional*, 2 vols. (1944); Helen McCadden, "Juan de Miralles and the American Revolution," *The Americas*, 29 (1973):359–375; Herminio Portell Vila, *Juan de Miralles: un habanero amigo de Jorge Washington* (1947).

Mobile, West Florida, Capture of (March 14, 1780)

Founded by the French, Mobile passed to British sovereignty by virtue of the Peace of Paris Treaty of 1763 and became part of British West Florida. It served as an army and navy post, which was auxiliary to the major garrison stationed at Pensacola. As the closest major British military post to Spanish Louisiana, it was an important contact site between Englishmen and Spaniards. After the outbreak of the Revolution, it also became a significant military objective for Louisiana governor Bernardo de Galvez. Once Galvez took Baton Rouge and the other British posts north of New Orleans on the Mississippi River in late 1789, he turned his attention to Mobile. In February 1780, he left New Orleans with approximately 750 men. By March 1, he had landed and made a base camp some three miles from the British post. He undertook a correspondence with the commander, Captain Elias Durnford, who refused to surrender without hostilities. Galvez accordingly began construction of artillery batteries and attacked on March 12. After several hours of devastating bombardment, Durnford began discussions for surrender. He formally delivered Mobile to Galvez on March 14. The fall of Mobile enabled the Spanish to press ahead with plans to attack Pensacola.

Light Townsend Cummins

REFERENCES

Francisco Borja Medina, *Jose de Espeleta, Gobernador de la Mobilia, 1780–81* (1980); John W. Caughey, *Bernardo de Galvez in Louisiana, 1776–1783* (1934); William S. And Hazel P. Coker, *The Siege of Mobile, 1780, in Maps* (1982); J. Barton Starr, *The American Revolution in West Florida* (1976); J. Leitch Wright, *The American Revolution in Florida* (1975).

Moncrieff, James (1744–1793)

British army officer. The son of James Moncrieff of Sauchop, Fifeshire, Moncrieff entered the Royal Military Academy at Woolwich on March 11, 1759, and was appointed practitioner engineer (ensign) on January 28, 1762. He was promoted to the rank of ensign in the 100th Foot (July 10, 1762) during the siege of Havana, Cuba. Moncrieff then saw further service in the West Indies and in East Florida. He was promoted to the rank of sub-engineer and lieutenant (December 4, 1770), and engineer and captain lieutenant (June 10, 1776).

He served with Lord Hugh Percy's forces on Staten Island in the autumn of 1776, and in 1777 he constructed a bridge over the Raritan River, New Jersey, for the passage of troops (a model of which survives at Woolwich). At Brandywine (September 11, 1777) he located a ford in that creek and guided the 4th Foot through it. It was during the southern campaigns that he rendered a series of particularly distinguished services in fortification and field action for which he was consistently under-rewarded despite the highest recommendations, a situation probably reflecting the low esteem in which military engineers were held by the eighteenth-century British government.

At Stono Ferry (June 20, 1779) Moncrieff joined in the pursuit of retreating rebels and was credited with personally capturing an ammunition wagon. He was responsible for the strengthening and extending of the fortifications of Savannah, and was in charge of landing guns and placing them in an incredibly short space of time prior to the Comte d'Estaing's attack. The French declared that Moncrieff had made his batteries spring up like mushrooms overnight. General Augustin Prevost wrote to Lord George Germain after the successful repulse of d'Estaing's greatly superior forces: "There is not an officer or soldier of this little army, capable of reflecting or judging, who will not regard as personal to himself any mark of Royal favour graciously conferred, through your Lordship, on Captain Moncrieff." As a result, Moncrieff was promoted brevet major dating from the delivery of the victory dispatches. He served as chief engineer during the siege of Charleston and General Sir Henry Clinton credited the success of the operations to "the zealous exertions of an engineer who understood his business," for which

Moncrieff was brevetted lieutenant colonel on September 27, 1780. He remained at Charleston in charge of the defenses. He was in charge of the export of some 800 slaves to the West Indies when the British evacuated Charleston, December 14, 1782, and he was accused of having benefited personally from the transaction.

He returned to England at the close of the war, and Moncrieff was employed in the Southern District, chiefly on the fortifications at Gosport. Promoted engineer-in-ordinary and regimental captain on October 1, 1784, he was appointed deputy quartermaster general of the army on July 14, 1790; a brevet promotion to colonel followed on November 18, 1790. In 1792–1793 he reported to the master general of the Ordnance (head of the artillery and engineering forces) on the defenses of the coast of Kent, and was on a committee dealing with the defenses of Chatham, one of the Royal Dockyards. On the outbreak of war with revolutionary France, Moncrieff was appointed quartermaster general of the forces sent to Holland under the Duke of York, serving as chief engineer at the siege of Valenciennes. He was promoted to regimental colonel of Royal Engineers on June 18, 1793. During a sortie by the besieged French garrison of Dunkirk on September 6, 1793, against the right wing of York's army, Moncrieff was mortally wounded, and died September 7, 1793. He was buried with full military honor at Ostend on September 10, symbolic of the growing prestige of army engineers.

De Witt Bailey

REFERENCES

Carl L. Baurmeister, *Revolution in America: Confidential Letters and Journals, 1776–1784,* trans. and ed. by Bernard A. Uhlendorf (1957); Sir Henry Clinton, *The American Rebellion, Sir Henry Clinton's Narrative of His Campaign, 1775–1781,* ed. by William B. Willcox (1954); *DNB*; Johann Ewald, *Diary of the American War. A Hessian Journal,* trans. and ed. by Joseph P. Tustin (1974).

Monks Corner, South Carolina, Action at (April 14, 1780) (Alternate spelling: Monck's)

In April 1780 Charleston was besieged by military and naval forces under the command of General Sir Henry Clinton. The harbor was sealed by the ships of Admiral Mariot Arbuthnot, and the peninsula was occupied by the British army. The only route still open for the Americans to receive supplies and reinforcements, and to use as a possible escape route, was to cross the Cooper River and turn northward toward Monks Corner, 30 miles to the northeast.

At Monks Corner, under the command of General Isaac Huger, was a mixed force of 500 American cavalry and infantry encamped near Biggin's Bridge. (A modern bridge across the Tail Race Canal now occupies this site.) From the town, a network of roads from the north served to bring troops and supplies (by way of present Route 41) to the banks of the Cooper River in Mount Pleasant, and to be ferried by boat to Charleston. Clinton knew that to force the city to capitulate, he had to take Monks Corner.

On April 11, 1780, Clinton learned of a large wagon train of supplies heading for Monks Corner, destined for Charleston. He ordered a combined infantry-cavalry raid to capture the supply wagons and to cut the route of escape for American troops.

The raiders, made up of 100 dragoons under the command of Lieutenant General Banastre Tarleton, and supported by a unit of mounted riflemen commanded by Major Patrick Ferguson, were joined by 1,400 infantry of the 33rd and 64th Regiments of Foot encamped at Goose Creek. The two regiments were commanded by Lieutenant James Webster.

Tarleton left the "Quarter House," a well-known tavern of the day, (located near the present intersection of Meeting Street and Dorchester Avenue) on April 12, and proceeded to Goose Creek. (U.S. Highway 52 follows Tarleton's route from Charleston, through Goose Creek, to Monks Corner.) Meeting with Webster, Tarleton left the infantry to follow at a slower pace, and he rode out the same night to cover the 15 miles to Monks Corner. Along the way, Tarleton's men captured a messenger en route to Charleston. Upon searching him, a letter was found that gave details of the American camp, and the disposition of Huger's forces.

Deciding on a night attack without waiting for the slower infantry, Tarleton's force moved toward the American positions. At about 3 a.m. on April 14, the British advance collided with Huger's guard. Sharp firing broke out, and the dragoons charged. Falling back before the overwhelming force, the guard fled toward their camp. So swift and surprising was the attack that Tarleton's cavalrymen had pounced upon the sleepy-eyed Americans before they had a chance to defend themselves.

Wielding sabers, the British horsemen cut down the American opposition. Some Americans managed to escape into the swamps, including Huger and the American cavalry command, Lieutenant Colonel William Washington.

Ferguson led his riflemen on foot across Biggin's Bridge with fixed bayonets to attack a small group of militiamen who were attempting to form a defense. But the militiamen scattered into the surrounding swamp. In less than an hour, Tarleton had accomplished his objective.

Casualties on the American side were 14 dead, along with 13 wounded. The entire wagon train destined for Charleston was captured intact, and 100 Americans, officers and enlisted men, were taken prisoners.

The British suffered only one officer and two enlisted men wounded. A major coup was the capture of 400 cavalry horses, which would replace those lost during the stormy passage at sea from New York.

The following day, Webster arrived in Monks Corner with additional British troops and crossed Biggin's Bridge, spreading out into the country, thereby cutting off all routes of escape from Charleston. The city surrendered 27 days later.

Gary M. Cope

REFERENCES

Warren Ripley, *South Carolina in the Revolution* (1983); Richard Wheeler, *Voices of 1776* (1972).

Monmouth, New Jersey, Battle of (June 28, 1778)

This was the last major battle of the War of Revolution to be fought in the North. It was contested for the better part of a day in the fields around and to the west of a small, East Jersey village called Freehold, the seat of Monmouth County. The weather was humid and extremely hot with summer temperatures regularly above 90 degrees. Since both sides left the field feeling satisfied at what had been accomplished, history has declared the battle a tactical draw.

Major General Henry Clinton arrived in Philadelphia from New York in early May 1778. He was replacing General William Howe as British commander of His Majesty's land forces in North America. In Philadelphia, Clinton found orders waiting from London. The news of the American-French alliance had changed the War of Revolution into a world war. New considerations now prevailed. Clinton was to withdraw from Philadelphia and concentrate his army in New York. From that base, Clinton could reinforce British forces in Canada, the West Indies, and Florida to protect them from possible French attacks. The British went on the defensive.

The whole Philadelphia adventure had been disillusioning for the British. There was some hope in 1777 that the American war effort would collapse with the capture of their capital city. That did not occur. The American government merely moved west to York, Pennsylvania, and continued their operations. Washington's army remained in the field and came out of their winter cantonment at Valley Forge trained and disciplined at the hands of an obscure German officer who called himself the Baron von Steuben. It was a very different and more dangerous force than Clinton confronted before.

Clinton was a callous, hardened, aggressive veteran officer. He was one of the few British generals who spoke German and who could actually converse with the allies directly. He also knew that the French fleet massing at Toulon would soon be in American waters. Given the time, it could block the British in Philadelphia, leaving them to the mercy of Washington's newly organized American army. Clinton had to move quickly.

One major problem he faced was to determine the best way to get his army and all of his baggage back to New York. In Philadelphia, there were several thousand Loyalists who feared American retribution and required British protection. They, too, had to be taken to New York. This was another complication that Clinton had to consider. The final decision was that the Loyalists, their baggage, the sick, some decimated Hessian regiments still shaken by the disaster at Fort Mercer the fall before, and others were placed in British ships bound for New York.

Clinton then decided to march his entire army and its baggage across the Jerseys to New York. He wanted to keep his total force together until the baggage train and the army safely reached New York. Then he would send out the detachments to their various new posts as ordered. The baggage train, which included military equip-

ment and booty taken from Philadelphia, numbered 1,500 wagons and stretched out for 12 miles. Clinton feared partisan harassment and needed all his infantry to protect the train.

By June 17, the British were ready to move. Three thousand Loyalists and the British fleet had already departed. The fleet succeeded in making it safely, missing Admiral Comte d'Estaing's tardy French fleet by three days. Marching south out of Philadelphia, the British crossed the Delaware River at Gloucester Point beginning at 3 a.m. on June 18. The operation took seven hours and ran smoothly. The covering force and boats were provided by Admiral "Black Dick" Howe.

That evening, after a march of eight miles, the British camped at Haddonfield. Clinton organized his force into two divisions. One he called his "gross." This division was commanded by General Wilhelm von Knyphausen, the experienced, senior German officer. Knyphausen's task was to accompany the baggage train to New York City. Knyphausen had two brigades of British infantry, the remaining Germans, and many of the Loyalist units.

General Lord Cornwallis commanded the other division, called "the advanced guard." This column was formed of the elite of the British army, including the guards battalions, three British infantry brigades, the British and German grenadiers, and most of the light infantry, dragoons, and rangers. It was with this force that Clinton planned to strike at Washington if the Americans followed the British through the Jerseys and sought a battle.

The whole month of June 1778 was a wet one with uncommonly high heat. By June 21, the British reformed at Mount Holly and moved from there to Burlington, Crosswicks, and on to Allentown. It was here that Clinton had to choose one of two routes. He could march straight toward New York across the Raritan River, or he could take an easterly course toward Sandy Hook, where the fleet could transfer his army to New York. The latter route was forty miles in length, the shorter of the two. It also protected his flanks as he moved toward safety on the coast. Clinton chose to move east to Sandy Hook.

In two columns, with Cornwallis moving north of the baggage train to screen it, Clinton left Allentown on June 25 and marched to Freehold. As Clinton moved deeper into the Jerseys, the harassment by Philemon Dickinson's Jersey militia and Daniel Morgan's 600-man force increased. Bridges were burned. Livestock was removed in the British path. Trees were felled into the road. Pickets were fired upon. The British struggled on in their retreat from Philadelphia.

As the British neared Freehold and the coast, the roads turned sandy and loose, making progress with the wagons difficult. The Americans filled in the wells, and water became scarce. The hot weather took its toll. Many became sick, and others deserted, including some 500 Germans who returned to Philadelphia to resume relationships begun during the occupation. Ominously from the west, rumors came in to Clinton that Washington's army was coming on in fast pursuit. Looting and pillaging as they moved, the British army reached Freehold on Friday, June 26.

Due to a rainstorm and the rigors of the march, Clinton rested his men on Saturday, June 27, and reconsidered it would not be long before the British reached the hills of Navesink and safety from American pursuit. Nothing would please Clinton more than fighting a general action against the Americans and turning this retrograde movement across Jersey into something like an English victory. If Washington attacked, Clinton was ready. But inspection of the ground around Freehold showed approaches that favored the defender and fields broken by three bogs (named the east, middle, and west morasses) that made maneuvering difficult and dangerous. Clinton did not anticipate an American attack at Freehold, but he wanted to be prepared.

Since May, Washington tried to discover British intentions. His spies were constantly out probing and questioning. Until he was sure, Washington decided to remain on the defensive. When Washington learned of Clinton's crossing of the Delaware, he knew Clinton's goal. The American army began moving north toward Coryell's Ferry on the Delaware River (today's New Hope), where they crossed on June 21. Morgan was sent ahead to assist General William Maxwell with his regular line Jersey brigade and the Jersey militia in both attacking Clinton's columns and keeping Washington informed of British movements. General Benedict Arnold entered Philadelphia to reestablish American control over the now wrecked city.

By June 25, Washington had reached Kingston. He was staying north of the British with the hills of Jersey behind him for cover if the British should turn against him and try to attack. It was at Kingston that Washington learned of Clinton's move to the east. The American pursuit began in earnest. Washington hurried his army after Clinton.

From 1775, Washington had commanded with the advice of military councils, in which his generals discussed military policy and participated in the decision-making process. Often the direction the army took was decided by a majority vote of generals, although Washington reserved the right to overrule the council if he thought it necessary. At Valley Forge and later, in the Jerseys, the generals debated what the Americans should do as the British left Philadelphia. General Charles Lee, recently returned from British captivity, was the loudest and most vocal of the generals in vehemently advising against attacking the British.

Lee felt that this British move was already a great American victory. It should not be risked by a defeat. French interest in the United States might lessen. Lee also believed that Americans could not stand up to regular British troops in battle. Linear warfare did not fit in with the native American talent for fighting in open order as dedicated individuals defending their country in the name of freedom. Lee believed it "criminal" to launch an attack.

On the other side, General Anthony Wayne, Nathanael Greene, and the Marquis de Lafayette were in favor of an immediate attack while Clinton was strung out along the Jersey roads. This was an opportunity that should not be missed. Washington seemed to side with this view, but there were other generals who agreed with Lee, such as Henry Knox and Lord Stirling, making the decision a difficult one for the commander-in-chief.

In the end, a compromise was reached. A strong force would be sent after the British to see if their rear guard could be cut off and destroyed, or if some other military advantage could be gained without risk. There would be no general attack. Lee took this to mean that whoever commanded the van—and he assumed it would be himself—would be permitted a wide latitude of attack. Washington took this to mean that the van would attack and Washington would fall on whatever opportunities were created. The other generals fell somewhere in between. The Americans went into battle lacking unity of command and a common understanding of how the battle would be fought.

General Charles Scott and 1,500 men were sent after Clinton. Then Wayne and 1,000 more men followed to support Scott. Lafayette was given the command after Lee turned it down. Then Lee reconsidered. With Maxwell, Dickinson, and Morgan added to Scott and Wayne, the van was a sizable force and was perhaps suited to the army's second in command after all. Washington agreed to the change and sent Lee along with additional troops to assume command. Lafayette was gracious in stepping aside.

On June 27, the American van reached Englishtown and stopped. They were six miles from Clinton's army. Washington, with a total force of 12,000 men, brought the rest of his army from Cranbury toward Englishtown for support. Twice during the night, Washington visited the van to discuss his view with Lee. Washington stressed that he wished Lee to attack the British in the morning as soon as they were on the march. Lee met with his brigadiers and told them that, since so much was uncertain concerning the British, there was no formal battle plan for the next day.

Dickinson had his militia close to the British on their northern flank, and Morgan was on the southern flank. Lee was waiting for word that the British were moving the next morning and then he would move. Morgan received orders from Lee that Morgan mistook to mean that the American attack would come Monday instead of Sunday. Because of this and other circumstances, Morgan's men did not play a role in the Battle of Monmouth. Lee never checked further with Morgan in the fighting.

Washington made a mistake in allowing Lee this command. Second in command by seniority and with a good record at Boston and Charleston early in the war, Lee had been a prisoner too long. The army had developed a great deal since he had been captured. Lee's strongly held beliefs ran directly against those of Washington's. In the rigid discipline of the eighteenth-century professional armies, in which Lee claimed experience, once the commanding general made his decision, the inferior officers were expected to carry them out. Evidently Lee felt he knew more than Washington and to obey the commander's orders would destroy the American army. This was the real problem. Lee saw Washington as

being weak, felt himself to be the superior officer, and he wished to pursue his own course.

Although Lee was not the first subordinate officer in history to doubt and act against his commander's wishes, one can question his professionalism as a soldier and commitment to the Revolution as the Americans saw it. Congress had appointed Washington as commander and until they change their views, Washington was responsible to them for the army. Lee was responsible to carry out Washington's orders. His request to command the van implicitly demanded this.

Whatever the decisions of the council, Washington had visited Lee twice in one night to insure that an attack would be carried out. Lee had his chance here to show his ability as second in command, develop a superior plan of attack, gain the commitment of his officers, and then carry out the offensive. If the attack clearly failed because the Americans were unable to stand up to the British regular line, then Lee could immediately point out to Congress that Washington was a weak and ignorant general who should be replaced, even by Lee himself.

But there was more to the situation than just Lee's opinions of the American line. This was Lee's first major field engagement of the war in which he held a command position. This was also Lee's first independent command. Finally, Lee commanded more men at Monmouth than at anytime prior in his career. Now the burden was on Lee to show his ability as a general officer in the field.

As a matter of comparison, Monmouth was also Clinton's first and only major field engagement of the war. He had performed well along the Hudson and in Rhode Island, but he had never before commanded such a large force in the field. On Sunday morning, June 28, Clinton ordered Knyphausen to march out of Freehold toward Middletown. At 4 a.m., Knyphausen moved his men and baggage train. Cornwallis stayed behind for another six hours and then left at 10 A.M. to follow Knyphausen. Knowing the Americans were near, Cornwallis moved very slowly.

At 4:30 A.M., Lee received word from the militia that the British were on the move. Lee ordered Colonel William Grayson, a 42-year-old Virginia lawyer, and his 600 men with Eleazer Oswald's artillery battery, forward toward Freehold to pursue the British. Due to a lack of guides,

Grayson got under way at 6 A.M. after an hour's delay.

Lee was not pleased with his command. He did not agree with Washington's orders. He did not know the position of the enemy although he could have used Morgan's veterans or Dickinson's militia to find out. He commanded officers he did not know and who did not know him. His command was mixed up, serving under officers who had been switched and shifted in the last few days. He had already expressed his lack of faith in his men and was in conflict with his officers such as Lafayette and Wayne. Nonetheless, Lee did not turn over his command.

Washington wished to avoid a general engagement, but he also wanted to make "an impression" on the British, particularly on their rear guard. As Lee moved out with his 4,000 effectives, Washington's main force was seven miles distant. Critics have since suggested that Washington was too far removed to support Lee. The question remains, how many men does it take to attack a rear guard, to take measure of the new American army in battle, and to allow the main British force to reach New York? Washington had maneuvered to do just this. He was positioned not to stop Clinton but to harass his rear. Otherwise, Washington would have moved farther north to hit Clinton's center along his line of march.

Between 7 and 8 A.M., Lee left his camp with Wayne moving first, followed by Scott and then Maxwell. Colonel Jackson and his 200 men left last as the rear guard. Some 700 men were left at Englishtown as the camp guard. As the American van marched, Lee received word from Dickinson that the British had not moved but were still in Freehold. Dickinson had picked up Cornwallis's 8,000 men still in the village. Knyphausen was on the road and moving. Lee stopped his force and sent Wayne ahead with Jackson's men to join Grayson and feel out the British. Lafayette took command of Wayne's troops.

Grayson's men had begun skirmishing with British pickets about a half mile past the Tennent Meeting House. A landmark on the battlefield, it was built in 1751, was named after William Tennent, a locally prominent minister, and is still in use today as a Presbyterian church. Dickinson, Wayne, Grayson, and Lee joined nearby to confer on the British location and strength. Meanwhile, some of Dickinson's militia were attacking the British baggage train along the road to Middletown.

At 10 A.M. Cornwallis began his march out of Freehold with 4,000 men, leaving some 3,600 men behind as the rear guard, including the British light infantry, dragoons, Queen's Rangers, the grenadiers, and two cannon. By 11 A.M. Lee had enough evidence that the British were leaving Freehold so that he ordered the 9th Pennsylvania Regiment forward to lead the van into the small village where the Monmouth County Court House was located. By 11:30 A.M. the Pennsylvanians had control of the village. The rest of Lee's men came up and took a short break in Freehold to eat and to recover. Already the heat and humidity were high and the men were suffering.

Lee now observed the British rear guard withdrawing and decided to attack and to destroy it. Just past noon, the Battle of Monmouth began as the 9th Pennsylvania received a charge of the light dragoons, repelled it, and then countercharged and repelled in return by the British artillery. Wayne brought up Jackson's men and Oswald's artillery for support. Skirmishing was now generally on a cleared field along the road to Middletown just north of Freehold.

Clinton was waiting for Washington to strike a blow and this appeared to be it. He ordered Cornwallis to turn around and to march back to Freehold. The British advanced in force on Lee with their two flanks "in the air," or exposed without protective cover or cavalry support. They would continue to fight this way all day with the Americans unable to take advantage of it. Morgan was in the right place to strike the British left as they returned to Freehold, but he never received the orders, and he spent the day at Wykoff's mills, four miles away.

Lee ordered an advance on the troops that were visible to him, which he considered to be the British rear guard. Wayne was ordered to halt the British advance east of the east morass (one of the three bogs on the battlefield), while Lee took Lafayette around the British right rear and caught them in a pincer movement. Wayne instead pushed the British line back, and Lee came out of his turning move to find Wayne where the British should have been. The Americans, as before, were stopped by British artillery covering their infantry withdrawal.

Now Lee could see what appeared to be the whole British army moving against him. Across

Briar Hill came the 3rd, 4th, and 5th British brigades to the support of the already present rear guard. Clinton noted Lee's right flank near Freehold "hanging in the air" and moved to turn it. Lee responded by sending Lafayette with several regiments to stop them. Lafayette went to the position assigned, found it unsuitable ground, and moved to a second position.

At this point, in the confusion of orders and moving troops, Lee had formed a line with Scott and Maxwell to face the British. Then Oswald's artillery received permission to retire to replenish its ammunition. With this move, thinking a retreat had been ordered, other units began to move back, including Scott's and Maxwell's troops. Wayne's men, taking shelter in the woods, had disappeared from Scott's view, merely confirming the retreat in his mind. Fearful of being outflanked and seeing what looked like the whole British army coming at them, the Americans began to retire.

By 1:30 P.M. Lee had ordered a retreat to Freehold to stop the British turning movement. Wayne's and Scott's men formed a line on a high rise of ground, where the battle monument stands today. Arriving in the village, Lee now saw the whole first division of the British army descending on him, some 8,000 troops. He realized he could not hold his ground, and he ordered another retreat to the ridge by the Carr House, to the west of the east morass.

By now his entire command was in total confusion. Scott retreated to the north of Weamaconk Creek and continued to Tennent Meeting House and on out of the battle. Wayne joined Lee at the Carr House. It was not a happy reunion. Lee ignored Wayne for the impetuous, imprudent actions Wayne had displayed on the field. Lee had about 2,000 men left of his command. Many men had left the field for the rear. Guided by Captain Wykoff of the Monmouth County militia, Lee positioned his next line on a ridge behind the Carr House. But this line also turned out to be a poor choice, and the retreat continued toward the west morass and the Tennent Meeting House.

By 2 P.M. Lee's force was retiring toward the causeway over the west morass with Wayne serving as the rear guard, holding off a persistent British pursuit. Lee's men were tired, thirsty, and hot. The officers did not know what was expected of them.

Lee refused to believe that he was responsible for the fluid state of the battle. He did not use his best soldiers to the best advantage. There was no plan of attack nor was there proper reconnaissance to ascertain Cornwallis's moves. Lee allowed Clinton to seize the initiative and to take control of the battle. Lee became a passive figure in the fighting. Lee's smaller force was placed in a situation that could easily have been avoided. Poor generalship produced this retreat. Lee was also passive in maintaining control over this inferiors. They operated on their own. Lee could not personally control a battlefield of this size by himself.

Another point to ponder is why Wayne, Lafayette, Scott, Maxwell, Grayson, and others all had problems obeying or understanding Lee's orders that day at Monmouth. Why did order arise from chaos with these same men after Washington assumed direct command? Was it a conspiracy of officers against Lee? Where is the evidence for that conclusion? There is none. The blame must lie elsewhere.

Washington had arrived at Tennent Meeting House around 1 P.M. and heard the sounds of gunfire. The main American army began to arrive from Englishtown. Then, around 2 to 3 P.M., the appearance of retreating men past the Tennent Meeting House stunned him. With some of the best American generals and with picked troops, Lee was supposed to have attacked the British rear. In a rage, Washington rode down the Tennent Road with his staff to find Lee. They met at a point near the causeway. Washington asked Lee to explain the confusion and the retreat. His anger was clear, and he silenced the normally volatile Lee.

Washington ordered Lee to organize his men for a defense in order to allow Washington to position the rest of his army on the hills beyond the west morass. Knowledgeable of the terrain, Lieutenant Colonel Rhea of the 2nd New Jersey aided Washington in placing his men. Grayson's men and Wayne's were formed into a line just to the east of the causeway to hold the British. Wayne took the left in the woods, and Grayson and other units from Lee's force with some artillery completed the position off to the right.

Clinton had the American army on the run and wished to take advantage of it. He brought his entire first division on the field, organized it into two lines, and advanced. The light infantry was on the right, the guards, grenadiers, and dragoons in the center, and the 3rd brigade of General Grey took the left. The 4th brigade and Hessian grenadiers formed the second line and the fifth baggage train on its way to safety; Clinton could have won victory here.

The British advanced and hit Wayne in the woods with such strength that Wayne was pushed back. The American line was flanked, but it rallied and reformed at a natural feature on the field to the east of the causeway, the hedgerow, where the 4th New York, 3rd Maryland, and 13th Pennsylvania regiments made a stand with Oswald's guns. Here they held out against the full pressure of the British line for 30 to 40 minutes, giving Washington enough time to develop his main battle line. Lee still believed that his actions throughout the day showed courage, coolness, and self-control. He had performed brilliantly, in his opinion.

Stirling's division came up on to Craig's Ridge and became the American left with the west morass to its front. Twelve guns were positioned in front of the American line to strengthen it. Greene's division marched to the American right and anchored its position on Coomb's Hill, where additional artillery was placed. Lafayette and part of Lee's force formed the reserve in the center. Von Steuben organized those of Lee's men who had returned to Englishtown.

Observing Washington's line, Clinton attacked the high point of Coomb's Hill and the American right first. The guards and several line regiments assaulted the position but were beaten back by the American artillery. Then the British grenadiers charged directly across the west morass, but they were stopped and thrown back with heavy losses.

Later, an additional probe was made by the Queen's Rangers and the light infantry to turn the American left flank from the Craig House area. The 42nd Regiment led the charge, and the British force was met with concentrated artillery and musketry fire to halt their advance. For an hour the battle raged, but American discipline and training learned at Valley Forge paid off. The British retreated.

Clinton brought up 16 cannon and began firing on the American lines, which brought a reply from the American artillery. For almost two hours, from 4 to 6 P.M., the artillery fire continued as the two armies watched. Not much damage was done by either side. This was the point in the battle when "Molly Pitcher" served water to the artillerymen in Stirling's batteries, including her husband, to help them serve the guns and to battle the heat of the day at the same time.

By 6:30 P.M. Clinton recalled his forces. Washington sent Wayne and some Pennsylvania regiments across the causeway again to test the British lines. The Pennsylvanians hit the grenadiers and forced them back until Clinton reinforced them with the 33rd Regiment of Foot and other units. Wayne was then forced back toward the hedgerow once more, where the Pennsylvanians received three vicious charges of the grenadiers without breaking. Lieutenant Colonel Henry Monckton of the 45th Regiment and commander of the 2nd Grenadier Battalion died in this action, and his body was fought over until finally the British fell back. The Americans claimed the body of the highest ranking British officer to die at Monmouth. (He was buried the next day at Tennent Meeting House with military honors.)

Eventually, after more severe fighting, Wayne retired once more back across the causeway, having met the best the British could field. The British resumed their withdrawal toward Freehold. Stirling sent General Enoch Poor and some New Hampshire troops out on the American left to probe the British lines. There was more hard fighting at Weamaconk Creek as the Americans hit the 3rd Brigade as it was crossing. This was the last major fighting of the battle, ending with nightfall and the British withdrawal.

General William Woodford's brigade and the North Carolina regiments were also sent out to join Poor, and this combined force advanced to ground near the Carr House. By 7:30 P.M., the Battle of Monmouth was finally over. The heat and humidity continued through the night. There was little relief. Washington was ready to resume the battle on Monday, June 29, but Clinton had given his men some time to rest and then marched them north to rejoin Knyphausen near Middletown. On June 30, the British reached the hills of Navesink and safety. From there, they moved to Sandy Hook, and the fleet ferried them across to New York without further bother.

Clinton believed that at Monmouth his rear guard was attacked on the march by the enemy's van. It turned upon them, drove them back to their guns, remained some time on the field until all advanced units returned, regrouped and

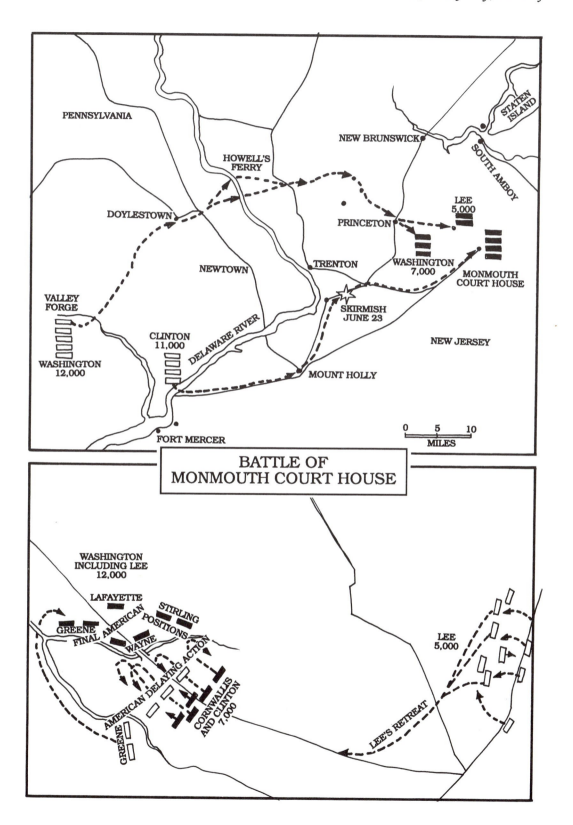

BATTLE OF
MONMOUTH COURT HOUSE

then rejoined the main army without being followed. He found the American claims of victory amusing. The British goal was to safely bring their baggage train and their army to New York. They did so. Monmouth stopped the American pursuit. He thought that it was a British victory.

Washington returned to Englishtown to establish his headquarters there. There was no general pursuit, although Morgan, embarrassed by his absence on the day of battle, and Maxwell were sent to follow the British into Sandy Hook. Von Steuben's system of linear warfare had worked. The American infantry stood face to face with their enemy in the accepted European tradition and fought them fiercely. They had nothing to be ashamed of. Greene and commissary Jeremiah Wadsworth had shown their professional styles in supplying the army as it moved from Pennsylvania to Monmouth. There was food and weaponry available. The Quartermaster and Commissary departments had improved to such an extent that a main American army could move quickly and effectively in the face of the enemy.

For the first time in the war, the whole of the main American army demonstrated the skill and maneuverability of a fighting machine. This was no longer a rabble in arms but a regular line force. The Americans, after their initial retreat, fought the British to a standstill and were ready to continue, when the British left the field. Since the Americans occupied the field, it was customary to declare them the victors. The British claimed that since the field meant nothing, the victory was a false one. Since both sides could claim a victory with some equity, militarily it should be considered a draw. Both sides achieved what they wanted.

The losses are difficult to determine accurately. Washington claimed to have buried some 240 British dead on the field. Casualty rates vary from 300 to 1,200 for the British. After a full day of such fighting, a count of 304 killed, 770 wounded, and 60 missing seems reasonable for the British. Perhaps their losses were in the 800 to 1,000 range. The Americans lost somewhat less, between 500 to 600 men, although one count has them losing 69 killed, 161 wounded, and 132 missing.

As for Lee, the more he pondered the battle, the more he believed that he had been mistreated by Washington. He demanded and was granted a court-martial. He conducted his own defense during the trial against three charges.

The first charge stated he did not attack as ordered on June 28. Washington had visited Lee twice the night before and attempted to clarify what he expected of Lee on the next day. Lee supposedly knew what he was to do. The second charge was that Lee performed in such a manner as to cause a disorderly, shameful, and unnecessary retreat before the enemy. Finally, he was accused of showing disrespect to Washington. After a month of testimony, he was suspended from command for a year. He never served in command again.

If Lee had reconnoitered properly, using the excellent troops at hand, he could have avoided most of the problems that he suffered that June day. He went into battle without a plan, since he knew little of the British dispositions. In the event, when Clinton turned with 8,000 men on Lee, a retreat would have been the probable result for the Americans. But Lee would never have been surprised if scouts had been used. Lee produced no plan for attack.

Washington should never have permitted Lee to command. Lee should never have gone into action unprepared and without a plan. That was his major mistake.

Paul J. Sanborn

REFERENCES

James Thomas Flexner, *George Washington in the American Revolution* (1968); Malcolm Gilman, *Monmouth Road to Glory* (1964); David G. Martin, "The Battle of Monmouth," *Strategy and Tactics*, 90 (1982); Paul David Nelson, *Anthony Wayne* (1985); Richard K. Showman, ed., *The Nathanael Green Papers*, 5 vols. (1978–?), *II*; Samuel S. Smith, *The Battle of Monmouth* (1964); William Stryker, *The Battle of Monmouth* (1970); Theodore Thayer, *The Making of a Scapegoat* (1976); Christopher Ward, *The War of Revolution* (1952); William B. Willcox, *Portrait of a General: General Clinton in the War of Independence* (1964).

Monroe, James (1758–1831)

Continental Army officer, fifth president of the United States. Because of his youth and the difficulty in raising troops at critical times, James Monroe played a minor role in the War of Independence. Nonetheless, he was an enthusiastic Patriot and fought in several major battles.

James Monroe was born in 1758 in Virginia, son of Spence and Elizabeth (Jones) Monroe. The family was not wealthy but lived in comfortable circumstances; James, like the sons of many Virginia gentlemen, spent considerable time hunting and riding in his youth. Both activities served him well in his later activities. In 1769 he began attending a school run by the Reverend Archibald Campbell, and in 1774 he entered William and Mary College. The college was located in Williamsburg, the capital of colonial Virginia, so the young student was in the midst of the conflict between Governor Lord Dunmore and the Patriot forces in 1774–1775. In 1775 the governor fled to a nearby British ship; a small group of Patriots, including Monroe, attacked the governor's palace in June and recovered military supplies that Dunmore had placed there. These items were then turned over to the militia.

In the spring of 1776, Monroe joined the 3rd Virginia Infantry and was soon commissioned a lieutenant. After training under General Andrew Lewis, this unit left for New York and joined Washington's troops at Manhattan in September. Monroe saw his first hostile action a few days later at Harlem Heights; his unit helped stall a British attack, and it was singled out for praise for bravery. Monroe remained with Washington's army during subsequent action at White Plains and as it retreated out of New York State.

Monroe was involved in his most significant war service at the crucial Battle of Trenton in late December 1776. He was one of Washington's troops to cross the icy Delaware River; he and Captain William Washington led a charge early in the fray that prevented the Hessian soldiers from mounting two cannon that would have threatened the success of this daring attack that helped restore morale and confidence in the American cause. Monroe nearly died here because he was hit in the shoulder by a musket ball; it severed an artery, and the young officer was saved only by the prompt action of a Dr. Riker, who had joined the troops the previous night to act as surgeon. Monroe's recovery from this wound lasted three months, by which time he had been promoted to captain.

He had no troops to command, however, and he was unsuccessful when he tried to recruit soldiers in Virginia. Backed with a letter from his maternal uncle, Judge Joseph Jones (a Member of the Virginia delegation in the Continental Congress), he went to Washington's headquarters seeking a position. Although he did not get a field command, he was in the Battles of Brandywine and Germantown, Pennsylvania. He did receive the rank of major and became an aide-de-camp to one of Washington's brigade commanders, William Alexander, generally known as Lord Stirling. Monroe later stated that his experience with Stirling on this larger scale of operations helped him years later in the War of 1812. Monroe then shared the discomforts of winter quarters at Valley Forge in 1777–1778. In June 1778 Monroe took part in his last engagement, the Battle of Monmouth Court House. He acted as adjutant to Stirling and his scouting was critical for the proper disposition of troops that prevented a successful British assault. He resigned from Stirling's staff in December 1778. There were too many officers available for him to get a command, but he did receive a commission as lieutenant colonel in a Virginia regiment; however, he was again unable to recruit the needed troops and returned to civilian life.

He then studied law under the guidance of Governor Thomas Jefferson. In 1780 he was appointed as a special military agent for Virginia and he was ordered to travel south to establish a communications system so that the Virginia officials would be kept informed of British military movements. After successfully accomplishing this, Monroe returned to his law studies but served briefly as a volunteer in November 1780. When the massive British invasion of Virginia came in 1781, he offered to serve again, but he was once more unable to get a command. Throughout these various military activities James Monroe had served without pay.

He was elected to the Virginia legislature in 1782 and to the Confederation Congress in 1783. After the war he was chosen as a member of the Virginia convention to ratify the constitution; after its adoption he was elected as a U.S. senator, minister to France, governor of Virginia, minister to Spain, and minister to England. He was appointed secretary of state in 1811; during the War of 1812, Monroe predicted that the British were planning to attack Washington, D.C. When that prediction proved correct, Monroe personally led a scouting party to ascertain the movement of the British troops, an action similar to his Revolutionary War service.

Madison also appointed him secretary of war. James Monroe was elected president twice, serving from 1817 to 1825. In his second election he was only one vote short of being the second president chosen unanimously. He died on July 4, 1831.

Lawrence R. Borne

REFERENCES

Harry Ammon, *James Monroe: The Quest for National Identity* (1971); W.P. Cresson, *James Monroe, 1758–1831: Chronology-Documents-Bibliographical Aids* (1969); Daniel C. Gilman, *James Monroe* (1989); Monroe Johnson, "James Monroe, Soldier," *William and Mary Quarterly*, 9 (1929):110–117.

Montagu, John

See Sandwich, 4th Earl of.

Montagu, Lord Charles Greville (1741–1784)

British army officer. Among the controversial figures of the American Revolution was Lord Charles Montagu, both a victim and a hero of his shortsightedness. Born on May 19, 1741, the son of Robert Montagu (the Duke of Manchester), Lord Charles graduated from Oxford in 1759, served in the House of Commons from 1762 to 1765, and was appointed governor of South Carolina in 1766.

Although he was absent from his province for most of his term of office, Montagu was well liked by Charlestown (Charleston) society, and he was successful during his governorship. But Montagu became a legend for his ineptitude in trying to stem the growing Revolutionary sentiments in South Carolina. Even his friend Peter Manigault felt that Montagu proved "it is not impossible for Man to be too great a Fool to make a good Governor." Four times he annoyed more than he defeated the radicals in the South Carolina House of Commons by dissolving the assembly. His unsuccessful attempt to defeat the radical members by moving the colonial assembly to less accessible Beaufort, South Carolina, may have directly inspired one of the grievances in the later Declaration of Independence. Ironically, Montagu, his obligations as governor aside, was actually in sympathy with the American positions on many issues. Montagu left for England in 1773, where an angry government forced him to resign. He was unable to obtain another governorship.

On December 12, 1780, Lord Charles was commissioned captain in the 88th Regiment of Foot, stationed in Jamaica. The governor of that colony sent him back to South Carolina to recruit loyal Americans and/or Americans being held as prisoners of war to serve as reinforcements for the British troops invading Nicaragua. However, upon his arrival, Montagu discovered that, far from having been subdued by the British army, South Carolina was still actively in the American Revolution. Recruitment of loyal Americans proved impractical, and Lord Cornwallis forbade any enlistments of American prisoners of war while British soldiers were still being held by the American army. The American prisoners of war continued to suffer and die aboard the British prison ships while Nisbet Balfour, the British commander of Charlestown, feared a breakout by the prisoners even more than an enemy attack.

Montagu was persistent, however, and when Cornwallis left the Carolinas with his army, Balfour felt free to allow the recruitment of the American prisoners. Montagu soon succeeded in enlisting enough men. He claimed that his humanity toward the prisoners of war helped his efforts, but His Lordship was apparently also aided by the threats and brutality from Balfour and his men. Montagu even tried (unsuccessfully) to enlist his old friend American general William Moultrie, offering Moultrie command over Montagu and the enlistees.

After a long and complicated odyssey across the Caribbean, Montagu and his recruits finally reached Jamaica on August 10, 1781. He was made lieutenant colonel commandant of the Duke of Cumberland Regiment, a unit created from his enlistees. They were never sent to Nicaragua but were used instead to defend Jamaica. Montagu's men received high praise from the governors of Jamaica. Other units were merged with his regiment, and he was allowed to travel to New York to obtain more recruits from the prison ships there.

En route to New York, however, Montagu was captured by the Americans and held on charges of having forced American prisoners of war to serve in the tropics, where the soldiers died from the climate. An investigation by General Nathanael Greene cleared Montagu, and he was allowed to proceed on his mission.

With the end of the American Revolution in 1782, Montagu's regiment was disbanded. With their pay and bonuses, these former prisoners of war could have returned to their homes in comfort. However, they instead chose to resettle with Montagu in Nova Scotia. Montagu died there on February 3, 1784. He remembers his regiment in his will. The men that he saved from the horrors of the prison ships placed an impressive memorial over his grave in St. Paul's Churchyard in Halifax.

Robert Scott Davis, Jr.

REFERENCES

Robert S. Davis, Jr., "Lord Montagu's Mission to Charlestown in 1781: American POWs for the King's Cause in Jamaica," *South Carolina Historical Magazine, 84* (1983):89–109; Alan. D. Watson, "The Beaufort Removal and the Revolutionary Impulse in South Carolina," *South Carolina Historical Magazine, 84* (1983):121–135.

Montgomery, Richard (1738–1775)

Continental Army officer. Montgomery had a significant impact on the American Revolution. Although his life and military career were brief, Montgomery established a unique association with the American Army. He represented a former British officer who settled in the colonies shortly before the Revolution, and was called upon subsequently to serve in the American Patriot cause. Unlike other professionally trained former British officers who readily sought military command in the Continental Army (Charles Lee and Horatio Gates, for example), Montgomery did not covet military appointment and responded reluctantly when urged to join the army. After his untimely death, Montgomery's fame continued to advance the Revolutionary cause by solidifying public support for the war effort.

Born in Ireland, the third son of a member of Parliament, he received his education at St. Andrews and Trinity colleges at Dublin. At the age of 18, Montgomery decided on a military career and entered the British army as an ensign in the 17th Foot. His service as a British officer spanned the Seven Years' War. Sent to Canada in 1757, he took part in the siege of Louisbourg, Cape Breton Island (Nova Scotia) in 1758 and was promoted to lieutenant. He subsequently served under General Jeffery Amherst in the suc-

cessful operations against Ticonderoga, Crown Point, and Montreal. Richard is sometimes confused with his oldest brother, Captain Alexander Montgomery, who served in the 43rd British Regiment in America during the war. Alexander became known as "Black Montgomery" because a disgruntled subordinate officer, Lieutenant Malcolm Fraser of the Highlanders, accused him of condoning an atrocity by his men wherein they killed and scalped French captives. In 1762, Montgomery received an advancement to captain, and was ordered to the West Indies. There, he participated in the capture of Martinique and Havana.

After the Treaty of Paris in 1763, Montgomery was stationed in New York. Two years later, he returned to England. During this time, he made friends with several of the liberal members of Parliament who sympathized with the colonies. This group included Isaac Barre, Edmund Burke, and Charles James Fox. Meanwhile, Montgomery became discontented by the lack of prospect for advancement in the peacetime British army. A majority on which he bid went to another officer. In disgust, Montgomery sold his captain commission on April 6, 1772, and made plans to return to America. Disappointed with his career as a British officer, he wanted to start a new life removed from the vexations of politics and public service. Montgomery sought solace and a new beginning in the colonies, where he intended to establish an idyllic life style for himself as a gentleman farmer. During his wartime service in America, the vastness of the county and the unlimited opportunities it offered impressed him. An enterprising gentleman, he reasoned, could readily accumulate land and eventually amass an estate.

Shortly after arriving at New York in late 1772 or early 1773, Montgomery purchased a 67-acre farmstead near Kings Bridge, some 13 miles north of New York City. While settling into his new surroundings during the first winter and spring, Montgomery became reacquainted with Janet Livingston. They had met briefly eight years before when he was an ambitious young officer during the war. After an unusually short courtship, Montgomery and Janet Livingston married on July 24, 1773. Her father, Robert R. Livingston, was the head of one of New York's most prominent families, and a Supreme Court judge of the province. After the marriage, Richard leased out his farm at Kings Bridge, and the

Montgomerys established their residence near Rhinebeck, New York, where Janet owned property.

The emerging events of 1775, which brought increasingly antagonistic relations between the colonies and England, interrupted the tranquil life of the Montgomerys. Although he had been in New York only two years, Montgomery's integrity became locally well known. On May 16, 1775, a constituency elected Montgomery to represent his county (Dutchess) in the New York Provincial Congress, even though he did not seek the office. Then, because of his reputation and previous military experience, the Provincial Congress nominated him for a general officer appointment in the Continental Army—again without his solicitation. On June 22, 1775, the Continental Congress appointed Montgomery as the second in rank of the eight brigadier generals designated at that time. Although the Livingston family, who were leaders of the New York Patriot movement, probably had some influence on Montgomery to once again confront politics and assume a military position, his final decision was a personal one that involved perceptions of honor and civic duty. He explained his rationale to his wife this way: "When I entered your family I was a stranger in your country . . . yet without my wish or knowledge they appoint me to the committee from Dutchess. The times were such I could not refuse however reluctant. . . . Now without consulting me they have made me general. In this capacity I may be of service for just cause. Can I refuse? . . . Honor calls on me." With some sadness, he left his new life to accept his commission and take up arms against England.

Washington made Montgomery second in command of an expedition led by Major General Philip Schuyler to defeat the British in Canada and gain the support of the Canadians toward the American cause. As a result of Schuyler's illness, field command of the expedition passed to Montgomery. The troops assigned to his force, largely fresh recruits with short-term enlistments, provided a challenge to Montgomery's leadership abilities. They were an undisciplined and inexperienced lot. Primarily through personal example, Montgomery managed to shape this armed group into an effective military organization during the Canadian operation. He was successful in capturing Fort Chambly, Fort St. Johns, and Montreal.

After receiving a promotion to major general, Montgomery marched his men along the St. Lawrence River to Quebec. There, they joined forces with the troops under Benedict Arnold, who had arrived via the Maine wilderness. Montgomery assumed overall command of an operation to capture Quebec, the last remaining and most important British stronghold in Canada. The combined force laid siege to Quebec in December 1775. Since the enlistment of most of his troops terminated at the end of the year, Montgomery decided on a daring plan of a direct assault of the well-protected city on December 31, hoping that audacity and surprise could offset the inadequacy of his forces. While leading his men during the storming of the city, Montgomery was shot and killed by a cannon blast from an outpost just before its defenders intended to retreat toward the inner city. After Montgomery's death and Arnold's receipt of a disabling wound, the attack on Quebec failed and the American campaign against the British in Canada faltered.

The British were almost as regretful of Montgomery's death as the Americans. General Sir Guy Carleton and other British officers who were guarding Quebec against Montgomery's advance had served with him earlier during the Seven Years' War. The British opponents recovered Montgomery's body and gave him a proper burial in Quebec. Montgomery was the first American general officer killed in the war. Joseph Warren (who had been appointed major general but had not yet been given his commission), died in action at Bunker Hill six months earlier. Montgomery's heroic sacrifice eclipsed that of Warren, as the Americans quickly elevated him to martyrdom in their struggle for independence.

The British political opposition party pointed to Montgomery as the epitome of virtuous American Revolutionaries. Soon after Montgomery's death, Edmund Burke delivered an eloquent and moving eulogy of him in the British Parliament. However, Prime Minister Lord Frederick North became agitated by this discourse and replied, "I cannot join in lamenting the death of Montgomery as a public loss. A curse on his virtues! They've undone this country. He was brave, he was noble, he was humane, he was generous; but still he was only a brave, able, humane, and generous rebel." To this, Charles James Fox retorted, "The term of rebel is no certain mark of disgrace. The great asserters of liberty, the saviors of their country, the benefactors of mankind in all ages, have all been called rebels."

In January 1776, Congress appointed a committee, including Benjamin Franklin, to "consider a proper method of paying a just tribute of gratitude to the memory of General Montgomery." The committee recommended that a monument be erected to Montgomery's memory. Congress approved the recommendation, and Benjamin Franklin made arrangements for the monument to be made in Paris. The war delayed finding a suitable location for erecting the memorial until 1787. At this time, the monument was erected with appropriate ceremony at St. Paul's Church in New York City, where it remains today. It stands as the first shrine dedicated by the government to an American Revolution hero. In 1818, American officials claimed Montgomery's remains from Quebec and ceremoniously reinterred them at St. Paul's Church.

The death of Montgomery did not discontinue his influence on the American Revolution. During a critical time when the colonists debated the issue of sustained armed revolt, Revolutionary Americans touted Montgomery's sacrifice to evoke patriotic spirit toward continuing the war. In 1776 a Patriot pamphlet appeared in Philadelphia under the title *A Dialogue Between the Ghost of General Montgomery and an American Delegate in a Wood Near Philadelphia*. This work is generally attributed to Thomas Paine, Revolutionary America's most influential pamphleteer. In 1777 Henry Hugh Brackenridge published a heroic tragedy, entitled *The Death of General Montgomery*. It was a dramatic poem clearly intended to arouse colonial sentiments against the British.

> The hapless fortune of the day is sunk!
> Montgomery slain, and wither'd every hope!
> Mysterious Providence, thy ways are just,
> And we submit in deep humility.
> But O let fire or pestilenced from Heaven,
> Avenge the butchery; let Englishmen,
> The cause and agents in this horrid war,
> In tenfold amplitude, meet gloomy death.

The Continental Congress also used Montgomery's death as a justification for expanding state commitment to the Revolutionary effort. In September 1776 Congress sent resolves to the states, raising quotas and increasing enlistment time for troops to be provided for the Continental Army. In a letter enclosed with the resolves, John Hancock, the president of Congress, stated that

> . . . the fall of the late General Montgomery before Quebec is undoubtedly to be ascribed to the limited time for which the troops were engaged; whose impatience to return home compelled him to make the attack contrary to the conviction of his own judgment. This fact alone furnishes a striking argument of the danger and impropriety of sending troops into the field under any restrictions as to the time of their enlistment. The noblest enterprise may be left unfinished by troops in such a predicament, or abandoned at the very moment success must have crowned the attempt.

There is a paucity of biographical studies pertaining to Montgomery in the literature. A book-length biography and several articles have been published. However, these sketches that have been produced on his life hardly do him justice. This situation is even more disconcerting since Montgomery's fame has endured with the passage of time. An examination of county designation records within the nation reflects the lasting permeation of Montgomery's life into the national consciousness. Traditionally, government officials select the name for a county from some well-known historical entity or personage. Excluding presidents and governors, Montgomery ranks fifth on the list of persons for whom the greatest number of counties was designated. Authorities have named some 16 counties throughout the nation after Montgomery. In addition, several cities throughout the United States, including the capital of Alabama, honor his name. It is somewhat ironic that Richard Montgomery, who was so well regarded by his contemporaries and whose death was so highly instrumental in forming general opinion during the Revolution, should now occupy such an obscure place in the historiography of that period.

Hal T. Shelton

REFERENCES

George W. Cullum, "Major-General Richard Montgomery," *Magazine of American History*, 11 (1884):273–299; John Ross Delafield, ed., "Janet Montgomery Reminiscences," *Dutchess County [N.Y.] Historical Society Year Book*, 15 (1930):47–76; Louise L. Hunt, *Biographical Notes Concerning General Richard Montgomery* (1876); Thomas P. Robinson, "Some Notes on Major-General Richard Montgomery," *New York History*, 37 (1956):388–398; A.L. Todd, *Richard Montgomery: Rebel of 1775* (1966).

Montresor, John (1736–1799)

British military officer. John Montresor was born at Gibraltar April 22, 1736, the son of James Gabriel Montresor, then chief engineer at that outpost. John presumably learned engineering from his father, for he did not receive formal training in the subject. His military service in North America had been extensive by the outbreak of the American Revolution.

John went with his father to America in 1754, where the elder Montresor has been assigned as chief engineer to Major General Edward Braddock. He obtained an ensigncy in the 48th Regiment of Foot in March 1755 and was appointed an additional engineer by Braddock in June. John Montresor was promoted lieutenant in the 48th on July 4, 1755, and he was wounded in Braddock's defeat on the Monongahela. His acting appointment as an engineer was continued by General William Shirley in 1756, and he worked on the fortifications of Fort Lydius (Fort Edward, New York). The 1757 campaign found him with Lord Loudon's expedition against Louisbourg, Cape Breton Island (Nova Scotia). Montresor received a commission as engineer and practitioner on May 19, 1758, thereby losing his lieutenancy in the 48th Regiment, an occurrence he protested. He accompanied General Jeffery Amherst in his successful expedition against Louisbourg that summer. Promotion to lieutenant and subengineer came on March 17, 1759. The final campaigns of the French and Indian War found John Montresor with Wolfe at Quebec in 1759 and with James Murray during his advance on Montreal in the summer of 1760.

John Montresor's services were equally energetic following the surrender of New France. He remained in Canada after 1760, assisting in mapping the new British conquest. In 1761 he explored the region between the St. Lawrence and the Kennebec River of Maine, the route later followed by Benedict Arnold on his 1775 march to Quebec. The Great Lakes Indian uprising of 1763 found Montresor ordered to Niagara and Detroit, then besieged by Chief Pontiac's warriors. While conveying reinforcements to Detroit late in August 1763, his vessel was cast away on the south shore of Lake Erie. Montresor fortified the wreck site and directed the survivors' successful defense against Indian attacks. He eventually reached Detroit, improved the fortifications of the post, and returned to New York for the winter. John Montresor again moved up the Great Lakes in 1764 and directed the construction of defenses on the Niagara Portage (including the first Fort Erie, Ontario) before continuing to Detroit as engineer for Colonel John Bradstreet's army.

During this phase of his military career, Montresor was assigned a variety of additional duties well beyond the normal activities of an engineer. These included his explorations, a successful overland carriage of dispatches between Quebec and Amherst's headquarters on Lake Champlain early in 1760, and partisan warfare at the head of small parties of troops in New York, Isle Royale, and Canada between 1756 and 1760. His activities against the Indians in 1763–1764 likewise presented an opportunity for Montresor to distinguish himself on independent commands, including a battalion of *Canadien* troops, the first ever employed in British service, from Oswego to Niagara in 1764.

With peace in America, Montresor busied himself at more conventional engineering duties. On March 1, 1764, shortly before his departure for Niagara, he married Frances Tucker in New York City, a union that eventually produced six children. In 1765 he was employed chiefly at Albany and New York, where he helped fortify old Fort George during the Stamp Act riots. Montresor was promoted engineer extraordinary and captain lieutenant on December 20, 1765, and traveled to England late in 1766. Following his return, he worked primarily from New York for the next few years. In 1768 he prepared plans for altering Fort Niagara, and in 1769–1770 he was sent to improve fortifications in the Bahamas and to survey the boundary between New York and New Jersey. Further work prior to the war included repairs to Castle William in Boston in 1770 and design of a new fort (later Fort Mifflin) below Philadelphia in 1771. In 1772 the Montresors had their portraits done by John S. Copley during the artist's visit to New York. The next few years were spent primarily at work in New York and Boston.

The rebellion in the American colonies found Montresor at Boston. He accompanied Percy's relief expedition to Lexington on April 19, 1775, and performed various duties in the garrison of Boston. He was appointed chief engineer in America on December 18, 1775, and received the rank of engineer in ordinary and captain on January 8, 1776. Montresor was present at Bunker Hill and was entrusted with the demolition of Castle William when Howe abandoned Boston in March 1776. John Montresor accompanied Howe's expedition to New York and fought in a number of engagements around Long Island and Manhattan in 1776. His final actions in America were in 1777 at the Battle of Brandywine, where he served as engineer, and at the reduction of the Mud Island fort, which he had designed and begun in 1771.

Despite his experience and position, Montresor does not seem to have been fully utilized in his capacity as chief engineer, perhaps, as suggested by some of his biographers, due to his lack of formal training. In October 1778, Montresor returned to England and retired from the army. His journals and memoranda of his services give an indication of his ill feelings and disappointment at not having received higher rank or greater recognition.

Montresor's earlier service did not prepare him for the ensuing two decades. Most of this time was spent in controversy, for in 1782 his engineering accounts were audited and many of his expenses disallowed. There were implications of misappropriation of funds and the amassing of a private fortune. Montresor did travel to the Continent in the 1780s and saw his elder sons enter military service, but much of his property was seized by the government, and he was confined to Maidstone Prison, England, where he died on June 26, 1799.

Brian Leigh Dunnigan

REFERENCES

R. Arthur Bowler, "John Montresor," *DCB*; British Army Lists. London, 1775–1778; G.D. Scull, ed., "The Montresor Journals," *Collections of the New York Historical Society for the Year 1881* (1882).

Moody, James (1744–1809)

Loyalist. Moody's background is obscure. In 1775 he was living on his father's farm in Sussex County, New Jersey. As a Loyalist he refused to take the required loyalty oath. Harassed for his Tory views, Moody fled to British lines with over 70 friends and relatives. He became an ensign and then a lieutenant in General Cortlandt Skinner's New Jersey Volunteers.

He led an adventurous life typified by daring raids on New Jersey farms. In retaliation for the confiscation of his estate, in May 1780 he plotted to kidnap several New Jersey politicians, including Governor William Livingston. Unsuccessful in that attempt, Moody captured 18 prominent residents of the state in early July. Captured by General Anthony Wayne at Liberty Pole Tavern in Teaneck, New Jersey, on July 21 he was removed to West Point, New York, where General Benedict Arnold, the commandant of the garrison, reputedly treated him harshly. Soon after, Moody was taken to Tappan, New Jersey, and from there to Steenrapie (present-day River Edge) to stand trial as a spy. On September 17 Moody escaped to British lines. Moody's next mission was to intercept some of Washington's correspondence, and after several attempts he succeeded. On another attempt, he tried to steal some documents from the Continental Congress. However, the mission was aborted, but his brother was captured in the endeavor and was executed in November 1781. Moody became so angry at New Jersey's reward for his capture that he offered a reward for the capture of Livingston.

Mentally depressed from the death of his brother, Moody sailed to England in January 1782, where he published his memoirs and where he appealed for compensation. The British government placed him on half-pay and awarded him monetary restitution for his services and for the loss of his property. Acquiring land in Nova Scotia, he settled near Sissiboo River in 1786. There he built mills and ships, becoming a community leader. Moody became a magistrate, a road commissioner, and he was elected to the House of Assembly in 1793 for successive terms. Moody is symbolic of the intensity of vendettas during the Revolution in New Jersey.

Richard L. Blanco

REFERENCES

DCB; E.A. Jones, *The Loyalists of New Jersey* (1927); [James Moody], *Lieutenant James Moody's Narrative* (1865); Carl F. Prince, et al., eds., *The Papers of William Livingston*, 5 vols. (1978–88), *4*; Lorenzo Sabine, *Biographical Sketches of Loyalists of the American Revolution*, 2 vols. (1864), *2*.

Moore, John (1753–?)

Loyalist. Had he survived the American Revolution and written a memoir, John Moore could have told the history of the war in the South from a unique Loyalist perspective. Certainly his views on why the Loyalist support for the king's cause failed would have been invaluable. Moore was born in what is now Gaston County, North Carolina, the son of Englishman John Moore. When the Revolution came, the younger Moore quit school to serve the king. Upon learning that a British army had captured Savannah, he organized more than 200 Loyalists in Tryon County and marched south to Georgia, seizing guns, horses, and rebel Colonel William Wofford along the way. However, his band was repulsed by one young man and a small group of women and children when they tried to assault Colonel John Thomas's house near Fair Forrest, South Carolina. En route, they joined the South Carolina Loyalists under Colonel James Boyd and continued together with Boyd in command and Moore as his second. After successfully evading and skirmishing with various militia, the Loyalists were defeated by Colonel Andrew Pickens at the Battle of Kettle Creek, Georgia, February 14, 1779.

During the battle, Moore disappeared and was at first thought by his followers and by the rebels to have been killed. He was soon prisoner at the jail in Ninety Six, South Carolina. By a writ of habeas corpus from South Carolina governor John Rutledge, he was removed from the jail and was finally within the British lines. The North Carolina Loyalist survivors of Kettle Creek were placed under his command in a unit called the North Carolina Volunteers. This outfit was never large, and by the summer of 1779 it had faded out of existence. After the unsuccessful French and American attack upon Savannah in October 1779, Moore and his men were sent in pursuit of the retreating rebels. Restored Royal Governor Sir James Wright made Moore a colonel in the Royal Georgia Militia, to organize the Loyalists in the areas of Georgia not yet under royal control.

When Lord Cornwallis began his march into the Carolina backcountry, Moore was a lieutenant colonel in Colonel John Hamilton's Royal North Carolina Regiment. Moore and Hamilton prematurely started a Loyalist uprising at Ramsour's Mill, North Carolina, near the home of Moore's father. They were badly defeated by the rebel militia there on June 20, 1780. Moore escaped, only to be arrested by Cornwallis. It was deemed impolitic to have Moore court-martialed, and he was released in time to participate and escape from the disastrous Loyalist defeat at King's Mountain, October 7, 1780. When the Georgia Loyalist militia of Colonel Thomas Waters was all but eliminated at the "Battle" of Hammond's Store, South Carolina, December 28, 1780, it seemed only natural that Moore was with them and again escaped.

John Moore could be described in many ways, including simply as a survivor. A family legend states that he eventually settled in Carlisle, England. More likely, he was captured in the last days of the Revolution and hanged. One Loyalist remembered that Moore died at the hands of Colonel Wade Hampton near the Wateree.

Robert Scott Davis, Jr.

REFERENCES

Lyman C. Draper, *King's Mountain and Its Heroes* (1881); Robert S. Davis, Jr., *Georgians in the Revolution* (1986).

Moore's Creek, North Carolina, Battle of (February 27, 1776)

In April 1775 North Carolina royal governor Josiah Martin wrote Lord Dartmouth, secretary of state for the colonies, that royal government in North Carolina was "absolutely impotent . . . nothing but the shadow of it is left." Events soon proved Martin right. On the last day of May, Martin, surrounded by increasingly hostile Patriots, spiked the guns at the governor's palace in New Bern and fled to Fort Johnston, located on the Cape Fear River near Brunswick. He then sent his family to New York and called a June 25 council meeting. Although attended by only three council members, the meeting did formally authorize Martin to issue commissions, to recruit militia, and to petition General Thomas Gage for funds to repair the fort. By that point, however, repair of the fort was a moot point. Hearing of the approach of Patriot forces Martin abandoned it for the sanctuary of the British sloop *Cruizer* on July 15. Three days later Martin watched in frustration as a "Savage and audacious mob" burned the fort.

Despite this opposition, Martin firmly believed that North Carolina was basically loyal and that a concerted demonstration of British strength would redeem the colony. With that in mind he conceived an ambitious plan. In a June 30 letter to Dartmouth, Martin boldly claimed to be able to immediately raise 3,000 Scotch Highlanders. With a supply of arms from Gage in Boston and a show of British regulars he would turn this into a 20,000-man force, with which he would "effectively restore order here and in South Carolina, and hold Virginia in such awe as to prevent that Province sending any succor to the northward."

To further plead his case, Martin sent North Carolina planter Alexander Schaw to London. Martin's proposal, Schaw's entreaties, and other correspondence from the colonies confirmed the rather benign picture held in London that North Carolina was predominantly loyal. Shortly before leaving office Dartmouth initiated a complex plan not only to secure North Carolina but to pacify the rest of the South. The plan called for seven regiments, under the command of General Lord Cornwallis, to sail to Cape Fear in a fleet commanded by Admiral Sir Peter Parker. Once there, they were to link up with a detachment of British regulars who would sail from Boston. The troops would land and supposedly would be greeted by the Loyalist army promised by Martin. After rolling over the Whig opposition in North Carolina, the expedition would move down the coast and pacify South Carolina. The plan, if it worked, would return British rule to much of the South.

Martin received final confirmation of this plan on January 3, 1776. One week later he issued a proclamation calling on all royal subjects to "unite and suppress" the "unnatural rebellion that has been excited . . . by traitorous and designing men." A place of rendezvous would be established, and the troops would march to Brunswick no later than February 15. There they would await the arrival of the British expedition.

Martin specifically addressed this proclamation to a number of prominent Highlanders in the colony. The Cape Fear region, particularly the area near Cross Creek (present-day Fayetteville), had been heavily settled by Scottish Highlanders. Martin was confident that he could count on their loyalty. Since July 1775, 80-year-old Lieutenant Colonel Donald MacDonald and Captain Alexander McLeod, both British regulars, had been recruiting these same Scotch for the Royal Highland Emigrant Brigade. In February, Martin appointed

MacDonald brigadier general of the militia and McLeod lieutenant colonel. The 300 recruits raised in 1775 by MacDonald and McLeod would serve as the core of the Loyalist army. Other well-known Loyalists, including Alexander McLean and Flora MacDonald's husband, Allan, were also involved in raising troops. Martin was equally confident that the former Regulators would flock to the royal standard, if for no other reason than to have revenge on their former eastern adversaries, most of whom were ardent Whigs. The British government helped recruitment by promising all who would sign up a package of benefits including 200 acres of land and 20 years tax exemption.

All of this activity did not escape the notice of the Patriot forces. Colonel James Moore's 1st North Carolina Continentals, 650 strong, were nearby, while Patriot militia were being mobilized throughout the colony. To Martin's surprise and dismay, the Whigs were particularly strong in the backcountry, an area he had previously thought largely immune from "seditious" thought.

The Highlander leaders met at Cross Creek on February 5. Assured that their ranks would soon be augmented by backcountry Loyalists, they decided not to wait for the arrival of the British but to mobilize immediately. Within days, some 1,400 Highlanders were encamped at Cross Creek, over half of whom were unarmed. However, the anticipated number of Regulators never materialized. Martin and his advisors had seriously overestimated their number, while the activities of the Whig militia broke up several Loyalist concentrations long before they could make it to Cross Creek. Barely 100 backcountry Loyalists joined the Highlanders.

On February 9, Moore learned that the Tories were collecting at Cross Creek. He immediately moved his troops to cut off the most direct route to the sea, stopping at Rockfish Creek Bridge, about seven miles from Cross Creek. He was soon reinforced by 450 militia under the various commands of Colonel Alexander Lillington, Colonel James Kenan, and Colonel James Ashe.

MacDonald began his march down Cape Fear toward the coast on February 18. The next day he found that his route, along the south side of Cape Fear, was blocked by Moore. In a bizarre sequence MacDonald and Moore then exchanged notes, each calling on the other to surrender.

The offers were refused. About this time some 20 Loyalists, announcing that "their courage was not Warproof," left for home. MacDonald, aware that Moore would soon receive more reinforcements, and feeling the noose tightening, deftly escaped on February 20. He slipped his troops around Moore, surreptitiously crossed the river, and burned or sunk his boats.

As soon as Moore realized he had been tricked, he ordered Richard Caswell to place his 600 militia at Corbett's Ferry on the Black River in another attempt to cut off MacDonald. Ashe and Lillington were ordered to reinforce Caswell while other troops were sent back to secure Cross Creek. Moore would give chase with the Continentals.

On February 23, MacDonald reached Corbett's Ferry. Caswell was entrenched on the far side. Once again MacDonald found his way blocked by an enemy force and once again he escaped. He bluffed an attack, using a handful of troops as decoys. Meanwhile, his men were constructing a temporary bridge, which they used to cross the Black River on the morning of February 26.

This would be only a temporary respite, however. Moore, who was in Elizabethtown when he received word of MacDonald's second escape, reacted quickly and ordered Caswell to the next logical river crossing. This was the bridge over the Widow Moore's Creek, some 18 miles northwest of Wilmington—a bridge MacDonald had to cross to reach his destination. Lillington and Caswell won the race, reaching the bridge on the evening of February 26. Caswell first had his troops dig in on the west side of the creek and then reconsidered, and then he moved to the east (far) side. Moore's Creek flows into the Black River about ten miles from where that river flows into Cape Fear. The narrow bridge was in a swampy area, at a point where the dark water was about 50 feet wide and 5 feet deep. Caswell was in overall command of about 950 troops, all militia.

The Loyalist force of about 1,500 reached the vicinity of Moore's Creek in the evening of February 26, some six miles from the bridge and Caswell. The hard marching had taken its toll on the elderly MacDonald, who fell ill and relinquished temporary command to McLeod. Learning of Caswell's defensive posture the decision was made by the Loyalists not to attempt another escape but to attack at daybreak on Feb-

ruary 27. This decision meant a fatiguing march through the swamp in the dark, a march begun at 1 A.M. that was only completed shortly before dawn.

Months of planning and weeks of marching ended in a battle that was decided in a few short minutes. In the semi-darkness of near dawn, the Highlanders, led by McLeod and Farquard Campbell, shouted "King George and Broad Swords," and rushed the bridge. They found that half the flooring of the bridge had been removed, and the girders had been greased with soap and tallow. The attackers were met with a withering fire, both from rifles and the two cannon at Caswell's disposal. A few Highlanders crossed the bridge, including McLeod and Campbell, but were killed before reaching the earthworks. Some were drowned in the murky water. Half-hearted efforts were made to rally the Loyalists, but to no avail. The Patriot forces quickly repaired the bridge, counterattacked, and spent the rest of the day capturing disheartened Loyalists. Among the captured was the ailing MacDonald, who took no part in the battle. Prisoners continued to be rounded up through the next day.

The Loyalists suffered a crushing defeat. At least 30 were killed, many more were wounded, and some 850 were captured. The Patriots also captured considerable material. Only one Patriot was killed and one wounded. Most of the captured Loyalists were quickly paroled, although the officers, including MacDonald, languished in jails for several months.

Martin regarded the setback as a "little check" that would have little consequence. Disagreeing with this rosy assessment was the expedition's overall commander General Sir Henry Clinton, who arrived from Boston on March 12. Expecting to find a large Loyalist army, he had little interest in challenging the entire Patriot militia of North Carolina. In any event Parker's fleet, delayed by storms, did not arrive until April 18. The British issued proclamations, made a reconnaissance in force, skirmished, and burned some rebel property, including the plantation of Patriot leader Robert Howe. Rather than give up the entire plan, the British fleet then left for their ill-fated attack on Charleston harbor.

The Patriot victory at Moore's Creek left the Patriots firmly in control in North Carolina, gave North Carolinian Patriots an inflated opinion of the capabilities of their militia, and it may have helped nudge the colony towards the decision for independence that would be made in the next months. The sullen Loyalists plotted revenge and largely bided their time, awaiting the next arrival of British forces. *See also:* MacDonald, Flora; North Carolina in the American Revolution

Jim Sumner

REFERENCES

Robert O. Demond, *The Loyalists in North Carolina During the Revolution* (1940); Charles E. Hatch, Jr., *The Battle of Moore's Creek Bridge* (1969); Duane Meyer, *The Highland Scots of North Carolina, 1732–1776* (1957); Hugh F. Rankin, "The Moore's Creek Bridge Campaign, 1776," *The North Carolina Historical Review*, 30 (1953):23–60; William L. Saunders, ed., *The Colonial Records of North Carolina*, X (1890); Vernon O. Stumpf, *Josiah Martin: The Last Royal Governor of North Carolina* (1986).

Moravian Indian Missions on the Muskingum River

Few events during the eight years of the Revolutionary War so stirred the resentment and anger of the Indian nations as the massacre of ninety Christian Indians at Gnadenhutten. Occurring just four months following the surrender of Cornwallis at Yorktown (October 19, 1781), the repercussions would occur throughout the next 30 years, especially in treaty discussions with the Indian nations. Even today, more than 200 years later, many of the incidents connected with the tragedy still stir controversy and at best remain a mystery to historians.

The Christian Indian mission of Gnadenhutten and its parent village of Schoenbrunn lay on the Muskingum River (now the Tuscarawas) in the northeastern section of the present state of Ohio. Both villages were settled in 1772.

Led by the Moravian missionary, David Zeisberger, 33 Delaware Indian converts left their village of Friedenstadt on the Beaver River in western Pennsylvania and arrived at the future site of Schoenbrunn on May 3, 1772. Five months later, another contingent of Mahican converts arrived in the valley from the recently abandoned mission of Friedenshutten on the Susquehanna River in eastern Pennsylvania. This contingent, led by Johann Schmick, settled eight miles down river from Schoenbrunn. Schmick became the missionary at Gnadenhutten and Zeisberger was the overall superintendent of both villages. The move had been planned the previous year in response to an invitation from Chief

Netawatwes, the head sachem of the Delaware nation, then living at Gekelemukpechunk (Kuh-Kee-luh-mook-pa-kunk) near present Newcomerstown, Ohio. In 1775, he moved his village to Goschachgunk (Ko-shock-ach-kunk) near present Coshocton, Ohio.

For the previous 27 years Zeisberger had worked first among the Iroquois nations and later among the Delawares and Mahicans in New York and Pennsylvania. Early in his career, he discovered that his missions should be removed from the influence of both native Indian villages and the ever-encroaching Euroamerican western migration. Unlike previous Protestant missionaries, Zeisberger's mission operation resembled a combination of both the Indian and white cultures—a half-way refuge from each. The traditional fall and winter huts, sugar gathering, and complete access to their native Indian relatives were freely permitted. However, native Indian witchcraft and clothing, dancing, polygamy, heathen festivals, games, and the use of liquor were forbidden.

Both villages prospered, and by the close of the year 1775 there were well over 400 Indian converts living at the 2 missions. Young apple and peach trees surrounded each village, and hundreds of acres of fenced plantations yearly grew corn, beans, squash, and pumpkins. Individual garden plots were located just behind every family home, and the carefully laid out streets were regularly swept clean.

In April 1776, at the insistence of Chief Netawatwes, Zeisberger founded another mission village three miles south of the new Delaware capital at Goschachgunk. Leaving his assistant, Johann Jungman, in charge at Schoenbrunn, Zeisberger and 35 of his converts began building the third mission, called Lichtenau.

The missions inevitably became involved in the American Revolution. British strategy called for the lieutenant governor, Henry Hamilton in Detroit, to create disturbances on the western frontier in the hope that Washington would divert troops from the eastern theater. Hamilton was successful in persuading the Shawnee, Wyandot, and Mingo tribes to join the British. However, the Delawares, through the efforts of Zeisberger, Netawatwes, and Chief White Eyes, remained neutral.

By the spring of 1777, with frequent war parties passing through the Schoenbrunn village, Zeisberger became concerned for the exposed condition of the converts living in this area. He ordered Jungman to abandon the town and to move all the villagers to Lichtenau. There were now over 300 converts living 3 miles from the native Delaware capital. Schmidt, and over 100 of his Christian Indians, remained at Gnadenhutten some 28 miles from Lichtenau.

Unfortunately, in the next three years Zeisberger's support among the Delaware council sharply deteriorated. The ancient chief Netawatwes died in the fall of 1776 and was replaced by his young, ineffective grandson, Gelelemend (Kuh-lay-luh-ment). White Eyes was killed by an American militiaman in October 1778, and Captain Pipe, the head chief of the Wolfe clan, defected to the English and moved his people to the upper Sandusky River in northwestern Ohio. Thus Zeisberger stood virtually alone among the advocates for neutrality at the Delaware council. Only the capture of Hamilton at Vincennes by George Rogers Clark on February 25, 1779, kept the remaining Delawares temporarily subdued for the next two years. By the early spring of 1779, it became obvious the converts would be in great peril at Lichtenau if the balance of the Delawares broke their neutrality and joined the British.

To protect his Christian flock against this eventuality, Zeisberger began to disband the Lichtenau congregation and remove them from their exposed position. In April 1779, he moved part of the converts back to a site near the old Schoenbrunn 35 miles from the Delaware capital (near present New Philadelphia, Ohio). The village was called New Schoenbrunn. The balance of the group, led by his assistant John Heckewelder, began a new mission, called Salem, just a few miles south of Gnadenhutten.

Despite Zeisberger's attempt to remain neutral, he continued to agonize over the many war parties who passed through the Moravian villages bound for depredations against the white western frontier settlements. On numerous occasions he was successful in deflecting some parties who accepted his advice and returned to their villages. During this interim period (1777–1781) he had been furnishing detailed intelligence to the commander at Fort Pitt, warning of the approach of British and Indian war parties. This caused inordinate Indian losses and inflamed the new British commander, Major Arent DePeyster, Hamilton's replacement at Detroit.

Early in the spring of 1781 the situation between the British and colonial antagonists became desperate. Colonel Daniel Brodhead, the commander of Fort Pitt, moved first. By forced march, he attacked the Delaware capital at Goschachgunk on April 19, killing almost 30 Delaware warriors and burning the village. The mission villages were spared because of Zeisberger's close association with the colonials over the past five years, but there was no longer any question regarding Delaware neutrality. They were now firmly in the camp of the British.

DePeyster, now fully convinced of Zeisberger's "duplicity," in August 1781 ordered the Wyandot chief Pomoacan (the Half-King) and Captain Pipe, the chief of the Wolfe clan of the Delawares, to remove the Moravians from the Muskingum Valley. To protect his interests and make sure the orders were followed to the letter, Captain Matthew Elliott, his deputy, accompanied the 250 Wyandots and Delawares. They arrived at Gnadenhutten on the hot summer morning of August 20. After several weeks of ineffectual negotiation, Matthew Elliott ordered Pomoacan to carry out his orders.

On the morning of September 11, over 400 converts from New Schoenbrunn and Salem were gathered together at Gnadenhutten. Zeisberger recorded that they broke camp, and "as if in a dream so as to hardly know our senses" they were forced to leave their beloved valley, most of their possessions, and all of the crops to begin the 100-mile forced march to the upper Sandusky River. Three beautiful and orderly little villages lay in scattered ruins with dead animals rotting in the streets and many of the crops and fences trampled and destroyed. Thus came to an end the first Moravian Christian missions in the Muskingum Valley. It would be 17 years before Zeisberger returned to found Goshen, the last of his many missions. Here he would finally be laid to rest in 1808 among the green hills he loved so dearly.

Arriving at the upper Sandusky on October 1, the converts were already in a near-starving condition. Pomoacan and his Wyandots, despite their promises, furnished little assistance. Had it not been for the Shawnee and several English traders, they would have starved.

The solution to their immediate problem lay 100 miles to the southeast, back in the valley of the Muskingum where acres of corn stood unharvested. Schebosh (the white man John Bull, Ziesberger's longtime friend and associate) agreed to take a small party, consisting mainly of his Indian family, and return to retrieve some of the crop. The Schebosh party left the Sandusky on October 15 and arrived 10 days later at the Muskingum. Two hours after arrival as they were gathering the corn, a party of 100 militiamen, led by Colonel David Williamson, arrived at the location, surrounded the harvesters, and forced them to return to Fort Henry (Wheeling). They were then taken to Fort Pitt, where all were released unharmed, much to the chagrin of the western settlers. Schebosh's letter of November 4 to Bethlehem (Pennsylvania) was the first information that Bethlehem had received of the converts' removal from the Muskingum.

Ten days after Schebosh's departure, Zeisberger and his assistants were summoned to Detroit by DePeyster to defend themselves against treason charges initiated by the Indian chiefs. Much to everyone's surprise, they were exonerated following the testimony of their bitter enemy, Captain Pipe, who exculpated them of all charges.

On November 22, the missionaries were back on the Sandusky with a small quantity of food furnished by the Detroit commander. But it was only a matter of time until the situation would again become desperate. From the middle of January and throughout February, over 150 of the converts began looking for food. Some traveled to the lower Sandusky to visit white traders, others went to the Shawnee. On February 7, a large part of over 100 departed again for the Muskingum. They arrived in the valley sometime during the third week in February 1782 and began gathering the unharvested corn at all three of the former village sites: New Schoenbrunn, Salem, and Gnadenhutten.

As the Moravian converts leisurely gathered their corn on the Muskingum, back among the white settlements, James Marshal, the county lieutenant for Washington County, called for the muster of 150 soldiers to mount an attack on the Muskingum villages. The men were to serve from March 1 until March 9. Not knowing the precise status of the Indians in this area, the objective was to deflect the future occupation of the former villages and to capture or kill any Indians they found in the area. The contingent was again commanded by Colonel David Williamson, a respected militia officer in the county.

The Williamson party arrived near the area on the evening of March 5. Most of the next morning was spent in planning their strategy for the day, knowing the Indians were in the villages. One group was to cross the river and surreptitiously pose as friends concerned for the Indians' safety; another was to enter the village and assume the same disguise.

As they approached the Gnadenhutten mission and began to cross the river, they discovered Schebosh's young son, Joseph, near the river. He was shot as he attempted to flee, the bullet breaking his arm. He was then tomahawked and scalped despite his plea as the son of a white man. The 16 men who had crossed the river proceeded downstream to the plantations, where they successfully convinced the harvesters to relinquish their weapons and return to the village. The second group, fearing the shot might alert the villagers, moved immediately to Gnadenhutten also posing as friends and protectors. On the evening of March 6, one of the villagers was instructed to accompany a party of the militia to Salem to bring in those converts. By noon on March 7 they returned to Gnadenhutten with the unarmed Salem contingent. The guise of hospitality was soon discarded, and the unarmed male converts were bound and placed in one of the buildings, the women and children in another. The balance of the day was spent in deciding their fate.

Williamson was rapidly losing control of his men. Throughout the long and protracted Indian wars most of the militia on this expedition had lost fathers, sons, daughters, brothers, and other relatives. And they had witnessed horrid murders and other depredations on an extensive scale. The thirst for revenge ran high. Only a strong hand of military discipline could have controlled the troops on this occasion. As with most militia contingents who were pioneer farmers and laborers, they cared little about army regulations or discipline. Williamson and his officers decided to submit the question to a vote. Those in favor of returning the prisoners to Fort Pitt took one step forward. Only 16 responded. The balance favored their destruction. The converts were all told to prepare for death the next day. All night long they sang and prayed.

Early the next morning they were led into two of the buildings, the men into one and the

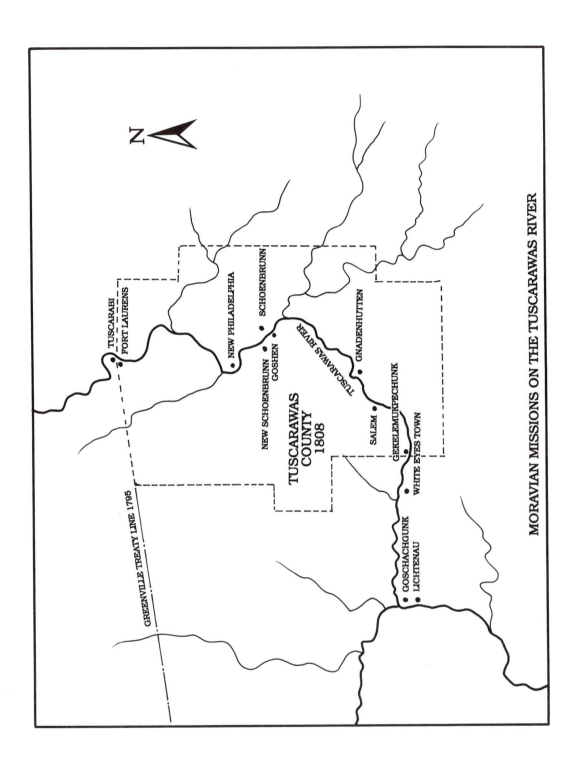

MORAVIAN MISSIONS ON THE TUSCARAWAS RIVER

women and children into another. One by one they were clubbed to death. Most were killed with a huge mallet found in the Cooper's House. Thus, 90 Christian Indians perished: 27 brethren, 24 sisters, 4 unbaptized adults, and 35 children. After burning both villages, the Williamson party returned to their homes.

Fortunately, the converts gathering corn at New Schoenbrunn had sent a messenger to Gnadenhutten the day before the massacre. The messenger discovered the body of young Schebosh and the tracks of the militia going toward Gnadenhutten. Returning to the valley, the New Schoenbrunn contingent immediately departed and escaped back to the Sandusky.

Two young boys survived the massacre. Thomas, who had been scalped and left for dead, escaped in the evening, and Jacob who had fled into the woods prior to the massacre and observed the proceedings from his hiding place. Both returned to the Sandusky and delivered to Zeisberger the only firsthand report of the massacre.

The tragic Williamson expedition against the Moravians did little to reduce the number of Indian excursions against the settlers in western Pennsylvania. Since most of the attacks were committed by Wyandots, Delawares, and Shawnees then living on the upper Sandusky and the Scioto, they continued unabated. Furthermore, the Gnadenhutten murders solved none of the pressing problems confronting the white settlers who committed murders.

Earl P. Olmstead

References

Eugene F. Bliss, *Diary of David Zeisberger* (1885); Cansol W. Butterfield, *Washington-Irvine Correspondence* (1885); Edmund De Schwienitz, *The Life and Times of David Zeisberger* (1870); Louis P. Kellogg, ed., *Frontier Retreat on the Upper Ohio, 1778–1781* (1917); George Knepper, *Ohio and Its People* (1989); Paul A.W. Wallace, ed., *Thirty Thousand Miles with John Heckenelder* (1958).

Morgan, Daniel (1736–1802)

Continental Army officer. Controversy and lack of information cloud various aspects of Daniel Morgan's life, including the date and place of his birth. Most sources list the former as 1736 but one suggests 1735. Biographers disagree about whether he was born in Hunterdon County, New Jersey, or in Bucks County, Pennsylvania. Morgan was probably related to Daniel Boone, but writers disagree on whether he was a cousin or an uncle of the famous Kentucky frontiersman. What is not in doubt is that Morgan became one of the outstanding military leaders for the Americans in the War of Independence despite his lack of formal education, influential family members, or prominent friends.

Whatever his origins and family background, Daniel Morgan left home while a teenager and journeyed to Winchester in Frederick County, Virginia, in 1753; he spent most of the rest of his life here except when he served in the military. He was tall (at least six feet), broad shouldered, and very athletic. He got a job driving a wagon and eventually bought his own; in 1755 he drove one of the supply wagons in the campaign of General Edward Braddock against the French forces at Fort Duquesne. Morgan was in the second detachment of Braddock's army so he was not present at the disastrous defeat when the French and Indians ambushed the British-American forces. Sometime during or shortly after this campaign Morgan knocked down a British officer who slapped him with a sword. This retaliation earned him a quick court-martial and a brutal flogging of several hundred lashes on his back. This beating certainly did not endear him to the British, but it did convince him not to resort to public whippings of soldiers when he was later in command of troops.

Later in 1755 he joined a local ranger company that was formed to counter Indian raids. He engaged in various military duties near Fort Ashby and Fort Edwards, north of Winchester. In 1756, he and one or two other soldiers were attacked while away from the forts. Here Daniel received his only battle wound when an Indian shot a musket ball that went through his neck and jaw; he survived this serious injury but lost several teeth and bore scars of the wound for the rest of his life. His actions for the next several years are in some dispute, but one source (Callahan) says he was appointed ensign in the Virginia militia in 1758 and a lieutenant in 1763. He was clearly in the military, whatever his rank, and showed bravery and competence at all times. He was involved also in a number of fights, brawls, and heavy drinking bouts, but this was typical of young men in frontier settings. What distinguished Morgan was that he was generally the best fighter, runner, and horseman in the many contests and competitions in which he engaged. He also continued to make a living driving a wagon, when not on military duty, and in later years, referred to himself as the "old wagoner."

He met Abigail Curry, daughter of a local farmer, about 1761 and began courting her; they apparently began a common-law marriage in 1763 and had two daughters, Nancy and Betsy. They were formally married in 1773. After 1763 Morgan settled down somewhat from his earlier wild activities. In 1771 he was made a captain in the militia in Frederick County; he enjoyed a mild degree of prosperity in the next few years as he and Abigail worked a farm that they had acquired.

In June 1774 Morgan and his company joined Major Angus McDonald's troops fighting the Shawnee Indians for control of the Ohio River country around Wheeling, Virginia. While he was not engaged in any spectacular or decisive battles in this conflict known as Dunmore's War, Daniel Morgan again showed courage and skill in several skirmishes.

The situation in America changed dramatically in 1775 when the War of Independence began. The Second Continental Congress prepared to fight the British and authorized the formation of several rifle companies. Morgan was chosen as captain of one of these that was raised in Frederick County, and he recruited ninety-six men in a short time. After a few weeks of preparation, they marched 600 miles to Cambridge, Massachusetts, in 3 weeks. These riflemen were held in awe by many Americans and British because of their skill in hitting targets 200 yards and more away. Their first task with the American army besieging Boston was sniping against British sentries and stragglers outside their lines.

Morgan's company was then chosen by lot to be one of three rifle companies to assist in the invasion of Canada through Maine; Benedict Arnold commanded the expedition, and he selected Morgan to lead all three companies. These rifle companies headed off as the advance party up the Kennebec River in September 1775. The American troops boated, marched, and dragged themselves 350 miles through the wilderness in a grueling campaign that nearly led to disaster for all. Morgan showed his toughness and dedication as he helped lead and push men forward. Arnold and a few men had to forge ahead and get supplies to save the rest of the soldiers. The

weakened and diminished force finally reached the St. Lawrence River in November. Morgan was with Arnold in the lead canoe crossing the river as they planned their attack on Quebec, the key city in Canada. The Americans were spotted, however, so the assault was delayed until another force, led by General Richard Montgomery, arrived after capturing Montreal and nearby forts. The joint forces besieged Quebec, then launched their attack in late December. Small units diverted British attention while the two main columns tried to break through the city's defenses; one of these was commanded by Montgomery and the other, which included Morgan, was led by Arnold. Montgomery was killed early in the battle, and his subordinates withdrew their troops without informing Arnold. Arnold's contingent was successful at first, but then he was seriously wounded. Morgan took over but with uncertain authority. At a crucial point in the fighting, he urged aggressive action that might have succeeded; the other officers insisted on caution, however, and the advantage was lost. Their soldiers were surrounded, and many, including Morgan, were captured. Their imprisonment at Quebec was relatively brief, and the prisoners fared well compared to their companions outside the fort who maintained a cold siege through the winter with an inadequate food supply. The prisoners were taken by ship to New Jersey in September 1776 and released on parole until exchanged for British prisoners. Morgan returned home and was formally exchanged in January 1777. He was appointed colonel of the 11th Virginia Regiment, but recruiting went slowly, some said because he was too insistent on selecting accurate marksmen. Nevertheless, the unit joined Washington's army in June. Morgan was then placed in command of a special corps of light infantry of approximately 500 Continental soldiers. He led them in several skirmishes in June and July against William Howe's troops in New Jersey. In August, Washington transferred Morgan's corps to the northern army to help General Horatio Gates try to stop the invasion from Canada by General John Burgoyne.

Burgoyne's position had been weakened somewhat by losses at Bennington and Fort Schuyler, but he still had substantial forces near Saratoga, New York. Morgan's corps was reinforced by 300 musketmen under Major Henry Dearborn; Morgan quickly impressed General

Gates as his men reconnoitered the British lines and harassed their scouts and Indians. The riflemen virtually closed off Burgoyne's sources of information by driving his scouts back into their own lines. Burgoyne finally advanced toward the American lines, and the Battle of Freeman's Farm was fought on September 19, with Morgan and Arnold leading the American attack. Morgan's riflemen shot most of the British artillery gunners and many officers. The British managed to hold their position but suffered nearly twice the casualties as the Americans. Despite being in the thick of the fight, Morgan's unit had only 15 casualties (4 killed).

Washington requested the return of the riflemen, but Gates convinced him that they should remain with the northern army. In the next several weeks Morgan's men proved their value with continued sniping against the British scouts. On October 7, Burgoyne resumed his march and Americans met him at the Battle of Bemis Heights. Morgan and his men were again in the thick of the fight as the advantages in the battle swayed back and forth. One of his riflemen performed one of the legendary feats of the war during this battle: Morgan detailed Timothy Murphy to try to pick off General Simon Fraser, a brave officer leading a contingent of troops. Murphy mortally wounded Fraser, and the British attack was soon broken.

After this loss at Bemis Heights, Burgoyne retreated and Gates was able to surround the British forces. On October 17, Burgoyne surrendered his army at Saratoga. The frontier riflemen had been a decisive factor in this key set of victories that led to the alliance with France a few months later.

Morgan's men now rejoined Washington's army, and they engaged in frequent reconnoitering and skirmishes in late 1777. They endured the hardships at Valley Forge the following winter and sent out numerous patrols during that time. Morgan's biggest problem personally was boredom since he was always eager for action. He was very impressed with Washington and ardently supported him when the strange events known as the Conway Cabal came to light.

In 1778 when British General Henry Clinton left Philadelphia, Morgan harassed the British troops along the road to Monmouth Court House, but he and his men were not in the main battle. Shortly after this he was given command of the 7th Regiment of a brigade and relinquished command of the rifle corps, which was disbanded later in the year. He had temporary command of the entire brigade and did well with the larger responsibilities this gave him. When General William Woodford returned to resume his command, Morgan reverted to the command of his regiment but felt ill at ease with the diminished responsibility. A new corps of light infantry was being formed, and he eagerly sought its command. When Anthony Wayne was instead given this position, Morgan was extremely disappointed and resigned in June 1779. Such resentment over loss of commands was a common problem for the American army throughout the war. It did not, however, signify any lessening of Morgan's support for the American cause. He returned to his farm and family but kept informed as well as possible on military matters. He suffered during these months from an ailment that bothered him for the rest of his life; it was variously described as sciatica and rheumatism.

In June 1780 he received word from Gates that he had been appointed head of the Southern Department of the army and that he wanted Morgan to serve under him. He met Gates and requested a promotion to brigadier general; he then started recruiting troops, but a relapse of his illness delayed his joining with Gates's army. Gates was badly defeated at the Battle of Camden in August, and Morgan decided to leave at once to join his old commander. He was short of money and had to lead an extra horse with him to sell for his traveling expenses. After he arrived, Gates sent him to assist General William Smallwood in harassing the troops of General Charles Cornwallis.

The British had formed two major light units in the South, those troops led by Major Patrick Ferguson, and those led by Lieutenant Colonel Banastre Tarleton. Ferguson's forces were virtually destroyed in October 1780 at King's Mountain, and Morgan thought he might have to face the hated Tarleton. He was known as "bloody Tarleton" for his slaughter of American troops trying to surrender at the Battle of Waxhaws in early 1780. Morgan was promoted to brigadier general in October, and Nathanael Greene arrived in December at Charlotte, North Carolina, as the replacement for Gates, badly discredited by the Camden debacle. Greene gave Morgan an independent command and told him to move southwest below the border of the two Carolinas, acting as he judged appropriate. Morgan recruited local militia, hoping to make his light force superior to that of Tarleton. As the new year opened, the stage was set for one of the most unusual battles in American history.

On January 6, 1781, Colonel Tarleton, leading 1,100 troops, began moving toward Morgan's position in northern South Carolina near an area called the Cowpens. Cornwallis followed Tarleton two days later. Morgan retreated to a position between the Pacolet and Broad rivers with the latter at his back. He had about 1,000 men, including some who had fought against Ferguson's forces at King's Mountain. He arranged his troops in three main lines with the cavalry in reserve at the rear. The first line in front of the cavalry was composed of Continentals and seasoned militia units; they were expected to stand fast under severe attack. The next line, 150 yards down the sloping terrain, was formed of the bulk of militia, led by Andrew Pickens; they were to fire 2 rounds after the British got within 50 yards, aiming especially for the officers. The front line—another 150 yards in advance—was made up of a small body of skirmishers, who were to open a scattered fire before falling back to join the militia. This combined group of skirmishers and militia was to retire in order behind the first line, after their two rounds, and act as additional reserves. Morgan was at his best the night before the attack, going from one group of militiamen to another explaining just what would be required during the battle. The men responded enthusiastically and assured the general they would do what was expected of them.

After marching for over a week, Tarleton had arrived at Morgan's previous camp; he learned of Morgan's retreat toward the Broad River, so he left camp at 3 A.M. on January 17 and moved ahead with his cavalry and infantry, leaving his wagons behind. Four hours later the two armies were in sight of each other, and Tarleton sent his dragoons forward to start the engagement. Morgan's skirmishers shot 15 men out of their saddles, but Tarleton advanced aggressively as his troops discarded much of their gear. Morgan's second line loosed a deadly volley, but the British then launched a bayonet charge. The militia began their retreat, but it broke down somewhat; the American cavalry, led by Lieutenant Colonel William Washington, held off the British horsemen, and the Continentals held firm. Although there was some confusion among the

Americans, they held steady and soon caught the British soldiers in a double envelopment. Washington's cavalry hit the British right flank, and the American militia attacked the enemy's left flank. The Continentals maintained their position and then launched a bayonet charge. Tarleton admitted later that his troops had been thrown into a "panic." They were thoroughly beaten but Tarleton himself escaped, set fire to his wagons, and raced back to rejoin Cornwallis. The British had over 100 killed and over 700 captured while total American casualties were under 80. Morgan's men also captured 2 field-pieces, 35 wagons, 100 horses, and 800 muskets. Tarleton's forces would never again be a decisive factor in the war; Greene was elated when he received word of the Cowpens victory, known as "the tactical masterpiece of the War for Independence." Eventually Greene learned the details of the troop arrangement from Morgan and he used similar tactics at the Battles of Guilford Court House and Eutaw Springs.

But Morgan's immediate problem was to preserve the victory by retreating before the advance of Cornwallis's main army. The Americans moved north quickly, covering 100 miles and crossing two rivers in five days. Cornwallis had started in pursuit on January 19; when he learned of Morgan's route, he destroyed huge quantities of his provisions, burning even his personal possessions. The British spared only salt, ammunition, medical supplies, and four ambulances. The chase was on, but the Americans were equal to the retreat as Morgan and Greene raced toward each other; Greene also directed his men to gather boats along the Dan River between North Carolina and Virginia, for retreat in that direction. The two generals met and just crossed the Yadkin River in front of Cornwallis. Morgan, suffering from rheumatism and hemorrhoids, still managed to lead his force 47 miles in 48 hours. As the combined armies continued the march toward the Dan River, Greene gave Morgan a leave of absence because of his health problems, and he headed home.

Morgan arrived in Frederick County in late February, where rest and cold baths gave him relief from his ailments. He was delighted to learn that Greene did escape from Cornwallis, but he fretted over the southern army and his inability to return to it. Like many soldiers he was strapped for money and wrote to officials for relief at this time. But Morgan always kept these problems in perspective and criticized those men who let them overcome their patriotism and support for the American cause. He even led a local militia unit to suppress a potential uprising in nearby Hampshire County.

His health improved, and he was preparing to rejoin Greene when he received a letter from the Marquis de Lafayette, who warned of an imminent invasion of Virginia by Cornwallis. The "old wagoner" went back into action, raising troops and gathering horses; he left in June to join Lafayette's army. He tried to force another battle with Tarleton but the latter veered away. Ill health again forced his retirement from active campaigning so he was not present at the decisive victory at Yorktown in October. He did take charge of caring for the British prisoners captured there; then, at age 46, he retired to peacetime pursuits.

By now Morgan was a well-respected citizen, and he lived a much quieter life than in his youth; this was apparently caused partly by his friendship with the Reverend Charles M. Thruston. Morgan was able to build a very large home, which he named Saratoga. Like many other soldiers, he argued with Congress over his back pay; he also had to request the medal that had been promised to him for the Cowpens victory. But he urged moderation to officers who protested too much as the war wound down (the Newburgh Addresses). He helped supervise the surveying of land for war veterans and received over 11,000 acres in Kentucky for his war service. He also purchased thousands of additional acres of land. His two daughters married Revolutionary War officers, Presley Neville and James Heard. He doted on his grandchildren (he had 19 or 20) and spent many hours telling them stories of his military activity. He apparently also had an illegitimate son, Willoughby, born in the mid-1780s. His mother is unknown, and Daniel seems to have kept his son's existence secret from his wife and daughters. Willoughby studied law in South Carolina, served in the War of 1812, and rose to the rank of lieutenant colonel.

Daniel Morgan's health continued to bother him in the early 1790s, and he turned down a commission as a brigadier general during the Indian troubles of the 1790s in the Ohio Valley. He remained well informed about political events and was an ardent supporter of President Washington and the Constitution. He identified the emerging Federalist faction with the national government and considered criticism or opposition to it to be the sign of disloyalty and anarchy. Part of the growing opposition came from hostility to national excise taxes; the major problem resulting from this hostility was the Whiskey Rebellion in 1794. Washington finally decided that troops were needed to force compliance with federal laws in western Pennsylvania, and Morgan was put in charge of a light corps from Virginia. While many supported him and the Federalist position, Morgan's political activities were not nearly as popular with people as were his military successes. He had little sympathy for the just complaints of the Pennsylvanians, but he did urge fair treatment and moderation toward the protesters. After the opposition movement collapsed, Morgan was left in charge of the 1,200 troops who remained in western Pennsylvania. He ran for the U.S. House of Representatives in 1795 (while still in command of troops) against Robin Rutherford but lost; his second campaign against the same Republican was successful two years later. He took his seat in the U.S. House of Representatives in May 1797 and supported the Federalist position steadily even though he seldom spoke in the debates.

He created a controversy when he issued orders to leaders of his militia unit to establish regular patrols. These orders were interpreted as attempts to intimidate the growing Republican groups; Morgan was pointedly criticized in the newspapers, and he apparently backed away from further action on this issue. Ill health led to his retirement in 1799, and a false report was circulated that he had died. He did go to live with his daughter in Winchester, where he joined the Presbyterian Church.

Despite the controversy over the Federalist views he held, Daniel Morgan has always been remembered and praised for his military contributions to the successful fight for independence. He had emphasized the thin skirmish line and individual marksmanship, and he had quickly recognized the value of light infantry. He had always treated enlisted men with sympathy and his rise in the officer ranks typified the American spirit and the difference between the European and American systems of promotion in the military. Few, if any, Americans had bettered his record as a battlefield tactician or in combining the peculiar talents of militiamen and partisans with Continental soldiers. And none, except possibly Benedict Arnold, had performed more spectacularly in leading men into action.

In 1801 he made his final will, leaving a large farm to his wife and the balance of his property equally divided between his two daughters. He died at age 66 on July 6, 1802. *See also*: Arnold's March to Quebec; Light Infantry (Continental)

Lawrence R. Borne

REFERENCES

George A. Billias, ed., *George Washington's Generals* (1964); North Callahan, *Rangers of the Revolution* (1961); Joseph F. Folsom, "General Daniel Morgan's Birthplace and Life," *New Jersey Historical Society Proceedings*, 14 (1929):277–92; James Graham, *The Life of General Daniel Morgan of the Virginia Line of the Army of the United States* (1859); Don Higginbotham, *Daniel Morgan: Revolutionary Riflemen* (1961).

Morgan, George (1742–1810)

American Indian agent. Born in Philadelphia in 1742, Morgan had a career as a frontiersman, land speculator, and Indian agent. As a young man he joined the Philadelphia firm of Baynton and Wharton, which specialized in the Indian trade. He became a full partner in 1763, married Baynton's daughter in 1764, and had 11 children with her. Baynton and Wharton lost heavily in Pontiac's War, however, and later went into receivership. As compensation, the firm received a land tract under the Treaty of Fort Stanwix in 1768. This grant provided the basis for establishing the Indiana Company. Morgan became secretary general and superintendent of the new company in 1766. He traveled into the Illinois country in search of trading opportunities, living there for a time and cultivating relations with the Indian tribes.

At the beginning of the Revolution, Congress created three departments, each with its own agent, to oversee relations with the Indians in the North, South, and the middle regions. In April 1776, Morgan was appointed Indian agent for the Middle Department at Fort Pitt. In that position, he worked assiduously and effectively in trying to keep the Delawares and other neighboring tribes neutral. He earned considerable respect among the Indians, and the Delawares honored him with the name Taimenend. He also argued consistently for an expedition to capture Detroit as the center of British influence among the western tribes.

Frustrated and in disagreement with much of congressional policy, Morgan resigned in 1779 and rejoined the Continental Army, where he attained the rank of colonel. At the end of the war he became an important landowner in New Jersey, settled in Princeton, and became a trustee of Princeton University. He was involved in several western land ventures after the Revolution and died in 1810.

Colin G. Calloway

REFERENCES

Randolph C. Downes, *Council Fires on the Upper Ohio* (1940); ———, "George Morgan, Indian Agent Extraordinary, 1776–1779," *Pennsylvania History* 1 (1934):202–216.

Morgan, John (1735–1789)

Continental Army physician. Born in Philadelphia, Morgan had a Welsh father who was a prosperous shopkeeper and landowner, and a Quaker mother. Information about young John's early schooling is unavailable, but it is recorded that in 1745 he was enrolled in the Reverend Samuel Finley's school in West Nottingham, Pennsylvania. In 1750 Morgan began his medical apprenticeship to Dr. John Redman, one of Philadelphia's foremost preceptors. Morgan learned to treat injuries to the bodily extremities, assisted in surgery, compounded drugs, and read the medical classics in his master's library. In March 1755 the bright Morgan was appointed apothecary to the Pennsylvania Hospital, the first such health care institution in North America, and in 1756 he earned his B.A. at the College of Philadelphia. Anxious to further his medical experience, Morgan enlisted in the Pennsylvania militia in 1756 and served as an ensign-surgeon, and later as a lieutenant, in several frontier posts in western Pennsylvania until 1760.

Like Dr. William Shippen, Jr., and other future medical luminaries from Pennsylvania such as Benjamin Rush, Morgan wished to enhance his scientific knowledge overseas. With letters of recommendation, Morgan sailed to England in May 1760. In London he became a hospital pupil at St. Thomas's, and he attended the lectures of Dr. William Hunter, the leading anatomist of the day. Hence Morgan had a solid background for future study—a classical education, an apprenticeship, hospital observation, along with laboratory dissection. He pursued advanced training at the University of Edinburgh, which probably had the best medical faculty in Europe. Here Morgan had classes in anatomy, chemistry, biology, and in the theory and practice of medicine by some of the great physicians located in the "Athens of the North." Morgan supplemented his classroom learning by "walking the wards" in the Royal Infirmary in Edinburgh. Thoroughly enjoying Edinburgh's cultural advantages, Morgan, who graduated with his M.D. in July 1762, began to formulate plans to raise the level of the medical profession at home. After making the Grand Tour of the Continent (1762–1764) and meeting some of Europe's medical and scientific elite, including the renowned Voltaire, Morgan returned to London in November 1764. Recognized in the medical community for his brilliance, Morgan was already the recipient of many honors—a correspondent of the Royal Academy of Surgery in Paris, a Fellow of the Royal Society, and a licentiate of the Royal College of Physicians of London, among others.

Departing for home in 1764, Morgan was determined to establish a medical school in Philadelphia, and he envisioned himself as its first professor. In England he had discussed his plans with Shippen. Shippen had offered anatomical lectures in the Quaker City (1762), and in 1765 his private classes on obstetrics and prenatal care constituted the first such instruction in America. But Shippen was not a skillful organizer compared to his more energetic and flamboyant colleague, Morgan. In May 1765 Morgan was elected to be professor of materia medica by the trustees of the College of Philadelphia at its budding medical school, but Morgan had deliberately slighted Shippen in planning the school and the curriculum. But Shippen's remarkable talents could not be overlooked, so he was appointed professor of anatomy at the fledgling school. Now the professional rivalry between the two intensified, for the haughty Morgan in his famous *Discourse* (1765) staked his claim as leader of the colonies' medical world. Hence the medical school opened in December 1765 with tense relationships between the two professors, who both wanted credit for founding the medical school (attached to the College of Philadelphia). Degrees in medicine, the bachelor's and the doctorate, were authorized. Shippen taught anatomy, and Morgan lectured on pharmacology and the theory and practice of medicine. For several years

Morgan and Shippen comprised the faculty until Adam Kuhn was appointed professor of botany, and Dr. Benjamin Rush professor of chemistry. Hence there were four professors compared to the seven medical professors at Edinburgh. Theoretical classroom instruction was supplemented in December 1766 by the practical instruction offered by Dr. Thomas Bond, who offered clinical instruction to pupils who followed him on his rounds of the Pennsylvania Hospital. The commencement in June 1768 of the first ten medical graduates from a North American institution was a significant event. Both Morgan and Shippen merited praise for their vision and dedication, but their competition for prestige seemed insatiable.

Morgan continued his distinguished teaching career and maintained a private practice to late 1775. A man of diversified interests, he was active in Philadelphia's cultural activities, won a prize for an essay on politics, read scientific papers, organized the Philadelphia Medical Society, and was active in the American Society of Philadelphia (both societies merged with the American Philosophical Society in 1768). Morgan was also interested in art, cultivating the silkworm, and broadening the base of iron production in late colonial America. Clearly, Morgan seemed destined to be one of America's great men of science and letters.

On July 25,1775, the Continental Congress appointed Dr. Benjamin Church, a prominent Boston physician, as director general of the Medical Department. In time, Church might have been able to shape his office into an efficient organization. However, he was soon disgraced and dismissed. Since early 1765 Church had been suspected of being a spy for General Thomas Gage, the British commander. Removed from his position in October, Church was tried, convicted, and exiled for treason.

To replace Church, Congress selected Morgan. Arriving at Cambridge on November 29, Morgan was challenged by the task of organizing hospitals, acquiring supplies, and improving the morale of his personnel. A haughty man, Morgan complicated his problems by antagonizing generals, delegates, and regimental surgeons. To his credit he appealed to the public for surgical dressings, he collected quantities of drugs, and he examined candidates for surgeoncies. Morgan's supervision of the inoculation of Patriot troops at the siege of Boston provided a model for the mass inoculation of soldiers the following year, to ward off smallpox, for the entire army.

After the British evacuation of Boston in March 1776, Washington moved his forces to protect New York City from an anticipated enemy attack that summer. Morgan shifted his staff to Manhattan, where again he displayed energy and imagination in anticipating medical needs. He forwarded stocks of drugs from New England to Manhattan, advertised for nurses and hospital orderlies, maintained careful accounting procedures, devised hospital diets, wrote instructions about the treatment of wounds, and attempted to explain his procedures to the military and to politicians. Morgan also established general hospitals in Manhattan at King's College (now Columbia University), the City Hospital, the Workhouse, the Exchange, and in vacated Loyalist homes in the Bowery.

Though the army had the experience of the British campaign with respect to preventive medicine, the officers were invariably uninformed about the ramifications of disease for their troops, particularly with respect to hygiene and sanitation. Furthermore, Morgan's arrangement for the treatment of casualties during combat had been virtually untested at Boston. Thus measures to shift staff quickly during combat and provisions to transfer casualties to the rear were incomplete.

Morgan's greatest difficulty, however, was with regimental surgeons, many of whom were poorly trained. Some were mere apprentices. Some surgeons fabricated medical excuses from duty for their townsmen; others falsified their records or never even reported the numbers of sick in their regiments to Morgan. In contrast to Morgan's instructions, regimental surgeons frequently detained the seriously ill in regimental hospitals instead of transferring them to Morgan's general hospitals. They complained to colonels and to Congress about Morgan's supposedly stingy disbursement of drugs and equipment. The temperamental Morgan castigated them as "unlettered, ignorant, crude to a degree scarcely to be imagined. Some of them have [never] seen an operation of surgery."

After the succession of American defeats from Long Island to White Plains, Washington crossed to the west side of the Hudson River. Dividing his army to hold Connecticut and the Hudson Highlands, he marched with the bat-tered remainder to New Jersey with the British close behind. During the retreat, Morgan's organization almost disintegrated. Some regiments lacked surgeons some untreated wounded actually bled to death. Morgan operated on casualties, he organized the evacuation of the sick from Long Island to Manhattan and then to New Jersey. He seemed to be everywhere—dispensing drugs, visiting patients, and establishing hospitals in whatever buildings were available. By mid-September, Morgan found sanctuaries for 1,000 patients at Hoboken and Weehawken. But when these centers were threatened by the fall of Fort Lee in November, Morgan had to move his sick to Hackensack. The flow of sick and wounded continued to inundate his temporary facilities and his overburdened staff. Again Morgan had to dispense his patients to Amboy, Elizabeth, Brunswick, Trenton, and Morristown. Threatened by invasion, New Jersey could not shelter all the casualties, so some 500 patients ended up at Fishkill and Peekskill on the Hudson; another 2,000 at Norwich and Stamford, Connecticut.

In such confusion the medical director was invariably blamed for defects in the handling of casualties. But Morgan was not at fault. Some nurses and orderlies fled; some regimental surgeons deserted. Desperate to evacuate Hoboken as the British neared, Morgan discovered that some panic-stricken militia had carried off every cart and wagon in the area. Even finding accommodations for his patients was difficult because some communities—fearing contagion and loss of property—protested vigorously about potential seizures of local houses for the troops.

During the retreat to the Delaware, Morgan faced still another problem—the emergence of Shippen, his archrival who challenged his authority. In July, Congress appointed Shippen as director of the flying camp in New Jersey. Shippen proceeded to organize facilities in Paramus, Fort Lee, Elizabeth, Perth Amboy, Trenton, and Brunswick. Confident that he could oust Morgan as director, Shippen began a crafty campaign to humiliate his old enemy. Dissatisfied with Morgan's performance, and deluged with complaints, Congress again reduced his power. It split Morgan's jurisdiction by restricting his authority to hospitals east of the Hudson and by authorizing Shippen to supervise hospitals west of the Hudson. As the American army retired through New Jersey in December, both doctors competed for staff, supplies, and hospital quarters; furthermore, they refused to assist each other in the crisis. Without even notifying Morgan, in late December the Medical Committee of Congress proposed that hospitals be established in Philadelphia and Bethlehem, Pennsylvania, under the authority of Pennsylvania's Committee of Public Safety. By then, Morgan was assailed on all sides as surgeons, generals, and delegates clamored for his removal. Arriving in Philadelphia on December 9, Morgan discovered that he had no staff, that Congress had fled to Baltimore, and that Washington was unwilling to enter into the dispute. By late December, as wagonloads of sick entered Philadelphia, Washington requested members of the clergy and local officials to find them quarters. In fact, when Washington prepared for his daring raid on Trenton in late December, he barely kept Morgan informed of developments.

After his victories at Trenton and Princeton, and during the winter cantonment at Morristown in 1776–1777, Washington pondered the need to improve the army. The Medical Department obviously needed new leadership, for Morgan was completely discredited. He was rebuked by scores of critics for excessive sickness rates, mistreatment of patients, corruption in the department, and for the demoralized condition of some regiments. Yet Morgan had been assigned a difficult task, and under the circumstances he had performed capably and professionally. But Morgan was targeted as the inevitable scapegoat. Without holding an inquiry into his conduct or providing Morgan with the opportunity the defend himself publicly, on January 9, 1777, Congress curtly dismissed him.

As part of the reorganization of the Medical Department, Shippen was appointed director general on April 11, 1777. Shippen administered the department in virtually the same fashion of his predecessor. Shippen deserves praise for supervising the inoculation of Washington's new troops in the spring of 1777. But in the Northern Department credit for the medical arrangements at Saratoga, New York, where General John Burgoyne's British army fought the Americans under General Horatio Gates, went to Dr. Jonathan Potts, the deputy director general of the Northern Department. His staff won the only commendation bestowed on medical men by Congress in the entire war.

Now it was Shippen's turn to feel the wrath of criticism. Shippen did not have sufficient wag-ons, stretcher-bearers, equipment, or emergency centers for pending battles. As a result, at Brandywine (September 11), and at Germantown (October 4), along with heavy casualties resulting from the defiant American defensive of the Delaware fortresses, medical facilities were overwhelmed with sick and wounded men. Virtually the same problems that had hampered Morgan in 1776 now impeded Shippen's attempts to ameliorate the plight of stricken soldiers. Because of the fluid nature of the campaign, the large number of casualties, and the lack of sanitation, the handling of the hospital was a disaster that autumn and winter. And to add to the difficulties confronting the medical staff was the fact that diseases—typhus, dysentery, and perhaps typhoid—struck the army hospitals located at some nine towns in Pennsylvania. Complaints about shortages of provisions, bedding, blankets, fuel, drugs, and clothing filled the pages of contemporary records, and the Medical Department was castigated again for contributing to the high incidence of sickness and death.

To such complaints, Shippen, who was handicapped by the near disintegration of the Quartermaster and Commissary Departments, acknowledged that the patients suffered needlessly, but he insisted that the fault was not his. Under a torrent of criticism for his supposedly inept, inhuman, and dishonest directorship, Shippen was subject to a congressional inquiry. In late January 1778 a congressional committee heard testimony from Shippen, Rush (who was emerging as Shippen's harshest critic), and other army doctors. Yet Shippen had Washington's confidence, he had influential friends in Congress, Rush lacked specific evidence about Shippen's supposed peculation, and the delegates hesitated to recommend measures that would embroil the department in further controversy. Thus, Shippen kept his job. The only major change was that Potts was named purveyor general of the Middle Department in an effort to improve the flow of hospital supplies. But henceforth the Medical Department would be regarded with suspicion and requests for money to operate the Department were intensely scrutinized. When Shippen submitted his budget in 1779, Congress halved it.

Now Rush, determined to hound his former professor from office, sought testimony and affidavits about Shippen's administration. In his effort to discredit Shippen, Rush was assisted by

Morgan, who also had been gathering evidence about his old rival.

Meanwhile at the Valley Forge hospital the medical staff made valiant efforts to maintain and to improve the health of the troops. But the credit went to men like Potts, William Brown, James Craik, Andrew Craigie, John Cochran, Samuel Kennedy, and Samuel Tilton, along with the invigorated Quartermaster Department under General Nathanael Greene. Shippen seemed to be totally involved in "paperwork." Even medical preparations for Monmouth in June 1778 were again uncoordinated. Shippen certainly knew a battle was pending, but, understandably, he was uncertain about where to locate army hospitals. And at the winter encampment at Morristown in the brutal winter of 1778–1779, men like Tilton and Cochran, not Shippen, won praise from the officers.

By 1780 the morale of the Medical Department was very low due to Shippen's hardship, to a two-year delay in back pay, and because medical officers were not given the same pension and land bounty benefits provided by Congress to line officers. Overshadowing such personnel matters was another congressional investigation underway about Shippen and the renewal of the Morgan-Shippen feud. Since his dismissal in 1777, Morgan attempted repeatedly to have Congress exonerate his conduct as medical director. After innumerable delays, a congressional committee investigated the matter and recommended that Morgan be exonerated. On June 18, 1779, Congress resolved that Morgan had "vindicated his conduct in every respect."

Now that his name was cleared, Morgan could pursue Shippen with a vengeance. He had Shippen formally charged with malpractice and misconduct, and he requested Congress to investigate the charges and to bring Shippen to trial. During the winter of 1779–1780 both Morgan and Shippen trudged through snowy Pennsylvania to gather depositions and potential witnesses. In the process they hurled such insults at each other that the venomous dispute demoralized the shaken Medical Department. Under the circumstances, Shippen had little time to supervise the department, his influence with Congress plummeted, budgetary requests were pigeonholed, and Cochran became de facto head of the department. On January 15, 1780, Washington ordered a court-martial of Shippen at Morristown. Shippen was charged on five counts.

The case began on March 14, and for several months some 60 medical men testified on behalf of Shippen or Morgan.

Morgan paraded his witnesses at Morristown until May 15. Then after a recess Shippen opened his defense in June. The five charges were trimmed to two—peculation and neglect of duty. (Apparently Shippen enriched himself by selling wine and sugar to the public from army hospital stores.) Whether he was actually indifferent to the suffering of his patients was difficult to ascertain. The court acquitted Shippen of all charges but labeled his conduct with respect to peculation in hospital stores as "highly improper and jointly reprehensible." Washington forwarded the verdict of the military court to Congress. In August, Congress voted to acquit Shippen, yet retained the same criticisms of his conduct held by the Morristown court. Though Morgan was indignant over the leniency of Congress, he finally had his victory, for what it was worth. Shippen's days as director general were numbered, and on June 3, 1787, he resigned, to be replaced by Cochran on October 6, 1781.

Inasmuch as Shippen's resignation tended to confirm Morgan's charges, Morgan saw fit to resume the vendetta by publishing another vitriolic pamphlet about his opponent. But the public was weary of this incessant bickering, and the controversy had exhausted the energies of both men. Morgan never recovered the vigor, brilliance, and imagination displayed in his previous years. His great days as leader of America's doctors were over; his career was virtually wrecked in this tragic and disgraceful episode that demeaned the medical profession. *See also:* Medicine, Military

Richard L. Blanco

REFERENCES

Whitfield J. Bell, Jr., *John Morgan. Continental Doctor* (1965); Richard L. Blanco, *Physician of the American Revolution. Jonathan Potts* (1979).

Morris, Gouverneur (1752–1816)

American statesman. Morris was born on January 31, 1752, at Morrisania, New York, the son of Lewis Morris, Jr., and his second wife Sarah Gouverneur. Gouverneur Morris had three stepbrothers, one stepsister, two older and two younger sisters. His family, large landholders, enjoyed high social and political status in pro-

vincial New Jersey and New York. Morris graduated from King's College (Columbia University
today) in 1768, then was admitted to the bar in
1771, and subsequently built a successful law
practice in New York City. Though at first he
had hoped for reconciliation with Great Britain,
as the Revolutionary crisis grew and though his
mother was a Loyalist and his half-brother Staats
Morris was a general in the British army,
Gouverneur sided with the Patriot cause. He sat
in the New York Provincial Congress (1775–
1777), supported the actions of the Continental
Congress, and helped draft the state constitution of New York in 1776–1777. Morris represented New York in the Continental Congress
in the years 1778 and 1779. He arrived at the
Continental Congress to relieve James Duane as
a delegate on January 20, 1778, when Congress
was meeting in York, Pennsylvania—moving
there in September 1777 in response to the threat
against Philadelphia from British general William Howe's army. During his attendance as a
New York delegate, the bulk of Morris's time
was spent in financial affairs, military matters,
and foreign relations.

On his first day of attendance he and Charles
Carroll of Carrollton, Maryland, were chosen as
additional members of a committee to consult
with George Washington, at Valley Forge, on
reorganization of the army. Originally, the members of the Board of War were to form the committee; but, since General Horatio Gates refused
to go to Valley Forge, Congress decided to exempt the other members of the board from duty
on the Committee, and elected Carroll and
Morris to replace Gates, Thomas Mifflin, and
Timothy Pickering. In this capacity, Morris spent
much time from January 24 into April 1778 consulting with Washington. He was one of the most
active and influential members of the Committee at Camp, which included Francis Dana, Joseph Reed, Nathaniel Folsom, and John Harvie.
Carroll did not attend, having returned home
because of his wife's illness.

Congress gave the committee wide duties related to its consultation with Washington. It was
to plan to redo the number of regiments in Continental service; to provide a list of meritorious
officers presently in service who could not be
connected with the regiments to be retained in
the new Continental military establishment; to
recommend to Congress needed appointments
of general officers; to remove officers in the civil

departments of the army for misconduct, inefficiency, or incompetence; and to appoint others
to replace them. The committee was to solve all
just causes for complaint about rank and to report to Congress their opinion concerning
needed reinforcements of the cavalry, infantry,
and artillery and how to obtain these reinforcements as well as to report what changes in the
regulations of army departments that would promote economies, discipline, and improved morale.

As a consequence of its tasks to review civil
departments for misconduct, inefficiency, and
incompetence, just four days after arriving in
camp, January 28, the committee wrote to Congress about the disastrous disarray of the Quartermaster Department: an audit called for the
removal of Quartermaster General Thomas
Mifflin, the committee recommending the appointment of Philip Schuyler in his place. This
nomination did not get through Congress, but
Mifflin was removed, and on March 2, 1778, as
newly suggested by the Committee at Camp,
Nathanael Greene was appointed quartermaster
general with Colonel John Cox and Charles
Pettit named Greene's assistants. Greene was
successful bringing order to procurement in time
to provide for the army at winter camp in
Morristown in 1780 when weather conditions
were much worse than at Valley Forge.

In a letter to the president of Congress, Henry
Laurens, dated February 5, 1778, the committee
put forth its proposals for reorganizing the army,
reducing the number of battalions, and reinforcing the cavalry, infantry, and artillery. Written
by Joseph Reed and signed by Francis Dana, the
original draft of this report was in Morris's hand.
The committee proposed a reduction of rank
and file in each battalion from 692 to 553 men
with 29 commissioned officers. The soldiers were
to be formed into nine companies, one of which
would be a company of light infantry. The 139-
man difference in each battalion would help fill
up the cavalry and artillery battalions. This plan
also included pay scales and rations for officers—the reduction in numbers producing a cost
saving relative to the old arrangements of $1,221
pay per month and 4,950 rations per month.
With a total of 4 artillery and 4 cavalry battalions and 90 battalions of infantry, the reorganized army would include 53,822 noncommissioned officers and men.

The plan was read in Congress on February

16. On February 26, Congress accepted the committee's general proposals, but delayed action on the details until the committee had returned from camp. On March 3, the committee wrote President Laurens a letter proposing the establishment of a corps of engineers and artificers amounting to two battalions of eight companies each with 100 men and officers in each company. The officers of this corps were to be skilled in mathematics, and the corps duties were to repair works damaged by enemy fire and to build new works. The committee admitted that forming a corps of engineers was as important as any of the other elements in their earlier proposal; but, at the time of their first report, they were not fully agreed on the matter. This letter was written by Morris and signed by Dana.

The committee's plan, revised to include an engineering department, was laid before Congress on May 18. It was debated for a number of days, and then on May 27 it was adopted without significant changes. Putting this reorganization into effect, however, took months. On July 9, Congress ordered Joseph Reed and Francis Dana to Washington's headquarters to complete the details of the new arrangements. In August, Roger Sherman and John Banister were added to this committee, but it was not until November 24 that the reorganization of the army was completed.

In order to encourage his veteran officers to remain in service, Washington had proposed to the Committee at Camp that Congress establish half-pay pensions for life for the Continental Army officers. Morris, in complete agreement with this approach, led the arguments in its favor on the floor of Congress. Substantial opposition to a peacetime military interest, however, blocked the life pensions in a vote on May 13; then on May 15 Congress compromised with a plan for half-pay pensions for seven years.

Concerning Morris's role in foreign affairs, on April 20, 1778, Congress formed a committee with Morris at its head to deal with Lord Frederick North's proposals for reconciliation between America and Great Britain. North, aware that America and France were close to completing a military alliance and also aware of what this portended for the Revolutionary War, proposed permitting American states to tax themselves and sending commissioners to America to negotiate a reconciliation. Congress regarded this to be a snare, and Morris was to point this out.

On April 22, Congress approved the committee's address on the subject, largely written by Morris, and called for its publication. The address first appeared in the *Pennsylvania Gazette* on April 24, then in pamphlet form as *Observations of the American Revolution*, published in 1779 and 1780. Morris's related *Address of the Congress to the Inhabitants of the United States*, published in 1778, was a commentary on the significance of the French alliance. In May, with Roger Sherman and Richard Henry Lee, Morris helped formulate the initial instructions to American peace commissioners. On September 14, 1778, Morris was chosen chairman of a committee to prepare a draft of instructions to Benjamin Franklin, minister plenipotentiary at the court of France. In the course of developing these instructions, Morris took it upon himself to consult with the French minister Conrad Alexandre Gerard in order to insure that the goals would be satisfactory to both nations.

Because of Morris's opposition to Governor George Clinton's policies, specifically with regard to land claims in Vermont, the New York State Legislature refused, in August 1779, to reelect him to another term in Congress. Consequently, Morris moved to Philadelphia, becoming a citizen of Pennsylvania, and embarked on a new phase in his Revolutionary War career. There, in February, March, and April 1780, he published remarkable essays on public finance under the pen name "An American." These essays brought his thinking to the attention of Robert Morris (no kin), who in February 1781 was to enter public office as superintendent of finance, or, in other words, as the first treasurer of the United States.

Gouverneur Morris's understanding of public finance and his nationalism were great contributions to the American Revolution and American history. On July 4, 1781, Robert Morris described the problems facing him as the head of the Department of Finance:

> The Derangement of our Money Affairs. The Enormity of our public Expenditures. The Confusion in all our Departments. The Languour of our general System. The complexity and consequent Inefficacy of our Operations. These are some, among the many, Reasons which have induced Congress to the Appointment of a Superintendent of Finance.

The new American republic had been locked for six years in a terrible and costly international struggle with the greatest military power in the world. The lowest year of the war was 1780, when the cause seemed doomed: Arnold had defected, troops mutinied, Congress officially had to admit that the Continental currency was worthless, and Horatio Gates's monumental defeat at Camden indicated the British could occupy the entire South. This low point in America's struggle stimulated steps to put new life into the war effort by tightening the Continental administration through replacement of congressional boards with single-headed executive departments, the primary one being the Office of Finance.

The superintendent, Robert Morris, was joined in that office by his alter ego, the witty and ebullient Gouverneur Morris. Wit and humor, in fact, was one of his contributions to the Revolutionary debate and history. Gouverneur's cultivated and individualistic intelligence complemented the financier's practical experience. He spoke French fluently as well and served as translator for the Finance Office. Doubling as the superintendent's cryptographer, he persuaded the Office of Foreign Affairs to discard the scrambled codes it had previously used for those of his own design. Numbers apparently held a special interest for him; he used them when devising new ciphers, spotted them throughout the proposals for American coinage he devised during the 1780s, and plotted annuity tables with them while Congress was considering pensions for Continental Army officers during the winter of 1782–1783. Gouverneur drafted many of the superintendent's letters and reports—the plan for establishing the Bank of North America (the quasi-national bank that became America's first commercial bank), the proposal for a mint and decimal coinage, and the seminal report on public credit. Gouverneur even composed communications of an intensely personal nature. "I could do nothing without him," Robert Morris told John Jay in 1783. Gouverneur's service in the Office of Finance ended on November 1, 1784, when the office was eliminated to be replaced by a revived Board of Treasury in 1785.

In collaboration with his friend, fellow governmental official, and intellectual mate, Robert Morris, Gouverneur developed a fiscal program and institutions intended to strengthen the federal government and to assert, ultimately, its superior authority over the state governments. Gouverneur, like Robert, conceived of America united in grandeur when most Americans thought of the interests on a local, state, or regional level. Though the program they devised in 1781–1782 collapsed in 1783 when local-oriented politicians refused to provide Congress with firm revenues in the form of import duties, it came to life again in the constitutional movement and in Hamilton's fiscal policies presented in his four treasury reports of 1790–1791.

In the Philadelphia Constitutional Convention of 1787 no one contributed more to the final product than Gouverneur Morris, and only Madison and James Wilson contributed as much. As Madison told Jared Sparks in 1831, the wording of the Constitution's final draft was Morris's. Though it cannot be documented, it seems likely, considering Morris's views and language power, that he was aware he was providing for enhancement of the national government's sphere when he wrote the so-called "elastic" and "contract" clauses. In addition, he reformulated the wording of the preamble stating the purposes of the Constitution by eliminating mention of the people as citizens of the various states, wording the Committee on Detail had requested, and by naming the people as the true sovereign, thereby reinforcing a principle that was certainly new under the sun.

That the United States adopted a decimal system of coinage should be attributed jointly to Gouverneur Morris and Thomas Jefferson. Morris proposed a decimal system of currency on January 15, 1782. In 1785, Jefferson took Morris's report, revised Morris's structure of coinage, and succeeded in getting Congress to adopt the plan; but, the idea of introducing a decimal system originated, Jefferson concurring, with Morris.

Morris has been marked as an arch conservative by the Beard-Becker school of American historians, predominant in the twentieth century between the wars, who tended to place nationalists of the Revolutionary era on the social-political right. In Gouverneur's case, this characterization resists revision stubbornly. That Morris was cynical, and unimpressed by the judgment of the average person is true. He also leaned toward strengthening executive government. Nevertheless, he was a major figure among a group of men who devised a system of government that, if it had roots in the past and in the

British constitution, was also extraordinarily new and historically unprecedented. Morris, in addition, was a civil libertarian. His argument for religious toleration and opposition to a special oath for Roman Catholics in the state constitutional convention of New York, 1776, was successful. His effort there to get the delegates to abolish slavery constitutionally, failed. He remained steadfast in his opposition to slavery, however. Years later on the floor of the Philadelphia Convention he offered a searing indictment of black slavery that carried far beyond its political ramifications into its morality.

> Upon what principle is it that the slaves shall be computed in the representation? Are they men? Then make them Citizens and let them vote. Are they property? Why then is no other property included? The Houses in this City are worth more than all the wretched slaves which cover the rice swamps of South Carolina. The admission of slaves into the Representation when fairly explained comes to this: that the inhabitant of Georgia and South Carolina who goes to the Coast of Africa, and in defiance of the most sacred laws of humanity tears away his fellow creatures from their dearest connections and damns them to the most cruel bondages, shall have more votes in a Government instituted for protection of the rights of mankind, than the Citizen of Pennsylvania and New Jersey who views with a laudable horror, so nefarious a practice.

This statement placed Gouverneur Morris among a growing number of persons in the Atlantic community of the eighteenth century that were morally outraged by slave labor systems. Partly for this reason and partly because of a commitment to traditional republican doubts about sustaining civic virtue in an expansive, culturally heterogeneous society, Morris, at the time of the peace negotiations, opposed acquisition of western lands. Historians have marked his opposition as representing the outlook of an Eastern mercantile reactionary unsympathetic with popular aspirations, but the heart of his concern was much more complex. He feared that empty western land open for migration would result in eventual disunion.

That the individualistic Morris, hardly socially rigid and certainly libertarian, detesting slavery, should be labeled conservative is misleading; it points up the simplified nature of such classifications when dealing with the American Revolutionary generation. Backward-looking values, which Morris shared, side by side with modern and liberal ones, permeated American republican thinking. Like the minds of the other founders, but probably to an even greater degree, his was an intriguing intellectual mixture of classic ideas and daring new principles and expectations.

In 1789 Morris traveled to Europe, to reside usually in France, as a business associate of Robert Morris. In 1790–1791, Washington sent him on a special mission to London in order to establish the groundwork for diplomatic ties and commercial agreement between the two nations. In 1792, Washington appointed him United States minister to France replacing Thomas Jefferson, who had returned home to fill the Cabinet post of foreign secretary. Morris resided in Paris, the only foreign envoy to remain there during The Terror, until 1794 when the French government requested his recall. He then traveled about Europe and Scotland, returning to New York in 1798. From 1800 to 1803, he served one term as a Federalist senator from New York. On December 25, 1809, he married the much younger Anne Cary Randolph, sister of Thomas Mann Randolph of Virginia. He was a canal commissioner of the state and supporter of the construction of the Erie Canal (1810–1813). He opposed the War of 1812 and, initially, sided with the extreme secessionists in the antiwar and states' rights Hartford Convention. Morris's son, Gouverneur, was born in February 1813. Morris died on November 6, 1816, at Morrisania, New York. *See also:* Nationalist Movement

Nelson S. Dearmont

REFERENCES

E. James Ferguson, John Catanzariti, Elizabeth M. Nuxoll, Mary A. Y. Gallagher, Nelson S. Dearmont, et al., eds., *The Papers of Robert Morris*, 7 vols. (1973–); Mary-Jo Kline, *Gouverneur Morris and the New Nation, 1775–1788* (1978); Andre Mauron, *Adrienne: The Life of the Marquise de La Fayette*, trans. by Gerard Hopkins (1961); Max M. Mintz, *Gouverneur Morris and the American Revolution* (1970); Paul H. Smith, et al., eds. *Letters of Delegates to Congress, 1774–1789*, 16 vols. (1975); Daniel Welthur, *Gouverneur Morris, Witness to Two Revolutions*, trans. by Elionore Deniston (1934).

Morris, Robert (1734–1806)

American statesman. Robert Morris is known primarily by his title "The Financier of the American Revolution," a reference both to his position as superintendent of finance of the United States from 1781 to 1784 and to his general role in raising money and supplies for the Continental government. He has many other claims to fame, however, and a few of notoriety. He was one of only two Founding Fathers to sign all three fundamental testaments of the American Revolution: the Declaration of Independence, the Articles of Confederation, and the United States Constitution. In the line of succession that includes Alexander Hamilton and Albert Gallatin, Morris may be considered the first of the three great Treasury secretaries who laid the financial foundations of the United States. He was also a powerful committee chairman in the Continental Congress, the first senator from Pennsylvania, an important figure in Pennsylvania politics, and one of the most prominent businessmen of his day. A bold and shrewd entrepreneur, and a forceful and energetic organizer and administrator, Morris exerted his greatest power during the earliest and then in the closing years of the War of Independence.

Born in Liverpool, England, January 31, 1734/1735 (1734 old style, 1735 new style), Robert Morris was the son of Robert Morris, a merchant, and Elizabeth Murphat, about whom nothing is known. In 1747 he arrived in America to join his father, by then a tobacco agent at Oxford, Maryland. Sent to Philadelphia for education and training under the care of Robert Greenway, he was apprenticed in 1748 in the mercantile house of Charles Willing of Philadelphia. In 1750 he inherited a moderate estate upon his father's accidental death. After undertaking various merchant voyages to the West Indies in 1756 and 1757, he became a partner of Thomas Willing in the firm of Willing and Morris. Marrying Mary White in 1769, he fathered seven children between 1769 and 1784.

Morris's involvement with the Revolutionary movement began in 1765 when he was among the merchants who opposed the Stamp Act and signed the nonimportation agreement. By 1775, Morris, as the active partner of Willing and Morris, was an export-import merchant with a far-flung international network of correspondents in Europe and the West Indies. Once he threw in his lot with the American Revolution,

he expanded his network still further and integrated it into the war effort. He was appointed vice president of the Council of Safety by the Pennsylvania Assembly and served as chairman of the subcommittee organizing the state's defense measures. On November 3, 1775, he was elected to the Second Continental Congress, serving until 1778. In August 1776 Morris signed the Declaration of Independence after initially disapproving the measure as premature.

Morris soon became Congress' chief commercial and financial agent. In 1775 and 1776 his firm received large contracts for importing war material for Congress and several states. As chairman of the Secret Committee of Trade, and an active member of the Committee of Secret Correspondence (later the Foreign Affairs Committee) and the Marine Committee, he was responsible for administering the Continental Congress' international procurement operations as well as much of its other international financial and naval affairs. In December 1776 he headed the congressional executive committee, which remained in Philadelphia during Congress' flight from the city. Dissolving his firm and leaving his partner Thomas Willing behind in Philadelphia during the British occupation of that city in 1777 and 1778, Morris sojourned at Mannheim, Pennsylvania, where, having obtained a leave of absence from Congress, he sought to straighten out the by then controversial and entangled Secret Committee accounts. Rarely attending Congress during its stay in York, Morris nevertheless served on the important committee to army headquarters appointed in November 1777, which sought to resolve the army's administrative and supply problems. In March 1778 he was among those who signed the Articles of Confederation.

During these years Morris and his wife, Mary White Morris, also assumed the social and diplomatic function of introducing foreign officers, merchants, and diplomats into American society, a role that they continued to play throughout the war. Their homes were social centers famous for tasteful furnishings and lavish entertaining.

Unlike many republicans of his day, Morris saw no inherent conflict between public and private interest, or between business and government. Nor did he see public and private interest as always and inevitably one and the same. At least when in office, he generally gave higher priority to public than to private good. Nevertheless, he had little faith in the prevalence of disinterested public virtue. Rather in all his dealings he sought mutuality or reciprocity of interest by bargaining or by contracts or by tying private interest to that of the public through various incentives. Morris's complex mixture of public and private affairs contributed greatly to the success of the war effort. Nevertheless, the potential conflict of interest was so great and so offensive to the ideology of "Republican Virtue" that he was subject to widespread public criticism and frequent investigation. This was particularly true during the partisan conflicts known collectively as the Deane-Lee affair, during which Morris's transactions with Silas Deane in Paris and his Secret Committee operations generally came under public scrutiny. During this period Morris also became a leader of Pennsylvania's "Republicans" or "Anticonstitutionalists," who sought to revise what they considered the excessively democratic or radical Pennsylvania Constitution. His conspicuous wealth and his party role, particularly his public opposition to depreciating paper money, price fixing, embargoes, and other economic controls, contributed to his investigation in July 1779 by a city price-regulation committee and to the mob action against Morris and his friends known as the "Fort Wilson Riot" of October 1779. Although no charges were proven against him, his reputation was somewhat tarnished during the period, and he acquired many inveterate opponents, particularly Arthur Lee and his friends, whose enmity was to follow him throughout his career.

From 1778 to 1781, ineligible for reelection to Congress under the terms of the Pennsylvania State Constitution, Morris served in the Pennsylvania Assembly and expanded his private business, especially in privateering and provisioning the French army and navy. By 1781 he had amassed such wealth and established such credit that he became the logical candidate for the superintendent of the Office of Finance, one of several executive departments established in the aftermath of military defeats in the South and the collapse of the Continental currency.

Until Morris could institutionalize the financial structures and the credit practices essential to restoring and preserving public credit, he placed his own personal credit and reputation as a merchant at the disposal of the United States Government. "My personal Credit, which thank Heaven I have preserved throughout all the tempests of the War, has been substituted for that which the Country lost," Morris declared in January 1782. "I am now striving to transfer that Credit to the Public and if I can regain for the United States the Confidence of Individuals so as that they will trust their property and exertions in the hands of Government, our Independence and Success are certain but without that Confidence we are nothing."

To finance the Yorktown campaign and for other public purposes, the financier began to issue "Morris's notes." Originally carrying no indication of public responsibility for their redemption, these notes circulated widely, in part because they were receivable for many taxes and because Morris could employ government revenues to redeem them. Morris, nevertheless, was considered personally liable for their redemption should government revenues prove inadequate. And he saw to it that arrangements for their redemption were in place before leaving office.

After Yorktown, Morris turned his attention more fully to his objective of reestablishing confidence in the United States and reestablishing Congress' public credit—its ability to borrow. This he proposed to do by redressing the scales of the Confederation in favor of the central government. His methods included: (1) funding the national debt with permanent and increasing domestic revenues vested in Congress by amendment to the Articles of Confederation, (2) erecting a system of Federal taxation to generate revenues on a timely and dependable basis, (3) keeping government expenditures in check by scrutinizing them for waste and extravagance, (4) initiating a competitive contract system for army procurement, and (5) establishing a national bank, the Bank of North America, that would create a stable currency in the form of bank notes, lend money to the government, and provide commercial credit to merchants and other businessmen.

Although Morris mobilized the public creditors, he could not persuade Congress to pass the funding plan that he presented on July 29, 1782, in a long letter to Congress containing every argument he and his assistant Gouverneur Morris could muster in favor of a package of federal taxes. Some states opposed all federal taxation on principle, others opposed some or all of the particular taxes suggested. Revenue from requisitions failed to arrive on schedule, and Morris's fund of procrastinating financial expedients was running low. The financier's efforts to get recalcitrant Rhode Island to ratify the impost of 1781, the fund on which he placed his chief reliance for reestablishing public credit sufficiently to secure the further loans he would need to meet his public commitments, were at an impasse. None of his nationalizing devices had secured constitutional reform, nor had they left him with enough revenue to meet his commitments.

Then in the fall of 1782, Morris had to contend with a crisis arising in the army. The major contracts he had devised to supply the army economically were on the verge of collapse because he had insufficient funds to meet his payments. Moreover, urgent messages arrived from General Washington that measures must be taken to provide the army with pay and to meet the various pledges made to the army. The financier temporarily met this crisis by negotiating on extended credit a new and considerably more expensive contract with the firm of Wadsworth and Carter to replace the previous West Point and moving army contracts for the rest of the year. He also took measures, the details of which he reported only to Washington, to import specie, some of which he intended to use to make payments to the army in cash. Morris persuaded Congress to seek additional foreign loans and renewed even more urgently his appeals to the states to meet their long overdue payments on Congress' specie requisitions. Finally, he pressed Rhode Island to come to an immediate decision on ratification of the impost of 1781.

His hopes were shattered in December 1782 by the arrival of official news that the Rhode Island legislature had formally and unanimously refused to ratify the impost. Congress, the financier, and Thomas Paine all sought vainly to reverse this decision. Virginia promptly repealed its ratification. The public creditors in Pennsylvania pressed the legislature for state assumption of payments of interest on the public debt, an approach that would strip the debt of its role as a potential cement to the Union. Although Congress persuaded the assembly to postpone such action at least until the next session, key leaders of the creditors' movement were merely biding their time. Convinced that congressional funding was doomed, they were determined to get past the financier's insistence on a national plan as soon as possible. All this bad news was

followed by the arrival of dispatches from Europe indicating that the French had so far refused to grant any further loans, that the financier was already overdrawn on previous loans, and that the recently opened Dutch loan was filling slowly.

Then, on December 31, 1782, a committee from the angry main army reached Philadelphia. Headed by General Alexander McDougall, and bearing a memorial that historian Forrest McDonald has likened to the ostensibly polite communications that precede a challenge to a duel, the committee's assignment was to lobby forcefully for army pay, commutation, and payment of half-pay pensions, and for the settlement and payment of army accounts. Clearly, Morris was now confronted simultaneously with a political, military, and financial crisis of daunting proportions.

At this juncture Morris sought permission from Congress for a further overdraft against potential French loans, pressing unsuccessfully to secure the sanction of the Chevalier de la Luzerne, minister of France, for the measure. He then committed himself to advancing in cash one month's pay to the army, a pledge he could not keep should no further foreign loans materialize. Whether this promise was primarily designed to appease the army or to provide a stronger argument to induce French advances is unclear. In any case Luzerne refused to cooperate. Then, on January 24, with a ringing declamation against being a "Minister of Injustice," the superintendent tendered his letter of resignation effective May 31, 1783, unless Congress adopted a satisfactory funding plan for paying the nation's debts.

At the same time, while protracted financial debates took place in Congress, he and Gouverneur Morris promoted efforts to unite the army and the public creditors behind his funding proposals so as to use their "influence" to assure their passage through Congress and ratification by the states. The drive, sometimes referred to as the "Newburgh Conspiracy," culminated in the appearance of the inflammatory Newburgh addresses at the main army encampment in New York. Both Robert and Gouverneur Morris were accused of using the army as political tools, of fomenting mutiny, even of encouraging a coup. Their exact roles in the army protests remain a subject of dispute among historians. Whatever the truth, the effort failed to secure ratification of a funding plan by all the states.

After a famous meeting with the army officers on March 15 at which he condemned the anonymous addresses circulated among the troops and pledged to make an appeal to Congress on behalf of army demands, Washington successfully contained the army discontent in New York. Passage of legislation for commutation of half-pay pensions for army officers and the settlement of army accounts soon followed. Also following quickly was enactment of a funding plan, but one so modified as to lose the financier's support. Nevertheless, in May, because of pressure from the army and from various unnamed "friends," Morris reached a compromise with Congress and agreed to stay on in office for the purpose of providing three months' pay to the disbanding army and meeting his other previous financial commitments. Finally, on November 1, 1784, after resources from a Dutch loan enabled him to pay off his remaining engagements, Morris turned in his commission as superintendent of finance. He commented upon leaving office:

> It gives me great pleasure to reflect that the Situation of public affairs is more prosperous than when that Commission was issued. The Sovereignty and Independence of America are acknowledged. May they be firmly established, and effectually secured! This can only be done by a just and vigorous Government. That these States therefore may be soon and long united under such a Government, is my ardent Wish and constant Prayer.

Although Morris had failed to achieve all of his goals during his administration as superintendent of finance, his policies contributed to the formation of a coalition of nationalist leaders in various states who ultimately led the way to the adoption of the United States Constitution. Morris, after serving in the Constitutional Convention, then helped the Washington administration to achieve many of his goals while serving as a Federalist senator under the new United States government. In the Senate, Morris supported most of Hamilton's financial programs, and was generally influential in the enactment of financial and commercial legislation. He also played a major role in the compromises that led to the removal of the nation's capital from New York to its temporary home at Philadelphia and to its ultimate destination on the Potomac.

After the war Morris also continued to promote American commerce. He was the major sponsor and financial backer of the first American ship to China, *The Empress of China*, and he continued to invest in subsequent China voyages. He also lobbied against the reimposition of British, French, and Spanish restrictions on American trade with their colonies. Unlike many American merchants who returned most of their trade into British channels at the moment of peace, Morris's continued to expand on the French and Dutch financial and commercial ties he had established during the war. His largest postwar venture was a tobacco contract with the Farmers General, holders of the monopoly of the French tobacco trade. This contract was widely opposed by Virginians, who believed it depressed their tobacco prices, and it was eventually overturned through the intervention of the Marquis de Lafayette and of Thomas Jefferson, the American minister to France. The contract involved Morris in substantial financial losses.

Robert sent Gouverneur Morris to France in 1789 as his agent to help resolve the financial difficulties resulting largely from his tobacco contract. Among the international transactions in which Gouverneur represented Robert Morris were efforts to refinance the American foreign war debt and to sell lands already owned by Robert or to be purchased by him under vast land speculation schemes. Robert's land speculations included the Holland Land Company, the Asylum Company, and the North American Land Company, and the early development plans for Washington, D.C.

Eventually, various losses and the inability to sustain the capital and credit necessary to finance such vast speculations brought on financial collapse and led to Morris's imprisonment for debt in 1798. Released after three years following passage of a federal bankruptcy law in 1800, Morris was supported until his death in 1806 by the proceeds of a small pension Gouverneur Morris had obtained from the Holland Land Company for Mary White Morris in compensation for her dower rights to a portion of her husband's property.

Elizabeth M. Nuxoll

REFERENCES

Edmund Cody Burnett, ed., *Letters to Members of the Continental Congress* (1921–1936), rpr. 1963; William Bell Clark and William James Morgan, et al., eds., *Naval Document of the American Revolution*, 8 vols. (1964–); *Deane Papers*, 5 vols., *Collection of the New York Historical Society* (1887–1891); E. James Ferguson, "The Nationalists of 1781–1783 and the Economic Interpretation of the Constitution," *Journal of American History*, 56 (1969):241–161; ———, *The Power of the Purse: A History of American Public Finance, 1776–1790* (1961); E. James Fergusson, John Catanzariti, Elizabeth M. Nuxoll, Mary A.Y. Gallagher, Nelson S. Dearmont, et al., eds., *The Papers of Robert Morris, 1781–1784*, 7 vols. to date (1973–); Worthington C. Ford, et al., eds., *Journals of the Continental Congress, 1774–1789* (1904–1937), rpr. 1968; Ellis Paxson Oberholtzer, *Robert Morris, Patriot and Financier* (1894), rpr. 1968; Paul H. Smith, et al., eds., *Letters of Delegates to Congress 1774–1789*, 15 vols. (1976–); William Graham Sumner, *The Financier and the Finances of the American Revolution* (1892), rpr. 1970; Clarence L. Ver Steeg, *Robert Morris, Revolutionary Finances with an Analysis of His Earlier Career* (1954), rpr. 1972 and 1976; Eleanor Young, *Forgotten Patriot Robert Morris* (1950).

Morristown, New Jersey, Cantonments (1777–1782)

During the War of Revolution, Morristown, New Jersey, became known as the military capital of the United States. Washington encamped his main army at this location twice during the war and placed detachments in the Morristown area during other winters. Morristown took its name from Lewis Morris, the first governor of New Jersey, and was the county seat of Morris County. Morristown came to symbolize the true meaning of the war, for this conflict was primarily a contest of waiting and surviving, rather than of fighting battles. The men who camped at Morristown experienced a test of character, endurance, and patience that sorely tried their emotional and physical resources.

The Morristown region was first settled about 1710 by New Englanders who came to this hilly and heavily wooded section of New Jersey to farm and mine the land for iron ore. Morristown during the 1770s was a little village of about 60 to 80 buildings sheltering approximately 250 people. The village was situated at the base of five hills the local people referred to as mountains. Farming and the iron industry composed the central elements of the local economy.

Following his victory at Trenton and Princeton, Washington brought his tired, ragged, and small army to Morristown at the suggestion of General Henry Knox to spend the winter of 1777. The men arrived on Monday evening, January 6, 1777. Snow was already on the ground. It was an eighteenth-century custom to marry on twelfth night, January 6. In the midst of their misery and exhaustion, it seems likely that many of the soldiers who had wives turned their thoughts to their families at home as they tried to make themselves comfortable. Certainly Washington joined them, since it was his eighteenth wedding anniversary, and on that day his wife, Martha, was far from Morristown. For the first few days the men were camped in the woods surrounding the village.

In time, the men found more suitable and permanent shelter. For this first encampment at Morristown, Washington placed the majority of his men in private homes and buildings in town and throughout the nearby countryside. In this way, the commander-in-chief hoped to fool the British as to how many men still served in the American army. It is doubtful that the British were fooled. According to the local legend, Washington made his headquarters in the three-storied, and imposing Arnold Tavern that stood on the border of the village green. The general used two rooms on the second floor.

Morristown was chosen for several reasons, one of which was its geographic location. The site placed Washington on the flank of the British army garrisoned in New York City. Running between the British and American armies was a 30-mile stretch of hills called the first and second Watchung Mountains. There were also other hills and some dangerous swampland, all of which together formed a fine defensive network to protect Washington from British attack.

A system of alarm beacons was constructed from the outposts close to the British to Morristown and on north to the Hudson Highlands (completed by 1779). Composed of poles 18 to 20 feet high with a platform for an open cage on top in which a lit fire would have signaled an alert, this arrangement provided more safeguards that Washington would not be caught by surprise. American occupation of Morristown also kept the communication lines open between Philadelphia and the northern states.

Another of Washington's main goals was to keep New Jersey free of British control. Camping at Morristown placed Washington's main army in a central position from which he could launch a quick response to any British invasion of the Jersies. Washington also felt the people in this part of the Jersies were both committed to the American cause and supportive of the army and its needs. In addition, the presence of the American army would protect the industrial base of the region from British destruction. The only drawback was that the region lacked enough farms and cleared land to feed the army, particularly in 1779 when over 10,000 men camped in the area for almost 7 months.

One of the local leaders in Morristown was Colonel Jacob Ford, Jr., who operated a powder mill on the Whippany River and the several iron furnaces. Ford was the leader of the eastern battalion of the Morris County militia, who died on January 11, 1777, of pneumonia contracted during the Princeton campaign. He was only 38 years old and left behind a widow and four children. Captain Caesar Rodney and his Delaware troops occupied the splendid Georgian Ford Mansion for several weeks before leaving for home as their enlistments expired.

During the weeks that followed, the army gradually became stabilized. As time passed, the usual frictions developed between the military and civilians, such as the soldiers insulting the inhabitants, plundering farmers' food stores and animal stock, cursing, gambling, and foraging for the army horses and oxen. Washington and his generals often found themselves caught in the middle, trying to settle some local complaint against the army.

The troops experienced the typical poor conditions that seemed to follow every American winter encampment. There was an acute lack of food, clothing, and pay. Health conditions were primitive. Smallpox broke out, and Washington took the risk of having the entire army inoculated by Dr. Nathaniel Bond and his assistants. Many got sick in the process, but smallpox did not destroy the army.

At one point in mid-March, fully 1,000 of the 5,000 men in Washington's army were incapacitated due to the effects of this medical procedure. Two thousand more were on the verge of going home, their short-term enlistments having expired. Washington had a total of 3,000 men in his effective force to counter a possible British attack.

In spite of all these problems, Washington continued to strengthen his position at Morristown. In late January, he had his men build an upper redoubt (which legend calls Fort Nonsense) on a hill 230 feet higher than the village, to help the guards keep watch for beacon fires from the Watchung Mountains signaling an enemy attack. Washington also persisted in recruiting a long-term three-year army from the states. In this way, the soldiers who survived their initial campaigning to become veterans would stay in the service long enough to make use of their experience.

Washington also had to utilize what men he had to pressure the British by maintaining an active system of outposts at such places as Elizabethtown, Paramus, Bound Brook, and Princeton. The Americans carried out a scorched earth policy so that the British foraging parties sent into the Jersies came back empty-handed. The British found themselves besieged in their garrisons and harassed whenever they ventured out of their lines.

With the spring, matters improved somewhat for the Americans; Martha Washington arrived from Mount Vernon in March to join her husband at camp. A social life began with the officers holding dances and receptions. The new levies began to arrive from the states, so that by May 20 Washington had 7,363 three-year men present for duty, organized in 38 regiments. Materials began arriving from France to equip the men. The army prepared to take the field. On May 28, Washington left Morristown behind and moved east toward the British to begin the campaign of 1777.

Two and a half years passed before the American army once more encamped at Morristown. During that time, much happened in the war. The cantonment at Valley Forge was fortunate in that the winter of 1777–1778 was rather mild. The following winter, 1778–1779, was also a mild one while the main American army spread their camps from Middlebrook (now Bound Brook), New Jersey, to Danbury, Connecticut. The war in the North had reached a stalemate that neither side could break.

The British, however, had achieved some success in the southern states. In 1779, the Americans and French had attempted a combined attack on Savannah, Georgia, which led to disaster. The admiral of the French fleet, d'Estaing, following this defeat, disappeared into the West

Indies. Washington waited in the North to learn of the French navy's intentions. When it became clear that the French were not sailing north, Washington ordered his army into winter quarters.

For 1779–1780, the American army wintered once more at Morristown. The men began arriving during the first week in December and the last were in by the end of the month. Some 10,800 men were under Washington's immediate command in 8 brigades. Colonel Edward Hand's four regiments, the New York Brigade, the 1st and 2nd Maryland, the 1st and 2nd Pennsylvania, and the 1st and 2nd Connecticut were marched to a wilderness area called Jockey Hollow, some four miles south of town.

In addition, General John Stark's brigade (1,270 men) camped on the eastern slope of Mount Kemble, while the New Jersey Brigade (1,314 men) stayed at "Ayre's Forge" on the Passaic River, both somewhat removed from the main camp site. Knox's artillery camped along the road to Mendham, one mile west of Jockey Hollow. The southern troops, including the North Carolina and Virginia lines would be sent south to assist repel the British invasion of South Carolina. The New England troops were encamped in the Hudson Highlands and in Connecticut.

The winter of 1779–1780 was known as "the hard winter" and was commonly believed to be the most severe of the entire century. The ground was already frozen and covered with almost two feet of snow when the army arrived at Jockey Hollow.

It was freezing cold as the men began to erect their "log house city." During this most bitter and prolonged winter of the century, it snowed four times in November, seven times in December, six times in January, four times in February, six times in March, and once in April. A total of 28 snowstorms hit the Jersies that season. The January 2–4 storm was notable in that it snowed four feet with high winds causing drifts of over six feet.

The image most Americans have of the snowy winter at Valley Forge actually belongs to the campground two years later at Morristown. The men struggled through the cold and snow to erect their huts. Six hundred acres of woodland were consumed to build the cabins. Each brigade was assigned a well-drained hillside where the parade ground and cabins were laid out. For each brigade a plot of ground 320 yards long by 100 yards deep was reserved. The huts rose on the hills with the private soldiers' cabins lower on the slopes and the officers' higher up. For each regiment in each brigade, the huts were arranged eight in a row, two to four feet apart, three to four rows deep.

The cabins housed 12 men each. They were uniformly built 14 feet wide and 16 feet long with a stone chimney erected in the middle of the back wall. Windows were cut into the cabins in the spring. Furniture such as tables, bunks, stools, and other items were fashioned by the men for the huts. The officers were forbidden to build their cabins until all the enlisted cabins were complete. When the building was finished, somewhere between 1,000 and 1,200 cabins stood at Jockey Hollow, mostly on the plantations of Peter Kemble and Henry Wick. For a time, Morristown became the sixth largest "city" in the United States. The returns for December 1779 show 14,628 men total in Washington's army with 12,053 present for duty.

One regulation that was strictly enforced concerned how the wood was divided up for the men to build their cabins and keep their fires burning all winter. The quartermasters laid out the plan of the camp such that the inhabitants of each cabin "owned" the wood to the width of their cabin and to the front of it for as far as they wished to go. The officers "owned" all the wood in the rear of the regiment as far as they needed to go.

The generals took quarters in the local homes. General Arthur St. Clair of the Pennsylvania Line lived with the Wicks. General William Smallwood of the Maryland Line lived with Peter Kemble, who was an ardent Tory and the father-in-law of General Thomas Gage of the British army. Washington moved in with Mrs. Theodosia Ford in the Ford Mansion. Mrs. Ford and her four children, ranging in age from eight to seventeen years old, lived in two rooms on the first floor. Washington and Martha, when she joined him December 31, lived on the second floor. Every other room and two newly built wooden structures were taken up by the servants and aides of the general and the Ford family. Washington's lifeguard lived in barracks across the road from the mansion. The crowded conditions at the Ford Mansion lasted for seven months.

This was a more professional and disciplined army than the one that had camped at Valley Forge. While some 1,000 men died of sickness and exposure at hospitals surrounding the Valley Forge cantonment, only 86 died at Morristown, in a much more severe winter and under much more difficult conditions. This time the huts were properly built according to the regulations and the sinks properly tended to for the term of the encampment.

The roads were frequently blocked by snow much of the time. Food could not be carted in to feed the men. The army actually almost starved to death on the hills of Morristown due to the severity of the weather, the lack of provisioning, and the collapse of the Continental currency, making purchases of necessary items to sustain life impossible.

The rivers froze solid, so supplies and heavy loads had to be carried on sleds across the ice. Washington called upon Congress, then the states, and finally on New Jersey in a desperate attempt to feed his men. The men were reduced to eating birch bark, shoes, and leather belts to survive. This critical situation of living from hand to mouth, and often not even that, lasted until May. The troops had extra clothing, little food, and no pay.

The cold was so bad that it froze the ink that the Baron Johann de Kalb was writing with as he did his paperwork by the fire inside his quarters. Money was so scarce in the army that Washington could not afford to pay his express riders to carry dispatches to Congress. It was during this winter of 1779 that the congressional paper money lost it effective value. A horse alone cost $20,000. The money was "not worth a continental." The local farmers of New Jersey carried out what was called "the London trade" of taking their produce to the British who paid for it in hard money. While Major Henry Lee and others attempted to stop this intercourse, the trade flourished.

Washington kept the soldiers busy to keep their minds off other matters. They drilled each day except in snowstorms. They did guard duty and were sent out on patrols. They performed fatigue duties. They maintained a watch on the British in New York by manning the outposts. They carried out a partisan war with parties of Loyalists or British coming out of New York in search of mischief or forage. Each day the men had mess, answered roll call, drilled, had inspec-

tion, went on guard or fatigue duty, and prepared for reviews and general inspection, which were two-day affairs for the brigades. Punishment, when called for, involved running the gauntlet or being lashed. For desertion or mutiny, the sentence was death.

In spite of Washington's orders, the men gambled a great deal. Some read, and others wrote home. Some prayed. Some of the musicians formed bands and put on concerts for the rank and file. Others made furniture, and some left camp to plunder the neighbors and citizens of Morris County to alleviate the severe shortages the army experienced. Many, however, deserted. Over 1,000 men left the army illegally that hard winter.

On the brighter side, Martha Washington was soon joined in camp by Kitty Greene and Lucy Knox. Some 34 officers and Washington each subscribed $400 to hold two dances in Morristown, one on February 23 and another on March 3. A third dance was held on April 24 to honor the visiting French minister. Many officers went on furlough home including the majority of the generals. At one point during the winter, Washington had only two brigadiers in camp. This placed a great deal of strain on Washington to get the work done that was necessary for the survival of the army.

For his staff, Washington had such aides as Robert Harrison, known as the "old secretary" at 35 years of age; Tench Tilghman of Maryland and Philadelphia, who would take the news of Yorktown to Congress in 1781; Alexander Hamilton, the young, hotheaded King's College graduate who would court Betsy Schuyler during the encampment and marry her the next December; James McHenry of Ireland, a physician who much later became secretary of war; and Richard Kidder Meade of Virginia. But all of these men, while dedicated and diligent, were too junior and too inexperienced to provide the type of assistance Washington needed.

On January 14–15, 1780, Lord Stirling led a force of 3,000 men with artillery on 500 sleighs to attack the British on Staten Island. Unfortunately, the British had advance warning of Stirling's proposed visit and retreated into their defenses in plenty of time. All Lord Stirling could do when he crossed over the ice to Staten Island was mill about for 24 hours before returning to the mainland.

The mission created some problems because many of the so-called Jersey militia were no more than plunderers and brigands who played the militia role to destroy, to rob, and to plunder the island. When Washington learned of this, he had as much of the plunder and items that could be identified to be returned to the British. But it was too late. The British struck back in retaliation by burning Newark Academy and Elizabethtown Meeting and Church. This failed raid resulted in one American soldier being killed and approximately 500 men "slightly frozen."

In April, the French minister to the United States arrived at Morristown with his party. It was important to impress the Chevalier de la Luzerne favorably so that French aid would continue to flow to America. On April 24, a parade and festivities were held in his honor along with a formal ball that evening with the officers. The troops performed well under von Steuben's critical eye. Luzerne inspected the entire American camp the next day and left for Philadelphia shortly thereafter convinced that there was hope for the American cause.

A member of the French minister's party, a Spanish representative named Juan de Miralles, became sick with the bilious fever at Morristown and was left behind to die on April 28 on the second floor across the hall from Washington's room in the Ford Mansion. He was given a full military funeral and buried in a Morristown churchyard with a Catholic ceremony.

From January to April, Benedict Arnold underwent a court-martial at Morristown in the Peter Dickerson Tavern for charges of misconduct in his military governorship of Philadelphia following the British departure in 1778. Of the four allegations lodged against him, he was acquitted of two and given a mild reprimand by Washington for the rest. Arnold was not satisfied with this outcome. By this time he had already communicated secretly with the British several times. The verdict of the court merely solidified his doubt about the American cause and helped lead to his treason in 1780.

Lafayette returned from France in May to rejoin the American army. He brought the good news that the French king was sending a force of 6,000 men and another fleet to American waters to help the Americans in their fight for liberty. This was welcome news for Washington. The British found out about the coming French force as soon as Washington, since Arnold sent this word across lines to the British through his contacts.

Following standard practice, Congress appointed a committee to visit camp and check with Washington on the state of the army. Philip Schuyler, John Mathews, and Nathaniel Peabody arrived in camp in April to serve as liaison between Congress and the army. They soon recommended that Congress do something to improve the conditions of the men before it was too late.

But it was already too late. On May 25, two Connecticut regiments returning to Morristown from an extended tour of outpost duty found no pay and no food waiting for them. Their morale was already low. The lack of money and meat fueled their anger. The 4th and 8th Connecticut formed 30 minutes after evening roll call after "growling like sore headed dogs" all day. They intended to march home, foraging for food on the way. Before leaving, they also intended "to tear their commissary to atoms." Colonel Return Jonathan Meigs of the Connecticut Line tried to reason with them. Someone bayoneted him in the side. But he was able to control the men and to send them back to their cabins.

The grumbling went on. Colonel Walter Stewart of the Pennsylvania Line came and talked with the men, encouraging them to follow their officers and realize why they were fighting and that their leaders shared in the same hardships as they did. Pennsylvania troops were brought over if necessary to put down the revolt, but eventually everything settled down, and the mutiny ended. However, the conditions causing it persisted. Congress was powerless to change things. The civilians and individual states were unwilling to help the men. The soldiers remained devoted to their cause and faithful to their officers but resented the unfair treatment they had received from the government.

The winter finally passed, and the season for campaigning arrived. The British captured Charleston, South Carolina, and General Wilhelm von Knyphausen invaded New Jersey from Staten Island in June. Washington and his army left their camp to respond to this British offensive. By June 25, the American army was marching to the Hudson Highlands from their winter campground at Morristown.

For the winter of 1780–1781, most of the American army camped at or near New Windsor above the Hudson Highlands. It was a mild winter. Washington sent General Anthony Wayne and his Pennsylvania Line to Morristown to occupy the huts of Colonel Hand's and the 1st Connecticut Brigade from the last encampment. Once more American troops would winter at Morristown on farmer Wick's plantation. Ten Pennsylvania regiments and their artillery came to the Jockey Hollow area and began to settle in.

It was not a happy group of men. There was little clothing or blankets. Morale was extremely low. There was no rum for the men to fortify themselves against the extremes of the climate. For a year, there had been no pay. Yet the most severe problem of all centered around the original enlistment terms that most of the men had agreed to when they had joined in 1777. They had been signed for three years or the duration of the war. The men saw that as three years or the end of the war, whichever came first. The officers saw it as three years or until the war ended. The difference in perspective was enough to lead to the greatest mutiny of the war. This was especially true when new recruits came to camp with bonus money and promises of land that far outdid what the veterans had been promised when they had joined years back.

General Anthony Wayne was well aware of these simmering problems and pleaded with the state officials to rectify the situation. The state, however, continued to neglect its men. It did nothing. But it did send agents with hard money, $25 per man, to persuade some six-month troops in the Pennsylvania Line to enlist for the duration. These agents arrived in camp January 1, 1781. That same day the Pennsylvania Line was to reorganize into six regiments from the original eleven. These two events only added to the confusion and upsetment.

The soldiers could not live on patriotism. By January 1, 1781, a soldier's annual pay was worth the equivalent of one dollar in hard money. Even then, the Pennsylvanians had not been paid. Washington had learned of this situation several months back. Knowing the men had some equity in their complaints over the length of enlistment issue, Washington still encouraged the officers in mid-1780 to try to reenlist the men whose time had expired. Many of the officers of the Pennsylvania Line had forced the men to sign without the bounty given by the state for new recruits. This pressure created a split in the Pennsylvania Line between the officers and men,

the veterans and newly signed, and the men and their state.

On January 1, 1781, General Wayne's thirty-sixth birthday, at 10 o'clock in the evening, a musket was discharged and a skyrocket soared into the air. Fully one half of the almost 2,500 men of the Pennsylvania formed, seized the artillery, roughed up a few officers, killed Captain Adam Bettin, and wounded Captain Tolbert and Lieutenant White, and began their march toward Pennsylvania to gain some satisfaction for their complaints. Wayne rushed to the scene along with Colonels Walter Stewart and Richard Butler to try to reason with the men. The soldiers would not change their minds. Fifteen hundred men marched for two days to present their case to their state officials.

This march required the services of as many oxen and horses as possible and led to the famous legend of Tempe Wick. Temperance Wick was the youngest of five children of Henry and Mary Wick, the apple farmers upon whose 1,400-acre plantation the Pennsylvanians were camped. Henry had died of pleurisy on December 21, 1780, and Mary Wick was sick herself. Tempe, 21 years old, had gone to a local physician for medicine for her mother. Upon her return, she was approached by several of the mutineers who wished to press her white horse into service. She persuaded them to allow her to return home first. Arriving home, Tempe supposedly hid her horse in her bedroom for several days until the danger of losing the horse had passed.

Led by a committee of sergeants, the men arrived in Princeton on Wednesday afternoon and camped on Colonel Morgan's plantation south of the college. The sergeants made their headquarters in Nassau Hall. John Williams of the 2nd Pennsylvania was the president of the council of sergeants. William Bowzer was the secretary. Wayne negotiated with the 12 sergeants of the council on January 5–6, while some 80 officers of the Pennsylvania Line who had armed themselves and followed their men were forced to remain several miles away in Pennington, such was the anger of the men.

General Henry Clinton found out about the mutiny before Washington did. At first the British gave some thought to invading New Jersey to take advantage of this rebel problem. Then Clinton decided to send two agents to talk the Pennsylvanians into coming over to the British side, where their grievances would be addressed. The agents, John Mason and his guide, James Ogden, were turned over to Wayne by the mutineers, and subsequently both were tried on January 10 and hanged the next day.

The Pennsylvania Executive Council sent Joseph Reed and General James Potter to deal with the men. The Continental Congress sent former general John Sullivan, the Reverend John Witherspoon, John Mathews, Samuel Atlee, and Theodorick Bland. It was Reed and Wayne who actually sat down and worked out the settlement with the sergeants. The rest of the politicians remained at Trenton. Generals St. Clair and Lafayette also passed through Princeton but did not play an active role in the final solution of the problem.

Reed arrived in Princeton on Sunday afternoon, January 7. On Monday, the sergeants had accepted Reed's proposals for release of the men who had served three full terms, back pay, clothing allowances, and other issues of concern. The justice of the men's cause, their firmness in presenting their arguments, and their loyalty to the cause impressed Reed, Wayne, and all those who dealt with this crisis. The complete settlement was agreed to by all parties in Trenton on January 10. The mutiny of the Pennsylvania Line turned out in the end to be an event of credit for the United States and led to the confusion of her enemies. Through every hardship, the men remained overwhelmingly loyal to the cause.

Although Wayne was sure his Pennsylvania command would disappear, 1,150 men remained in the regiments after those who had served their full time, or said they had, were allowed to leave for home. All mutineers were granted full amnesty. Prompt action was promised on back pay and clothing allotments. The entire line was furloughed until March 15 and was reduced to three battalions. They served out the remainder of the war in that organization.

The rest of the American army watched the Pennsylvanians with great interest, especially the New Jersey Line. The settlement of the Pennsylvania mutiny prompted the New Jersey brigade stationed at Pompton to revolt on January 20. At that time, General Elias Dayton, the Jersey brigade commander, was away from camp and his second in command, Colonel Israel Shreve was fat, incompetent, and slow of thought.

Dayton rushed back to his men to keep the revolt from spreading.

This time, Washington acted firmly and quickly. On January 27, he sent General Robert Howe with 550 trusted New England troops to surround the Jersey mutineers, about 200 in number, and to quell the uprising. Two of the mutiny's leaders were executed and Sergeant George Grant was pardoned. The New Jersey brigade was marched on February 7 to Jockey Hollow and placed in the cabins recently occupied by the Pennsylvania Line. On July 8, 1781, they were marched to King's Bridge on the Hudson.

The final camp of the Continental Army at Morristown came the next winter when General Dayton brought the two Jersey regiments of about 700 men in his brigade back to Morristown on December 7, 1781. The Jersey brigade camped there until August 29, 1782. By September 1, 1782, the last American troops had departed, and Morristown ceased to play its role in the War of Revolution. The site passed into history.

In 1933, Morristown, including Fort Nonsense, the Ford Mansion, and Jockey Hollow with the Wick farm became the First National Historical Park in the United States. Today the park memorializes the suffering and devotion of the faithful men who formed the Continental Army as it fought a war of posts and endurance against the British, and who struggled to survive the neglect of their fellow citizens, in the name of freedom. *See also*: Valley Forge, Pennsylvania, the Encampment of

Paul J. Sanborn

REFERENCES

Mary Ann Cataldo and Judi Benvenuti, *Morristown, the War Years* (1979); Don Higginbotham, *The War of American Independence* (1971); Douglas S. Freeman, *George Washington, a Biography*, 7 vols. (1948–57); Joseph Plumb Martin, *Private Yankee Doodle* (1962); Paul David Nelson, *Anthony Wayne* (1985); Charles Royster, *A Revolutionary People at War* (1979); George F. Scheer and Russell F. Weigley, *Morristown* (1983); Samuel S. Smith, *Winter at Morristown, 1779–80, The Darkest Hour* (1979); Bruce W. Stewart, *Morristown, Crucible of the American Revolution* (1975); Carl Van Doren, *Mutiny in January* (1943); Melvin J. Weig, *Morristown* (1950).

Mount Independence, Vermont

A formidable 300-acre peninsula located on the eastern shore of Lake Champlain in Orwell, Vermont, Mount Independence has the distinction of being the only major Revolutionary War fortification built on Vermont soil, and together with the neighboring site of Fort Ticonderoga, it was the key military installation designed to halt the advance of British forces from Canada during the early years of the Revolution. However, Ticonderoga was a holdover from the conflicts between the French and British in the 1750s, and its southerly facing cannon were quite useless against a northern enemy. This contrasted with the cannon batteries at Mount Independence, which were built specifically for the Revolution, making this strategically vital to American defenses in the North.

Mount Independence was selected for an outpost by General Philip Schuyler and his officers in the spring of 1776, and the clearing of trees and construction of fortifications was placed under the command of Colonel Jeduthan Baldwin, later assisted by Thaddeus Kosciuszko. Beginning that July, batteries were placed on the shore of Lake Champlain and on the cliffs above, and the site was christened "Mount Independence" on July 28 following a reading of the Declaration of Independence to the assembled troops. A star-shaped palisade fort was constructed that November on the highest part of the "Mount," and other structures included barracks, houses, huts, tents, lookout posts, artificers' shops, one or more regimental hospitals, five blockhouses, batteries, and a crane used for hoisting cargo from the beach below. Of special significance was the construction of a 250-foot general hospital on the Mount, of which there were only three in the Northern Medical Department. Jonathan Potts, a 1768 graduate of the new Philadelphia Medical College, was the doctor in charge. Equally important was the construction of a massive 1,600-foot floating bridge across Lake Champlain, connecting Mount Independence with Fort Ticonderoga on the New York shore, a distance of one-quarter mile.

The American troops that occupied Mount Independence may have numbered as many as 12,000 or 13,000 men, organized into three brigades. These were Continental soldiers and militia from the colonies of Massachusetts, New Hampshire, Connecticut, New Jersey, and Pennsylvania, and they remained at full strength into the fall of 1776. It was on October 28 that the fortifications proved their worth when a British fleet under Sir Guy Carleton, fresh from the Battle of Valcour Island, sailed within three miles of the Mount. Finding American forces to be at peak strength, the British chose not to fight and returned to Canada for the winter, clearly failing in their objective to separate New York from the New England colonies. The construction of Mount Independence at one of the narrowest choke points on Lake Champlain thus delayed the British advance for nearly a year.

By the late fall of 1776, many of the men went home, leaving a garrison of no more than 2,000 to 3,000 soldiers. Colonel Anthony Wayne of the 4th Pennsylvania was the senior officer in charge through the fall and winter of 1776–1777—at which time many men froze to death— but he was later replaced by General Arthur St. Clair who assumed command in June 1777. St. Clair was still in command on July 5–6 when an army of 8,000 British, German, and Canadian troops, led by General John Burgoyne, successfully drove the Americans from the Mount and captured large quantities of American provisions and ordnance. The retreating Americans were pursued as far as Hubbardton (July 7), but most survived and fought Burgoyne again that September in Saratoga. St. Clair's decision to abandon the Mount Independence/Fort Ticonderoga complex without fighting became a major scandal in Congress, but it was ultimately determined that he had lacked sufficient troops with which to hold his position. St. Clair was acquitted with highest honors at his court-martial trial in 1778.

After American forces abandoned Mount Independence, German "Brunswicker" troops then occupied a line of blockhouses along the eastern side of the Mount to prevent the return of the Americans. Colonel John Brown did, in fact, make a diversionary attack upon the Mount on September 18, 1777, while other American forces were attacking Fort Ticonderoga. Later, when the German garrison received word of Burgoyne's defeat at Saratoga, this last vestige of Burgoyne's army burned all buildings on the Mount on November 8, 1777, and retreated to Canada. Mount Independence has not been built upon since that time, and it has survived until today as an unusually intact—and fragile—set of foundations representing just one year in the American Revolution.

David R. Starbuck

REFERENCES

Jeduthan Baldwin, *The Revolutionary Journal of Col. Jeduthan Baldwin 1775–1778* (1906); Thomas Furcron, "Mount Independence," *The Bulletin of the Fort Ticonderoga Museum, 9* (1954):230–248; Anthony Wayne, "The Wayne Orderly Book," *The Bulletin of the Fort Ticonderoga Museum, 11* (1963):93–112; *12* (1964):125–134, 177–205; John A. Williams, "Mount Independence in Time of War, 1776–1783," *Vermont History, 35* (1965):89–108.

Moylan, Stephan (1737–1811)

Continental Army officer. Moylan was born in Cork, Ireland, to a wealthy Catholic family. Educated in France, he worked three years in Lisbon before arriving in Philadelphia.

On August 11, 1775, he became muster-master general. Early in 1776 Moylan became secretary to Washington, and in June he succeeded Thomas Mifflin as quartermaster general at the rank of colonel. Moylan was unsuccessful in this post due to reasons beyond his control, and he resigned the position in September 1776.

Thereafter Moylan served with the 4th Continental Dragoons as a colonel. He fought at Monmouth and at Bull's Ferry (July 1780). Whether he joined the fighting in the Carolinas or served with Lafayette in Virginia is uncertain. He was in the field at the conclusion of the Yorktown campaign. In 1793 he was appointed commissioner of loans in Philadelphia, and in 1796 Moylan was elected president of the Friendly Sons of St. Patrick.

Richard L. Blanco

REFERENCES

Frank Monaghan, "Stephen Moylan in the American Revolution," *Studies, 19* (1930):481–486; [Stephen Moylan], "Selections from the Correspondence of Col. Stephen Moylan," *Pennsylvania Magazine of History & Biography, 37* (1913):341–360.

Muhlenberg, John Peter Gabriel (1746–1807)

Continental Army officer. Muhlenberg was one of several clergymen who rallied to the patriotic cause and served in the Continental Army and Navy. However, unlike most he chose to serve as a line officer rather than as a chaplain.

And this he did with distinction, rising to the rank of major general.

Born in Trappe, Pennsylvania, to the most prominent Lutheran pastor in the colonies, Muhlenberg was sent with his brothers to study for the ministry at their father's alma mater in Halle, Germany. Peter, however, became restless and enlisted with a band of German dragoons on a recruiting visit to the community. Although he became secretary of the regiment, due to his parents' disapproval, he allowed them to secure his early release in 1767 from the dragoons. This was done with the assistance of a British colonel, as the unit was in their employ.

Upon his return to America he resumed his theological studies in earnest, with the result that he was ordained a pastor of the Lutheran church. He served as a pastor for the following eight years. In order to serve officially as pastor of a congregation of German immigrants in the state of Virginia, he traveled to England to secure an Anglican (Episcopal) ordination. Nevertheless, the fact that he retained his Lutheran ties is evidenced by his lifelong association with a Lutheran congregation in Philadelphia even after he demitted the ministry.

His final sermon in Woodstock, Virginia, has been immortalized by one of Pennsylvania's two statues featured in the national capital. Calling on his parishioners to affirm the Revolutionary cause, he proclaimed "there is a time to preach and a time to fight, and now is the time to fight!" With this he threw off his clerical garb to reveal the uniform of a Continental colonel. That day he recruited over 300 members of his congregation to join him in the 8th Virginia Regiment of German-Americans. In the words of the poet Thomas Buchanan:

> The pastor rose: the prayer was strong;
> The psalm was warrior David's song . . .
> Then swept his kindling glance of fire
> From startled pew to breathless choir,
> When suddenly his mantle wide
> His hands impatient flung aside,
> And, lo! he met their wondering eyes
> Complete in all a warrior's guise.

Colonel Muhlenberg and his new recruits were immediately dispatched to aid Lee in Charleston, as "of all the Virginia regiments this was the most complete, the best armed, best clothed and best equipped for immediate service." General Lee praised Muhlenberg's force, saying his troops were "alert, zealous and spirited."

While defending the coasts of South Carolina and Georgia, his men greeted news of the Declaration of Independence with great enthusiasm. Upon their return to Virginia, he was promoted in February 1777 to brigadier general and put in command of the Virginia Line. Called to join Washington at Morristown, they arrived in time to perform well on the field at Brandywine, Germantown, and Monmouth. At the battle of Stony Point, Muhlenberg was second in command.

At the close of the year the Virginia Line was ordered to the defense of Charleston. Meanwhile, Muhlenberg was charged with the defense of Virginia. Throughout 1780 he energetically recruited companies for General Nathanael Greene. In September 1783, before news of peace reached the colonies, he was breveted a major general.

With the end of the war, he retired from the military to his home state of Pennsylvania, where he continued to serve his nation in a civil capacity. After serving as a member of the state's Supreme Executive Committee, he became vice president of the commonwealth (1785–1788) while Franklin was the president. He was one of the state's representatives to the First, Third, and Sixth Congresses. Following a term as a United States senator, he ended his political career in an appointed position under President Jefferson. *See also*: Lutherans in the American Revolution

Robert C. Stroud

REFERENCES

William J. Finck, *Lutheran Landmarks and Pioneers in America* (1913); Charles W. Heathcote, "General John Peter Gabriel Muhlenberg," *Picket Post*, 42 (1953):4–10; Edward W. Hocken, *The Fighting Parson and the American Revolution* (1936); John N. Selby, *The Revolution in Virginia* (1982); A. R. Wentz, *A Basic History of Lutheranism in America* (1964).

Murphy, Timothy (1751–1818)

American soldier, frontiersman. "Sure-shot Tim," Timothy Murphy, through his amazing feats of marksmanship and bravery became a legend of the Revolution. Unable to read or write and never promoted beyond sergeant, he nevertheless exerted a singular personal influence on several campaigns on the war, if he actually accomplished all the exploits attributed to him. Murphy's life, like other frontiersmen of American history, has been mixed with myth to a point where it is difficult to distinguish fact from fiction. With his comrade in arms David Elerson, he fought against the British in the Morgan's "Corps of Riflemen," most notably at Saratoga, and served as a scout in the militia in the savage conflict that raged on the frontier of New York.

Murphy was born in 1751, of Irish immigrant parents, at Minisink, New Jersey, in the Delaware Gap. At an early age his parents moved to Shamokin Flats (Sunbury) in the Wyoming Valley of Pennsylvania. He grew up on the frontier hardened to life outdoors and knowledgeable in the ways of the Indians. In manhood Murphy was not tall but was powerfully built and swift of foot. Dark skinned with black eyes and jet black hair, his manner was rough and his speech profane, but it was said he was good at heart. When fighting broke out with the British, Murphy was in Pennsylvania employed as an axeman by surveyors.

After Lexington, Murphy joined Captain Lowden's Company of the Pennsylvanian Battalion of Riflemen in Northumberland, his home county. Legend has it that he carried a "Golcher rifle," made by a Pennsylvanian gunsmith of the same name. It is, however, more likely that this curious, double-barrelled gun was actually made after 1800. Murphy was involved in skirmishes with the British outside Boston in the fall of 1775 and was present at the Battle of Long Island in 1776. When his enlistment expired, Murphy joined Captain James Parr's company of the 1st Pennsylvania Regiment and from 1776–1777 served in a succession of Pennsylvania Line regiments. He was at Trenton and Princeton and fought in the spring campaign of 1777 in New Jersey.

In July 1777 Murphy was drafted into Captain Parr's 6th company of Colonel Daniel Morgan's newly formed elite "Rifle Corps." The "Corps" was soon sent by George Washington to reinforce General Horatio Gates's army. In the battles with the forces under the command of Lieutenant General John Burgoyne, Murphy and his comrades were given great freedom to rove and skirmish against the British outposts. They harassed the enemy by shooting officers, cutting off forage parties, and intercepting supplies. In one incident Murphy forced the countersign from a captured sentry and used it to take a British officer prisoner in his own tent. He has been credited with the mortal wounding of Brigadier General Simon Fraser at Saratoga on October 7, probably Murphy's most famous feat of arms. It was said, at the urging of Major General Benedict Arnold, Morgan took Murphy and a few other sharpshooters aside and told them: "That gallant officer is General Fraser I admire and honour him, but it is necessary he should die, victory for the enemy depends on him. Take your station in that clump of bushes and do your duty." The other riflemen fired without effect, but Murphy, settled his gun in the fork of a tree and, at a range of 200 yards, began shooting. He missed on the first two shots, but the third round found its mark. The fatally wounded Fraser was escorted off the field and died the next morning. Murphy was also said to be responsible for the death of Sir Francis Carr Clerke, Burgoyne's aide-de-camp. Clerke was shot the same day as Fraser and died on the night of October 7–8, a prisoner in Gates's camp.

With the close of the campaign Morgan's "Rifle Corps" returned to the army headquarters outside Philadelphia. In late November 1777, Murphy joined the 7th Pennsylvania Line encamped at Valley Forge, but in June 1778 he rejoined his old regiment. Morgan's riflemen did not actually participate in the fighting at Monmouth, June 28, 1778, but while on a reconnaissance patrol after the battle Murphy, assisted by Elerson and two others, captured the private coach of a British general.

In July 1778, Murphy was sent in a company of rifles under Captain Parr to the Schoharie Valley area of New York (Albany and Tryon counties). In the bloody war of raid and counterraid, reprisal and counterreprisal in frontier New York and Pennsylvania, Murphy earned a reputation as a ruthless Indian fighter. In August 1778 he and Elerson assassinated Christian Service, a local Tory who had assisted Loyalist raiders. Parr's company was involved in many of the battles on the frontier. In revenge for German Flats they helped burn the Indian town of Unadilla on October 8, 1778. In November 1778, Murphy barely escaped with his life from a large party of Indians. He was to have several other close brushes with death during the war. As a leader of the scouts of the "Rifle Corps," Murphy reconnoitered for the armies that campaigned in New York against the Indians. With his company, Murphy was in Colonel Goose Van Schaick's expedition to western New York in April 1779, a revenge excursion against the Onondagas. He and his company joined General John Sullivan at Tioga and fought against the Iroquois and British at Newtown, August 29, 1779. On September 13 Lieutenant Thomas Boyd of the "Corps," while on a scout to the Indian town of Genesee, was caught in an ambush. Twenty-two of his men were killed, Murphy and another rifleman the only ones to escape. Boyd and a sergeant named Parker were captured, then taken to Little Beard's town to be tortured and finally decapitated. Murphy, himself, almost ended up the same way. While on a scout in the Delaware Forts in the spring of 1780, he and Captain Alexander Harper were captured by 11 Iroquois warriors who intended to take them to the Indian town of Oquaga. At night, after the party had camped the two men, bound together, waited for their chance to act. They were able to release themselves when the Indians, who had been drinking heavily, fell asleep. Murphy and Harper removed the weapons of the Indians and silently killed them, one by one. A single Iroquois escaped alive.

In September 1780, Tory leader Sir John Johnson left his base in Canada on a raid into the Schoharie Valley. Johnson's raid was to be the scene of Murphy's most impressive feat of the entire Revolution. Johnson had 500 to 800 British regulars and Loyalists, a company of Hessian jaegers, 500 Indians under Joseph Brant and Cornplanter, and some light artillery. A trio of crude fortifications (the Lower, Middle, and Upper Forts) and their small garrisons protected the Schoharie Valley. Johnson entered the valley from southwest and passed by the Upper Fort on the night of October 15. As they went the raiders burnt houses and barns and killed or carried off livestock, arriving outside the Middle Fort the next morning. The Middle Fort consisted of a crude stockade made of hewn timber and earth surrounding several strong stone houses. Inside were about 200 soldiers: 150 state militia ("three months' men") under Major Melanchthon Woolsey, in overall command; and 50 local militia, commanded by Colonel Bartholmew Vrooman. Also among the garrison was Murphy who with the scouts had first detected Johnson's entry into the valley.

On the morning of October 16, Johnson slowly invested the Middle Fort. Four hours later he began a cannonade, but found his artillery was too light to be truly effective. Frustrated, he decided to attempt to negotiate the fort's surrender by offering protection for the garrison. As the flag, carried by Captain Andrew Thompson of Butler's Rangers, approached the fort it was fired on by Murphy and Elerson. Murphy, who could expect little mercy from Brant's Iroquois, had no faith that Woolsey would resist Johnson's demand to capitulate. Woolsey immediately ordered Murphy arrested, but no man in the garrison acted. On the contrary they rallied around the insubordinate rifleman. Johnson sent a white flag a second time, but the determined Murphy again fired on it. When Woolsey ordered a white flag run up on the fort's flagstaff Murphy declared he would shoot anyone who obeyed. He fired on a third flag sent by Johnson. Exasperated, Woolsey demanded to know, "who dared disobey his orders," and in reply Murphy responded, "I fired on that flag." When finally, Woolsey threatened him with death, if he repeated the act, Murphy said, "Major Woolsey, sooner than see that flag enter this fort, I'll send a bullet through your heart." Murphy, backed by the militia, won the day and Woolsey relented yielding the command to Vrooman. In shame, Woolsey hid in the cellar below the kitchen where the powder was stored. Johnson and his officers, unaware of the disorder inside the fort, decided to raise the siege and after a half-hearted attempt at the Lower Fort (in which Murphy, Elerson, and other militiamen assisted in the defense) exited the valley. As Johnson went, he left a trail of destruction and desolation in his wake. It is said that shortly after this raid, perhaps in a fit of revenge, Murphy skinned the leg of an Indian whom he had killed and drew this grisly trophy over his own limb.

In April 1781 Murphy joined the 3rd Regiment of the Pennsylvania Line and in May marched to New York under Brigadier General Anthony Wayne. He was in action at Green Spring, Virginia (July 6, 1781), and present at the surrender at Yorktown, after which he was mustered out of the regiment and returned to the Schoharie Valley in October 1781. Murphy continued to fight as a militiaman in frontier skirmishes against the Indians and Loyalists until the end of the Revolution. His war service ended fittingly when he was presented to George Washington on August 3, 1783.

He had met and married Margaretha "Peggy" Feeck at the Upper Fort just before Sullivan's Iroquois expedition of 1779 (her parents' home was enclosed in the Upper Fort). They were married on October 1, 1780, despite the protests of Peggy's father, John Feeck, who did not believe a poor soldier like Murphy was a suitable match for his daughter. The couple had six children before Peggy died September 7, 1807. Murphy was remarried to Mary Robertson in 1812 and had four children by her, including one they named George Washington. Murphy farmed his father-in-law Feeck's land and later acquired a large amount of real estate including a number of farms and a grist mill. He became involved in local politics and became something of a political power.

Murphy died of throat cancer June 27, 1818, at the age of 67 and was buried within the Middle Fort at Fultonham. He was later reburied at Middleburgh, New York.

Murphy proved that the Revolution was perhaps a war where a single, simple soldier was still able to alter the tide of a battle, as he did at Bemis Heights and at the Middle Fort. His exploits in the border warfare in New York bear witness to the stark brutality of that conflict. Forgotten today, Murphy deserves to be remembered, like Daniel Boone, as one of the great frontiersmen of the American Revolution.

Brian E. Hubner

REFERENCES

James Dearing, "How an Irishman Turned the Tide at Saratoga," *Journal of the Irish American Society,* *10*(1911):109–113; Daniel F. Mowery, "Timothy Murphy," *Northumberland County Historical Society. Proceedings,* 9(1937):83–91; Michael J. O'Brien, *Timothy Murphy: Hero of the American Revolution* (1941); William Sibsy, *Life and Adventures of Timothy Murphy the Benefactor of Schoharie . . .* (1839), rpr. 1863; Jeptha R. Simms, *History of Schoharie County, and Border Wars of New York; containing also a sketch of the Causes Which led to the American Revolution and Interesting Memoranda of the Mohawk Valley. Together with Much other Historical and Miscellaneous Matters, Never Before Published,* vol. 1 (1845).

Murray, John, 4th Earl of Dunmore. *Known as* Lord Dunmore (1732–1809)

Royal governor of Virginia. Although initially well received in his colony, Lord Dunmore failed to retain the popular support necessary for coping with Virginia's growing Revolutionary movement. His self-interested enthusiasm for Virginia's western expansion on the eve of the American Revolution led him to neglect the cultivation of political moderates and the reporting of conditions in his colony, a dereliction of duty that contributed to the speedy collapse of royal authority in Virginia. As tensions spilled over into violence, Dunmore attempted to restore the King's authority in Virginia by force, leading Loyalist militia, liberated slaves, naval vessels, royal soldiers, and marines on a number of raids and skirmishes. By the summer of 1776, however, Virginians forced Dunmore and his followers out of the colony. He spent most of the remaining war years in England and exerted little further influence on the course of the Revolutionary War.

Dunmore was born about 1730. He entered the Royal Army in 1749 and retained his commission until 1760, when he resigned to enter politics. Chosen to serve as one of the 16 peers representing the Scottish nobles in Britain's House of Lords, Dunmore pursued an unexceptional political career. In votes and rare debates, he took moderate stands on issues concerning the American colonies.

Appointed as governor of New York in January 1770, Dunmore went to America to secure fortunes for himself and his heirs. This was no small task, since he and his wife Charlotte—daughter of the earl of Galloway—had four daughters and five sons. Dunmore proved equal to the challenge, however. Only a few months after arriving at his new post in October 1770, the new governor secured over 50,000 acres of land around Lake Champlain.

Dunmore's relations with the New York elite were mixed. He befriended the influential Sir William Johnson, England's Indian superintendent for the northern colonies. As an active expansionist Dunmore was also popular with New York's land speculators, but he quarreled with his lieutenant governor, Cadwallader Colden, over the distribution of official salaries, thus alienating a powerful interest in New York politics.

In the winter of 1771, having held office only a few months, Dunmore was reassigned to the governorship of Virginia. These new orders were intended as a promotion with an increased salary, for Virginia was Britain's wealthiest and most populous mainland colony. Dunmore fought the transfer, however, out of reluctance to abandon his northern land speculations. Even after his last appeal was denied, the earl delayed his departure from New York for months.

Dunmore arrived at the colonial capital of Williamsburg in late September 1771. As in New York, he offended some Virginia leaders, but others, including George Washington, found the governor agreeable to their interests, western expansion chief among them. To Dunmore, the acquisition of western lands offered a means of building his personal fortune while cementing new political alliances with elite Virginians. The governor therefore repeatedly disobeyed instructions from England by authorizing surveys of western land—including 100,000 acres for his sons—and by establishing new frontier governments.

Virginia's northwesterly expansion inflamed old tensions with western Indians. By the spring of 1774 these tensions burst into an open conflict known as Dunmore's War, which pitted Virginian's against tribes living north of the Ohio River. In the early fall of 1774, Dunmore led an invasion into modern Ohio, and on October 19 forced his Indian opponents to accept a peace treaty acknowledging Virginia's claims to all territory south and east of the Ohio River. Virginians applauded Dunmore's martial success and greeted the governor warmly when he returned to Williamsburg in early December 1774.

But beneath Dunmore's apparent popularity lay more fundamental tensions that could not be defused by the glories of a speedy campaign against the Indians. When Dunmore had first sought colonial funding for his campaign, Virginia's House of Burgesses refused to consider the matter. Instead, the assembled legislators focused on the imperial crisis following the Boston Tea Party. The burgesses had signaled their opposition to Parliament's Boston Port Act by voting a day of fasting and prayer, upon which Dunmore dissolved the assembly. Unable to obtain funding from the burgesses, the governor financed his expedition by promising loot to frontier militia units.

Once the Indian war was over, Dunmore hurt the Crown's cause by not dealing more diplomatically with Virginia's elite. Beyond this important failure, he also neglected to keep his superiors informed of the emerging resistance movement in Virginia. British policymakers thus remained ignorant of the extent of Virginia's support for Boston until February 1775. But if Dunmore offered little advice to England, the Crown in turn sent only limited instructions to him. As a result, the governor was left to deal as he saw fit with restless but not necessarily rebellious Virginians. Unfortunately for the Crown, Dunmore's judgment was unequal to this challenge. From the spring of 1775 through his final departure from Virginia in the summer of 1776, Dunmore consistently selected inappropriate courses of action that only served to alienate most of his potential supporters.

Dunmore made the first of his major errors in April 1775. Acting on his fears that insurgents might break into the colonial magazine at Williamsburg, Dunmore ordered Royal Marines to transfer gunpowder from the magazine to a warship in the York River. A marine detachment carried out the governor's orders in the early morning darkness of April 21, but the precaution cost the royal interest dearly. Virginians of all political descriptions—moderates as well as radicals—were outraged, and news of British raids on Lexington and Concord just two days earlier made Dunmore's ill-timed move seem part of an imperial conspiracy. Tempers continued to rise through May 1775. Finally in June, Dunmore and his family fled the Governor's Palace in Williamsburg to take refuge aboard the HMS *Fowey*.

Following his flight, Dunmore spent 14 more months in Virginia, alternately floating upon and encamped around the Chesapeake Bay. His first landing was at the mouth of the bay, where Dunmore spent the summer of 1775 assembling a military force around the towns of Norfolk and Portsmouth, and planning to raise an army among his frontier supporters. The latter project collapsed in November with the capture of Loyalist Dr. John Connolly, who hoped to lead a force from the west to a rendezvous with Dunmore on the Potomac River. Despite this setback, Dunmore enjoyed other military victories during the fall with a series of raids against Virginian supply collections that captured over 70 cannon, as well as a variety of other military equipment.

The success of these raids led Dunmore to proclaim on November 15, 1775, that Virginia was in a state of rebellion. In contemporary English usage, this proclamation required loyal subjects to help suppress the revolt. Beyond this conventional definition of raising the King's standard, Dunmore took the radical step of declaring the freedom of all able-bodied male slaves belonging to rebels, if those slaves would run away and join Dunmore's army. Several hundred accepted the governor's offer, forming the Ethiopian Regiment under command of Thomas Byrd, son of William Byrd III of Virginia. In response, Virginians threatened slaves with execution if recaptured under arms, but in practice most Black prisoners of war were condemned to labor in the lead mines of southwest Virginia or sold to the West Indies.

For about three weeks after raising the King's standard, Dunmore enjoyed great success recruiting whites as well as Blacks, with some 3,000 inhabitants from around Norfolk and Portsmouth taking an oath of allegiance to the Crown. This achievement was short-lived, however, thanks to the American victory at Great Bridge on December 9. The loss of Great Bridge made it impossible for Dunmore to defend his fortifications around Norfolk, and so the governor, his army, and a large number of Loyalists withdrew to ships anchored just off Norfolk in Hampton Roads.

This royal flotilla lay quiet for several weeks while Virginia troops occupied Norfolk and harassed British foraging parties. Fighting resumed on January 1, 1776, when the Royal Navy began bombarding American positions in Norfolk, and Dunmore sent a landing party to set fire to selected buildings ashore. Virginia troops seized on this action as a pretext to loot and burn much of the town. On orders of the American commander, Colonel Robert Howe, the remainder of Norfolk was put to the torch in early February. Contemporaries blamed Dunmore for the destruction of Norfolk, despite the fact that most of the loss came at American hands.

After the burning of Norfolk, Dunmore put his forces into winter quarters at Tucker's Point, across the Elizabeth River from the ruined town. The governor remained there until late May, when the threat of American fireships forced him to evacuate the Tucker's Point position. A flotilla of almost 100 vessels carried Dunmore's refugees north up the Chesapeake Bay. On May 27, 1776, Dunmore landed on Gwynn's Island, located at the Piankatank River's mouth on the western shore of the Chesapeake Bay.

The shift to Gwynn's Island began the final stage in the extinction of royal authority in Virginia, although this climax was not immediately obvious. Dunmore intended the post to provide a convenient rallying point for nearby Loyalists, an expectation fulfilled by about 200 recruits to the Queen's Own Loyal Regiment. Gwynn's Island also offered an anchorage for any British ships bearing reinforcements, but as time passed these did not materialize. Instead, Virginia troops under the command of Colonel William Daingerfield and Colonel Hugh Mercer began to appear on the mainland, separated from Dunmore's increasingly sickly force by only a few hundred yards of intermittently fordable water.

Dunmore's artillery and naval fire support held the threat of an American assault at bay for a time, but by July the governor's position was all but untenable. In that month, Dunmore's former subordinate from the 1774 Indian war, General Andrew Lewis, brought a variety of cannon from Williamsburg and bombarded Dunmore's naval vessels. Faced with the likelihood of an American assault under cover of these new guns, Dunmore evacuated Gwynn's Island. After landing briefly on St. George's Island and later near Dumfries to load fresh water, Dunmore led his decimated flotilla out of the Chesapeake Bay on August 7. Once offshore, Dunmore set a course for British-occupied New York; most of the other vessels chose instead to proceed to Florida.

Dunmore never returned to Virginia. In November 1776 he sailed to England, where he eventually resumed his seat in the House of Lords. In early 1781 Dunmore was ordered to raise a Loyalist force and return to his old colony in the wake of Lord Cornwallis's invasion of Virginia. By the time Dunmore crossed the Atlantic, however, Cornwallis had surrendered at Yorktown, and no hope survived of reclaiming the old office.

Dunmore landed in Charleston, South Carolina, where he remained into the spring of 1782, planning a new invasion of Virginia. This scheme collapsed in the face of the accelerating peace movement, and Dunmore returned to England. There the earl became a vigorous spokesman on behalf of Loyalist refugees seeking compensation for damages suffered during the war. Dunmore's own claims for losses, which totaled almost £33,000, were paid in full by the British government.

In 1786 Dunmore was appointed governor of the Bahama Islands, which had become a major habitation for American Loyalists. His administration was marked by the same adventurism and lavish spending that characterized his Virginia tenure. Disputes over irregular public accounts, combined with shifting political alliances in England, and the scandalous secret marriage of Dunmore's daughter to a younger son of George III, led to the earl's dismissal as governor of the Bahamas in 1796. He returned to an English retirement and died in February 1809.

As Virginia's last royal governor, Dunmore played a central role in bringing on the Revolution in that colony. By concentrating his energies on western expansion and the Indian conflict of 1774, he neglected the maintenance of political ties binding many elite Virginians to Britain. Similar carelessness in official correspondence left Dunmore's superiors in the royal government unaware of Virginia's growing opposition to imperial policy. Any hope that moderate Virginians might continue to support reconciliation collapsed in November 1775 when Dunmore's heavy-handed proclamation declared freedom for slaves of rebellious masters. His military activities in the Chesapeake Bay from the summer of 1775 to the summer of 1776 suggested that a full-scale invasion from Britain was due at any moment, thus providing American radicals with an overwhelming propaganda advantage. At the same time, Dunmore's failure to secure the strategic Great Bridge and to hold the base on Gwynn's Island led to retreats that gravely undermined British credibility among Virginia Loyalists. No royal governor could have retained control of Virginia as the Revolution accelerated, but a man more prudent than Dunmore might well have delayed and diverted that colony's march to independence. *See also*: Dunmore's Proclamation; Virginia in the American Revolution

Turk McClesky

REFERENCES

Richard Orr Curry, "Lord Dunmore and the West: A Re-Evaluation," *West Virginia History*, 19 (1958):231–243; Benjamin Quarles, "Lord Dunmore as Liberator," *William and Mary Quarterly*, 3rd ser., 15 (1958):494–507; John E. Selby, *Dunmore* (1977); Reuben Gold Thwaites and Louise Phelps Kellogg, eds., *Documentary History of Dunmore's War*, 1774 (1905); J. Leitch Wright, Jr., "Lord Dunmore's Loyalist Asylum in the Floridas," *Florida Historical Quarterly*, 49 (1970–71):370–379.

Music, Military

During the American Revolution, music was used in the pageantry of military ceremonies to dramatize an event, to communicate orders, and to maintain the pace of troops on the march. Furthermore, military music had other functions—to provide a sense of awe and pride in a national army (Continental, British, French, or that of a German state), to signal shifts in tactics on the battlefield, and to provide entertainment for both soldiers and noncombatants.

In a period when royal and aristocratic patronage was the basis of a musician's livelihood, the European crowned heads had the most talented musicians of the time at their disposal. In France, for instance, no story of military music can overlook the contributions of the celebrated Jean-Baptiste Lully, who was for many years the *surintendant de la musique* to King Louis XIV, the renowned Sun King. Under Lully, military music became an essential part of *l'armée royale*. Lully not only enlarged the size of military bands but he also composed music for individual French army units. The military compositions of Lully best remembered today are those composed for the French cavalry, thanks largely to a rare recording by Adjutant-Chef Trompette-Major Albert Grosse and the mounted band of the famed French Garde Republicaine in the 1960s. Although the only French cavalry to serve in the American Revolution were the mounted hussars of the duc de Lauzun's Legion, the musical creations of Lully demonstrate the degree the French Bourbon Monarchy stressed military music as a symbol of its pomp and power.

Lully composed some of his most rousing pieces for the *Maison du Roi*, the troops of the French king that corresponded to King George III's Household Brigades. Among the royal units that Lully wrote for were the Grey Musketeers and the Black Musketeers, who received their names from the color of their splendid horses. Two other military formations for which Lully wrote marches were affiliated with the monarchy but were not actually part of the prestigious *Maison du Roi*, the Dragoons of the King and the Queen's Dragoons. The "Marche des Dragons du Roi," the "March of the King's Dragoons," was written by Lully at the express request of the regiment's officers in 1675, at the time when the army of Louis XIV was embroiled in the hard-fought war against the Dutch. The com-

position became so popular that its use spread throughout the regiments of the French cavalry and was still most likely in vogue when France entered the war on the side of the United States in 1778.

The British monarchy was not to be outdone by the French in its patronage of the great musical minds of the day. (In his classic work *Military Music of the American Revolution*, Raoul F. Camus makes the assertion that French music played a clear role in the development of that of England, due to the close diplomatic relationship between Louis XIV and Charles II of England.) King George II of England employed the great George Friedrich Handel to create works extolling the monarchy. In 1749, to commemorate the Peace of Aix-la-Chapelle, which brought to an end the War of the Austrian Succession, Handel penned the lusty "Fireworks Music," which enlisted the services of musicians of the regiments stationed in London, most likely from the Brigade of Guards, in a "Wagnerian" performance.

Of all the troops of France and England, none indeed was more resplendent in their uniforms than were the bandsmen. In the competition for the more resplendent band, the French army seemed to have taken the lead. A description of a drummer of the Soissonais Regiment, which thrilled the citizens of Philadelphia as it marched through their city on its way south to Yorktown in September 1781, gives an impressive picture of a French musician's dress:

> Drummers' coats were royal blue faced with the regimental color [crimson for the Soissonais] and liberally decorated with 'royal lace,' crimson with 2 white chain design. (Elting 1974)

The musicians in all the French infantry wore the same uniform, in the design called the "royal livery." Even those who served in the French marines, the *Corps Royale de Marine*, were issued the same uniform, although the marines were distinguished by an anchor on their buttons, while the infantry, like the Soissonais and Bourbonnais, had their regimental numbers on their uniform buttons (that of the Soissonais was "41"). This impressive chain design stretched down both sleeves of the uniform coat and onto the body of the coat itself. At the celebration of the Bicentennial of the United States Constitution in September 1987, a drummer of the military reenactment Bourbonnais Regiment wore this coat, complemented by the traditional white waistcoat, breeches, and gaiters, while on parade in front of Philadelphia's Independence Hall.

The sumptuousness of the royal livery and the professionalism of the musicmakers themselves were recognized by both sides at the surrender of the British to the French and Americans under George Washington at Yorktown on October 19, 1781. John Doehla, a sergeant with the Germans, who laid down their arms with General Charles Cornwallis's British, later recalled, as quoted by Camus,

> On the right wing of each French regiment was gorgeously paraded a rich standard of white silk, with three golden *fleurs de lis* embroidered on it. Beyond these standards stood the drummers and fifers, and in front of them the band, which played delightfully.

Dr. James Thacher, a surgeon who had soldiered on with the American army throughout the war remembered:

> The French troops, in complete uniform, displayed a martial and noble appearance, their band of music . . . is a delightful novelty, and produced while marching to the [surrender] ground a most enchanting effect.

As with the French army bands, the uniforms worn by those of their British adversaries were carefully regulated, the British by the royal clothing warrant of 1768, the French (at least those formations like the Soissonais who sailed to Newport, Rhode Island, with Rochambeau in 1780) according to the 1779 uniform regulations. In the British army, drummers and fifers were clothed in the color of the regiment's "facing color" (that is, the color on the lapels and coattails identifying the unit). For example, the musicians were garbed in coats in the 35th Regiment of Infantry of a brownish-yellow, the facing color of the 35th. In the 43rd British Reenactment Regiment, fifer Tom Maguire and drum major Larry Schmidt wore white coats, the facing color of the 43rd being white. British musicians wore bearskin caps, it should be noted, while French musicmakers had the traditional three-cornered hats.

It is interesting to note some contemporary comments that have come down to us regarding British bands of the day. In 1774, the 3rd Regiment, which would see action in the South during the war: "A trumpet is used to call back the Light Infantry to the battalion. 9 Musicians." Of

the 17th Regiment, which would fight at Princeton and at Brandywine, a 1772 inspection return noted: "Drummers and Fifes handsome and well-dressed—played well. Band of Music good and handsomely dressed." The 49th Regiment, which was in combat at Long Island and White Plains had "A band of music. Grenadiers and Drummers have black bearskins."

Uniform remarks have purposely been reserved for the infantry of France and England because, except for Lauzun's cavalry, no French mounted units came to America, and only two British cavalry regiments, the 16th and 17th Light Dragoons, served in the war. And even these two fine units later lost their organizational identity when they became amalgamated in Colonel Banastre Tarleton's British Legion later during the conflict.

Of the instruments used by the bandsmen, in addition to the better-known fifes and drums, there were also oboes, bassoons, horns, trumpets, and sometimes "jingling johnnies," which were bells mounted on staffs, in imitation of the bands of the exotic Ottoman Turks. In the famed British Highland regiments, the pipers took the place of the fifers. Except for the Highland pipes, music instruments were generally the same for the English, French, and American "bands of musick."

Insofar as the Continental Army was concerned, the United States was the youngest state of these three main combatants, and it had less of its own music on which to draw compared to the two monarchies and the German states. Therefore, American "musick" tended to enshrine the young nation's accomplishments and newfound freedom rather than any longstanding dynastic legacy.

One such song praising American liberty was called "Chester." Composed by Walter Billings, better known at the time for his sacred music, it is named after the city in Pennsylvania to which Washington's army withdrew following its defeat by the British General William Howe at Brandywine in October 1777. It reads:

> Let tyrants shake their iron rod,
> And slavery clank her galling chains;
> We fear them not;—we trust in God—
> New England's God forever reigns.
>
> Howe and Burgoyne and Clinton, too
> With Prescott and Cornwallis join'd,
> Together plot our overthrow,
> In one Infernal league combin'd.

Where God inspired us for the fight,
Their ranks were broke, their lines were
    forc'd,
Their ships were scatter'd in our sight,
Or Swiftly driven from our coast.

The Foe comes on with haughty stride,
Our troops advance with martial noise,
Their Vet'rans flee before our youth
And Gen'rals yield to beardless boys.

What grateful off'ring shall we bring
What shall we render to the Lord,
Loud Hallelujahs let us sing,
And praise His name on ev'ry chord.

"Chester" actually predated the Revolution, having been written by Billings in 1770. According to George P. Carroll, former Director of Music for the Company of Military Historians, this tune may "have been the most popular American song of the War."

Other pieces of martial music written to buttress support for the Patriot cause praised famous generals and battlefield triumphs. "God Save Great Washington" really initiated the development of Washington as the symbolic premier American of his age. Amusingly enough, the music for the composition was the British hymn "God Save the King," an early example of "liberating" something from the enemy for Patriot use. "Stony Point" was an impressive fife and drum tune composed to mark General Anthony Wayne's storming of the British fortification above the Hudson River in July 1779 at Stony Point.

Contemporary mention of American military bands begins in 1776. An early booster of American military music was General Andrew Lewis, in command of Continental troops at Williamsburg, Virginia. Lewis appointed a drum major and fife major, Raoul Camus relates, and ordered them to "practice the young Fifers & Drummers between the hours of 11 and 1 o'clock every day." Other Continental units known for their tunesmiths were the 3rd Continental Artillery Regiment, Samuel Webb's Additional Regiment, and Christian Febiger's Infantry Regiment.

It is interesting to note that Webb's regiment represents another example of wartime "liberation." Webb's Continentals were garbed in coats shipped from England—red coats of course—that were taken off a British supply ship waylaid by an American privateer on its course for the British-held New York City.

Febiger, who constantly requested aid to improve his band and may have been the first American to request "Federal" funds for the arts, wrote:

> The men are enlisted to serve as musicians or fifers and do duty as such. Their music had more influence on the minds and motions of the militia last summer in this state [Virginia] than the oratory of [the great ancient Roman] Cicero, and in the recruiting business they are at least as useful as a well-spoken recruiting Sergeant.

Febiger received little government support for his regimental band (that of the 2nd Virginia), and hence, he relied heavily on his own money to keep the band functioning. The band in 1782 numbered nine musicians. Colonel Febiger was so dedicated to having an excellent "band of musick" that at one time he turned in 21 fifes for being out of key.

It appears that the band of the 3rd Artillery, whose colonel was Massachusetts' John Crane, was considered the most accomplished in Washington's army. Crane's band is known to have acquired clarinets as well as bassoons, oboes, and horns, and may have received support from the entire Brigade of Artillery. Lieutenant John Hiwell of the band was appointed Inspector and Superintendent of music for the entire army in August 1778, as testimony to the band's professionalism and virtuosity. In February 1783 the 3rd Artillery's "band of musick" played a concert at Portsmouth, New Hampshire, which featured "several overtures, symphonies, military music, several songs, and several duettos [duettes?] on the French horn," according to the New Hampshire *Gazette* for February 15, 1783.

In addition to these bands, the best known of Continental Army bands, other formations had their music too. Colonel Henry Jackson's regimental "musicianers" were on hand to play for the Christmas festivities in 1778, when the Continentals were in camp around Middlebrook, New Jersey. In return for their music festival, the bandsmen were rewarded with "Provisions, and one Gill of West India Rum per day and more when he may find it Necessary." In return for its role in this Yuletide celebration, Webb's band received new coats of white or yellow as Christmas gifts.

Far more than today, when military singing is almost a lost art (except for formal choirs), military songs and marches of the Revolutionary period, like the later Civil War, expressed the hopes and lives and feelings of the fighting men. Such songs could be stirring expressions of fierce regimental pride like the "British Grenadiers" or the sort of humorous songs the French army enjoyed. (One musical "hit" of Louis XIV's time, "L'Oignon Frit," told how French soldiers loved onions "frit a l'huile"—fried in oil, deep-fried as we would call it today.)

Another French favorite mocked the famous British commander John Churchill, First Duke of Marlborough. Called "Malbrouck s'-en-va-t'en-guerre," it went something like this:

Malbrouck s'-en-va-t'en guerre
Malbrouck s'-en-va-t'en guerre
Mirontons, mirontons, mirontons,
Mirontons, mirontons, mirontons,
Malbrouck s'-en-va-t'en guerre

Ne sais que reviendra
Ne sais que reviendra
Mirontons, mirontons, mirontons,
Mirontons, mirontons, mirontons,
Malbrouck s'-en-va-t'en guerre.

A rough translation would be as follows:

Marlborough has gone to war,
repeat
nonsense line (mirontons)
nonsense line
Marlborough has gone to war.

I don't know when he'll come back
repeat
nonsense line
nonsense line
Marlborough has gone to war.

For sheer pomp and circumstance, nothing has ever surpassed the "British Grenadiers":

Some talk of Alexander, and some of Hercules,
Of Hector and Lysander, and such
great names as these;
But of all the world's brave heroes there's
none that can compare
With a tow, row, row, row, row, row
To the British Grenadiers.

Whene'ever we are commanded to storm
the palisades,
Our leaders march with fuses, and we with
hand grenades;
We throw them from the glacis, about the
enemy's ears,
With a tow, row, row, row, row, row
To the British Grenadiers.

And when the siege is over, we to the town
repair,

The townsmen cry, "Hurrah, boys, here
comes a Grenadier;
Here comes the Grenadiers, my boys, who
know no doubts and fears!"
With a tow, row, row, row, row, row
To the British Grenadiers.

Then let us fill a bumper, and drink the
health of those
Who carry caps and pouches, and wear the
louped clothes;
May they and their commanders live happy
all their years,
With a tow, row, row, row, row, row
To the British Grenadiers.

(The official version of the "British Grenadiers," from the Horse Guards in London, substitutes "and some of Militades" for "and such great names as these.")

The earliest version of the "British Grenadiers" dates from about 1685 when grenadiers were used as special storm troops to attack enemy fortifications with primitive hand grenades. During the Revolution, grenadiers were still big and hardy men and were used for the toughest combat assignments. Memories of the brave lads who wore "the louped clothes" in the Duke of Marlborough's time are still kept strong in today's British army. During the "Trooping of the Color" ceremony on Queen Elizabeth II's birthday, when the color (the flag) is marched out into the center of the parade ground, the massed bands of the Horse Guards and the Foot Guards (of which the Grenadier Guards is first in precedence) break into a thundering rendition of the "British Grenadiers."

The most interesting of the songs performed to stiffen the soldiers' resolve in the face of the foe was "The White Cockade." According to George Carroll, when the Minutemen contingent from Acton, Massachusetts, met the "redcoats" at Concord, on April 19, 1775, the two Acton fifers, commanded by Major John Butterick, struck up "The White Cockade." Although not an American tune like "Yankee Doodle," "The White Cockade" had a hearty pedigree as a song of defiance against the British. It began as a song of Stuart resistance in England to the Hanoverian Georges and became the unofficial national anthem of the Irish, who fought the British both at home in the Jacobite War of 1688–1690 in Ireland and later in the legendary Irish Brigade in the service of France, the "Wild Geese." Due to the text, "The White Cockade" might date from the Jacobite Rebellion of 1745, when "Bonnie Prince Charlie" (Charles Edward Stuart) invaded the British Isles to regain the throne of his father, James II.

> King Charles he is King James's son,
> And from a royal line is sprung;
> Then up with shout, and out with blade,
> And We'll raise once more the white cockade.
> Oh! my dear, my fair-haired youth,
> Thou yet has hearts of fire and truth;
> Then up with shout, and out with blade,
> We'll raise once more the white cockade.
>
> My young mens' hearts are dark with woe,
> On my virgins' cheeks the grief-drops flow;
> The sun scarce lights the sorrowing day,
> Since our rightful prince went far away.
> He's gone, the stranger holds his throne,
> The royal bird far off is flown;
> But up with shout, and out with blade—
> We'll stand or fall with the white cockade.
>
> Nor more the cuckoo hails the spring,
> The woods no more with the staunch hounds ring;
> The song from the glen, so sweet before,
> Is hushed since our Charles has left our shore.
> The Prince is gone; but soon he will come,
> With trumpet sounds and with beat of drum;
> Then up with shout, and out with blade;
> Huzza for the right and the white cockade!

(The song may actually have been written after "Bonnie Prince Charlie" was defeated by the Duke of Cumberland at Culloden Moor in 1746 and "went far away"—back to painful exile in France. At any rate, on the day of Concord, many Britishers had reason to rue hearing "The White Cockade.")

The white cockade was the emblem worn by the Irish troops in their three-cornered hats, and also by their French comrades in arms. When the Comte de Rochambeau brought his fighting French over to support the Patriot cause in 1780, General Washington ordered that all American troops would henceforth sport a white cockade over their usual black one to honor the French alliance. This must have been no small source of pride to the thousands of Irish serving in the Continental Army.

By the time Rochambeau disembarked at Newport, Rhode Island, Continental Army musicians were certainly more fittingly accoutered than the daring fifers of Acton. Acting on congressional authority, Washington issued a General Order regarding the soldiers' clothing on October 2, 1779. Basically, a blue uniform was to be worn by all Continental and state regiments, with the color of the facings identifying the state of the infantry regiments, and the artillery and cavalry distinguished by scarlet and white, respectively.

In spite of the General Orders, due to supply problems it was often very hard to dress soldiers in the manner stipulated in the regulations. Ironically, the best source of information on how the musicians and the other soldiers actually looked appears in printed descriptions of army deserters found in contemporary newspapers, for the periods both before and after the uniform order:

> "A drummer wearing a new hat, blue regimental coat, white breeches." (Colonel David Gilman's New Hampshire regiment, in the Portsmouth, New Hampshire, *Freeman's Journal*, August 31, 1776)

> "Scarlet coat faced with black, leather breeches, white shoes, a beaver hat [worn by a drummer]." (Colonel Gamaliel Bradford's 14th Massachusetts Continental Regiment, in the *Boston Gazette*, February 3, 1777)

> "Blue coat with yellow facings, and a drummer's cap." (Colonel William Russell's 13th Virginia Continental Regiment, in the *Pennsylvania Evening Post*, August 16, 1777)

As in the British army, Continental musicians seem to have worn usually uniforms of "reversed colors": if a regiment's coat was blue with yellow facings, then a musician's coat might be yellow with blue facings.

Although desertion continued to plague the American "musick," sometimes recruits came from unlikely sources. One English traveler noted dejectedly in 1778:

> I am sorry to inform you that the Americans are too successful in enticing our soldiers to desert; a few days since the whole band of the 62nd Regt. excepting the Master, deserted in a body, and are now playing to an American Regt. in Boston.

Along with the other functions executed by musicians in all the three armies studied for this essay, they also carried out the utilitarian one of announcing orders both in camp and on the field of battle. One important point to note is that, in the cavalry and light infantry companies, orders were usually given by bugle horns or trumpets, since these types of troops fought in far more dispersed formations than did the regular troops like the grenadiers. Furthermore, orders played out on fife or drum simply did not carry as far as those given by trumpets or bugles.

In camp, all the parts of a soldier's day were marked by the tuneful commands, the whistle of five, the rattle drums, or the clear calls of the trumpet. The use of music to give orders in the Continental forces was codified in General Baron von Steuben's celebrated regulations. To rise up the troops in the morning, the Baron used the British call to reveille: "the reveille is beat at day-break, and is the signal for the soldiers to rise, and the sentries to leave off challenging [from the night before]." Most aspects of military life were provided for in music, from collecting firewood to calling meetings of officers and noncommissioned officers. If the troops were to prepare for battle, the drums would roll out the stirring "To Arms." In combat, when the time came for an attack with cold steel, the "British Reveille" would sound out again—for it had another, more ominous, title "The Points of War"—the bayonets. Emulating the British, the tune "The British Grenadiers" was used by the Americans to order an advance, at least in music adopted by General Henry Knox for his artillery in 1779.

In combat, although the infantry often took the brunt of the fighting, it was the cavalry that had the role of delivering the final blow. However, a sometimes fatal flaw to cavalry maneuvers was a very simple one: cavalry did not know how to stop charging. At the Battle of Waterloo in 1815, the British Union Brigade was successful in riding over the French artillery, but it was then cut to pieces because its officers could not recall their men to the safety of their own lines. For this reason, the call to rally after a charge might be considered the most important of cavalry trumpet or bugle calls in action; in the French cavalry, this command was the *ralliement* and has been defined by Albert Gossez as the order that "served to reassemble the squadrons [*peletons*] after the charge."

When on the march, it was up to the music not only to keep up the step of the troops but also to bolster their morale. Grenadiers and light infantry marched at a faster pace than the rest of the infantry, interestingly enough; "The British Grenadiers" was at a quick 2/4 time. Little could enliven the pace of tired men on a long, dusty march than a merry fife and drum piece. One such tune was known as "Mrs. Casey," popular in the British army, and most likely in the Ameri-

can as well. Indeed, a great number of marches as well as military orders given by music were shared by these two opposing forces. "Roslin Castle" was used as a funeral dirge by both armies, and "The Rogue's March" was common in British and American camps to drum out of camp deserters, other malefactors, and whores. The only apparent difference was that the refrain "poor old soldier" in "The Rogue's March" became "poor old Tory" in the Yankee version. Both the "Quick Scotch" and the slower-paced "Scotch" were used as reveilles in American and British encampments.

A fascinating point about music played on the march, as well as at many other times, was its unmilitary nature. Perhaps it reflected, as today, the very small part of a soldier's career that was actually spent in combat—or perhaps a strong desire to forget the actual fighting and bloodshed. Many English regimental marches had their origin in tunes popular in the counties in which the units were raised. "The Warwickshire Lads," composed for the 1769 Shakespeare celebration at Stratford-on-Avon, enjoyed a following among units raised in the county of Warwickshire, such as the 6th Foot, which in 1776 arrived in New York City, only to be divided up among other formations. The 25th Foot, the Edinburgh Regiment, which saw action at Gibraltar, marched to the old Scots classic "Blue Bonnets Over the Border." The 26th Foot swung along to the jaunty "Within a Mile of Edinboro' Town," being likewise a Scottish regiment; the 26th was blooded at Monmouth in 1778.

French marches, at least until the martial First Empire of Napoleon, also had an unmilitary flair. A longtime favorite was "Aupres de ma blonde ("After my Blonde"), as was the aforementioned "L'Oignon Frit." Other French pieces were the "Chevaliers de la Table Ronde" ("The Knights of the Round Table"), "La Joie du Soldat" ("A Soldier's Joy"), and a tune that reflected the years when Canada had been ruled by France, before Canada fell to England in the French and Indian War, "Un Canadien Errant" ("The Wandering Canadian"). What list of Gallic tunes could but end with another salute to feminine beauty— "La Belle Catherine" ("The Beautiful Catherine")?

Of American songs, "The Girl I Left Behind Me" had British roots, dating from about the time of the French and Indian War, when the

English raised regiments at a time when they feared invasion from France. A song from the French and Indian War, "Over the Hills and Far Away," which may still have been played by Continental musicians, was derived directly from a British tune of the same name that was a musical "hit" with British fighting men under the Duke of Marlborough. A comparison of the two songs is interesting, to show how a song's lyrics could be modified to keep up with the changing times. First, the old version of "Over the Hills and Far Away" from Marlborough's time:

Hark now the drums beat up again,
For all true soldier gentlemen
Then let us 'list and march, I say,
Over the hills and far away.

Chorus
Over the hills and o'er the main,
To Flanders, Portugal and Spain,
Queen Anne commands and we'll obey
Over the hills and far away.

All gentlemen that have a mind
To serve the queen that's good and kind
Come 'list and enter into pay,
Then over the hills and far away.

Chorus
No more from sound of drums retreat
When Marlborough and Galway beat
The French and Spaniards every day—
Went over the hills and far away!

(The line where the French and Spaniards "went over the hills" to flee from the British commanders Marlborough and Galway may be the origin of the expression "going over the hill"—meaning to desert.)

Now, the French and Indian War song:

Over the hills with heart we go,
To fight the proud insulting foe,
Our country calls and we'll obey
Over the hills and far away.

Over the mountain's dreary waste,
To meet the enemy we haste,
Our king commands and we'll obey,
Over the hills and far away.

Whoe'er is bold, whoe'er is free
Will join and come along with me,
To drive the French without delay
Over the hills and far away.

On fair Ohio's banks we stand,
Musket and bayonet in hand,
The French are beat, they dare not stay,
But take to their heels, and run away.

Over the rocks and over the steep,
Over the waters, wide and deep,
We'll drive the French without delay
Over the hills and far away.

Of course, no coverage of American marching songs would be complete without the godfather of them all, "Yankee Doodle." Apparently, the song was first written in England during the English Civil War by the Cavaliers to mock the sober Puritan Roundheads; later on, British redcoats used it to humiliate the Americans in the early days of the Revolution. Nevertheless, Washington's Continentals brazenly adopted it as their own, presumably with modernized verses, dating when Washington took command in 1775:

Fath'r and I went down to camp,
Along with Captain Good-'in,
And there we saw the men and boys
As thick as hasty pud-din'.

Chorus
Yankee Doodle keep it up,
Yankee Doodle dandy,
Mind the music and the step,
And with the girls be handy.

And there we see a thousand men,
As rich as Squire David;
And what they wasted ev'ry day,
I wish it could be saved.

Chorus
And there was Captain Washington
Upon a slapping stallion,
A giving orders to his men,
I guess there was a million.

Chorus
And then the feathers on his hat,
They looked so very fine, ah!
I wanted peskily to get
To give to my Jemima.

Chorus
And there I see a swamping gun,
Large as a log of maple
Upon a mighty little cart;
A load for father's cattle.

Chorus
And every time they fired it off,
It took a horn of powder;   [a cannon]
It made a noise like father's gun,
Only a nation louder.

Chorus
And there I see a little keg,
Its head all made of leather,

They knocked upon 't with little sticks   [a drum]
To call the folks together.

Chorus
And Cap'n Davis had a gun,
He kind o'clapt his hand on 't
               [putting a bayonet on a musket]
And stuck a crooked stabbing iron
Upon the little end on 't.

Chorus
The troopers, too, would gallop up
And fire in our faces;
It scared me almost half to death   [cavalry drill]
To see them run such races.

Chorus
It scared me so I hooked it off   [hooked it off—ran]
Nor stopped, as I remember.
Nor turned about til I got home,
Locked up in my mother's chamber.

Chorus

From memorializing a European dynasty to quickening a soldier's leaden pace on an exhausting march, to waking a soldier in the morning to putting him to sleep at night, military music was as much a part of a Revolutionary War soldier's life as his hat or his musket. It gave him pride in his country and army, the courage to carry on in the face of great odds, and a laugh or a smile when he needed it. For a soldier in the Revolution, military music was very important.

Endnote

It should be noted that the trumpeters of the British Light Dragoons were issued three-cornered hats with feathers atop them rather than the jockey hat-type helmets worn by the rest of their regiments. Drums, in fact, seem to have been issued to the musicians instead of trumpets before roughly the mid-1760s. According to Captain Hinde, in his authoritative *The Discipline of the Light Horse* (1778), the musicians, as cited by Hew Strachan,

> When they are dismounted, form a band of music, consisting of two French horns, two clarinets, and two bassoons, and also one fife to a Regiment; but when mounted, the trumpets only found.

Apparently, as in all uniforms, there were exceptions to the rule. An inspection return for the Light Company of the 4th King's Own Regiment of Foot (infantry) had trumpeters wearing hats in lieu of bearskin caps. In the reenactment 43rd Foot in 1988 hats instead of caps were also permitted for the musicians. All so-called royal regiments in the British army had blue facings, like the 4th. Interestingly enough, drummers and fifers of the 13th and 25th regiments seem to have been crowned with *white* bearskin caps!

John F. Murphy, Jr.

REFERENCES

Russell Ames, *The Story of American Folk Song* (1960); Major R. Barnes, *The British Army of 1914* (1968); ———, *The Soldiers of London* (1968); Michael Barthorp, *British Cavalry Uniforms Since 1660* (1984); Oscar Brand, *Songs of '76: A Folksinger's History of the Revolution* (1972); Raoul F. Camus, *Military Music of the American Revolution* (1976); Burke Davis, *America's First Army* (1962); Col. John R. Elting, ed., *Military Uniforms in America: The Era of the American Revolution, 1755–1795* (1974); Lilane and Fred Funcken, *L'Uniforme et les Armes des Soldats de la Guerre en Dentelle*, 2 vols. (1975–6); Kathleen Hoagland, *1000 Years of Irish Poetry* (1975); Philip R.N. Katcher, *Encyclopedia of British, Provincial, and German Army Units, 1775–1783* (1973); ———, *Uniforms of the Continental Army* (1981); Lt. Charles M. Lefferts, *Uniforms of the American, British, French, and German Armies of the War of the American Revolution, 1775–1783* (n.d.); Alan Lomax, *Folk Songs of North America* (1960); John Mollo, *Uniforms of the American Revolution* (1975); National Society of Colonial Dames of America, *American War Songs* (1925); Michel Petard, "L'Evolution du Costume Militaire [1775–1779]," *Tradition*, 9 (1987):23–7; Harold L. Peterson, *The Book of the Continental Soldier* (1968); Private correspondence from Colonel Martel, Curator, Musee de' l'Armee, Paris, France, 1976–1979, on French military music; Hew Strachan, *British Military Uniforms, 1768–96: The Dress of the British Army from Official Sources* (1975); James Thacher, *Military Journal of the American Revolution* (1969); Richard Wheeler, *Voices of 1776* (1972); Robert and Christopher Wilkinson-Lathan, *Infantry Uniforms Including Artillery and Other Supporting Corps of Britain and the Commonwealth, 1742–1855* (1969); Lewis Winstock, *Songs and Music of the Redcoats, 1642–1902* (1972).

DISCOGRAPHY

"A Concert of Military Music." Fifes and Drums of Colonial Williamsburg. Colonial Williamsburg Foundation (1978).

"Marches et Fanfares de la Cavalerie." Fanfare de Cavalerie de la Garde Republicaine. Vogue Records (n.d.).

"Marches of the Vanishing Regiments." Band of the Royal School of Music, Kneller Hall. BBC Record (1968–9).

"Military Music in America: Fife and Drum Music of the American Revolution." Company of Military Collectors & Historians (n.d.).

"Songs and Music of the Redcoats, 1642–1902." Martin Wyndham-Read. The Druids, Gerry Fox, Band of the Scots Guards. Argo Records (n.d.).

"Vive la Compagnie!" Tippecanoe Ancient Fife and Drum Corps (n.d.).

Musket

A smoothbore long-barrelled full-stocked longarm used by infantry from the sixteenth to the nineteenth centuries. By the time of the Revolution these were all of flintlock ignition and fitted with a steel ramrod (except some older unconverted British arms with wood rammers used to arm the Loyalists), sling swivels, and a socket bayonet. British patterns have their barrel held to the stock by three pins and the upper sling swivel screw, while French and German models use three bands, the upper band normally having two straps across the barrel.

Great Britain

British muskets as used by the regular and Loyalist troops, and as captured from them by the Americans, were of three basic types: the Long Land Pattern with a 46-inch barrel, the Short Land Pattern with a 42-inch barrel, and the Marine or Militia musket also with a 42-inch barrel. Short Land muskets made until 1775 have a rounded-surface sideplate; those after 1775 have a flat plate of the same outline. From 1778 the locks of the Short Land musket have two screws showing behind the cock, a teardrop finial on the feather-spring, and no engraving on the top jaw or back of the steel. From 1779 the second brass rammer pipe was made with a straight, tapering flare toward the front. The Long Land Pattern was carried by the Guards Brigade sent to America. All other infantry regiments, with possible individual exceptions within regiments for logistic reasons, carried the Short Land Pattern, which had been officially adopted for all line infantry in 1768. The marines carried the Marine or Militia musket, which resembles the Short Land but lacks a thumbpiece at the wrist and has a screw through the buttplate tang rather than a transverse pin. Loyalist troops were often equipped with older arms, many still having wooden rammers, and these would have included Long and Short Land, Marine or Militia, and perhaps even Short Land Dragoon muskets with wood rammers, as well as Short Land muskets made in Liege beginning in 1778. The Royal Navy had fixed allowances of Sea Service muskets on each rating of vessel. These muskets have 37-inch pin-held 0.78 caliber barrels; the lockplate and ring-neck cock are flat with a bevelled edge. The brass furniture included are flat sideplate and buttplate, with two rammer pipes (no tailpipe) and a rounded trigger guard with a bulbous front finial. They take a standard socket bayonet and have a wooden rammer. All regulation British military arms will bear the king's proofmarks on the barrel [two marks formed of (1) a crown over GR over a broad arrow and (2) a crown over crossed sceptres; and the Government ownership mark stamped on the lockplate below the pan, of a crown over the broad arrow; and the Ordnance Storekeeper's mark struck into the right side of the butt of a crown over the script letters GR addorsed]. In addition the stock will bear inspector's crowned numerals and contractor's names or initials, and similar crowned numerals will be found on the barrel and inside the lockplate. Engraved on the lockplate ahead of the cock will be the royal cipher of a crown over GR and across the tail of the plate either a lockmaker's name and date (before 1764) or TOWER.

France

The French troops sent to America in 1779 carried chiefly the Model 1763-66 musket (actually the lightweight version of the Model 1763 introduced in 1766 but still marked on the barrel tang with the earlier date) and a very small scattering of various low-production models up to that of 1774. All of these were a nominal 0.69 caliber, taking a spherical ball of 0.66" diameter and a charge of 7 drams 4^1/2 grains (197 grains). The barrel was 44 ^{3}/4 inches long and secured by 3 flat bands, the upper one having 2 straps over the barrel with a blade front sight on the rear strap. The lock and ring-neck cock are flat with a beveled edge. The furniture was iron, another difference between the French and the British, German, and Spanish muskets, which had brass furniture. All had steel rammers. The French navy used the Model 1763–66 musket with all brass furniture. French regulation arms will bear the name of the national armory at which they were manufactured engraved on the lockplate (Charleville, Maubeuge, St. Etienne,

Tulle), with appropriate proofmarks for that armory on the barrel.

United States

The rebel armies were equipped with a mixture of captured British and Hessian, and French regulation arms, as well as copies of the British Short Land Pattern stocked up for the various Committees of Safety by local gunsmiths using a combination of old parts and newly homemade parts; they also obtained arms made in Liege and Holland, usually following contemporary Dutch and German patterns and large numbers of old, surplus arms supplied to American buyers by various commercial firms. Many of these arms were stamped or branded on metal and wood with the markings of the various states, or with "US" or "U.States" on government-purchased arms. There is considerable question among scholars as to how much of this marking was done during the Revolution, and how much during the 1780s and 1790s. Some British arms had remained in the colonies after the peace of 1783, but most of those obtained by the rebels were captured in British supply vessels by American privateers. Muskets made or restocked in America were almost all based on pin-fastened British patterns and will have American black walnut, maple, or cherry stocks; some used old or captured regulation British furniture and locks, while others incorporated simpler and cruder designs of brass mounts. Normally these muskets are not signed.

Spain

The Spanish forces based at New Orleans and sent from Cuba after her declaration of war on June 21, 1779, were armed with the Model 1757 Infantry musket. Whether any of the Spanish colonial militia forces would have been armed with the earlier Model 1722 Infantry musket is questionable, given the generally inadequate storage and maintenance facilities in harsh climatic conditions. Model 1722 muskets have a 43 3/4-inch 0.70 caliber barrel held by three flat bands, with the breech section octagonal to just forward of the lower band. The double-strap top band is held by a round pin-spring, and the rammer guide on the underside is straight, not flared. The lower band strap is narrower over the barrel, and the middle band, which holds the upper sling swivel, is wider than the later model.

The lock has a round pan with no pan bridle and is flat with a beveled edge and has no groove across the tail. The stock is of the conventional "hand-rail" design, with no carving at the barrel tang. The brass furniture is rounded, except for the flat, beveled-edge S-pattern sideplate. The Model 1757 musket has a 43 3/4-inch 0.70 caliber round barrel, the breech area octagonal only for a few inches ahead of the lock area, with a front sight that doubles as bayonet stud. The barrel is held by three flat brass bands, the two lower held by friction, the upper band with two straps and a flare on the underside as a guide for the iron rammer, held by a flat pin-spring on the right side. Sling swivels are mounted through the middle band and at the lower end of the trigger guard tang. The walnut stock has an apron carved around the barrel tang, and the conventional "hand-rail" butt, with a groove along each side of the comb. The furniture is brass and is flat with beveled edges, the elaborate sideplate having a third screw at the tail. The lockplate and cock are also flat with beveled edges, the pan is faceted and has a bridle, and the cock-screw has a large ring-head. Spanish lock markings include a small crown with a date stamped beneath it, and sometimes contractor's initials.

De Witt Bailey

REFERENCES

De Witt Bailey, *British Military Longarms 1715–1865* (1986); Howard L. Blackmore, *British Military Firearms 1656–1850* (1961); Jean Boudriot, *Armes a Feu Francaises Modeles d'Ordonnance* (1961–63); Juan L. Calvo, *Armamento Reglamentario y Auxiliar de Ejercito Espanol*, Vol. 1 (1975); Warren Moore, *Weapons of the American Revolution* (1967); George C. Neumann, *The History of Weapons of the American Revolution* (1967).

Musketoon

A short heavy-barrelled smoothbore shoulder arm, originally meaning "short musket" but often used interchangeably with Blunderbuss. Naval and military (as opposed to maritime and civilian) usage in the eighteenth century generally referred to short heavy-barrelled arms with a slightly flared muzzle, used as boat guns. The French word *mousqueton* means carbine, a totally different type of weapon.

Musketoons were used by the navies that participated in the Revolution, often with a swivel shaped like an oarlock through the fore-end.

De Witt Bailey

REFERENCE

De Witt Bailey, *British Military Longarms 1715–1865* (1986).

Musketry

The term "musketry" indicates the military use of the musket to achieve controlled mass firepower, based on the use of linear tactics and firing by volleys. Linear tactics involved deploying of the regiments in as wide a front as numbers, terrain, and enemy numbers would allow, to maximize the number of muskets that could be fired.

In the British army a system of firing by Grand Divisions, based on the tactical unit of the platoon, was used. The regiment or battalion of eight companies (light infantry and grenadiers were brigaded separately in America) was divided into 12 platoons, each with an officer and sergeant. These platoons were formed into four Grand Divisions, each having three platoons, with a captain, a lieutenant, and an ensign in charge. The platoons were arranged in a symmetrical order in the firing line, and firing could be either by Grand Divisions (in the order 1,3,4,2 from the left of the line), or by platoons commenced at either end of the line, or from the center working outward in each direction. The object was to keep some part of the enemy line always under fire, and to have some part of one's own line always ready to fire. In practice this elaborate system (as well as all others) deteriorated very quickly in combat conditions. It depended heavily upon the amount and quality of training to which the troops had been subjected. Highly trained, disciplined troops could, under combat conditions, deliver at the most three volleys according to the manual, but after, the noise of battle obscured verbal commands from company officers and noncommissioned officers, and often even drum commands to a large extent, and firing was "at will," and as rapidly as the individual could manage until (a) his ammunition ran out, (b) his musket ceased to function, or (c) a bayonet charge was ordered. When advancing or retreating, firing was either by individual or ranks. Having fired, the foremost rank would stand fast and the rear rank advance through the intervals, form line, and fire, with the process being repeated until the enemy line broke or a charge was ordered. Although General Howe stated in General Orders while the British army was in Boston that three ranks would be the standard tactical deployment formation, all available evidence suggests that he and his successors used two ranks in action.

The German auxiliary troops, which were specially raised for service with the British forces in North America, adapted their maneuvers and firings to those of the British, including the line of two ranks.

The French army had used three ranks since the early 1750s with a variety of fire systems based on regimental preference. Throughout the first half of the eighteenth century firepower had been played down by all French military writers, and certainly by field commanders, largely because of the lack of discipline and training of most French regiments, and the resulting emphasis on movement and shock tactics in place of firepower. There was no fire training until after 1748. Regulations of 1755, 1764, and 1766 specified fire by section, platoon, quarter-rank, half-rank, and battalion. The Instruction of May 30, 1775, was the first to prescribe fire drill for the troops, at distances from 100 to 220 yards, but it was accompanied by a very small ammunition allowance. The final drill instruction of the ancien régime, the Ordinance of June 1, 1776, abolished the variety of firings and specified fire by files, beginning with the first file on the right of each platoon, progressing by files to the left, for one firing only; thereafter "at will." This reflects acceptance of battlefield conditions. There was also firing by half-battalions and battalions, ahead and to the rear. How far any of these official instructions had superseded regimental preferences in the regiments sent to America is unclear.

In the Continental Army musketry training, prior to the appearance of Baron von Steuben's initial "Instructions" in 1778 and his official "Regulations for the Order and Discipline of the Troops of the United States" in early 1779, was based on older British manuals such as Bland's "Treatise of Military Discipline" (1738–1762) and Windham's "A Plan of Discipline Composed for the Use of the County of Norfolk" (1759), and the most recent official British "Manual Exercise" of 1764. Timothy Pickering's simplified version of the 1764 manual was adopted for Massachusetts militia in 1776. Von Steuben's manual was an amalgam of the French regulations of 1755 and 1766, the Prussian (English translation of 1759), the British 1764 Manual, and Pickering's of 1775. Two ranks was the standard formation for maneuvering and from which firing was performed either by platoons or ranks.

De Witt Bailey

REFERENCES

De Witt Bailey, *British Military Longarms 1715–1865* (1986); Howard L. Blackmore, *British Military Firearms 1656–1850*(1961); Warren Moore, *Weapons of the American Revolution* (1967); George C. Neumann, *The History of the Weapons of the American Revolution* (1967).

Mutiny in Philadelphia, Pennsylvania (June 1783)

The year 1783 should have been a joyful one for the infant United States. A newly created nation had humbled the mightiest empire in eighteenth-century Europe during the peace negotiations in Paris after nearly eight years of bloody warfare. Yet America was gripped in the throngs of political and financial chaos. In order to limit the rapidly expanding national debt, the Confederation Congress, in session in the country's largest city of Philadelphia, ordered Washington to begin furloughing his troops even though the definite peace would not be ratified between all the concerned parties for many months. However, the commander-in-chief insisted that his men should leave the service of their country with at least three months' pay in their pockets. The national treasury, though, did not have the funds to support Washington's promises, and appeals to the states for assistance produced few results. Superintendent of Finance Robert Morris felt compelled to issue his own bank notes to the soldiers; they had the nickname "Short Bob" or "Long Bob" notes in his honor and were redeemable by the states in various durations of time depending on their designation. Congress, on the other hand, had attempted to placate the soldiers by permitting them to retain their weapons as a parting gift. However, growing discontentment was spreading throughout the Continental command because of the insensitivity to the army.

The first hint of trouble occurred on June 13 when the sergeants, in command of the local Philadelphia garrison, conducted a protest demonstration on the very doorstep of the Confederation Congress, the Pennsylvania State House or as it is known today, Independence Hall. These noncommissioned officers refused to accept their discharge until they received their overdue pay. James Madison noted that the Congress took little notice of this "mutinous memorial from the Sergeants."

The soldiers' exasperation over their reimbursement also manifested itself among the troops of the Pennsylvania Line stationed in Lancaster of their home state. A small number, between 50 to 80 enlisted men, refused to heed the orders of their commanding officer, Colonel Richard Butler. On June 17 this small group began a march on the government in Philadelphia to express their grievances. They vowed "to cooperate with the men in the city [the Philadelphia Garrison]" and "to procure their pay." Butler vainly tried to appease his men with promises, but to no avail. Butler sent officers after the marching troops to warn them that if they pressed on they would be sent back empty-handed and their "appearance in Philadelphia . . . will be justly construed into menace, rather than a proper mode of seeking justice."

On June 19, a letter from Butler reached John Dickinson, the president of the Supreme Executive Council of Pennsylvania, warning of the mutinous troops headed in his direction. It was his council's duty to maintain local law and order, which included preserving the safety and protection of the Continental or Confederation Congress. Dickinson "immediately transmitted" Butler's warnings to the Congress, which was meeting downstairs from his Pennsylvania State House council chamber in the former colonial assembly room.

The Congress quickly formed a committee consisting of Alexander Hamilton, Oliver Ellsworth, and Richard Peters to probe this matter. The committee decided that this action was indeed a serious threat to the government. They strongly recommended that Dickinson summon the state militia to intercept the mutineers before they reached the city and joined forces with the potentially rebellious local troops. Hamilton, a former Continental Army officer and aide to Washington, believed that there must be a strong show of force to avoid repetitions of the violent scenes of the mutiny of Morristown in 1781. However, the somewhat frightened council was unwilling to support the committee's recommendations unless these rebellious troops committed some sort of outrage, like harming congressmen.

During Pennsylvania's vacillation, Hamilton dispatched the assistant secretary of war, Major William Jackson, "to meet" the mutineers before their arrival in the capital city. Jackson was to "assure them of the best intentions in congress to do them justice" and to offer them fair treatment if they returned to their officer's control in Lancaster. He was even to offer the men provisions, "if they would remain where they are" at that moment, but the soldiers continued to march. As this news filtered into Philadelphia, alarming rumors spread among the populace; the Bank of North America would be robbed, shops and private homes would be looted, and the congressmen and state officials would be slaughtered in their very seats.

The Pennsylvania state officials still took no apparent action as they continued to believe that the rapidly approaching troops could be appeased. Instructions were issued that these soldiers were to be peacefully received in the Northern Liberties' Barracks. On June 20, the mutineers finally arrived and entered the barracks without violence. However, the fears of the congressional committee had come to pass. The mutineers' ranks swelled with the addition of several companies of veterans and members of the city's garrison. The small, 80-man revolt had surged into an approximately 500-man revolution. It had been these veteran troops' loyalty that General Arthur St. Clair, of the same Pennsylvania Line, and congressional president Elias Boudinot had been counting on to maintain order. However, as it was Friday afternoon, the Congress adjourned for what they believed would be a weekend's rest until Monday morning.

However, this weekend reprieve did not last long. As Boudinot received reports of the swelled numbers of mutineers, he summoned a special session of the Congress for one o'clock, Saturday afternoon in the state house. There representatives from 6 states, not enough for a quorum, gathered at this site only to discover that some 300 rebellious soldiers had surrounded the building. Led by their sergeants, these soldiers alleged that "the officers in general have forsaken us and refuse to take any further command." To secure this government structure, the mutineers posted sentinels at the doors and win-

dows. Congressman James Madison observed that these men were drunk on "spiritous drink" from a nearby "Tippling House." The soldiers threatened congressman and councilman alike, and in one instance, one mutineer pressed his bayonet on a delegate's chest. In the meantime, a gathering crowd of citizens shouted encouragingly to the soldiers with "stand for your rights," so it was quite clear whose side the general populace supported. One can only imagine the effect of having 300 men, armed with weapons looted from the state magazine and arsenal, on these government officials. Though the mutineers never attempted to enter the state house by force, the Supreme Executive Council still demonstrated its lack of courage by hesitating to react in this volatile situation.

Dickinson entered the congressional meeting to share with the representatives the written demands made on his council by the troops. They were delivered by St. Clair, who was later ordered by the Congress to adopt "such measures as he might think best calculated to draw them off to their barracks." In brief, the men wanted the "authority to appoint commissioned officers to command" them and they would, in turn, redress the soldiers' grievances with "full power to adopt such measures as they may judge most likely to procure us justice." They further demanded that the council "immediately issue such authority and deliver it" or they would "instantly let in those injured soldiers" upon them and "abide the consequences." Twenty minutes were given for a decision. Not to be intimidated by such threats the Supreme Executive Council unanimously rejected the proposals.

This drama at the state house lasted a considerable amount of time. Boudinot wrote his brother Elisha, that the Congress was kept "prisoner in manner three hours, though they offered no insults personally, to my great mortification, not a single citizen came to our assistance." Finally, the assembled representatives of the state and national governments departed from their respective chamber and walked through the cordon of hostile troops. The soldiers did not break discipline, and only insults were hurled at the officials. St. Clair persuaded some of the men to return to their barracks with the promise that they could designate their own officers to represent them in dealing with the council. This agreement was in contrast to the decision made by the state officials. At this point, there was still no violence in Philadelphia, however, and the mutineers still commanded the streets by holding the powder house, several arsenals, and a few pieces of artillery.

Before exiting, Boudinot decided to hold another afternoon session in the relative safety of the First Continental Congress' meeting site, Carpenters' Hall. He also notified Washington, with the remaining Continental Army at Newburgh, New York, of the serious events which had taken place. In his letter, Boudinot was of the opinion that "the worst is yet to come." He requested Washington to "direct some of your best troops on which you can depend under these circumstances, towards this city." The message, though, would not reach the commander-in-chief for several days.

Congress, now finally having at least a quorum, formally called upon the state of Pennsylvania for protection. It requested that the state militia be summoned to quell the rebellious troops and to disarm them. The council was still not moved to action by these requests. When pressed as to whether the militia should have been called, Colonel Shee, the senior commander, reported "that it would be imprudent to call upon the militia now as we are convinced that it would be ineffectual." The state arsenals and magazines were still in the possession of the mutineers so it can only be estimated if the militia could have been properly armed, although Hamilton contended that sufficient weapons were suitable for the militia.

The Congress seemed to have been pushed to the breaking point. A resolution indicating firmness was adopted because "the authority of the United States [has] been grossly insulted by the disorderly and menacing appearance of a body of soldiers." It continued "that effectual measures be immediately taken for supporting the public authority." Later, Dr. Benjamin Rush observed that when the Congress' resolution was printed as a proclamation on a public handbill and distributed, it "has been torn down and otherwise insulted by the common people." He believed the "universal cry was the men had been neglected and injured" while in the service of their country. For this moment, however, these congressional decisions were kept secret until another joint governmental conference could be held.

Hamilton and his committee were directed by Congress to explain to the Pennsylvania government what "effectual measures" meant in their resolution. If there was "not satisfactory ground for expecting adequate and prompt exertions of this state for supporting the dignity of the federal government," then the Congress would remove the national capital to either Princeton or Trenton. The council reacted by summoning the militia, for Philadelphia could lose the prospect of becoming the national seat of government.

Dickinson called a special council meeting on Sunday morning at his home. Hamilton and Ellsworth attended and formally presented the congressional resolution. Pennsylvania was unmistakably informed that the national government would withdraw from Philadelphia unless adequate protection could be provided for its members. The council continued to contend that requesting the services of the militia, without the confidence of having a sufficient force, would only antagonize the mutineers. They might then commit violence that until now, through appeasement, had been avoided. These views that the militia would not adequately respond were essentially correct. Rush noted that when an experiment was attempted and some units were summoned, "only thirteen men assembled at the parade of Colonel Reed's battalion." The council hinted that the militia would probably react positively once "some outrage was committed by the troops," but until then, the citizens regarded the mutineers as objects of pity rather than resentment. The Congress had their answer to the request for protection. Pennsylvania would continue to stall in the hope that the mutineers would acquiesce or until Washington's loyal troops arrived to restore order.

As the new week began, another joint governmental meeting was held in the state house with the same requests and responses by each concerned party. Hamilton asked Dickinson to place the council's negative replies in writing for the public record, but he was refused. Hamilton promised that he would carry out his promise to strongly recommend that the national capital be transferred to New Jersey, but still to no avail. He only had to walk downstairs to report to the Congress of the council's continuing response. He stated that they regretted the insults to the members of the national government; however, he believed "themselves had a principal share in it." Pennsylvania's congressional delegation rebuked Hamilton for his comments and offered a watered-down resolution, one not blaming the council and noting they too had suffered by this entire affair.

During the day, it appeared the policy of appeasement was indeed working. There had been no large-scale destruction or public demonstrations as most of the troops remained in their barracks. However, as Boudinot had predicted, the worst was yet to come.

The soldiers' actions on Tuesday shattered the city's relative peace and quiet as they became more threatening. The mutineers once again surrounded the state house and sent in their six selected officers to negotiate with St. Clair and the council. The commanding sergeants, having turned the inhabitants of the government quarter into virtual hostages, threatened them all with death. "Every effort in your power must be exerted to bring about the most ample justice . . . should you not . . . do all yours, death is inevitably your fate."

To prevent their premature death, Hamilton's committee urged the Congress to meet in two days in Princeton. Boudinot welcomed the possibility of having the national capital in his home state. He wished "Jersey to show her readiness on this occasion as it may fix Congress as to their permanent residence." He officially ratified the transfer and issued the previously secret proclamation to the populace.

At approximately the same time the Congress was packing its bags, General Washington finally received Boudinot's letter informing him of the mutiny. The commander-in-chief's feelings were quite apparent at this news. "It was not until three o'clock this afternoon that I had the first intimation of the infamous and outrageous mutiny of the Pennsylvania troops." He immediately ordered some 1,500 loyal troops, a large portion of his remaining command, "which would comprise this gallant little army," to Philadelphia. Selected for command of this force was Major General Robert Howe, who had been instrumental in crushing previous mutinies, with orders to suppress the revolt using any means at his discretion unless countermanded by the Congress. Washington defended the integrity of the Continental Army by contending that the mutineers were "recruits and soldiers of a day." They have not "born the heat and burdens of the War" not "suffered and bled without a murmur." They have not "patiently endured hunger, nakedness and cold," but have actually "very few hardships

to complain of." It appeared that Washington was expressing his concern that Congress might harden in opposition to the legitimate requests of the loyal veteran regiments. Congressman John Montgomery, of the mutineers' home state, shared Washington's opinions on the Lancaster troops who had recently received a nine pound enlistment bounty, "a suit of clothes and their arms; most of whom had been in service not more than five months and had never been in action." He called them "the offscourings and filth of the earth."

At last, finally aroused by the departure of the Congress and finding the soldiers still "in a very tumultuous disposition," the Supreme Executive Council convinced itself to adopt the strong measure Hamilton had urged from the onslaught. Robert Morris sent for the president of the Bank of North America, Thomas Willings, when intelligence was obtained that this financial institution was to be attacked and robbed. Willings was requested to place the bank into a position of defense. The council finally decided "that the militia officers be directed to call for as many of their respected commands as possible." As these measures seemed to be successful, they became almost bold in comparison to their previous inaction. They refused to "take the proposals now made by the soldiers into consideration unless they put themselves under the command of their officers, and make a full and satisfactory submission to the Congress." The troops replied, through their liaison, that they did not think "they had offended Congress on Saturday, as their intention was to apply to Council." However, the mutiny was beginning to disintegrate. The militia officers had managed to muster about 500 men, and news that Washington was sending a large army was spreading throughout Philadelphia. The leaders of the mutiny had seen fit to desert their followers, and the city's sheriff was ordered "to take effectual measures for apprehending" them. Without their leaders, with the militia growing in strength, and Howe's army marching south, the mutineers began to capitulate and to lay down their arms to offer "dutiful submission to the offended majesty of the United States." After an address by Dickinson, the men were persuaded to follow their officers and to return to Lancaster.

During the next week, Philadelphia began to return to relative calm as the loyal Continental troops finally arrived. Two sergeants of the

Lancaster troops were sentenced to be shot while four others were to receive corporal punishment. All were subsequently pardoned by the Congress and released.

The incident now seemed closed. The Pennsylvania authorities and Philadelphia itself wanted the national capital to be in Philadelphia. The local newspapers sought to minimize the danger of the mutiny, to vindicate the city and state authorities, and to place all the blame for this affair on the Congress, and particularly on Hamilton. It was hinted that this move to Princeton was part of a grand scheme of Hamilton's to bring the national capital closer to his own New York City, where it ultimately would shift after the British departed. It is clear that Philadelphia wanted the Congress to return, but Oliver Ellsworth felt that "they will hardly return to Philadelphia, without some assurance of protection, or even then with the intention to stay longer than till accommodations shall be elsewhere prepared for a fixed residence." As a proud resident of the city, Rush expressed his opinion that if Congress remained "one week longer at Princeton feeding one another with ideas of insulted and wounded dignity, you may lose Pennsylvania from your wise plans of Continental revenue." He further pleaded that "three wrongs will not make one right. The soldiers did wrong in revolting, the Council did wrong in not calling out the militia, and the Congress are doing wrong in remaining in Princeton. The two formers have come right. Congress alone perseveres in the wrong." John Montgomery countered, "Will you proud Philadelphians condescend to invite them or will you rather say they went without our knowledge and they may return without an invitation?"

It is quite clear that the Confederation Congress and the Pennsylvania government had suffered a fatal wound from this entire affair. It was an injury from which neither could possibly recover. The two governments had publicly argued, they could not agree on how to end the mutiny, and they ultimately disgraced themselves in many of the populace's eyes. Each demonstrated its weaknesses and its limitations during the entire affair. The final result of the mutiny would occur a few years later with the ending of the existing national government, controlled by the Articles of Confederation, and the establishment of the federal system through the Constitutional Convention of 1787. Pennsylvania also followed this example and benefited. In 1790 it adopted a new state constitution, which continues to function to this day.

Andrew A. Zellers-Frederick

REFERENCES

Edmund C. Burnett, ed., *Letters to Members of the Continental Congress*, 8 vols. (1921–26), 7; Worthington C. Ford, ed., *Journals of the Continental Congress, 1774–1789*, 34 vols. (1904–37), 24; Virginia Moore, *The Madisons* (1979); Pennsylvania Archives, Vol. X (1854); Thomas Scarf and Thompson Wescott, *History of Philadelphia, 1609–1884*, 3 vols. (1884), 1.

Mutiny of the Connecticut Line (May 25, 1780)

After wintering at Morristown, New Jersey, two regiments of the Connecticut Line complained about back pay and the lack of meat. On May 25 in a related development, 11 men (none of whom were from Connecticut regiments) who had been sentenced to death for desertion were to be executed the following day. The two rebellious Connecticut regiments prepared to march off in order to find food, without authorization. Colonel Return Jonathan Meigs of the 6th Connecticut was hit on the head by a soldier during an argument. After Meigs and two Pennsylvania Line colonels pleaded with the troops, the men returned to their huts. The mutiny simmered down. On May 26, four of the eleven men sentenced to die were executed; the rest were pardoned. The two Connecticut regiments were soon posted for duty at West Point.

Richard L. Blanco

REFERENCES

James C. Neagles, *Summer Soldiers. A Survey and Index of Revolutionary War Courts-Martial* (1986); James Thacher, *A Military Journal During the American Revolutionary War* (1827); Carl Van Doren, *Mutiny in January* (1943).

Mutiny of the New Jersey Line (January 20–21, 1781)

Although the mutiny of the Pennsylvania Line at Morristown, New Jersey, on January 1, 1781, was quelled within a few weeks of prolonged negotiations between disaffected army sergeants and General Anthony Wayne along with Joseph Reed, the example triggered another rebellion. On January 20–21, about 200 New Jersey Continentals, encamped at Pompton, New Jersey, initiated a mutiny. Suffering from insufficient provisions and inadequate shelter, the demoralized men demanded improvements in their conditions of service as well as back pay and earned discharges. The troops recently had received $5 in specie as a token payment for long overdue pay, but they were indignant over the unresolved issues of bounties and enlistment terms that were offered to new recruits.

Washington acted quickly. He ordered General Robert Howe with 500 New England troops to march from West Point to the Jersey encampment in order to coerce the mutineers. Washington also directed Colonel Israel Shreve to bring dependable New Jersey regulars to compel the disgruntled men to return to duty; he also requested Governor William Livingston to call out the state militia. Washington was worried about the possible reduction of manpower at his disposal and about the ramifications of a second major mutiny within a month for the army.

On January 27, Lieutenant Colonel Francis Barber and a detachment of New Jersey troops subdued the rebels in their camp. Barber ordered the mutineers to assemble without their weapons. Hesitating briefly, the men complied. Following Washington's orders, Barber identified three leaders of the revolt and had them court-martialed. The men were convicted on their camp site and were sentenced to death. Then Barber determined which of the rebel soldiers had been the strongest supporters of the condemned men. He selected 12 and ordered them to form a firing squad. After the first two men were killed by their own comrades at arms, Barber reprieved the third. Apparently, Washington dealt more harshly with the New Jersey troops compared to the Pennsylvania Line because he feared that the example of another mutiny would spark still another mutiny and because the New Jersey Line, less experienced in service and less cohesive than the veteran Pennsylvania troops, were more pliable.

Compared to the concessions granted to the mutinous Pennsylvania troops, the New Jersey soldiers received few immediate gains. Washington could not alleviate their distress immediately nor could he improve their financial problems because of chronic inflation. Yet the New Jersey Legislature soon enacted a law to compensate troops for price increases. In Congress, delegates considered measures to improve the welfare of the soldiers. Determined to place the nation on a firmer credit and currency basis, the delegates appointed Robert Morris as Superintendent of the Department of Finance.

As a result of Washington's firmness in handling this incident and the efforts of the politicians to improve troop morale, the danger passed. Whether conditions for the men actually improved in 1781 or whether the soldiers were too physically and mentally fatigued to protest over their plight is debatable. There were no more major uprisings among Washington's regulars for the rest of the war.

Richard L. Blanco

REFERENCES

Mark Edward Lender, *The Enlisted Line: The Continental Soldier of New Jersey*, unpublished Ph.D. Dissertation, Rutgers, the State University (1975); Leonard Lundin, *Cockpit of Revolution: The War for Independence in New Jersey* (1940); James Kirby Martin, "A Most Undisciplined, Profligate Crew ..." in Ronald Hoffman and Peter J. Albert, *Arms and Independence* (1984); Carl E. Prince, et al., eds. *The Papers of William Livingston*, 5 vols. (1978–88), 4.

Mutiny of the New York Line (June 1780)

While stationed at Fort Stanwix on the Mohawk River, New York, 31 men of the 1st New York Regiment became disgruntled about back pay and clothing issues. They marched off as if to desert to the British posted at Oswegatchie (Ogdenburg) on the St. Lawrence River. Assisted by Oneida Indians, Lieutenant Abraham Handenbergh of the Continentals managed to overtake them. Thirteen of the deserters were shot by the Indians. The remainder presumably escaped to the enemy. As one authority remarked: "This is probably the only time in the history of the American army when an officer used Indians to kill white soldiers."

Richard L. Blanco

REFERENCES

James C. Neagles, *Summer Soldiers: A Survey and Index of Revolutionary War Courts-Martial* (1986); Carl Van Doren, *Mutiny in January* (1943).

Mutiny of the Pennsylvania Line (January, 1781)

In the autumn of 1780, General Anthony Wayne pleaded with members of the Pennsylvania Assembly to rectify the complaints of his troops. The demoralized men lacked uniforms, blankets, and provisions, and they grumbled about a needed settlement of back pay in hard currency. Evidently their enthusiasm for republican ideals, that so typified the early war years had eroded.

On December 16, the assembly enacted a bill which provided that the regulars receive their pay for the last three years in specie. But the new law would take months to implement. As the Pennsylvania troops marched from New York to their familiar winter cantonment at Morristown, New Jersey, in November they were sullen and disgruntled over their plight. They still lacked shoes, blankets, and rum; the payment of hard cash seemed months ahead. Furthermore, the troops were embittered about their terms of service. They had enlisted for three years. But due to the vagueness in the wording of the enlistment articles, it could have been interpreted to mean for the duration of the war.

On January 1, 1781, the Pennsylvania Line revolted. In the action one officer was killed, two officers were seriously wounded, and many others had been mauled by the angry men. Some troops also were casualties in the melee. The mutineers seized the artillery and marched away with fixed bayonets to Princeton. From his headquarters at Mount Kemble, New Jersey, Wayne notified Washington of the uprising on January 2. He also requested the mutineers to select a man from each regiment to present the soldiers' grievances, and he urged President Joseph Reed of the Assembly to negotiate with the rebels. Wayne took his reliable regiments to Princeton, where the mutineers were encamped. Washington commended Wayne for his duty. Although Washington was tempted to journey to Princeton to oversee the proceedings, he decided to remain at New Windsor, New York, in order to ascertain the morale of the men in his command.

At Princeton a committee of sergeants presented their demands—that the troops be fed and clothed; that they receive their back pay for one year immediately, and in specie; and that soldiers who had enlisted for, and served for, three years be discharged. Wayne lacked the authority to comply with these terms, so he recommended that Reed and members of the Executive Council meet in Princeton with the mutineers. Reed immediately agreed to negotiate, and the mutineers promised not to march onto Philadelphia. Though Wayne fretted that some troops might desert to the enemy he was relieved to learn that when two British agents appeared in camp with promises of rewards and clemency from General Sir Henry Clinton, the troops seized Clinton's emissaries and imprisoned them.

On January 7, Wayne acted on Reed's suggestion that the troops move to Trenton for the discussions with the politicians. Ostensibly the reason was the troops could be provisioned there. But a less obvious factor was that by inducing the men to come to Trenton, Pennsylvania's statesmen could maintain some sense of dignity in the affair by having the troops come to them. By January 9, negotiations were underway in Trenton. Wayne became increasingly unsympathetic to the mutineers and urged Washington to dismiss them from the service. But Washington was worried that if the men were discharged, his manpower would be depleted. In addition, he was concerned that Reed's committee would be too lenient with the mutineers.

By January 9 a settlement was reached between Reed and the sergeants. The troops were promised shoes, shirts, and overalls, which had been collected by a citizens' committee headed by Esther Reed and Sarah Bache in Philadelphia for shipment to Trenton. Governor William Livingston promised to send meat for the hungry men. Secondly, all Pennsylvania troops were to receive pay warrants, which the state was obligated to redeem. Third, a committee of three men to be appointed by Reed and the council would conduct a hearing to determine who should be discharged. Those men who had enlisted for three years or for the duration of the war were eligible to present themselves. Those soldiers who presented written proof or who took an oath about the validity of their three-year enlistments were to be discharged. The agreement clearly favored the mutineers because the civil authorities were helpless against the power of the troops and because Washington did not use force to quell the mutiny.

On January 10, the sergeants turned over to Wayne the two British agents who were soon after executed. In the following weeks, Wayne watched in dismay as his regiments (consisting of some 1,467 men) dwindled to 1,317 as the three-year men went home. The remaining Pennsylvania troops who had mutinied were furloughed until March 1781. On January 24, Congress approved Wayne's recommendation of a general amnesty to the mutineers, for it had few feasible options.

The incident is significant because it was the most famous mutiny in the American army during the war and because it sparked another mutiny in January 1781 by the New Jersey Line. Furthermore, the event demonstrated Washington's ambivalence in this matter—whether to use force to suppress the mutiny or whether to accept arrangements devised by civil authorities who could be too lenient in dealing with the military. In Congress, the news of the mutiny stimulated further discussions about the means to stabilize the economy and about measures to improve the welfare of the troops.

Richard L. Blanco

REFERENCES

Larry Gragg, "Mutiny in Washington's Army," *American History Illustrated*, 11 (1974):34–45; Paul V. Lutz, "Rebellion Among the Rebels," *Manuscripts*, 19 (1967):10–16; Paul David Nelson, *Anthony Wayne, Soldier of the Republic* (1985); Carle E. Prince, et al., eds., *The Papers of William Livingston*, 5 vols. (1978–88), 4; Carl Van Doren, *Mutiny in January: The Story of a Crisis in the Continental Army* (1943)

Nancy, Capture of the (November 29, 1775)

The *Nancy* was a British ordnance transport captured on November 29, 1775, by the armed schooner *Lee* (Captain John Manley), one of the vessels of George Washington's makeshift naval force. The Americans were aware that the unarmed brigantine had become separated from the rest of her convoy in a storm and that the British were looking for her. A British frigate had actually found the *Nancy* first, only to lose her again. Manley took the British vessel by surprise (her crew thought the *Lee* was a pilot boat come to guide her into Boston). The loss of the *Nancy* was a blow to British forces at Boston and a gain of considerable magnitude for the colonials. Although she carried little powder, her capture provided the Americans with 2,000 muskets, 31 tons of musket shot, 3,000 round shot, 100,000 musket flints, and a considerable quantity of cartridges as well as a bronze 13-inch mortar susbsequently dubbed "The Congress." It was by far the most important American acquisition of British arms at sea during the war.

Spencer Tucker

REFERENCES

William B. Clark and William James Morgan, eds., *Naval Documents of the American Revolution*, 8 vols. (1965–), *2*, *3*; Nathan Miller, *Sea of Glory. The Continental Navy Fights for Independence 1775–1783* (1974).

Nationalist Movement (1780–1784)

In 1780, faced by devastating military defeats in the South and military stalemate in the North, and confronted by the collapse of the Continental currency and with it of public credit, a new group of leaders came to power committed to strengthening central power sufficiently to win the war and to ensure American independence. Disillusioned with the prospect for victory through "revolutionary virtue" and "enthusiasm," which were widely perceived as having run their course, the group commonly referred to as "nationalists" favored reliance on a professionalized and adequately rewarded Continental army, rather than militia service, and administrative reform stressing increased executive authority and individual rather than collective responsibility and accountability. Some members of the group even advocated the assumption of temporary dictatorial authority by specific leaders until the emergency passed. Although some studies of the Confederation period depict this movement as a conservative, aristocratic, even counterrevolutionary one, at bottom they agree with the more recent scholarly emphasis asserting that the consensus on which "nationalists" came to power was grounded primarily in financial collapse and in the desperate military situation. It derived from a wish to win the war. One inherent dilemma for the "nationalists" arose from this situation. Every success they achieved in overcoming the military-financial crisis that existed in 1780 would erode the basis for their power.

There have been numerous semantic controversies over the use of the terms "nationalist" and "party" for this movement, and to the applicability of the terms to particular leaders. Clearly there was no "nationalist party" in the sense of a formalized and disciplined organization. Nevertheless, in 1780–1781, almost everyone who had served for several years in Congress, in the army or its administrative departments, or in diplomatic service, was to some extent a nationalist, since all had had long experience with the periods of disunion. At the same time, all were also "federalists" in the sense of believing in a division of powers between the states and the central government. Despite the charges of some opponents, none were in fact full consolidationists, interested in permanently abolishing the role of the states in favor of a highly centralized national government. They merely differed from their more parochial opponents in their belief that the balance had tipped too far in the direction of the states and needed to be redressed. They differed among themselves both in the extent to which the balance needed to be reversed and in the best strategy for accomplishing it. Their perceptions on both points also varied with the circumstances confronting them at a particular time. Almost all agreed that some form of reliable Continental revenue was essential to both Continental union and credit, and most adhered to a Continental impost (a tax on imports) as the most practicable first step in that direction. Most also were anxious to obtain additional foreign support, particularly from France, and saw a stronger government as needed to inspire the necessary confidence abroad. Intent on restoring confidence in government and the economy, many also opposed depreciating paper money and economic controls such as price regulation, trade embargoes, and legal tender laws. Leaders of the "nationalists" included Robert Morris, Gouverneur Morris, George Washington, Alexander Hamilton, James Duane, James Madison, James Wilson, and Philip Schuyler. Thomas Paine was enlisted to write in favor of many of the "nationalist" policies.

There were two fundamental obstacles to the accomplishment of nationalist goals. The first was the structure of the Confederation under the newly ratified Articles of Confederation. Congressmen were elected annually by the various state legislatures, and no congressman was to serve for more than three consecutive years. Congress could not tax, but it could only requisition (request) money from the states. Although the states were presumably bound to comply, Congress had no way to force them to do so. All amendments to the Articles required ratification by every state. Support from all the state legislatures would be needed to obtain any type of constitutional reform, including any kind of Continental taxation. Moreover, major issues in Congress, including all revenue measures, required the vote of nine states. Therefore, any party adhering to a "nationalist" perspective would have to exert dominant influence within nine states to secure passage of ordinary revenue measures, and within every state in the Union to obtain constitutional reform, including enactment of federal taxation. Loss of influence even for a year or two within one or two states could change the configuration of Congress and undo policies on which consensus had previously existed. What party known to later American history could have succeeded under such a constitutional structure?

On the other hand, parochially minded or states' rights partisans needed only to influence one or two state legislatures to defeat the mainstays of the "nationalist" program, a lesson made painfully apparent during Robert Morris's financial administration by Rhode Island's rejection of the impost.

Worse still was the fact that because of the fundamental ideological concepts of the American Revolution, the idea of attempting even to influence much less coerce the various states was anathema. The ideology of the Revolution had long fulminated against the dangers of the British central government; Revolutionary propaganda had pointed out in detail all the dangerous techniques a central government would use to usurp power. The better any centralizing power was at applying these techniques, the more dangerous it would appear to many Americans.

Much has been said about the effectiveness of the parochialists in achieving their objectives, particularly at the state level. But it must be added that the faction's task was far simpler than that of the "nationalists." All that was really needed to defeat the "nationalist" program was to gain support in a few state legislatures. Given the long-established Revolutionary propaganda network into which it could feed and the ideological heritage available, dissemination of anti-nationalist views was an easy task. Moreover, use of the press and chains of correspondence for such purposes had a long and honorable tradition in the states, while similar techniques used by the central government or its agents (or "tools") were traditionally regarded as manifestations of corrupt and dangerous influence. Thus, Thomas Paine's "nationalist" writings aroused a storm of criticism, particularly in New England.

Among the centralizing devices the "nationalists" employed to overcome localist tendencies and radical republican ideology were various financial techniques, particularly centralized management of the national debt and the creation of a national bank, patronage, and the creation and manipulation of national pressure groups, including the public creditors and the army. Others included frequent use of the press, and the promotion of national symbols, such as the renewed effort to create a national coinage with appropriate messages incorporated into their design.

Constitutional reform through the impost and funding plan failed in 1783 and 1784, and the alternate suggestions for a constitutional convention probably could have accomplished little then. The arrival of peace had undercut the sense of danger; war no longer served as a cement to the Union. Thomas Paine was no doubt right when he said he abandoned some of his constitutional proposals because the times were not bad enough yet to be put right. Prominent "nationalists" largely left office and returned to the private sector by 1784.

Nevertheless, after the nation experienced troubled times during the mid-1780s, the group's fortunes changed. Working with many of the same ideas, the same writers, the same networks, the same pressure groups, but in more propitious times, the "nationalists," now evolved into "Federalists," succeeded in accomplishing many of their objectives in 1787 with the adoption of the new United States Constitution, or shortly thereafter under the new United States Government.

Elizabeth M. Nuxoll

REFERENCES

E. Wayne Carp, *To Starve the Army at Pleasure: Continental Army Administration and American Political Culture, 1775–1783* (1984); E. James Ferguson, *The Power of the Purse: A History of America's Public Finance, 1776–1790* (1961); ———, "The Nationalists of 1781–1783 and the Economic Interpretation of the Constitution," *Journal of American History*, 56 (1969); 241–261; E. James Ferguson, John Catanzariti, Elizabeth M. Nuxoll, Mary A. Y. Gallagher, Nelson S. Dearmont et al., eds., *The Papers of Robert Morris, 1781–1784*, 7 vols. (1973–); H. James Henderson, *Party Politics in the Continental Congress* (1974); Merrill Jensen, *The New Nation: A History of the United States During the Confederation, 1781–1789* (1950); Jackson T. Main, *Political Parties Before the Constitution* (1973).

Naval Gunnery

Handling and firing guns at sea was no easy task. It was carried out in a minimum of space under conditions of great noise and confusion. To be effective in battle, crews had to be well trained.

The basic implements for serving guns consisted of the rammer, sponge, worm, ladle, priming wire, and boring bit. The rammer was used to seat both the powder cartridge and the shot. The sponge was used to clean the gun between firings in order to remove any bits of burning debris that might ignite a powder cartridge prematurely. The worm, which might be mounted in the sponge, was a metal corkscrew to extract the wad and cartridge from the bore if that proved necessary. The ladle was a cylindrical copper spoon used to load loose powder into the gun if there was no cartridge; it could also be used to reverse the process. Priming wires were used to clear the inside of the touchhole. Boring bits removed obstructions from the vent.

Other service equipment included staffs to hold the match, match tubs, and crowbars. Handspikes (or handspecs) were used to elevate the breech of the gun to shift the carriage. There were also passing boxes for cartridges, fire buckets, lanterns, wet swabs, and battle axes.

The first step in preparing a cannon for firing was to load it with powder. At first, this was simply loose powder introduced by means of a ladle. By the time of the Revolution, the powder was packed in cartridges. By the mid-eighteenth century, powder had improved to the point that the amount of the charge had been reduced from the earlier two-thirds weight of the ball to one-half. By the 1770s the weight was less than a half, and early in the next century, was set at one-third.

Subsequent powder charges were smaller as the gun grew hotter, for the heat increased the strength of the powder. Another reason for reducing subsequent charges was to increase splintering in the target vessel. Battles in the age of fighting sail were usually won by man-killing rather than ship-killing. Wooden splinters were the chief casualty producers, and the desired velocity was one that would just penetrate wood and would produce a shower of splinters rather than pass through to leave a clean hole.

Sinking a ship by holing it during an engagement was unusual. If a vessel was sunk it was usually the result of the explosion of a powder magazine. More often, captains surrendered as the result of excessive casualties in their crews.

The powder cartridge was seated at the bottom of the bore by means of the rammer. A wad might then be inserted, especially if the gun was to be kept loaded for any period of time. A second wad could be placed over the shot to keep it from rolling away from the charge. This also prevented the shot from causing friction that could set off the powder.

After the gun was fully loaded, a priming wire was inserted into the touchhole to pierce the cartridge and to insure that the touchhole was open and free of debris. To prime the gun, fine grain powder was poured in the touchhole until it accumulated at the top.

The gun on its carriage was then sighted on the target. Handspikes were levered under the inner ends of the carriage brackets to raise the breech so that the wooden elevating edge, known as the quoin, was positioned properly. Lateral movement was accomplished by the crew pulling on the side tackles, which were fastened to bolts on the bracket horns of the carriage and ran to the ship's side.

The carriage had to recoil or else it would be destroyed. The amount of recoil was limited by a stout rope known as breeching. It was secured around the neck of the cascabel and through ringbolts on the sides of the carriage. Its ends were clinched to other ringbolts set in the bulwarks on either side of the gun port. When a gun was fired it recoiled the length of the breeching. With its muzzle about a foot inside the port, the gun was in position to be loaded.

Even with breeching, the recoil of a carriage was not always predictable, especially in oblique or off-the-beam firing. For that reason, gun crews had to be extremely vigilant. Even so, injuries were frequent.

Once loaded, the gun was "run out" by means of side tackles secured to the sides of the carriage and then to the bulwarks. The train tackle attached to the rear of the carriage checked lateral movement. It could also be used to bring the gun in for loading if necessary and to hold the gun in position during loading.

Cannon of the era of the American Revolution were fired by means of a match. A slow match was made of hemp or cotton rope. It was supplied to each gun and was wound around a wooden staff known as a linstock. The linstock had a pointed metal end and was either stuck in the deck or in the match cup supplied to each gun.

Slow match was used to light port fire or quick match, a short length of flammable material that provided more rapid and reliable ignition of the charge. It burned more quickly and with a much more intense fire than slow match. Its end was pinched off after each use. Port fire was made of saltpeter or niter, sulphur, and mealed powder, all contained in a paper casing.

At first, priming was accomplished by filling the vent with loose powder from a powder horn. This was not altogether satisfactory, because the loose powder tended to erode the vent. Goose quills, packed ahead of time with powder and having an expanded area at the top, provided a solution. Both tubes and gun locks, a sure and precise ignition system, had been tried in English warships by the end of the Seven Years' War (1756–1763). There was, however, general opposition to their use. The old match continued to be the preferred method until near the end of the War of the American Revolution, when Captain Sir Charles Douglas of the Royal Navy personally outfitted the guns of the *Duke* and the *Formidable* with locks and tubes and proved their worth in the April 1782 Battle of the Saints against the French.

In the era of the American Revolution gun sights were virtually unknown at sea. Gunners aimed simply by sighting along the axis of the gun, which more often than not caused the shot to go high (the result of the dispart, or difference in the diameter of the gun at breech and muzzle). In the age of fighting sail, however, most sea engagements were at extremely close range, many of them yardarm to yardarm. In such circumstances it was difficult even for a poorly trained crew to miss the target.

The basic projectile of the era was solid round shot. There was also grapeshot. The latter consisted of a number of smaller balls (usually nine) placed around a central spool, the whole being covered with canvas and secured with cord so that it resembled a bunch of grapes. Grapeshot was used at close range against personnel and to damage rigging. Dismantling shot, which came in a variety of types, was used to bring down the lighter spars and rigging of an enemy vessel. It might consist of two round shot connected with a length of chain.

Guns were also fired double-shotted, usually in the first broadsides of an action.

Gunnery drill depended on individual captains, and commands varied widely even on the same ship. The rapidity of firing depended on the manual strength of the gun crew and their training. *See also*: Douglas, Charles; Navies of the American Revolution

Spencer Tucker

REFERENCES

Brian Lavery, *The Arming and Fitting of English Ships of War, 1600–1815* (1987); Peter Padfield, *Guns at Sea* (1974); Spencer C. Tucker, *Arming the Fleet. U.S. Naval Ordnance in the Muzzle-loading Era* (1989).

Naval Ordnance (British, French, American)

Warships of the period of the American Revolution were categorized according to rate, a rough reflection of the number of cannon they carried, First-rates were the largest ships and carried 100 guns or more. The most common large warship by the time of the Revolution, however, was the 74-gun third-rate. Ordnance totals included only the heavy cannon; excluded were carronades, light howitzers, and mortars employed in the fighting tops (and usually known, in American service, as "coehorns"), and swivel guns intended for antipersonnel use and mounted in the rails of smaller warships or carried on boats.

Although the British and French navies established regulations specifying the type and number of guns to be carried aboard different rates of warships, in actual practice armament varied considerably from ship to ship. Warships could easily exceed their rate, and often did so, even though this could adversely affect sailing quality. Armament also changed a great deal throughout the life of a vessel. Captains flouted regulations in order to have what they considered the most effective ordnance mix on their vessels. Furthermore, because this was an age of slow technological change, the life of a gun was usually determined not by length of time in service but the number of rounds it had fired. Many ships kept older pieces in place, as in the case of lighter bronze guns as opposed to newer pieces in iron. All of the preceding was particularly true of the American warships of the Revolutionary War, when nonstandardization was the rule rather than the exception. Indeed, for the United States Navy, this continued to be the case until well into the nineteenth century.

Most guns were mounted on truck carriages and positioned on both the port and starboard sides of a warship. Sloops had all their guns on one deck. The larger frigates and liners carried their ordnance arranged in tiers. On the gun deck(s) the cannon pointed through square gun ports cut in the sides of the ship, and on the upper deck through ports in the bulwarks. Strongly constructed bulwarks on the upper decks helped protect the crews who worked the guns during battle, as did hammocks stored in netting above the bulwarks. Crews working the open deck were, however, vulnerable to plunging fire from the weapons of marines and sailors who fired down at them from the tops of opposing vessels.

For purposes of ship stability, the largest guns aboard ship were carried on the lowest deck. Although a few long guns were available to fire forward and astern for chase purposes, most of the cannon on a warship were arranged to fire broadsides. In order to engage an opponent effectively, therefore, warships had to be broadside to their targets. This influenced the tactics of the day, which for battle fleets meant line ahead formation with the two sides banging away at each other at very close range until opposing vessels "struck," or surrendered.

By the time of the American Revolution iron had won out over bronze as the metal of choice for naval cannon, although large mortars for shore bombardment work were still of bronze and there were even some large bronze long guns still aboard warships. The number of bronze naval guns had dramatically declined in the course of the eighteenth century, however. For example, France had a total of 771 bronze naval guns in 1719 but only 136 by 1768. Because of their relatively paucity of numbers at sea, bronze guns will not be discussed here.

Individual cannon were denominated by the size of their solid round shot—a 32-pounder gun fired a ball weighing approximately 32 pounds. Artillery at sea was basically of the cannon type. The one exception to this was a short, light piece known as the carronade. It fired its shot at less windage and lower charge than a long gun of the same caliber. While they lacked the range of cannon, carronades were very destructive at short range. Their relative lightness meant that the warship's weight of broadside could be greatly increased. The Royal Navy was the first to introduce the carronade aboard its warships, and the first regulation governing its numbers for each class of warship was in 1779. The French did not adopt the carronade until 1794; neither was it available to the Americans in the American Revolution, although it was widely used aboard American vessels in the War of 1812.

Cannon varied considerably in length. French guns of the period immediately before the American Revolution were approximately 18.3 calibers in length for a 36-pounder, while a 6-pounder was about 23 calibers. British guns of the period ranged from approximately 17 calibers for a 42-pounder to 23 calibers for a 6-pounder. It should be pointed out, however, that the same caliber guns were often made in different lengths, depending on their use and place in a ship. Too short a bore adversely affected range, and the muzzle-blast from a short gun could injure the ship's side if it were fired obliquely. Most American naval officers preferred guns in excess of 18 calibers. In the naval terminology of all three countries, length of gun meant the distance from the rear of the breech ring to the front of the muzzle. This excluded the cascabel.

Broadside cannon were mounted on wooden carriages that rolled on four wooden wheels known as trucks. All carriage dimensions were in direct proportion to the shot diameter of the gun they carried.

British Naval Ordnance

British warships were ordered by ordnances, or establishments, that of 1745 being the last put in effect. Thereafter there was never any regular establishment as far as the dimensions of vessels were concerned; instead, ships were built around a specific armament. This was especially true of the new class of 74-gun ships introduced in the 1750s, the most common type of ship of the line until well after 1815.

The largest cannon carried aboard British warships were 42-pounders, but these were found only on the lower deck of first-rates. The ordnance establishment of 1762 (excluding $^1/_2$-pounder swivels) for the Royal Navy is found in Table 1.

Concerning the guns themselves, Clowes gives measurements for individual guns in the establishment of 1743 (weight is expressed in cwt, or units of 112 pounds; windage is the difference between the diameter of the ball and that of the bore; the length and weight of the 4-pounder, not given by Clowes, is taken from Muller). This is representative of British guns of the period of the American Revolution. The dimensions are found in Table 2.

TABLE 1

Size of cannon	42	32	24	18	12	9	6	4	3
Type of warship	Number of cannon								
First-rates (100 guns), large	30		28		30		12		
First-rates (100 guns), small	28		28		28		16		
Second-rates (90 guns)		26		26	26		12		
Third-rates (80 guns)		26		26		24	4		
Third-rates (74-guns), large		28	30			16			
Third-rates (74 guns), smaller		28		28		18			
Third-rates (64 guns)			26		26		12		
Fourth-rates (50 guns)			22		22		6		
Fifth-rates (44 guns)				20		22	2		
Fifth-rates (36 guns)					26		10		
Fifth-rates (32 guns)					26		6		
Sixth-rates (28 guns)						24			4
Sixth-rates (24 guns)						22			2
Sixth-rates (20 guns)						20			
14-gun sloops							14		

TABLE 2

	length (ft-in)	weight (cwt)	caliber (in)	service charge (lbs-ozs)	windage (in)
42-pdr	10-0	65	7.03	17-0	.35
32-pdr	9-6	55	6.43	14-0	.33
24-pdr	9-6	50	5.84	11-0	.30
"	9-0	46	"	"	"
18-pdr	9-6	42	5.3	9-0	.27
"	9-0	39	"	"	"
12-pdr	9-6	36	4.64	6-0	.24
"	9-0	32	"	"	"
"	8-6	31	"	"	"
9-pdr	9-0	28.5	4.22	4-8	.22
"	8-6	27	"	"	"
"	8-0	26	"	"	"
"	7-6	24	"	"	"
"	7-6	23	"	"	"
6-pdr	9-0	24.5	3.67	3-0	.19
"	8-6	22	"	"	"
"	8-0	21	"	"	"
"	7-6	20	"	"	"
"	7-0	19	"	"	"
"	6-6	17	"	"	"
4-pdr	6-0	12.5	3.22	2-0	.18
3-pdr	4-6	7	2.91	1-8	.14
"	7-0				

TABLE 3

Size of cannon	36	24	28	12	8	6	4
Type of warship	Number of cannon						
100 guns	30	32		32	16		
80 guns	30	32		18			
74 guns, early, 152–154 feet		26		28	16	4	
74 guns, after 1752, 166 feet		28		30	16		
74 guns, after 1762, 172–175 feet		28		30	16		
64 guns, early, 136–145 feet			24		26		12
64 guns, after 1735, 144 to 154 feet			26		28		8
60–50 guns	main battery of 22 to 24 18-pdrs						
frigates (1772)				26			

TABLE 4

	Length (inches)	Weight (approx)	Powder charge	bore diameter (inches)	shot diameter (inches)
36-pdr	121.50	8540	15.82	6.891	6.595
24-pdr	121.50	6400	10.42	6.017	5.758
18-pdr	115.10	5180	7.90	5.470	5.239
12-pdr	108.71	3910	5.61	4.774	4.574
8-pdr	102.31	2610	5.58	4.175	3.987
6-pdr	95.92	2020	3.60	3.790	3.627
4-pdr	76.74	1250	2.26	3.308	3.168

French Naval Ordnance

In 1763 French vessels, classified according to the number of their guns, were those of 116, 100, 90, 80, 74, 64, and 50 guns. The number of ships of 50 to 60 guns, utilized for police actions and general intelligence gathering, declined in the course of the eighteenth century. There were ten before the Seven Years' War; they disappeared entirely after the War of the American Revolution, replaced by frigates.

Typical French armaments of the period are found in Table 3.

Table 4 gives principal dimensions for French iron naval guns in 1721 (weights are converted from French pounds and lengths from French feet, inches, lines, and points).

In 1733, the proportions of 1721 were changed, as the guns were considered too heavy and their tulip muzzle too unwieldy for the gun ports. Proportions were established for the 4-, 6-, and 8-pounders as 11 calibers at the vent or touchhole, 9 before the trunnions, and 7 at the chase astragal. For those of 12-, 18-, 24-, and 36-pounders, their dimensions were 10.5 calibers at the vent, 8.5 before the trunnions, and 6.5 at the chase astragal. Approximate weights of the new guns (in American pounds) were as follows: 35-pounder, 8,155; 24-pounder, 6,050; 18-pounder, 4,840; 12-pounder, 3,520; 8-pounder, 2,420; 6-pounder, 1,870; and 4-pounder, 1,210.

There was further modification in design in 1758 as a result of the Seven Years' War. The only change in length was that the 36-pounder was increased from 119.69 inches to 125.98 inches. Wall thickness was also slightly reduced, resulting in a savings of weight.

British guns of this period were generally shorter than those of the French and this led to the decision in 1766 to reduce the length significantly. New French naval guns were to be decreased as follows:

36-pounder, from 125.98 inches to 113.39 inches
24-pounder, from 119.69 inches to 107.09 inches
18-pounder, from 113.39 inches to 100.79 inches
12-pounder, from 107.09 inches to 94.49 inches
8-pounder, from 100.79 inches to 86.22 inches
6-pounder, from 88.19 inches to 79.53 inches
4-pounder, from 75.59 inches to 69.29 inches

These lengths were still considered excessive for certain types of warships. In 1778, the last change before the American Revolution, shorter 12-, 8-, 6-, and 4-pounders were designed, especially for new frigates to be constructed at Saint-Malo.

American Naval Ordnance

Most of the vessels on the American side during the Revolution were quite small. The largest were frigates. One 74-gun ship, the *America* of 1782, was launched. The first American-built ship of the line, she was presented as a gift to France.

Not only were guns aboard the American frigates smaller in caliber than the largest guns in use by British and French, but as might be expected for a nation with no established armaments industry nor naval tradition, armaments were extremely eclectic. There was simply no standardized or uniform armament aboard American vessels of the Revolution. When Jovial Coit took command of the *Harrison*, he described her armament as

> 4 four pounders, brought into this country by the company of Lords Say and Seal, to Saybrook when they first came, a pair of coehorns that Noah had in the Ark; one of which lacks a touch-hole, having hardened steel drove therein, that she might not be of service to Sir Edmond Andros—six Swivels, the first that ever were landed in Plymouth, and never fired since.

Since cannon were in short supply the Americans made do with whatever was available. This was the case for the *Alliance* and the *Confederacy*, two frigates built in 1777. All their guns were to have been produced by Salisbury Furnace in Connecticut. This did not work out and so the contract was given to John Brown of Rhode Island. He was also unsuccessful in delivering the guns. The *Confederacy* went to sea armed with two 6-pounders taken from the wreck of the *Columbus*, a 12-pounder borrowed from the army, and other 12-pounders taken from the captured British galley *Pigot*. Some warships had to wait for months to receive their armaments. There was no such problem for the privateers; their guns, even the larger sizes, were always more easily obtained.

Cannon used in American warships during the Revolutionary War were cast by American founders, borrowed from land fortifications, purchased in the West Indies, obtained from France or other European states, or captured from the English.

Much of the armament of Brigadier General Benedict Arnold's 1776 Lake Champlain fleet came from the land forts of Ticonderoga and Crown Point. These were older guns of varied national background. Among the most famous of American cannon of the Revolution are those from the gondola *Philadelphia*, part of Arnold's flotilla, and now in the Smithsonian Institution. Her 12-pounder slide-mounted bow gun and two truck carriage-mounted 9-pounders that fired in broadsides are believed to be of older Swedish manufacture. A few American vessels, such as the *Queen of France* and the *Hague*, were armed with modern ordnance; these two got their guns directly from French arsenals. These is no record of French ordnance on board American naval vessels other than on those actually fitted out in France.

With the exception of swivels and coehorns, all ordnance used by the Americans were long guns. The largest cannon in use at sea by the Americans in the war were the old 18-pounders obtained in France and mounted in the *Bonhomme Richard*; at least one of these blew up during the battle with the *Serapis*. The largest cannon in common use in the Continental Navy were 12-pounders. Some 12-pounders, cast at Salisbury Furnace and described as "short & fit only for Ship Cannon," weighed 23 or 24 hundred weight (2,576 to 2,688 pounds).

The dearth of guns of the American Revolution identified as manufactured in this country makes statements about them difficult, but it is believed that most were copied from British rather than French designs. *See also*: Cannon founders (American)

Spencer Tucker

REFERENCES

Jean Boudriot, "L'Artillerie de Mer de la Marine Francaise, 1674–1856," *Triton* (No. 845, 1er Trimestre, 1968) supplement to *Neputnia* No. 89; William L. Clowes, *The Royal Navy, A History: From the Earliest Times to the Present*, 7 vols, (1897–1903) 3, 4; L. Denoix and J. N. Muracciole, "Historique de l'Artillerie de la Marine de ses origines a 1870," *Memorial de l'artillerie francaise*, XXXVIII (No. 4) (1963); Brian Lavery, *The Arming and Fitting of English Ships of War, 1600–1815* (1987); John Muller, *A Treatise of Artillery* (1759); Spencer C. Tucker, *Arming the Fleet. U.S. Naval Ordnance in the Muzzle-loading Era* (1989).

Naval Pay

Congress established the Continental Navy and set its pay scales in November 1775. According to the earliest schedule, monthly wages ranged from $32 for ship captains to $6.67 for ordinary seamen. It was not long before Congress recognized that these wages were not high enough and raised the salary for captains to $125 per month, and ordinary sailors to $8. Expecting that the navy's primary function would be to harass British shipping, the delegates assumed that income from the sale of prizes, shared between the United States and the crews according to formula, would be sufficient to cover the costs of pay and subsistence. According to naval regulations, pay was not due until the end of the enlistment.

The cost of outfitting vessels was extremely high. Although it hoped to create a 13-frigate navy, Congress never had resources to put more than a few ships under its flag at any one time. However, it was a struggle to man even these. Opportunities for more lucrative employment on privateers and more attractive bounties for enlisting in the army drastically limited the pool of experienced sailors for the navy to draw upon. As the war went on, the numbers of Americans captured by the British diminished the supply of seasoned seamen even further. In such a market, the government's ability to provide reliable and adequate naval pay or its willingness to assign its vessels to cruise for prizes was a barometer of what recruiting drives would produce, and what the navy could be expected to achieve.

Seamen enlisted either for the year or for the cruise, and expected to receive an enlistment bounty to tide their families over until they returned or managed to send home some portion of their prize money. For the first six years of the war, the bounty was paid in paper money, the value of which eventually depreciated to the point where it offered no incentive to enlistment. Thereafter, only a more substantial incentive, such as the opportunity to serve under a popular captain, attracted seasoned sailors. When recruiting drives were not productive, captains resorted to impressment, hired on slaves or untrained youth, or filled their ranks with captured British seamen. None of these expedients provided them with crews with which they could confidently brave a stormy sea or could do battle with the enemy. As a result, naval operations became more and more irregular.

By 1780, the Continental currency had completely collapsed, and it was clear that the government had to be reformed and its finances set on a firmer foundation before the war effort could be effectively resumed. In July of that year, Congress decided to pay naval wages in cash, and raised enlistment bounties to $20—but it lacked the means to carry out its plan. Early in 1781, Congress created the position of superintendent of finance, and named Robert Morris to fill it. In September of that same year, having failed to find a suitable candidate for agent of marine (secretary of the navy), Congress named Morris to act in that capacity as well. Calls for funds to meet naval expenses and his vision of the navy's potential role in improving the nation's finances had drawn him into naval affairs even before he officially assumed the position, however.

In July 1781, Morris confronted the consequences of inadequate naval pay when he took jurisdiction over the frigate *Trumbull*, which had been inactive for a number of months because there were no funds to outfit her and to pay her crew. He planned to send the ship to Havana on a secret mission to raise desperately needed capital for the Bank of North America. Enlistment efforts faltered, and she was forced to take on captive British seamen who refused to fight when she was attacked. The *Trumbull* was captured by a British frigate soon after she left port.

Morris's ability to provide funds for recruitment and salaries were further drained when Congress ordered him to provide some salary for officers who had been captured and imprisoned by the British or left without assignment because few positions were available. To do so, he was compelled to raise funds by selling off surplus naval stores. After the *Trumbull*'s loss, there were only two Continental frigates fit for active duty, the *Alliance* and the *Deane*. Even though ordered to cruise for prizes, their crews refused to reenlist until they were given some of their back pay. Although he refused as a matter of policy to use current revenues to pay debts contracted before his administration began, Morris realized the *Alliance* would never go to sea unless he agreed to apply the Continental share of prizes taken on the cruise to pay back wages. He set the stage for future trouble, however, when, at the last minute, he assigned her to bring Marquis de Lafayette to France to appeal for loans to support the war effort, and forbade her captain, John Barry, to cruise for prizes until the Marquis was safely ashore. Barry had to enlist 37 Frenchmen on the outward voyage to complete his crew. He reached France after a short voyage in January 1782, cruised for prizes until mid-March, and returned home empty-handed, with angry officers and crew, at the end of May.

The *Deane* was not manned until March 10, 1782. During a short but successful cruise in the West Indies, she took five prizes, most of the proceeds from which were divided among her men. Believing that the crew got too large a share of the profits from captures that involved little risk, Morris persuaded Congress to adopt a revision of the rules for distributing prizes, which put more money for certain types of prizes in the government's hands but pledged it to pay current wages promptly, which would have worked in favor of the crews, since there were often lengthy delays before proceeds from the sale of prizes reached the sailors who had earned them.

As the *Deane* returned to port, however, mutiny broke out on the *Alliance*. Even before it erupted, the ship's officers, many of whom had received little salary since the beginning of their enlistments, had written to Morris to demand pay. Since no prizes had been taken on her recent cruise, Morris unwisely considered himself released from his promise to provide back pay out of the Continental share. He was, however, astute enough to realize that the ship would not leave port again unless he issued at least two months' pay to the officers and crews of both frigates.

Barry sailed again on August 4, 1782, under orders to cruise for prizes, and fortune blessed his voyage. By the time he reached France, he had sent a total of nine ships into American and French ports. Soon after he berthed at L'Orient, he was joined by the *General Washington*, a packet vessel Morris had recently purchased. Treasury records on this ship indicate only that the naval paymaster was authorized to make "disbursements," probably enlistment bounties sizable enough to persuade men to enlist under "no cruising" orders. Whatever the amount, the *Alliance* officers became convinced by comparing notes with those of the *General Washington* that the time had come to demand back pay from the Continental share of the prizes they had just taken. This, Barry considered himself unable to

authorize, although he promised to support any just demand before Morris when the ship returned to America. As proceeds from the sales were made available, he also paid out a portion of the crew's prize shares. This was not enough to satisfy his officers, however, and they refused to board the ship. Barry formally charged them with disobedience and left them to make their way back home to face court-martials on their arrival. After instructing the American agent in France to ship home the rest of the crew's share of prize money in the form of merchandise, Barry took on officers where he could, and sailed for the West Indies.

Another reflection of the problems derived from the government's inability to pay wages promptly was the abuse of "officers' privilege." Various arrangements in which trade was used to supplement seamen's wages were commonplace in the eighteenth century. Merchant vessels allocated cargo space to allow officers, and sometimes crew, to ship goods on their own account and, since most American officers had been recruited from commercial service, they were accustomed to the practice. Despite attempts to regulate it, captains sailing for a penniless government frequently reverted to mercantile practice, even though added weight decreased their vessel's maneuverability and increased the risk of loss or capture. Several captains loaded their ships so heavily with private goods that their missions were severely compromised. One Continental frigate, the *Confederacy*, was rumored to have been lost because of this, and the *Duc de Lauzun*, a public vessel Morris had acquired to bring much-needed silver from Havana on public account, carried such a heavy cargo of private goods that it narrowly escaped capture by British men-of-war blockading the American coast.

The *Lauzun* and the *General Washington*, which had just returned from Europe carrying the provisional treaty ending hostilities with Britain, both made port at Philadelphia in March 1783. Rumors circulated that they had come in heavily laden with private goods. Congress ordered Morris to investigate, and he verified the accuracy of the charges. Although he set strict limits on the amount of private cargo that could be carried on public vessels in the future and severely reprimanded both captains, he imposed no further penalty.

When the *Alliance*, which had convoyed the *Du de Lauzun*, brought the public money safely past the British cruisers and made port in Rhode Island, Morris ordered her men paid off in silver for the entire period of their service under his administration. This was the only crew so favored in the entire course of the war. In the months that followed, the officers who had left the ship in France when Barry refused to give them back pay, arrived in the United States to face trial. The court, composed of officers who had also suffered from the Continent's poverty, deprived them of their commissions but upheld their right to pay and prize money earned before that time.

For most of the war, the most substantial earnings realized by the officers and men of the Continental Navy came from prize shares and from trade. While luck might favor a particular voyage, many prizes did not always insure a good return, as proceeds from their sale were often tied up in litigation for months and years. Sailors, like their counterparts in the army, derived little benefit from the salaries Congress had voted to establish. At the beginning of the war, they were paid in paper currency, which rapidly depreciated. As the war progressed, they refused to enlist when vessels were not assigned to cruise, or came to depend more and more heavily on income from prizes or trade to support themselves and their families. In desperation, they mutinied in protest. While it could not countenance such breaches of discipline, Congress, fundamentally unable to afford a navy throughout the war, nevertheless recognized the validity of their grievances, and generally refrained from imposing the maximum penalty. *See also*: Army pay

Mary A.Y. Gallagher

REFERENCES

William Bell Clark, *Gallant John Barry, 1745–1803: The Story of a Naval Hero of Two Wars* (1938); E. James Ferguson, John Catanzariti, et al., eds., *The Papers of Robert Morris*, 7 vols. (1973–); William M. Fowler, Jr., *Rebels under Sail: The American Navy during the Revolution* (1976); Martin I.J. Griffin, *Commodore John Barry* (1903); *Journals of the Continental Congress* (1904–1937); Charles Oscar Paullin, *The Navy of the American Revolution* (1971).

Naval Stores (British)

Products such as tar, turpentine, pitch, and rosin that come from resinous conifers are essential for the construction and maintenance of wooden sailing vessels. Naval stores and ship timber, which includes lumber and masts, were crucial items for any eighteenth-century navy. The British naval failure in the American Revolutionary War was due to many factors, and one of these was Britain's inability to obtain an adequate supply of such products to maintain her ships properly.

Britain was not self-sufficient in naval stores. Her primary source of these items until 1776 were her North American colonies. With the Revolution, naval stores and ship timber exports to Britain were cut off. British tar imports from 1766 to 1783 demonstrate the effectiveness of this embargo on the British navy. From 1766 to 1774, the American colonies supplied nearly 90 percent of Britain's tar. From 1775 to 1783 American tar exports to Britain declined, and Britain was never able to fully make up for this loss. Imports in 1776 and 1777 were extremely low, and the average imports from 1775 to 1783 were 36,000 barrels or 29 percent below the earlier eight-year period. This decrease in supply came at the same time as demand rose, and the end result was a continual deterioration of British hulls due to worm damage and marine fouling. Similar shortages of pitch, rosin, and turpentine further undermined the seaworthiness of British ships.

Replacing this rotted, worm-infested wood with new timber was also a problem during the Revolutionary War. Great Britain, which had suffered timber shortages since the days of Cromwell, had cut down its remaining oak forests during the Seven Years' War, so she had very little British timber for this purpose. Timber had to be imported. Most of this timber came from the Baltic, which also supplied Britain's foes.

A third major shortfall was the lack of masts. Only the American colonies were able to supply great masts of over 27 inches in diameter. On January 1, 1775, Britain's naval yards had 397 large American masts in stock, which equated to a three-year supply. American mast shipments ended on July 31, 1775, and by 1778 all the great masts had been mounted. Britain was thereby forced to import smaller Baltic masts, and from 1778 to 1782, 996 masts over 21 inches in diameter were imported from Russia. Although mast supply continued, problems arose from using these smaller masts. Since 1653, Great Britain had utilized the great American masts on her largest sailing vessels. Now, with no large masts,

Britain had to relearn the lost art of piecing together small trees into large, composite masts. A slight error in constructing this laminate mast could either weaken the mast or result in slower speed for the vessel. Numerous masts pieced together in 1778 and 1779 were improperly proportioned, and it was not until 1780 that the lost art was relearned. Even so, timber for composite masts was in short supply until 1782, and the American and West Indies ports never had an adequate number during the entire war.

Due to these factors, as well as to internal mismanagement of dockyards, the British navy was in poor condition when the French entered the war in 1778. In January 1778, Lord Sandwich claimed there were 35 seaworthy ships available at the dockyards and another seven could be readied for service in two weeks. Yet, two months later Admiral Augustus Keppel found "only six ships fit to meet a seaman's eye." It was not until June, two months after the French fleet had sailed, that the promised British ships were deemed seaworthy and set to sea.

Similar problems dogged the British navy throughout the war. While French Admiral d'Estaing sailed safely across the Atlantic, Lord John Byron's 13 vessels, which had been chasing their Gallic foe, were driven back to Britain with broken masts after encountering a fierce storm. Lord Byron finally caught up with the numerically inferior French and blockaded them in Boston, but in October, another gale damaged British masts and forced them to put in at Newport for repairs. Admiral d'Estaing was thereby able to sail his sturdy ships to the West Indies and seize Grenada without any British naval interference.

British commanders in the West Indies realized naval stores were in critical supply. In 1778, Admiral Young complained he was "now in want of Naval Stores of all kinds." The same year, Admiral Samuel Barrington similarly commented, "There appears to be a want of every kind of stores and masts in particular, there not being one fit for a frigate or any ship of a larger class." In 1780 an autumn storm dismantled many British ships and Commissioner Laforey incanted a familiar refrain, "What we shall do for masts, sails, and stores to repair all these damages we know of, and those we have yet to learn, I know not."

These critical shortages contributed to the most significant British naval defeat of the war.

On September 5, 1781, Admiral Thomas Graves failed to defeat a superior French fleet in the Chesapeake Bay. Instead of renewing the battle, the undefeated Graves retreated to New York City since his ships "had not speed enough in so mutilated a state to attack" the French. While the British fleet refitted and Admiral Graves lamented about "the excessive want of stores and provisions and the immense repairs wanted for a crazy and shattered squadron," General Lord Cornwallis surrendered to the superior Franco-American army at Yorktown. This battle determined the outcome of the war, and, appropriately, a fleet beset by the lack of naval stores and timbers contributed to the British defeat.

The British navy performed poorly during the American Revolutionary War. The Royal Navy lost 66 ships due to foundering, which was primarily caused by using unseasoned timber. One of these ships that foundered was the *Royal George*, a 100-gun ship of the line, which lost its unseasoned bottom as well as its crew. Such inexcusable disasters as well as the general unseaworthiness of British ships can be attributed to the lack of naval stores and masts, and this was a contributory cause of Britain's eventual defeat.

David C. Farner

REFERENCES

Robert Greenhalgh Albion, *Forests and Sea Power* (1926); Kustaa Hautala, *European and American Tar in the English Market During the Eighteenth and Early Nineteenth Centuries* (1963); W.M. James, *The British Navy in Adversity* (1926); Arthur R.M. Lower, *Great Britain's Woodyard* (1973); Frank Spencer, "Lord Sandwich, Russian Masts and American Independence," *Mariner's Mirror, 44* (1958):116–127.

Navarro, Diego Jose (? – ?)

Spanish colonial administrator, Spanish military officer. A native of Spain, Navarro rose to the rank of field marshal in the Spanish army. He served as captain general of Cuba from June 12, 1777, until February 12, 1782. In this capacity, he was the regional military commander for the Spanish territories closest in proximity to North America: Cuba, Louisiana, and the Caribbean Islands. He directed espionage activities that targeted events in the rebellious colonies, most importantly directing the operations of Juan de Miralles and Luciano de Herrera. He also furnished most of the military supplies that Spain made available at New Orleans to the Continental Congress. Navarro also served as the military superior of Bernardo de Galvez. In so doing, he supplied most of the support in material and additional troops used in the attacks on Mobile and Pensacola.

Light Townsend Cummins

REFERENCES

Kathryn Abbey, "Efforts of Spain to Maintain Sources of Information in British Colonies before 1779," *Mississippi Valley Historical Review*, 15 (1928):56–68; Light T. Cummins, "Spanish Espionage in the South During the American Revolution," *Southern Studies*, 29 (1980):39–49; Herminio Portell Vila, *Historia de Cuba en sus relaciones con los Estados Unidos y Espana*, 4 vols. (1938); ———, "Primeros relaciones entre Cuba y los Estados Unidos," *Universidad de Havana*, 2 (1937): 21–47; J. Leitch Wright, *Florida in the American Revolution* (1975).

Navies of the American Revolution

Background

By 1775, the wooden sailing warship had reached a high degree of maturity, the result of over 200 years of continuous development. Although further advances in the art of naval ship design and construction were still to come in the remaining half-century of the "age of fighting sail," these improvements were mostly evolutionary in nature, rather than revolutionary. Thus the warships that fought in the American War of Independence are excellent examples of naval warfare at the height of the age of fighting sail.

Every navy had several distinct tactical and strategic missions, such as winning battles, or scouting, or carrying dispatches. As is the case with modern navies, no single ship type could efficiently accomplish all the roles, and vessels that were optimized to perform individual tasks quickly developed. By the time of the American Revolution, three major types of warships had developed to fill the available roles. These three were the ship of the line, the frigate, and the corvette.

Ships possessing two or three complete gun decks (see under the head "Methods of Calculating Fighting Power") were the battleships of the age of sail. They were called ships of the line

because sea battles were typically fought by groups of ships in line, one behind the other. This formation made sense for sailing warships, since the vast majority of their guns were mounted along the ships' sides, rather than in the bow or stern. The long single line, variously called the line of battle, line astern, or line ahead, was therefore the most efficient way to use a sailing fleet's firepower.

Every ship in the line was supposed to be powerful enough to fight any ship in the enemy line, or the weaker ship would create a weak link in the line that could be exploited by the enemy. Any ship strong enough to "lie in the line" thus became known by the appellation "ship of the line" (SOL). SOLs were further divided into three-deckers and two-deckers.

The three-decked SOL was the most powerful type of warship in existence during the American Revolution. They were specifically designed to contain more firepower in a single hull than any other type of vessel, and mounted from 80 to 120 guns. Such concentrated firepower made three-deckers useful as strong points in the line of battle, and admirals normally used them as flagships because they gave the admiral direct control over as much fighting force as possible—a critical consideration in an age of unreliable ship-to-ship communications. (Signal flags were often invisible on a smoke-shrouded battlefield, and were obviously useless in a fog or at night.) Three-deckers also had more space than the smaller two-deckers for an admiral and his staff.

Three-deckers had some disadvantages, of course. Because they were designed to carry the maximum number of guns, many desirable nautical qualities had to be subordinated to this requirement. Three-deckers were very broad and deep-drafted for their length, and were therefore generally slower, less maneuverable and less weatherly than two-deckers. The freeboard of the lowest gun deck was less than most two-deckers, and this affected tactics, as the two-deckers could open their lower-deck gun ports in weather that forced the three-deckers to keep their lower-deck gun ports closed. Three-deckers also cost significantly more per ton to construct and maintain.

These limitations combined to make three-deckers quite rare in most navies, and nonexistent in many. The experience of war showed their usefulness, however, and their number tended to increase as a result.

SOLs with two gun decks were the backbone of every major navy. These ships, mounting from 60 to 80 guns, made up the vast majority of every navy's battle fleet. They were the ideal compromise: strong enough to stand up to any SOL (even a three-decker, for a short time), yet much cheaper to build, equip, maintain, and man than the larger ships.

By the time of the American Revolution, the standard types of two-decked SOLs were the 64-gun and the 74-gun. These had evolved from the 60- and 70-gun SOLs, respectively, and many of the earlier type still existed. In addition, a very large and powerful two-decker 80 existed in the French and Spanish navies. The gradual trend toward larger and more powerful two-deckers made smaller types of three-deckers obsolescent. The small three-deckers were sometimes less powerful than the large two-deckers, while having all the disadvantages mentioned above.

Most navies operated smaller ships mounting between 50 and 58 guns on two complete gun decks. These obsolescent ships were not called ships of the line, because they were thought to be too weak to fight in the line of battle. In fact, these small two-deckers often did fight in the line, especially in less critical theaters such as the Indian Ocean or the North Sea. For this reason they are included in Table 1, SOLs in Active Service. These ships held an anomalous position; they were too slow to run away from SOLs, and too weak to fight them. (See Table 1.)

The classical definition of the frigate was a warship mounting a single complete row of guns on the gun deck and another partial row of guns on the forecastle and quarterdeck, totaling from 26 to 40 guns. Frigates were the jacks-of-all-trades of the sailing fleets, performing duties as commerce raiders, message carriers, convoy escorts, and fleet scouts. Frigates at one time or another undertook every possible naval mission, and they were as necessary to a navy as SOLs. In fact, frigates occasionally fought in the line of battle, but this was normally an act of desperation, as they were simply not powerful enough to slug it out with SOLs one on one with any expectation of success. Frigates were often nearly as long as SOLs, but were much narrower and less deep-drafted than the larger ships, which made them faster under most conditions. As SOLs were analogous to battleships, so frigates

were comparable to twentieth-century cruisers. Most navies maintained roughly the same number of frigates as SOLs in active service during wartime.

The term "frigate" was in use as early as 1660, but the word did not achieve the meaning described above until about 1740, when the first true frigates were built. Many historians have erred by calling very small two-deckers (such as the British 44) frigates, even though these ships were not designed as frigates and were unable to perform many frigate missions.

The frigate evolved rapidly during the American War of Independence. At the start of the war the standard frigate in every major navy mounted 8- to 12-pounder long guns on the gun deck. The smaller ships, mounting only 8- or 9-pounder guns, were soon found to be obsolete, and declined precipitously in numbers as the war went on. By 1780 or so the 12-pounder frigate was the standard type in all the navies. Toward the end of the war, several nations experimented with very large frigates armed with 18-pounder long guns on the gun deck. This tremendous advantage in firepower—50 percent—gave them a decisive advantage over all other frigates. By 1783 several had been built, and they became the standard frigate type during the French Revolutionary and Napoleonic wars.

The smallest type of warships came in a bewildering variety of hull and rigging configurations and names, being variously called post-ships, corvettes, sloops of war, brig-sloops, gun-brigs, cutters, chasse-marees, luggers, schooners, and so forth. The modern term for ships of this type is corvette, and that name is used here. Corvettes carried all their guns on one deck, mounting none at all on the forecastle and quarterdeck. Corvettes were useful for tasks that either did not require the force of an SOL or frigate, or that placed a premium on shallow draft. They were ideal for commerce raiding against defenseless merchantmen or carrying messages, thus freeing valuable frigates for more important tasks.

Corvettes were usually armed with 3- to 9-pounder long guns. They carried from 4 to 24 cannon, but usually mounted 10 to 20 guns.

Corvettes were small ships, usually less than 100 feet in length, and they were also much more lightly constructed than frigates and SOLs. Corvettes also carried a tremendous amount of rigging in order to make them as fast as possible.

These factors made corvettes inherently unstable and fragile. Thus corvettes sometimes capsized in sudden gusts of wind, or were staved in by large waves during storms. In fact, more corvettes were lost due to weather-related causes than were lost to enemy action.

Another problem related to the small size of corvettes was that they were only faster than larger ships in light winds and smooth seas. In stronger winds, the larger ships were faster, because they were not as affected by the heavier seas, and they often captured corvettes in heavy weather.

All sailing warships were a compromise between the conflicting demands of seaworthiness and of combat. To cite just one example, a relatively broad, deep, and bluff shape was best for carrying the heavy weight of the guns, but a long and narrow shape was best for speed. This and many other contradictory demands often worked directly against one another, and reconciling them to produce a nicely balanced warship design required not only practical shipbuilding experience but also a sophisticated understanding of their mathematical interrelationships. Unfortunately, many of the mathematical tools necessary to reduce this tremendously complex process to a series of formulas did not yet exist. This made warship design as much an art as a science, although many naval architects did receive some sort of formal training in this period, particularly in France. In Britain, on the other hand, ship design theory was less studied, so that virtually all merchant shipbuilders, and most naval shipwrights as well, relied mainly on time-honored "rules of thumb."

This lack of certainty in the art of warship design meant that one of the easiest ways to produce a good ship was to copy an existing ship that was known to possess the qualities desired. Perhaps one or two slight changes would be made, to see what effect they might have, but often enough the ship was just copied outright. The British did most of the copying, both because the state of naval architecture was less advanced in Britain than in France or Spain, and also because the British captured so many more ships than any other nation that they naturally had a much better chance of obtaining and identifying a superior foreign design.

Many popular histories of the age of sail emphasize the apparently great longevity of the wooden warships of the period. Authors often cite examples such as HMS *Victory* (launched in 1765, and 40 years old at Trafalgar) to show how long-lived sailing men-of-war were, but she (and others like her) were exceptions to the rule. Many factors conspired to wear out vessels much more quickly than is usually understood. A major factor was the strain on a ship's frame from the constant pounding of wind and wave. Another element was the action of parasites like the Teredo, or shipworm, which fed on the wood of a ship's hull.

The active career of a typical SOL was only 12 to 15 years. After this period extensive repair work was necessary, often costing more than the original construction of the ship. This lifespan does not include time spent laid up "in ordinary," with all the guns and most of the other stores removed, or the years after a ship's active cruising days were over, when a vessel could still be used for other tasks that were less stressful on the ship's structure.

One reason this misconception has arisen is that navies of the period often undertook extensive repairs of old ships to prolong their life. These repairs ranged from replacing individual old or rotten timbers ("refits" or "minor repairs") to replacing the entire outer skin and decks, retaining only the ship's frame ("major repairs"). Rebuilding went even further. A ship being rebuilt was completely taken apart ("broken up"). Then some of her more sound timbers were used in the construction of an entirely new vessel (retaining the same name), which often had little or no resemblance to the original vessel. This practice was often used to evade budgetary or other prohibitions about building new ships.

Ships were either in ordinary or in commission. When a ship was placed in ordinary, her guns, stores, upper masts (topmasts and topgallants) and all yards were removed, and she had no crew. A ship that was commissioned had some officers and at least a partial crew appointed to her. If the ship was to see active service (i.e., go to sea), the cadre crew's first duties were to see to the rigging, arming, and provisioning of the ship, while the rest of the crew was obtained. However, a ship in commission could also serve productively without being ready or able to go to sea. Such duties included blockship, guardship, hospital ship, prison hulk, and sheer hulk. All of these missions required the ship to be commissioned, and the use of the term "commissioned" to describe both categories of warship usage has caused tremendous confusion for historians trying to determine the real naval might of states of the age of sail. As an example of the problems that could arise, the British navy list showed 174 SOLs at the end of the Revolution, but of this number only about 90 were in active service.

British Navy (Royal Navy)

In 1775 the British navy was the world's largest, and was blessed with an excellent cadre of the battle-trained officers who had experienced victory after victory during the Seven Years' War, which had ended only a dozen years previously. Unfortunately, the intervening years of peace had not been kind to the navy: a parsimonious Parliament and several mediocre First Lords of the Admiralty had allowed the navy's vessels to deteriorate to an alarming extent. Few ships were constructed, while many old and rotten ships reached the end of their useful lives and were broken up or otherwise disposed of. Other ships that were still useful were not repaired on a timely basis, so that they gradually became rotten.

As a result of these false economies, the British navy was unready for the naval war that commenced with France's entry into hostilities in July 1778. Although many new ships were built and others repaired or rebuilt during the war, it was not enough to overcome the years of neglect. Even several notable victories only served to change the outcome of the war from a clear British defeat to a near draw. What the war proved above all else was that the British navy was unable to decisively defeat the numerically superior naval forces of the four opposing sea powers (counting the United States). The results of this discovery were reflected in the Treaty of Versailles. The British reluctantly acknowledged American independence, ceded Minorca and Florida to the Spanish, and made several small concessions to France and the Netherlands.

A major problem that plagued the navy for much of the century was the very high level of conservatism among British shipwrights. This resulted in British ships being smaller and therefore usually slower than their foreign equivalents. This matter is discussed more fully below.

The level of politicism in the officer corps was another problem that rendered the navy less effective than in previous and later wars. The American war was not universally popular in Britain, and many able officers refused to serve an administration that held opposing political views, forcing the government to appoint less competent officers with more politically palatable views instead.

Despite these problems, the British were more innovative than the French in several ways. For example, the British were the first to adopt two very important innovations on a wide scale. These were coppering and the carronade.

Ever since wooden ships went to sea, the shipworm had been a serious nuisance. This worm ate the wood of a ship's hull, leaving a fatally weakened structure behind, which would eventually collapse (as happened to the *Royal Oak* at Spithead in 1782). Many remedies had been tried to eliminate this menace, but the final solution proved to be the fitting of copper sheets over the underwater portions of the ship's hull. The copper was poisonous to the worms, and had the additional side benefit of keeping the ship's bottom much cleaner than before. This gave coppered ships a significant speed advantage over uncoppered ships.

The first ship to be coppered was the frigate *Alarm*, in 1761. The experiment was so successful that a crash program to fit every warship with copper bottoms was undertaken in 1778. By 1783 the vast majority of British warships had been so fitted. The enemy powers were much slower in coppering their ships, and the resulting British speed advantage proved to be operationally important several times during the war.

The other major British innovation was the carronade. In 1774 a new type of gun, called the "smasher," was invented at Carron, Scotland. This gun was the first of a new type of naval ordnance, which quickly acquired the name of carronade. Carronades had the same relationship to the standard naval long guns that shotguns have to rifles: the carronade excelled at point-blank combat (up to 300 or 400 yards), but it was ineffective at longer distances.

Carronades had many advantages compared to long guns. Carronades were much lighter; a 32-pounder carronade weighed about the same as a 6-pounder long gun, but required fewer men and less space to operate, and was more accurate (up to the limits of its range). And the impact of a 32-pound shot was much more deadly than that of a small 6-pound ball.

These were powerful advantages. The space and weight advantages allowed carronades to be placed where no long guns could previously be mounted, increasing the ship's firepower and number of guns. Finally, most naval combat took place at short ranges anyway, where the carronade was much more efficient than the same weight of long guns, thus removing the last objection to the new weapon. These arguments were persuasive enough to cause the use of carronades to spread rapidly throughout the British navy during the war. The first weapons were installed in 1779, and in July of that year the Admiralty issued an order assigning carronades to all naval vessels, at the discretion of the ship's captain. By January 1781, 429 ships of the British navy carried a total of 604 carronades. By 1783 there was hardly a Royal Navy ship that did not carry at least a few, and some vessels (usually corvettes) had been rearmed entirely with carronades.

The carronade was especially well suited to the British style of naval combat, which emphasized the value of close action. The French naval doctrine of the period specified that the enemy should be engaged at longer ranges, and was, therefore, not so well suited for the carronade. Perhaps for this reason, only the British navy made any use of the carronade during the war.

British warships were notorious throughout the eighteenth century for being generally smaller and slower than their French and Spanish opponents. This unhappy state of affairs resulted from the conservatism of the British naval bureaucracy, which enforced a set of rules known as the establishments. The establishments dictated the precise dimensions and armament for every class of British warship, and deviation was discouraged and sometimes prohibited. Standardization was not intrinsically bad, as the experience of the French navy showed, but the British were much too conservative in their size and tonnage limits. These limits were gradually raised, and the worst excesses of this system were past by the time of the American war, but it took until the end of the century before British ships achieved parity with equivalent French ships.

There were more three-deckers in the British navy than in all other navies in the world in 1775. Because of the initial nature of the war, and then due to the necessity to build as many ships as quickly as possible, only one three-decker was built and completed during the war, while her opponents completed six.

The most outstanding example of British naval conservatism in this period is that nation's curious attachment to two classes of very small

two-deckers, rated at 50 and 44 guns. The 50's were obsolescent by 1775, but their continued existence could be partially justified by the argument that they could still fight in the line in emergencies, or in peripheral theaters (as actually occurred). They were also very economical ways to obtain miniature SOLs for use as station flagships in times of peace. Perhaps for these reasons, the British continued to build 50's until 1790.

No such reasons can be given for the continued construction of the useless 44's. They were too small to fight in the line of battle, but generally too slow to act as frigates. Despite these very serious drawbacks, Britain built over a dozen of them during the war. One reason for building the 44's may have been the peculiar nature of the American rebellion. In 1775 the colonists had no navy at all, but had a very long coastline, with many bays and navigable rivers. SOLs were too deep-drafted to be useful in these waters, and it was apparently thought that the 44's would be useful as they required less water than SOLs. This explanation is reasonable as far as it goes, but fails to explain why the British did not instead build more true frigates; they were even more shallow-drafted than the ungainly 44's.

In comparison to Britain's outstanding conservatism with the small two-deckers, her policy with regard to frigates was relatively enlightened. In 1775 the ratio of 18-pounder to 12-pounder frigates to 9-pounder frigates was about 1:12:8. By January 1783, the ratio had changed to 1:3:2. The British were actually even with or slightly ahead of the French in their adoption of the 18-pounder frigate.

French Navy

When the French entered the war against Britain on the side of the rebellious American colonies in July 1778, the French navy was more prepared for war than it had been since the glorious days of Anne-Hilarion de Tourville, nearly a century before.

This was a remarkable achievement, because the French navy had been largely destroyed during the Seven Year's War (1756–1763). A series of battles in 1759, of which the most important was Quiberon Bay, resulted in the loss of 35 SOLs of the French navy, either captured by the British or destroyed. This was nearly half of all the SOLs available to France, and such an enormous loss rendered the French navy impotent for the remainder of the war.

However, the reconstruction of the French navy began almost immediately. The catalyst was the appointment of the Duke de Choiseul as Minister of the Navy in 1761. This able man understood the importance of sea power, and was determined to create a navy for France that would, with Spanish help, be able to meet the fleets of England on even terms. In the next decade the French fleet was completely rejuvenated, and by 1770 a modern fleet of SOLs and frigates existed. Equally important, the dockyards had been well stocked with all of the many materials necessary for the upkeep of a large navy.

Choiseul was dismissed from office in 1770, and from that year until the death of Louis XV in 1774 the rebuilding program languished. The beginning of the American Revolution in 1775 prompted renewed attention to the condition of the French navy, and over the next three years almost all the existing warships underwent repairs or reconstruction in order to ready them for war. By 1778 the navy was at a high state of readiness, and could for a limited time—months, or perhaps a year at the most—count on having nearly the same numbers of SOLs available as the British navy. After this time, Britain's greater economic resources would allow her to build and man more SOLs than France alone could hope to match. The French government was well aware of this, and for this reason made every effort to entice Spain to join the war against Britain.

French participation in the American Revolution lasted from July 1778 to January 1783. These five years of war represented the zenith of French seapower in the age of sail. By dint of an enormous financial effort (which drove France deeply into debt and thereby played a significant role in the onset of the French Revolution), France was able to keep a large and formidable fleet at sea, rising from 52 SOLs at the start of the war to over 70 by 1782 (see Table 1). The French navy enjoyed good fortune during the first four years of warfare, and only one French SOL, the *Prothee* (64 guns) was lost to enemy action, although others were lost to accidental causes. But in 1782 this good fortune disappeared, and no fewer than 15 SOLs were lost to enemy action or to the hazards of the sea in that year; 8 were lost in a span of only 10 days (see Table 1). These cumulative losses seriously weak-

ened the French navy, and doubtless hastened the end of the war, for France could not easily replace these ships.

Although the French navy enjoyed more success in this war than in any other since the times of Tourville, it was not without serious problems. Two in particular hampered the French navy's performance in the American war.

First, there was a sharp division between the noble class of naval officers—the Corps de la Marine—and the non-noble class. This vicious practice not only prevented many able but non-noble officers from rising to positions of responsibility, but also led to a curiously democratic view of orders. Orders from one noble to another were apparently apt to be discussed, rather than rigorously obeyed as in the British navy, because every noble felt himself the equal of every other noble. This divisive behavior is illustrated well by the troubles of Admiral Pierre Suffren with his subordinate commanders in his Indian Ocean campaign. There were several attempts at reform before the war, but all they succeeded in doing was to create a period of administrative turbulence that had the eventual effect of strengthening the hand of the Corps de la Marine.

The second problem was the lack of sea time that most French officers received in peacetime. Whereas the British navy still maintained a sizable cadre of ships and crews during peacetime, which served to maintain the specialized nautical skills of the officers, the French navy maintained a much smaller number of such ships, and therefore had a much smaller cadre of experienced officers when war came. Partly as a result, French skill in shiphandling and fleet evolutions was in general not up to the level of their British enemies, although the disparity was not great.

All French naval architects in the eighteenth century received a good deal of instruction in the mathematics of warship design, and it is hardly a coincidence that French warships were widely considered to be superior to those of every other nation for most of the century. The theoretical grounding that French ship designers received helped them to be more willing to experiment , and the result was a series of excellent warships that were usually larger and faster than their British counterparts.

The experiences of war tempered theories of ship design with empirical data, demonstrating clearly which ship types were most useful. These types were reproduced, while those that proved lacking in some way were quickly abandoned. As a result of this flexibility, the composition of the French navy during the war years underwent a gradual but quite marked change. In particular, the historical trend toward larger and larger ships within the same types continued and perhaps accelerated during the war.

One notable trend was the emergence of the three-decker as a major line of development. For most of the eighteenth century the French navy possessed either one or no three-deckers. At the start of the war in July 1778, France had only two three-deckers available, the *Ville de Paris* (90 guns) and the *Bretagne* (110 guns). Their early experiences in the war, particularly the battle of Ushant, convinced them of the utility of very large ships, and in 1779 the French laid down another 4 three-deckers, all rated at 110 guns and all launched within the remarkably short period of about a year. These huge vessels went into active service in 1780 and 1781, and tripled the number of three-deckers in the French navy. At the same time the *Ville de Paris* was upgunned by the addition of 14 guns to her forecastle and quarterdeck, thus making her a 104.

The composition of the two-decker force also changed dramatically. At the start of the war, the ratio between 74's and the smaller 64's was just about 1:1. By the end of the war, however, the ratio had increased to almost 2:1. This change was the natural consequence of the enormous superiority of the 74's, which were generally faster and more seaworthy than the 64's, and which were also much more heavily armed . After the end of the war the phase-out of the 64's continued, and none remained by the outbreak of the French Revolution in 1789.

Just as the French navy recognized the obsolescence of the 64's, they also realized that the 50-gun ship was hopelessly outclassed and did not build any after the Seven Years' War. As a result, only four 50's served in the French navy at any one time during the American war, and two of these were captured British ships.

Two major types of frigates served in the French navy during the American Revolution; the *fregates de 12* and the *fregates de 8*. These designations indicated ships armed with 12-pounder or 8-pounder long guns on the gun deck. Both types typically carried around 30 to 32 guns total. The 8-pounder frigates proved to be too lightly armed to fulfill a frigate's role (like the British 9-pounder frigates), and were phased out relatively rapidly during the war. By January 31, 1780, there were fifty-one 12-pounder frigates on the navy list, but only seven 8-pounder frigates.

In 1781 the *Venus*, the first of a new type of frigate, the *fregate de 18*, was launched at Brest. Seven others were launched before the end of the war. These powerful frigates mounted 18-pounder long guns on the gun deck, and thus had an enormously greater broadside than any previous frigates. This advantage made them the standard frigate type by the Napoleonic wars.

Spanish Navy

The Spanish navy was a comparatively recent creation, having only been created as a national navy in 1714. Prior to that all the naval forces of Spain had belonged to various regional or provincial fleets. The new national organization was inherently more efficient, but the Spanish navy remained distinctly inferior to both the British and French navies during the eighteenth century.

The size of the Spanish navy was not the problem; by 1775 Spain had the third largest fleet in the world. The ships themselves were not the problem either; they were usually of excellent design and construction, partly due to the large number of English and Irish shipwrights (such as Matthew Mullen) who had been recruited to manage Spain's shipyards.

The navy's problems lay in other areas, such as the lack of a professionally competent officer corps, the inefficiency and corruption of the Spanish Ministry of Marine, the lack of suitable naval stores (e.g., ropes and sails), poor-quality guns, and crews who were often convicts and raw landsmen. British officers were able to produce well-trained sailors from the same unlikely raw material, but Spanish officers were generally unable to duplicate this performance. Further disadvantages included Spain's primarily agricultural rather than industrial economy and her lackluster naval tradition.

Given these disadvantages, it is not surprising that Spanish naval vessels were generally considered to be less efficient than British, French, or Dutch ships.

Despite the lack of Spanish maritime competence, the sheer size of the Spanish navy made it enormously important to the allied war effort against Britain. Neither France nor Spain could individually win a maritime war with Britain, but their combined fleets were significantly larger than the British navy (see Table 1). In the summer of 1779 a Franco-Spanish armada of 30 French and 36 Spanish SOLs sortied into the English Channel. The opposing British fleet was able to muster only 35 SOLs, despite the imminent danger of French invasion, and was so heavily outnumbered that it was forced to seek refuge in port, leaving the allied fleet in control of the Channel for a brief period. Although the allies were unable to use this advantage to execute the long-planned invasion of England, the importance of the Spanish contribution—over half the total force—is clear.

Spanish warships, like those of France, were well designed, generally much larger than British ships carrying the same number of guns, and well built. Indeed, Spanish ships often displayed astonishing longevity. For example, the *Rayo* (80 guns), launched in 1749, was still serving at Trafalgar, in 1805, where she was the oldest ship present. The *Fenix* also of 80 guns, was launched in the same year as the *Rayo*, and served in the Spanish and then British navies from that year until 1813. The main reason for this durability appears to have been the use of mahogany and other tropical hardwoods from the Spanish colonies in the Americas. Over one-third of all Spanish SOLs built in the eighteenth century were built at Havana, Cuba, partly because of the ready supply of such excellent raw materials.

Another reason for the long lives of many Spanish ships may have been the Spanish navy's policy of undergunning their ships, compared to the British and French navies. Many types of Spanish warships mounted guns one caliber smaller than the French or British would use on a deck. Examples include the 70, which carried only 24-pounders on the lower gun deck, compared to 32-pounders and 36-pounders for British and French 70's respectively. The other major example of undergunning was the 34-gun frigate. This ship appears to have been armed like equivalent French and British frigates, but what the Ship Armaments section does not show is that the 34's were as large as British or French 18-pounders frigates. The British often added guns to captured 34's and rated them as 36's, and this is another indication of their ability to mount more guns than the Spanish did.

This consistent pattern of weak armament was a clear disadvantage in battle, but the lighter guns also put less strain on the ship's structure, and this, combined with the naturally large size of Spanish naval vessels, must have had some beneficial effect on the ships' lifespans.

For most of the eighteenth century the Spanish, like the French, had concentrated on two-deckers, building only one three-decker before 1769. The launching of the 120-gun *Santisima Trinidad* in that year began a new trend in the Spanish navy. Another three-decker, the *Purisima Concepcion* (112 guns), was launched in 1779, and the *San Josef* of the same force was launched in 1783. These ships proved to be quite successful, and another nine 112's were built in the decade after the war.

Before the *Santisima Trinidad*, the most powerful ships in the navy were the 80-gun two-deckers. The *Fenix* was a very old ship and mounted only 24-pounders on her lower gun deck, but most of the others carried the weaponry shown in the Ship Armaments section. A half-dozen of these ships were built in the decade between 1765 and 1775, and as many as eight were operational simultaneously during the war. The success of the three-deckers resulted in the larger ships taking the place of the 80's, and no more 80's were launched until 1795.

The standard SOLs in the Spanish navy during the American Revolution were the 70's and 60's. As mentioned above, both types were weakly armed compared to their British equivalents (i.e., 74's and 64's), and this weakness was one of the reasons that Spanish squadrons and fleets were never as formidable as the mere number of ships would indicate.

The only frigate type to serve in significant numbers in this period was the 34. This class of ship was very large for the number and caliber of guns carried, or, to put it another way, was poorly armed for its size. On the other hand, 34's were much appreciated for their sailing qualities.

The Netherlands Navy

The Netherlands became a reluctant member of the anti-British alliance when Great Britain recalled her ambassador and initiated hostilities on December 20, 1780. Britain took this drastic step to prevent Dutch participation in the League of Armed Neutrality (then being formed under the aegis of Tsarina Catherine II of Russia). The United Provinces thus became the last of the combatants to enter the American Revolution.

The Dutch navy entered this war in a completely unprepared state, for economic, geographic, and political reasons. The economic reason was simply that, by 1775, the Netherlands was no longer the world's preeminent seafaring power, as it had been during the seventeenth century. As other nations sent their own fleets of merchantmen to sea, the Netherlands gradually lost its lucrative role as middleman of the world. Lacking significant natural resources to compensate for this relative decline in trade, the economy of the United Provinces languished in a state of stagnation and decline after about 1730, while at the same time the trade of Britain, France, and the future United States was growing swiftly. This economic decline made it difficult for the Dutch to maintain a first-class fleet.

Geography also worked against the Netherlands. First, the United Provinces were small in area compared to France or Great Britain, and thus had a smaller population base to furnish the sailors for the fleet. Second, the trade lanes from the Dutch ports to the rest of the world had to pass down the English Channel, thereby being vulnerable to both French and British pressures. Third, the shallow waters of the Zuider Zee and the Rhine estuary, and the siltation problems of all the major Dutch ports, meant that the size of Dutch warships was strictly limited. Thus, as warships inevitably increased in size during the eighteenth century, the Dutch were less and less able to compete. Last, the proximity of France forced the Dutch to maintain an army as well as a fleet, and this division of effort naturally hurt the size and readiness of the fleet.

The Netherlands were also divided politically, between pro-French and pro-British camps. Since the pro-British faction included the Stadholder, William V, and many other notables, the United Provinces were hardly united in their support of a strong navy (which was by implication anti-British). Another political problem was the lack of unity of the seven United Provinces. The seven provinces were not a nation at all, in the sense that France or Spain were nations. Instead the provinces were a sort of federation, with a nearly unmanageable political structure. A symptom of this disunity was the division of the Dutch navy into five effectively independent "admiralties." These five naval administrative organizations often disagreed with one another, and their wranglings made a coherent national naval strategy almost impossible.

All of these disadvantages ensured that the Netherlands could only claim the status of a second-rate naval power by the time of the American Revolution. However, the Dutch weakness in number of ships was somewhat compensated for by their natural affinity for the sea. The Dutch, unlike the Spanish and the French, had a long tradition of success at sea, dating back to the "sea beggars" at the time of Dutch independence from Spain, and reinforced by the exploits of the first Anglo-Dutch wars, when great fleets under Tromp and De Ruyter had fought the British to a draw, and the flames of burning British ships could be seen in London. The Dutch acquitted themselves reasonably well against a somewhat superior British squadron in the Battle of Dogger Bank, the only major naval action fought by the Dutch in the war of the American Revolution. Most importantly, the addition of the Dutch to the ranks of the enemies of Britain forced the British to tie down ships and men that were desperately needed elsewhere to cover the important trade with the Baltic that had to traverse the North Sea.

After their entry into the war, the Dutch undertook a massive rearmament program. The plan was to build 33 new SOLs (three 70's, nineteen 60's, and eleven 50's) and 22 new frigates. If the United Provinces had been able to construct and man such a force, it would have had a dramatic effect on the course of the naval war, but it is unlikely that such a massive shipbuilding program would actually have been completed, given the war, despite losing several SOLs to enemy action. The SOLs in Active Service table (Table 1) shows the extent of the growth; the number of SOLs ready for active service was only 11 in December 1780, 14 on April 1, 1781, 19 on April 1, 1782, and 25 is a reasonable estimate for 1783, if the war had continued.

The Dutch had the same official rating convention as the other powers, and their SOLs were nominally ranked as 50's, 60's, and 70's. However, all histories of the war usually refer to ships by the exact number of guns carried at the time. This could be very confusing, as a ship might carry a few more or less guns at various points during her career. For example, the *Wreker* (launched in 1783), was ranked as a 70, 74, 76, and an 80 at various times during her long ca-

TABLE 1

Ships of the line in active service, 1778–1782

BRITISH

Ship Type	7/1/1778	7/1/1779	7/1/1780	4/1/1781	4/1/1782
100 guns	1	3	3	3	3
98	-	3	6	6	7
90	7	5	5	5	3
80	1	1	2	3	4
74	27	37	42	38	36
70	1	1	1	2	2
64	19	23	26	21	24
60	2	4	4	4	1
50	8	13	12	12	14
Totals:	66	90	101	94	94

FRENCH

Ship Type	7/1/1778	7/1/1779	7/1/1780	4/1/1781	4/1/1782	4/22/1782
110 guns	1	1	4	5	3	3
90/104	1	1	1	1	1	-
80	5	6	6	5	6	6
74	20	29	32	32	36	32
70	1	1	1	1	1	1
64	19	21	20	22	21	18
60	1	1	1	1	1	1
50	4	3	4	3	4	4
Totals:	52	63	69	70	73	65

SPANISH

Ship Type	7/1/1779	7/1/1780	4/1/1781	4/1/1782
120 guns	1	1	1	1
112	-	1	1	1
80	7	7	8	8
70	42	31	35	33
64	3	3	3	3
60	4	4	5	7
54	1	1	1	1
Totals:	58	48	54	54

DUTCH

Ship Type	12/1780	4/1/1781	4/1/1782
77 guns	?	1	1
60–68	?	5	8
50–56	?	8	10
Totals:	11	14	19

reer. Fortunately, Dutch SOLs fell into three clearly defined categories during the war, and they are here called 74, 64, and 54, as these are the most commonly found labels for them.

The composition of the Dutch navy was quite different from that of the three major seapowers. The Dutch navy was inferior both numerically and in the size of individual ships. The Dutch navy contained only one ship rated at over 64 guns, the *Admiraal-Generaal*, a 74, and the greatest portion of the navy consisted of 54's. These small two-deckers were very lightly gunned—even the flimsy British and French 50's were more heavily armed. One would logically expect a 50 to be inferior in force to a 54. However, in the case of the Dutch 54 and British 50 the actual ratio of force was the reverse, as the total weight of broadside shows.

The 54 was an exception. The other types of Dutch naval vessels did not suffer from the problem of undergunning, and were actually rather heavily armed compared to their foreign counterparts, given the difference between the Dutch and English pounds.

American Navy

In 1775 the American colonies were barely a century and a half old; but in that time, the colonies had grown tremendously, such that a large percentage of the British Empire's cargo was carried in American merchant ships. This large merchant fleet did not, however, give the rebellious colonies an equivalent naval capability. Unlike armies, navies required a very complex supporting infrastructure, including dockyards with specialized naval stores, shipyards to build the warships, and a competent and organized bureaucracy to ensure the smooth flow of men, material, and money. Such entities could not be created in only a month or two; the British navy had been working on the problems of naval administration for well over a century by the start of the American Revolution, and still encountered problems during the war.

The rebels did not have years to organize their navy. Instead, the colonists were faced with the almost impossible task of creating a navy from scratch when they declared their independence from Great Britain. It is not surprising that the rebels failed; rather it is amazing that they accomplished anything at all.

The first warships of the young nation were converted merchant ships; the first officers were taken from the merchant marine or were political appointees. Some of the new captains—John Paul Jones and Nicholas Biddle come to mind—were charismatic leaders with courage and brilliance, and were equal to the best foreign captains. Many more officers, however, proved entirely lacking in the required skills, and were as bad as the worst officers in other navies. Hardly any of the first group of officers had any prior combat experience.

American warships came from three sources: the Continental (national) Navy, the various states' navies, and privateers. The Continental Navy was raised by decree of the Continental Congress, and was intended to be a regular navy, modeled on the lines of the British Royal Navy. Most of the states also raised their own navies, using them mainly for coast defense. Lastly, private citizens could obtain letters of marque. These were licenses allowing them legally to capture enemy ships ("prizes") and make whatever profit from their prizes that they could. It was a lucrative but risky business; while some entrepreneurs made their fortunes seizing and selling British merchant ships and crew, many others were captured, and languished in British prison hulks.

Despite their best efforts, the American naval forces in the end had virtually no effect upon the British conduct of the war, and the gallant fleet of 1777 had dwindled to only a few ships by 1783. The rebellious colonies were dependent upon France and other outside sources for the military supplies that made it possible for them to field armies against the British, but is was the French navy, not American warships, that provided the naval support that was the essential precondition for American independence.

On December 13, 1775, Continental Congress authorized the construction of thirteen frigates, one to represent each of the rebellious colonies. These frigates were to form the backbone of the new American navy. These ships were in general larger than British ships of the same type, and appear to have been generally well-designed ships, despite their shipwrights' lack of experience in designing warships. Six of the 13 were captured or burnt to avoid capture before ever getting to sea. All of the remaining seven were destroyed or captured by July 1781, and most of them accomplished little before meeting their fates.

Before the first batch of frigates had been completed, Congress passed a new naval act calling for the construction of three 74-gun SOLs and five 36-gun frigates, in addition to smaller ships. This was a grandiose plan that was soon shown to be completely impractical, and in the end only the *America* (74 guns) and the *Alliance* (36 guns) were ever completed.

The *America* was laid down in 1777 at Portsmouth, New Hampshire. Her construction took five years—an extraordinarily long time by wartime standards. The reason for the delay was not technical but financial. As the war went on Congress found itself in increasingly desperate financial straits, and money for a ship of the line was hard to obtain. The whole project turned into a nightmare, and it is something of a miracle that she was ever launched. But construction straggled along, and was somewhat accelerated by the appointment of John Paul Jones to be her first captain. He never got to take her to sea, though; immediately after launch on November 5, 1782, she was given to France. The ostensible reason for the gift was to replace the *Magnifique* (74 guns) which had run aground and became a total wreck in Boston harbor earlier in the same year, but another reason may have been that Congress, finding it increasingly difficult to borrow money, snapped at this chance of getting rid of the *America*. The French found the *America* to be a poorly designed SOL (undoubtedly the result of American lack of design experience with very large warships), and she was laid up almost immediately.

Probably the most famous ship in the American navy was the *Bonhomme Richard*. She was originally the *Duc de Duras*, an old East Indiaman. These were very large and stoutly constructed merchantmen, designed expressly to withstand the rigors of long voyages between Europe and the Indian Ocean, as their name suggests. John Paul Jones armed her with six old 18-pounders, twenty-six 12-pounders, and eight 9-pounders, and took her out of Brest as the commodore of a small Franco-American combined squadron. Meeting a British convoy on September 23, 1779, Jones captured the British warship *Serapis*, with 44 guns (of much superior force) in an epic fight.

Methods of Calculating Fighting Power

There were several methods of calculating the fighting ability of a warship in the age of fighting sail. The two usual methods were the total number of guns mounted and the number of complete gun decks the ship had. In addition, there was a third, traditional way, the use of rates.

A universally used method of calculating a naval vessel's combat value was the number of cannon the ship carried. In fact, the number of guns was so generally used as the standard measurement of a warship's fighting power that it was usually included with the ship's name whenever the ship was mentioned in reports or histories, as follows: "HMS *Victory*, 100."

The assumption is that a ship's combat capability was related to the total number of guns mounted. This was approximately correct, but there were two problems that have bedeviled students of this era.

First, in many cases the number of guns was not an accurate measure of a ship's fighting power. Preceding sections have mentioned several examples. The lesson to be learned from these examples is that the most accurate measure of a ship's fighting power was the weight of the broadside, not the number of guns. Ships with more guns naturally tended to have larger calibers of guns as well, but this relationship was far from exact.

The second problem is that the number of guns often changed as ships went through refits, aged, and so on. Things really got fouled up when the carronade appeared, because they were not counted as part of the ship's armament. By the war's end, most British warships carried several carronades, and thus had more total guns than was the official number. This divergence has caused students of the period much heartache, because it became impossible to discern a ship's real force merely by knowing her numerical gun rating. Whereas a 74-gun SOL previously had exactly one armament configuration, she might mount any number of carronades, or none, depending on her captain's whim. The problem became worse during the Napoleonic wars, and was not corrected until 1812, when carronades finally became officially counted as part of a ship's armament in the British navy.

A less specific measurement of a warship's fighting power was the number of gun decks the ship possessed. A gun deck was any deck of the ship that was completely lined with guns, from bow to stern. The number of complete gun decks a warship might possess ranged from one to three. For example, a three-decker carried her main armament on three complete gun decks; other, lighter guns might be located on the forecastle and quarterdeck, and even on the poop, but the number of complete decks of guns determined the ship's approximate fighting power. A ship with three gun decks could usually carry more guns than a ship with two gun decks, and would thus be more powerful, assuming that the sizes of the guns aboard both ships were identical.

Naval ships were also grouped into categories of nominally similar fighting power called rates. When first instituted, the rates divided warships into types in a reasonably logical manner, but the rates became outdated as warships grew in size, and by 1775 they were essentially meaningless. For this reason rates are not used in this article, although they are often mentioned in histories of the era.

Ships Armaments

The following table shows the armaments of the SOLs and frigates of the British, French, Spanish and Dutch navies. The armament of American warships is not listed, because their armament was a heterogenous mix of different calibers. The casting of naval cannon was already a very specialized art by 1775, and the colonial foundries lacked the skills to produce naval guns in either the quantity or quality nec-

essary. To make up the gap, the Americans had to resort to captured British guns, purchased French guns, and whatever could be scrounged from old forts. The frigate *Boston*, 24, is a good example of the heterogenous nature of American warship armament. She went to sea with the following armament: five 5 12-pounders, nineteen 9-pounders, two 6-pounders, and four 4-pounders.

The table shows only the nominal or standard armament of each type of ship: actual armaments often varied quite a bit, especially for British ships after 1778, when carronades came into use. Nonetheless, these figures at least serve as some basis for comparison of the ships to each other. Carronades are not generally listed because the number mounted varied so much from ship to ship.

Each column of the table shows the armament for a single deck of the ship, with the number of guns on the left and their caliber (size of shot) in pounds on the right. The meaning of the column headings is shown below. Frigates have their single gun deck listed under the upper gun deck, because that was official British parlance. The rightmost column contains the figure for the total weight of shot thrown in a single broadside (i.e., half of the ship's guns). This figure is more important than the actual number of guns in determining a ship's real fighting value because it shows the tremendous importance of large guns and conversely shows how unimportant the smaller calibers of guns were. A comparison of the total number of guns against the broadside weight for various ship types will show the difference between the apparent and the true firepower of each ship.

The table confirms that the system of ranking ships by the number of guns worked in most cases. A few deceptive cases stand out, such as the British and French 80-gun SOLs. Although mounting exactly the same number of guns, the French ship possesses a broadside almost 40 percent heavier than the British ship. The reason is obvious once the calibers of the guns are noted; the British ship is armed largely with 18-, 9-, and 4-pounder cannon, while the French vessel is mostly armed with 36- and 24-pounders. That the French 80 was a very powerful ship is espe-

TABLE 2

Armaments of ships of the line and frigates

Ship Type	(Guns)					
	LGD	MGD	UGD	QD/FC	Nom. Bdsd.	Eng. Wgt.
BRITAIN						
Three-decked SOLs:						
100	28-32 pdrs.	28-24pdrs.	28-12pdrs.	16-6 pdrs.	1000	1000
90/98 (new)	28-32	30-18	30-12	2-9	907	907
90 (old)	26-32	26-18	26-12	12-6	842	842
80	26-32	26-18	24-9	4-6	770	770
Two-decked SOLs						
74	28-32	-	28-18	18-9	781	781
70	26-32	-	28-18	16-9	740	740
64	26-24	-	26-18	12-6	582	582
60	24-24	-	26-11	10-6	474	474
50 ("two-decker")	22-24	-	22-12	6-6	414	414
44 ("two-decker")	20-18	-	22-9	2-6	285	285
Frigates						
38 *(Flora)*	-	-	26-18	10-9,6-18c	333	333
32	-	-	26-12	6-6	174	174
28	-	-	24-9	4-3	114	114

cially clear when one notes that it possessed a heavier broadside than even the British 100, the largest of the British warships.

Unfortunately, the weight of a "pound" varied from country to country. 36 French pounds weighed almost exactly 39 English pounds, an 8 percent difference, while the Amsterdam pound presumably used by the Dutch was about 9 percent heavier than the British pound. The Spanish pound was nearly identical to the British pound. These differences in the actual weights of the broadside are shown in the rightmost column, and should be considered the most accurate statement of relative force between the ships shown on the table.

Key to Column Headings

Ship Type: The official rating of the ship, in number of guns. This is occasionally different from the actual number of guns mounted. Two numbers separated by a slash means that the same ships were referred to by two numbers, usually indicating minor armament modifications. Ship names are included when the ship was in some way exceptional (usually because it was the only one of its type). Other useful information may also be listed after the gun rating.

LGD: Lower Gun Deck (also called simply Gun Deck).

MGD: Middle Gun Deck.

UGD: Upper Gun Deck.

QD/FC: The quarterdeck and forecastle.

Nom.Bdsd.: The weight of a single discharge of half of the ship's guns (i.e., all the guns on one side). This figure is rendered in the native pounds of the country under which it is listed. Note: A small "c" after a gun weight means that the guns are carronades.

Eng. Wgt.: The weight of the broadside in English pounds (rounded to the nearest pound).

Armaments of ships of the line and frigates (cont'd)

Ship Type	(Guns)					
	LGD	MGD	UGD	QD/FC	Nom. Bdsd.	Eng. Wgt.
FRANCE						
Three-decked SOLs						
110	30-36 pdrs.	32-24 pdrs.	32-12 pdrs.	16-8 pdrs.	1236	1335
104 (*Ville de Paris*)	30-36	30-24	30-12	14-8	1136	1227
90 (*Ville de Paris*)	30-36	30-24	30-12	-	1080	1166
Two-decked SOLs						
80	30-36	-	32-24	18-12	1077	1163
74	28-36	-	30-18	16-8	876	946
70 (*Dauphin-Royal*)	26-36	-	28-18	16-8	822	888
64	26-24	-	28-12	10-8	520	562
60 (*St. Michel*)	24-24	-	26-12	14-6	486	525
50 ("two-decker")	24-24	-	26-12	-	444	480
Frigates						
36 (*fregates de 18*)	-	-	28-18	8-8	284	307
32 (*fregates de 12*)	-	-	26-12	6-6	174	188
26/30 (*fregates de 8*)	-	-	26-8	4-4	136	147
SPAIN						
Three-decked SOLs						
120 (*Santisima Trinidad*)	30-36 pdrs.	32-24 pdrs.	32-12 pdrs.	26-8 pdrs.	1220	1232
112 (*Purisima Concepcion*)	30-36	32-24	32-12	18-8	1188	1200
Two-decked SOLs						
80	30-36	-	32-18	18-12	936	945
70/74	28-24	-	30-18	12/18-8	654	661
60/64	26-24	-	26-12	8/12-8	500	505
Frigates						
34	-	-	26-12	8-6	180	182
THE NETHERLANDS						
Two-decked SOLs						
74 (*Admiraal-Generaal*)	28-36 pdrs.	-	28-18 prs	20-8 pdrs.	834	909
64/68	26-24	-	26-18	14-8	602	656
54 ("two-decker")	24-18	-	24-12	6-6	378	412
Frigates						
40 (*Argo*)	-	-	28-18	12-6	288	314
36	-	-	26-12	10-6	186	203

Mark A. Campbell and Jack Greene

REFERENCES

Jean Boudriot, *The Seventy-Four Gun Ship*, trans. by David Roberts, 4 vols. (1980–86); Howard Chapelle, *The History of the American Sailing Navy* (1944); Wiliam L. Clowes, *The Royal Navy: A History from the Earliest Times to the Present*, 7 vols. (1897–1903), 3; Brian Lavary, *The Arming and Fitting of English Ships of War, 1600–1815* (1987); ———, *The Ships of the Line*, 2 vols. (1983).

Navigation and Tactics at Sea

Time has brought an aura of mystery and romance to the vessels and seamen of the Age of Sail. Paintings of smoke-wreathed ships with billowing sails evoke images of a time when beauty and utility merged. The truth was far from that. The vessels were slow in speed and difficult to handle. As far as the crews were concerned, they were cramped and malodorous wooden forts, where the crew could be trapped for years. The commanders faced many of the problems found in today's navies, but had none of the modern advances in command, control, and communication. These vessels were kept in action through skill, knowledge, discipline, and endurance.

Handling a square-rigged vessel is an exact art that leaves no room for mistakes. The captain had the responsibility for everything that occurred on his vessel. It is through the perspective of the decisions and responsibilities of this man that the handling of one of these vessels in battle is best understood. The square-rigged naval vessel was a complicated machine, and while one man held the burden of command, no one person could see all that was going on simultaneously. The captain had to navigate the ship, interpret the signals, and follow strategies and tactics laid out by shoreside officials. While junior officers would assist and skilled tasks were left to the warrant officers, the captain was very much alone in command.

One of the first priorities of the captain of an eighteenth-century naval vessel was order, both internal and external. A square-rigged man-of-war was a community where there was no space and no privacy; the only way to keep order was harsh discipline. Many of the seamen had been forced into service. There were others who were little more than hardened criminals. The combination of long voyages, poor food, and cramped quarters produced conditions in which tempers could flare over the slightest offense. These warships needed large crews in order to fight, but routine sailing required fewer crewmen. For instance, a 100-gun ship of the line could require 850 or more men, but only 10 percent of these personnel were needed to sail her. The remaining 90 percent were needed to man guns, to pass powder, and to repair the vessel. Many of these crewmembers could not be engaged in anything other than "busy work," therefore compounding the problems of command. Strangely enough, disease was not usually as prevalent a problem as we would think today, in spite of the crowding and oftentimes poor food. To aid the captain, the marine force was used as the ultimate weapon of discipline. These personnel formed an armed unit that could be counted on to protect the ship against potential disorder. The fact that there were so few instances of mutiny or major disturbances is a tribute to the command abilities of the captains.

External order was maintained by a series of instructions for fighting, and various coded signals. The "Fighting Instructions," as the much maligned and often ignored Royal Navy instructions were entitled, provided a set of directions that sought to provide concentrated firepower against an opponent. During the entire period of fighting sail, the main armament was concentrated on the broadside. To use these guns effectively, the vessels were best brought into action in "line ahead," that is, one after another, firing at the enemy vessels, presumably also in line. While the maneuver would appear to be an easy one, the varying rates of advance, caused by the lack of uniformity in rigging or hull form, the fouling of the bottom by marine growth (coppering bottoms was a Royal Navy practice, but not universal), and the vagaries of the wind over the miles that might separate a fleet, would make it almost impossible for a practical fleet to approach in order. A fleet less practiced, or one hastily thrown together, did not have the slightest hope of keeping station. Keeping station was not a problem for many of the smaller vessels, known as frigates and sloops, which did the most fighting. These fought as part of commerce-raiding expeditions or defending merchant vessels convoys, and frequently fought alone as single ships. Only the largest and most heavily armed vessels, called ships of the line, normally mounting 60 or more guns, could fight in the often brutal, formal fleet actions. Even these vessels were not large by today's standards. A typical three (gun) deck vessel had a length of approximately 200 feet and a breadth of around 50 feet. In all of these vessels the pressure of the large sail area was counterbalanced by iron, lead, and stone carried at or near the bottom of the vessel. This ballast gave these craft a draft of 20 feet or so, deep in comparison to their size. Even with this weight, the lower gunports on the side away from the wind (called the lee side) would be unusable in any size breeze. The ships of the line were costly to build, supply, and man. They required perhaps 2,000 trees and usually many years to complete. A ship of the line might also have close to 900 crew on the average, while a sloop would need only 200 or so men.

The captain also had to consider what the loss of his vessel could mean and how well it was maintained. The very expense of maintaining a navy caused the countries who had them to be conservative with their use and sometimes sparing with required upkeep and maintenance. Wartime would bring about rapid expansion and construction or repairs and forced the use of green or not properly seasoned wood. While this solved an immediate problem, it would often mean that the vessel would experience rot and deterioration in service. The problem of deterioration plagued all the navies of the Revolution and forced many vessels to enter combat weaker than their size indicated, as the ship's timbers could no longer carry the weight of their full complement of guns. The amount of deterioration and the expense of vessel operations could and did effect the outcome of battle. The captain knew that timber sides of four inches in thickness could withstand brutal punishment, but the greatest danger to these vessels was fire. In many cases the captains passed up opportunities in battle for fear of losing a ship to fire.

Discipline, courage, and order alone would not give the captain a fighting ship. Teamwork was essential. The captain was forced to walk a very narrow line between sufficient and excessive discipline. The complexity of handling and fighting a vessel under sail required the crew to know and perform their jobs under the worst conditions. The better drilled and, therefore, more cohesive crews had more potential to be victorious. The captain who could get concentrated, rapid, and steady fire would have the advantage over a vessel that fought without control. Knowledge of the vessel was essential. Each member of the crew had a task, and each had to know that task. Hours were spent memorizing every line and job, until each person could perform tasks perfectly. Constant drills were provided to insure the crews had the skills necessary to carry out orders.

Gunnery was another problem. The gunners had a selection of shot, designed to be used to exploit an opponent's weaknesses. It was similar to the fortress artillery ashore and used much of the same ammunition. The gunners could clear an opponent's deck with grape (small balls in bags), and canister (small balls in a powder-filled

can, which was designed to explode). Bar shot and chain shot were fired to cut and tangle rigging, and heated or hot shot was used to set fires. By far the most common shot fired was the solid shot. This was used to batter the hull and possibly hole it below the waterline. The solid ball was also a serious hazard to the gun crews as each shot that hit splintered the interior planking, which, in turn, caused serious wounds. Heated shot, which on the surface would appear to be the most effective in destroying an enemy's ship, was not preferred as frequently because the object of battle was to capture the opponent's vessel. The captain had to place a great deal of trust in his gunner to insure that the proper and ordered load was fired at the best time for the most telling effect.

The skill of the warrant officer, known as the master, in handling the sails according to the tactical plan of the captain would determine how effective the vessel would be in combat. Even with all sails set, these vessels were slow and cumbersome. A ship of the line did well to make six knots (i.e., six nautical miles per hour) sailing on its best course, that is with the wind from astern. The square rig of these vessels constrained them from streering closer than 70 degrees either side of the wind's direction (upwind). If it was necessary to travel against the wind (called "beat to windward"), requiring the ship to sail in a series of zigzag maneuvers, a ship of the line did well to make one knot. When stripped for action these ships were even slower. When entering combat only the upper (smaller) square sails and the smaller fore and aft (triangular) sails were carried. No matter what the strategy and tactics applied, the actual approach of vessels in battle was never quick and days could go by before the guns were in range.

Small course and speed changes were made by adjusting some or all of the sails, to get the maximum or lessen efficiency in order to keep station. These sail adjustments, along with practiced use of the rudder and intimate knowledge of the vessel, allowed stations to be kept. Even so, the differing characteristics of the vessels and the condition of the hulls made formation sailing difficult.

In order to change course more than a few degrees or to make progress against the wind, the head or the stern of the vessel would have to be brought through the wind, so as to place the wind on the opposite side. To do this there were three basic maneuvers available. The first of these maneuvers, "tacking," was used to make progress against the wind. In this maneuver, the bow was forced up into the wind and the vessel's momentum was relied on to bring the bow through. The sails and lines had to be shifted to the opposite side during this time. This could be a fast and economical maneuver, but it was dangerous, as it had to be performed smoothly. If all sway was lost, the vessel became "in irons" (the sails were not filled and just shook, thus providing no propulsion or steering force), and the sails then had to be "backed" (filled in reverse) or if possible, the bow was allowed to fall back on the old course and the maneuver was attempted again, once momentum was restored. Another danger was the real possibility that the sails could fill in reverse. The masts, braced for wind pressure from astern and the sides, could break under the strain. In battle, damage or the reduced amount of sail carried could make tacking an impossible maneuver to accomplish.

"Wearing ship," that is, bringing the wind around the stern, was a safer maneuver for a damaged vessel or one that found herself buffeted by strong winds and high seas. In this maneuver the vessel's stern was brought through the wind. This cost a great deal of ground and therefore reduced the vessel's advance toward its objective. It did allow the vessel to remain under control during the maneuver, however, and for a heavily damaged vessel this might be the only safe maneuver.

The vessel could also employ a maneuver known as "boxhauling." Here the sails were allowed to fill in reverse, allowing the vessel to sail a slight distance backward. This could be done to slow a vessel, perform a tight turn, or restore lost motion. Under control and in the right circumstances this maneuver was safe, but for a sail vessel with damage it was dangerous. The skill of the master and the personnel that he directed could make or break a captain's tactical plan. One final consideration the captain had to make was whether or not the vessel would be underway at all. A number of engagements were actually fought with one side or the other at anchor (St. Kitts, January 25–26, 1782).

In addition to the internal and structural problems, the captain had to consider nature. While the national government could determine what the targets would be for the fleet and the objectives of a campaign, the weather determined when these objectives could be pursued. This was good for both sides. The side who had to defend could predict when they would be attacked, and the attacking side would watch for breaks in climatic patterns to try and surprise the defenders with an attack when they least expected it. A good example of this is the naval campaigns fought off the Atlantic coast and in the Carribean. In the summer and early fall, the fleets would be stationed off the Atlantic Coast of North America, avoiding the hurricane season in the Caribbean. In late fall and winter, they would shift to the Caribbean and avoid the coastal storms of the North Atlantic.

The weather and seas could affect the overall outcome of a battle, changing a loser to a winner with a single windshift. When there were light winds, the approach for battle was measured in feet per hour and not miles. The large underbody mentioned earlier allowed ocean currents to affect the ships. It was not uncommon, in light breezes, for one of these vessels to be prevented by the current from completing a maneuver. Sometimes a warship was forced to use its small boats to pull the vessel through. A commander had to consider where his vessel or fleet could best be placed to handle any potential weather problem and still carry out the battle plan.

There were two schools of thought on use of the weather in naval tactics. The first required the commander to assemble the fleet into a position known as the "Weather Gauge." Here the fleet was maneuvered to be upwind of the opponent so that it might come down on the opponent from the same direction as the wind. This had some advantages. The first was that the attacking fleet would have the wind behind it and therefore would have more room and ease to maneuver. The attacker would then be able to play a game of psychological warfare with his opponent until he was ready to attack. In addition, the last part of the attacker's approach would blanket the wind, thus slowing the opponent. The defender could only narrow the gap between them and the attacker by a long series of slow maneuvers upwind. Secondly, the smoke from the gun discharges would roll down, masking the enemy's signals and causing confusion in his ranks, while (in theory) leaving the attacker's signals clear. Another advantage was that, with a stiff breeze, the vessels downwind would have their undersides exposed due to the heeling caused by the wind, while the attacker's vessels would not have this vulnerable area exposed. For the British this matched their desire to crush the enemy fleet, and so the Weather Gauge was their chosen position. The wind, however, could be fickle, and an attack plan could be ruined by a wind shift that would alter this position.

The other school of thought on attack was to take the lee or downwind position. From the previous paragraph it would appear that this was a more vulnerable position. However, it also had advantages. The lee position allowed a vessel to turn easily and run downwind and, therefore, escape. The smoke of battle could provide a screen to allow vessels to maneuver away before steps could be taken to stop them. The heel of the vessel in a heavy wind, claimed as an advantage by the proponents of the Weather Gauge, could be an advantage for the vessels to leeward. The vessels downwind would not have any of their guns on the engaged side masked by being too close to the water and would, therefore, be able to bring the full complement to bear. These guns would also be able to more easily hit the rigging of the vessels to windward (upwind), which would slow their approach. The advantages of both positions were argued throughout the period known as the Age of Fighting Sail, and the argument was never settled. Britain preferred the Weather Gauge and the French found the leeward position to their advantage.

When working with other vessels in his fleet the captain had to communicate; however, communication between vessels was at best poor. Though new codes existed that made more efficient use of the signal flags, they were not widely used. Oftentimes, in fact, each commander had his own signal book. When new ships joined a fleet or squadron, they might not have the right codes. In any case, the signals were difficult to read. The smoke from gun discharges tended to mask the signals, so to improve communications, the flagship (the commander's vessel) was to be in the center. In theory, therefore, the signals could be passed up and down the line in half the time. Adding to the problem of communication between ships was that the two ends of a fleet would also be commanded by an admiral, who might or might not agree with the fleet commander. More often than not, the signals were ignored allegedly because the rigging or smoke obscured the flags. One way the commanders improved communications was to station frigates on the far side of the fleet; signals were then passed from the flagship down the line of frigates. But many of the same problems persisted. At times, things would be so bad that a vessel was sent back to ask what was wanted, and in some instances a boat had to be rowed over with a message. The best communication resulted when the officers and crews of a fleet had practiced together previously as one. In that way, the men knew their commander's style of battle and could anticipate his orders.

Two further considerations affected the way the captains performed. National policy shaped how a navy would fight. The Royal Navy reflected the national will to control the seas, and so fought aggressively to destroy the opposition. The French fought from a position of naval weakness, which had developed over the preceding years, so they fought to cripple their opponent before their opponent destroyed them. Thus the French endeavored to keep a "fleet in being" so as to tie down the British so they would not threaten French dominance on land. These policies affected the way that the fleets tactically deployed and even the way they pressed their attacks. As well, the system of prize money that had long been part of naval tradition complicated an action. Any vessel that assisted in the capture of another vessel was entitled to money awarded by a court to the crew (and the admiral) by a somewhat shifting and complicated formula. This hope of prize money did play a part in getting the volunteers to join and in keeping the less willing members of the crew in line. Therefore, on occasion, capture rather than destruction of a vessel was uppermost in the minds of a crew, and thus an advantage was sometimes lost for monetary gain.

All of these thoughts and problems were the burden of the captain, but when the enemy was sighted, the ship had to be prepared and make the best of what was on hand. Once an enemy was sighted, frequently by a lookout who spotted masts on the horizon, the ship had to be prepared for battle. The position of the fleet when an enemy was sighted would contribute to the length of time the approach would take. Even with an advantageous position, the speed difference might be as little as half a knot. The position that the fleets had in respect to the sun was also important. Vessels that approached with the sun behind them would have the opposing fleet blinded and lit by the sun.

During the approach, normal shipboard routine was maintained. It was a source of pride to prepare the ship for battle in as short a period as possible. (When "general quarters" was beaten by the drummers signaling that preparation for combat was to be made, most Royal Navy ships could be readied for action in 20 minutes.) As part of this preparation, all but the necessary sails to maneuver a vessel in combat were taken down. If they were too large to take down, they would be furled. This served two purposes, the first was that the vessel could be handled by a smaller sail crew, and second, the possibility of the rigging aloft catching fire or putting undue strain on damaged masts would be minimized. Below decks, each man had a task. Some cleared guns and ran them out, while others stowed away the furnishings of the captain's cabin. In other areas the surgeon and his assistants set up the hospital. In the magazines, where the powder was kept, the gunner's mates passed powder cartridges to young boys, known as "powder monkeys," who would then race along the gun decks to supply the guns. Part of the preparation required placing wet safety blankets over the powder access doors to prevent a spark from penetrating the magazine. On the main deck, to lessen the chance of loss, livestock and valuables were placed in boats that were lowered over the ship's side and were recovered later. Marines manned the rigging and rails with muskets and grenades in order to sweep the personnel from an enemy's deck and to allow boarding. The captain attended to the details and insured that his officers and warrants were carrying out his orders. All through the vessel hand weapons such as axes, cutlasses, and pistols were accessible to arm boarding parties or to repel boarders.

The vessels in a fleet action used this time to communicate by signals. Frequently, the captains met aboard the flagship to determine how they would fight the battle. The maneuvers would be based on those discussed in the fighting instructions. There were opposing schools of thought on how to fight. No one argued against the fact that the line ahead formation was best. This allowed proper and concentrated use of the vessel's firepower arranged down each side. This rigid formation also prevented the friendly vessels from fouling each other's maneuvers and fire. Throughout the entire Age of Fighting Sail, there was a great deal of controversy over whether the formal or melee tactics were the best way to defeat an enemy.

In formal tactics the vessels of the fleet were to keep in line of battle, one immediately following another at set intervals. To keep this line was all important. This tactic could be employed where the vessels were running parallel or approaching from opposite positions. When running parallel, the advantage was that the guns could be brought to bear for a longer period of time and the vessels could support each other. The firepower of the fleet could, at least in theory, be equally distributed along the line. Success depended on good gunnery and tough ships and crews. There were two disadvantages above all the problems we have previously reviewed. The first was that a determined or faster opponent could work into a position where his fleet could cut across the top of your line. This maneuver was known as crossing the "T." This would allow concentrated fire on the first ships in your line and effectively wreck your line of battle. In addition, the very nature of formality of the line of battle stifled any initiative and therefore heightened the caution of the individual ship commanders. These formations frequently yielded inconclusive results.

In the melee school of tactics, the initial approach was similar; the idea was to use initiative and to mass firepower on a portion of the enemy's line in order to disable it more quickly. The enemy's line could also be "doubled," that is, the attacker could sail around his opponent's ships and then maneuver to reach the opposite side of the enemy. The attacker also had the option of dividing his ships, or splitting one's line, and having his vessels bombard the enemy on both sides. Another tactic was "breaking." Here vessels would penetrate the enemy's line, effectively breaking up his line of battle into small, disoriented groups. The enemy's firepower could then be overwhelmed.

While the conference before battle could present all sorts of excellent textbook solutions and many paper victories, it was the captain and the crew he commanded that determined what really would happen. As he returned to his ship or put down the message, the key to the outcome of combat was his initiative and aggressiveness.

After a flurry of preparation, the waiting continued until the vessels drew into gun range.

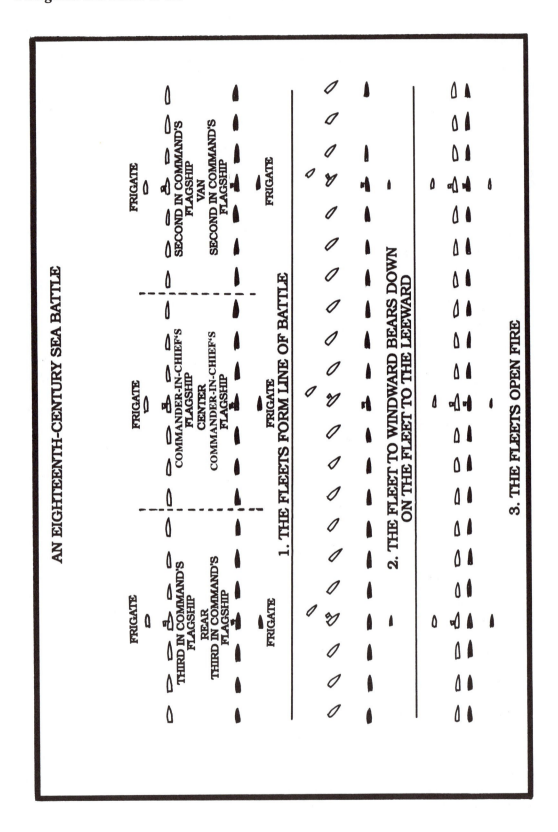

AN EIGHTEENTH-CENTURY SEA BATTLE

FRIGATE

SECOND IN COMMAND'S
FLAGSHIP
VAN
SECOND IN COMMAND'S
FLAGSHIP

FRIGATE

FRIGATE

COMMANDER-IN-CHIEF'S
FLAGSHIP
CENTER
COMMANDER-IN-CHIEF'S
FLAGSHIP

FRIGATE

FRIGATE

THIRD IN COMMAND'S
FLAGSHIP
REAR
THIRD IN COMMAND'S
FLAGSHIP

FRIGATE

1. THE FLEETS FORM LINE OF BATTLE

2. THE FLEET TO WINDWARD BEARS DOWN
ON THE FLEET TO THE LEEWARD

3. THE FLEETS OPEN FIRE

Once the battle joined and the guns fired, the decks filled with fire, smoke, and heat. As enemy fire struck a vessel, wood splintered, and lines and sails dislodged, wounding or killing those serving the guns. Crews struggled to reload and fire again in order to get the most out of the few minutes they might be in gun range. If the wind allowed, the vessel was maneuvered in close in attempt to foul the other vessel's rigging. At that time, any subtlety of tactics and maneuver was lost. The battle could became an all-out test of wills if opposing vessels grappled alongside each other and locked together in hand-to-hand combat. The crews slugged it out for possession of the decks. Frequently guns continued to fire at point-blank range until the colors (flags) were lowered and the vessel surrendered. The fighting could be so fierce that the victor's vessel would be destroyed, due to damage below the waterline or due to fire. In many cases the efforts of the uninjured members of both crews were required to insure that at least one of the vessels would survive. After a victory the crews of both the winning and losing sides had to separate the vessels in order to prevent the better of the two from being dragged under by an extensively damaged one.

After the battle, damage was repaired and the vessel returned to action as far as it was possible. The crew might have to find a friendly port to put in and repair the damage before setting out on a further cruise or returning home. Once the battle excitement died away, the routine of sailing began once again. The vessel would once again watch and wait—perhaps for months and even years—for another chance at action.

Throughout the Age of Sail, the captain was the key to the handling of a vessel in battle. He set the tone and aggressiveness of his vessel. He and he alone was the secret to handling a vessel under sail in action. How fast the vessel would again see action depended on how the captain handled the strain of combat and interpreted his orders. For us to completely understand a naval battle of that age, we must first study the captains—what they faced and how they thought.

George John Munkenbeck, Jr.

REFERENCES

Jack Coggins, *Ships and Seamen of the American Revolution* (1969); R. Ernest Dupuy, Gay Hammerman, Grace P. Hayes, *The American Revolution: A Global*

War (1977); Thomas E. Greiss, *The Dawn of Modern Warfare* (1984); Anthony Preston, David Lyon, John H. Batchelor, *Navies of the American Revolution* (1975); C. Keith Wilbur, *Picture Book of the Revolution's Privateers* (1973).

Nelson, Thomas, Jr. (1739–1789)

Militia officer, governor of Virginia. The scion of planter aristocracy in Virginia, Nelson was educated by tutors at the family estate in Yorktown and at Cambridge University, England. Generally conservative on political issues, he served in the House of Burgesses and on the King's Council for the colony.

Appointed colonel of the 2nd Virginia Regiment, in July 1776 he resigned to serve in Congress. Due to illness, however, Nelson left Congress in May 1777. Made brigadier general in the Virginia militia (August 1779), he played a major role in thwarting British expeditions under General Edward Mathew and under General Alexander Leslie in the Tidewater. Nelson also served in the House of Delegates (1779–80), where he became a leader. He also found time to be on the board of visitors for William and Mary College (1779). In June 1781, under the pressure of invasion by enemy forces under General Benedict Arnold and under Lord Cornwallis, the state's voters elected Nelson as governor to succeed Thomas Jefferson. Less concerned with philosophical matters, Nelson became a capable war governor during his brief term, and unlike Jefferson, he was provided with dictatorial powers. He acquired weapons and provisions, suppressed Loyalists, impressed goods, tightened control of the militia, decreed martial law, recruited for the army, and handled the transfer of prisoners of war. He left the capitol at Richmond to join the Marquis de Lafayette (September 1781), and at the siege of Yorktown he watched the destruction of his home by American cannon fire. He did not finish his term as governor. Destitute at the end of the war, he died a debtor. *See also*: Virginia in the American Revolution

Richard L. Blanco

REFERENCES

Julian P. Boyd, et al., eds., *Papers of Thomas Jefferson*, 6 vols. (1950–52), 4; Emory G. Evans, *Thomas Nelson of Yorktown* (1975).

Neptune, Francis Joseph
(c. 1748–?)

Passamaguoddy Indian Chief. The son of Passamaguoddy Indian chief Jean Baptiste Neptune, Francis Joseph Neptune became known as "Governor Francis." Although he did not become the leader of the Passamaguoddies until after the death of his father in 1778, he is remembered as a powerful and popular chief. Thirty years ago, old men still told stories about him with as much enthusiasm as if the events had happened the day before. One story explained how Francis was the winner of a terrible fight with a Micmac chief who had taken the form of a giant sea monster. Another was about him as a 15-year-old boy, when he performed what men said was an impossible musket shot, the killing of a British officer of HMS *Mermaid*, a warship that had come into Machias River during the Revolution. This story has been so popular that it has been included in the Passamaguoddy literature series used in the Passamaguoddy culture classes.

A British officer was pacing up and down the deck in his red coat as the vessel was slowly making its way up the river. The plan was to burn the homes of the Americans along the river. About 40 or 50 Indians were dispatched to stop the ship's progress up the river. When the Indians saw the officer, they were still at such a distance from the ship that the older men agreed that they were beyond musket range. The young Francis knew that he could shoot him and so persisted until he was given a musket. He took careful aim and fired. The British officer fell, dead. This resulted in considerable confusion among the ship's crew and they retreated. Colonel John Allan included the incident in his report. In 1850 Francis's son, Governor John Francis, obtained written testimony of his father's act from the sons of several Machias residents whose fathers were said to have witnessed it.

On July 10, 1778, when Allan was at Passamaguoddy, he designated Francis Joseph Neptune and Joseph Tomma as the persons responsible for distributing provisions provided by Massachusetts Bay for the Indians.

About 1850, in an undated petition, Francis's son, Governor John Francis, asked the federal government to grant the bounty land "to which heirs of revolutionary Soldiers are entitled" stating that his "father, Francis Joseph, served with the Americans in the Revolutionary War, and although he served the American cause faithfully during the war, he did not receive any compensation for his services from the United States." Perhaps if he had tried much earlier, his petition would have been granted.

"Frans. Jost. Nepton" headed Allan's list of Indians at "Scoodick on the Lakes . . . that are and have been in the Service of the United States by order of Col. Allen . . . July 28, 1780." These Indians were to receive the regular pay of soldiers while in the service of the United States.

In 1796 the Maine–New Brunswick border was finally settled. Francis was asked to send guides to those who were officially to establish the border. The Passamaguoddy played an important role in the Maine–New Brunswick border settlement.

The Indians had been ignored in the peace treaty following the Revolution. In 1796, when it was apparent that the American victory would not be challenged and that the new governments were stable, Governor Francis Joseph and several others went to Boston and negotiated a treaty with Massachusetts for a reservation of 23,000 acres, fishing rights on the Schoodic Lakes, and 10 acres at Pleasant Point, Maine. The Passamaguoddy Indians are still living on these reserves. The ideals concerning land and liberties that had inspired the Revolution were also important to the Maine Indians.

Nicholas N. Smith

REFERENCES

Bruce W. Belmore, *Early Princeton, Maine* (1945); Fannie Hardie Eckstorm, *Old John Neptune and Other Maine Indian Shamans* (1945); Frederick Kidder, *Military Operations in Eastern Maine and Nova Scotia During the Revolution* (1971); William H. Kilby, *Eastport, Me.* (1888); "Treaty with Passamaguoddy Tribe of Indians, by Commonwealth of Massachusetts, Sept. 29, 1794, *Resolves of the General Court of Commonwealth of Massachusetts* (1794): 46–47.

"Neutral Ground"

See Armand's Legion; Greene, Christopher.

Newburgh Conspiracy
(January–March 1783)

The disaster at Yorktown helped propel the Rockingham ministry to power in England. Lord Frederick North was forced to step down as prime minister. Peace talks began. General Sir Henry Clinton was replaced in command at New York City by a general many then (and now) considered to be the best British general in North America, Sir Guy Carleton. A tenuous cease-fire was agreed upon between the Americans and the British that lasted until the cessation of fighting was finally announced on April 19, 1783. Lord Charles Cornwallis's surrender did not end the War of Revolution. Washington and his army were forced to stay in the field another 18 months.

During this unsettled time between Yorktown and final peace, the American army was at its professional best, thanks to the efforts of the Baron Friedrich von Steuben. Drill and discipline reached their highest levels of the war. Washington could field a small but respectable regular army. The men were mostly veterans with more than two years' active service.

The Americans came to New Windsor, New York, for their final cantonment of the war. It was here, close to the Hudson River in the foothills to the north of the Hudson Highlands, some 60 miles north of New York City and a dozen miles removed from the fortifications of West Point, that the final scenes of the war were played out. The soldiers began arriving in the summer of 1782 and disbanded from New Windsor the following summer of 1783, never to assemble again. The 8,000 to 10,000 men of the Continental Army made this their last common effort.

The grounds at New Windsor were approximately 2½ miles square with nearly 800 cabins, each housing 16 men. Gone were the days of Valley Forge, when the discipline was lax and the men inexperienced. This cantonment was constructed with a certain style that impressed even the most veteran observers. The cabins were constructed in accordance with Washington's orders with a regularity, convenience, and even a degree of elegance that insured a low sickness rate and high morale among the troops. Many of the structures were built of both logs and stone.

At this time, General Horatio Gates rejoined the American army. As Washington's second in command at New Windsor, he was placed in charge of building the encampment. He did an excellent job supervising the work. Gates made his headquarters at the Ellison house nearby.

Gates also directed the construction of a large building, 110 feet by 30 feet, on Snake Hill. It had a cupola and flagstaff on the roof, rows of benches inside, a gallery for speakers or an orchestra, and four small rooms for quartermaster and commissary use. Dedicated by Chaplain Israel Evans on February 6, 1783, it was named "The Temple of Virtue" by Colonel Edward Hand. Later, the name was shortened to "the Temple."

Close by, in the river port town of Newburgh, George Washington made his headquarters at the Hasbrouck house. Arriving March 31–April 1, 1782, Washington stayed in this house until August 19, 1783, making it the headquarters he used for the longest period of time of the hundred places he stayed during the war. Martha, his wife, stayed with him for much of the time Washington was in Newburgh.

Jonathan Hasbrouck, who died in 1780, had been a militia colonel in the American service. His widow, Tryntje, and his daughters moved into other quarters to allow Washington use of the house. The army erected a number of buildings, such as a stable, boat house, privy, and guard house to supplement the headquarters building. Washington's Life Guard built their own barracks nearby. All told, Washington stayed in the Dutch-style fieldstone house for 16½ months.

During the New Windsor cantonment, a number of important events took place that gave this period of the war significance. The first came in May 1782 when Colonel Lewis Nicola, an Irish-born Huguenot in the American army, called for the general who had led the army in war to lead the country in peace as king. The substitution would have been King George I for King George III. Nicola suggested in his letter to Washington that Washington, like Oliver Cromwell, seize power with the support of his officers. Nicola, and many others, saw anarchy in the future. The Articles of Confederation were weak. Democracy had never worked in a country so large. Many people lacked confidence in the new system. A strong hand was needed to provide a stable government.

Washington responded to this offer quickly and firmly. He turned down the offer flat. He viewed the idea of being king with "abhorrence and reprehend[ed] with severity" Nicola for having even thought about such a possibility. "You could not have found a person to whom your schemes are more disagreeable." Washington continued to support the civilian government and refused the temptation of taking power when it was offered to him.

A more ominous event that developed during the New Windsor encampment became known as the Newburgh Conspiracy. The imminence of a peace settlement made the army restive, particularly the officers. Congress had not dealt with them fairly and had refused to settle past claims and future benefits. The officers were concerned over pay issues, supply and equipment owed them, and the demobilization process. Informal meetings and common discontent led to a concerted plan of action.

General Alexander McDougall and Colonels Matthais Ogden and John Brooks rode to Philadelphia to place before Congress a grand memorial. McDougall was an excellent choice. He had Washington's support. Washington was angry over the treatment of the officers by Congress. But he also knew that Congress was helpless without a source of revenue and that the states were unwilling to provide one. McDougall was a man who saw both sides of an issue.

The general's priority was a pension for the officers, although Congress was against that measure. Such a pension for the officers was too expensive, would have caused a rise in taxes, would have created a class of idle pensioners, and was unjustified on the grounds of merit. So the lines were drawn.

Yet Congress had already granted officers pensions beginning October 21, 1780, when they were to have been discharged from active service. The actuaries had told Congress that the officers would live an average of 12 years after discharge. Congress offered a life pension at half-pay or one that could have been commuted to full pay for five years. (Washington requested seven years.) Congress hoped that this alternative would tempt the officer corps, and Congress would get off cheaply by paying five years' full pay, which was actually ten half-years, a full year's pay less than the twelve years officers were predicted to live. Somehow this all reflected poorly on politicians who thought so little of the men who had led their army.

Washington had intended to winter that year at Mount Vernon, but the unrest among his troops required that he stay in New York. Congress had wished Washington to disband part of his army in 1782 and to send the men home empty-handed. The country was bankrupt. Many saw the army as a threat to the country's liberty.

People wanted the army to disappear, now that the fighting seemed to be over. A period of political confusion, procrastination, and conflict had begun.

McDougall and his party arrived in Philadelphia on December 29, 1782, and stayed at the Indian Queen Tavern. Their petition to Congress requested back pay, clothing, ration and forage allowances for officers, and the half-pay pension measure. The whole officer corps of the northern army at New Windsor stood behind this petition.

The petition was presented to Congress on January 6, and it was immediately referred to committee. It read in part that the officers had suffered all that men could bear. Their property was expended and their private resources were at an end. On January 13, McDougall met with the congressional committee. He used strong and vivid language to describe the condition and perspective of the officer corps. The committee was moved by his commentary but was powerless.

Hopes had been placed on a 5 percent impost that all the states but Rhode Island had agreed to. Then, to destroy all plans, Virginia changed her vote and sided with Rhode Island. The impost tax that would have brought money into the empty treasury was now a dead issue. Congress then basically did nothing but place the burden of paying the officers on Robert Morris, the superintendent of finance, who had neither money nor means of gaining more loans at this late stage in the war.

On January 22, Alexander Hamilton, then a member of Congress from New York, wrote the committee report for the consideration of the whole. After eight days of discussion, the committee had agreed with the army's demands and requested Congress to act. In its bankrupt condition, there was nothing Congress could do.

While Congress feared the military, the military despised the civilians. A breach had grown between the people and their army. The officers saw the civilians and politicians in safe positions, receiving their pay and in some cases benefiting from war contracts. The officers, on the other hand, had risked their lives and fortunes for the country and were being ignored.

Additionally, there were two major factions in Congress. The Nationalists believed that Congress was too weak and the states had not done their job in supporting national interests. The States' Righters were afraid of losing local power and control of government to the national Congress. They hesitated to supply their own state troops, raise taxes, or support Congress. The Nationalists in Congress saw the army as a tool to force the local interest faction to support the Nationalist cause.

The immediate result of McDougall's mission was that Congress granted one part of the petition. The officers were to be given one month's pay, somehow to be raised by Robert Morris, the superintendent of finance. With discharge in sight, and justice on their side, for the officer corps the First Newburgh Address appeared in camp on March 10 in response to Congress' decision.

It has been said that the plot was planned in Philadelphia by Nationalist congressmen and hatched in Newburgh by officers who wanted a reward for their years of service. Alexander Hamilton wrote to Washington to inform him that McDougall's petition would inflame the officers, and to suggest that Washington use his power to threaten Congress, to scare it into acting for the benefit of both the army and the national government. When Washington refused to participate in this little maneuver, the Nationalists' attention may have turned to General Horatio Gates.

Although Gates was for states' rights and had little in common with the Nationalists, it is evident that Gates played some role in the conspiracy, since he allowed most of his staff to perform active roles without stopping them. Gates positioned himself as the opportunist once again. No matter what the outcome of this officer plot, Gates would have been in place to go either way, without hurting his reputation.

The First Newburgh Address was written by Major John Armstrong, a 26-year-old aide of Gates. Having joined the army in 1775, Armstrong was a Patriot who went on to be Pennsylvania's secretary of state and a United States senator, and who even fought in the War of 1812. But he was angry now with Congress. The Address was copied by Captain Christopher Richmond, also of Gate's staff. It was distributed by Richmond, Walter Stewart, a former Gates aide and now northern army inspector general, and Major William Barber of Friedrich von Steuben's staff. It was published at the time anonymously.

The Address called for a meeting of all officers the next day in the Temple. It said that one's

faith in one's country had its limits as well as its temper and that there were points beyond which neither can be stretched without sinking into cowardice or playing into credulity. "To be tame and unprovoked when injuries press hard upon you, is more than weakness . . . that suffering courage of yours was active once." Was the country grateful for what that courage had won? Or is it rather a country that freely tramples upon the rights of officers? The document had a blunt tone, warning officers not to listen to the counsel of the one who would call for moderation (Washington). Decisive action was called for in order to force Congress to show its gratitude.

The Address threatened to have the army remain in the field if peace came, or to go off into the interior of the country if the war continued, until the demands of the officers were met. This move could very well have reversed the entire Revolution and brought about a military coup of the government.

The broad issue of financial security and justice for the officers had divided the army. While all officers were upset over the treatment they had received from Congress, many still agreed with Washington, who remained the voice of moderation. Before the army disbanded, they wished to pressure Congress to meet their just demands. Henry Knox and McDougall were of this group. On the other hand there were the officers who wished to assert the full power of the army and to attempt a coup d'etat against Congress. This group was led by Gate's staff, if not by Gates himself.

Washington was outraged but not surprised by this address. He immediately began gathering allies, such as Knox and other moderates. The next day, Tuesday, March 11, in the general orders, Washington called the Newburgh Address "disorderly and irregular." Washington requested a meeting on Saturday, March 15, at the Temple, stating that he would not attend so that the officers could speak their minds freely. Gates, as the ranking officer, would be in charge.

Gates's group was fooled by this offer and agreed to wait until Saturday. A Second Newburgh Address was published, accepting the new meeting date and calling on the officers to remain active in their opposition to Congress. Washington now, as always, became the central figure in this drama. The officers realized, as did the Nationalists in Congress such as Gouverneur Morris, Alexander Hamilton, and Robert Morris, that the private soldiers would more than likely never follow an officers' revolt. The soldiers wanted their pay and demobilization. Why should they fight for the benefits of officers? It was Washington who would allow the officers to save face and extricate them from the dangerous position they had taken. At the same time, Congress would be threatened enough to take some action to force the states into line.

Saturday, March 15, 1783, came and the officers duly gathered in the Temple at noon. They were in an angry mood and became even more incensed when Washington rode up and entered the building uninvited. Washington apologized for being there and requested permission to speak. Gates, in the speaker's chair, recognized the commander-in-chief, and Washington addressed his officers.

Visibly agitated, he read a prepared statement. Such was the danger of the moment, Washington could not afford to miss a thought or express an idea unclearly. Everything was planned carefully and staged effectively. First, he said it was not his original intention to be there (although it was), but he felt it necessary to give his personal sentiments to the men.

Washington called this movement not one of redress but a drive for power, perhaps even leading to the overthrow of civilian government. Its "insidious designs" were known to the commander. Washington urged patience. He asked the officers to use reason rather than passion to guide their actions. He asked them not to turn on the country in the extreme hour of her distress. He criticized the idea that Congress was guilty of "premeditated injustice." He pleaded with them to do nothing that would lessen the dignity and sully the glory they had won in the contest of this war. Washington attempted to persuade the officers to keep the army's record as the nation's guardian of republican liberty intact by not attempting to coerce a free government.

Washington saw that he was not winning the officers over to his position. They were still angry and upset at what he had said and that he had come to their meeting. In order to substantiate his claims that Congress was not working against them, Washington wished to read a letter he had received from Joseph Jones, a congressman from Virginia. Written in a difficult scrawl and such was his excitement, Washington could not make out the words and fumbled

in speaking. He then brought out a pair of reading spectacles made for him by David Rittenhouse of Philadelphia. Only his immediate military family had seen him use these before. A rustle went through the room. Washington placed the glasses on his nose and then said to his officers: "Gentlemen, you must pardon me. I have grown gray in your service and now find myself going blind as well." He then proceeded to read Jones's letter detailing the problems faced and making the promise that Congress would support the officers in the end.

Washington then left the meeting, mounted his horse, and rode from the area. Many of the officers were visibly moved by Washington's gesture with the glasses. There followed 30 minutes of debate and discussion with Timothy Pickering leading the opposition against Washington's case. Gates did not take an active role in the discussion. Washington's most trusted officers then took charge and the conspiracy was over.

Knox came forth to lead the committee that agreed upon five resolutions. They thanked McDougall for his efforts in Philadelphia. Washington was also given a note of thanks. The officers then expressed their confidence in Congress and repudiated the "infamous propositions . . . in a late anonymous address." The officers also approved commutation of the pensions as developed by Congress.

In the end, the officers heeded Washington's call to exemplify patriotism as leaders of the Revolution. Many wept and all were moved by Washington's gesture at the meeting. The general had verbalized for everyone the suffering and sacrifices they had made to establish republican virtue. They did not wish to tarnish their military pride. It was generally realized that the officers would only lose their hard-earned reputations by any such manuevering against Congress, a government they had helped to establish in the first place. Many were still bitter, but most were once again behind Washington.

In this action called the Newburgh Conspiracy, Washington spared the United States a military coup, asserted the strength of his personal leadership over his officers and men, and set the highest example of selfless behavior, one that was followed by his officers.

On the other side, Congress gave in completely when faced with the threat of military action. After receiving Washington's letter of

March 17, 1783, that described the events at New Windsor, Congress agreed to commutation of half-pay for life to full pay for five years for officers of state line units who chose that option. The March 21 vote in Congress made McDougall's mission a success, but the Nationalists were still not victors in Congress. That victory would only come in 1787 with the writing of the new constitution.

As with most such conspiracies, no one will every really know what went on in Newburgh that winter. Gates either lost his nerve at the last moment or decided to change his mind. The actions of Gates and his staff, however, violated the Articles of War, and Gates was open to charges of mutiny, whatever his role or intentions. In late March, however, Gates left the army and New Windsor to return to his mortally ill wife in Virginia. Washington saw Gates at the core of this crisis. Fortunately for the Americans, the affair died on March 15. No action was ever taken against Gates.

The next month, on April 19, 1783, a ceremony was held to mark the end of hostilities between the United States and Great Britain. At noon, the congressional proclamation to end the fighting was read to the troops, followed by three loud huzzas, a prayer offered by the Reverend Mr. Ganno and an anthem, "Independence" by Billings. From that date on, the Continental Army melted away in small groups. The cantonment at New Windsor came to an end. The huts were later auctioned off and traces of the campground eventually disappeared.

The final scene at New Windsor was played out on May 10, 1783, when the Society of the Cincinnati was formed at the Temple by officers of the American army. Knox was instrumental in developing this society of officers who would, like the ancient Roman hero from whom the society took its name, go back to their farms now that the war was over. They would, however, cherish their military glory by meeting from time to time. Washington was elected the first president general. It was formed as a perpetual society with membership being passed to the oldest son.

From Newburgh, Washington rode to Princeton, New Jersey, in August 1783 to meet with Congress. Congressmen had fled there from Philadelphia over other military demands for satisfaction they could not meet. Then Washington moved to New York to take command of

that city as General Sir Guy Carleton and his British army evacuated in November. New Windsor had passed from the War of Revolution.

Paul J. Sanborn

REFERENCES

Edmund C. Burnett, *The Continental Congress* (1941); Roger J. Champagne, *Alexander McDougall and the American Revolution in New York* (1975); James T. Flexner, *George Washington in the American Revolution* (1968); Don Higginbotham, *The War of American Independence* (1971); Richard H. Kohn, "Inside History of Newburgh," *William and Mary Quarterly*, 27 (1970):187–220; Owen F. Lewis, *Washington's Final Victory* (1967); James K. Martin and Mark E. Lender, *A Respectable Army* (1982); Lynn Montross, *Rag, Tag, and Bobtail* (1952); Paul David Nelson, *General Horatio Gates* (1976); Charles Royster, *A Revolutionary People at War* (1979); C. Edward Skeen, "The Newburgh Conspiracy Reconsidered," *William and Mary Quarterly, 31* (1974):273–290.

New Hampshire Continentals

Before there was a Continental Army there was a New England Army. When the news of the fighting at Concord and Lexington (April 19, 1775) spread throughout the region, many men took their muskets and headed for Boston. Within a few days, an army had gathered on the hills outside of that town.

Organizing these men was difficult. They had come from all over New England, but many of them returned home within a few days. As some of them left, others arrived. There was constant confusion in the camps as the army attempted to organize itself while maintaining the siege of the British in Boston.

As the men were gathering, the Massachusetts Provincial Congress acted. Within a few days it authorized the formation of a 30,000-man "Army of Observation" and sent representatives to New Hampshire, Rhode Island, and Connecticut to seek their aid. Meanwhile, the Massachusetts Committee of Safety authorized Paul Dudley Sargent of Amherst, New Hampshire, to enlist a regiment from among New Hampshire men who were already in Massachusetts.

Among the earliest of these to arrive were some 60 men from Nottingham, New Hampshire. They reached Cambridge on the morning of April 21, having marched 45 miles in 20 hours.

By the next morning John Stark had gathered about 300 men at Chelsea, Massachusetts. Within a few days there may have been as many as 2,000 New Hampshire men in and around Cambridge, joining regiments being organized by Sargent, Stark, and James Reed of Fitzwilliam, New Hampshire.

All three of these men were leaders in their communities, and Stark and Reed were veterans of the French and Indian War. Their ability to enlist men into their regiments depended largely on their reputations. Stark, a woodsman and soldier who had been a captain in Rogers' Rangers during the French and Indian War, was the best known of the three. Before long, his regiment grew to more than 800 men organized into 14 companies. Reed and Sargent each raised an additional four companies.

The New Hampshire Provincial Congress met in Exeter on April 21 and appointed Nathanial Folsom, a militia colonel and veteran of the French and Indian War, to command the New Hampshire troops in Massachusetts. The Congress voted not to discourage New Hampshire men from enlisting in Massachusetts regiments but, because only 34 towns were represented, it delayed raising any troops on their own authority.

The congress that met in May included 133 representatives from 101 towns. It quickly voted to raise 2,000 troops, organized in three regiments, to serve until the end of December. It then commissioned Folsom as general of the New Hampshire troops and Stark, Reed, and Enoch Poor of Exeter as colonels to command the three regiments. Stark's and Reed's regiments, the 1st and 3rd, respectively, were already organized in Massachusetts. Poor's regiment, designated the 2nd New Hampshire, was organized in and around Portsmouth and Exeter. Some of Stark's men were added to Reed's regiment so that each regiment contained ten companies. (Sargent was not offered a New Hampshire commission and the companies he raised became part of the 8th Massachusetts, which he commanded.)

Most of the men who joined these regiments, enlisting for the rest of the year, were in their late teens or twenties. They described themselves as farmers, husbandmen, or yeomen. There were also some craftsmen, some who were in their fifties, and some in their early teens. In a typical company, Captain Hezekiah Hutchins's of Reed's regiment, there were 44 farmers, 5 cordwainers, 4 joiners, 3 tailors, 2 blacksmiths, a weaver, a mariner, a gunsmith, a turner, a tanner, and a miller. Forty-seven of these men were between 17 and 29. Both the youngest, 15-year-old Robert Hale, and the oldest, 50-year-old Samuel Stevens, described themselves as yeomen.

Folsom wanted an artillery company as part of his brigade, but New Hampshire could not find officers qualified to command one. Cannon were available, however, and in June, three 24-pounders were sent to Massachusetts.

Folsom and Stark spent some time in the spring of 1775 engaged in a quarrel over seniority. Stark, who thought that he should have been commissioned as general, for a time refused to receive orders from Folsom. At one point, Stark threatened to take his pack and go home. After the Provincial Congress intervened, the two men settled their dispute, and Stark submitted to Folsom's authority. There were long-term results, however, and when the Continental Congress commissioned generals for the army, Folsom was passed over and John Sullivan was commissioned as brigadier general from New Hampshire.

As the siege of Boston developed, the two New Hampshire regiments were on the left of the American line—Stark at Winter Hill in Medford and Reed near Charlestown Neck. The morning after Massachusetts troops started to fortify Bunker Hill, Stark's and Reed's regiments were among the reinforcements ordered forward.

Before the troops could take up their position they had to make up cartridges. Each man was issued one flint, powder, and lead from a nearby church's organ pipes, enough to make fifteen cartridges each. The two regiments, led by Stark, marched across Charlestown Neck and took up a position on the left of the American line, extending it down to the water's edge. There, three times they repulsed the charge of the British light infantry companies. When the British finally overcame the Americans in the redoubt, the troops on the left, the two New Hampshire regiments, and Captain Thomas Knowlton's Connecticut regiment, fought as a rear guard until the Americans cleared the Charlestown Peninsula.

When news of the battle reached New Hampshire, the Committee of Safety ordered Poor's 2nd New Hampshire, except one company, kept back as a garrison at Hampton, New Hampshire, to march to Cambridge. By the time all three New Hampshire regiments were assembled in Cambridge, Washington had arrived to take command of what was now the Continental Army and John Sullivan had replaced Folsom as commander of the New Hampshire troops.

The New Hampshire regiments that Washington found were each organized as a single battalion of ten companies. Each regiment was commanded by a colonel, assisted by a lieutenant colonel, a major, an adjutant, a quartermaster, and a surgeon and surgeon's mate. Poor's 2nd New Hampshire included a quartermaster sergeant and a sergeant major. There was one chaplain who served all three regiments. Each of the companies was commanded by a captain, assisted by a first lieutenant and a second lieutenant. Each company had four sergeants, four corporals, a drummer, a fifer, and about fifty privates. These regiments were rarely at full strength. The earliest surviving monthly strength report, July 1775, shows a grand total for all three regiments of 1,712 officers and men.

The three New Hampshire regiments were in John Sullivan's brigade, part of Major General Charles Lee's division. Lee's division held the left of the American lines. They were busy throughout the summer and fall, strengthening their fortifications and skirmishing with the British.

In September, Washington called for volunteers for an expedition led by Benedict Arnold to go up the Kennebec River and to assault Quebec. Many of the more adventurous men in the army volunteered. Captain Henry Dearborn quickly formed a company of 77 men drawn from all three New Hampshire regiments, but principally from Stark's. An additional 11 men from Reed's regiment joined the company led by Captain Samuel Ward, Jr., of Rhode Island.

Around Boston the siege went on. Both order and organization were increasing in the army. The soldiers were being fed and housed, and they continued to extend their lines around Boston and to skirmish with the British. There were problems, however. Powder was still scarce and most of the regiments were enlisted only until the end of the year.

Congress, taking Washington's advice, voted to reorganize the army into 26 regiments. New Hampshire's quota was three regiments. The new regiments were a single battalion of eight strong companies. Each regiment was commanded by a colonel, assisted by a lieutenant colonel and a major. The staff consisted of an adjutant, a quartermaster, a paymaster, a surgeon and a surgeon's mate, a chaplain, a sergeant major, a quartermaster sergeant, a drum major, and a fife major. Each company was commanded by a captain, assisted by a first lieutenant, a second lieutenant, and an ensign. The companies had four sergeants, four corporals, a drummer, a fifer, and 76 privates each.

As part of the reorganization, the regiments lost their provincial designations and were renumbered as Continental regiments, based on the seniority of the colonel. Reed's 3rd New Hampshire became the 2nd Continental, Stark's 1st New Hampshire became the 5th Continental, and Poor's 2nd New Hampshire became the 8th Continental Regiment.

Fifty-two of the officers and many of the enlisted men who were serving in the New Hampshire regiments reenlisted for another year. None of these regiments was ever up to full strength (733 officers and enlisted men), but by the end of January Reed had 581, Stark had 571, and Poor had 600 officers and men on their rolls.

The British evacuated Boston on March 17, 1776, and Washington turned his attention to New York City. He saw it as one of the keys to the continent. As the army was moving to New York, the Continental Congress, expecting British reinforcements for Canada, asked Washington to send reinforcements there. He responded, ordering John Sullivan to the north with reinforcements, including the three New Hampshire regiments. Poor marched first, on April 15, followed by Reed and Stark on April 27.

They arrived to find the army defeated, diseased, and in retreat. (Among the defeats was the capture of most of Colonel Timothy Bedel's regiment at the Cedars, outside of Montreal. Bedel's regiment, originally three companies of rangers from New Hampshire, was expanded to eight companies and taken into the Continental service early in 1776.) Reed was sent to Montreal, Poor to St. Johns, and Stark to Sorel. They arrived in Canada in time to be caught up in the disaster at Trois Rivieres and the retreat to Ile aux Noix. Henry Blake, a fifer in Stark's regiment, described the retreat in a diary.

(June) 19th The most part of my company, including myself, were inoculated for the small pox. Thursday, the 20th, marched from

Oil of Nox and got out of the bounds of Canada, and pitched our tents beside of the lake. . . .

July 1st, 1776, Lieutenant Karr died with the small pox. Tuesday, July 2, the schooners with the remainder of our forces, arrived at Crown Point some time on the night. We moved Sergt Kimball out of the camp into a house to be nursed, for he was bad with the small pox. Friday, the 5th, Sergt. Kimball died about sunset with the small pox. The same day I had the small pox break out on me. Saturday, the 6th, we buried Sergt Phineas Kimball this forenoon. . . . Saturday, 13th, Duty Stickney died with the small pox and was buried the same day. Wednesday, July 17th, our regiment moved from crown point to Ticonderoga. . . . Sunday, the 21st, Corporal Joseph Bayley died with the small pox and was buried. Monday, 22d, Lieut Hardy and about 30 sick men of our company, set out for the hospital at Fort George. . . . Friday, 26th, among the men that went over Lake George, Jacob Bradbury died before they landed and John Putney died the day after.

Henry Blake survived but many others did not. By August 24 Stark's regiment was down to 254 officers and men present and fit for duty. Poor's regiment was down to 228 and Reed's to 254. Their combined sick list was over 500. Among the sick was James Reed, who had been promoted to brigadier general earlier in the month. (Reed went blind from smallpox early in September and had to retire from the army.) By the end of October the three New Hampshire regiments could muster only 605 officers and enlisted men present and fit for duty.

Although the American fleet under General Benedict Arnold was defeated in the Battle of Valcour Island, it was too late in the year for the British to attempt to capture Fort Ticonderoga. The campaign was over. The British returned to Canada and Washington ordered General Horatio Gates, who had commanded the Northern Army since July, to join him, bringing with him most of his Continentals.

Gates, with seven regiments from the Northern Army, including the New Hampshire regiments, marched over 200 miles, reaching Washington late in December. By this time Washington's forces were down to 6,104 officers and men present and fit for duty. The reinforcements from the Northern Army may have added as many as 600 men to the total.

A few days after reaching Washington, the New Hampshire regiments, now part of Sullivan's Division, were across the Delaware with Washington, attacking Trenton. Sullivan's Division, on Washington's right flank, attacked along the River Road. Forcing his way into the lower part of the town, Stark shouted for his men to follow him and led a charge. His troops, using their bayonets, sent the Hessians reeling through the town. Sullivan sent a brigade to hold the bridge over Assunpink Creek, and the Hessians' retreat was blocked. By 9 A.M. on the morning of December 26, the fight was over.

The enlistments of most of the New England regiments expired on December 30, but Washington had another stroke in mind. To carry it out he needed to hold the army together. Calling individual regiments together on their parade ground, he offered a bounty of ten dollars to each Continental who would stay for another six weeks. The regimental officers added their own appeal. Stark promised his regiment that he would sell his own property to pay their bounty if Congress refused to honor Washington's pledge. Almost all the fit men, about 1,200 in 20 New England regiments, stayed.

Washington recrossed the Delaware with about 1,600 soldiers. On January 3, 1777, he struck the British at Princeton. By January 7 he reached Morristown, New Jersey, where the remnants of the army went into winter quarters. By the middle of February the remaining New Englanders, their extended enlistments having expired, returned to their homes. Those officers who were not worn out or discouraged returned home to recruit new soliders who would enlist for three years or for the rest of the war.

Stark, Poor, and Alexander Scammel returned to New Hampshire to recruit the three regiments that were New Hampshire's quota. During the winter, Congress promoted Poor to brigadier general. Stark, who had been senior to Poor, angrily resigned. Stark's old regiment, once again designated the 1st New Hampshire, was commanded by Colonel Joseph Cilley; Poor's, now the 2nd New Hampshire, by Colonel Nathan Hale; and Reed's, now the 3rd New Hampshire, by Colonel Alexander Scammel. (Cilley had started the war as major in Poor's regiment and Hale as major in Reed's.) These three regiments were recruited during the winter and spring of 1777. By June 28, about two-thirds complete, they assembled at Ticonderoga. (New Hampshire also raised, on the Continental establishment, two companies of rangers, commanded by Major Benjamin Whitcomb and an infantry regiment commanded by Colonel Pierse Long.)

All that spring the Northern Army had been gathering. General Arthur St. Clair commanded the garrison at Ticonderoga, some 2,500 men including the three New Hampshire regiments. St. Clair had too few men who were too poorly equipped to hold the fort for long. When the British, commanded by General John Burgoyne, mounted cannon on the summit of Sugar Loaf Hill, St. Clair abandoned the fort and retreated.

The retreat began. At 1 A.M. on the morning of July 6, the 1st New Hampshire struck their tents and assembled with packs and provisions. They quickly marched from Ticonderoga, over the floating bridge, to Mount Independence. There they saw provisions lying around, clothing chests broken open, and confusion everywhere.

St. Clair led most of his force away from Ticonderoga toward Hubbarton and Castleton, Vermont, and on to Fort Edward, New York. Long, with the remains of Arnold's fleet, and some 200 bateaux, escorted the sick and as much of the supplies as he could carry down Lake Champlain to Skenesboro.

The British pursuit began earlier than the Americans expected. Early in the morning of July 7, 1777, the British caught up with St. Clair's rear guard; Warner's regiment, the 11th Massachusetts, and the 2nd New Hampshire. The British struck the 2nd New Hampshire first. Ebenezer Fletcher, a 16-year-old fifer in the 2nd New Hampshire, was just recovering from the measles. This was his first taste of battle.

> The morning after our retreat, orders came very early for the troops to refresh and be ready for marching. Some were eating, some were cooking, and all in a very unfit posture for battle. Just as the sun rose, there was a cry, "*the enemy are upon us*." Looking round I saw the enemy in line of battle. Orders came to lay down our packs and be ready for action. The fire instantly began. We were but few in number compared to the enemy. At the commencement of the battle, many of our party retreated back into the woods. Capt. Carr came up and says, "My lads advance, we shall beat them yet." A few of us followed him in view of the enemy. Every

> man was trying to secure himself behind girdled trees, which were standing in the place of action. I made a shelter for myself and discharged my piece. Having loaded again and taken aim, my piece missed fire. I brought the same a second time to my face; but before I had time to discharge it, I received a musket ball in the small of my back, and fell with my gun cocked.

After a short, sharp battle, the 2nd New Hampshire broke. The British captured Fletcher, over 200 of his comrades, including Colonel Hale, and both of the 2nd New Hampshire's flags.

Meanwhile, Long had landed at Skenesboro. Two hours after he landed, the pursuing British fleet sailed up. Long lost much of his baggage and all his artillery, but he was able to burn the fort and barracks and most of his boats before continuing the retreat to Fort Ann. There, reinforced by some New York militia, Long turned and skirmished with the British advance guard. Fearing British reinforcements, Long broke off the action after two hours, burned Fort Ann, and continued retreating to Fort Edward. After Hubbardton, St. Clair marched to Rutland, Vermont, and then to Fort Edward, arriving there on July 12.

The retreat continued from Fort Edward, first to Moses Creek and then to Van Schaick's Island. Poor, in command of the New Hampshire Continentals, was sent to guard London's Ferry, three miles up the Mohawk River.

By this time Gates had replaced Schuyler. When Gates arrived, on August 19, he found just over 6,000 men in five brigades, present for duty. Poor's, with almost 1,300 men, was the largest. Early in September, Gates moved forward to Stillwater, New York, and fortified Bemis Heights.

On the morning of September 19, 1777, Burgoyne advanced, bringing on the first Battle of Saratoga, or Freeman's Farm. The 1st, 2nd, and 3rd New Hampshire were in Arnold's Division, which also included two regiments of New York Continentals, Daniel Morgan's riflemen with Dearborn's light infantry, and militia from Connecticut, on the left of the American line.

Arnold sent in Morgan and Dearborn to oppose the British. As the battle developed, Arnold ordered Cilley's 1st New Hampshire forward on Morgan's left. Lieutenant Thomas Blake of the 1st New Hampshire charged the British line with Cilley.

About 12 o'clock the first N. Hampshire Regt marched out to meet the enemy. We met them about one mile from our encampment, where the engagement began very closely, and continued about 20 minutes, in which time we lost so many men, and received no reinforcement, that we were obliged to retreat, but before we got to the encampment we met two regiments [The remains of the 2nd New Hampshire, commanded by its lieutenant colonel, Winborn Adams, and the 3rd New Hampshire] coming out as a reinforcement, when we returned and renewed the attack which continued very warm until dark at which time we withdrew and retired to our encampment.

In this engagement the enemy had two fieldpieces in the field, which we took three or four times, but as it was in the woods, they were not removed.

Soon all of Arnold's Division was engaged, and heavy fighting continued. When the Americans withdrew to their camp the British camped on the battlefield.

On the morning of October 7, Burgoyne once more advanced. Gates ordered Morgan and Dearborn to attack the British right and Poor to assault their left. The three New Hampshire regiments formed about 3:30 P.M. and attacked about 4 P.M.

Poor advanced up a slope toward the British line, the Continentals holding their fire. The British fired a volley and charged with the bayonet. The Continentals broke the British charge with musket fire and charged forward themselves. After a sharp fight, the British broke, retreating in disorder. Cilley, exultant at their success, was whooping it up while astride a captured British 12-pounder gun.

The British retreated during the night. By October 13 they were completely surrounded. On October 17 the British marched out of their lines, piled their arms in front of the victorious Americans, and marched off to captivity.

Although the Continentals were not in uniform they had a military bearing. Their muskets, a mixture of French, British, and German, were all tipped with bayonets. Their cartridge boxes, of various sizes and capacities, were filled with cartridges, and they no longer had to manipulate loose powder in a powder horn and bullets in a bullet pouch during the confusion of battle. (Several pieces of military equipment carried by New Hampshire soldiers in the Revolu-

tion, including the flags the 2nd New Hampshire lost at Hubbardton, may be seen in the museum collections of the New Hampshire Historical Society.)

Within a few days after the British surrender most of the Continentals were marching south to join Washington. By November 2, Poor's Brigade reached Fishkill, New York, where it camped for a few days. As the brigade was preparing to cross the Hudson River the men refused to march. They had not been paid for months and were demanding their money before they would cross the river. There was a scuffle and before order was restored a captain shot a private and was in turn killed by a second soldier. The officers soon restored order and the brigade crossed the river at King's Ferry.

The New Hampshire Continentals reached Washington's army at White Marsh, Pennsylvania, on November 21, 1777. They were with the army as Washington skirmished with the British outside of Philadelphia, attempting to provoke an attack. Too weak to attack them, Washington marched for Valley Forge.

The army reached Valley Forge on December 19, and began to build huts for the winter. The work went slowly. As late as December 31, the 3rd New Hampshire was still living in tents. By this time the effective strength of the 1st New Hampshire was 241; the 2nd New Hampshire, 172; and the 3rd New Hampshire, 237. Their sick rate was almost 39 percent. (The location of Poor's Brigade camp can be seen midway between the National Memorial Arch and the statue of General Anthony Wayne at the Valley Forge National Historical Park.)

In February the brigade built breastworks in front of its huts and saw the arrival of General Friedrich von Steuben in the camp. As the winter wore on and turned into spring the regiments grew smaller. By March, the three regiments of New Hampshire Continentals totaled 177 officers and men present and fit for duty. They had 509 soldiers sick and 35 without clothes. Eleven men had died during the month and two had deserted. On the positive side, there were three new recruits.

While the army was at Valley Forge all the infantry regiments were reorganized. A light infantry company was added to each regiment, but companies became smaller; the total number of officers and men in each regiment was cut from 732 to 582. Each of the field officers also commanded a company, and three of the lieutenants served additional duty as adjutant, quartermaster, and paymaster. In the field, the light infantry companies were usually detached from their regiments to form temporary light infantry battalions.

As spring continued the sick returned to duty, the troops got uniforms, and the army, under von Steuben's instruction, learned to drill. From New Hampshire, the state sent 200 uniforms, and by the end of April all the New Hampshire troops had clothes and the number of sick was decreasing. In May, the men got an outing of sorts. Poor's Brigade was part of a force that Washington sent under LaFayette to form an outpost at Barren Hill, part way between Valley Forge and Philadelphia.

The army moved out of their huts and pitched their tents in front of their lines on June 10. A few days later the New Hampshire troops, now in General Charles Lee's Division, marched in pursuit of the British.

The weather turned hot in late June as Washington pursued the British across New Jersey, and water was scarce. The 1st New Hampshire, part of Poor's Brigade, reached Englishtown, New Jersey, on the morning of June 28. They dropped their packs and coats there, and continued forward, marching as quickly as possible.

The Battle of Monmouth was a confusing struggle, fought over difficult terrain, in heatstroke-inducing weather. Poor's Brigade was on the American left during the climactic British assaults. After beating off the last British assault, Washington attempted to pursue them as they retreated. He ordered Poor from his left and another brigade from his right to advance. The men went forward for about a mile but were so exhausted from the heat and the march that the pursuit petered out. Poor bivouacked that night on the battlefield between the West and Middle ravines.

After the battle, the army rested for two days and then resumed the march for New York. Poor's Brigade reached White Plains on July 24 and camped, part of the garrison there. They stayed at White Plains until September 11, when the brigade marched for Danbury, Connecticut, reaching that place on September 18. While the brigade was at Danbury they caught two New Hampshire men with a large sum of counterfeit money. Henry Dearborn was on the court-martial that tried them. Both men confessed to be-

ing British spies and were condemned to die. They were hanged at Hartford, Connecticut, on November 4.

A few days later, on October 17, 1778, the troops celebrated the anniversary of Burgoyne's surrender. Israel Evans, the Poor's Brigade chaplain, preached and then there was a dinner for all the officers. After the dinner there were 13 toasts, each followed by the firing of a cannon. The next morning the officers sobered up, and on the following day the brigade marched for Hartford, Connecticut.

The brigade camped near Hartford from October 24 to November 20 and then marched to Simsbury, Connecticut. There, they took over as escort for some of Burgoyne's German troops who were being sent to Virginia. They escorted the Germans as far as New Milford, Connecticut, where they turned them over to militia who would guard them farther on.

The brigade then marched for Redding, Connecticut, where they built huts for their winter quarters. They stayed there until May 1779 when they marched to Peekskill, New York. They had only been at Peekskill a few days when they were ordered to be ready to march on short notice. After drawing camp equipment they prepared to march to Easton, Pennsylvania. The 1st New Hampshire started on May 9 and the 2nd and 3rd New Hampshire followed on May 17. Easton was the rendezvous for a force that General John Sullivan was to lead against the Indians of the Six Nations.

Sullivan's Division slowly assembled at Easton and then marched to the Wyoming Valley (near present-day Wilkes-Barre, Pennsylvania). They left Wyoming at the end of July and headed into the Iroquois country in western New York. Ebenezer Fletcher, now healed of his wound and returned to his regiment, called the expedition "a long and tedious march . . . where we drove the savages before us, burnt their huts, [and] destroyed their corn." The only action occurred near the Indian village of Newtown. There, on August 29, the Indians and Tories tried to ambush Sullivan's Division.

The Americans discovered the ambush and while part of the division formed in front of the Indians' breastwork, Poor's Brigade and the riflemen moved around to the left. Supported by James Clinton's Brigade, Poor marched into the Indian's rear. In the 1st New Hampshire, Thomas Blake heard the Indians give "a most hideous yell which resounded in the mountains as if covered with them." The brigade advanced up the mountain with fixed bayonets and fired a volley at the enemy. After a short, sharp fight the Indians and their allies fled.

Sullivan's Division continued its march as far as Genesee, New York, which they burned on September 15. A month later the troops were back in Easton. By early December, the New Hampshire regiments were near Danbury, Connecticut, building huts for their winter quarters. They spent the winter there and in the spring of 1780, joined the garrison at West Point. Later that year they rejoined the main army in New Jersey. When Benedict Arnold's treason was discovered, Washington rushed four brigades, including the New Hampshire brigade, to West Point.

The New Hampshire regiments were in a state of flux during 1780. Poor left to command a brigade of light infantry on August 4. The New Hampshire Brigade was then commanded by Colonel Moses Hazen, who had become the senior colonel in the brigade when his 2nd Canadian Regiment was added to it. (After suffering from what Dearborn described as "bilious fever" for 13 days, Poor died on September 8, 1780.) John Stark, who had been appointed a Continental brigadier general as a reward for his victory at Bennington, took command of the brigade in December 1780.

Besides changes in command there were also changes among the rank and file. Many of the men had enlisted for three years in the spring of 1777, and their enlistments were expiring. The three regiments discharged 499 soldiers between February and July. Enlistments were slow, only 104 between February and June. In July 1780, 437 men joined and in August 143 more, but most of these had only six-month enlistments. They had enlisted under the terms of a resolution passed by the New Hampshire General Assembly to raise 600 men for the New Hampshire Continental regiments to serve until the end of December.

The New Hampshire troops remained in and around West Point through May 1781. They then moved down the Hudson River, first to Peekskill and then to Dobbs Ferry. Stark left the brigade in June when Washington sent him to command the Northern Department, headquartered at Albany.

That August, Washington reorganized his command for the march to Yorktown. He formed five light infantry battalions from the light infantry companies of the New England, New York, and New Jersey Continental regiments. The two New Hampshire light infantry companies were part of Alexander Scammell's battalion in Hazen's Brigade. They were among the troops that marched south to Yorktown.

When the main army marched south, the forces remaining behind were commanded by Major General William Heath. Their task was to contain the British in New York City.

On October 10, 1781, Heath sent the 2nd New Hampshire, a regiment he described as "weak in numbers, but excellent troops," and a fieldpiece to reinforce Stark. Four days later Heath ordered the 1st New Hampshire along with the 10th Massachusetts and an artillery detachment to follow them. The New Hampshire regiments remained along the Hudson and Mohawk rivers throughout that summer and fall and into the winter.

As fall moved into winter the condition of the troops grew worse. The troops were short of blankets, and only 36 of the "three years or during the war" men in the two regiments had enough clothes to be fit for duty. Stark called the only tailor in the two regiments "a drunken rascal, that could be hardly compelled to make three coats in a winter." In such conditions it is not surprising that some of the men mutinied. Stark, with "the seasonable interposition of the officers . . . quelled [it] very easily."

The regiments continued to garrison the northern frontier. They kept scouting parties out along Lakes George and Champlain and along the Mohawk River. In November 1782, after having been on the frontier for over a year, they rejoined the main army at Newburgh.

The New Hampshire troops remained with the main army for the remainder of their service. In March 1783, as the war was winding down and peace commissioners were meeting in Europe, the two regiments were reorganized as the New Hampshire Regiment, commanded by George Reid and the New Hampshire Battalion commanded by Major William Scott. The following June they were further consolidated. Those men who had enlisted "for the war" were furloughed. Those who had enlisted for three years were organized as the New Hampshire Battalion. The battalion, commanded by Reid, was made up of five companies, and totaled 376 officers and enlisted men. They were among the Continentals who marched into New York when the last British troops evacuated the city on November 25, 1783.

Reid had joined the 1st New Hampshire on April 23, 1775. As a captain in command of the 10th Company he had walked on to Bunker Hill with Stark. He was promoted to major on November 8, 1776, and to lieutenant colonel on April 2, 1777. In March 1778, he succeeded to command of the 2nd New Hampshire as lieutenant colonel commandant. He commanded the New Hampshire Battalion of the Continental Line, the last of New Hampshire's Continentals, when it was disbanded at New Windsor, New York, on January 1, 1784.

Between April 21, 1775, and January 1, 1784, the New Hampshire Continentals marched and fought from Canada to Virginia. The list of their campaigns includes the siege of Boston, the invasion of Canada, the defense of Canada, fighting at Lake Champlain, Trenton-Princeton, Saratoga, Philadelphia-Monmouth, the Sullivan-Clinton campaign, Yorktown, and service in the Northern Department in 1781.

Now the war was over. The men, their discharges in their pockets, their muskets on their shoulders, and their pay in arrears, went home. *See also*: New Hampshire in the American Revolution

Walter A. Ryan

REFERENCES

Fred Anderson Berg, *Encyclopedia of Continental Army Units* (1972); Lloyd A. Brown and Howard H. Peckham, eds., *Revolutionary War Journals of Henry Dearborn, 1775–1783* (1971); Charles I. Bushnell, ed., *The Narrative of Ebenezer Fletcher, a Soldier of the Revolution* (1970); Frederic Kidder, *History of the First New Hampshire Regiment in the War of the Revolution* (1973); Charles H. Lesser, *The Sinews of Independence* (1976); Chandler E. Potter, *The Military History of the State of New Hampshire, 1623–1861* (1972); Charles Royster, *A Revolutionary People at War* (1979); Caleb Stark, *Memoir and Official Correspondence of General John Stark* (1972); Robert K. Wright, Jr., *The Continental Army* (1989).

New Hampshire in the American Revolution

When John Wentworth was appointed governor of New Hampshire in 1767, the people welcomed him with the hope that he remain in office for many terms. He was a member of one of the oldest and most powerful families in New Hampshire and the third Wentworth to serve as governor or lieutenant governor.

During the years leading up to the Revolution, New Hampshire was one of the more moderate provinces. No delegation from New Hampshire attended the Stamp Act Congress. In Portsmouth, the capital and major port, the town meeting refused to adopt a nonimportation agreement. By the summer of 1773, Wentworth felt the crisis had passed and that the royal governor and his administration were secure in New Hampshire.

By the spring of 1774, Parliament had passed the Tea Act and the Tea Party had taken place in Boston. The previous February Wentworth dissolved the New Hampshire House of Representatives when the members discussed letters received from Massachusetts, Connecticut, and Maryland opposing British attempts to tax the colonies. A new assembly, elected in May, was dissolved by the governor when it appointed a Committee of Correspondence.

After the assembly was dissolved, the New Hampshire Committee of Correspondence received a circular letter from Virginia calling for a Continental Congress. The committee called the members of the assembly back into session, but they had no sooner gathered in the assembly chamber when Wentworth, accompanied by Sheriff John Parker, appeared. Wentworth told the members that their meeting was illegal and ordered the sheriff to disperse them. The members left but only to go to a nearby tavern. There they issued a call for a provincial congress to meet at Exeter.

Less than two weeks later, the ship *Grosvenor*, carrying tea, arrived in Portsmouth harbor. The tea, 27 chests of it, was landed secretly during the night of June 25. Although the popular leaders were caught off guard, they quickly called a town meeting at which they convinced Edward Parry, the owner of the tea, to reexport it to Halifax, Nova Scotia.

The first Provincial Congress, the first organized Revolutionary activity in New Hampshire, met on July 21, less than a month after the tea had been sent away. Eighty-five delegates, most of them elected from towns in the seacoast area, chose Nathaniel Folsom and John Sullivan as New Hampshire's delegates to the First Continental Congress. The Congress then appropriated 200 pounds for Folsom's and Sullivan's expenses and appointed John Giddings treasurer to handle the money. The delegates chose John Wentworth (speaker of the house and a relative of the governor), Meshech Weare, Josiah Bartlett, Christopher Toppan, and John Pickering, Jr., as a committee to write Folsom and Sullivan's instructions and to act for the Congress after it adjourned.

Although the popular leaders were now organized, Wentworth still felt that New Hampshire was "much more moderate than any other [province] to the southward." More trouble was brewing, however. The ship *Fox* arrived in Portsmouth on September 8, carrying among other cargo 30 chests of tea, consigned to Parry. This time a mob gathered and stoned Parry's house. Once again a compromise was reached, and the tea was reshipped to Halifax.

A more serious challenge to Wentworth took place in October, and this time it was Wentworth who precipitated it. The British troops in Boston were in need of barracks, but General Thomas Gage could not find any carpenters in Boston who would work for the British army. He asked Wentworth for help. Wentworth knew that the people in New Hampshire were as opposed to helping the British army as those in Massachusetts. Still, Wentworth, as the royal governor, felt that he had an obligation to help.

Wentworth could have consulted with the council and have advertised openly for carpenters. If he had done so, however, he would not have recruited any carpenters and would have diminished his already shaky authority. Instead, he worked through an agent, Nicholas Austin, of Middleton. Austin hired the carpenters and sent them to Boston without telling them what they would be building. When the secret came out, the local committee of correspondence forced Austin to apologize on his knees before them. In Portsmouth, Wentworth was censured as an "enemy to the community" by the New Hampshire Committee of Ways and Means.

Soon, what had been primarily a political conflict became more violent. An order in council had been published prohibiting the export of gunpowder and other military stores to the colonies. On December 13, Paul Revere rode into Portsmouth from Boston, carrying the rumor that British troops were coming from Boston to garrison Fort William and Mary and secure the powder and arms stored there.

The next day over 400 men gathered in Portsmouth. Led by Thomas Pickering and John Langdon, they marched to New Castle Island and assaulted the fort. The garrison, Captain John Cochran, and five privates fired some of their cannon but were soon overpowered. The Patriots hauled down the flag, held the commander and his men prisoner, and carried off about 100 barrels of gunpowder. The next day another group of men led by John Sullivan came and carried off all of the muskets and 16 of the lighter cannon.

The booty, guarded by a group of men led by Nathaniel Folsom, was stored most of the next day at the river's edge in Portsmouth. As soon as the tide was right it was all taken upriver and hidden in several towns around Great Bay.

Wentworth was powerless. When he called on the provincial militia, no one turned out. When he and the members of the council tried to get to the fort he could not find a single man to launch his barge and row them to the fort. The royal government had collapsed, and Wentworth feared that he and his family would become the target of mob violence.

All that Wentworth could do in the aftermath of the raid on the fort was to issue a proclamation and call for troops. In the proclamation, he called on the provincial authorities to find and jail the men who had taken part in the raid. Finding them was no problem. Everyone from Wentworth on down knew who they were. The problem was that no royal official dared to take action against any of them. Regarding troops, General Gage could spare none. The only force available, two ships, the *Canceaux* and the *Scarborough*, were sent by Admiral Samuel Graves. The ships anchored off Portsmouth, and the Royal government in New Hampshire was secure within the range of their guns.

On January 25, 1775, a second Provincial Congress met at Exeter. The Congress appointed Sullivan and Langdon as New Hampshire's delegates to the Continental Congress and appointed a committee of correspondence. Finally, they passed a series of resolutions: they encouraged the people of New Hampshire to obey the law, to follow the recommendations of the Continental Congress, to boycott tea, and to support the people of Boston. The Congress recognized that "the Militia upon this Continent, if properly disciplined, would be able to do great service in its defense" and so called on the militia to arm themselves and practice their drill.

Wentworth realized that the Provincial Congress was becoming the real government of New Hampshire, but he would not give up. He attempted to restore royal authority in New Hampshire by ordering elections for a new assembly. Wentworth hoped that he would be able to conjure up a loyalist assembly and to that end he extended representation to three thinly settled frontier towns dominated by his friends. He also made plans to arrest any assemblyman who had taken part in the raid on Fort William and Mary. Between the time that the elections were held and the time that the assembly first met, fighting broke out in Massachusetts at Lexington and Concord and a third Provincial Congress was elected in New Hampshire. Many of the assemblymen were also members of the Provincial Congress. This third Provincial Congress appointed Folsom to command the New Hampshire troops that had gone to Massachusetts following the fighting at Concord and Lexington.

When the assembly convened on May 3, 1775, Wentworth's worst fears were realized. Active Patriots, including Folsom, John Langdon, and his brother, Woodbury, made up about one-third of the assembly. Wentworth could not make the planned arrests. He had no armed force on which he could rely. When the assembly refused to seat the delegates from the three frontier towns, Wentworth adjourned it to June 12.

On June 13, 1775, Wentworth was dining with John Fenton, one of the delegates that the assembly had refused to seat, when a mob surrounded the house and demanded Fenton. At first Wentworth refused, but when the mob drew up a cannon he handed Fenton over. That night Wentworth, his wife, and their young son abandoned their house and escaped to Fort William and Mary. There he and his family lived in a house with a leaky roof, protected by the guns of the HMS *Scarborough*. In August, when the *Scarborough* sailed for Boston, Wentworth, his wife, and their infant son were aboard.

Wentworth returned to New Hampshire only once. On September 21, 1775, he chartered a schooner at Boston and sailed to the town of Gosport on the Isles of Shoals. There, he prorogued the New Hampshire Assembly to April 24, 1776. This was the last act of the royal government of the province of New Hampshire. The assembly never met.

Even before Wentworth left New Hampshire, the royal government had almost ceased functioning. The Revolutionary party was in control, and political authority was in the hands of the Provincial Congress and local committees of safety.

A fourth Provincial Congress met on May 17, 1775. This Congress raised the 2,000 men who became the New Hampshire Continentals and requested that the Continental Congress devise some procedure under which New Hampshire might set up a civil government. On November 3, 1775, the Continental Congress resolved that New Hampshire should organize a government "to secure peace and good order . . . during the continuance of the dispute" with Great Britain.

Even before the Provincial Congress heard from the Continental Congress, it acted. A fifth Provincial Congress, with expanded representation, was to be elected. This congress would have the authority to set up a civil government for New Hampshire and to resolve itself into a house of representatives. It quickly did so.

New Hampshire's first constitution, adopted January 5, 1776, was a temporary document to last only for the duration of the war. It preceded the Declaration of Independence and looked forward to a reconciliation between the colonies and Great Britain. Nevertheless, it was, and was seen at the time, as marking a distinct break with the past.

During the Revolution the civilian leadership of New Hampshire faced three major challenges—to establish an effective government that would be accepted by the people of New Hampshire, to hold the state together, and to further the war by suppressing Tories and raising and paying troops, both Continentals and militia.

The constitution set up a house of representatives and a council, but contained no provision for a governor. Because the legislature could not remain constantly in session, the members appointed a Committee of Safety, a body not mentioned in the constitution, to act when they were in recess. The Committee of Safety quickly became the executive arm of the government.

Although the structure of the government was unwieldy, the people of New Hampshire were fortunate in the quality of the political leadership that arose. Meshech Weare, president of the council and chief justice of the superior court, was also chairman of the Committee of Safety. Weare, Josiah Bartlett (a member of the council), and John Dudley, from the House of Representatives, were the most active members of the Committee of Safety. All three men remained in office throughout the war and provided both continuous and energetic executive leadership.

Weare was popular and well respected, but the government that he headed was not universally approved. Many leaders of the old colonial elite, especially in the Portsmouth area, condemned the plural officeholding that was characteristic of the Revolutionary government. The use of the Committee of Safety as the executive branch inextricably intermixed the executive and legislative functions of government. Not only Weare, but Josiah Bartlett, John Dudley, Nathaniel Folsom, Ebenezer Thompson, and Matthew Thornton were both legislators and judges.

In the towns along the upper Connecticut River, many people were unhappy with the method of representation adopted by the Revolutionary government. In the colonial House of Representatives, the royal governor determined the right of a town to elect a representative. The Revolutionary House of Representatives was apportioned by town, but towns having fewer than 100 voters were grouped together to elect a single representative.

The towns on both sides of the Connecticut River were recently settled by people from Connecticut. There they were accustomed to a government where each town, no matter its population, had its own representative. The people in these towns, lead by Eleazer Wheelock, president of Dartmouth College, and Bezaleel Woodward, a faculty member there, feared that they would be dominated by representatives from the populous seacoast area.

Weare and his associates responded to these varied objections in two ways. They supported a movement that had been gaining strength to write a new constitution and they tried to conciliate the people along the Connecticut River.

Weare saw the need for a permanent constitution and hoped that when one was adopted it would have an independent executive. The New Hampshire Constitutional Convention, which met in Concord in June 1778, produced a document that differed little from the temporary constitution of 1776. It kept executive authority in the council and assembly and strictly limited plu-

ral officeholding. This was a combination of provisions of which Weare could not have approved. The provision-making representation proportional to population did not appeal to the people in the upper Connecticut River valley. Many of the towns in that region refused even to vote on the proposed constitution.

Not only Weare and his associates, but also a majority of the voters, opposed the work of the convention. The whole subject of constitution making remained quiet in New Hampshire until 1781. In that year a new convention was elected and ordered to stay in session, revising its work as necessary, until the voters accepted a constitution.

The convention adopted a very conservative plan and promptly saw the people reject it. Based on the Massachusetts Constitution and the Essex Resolves, it featured a strong governor, a 50-member house of representatives, and a 12-member senate. The members of the House were to be elected from the counties, proportional to population, by delegates elected in the individual towns. Senators were to be elected from the counties in proportion to that county's taxable wealth.

The convention members revised their work. They did away with indirect election of the House of Representatives and instead allowed each town or group of towns with 150 voters to elect one representative. Towns having an additional 300 voters could elect a second. This constitution also was rejected. One observer noted that "we have a constitution as often as we have an almanac."

The convention met yet again. It changed the title of the executive from governor to president. The president was limited by not having a veto, by having to preside over the Senate, and by a council, elected by the legislature from among the legislators. This, together with an extensive Bill of Rights, evidently convinced enough of the voters. They adopted the constitution on October 31, 1783. It went into effect on the first Wednesday in June 1784, replacing the temporary wartime constitution two years and eight months after the British surrendered at Yorktown.

While the form of government that New Hampshire would have was being debated, the geographic extent of New Hampshire was also in question. By the end of 1776, the College Party, as the leaders in the towns in the upper

Connecticut River valley were known, refused to recognize the authority of the government in Exeter. They were firm believers in the adage, "one town, one vote." They argued that with the Revolution all of the towns in western New Hampshire were in a state of nature and could join together to form a state in any combination agreeable to themselves. They based their arguments more on an intense localism, fueled in part by the topography of New Hampshire, than on any constitutional theories.

Weare tried to conciliate these western rebels. A weekly post rider went between Exeter and Fort Number Four on the Connecticut River. The New Hampshire Assembly voted to expand a town's representation as its population grew. Wheelock and Woodward received justice of the peace commissions, and Woodward was appointed to the Grafton County Court.

Politics took a back seat to war in the summer of 1777, but as soon as General John Burgoyne had surrendered it was politics as usual along the river once more. The New Hampshire Grants, the territory between the Connecticut River and Lake Champlain, declared its independence as the state of Vermont in July 1777.

Shortly thereafter the leaders of the College Party worked out a plan. They would join Vermont and then with the help of their neighbors just across the river would wrest control of the new state from the hands of the Allen brothers. The Vermont Assembly, which met in June 1778, at first hesitated to accept the New Hampshire towns. Then, when several towns in eastern Vermont threatened to secede to join their New Hampshire neighbors, 16 New Hampshire towns were allowed into the fold.

The news reached Weare quickly. As soon as he found out what had happened, Weare wrote to the Continental Congress. Calling it the "Ideal State of Vermont who now exercise a pretended jurisdiction there," Weare asked the Congress to help settle the dispute before any blood was shed. Weare, astonished that Vermont would add to its difficulties, warned Thomas Chittenden, Vermont's governor, that New Hampshire would send help if New Hampshire Loyalists requested it.

The Vermont leaders were in a quandary. They did not want the New Hampshire towns, but neither did they want to lose the Vermont towns along the west bank of the Connecticut River. Chittenden promised Weare not to impinge on New Hampshire's rights. He also sent Ethan Allen to Philadelphia to lobby Congress. While in Philadelphia, Allen met with Bartlett, then a New Hampshire delegate to the Continental Congress. Allen disavowed the annexation of the New Hampshire towns and asked Bartlett to hold off any discussion of the matter in Congress.

That October, the Vermont Assembly refused to organize the New Hampshire towns as a county in Vermont. With that, Vermont's deputy governor, two counselors, and 24 members of the assembly, all from Connecticut River valley towns on both sides of the river, withdrew from Vermont and proclaimed the state of New Connecticut.

In December, delegates from 14 New Hampshire towns and eight Vermont towns met at Cornish, New Hampshire. The Cornish Convention offered three choices to settle their dispute with New Hampshire—negotiation to settle a boundary between them, submit the matter to Congress, or unite all the territory west of the Connecticut River to New Hampshire. In June 1779, the New Hampshire Assembly voted to claim the territory of Vermont but not to press the claim if Congress recognized Vermont as a separate state. Before long all three adjacent states, New Hampshire, Massachusetts, and New York, laid claim to the territory of Vermont.

Faced with conflicting claims, Congress took no action. In New Hampshire, some leaders, including John Sullivan, opposed any expansion west of the Connecticut River. Others, including Woodbury Langdon and Nathaniel Peabody, pressed New Hampshire's claims. Along the river the leaders of the College Party called for another convention, this time to meet at Charlestown, New Hampshire, in January 1781. Delegates from 43 towns attended.

In a confused meeting the Charlestown convention first voted to unite with New Hampshire. Then, after intense lobbying by Ira Allen, they reconsidered and voted to join Vermont. Thirty-six New Hampshire towns in Cheshire and Grafton counties joined Vermont at this time.

Vermont pressed its claim. Counties were established. Judges were appointed, and courts sat. The militia was organized. Soon some as supporters of New Hampshire refused to obey Vermont officials and civil war seemed about to break out.

In Chesterfield, New Hampshire, a group of New Hampshire's supporters were meeting at Nathaniel Bingham's house when Samuel Davis, the Vermont constable, burst in. Davis started to serve a writ on James Robinson, but Bingham interrupted and told Davis to leave. Davis then took out a book and started to read the Riot Act. John Grandy threatened to kick the book into the fire and Davis left. A few days later Bingham and Grandy were arrested and, when they refused to post bail in a Vermont court, were jailed in Charlestown. When Enoch Hale, the Cheshire County sheriff, tried to free the two men, he too was jailed.

The New Hampshire Committee of Safety was busy. It issued warrants for the arrest of several Vermont officials who had been acting in New Hampshire and ordered Moses Kelly, the Hillsborough county sheriff, to free the three men in Charlestown jail. The militia in Hillsborough and Cheshire counties was ordered to be ready to assist Kelly.

Governor Chittenden of Vermont threatened to meet force with force. At the same time, he sent Ira Allen to Exeter to meet with the New Hampshire Committee of Safety. Allen met with Bartlett (Bartlett had served in Congress from May to November 1778. At this time he was back in New Hampshire. He met with Allen because Weare was absent, injured from a fall from his horse) but was unable to make any headway. Both Bartlett and Weare refused to negotiate while Vermont claimed any territory east of the Connecticut River.

Soon some of the arrest warrants issued by the New Hampshire Committee of Safety were being carried out. Nathaniel Prentice, one of the magistrates who had ordered Hale jailed, had himself been arrested and was in jail in Exeter. Another Vermont magistrate, Samuel King, had been arrested but was freed by a mob as he was being taken through Keene. After King had been freed, the mob, some of whom had been drinking, rampaged through the area, driving many New Hampshire supporters from their homes. Meanwhile, the New Hampshire Assembly gave the people along the Connecticut River 40 days to take an oath of allegiance to New Hampshire and authorized the Committee of Safety to raise 1,000 militia to be commanded by John Sullivan to restore order in the area.

Pressed by New Hampshire, by a congressional resolution refusing to discuss recognition of Vermont as a state unless it withdrew from its recent annexations (Vermont was also claiming several towns in northeastern New York), and by a letter from George Washington to Chittenden advising Vermont to limit itself to the territory between Lake Champlain and the Connecticut River, Vermont withdrew. At a midwinter meeting held at Bennington, the Vermont Assembly defined Vermont as being west of the Connecticut River and east of Lake Champlain.

With that action, the revolt in New Hampshire's western towns petered out. A mob led by Samuel Davis disrupted the inferior court sitting in Keene in September 1782, but Davis and other ringleaders were arrested and brought before the superior court in Keene a month later. A second mob of over 200 men tried to prevent the superior court from meeting. The judges were not intimidated, and the court sat as scheduled. The court found Davis and his associates guilty but suspended their sentences upon their promise of good behavior.

Weare always dealt with the dissidents in the Connecticut River valley towns with both firmness and conciliation. He worked to maintain both the territorial and the political integrity of New Hampshire. When the dissidents made constitutional arguments, Weare responded to them within the limits of the Revolutionary ideology. When the revolt ended, the first appointments in the local courts and militia went to men who had supported New Hampshire. Before long, however, local leaders who had supported Vermont were included. Bezaleel Woodward was reappointed as a justice of the peace in 1783. When he appeared as an assemblyman, elected to represent Hanover in the New Hampshire Assembly in 1784, the rebellion was well and truly over.

The most important task faced by all state governments during the Revolution was supporting the war. Weare and his associates, in common with civilian leaders in other states, faced three major problems directly related to making war—recruiting soldiers, controlling dissenters, and raising money.

In the first flush of enthusiasm following the fighting at Concord and Lexington, many New Hampshire men took their muskets and flocked to the hills outside of Boston. In New Hampshire the Provincial Congress soon voted to raise 2,000 men and to organize them into three regiments. Although many of the men who took the road to Boston only stayed a few days, enough were willing to remain to form two regiments. The third regiment was organized in New Hampshire. These three regiments, which became the New Hampshire Continentals, served through 1780, when they were consolidated into two. The state never was able to fill these regiments, however, and in December 1780, just before the consolidation, they contained just 591 officers and men.

During the war, New Hampshire also raised state troops and militia for local defense and to meet specific short-term needs. Throughout the war, New Hampshire maintained a garrison, usually one or two companies, at the forts at the mouth of Portsmouth harbor. The state also kept one or more detachments of scouts or rangers along the upper Connecticut River for much of the war.

In addition to these duties, which were primarily for local defense, the militia was also called upon for service outside of the state. In the winter of 1775, 16 companies were raised to garrison the lines outside of Boston while the Continental Army was being reorganized. During the Canadian campaign of 1776, Timothy Bedel's Regiment served with the northern army.

The year 1777, as Burgoyne was advancing toward Saratoga, saw the greatest outpouring of New Hampshire militia. Pierse Long's Regiment was ordered to Fort Ticonderoga in February. In May and June three more regiments and parts of nine others followed him. In July, John Stark raised a brigade of New Hampshire militia that formed the core of the troops at the Battle of Bennington. Another brigade, commanded by General William Whipple, was with the northern army at Saratoga.

New Hampshire militia also served in Rhode Island. Joseph Senter's Regiment was there from June 1777 through the end of the year. A brigade, led by Whipple, was part of John Sullivan's force there during the summer and fall of 1778. A regiment led by Hercules Mooney served there in the summer and fall of 1779.

In 1780, two regiments of New Hampshire militia were part of the garrison at West Point in the wake of Benedict Arnold's treason. During the final years of the war the militia was called out for emergency service to repel British and Indian raiding parties that came down into New England from Canada.

The militia also served as an internal police force. During the early part of the Revolution local militia companies were often used to enforce the decisions of local committees of safety. On January 17, 1777, the New Hampshire legislature, in what was the first of a series of acts designed to control and to punish Tories, gave anyone who opposed the Revolution 90 days to sell their property and leave the state. That summer, as Burgoyne's army was advancing, the Committee of Safety acted to imprison suspected Tories and allowed colonels of the militia regiments to disarm those who were not imprisoned.

The legislature passed a Proscription Act in November 1778, which listed 76 Tories by name and applied to any others who should desert to the British. Nine days later it passed a Confiscation Act. Confiscation applied to 28 named people and to any others who might actively aid the British in the war. John Wentworth headed both lists.

Loyalty oaths were used throughout the Revolution to separate Patriots from Tories. The Association Test, which required the signers to promise "to the utmost of our Power, at the Risque of our Lives and Fortunes, with Arms, oppose the Hostile Proceedings of the British Fleets and Armies against the United American Colonies," was presented to all adult males in New Hampshire in 1776. At least 773 people, some of whom were Quakers, refused to sign. In 1781 and 1782, loyalty oaths, aimed at both Tories and partisans of Vermont in the Connecticut River valley, were required before one could bring a suit in court, serve as a juror or as a public official, have a tavern license, or vote. During the Revolution perhaps as many as 100 Tories, with their families, left the state.

The Revolutionary War never stopped because of either a lack of money or a lack of supplies. Still, finding the money to purchase weapons and supplies and to pay the soldiers was a constant struggle for the leaders of the Revolution. Drawing on their colonial experience, New Hampshire, along with the Continental Congress and other states, printed paper money to pay for the Revolution.

Before the Revolution ended, New Hampshire issued more than 151,000 pounds in paper currency. In addition, paper currency issued by the Continental Congress was circulating in the state. When the British province of New Hampshire had issued paper currency there had been some inflation but it was held in check by the expectation that the British government would reimburse the province for most of its war expenses. During the Revolution there was no such expectation. As a result, as more money was printed its value dropped precipitously.

Weare and his associates tried several methods to deal with these economic problems but they never did succeed in solving them. Laws requiring creditors to accept repayment in the paper currency were passed. Price and wage scales were established. None of these methods worked. By 1781, the currency was practically worthless, and requisitions for the Continental Army were being collected in beef and rum.

New Hampshire repealed its laws enforcing the use of the paper money by the fall of 1781. After that, only gold and silver coin were legal tender. Taxes were payable in coin, cattle, or merchandise. This worked better than any previous method of raising money, and by 1783 the resumption of trade was bringing coin back into the state.

Weare had spent his health leading New Hampshire through the Revolution. He had been 62 years old in 1776. He served throughout the Revolution as president of the council, chairman of the Committee of Safety, and chief justice. Weare guided New Hampshire through its Revolutionary journey by a mixture of diligence, prudence, and strength of character. Worn out, he resigned his offices in 1785. He died in his unpainted farmhouse in Hampton Falls, New Hampshire, January 15, 1786, at age 73.

Walter A. Ryan

REFERENCES

Jere R. Daniell, *Experiment in Republicanism* (1970); Franck C. Mevers, ed., *The Papers of Josiah Bartlett* (1979); Peter E. Randall, *New Hampshire: Years of Revolution 1774–1783* (1976); Richard Francis Upton, *Revolutionary New Hampshire* (1971).

New Jersey in the American Revolution

Warfare between British and Patriot troops did not begin in New Jersey until June 29, 1776. Six British men-of-war ran aground the American brig *Nancy* off Cape May. As crews took control of the vessel, shots killed one American, initiating New Jersey into the violence of war. As "cockpit of the revolution," New Jersey experienced unceasing conflict for the next six years. Struggle between Washington's army, stationed in New Jersey intermittently from 1776 until 1780 and British troops, headquartered in New York City for much of the war, exacerbated local tensions and created long-harbored hatred between Whigs, Tories, and neutrals. Much of eastern New Jersey lay within a "neutral zone," a broad arc controlled more by gangs of escaped slaves, white vigilantes, and bandits, than by competing armies. Southern New Jersey, better known as West Jersey, also experienced obnoxious raiding because it was close to Philadelphia. Although the Society of Friends, officially neutral in war, was dominant among the population in West Jersey, guerrilla warfare was constant.

Prelude to warfare in New Jersey was historic. Personal affiliation depended on a complex of factors. Class tensions emerged in the late 1740s in a series of land riots that recurred as anti-lawyer protests in pre-Revolutionary years. Ethnic conflict flared between the politically dominant English and traditional foes including Scotch-Irish, Dutch, and Germans. Anglicans desiring establishment of a bishopric in the late 1760s ran afoul of Presbyterians in Essex County, pietistic Dutch Reformed in Bergen and Monmouth counties, nonconformist Congregationalists from New England in Monmouth, and Quakers and German Lutherans in West Jersey. Much of the colony went unchurched and viewed Anglican policies as undesired state intervention. The Dutch Reformed, in particular, regarded the Anglican Society of the Propagation of the Gospel in Foreign Parts (S.P.G.) as unwarranted interference with slaveholding. Quakers spearheaded abolitionist movements, though slaveholders quickly thwarted any legislative attempts to end slavery. Black bondage was an important labor supply in the colony, and laws governing slaves were among the harshest in North America. Fugitive slaves, conspiracies, and frolicks were unceasing threats. Slaves' restiveness increased dramatically in the early 1770s, and county sheriffs were ordered to disarm slaves and enact strict curfews.

Economically, widespread bankruptcies, local crop failures, and new elaborations of the British imperial system created new distress in the 1770s. Fledgling iron foundries hampered by enumerated commodities restrictions suffered under British rules. Trade with the West Indies curtailed by navigation acts reappeared as piracy. Despite restrictions on land purchases, wealthy speculators built up vast estates on the frontier. Smoldering hostilities against government broke out in riots in 1769 and 1770. "Liberty boy" mobs in Essex and Monmouth counties burned the homes of lawyers and stormed courthouses. Clashes showed strains between the conservative political elite and the radical popular will.

Local animosities outweighed imperial debates. A small, dependent agrarian colony, New Jersey was secure in British Empire. Older political disputes, including stationing of troops and paper money controversy were resolved by 1774. Governor William Franklin, son of Benjamin, used administrative acumen and clear understanding of the needs of the colony to foster loyalty.

Most pre-Revolutionary action was inchoate. A moderate political stance meant New Jersey lacked Revolutionary or separatist movement. Even after bloodshed at Lexington-Concord, New Jersey citizens were reluctant to talk openly of independence. The colony lacked newspapers to disseminate propaganda, it had no large mercantile class to invoke stringent economic sanctions, and pervasive Quaker pacifism inhibited radical development. Rather, violence, once imposed from without by national armies, fed upon long-term local disputes.

As pre-Revolutionary tumult quickened, affiliation divided along ethnic, religious, and professional lines. Chief among Loyalists were Governor Franklin; wealthy landowners Cortlandt and Stephen Skinner; chief justice of the colony, Frederick Smythe, and important merchants Peter Kemble and James Parker. More ordinary loyal citizens included James Moody, a farmer from Sussex County, grocers William Dumayne and Thomas Gumersall of Elizabeth Town, lawyers Daniel Issac Brown of Hackensack and Bernardus LaGrange of Raritan. Nearly every Anglican cleric in the province remained loyal, as did a few Dutch Reformed. Less orthodox Quakers favored the English in opposition to the denomination's general neutrality. It was generally accepted that the colony's black slaves supported the British, believing that emancipation would follow English victory. Blacks became an important military force in the war years.

Whigs came from all levels of society. Key figures were Lord Stirling (William Alexander),

his brother-in-law John Stevens, lawyers Richard Stockton and Francis Hopkinson, ironmaster John Jacob Faesch, slave dealer Thomas Brown of Bergen County, and the Neilsons and Schurmans of New Brunswick. Andrew Sinnickson, the wealthiest descendant of Swedish colonists, and John Burrowes, the "Corn King" of Middletown Point, vigorously supported the American side. Intellectuals siding with the Whigs included John Witherspoon, president of the College of New Jersey, poet Phillip Freneau, and William Livingston, essayist, lawyer and soon-to-be first state governor.

The pacifist Society of Friends was the most famous of neutrals. Others included farmers within the "neutral zone" who traded with both sides and precariously balanced political favor with occupying forces. Many citizens followed this principle and wore Continental uniforms when Whigs arrived, then later wore British red as the king's army took control.

After May 1775, "associations" of county officials and government by the New Jersey Provincial Congress supplanted the colonial assembly as the political authority. Governor Franklin was arrested and deported to imprisonment in Connecticut. In June 1776 Revolutionary leaders elected five delegates to the Continental Congress, with a mandate to declare independence if necessary. While the Declaration of Independence was debated in Philadelphia, a Revolutionary constitution was adopted in New Jersey. This document ended the king's civil authority, although admitting the possibility of reconciliation, for it called for the election of a new assembly and legislative council the next month to elect a governor. As skirmishes broke out along the coast, New Jersey sent three battalions for Continental service in defense of New York. Detachments of militia apprehended Tories opposing the new government in Hunterdon County. In Monmouth County, the Shrewsbury Township Committee ordered Colonel Samuel Breeze to arrest all blacks meeting at unlicensed taverns and to confiscate guns from slaves. Loyalists in Shrewsbury kept communications open with the British in New York. Whigs denounced Tories as "enemies to the Rights of America." Nonetheless, political cleavages appeared in every county in the state.

On August 31, 1776, a joint session of the legislature elected William Livingston governor of the new state. In his address Livingston lamented the necessity of independence but avowed that the Crown tyranny implemented by arriving British forces must be met by unity. Livingston told the assembly that "it is absolutely necessary to turn our first Attention to the operations of War." He then ordered that the militia be paid immediately, and extended their terms of service.

Despite Livingston's vigilance, the assembly was slow to move. Provincial forces lacked leadership, experience, and ammunition. Most were raw recruits who vacillated between extremes of overconfidence and panic. Although 2,000 militia were exhorted to turn out, by August few could be found. General George Washington worried openly about new Jersey's determination. Mosquitoes, desertions, and lack of equipment and shelter further hampered enlistments. Desertion into the British lines became rampant.

Fortunately, the theater of war began on Long Island, where General William Howe's 20,000 British and Hessian troops overwhelmed American defenders on August 27, 1776. After Washington retreated through New York City and Manhattan Heights across the Hudson River to New Jersey, independence seemed very precarious. Eastern New Jersey quickly felt the brunt of the advancing English army. By early September, three British warships enabled Howe to capture the American post at Paulus Hook and complete English domination over New York Bay. Unexpectedly, the British dawdled, declined to complete the operation and allowed the Americans to escape into Bergen County.

New Jersey remained fairly quiet for two months. Washington and Lord Stirling took up headquarters at Hackensack while the British completed the occupation of New York City. Reconciliation meetings held on Staten Island proved fruitless. In early November the British inflicted severe losses on Washington's army on upper Manhattan Island. On November 19, Cornwallis headed 4,500 men in an assault on Fort Lee and forced Americans to evacuate, leaving behind badly needed military supplies.

The next month saw a virtual rout of American forces across New Jersey. Nathanael Greene and Washington joined forces at Hackensack, and with Cornwallis in hot pursuit, retreated rapidly through the state. Few recruits joined the disorganized Patriots. With the Revolution in disarray, formerly intimidated Tories in Bergen and Essex counties paraded their sympa-

thies. As British troops advanced, slaves abandoned their masters for freedom in service to the king. Washington completed his retreat into Pennsylvania on December 2, while Congress, in terror of capture by British, fled to Baltimore and left him with near dictatorial powers. William Livingston ordered all the militias out from counties north of Monmouth and Burlington but to no avail.

New Jersey's lack of ardor for the Revolution stemmed from pragmatic views of citizens. Without any national vision and with local concerns paramount, the arrival of the imposing redcoats seemed to doom the pretentions of the Americans. The advancing British heard cheers from inhabitants as far west as the outskirts of Trenton. Cortlandt Skinner raised several hundred recruits in a loyal militia. Prominent Loyalists administered oaths of allegiance in Monmouth and Bergen counties. In the south, Quakers remained aloof to the American side. As Washington and his army fled into Pennsylvania, the British conquest of New Jersey was temporarily complete. One disquieting note was the anger of citizens at the depredations and looting by the British forces. Many previously neutral New Jerseyans developed a thorough dislike for the British.

Their backs to the wall, the American benefited once again from the unaggressive strategy of General Howe. Rather than chase Washington, he chose to occupy Trenton and did not even attempt to impress timber in a Loyalist stronghold to build rafts to pursue the Americans. In every step of the campaign Howe failed to deliver the knockout punch open to him. The plodding British army allowed the Americans to slip away in Bergen County, at New Brunswick, and at Trenton. Howe had some affection for the former colonies and hesitated in their complete destruction.

Washington responded to the crisis with forceful action. After Howe sent the bulk of his army to New York on December 13 and left only garrisons at Trenton, Princeton, Bordentown, Perth Amboy, and New Brunswick, Washington moved to restore American confidence. Learning that the Hessian garrison at Trenton was unprepared for attack, Washington led a three-pronged force on December 26 across the ice-choked Delaware and routed the surprised Hessians in one hour. Quickly, the Patriots rounded up nearly 1,000 prisoners and occupied

Trenton. On January 2, 1777, Washington repeated his virtuosity by outflanking Cornwallis's army at Princeton and establishing an American presence in New Jersey, lifting Patriot morale enormously. Washington then stationed his troops for the winter at Morristown. With the British momentum stalled, and memories of the previous months' terror ablaze, New Jersey's militias filled their quotas as never before.

As the two armies waited out the winter, local battle took precedent. Patriots and Tories plundered each other as military control wavered. Governor Livingston made proclamations against looting, but with the state government still weak, his words had little effect. The British leadership, encamped in luxury in Perth Amboy, was indifferent to the internecine conflict. New Brunswick, headquarters for Lord Cornwallis, became a pale imitation of the gay society of New York, itself but a provincial imitation of London. To disturb the British, Washington ordered constant patrols to prevent traffic in provisions, livestock, and forage. Warfare descended into daily clashes designed to secure or prevent the sale of necessities. Gradually, the American strategy showed effectiveness, and outbreaks of scurvy decimated the Hessians. Horses lacking hay died or became too weak to pull heavy wagons. Fuel became scarce in Perth Amboy, and smallpox appeared.

The war of attrition hampered the Americans as well. The farmer militias were loathe to turn out during planting season. Desertions inspired by hard English specie were a severe problem. Even with Livingston's constant appeals, provisions for the Patriots were low, and clothing was scarce, though not as much as in Valley Forge a year later. Washington's plan to inoculate the army against smallpox frightened local citizens in Morristown. Military mores including gambling and casual profanity irritated the population. Another problem lay with the Society of Friends. Local military leaders urged Livingston, who was sympathetic to Quaker ideals, to fine them for refusing to march with the militia. With Washington's support, Livingston was able to refuse such demands.

The advance and retreat of the two armies, county militias, and guerrilla raiders made life uncomfortable in towns near the fighting. Troops depended on plunder and had little sympathy for the citizenry. There was more to fear from the British, but life near the American lines

was not easy either. Even distant from the theater of war, farmers found cattle and wagons confiscated. At times payment was made, but often raiders hardly bothered with reasons or promises of compensation. Both sides used such depredations as propaganda. These reports scarcely altered affiliation. At the beginning of 1777, most of Bergen County was Tory, as was Monmouth. The Whigs were strongest in the south and in Presbyterian Essex and Middlesex counties. In January 1777, Washington and Livingston made the drastic move of ordering the arrest and confinement of Tories.

The Constitution of 1776 did little to level franchise requirements. Making the governing council elective rather than appointive aimed less at preserving the advantages than avoiding the evils of the past. New Jersey retained deferential politics with heavy property requirements for officeholding. The council and assembly continued the appointment of the executive and judicial branches and had the power of impeachment. The Constitution also added a Bill of Rights retaining trial by jury, freedom of religion, and disallowed tax support for any denomination. The Constitution was not submitted to the voters for ratification. Wartime exigencies created extraordinary powers, and the Constitution was renewed.

Despite official consensus, factions raged within the new government between groups led by Livingston and Abraham Clark. Livingston was close to the military command and favored centralized government. Clark, in contrast, viewed Washington with suspicion and was a major theoretician of new democratic ideals. He was tireless in his attendance at Congress. Livingston continued as executive, and though rebuffed in his attempt in 1778 to end slavery, he remained a popular governor. Livingston had to head off more extreme reaction to Tories. In early 1778 David Forman of Monmouth County organized the Association for Retaliation, a band of violent Whigs. Livingston had to prosecute Forman for creating an illegal vigilante government, while at the same time retain the loyalty of the beleaguered Patriots of Monmouth.

New Jersey continued to be the center of the war. Washington opened the 1777 campaign in New Jersey with determination. Believing the British were still shaken by the losses at Trenton and Princeton, Washington hoped to drive them from the state. Prowling American detachments bothered British forces, but the American army lost many men to agricultural demands. Washington's forces were insufficient at the beginning of May 1777 to expect the success of major undertakings. Meanwhile, the British bolstered their forces with arrivals from Rhode Island, bringing their estimated numbers to over 10,000. Despite the numerical imbalance, General Howe's indecision cost the British opportunities to crush the Americans. Even as the Crown forces repulsed American raiders at Perth Amboy in May, Howe decided against a march across New Jersey to the Delaware. He preferred to attain his goal of Philadelphia by sea. Still, intelligence reached Washington that the British had extended their lines beyond occupied towns and that a general invasion of New Jersey was still feasible. The American general's spies informed him of British movements on Staten Island, near Perth Amboy, and a coalescence of troops near New Brunswick suggested that the British could move across Jersey at any time.

Washington was forced to await British action. By early June his position improved as reinforcements arrived. On June 9, 1977, it was clear that the major British effort was nigh. On the night of June 13, the entire British army, now nearly 11,000 strong, marched from New Brunswick to Somerset Court House, where American guerrillas caused some damage. The American forces watched as Howe's army tried to lure them into a major conflict on the lowlands. American guerrillas, composed of farmers no longer fearful of the king's army distracted the English with small raids. After five days of feinting, Howe retired his massive force back to New Brunswick, wreaking vengeance on civilians.

Washington's forces rejoiced, prematurely. The British forces, especially Hessians, made aggressive sorties against the Americans resulting in heavy casualties on both sides. Unexpectedly, Howe's army retreated and evacuated Perth Amboy for New York. Howe received immense criticism for the conduct of his army, and after his departure on June 30 he would never return to New Jersey.

The surprise British retreat greatly bolstered American hopes in New Jersey. By July 1, most New Jersey militiamen were discharged with thanks consisting of several wagonloads of meat and flour distributed among the inhabitants near the most recent battles. Tories felt deeply disappointed by Howe's mysterious actions. Despite the general British retreat from New Jersey, Washington remained, watching Howe's army across the Hudson and wondering what the next British move might be. Washington worried about being enticed into a northern campaign that would leave Jersey open to an easy British invasion. Reluctantly, Washington began to move north to defend the highland forts of the Pallisades, when news of a British invasion brought him hurrying back.

On July 20, 1777, over 160 vessels of the royal fleet fell down from Staten Island to Sandy Hook Bay. Howe attempted a ruse to deflect American attention from his real intentions to invade Philadelphia. As Washington, suspecting a trick, moved quickly to defend southern Jersey, its northern borders lay undefended. Sir Henry Clinton, left to defend British forces on Staten Island, launched a small invasion across Bergen and part of Essex County to little resistance. As Washington tried unsuccessfully to defend Philadelphia, Clinton wreaked havoc in East Jersey. Livingston, Forman, and General Philemon Dickenson struggled against public apathy and despair. The militia was only inspired when defending their local territory. Bothered on the northern flank and anxiously trying to stem the main British army and navy at Philadelphia, the American forces faced desperation. The peaceful interlude of the previous month gave way to full-scale warfare in late July 1777.

Washington concentrated most of his efforts at Fort Mifflin on Mud Island in the middle of the Delaware just below Philadelphia. As Fort Mifflin was considered impregnable, work began on supportive resistance at Billingsport on the Jersey shore. Howe then outflanked the Americans and took Philadelphia by land. Fort Mifflin, however, assured that the Americans could keep the Delaware closed to British shipping. Soon, however, a British detachment of 1,500 men routed the Americans, took Billingsport, and forced a Patriot retreat back into New Jersey. Washington attempted to regain momentum at Germantown on October 4 and to strengthen American defenses at Red Bank, New Jersey. The beseiged American garrison at Fort Mifflin, exhausted by overwork at the damp, unhealthy fort, worried about the menacing British forces surrounding them. A first major effort to level the fort in the second week of October only weakened the garrison. Three weeks later Hessians attempting to overwhelm the fort were routed. Even so, Washington's request to Livingston to relieve the heroic soldiers at Fort Mifflin went unheeded. Livingston, just finishing his first term, lacked power to send a militia. Fortunately for the Americans, Forman with 100 men from Monmouth rushed to the aid of the fort. Forman had been unable to recruit one soldier from the southern counties.

The principal American aim of closing the Delaware did not remain accomplished for long. A second major attack by the British nearly succeeded but was hampered by heavy rainfall. Not until they began to ascend the smaller Tinecum channel in lighter boats could the British reinforce Philadelphia. Protected by batteries on Province and Carpenter's Islands, the British were able to outmaneuver the Americans. As British flatboats brought supplies and munitions, their navy and army began a cannonade against Fort Mifflin. After six days of bombardment, the last American survivors abandoned the fort and rowed over to the shelter of Red Bank, New Jersey. Shortly after Fort Mercer, a second American stronghold fell to British guns. Howe and his men had achieved their greatest triumph, but New Jersey remained American. In the state, opposition to the British army and king was growing firmer and better organized.

As the Americans grew more secure in their control of New Jersey, they began to crack down on Tories. Sporadic arrests and savage reprisals angered adherents of the Crown in the state. As the winter wore on, the southern counties experienced what the north had long known. The proximity of armies brought misery. The British army used any pretext to arrest Patriot families and to destroy their property. The American militia lived off the spoils of war. Little attention was given to discipline. In the northeastern counties only Bergen County farmers were able to avoid kidnappings, ambushes, and raids.

Clandestine trading with the English occurred even in Elizabeth Town, home of Livingston and Clark. Despite legislation enacted in 1777 making unlicensed presence behind enemy lines a capital offense, the prohibition was ineffective. The British constantly used "flags of truce" to engage in espionage. American respect for elite Loyalists proved a mistaken policy. Captain Archibald Kennedy, a paroled landowner, became a notorious spy. Busy Tories and a deterioration of public morale tarnished whatever

glamour left over from the beginning of the war. Even though British guns were fairly remote, more so than a year before, dissent became rampant among the Whigs. Widespread criticism, much of it accurate, denounced military corruption and inefficiency. By February 1778 the starving American forces at Valley Forge mirrored the Patriot will across New Jersey.

Livingston complied as best he could with Washington's desperate pleas for help in the painful winter of 1777–1778. Appalling conditions sponsored little hope for the coming year. The state suffered from guerrilla activity in the north and south, constant threats of British raids, defeatest propaganda, low morale, corruption, and the scandal of illicit trade with the English.

As the campaign of the summer of 1778 loomed, Americans were roused to great indignation by a murderous raid at Hancock's Creek near the Delaware River. British raiders bayoneted every American prisoner, inspiring deep animosity and setting off a chain of reprisals against Tories. A similar British victory at Bordentown, New Jersey, was Pyrrhic as it resulted more in the exasperation of the inhabitants than any logistical gain. Nor did Howe's replacement by Sir Henry Clinton bear much hope. Rather than regain American confidence, the British planned to ravage the American coastline from Massachusetts to New York. Livingston, suspecting such a plan, warned of fierce days ahead.

Clinton proposed to accomplish the sacking of America even if it meant evacuating Philadelphia and marching his troops overland to New York City. Following a circuitous path, the massive force took nine days to accomplish passage, at times annoyed by sniping from the New Jersey militia. En route, Clinton's army attracted numerous slaves wishing freedom from their Patriot masters. As the British plodded on under a blazing sun, Washington puzzled over the correct response. Permitting the sluggish giant to cross unmolested was admitting weakness. On the other hand, risking defeat on the lowlands of the state was foolhardy. After several feints at the British, the Americans made a last strike near Freehold at the Monmouth Court House on June 28. As Washington approached, he was amazed to find that General Charles Lee, his local command, had given no order to fight as the British attacked. The commander-in-chief took control, rallied his men and was able to turn a disgraceful

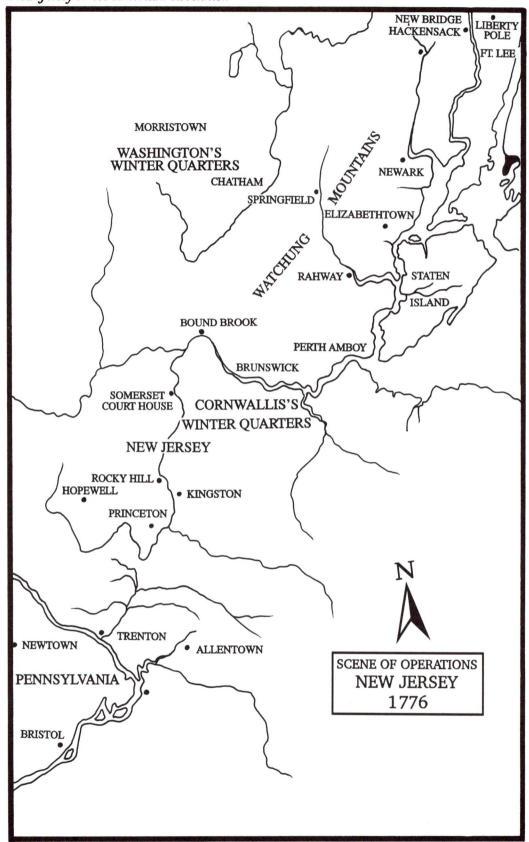

NEW BRIDGE
HACKENSACK
LIBERTY POLE
FT. LEE

MORRISTOWN

WASHINGTON'S
WINTER QUARTERS

CHATHAM

SPRINGFIELD

NEWARK

ELIZABETHTOWN

WATCHUNG MOUNTAINS

RAHWAY

STATEN
ISLAND

BOUND BROOK

PERTH AMBOY

BRUNSWICK

SOMERSET
COURT HOUSE

CORNWALLIS'S
WINTER QUARTERS

NEW JERSEY

ROCKY HILL
HOPEWELL

KINGSTON

PRINCETON

N

TRENTON

NEWTOWN

ALLENTOWN

PENNSYLVANIA

BRISTOL

SCENE OF OPERATIONS
NEW JERSEY
1776

rout into a stalemate. The British were able to escape into Sandy Hook and New York City and were now poised to ravage East Jersey.

After the Battle of Monmouth, there were no major conflicts in New Jersey until the skirmish at Springfield in June 1780. Washington returned to the state for two winter camps, but principal military operations essentially moved southward. Warfare was conducted on the local level between Tories, Patriots, and marauding gangs of escaped slaves and Pine Barrens robbers. Off the coast, privateers operating from Little Egg Harbor and Toms River attacked anything under sail. The only vessels to make New York Port were the heavily guarded. The British retaliated against pirates by periodic raids, which burned and sacked coastal towns. The large profits of privateering kept British revenge from any major success.

In 1779 former Governor William Franklin organized Tories into the Associated Loyalists. This group was intent upon regaining land confiscated during the war and harbored vain hopes of effecting military victory. Their greatest successes were the combined efforts of the Queen's Rangers under Colonel John Simcoe and the black raider Colonel Tye, once a slave to John Corlies of Shrewsbury in Monmouth County. Tye, often joined by Simcoe, raided Monmouth County Patriots with impunity, carrying off livestock, plate, and prisoners on numerous occasions in 1779 and 1780. In June 1780 British General Wilhelm von Knyphausen conducted a fruitless foray against American forces at Springfield. Tye and his men softened Patriot defenses in preparation for the main attack. Tye kept up the pressure over the summer of 1780 and captured over 20 Monmouth County militia. Killed in a raid on Josiah Huddy's home in September 1780, Tye represented the powerful claims blacks made for freedom in New Jersey.

Huddy was the focus of a final raid in 1781. Captured by the Associated Loyalists and hung on the beach in retaliation, Huddy in death became the focus of Patriot anger. Even after the defeat of Cornwallis at Yorktown, the Huddy incident caused tense relations between Americans and Tories around New Jersey.

The war's conclusion left deep scars on New Jersey. Several counties passed exclusion acts against Tories; class antagonisms remained from prewar days; and New Jersey currency fluctuated wildly in the early 1780s. Independence brought a degree of stability largely through the unceasing efforts of Livingston, but major areas of change including universal suffrage and abolition of slavery lay in the future. New Jersey's role in the new republic was often defensive in attempting to retain the powers of the small states.

Graham Hodges

REFERENCES

Larry Gerlach, *New Jersey in the American Revolution, 1763–1783. A Documentary History* (1975); ——— *Prologue to Independence. New Jersey in the Coming of the American Revolution* (1976); Adrian C. Leiby, *The Revolutionary War in the Hackensack Valley. The Jersey Dutch and the Neutral Ground* (1960); Leonard Lundlin, *Cockpit of the Revolution. The War for Independence in New Jersey* (1940); Carl Prince, et al., eds., *The Papers of William Livingston*, 5 vols. (1977–1990).

New Orleans, Louisiana

Situated near the mouth of the Mississippi River, New Orleans was the capital of Spanish Louisiana, and it served as an important contact point between rebel Americans and Spaniards during the Revolution. Founded by Bienville in 1718, New Orleans passed to Spain by virtue of the Peace of Paris in 1763. The first Spanish attempt to establish a colonial government under Antonio de Ulloa failed in 1767 when an irate mob of Creole settlers forced him to flee the province. In 1769, General Alegandro O'Reilly firmly planted the flag of Spain on the lower Mississippi River when he brought enough troops to the colony to insure establishment of a firm government.

Although O'Reilly and his successors (most notably Luis de Unzaga and Bernardo de Galvez) made efforts to end contraband trade with nearby British in West Florida, in reality they tolerated a growing number of Anglo merchants who came to New Orleans in order to trade. The Spanish government needed these traders so that a viable economy could be maintained. During the 1770s and early 1780s, this growing Anglo-American merchant population included Oliver Pollock, James Rumsey, Evan Jones, Thomas Power, Daniel Clark, Sr., and Daniel Clark, Jr. They were partisans of the American cause during the Revolution and did much to insure that supplies needed by the rebels could be secured at New Orleans. As well, New Orleans became a safe refuge for American shipping, which sought secure anchorage and safety from British privateers in the region. After 1777, when Bernardo de Galvez became governor, the Spanish at New Orleans openly sympathized with the Americans, and gave Anglo merchants at New Orleans had a relatively free hand in support of the American cause. The net effect of this activity was to awaken the interest of east coast mercantile firms, especially at Philadelphia and Baltimore, in the profit that could be secured in trade with the lower Mississippi River. In many respects, the Anglo merchants at New Orleans during the American Revolution became the commercial precursors to the Louisiana Purchase.

Light Townsend Cummins

REFERENCES

Jose Rodulfo Boeta, *Bernardo de Galvez* (1976); John W. Caughey, *Bernardo de Galvez in Louisiana, 1776–1783* (1934); Light T. Cummins, "Anglo Merchants and Capital Migration in Spanish Colonial New Orleans, 1763–1803," *Gulf Coast Historical Review 4*, (1982): 7–28; ———, "Spanish Imperial Policy in the Lower Mississippi during the American Revolution " *Louisiana Review, 11* (1979):33–45; James A. James, *Oliver Pollock: Life and Times of an Unknown Patriot* (1937).

Newport, Rhode Island, Siege of (August 1778)

At the beginning of the American Revolution, Newport, Rhode Island, was a flourishing commercial center with a population of some 11,000, one of the half-dozen largest cities in the United States. Because of its strategic location between Massachusetts and New York, seaborne British forces attacked Newport and captured it in early December 1776. During their occupation these troops caused so much damage and destruction to ships, buildings, foodstuffs, and other supplies in the area that more than 4,000 inhabitants fled the city before the eventual British withdrawal in late October 1779. Such misconduct led one of their own officers, Captain Frederick Mackenzie of the Royal Welch Fusiliers, to conclude that these "excesses . . . have thrown great disgrace on our arms."

More than a year before the British evacuation, Newport was the site of the first attempt at military cooperation between elements of the American army and their new French allies. In April 1778, two months after the signing of the

Franco-American alliance, the Comte d'Estaing left the French port of Toulon in command of a naval squadron and 3,500 to 4,000 infantry. The expedition reached the Delaware coast on July 7–8, then sailed for New York, anchoring near Sandy Hook on July 11. British strength at New York, together with the inability of the deep-bottomed French vessels to cross local sandbars safely, discouraged d'Estaing and frustrated Washington's pet project, a direct attack on New York. After a week and a half of inaction the French sailed for Rhode Island, arriving off Newport on July 29.

From the start of operations, difficulties plagued the allies. D'Estaing's men, at sea for three and a half months, were suffering from severe shortages of provisions and widespread disease, especially scurvy. They were anxious to land and engage the enemy. General John Sullivan, the American commander, was still in the process of assembling his forces; militiamen were marching from various localities in southern New England, and Lafayette was en route with two brigades of Continentals. Furthermore, with a prior military career that included defeats at Staten Island, Brandywine, and Germantown, Sullivan was desperate for a victory and wanted to delay any action until he had a decisive advantage. On the other hand, the British garrison at Newport, under the orders of General Richard Pigot, was receiving substantial reinforcements from New York that would raise its strength to some 6,000 men. Finally, the allied commanders differed between themselves. Sullivan was suspicious of French arrogance; d'Estaing was wary of American incompetence. Even the time and place of attack were matters of disagreement. When the French began to land troops on Conanicut Island, west of Newport, on the morning of August 9, the Americans launched their attack on the British before all the French were ashore. More importantly, later the same day an English fleet under Admiral Richard Howe appeared on the horizon. D'Estaing immediately began to reembark his land forces and set sail the next day to avoid being caught at anchor and to confront Howe, after promising Sullivan to return as soon as possible.

Following limited action at long range, the opposing fleets were struck by a gale that damaged and scattered the ships on both sides. Howe withdrew to New York for repairs. D'Estaing's squadron reached Newport on August 20, only to announce that the French were departing for Boston to refit. Meanwhile, Sullivan, whose forces had reached 10,000 officers and men, prepared to open the siege unaided. On August 12–13, however, the same storm that ravaged the two fleets struck the unprotected American troops and damaged their supplies. D'Estaing's departure for Massachusetts on August 22 dealt Sullivan's hopes a more severe blow and bitterly disappointed and angered him. Later the same day Sullivan and his officers drew up a protest against the French conduct (which Lafayette refused to sign) and sent it on to Boston. In his general orders of August 24, the American commander assured his troops that alone they could achieve what their "Allies refuse to assist in obtaining."

The controversy created by Sullivan's charges soon overshadowed the fate of Newport. Lafayette rode nonstop to Boston to urge d'Estaing to do something; the admiral reiterated that his ships were in dire need of repair, but offered to march his ground forces to Newport overland. Even before Lafayette could return, the Americans began pulling back from Newport, and on August 30 Sullivan ordered a general retreat to Tiverton on the mainland, a withdrawal completed by the morning of the next day. Even before these developments, official efforts were being made by Congress and the Rhode Island legislature to "hush up" the disagreement; however, public opinion was incensed at what was considered betrayal by the French.

By August 28, the three most seriously damaged of d'Estaing's vessels were in the inner harbor of Boston, while the remainder of the fleet took positions at Nantasket Road and his troops began fortifying a number of the islands in Boston Bay. Public welcomes, formal dinners, friendly visits by local notables, and favorable articles in Boston newspapers all ignored the recent unpleasantness and emphasized amity with the French. Sullivan himself modified his position and downplayed his disagreement with d'Estaing. Official cordiality, however, could not eradicate popular resentment.

During the evening of September 8, a dockside riot broke out around a bakery set up by the French; when they intervened to restore order, two French naval officers were wounded, one of whom died a week later. Local authorities offered a reward for information on the perpetrators and blamed the violence on British deserters serving on an American privateer, although no one was ever charged. Again, American officials attempted to minimize the importance of the affair and the Boston press largely ignored it. For his part, d'Estaing was conciliatory; he and his officers continued to participate prominently in various public festivities and social gatherings. Although formal appearances were to the contrary, friction continued and other incidents occurred between Americans and French, although on a smaller, less violent scale. When d'Estaing's forces departed for the West Indies on November 4, few Americans sincerely regretted it.

On the whole, the siege of Newport and its aftermath augured ill for cooperation between the two new allies. *See also*: Rhode Island campaign of 1778; Rhode Island in the American Revolution

Sam Scott

REFERENCES

Paul F. Dearden, "The Siege of Newport: Inauspicious Dawn of Alliance," *Rhode Island History*, 29 (1970):17–35; Frederick Mackenzie, *Diary of Frederick Mackenzie*, 2 vols. (1930) rpt. 1968; Fitz-Henry Smith, Jr., "The French at Boston during the Revolution, With Particular Reference to the French Fleets and the Fortifications in the Harbor," *The Bostonian Society Publications, 10*(1913):9–75; William C. Stinchcombe, *The American Revolution and the French Alliance* (1969); Charles P. Whittemore, *A General of the Revolution: John Sullivan of New Hampshire* (1961).

Newtown, New York, Battle of

See Sullivan-Clinton Expedition to Iroquois Country.

New Windsor, New York, Cantonment

See Newburgh Conspiracy.

New York City, British Occupation of

In 1775, when the British government decided to evacuate Boston, it also made preparations to send a large army to occupy New York

City. New York's harbor was the best on the east coast and would afford the Royal Navy a safe haven during winter as well as an ideal staging area from which to harass other coastal communities. The Hudson River provided excellent lines of communication with both Canada and the American interior. There were also, or so it was believed, large numbers of Loyalist residents who could be induced to fight on the British side. Moreover, the city's hinterland had valuable stores of grain, fresh vegetables, animal fodder, fuel, horses, and other resources that the military would need for its operations against the rebels.

The British navy anchored off Staten Island, New York, on June 29, 1776, and the army subdued the island three days later. On August 22, General Sir William Howe, commander-in-chief of the British army in America, landed 15,000 troops on nearby Long Island. On August 27 he handily defeated Washington at the Battle of Long Island and quickly reestablished royal authority over that island and its residents. On September 15, Howe also captured New York City; and on November 16, he seized Fort Washington and thereby gained control over the whole of Manhattan Island.

It was a good start. Nevertheless, if the British were to persuade residents to cooperate wholeheartedly in the war effort, they needed to pursue a policy of reconciliation and win the minds and hearts of the inhabitants living in British-occupied New York. Regrettably, the military failed from the outset to pay sufficient heed to civil-military relations. Instead of immediately restoring civilian rule, it stretched the meaning and intent of the Prohibitory Act of 1775 and used it to justify instituting martial law. In September 1776, Howe and his brother, Admiral Richard Lord Howe, the king's Commissioners for Restoring Peace, reappointed William Tryon governor of New York; but they commanded him to keep the civil government dormant, thereby leaving direction of public affairs in military hands. As a result, the elections, held every fall to choose members of the city council, were suspended during the occupation. Other municipal officials also ceased functioning, and no provision was made for trial by jury. David Mathews, who had been major since February 1776, was permitted to retain his title, but real power was turned over to a military commandant who took charge of city affairs. In December 1777, Major

General James Robertson, who was commandant at that time, appointed a city vestry, composed of civilians, to assist the poor, rent houses in town, and oversee street cleaning and lamp lighting. In May 1778 his successor, Major General Valentine Jones, established a quasi-civilian body, the Department of Police, with authority to maintain law and order and to regulate the local economy.

Inhabitants in the adjacent rural areas of British-occupied New York also suffered from what one sympathetic observer termed "a thorough Despotism." For example, the people of Queens County, which was located on Long Island, petitioned Tryon in October 1776 for the reinstitution of civil government, but he was powerless to act. Moreover, even though the Howes demanded that martial law remain in effect, they neglected to establish a consistent policy of enforcement in the county. In matters pertaining to the war's conduct, Colonel Archibald Hamilton, commander of the county militia, had general oversight. Not only were the militia officers under his direction; so too were the local justices of the peace. The latter were likewise required to aid the Commissary, Quartermaster, and Barrackmaster departments whenever necessary. In the beginning, justices on occasion summoned residents together to ascertain how the army's demands were to be satisfied, but by 1779 decisions were also being reached at meetings of the justices and militia officers, who then enforced what they had decided upon. Surprisingly, most of the prewar governmental institutions in the county continued operating. The towns held their yearly meetings and elected local officials. The county board of supervisors still convened; the mortgage office stayed opened; and land conveyances were recorded. A noncombatant could not sue a soldier, but the Queens County Court of Common Pleas adjudicated civil disputes until 1779, and justices of the peace discharged at least some of their lawful responsibilities. However, local officials could not interfere with military operations or question British authority. In sum, they had become collaborators who could with impunity be ignored or overruled.

The Howes realized that promoting reconciliation was a vital part of the war effort. But they prohibited the restoration of civil authority in 1776, because they assumed that the conquest of New York City would result in the prompt demise of the rebellion throughout the province and that they should await that moment to act. In fact, Howe was so certain of success in 1776 that he neglected to mobilize local Loyalists. However, even after it became obvious that hostilities would persist for at least another year, the Howes continued to find excuses for not ending martial law. They claimed, for example, that civil government would only be beneficial if it were restored to the entire province at the same time, so that the legislature could be called into session. Responsible both for waging the war and winning the peace, they evidently determined that the former was the more important objective. Reviving civil authority would impede prosecution of the war, imperil a quick victory, and possibly impair their reputations. Nonetheless, the need to quell a rebellion 3,000 miles from home, the demands that the army made on noncombatants for assistance, and the inability of civilian authorities to check military abuses ultimately culminated in the alienation of the local population and in pleas by area residents for the reinstitution of civilian rule.

New York City merchants were among the first to complain. Although they profited during the occupation from army contracts, privateering, and smuggling, they were still angered by the way British authorities regulated trade. The Prohibitory Act permitted traders to import goods from Britain but prohibited them from exporting any merchandise whatsoever without a license from either the commander-in-chief or the king's Commissioners for Restoring Peace. As events turned out, few permits were issued during the first years of the war. Moreover, no ship could depart the harbor until its captain had received authorization to load the vessel, had provided authorities with a sworn statement enumerating the types and quantities of goods to be shipped, and had obtained a certificate from the Superintendent of Imports and Exports declaring that all regulations established by the commander-in-chief had been obeyed. Similar requirements were in effect for small craft plying the waters between Manhattan, Staten, and Long islands. Although these procedures were not always strictly enforced, failure to abide by any of them could result in seizure of the ship and its cargo. Beginning in September 1778 merchants were permitted to export wares to Britain, but the rules regulating commerce necessarily became both more numerous and more onerous.

Housing, of course, was another problem. Although perhaps as much as 90 percent of the population evacuated New York City before Howe recaptured it, the arrival of about 30,000 British soldiers and a large contingent of Loyalist refugees quickly overtaxed the city's ability to accommodate them. Moreover, a fire that broke out in town on the night of September 20, 1776, destroyed about one-quarter of the housing stock. Howe consequently confiscated every building in the city owned by people in rebellion and authorized the barrackmaster general to seize any vacant house or store that could be employed in the king's service. The real estate so appropriated was estimated to be worth £575,000. Complicating matters was the fact that the buildings required for army use had, as much as possible, to be centralized in a specific geographic locale so they could be defended against sabotage. In consequence, the military was also given the first choice of dwellings and warehouses throughout the city. Local Tories, as a result, were often evicted from their homes and property, sometimes for the convenience of an officer who already had another residence. Inadequately compensated for their losses, the Loyalists soon became discontented.

The situation eased somewhat as time passed, and most of the soldiers were transferred to northern Manhattan, Staten Island, and Queens County. But that development only alienated people in the rural areas. In winter, troops were frequently quartered in private residences. An army officer and a community leader would visit each home to determine how many redcoats were to be billeted there. Ten or twelve soldiers were usually boarded off in a section of the dwelling, and their treatment of inhabitants often caused consternation. Farmers had to lock their animals in the barn or house to forestall thievery by redcoats, who were always on the prowl for food. The boredom of military life also led to frequent bouts of drunkenness and the destruction of property.

In July 1780 Philip Livingston was named Superintendent of Derelict Properties on Long Island and was ordered to seize the lands of absentee rebels, which were to be allocated, whenever possible, to refugee families. Confiscated property also could be rented out, and the proceeds were earmarked for the support of destitute Loyalist refugees. In Queens County, for example, Livingston assigned 2,807 acres, the land of more than 40 residents, to 468 refugees. Ten other estates were leased to raise relief funds. Unfortunately, not only was favoritism displayed toward particular lessees in the rent they were charged, but the superintendent also exceeded his authority by appropriating the property of persons who were not rebels. Because aggrieved property owners could not testify in their own behalf, they had no legal recourse. In the end, Livingston's abuse of power only persuaded civilians that the military was insisting upon martial law so that royal officials could engage in corruption without fear of prosecution in the civil courts.

Supplying the army, Loyalist refugees, and civilians with food caused as many headaches as the housing shortage. The largest portion of the foodstuffs was shipped to New York City from Britain and Ireland. However, provisions were also acquired by dispatching foraging parties into enemy territory, by participating in illegal trade with Americans, and by purchasing supplies from the rural areas under British control. Tragically, the city frequently experienced shortages of food, and noncombatants were the first to suffer. The cost of living shot up 300 percent during the war, and the commander-in-chief was compelled not only to set the prices but also to determine how much food each family could buy. Although the victuals transported from Europe were meant for the soldiers, military officials were sometimes forced to sell rations to civilians to spare them undue distress.

The rural counties of British-occupied New York also suffered because of corruption in the Commissary Department. When American forces fled Long Island in August 1776, they abandoned cattle that they had impounded from local residents. Although Howe announced that these animals would be given back to their rightful owners, only the cows and lean calves were actually returned. The Commissary Department appropriated the rest but promised that residents would be reimbursed for their property. However, the owners were later denied payment. Commissary officials cursed a few for being rebels, threatened some with jail, and informed others that recompense must come from the Americans. The department then billed the Treasury for the animals, and royal officials pocketed the money.

Similar abuses persisted throughout the war. Commissary officials at times employed intimidation to seize supplies without payment or at prices below those established by the commander-in-chief; the Crown nonetheless paid the higher fixed price. Little imagination was required to falsify financial records in order to defraud the government. Commissary employees often compelled inhabitants to sign blank receipts to secure payment for victuals the army had appropriated; if a farmer refused, he was not paid. Corrupt officials then made a profit by writing in inflated sums of money before they handed the receipts over to military authorities for reimbursement. Such practices not only cost the Treasury money but convinced residents that the British and not the Americans were the real enemy.

The effort to furnish New York City with fuel for heating and cooking followed a pattern similar to that just outlined for foodstuffs. At first, uncultivated land near town and wood cut from the estates of absentee rebels, supplemented by coal from Cape Breton Island, largely met British needs. But as the war dragged on and New York experienced a few harsh winters, the price of fuel increased dramatically, and occupation officials were required to set prices. Again, the civilian population suffered the most, for the Barrackmaster Department impounded private supplies of all types for the army's use. Eventually, military authorities were forced to turn to Staten and Long islands to satisfy the city's insatiable demand for fuel, and the results were predictable. Licensed contractors laid bare entire farms with little concern for future needs. The barrackmaster exercised little supervision over these licensees, who at times cut their quotas from the most accessible land without regard for ownership. Farmers protested. But the lumbermen were gone and officials apathetic, for the Barrackmaster Department was sharing in the spoils. Wood acquired from rebel land was free, except for cutting and transportation costs. Unprincipled officials, however, sold these supplies to the government at the market price.

Similar tales could be recounted about how royal officials requisitioned other kinds of supplies for the military's use. Greed was certainly a cause for the mismanagement that was so evident, but so too was the negative attitude toward Americans that so many British military officers shared. Some resented the drubbing their army had suffered at Lexington and Concord and took advantage of every opportunity afforded them at New York to get revenge. Others were convinced that all Americans were rebels and treated them accordingly. Moreover, army officers came from the British upper class and believed the colonists to be social inferiors, greedy, and ill-bred. As one officer explained it, Americans were such "a Leveling, underbred, Artful, Race of people that we Cannot Associate with them. Void of principle, their whole Conversation is turn'd on their Interest, and as to gratitude they have no such word in their dictionary and either cant or wont understand what it means." Under the circumstances, officers had little sympathy for the demands made by New Yorkers that they be paid a fair price for the supplies the military appropriated and that they be treated with the respect due them as subjects of the king. In short, army officers remained ignorant of, or insensitive to, the advantages that would have accrued to their own side if they had only cultivated the support of Loyalists and neutrals by pursuing a policy of reconciliation. Not only did officers mistreat residents, but their distaste for Americans also filtered down to the rank and file and provided ordinary soldiers with all the justification they needed to abuse and plunder the civilian population. As a result, public dissatisfaction with the army increased over time, and demands for the restoration of civil government grew more incessant.

Burgoyne's defeat at Saratoga in October 1777 and fear of a Franco-American alliance finally persuaded the British government to pay greater heed to the war's political dimension. As a result, in February 1778 it established a new peace commission headed by Frederick Howard, fifth earl of Carlisle. Although the Carlisle Commission had authority to terminate martial law in British-occupied New York, it refused to do so, for the military adamantly opposed the idea. However, because of their experiences in America, two of the commissioners, on their return home, argued before a cabinet council that civilian rule should be restored. Lord George Germain, who was secretary of state for the American Department, concurred, and in May 1779 the government named General James Robertson governor of New York. He was directed to revive civil government as soon as General Sir Henry Clinton, who had replaced Howe as army commander-in-chief, declared New York to be at the king's peace. Moreover, in July 1779, the ministry appointed Clinton sole peace com-

missioner and instructed him to restore civil authority in New York. To meet criticisms of military misconduct, a civilian-military council was created to advise him. However, it had no authority to act independently.

Unfortunately for the government, Clinton opposed its new civil policy. First, he was concerned, like Howe before him, that civilian officials might impede military operations. Second, he was afraid that once the civil law courts had reopened, civilians would begin to file suits against officers and enlisted men for the crimes they had perpetrated over the past several years. As a result, when Robertson was sworn into office in March 1780, the commander-in-chief would not allow him to revive civil government. In fact, Clinton confided to a friend in Britain two months later that he would resign rather than end martial law. Finally, in June, he asked Germain if he could "partially" restore civil authority, for "to open the Courts of Civil Law would increase the Confusion, and be productive of many other bad Consequences. In the months that followed, Robertson won permission to perform his civil duties in a military capacity under orders issued by Clinton.

In July 1780, for example, the governor, with Clinton's approbation, appointed George Duncan Ludlow superintendent of the newly created Court of Police on Long Island. The superintendent had power to maintain law and order; and all other civilian officials on the island were required to assist him and obey his decrees. Although Robertson extolled the Court of Police as a partial restoration of civil government, it represented nothing more than martial law under a new guise. Trial by jury was not restored, and the superintendent was directly responsible to military authorities.

Nor did corruption end. Robertson and Ludlow reportedly began profiting from the new arrangement by taking control of the smuggling going on between Long Island and New England. Both Howe and Clinton had issued proclamations prohibiting the export of goods out of British-occupied New York without a license from the Superintendent of Imports and Exports. Requests for these permits eventually became so numerous that each applicant had to submit a recommendation corroborating his loyalty to the Crown. Although permits could not be issued for trade with areas in rebellion, an illicit commerce with New England existed, and the governor evidently wanted to capitalize on it. He therefore had the power of issuing recommendations vested in Ludlow, who then began assessing an unauthorized fee for the recommendations. These now also served as unofficial permits for the illegal trade with New England.

In the end, the debate over whether civil authority should be restored in New York deteriorated into a personal feud between Clinton and Robertson. Each sought to place responsibility for the failure of the government's civil policy on the other. Although the governor was illegally profiting by the continuation of martial law, he publicly blamed the commander-in-chief. Clinton, however, strongly suspected that Robertson's enthusiasm for civil government would persist only so long as his own opposition continued. So certain of this was he that he artfully offered in 1782, after the British defeat at Yorktown, to reestablish civilian rule in order to expose the governor's duplicity. Clinton believed himself vindicated when the governor's Council recommended that martial law be continued: reviving civil government would necessitate calling the Assembly, and that step might embarrass the government if it decided, because of Yorktown, to evacuate New York.

Even if civil government had been restored in 1782, it was too late to win the minds and hearts of the people. It is true that a large number of Tories fled New York City either during the Revolution or at its end, but it is impossible to determine what percentage of these people had been prewar residents of what became British-occupied New York between 1776 and 1783. In Queens County, one area for which there is some hard evidence, only about 5 to 6 percent of the prewar population became Loyalist exiles. However, those whom remained behind in 1783, when the British evacuated the city and the surrounding areas, quickly made their peace with the new state government. No "fifth column" dedicated to reunion with the Mother Country ever emerged in New York. The long hard years of military occupation had prepared Loyalists and neutrals alike for American independence.
See also: Robertson, James

Joseph S. Tiedemann

REFERENCES

Oscar Theodore Barck, Jr., *New York City during the War for Independence with Special Reference to the Period of British Occupation* (1931); Milton M. Klein, "An Experiment That Failed: General James Robertson and Civil Government in British New York, 1779–1783," *New York History*, 61 (1980):229–54; Milton M. Klein and Ronald W. Howard, eds., *The Twilight of British Rule in Revolutionary America: The New York Letter Book of General James Robertson, 1780–1783* (1983); Philip Ranlet, *The New York Loyalists* (1986); and Joseph S. Tiedemann, "Patriots by Default: Queens County, New York, and the British Army, 1776–1783," *William and Mary Quarterly*, 43 (1986):35–63.

New York Continentals

On June 14, 1775, in response to requests from Massachusetts Patriot leaders, the Continental Congress adopted and took command of the New England troops that encircled Boston. This act created the first American standing army, the Continental Army, under the "General and Commander-in-chief of all the Continental Forces," George Washington of Virginia. The call by Congress for each of the rebellious states to raise regiments for service was quickly answered by New York, which had units on the way to the Canadian frontier by the end of July. During the course of the Revolutionary War, the army raised by New York, the New York Continental Line, was transformed from a disorganized, motley group of farmers, laborers, and artisans into a respected and disciplined fighting force, among the best and most efficient in the Continental Army.

By August 1775, New York had raised over 2,000 troops for a six-month tour of duty. The men who enlisted in the army had little or no military experience, except for what was required by local militia duty, and for the first few months of the war, they received little additional training. Only those who were "able-bodied, healthy and a good marcher" and of high "moral character" were to be enlisted, but it is clear that these strict guidelines were not always followed. The initial terms of enlistment could not be considered very enticing—53 shillings and 2 pence per month pay (about two pounds sterling) with a 10 pence allowance for those recruits who supplied their own arms. In addition, each soldier was to receive a canteen, coat, felt hat, tomahawk, and knapsack. Although the initial congressional plan had called for New York to raise 3,000 men, the actual number enlisted was closer to 2,000. These men were organized into four regiments under the command of Colonels James

Clinton, Alexander McDougall, Goose Van Shaik, and James Holmes. Each regiment was organized into 10 companies of 72 men with two lieutenants and one captain in command.

Within a few weeks of the intial muster, the 1st New York Regiment was sent north to participate in the proposed invasion of Canada. Like their New England counterparts, these young New York recruits had received virtually no training, and their only real brush with military discipline was their forced march from New York City to Albany. Their entrance to camp was underwhelming. Major General Philip Schuyler, commander of the invasion force, while commenting on a group of deserters stated that "if those who are gone are like some that remain, we have gained by their going off." Schuyler's comments were premature. Although the New York soldiers of 1775 certainly paled in comparison to their British opposition and even to the New York Line of the late 1770s, these men were certainly high in spirit and energy, if not discipline and organization.

On August 28, under the command of General Richard Montgomery, the invasion force left Fort Ticonderoga. The troops consisted primarily of the 1st New York Regiment and David Waterbury's Connecticut Regiment. The invading army became unexpectanly bogged down in the siege of St. Johns Fort, and it did not reach Montreal until November 13. On that day, the city surrendered after offering no resistance. The destination of the invading force remained Quebec, which was under the command of Governor Guy Carleton. On December 2, Montgomery laid siege to Quebec, but with the onset of winter, plans were approved to attack the city. On December 31, during a blinding snowstorm, Montgomery led the 1st New York Regiment in a frontal assault on the city, which was beaten back. Among the first killed was Montgomery, who came to be lauded as a martyr of the New York Line.

At the beginning of December, before the assault on Quebec, the enlistment period for the troops had expired. Although most of the men were persuaded to reenlist for an additional six months, this problem plagued the Continental Army during the first year of its existence. The Continental Army had no declared aims or firmly set organization. The New York Line was initially recruited to safeguard and defend its own territory—New York. Many soldiers were alarmed to discover that they would be serving in an armed expedition against Canada. Furthermore with terms of enlistment set for only six months, there was no time for adequate training or long-range goals. Additionally, there was little or no opportunity to build a cadre of veteran troops. Here it is important to recall that colonial Americans had no experience in serving in a regular army. The most respected republican theorists of the day, such as the radical Whig thinkers and the commonwealth man, repeatedly warned of the threats that a standing army served to a good republican citizenry. These threats were very real and much discussed, and explain much of the reluctance on the part of colonial Americans to sanction and support a standing army.

By April 1776, with the second period of enlistment set to expire, most of the existing New York Line felt that they had done their duty and refused to reenlist. These men had seen combat and had taken part in the exhausting and unsuccessful siege on Quebec. Having originally planned to serve only six months, they ended up serving between ten and twelve months. Many of these men were farmers and agricultural laborers and were not trained as professionals. Regardless of their ardor for the cause, their enthusiasm did not include fighting against the world's best trained army. Much of the blame for the inability to maintain a cohesive fighting force in New York must rest with the Provincial Congress and, ultimately, the Continental Congress.

In January 1776 Congress resolved that New York should raise a new unit for service in Canada. Known as Nicholson's New York Regiment, this detachment was commanded by Colonel John Nicholson and was composed primarily of recruits from the failed Canadian invasion. In March, the Continental Congress asked for four new regiments, the 2nd Continental Establishment. These four New York regiments were organized to serve with the main Continental Army, not on the Canadian front with Nicholson's Regiment. These regiments were raised to serve until the end of 1776, which, of course, would simply necessitate a third major reorganization at the end of the year. There were two reasons that Congress called for this. First, Congress simply did not foresee the conflict lasting beyond the year's end. Second, and equally important, it was very hard to enlist recruits for longer than a few months at a time. These recruits received little more training than the New York Line of 1775, although they saw considerably more action as a central part of Washington's Continental Army, at Long Island, Manhattan, and Morristown.

In June 1776 Congress authorized the 5th New York Regiment to be organized under the command of Lewis DuBois. Unlike the other regiments of the New York Line, the 5th New York was ordered to serve with the northern army, primarily in upstate New York. Most of the regiment's service was in garrison duty in forts along the frontier and on the Hudson. In October 1777, General Henry Clinton's expedition up the Hudson smashed DuBois's regiment at Fort Montgomery, capturing most of the troops. This was probably the single most important defeat in the history of the New York Line.

In late 1776 the Continental Congress was forced by military necessity to organize an army to last the duration of the conflict. Recruiting began in late 1776, with four additional New York units to be organized around the four regiments of 1776. The standard term of service for the new regiment was three years, not one year or just six months. Congress offered a bounty of $20 and a 100-acre grant of land, but it was still difficult to obtain recruits since civilians trying to avoid military service were offering higher bounties than the Continental Army.

The four New York regiments reorganized in 1777 served through the war until 1781. These regiments are the first that can be considered an army in the traditional sense, with long periods of enlistment and high levels of proficiency in drill and combat. For much of 1777, parts of the 1st New York Line were involved in garrison duty on the western frontier, while the 2nd, 4th, and rest of the 1st were stationed with Washington's main Continental Army. The 3rd New York Line and scattered battalions from the other three regiments composed a large part of the northern army under Schuyler and later General Horatio Gates. This regiment, and several other New York detachments were integral in fighting and defeating the British at Saratoga.

After Saratoga, the northern army dwindled in size and significance, and most of the New York army was put under the command of Washington. The winter of 1777–1778, known best for the fierce winter at Valley Forge, was also the first truly organized training period for the New York Continental Line. It was at Valley Forge that Baron von Steuben served as training officer, instructing the recruits in the European training skills, drills, parade, and battle formations. Steuben's methods, however, were not those of Prussian discipline that so many historians have described, but an adaptation of this to the American situation. Continentals were not like the European armies who could be commanded and held in check only through fear. The greatest motivation among American soldiers was that of self-determination, autonomy, and public spiritedness, and von Steuben used these ideas in his plan of discipline. One of his main changes in discipline was to have Continental officers train their own men to avoid distancing the troops from their officers. Officers were to gain the love and loyalty of their men not through informality but through diligence and kindness. The only type of punishment von Steuben prescribed in his *Regulations for the Order and Discipline of the Troops of the United States* was confinement to quarters—not the 500 lashes promoted by Washington. The New York Line did not master von Steuben's European maneuvers and drill until near the end of the war—they were simply unaccustomed to it and were not certain of its importance.

Throughout 1778–1779, the same problems continued to plague the New York Line. The worst of these was supply problems. Proper food, clothing, and ammunition were always in short supply. Low morale and plundering by the troops often resulted from these conditions. Little could be done about the first except to win battles, but the second could be, and often was, dealt with severely by Continental authorities. An additional problem was soldiers' pay, which was continually in arrears. Even when the soldiers were paid, it was often in inflated Continental currency, which had depreciated to the point that it was virtually worthless. Not only did enlistees suffer during the war, however, so too did officers. Many of the officers in the New York Continental Line held their position as a result of patronage on the part of some benefactor. This led to often violent jealousies among army officers who felt that they were being bypassed or overlooked. The number of fights and duels among officers was astounding, and this pattern continued right up until the end of the war.

However, 1778 and 1779 did see military successes for the New York Line. Although the Battle of Monmouth was generally indecisive, at the end of the day-long battle, the Continental Army held the field. The New York Line achieved great military success under the command of General John Sullivan in his expedition to destroy Indian settlements in western New York. The year 1780 witnessed long periods of garrison duty for the 1st and 2nd regiments, one of the most tedious and tiring aspects of military duty. However, during 1780 the New York Line underwent substantial reorganization, when the 3rd and 4th New York were incorporated into the 1st and 2nd regiments, respectively. It was in this newly reorganized form that the renamed New York Brigade was incorporated into General Washington's main Continental Army. By this time, the New York Line was only about one-third the size it had been in 1776, but most other states suffered similar problems in recruitment. During 1781 the New York Line left the northeast for the first time during the war, and proceeded with Washington to the Chesapeake and Yorktown.

The New York Line saw very limited action after Yorktown. As enlistments ran out, no new efforts were made to recruit in great numbers. The only major action in New York between Yorktown and the Peace of Paris took place in the Mohawk Valley, and even this was just sporadic activity, although several hundred regulars of the New York Line were employed on raiding expeditions against the Iroquois. The line was gradually disestablished throughout the 1780s along with most of the Continental establishments.

Much has been written recently about the composition of the Continental Army. Many historians have asserted that the Continental Army was made up of foreign recruits—men who were poor and landless and joined because of economic necessity. For the New York Line, in 1775 and 1776 at least, this was not true. An analysis of available muster rolls has determined that almost 80 percent of the New York troops were American born and close to 50 percent were born in New York. The soldiers were young; over half of the recruits were under 24. In the first years of the war, the recruits seem to have been a fairly accurate representation of New York society. However, after 1776, this changed substantially, as the New York Line was becoming composed of the poorest elements in New York. Quite simply, farmers and artisans could not afford to join the army for an entire year, let alone for a three-year enlistment. Agricultural and urban laborers, however, probably found this to be just as profitable to working in depressed New York.

Why these young men joined the army to fight is, however, a more complex problem. The lack of economic opportunities in many New York areas probably accelerated the enlistment process and, at certain times, swelled the ranks. However, this should not overshadow the Revolutionary commitment the Continentals shared, their belief in republicanism and in the independence movement.

Thomas S. Wermuth

REFERENCES

Fred Berg, *Encyclopedia of the Continental Army* (1974); T.W. Egly, *History of the First New York Regiment, 1775–1783* (1981); Mark Lender and James Kirby Martin, *A Respectable Army: Military Origins of the Republic* (1982); Charles Royster, *A Revolutionary People at War* (1979).

New York Fire (September 21, 1776)

On September 12, 1776, Washington made the fateful decision to cut his losses and to withdraw his defeated army from New York City. The city was in chaos; thousands of Patriots fled, and their houses and shops were looted by rejoicing Loyalists. In the early morning of September 21 a fire broke out and, fanned by a high wind, it consumed nearly one-third of the city. It has never been conclusively proved that the fire was the result of arson, but British and Loyalists alike were convinced that the rebels had made one final attempt to turn their triumph into a Pyrrhic victory.

British authorities arrested about 200 suspects over the next few weeks, trying to pin the crime on "New-England incendiaries" such as one Captain Fellows, who was carrying matches and a large sum of money when apprehended. Patriot leaders, including Washington, expressed satisfaction at the news of the fire, but there is no evidence that they ordered it.

In October 1783, in the last months of the British occupation, Sir Guy Carleton investigated the fire again and turned up ample evidence that it had been arson. But seven years had passed; the principal witnesses were gone, and stories about the fire had been augmented into legends. And Carleton interviewed only Loyalists.

Tom Martin

REFERENCES

Catherine S. Crary, *The Price of Loyalty: Tory Writings from the Revolutionary Era* (1973); Philip Ranlet, *The New York Loyalists* (1986).

New York, Frontier Warfare in (1777–1782)

Western New York was in many ways the true cockpit of the war. British-held Canada and the Old Northwest lay beyond the frontier, and the border region itself was occupied by the unpredictable and volatile Iroquois Confederation and its allies. The vulnerable line of the Hudson and Lake Champlain was a natural highway between Montreal and New York, and it divided New England from the rest of the colonies. At the outbreak of the war, much of this region was included within Tryon County, a vast principality under the virtual control of the Johnson family. The county extended from near Albany north to the St. Lawrence and west to the Iroquois country. It was forested and was sparsely settled by migrant New Englanders and recent arrivals from the Scottish Highlands and the German Palatinate—all of them fiercely independent. Relations with the Indians were generally good, and the majority of the settlers were Loyalists. Before Lieutenant Colonel Barry St. Leger's defeat at Fort Stanwix, the nerve center of the region was Johnson Hall (near present Amsterdam), but as early as June 1775 the Johnsons and their retainers prudently had moved west to Niagara. During the American invasion of Canada in 1776 Colonel John Butler was slowly organizing the tribes and the displaced Tories into a fighting force at Fort Niagara. Only the Oneidas and Tuscaroras supported the rebels; throughout much of this period they served as a buffer between the Loyalist raiders and the Patriot settlements.

The great council held at Oswego in July 1777 decided the region's fate for the next five years. The 300-year-old Iroquois Confederation was broken, but most of the tribes followed the Mohawk war chief Joseph Brant to the British side. At the same time General John Burgoyne attempted his invasion of New York via the Lake Champlain–Hudson route. St. Leger's expedition out of Oswego, intended to reinforce Burgoyne, was turned back at Fort Stanwix and Oriskany in August. Then Burgoyne was defeated at Saratoga (October 1777), the diplomatic turning point of the war. As a result, more Loyalist settlers fled to Niagara, and Patriot forces took control of the Mohawk Valley. Those settlers who remained behind provided grain for the Patriot army. But after Saratoga, the military situation on the New York frontier deteriorated into a series of raids and counterraids, with the farmers as targets, and with the Indians often playing the decisive role. This period, lasting into 1782, is known as the "Border Warfare" in New York.

On the Loyalist side, three major forces now began to coalesce. Sir John Johnson, heir of the "Mohawk baronet," organized his Royal Greens regiment from among the refugees at Niagara who had been his tenants and retainers. His rival John Butler, another great landowner and former deputy Indian superintendent for Canada, raised Butler's Rangers at Niagara. Joseph Brant commanded the loyalty of hundreds of Iroquois warriors, and he often fought alongside Johnson or Butler. In addition, Brant had a small but fanatic band of white followers, known as Brant's Volunteers. Together these forces, with many irregulars and sometimes supported by British troops, harried the frontier from the St. Lawrence to Kentucky over the next four years.

The Wyoming Valley is a segment of the Susquehanna Valley, including modern Wilkes-Barre, and was originally claimed by both Pennsylvania and Connecticut. On July 3, 1778, the border warfare began in earnest. A force of some 1,000 Indians and Loyalists under John Butler descended upon Fort Wintermoot and fought a short, fierce battle with the New York militia, who were outnumbered three to one. The Patriots were scattered, and during the night of July 3–4 a number of women, children, and other noncombatants were slaughtered. Much of the killing was done by Senecas under Sayengaraghta, who believed their lands had been stolen by whites. According to Butler, 227 scalps and only five prisoners were taken. Some of those who escaped died later in the wilderness from exposure to the elements. Others made it to the village of Minisink, where they described the massacre. More than 1,000 houses had been burned and most of the cattle were stolen. The atrocity stories were played up in lurid detail by the Patriot press; later the Scottish poet Thomas Campbell wrote a poem about the incident, "Gertrude of Wyoming." In particular, rumor blamed Joseph Brant for the massacre; but he was 80 miles away at Unadilla. Years later Campbell apologized in person to Brant.

The Loyalists held the valley for a month, but withdrew when the militia regrouped and advanced up the Susquehanna. In September, a small Patriot force burned some Indian villages on the east branch of the river, and it recovered some of the loot taken from their Wyoming homesteads.

In the meantime, Brant was active. His Mohawk warriors destroyed the tiny settlement of Andrewstown (Andrustown, now Jordanville) and Springfield on July 18. The purpose of the raid was to secure provisions; it had no military significance. But it added to the dimension of terror on the frontier and caused another wave of refugees. Brant then lay low for some weeks, hoping for reinforcements from Butler before he attacked the large village of German Flats. The help did not come but Brant attacked anyway, on September 17. Scots had seen him coming. When Brant reached the town, he found that the inhabitants were defending themselves inside Forts Dayton and Herkimer. The Mohawks destroyed the settlement and seized cattle but they were unable to capture these posts.

In early October, Pennsylvania troops under Colonel Thomas Hartley destroyed the important Seneca towns of Tioga and Oquaga, in retaliation for the Wyoming incident. These Senecas had not been at Wyoming and were enraged by what they considered an unprovoked attack. They now joined John Butler's men, who were preparing another major raid. The attack on Cherry Valley was not merely punitive; it was part of Butler's strategy to isolate Fort Stanwix and to regain control of the Mohawk Valley. Butler's son, Walter Butler, led the Rangers out of Niagara, and he joined forces with Brant's Mohawks at Geneseo in late October. The raiders required several weeks to traverse the 200 miles to Cherry Valley, a rich but sparsely settled area east of Lake Otsego. The Senecas joined them en route. On the morning of November 11, in the wake of a heavy snowfall, the Tories descended on the unsuspecting settlers, who numbered no more than 300. In addition to

the Continental soldiers at nearby Fort Alden who were slaughtered, more than 30 women and children were murdered. Butler, an arrogant young man who pictured himself as a great commander, proved unable to stop the Indians from massacring the noncombatants. In succeeding months rumor blamed "the Monster Brant" for the killings, but in fact he had intervened to save the lives of many civilians. One of Butler's Rangers later wrote that the Indians "exerted the most horrid barbarities, the blody seen is almost past discription."

The Cherry Valley raid was a success in that it secured Loyalist control of the Mohawk region. But it also convinced the Americans that a massive counterattack was essential. Accordingly, Sullivan's expedition was planned during that winter and was set in motion in May 1779.

During the winter of 1778–1779 public outrage against the border raids mounted. Washington had been unable to send regular troops for the defense of the New York frontier, but by the end of the winter the military situation had stabilized and plans were made for a major offensive against the Loyalists and their Iroquois allies. Washington even sent questionnaires to the officers in the region to try to ascertain the exact state of affairs. After General Horatio Gates turned down the opportunity to command, the leadership of the expedition went to Major General John Sullivan. An army of 2,500 was assembled at Easton, Pennsylvania, in May, and on June 18 it began its advance up the Wyoming Valley. Observing the remains of the previous summer's destruction by the Indians and Loyalists, the Continentals became grimly determined to end the Tory threat once and for all. A few weeks earlier, Brigadier General James Clinton (based at Canajoharie) had led 1,500 men on a successful raid from Fort Stanwix through the Onondaga country to Oswego and back, and then southeast to the portages between Canajoharie and Lake Otsego, where he waited for Sullivan for seven weeks. The plan was for a joint westward thrust, perhaps as far as Niagara. Sullivan reached the ruined Seneca village of Tioga on August 11 and built a small fort there. On August 13, he burned the lower Chemung settlements. Throughout that week, Sullivan's forces were shadowed by Joseph Brant, who was trying desperately to assemble a large enough force to challenge the Americans. Likewise on August 11, Colonel Daniel Brodhead set out from Pittsburgh with 600 men, hoping to join Sullivan for the attack on Niagara. Claiming later that his guides did not know the way, Brodhead turned back after burning ten villages and was back in Pittsburgh the same day that Clinton joined Sullivan.

The Indians and the Loyalists, in the meantime, were thrown into confusion by rumors. News came that a French army had captured Vincennes, and that Detroit was its next target. Brodhead's advance was reported, but it was not known in New York that he had turned back. The British authorities in Canada, though realizing that the rumors were exaggerated, did not know how to react to these threats. Apparently too far away from Butler that summer to be aware of the evolving defensive strategy against Sullivan, Brant nevertheless distracted the Americans on July 19 by raiding the village of Minisink, south of the Catskills. A battle was fought with the local militia, and Brant withdrew on July 22, cutting westward in front of Sullivan's line of advance.

By the third week of August, Brant's 800 Indians and Tories were assembled near Chemung and Newtown (Elmira), near where the Susquehanna enters Pennsylvania. He was determined to make a stand but had to wait for Butler's help. Butler had been delayed in Seneca country, but by August 28 he caught up with Brant. Butler's Rangers numbered only about 250 in addition to a handful of British regulars. Butler advised against attacking Sullivan, who now had about 4,000 men. But the Indians were already hastily throwing up breastworks, and the next morning Sullivan hit Newtown. Casualties in the decisive battle of Newtown were not heavy, but the Indians and Loyalists were scattered. The way was now clear for a leisurely advance north by the Patriots and then west through Iroquois country. During the next two weeks, Sullivan laid waste a broad stretch of territory south of the Finger Lakes and reached Genesee on September 14. The Loyalists had regrouped under Walter Butler, and they captured an advance party led by Lieutenant Thomas Boyd on September 13. Boyd and a sergeant were questioned by Butler and then they were tortured to death by the Indians.

Sullivan had now overextended his force, and when Brodhead did not appear, Sullivan knew that he could not march onto Niagara. As many observers have pointed out, this was a serious mistake. He had infuriated the Iroquois by devastating their heartland, but he left their military base at Niagara unscathed. Sullivan's withdrawal was as slow and destructive as his advance. He was back at Tioga by the end of the month. The Indians had been whipped to a new fury, and the reprisals were soon forthcoming.

Before the winter of 1779–1780 was over, the Loyalists, Indians, and British regulars had ravaged the Oneida nation and driven the survivors eastward as far as Schenectady. The American high command had hoped that Sullivan's expedition would frighten the Iroquois into making peace, but it now appeared that the purpose of the mission had backfired. A series of raids in March and April wiped out Skenesboro, Harpersfield, and Minisink (for the second time). Brant had hoped to reduce the important Upper Fort on the Schoharie Valley, but his captives told him (falsely) that it was garrisoned by 300 Continentals. A raid on Sacandaga failed, but on April 24, Cherry Valley was again put to the torch. All this was preliminary to a larger offensive under the command of Sir John Johnson, who led 400 volunteers and 200 Indians down the Mohawk in mid-May. He had approached unseen from Canada, by way of Crown Point.

On May 21, Johnson occupied the settlements around Johnstown. The next day, a party of Mohawks burned the village of Caughnawaga. Over the next several days, a number of small raids were launched out of Johnstown. On May 27 he set out for Crown Point, laden with prisoners, booty, and the families of many of his Loyalist volunteers.

Joseph Brant was then at Niagara, reassembling his forces. In June and July he moved across the scorched lands of the Six Nations, planning to pillage Oneida settlements. In August, with 500 men, he fell upon the village of Canajoharie and sacked it. Halting there, he then divided his men into seven small parties to attack Cherry Valley, German Flats, and other rebel towns where Oneidas had taken refuge. Then he headed back to Niagara. In September, he was at Oswego with Johnson. General Sir Frederick Haldimand, pleased with Johnson's May campaign, had ordered a follow-up, perhaps timed to coincide with Benedict Arnold's planned surrender of West Point. Brant joined forces with the Seneca chief Cornplanter and then met Johnson at Unadilla, creating a sizable force (estimates range from 800 to 1,500 men). On October 15, 16, and 17 this army swept through the Schoharie Valley, burning and pillaging, and it then moved on to Fort Hunter, where considerable property was destroyed. The next day Johnson advanced up both banks of the Mohawk, destroying farms and settlements between the fort and Canajoharie. Stopping briefly at Palatine, he crossed the Mohawk at Keder's Rifts and proceeded to Klock's Field (Fox's Mill), where the American pursuers caught up with Brant.

Upon learning of Johnson's advance, General Robert Van Rensselaer hastily assembled some 500 militia and set out in pursuit; Governor Clinton followed behind with reinforcements. Without waiting for Van Rensselaer, Colonel John Brown attacked Johnson's forces at Fort Paris in Stone Arabia with 130 men. Brown and 40 of his men were killed, and Johnson then burned Stone Arabia. In the meantime, Van Rensselaer was joined by 300 to 400 militia and 40 Oneidas under Colonel Lewis DuBois, bringing the Patriot forces to about 850. A night of confused fighting followed (October 19). The Tories withdrew toward Lake Onondaga, and luckily captured an American party that had been sent out from Fort Stanwix to burn the boats that the raiders had left on the lake. They were back at Oswego by October 26.

During October, British regulars out of Canada also harassed upper New England. The village of Royalton in the upper Connecticut Valley was partially destroyed by the 53rd Regiment. Approaching by way of Fort George, another contingent raided Ball's Town (Ballston) near Schenectady and harried the region north of Albany.

After escaping from the Continentals at Klock's Field, Brant and the Butlers wintered at Niagara. In the spring Brant went west to Detroit, and spent the summer of 1781 campaigning in the Ohio country. But before the snow had melted that spring, the Loyalists were back in the Mohawk country. Because the Oneida communities had all been destroyed and could no longer offer protection or warning, the valley was now particularly vulnerable. German Flats and Cherry Valley were raided yet again, Fort Stanwix suffered both fire and flood that spring, and two militia units were captured while trying to provision it. Accordingly the famous post was abandoned in May, but the Loyalists did not occupy it permanently.

In June, Colonel Marinus Willett, a veteran of the New York frontier, arrived with 400 fresh troops to defend the region. This proved to be an almost impossible task. There were too many small settlements scattered over too great an area, and the Indians or Tories could appear anywhere. Willett established his headquarters at Canajoharie, and parceled out his troops to Ball's Town, Catskill, and Fort Herkimer. The settlers in the borderlands, though still numbering about 5,000, were of little value; the number of men fit for militia duty had declined by two-thirds since the beginning of the war.

On July 9, John Doxtader led a small corps of Tories against Currytown, four miles from Canajoharie. Later reports said that 350 Indians were with him, but this seems exaggerated. Whatever his numbers, it was audacious of Doxtader to strike so close to Willett. Willett set out in pursuit and that night surrounded the Indians in their camp at Sharon Springs Swamp. About 40 were killed, and the rest escaped.

On August 6, John Christian Shell and his family held off an attack by 60 Indians and Highlander Loyalists under Donald McDonald, a retainer of Sir John Johnson. The Shells wounded and captured McDonald, who died the next day. The tiny settlement known as Shell's Bush was five miles north of Fort Dayton.

During late August, a large Loyalist-Indian force under Captain William Caldwell ravaged western Ulster County, but the militia drove them away. Caldwell incurred heavy losses in a skirmish at Wawarsing. Minor raids continued into the autumn, but there was no apparent general strategy, and the border warfare was clearly winding down.

In October 1781 the British made one final concerted effort on the New York frontier. Major John Ross and Walter Butler set out from Oswego with 130 Indians and 570 Tories and regulars on October 16, burning several farms and villages along the Mohawk east of Warrenbush. They then withdrew, probably because expected reinforcements from Sir John Johnson did not arrive. The weather was bad, and Ross knew that the Continentals were not far away. Indeed, Willett caught up with the expeditions at Johnstown, when it had halted on the night of October 25. Willett attacked, but his troops inexplicably panicked and fled. But the Loyalists also withdrew, leaving behind much of their baggage. Willett lost 40 men, but his force killed 50 of the invaders, and captured 50 more. He then withdrew to German Flats, cutting Ross and Butler off from the boats they had left on Oneida Creek. At the same time 60 fresh Oneida warriors joined the Americans.

Ross and Butler moved away slowly, searching for a path northward to Canada rather than back to Lake Oneida. After a three-day delay, Willett pursued, marching 20 miles through a snowstorm on October 29. The next day a skirmish was fought across the fords of West Canada Creek (Jerseyfield). Walter Butler's body was found afterward in the shallows. Ross fled, but Willett gave up the chase a day later.

Ross's expedition, which had begun with such high hopes, ended in debacle. The Indians, the Loyalists and the regulars all blamed one another for the failure. The war was in fact over (the surrender at Yorktown had occurred two weeks earlier), but scattered raids continued during the spring and summer of 1782. Joseph Brant attacked Fort Herkimer in July, and burned some houses around Fort Dayton. General Sir Guy Carleton, now commanding in New York City, had promised the American government a cessation of hostilities; but Brant was not aware of this. Throughout the autumn the Iroquois and the Loyalists at Oswego and Niagara waited for further instructions. Long before news of the peace came, the Indians and Loyalists had given up their border warfare for they were beginning to build permanent settlements in Canada.

Tom Martin

REFERENCES

Robert McCluer Calhoon, *The Loyalists in Revolutionary America, 1760–1781* (1973); Isabel Thompson Kelsay, *Joseph Brant, 1743–1807: Man of Two Worlds* (1984); Howard Swiggett, *War out of Niagara: Walter Butler and the Tory Rangers* (1933).

New York in the American Revolution

Two ironies ruled New York's entrance into the American Revolution. Although committees of correspondence supplanted royal government by late 1774, New York was among the last colonies to sign the Declaration of Independence. While the pre-Revolutionary politics of New York were often radical, its first constitution, enacted under fire in 1777, was conservative. Because of its strategic position as the axle of the

North American colonies and possession of the best port on the continent, New York was focus of much military action. New York City was occupied by the British in October 1776 and their evacuation on November 25, 1783, marked the end of the war.

New York's road to revolution began deep in its past. Ethnic divisions between the politically dominant English and the first colonizers, the Dutch, and religious divisions between Anglicans, Dutch Reformed, Lutheran, Presbyterians, and Society of Friends affected political affairs. Beginning with the Leisler Revolt in 1689, New York's plebeian population asserted itself within the limits of colonial rule. Political parties centered around key families, including the DeLanceys, Livingstons, and Morrises, who vied for favor with royal governors and with middling mechanics and farmers. In the city, mobs influenced assembly voting early in the eighteenth century and accelerated that impact as the Revolution neared. In the countryside, paternalistic relations between major landowners and their tenants were rapidly transformed from semifeudalism to capitalism in the decades before the conflict. These transitions meant New York's common folk developed a class-based, nonconformist tradition, while the hierarchy of politics remained rigid.

Two groups not within formal politics, the Iroquois nation and African-American slaves, deeply affected the conduct of law and society. The Iroquois effectively stymied economic and demographic growth into northwestern New York, while black slaves showed readiness to rebel in famous conspiracies in 1712 and 1741 and in countless individual rebellions. New York's slave codes were the harshest of the northern colonies. When the Revolution came, American Indians and African-Americans chose allegiance to the Crown based upon historic ties.

The pace of the Revolution stepped up sharply in the 1760s. Beset by economic depression and resentful British troops who were quartered in the city and angry at the passive assembly, mobs protested the Stamp Act of 1765 with ritual destruction of the property of officeholders. The "people out of doors" intimidated the assembly and instituted an embargo of British goods. New popular leaders like Alexander MacDougall, Isaac Sears, John Lamb, and Joseph Allicotte challenged Crown officials and local assemblymen. Although New York was not as badly affected by the depression of the 1760s as was Boston, widening economic inequities eroded deferential politics prized by colonial rulers. The announcement in 1766 that Parliament had rescinded the Stamp Act brought joyful celebration and sustained rituals of revolution that mechanics and tradesmen annually celebrated at tavern dinners and in parades. Anti-theater riots demonstrated the conservative side of the mob. Alexander MacDougall created further controversy in 1768 when the government charged him with libel. Jailed, he became known as the "Wilkes of America," to the Sons of Liberty, as the mobs became more officially known. Allicotte and Sears pursued nonimportation with zeal, publishing the names of uncooperative merchants and boarding ships in the harbor to inspect for contraband.

In the countryside new capitalist relations and ethnic conflicts resulted in land riots. Part of the emerging populist response throughout the western borders of British North America, land rioters in the Hudson Valley responded to threats of dispossession. Tenants on the massive Livingston estate marched on the manor house demanding an end to taxes. Farther north, New Englanders were reported to be squatting on land near Crown Point, declaring that possession was 11 points in the law. Attempts to quell violence in each of these instances resulted in the beating of sheriffs.

Assembly elections in 1768 and 1769 brought no consensus to politics. By 1770 the pace of insurrection quickened. Animosities between English troops and tradesmen worsened in New York City. On January 15, 1770, soldiers tried unsuccessfully to cut down a Liberty Pole outside Montangne's Tavern near the Commons in New York City. After two days of street brawls, they finally succeeded in chopping up the pole. Not until the troops were restricted to their barracks was calm restored. Four years later, New York had its own tea party when crowds boarded the ship *London* and dumped tea into the harbor.

Political order also declined in rural areas. Rioters disguising themselves by blackening their faces assaulted constables, destroyed jails, and freed prisoners. Confrontations with authorities across the northern counties of the colony continued through the early 1770s. The Green Mountain Boys formed a rural counterpart of the city's Liberty Boys. Led by Ethan Allen, they warned sheriffs in Cumberland County against

executing evictions, interfered with private disputes, and rescued prisoners held for debt. In city and countryside, rioters supplanted Crown and colonial authority. The gulf between the rioters and Crown authority was so vast in part because of the limited suffrage in the colony. Family parties, proprietorship of offices, and long-term incumbencies held little opportunity for the expansion of legitimate republicanism.

Some legitimate opposition existed. The Zenger Affair of 1734 inspired a legacy of republican opposition. In the 1750s William Livingston, John Morin Scott, and William Smith, Jr., published the *Independent Reflector*, an articulate provincial voice challenging civic and religious orthodoxy. In the 1760s Scott wrote a series of essays opposing the Stamp Act and arguing that the colonial assembly, not Parliament, should impose taxes.

Popular opposition, revolt in the northern colonies and the rise of a provincial leadership class all came together in the tumultuous year of 1775. Committees of Safety became political structures that spread over the whole province. As news of the war in Boston thundered through New York, committees in Albany, for example, established their own police force, took command of the militia, made preparations for war and interfered with the royal mail. The committee prepared for provincial elections and listened to the advice of the Continental Congress. Along with military concerns, it controlled prices and the practice of medicine.

In New York City the street turmoil produced leadership and followers, just as it had in the 1760s. Judge William Smith noted in his *Diary* that "The taverns are filled with politicians every night. . . . Armed parties summon the town publicly to come and take arms and learn the manual exercise. . . . Sears. . . with 360 armed men waited on Eliot the collector, and got the keys of the Custom House to shut up the port." Anxious Loyalists including John Watts, Colonel Roger Morris, and others left quickly for England, leaving behind fortunes in real estate. Loyalists James DeLancey and newspaperman James Rivington escaped danger only by apologetic appeals to the crowd. In April 1775 the Committee of Sixty withdrew in favor of a larger body of one hundred, which began a career as the Revolutionary government of the city. In May the New York Provincial Congress delegates from the city and northern counties met in New

York to form a state legislature. Radicals Sears, MacDougall, and Scott dominated the meeting and strongly opposed any reconciliation with England.

In the early summer talk turned to marching as state militias mustered in New York City. Needing weapons and powder and noting that the British had prudently removed five companies of troops to the warship *Asia*, mobs raided powderhouses at Turtle Bay. The committee sponsored powder mills and gunsmiths. Even though the Provincial Congress hesitated to seize guns and cannon from the British, old ship cannon around the docks were removed to Kingsbridge to guard the approaches from Connecticut and upper New York. When he arrived on June 25, General George Washington received a tumultuous welcome from the city. In contrast, Governor William Tryon found welcome only from the mayor, Anglican ministers, and assemblymen. While Washington had popular favor, the English governor held power in name only.

As New York prepared for revolution, colonial political splits reappeared in new guises. Radical Whigs emerged from the Liberty Boys and land rioters of the previous ten years. Derived from artisan, semiskilled, and mariner classes, these Whigs represented both an upwardly mobile political group and those occupations most damaged by ten years of cyclical depression. Ethnically, warm Whigs were Scotch-Irish, some Dutch, and Americans of several generations. More conservative Whigs came from the political gentry, usually apart from the Anglican leadership. The Presbyterian Livingstons and Morrisses and their allies including John Jay, James Duane, and Philip Schuyler perceived the inevitability of revolution and were determined to rein in, if possible, radical tendencies to preserve their place in the new order. Hope for reconciliation with England was never far beneath the surface.

New York's Loyalists were more mixed than initially might appear. Some choices faithful to the Crown were not surprising. Virtually every Anglican priest remained loyal, as did most of their parishioners. Most of the colonial officeholders and families with close ties to colonial leadership joined the Tory ranks. Judges, councilors, and assemblymen were primarily loyal. Major landowners such as the DeLanceys, James Jauncey, and Hugh Wallace, who owed power, honor, and wealth to their ties with the Mother Country, followed the career path they knew best. Great merchants stayed loyal whether politically active or not. Foreign birth contributed to this choice even if self-interest was not obvious. Working-class carters with ties to the Anglican church or with the DeLanceys followed the patronage route. Recent Scotch-Irish tenants of Loyalist Sir William Johnson adopted his politics.

Disaffection from the Crown took extreme routes. Shortly after New Yorkers signed the Declaration of Independence, Cumberland and Gloucester counties broke away to form Vermont. Displeased with the Whig decision to continue quit-rents after independence and to impose taxes for the building of courthouses, and aware that many moderate Whigs were speculating in land, Vermonters met in July 1776. They lumped together monarchial government and provincial authority and declared independence. By early 1777 Vermonters established a constitution that borrowed heavily from Pennsylvania's radical document. Vermont created a single-house legislature, lacked a governor, set procedures for direct popular involvement, and abolished slavery.

By the end of 1776 the southern district of New York City was under military occupation. A wide arc around New York City became known as the "neutral zone" as the two armies and guerrilla bands of escaped slaves and rootless whites vied for control. The Hudson Valley region splintered into factions. In the northeast, Vermonters created a new political entity. Except in New York City, where the British army gave it a facade of legitimacy, the colonial political order was dead. In no other place in the colony did Crown officials hold any real power.

The death of the colonial order became official in 1777 when New Yorkers established a new constitution. Although threatened by the proximity of General John Burgoyne's army, and preempted by the revolution in Vermont, the first state legislature established a bicameral house, apportioned membership for the house and senate, set fairly tough suffrage qualifications, and prepared for a gubernatorial election. Political realism emanating from military danger and a highly fragmented social order dictated consensus if possible. Many of the delegates were newcomers, including firebrand Sons of Liberty from New York City or up-province politicians never before possessed of real power. No one came from the breakaway Vermont region. The only delegates with any coherent self-image were conservative landlords and merchants determined to direct the course of the Revolution. As the new government fled from hiding place to new refuge over the winter of 1776, the conservatives gained the upper hand.

If conservative Whigs appeared victorious in channeling the Revolution in 1776, the surprise victory of George Clinton in the first gubernatorial election the next year showed the continued strength of radical Patriots. Clinton, an Ulster lawyer, former assemblyman, and defender of Alexander MacDougall in the late 1760s, was by 1777 a brigadier general in the state milita and Continental Army. Clinton was opposed by Philip Schuyler of Albany and John Morin Scott, who lacked a power base as New York City lay under British occupation. Schuyler was heavily favored, but Clinton had the advantage of being an outsider with key insider connections. He won in the fragmented election, with strong support from the mid-Hudson region and a significant minority in Schuyler's Albany.

Clinton joined the new assembly and senate meeting for the first time in September 1777. Of 290 assemblymen, only six were veterans of the colonial body. However, 85 had experience in the Revolutionary congresses, and 94 served on Revolutionary committees. In the Senate, experience was slightly more widespread, but with few colonial officers deserting the Crown, there was ample room for new, wartime experience. A second reason for the advent of newcomers in both halls was their increased size of officeholders, as the state nearly doubled the number of colonial legislators. Many had been local officeholders who were now elevated to state tenure. Overall, members of the assembly or senate were less wealthy, less educated, and less cosmopolitan than their predecessors in the Colonial era.

In the next few years Clinton astutely managed power and restrained the influence of the conservative Whigs over issues of taxation, committee membership, treatment of Tories, and use of paper money. Clinton was governing a beseiged, wartorn state. He had three objectives. First was to keep the army and militia in the field and to prevent the loss of any more territory to the British. The second was to raise the supplies needed by the army. The third was to undo the secession of Vermont. The first two objectives required a delicate balance of taxation and encouragement of the state's economy, for without some ability to resist economic crisis, the will to combat the British would be lost. Necessarily, Clinton formed a coalition that pushed through taxation policies levying the same rates on improved and unimproved land. Clinton was able to carry this coalition because few wished to argue in the midst of a war. Legislators also recognized that higher issues were at stake than local quarrels. Third, all understood that the coalition was temporary.

Clinton was able to establish power and win election to four terms through important lessons learned during the Revolution. He controlled patronage, led the newcomers, and was able to identify opposition as undermining the Revolution. He repudiated his ties with the older, conservative elite and moved toward identification with the legislative and popular radicals. That wartime radicalism was a coalition of three sources. First were insurgent politicians who mediated landlord-tenant strife in Albany, Dutchess, and Westchester counties. Second were Patriots from the west bank of the Hudson, and third were former Sons of Liberty, mechanics, small merchants, carters, and mariners from New York City. This coalition controlled the assembly and Senate during the early 1780s and pushed through Revolutionary measures and retaliation against Tories.

One key issue that received little radical support was the abolition of slavery. New Yorkers owned the greatest number of slaves north of the Chesapeake. Dutch subsistence farmers and Anglican merchants and their wives depended heavily upon black slave labor. The Dutch and English developed a paternalist vision of their slaves and strongly felt that abolition was inappropriate. Further, Lord Dunmore's clarion call in Virginia to slaves to abandon their masters and to join the British forces terrified northerners as well as southern planters. Outside of the Society of Friends, which was gradually eliminating slave-holders from its membership, no denomination took a principled stand against slavery. With economic, social, and religious custom favoring the retention of slavery, abolitionism received little support. As a result, blacks took any opportunity to flee to the advancing British army. During the eight years of the war, as many slaves fled their masters as was recorded in the previous 60 years. Although some free blacks or slaves fought for the Patriots as substitutes for their masters, it was commonly recognized that African-Americans in New York supported the British, believing that freedom would come with a Crown victory.

Similarly, the Iroquois nation supported the English. Careful to avoid constant alliances during the Colonial period and strong enough to enforce a proclamation line limiting white western settlements as recently as 1768, the Iroquois became alarmed by the land-hungry Whigs. Dunmore's War, designed to force the Shawnee to cede the Ohio River region to Virginia, aroused fears among the Iroquois to the north. Meeting with Sir William Johnson, the English advisor closest to the Indians, Iroquois leaders attributed their own anger to younger men and demanded Johnson curb the reckless and "lawless" whites intent upon seizing land beyond the territorial barriers fixed at Fort Stanwix in 1768. As hostilities quickened in 1775, Iroquois fortunes, particularly the Mohawk's, became entangled with the Johnson's. Sir John Johnson, son of William, aroused enmity from Americans by his loyalism. Philip Schuyler proceeded in January 1776 with a force of 700 men to confront Sir John at Johnstown. While the Mohawks were sent a courtesy message of the advance, they were not permitted much participation in the negotiations. Johnson's refusal to remain confined on parole to a restricted area of Tryon County, coupled with the Americans' summary treatment of the Mohawks, pushed the Indian nation closer to alliance with the English.

For a time, the Iroquois maintained an uneasy neutrality. The British were far more aggressive, however, in recruitment of the Indians than the Americans, who showed little interest in enlisting them. The cost of maintaining a friendship and the responsibility of curbing white land hunger was more than the Patriots could assume. By July 1776, the English wooed Joseph Brant, the warrior chief of the Mohawks, into an alliance. Brant was unaware that the English regarded Indian nations as under Crown dominion. In a council at Onoquaga near the Susquehanna River, Brant convinced other Indian leaders to side with the British. After receiving a wampum belt of agreement, Brant spent the rest of the year and early 1777 traveling around the state encouraging other Indians to support the king. The Iroquois proved helpful to the British

almost immediately. The stalemated Battle of Oriskany in August 1777 pushed the Indians into the Loyalist camp. Six hundred to eight hundred Indians joined the British in preventing the Americans from relieving a besieged fort. Both sides suffered heavy losses.

The year 1778 saw frequent border warfare between the Indians and Americans. With the exception of some Tuscaroras and about half the Oneidas, nearly all Indians sided with the British. In May 1778 Indian raiders plundered and burned Cobleskill. Succeeding raids against German Flats, Unadilla, and the massacre at Cherry Valley in November 1778 characterized Indian forays against white settlements.

By 1779 American forces were strong enough to retaliate. General James Clinton and about 600 men pushed across the state to punish the Indians. Patriot forces from the south and west joined General John Sullivan's advance. The three wings joined in the Genesee territory by the end of the summer of 1779 and succeeded in laying waste to several Indian towns, destroying crops and livestock, and inflicting a terrible retribution upon the Iroquois confederacy.

Although it badly damaged the Confederacy, Indian raids continued in 1780 and 1781. Marauding parties of Tories and Indians battled Americans across the Mohawk region. Raids over several years cost Tryon County alone 700 buildings destroyed, 150,000 bushels of wheat burned, 12,000 farms abandoned, and left 380 widows and 2,000 fatherless children. The Americans broke the Indian ability to continue raids in the last battle on New York soil at Johnstown in October 1781. Shortly before Lord Charles Cornwallis lost at Yorktown, Colonel Marinus Willett and 400 men decisively defeated a larger army of Loyalists and Indians. The overall defeat of the English cost the Iroquois dearly and when the British ceded their lands to the Americans in the Peace Treaty of 1783, the Indians lost vast tracts of land.

The Iroquois were not the only local losers in the Revolution. A key means of defining the new order and creating a partisan culture were the Confiscation Acts. Shortly after independence, local committees began defining citizenship. They arrested people who refused Continental currency. The Revolutionaries required people to swear allegiance to the new nation, thus identifying friends and enemies. The third Provincial Congress of 1776 set up committees to detect conspiracies with powers to arrest, confine, and even exile offenders. By late 1779 the legislature became more active and began punishing the Revolution's enemies. It voided licenses to practice law granted before 1776, with readmission to the bar based upon a jury decision. More dramatic was the Forfeitures Act of October 1779. This legislation declared that Loyalists had "forfeited all Right to the Protection of this State," and banished 70 for treason from the state under penalty of death. Their property was seized and sold. Subsequent laws made Loyalist writings and speeches felonies. At the close of the war the Trespass Act permitted landowners in the occupied zones to sue for damages against anyone who had used the property during the war, even if required to do so by British authorities. This series of laws gave New York a reputation as being very severe to the enemies of the Revolution. Creating an inequality before law between Loyalist and Patriot, the laws also secured the Revolution by rewarding friends, forcing important royalists into exile, and silencing those who stayed behind.

Until November 1783 New York City remained under British rule despite the defeat of Cornwallis at Yorktown. More than 50,000 people, or twice the population of the city in 1775, crammed into the devastated city. Nearly destroyed by fires in 1776 and 1778, the city was the asylum for Loyalist refugees, the British army, and thousands of runaway slaves. The class dimensions of the city were vast. British officers threw expensive parties and gambled at horse races. At the same time, crime was rampant and thousands lived on the brink of starvation, especially during the harsh winter of 1779–1780. Desperate Loyalists, hoping to serve the king and regain their confiscated land, found the English disinterested in their applications. Not until 1779 were the Associated Loyalists permitted to begin raids within the "neutral ground." These guerilla actions did some good and helped supply the beleaguered urban population. They also raised the deep animosity between Patriot and Tory. The execution of Josiah Huddy of New Jersey, a Monmouth County Patriot, is illustrative. Huddy was famous for his depredations against Tories. In September 1780 Colonel Tye, an escaped slave who organized his own band of guerrillas, succeeded in capturing Huddy at his home. On the way to Sandy Hook, Huddy escaped, and Tye was killed. Two years later the Associated Loyalists recaptured Huddy, brought him to the shores of Monmouth and hung him. The Americans demanded revenge, and an innocent English officer was almost hung in retaliation. The execution nearly brought a halt to the peace process.

Huddy's execution exemplified the nasty conflict around New York City after Yorktown. Loyalists and slaves repeatedly raided towns within the "neutral ground." As George Washington returned from the glorious victory at Yorktown and General Sir Guy Carleton, commander-in-chief of British forces, negotiated a peace treaty, the forays showed the unceasing enmity on the local level. One difficult point in the negotiations between Washington and Carleton was the status of 3,000 to 4,000 blacks in New York City. Washington presumed that many of them would be returned to their Patriot masters. In contrast, Carleton believed that the blacks, having come to the British lines invited by English commanders, were entitled to their freedom. Carleton won the argument, and 3,000 former slaves left New York along with about 30,000 white Loyalists in the evacuation of New York City during 1783.

The Americans regained the city on November 25, 1783. Washington and his army, accompanied by Clinton, marched down the Bowery to the tip of Manhattan. After a British flag atop a greased pole was replaced by an American flag, the city became part of the new nation.

The war had been harsh to New York. Ninety-two battles in the Revolution were fought in New York. No other state faced such constant triangular warfare among Patriots, Loyalists, and the British. New York City was the only capital under the British flag throughout the entire war. The city's population was 20,000 in 1775, swelled to 50,000 during the war, but dropped to 10,000 at its close. The state's population of 185,000 placed it only eighth in the Union. Its strategic position gave it importance but caused terrible human loss.

Graham Hodges

REFERENCES

Edward Countryman, *A People in Revolution. The American Revolution and Political Society in New York, 1760–1790* (1982); Barbara Graymont, *The Iroquois in the American Revolution* (1972); Janice Potter, *The Liberty We Seek: Loyalist Ideology in Colonial New York and Massachusetts* (1983); Philip Ranlet, *The New York Loyalists* (1986); Thomas

Jefferson Wertenbaker, *Father Knickerbocker Rebels* (1948); Alfred F. Young, *The Democratic Republican of New York: The Origins, 1763–1797* (1967).

New York Volunteers

This Loyalist unit originated through the efforts of Governor William Tryon of New York. Early in 1776 he actively recruited Scottish emigrants in the New York area and by May had enough men to form two companies. He sent the recruits to Halifax, where General William Howe offically formed them into the 1st and 2nd New York Provincial companies on June 1. The 1st Company was commanded by Captain Archibald Campbell and the 2nd was placed under Captain Alexander Grant. Howe dated their commissions from January 1776 and made Campbell senior by one day.

The New Yorkers sailed with the British army on June 10, arriving at New York by the end of the month. The two companies participated in the Battle of Long Island as well as in the balance of the campaign for New York City.

When Campbell died during a minor operation early in 1777, the command of both companies devolved upon Grant. Shortly after, recruiting was expanded, and the unit, now at least four companies, was designated the New York Volunteers with Grant being promoted to major commanding.

The Volunteers participated in the expedition of Sir Henry Clinton against Forts Montgomery and Clinton in the Hudson Highlands in October 1777. During the assault on Fort Montgomery, Major Grant was killed, and in November, George Turnbull was named lieutenant colonel commandant of the regiment.

During 1778 the Volunteers remained in the New York garrison, where they numbered 198 in January and 271 by August. On November 26, 1778, the New Yorkers sailed as part of the expedition bound for Savannah under Lieutenant Colonel Archibald Campbell of the 71st Foot. By the end of December the city had fallen.

For the remainder of 1779 the Volunteers operated in Georgia, with 150 participating in the defense of Savannah during the failed Franco-American siege of September–October. Meanwhile, on May 2 the Volunteers had been named the 3rd American Regiment. This made them a permanent unit on the newly formed American establishment, enhancing the status of the officers and men.

Early in 1780, the Volunteers were sent to the siege of Charleston as part of a reinforcement for Clinton. They arrived from Georgia in the middle of March, joining a group of 170 Volunteers that had come with Clinton from New York. These men were probably the infantry portion of Emmerich's Chasseurs, who were disbanded on August 31, 1779, and who had been assigned to the New York Volunteers.

Also sailing with Clinton was a rifle company under Captain John Althaus, formerly of Emmerich's, and now belonging to the Volunteers. However, the riflemen never had the opportunity to participate in the siege. They were on the transport *Anna*, which was dismasted and spent over eight weeks being swept across the Atlantic to England. They did not return to New York until October 1780.

The Volunteers remained with the southern army when Clinton returned to New York, and engaged the rebels again in August at Rocky Mount, South Carolina. At that time 150 of them were attacked by Thomas Sumter with about 600 men, but the Yorkers successfully resisted for eight hours before the rebels withdrew.

Turnbull received permission from Cornwallis to return to New York for health reasons in November, and Lieutenant Colonel Welbore E. Doyle of the Volunteers of Ireland took over field command of the New Yorkers. At least part of the unit was soon converted to mounted infantry for outpost duty, but with the further deterioration of the situation in South Carolina the regiment was reassembled at Camden. Here on April 25, 1781, the Volunteers participated in Lord Francis Rawdon's victory over the rebels under Nathanel Greene at Hobkirk's Hill.

On May 9 Rawdon evacuated Camden and moved toward the coast. At Orangeburg he joined a force under Lieutenant Colonel Alexander Stewart of the 3rd Foot, whom he left in command there while he proceeded on to Charleston. Part of Stewart's force included 47 New York Volunteers, and they were with him when he defeated Greene at Eutaw Springs on September 8, 1781. The battle was saved for the British mainly because the detachment of Volunteers under Major Sheridan held a critical strong point in their camp and refused to be driven out.

The regiment spent the rest of its time in the South at Charleston doing garrison duty, the outstanding exception being participation in an extensive raid into the countryside in February 1782. When the city was evacuated in December, 211 New York Volunteers returned home. They landed in New York on January 3, 1783.

Because it was the only regiment of the five comprising the American establishment that was not eventually added to the British establishment, Turnbull made a representation to Sir Guy Carleton on August 18, 1783, for regular status for his men. However, the plea was not successful, and by the end of the year the unit, now reduced to 161, had been transported to Nova Scotia for reduction.

The regiment is known to have had a light infantry company since caps were provided for it in 1780. The only other clear uniform details date from 1783, where one source states "Red Coat, Buff Lappel Variety Trimming," and a second shows red coat and blue facings. Buttons marked "NYV" exist for both officers and men.

Walter T. Dornfest

REFERENCES

Archibald Campbell, *Journal of an Expedition Against the Rebels of Georgia in North America*, ed. by Colin Campbell (1981); Philip Klingle, "Soldiers of Kings," *Journal of Long Island History*, 12 (1976): 22–35; Eric I. Manders, *The Battle of Long Island* (1978); Christoper Ward, *War of the Revolution*, ed. by John R. Alden (1952).

Niagara Portage

Perhaps the single most critical point for British forces attempting to retain control of the Upper Great Lakes was the portage around Niagara Falls. British communications with the Upper Great Lakes posts, as well as with the Illinois country, relied on this route. Over the Niagara Portage passed the troops, military supplies, trade goods, and Indian presents needed for the war in the west. A return traffic of furs bound for Montreal continued throughout the conflict.

The four Upper Great Lakes—Superior, Michigan, Huron, and Erie—are drained by the Niagara River. This empties into Lake Ontario. During its roughly 30-mile course between Lakes Erie and Ontario, the Niagara River drops 400 feet in a series of rapids and the 182-foot leap over Niagara Falls. Although the cataracts pre-sented a barrier to water transportation, the Niagara River also provided the most direct route to the northern interior of the continent.

The portage began at the mouth of the Niagara Gorge (Lewiston, New York), six miles above Lake Ontario. There, boats and goods were hauled up the steep riverbank from the lower Niagara River and dragged up the Niagara escarpment for a total lift of more than 300 feet. It was then a relatively level carry for eight miles to a point above the falls (Niagara Falls, New York), where boats could be returned to the water to proceed to Lake Erie.

The French gained effective control of the portage in 1726 with the completion of Fort Niagara. They improved the portage route and established posts at its head and foot. The British took Fort Niagara and the portage in 1759. They reestablished the post at the head of the portage in 1760, calling it the "Upper Landing" or "Little Niagara." A fortified storehouse was built at the foot of the portage—the "Lower Landing"—two years later. Both were improved during the Indian uprising of 1763–64, and the upper stockade was named Fort Schlosser. A Seneca attack on the portage in September 1763 resulted in additional fortification of the Niagara Portage during John Bradstreet's 1764 expedition to Detroit. In addition to temporary defenses along the road, a new post was built on the shore of Lake Erie and christened Fort Erie.

After 1764 there was reductions in the military posts on the portage. By 1765, the operation of the portage had been contracted to the partnership of Francis Pfister and John Stedman. Formerly, the military had moved its own supplies and private traders had fended for themselves. Under the new agreement, Pfister and Stedman would transport government supplies and, in return, receive the concession to move all private goods. This arrangement would continue through the American Revolution. Military operation of the portage was further reduced in 1766 when all posts other than Fort Niagara and Fort Erie were abandoned and government teams and equipment turned over to the contractors. Pfister and Stedman based themselves at Fort Schlosser and did very well by their arrangement. Pfister departed Niagara in 1773, although he apparently retained an interest in the partnership. Stedman's contract was renewed regularly. In 1781 he passed the business to his brother, Philip, and eventually to his nephew,

Philip, Jr. The Stedmans' operation continued until about 1790 when the portage was moved to the west bank of the Niagara River in anticipation of an American occupation of Fort Niagara.

The outbreak of war in 1775 renewed military concerns for the portage. Fort Schlosser was reoccupied by a small detachment from Fort Niagara. A guard also was maintained at the Lower Landing to protect supplies in transit. The aging stockade and buildings of Fort Schlosser were replaced in 1779, and Fort Erie was repaired following heavy storm damage the same year. The flow of goods and personnel continued uninterrupted throughout the conflict, however. Sailing vessels of the Naval Department ascended the river to the Lower Landing and discharged their cargoes. These were carried overland to Fort Schlosser, reloaded into small boats and then further transshipped to the Lake Erie sailing vessels at Fort Erie. *See also*: Great Lakes Posts

Brian Leigh Dunnigan

REFERENCES

Brian Leigh Dunnigan, "Portaging Niagara," *Inland Seas*, 42 (1986): 177–83, 216–33; David Owen, *Fort Erie, 1764–1823: An Historical Guide* (1985); Frank Severance, *An Old Frontier of France*, 2 vols. (1917); Paul L. Stevens, *A King's Colonel at Niagara, 1774–1778: Lt. Col. John Caldwell and the Beginnings of the American Revolution on the New York Frontier* (1987).

Nicholas, Samuel (1744–1790)

Continental Marine officer. Samuel Nicholas was born in Philadelphia about 1744 to Anthony, a blacksmith, and Mary. He attended the Academy of Philadelphia, which became the University of Pennsylvania, from January 1, 1752, until December 17, 1759. Before the outbreak of the Revolution, he was a tavernkeeper at the Sign of the Commission Waggon which was owned by his mother-in-law.

Nicholas received the first officer's commissions in the newly created Continental Navy, that of captain in the Continental Marines on November 28, 1775. Congress, on November 10, 1775, authorized the creation of two battalions of marines to serve with the navy. Captain Nicholas's first duty was to begin recruiting.

The first marines were enlisted by Captain Nicholas in Philadelphia between December 6, 1775, and January 14, 1776. In 40 days, Nicholas managed to sign up 60 men to serve aboard the *Alfred*, a ship recently converted from a merchantman. The *Alfred* served as Commodore Esek Hopkins's flagship for the first Continental squadron, which sailed to New Providence Island for its first mission.

Nicholas led the landing party that consisted of 200 marines and 50 sailors. The landing was unopposed, and Nicholas successfully captured the two forts defending the island. He arrived back in New London with the squadron on April 8, 1776.

Hopkins sent Nicholas to Congress with the dispatches about his cruise. Once there, Nicholas was detached from the *Alfred* and promoted to major on June 25, 1776. He remained in Philadelphia to recruit and to train marines that were needed for the new frigates that were being built.

In December 1776 Major Nicholas received new orders. He was to proceed to New Jersey, with three of the four companies in Philadelphia, and there to join Colonel John Cadwalader's Philadelphia brigade. Nicholas had a total of 80 men, and his unit participated in the Second Battle of Trenton (Assunpink Creek) and in the Battle of Princeton.

In March 1777 Major Nicholas returned to Philadelphia, where he executed orders for the Board of Admiralty until 1780. In September 1777 Nicholas was sent to Lebanon, Connecticut, to obtain arms and ammunition for the army. He was also assigned several other duties including that of being authorized to sign Continental currency (August 8, 1778) and Continental bills of credit (May 29, 1779). In August 1778 Major Nicholas transported one million silver crowns on loan from France via Boston to Philadelphia, carefully avoiding the British garrison at New York.

On August 10, 1781, Nicholas requested duty at sea aboard the new frigate *America*. He also requested that pay and prize money be paid him. His request to return to sea was denied, but he was reimbursed up to August 25, 1781, at which time he was considered retired. In November 1781, even though retired, Nicholas sat on a board of inquiry into the loss of the frigate *Trumbull*.

Nicholas was the highest ranking marine officer during the war. His duties as muster master gave legitimacy to the claim that he was the first commandant of the Marine Corps. After his service, Nicholas returned to his tavernkeeping, and died on August 27, 1790, in Philadelphia.

Marc Genberg

REFERENCES

Michael Calvert, *A Dictionary of Battles (1715–1815)* (1979); Allen R. Millett, *Semper Fiedelis* (1980); Edwin H. Simmons, *The United States Marines 1775–1975* (1974); Charles R. Smith, *Marines in the Revolution* (1975).

Nicola, Lewis (1717–1807)

Continental Army officer. Lewis Nicola, colonial editor and Revolutionary tactician and military officer, was born in 1717 in France, the descendent of Huguenots. He attended school in Ireland, where he subsequently served as a military officer for almost 30 years. He moved from Dublin to Philadelphia in 1766.

Philadelphia records indicate that he performed some surveying services in addition to working as a merchant. In September 1767 Nicola developed a circulating library for the city, providing patrons the opportunity to choose and rent from more than 1,000 volumes—domestic and imported—of poetry, drama, histories, and French works for several dollars annually. When Nicola arrived, Philadelphia had not had a magazine for approximately ten years, and he decided to create his own journal, serving as editor of *The American Magazine, or General Repository*.

Emphasizing the publication of scientific articles, commentaries on political science, and criticisms of abuses by the European aristocracy in biographical and historical sketches concluding with morals, Nicola strived to produce a secular publication. The magazine had a wide circulation throughout the colonies, and Nicola endeavored to teach colonists with this general interest magazine, stressing its practical yet entertaining aspects. He also hoped to improve the quality of colonial periodicals as well as their audience by concentrating on intellectual topics—for example, the first issue included an "Essay on the Importance of Natural History"—subjects that few colonial publications had broached. Attempting to make science seem accessible to the colonists regardless of their education or prior experiences, Nicola stressed to

his readers that many scientific findings had been discovered by chance and not necessarily by a well-educated individual. He published a total of nine issues in 1769 before ceasing publication. Unfortunately, many of his critics deemed the magazine unsuccessful.

Interested in further scientific work, Nicola was a member of a local Philadelphia science organization patterned after and named for Benjamin Franklin's Junto. The group collected scientific equipment and sought "Mutual Improvement in Useful Knowledge," hosting a diverse membership that included clock maker Owen Biddle, naturalist John Bartram's sons Isaac and Moses, and Dr. John Morgan. In a reorganization the group was renamed the American Society for Promoting and Propagating Useful Knowledge, Held at Philadelphia—better known as the American Society. Although they were bitter rivals, the American Society, with Nicola as a negotiator, and the American Philosophical Society agreed to merge into a group adopting the latter's name in 1769. Nicola served as a curator for the American Philosophical Society. He also published the Society's *Transactions*, editing and writing informative scientific articles in appendices of *The American Magazine, or General Repository*.

Nicola believed that civil positions could be used for both personal benefit and public improvement, diligently applying himself to civic offices. In 1774 Nicola became a justice of the peace in Northampton County, Pennsylvania, where he lived with his wife and daughters. Interested in improving the militia for public security, Nicola published three military handbooks: *A Treatise of Military Exercise, Calculated for the Use of the Americans* (1776) and translations from the French of Louis André de La Mamie de Clairac's *L'Ingénieur de Campagne [Field Engineer]* (1776) and Grandmaison's *A Treatise, on the Military Service, of Light Horse and Light Infantry* (1777). In his own treatise Nicola recommended avoiding "pitched battles with veteran troops" and advised the militia to use "woods and swampy grounds" and fences so that they could attack "on all sides day and night, officers and men killed or wounded without perceiving their enemies.

Nicola did not believe that lengthy training periods or strict discipline was necessary to maintain order and keep soldiers committed, stressing that "men, who, compelled by the unhappy state of the times, take up arms to defend their liberties, with a design to lay them down as soon as the end proposed is obtained." His manual was widely used by Revolutionary soldiers because of its simplicity and uncomplicated explanations of how to fire weapons and maneuver on the battlefield. Nicola, eager to improve military methods, recommended that riflemen be exempt from regular drill, arguing that they had a specialized role distinct and separate from ordinary, rote battlefield maneuvers and needed to be prepared differently for their particular objectives.

In 1776 Nicola became the barrackmaster of Philadelphia as well as town major from late 1776 until 1782, being in charge of the home guards. He also recruited officers. A skilled cartographer, Nicola helped create a map depicting the British occupation of Philadelphia from 1777 to 1778. Nicola requested that a military government be established in Philadelphia because he disliked Benedict Arnold's leadership following the British withdrawal; Nicola also recommended that he be named as military governor in charge of the new government. However, his superiors did not accept his suggestions.

Instead, in the summer of 1777, Congress established a Corps of Invalids and appointed Nicola as commander of this regiment of invalid veterans and officers, who were disabled for field service but who could perform necessary camp and guard tasks for various encampments. Congress assigned Nicola the rank of colonel, and he also trained recruits. The veterans in the Corps of Invalids instructed younger officers, and Nicola's French influence molded future professional military training at the national army academy at West Point. General Washington began transferring Nicola's corps to West Point in 1778.

By 1781 Nicola's men were stationed at the West Point fort. In May 1782 he proposed to General George Washington that a monarchial government with Washington as king (or holding a similar title altered for popular acceptance) be formed. Although other factions with which Nicola was not aligned also supported a monarchy, an upset Washington demanded an apology, admonishing Nicola, who asked for the commander-in-chief's pardon. Nicola's suggestion was kept secret during the American Revolution—although he was criticized when it later was revealed—and in November 1783 he was

promoted to the rank of brigadier general. Nicola was released from command of the Invalid Regiment in June 1783.

As a veteran Nicola gained membership in the Society of the Cincinnati, in which he held leadership positions until he moved to a remote part of the state. In 1788 he returned to Philadelphia, where he continued to have administrative responsibility, as manager of the city's workhouse. Often designated officially in records with the surname Nicholas, in the 1790s Nicola inspected the state's militia brigades while earning income as a merchant. In 1798 he moved to Alexandria, Virginia, where, nine years later, he died on August 9, 1807.

Elizabeth D. Schafer

REFERENCES

Carl and Jessica Bridenbaugh, *Rebels and Gentlemen: Philadelphia in the Age of Franklin* (1942); *DAB*; J.C. Fitzpatrick, "The Invalid Regiment and Its Colonel," *The Spirit of the Revolution* (1924); Charles Royster, *A Revolutionary People at War: The Continental Army and American Character, 1775–1783* (1979).

Nicolson, James

See Continental Navy.

Ninety Six, South Carolina, Battle of (November 18–22, 1775)

The courthouse village of Ninety Six was the scene of the first battle of the American Revolution in the southern colonies. Established in 1772 as the judicial center for the South Carolina frontier, the village included a courthouse and brick jail surrounded by a dozen residences. It was located astride the Cherokee Path, the major trade route between the Cherokee Indians and Charleston. For three days, from November 19–21, 1775, Patriot and Loyalist militia fought a battle that marked the beginning of a civil war in the province, a struggle that continued until 1783.

Tension had been building in the backcountry since June 1775 when the South Carolina Provincial Congress created a provisional government under The Association. The Patriot decision to organize three militia regiments aroused the suspicion of backcountry Tories. Colonel Thomas Fletchell, commander of the Upper

Saluda royal militia, joined with Joseph Robinson, Moses Kirkland, and Robert Cunningham to defy the Patriot government. Fletchell persuaded the men under his command to stand fast in their allegiance to the king. When Patriot militia seized the magazine and two brass cannon at Fort Charlotte on the Savannah River, a force of 200 Loyalists, commanded by Joseph Robinson, marched to Ninety Six, where the supplies were stored, and carried away all munitions except the cannon.

Loyalist sentiment was increasing in the backcountry, and an effort to promote the Patriot cause seemed essential. On July 23, Patriot leaders dispatched William Henry Drayton, accompanied by the Reverends William Tennent and Oliver Hart, to the backcountry "to settle all political disputes between the people." In a series of public meetings, the Patriot missionaries preached rebellion with evangelical fervor to unresponsive audiences. When persuasion failed, Drayton was authorized to muster Patriot militia and to arrest the Tory ringleaders. From his headquarters, Drayton outlined his strategy to his superiors in Charleston. He would march "into the heart of Fletchall's quarters" and thought "this cruel opposition . . . will be rooted out without risk to our side." Before Drayton could execute his plan, however, Fletchall's Loyalist army materialized only four miles from Ninety Six. The eruption of full-scale civil war in the backcountry seemed imminent. Bloodshed was prevented when Fletchell, to the dismay of many associates, agreed to a conference with Drayton. On September 16, 1775, the two men negotiated an agreement to preserve the peace. The Loyalists promised never to join any British force that might invade the colony, while Drayton guaranteed the lives and property of those who rejected The Association.

Peace in the backcountry might have been preserved had the Council of Safety not ordered the arrest of Robert Cunningham and dispatched a wagonload of munitions to the Cherokee villages. Cunningham's arrest for "uttering seditious words" and his indefinite imprisonment in Charleston was a clear threat to all Loyalists. Further, the Patriot decision to send munitions to the Cherokees inspired a rumor that the Indians would attack Loyalists on the frontier. Patrick Cunningham assumed the mantle of Loyalist leadership. Unable to free his older brother, he led a raiding party to intercept and seize the ammunition wagon bound for Keowee.

Colonel Andrew Williamson, commanding the Patriot militia in the Ninety Six District, planned to strike the Loyalists who supported Cunningham and Fletchell. Before he could march on Fletchall's stronghold near Fair Forest, Williamson learned that a Loyalist force of 1,800 men was en route to Ninety Six.

On November 18, Williamson moved his 563 militiamen to protect Ninety Six. He arrived on Sunday morning and took up a position on John Savage's plantation about 200 yards west of the courthouse and jail. The Patriots constructed a crude fort "of old fence rails joined to a barn and some outhouses." Some parts of this rustic fortification were made of bales of "straw with some beeves' hides." Before the fortified camp could be completed, the Loyalist army appeared, led by Cunningham and Joseph Robinson. When a brief conference failed to reach a settlement, fighting broke out with Patriot and Loyalist militia firing "rifles and muskets, from behind houses, trees, logs, stumps and fences."

Darkness silenced the muskets, but heavy firing resumed at dawn. In an attempt to drive the Patriots from their defenses, the Loyalists "set fire to the fences and old grass in the fields" around the fort, an effort that failed because "the ground was too wet." When that tactic proved ineffective, the Loyalists constructed a mantelet, "a kind of rolling battery" fixed on a wagon frame, to use as a shield to approach the Patriot lines for an assault. The mantelet did not operate properly, perhaps because it did not provide sufficient protection against the three swivel cannon of the Patriots.

On November 21, with his gunpowder nearly exhausted, Williamson conferred with his officers and planned a midnight attack against the Loyalist siege lines. About sunset, before the Patriots were prepared to execute their sally, the Loyalists signaled with a white flag from a window in the jail and requested an end to fighting. Williamson agreed to meet Patrick Cunningham outside the stockade under a flag of truce. A two-hour conference produced no agreement, except that representatives of both forces would continue their negotiations at a house in Ninety Six the following morning.

The next day, Williamson and Cunningham quickly settled the terms of a treaty. Hostilities would cease and both armies would be disbanded. The Patriots agreed to destroy their fortifications and all prisoners captured by either side would be set free. All militia were allowed to return to their homes without interference. Both parties agreed to a 20-day truce to permit each faction to confer with leaders in Charleston.

Both Loyalists and Patriots found advantages in this agreement. The Loyalists may have learned that Colonel Richard Richardson was advancing from the Low Country with a Patriot force which would end their numerical superiority. Moreover, Emanuel Miller, a deserter from the Patriot garrison, warned Cunningham of the midnight attack that was imminent.

The Patriots were anxious to arrange a truce because they were short on gunpowder and ammunition. As Williamson reported to the Council, the truce "was lucky for us, was we had not above thirty pounds of powder."

The Battle of Ninety Six, the first Revolutionary engagement in the southern colonies, produced few casualties and came to an inconclusive end. It was however, the beginning of a vicious civil war that continued in the southern provinces until after Yorktown.

Marvin L. Cann

REFERENCES

Robert D. Bass, *Ninety Six: The Struggle for the South Carolina Back Country* (1976); Marvin L. Cann, "Prelude to War: The Final Battle of Ninety Six, November 19–21, 1775," *South Carolina Historical Magazine*, 76 (1976): 197–214.

Ninety Six, South Carolina, Siege of (May 22–June 19, 1781)

The courthouse village of Ninety Six, located on a ridge south of the Saluda River in the South Carolina backcountry, was the scene of one of the longest sieges conducted by American forces during the Revolutionary War.

After the British captured Charleston in May 1780, Lord Charles Cornwallis garrisoned a chain of posts in the interior including large strategic forts at Augusta, Camden, Georgetown, and Ninety Six with small supporting posts at Forts Motte, Granby, Watson, and Orangeburg. He expected these garrisons to repel any Patriot attack, to recruit Loyalist volunteers, and to furnish supplies for offensive operations into Virginia.

The principal fortress was established at Ninety Six, the westernmost outpost that guarded vital lines of communication to the Cherokee Nation and between Augusta and Charlotte. Ninety Six was centered in a region where many inhabitants were sympathetic to the British cause and where a strong Loyalist regiment might be raised.

To command this strategic fort, Cornwallis selected Colonel John Harris Cruger, a prominent New York Loyalist, who came to Ninety Six with his 2nd Battalion of New York Volunteers. The garrison also included a battalion of Loyalist militia from New Jersey under Lieutenant Colonel Isaac Allen and 200 South Carolina Loyalist militia led by Richard King. In his letter of instructions to Cruger, Cornwallis underscored the critical nature of the assignment and warned that "keeping possession of the backcountry is of utmost importance, indeed the success of the war in the Southern District depends totally upon it."

By September 1780 Cruger began the fortification system that made Ninety Six one of the strongest British positions in the South. First, the garrison built a palisade and ditch around the village with blockhouses protecting the Island Ford and Charleston roads. An earthen redoubt was added around the brick jail, yet Cruger considered the fortifications inadequate. He urged Cornwallis to dispatch an engineer to add "the nice touches and compleat arrangement of things." In November, Cornwallis sent his staff engineer, Lieutenant Henry Haldane, to inspect the defenses at Ninety Six. Haldane "found the works in a much better state than expected" and recommended only two additions. On a line 30 yards from the ditch, he indicated the proper location for an abatis; and, in an area adjoining the northeastern corner of the town stockade, he laid out a regular earthen fort in the shape of an eight-point star, with walls 12 feet high and protected by a deep ditch and abatis.

Cruger later added a small stockade fort, with palisade lines joining outbuildings on land held by James Holmes. This small redoubt stood on the high ground 200 yards west of the jail to protect the garrison's only water supply, which came from a stream in a ravine below the village. Holmes was connected to the town defenses by a *caponier*, or communications trench.

In the spring of 1781, American general Nathanael Greene led his forces in a war of the outposts. By late May, all British posts west of Charleston had been captured except Augusta and Ninety Six. Sending Colonels Henry Lee and Francis Marion to attack Augusta, Greene marched to Ninety Six with a corps of 974 men from Maryland, Virginia, North Carolina, and Delaware.

The American army encamped before Ninety Six on the night of May 22, 1781. Accompanied by his chief engineer, Count Thaddeus Kosciuszko, Greene reconnoitered the British post to plan the attack. Kosciuszko urged an attack by siege, and Greene agreed.

The Patriots constructed an artillery battery about 130 yards from the Star Redoubt to support a siege trench that they opened only 70 yards from the Star Redoubt. This rash attempt to begin a siege so near a regular fortification caused a disaster. Early on May 23, Cruger mounted his cannon on a platform in the Star. Under heavy barrages and "incessant platoons of musketry," a 30-man sortie attacked the American sappers. The Americans suffered serious casualties and lost their entrenching tools to the British. The sally party had only one casualty, Lieutenant John Roney of the New York Volunteers, who was mortally wounded.

Greene promptly withdrew to a position two hundred yards from the Star and began digging a system of approach trenches and parallels which allowed his troops, slowly but under cover, to move toward the Star Redoubt. Construction of the siegeworks and cannon batteries required exhausting labor. Kosciuszko complained that the "Ground was very hard and approached very much to Soft Stone." With 12-days of backbreaking work by American sappers, the siegeworks were just outside the abatis, about 30 yards from the defensive ditch, and American fatigue parties were subjected to a withering and deadly fire. To counter this hazard, Greene ordered construction of a log tower, which was completed on June 2. Patriot marksmen, firing from the tower, silenced the British muskets and forced the defenders to stay below the parapet. Green reported that "not a man could shew his head but he was immediately shot down."

Cruger raised the parapet three feet with sandbags and tried to burn the log tower. His men fired heated cannon balls into the tower, but since the logs were green and there were no proper furnaces for heating shot, the attempt failed.

On June 8, Lee joined the army at Ninety Six after a successful attack at Augusta. Greene ordered the Virginia Legion to open siegeworks against Holmes Fort. Despite nightly sorties from the fort that resulted in bitter fighting and mounting causalities on both sides, by June 12 Lee was able to enfilade the ravine below Holmes Fort with cannon and rifle fire. This deprived the garrison of water and, in the intense June heat, caused great suffering. Until the siege ended seven days later, the only water available to the garrison was brought into the lines at night by naked slaves who slipped into the ravine and returned with a few pails, which were carefully rationed.

Meanwhile, the attack against the Star Redoubt continued. American sappers cut through the abatis and extended assault trenches to within six feet of the ditch. Greene also set engineers to work on a mine, or tunnel, which was intended to run beneath the defensive ditch and under the wall of the redoubt. A chamber at the end of the mine was to be packed with gunpowder and exploded to breach the wall, opening the way for a Patriot assault. Greene was forced by circumstances to lift the siege before the mine was completed.

From the beginning of the 28-day siege of Fort Ninety Six, Greene feared that British reinforcements might interrupt his attack before the garrison surrendered. His concern was well founded. On June 3, three regiments of Irish Guards arrived in Charleston to reinforce Lord Francis Rawdon. With 2,000 fresh troops, Rawdon marched to relieve Ninety Six. On June 17, word of Rawdon's approach reached the beleaguered garrison when a Loyalist farmer dashed into the fort on horseback with the news that Rawdon was near the Saluda River, hardly more than a day's march from the fort.

Since siege tactics had failed to breach the defenses at Ninety Six, Greene reluctantly ordered an assault, signaling the attack at noon on June 18, 1781. This frontal assault against the Star Redoubt was bloody and brief.

The Virginia Legion and Delaware infantry stormed the stockade fort on the right and drove the defenders from Holmes Redoubt, but the attack on the Star failed. Under a "furious cannonade," 50 Patriots of the forlorn hope entered the ditch to pull down the sandbags topping the parapet with grappling hooks so that the main body of troops might scale the wall. Cruger's men could not aim at the assault party without being exposed to lethal fire. Cruger sent two sally parties to drive the Americans from the ditch. These volunteers circled the ditch and charged the Americans from both sides with fixed bayonets. About 40 Patriots were killed or wounded, and the force of the assault was broken.

Since he was unable to capture Fort Ninety Six and did not dare contest Lord Rawdon's reinforcements in the open, Greene lifted the siege and retreated beyond the Saluda River.

The relief expedition reached Ninety Six on June 21, exhausted by the forced march in the hot and humid Carolina summer. Rawdon had few options. Fort Ninety Six was isolated in the interior, nearly 200 miles from the closest British base. An effective garrison could not be maintained there, and it was too far from Charleston to be saved from another Patriot attack. Consequently, Rawdon decided to abandon Ninety Six and the backcountry. He demolished the fortifications, burned the village, and gathered neighborhood Loyalists who wanted British protection before returning to Charleston. With the evacuation from Ninety Six, the British lost their final stronghold in the southern interior and were confined to a small coastal enclave until the war ended.

Marvin L. Cann

REFERENCES

Robert D. Bass, *Ninety Six: The Struggle for the South Carolina Back Country* (1975); Marvin L. Cann, "War in the Back Country: The Siege of Ninety Six, May 22–June 19, 1781." *South Carolina Historical Magazine*, 71 (1971). 1–24.

Nixon, John (1725–1815)

Continental Army officer. Nixon was from Framingham, Massachusetts. He participated in several campaigns during the French and Indian War. At the Battle of Concord (April 19, 1775) Nixon served as a militia colonel. At Bunker Hill (June 17, 1775) he was wounded. Nixon was in the New York campaign and performed ably at Harlem Heights. He became a Continental colonel and in August 1776 a brigadier general. He led a brigade on the Delaware to assist in the capture of Trenton, but his unit was unable to cross the river on December 25, 1775.

Nixon marched his regiment to Saratoga. There he helped to defend the American right wing on the Hudson River. During the battle, Nixon suffered severe injuries to an eye and an ear. Apparently his last important military duty was to guard part of the Convention Army marched to Cambridge. Due to poor health, he resigned from the army in September 1780.

Richard L. Blanco

REFERENCES

DAB; John H. Merriam, "The Military Record of Brigadier General John Nixon of Massachusetts," *American Antiquarian Society Proceedings, 36* (1926) :38–70.

Norfolk, Virginia, the Burning of (January 1, 1776)

After Lord Dunmore evacuated Great Bridge and Norfolk he found sanctuary within a squadron of five British naval vessels anchored off the coast. General Robert Howe, commander of the Virginian troops, feared a British attack on his camp. In need of water and provisions for his force and determined to have revenge on the rebels, Dunmore ordered the bombardment of the docks, the burning of the town, and the seizure of supplies. The actual degree of damage caused by the British was minimal (about 50 buildings). What is unique about this incident was its propaganda value for the Patriot cause. Howe, anxious to retaliate on the port because of its Loyalist sympathies, let the town burn. Then American troops set fire to supposedly Tory dwellings. The burning and looting by the Americans lasted three days, and another 860 structures were destroyed. However, the truth was concealed, and for decades the American public blamed Dunmore for the devastation of this Virginia port.

Richard L. Blanco

REFERENCES

David John Mays, ed., *The Letters and Papers of Edmund Pendleton, 1734–1803*, 2 vols. (1967); John Selby, *The Revolution in Virginia 1775–1783* (1989).

North, Frederick Lord, 2nd Earl of Guilford (1732–1792)

British statesman. Lord North was Prime Minister of England during the American Revolution and a leading British politician during the entire period of conflict with the American colonies. He was chief spokesman for the government in the House of Commons from 1768 to 1782, and he was head of the cabinet and Lord Treasurer from 1770 to 1782. He faced numerous domestic and foreign problems, but his ministry was primarily occupied with the America situation. He consistently supported Britain's efforts to maintain sovereignty over its American colonies. For nearly two centuries his incompetence and corruption were considered responsible for the breakup of the first British Empire. Recently his reputation has been revived, and his ability as a politician and his personal integrity have been reestablished.

Lord North was born on April 13, 1732, in London. His father was Francis North, first Earl of Guilford, an intimate friend of the Prince of Wales, father of George III. Francis North was on good terms with his son throughout his life, but he severely restricted Lord North's allowance, causing him financial difficulties. Lord North's mother was Lady Lucy Montagu, daughter of the second Earl of Halifax. She died in 1734, and Lord North had two stepmothers with whom he enjoyed cordial relations. One of his stepbrothers was Lord Lewisham, second Earl of Dartmouth, who became North's closest personal friend. He grew up in a happy family atmosphere.

Lord North went to Eton in 1742 and then to Trinity College, Oxford, where he received an M.A. in 1750. After leaving university, North and Lewisham spent three years traveling on the continent. They visited Germany, Italy, and France; not a breath of scandal accompanied their journeys. In May 1756 North married the heiress Anne Speke. They had an especially happy marriage, producing seven children. The only cloud in their married life was lack of money because Anne's inheritance did not materialize. They did not have the funds to live like other members of their class, and they could not participate in fashionable social life. In order to support his family, it was necessary for North to pursue a political career.

A life in politics was natural for North. He was born into the British oligarchy that controlled eighteenth-century politics. He was related to nearly all important political figures of the period, both in the government and in the opposition. His godfather was the Prince of Wales, and George III was one of his childhood playmates. Because of his close personal relations and strong physical resemblance to members of the royal family, North was plagued throughout his life with rumors that he was actually George III's half-brother. When North returned from Europe in 1754, his father secured him the parliamentary seat of Banbury, which North held until his succession to the earldom in 1790. North entered the Commons determined to achieve government office and political preferment from his various relatives, friends, and colleagues. His pursuit of office was helped by his good education, his excellent manners, his sense of humor, his reputation as a man of integrity, his debating skills, and his ability to understand government finance.

North entered the Commons as a protégé of the Duke of Newcastle. He made several successful speeches in the House, and by 1760 he was known as a coming man. He received several minor appointments, which provided him with needed income. In 1759 Newcastle appointed him to the Treasury Board, and he remained on the Board through several ministries because of the good will of George III. During the early years of his political life, financial needs usually dictated that North support the ministry in office, though his political allegiance would not allow him to accept office from the Marquis of Rockingham in 1765. North was opposed to repeal of the Stamp Act and believed that the American problem should be handled with firmness. In 1766 Chatham appointed North joint-paymaster for the forces and made him a member of the Privy Council, more than doubling his income and increasing his political influence. By 1767 he was attending cabinet meetings and was one of the chief spokesman for the government in the House of Commons.

He had been suggested as a possible Chancellor of the Exchequer as early as 1765, but he was not appointed to the office until 1767, upon the death of Charles Townshend. North did not want the appointment because he would lose 1,000 pounds sterling of income when he gave up the paymastership. But the king let it be known that North would have no office at all if he refused to become Chancellor of the Exchequer. The government needed North as Chancellor because of his financial and budgetary knowledge and because of his skills as a debater. He better than anyone else was able to argue persuasively the government's position, and from 1767 until 1782 North was the leader of the House of Commons. North quickly demonstrated his skillful management of the House with his successful handling of the Middlesex election and the case of John Wilkes. He gained prestige in the House and the king's confidence, but his stand against the popular hero Wilkes gained him no support outside of Parliament or in America.

Relations with the American colonies were difficult when he first came to office because the government was attempting to enforce the Townshend Duties. North apparently had nothing to do with imposition of the duties in 1767, but as Chancellor of the Exchequer in the Duke of Grafton's ministry the duties became part of his American policy. From the beginning North showed reluctance to maintain the taxes, in part because of nonimportation but also because he considered them to be "uncommercial." However, he unequivocally supported the right of parliamentary taxation of the colonies and believed the colonists should submit to the will of the British government. He supported sending troops to Boston to establish order and aid in compliance, and he agreed with Townshend's policy of establishing an American civil list that would place colonial officials under the control of the British government. In 1769 he voted with the majority of the cabinet to retain the Townshend Duties.

Grafton's government, weakened by conflict over American policy and the Wilkes affair, was forced to resign in early 1770. George III immediately let it be known that he preferred to have Lord North as leader of the next government. When North had assured himself that he had a majority of votes in the House Commons, he agreed to become First Lord of the Treasury, head of the ministry and move to Downing Street. He retained his position as Chancellor of the Exchequer, therefore controlling all aspects of governmental finance until 1782 when his ministry was forced to resign. Some people expressed surprise that he was chosen to lead the government, but many more concluded that he was the obvious choice. Clearly the government would be more successful if its leader was in the House of Commons, and North had been chief spokesman in the House for more than two years. His popularity in the House was both personal and political. In addition, there were no other candidates for the office who had the king's support. By April 1770 North had consolidated his position among the independent members of Parliament and could assure the government a majority of 70 votes.

The survival of North's government for 12 years was based on a number of factors. Much of North's political success resulted from his personal qualities. His knowledge of finance was superior to anyone else's, and therefore he was able to withstand attack in this pivotal area of policy. His debating skills were unsurpassed. He was not a great orator, never achieving the rhetorical levels of Fox or Chatham. But he could win debates with clear enunciation of his position and through his ability to trip up speakers who attempted to appear clever and witty. He often used self-deprecation and then gently ridiculed his opponents. He had a prodigious memory that provided him with detail and fact that he could use effectively even when speaking extemporaneously. He always presented his ideas as practical, managing to paint his opponents as unrealistic. He was willing to compromise in ways that assured victory for the government. In addition, he was personally popular. Despite his piglike face, bulging eyes, and floundering body, he was naturally charming and good tempered. He never became angry. Even his political enemies had to admit that they liked Lord North as a person. His pleasing personality helped to attract and retain the allegiance of the pivotal country members through various crises, until his failed American policy would no longer be tolerated by the country.

North's success in government was also due to the disarray of the opposition. There was personal conflict among many of the leaders. The opposition was also divided over policy, especially about radicalism and reform of the House of Commons. Nearly all the opposition leaders were in the House of Lords, thus strengthening North's influence in the lower House.

North used patronage to maintain a majority in the House of Commons. His close association with the king gave him the ability to award pensions and offices that would reward government supporters and cement their loyalty to the ministry. He did not have enough patronage to go around, however, and such rewards were only one of the tools that he used to maintain his government in power.

Of immense importance to Lord North's

position was the support of the king. No late eighteenth-century ministry could endure for 12 years without the backing of George III. The close relationship between North and the king was based upon a long friendship, a similarity of views, and mutual need. George III needed North's skills in government to maintain a stable ministry, and North needed the king's support to stay in office and to provide him with the patronage he needed to support his family. The king rewarded his minister with honors, such as the Order of the Garter, and with lucrative offices, such as lifetime Wardenship of the Cinque Ports. In addition, in 1777 George III assumed North's debts of eighteen thousand pounds sterling, thus binding the minister to the king's service for as long as the king required him. North consulted George III far more often than any Prime Minister before him, and George continually offered volumes of advice to North and the other members of the cabinet. Their relationship was so close that the opposition and many historians have viewed North as a lackey in George III's attempt to establish royal dominance of British politics. But North was no lackey. He listened to the king and weighed his advice, but his policies were determined by many considerations. Usually North adopted policies that would be supported by the House of Commons. Like all good Whigs, North believed in the supremacy of the British Parliament, that Parliament was responsible only to itself even if it meant opposition to the throne. Thus in 1763 North supported Grenville's attacks on Lord Bute, and in 1783 he formed a coalition government with the king's personal enemy Charles James Fox. It was North's belief in parliamentary sovereignty that also caused him to pursue a firm policy toward the American colonies, even if it meant going to war.

Another frequent criticism of Lord North from both contemporaries and historians has been that he was a weak and indecisive Prime Minister. Other cabinet members complained that he did not accept his role as leader of the government. There were continual accounts of cabinet meetings held after dinner at which North was unprepared and uninterested, allowing policy to be determined in a slapdash manner with no formal record of what had taken place. He seldom intervened in the running of individual government departments, with the result that contradictory policies might be pur-

sued by different cabinet ministers. He would not control ministers, like Lord Sandwich and Lord Germain, who violently criticized each other. At times it seemed that his government was one of chaos. In the second half of his ministry he was often unable to make crucial decisions about policy and personnel, to the despair of the king and government supporters. At times North responded to charges of poor leadership by arguing that he was not a Prime Minister, that there was no such office in the British constitution. He refused to call himself Prime Minister, and seemed to take pride in his ability to say that he did not interfere in the running of departments other than the Treasury and Exchequer. He ran the cabinet by consensus, but at times he did exercise sufficient leadership to justify the title Prime Minister. However, he was more likely to avoid dominating his government. In part this was because of the debilitating amount of work he had as leader in the Commons and as chief financial minister. He was always tired, frequently sleeping during parliamentary debate and cabinet meetings. But he also avoided confrontation and controversy by hiding behind his claim of departmental responsibility. He was prone to indecision in difficult situations, consulting with many and prolonging inactivity. At times he fell into deep depressions that were brought on by personal and political crises—the death of a favorite child or Burgoyne's surrender at Saratoga. During these depressions he would beg the king to release him from office. Over a period of weeks or months his depression would abate, he would remain in office, and he would finally make the crucial decisions. However, government had been paralyzed while he recovered and complaints of lack of decisive leadership were justified.

Despite periods of depression and indecision, North remained in office for 12 years, much of the time fulfilling his role admirably and relishing the political game, which he dominated. He enjoyed the approval of the House of Commons and the affection of the king. Though his policies were occasionally rejected by Parliament, he was the only man who seemed capable of running the government during the 1770's. He attempted to bring moderation and stability to government, and his great grief was that he was forced by events to plunge England into war with the American colonies, France, and Spain.

When he formed his government in 1770, North hoped to be able to solve the American problem with a policy of conciliation and firmness. In order to demonstrate the good will of the Mother Country, British troops were removed from Boston to Castle William, and the New York Assembly was allowed to issue bills of credit. Most importantly, he proposed to repeal all the Townshend Duties except for the tax on tea. This would eliminate the bulk of American grievances. He did not believe that the British government should capitulate entirely, so the tea tax remained to demonstrate parliamentary sovereignty. North argued that the tea tax was a "commercial" tax because tea was not of English manufacture and it was a luxury. North also knew that the House of Commons would not accept any government policy that backed down from asserting the right of parliamentary taxation. North anticipated that money from the tea tax would provide a civil list that would gradually allow the British government more control over colonial affairs. North's policy was successful; the Americans abandoned nonimportation, the House of Commons retained the appearance of supremacy over its Empire, and American affairs receded from the public agenda.

North was serious in his approach to the American question because he believed, like most Englishmen, that the American colonies were essential to English trade and prosperity. He thought that maintenance of the American empire was essential to England's stature as a great nation. For this reason he was willing to conciliate and compromise with the Americans, if that meant continued trade and peaceful relations. But because of America's importance to British prosperity, North was not willing to allow the Americans control of their own trade and economy. North was convinced that Britain's economic health depended on the American economy; therefore, he continually affirmed that the British Parliament must have ultimate control over the American colonies.

North's American policy proved satisfactory until 1773, but disintegrated with passage of the Tea Act of 1773. Though a number of American radicals believed that the Tea Act was a plot to impose coercion on the American colonies, North had no such intention. His problem in 1773 was the financial ruin of the East India Company, and his goals were to end the abuses of mismanagement and put the company on a sound financial footing. One of the provisions of his plan to save the company was to allow it to sell its tea in America without the use of middlemen. North would not rescind the Townshend duty on tea, knowing that the majority in Commons would reject the idea, but he believed Americans would continue to buy taxed English tea as they had since 1770. The American response, particularly to the Boston Tea Party, seems to have truly surprised and angered North. He resolved to demonstrate the supremacy of parliamentary legislative authority to all Americans. He believed that a show of force would pacify America, and that failure of the British government to respond firmly to the outrage in Boston would further erode imperial control. North had no choice but to respond with force. The House of Commons was furious at Boston's defiance, and North could not have remained in power if he had wavered in his resolve to demonstrate English authority. The Coercive Acts were the instruments of his policy of firm response; they would punish Boston for the destruction of the tea and give the British government administrative control over future events in Massachusetts. North expected Massachusetts to capitulate in the face of British resolve, believing that American commercial interests would disavow radicals like Adams and Hancock in order to reestablish trade. North was wrong, and the American colonists rallied around Massachusetts.

In early 1775 North returned to his earlier policy of combining force and conciliation. Passage of the New England Restraining Act was an aspect of his policy of firm response; offering his olive branch to the American colonies, in which he promised not to execute Parliament's right to tax the colonies if their legislatures would vote sufficient funds to provide for the common defense, was his attempt at conciliation. This time his policy of conciliation failed to pacify the colonists. Events in America outran North's capacity to manage them. After receiving word of the Battle of Bunker Hill, North informed the king that the American situation had to be treated as a foreign war. The minister that had hoped to provide imperial stability and prosperity found that he had been unable to prevent a colonial rebellion.

The failure of his American policy colored North's response to subsequent events, never allowing him to approach American affairs with optimism. He never seemed to understand why his American policy had failed, and his confusion about the American situation may have led him to doubt his ability to devise a successful American strategy. His pessimism was reinforced by the lack of fervor in England toward the war. The Commons did not want to vote much money, and there were few volunteers to fight the American rebels. He received no guidance from the opposition in formulating a new policy. They provided no insight into imperial governance, merely disclaiming against North's incompetence, his despotism or his pandering to royal influence. North did not want war, but he saw no alternative. North was personally and politically committed to the maintenance of parliamentary sovereignty, and he could only maintain sovereignty through war. No other policy would have carried a majority in the House of Commons in 1775.

Perhaps because of his own pessimism as well as doubts about his ability in military matters, Lord North gave control of conduct of the war to other members of the cabinet, primarily the new American secretary Lord George Germain. North offered opinions on American campaigns, but he largely confined his involvement to defending government policy in the House of Commons and to financial aspects of fighting the war.

His main problem was finding the money necessary to wage a full-scale war across the Atlantic. The war could not be fought out of current revenue, so it was necessary for North to float annual loans to meet military and naval expenses. The loans were increasingly difficult to negotiate as the war dragged on and the national debt increased. North successfully borrowed 57.5 million pounds but at ever higher interest, which aroused great criticism in the Commons among both opposition and country members. As interest on the debt increased, North was forced to raise taxes, which decreased the popularity of both the war and his ministry. North also had to handle military contracts and government suppliers. He made do with the existing system, but was appalled at the waste and corruption that existed. He instituted a number of studies and commissions of inquiry, which proposed reforms that were implemented by William Pitt during his ministry. North was forced to defend his government against continual charges of mismanagement and corruption. Surviving records provide no evidence that he ever personally benefited from any of the fraud, though some of his friends and political allies did.

As North involved himself in financial matters, military operations failed to bring an end to the war. Burgoyne's surrender at Saratoga was a devastating blow to North because he, like the rest of the ministry, had pinned their hopes on a successful campaign in 1777. Saratoga forced North to face the failure of his government's policies, and his response was to decry his own weaknesses, to declare himself unfit to run the war and to ask the king to allow him to resign. He remained in office four years following Saratoga, but he never believed he could bring the war to a successful conclusion. There is little evidence of his personal involvement in military decisions after 1777 except to approve strategy such as launching a southern campaign. He attended cabinet meetings and defended the government in Parliament and to George III. He remained occupied with financial matters and with maintaining a parliamentary majority, allowing his ministers to take the lead in formulating British policy against America and her allies. The documentary record substantiates charges from contemporaries and historians that he failed to give overall leadership to administration of the war.

North and his cabinet faced serious problems between 1778 and their fall from power in 1782. American strategy needed constant revision. The French and Spanish were endangering other imperial possessions and were sailing in the English Channel, threatening the safety of the English coast and English shipping. England found herself isolated in world affairs, and North had to address himself continually to questions of foreign affairs. Ireland and India erupted in rebellion, suggesting that the entire Empire might be crumbling under North's leadership. The situation in Parliament also deteriorated. Criticism from the opposition increased inside Parliament and agitation for reform increased outside. Finally in 1780 discontent about North and his ministry coalesced in Dunning's famous resolution that "the influence of the crown has increased, is increasing, and ought to be diminished," demonstrating that there was a lack of confidence in North's ministry. But North remained in office, aided by the Gordon Riots, the fall of Charleston, and a resolute policy toward Ireland and India. He retained the support of the independent members, who found no alternate leader who represented their political beliefs better than North.

Only when Cornwallis surrendered at Yorktown was the burden of war too great to allow North to continue as Prime Minister. According to accounts, North received the news from Yorktown on November 25, 1781, with the statement, "Oh God! It is all over." North recognized that the load of taxes and unfunded debt were unbearable to the country in the face of an unsuccessful war. His own ministry was too compromised by its war policy to continue in office and negotiate a peace settlement. He was forced to hold his ministry together for a few months because the king refused to accept the idea of American independence and would not allow him to resign. As votes were taken on various measures, North's majority in the Commons gradually disappeared. Finally on March 20, 1782, it was clear that the House would vote no confidence in North, and to avoid the shame of that vote, George III allowed him to resign. George rudely dismissed his friend and servant with the words, "Remember, my Lord, that it is you who desert me, not I you." The king then pettily refused to pay the election debts North had taken out on the king's behalf in 1780, leaving North burdened with the threat of financial insolvency.

North remained a powerful force in the House of Commons because he had almost one hundred followers who continued to vote with him in opposition. North opposed Lord Shelburne's peace plan and joined forces with his former political enemy Charles James Fox. In 1783 they formed a coalition forcing Shelburne out of office and foisting themselves on an angry George III. Through political maneuvering in the House of Lords, George was able to defeat the Fox-North coalition and replace it with the Younger Pitt's first ministry. North continued in the House of Commons in steady opposition to Pitt's government until 1790 but his followers gradually disappeared; in 1788 he only controlled about 20 votes in the House. He continued to see himself as a champion of parliamentary government, but his reputation was destroyed. To most Englishmen, he was the minister who had lost America.

In 1790 his father died, and he became the Earl of Guilford. His financial problems were now solved, but his succession came too late in life for him to receive much benefit. He was already completely blind and his health was failing. He died on August 5, 1792, having acknowledged that he had made political mistakes but fearful that history would judge him more harshly than he deserved. Posterity has not been kind. For 200 years Englishmen regarded him as responsible for the loss of the American colonies, and Americans viewed him as the man whose tyrannical policies forced them into revolution. Only recently have historians applauded his efficient handling of administrative and financial problems, anticipating many reforms upon which rest the reputation of William Pitt. Many acknowledge that North's policies were the only ones acceptable to the House of Commons in the 1780s and that probably no one could have saved the Empire. However, Lord North bears the political responsibility for the loss of the first British Empire.

Allida McKinley

REFERENCES

Herbert Butterfield, *George III, Lord North and the People 1778–80* (1949); John Cannon, *The Fox-North Coalition: Crisis of the Constitution, 1782–1784* (1969); Charles Daniel Smith, *The Early Career of Lord North the Prime Minister* (1979); Peter D.G. Thomas, *Lord North* (1976).

North Carolina in the American Revolution

North Carolina entered the Revolution as a rural, agricultural, heterogeneous colony. It was also showing the effects of a massive population explosion that strained the government's capacity to govern, exacerbated sectional tensions, and populated the colony with a remarkably diverse population. Although population figures for this period are imprecise, it is generally estimated that North Carolina had barely 30,000 white people in 1730, almost all confined to the eastern edge of the colony. Four decades later, North Carolina's population had reached a total variously estimated anywhere from 250,000 to 340,000. Beginning around 1750 much of this influx came down the Great Wagon Road into the North Carolina backcountry, lured by land that was cheap, fertile, and readily available.

Scotch-Irish Presbyterians, Lutheran and Reformed Germans, and Moravians (especially in the area around Salem), mixed with English settlers coming from the eastern part of the colony, from South Carolina, and from the Virginia Tidewater to populate the backcountry. Scottish Highlanders settled in the Cape Fear region near Cross Creek (present-day Fayetteville), particularly after the Highlander defeat in 1746 at the Battle of Culloden.

Nonetheless, the 1790 census indicated that most North Carolinians had English surnames, although doubtless some non-English settlers had anglicized their names by that point. Settlers of English descent dominated the eastern part of North Carolina, which had been settled since the 1650s, and were present throughout the colony. Many of the English speakers were Baptists, Methodists, Quakers, and other dissenters. Thus the Church of England, although legally established, was weak.

Black slaves made up an increasing portion of the colony, possibly as many as 80,000 by the beginning of the Revolution. They were located mostly in the eastern part of North Carolina. Over half of New Hanover County's population in 1780 were slaves, while several other eastern counties approached that figure. Slaveholding was concentrated in areas where planters produced for the market. Manumission was difficult in colonial North Carolina, and the number of free blacks was small.

Generations of war, disease, and outmigration had depleted the native Americans of North Carolina's nonmountain regions, leaving them little threat to white settlement of the backcountry. At the western edge of white settlement, however, were the more numerous and more dangerous Cherokees, who combined with the physical barrier of the Appalachian Mountains to present formidable obstacles to western expansion. Yet prior to the Revolution some settlers had disregarded British restrictions and settled west of the mountains.

Most North Carolinians made their living by farming. Virtually every farmer in the interior practiced subsistence agriculture. Numerous visitors commented on the large number of free-ranging livestock. Many also commented on the alleged backwardness of much of the colony. In the words of historian Alice Mathews, the average North Carolinian was "indebted, lived in a small frame house or log cabin, was often deemed slovenly and lazy by contemporary visitors, and had little contact with the outside world." Geography was a major factor holding back the economic growth of the colony. A series of barrier islands, known as the Outer Banks, restricted coastal traffic. Transportation from the coast to the interior was poor, while several major river systems ended up in Virginia or South Carolina. The Moravians, for example, regularly sent trade goods to distant Charleston, rather than to the inaccessible ports of the North Carolina coast.

Nonetheless, it would be a mistake to think of North Carolina in this period as nothing but a frontier of small farmers. Large planters were scattered throughout the eastern portion of the colony, while well-to-do merchants were situated in such modest but locally important towns as New Bern, Edenton, Wilmington, Brunswick, Halifax, Cross Creek, and Bath. The Cape Fear River provided the colony's best coastal access to the interior. Alone of North Carolina's major rivers, it emptied directly into the Atlantic Ocean. By 1770 Cross Creek had emerged as the hub of the Cape Fear region's inland trade, while Wilmington was in the process of supplanting Brunswick as the primary port on the Cape Fear, in large part because it was located further upriver than its rival and was thus better protected from bad weather and hostile invasion.

North Carolina's largest export was naval stores, specifically turpentine, tar, pitch, and rosin produced from the east's abundant supply of pine trees. The largest producers of naval stores relied heavily on slaves. Since the British navy was the single largest purchaser of North Carolina's largest export, the approach of hostilities had serious implications for this valuable crop. The east also exported lumber, especially sawn lumber, staves, and shingles. The Cape Fear region was filled with sawmills, while shingles were a major export of the Albemarle region. Another major export was foodstuffs, including corn, pork, beef, fish, wheat, peas, and beans. Much of this was exported to the West Indies. Tobacco was also a major export, although not to the extent of Virginia or Maryland. A large proportion of North Carolina's tobacco crop was grown in the northeast part of the colony and exported by way of Virginia ports. Even so some 1,500,000 pounds of tobacco were shipped from North Carolina ports. Rice and indigo were grown in the lower Cape Fear region and were heavily associated with slavery. North Carolina sent the largest amount of its exports to other colonies, followed by the British Isles, then the West Indies.

Imports from Britain and the other colonies included manufactured goods, salt, refined sugar, spices, beverages, rum, and molasses. Some planters and merchants amassed fortunes and constituted the colony's elite, along with a small professional class. The bulk of this elite was located in the eastern part of North Carolina. Furthermore, the eastern counties were overrepresented in the colonial assembly, adding to sectional animosities.

Thus North Carolina had reasons to be cautious in moving away from Great Britain. The colony was fully integrated into the colonial trading network and relied on the manufactured goods most easily obtained from Great Britain. The huge influx of Scotch and Germans had not been fully assimilated, the Cherokees were poised menacingly on the colony's perimeter, always subject to British encouragement, and rumors of British aims to free and arm the slaves sent shivers up countless spines. Yet North Carolinians, like other colonists, were determined to fight for their rights as Englishmen. As events progressed the colony's caution gave way to its determination.

Perhaps most cautioning was the Regulator controversy, which had inflamed the backcountry in the decade preceding the Revolution. Nineteenth-century historians regarded the Regulators as harbingers of the Revolution. Although present historians have long since discarded that sentiment, it is less clear what the Regulators were. Some argue that the crisis was largely a sectional one, drawn along east–west lines. Others see it as class warfare. Still others see it as status anxiety by eastern planters worried about the growing power of the backcountry.

The Regulators were backcountry farmers who protested a series of government abuses, specifically a regressive tax system that relied largely on poll taxes, fees, and duties, and the abuses of appointed judicial and administrative officials who routinely awarded public contracts to friends, charged exorbitant fees, and used the legal system to extort money and line their pockets. Many farmers were unable to pay these taxes and fees and as a result lost their land to corrupt officials. Few argued that the Regulators did not have legitimate grievances. William Tryon, royal governor from 1765 until 1771, estimated that county sheriffs had embezzled over half the money due the government between 1754 and 1767.

The Regulator movement began in 1766 and was formally organized in 1768. At first they confined their protests to such lawful attempts at redress as publishing pamphlets, attempting to elect farmers to the General Assembly, and lobbying the governor and the General Assembly. None of these avenues was successful. Eventually, the Regulators turned to more drastic measures, including refusing to pay taxes, confronting officials, and breaking up court sessions. By 1768 the movement had turned violent. The Regulators resorted to riots, beatings, jail burnings, and forced court closings to press their case, all to no avail.

Governor Tryon was not unsympathetic to the Regulators, at least during the early phase of the controversy. His attention was no doubt diverted by the increasing crisis in British–colonial relations, particularly the Townshend Act controversy. However, as events became more violent, Tryon became more determined to enforce the laws, however inequitable they might be. In December 1770 the legislature passed several conciliatory measures, including fee regulation and the establishment of four new western counties. However, the next month the legislature passed the Johnston Riot Act, which imposed harsh penalties on rioters and granted the governor the right to take whatever steps were necessary to ensure tranquility. The act infuriated the Regulators, who continued their protests. In the spring of 1771 Governor Tryon marched the militia into the heart of Regulator country in order to guarantee court sessions. On May 16, 1771, the two sides met on the banks of Alamance Creek. Tryon commanded over 1,100 militia against 2,000 to 3,000 poorly disciplined, poorly armed Regulators. Tryon crushed the Regulators in the two-hour Battle of Alamance. The Regulators lost about 20 killed and 100 wounded, while the militia lost 9 dead and 61 wounded. Seven Regulators were hanged, one after the battle, the rest after a court-martial. Over 6,000 Regulators received pardons by signing oaths of allegiance, while a handful fled westward.

Governor Tryon left shortly afterward to become governor of New York. He was replaced by Josiah Martin, a 34-year-old professional soldier. Martin was honest, hardworking, and intelligent. He was also stubborn, intolerant, devoted to royal prerogatives, and completely unwilling to compromise with his increasingly numerous opponents. His tenure in North Carolina would be stormy.

Although largely an internal affair, the Regulator controversy took place in the context of deteriorating relations between the colonies and England. Cautious North Carolina did not play a leading role in these developments but did offer general support to colonial opposition to the Stamp Act, the Townshend Act, and the Coercive Act. Opposition to the Stamp Act was especially violent in the lower Cape Fear region. In November 1765 after several demonstrations, the Sons of Liberty forced the resignation of the Wilmington stamp master. That same month many of these same men refused to allow the landing of stamps in Brunswick. The following February an armed mob sabotaged efforts to enforce the Stamp Act in Brunswick and forced the resignation of the comptroller of customs. During the Townshend Act crisis the assembly met illegally and formed a nonimportation association, under the leadership of Speaker of the House John Harvey.

In December 1773 North Carolina established a Committee of Correspondence, in response to a request from Virginia that each colony establish such a group in order to coordinate responses to British moves. The first members of the committee were Harvey, Robert Howe, Richard Caswell, Edward Vail, John Ashe, Joseph Hewes, and Samuel Johnston. These men would continue to be leaders in the struggle against England. At the same time the General Assembly was clashing with Governor Martin over the colony's court system. This struggle, which was unrelated to the larger questions concerning the Crown and the colonies, nonetheless resulted in increasing tensions between Martin and the legislature.

These tensions worsened in 1774, when Governor Martin refused to call the legislature into session for the purpose of electing delegates to the Continental Congress. Instead Harvey called what became known as the First Provincial Congress, the first of five extralegal assemblies that moved the state from colony to commonwealth over the next two years. They met in New Bern from August 25 to August 27 and elected William Hooper, Richard Caswell, and Joseph Hewes as delegates to the First Continental Congress. They also criticized recent acts of Parliament, endorsed economic measures against England, recommended the establishment of local com-

mittees of safety, and authorized Harvey to call another congress at his discretion. However, North Carolina was still not ready for a clean break. The Congress continued to profess its continued loyalty to the Crown.

Harvey called the colony's Second Provincial Congress to meet at New Bern on April 3, 1775. In the meantime, Governor Martin had called for the colonial assembly to meet in New Bern on April 4, hoping that the legitimate assembly would undermine the extralegal one. As it turned out voters elected an almost identical membership to both groups. The two assemblies ran in conjunction until April 7, when the Congress adjourned. An angry Martin dissolved the assembly the following day. This would be North Carolina's last royal assembly. The Congress elected Hewes, Hooper, and Caswell again to be delegates to the Continental Congress, further endorsed committees of safety, and established a Council of Safety for the colony. The patriotic fervor of the group can be seen by the reaction to the one member who declined to endorse their actions. "It is manifest," the Congress maintained, that "his intentions are inimical to the Cause of American Liberty, and we do hold him up as a proper object of Contempt to the Continent, and recommend that every person break off all connection and have no further commercial Intercourse or Dealings with him."

Many counties and towns did organize safety committees during this period. These committees furthered the radical cause by enforcing the dictates of the Continental and Provincial congresses, publicizing the cause, and punishing backsliders. The committees generally acted as judge and jury to alleged non-Patriots.

North Carolina's Second Provincial Congress dissolved only days before the fighting began in Massachusetts, although news of this momentous event did not reach most of North Carolina until the middle of May. The sickly Harvey died in early May. However, the previous Provincial Congress had prepared for such an eventuality by giving Samuel Johnston the right to call another provincial congress, should Harvey be unable to fulfill that duty. On May 31 citizens in Mecklenburg County adopted the so-called "Mecklenburg Resolves," which declared all commissions granted by the king to be null and void in the county, graphic evidence of how far Revolutionary sentiment had gone in that Scotch-Irish stronghold. That same day, Martin fled New Bern for Fort Johnston , located at the mouth of the Cape Fear River, and desperately attempted to stem the tide of revolution. Late in June, Martin wrote the Earl of Dartmouth that royal government in North Carolina "is here as absolutely prostrate as impotent, and nothing but the shadow is left." In the early morning hours of July 19, he received word that some 500 local militia, led by Howe, Ashe, and Cornelius Harnett, were advancing on the fort. Martin fled again, this time to the British warship *Cruizer*, which was anchored offshore. Shortly afterward, the deserted fort was burned.

The General Assembly was scheduled to meet in New Bern on July 12. Martin prorogued it until September, then decided to not call it. On August 8 Martin issued his so-called "Fiery Proclamation," in which he denounced recent events in the strongest possible terms and lambasted Revolutionary leaders as being motivated by "their own lust for power and lawless ambition."

Samuel Johnston called the Third Provincial Congress, which met in Hillsborough from August 20 to September 10, 1775. The decision to meet in the heart of Regulator territory has been variously interpreted as an attempt to intimidate those potential opponents of the radicals, or an attempt to attract them to the cause. This congress was largely devoted to putting North Carolina on a war footing and establishing a provisional government. Although denounced by Martin as unrepresentative, the Congress consisted of 184 delegates representing every county and town in North Carolina. The Congress continued to profess loyalty to the Crown, while criticizing both Parliament and Governor Martin. The group authorized two 500-man regiments for the Continental Line, one commanded by Colonel James Moore and the other by Colonel Robert Howe. They also authorized six battalions of minutemen, one from each of North Carolina's military districts.

In the absence of effective government, the Congress established a 13-man provincial council, and a popularly elected safety committee in each of the colony's military districts. They authorized $125,000 to be issued in bills of credit and levied a poll tax of two shillings. Determined not to burn bridges unnecessarily, they sent delegations to court both the Regulators and the Highlanders, both believed to be loyal to the Crown, and rejected Benjamin Franklin's call for a colonial confederation.

Despite the efforts of the Whigs, a substantial number of North Carolinians did remain loyal to the crown. Indeed, Martin was convinced that the majority of North Carolinians were loyal, with only a few mischievous radicals making trouble. He was particularly convinced of the loyalty of the Highlanders and former Regulators, the two groups who concerned the Whigs. Martin was so sure that he proposed to his superiors a complicated plan to crush the rebellion in the Carolinas. He confidently expected to be able to raise 3,000 Highland Scots, 3,000 Regulators, and 3,000 assorted other Tories to fight for the Crown. They would link up on the North Carolina coast with regulars from the British Isles, British troops from Boston, and a British fleet. After the rendezvous they would sweep through North Carolina, and then South Carolina and Virginia, ending the rebellion in the South.

Martin's ambitious plans came to naught. Loyalist partisans were able to raise only a fraction of the 3,000 Highlanders predicted by Martin. In the backcountry, many former Regulators resisted Martin's call to fight for the Crown, while Whig troops broke up the small concentrations of those who did mobilize, preventing most from ever reaching the coast. Throughout the war Martin and the British would overrate the loyalism of the former Regulators. The Highlanders and other Loyalists who did respond were decisively defeated at the Battle of Moore's Creek in February 1776. The rendezvous never took place.

The Loyalist defeat at Moore's Creek emboldened the Whig cause, chastened the Loyalists, and undermined Martin's credibility with the British. The armed conflict also ended any hope of accommodation with the Crown. When the Fourth Provincial Congress met at Halifax from April 4 through May 15, 1776, independence rather than reconciliation was the order of business. It was this assembly that produced the so-called "Halifax Resolves." On April 12 the assemblage unanimously authorized North Carolina delegates in the Continental Congress to "be empowered to concur with the delegates of the other Colonies in declaring Independency, and forming foreign alliances." The group also refined army maintenance, issued more bills of credit, and appointed a nine-man Council of Safety to serve as the executive branch of government. Cornelius Harnett was elected council president.

However, this congress decided not to establish a state constitution, delaying that decision until the fall. Accordingly, the council called for an October 15 election to select delegates for a congress that would produce "the Corner Stone of all Law, the state's first constitution. The election was hotly contested and showed the fissures that divided the Whigs. Voters elected 183 delegates. Although the political leanings of all the delegates are not known, it appears that the convention was about evenly divided between conservatives who favored a strong executive, an independent judiciary, and strict property qualifications for voting, and radicals who favored a strong legislature, a weak executive, and modest property requirements for voting. Enough moderate delegates were elected to hold the balance of power.

The Fifth (and final) Provincial Congress was held at Halifax, from November 12 to December 23, 1776. A committee of 28 delegates drafted the constitution. Influenced by colonial experiences, a quick study of other recent state constitutions, instructions from several counties, and John Adams's essay, "Thoughts on Government," these men produced a compromise government more liberal than that of the royal period, although conservative in many respects.

The North Carolina constitution provided for the basic three branches of government. Mindful of years of disputes with royal governors and judges, the constitution made the bicameral legislature considerably more powerful than the other two branches. The legislature would appoint the governor to a one-year term; a governor could only hold that office for three years in a six-year period. The legislature also gained the power to name other government officials, the seven members of the council of state, principal judicial posts, and generals in the state militia.

The constitution provided moderate property qualifications for voting. Free men (including blacks) who paid taxes could vote for members of the House of Commons, but ownership of 50 acres was required to vote for the state senate. House members were required to own 100 acres of land, senators 300 acres. The governor was required to own property worth at least 1,000 pounds. The Church of England was disestablished, while statewide officeholding was restricted to Protestants. A Declaration of Rights

consisted of 25 articles designed to protect the rights of citizens. Moderate Richard Caswell was elected interim governor. The constitution was adopted by the Congress at large but was not submitted to the electorate for ratification.

The first state legislature met at New Bern on April 7, 1777. They quickly confirmed Caswell as governor and began steps to consolidate control of the state. Although the Battle of Moore's Creek ended for a time direct military opposition by Tories, the state still possessed a large number of Loyalists, Highland Scots in particular. They spoke against the Revolution, refused to accept money, and bided their time until the return of the king's forces. In response the legislature established a state militia, moved to confiscate Tory property, and established loyalty oaths. Some Loyalists, including several merchants, refused to take the oath and left the state. The legislature also voted an ad valorem tax on land, slaves, and other property; instituted poll taxes; and borrowed money to finance the government.

As the war shifted south, military preparedness took legislative priority. The weakness of the governor hampered the state's defensive efforts. In 1780 Governor Abner Nash asked the legislature for a Board of War to advise him on military matters. Alexander Martin, John Penn, and Oroondates Davis were appointed. The board, especially Penn, took such an active control of military operations that the aggrieved Nash threatened to resign. The following year the legislature replaced the board with a three-member Council Extraordinary—Caswell, Alexander Martin, and Allen Jones. This council was given the power to do whatever was necessary to defend the security of the state. The citizenry routinely disregarded the council, to the detriment of the state's war effort.

North Carolina was the site of hostilities for much of 1780 and 1781. Although the two invasions of Cornwallis and Nathanael Greene's masterful campaign have drawn much attention, these regular army conflicts were only a small part of the struggle. In January 1781 Wilmington was captured by Major James Craig. His forces occupied that valuable port city for most of the year and used it as a base for raids into the interior. For most of this period the state was a civil war battleground between Whigs and Loyalists. There were some major pitched battles, most notably the Battle of Ramsour's Mill on June 20,

1780. Predominantly, however, the fighting consisted of vicious, small-scale fighting and raiding involving state militia and partisan bands of both persuasions. Both sides committed depredations, as many partisans seemed more interested in looting or revenge than ideology.

Several of these fights struck directly at the state's ability to govern. In July 1781 Loyalist leader David Fanning raided the Chatham County seat of Pittsboro to stop a court-martial of Loyalists, taking as prisoners several members of the General Assembly, court officials, and militia officers. On September 12 Fanning raided the temporary capital of Hillsborough. He escaped with 200 prisoners, including Governor Thomas Burke, his council, Continental officers, and legislators. This fighting continued until the spring of 1782, when Fanning finally left the state.

In 1783 the General Assembly pardoned most Loyalists. There were five groups of exceptions: British officers, 68 men named in the Confiscation Act of 1779, those absent from the state the previous 12 months, those guilty of major crimes, and a handful of especially objectionable Loyalists, such as David Fanning. Many loyalists returned to the state, not always meeting a favorable reception. Others left for Canada.

The Revolution's impact was not confined to politics and the military. North Carolina's old commercial order largely collapsed. The loss of traditional markets and the interference of British war vessels severely handicapped trade. As much as possible the state tried to conduct business as usual. The 1776 Congress and the 1778 legislature declared in force all unexpired previous North Carolina laws not inconsistent with independence. The Congress of 1776 appointed a collector for each of five ports of entry and established an admiralty court with jurisdiction over British vessels seized on high seas. Yet commercial regulations were unenforced, warehouses went unrepaired, commodities uninspected, duties uncollected. The fabled dangers of the North Carolina coast did keep the British navy at bay and enabled the state to maintain some valuable oceangoing commerce.

New trade routes were opened up to France, Bermuda, and non-British West Indies, particularly St. Eustatius, Martinique, Hispaniola, and St. Croix. Merchants and agents of the government sought war supplies and such products as salt, sugar, clothing, and tools. Traditional exports such as naval stores, provisions, and lumber declined, while tobacco increased in importance as an export. In addition to the shortage of staples, the average North Carolinian was plagued by profiteering, inflation, and a widespread reluctance to accept paper money. Historian Christopher Crittenden has written of an "orgy of spending and speculation" that undermined the economy. Trade was especially disrupted in the backcountry. In 1780 the General Assembly, decrying "the wicked arts of a set of men called speculators; who regardless of everything but their own illicit gain spread themselves over the country forestalling and engrossing the necessary articles of life and commerce," passed a series of acts designed to curtail speculation. The legislation was notably unsuccessful. Yet, North Carolina's relative self-suffiency probably enabled it to survive the economic difficulties of the period with more ease than many of its sister states.

The war wrought other changes. As in other states, the disestablished Church of England became associated with loyalism and disappeared, replaced by the Episcopal denomination. Religious leaders of all denominations bemoaned a collapse in morals and piety brought on by the conflict. Returning soldiers constituted an interest group that had to be satisfied. The Bonus Act of 1780, supplemented in 1782, set aside a military reservation in the western part of the state, granting lands ranging from 640 acres for a private to 12,000 acres for a brigadier general. This furthered settlement across western North Carolina, a portion of which later became the short-lived and unofficial state of Franklin. In 1789 North Carolina ceded much of this land to the United States government, where it eventually became the state of Tennessee. The Cherokees, defeated in the early part of the war by a combined multistate expedition, were too weak to deflect this new surge of white settlement. Cruelly disappointed was the state's black population, some of whom fought for independence. Despite the implications of the Declaration of Independence, most blacks remained slaves and free blacks remained second-class citizens.

It is not easy to chart changes wrought by the Revolution in North Carolina's social system. Historian Alice Mathews, who has made the most careful study of the subject, concludes that "once the fighting had stopped, and North Carolinians had again settled down to peacetime endeavors, their society appeared much as it had before the war." During the war ordinary life was disrupted by the difficulty in obtaining such basics as salt and sugar, the disorder of trade, inflation, the closing of schools and churches, and the raising of armies, not to mention armed conflict, property destruction, and death. There was no newspaper published in the state after 1778, while postal traffic virtually ceased for much of the war. Yet, North Carolina economy and society recovered quickly after the war.

Many of the divisions of colonial society remained well after the revolution. Although the state's political base had broadened somewhat, political life was still dominated by an economic and social elite. Class lines remained visible and important. East–west sectional divisions remained, although they were somewhat alleviated by the 1792 establishment of the state capital in the newly created and more centrally located town of Raleigh. Conservatives and radicals continued to search for the proper way to define the character of their new commonwealth.

Jim Sumner

REFERENCES

Lindley S. Butler, *North Carolina and the Coming of the Revolution, 1763–1776* (1976); Robert M. Calhoon, *Religion and the American Revolution in North Carolina* (1976); Charles Christopher Crittenden, *The Commerce of North Carolina, 1763–1789* (1936); Jeffrey J. Crow, *The Black Experience in Revolutionary North Carolina* (1977) Robert O. DeMond, *The Loyalists in North Carolina During the Revolution* (1940); Robert L. Ganyard, *The Emergence of North Carolina's Revolutionary State Government* (1978); Alice E. Mathews, *Society in Revolutionary North Carolina* (1976); Vernon O. Stumpf, *Josiah Martin; The Last Royal Governor of North Carolina* (1986); Carole Troxler, *The Loyalist Experience in North Carolina* (1976); Harry L. Watson, *An Independent People: The Way We Lived in North Carolina, 1770–1820* (1983).

O'Brien, Jeremiah (1744–1818)

Privateer. Born in Kittery, Massachusetts (now Maine), O'Brien grew up in Machias and worked in his father's lumber business. On June 2, 1775, the schooner HMS *Margaretta* arrived with two sloops to load timber for British barracks in Boston. O'Brien urged the British commander to reconsider such an action. After his warning was disregarded, on June 11 O'Brien led 40 men to capture the *Margaretta* and a sloop. This incident was the first naval engagement by American forces in the Revolution.

O'Brien then refitted the *Unity*, the captured sloop, with guns from the *Margaretta*. On July 11, he captured a British schooner and a tender off Machias. Soon after, O'Brien led in the defense of Machias, which was attacked by an enemy force from Halifax. His two ships were commissioned as the first ships in the Massachusetts navy. He became a privateer and took several prizes in 1776 and 1777. In 1777 he captured the *Scarborough*. Commanding the *Hannibal* in 1780, O'Brien was captured and confined in Mill Prison, England. He managed to escape to France and then to America in 1781. Appointed collector of customs in Machias (1811), O'Brien was the first American naval hero of the war. *See also: Margaretta* Affair

Richard L. Blanco

REFERENCES

Henry Steel Commanger and Robert B. Morris, eds., *The Spirit of Seventy-Six—The Story of the American Revolution as Told by Participants* (1983); *DAB*; William L. Fowler, *Rebels Under Sail—The American Navy During the Revolution* (1976); John F. Miller, *American Ships of the Colonial and Revolutionary Period* (1978); Nathan Miller, *Sea of Glory. The Continental Navy Fights for Independence* (1974); Andrew S. Sherman, *Life of Captain Jeremiah O'Brien, Machias, Maine . . .* (1902).

Oconostota (Great Warrior) (c. 1712–1783)

Cherokee Indian chief. Oconostota was a leading Cherokee warrior and spokesman in the mid-eighteenth century who became a major advocate of peace with the whites in the 1760s. He first appeared in historical literature in 1736, when he supported a French delegation that visited the Overhill Cherokee towns. Two years later, Oconostota blamed the English for his disfigurement caused by smallpox. For the next two decades he continued to court the French.

In August 1754, Oconostota and other Cherokee chiefs, unhappy over trading with South Carolina, attempted unsuccessfully to break that state's monopoly by opening commercial ties with Virginia. In 1755 he led 500 warriors to a decisive victory over the Creeks at the Battle of Taliwa, forcing the losers to leave northern Georgia to the Cherokees.

Although Oconostota was not a great orator, he had enough stature within the tribe to head delegations. In 1759 he led a large group of Cherokee chiefs to Charleston in an attempt to prevent the outbreak of war between the Cherokees and the whites. South Carolina Governor Lyttleton ignored the peaceful intentions of these leaders, took them hostage, and marched the group to Fort Prince George. There he demanded that the tribe surrender the Indians who murdered 24 whites in exchange for the release of the chiefs. Eventually, Little Carpenter, a great eighteenth-century peace chief, secured the release of a few, leaving 24. Oconostota was one of the chiefs released, and he soon led an attack on Fort Prince George, which resulted in the immediate execution of the remaining hostages. This attack on the fort brought a punitive expedition under Archibald Montgomery, who destroyed many of the Lower Towns in 1760. Oconostota and his warriors repulsed Montgomery at Etchoe about six miles south of Franklin, North Carolina, on June 1. Believing that he had sufficiently chastised the Cherokees, Montgomery returned to Charleston.

Oconostota then began a siege of Fort Loudoun in Tennessee, which surrendered in early August. Although the Cherokees promised that the garrison could march away unmolested, they later attacked the retreating soldiers, killing a number exactly equal to the number of hostages killed at Fort Prince George.

Great Warrior traveled to New Orleans in 1776, where he received a French commission but failed to bring back needed supplies for war. In the spring of 1761, Colonel James Grant led approximately 2,400 men into Cherokee country. Grant's scouts detected a Cherokee ambush near the location where Montgomery had been attacked. Grant avoided the ambush and was successful against the Cherokees. He became the first white man to invade the Middle Settlements,

where he destroyed at least 15 towns and over 1,500 acres of corn.

Although the Cherokee War was disastrous for the tribe, it raised the status of Oconostota, who by 1764 was the effective head of the Cherokees. In 1768 Great Warrior led a delegation of Cherokees to the Iroquois, and later that year he and other leaders agreed to a new boundary line with Virginia. The ink was barely dry on the treaty before whites began crossing over the boundary and Virginia began requesting more land. Oconostota replied, "We shall give no part of our land away unless we are paid for it and indeed we want to keep the Virginians at as great a distance as possible as they are generally bad men and love to steal horses and hunt deer. . . . But what are a few goods in comparison to good land. The land will last forever."

In the early 1770s Oconostota declined a proposal from northern Indians to cooperate in an attack on the whites. In late 1773 Great Warrior visited Charleston, where, because of his status among the Cherokees, he was inducted into St. Andrews Society, a fraternal organization of Scots founded in 1729. The following year Oconostota prevented young warriors from joining the Shawnees in another proposed attack on whites. In the spring of 1775, Oconostota, preferring land cessions to war, was one of the signatories on a deed to North Carolina lawyer Richard Henderson, which turned over 20 million acres primarily in middle Tennessee and most of Kentucky.

In July 1776 young Cherokee warriors led a series of attacks on the Watauga, Holston, and Carter Valley settlements in present-day eastern Tennessee. A series of raids were also launched on the Carolina and Georgia frontiers. The Americans retaliated in the fall. William Christian devastated the Oconostota's Overhill Towns, and the Cherokees agreed to sign a peace the following spring. At that treaty, Long Island of the Holston, the Cherokees ceded additional land to Virginia. When a Cherokee was accidentally killed at the meeting, and it appeared that negotiations might end, Oconostota insisted that the conference continue.

Although the Cherokees were technically at peace for the next three years, young warriors under the leadership of Dragging Canoe broke away from the tribe and resettled at Chickamauga. These Cherokees continued to attack the Virginia and Carolina frontiers. Whites blamed all Cherokees for these incursions, and Oconostota was obliged to ask for peace again in May 1779. Encouraged by British successes in the South, the Cherokees rejoined the Revolution briefly during the following year, but punitive expeditions by Colonel John Sevier and Arthur Campbell soon ended Cherokee activity.

In July 1782, Oconostota resigned his authority, designating his son, Tuckesee, as his successor, but the Cherokees found Tuckesee unacceptable. In the spring of 1783, Oconostota died. Oconostota's grave was discovered in 1972, and he was reinterred in 1987 near the Sequoyah Museum in Vonore, Tennessee.

William L. Anderson

REFERENCES

John P. Brown, *Old Frontiers: The Story of the Cherokee Indians from Earliest Times to the Date of Their Removal, 1838* (1938); David H. Corkran, *The Cherokee Frontier: Conflict and Survival, 1740–62* (1962); James C. Kelly, "Oconostota," *Journal of American Studies 3* (1979): 221–238; Grace Steele Woodward, *The Cherokees* (1963).

O'Hara, Charles (1740–1802)

British army officer. Born the illegitimate son of James O'Hara, who was both colonel of the Coldstream Guards and the second Lord Tyrawley, Charles O'Hara was educated at the Westminster School and was appointed cornet in the 3rd Dragoons when he was but 12 years old, on December 23, 1752.

With his father's influence, O'Hara gained appointment as lieutenant and captain in the Coldstream Guards on January 14, 1756. He served as aide-de-camp to the Marquis of Granley in Germany shortly after the Battle of Minden. Later O'Hara served as quartermaster general of troops under Lord Tyrawley in Portugal in the brief campaign of 1762, with the brevet rank of lieutenant colonel.

By July 1766, O'Hara was commandant of the garrison at Goreé, Senegal, in Africa, and lieutenant colonel commandant of the Africa Corps, a unit composed of soldiers who agreed to serve for life in Africa in return for amnesty for their past military crimes.

O'Hara was promoted to lieutenant colonel in the Coldstream Guards in 1769 and to brevet colonel in 1779. He eventually replaced General Thomas Gage as colonel of the 22nd Regiment of Foot on March 18, 1782.

A dark, handsome, mannerly Irishman, with bright, shining teeth, O'Hara was fluent in French and gifted in the art of conversation. He was well known in London society and was a personal friend of Horace Walpole. A veteran of campaigns in Europe and Africa, he followed his Guards Regiment to North America after some service in Ireland.

Colonel O'Hara was part of a three-officer commission that met with American officers at Newtown in Bucks County, Pennsylvania, on April 6, 1778, to negotiate a prisoner exchange, before the campaign of 1778 opened. O'Hara was also one of the officers who subscribed funds to the support of General William Howe's farewell banquet, the Meschianza, in Philadelphia.

Following the Battle of Monmouth and the British army's return to New York, General Henry Clinton placed O'Hara in command at Sandy Hook to defend New York harbor from French naval attack. Clinton seems to have later regretted this appointment, but he does say that O'Hara was well known to Admiral Richard Howe and other leading British officers. They at least seemed to have a high regard for the obliging Irishman. In any event, from 1778 to 1780, O'Hara remained part of the garrison in New York City.

In October 1780, Charles O'Hara, an outstanding leader and one of Lord Charles Cornwallis's few intimates, was appointed brigadier general and sent to the southern army in command of the Brigade of Guards. There were three Guards regiments in the British army of the time. The first was called the Grenadier Guards, the second was the Coldstream Guards, and the third regiment was the Scots Guards.

These three units, along with the Horse Guards, were responsible for guarding the life of the king and his family. The oldest corps in the army, they were all picked men. For service in quelling the rebellion in North America, 15 men were selected from each of the 64 companies in the Household Infantry to form a Brigade of Guards. The Guards saw their first action in the war at the storming of Fort Washington in late 1776.

It was these elite troops, over 500 in number, that O'Hara led as the van of Cornwallis's pursuit of General Nathanael Greene's American army on the famous race across North Carolina to the Dan River. On February 1, 1781, at Cowan's Ford, O'Hara and the guards were the first to cross the Catawba River as Cornwallis flanked the North Carolina militia of General William Davidson. O'Hara was unhorsed under fire in the confusion of crossing the river. Davidson was shot in the head and killed. In spite of all this, Greene's army escaped to continue their retreat. Cornwallis burned his baggage train and, with a light but unsupplied force, raced after Greene.

O'Hara later described Cornwallis's intentions to the Duke of Grafton in a letter dated April 20, 1781:

> In this situation, without baggage, necessaries, or provisions of any sort for officers or soldiers, in the most barren, inhospitable, unhealthy part of the North America, opposed to the most savage, inveterate, perfidious, cruel enemy, with zeal and with bayonets only, it was resolved to follow Greene's army to the end of the world.

Greene's men won the race to the Dan River and gained safety in Virginia. A short time later, Greene recrossed the Dan and offered battle to Cornwallis at Guilford Court House, North Carolina. On March 15, 1781, the two armies collided.

In one of the largest and bloodiest battles of the southern campaign, Cornwallis fought his way through two lines of Greene's men. Then the British closed with Greene's third and main battle line. O'Hara led the 2nd Battalion of Guards and Grenadiers in the vicious fighting with Greene's regulars in the slight valley in front of the American third line.

O'Hara was wounded severely in the thigh and chest during the fighting. So close was the contest that Cornwallis was forced to have his artillery fire grapeshot into the struggling mass of men so that the British could extricate themselves and preserve their army. In the end, the British held the field, but in so doing, they paid a high human cost.

With almost a third of his army lost as casualties at Guilford, Cornwallis made his way for the coast. The British arrived at Wilmington, North Carolina, on April 7 to recover, resupply, and refit. O'Hara made it there by horse litter. Although his wounds were serious, O'Hara survived and stayed at the side of his commander and friend.

As Cornwallis saw it, Virginia had to be taken out of the war in order for the British to control the southern colonies. Therefore, once his army was rested, Cornwallis invaded Virginia. O'Hara was probably in agreement with this decision, as he later wrote that the North Carolina campaign had not produced one substantial benefit to Great Britain but had completely worn out the king's soldiers and totally destroyed Cornwallis's army.

However, Cornwallis's plans did not turn out well. By September, the British found themselves trapped in the town of York, by a combined French and American land force, with the sea routes closed off by a French fleet. Without support from Clinton in New York, Cornwallis was forced to surrender his army on October 19, 1781.

Tradition places O'Hara, the only other general officer in Cornwallis's army besides Cornwallis himself, leading the British and German forces out to surrender. That evening, O'Hara was dined by the French officers, where he showed his poise and diplomacy in the face of defeat.

In his correspondence, Cornwallis characterized O'Hara's contributions to the southern campaign of 1780–1781 by stating, "His zealous services under my command, the pains he took and the success he met with in reconciling the guards to every kind of hardship, give him a just claim, independent of old friendship, on my very strongest recommendations in his favour."

O'Hara was exchanged by the Americans on February 9, 1782. In the meantime, he had been promoted to the rank of major general. In May 1782, O'Hara led two regiments to Jamaica and Antigua, as reinforcements from the garrison at New York City.

In 1784, O'Hara returned home for a time, but debts he had incurred soon forced him to go abroad. He served as major general on staff at Gibraltar from 1787 to 1790, when he once again returned to England. In 1791, O'Hara became colonel of the 74th Highlanders Regiment. The following year, he was posted to Gibraltar as lieutenant governor and was promoted to the rank of lieutenant general in 1793.

That year O'Hara served in command of the British troops at Fort Mulgrave near Toulon, France, during the French Revolution. He was taken prisoner by the French and held in Paris. In August 1795, O'Hara was exchanged for General Jean Baptiste Rochambeau. Upon his return to England, O'Hara was appointed governor of Gibraltar, a position he dearly wanted.

O'Hara was made a full general in 1798. Since he was a fine leader and an excellent administrator, his term as governor of Gibraltar was a good one. Although he was a strict disciplinarian, he was popular with his men. Known in society for his hospitality, wit, companionship, and the gift of speech, he was much in demand at parties, receptions, and routs. O'Hara was extremely popular with the ladies. Part of his charm, no doubt, came from a combination of the outdated styles of dress he affected in public and his courtly mannerisms. He eventually became known as "the cock of the rock."

General Charles O'Hara died at Gibraltar on February 21, 1802. In spite of earlier monetary problems, he died wealthy and left 70,000 pounds sterling to two ladies of Gibraltar to care for their needs and those of his illegitimate children.

Paul J. Sanborn

REFERENCES

Edward E. Curtis, *The Organization of the British Army in the American Revolution* (1969); Burke Davis, *The Campaign That Won America* (1970); *DAB*; Don Higginbotham, *The War of American Independence* (1971); Philip R.N. Katcher, *Encyclopedia of British, Provincial and German Army Units, 1775–1783* (1973); Baron Ludwig Von Closen, *Revolutionary Journal* (1958); Christopher Ward, *The War of Revolution* (1958); Franklin and Mary Wickwire, *Cornwallis: The American Adventure* (1970).

Oliver, Peter

See Massachusetts in the American Revolution.

Origins of the American Revolution

See individual entries on Connecticut, Georgia, Florida, Massachusetts, New Hampshire, New Jersey, New York, North Carolina, Rhode Island, South Carolina, Virginia in the American Revolution.

Oriskany, New York, Battle of (August 6, 1777)

Nicholas Herkimer, chairman of the Tryon County Committee of Safety and brigadier general of militia, learned on July 30 from a friendly Oneida Indian that Colonel Barry St. Leger's expedition was nearing Fort Stanwix. He immediately ordered the county's militia to rendezvous at Fort Dayton, and on August 4, with 800 militiamen and some 400 oxcarts, Herkimer left Fort Dayton for the besieged garrison at Stanwix 30 miles upriver. Sixty Oneida Indians joined him on the march and acted as scouts for the Americans. Despite the burdensome oxcarts, the relief column moved quickly, advancing to within ten miles of Stanwix by the following evening. Herkimer sent several runners forward to inform the fort's commander, Colonel Peter Gansevoort, of his presence. He also asked Gansevoort to fire three cannon the next morning to acknowledge receipt of his message and to coordinate a sortie out of the fort as the relief column approached.

On the morning of August 6, a stormy council of war took place in Herkimer's camp. Unwilling to move until he heard the three shots from the fort, Herkimer refused to advance. His subordinates, full of fight, wanted to push forward immediately. In the angry debate that ensued, the regimental commanders went so far as to impugn Herkimer's character by denouncing him as a coward and a Tory (in part because his brother was serving with St. Leger). Although he continued to remonstrate against a rash move, Herkimer reluctantly ordered the advance. He insisted, however, that special precautions be taken to protect the flanks. Unfortunately, failure to attend to the column's security soon led to tragedy.

When St. Leger learned of the approach of Herkimer's relief column, he quickly moved to oppose it. Having detached so many of his white troops to work details, he had to scramble to assemble an adequate force. He realized he would be outnumbered, so he sought an opportunity to ambush the Americans. On the road to Stanwix, six miles from the fort and two miles northwest of Oriskany village, he found a narrow defile ideally suited to his purposes. The road ran through a ravine with steep sides and a marshy bottom that could be traversed only on a crude log causeway; also, the undergrowth and hemlock on each side of the path provided ideal concealment. The ambush was laid on the western end of the ravine with parts of John Johnson's Royal Greens and John Butler's Tory Rangers across the head of the column, and Joseph Brant's Indians placed along the flanks. The plan called for the whites to check Herkimer's advance, while the Indians pressed the flanks and closed on the rear to encircle and overwhelm the Americans.

About ten o'clock on the morning of August 6, Herkimer's column descended into the ravine. The Oneida scouts moved in advance but for some reason failed to discover the ambush. Herkimer, mounted on a white horse, rode at the head of 600 militiamen marching in columns of twos (perhaps to dispel charges of cowardice). They were followed by the 400 oxcarts and a rear guard of 200 men under the command of Colonel Visscher. Stretching almost a mile through the wilderness, the column unsuspectingly entered the trap. The main body and the oxcarts were struggling through the ravine when Indians struck, albeit prematurely. They attacked at the rear of the oxcarts and cut the rear guard off from the main body. As Visscher's men turned and fled, some of the Indians pursued while other sealed off the main column, completing its encirclement. Herkimer heard the firing far behind him and turned to investigate, but found the road blocked. At that moment, the entire column came under attack as the Tories in the front and the Indians on the flanks opened fire. Thrown into disorder by fire from concealed positions and by the cramped conditions in the ravine, the Americans suddenly found themselves battling for their very survival. Confusion reigned as fire poured in from all sides and the Indians rushed forward to wage hand-to-hand combat. While the Americans struggled to reach higher ground and to form a crude defensive perimeter, Herkimer coolly directed his men as best as he could. Wounded in the leg early on and his horse dead, Herkimer was carried into the militiamen's circle, propped up against a tree, and placed on his saddle. He refused to seek cover and instead calmly smoked his pipe while the battle raged around him. Herkimer's coolness undoubtedly heartened his men, but it did not diminish the gravity of their situation. Forty-five minutes after the battle began, a violent thunderstorm broke, wetting the combatants' powder and bringing an abrupt cessation to the fighting.

The Americans used the one-hour respite to reorganize their defense and, most importantly, to change their tactics. Herkimer ordered his men to fight in twos in order to counter the favorite Indian tactic of rushing forward as soon as an American had fired and cutting him down

before he could reload. Only one would fire at a time, so while he reloaded, his partner could hold off an enemy who charged. As a result, when the battle resumed, the Americans were well prepared to meet the Indian onslaught. Fierce hand-to-hand fighting raged not only between whites and Indians but among the whites as well. Tories and Patriots from Tryon County fought savagely at close quarters with knives, bayonets, and clubbed muskets. When Tory reinforcements arrived on the field, John Butler employed a ruse to try and turn the tide. He ordered a detachment from the Royal Greens to turn their coats inside out and approach Herkimer's men from the direction of the fort under the guise of a sortie from Stanwix. Only the keen eye of Captain Gardenier thwarted this trickery, for he recognized a former neighbor who was a Tory and ordered his men to open fire. The brutal combat continued for hours, but as the Indians gradually tired and lost interest, the Tories decided to break off contact. The Indians and Tories left the field to the beleaguered Americans, who were unable and unwilling to pursue. Instead, Herkimer and his survivors began making their way back to Fort Dayton.

The Battle of Oriskany had raged for perhaps six hours with both sides suffering severely. Reports of casualties varied wildly and prevent a definitive accounting of this bloody encounter; nevertheless, Oriskany ranks as one of the bloodiest battles of the war in proportion to the numbers engaged. It is possible that at least 150 fell on each side, and the cost may well have been even higher for the Americans. Nicholas Herkimer died ten days after the battle when bleeding from his amputated leg could not be stopped. Although Herkimer's men failed to relieve Fort Stanwix, the fierceness of the Battle of Oriskany had a telling impact on St. Leger's expedition. The fact that the Indians did much of the fighting and suffered heavily, plus St. Leger's failure to protect their camps during the battle, greatly angered his Indian allies and contributed to their willingness to forsake him later in the month.

Ralph L. Eckert

References

Anon., *Memorial of the Centennial Celebration of the Battle of Oriskany, August 6, 1877* (1878); Henry B. Dawson, *Battles of the United States . . .* (1858); Hoffman Nickerson, *The Turning Point of the Revo-*

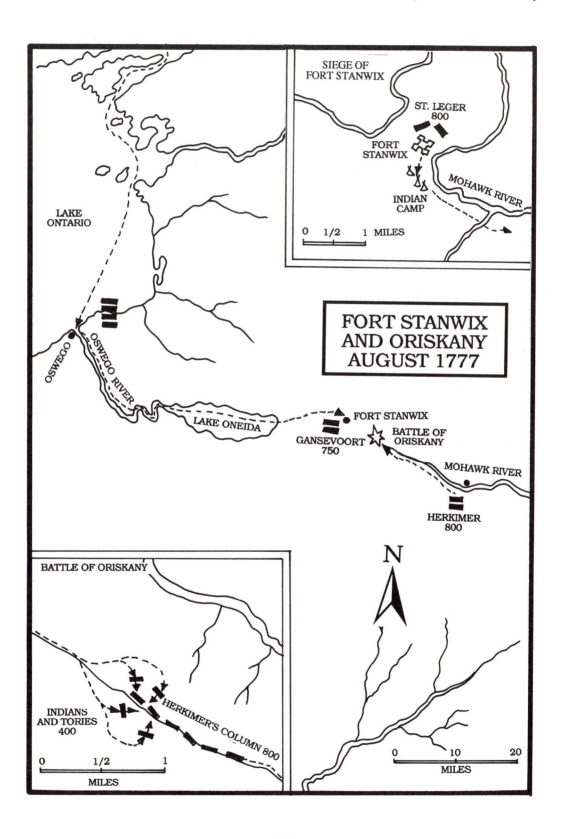

SIEGE OF
FORT STANWIX

ST. LEGER
800

FORT
STANWIX

MOHAWK RIVER

INDIAN
CAMP

0   1/2   1   MILES

LAKE
ONTARIO

OSWEGO

OSWEGO RIVER

LAKE ONEIDA

GANSEVOORT
750

FORT STANWIX
AND ORISKANY
AUGUST 1777

FORT STANWIX

BATTLE OF
ORISKANY

MOHAWK RIVER

HERKIMER
800

BATTLE OF ORISKANY

INDIANS
AND TORIES
400

HERKIMER'S COLUMN 800

0   1/2   1
MILES

N

0   10   20
MILES

lution or Burgoyne in America (1928); John Albert Scott, *Fort Stanwix (Fort Schuyler) and Oriskany* . . . (1927); Howard Swiggert, *War Out of Niagara: Walter Butler and the Tory Rangers* (1933).

Oswald, Eleazer (1755–1795)

Continental Army officer. Eleazer Oswald, a relative of British diplomat Richard Oswald, immigrated to America about 1770. He served under Benedict Arnold at Ticonderoga, and became his secretary. At Quebec, Oswald assumed command of the ill-fated American attack after Arnold was wounded. Oswald, too, was later wounded in the fight, and on December 31, 1775, he was captured, along with Captain John Lamb. The two became lifelong friends.

Following Oswald's exchange, he received a commission as a lieutenant colonel on January 1, 1777, and was appointed second in command of Lamb's 2nd Continental Artillery Regiment. He distinguished himself under Arnold at Campo Hill during the raid on Danbury in April 1777. At Monmouth, on June 28, 1777, Oswald was the second ranking American artillery commander after General Henry Knox. Commanding four fieldpieces in the front of the American column, Oswald twice was cut off from friendly infantry support and lost one of his guns in the process; but he held his position. Knox later wrote to Lamb describing the battle, and called Oswald "one of the best officers of the Army."

Oswald resigned his commission immediately after Monmouth, in the midst of the general squabble over relative rank and seniority that followed the 1778 reorganization of the army. He went into a publishing partnership with William Goddard and printed the *Maryland Journal*. His publication of General Charles Lee's attacks on Washington resulted in a public demonstration against him. Between 1782 and 1787 he published a number of increasingly partisan and strident newspapers. He was an opponent of the proposed Constitution, and he helped John Lamb defend his house when it came under attack by a Federalist mob. Oswald was a strong opponent of all Alexander Hamilton's policies. In 1789 he challenged Hamilton to a duel, but later withdrew the challenge when friends intervened.

In 1792 Oswald went to England on business. Shortly after, he surfaced in France as a colonel of artillery in the Republican Army, and commanded a regiment under General Charles Dumouriez at the battle of Jemmapes. At that time France had ample skilled artillery officers. The French had a strong artillery tradition and a fair-sized pool of Gribeauval-trained officers, one of whom was Napoleon. The French, therefore, must have been very impressed with Oswald's skill as an artilleryman.

The French government later sent Oswald to Ireland on a secret mission to evaluate the possibility of success of a proposed French invasion. Oswald made his report to the French Minister of Foreign Affairs, but he received neither response nor further instructions. When Oswald finally returned to the United States in 1794, he continued to wear his French uniform, which further inflamed his old political opponents. The following year, Oswald contracted yellow fever and died while attending to John Lamb's son-in-law, who was stricken with the same disease.

David T. Zabecki

REFERENCES

Issac Q. Leake, *Memoir of the Life and Times of General John Lamb* (1857), rpr. 1970; James G. Wilson and John Fiske, *Appleton's Cyclopaedia of American Biography*, 6 vols. (1886–89), 4.

Otto, Bodo (1711–1787)

Continental Army physician. On July 20, 1711, in Hanover, Germany, Bodo Otto was born, the son of Christopher Otto, who served as both forester for the Oberg family and local tax collector, and his wife, Maria Magdalena Menechen. Baron Bodo von Oberg was Otto's godfather and namesake. When Otto was 13, his father arranged for him to be an apprentice to a surgeon at Hildesheim. Otto continued his training as assistant to surgeons at Hamburg and with army service, providing peacetime medical assistance for the Duke of Celle's Dragoons. In the city of Luneberg, Otto passed surgeon examinations, qualifying him as physician. He married Elizabeth Sanchen; she gave birth to a daughter, Mary Elizabeth, in 1737 and died the following year. In 1742 Otto married Catharina Dorothea Dahncken, with whom he had four children: Frederick Christopher (1743), Dorothea Sophia (1744), Bodo, Jr. (1748), and John Augustus (1751).

Otto functioned as chief surgeon first for the Fortress of Kalkberg, treating prisoners and invalids, then for the District of Scharzfels. Although he already was certified as a physician, Otto attended classes at the University of Gottingen. Several years after his father died, Otto decided to migrate to the colonies, swearing an oath of allegiance to Pennsylvania and settling near Philadelphia in 1755. A devoutly religious man, Otto worked closely with German immigrants who had similar beliefs and established his medical practice in Germantown. He then moved to New Jersey in 1760, living there for several years.

When his wife died in 1765, Otto returned to Philadelphia, and in the next year, he married his third wife, Maria Margaretta Paris. He was a member of the American Philosophical Society and helped found the German Academy, which was structured similarly to Halle University. He moved once again to own the Reading Apothecary Shop, where he personally prepared pharmaceuticals for his clients. Otto's sons trained as doctors and were active in the Sons of Liberty. Otto also became an ardent supporter of the Revolution.

As a member of the Berks County Controlling Committee and Pennsylvania Provincial Conference, Otto became the war surgeon for local troops but lost crucial medicine and supplies that he owned while fleeing during the Battle of Long Island. He served in various field and hospital-physician positions—as Chief of the Bettering House Hospital in Philadelphia, at Trenton Hospital, and Fulling Mill Hospital at Bethlehem—before, as director of the medical district, assuming leadership of the Yellow Springs Hospital, site of Valley Forge Medical Department headquarters. Otto took another oath of allegiance at Valley Forge.

He communicated well with Lutherans and other religious groups whose buildings were used for hospital functions, facilitating civilian-military relations and enabling some confiscated church property to be returned. Otto was in charge of soldiers that were chronically ill or whose severe wounds required rehabilitation. His three sons assisted him at the hospital. Although Yellow Springs was noted as one of the best-maintained Revolutionary hospitals, Otto constantly appealed for unavailable pharmaceuticals, equipment, and comforts for the patients.

During the Revolution, Otto served as a witness for Dr. William Shippen, Jr., Director General of Hospitals, when Drs. Benjamin Rush and John Morgan attempted to court-martial him. Shippen complimented Otto for his efforts to keep his hospitals well supplied and noted that no soldiers had complained of their treatment at Yellow Springs. Rush and Morgan argued that Otto's support for Shippen was false and slanderous, questioning his judgment and attacking his lack of fluency with the English language. They claimed that Otto was vulnerable to Shippen's manipulation, but Otto defended his testimony, stating, "For my own conduct as a public officer, I am, and at all times expect, to be held accountable at a proper tribunal, and I rest assured that my character in private life will ever be proof against the darts of slander and efforts of malice."

In 1780 Congress reorganized the Medical Department, and Otto received the rank of Hospital Physician and Surgeon. In September 1781 Yellow Springs Hospital was closed, and Dr. John Cochran ordered Otto to send remaining patients to the Bettering House Hospital in Philadelphia. Otto served as chief of that institution and returned to Philadelphia. Otto was officially discharged from military service in January 1782; he reestablished his medical practice and apothecary in Philadelphia that same year.

Otto campaigned for veterans' benefits. He and his sons had accepted certificates of indebtedness equal to five years' pay at retiring rank but never received any reimbursement. Revolutionary financier Haym Solomon aided Otto financially as his attorney by exchanging Otto's certificate for a loan. In the state assembly Otto spoke out for Pennsylvanian officers discriminated against in benefits. Otto briefly practiced medicine in Baltimore, Maryland, before returning to Reading, Pennsylvania, where he died in 1787.

Elizabeth D. Schafer

REFERENCES

Louis C. Duncan, *Medical Men in the American Revolution* (1931); James E. Gibson, *Dr. Bodo Otto and the Medical Background of the American Revolution* (1937).

Paine, Robert Treat (1731–1814)

American statesman. Born in Boston on March 11, 1731, Robert Treat Paine became a signer of the Declaration of Independence and a prominent New England jurist. Paine was educated at Harvard College, where he studied theology and law; he was admitted to the bar in 1757 and practiced law in Portland, Maine, and later in Taunton, Massachusetts. In 1770, Paine married Sally Cobb; they had eight children including the poet Robert Treat Paine (1773–1811).

Paine assisted in the prosecution of the Boston Massacre case and represented Massachusetts in the First and Second Continental Congresses. In addition to signing the Declaration of Independence, July 4, 1776, Paine was a signatory of the "Olive Branch Petition," which had been directed to George III in 1775. During the late 1770s, Paine served as the attorney general in Massachusetts.

Paine was appointed twice to the Massachusetts Supreme Court by his friend, Governor John Hancock; Paine served on this court from 1790 to 1804. Paine consistently allied himself with Hancock in disputes with Samuel and John Adams. Robert Treat Paine contributed to the establishment of the American Academy of Arts and Sciences (1780). He died on May 11, 1814, in Boston.

William T. Walker

REFERENCES

Ralph Davol, *Two Men of Taunton* (1912); John Sanderson, *Biographies of the Signers to the Declaration of Independence*; Sarah Paine and C.H. Pope, *Paine Ancestry* (1912).

Paine, Thomas (1737–1809)

American political theorist. Theoretician and propagandist of the American Revolution, deist, and author of *Common Sense*, *The Age of Reason*, and *The Rights of Man*. Paine was born January 29, 1737, at Thetford, Norfolk, England. Paine was the son of Joseph Paine, a working-class Quaker corset maker, and Frances Cocke Paine, the daughter of an Anglican attorney. Paine's formal education was limited; in 1750, at the age of 13, he terminated his schooling and began to work with his father. During the next two decades, Paine worked in a variety of jobs including teacher, grocer, and exciseman. He was married twice; Paine's first wife, Mary Lambert, died on September 27, 1759—less than one year after they were married. In 1771 Paine married Elizabeth Olive; they separated in 1774. The instability of his personal life was matched by Paine's dissatisfaction and performance as an exciseman. On two occasions Paine was dismissed; the second occasion resulted in bankruptcy and in Paine emerging as an advocate for the grievances of the excisemen. In 1772 Paine wrote *The Case of the Officers of Excise* in which he argued for a salary increment. Shortly thereafter, Paine met Benjamin Franklin and obtained a favorable letter of recommendation prior to sailing for the colonies.

On November 30, 1774, Thomas Paine arrived in Philadelphia; he found employment by writing for the *Pennsylvania Magazine* and quickly became identified as abolitionist and political revolutionary. On January 10, 1776, Paine's pamphlet *Common Sense* was published and established Paine's reputation as a principal theoretician of the American Revolution. It urged the immediate declaration of independence, not merely as a striking practical gesture that would unite the colonies and would secure French and Spanish aid, but as a the fulfillment of America's moral obligation to the world. Paine contended that "The sun never shone on a cause of greater worth." *Common Sense* was critically acclaimed; some historians maintain that 500,000 copies were sold. In 1777 Paine began to publish a series of pieces in the *Pennsylvania Journal* under the title of the "Crisis" series; a total of 12 articles appeared in this series, the most significant being "The Crisis Extraordinary," which outlined a plan for the financing of the Revolutionary War. During the late 1770s Paine served as secretary to the Congress and as clerk of the Pennsylvania Assembly; his reputation was tarnished by his mismanagement of confidential information in the Beaumarchais affair—the agent for the delivery of French aid prior to the French declaration of war against Britain. In 1780 Paine published "Public Good," which expanded on the themes of *Common Sense* and condemned Virginia's claims in the west.

With the end of the war Paine found that he was unemployed. For his war efforts he received a farm in New Rochelle, New York. During the early 1780s Paine resided in Bordentown, New Jersey, wrote, and worked on a project to build an iron bridge. In 1796 Paine published *Disser-*

tations on Government, The Affairs of the Bank, and Paper-Money, which was a polemic denouncing paper money as inherently inflationary. In the following year Paine traveled to Europe to acquire support for his iron bridge project. Between 1787 and 1789 Paine wandered back and forth between England and France, discussed politics with Edmund Burke and the Marquis de Condorcet, and built his bridge. In the fall of 1789, Paine went to Paris to investigate the status of the new National Assembly; between 1789 and 1792 Paine made several trips to England in an effort to assist in the spreading of the French Revolution. In response to Edmund Burke's *Reflections on the Revolution in France* (1790), Paine wrote the first part of *The Rights of Man* (1791); the second part was published in 1792. In *The Rights of Man*, Paine defended the extreme measures of the French revolutionary regime in advancing the cause of the revolution, and argued that it was the responsibility of governments to "guarantee" the natural rights of man. He identified these natural rights as liberty, property, security, and resistance to oppression; Paine asserted that all men are created equal in their claim to these rights and that only a republic could sustain them. Paine argued that all nations required a written constitution which guaranteed these rights and which provided for manhood suffrage and limitations on the executive, legislative, and judicial governors of the republic. Paine urged the English to overthrow George III and to join in the revolutionary movement. While *The Rights of Man* was applauded by English radicals, it resulted in Paine being charged *in absentia* for treason and declared an outlaw in 1792. During the same year, Paine was made a French citizen during the last month in the history of the National Assembly. His French citizenship was revoked by the Convention (1793) during the antiforeign hysteria caused by the outbreak of war with Prussia and Austria. Paine was imprisoned (December 1793–November 1794) in Luxembourg; he was released after the Thermidorean Reaction, French military victories, and the initiation of the movement that would lead to the establishment of the more conservative Directory in 1795. During his confinement, Paine wrote *The Age of Reason*, which was published in two parts in 1794 and 1796. In this book Paine advanced an "enlightened" explanation of reality that was characteristically mathematical and scientific in its argumentation. *The*

ty as a myth
Testaments
time, Paine
of for the
onal deist
e natural

Paris
les of
rian
n."
hi-
le-
e

French seamen and with French officials at St
Pierre and Miquelon. Regarding the fishing area
as a "nursery" for British seamen, and hence for
the Royal Navy, Palliser exerted increasing control over British fishermen in the area. He also
explored the coast of Labrador, assisted Moravian
missionaries in their conversion of the Inuit,
stimulated the fur trade, and assisted Captain
James Cook, who surveyed Newfoundland waters in 1763. Replaced by Admiral John Byron
in 1768, Palliser returned to England. He was
appointed Comptroller of the Navy and in this
capacity he outfitted Cook's expedition to the
Pacific. Palliser became an MP in 1774, a rear
admiral in 1775, and a Lord of the Admiralty.
In early 1775 Palliser supervised the loading
transports and vituallers that were sent to re-
the siege of Quebec under Sir Charles
s. In 1778 Palliser was a vice admiral and
mmand of the home fleet under Ad-
us Keppel. After the indecisive en-
the French off Ushant (July 27,
as criticized for errors in tactics
g with Keppel's orders. The
political issue in Parliament,
urt-martial investigation
cer corps into supporters
London mob pillaged
his parliamentary seat.
sinecure, governor
0). Palliser served
84) and became
istrator, Palliser
Cape Palliser
him. See also:
le of
L. Blanco

ir,

and Quincy families. He attended the Suffolk Convention and the Massachusetts Provincial Congress.

Appointed a captain in the 2nd Massachusetts Regiment in 1774, Palmer served at Bunker Hill and at the siege of Boston, becoming a lieutenant colonel and then colonel. After the British evacuation of Boston in March 1776, Palmer, now a brigadier general, helped to organize the colony's militia and to oversee the coastal defenses.

In February 1777 Palmer led a small force recapture Newport, Rhode Island, from the emy, but the effort failed. Washington the ignated Major General Joseph Spencer necticut to command an amphibious from Tiverton, Rhode Island, with N troops. Palmer, as second in comm calling out the Massachusetts r for the operation scheduled for men became restless with ir serted, and the British learn ing attack. Palmer's majo boats for the assault, bu and carpenters many of worthy. In addition, t towropes, and pro objections, Spence attack from Fo Hogland Ferry it was soon a for October plummetin were mu

A co dered Con Afte Palm The ge

commercia
as a cler!
Charles
he w
and
pla
Fl

Age of Reason denounced Christian
and condemned the Old and New
as inconsistent. However, at the same
argued that God does exist; the pro
existence of Paine's God is the traditi
argument involved with creation and th
order.

Between 1795 and 1802 Paine lived in
and published *Dissertation on First-Princi*
Government (1795) and two essays, "Agra
Justice" and "Letter to George Washingt
He assisted in the establishment of the Theo
lanthropists, a group dedicated to advancing ɑ
ism and discrediting Christianity. In 1802 Pai
returned to the United States, where his reputation as a controversial figure had been sustained.
Between 1802 and his death in 1809, Paine lived
in New York, New Rochelle, and Bordentown;
these were years of decline in health and were
devoid of serious work. Thomas Paine died on
June 8, 1809, and was buried on his farm in New
Rochelle. In 1819 William Cobbett had Paine's
remains removed and transported to England,
where he intended to inter them in a memorial
monument. Cobbett's plan was never realized,
and after Cobbett's death (1835), the remnants
of Paine's body were acquired by a furniture
dealer in 1844; there is no further record on the
disposition of the bones.

William T. Walker

REFERENCES

A. Owen Aldridge, *Thomas Paine's American Ideology*
(1984); ———, *Man of Reason: The Life of Thomas*
Paine (1959); Marilyn Butler, ed., *Burke, Paine,*
Godwin, and the Revolution Controversy (1984); E.
Foner, *Tom Paine and Revolutionary America* (1976);
Bruce Kuklick, ed., *Paine, Political Writings* (1989);
Mark Philip, *Paine* (1980).

Palliser, Hugh (c. 1722–1796)

British navy officer. Palliser was born to a
family of landed gentry in England. Joining the
Royal Navy at 11 years of age, he became a lieutenant in 1741 and a captain in 1746. During the
War of the Austrian Succession he was wounded
in action. During the Seven Years' War he helped
to blockade French ports and he served in North
American waters off Louisbourg and Newfoundland. Appointed a commodore and governor of
Newfoundland, Palliser implemented the terms
of the Treaty of Paris (1763) regarding French
fishing rights. He dealt tactfully but firmly with

of ɩ
lieve
Dougla
third in cc
miral August
gagement with
1778), Palliser w
and for disagreeii
incident became a ɩ
and the resulting cc
tended to split the off
of each admiral. After ɑ
his home, Palliser resigned ɩ
He ended his career with ɑ
of Greenwich Hospital (178
again in Parliament (1780–1ʔ
admiral in 1787. A capable admir.
was honored by the naming of
(Cook Strait, New Zealand) after
Keppel-Palliser Affair; Ushant, Batt.

Richaru

REFERENCES

CDB; J.H. Broomfeld, "The Keppel-Palliser
1778–1779," *Mariners' Mirror,* 47(1961):19
W.H. Whitelog, "Governor Hugh Pallis
the Newfoundland and Labrador Fisher,
1768," *Canadian Historical Review, 50* (196
163.

Palmer, Joseph (1716–178ƨ

Continental officer. Palmer migr
England to Boston in 1746. Unsucces
manufacturing enterprise, he had bett
trade and realty. Settling at Braintre
chusetts, Palmer was acquainted with

activities of the southeast, serving
to John Gordon and Company of
ton from 1765 until 1772. In that year,
appointed as one of Gordon's attorneys
managed Gordon's mercantile interests and
ntations in both South Carolina and East
orida. During this time, Panton himself acquired sizable landholdings in South Carolina.
He also became acquainted with the leading
Carolina merchants and others involved in the
southern Indian trade, including John Stuart,
Superintendent of Indian Affairs in the South.
Panton remained loyal to Great Britain when
the Revolutionary War broke out. In 1775, he
joined the numerous Loyalists in South Carolina and Georgia who found it expedient to relocate to East Florida.

In East Florida, Superintendent Stuart and
Governor Patrick Tonyn were anxious to ensure Creek Indian loyalty to the Crown by providing adequate supplies of trade goods. The East
Florida–Creek trade had always been limited,
and Augusta, Georgia, had been the staging point
for most trading paths into the southeastern
backcountry. In light of Patriot control of
Charleston and Augusta, it became imperative
to make St. Augustine the port of entry for British trade goods destined for the southeastern
Indians and to establish official trading stations.
Panton's experience and connections soon led
to his appointment as manager of the East Florida
Indian Trade.

Prior to the Revolution, the most successful
Indian traders in East Florida had been James
Spalding and his partner Roger Kelsall. Around
1775, Panton entered a partnership with Thomas Forbes and the two did business with
Spalding and Kelsall. As the war progressed,
Panton and Forbes came to control the majority
of the East Florida trade in addition to handling
the distribution of British presents to the southern tribes. With the retrocession of Florida to
Spain, Spalding and Kelsall retired to the Bahamas. About the same time, Panton and Forbes
joined forces with John Leslie, William
Alexander, and Charles McLatchy to form
Panton, Leslie and Company. McLatchy had
been Spalding-Kelsall's chief storekeeper. Panton
and his new company became the only viable
Indian trading company in East Florida.

Alexander and Forbes relocated to the Bahamas to further the company's fortunes in that
quarter, while Panton and McLatchy remained

to
en-
des-
f Con-
operation
ew England
and, erred by
ilitia too early
October 16. The
activity, some de-
ed of the forthcom-
r task was to acquire
due to a lack of tools
the boats were not sea-
ere was a scarcity of tents,
isions. Ignoring Palmer's
r on October 17 ordered an
land Ferry and a feint from
. The expedition was a fiasco, and
borted. Another attempt planned
22 was called off due to sickness and
g morale. On October 28 the men
tered and sent home.

rt of inquiry held in Massachusetts or-
lmer to be tried by court-martial, but
assumed responsibility for the matter.
months of testimony both Spencer and
ere exonerated and the case was closed.
ression remains that two incompetent
mismanaged a difficult undertaking.

Richard L. Blanco

CE

. Shipton, "General Joseph Palmer, Scape-
he Rhode Island Fiasco, October, 1777,"
land Quarterly, 39 (1966):498–512.

, William (c. 1740s–1801)

trader. William Panton, a native of
rrived in Charleston, South Carolina,
quickly became acquainted with the

in East Florida. During the transition of power in East Florida, Panton used his contacts with British governor Tonyn, Superintendent Brown, and Creek headman Alexander McGillivray in a bid to obtain concessions for his company under the new Spanish regime. Meanwhile, Panton's partner, Thomas Forbes, lobbied the Spanish ambassador in London. The Spanish were aware that a well-established trade would be essential in establishing peaceful relations with the southeastern tribes. The partners argued that their trade contacts and experience would be invaluable to the new Spanish regime. They were eventually successful, and since St. Augustine was isolated from the upper Creeks, Choctaw, and Chickasaw, Panton, Leslie and Company extended their operation to Spanish Pensacola and Mobile. For his efforts in promoting the interests of Panton, Leslie and Company, Creek headman Alexander McGillivray was made a silent partner in the firm. In the postwar period, Panton, Leslie and Company became the leading trade enterprise in the Spanish Floridas. William Panton died on February 26, 1801. The company's successor, John Forbes & Company, continued to dominate the southern Indian trade and commerce along the Gulf Coast until the 1840s.

Kathryn Braund

REFERENCES

William S. Coker and Thomas D. Watson, *Indian Traders of the Southeastern Spanish Borderlands: Panton, Leslie & Company and John Forbes & Company, 1783–1847* (1986); Marie T. Greenslade, "William Panton," *Florida Historical Quarterly*, 14 (1935):107–29; Thomas D. Watson, "Continuity in Commerce: Development of the Panton, Leslie and Company Trade Monopoly in West Florida," *Florida Historical Quarterly*, 54 (April 1976):548–64; J. Leitch Wright, Jr., "The Queen's Redoubt Explosion in the Lives of William A. Bowles, John Miller and William Panton," in *Anglo-Spanish Confrontation on the Gulf Coast During the American Revolution*, ed. by William S. Coker and Robert R. Rea (1982).

Paoli "Massacre" (Pennsylvania) (September 20–21, 1777)

In the summer of 1777, General Sir William Howe had assembled a large British force in New York City with the intent of invading Pennsylvania through Maryland in order to capture the rebel capital at Philadelphia. It was his belief that such a victory, coupled with General John Burgoyne's assured success in cutting the Hudson River–Lake Champlain waterway, would guarantee the collapse of the rebel forces and bring all of His Majesty's colonies in North America back into the Empire. Waiting until late in the season to ensure that Burgoyne was making suitable progress in his campaign, Howe and his army of 18,000 British and German troops sailed from New York and landed at Head of Elk, Maryland, proceeding to march northward toward Philadelphia.

Washington, positioned in the Jerseys, watched Howe's movements closely and eventually realized the British intention was to capture Philadelphia. This city, with the largest population in the United States, could not be surrendered without a fight. Washington's army moved south and shielded Philadelphia by taking a strong position in Delaware. Noting this, Howe veered to his left, attempting to get around the American right flank. As both opposing armies moved, they collided in the first major battle of the Pennsylvania campaign along the banks of Brandywine Creek. The American army gave a good account of itself, but it was flanked and finally forced from the field. The retreat was a controlled one, however. Washington's army was beaten but not disheartened.

Howe took five days to recover and rest his force after Brandywine and then decided to maneuver Washington out of position by threatening the American supply bases in the Reading–Valley Forge region of Pennsylvania. Washington did not have enough strength to cover both the capital and his supply centers. He chose to cover his supply sources. Philadelphia after all was only a city, easily surrendered and, perhaps, easily recovered.

As Howe moved northward into the Great Valley of Chester County, Washington positioned his army to block the way in a line from the White Horse Tavern to the Goshen Meeting House. A battle developed on September 16, 1777, but got no further than the preliminaries before a strong rainstorm ended all thoughts of fighting. Washington retreated to Yellow Springs to resupply and reorganize his force while Howe continued on his way to Tredyffrin Township, where camp was made.

From his position, Howe burned the forge and mills along Valley Creek and destroyed valuable rebel military supplies stored there. The British army was cut off from its supply base stored in the British fleet, so the army was living off the land as they marched. Much suffering on the part of both Tory and rebel landowners resulted as the British seized the food and supplies they needed in Chester County.

To counter this invasion, Washington ordered General Anthony Wayne and his two brigades of Pennsylvania Line to take up a position behind the British army, to harass them whenever possible, and, perhaps, even to capture the British baggage train in the confusion when Howe began to cross the Schuylkill River. Wayne was a native of this area of Pennsylvania, having been born and raised at Waynesborough, an estate not more than three miles from where Wayne would eventually establish his "hidden" camp. Knowing all the roads and secret paths, Wayne decided to place his troops on the fields of a Tory farmer named Griffith. He had approximately 1,500 troops, four cannon, and eight baggage wagons with him. He took his position on September 19 and watched the British closely.

Wayne believed that Washington would bring the rest of the American army to the northern side of the Schuylkill River and would hit Howe as the British tried to ford that stream. This would allow General William Maxwell, who never did play a part in this operation, and Wayne to attack the British rear, thus trapping the enemy in the Great Valley and winning a great victory. Washington, however, found his army worn from the results of weeks of campaigning. Over 1,000 of his men had no shoes. The Americans could not yet march to stop Howe. Wayne was left to his own devices. Messages from Washington to Wayne informing him of this situation were captured by the British.

Wayne had ten of his own cattle slaughtered to feed his men. He marched his force from their camp toward the British to see if he could catch the enemy in motion. The Pennsylvanians then marched back to the secret camp. Wayne waited. September 20 passed. A cold, light rain began to fall. Wayne eventually learned that Howe intended to cross over the Schuylkill River the next day, and Wayne decided to take advantage of this move.

But the British were not idle either. Howe had discovered Wayne's position. Local Tories had informed Howe, and Howe's scouts could certainly have picked up talk in the local taverns

about Wayne's men and where they were stationed. Howe decided to act first to eliminate this threat to his rear.

Assigning the overall command to one of his best tactical generals, Major General Charles Grey, Howe wanted Wayne's force destroyed before the British began crossing the river. Grey prepared his force, taking with him the light infantry, the 44th and 42nd Regiments of Foot, along with some of the 16th Dragoons. Colonel Thomas Musgrave would supplement this attacking force with the 55th and 40th regiments by trying to cut off the American retreat. Grey instructed his men to remove their charges from their weapons. Those weapons that could not be unloaded should have their flints removed. These precautions would prevent a weapon from firing before the attack, thus warning the Americans of the British approach. Unfortunately this order later became known in the American camp, and General Grey earned the rather severe nickname "No Flint" Grey for the rest of his time in the Revolutionary War. It was not deserved. Wayne himself would use the same tactics at Stony Point in 1779 and both the French and American light infantry would do the same at Yorktown in the storming of Redoubts 9 and 10 in 1781, just to mention two examples. It was a sign of good leadership and military management rather than illegal gamesmanship to remove the flints of loaded weapons for a surprise attack.

Leaving the British camp at 10 P.M., Grey led his men along the Swede's Ford Road toward the American camp. The British knew where Wayne was camped but did not know the layout of the camp itself. The light infantry led the way, followed by the 44th Regiment. The 42nd Black Watch Regiment came in reserve. Moving separately from Grey's force, Musgrave's two regiments took position at the Paoli Tavern to cut off Wayne's retreat toward Washington, although this positioning is hard to understand since any American retreat would have to run over the attacking British force in order to come in Musgrave's direction. Musgrave evidently sent a detachment to Waynesborough to search for Wayne. The British did not succeed in finding Wayne at home.

At the same time that the British were leaving their camp under Grey, Wayne received word from Morgan Jones, the father of Wayne's chaplain, David Jones, that the British knew Wayne's position and would attack that very night. A servant boy of a Mr. Clayton's had been in the British camp and overheard the soldiers talking. Upon being released, the servant came directly to Clayton and then to Jones. These local men warned Wayne and gave him several hours to prepare his men. Wayne ordered additional pickets and videttes posted, two other roads covered, and the men in his force made aware of the British possible approach. The Pennsylvanians were ordered to prepare their arms, put their cartridge boxes under their coats, and to lie down on their weapons to protect them from the rain. Wayne then waited to see what would come.

Grey, accompanied by his aide, Captain John André, was taking no chances. As his force moved along the Swede's Ford Road, he gathered up every resident along the line of march so that no one would slip out and warn Wayne of the British approach. As the British dragoons came to the turn to the south off the Swede's Ford Road, the first shots of the night were fired by the American videttes posted at that point. Discharging their weapons, the Americans rode off, presumably to warn Wayne. The British pushed on, crossing the Lancaster Wagon Road and passing near the Admiral Warren Tavern. It was here that a local blacksmith was roused to guide Grey and his troops up the ridge in their final approach to the American camp. Grey himself came to the front of his first troops, the light infantry, and sent them through the woods and on into the American camp with a cheer. The British ran over two pickets who had time to fire their weapons before being overwhelmed.

All this firing of weapons and the riding of videttes should have warned Wayne that the intelligence he had received earlier in the evening might be true. There may have been doubt in his mind, since General William Smallwood, with 1,500 additional soldiers from Maryland and Delaware, was under orders to join Wayne in the British rear in order to assist in the harassment the next day. Could this be Smallwood's force?

Finally, at some point in the British approach up the ridge toward Wayne's camp, Wayne sounded the alarm and got his light infantry and 1st Pennsylvania Regiment up to receive the attack. At 1 A.M. the British struck Wayne, coming through the woods to his immediate front, yelling and screaming. Although this is still debated today, the British probably did not fire, but used the American fire and campfires to good advantage to locate the Americans and kill them with the bayonet only.

Wayne was able to get his entire artillery train off, although one of the gun carriages broke and needed repair. It could not have been a complete surprise on the American line. At least two bodies of troops were ready to reply and did so to the British attack. Wayne evidently realizing his force numbered only a tenth of Howe's army and would be struck by a force at least equal to that of his own. He had already determined to order a retreat and gave the orders for this process to begin. Colonel Richard Humpton of the 11th Pennsylvania was second in command to Wayne and was ordered to have the troops assemble, wheel by section to the right, and march off by the left along the Indian King Road toward the White Horse Tavern.

In the event, Humpton acted slowly. The regiments in the two brigades split into two groups. The 2nd and 7th Pennsylvania regiments passed on the wrong side of the now dying campfires so that the British could see them clearly silhouetted against the light while the British enjoyed the benefit of the dark. It was these two regiments that received the most British attention that night and thus suffered the most casualties. Wayne intended no stand be made and took special pains to hasten the departure of the remainder of his force, using the light infantry and 1st Pennsylvania as a rear guard. In time, the 4th Pennsylvania would be called back to provide additional help in covering the withdrawal.

The British light infantry did most of the execution that night. Trained to yell and cheer in order to unnerve the enemy, they did their duty with dispatch. A legend has it that they even knew the American password for the night, which if true, would explain how they were able to approach so close to the American pickets so as to overwhelm them. It was this sentence they screamed as they raced through the camp: "Here we come and there they go." They concentrated though on the tents and shelters and what troops they could see in the light of the campfires. Thus most of Wayne's force escaped unharmed but shaken. Wayne and his covering force stayed on the right, where the British just chanced to come out of the woods in the first place, and held off any of the British bent on going beyond the campsite.

Unfortunately for the Americans, the retreat was not a particularly organized one. Many of the Pennsylvanians panicked. Some wound up in Downingtown by sunrise. Lieutenant Samuel Brady of the 6th Pennsylvania wound up in a swamp, where he hid, assuming he was alone and safe from pursuit. When morning came and he looked about, he found himself with 55 others who had taken the same route to safety. He organized them and marched them to rejoin Wayne at the Red Lion Tavern. Smallwood's men were marching along the Indian King Road to join Wayne at the precise time that Grey's men struck the American camp. They were about a mile from Wayne when the fleeing Pennsylvanians came down the road and proved more than enough to shake the fortitude of the Maryland and Delaware troops and all soon joined in the retreat. It took many miles to bring them all back to order.

Since Howe planned to cross the Schuylkill that very day, September 21, Grey recalled his force quickly, finished up the destruction of the camp and began a quick march back to the main British camp, picking up Musgrave at the Paoli Tavern along the way. With them, the British carried 71 prisoners, 40 of whom were so seriously wounded they were left at homes along the line of march. André claimed over 200 American dead were left on the field. The British also claimed to have captured all eight of Wayne's wagons.

The next day local farmers came to the field of battle and discovered 53 dead Americans. These they buried on a neighboring farm since Griffith, a Tory, refused to allow them burial on his farm. Later another dead American was found and buried with the others. Historians have argued over the exact number of casualties on both sides at Paoli. The consensus seems to be 150 American dead and wounded and another 40 captured. The British claimed 6 killed and 22 wounded. It is hard to say if these British totals are correct, but the sense of the battle indicates the totals may very well be close in this case.

Wayne sent letters to Washington and to his wife, Polly, from the Red Lion Tavern, where Lionville, Pennsylvania, is today, describing in the best possible light what had occurred. Wayne spent a day tending to his wounded and gathering his force about him. Then he set out to rejoin the main American army. In time, he requested a court-martial in order to set the record straight about Paoli. The court-martial met from October 25 to October 30, 1777, under the direction of General John Sullivan. The verdict was announced on November 1 in the general orders of the day. Wayne was acquitted unanimously of the charges of being negligent in the performance of his duties.

Congress, hearing that Howe was to cross the Schuylkill and take Philadelphia without any additional interference from Washington, fled their capital city into the Jersies and would eventually wind up in Lancaster/York, Pennsylvania. The Liberty Bell and other city bells were taken from their towers and removed to Allentown so that the British would not melt them down into cannon balls. The British light infantry, in order to let people know it was their force that defeated Wayne by surprise, began wearing red feathers in their helmets (or so the legend goes). Wayne and his men got their chance for revenge on a following Saturday in October at Germantown. Though American officers tried to restrain the men, many British were bayoneted even after surrendering in return for the same British actions at Paoli. Wayne would become a better general officer for his experience at Paoli. In time, he would become one of Washington's best tactical generals and would become the commander-in-chief of the United States Army during Washington's presidency in the 1790s.

The Paoli Tavern, a spot where Wayne drank many a toast to the rebel cause of liberty before the war, no longer stands today. It took its name from Pasquale Paoli, a Corsican patriot against the French. The American camp was located on Griffith's farm, part of which is today the campus of Malvern Preparatory School. The monument and burial grounds of the American troops killed at Paoli are located in the borough of Malvern and stand in Memorial Park. The Admiral Warren Tavern still operates today as a restaurant, having been restored to its colonial style. Since Wayne's camp was but a mile from this tavern and two miles from the Paoli, the incident should be called the Warren "Massacre."

Of course it was not a "massacre" in any sense of the word. It was instead a cunning move by Howe and an effective night action by Grey to eliminate a threat to the British rear before they crossed a river. Nothing done that night by the British was illegal or immoral or against the "rules of warfare." It was no more immoral than the

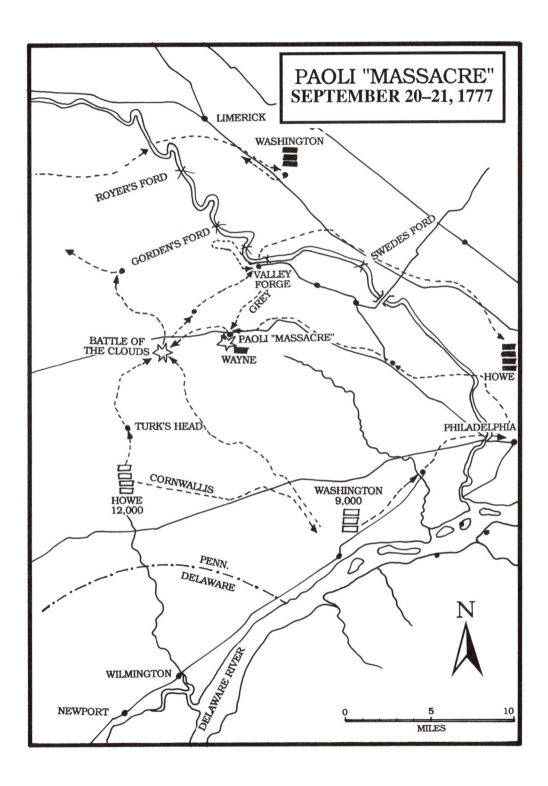

PAOLI "MASSACRE"
SEPTEMBER 20–21, 1777

LIMERICK

WASHINGTON

ROYER'S FORD

GORDEN'S FORD

SWEDES FORD

VALLEY FORGE

GREY

PAOLI "MASSACRE"

BATTLE OF THE CLOUDS

WAYNE

HOWE

TURK'S HEAD

PHILADELPHIA

CORNWALLIS

HOWE 12,000

WASHINGTON 9,000

PENN.

DELAWARE

WILMINGTON

NEWPORT

DELAWARE RIVER

N

0   5   10
MILES

common American practice in the war of aiming directly at particular soldiers in battle, particularly officers. But the American propagandists created the title and forced the issue, and "massacre" it has been ever since, though less than 10 percent of Wayne's force were casualties.

Paul J. Sanborn

REFERENCES

John André, *Major André's Journal*, ed. by Henry Cabot Lodge (1903), rpr. 1968; Donald Grey Brownlow, *A Documentary History of the Paoli "Massacre"* (1952); Douglas S. Freeman, *George Washington* (1957); Paul David Nelson, *Anthony Wayne* (1985); John F. Reed, *Campaign to Valley Forge* (1985); Charles J. Stille, *Anthony Wayne and the Pennsylvania Line* (1893), rpr. 1988.

Parker, John (1725–1775)

Massachusetts militia officer. Born in Lexington, Massachusetts, Parker was a veteran of the French and Indian War, a farmer, and a mechanic. On April 18, 1775, Captain Parker placed his 130 minutemen on the village green in Lexington. Nearby was the home of the Reverend Jonas Clarke, where Samuel Adams and John Hancock were hiding. Parker awaited the arrival of a British force under Lieutenant Colonel Francis Smith and Major John Pitcairn. After a long wait that night, Parker ordered his men to rest, and he went to Buckman's Tavern for refreshments.

By daybreak news of the advance guard of redcoats under Pitcairn arrived in the village. Adams and Hancock fled; Parker had a drummer sound the alarm, and about 70 men turned out to confront the British. About 40 more individuals were spectators. What occurred next and who fired the first shot are subjects of dispute. It is doubted if Parker said, "Stand your ground. Don't fire unless fired upon. But if they mean to have a war, let it begin here." In any case the statement attributed to the leader of the minutemen provided useful propaganda for the Revolutionary cause. Eight Americans were killed and nine were wounded in this skirmish, which ignited the war.

Parker and his men later joined the rest of the Massachusetts militia in harassing the British column in its retreat from Concord. Parker served at the siege of Boston, but he became ill and died September 17, 1775.

Richard L. Blanco

REFERENCES

Allen French, *The Day of Lexington and Concord* (1925); John R. Galvin, *The Minute Men* (1987); Robert A. Gross, *The Minute Men and Their World* (1976); Arthur A. Tourtellot, *Lexington and Concord* (1963).

Parker's Ferry, South Carolina, Action at (August 31, 1781)

Patriot militia captain William Harden of South Carolina had two major problems facing him—pressure from 300 to 400 Loyalist militiamen and desertions and refusals to reenlist from many of his men, who were frightened after the execution of Isaac Hayne or who were tired of the ravages of war. To counter this low ebb in morale, Harden requested assistance from Francis Marion, the "Swamp Fox," who was in camp 100 miles away at Peyree's Plantation in St. Stephens Parish. Marion was to attack a British force under a Major Charles Fraser at Parker's Ferry on the Edisto River in Colleton County. Captain George Cooper, meanwhile, was to create a diversion by attacking British forces near Dorchester and Monck's Corner.

Marion and his 200 men hid in a swamp along the road leading to the ferry. They then opened fire on Fraser's force, which soon retreated. There was little pursuit from the Americans, who were short on ammunition and who retired upon the approach of a British infantry detachment.

Harold Campbell

REFERENCES

Edward McCrady, *History of South Carolina in the Revolution, 1780–1783* (1902); Warren Ripley, *Battleground: South Carolina in the Revolution* (1983).

Parkers of the Royal Navy

During the American Revolution, the name Parker became synonymous with the British navy. At least three men of that name were major officers.

Hyde Parker (1714–1782) had already served several years as a merchant seaman before becoming an officer in the Royal Navy at age 24. By 1749, he was a captain. Even in peacetime, Parker had a lively career—in 1753 protecting North Atlantic fisheries and fighting smugglers, in 1756 arranging the release of all European slaves in Morocco, and in 1759 serving off the coast of France under Admiral Lord Richard

Howe. When what the Americans knew as the French and Indian War heated up, Hyde Parker was sent to the East Indies, where he served in campaigns from India to the Phillippines. In 1764, he returned to England and retired from the navy for 12 years.

The American Revolution brought him back into the service. Starting in 1776, he served as a rear admiral under Vice Admiral John Byron and saw action in the West Indies. Parker was promoted to vice admiral in 1780 and given the command of a Baltic squadron. As such, his ships fought an equal Dutch fleet to a draw after heavy fighting. Admiral Hyde Parker, made a baron upon the death of his older brother (also named Hyde), was lost at sea with his ship in 1782.

Still another Hyde Parker (1739–1807) was the son of the above admiral. He also joined the navy, and by 1776 the younger Hyde Parker was serving in the North American station. As such, he successfully overcame the obstacles invented by Benjamin Franklin for blocking the North River (Hudson), and he captured two gun boats. For this victory, he was knighted. He also served with distinction at Rhode Island and Savannah.

On October 4, 1780, his ship was wrecked in a hurricane off the coast of Cuba. He and the other survivors entrenched and sent to Jamaica for help. They were soon rescued. In 1782, Parker sailed to the relief of Gibraltar, and in the wars with France in the 1790s, he served in numerous actions in the Mediterranean as an admiral. As commander-in-chief of Jamaica (1796–1800), his fleet captured several prizes. His last campaign was against the Dutch in 1800, and it is best remembered for the successes of his second in command, Horatio Nelson. Parker retired soon after and died March 16, 1807.

Peter Parker (1721–1811) was the son of Rear Admiral Christopher Parker (d. 1765). He first went to sea under his father and was a captain by 1747. In 1757, he served in the fighting in the West Indies and was knighted in 1772. However, most of his time from 1762 to 1775 was spent in England awaiting another command. When he was given charge of a fleet in North America, he commanded in the unsuccessful assault upon Sullivan Island, near Charlestown, South Carolina, on June 26, 1776. Parker met with greater success in the reduction of Long Island later that year, under Lord Howe. In 1777, he was promoted to rear admiral and commander-in-chief of Jamaica. Two years later he was promoted to vice admiral, in 1782 was made a baronet, and in 1787 was made a full admiral. Sir Peter Parker is chiefly remembered as a patron of young Horatio Nelson, but their relationship has been overstated. Parker died in London, December 21, 1811.

Robert Scott Davis, Jr.

REFERENCE
DNB.

Parsons, Samuel Holden (1737–1789)

Continental Army officer. The son of a clergyman, Parsons was raised in Connecticut and Massachusetts. After graduating from Harvard (1756) he studied law and was admitted to the bar in Massachusetts (1759). Parsons served in the assembly, and in 1773 he was appointed a king's attorney. Made a major in the militia (1770), Parsons became a colonel in 1775 and was given that rank in the Continental Army.

Parsons saw action at the siege of Boston. Promoted to brigadier general, Parsons led troops at Kip's Bay. Thereafter he was stationed in the Hudson Highlands and in New Jersey, where he had recruiting duties in 1777. During the winter of 1778–1779 Parsons was posted to West Point. In July 1779 he led a force that harassed the British on their raid of Norfolk, Connecticut. Promoted to major general (October 1780), Parsons performed well in an action at Morrisana (January 22–23, 1781). Worried about his investments in depreciated government securities, Parsons complained bitterly. Though approached by a British agent, Parsons never contemplated treason.

Resigning from the army in July 1782 he returned to his law practice in Middletown, Connecticut. By March 1787 he became a director for the Ohio Company. That year he was appointed a judge of the Northwest Territory, and in 1788 he moved to Adelphia (Marietta, Ohio). Granted 24,000 acres of land for his war services, Parsons visited his holdings in the Western Reserve of Connecticut along Lake Erie. Soon after, he died on the Big Beaver River when his canoe capsized.

Richard L. Blanco

REFERENCES

DAB; Charles S. Hall, *Life and Letters of Samuel Holden Parsons* (1905); George B. Loring, "Vindication of General Samuel Holden Parsons," *Magazine of American History, 20* (1888):286–303.

Pattison, James (1723–1805)

British army officer. James Pattison was the second son of a London merchant. He received his commission as a lieutenant fireworker on April 1, 1740. In 1747 he assumed his first command when he raised a company of miners at Woolwich. Two years later his unit was converted to an artillery company. He held company command until 1759, when he was promoted to major. In 1762 he commanded the Royal Artillery companies sent to Portugal, and in 1769 he went to Venice to supervise the organization of the Venetian Artillery. This last assignment earned him a reputation as something of a diplomat.

When the commander of the 4th Battalion, Royal Artillery (R.A.) died in England, Pattison succeeded to its command on April 25, 1777, with the rank of colonel. He immediately left for America to assume active command of the battalion, which until then had functioned under the direction of second in command Colonel Samuel Cleaveland. When Pattison reached New York on September 24 he received the "local rank" of brigadier. Sir Henry Clinton later promoted him to major general on February 19, 1779.

The commander of the 4th Battalion, R.A. also functioned as the overall British Artillery commander in America (but not in Canada). In addition to those assignments, Pattison also became commandant of New York City. Most of his time in America seems to have been taken up with that task, which included command of the city's militia and the organization and management of the city's fortifications. On at least one occasion, he did command in the field when he led the artillery during General James Paterson's operations against Stony Point and Verplancks Point in June 1779.

While commandant of New York City, Pattison developed some interesting insights on the war. Writing to his brother in 1777, Pattison noted: "I own I had very mistaken notions myself when in England of reducing America to obedience by conquest. I have totally changed my sentiments, not that I would wish them to be known but to yourself, as it might not be prudent for me to declare them. . . . We have not only armies to combat with, but a whole country, where every man, woman, and even child is your enemy, and, in fact, do in one shape or another act as such."

Pattison returned to England on October 4, 1780. Although he left America for reasons of health, he lived for another 25 years, serving twice as the commandant of the Woolwich Garrison and also as the governor of the Royal Military Academy.

David T. Zabecki

REFERENCES

James Alex Browne, *England's Artillerymen* (1865); Captain Francis Duncan, *History of the Royal Regiment of Artillery*, Vol. I (1872); John Kane, *List of Officers of the Royal Regiment of Artillery*, 4th ed. (1890).

Paulus Hook, New Jersey, Raid on (August 18–19, 1779) (Alternate spelling: Powles)

Now part of Jersey City, Paulus Hook was the New Jersey terminus of the ferry from New York City. An island at high tide, this low point of land was connected to the mainland by a long causeway across a swamp. The fort was 11 miles south of Fort Constitution; it guarded the lower Hudson River; and it was bounded by the natural moat of the Hackensack River. The nearest bridge connecting this isthmus to the mainland was 12 miles away. Held by the British since late 1776, this post was protected by a drawbridge, a heavy gate, a palisade, redoubts, a storehouse, and three cannon. The 300 troops there appeared to be safe from attack, and with a Royal Navy sloop off shore with 50 marines, and with British regulars available from Manhattan on quick notice, the place seemed impregnable. General Henry Clinton used it to check any American raiders in the area and as a base for expeditions inland by British troops.

The task of raiding this position was assigned to Major Henry Lee and his 2nd Partisan Corps of some 200 men. "Light-Horse" Harry Lee was famous for his stealth and skill in such operations, and he was particularly embittered because he and his corps had not shared in the glory bestowed upon Anthony Wayne for storming

Stony Point (July 16, 1779). Hence he sought an objective that required his special skills—daring, meticulous planning, and careful consideration of tides and hours of darkness. He planned to capture the entire garrison but not to retain the post.

From Paramus, New Jersey, Lee had detailed information from Captain Allen McLean of his corps about enemy dispositions, and he made preparations with Captain Henry Peyton to have boats available on the Hackensack River in order to elude British pursuit. Dividing his men into three groups, Lee led his men in the darkness to Paulus Hook. Unfortunately for Lee, about one-half of his troops lost their way so that the scheduled attack was delayed about four hours, just before rising tide. With bayonets fixed and muskets loaded but not primed, the Americans crossed the swamp and adjacent creeks. Although British sentries sounded the alarm, Lee's "forlorn hope" of volunteers waded through the ditches, scaled the palisades, pushed through the abatis, and attacked the redoubt. Without firing a shot the corps killed 50 British with the bayonet and captured about 150 more. But 50 German Auxiliaries who had retreated to a blockhouse fought on and refused to surrender. The affair was over in 30 minutes, but there was no time to capture the Germans, nor to spike the guns.

In Manhattan the British were aroused quickly. Lee had to evacuate with his prisoners before the enemy could trap his men between the Hudson and the Hackensack. After a harrowing five-mile march to the rendezvous, Lee's men were dismayed by the fact that the anticipated boats were not there. Assuming that the operation had been canceled, Peyton had taken the boats back to Newark. Lee's men had to continue their march with the enemy now in close pursuit. The British caught up with them at Liberty Pole Tavern (Englewood, New Jersey) but a contingent of General William Alexander's troops helped Lee's corps to repel the attack.

The news of this daring exploit heartened the nation. Although the assault had minor military consequences, the propaganda value of this deed was inestimable and it demonstrated to Clinton that even his supposedly impregnable outposts were vulnerable to attack. The irony of this remarkable adventure for the glory-seeking Lee is that he was subject to court-martial on eight charges related to the operation by officers jealous of the autonomy given him by Washington. Lee was acquitted on September 29. Soon after, Congress provided a bonus to his men, promoted some of the corps lieutenants, congratulated Lee for his heroism, and ordered a special medal

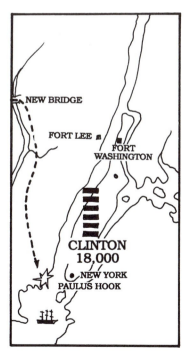

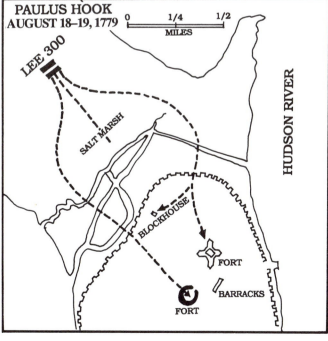

struck in his honor. But Lee was denied the colonelcy that he desired.

Richard L. Blanco

REFERENCES

Noel B. Gerson, *Light-Horse Harry* (1966); Charles Royster, *Light-Horse Harry Lee and the Legacy of the American Revolution* (1981); Bernard A. Uhlendorf, ed. and trans., *Revolution in America: Baurmeister Journals . . .* (1957); Christopher Ward, 2 vols. *The War of the American Revolution* (1952), 2.

Peace Commission of the Howe Brothers

See Howe, Richard Lord.

Peace Treaty of September 3, 1783

See Diplomacy of the American Revolution.

Peale, Charles Willson (1741–1827)

American painter. Charles Willson Peale, portrait painter, naturalist, and Patriot, was born in Maryland, the son of Charles Peale, a native of England and a schoolmaster. Peale was originally trained as a saddler, but his activities as a member of the Sons of Freedom during the Stamp Act crisis forced him to give up this vocation. After attempting some portraits on his own and receiving a few lessons from the painter John Hesselius, he met the artist John Singleton Copley in Boston on a trip to New England. Back in Maryland, a group of men raised a subscription to send the promising artist to London to study painting and to investigate what proved to be a spurious legacy. He became a pupil of Benjamin West, the American artist residing in London from 1767 through 1769.

Peale then pursued his painting career in Maryland until he moved to Philadelphia in 1776. There he joined the city militia as a private. He was active in recruiting volunteers and was elected a lieutenant. When the unit was activated in December 1776 he saw action at the Battles of Trenton and Princeton and was commissioned captain of the 4th Battalion or Regiment of Foot and continued with them until the British left Philadelphia. Peale served on military and civil committees, was chairman of the Constitutional Society, and in 1779 was elected one of the Philadelphia representatives in the Pennsylvania General Assembly.

During this period, he painted many portraits of his fellow officers in miniature, which he later replicated in life size to hang in his museum. This museum, which he first opened in his house, was located in the Hall of the American Philosophical Society from 1794 to 1802. At this time, he was permitted to place the museum in the State House (Independence Hall) in Philadelphia, where it remained until its dissolution in 1854. Here were hung in long rows above the natural history display cases his portraits of the Revolutionary heroes and political figures. The bulk of this collection was purchased by the City of Philadelphia at the time the museum closed and now is on display at Independence National Historical Park.

Peale painted the first life portrait of George Washington at Mount Vernon in 1772, in which Washington wears the uniform of a colonel in the Virginia militia. All in all, Washington sat for Peale seven times, and from these Peale produced at least 60 portraits. The last sitting was in 1795 during Washington's presidency.

In addition to his own art, history, and natural history museum, Peale was largely responsible for the establishment of the Pennsylvania Academy of Fine Arts in 1805.

Peale was married three times and fathered 12 children who survived to adulthood, many of whom were artists in their own right. His son Rembrandt Peale (1778–1860) was also a portrait painter who painted a number of Revolutionary figures later in their lives. Peale believed that anyone could be trained as an artist. In addition to his children, he trained his brother James Peale (1749–1831) and his nephew, Charles Peale Polk (1767–1822), as portrait painters. Both of them later painted portraits of Revolutionary figures. The portraits they painted have often been confused with those of Peale himself.

Robert G. Stewart

REFERENCES

Lillian B. Miller, ed. *The Selected Papers of Charles Willson Peale and His Family*, vol. I, *Charles Willson Peale: Artist in Revolutionary America 1735–1791* (1983), vol. II, *Charles Willson Peale: The Artist as Museum Keeper 1793–1810* (1988); E.P. Richardson, Brooke Hindle, and L.B. Miller, *Charles Willson Peale and His World* (1982); Charles Coleman Sellers, *Charles Willsom Peale: A Biography* (1969);

————, *Portraits and Miniatures by Charles Willson Peale, Transactions of the American Philosophical Society*, *42*, Part I (1952) and *49*, Supplement, Part 3 (1969).

Peekskill, New York, Raid on (March 23, 1777)

A British raiding party (the second in two months) consisting of approximately 500 redcoats with four light fieldpieces came ashore from several transports guarded by a frigate to destroy this Revolutionary supply base, an important link to the installations guarding the strategic Hudson River. Brigadier General Alexander McDougall with a garrison of half this size withdrew and burned stores. A Patriot force of 80 men under Lieutenant Colonel Marinus Willett arrived from Fort Constitution and boldly engaged the raiders the next day. The British suffered 15 casualties before they withdrew, and the rebels had two killed and five wounded.

The disquieting news of this successful raid and the destruction of much needed supplies made George Washington take action. Worried about future sallies against the posts on the Hudson River, he ordered Major General William Heath to send eight regiments to Peekskill. In retrospect, this raid was not a harbinger of future military actions by the British, and the rebel cause suffered no permanent damage with the losses at Peekskill.

Harold J. Weiss, Jr.

REFERENCES

William Abbatt, ed., *Memoirs of Major-General William Heat, by Himself*, new ed. (1901); John E. Ferling, *The First of Men: A Life of George Washington* (1988); Douglas S. Freeman, *George Washington: A Biography*, 7 vols. (1948–57), *4*; Howard H. Peckham, ed., *The Toll of Independence: Engagements and Battle Casualties of the American Revolution* (1974).

Pell's Point, New York, Battle of (October 18, 1776) (Alternate names: Eastchester, Pelham, Pelham's Bay, Split Rock)

This battle was a delaying action on the part of the Americans, expertly carried out, to force the British van to wait until the main body of British came to its support. The delay permitted Washington's army to escape being encircled or being cut off in its retreat from Harlem Heights to White Plains in the New York campaign of 1776. Because of its strategic implications, the numbers engaged, the duration of the engagement and its results, the Battle of Pell's Point deserves to be ranked as a major and significant action of the War of Revolution.

The British and the Americans faced each other at Harlem Heights on the northern portion of Manhattan Island for almost a month following the Battle of Harlem Heights. General William Howe did little. He did not wish to assault the American positions and took his time plotting out his next move. It came in mid-October, and when it did, it was a quick and decisive move. Howe decided to use his favorite flanking technique once more, as he had at the Battle of Long Island.

While Lord Hugh Percy of Lexington-Concord fame held the attention of the Americans, Howe sent a large portion of his army on an amphibious operation using the East River to land at Throg's Neck behind the American lines on October 12. It was Howe's intention to capture King's Bridge, Washington's sole retreat route from Manhattan Island to the north, or to force Washington into battle. It was also possible to cut Washington's army off from its supply bases in Connecticut or to force Washington to flee from the New York City area entirely.

At first, Washington did little except to bottle up Howe at Throg's Neck, actually an island at anytime but at low tide. The Americans were working to strengthen Fort Washington and were trying to block off the Hudson River from British shipping. Washington needed more time before exposing Fort Washington to attack.

Finally, with about 13,000 men, Washington began moving north toward White Plains, the newly selected American defensive position. The British had passed Forts Lee and Washington and the blockage in the Hudson without damage. Their ships had sailed north to Tarrytown with troops. The British at Throg's Neck could break out and join up with those at Tarrytown to trap Washington's entire army and force his surrender. He could wait no longer. On October 18, the brigade of General William Alexander (Lord Stirling) made the 18-mile march in four hours to White Plains. The rest of the American army followed over the next four days at a much slower pace. Twenty-eight hundred men were left behind to garrison Fort Washington.

Frustrated at Throg's Neck, with 4,000 Americans holding him in check for six days, Howe decided to make another landing, this time three miles north at Pell's Point. This second flanking movement would make use of a peninsula, a part of the mainland, and would permit the British, if their luck held out, to catch Washington's army spread out on the line of march toward White Plains.

General Sir William Clinton and Lord Cornwallis cooperated in leading this landing at Pell's Point. The major portion of the British force was four German regiments of Friedrich von Stirn's brigade, numbering approximately 3,000 men. Some light infantry, grenadiers, and dismounted dragoons of the 16th Light Horse were also along. The American commander on the scene, Colonel John Glover, estimated he faced about 4,000 men. Leaving Throg's Neck at 2 A.M. on Friday, October 18, they achieved complete surprise. The landing went without a hitch, unopposed.

The only American troops in the area were under the command of John Glover, a short, stocky Massachusetts officer in charge of a brigade of four Massachusetts Continental regiments. They had been in position at Eastchester guarding the Old Post Road for four days. On the morning of October 18, Glover went to his observation rock with his glass and looked out into Pelham Bay and saw the British fleet landing the troops. He had the alarm sounded and sent word immediately to General Charles Lee to alert that officer to the British move. Lee either never received the message or never acted upon it. Glover was left to bring this affair to its conclusion alone with his brigade of 750 men and three guns.

The odds against Glover were five to one. This was his first independent command. He did not hesitate but went instantly into action. He held his own regiment of 180 men, the 14th Continentals, as his reserve along with the three cannon, which would be of little use in the broken countryside over which the action would be contested. The reserve regiment and three cannon would serve as his final line, positioned on the far side of Hutchinson's Creek with the planks of the bridge over the creek removed for additional safety.

With his other three regiments, and skirmishers out in front, he hurried down from his campground to delay the British advance. The only way for the British to reach the vital Boston–New York Post Road in Glover's rear was along Split Rock Road. (This road was named after a huge split rock that was an ancient Indian landmark that still exists today, although it is in the median strip of the New England Thruway near Exit 6, where it is preserved but difficult to appreciate.) Glover placed his three regiments along Split Rock Road at staggered intervals on opposite sides of the road.

The British had to march down the roadway. The fields to either side of the road were broken by stone fences and the road itself was bordered on both sides with the same kind of fences. For defense, this was excellent ground. Glover developed a gauntlet for the British and had his men behind stone walls that provided good cover and he encouraged confidence in the troops. The first regiment placed was that of Colonel Joseph Reed, the 13th Continental, with 226 men. It stood to the left of the road nearest to the split rock. Glover planned for a rotating regimental fire. As the British brought pressure to bear on each regiment in turn, that regiment would withdraw under cover of the next regiment behind. Much of the battle was fought near and around the split rock itself.

Once his three regiments were in position along the road, Glover took 40 men of his advanced troops and went out after the British skirmishers. The Americans attacked and exchanged five full vollies with the enemy before falling back. The British, sensing a victory, gave a shout and rushed forward after the fleeing Americans. At a distance of a perfect 30 yards for complete accuracy with the muskets, Reed's men rose from behind their stone wall and fired point-blank into the oncoming British. A sheet of flame from 200 men blasted the British back in confusion. They went running back down the hill whence they had come.

A lull settled over the field for over an hour while the British brought the rest of their units to the front to force the issue. Then, firing their six cannon without effect, the British came on to attack Reed's regiment. The Americans waited until the British drew within 50 yards, still an excellent distance, and then cut loose with another volley. The British were hurt badly; they faltered but then fired back. Both sides proceeded to exchange seven rounds at 50 yards until Glover ordered Reed to move his men to the rear.

Once again, the British sensed victory and came charging after Reed's withdrawing regiment. Cheering and shouting, they rushed forward to finish off Reed. It was then that the second American regiment, Colonel William Shepard's 3rd Continentals, rose up out of their stone wall fence on the right side of the road, and poured a vicious volley directly into the surging British ranks. The British were stopped in their tracks and fell back in confusion. Reed's men retreated in safety.

Shepard's 200 men then began to fire in rolling vollies, section by section, up and down the American line, so that a continual stream of lead flew toward the British. This was the hottest fighting of the day. A fierce and bloody contest developed as Shepard's men let loose with 17 full vollies into the British, who refused to run before the rebels and forced themselves into repeated attempts to break Shepard's line. Colonel Shepard, a hardened veteran of the French and Indian War, was wounded in the neck, but his regiment maintained its line until Glover withdrew them. By now, after regrouping and bringing up more troops, the British were in such strength that a withdrawal was necessary to save Shepard's regiment.

Now it was Colonel Loammi Baldwin (who later helped develop the apple named after him) and his 234 men of the 26th Continentals that rose up from their stone wall and poured more lead into the advancing British line. Once again, the British were thrown into confusion, fell back in retreat, and regrouped. For a delaying action, there can be no more vicious and bloody example in the entire War of Revolution.

How long this process would have continued is hard to say. It was at this point, though, that Cornwallis appeared in the rear of Glover's force, flanking the Americans by heading for the bridge over Hutchinson's Creek. This threat caused Glover to break off the action and withdraw his three regiments to avoid being cut off. The Americans retired in the face of British pressure under control and without panic. It was no rout. Proud of themselves and having done great damage to the enemy, the men were reluctant to leave the field. The total American brigade formed with its reserve on top of the hill where the morning's encampment had been, after having to wade the creek. The three American cannon provided cover for the retreat.

The British came up and fired their artillery against the American position for the rest of the day. There were no further British infantry attacks. The Americans returned the fire but little damage was done on either side. When darkness came, the Americans fell back three miles to Dobbs Ferry and camped, greatly fatigued but satisfied with the results of the day; Clinton and Cornwallis did not pursue. Clinton actually believed that he had faced some 14,000 Americans during the day's action.

Howe likewise overestimated the number of American Patriots involved in the action. He admitted to 3 killed and 20 wounded, ignoring the German's casualties who had composed 75 percent of the British force in the battle. Some deserters claimed the British had actually suffered around 800 casualties with 200 killed on the spot. Glover's men had fired 25 full vollies into the enemy at 50 yards or less. The Americans had fought calmly and with style. American losses were put at 6 killed and 13 wounded, including Colonel Shepard. Many of the German casualties were housed in St. Paul's Episcopal Church, still standing on Columbus Avenue near 233rd Street in the Bronx.

Washington gained the time he needed to withdraw to the new American lines at White Plains. It took Howe two days to recover enough to resume his maneuvering. If Howe had chased Glover, he could have captured the Post Road and gone on to White Plains or trapped Washington to the south. The Battle of Pell's Point delayed him enough to keep these eventualities from happening.

Washington and General Charles Lee both congratulated Glover for his excellent strategic and tactical accomplishment in this action. Glover had once again saved the American army from disaster.

Paul J. Sanborn

REFERENCES

William Abbatt, *The Battle of Pell's Point* (1901); George A. Billias, *General John Glover* (1960); ———, "Pelham Bay: A Forgotten Battle," in *New York Historical Society Narratives of the Revolution in New York* (1975); Bruce Bliven, Jr., *Battle for Manhattan* (1964); Christopher Ward, *The War of Revolution*, 2 vols., (1952), *1*.

Pennsylvania Rifle

This is the modern academic generic term for the American-made long-barrelled maple-stocked rifle, reflecting the most well-known area of manufacture of these weapons. The older term, "Kentucky rifle," referred to the area in which they saw frequent and dramatic use primarily after the Revolution. There is increasing evidence that this type of rifle was widely manufactured in Virginia and the Carolinas as early as it was in western Pennsylvania. The appearance of this rifle is now placed in the 1740s, the earlier date of the mid-1720s lacking clear evidence. Its production and development appear directly related to the settlement of Germanic immigrants. *See also*: Rifle (America); Riflemen

De Witt Bailey

REFERENCES

De Witt Bailey, "The Rifle in the American War, 1775–1783," *Guns Review*, 9 (1969):8–12; Joe D. Huddleston, *Colonial Riflemen in the American Revolution* (1978); Warren Moore, *Weapons of the American Revolution* (1967).

Penobscot Expedition (July 19–August 15, 1779)

The Penobscot expedition of the summer of 1779 was an attempt by the citizens of Massachusetts to reduce a British fort on the Penobscot River in Massachusetts (now part of Maine). It was the largest naval expedition mounted by the Americans during the Revolutionary War, indeed the largest amphibious assault until the landing of Americans under Winfield Scott at Veracruz during the Mexican War. It also turned out to be the Americans' worst naval disaster of the entire war.

In June 1779 a detachment of approximately 700 British from the 7th and 82nd Infantry regiments, under command of Brigadier General Francis McLean, sailed from Halifax. They were accompanied by the sloops *North* (20 guns), *Albany* (18 guns), and *Nautilus* (18 guns), under the command of Captain Henry Mowat, who had burned Falmouth in 1775. The British force entered Penobscot Bay, 180 miles from Boston, and on June 17 landed on the Bagaduce peninsula, now Castine, Maine, to construct a fort. The spot selected was a peninsula jutting out into Penobscot Bay and controlling it. The British soon constructed a small redoubt named Fort George on cleared ground at the top of a high bluff. Provisions and artillery all had to be man-handled about a quarter-mile from the shore to the fort, so work was slow.

The British intended the new fort to bring a number of benefits. For some time they had been relying on timber from Penobscot Bay to repair and refit their ships at Halifax. A fortification on the bay would provide security for mast ships, while preventing the Americans from obtaining timber from Maine. In addition it would provide a new home for Loyalists then under British protection in Nova Scotia, and it could serve as a base for British cruisers operating against the New England coast.

New England had been free of British troops since the evacuation of Boston in 1776, and the news of a new British fort was received with considerable alarm. The Massachusetts General Court was then in session, and it soon authorized an operation to dislodge the invaders. Speed was essential if the British were to be defeated before they could strengthen their position. The Massachusetts State Board of War was in charge of the expedition. A call went out for 1,500 militiamen to serve under Brigadier General Solomon Lovell. General Peleg Wadsworth was second in command and Lieutenant Colonel Paul Revere was in charge of the artillery. Since so many locals were already in the Continental Army, the militiamen who volunteered for the expedition were hardly the best; many were either boys or old men, and in any case, only about 900 volunteered. Their weapons were also of uneven quality.

To transport the expedition to Maine there was a sizable force of state-owned vessels and privateers. The Continental Congress granted permission for the expedition to use the three remaining federal ships at Boston, the frigate *Warren* (32 guns), commanded by Dudley Saltonstall; the sloop *Providence* (12 guns), under Hoystead Hacker; and the brig *Diligence* (14 guns), recently captured from the British and commanded by Lieutenant Philip Brown. There were also three 14-gun brigs of the Massachusetts Navy, the *Hazard*, *Active*, and *Tyrannicide*; one New Hampshire vessel, the 20-gun *Hampden*; 10 privateers (*Sally*, *Putnam*, *Hector*, *Revenge*, *Vengeance*, *Black Prince*, *Sky Rocket*, *Defence*, *Pallas*, and *Hunter*), and 24 transports and supply vessels. In all, these ships mounted some 344 guns of various types, although most of them were light, They also carried about 300 marines—half from the Continental Navy and the rest from Massachusetts. Saltonstall, the senior Continental officer, was made commodore of the naval elements. The entire expense of the expedition was borne by Massachusetts.

In order to raise seamen for the expedition, Massachusetts imposed a 40-day embargo on merchant shipping. There was a universal expectation that the expedition would be brief, easy, and successful. Saltonstall's instructions were "to take every measure & use your utmost Endeavours to Captivate, Kill or Destroy the Enemies whole Force both by Sea & Land, & the most effectually to answer that purpose, you are to Consult measures & preserve the greatest harmony with the Command of the Land Forces, that the navy & army may Cooperate & assist each other." Unfortunately, the latter injunction was ignored and disaster was the result.

The expedition sailed from Boston on July 19, and it put into Boothbay Harbour (Maine) for reinforcements. The full complement of men was not made up, but the fleet sailed for Bagaduce on July 24. It was impossible to conceal the preparations for such a large undertaking; when the American force arrived in Penobscot Bay, the British had already been forewarned and were prepared. General McLean had requested help from New York; he had also ordered work expedited on Fort George and the construction of secondary batteries on the Bagaduce peninsula and nearby Nautilus Island. Captain Mowat had moored the three sloops close to the harbor entrance, with the transports behind them.

Late on July 24 the British garrison at Fort George sighted the American fleet coming up Penobscot Bay. If the Americans had mounted an immediate, determined attack, in all probability it would have been successful. Instead, the operation was marked by one delay after another.

The attack began on July 25 at 3 P.M. Nine of the American vessels, in three divisions, made for the British line, hove to, and engaged them over a two-hour period. The exchange of fire was largely ineffectual. While that was in progress, General Lovell, in his words, tried "to make a lodgment on Majorbagaduce, but the wind springing up very strong, I was obliged to desist, lest the first division might suffer before they could be supported by the second."

Early on July 26, about 150 marines, led by Captain John Welsh of the *Warren* and covered by the guns of the flotilla, landed on Nautilus Island directly opposite the British fort and commanding the mouth of the harbor. The Americans drove off its defenders and captured four pieces of artillery and some ammunition. Despite bad weather, they also managed to get some heavier guns ashore. Revere's artillerymen mounted two 18-pounders and a 12-pounder to cover the British anchorage; Mowat responded by moving his vessels farther up the harbor to get them out of range.

The Americans spent July 27 reconnoitering the British position, a costly and unnecessary delay that gave the British additional time to prepare. Some of the subordinate naval officers recognized this and presented a petition to Saltonstall in which they called for "the most speedy Exertions . . . to accomplish the design we came upon. We think Delays in the present Case are extremely dangerous, as our Enemies are daily Fortifying and Strengthening themselves & are stimulated so to do, being in daily Expectation of Reinforcement."

At 3:00 on the morning of July 28, the *Tyrannicide* opened fire into the woods to clear the enemy from the landing site on the western or bay side of the peninsula. The American battery on Nautilus Island also carried on a long-range duel with the cannon on Mowat's sloops. The landing was covered by the guns of two ships and three brigs, all of which came close to shore and fired into the woods until the landings began. The Americans came ashore in three divisions—marines on the right, militia under Colonel Mitchell on the left, and militia under Colonel McCobb with the artillery in the center. The marines met the stiffest resistance, and were attacked as soon as they landed. The British were able to fire down on the Americans from a steep bluff, but the marines drove the British infantry back to Fort George. The British sustained 12 dead on the spot, 8 wounded, and about 10 prisoners. The Americans lost about 35 killed and wounded. That afternoon the Americans captured a battery of three 6-pounders that the British had abandoned. The attackers immediately began constructing a battery on high ground near the fort.

At this point the naval–ground force cooperation, vital for the success of the operation, collapsed. Despite the fact that his troops were only 600 yards from their objective, Lovell refused to order another assault, insisting that Saltonstall's vessels first defeat the enemy sloops. Lovell believed that, with the British protected by earth and log entrenchments, the American ground force would be insufficient to carry the fort as long as the British ashore were supported by Mowat's sloops. Despite an agreement that the ships would attack the British squadron on July 29, Saltonstall refused to order it, even though he had overwhelming naval superiority. He insisted that Fort George be taken before he ordered an attack against the ships.

Neither American commander budged. The only hope for success was that the operation be completed quickly. Instead, it turned into a prolonged siege. When the Americans arrived, Fort George had consisted of a northern wall four feet high, low stone walls to the east and west, and no wall at the rear. The British were able, during the delay, to improve this significantly. Still, it was a near-run thing for the fort's defenders. The Americans were on the verge of a final land assault when a British relief force arrived. Many of Saltonstall's captains, fearful that the British would bottle them up in the bay, pleaded with him for an immediate attack. With the siege now dragging into weeks, the Naval Board in Boston sent Saltonstall a message, dated August 12, that read in part:

> We have for sometime been at loss to know why the enemy's ships have not been attacked ... it is agreed on all hands that they are at all times in your power. . . . It is therefore our orders that as soon as you receive this you are to take the most effectual measures for the capture or destruction of the enemy's ships, and with the greatest dispatch the nature and situation of things will admit of.

This might have pressured Saltonstall into action, but it came too late. On July 28, Commodore Sir George Collier at New York had received word of the American expedition. He quickly commandeered every ship at his disposal and sailed from Sandy Hook on August 3, leaving New York undefended in order to take maximum naval strength to Penobscot Bay. Collier had his flag in the *Raisonable* (64 guns). He also had the 32-gun frigates *Blonde* and *Virginia* (a former American frigate, captured the year before), the *Greyhound* (28 guns), the *Camilla* (20 guns) and *Galatea* (20 guns), and the sloop *Otter* (14 guns).

On August 13, the *Active* and the *Diligent*, which had been patrolling the mouth of the bay since July 30 in order to provide the earliest possible warning of an enemy approach, brought word of strange sails approaching. The British squadron, delayed by fog, had arrived.

During the night of August 13, the Americans hastily reembarked their troops. There was confusion and panic as the troops abandoned cannon and equipment and made for the transports. In a command meeting aboard the *Warren* some of the captains called for a stand by drawing up their vessels in a crescent and raking the British warships as they came up the bay single file. They hoped to be able to damage enough of the British tops to allow some of their ships to escape. Saltonstall appeared to agree and then lost his nerve. The next day he signaled that it was every man for himself. All discipline was lost in a mad rush for safety. Only two American vessels, the *Defence* and the *Hunter*, attempted to get to sea down the passage between Long Island and the western shore of the bay; Collier captured the *Hunter*, and the *Defence* was destroyed. As night fell, the rest of the fleet ran upriver. Lacking pilots, the British ships anchored for the night. Throughout the night the British heard explosions and saw flames as the Americans ran their ships aground and set them afire rather than have them fall into enemy hands. Seamen and soldiers alike then fled into the woods and set out on foot to try to get to Providence and Boston. Lovell wrote in his journal. "To attempt to give a description of this terrible Day is out of my Power. . . .Transports on fire. Men of war blowing up . . . and as much confusion as can possibly be conceived."

The next day the British moved upriver and everywhere saw evidence of the burned American vessels. Only the *Hunter* and the 22-gun ship *Hampden*, taken before she could enter the Penobscot River, escaped destruction.

A 400-man Continental Army regiment, detailed for service at Penobscot Bay, did not get underway to Bagaduce until after the arrival of the British. On August 19, immediately on learning of the defeat, the ships carrying the regiment put into Portsmouth to avoid capture by Collier's warships.

In all, nearly 500 Americans were killed or taken prisoner. Lack of training and inexperience were partly to blame for the disaster, but the main failure was one of command. Shortly

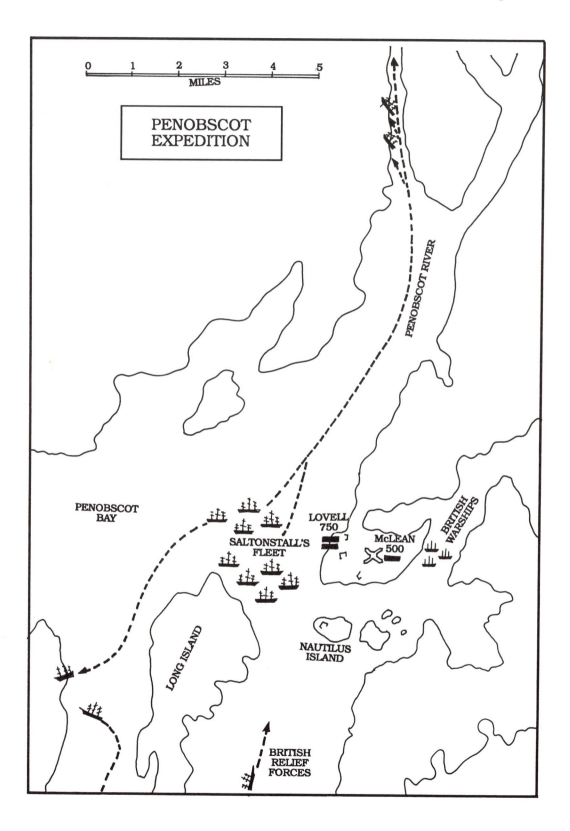

afterward, a committee of the Massachusetts House of Representatives investigated the causes of the expedition's failure. Perhaps with the partial intention of establishing a claim on Congress for reimbursement (Congress later approved restoration of $2 million of the purported $7 million to $8 million loss sustained by Massachusetts), the investigating committee saddled Saltonstall with most of the blame. It held that "The principal reason for the failure was the want of proper spirit and energy on the part of the Commodore." Indeed, if the small British squadron had been dealt with at the outset and proper support given the troops ashore, General Lovell should have been able to take the half-finished British position and establish military control of the region. A few weeks after the committee report, Saltonstall was tried by court-martial aboard the frigate *Deane* in Boston harbor and was dismissed from the Continental Navy. He later became a successful privateersman and merchant. The same Massachusetts investigating committee also heard charges against Paul Revere. Many of the officers who had been on the expedition accused him of cowardice. He had not gone ashore with his men during the July 28 assault, instead waiting until the high ground was secured. They also charged him with not being on shore to supervise his men during much of the siege. Revere appealed the verdict of misconduct rendered by the committee, but a new hearing by the Massachusetts House of Representatives reaffirmed it. All was not amicable on the British side. Mowat was enraged that Collier would not let him carry the dispatches announcing the victory; and Collier must have been less than pleased to learn on his return to New York that Vice Admiral Marriot Arbuthnot had arrived to replace him. The British continued to hold Bagaduce, and it was the last fortification they abandoned at the end of the Revolutionary War.

The Penobscot Bay expedition illustrates the absolute necessity for coordination in a land–sea expedition. It also is a clear example of the great advantage the British possessed during most of the war in the Royal Navy.

Spencer Tucker

REFERENCES

Gardner W. Allen, *A Naval History of the American Revolution, Vol. II* (1913), rpr. 1970; Russell Bellico, "The Great Penobscot Blunder, "*American History Illustrated,* 13 (8), (1978): 4–9; Russell Bourne, "The Penobscot Fiasco" *American Heritage,* 25 (6), (1974) : 28–33, 100–101; Nathan Miller, *Sea of Glory. The Continental Navy Fights for Independence, 1775–1783* (1974); David Syrett, *The Royal Navy in American Waters 1775–1783* (1989).

Pensacola, West Florida, Capture of (May 9, 1781)

Pensacola served as the capital of British West Florida from 1781 until it fell to Spain in this battle. As such, it was Great Britain's major army and navy garrison in the northern Gulf of Mexico. The Spanish attack culminated a two-year process by which Bernardo de Galvez and his army earlier took Baton Rouge (1779) and Mobile (1780) as preludes to the major assault against the West Florida capital, where Governor Peter Chester served as head of the colony and General John Campbell commanded the garrison. The British governor of Jamaica, to which Pensacola was attached as an outlying command, attempted unsuccessfully to reinforce Campbell's troops after the Spanish capture of Mobile. The failure to do so made Pensacola an attractive target for the Spanish, whose 1780 plans to take the town were dashed by a hurricane that scattered the attacking expedition. Galvez commanded an ambitious expedition that sailed from Havana and New Orleans in the early spring of 1781, arriving at Santa Rosa Island off Escambia Bay in March. Using the island as a base camp, Galvez sailed his major force onto the mainland. Campbell agreed to retire his troops to Fort George in return for Galvez's promise not to bombard the town of Pensacola itself. The Spanish siege of the fort began the last week of April. A lucky shot from a Spanish gun emplacement on the afternoon of May 8 brought the siege to a sudden and decisive end when a shell ignited the main British ammunition dump inside the fort. The spectacular explosion that resulted killed over 100 men and wounded many more. Campbell had little choice but to surrender, which he did the following day. Galvez took over 1,000 British prisoners, all of whom were paroled and returned to England. Pensacola, as a result of this battle, would remain in Spanish hands for the rest of the Colonial era. It eventually passed into possession of the United States by virtue of the Adams-Onis Treaty of 1819.

Light Townsend Cummins

REFERENCES

John W. Caughey, *Bernardo de Galvez in Louisiana, 1776–1783* (1934); William S. Coker and Robert R. Rea, *Anglo-Spanish Confrontation on the Gulf Coast During the American Revolution* (1982); Virginia Parks, ed., *Siege: Spain and Britain: Battle of Pensacola, March 9–May 8, 1781* (1981); N. Orwin Rush, *The Battle of Pensacola* (1966); J. Barton Starr, *The American Revolution in West Florida* (1976).

Percy, Hugh (1742–1817)

British army officer. Born August 28, 1742, Hugh Percy was the eldest son of Hugh Smithson, the 1st Duke of Northumberland. He was breveted ensign in the 24th Foot May 1, 1759, exchanging into the 85th Foot as captain August 6, 1759. He served in Prince Ferdinand of Brunswick's allied army at the battles of Bergen and Minden. He was made lieutenant colonel commandant of the 111th Foot April 16, 1762. Later that year Percy was gazetted captain and lieutenant colonel in the Grenadier Guards. In May 1763, he was elected M.P. for Westminster, which he represented until he succeeded to the peerage in 1776. Percy was promoted to colonel and appointed an aide-de-camp to the king October 26, 1764. He married the Earl of Bute's daughter, Lady Anne Stuart on July 3, 1764 (divorced 1779), and Frances Julia Burrell on May 25, 1779. Percy was colonel of the 5th Foot (November 1768) and was criticized at the time as having gained the position by the influence of his marriage. He succeeded as Baron Percy with the courtesy title of "Earl" (his father being a duke), on the death of his mother, December 5, 1776.

Despite opposing the government's American policy and the idea of war against the colonies, he offered to command troops in America, and went to Boston in the spring of 1774, where General Thomas Gage placed him in command of the British camp. He led a relief column out of Boston after the Battles at Lexington and Concord on April 19, 1775, marching 30 miles in 10 hours; its timely arrival made possible the return of the British forces to Boston, although under a constant harassing fire. Percy did not lead his regiment, the 5th Foot (in which he was extremely popular), at the Battle of Breed's Hill, either due to illness or a tactical disagreement with General William Howe. Percy's constitu-

tion had been weak from childhood, so either or both reasons may have applied. His management of the relief column gained him appointment as local (in America) major general July 11, 1775, and on September 29, that rank in the army was confirmed. He commanded a division in General William Howe's right wing at the Battle of Long Island (August 27, 1776), and supported Howe's decision not to attack Washington's position at Brooklyn. In the attack on Fort Washington, November 16, 1776, Percy led a division and was the first into the rebel lines. He accompanied General Sir Henry Clinton on the expedition to occupy Rhode Island in December 1776, and remained in command when Clinton went on leave to England.

Early in January 1777 Howe wrote Percy asking for forage to be sent to New York, and when Percy took six weeks to reply that spare forage was not available, Howe replied with a variety of criticisms relating to the Rhode Island operation, several of which were not Percy's responsibility. Early in March Percy requested permission to resign, which was granted. The loss of such a capable and popular subordinate commander increased the problems already prevalent in the British command structure. Percy was popular not only with the public and the press, but with his regiment, who had requested and received permission to style themselves the "Northumberland Fusiliers." Percy paid unusual attention to feeding and clothing his men, and after Breed's Hill the widows of those killed were sent back to England at his expense, with an extra sum of money on landing.

On November 1, 1784, Percy received command of the 2nd Troops Horse Grenadier Guards, which became the 2nd Life Guards in June 1788. He succeeded his father as the 2nd Duke of Northumberland on June 6, 1786, at which time he became lord lieutenant and vice admiral of Northumberland. He was promoted to general in the army on October 12, 1793, and took command of the Percy Tenantry, a local yeomanry regiment based on his estates, in 1798. He served as colonel of the Horse Guards from 1806 to 1812. He seems to have developed pronounced political views and developed them in political in-fighting from the 1780s, generally in opposition to William Pitt the Younger and his policies. As a result he never again held any significant political or military position. His delicate constitution and gout made him irritable and very difficult to work with. He died July 10, 1817.

De Witt Bailey

REFERENCES

Sir Henry Clinton, *The American Campaign. Sir Henry Clinton's Narrative of His Campaign, 1775–1782*, ed. by William B. Willcox (1954); *DNB*; Ira Gruber, *The Howe Brothers and the American Revolution* (1972); Christopher Ward, *The War of the American Revolution*, ed. by John Richard Alden, 2 vols. (1957), *1*.

Petty Fitzmaurice, William, 2nd Earl of Shelburne.

See Shelburne, 2nd Earl of.

Philadelphia, Pennsylvania, British Occupation of (Winter 1777–1778)

On September 25, 1777, Philadelphia had been the capital city of the newly proclaimed United States of America for almost 15 months. For the first time, it was about to be occupied by an enemy army. General Sir William Howe and his British army were prepared to take possession the following day.

At the time, the city's population stood at nearly 22,000 people, 17,000 of whom were women and children. There were 5,470 houses, nearly 600 of which were vacant, their occupants having fled the city. Many of the 300 or so businesses were empty of goods. Most of those who followed the American cause, especially the men, had departed from the city, or were in hiding. The remaining people were Loyalists, neutrals, or too poor to move. Many of the neutrals were Quakers.

Joseph Galloway had been a leading politician in Pennsylvania before the war, rising to the position of speaker of the colony's assembly. In 1774, he had been an active member of the First Continental Congress. But, when the radicals gained control of the proceedings, Galloway found it impossible to follow their lead. He had remained loyal to his king.

During Howe's Pennsylvania campaign, Galloway had provided valuable services guiding the British through Pennsylvania toward Philadelphia. Finally the time had come for Joseph Galloway to reenter the city where he had spent so much of his life.

At Galloway's request, Thomas Willing, a close friend and fellow Loyalist, informed the inhabitants of Philadelphia to remain quietly and peaceably in their own dwellings and no one would be molested. The citizens of the city formed patrols to walk the street and to stop arsonists from burning the city as New York had been burned the year before. Two such criminals were caught before they could light their fires.

September 26 dawned sunny, bright, and clear. At 8:30 A.M. General Cornwallis led the British and German grenadiers, the dragoons, and the artillery into the city in a triumphant entry. The troops looked their best with their uniforms bright and their brass polished. At 10 A.M. the British took official possession of Philadelphia at the State House Square amidst the acclamation of some thousands of women and children, and a few men. The bands played "God Save Our Great King George Our King," and Philadelphia became a garrison city for the next eight and a half months. Along with Cornwallis had come many of the city's leading Loyalists such as Enoch Story, William and Andrew Allen, and Joseph Galloway. Howe and the main part of the British army remained in camp at Germantown, some six miles outside the city.

At first, the people generally welcomed the British. Many were very unhappy at the high-handed ways of Congress and the Americans who confiscated what they needed and paid in paper rather than in good, hard currency. Too many demands had been made and too little given in return. For many, times were improving. But the British faced many problems in Philadelphia.

The Americans had carried off most of the supplies and food in the city as they evacuated it. The vessels and boats were removed from the Delaware River so that trade had virtually stopped. Blankets, carpets, clothing, lead, leaden pipes, and all the bells of the city had been removed. Four thousand head of cattle had been taken from the pastures surrounding the city, along with most of the horses. The Americans had even cut the hay and ruined the meadows to eliminate forage.

All of these problems had to be dealt with along with the very real military ones. The Americans had the Delaware River blocked at Forts Mifflin and Mercer. The British were very low on supplies and had to open the river so that the British fleet could bring the necessary goods to the city. Then there was Washington's army. It did not remain dormant. It relentlessly harassed and probed at the British lines from October until the following June.

The Americans attempted to cut Philadelphia off from the countryside. There were constant and continual skirmishes. It is sheer myth to think that Howe and his army relaxed the winter months away in comfort in Philadelphia while the Americans wallowed in their misery at Valley Forge until spring. Nothing could be further from the truth.

Before December 19, 1777, Washington was constantly testing and threatening Howe. The British often returned the favor. Later, during the cantonment period that winter, the two main armies remained in their respective camps. However, there was rarely a time that detachments from both armies were not out in the no-man's land between the two armies in some raid or skirmish.

General Howe decided to establish a civil government in the city that would be composed of the better sort of loyal citizens, many of whom had accompanied the army in its campaign to regain Philadelphia. In actuality, it was all pretense. The military had to control the city, beleaguered as it was from the outside and beset with severe problems from the inside. There was no practical way that Howe could afford to deal with the conflicts that he already had and add attempts at working with a civilian government.

Yet there was something to be said for appearance over substance, especially in the eyes of the citizens. Howe wished to bring the colonists back to British rule. Military rule is by definition harsh at best, considering the conditions under which it must operate. With this in mind, Samuel Shoemaker was appointed mayor of the city and Joseph Galloway, by proclamation of Howe on December 4, was created "Superintended General of Police in the City and Its Environs and Superintendent of Imports and Exports to and from Philadelphia." In fact, however, the military always had the last say.

Shoemaker was a true figurehead, useful for ceremony and little else. He also served as one of Galloway's magistrates. In his role as trade director, Galloway worked closely with his counterpart in New York City, Andrew Elliot, to restart commerce and trade in Philadelphia as soon as possible. As police commissioner, Galloway and his magistrates struggled to maintain order

in the city throughout the British occupation period. In both roles, he met with mixed success and found himself frustrated at every turn.

After the river had been opened and the Battle of Germantown had been fought, Philadelphia truly became a garrison city. Troops were placed in barracks, public buildings, encampments, and in several of the empty houses. The officers rented space in homes with the general officers occupying the better mansions of the city. General Charles Grey and his aide, captain John André, took over Benjamin Franklin's house while General Wilhelm von Knyphausen stayed in the American general John Cadwalader's house on Second Street. Howe made his headquarters at former royal governor Richard Penn's house on Market Street. Respect for private property during the occupation varied among the officers.

Since the British were under daily harassment from the Americans, they fortified the city with a series of redoubts and entrenchments, particularly facing to the north. The repeated attacks forced the British to be always on the alert. This added pressure to the internal situation in the city. It was necessary to exercise the troops not on guard. Any open space or common area was put to use in drilling and training.

For the people of the city, business started up once more and everyone tried to get things back to normal. But there was profiteering, high prices, poor quality of goods in the stores, a severe lack of fuel, and a shortage of food, particularly dairy products. Things eased a bit once trade opened with New York and once the fleet opened the river; the merchants resumed their activities and food slipped past the American patrols. It must be noted that there was never a period of plenty during that entire winter in Philadelphia.

Joseph Galloway took his duties seriously and tried his best to deal with trade problems, crime, and the plight of the poor. He and the police even took up a subscription in February to help the poor of the city survive until spring. He worked to eliminate the black market, tried to protect the civilians from the soldiers, and tried to keep the city safe and clean. As he began to realize the extent of his superficial role, the gap widened between him and General Howe.

Unfortunately, the British and German licentiousness increased as the weeks passed and the pressures of being held in Philadelphia built up. The civilians suffered greatly from this behavior of the troops. As the incidents increased between military and civilians, Howe dropped all pretense and openly took over control of the city. A curfew was declared, and commercial matters were placed under British supervision.

On a daily basis, courts-martial were held due to the conduct of the occupation army in the city. They were held in the state house, the old jail, public buildings, and various taverns. A regular court-martial board consisted of three generals and ten captains. The officers were kept busy all winter. Punishment ranged from the death penalty to anywhere from 400 to 1,000 lashes.

Still the soldiers looted, robbed, fought with the people, and committed other crimes. There were also a number of civilian criminals who took advantage of the situation to add to the confusion. They, too, were tried by the military courts. It was martial law in Philadelphia, and the old days of American rule began to look better to many.

Galloway and his unarmed civilian magistrates were held in contempt by many of the military and the toughs of the city. There were acts of vandalism, constant frictions between groups of locals and the soldiers, and many felonies to be dealt with. No one was allowed on the streets from 8:30 P.M. to dawn without a lantern lit. In addition, Galloway had to deal with internal security from American spies and secret enemies in the city.

As a part of his duties, Galloway identified these spies, directed his own unit of about 80 spies out watching Washington at Valley Forge, and administered the Loyalist oath to city residents. George Harding assisted Galloway in finding spies. Abraham Carlisle granted passports in and out of the city. George Roberts and James Reynolds, among others, enforced the curfew during the nightwatch.

During the occupation there were a number of entertainments and parties held for the amusement of the officers and their guests. The officers themselves put on several plays, and in the end, as General Howe left for England, a massive party was held at the Wharton estate to honor his departure. It is this image that seems to have stuck in the minds of many Americans rather than the reality of the situation for the typical Philadelphian and British soldier.

Howe had asked to be recalled to England in the fall, and he finally obtained permission late that winter. In May, he would return to defend his conduct of the war to the king and Parliament. The British also learned while they occupied Philadelphia that the French openly had allied themselves with the rebels. This meant that French sea power could critically disrupt British plans.

It was decided to evacuate Philadelphia. Galloway was dismayed and angry. He argued that Philadelphia must be held because it was centrally located in the colonies and vital for British control. It was a key manufacturing district that the British could not afford to lose or return to the Americans. It was a fertile region for food and other supplies that must be denied to Washington and his men. There were valuable shipyards along the Delaware that the British must control. Finally, it was a poor move for the morale of the Loyalists throughout the colonies to lose this city at this time after three long years of war.

In spite of these arguments, Galloway lost. He and his daughter, Elizabeth, left with the British army and returned to New York and from there to England, where he spent the last of his days attacking Howe and the British ministry in their conduct of the war. He never returned to Philadelphia, dying in England in 1803.

In June 1778, when the British evacuated the city, some 500 Philadelphia women who had taken up with British and German soldiers during the occupation accompanied the army. An additional 1,648 women and 539 children who previously had been following the British army also left with them for New York.

The city of Philadelphia was left a mess by the departing army. There was debris and filth present everywhere. The stench was unbearable. The first thing the people had to do, whether they were there already or returning to reclaim their homes, was to clean up the mess left behind. General Benedict Arnold, limping from his leg wound taken at the Battle of Bemis Heights, was appointed military governor of Philadelphia until the city government was reestablished. His tenure lasted until March 1779. The Americans returned to a city that was filled with destroyed property. But the rebuilding process began immediately, and in a short time, Philadelphia was livable once more. It was never taken again during the war.

Paul J. Sanborn

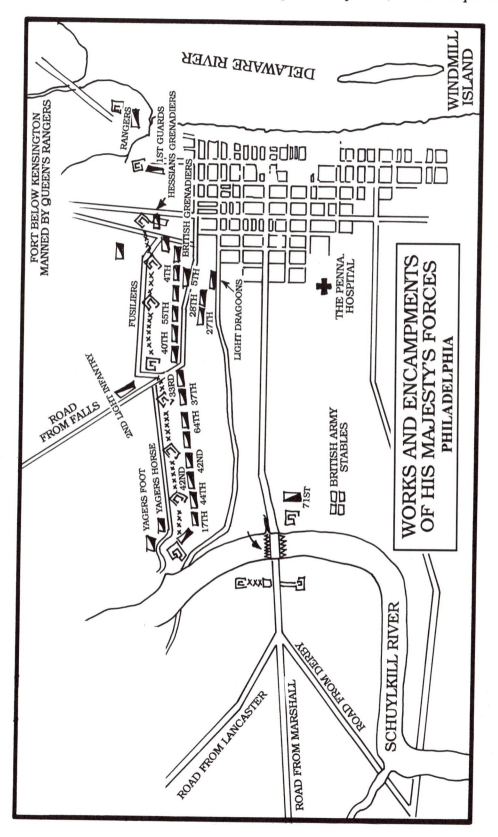

WORKS AND ENCAMPMENTS OF HIS MAJESTY'S FORCES PHILADELPHIA

DELAWARE RIVER

WINDMILL ISLAND

FORT BELOW KENSINGTON MANNED BY QUEEN'S RANGERS

RANGERS

1ST GUARDS

HESSIANS GRENADIERS

BRITISH GRENADIERS

FUSILIERS

4TH

55TH

40TH

28TH 5TH

27TH

LIGHT DRAGOONS

THE PENNA. HOSPITAL

ROAD FROM FALLS

2ND LIGHT INFANTRY

33RD

YAGERS FOOT

YAGERS HORSE

42ND

64TH 37TH

44TH 42ND

17TH

71ST

BRITISH ARMY STABLES

SCHUYLKILL RIVER

ROAD FROM LANCASTER

ROAD FROM MARSHALL

ROAD FROM DERBY

REFERENCES

David R. Boldt, ed., *The Founding City* (1978); John E. Ferling, *The Loyalist Mind* (1977); John W. Jackson, *With the British Army in Philadelphia* (1979); John F. Reed, *Campaign to Valley Forge* (1965); Russell F. Weigley, ed., *Philadelphia: A 300 Year History* (1982).

Phillips, William (1731–1781)

British army officer. William Phillips began his military career as a gentleman cadet on August 1, 1746. The following January 2, at the age of 15, he was commissioned a lieutenant fireworker. From April 1750 to May 1756 he held the appointment of quartermaster of the Royal Regiment of Artillery. In 1756 he also received his promotion to first lieutenant in April and his promotion to captain in May, jumping over the rank of captain lieutenant. He was then selected over the heads of many senior captains to command the company of artillery being sent against the French at Minorca during the Seven Years' War. His rapid advancement produced a good deal of resentment within the regiment.

In 1758 he went to Germany, where he took command of three Royal Artillery (R.A.) companies attached to the army of Prince Ferdinand of Brunswick. One of his subordinate company commanders was Captain Forbes Macbean, who would later serve as his second in command of Royal Artillery in Canada during the Revolution. At the Battle of Minden in 1759, and again at Warburg in 1760, Phillips brought his guns into the action at a full gallop. In those days that was considered an impossible maneuver because of the poor mobility of cannon. This feat alone firmly established him as one of the R.A.'s great heroes. While in Germany Phillips also established the R.A.'s first musical band.

Phillips went to North America for the first time in 1768 to assume command of an artillery company at Niagara. In 1771 he went back to England to raise a new company in the R.A.'s 4th Battalion, and in 1773 he brought that company to Montreal. In 1760, Phillips was promoted to the rank of lieutenant colonel in the British army, and in 1772 he became a full colonel. All the while, however, he remained only a captain in the regiment. He finally received his promotion to major in the Royal Artillery on April 25, 1777, but the following August 29, he also became a major general in the British army.

During Burgoyne's offensive in 1777 in northern New York, Phillips served as second in command of the combined British-German force as well as its artillery commander. He played a key role in the capture of Fort Ticonderoga when he put four British 12-pounders on top of Mount Defiance, fulfilling the earlier predictions of American engineer Tadeusz Kosciuszko. Most of Ticonderoga's defenders thought that such a feat was impossible; but Phillips noted, "Where a goat can go, a man can go, and where a man can go, he can drag a gun."

At both Freeman's Farm and Saratoga, Phillips commanded the British left wing and aggressively employed the artillery with telling effect. At one critical point he restored a crumbling situation by personally assuming control of the 20th Regiment of Foot. After the British surrender, Burgoyne was allowed to return to England on April 5, 1778, and Phillips became the senior officer of the so-called Convention Army.

During the period of his captivity, Phillips gained a reputation for arrogance among the Americans. When British lieutenant Richard Brown was shot and killed by an American sentry on June 17, 1778, Phillips tried to turn it into a major incident, claiming that the British officer had been murdered. In November 1779 Phillips was allowed to go free on parole, and on October 13, 1780, he was formally exchanged for American major general Benjamin Lincoln.

Rather than returning Phillips to the artillery, General Sir Henry Clinton placed him in command of a 2,000-man force with orders to prevent the French under Rochambeau from linking up with Lafayette. Phillips thus became the first (but certainly not the last) Royal Artillery officer to have full command over a major British force in the field.

Phillips and his troops landed at Williamsburg on April 20, 1781, and linked up with a smaller British force under General Benedict Arnold, who now served with the British. Phillips then assumed overall command of the 3,500-strong force and started it moving toward Petersburg to link up with Cornwallis. During this march the artillery in Arnold's column fought it's amazing engagement against the American naval squadron at Osborne's Landing. On April 30, Phillips seized and destroyed a large quantity of American stores at Manchester; but shortly after that, he came down with typhoid fever. Phillips tried to hold on to his command as long as he could, issuing orders from his bed in an ambulance wagon; but he died on May 13, 1781, just after his army entered Petersburg.

Opinions on Phillips tend to divide evenly along partisan lines. Royal Artillery historian Captain Francis Duncan called him "a model for artillerymen to imitate, in gallantry, ability, and progress." Thomas Jefferson, who once entertained Phillips at Monticello during the latter's captivity, called him, "the proudest man of the proudest nation on earth."

David T. Zabecki

REFERENCES

James Alex Browne, *England's Artillerymen* (1865); Captain Francis Duncan, *History of the Royal Regiment of Artillery*, Vol. I (1872); John Kane, *List of Officers of the Royal Regiment of Artillery*, 4th ed. (1890).

Pickens, Andrew (1739–1817)

South Carolina militia officer. In the great mass of southern colonial frontiersmen whom chroniclers like the Reverend Woodmason were so quick to criticize as little better than savages, were many families from whom state and national leaders would emerge during the American Revolution. Arguably the most notable of these men to rise to the top because of the war was Andrew Pickens of South Carolina. His family was among the Huguenots and Scots-Irish who settled in Northern Ireland and then migrated to Pennsylvania and down trails like the Great Wagon roads, along the Indian frontiers of the South, before the Revolution. His grandfather had fled France following the Revocation of the Edict of Nantes and settled in Scotland, Northern Ireland, and then Pennsylvania.

Andrew Pickens was born in Paxton Township, Pennsylvania, to Andrew and Anne Davis Pickens on September 19, 1739. As a child Andrew lived in Augusta County, Virginia; Anson County, North Carolina; and finally the Waxhaw area of South Carolina, where his father died about 1756. His first military campaign was in the Cherokee War of 1760–1761, when he serve as a company officer in the South Carolina regiment raised by Lieutenant Governor William Bull. During this campaign, Pickens would remember, "I learned something of british cruelty which I always abhorred." After the victory over

the Cherokees, he moved to the Long Cane, South Carolina, settlement, married, started a family, and became a landowner, an Indian trader, and a minor local official.

The Long Cane settlement was divided by the politics of the coming rebellion and ultimately produced many of the South Carolina leaders of both sides in the Revolution. Andrew Pickens cast his lot with the rebels and never went back. In 1775, he was already a captain of a company of volunteers. Under the command of Andrew Williamson, Pickens was involved in suppressing the Loyalists, who were led by such men as Moses Kirkland, Joseph Robinson, Thomas Fletchall, and the Cunninghams—Robert, Patrick, and William. In November 1775, Pickens was among the men under Williamson besieged near Ninety Six, South Carolina, in what was the first land battle in South Carolina during the Revolution. Williamson succeeded, as much by negotiation as firepower, in dispersing the Loyalists. Pickens also served under Williamson in the campaigns against the Cherokees in 1776 that devastated the Indians. On August 12, 1776, he and 35 of his men were surrounded by Cherokees and won a desperate fight at close quarters near Tamasee. Pickens also served in General Andrew Williamson's brigade in the unsuccessful American invasion of British East Florida in 1778.

British forces captured Savannah, Georgia, in December 1778 and by the following February had overrun that entire state. While Williamson and much of his militia brigade were defending the South Carolina backcountry from the British troops in Augusta, Georgia, Pickens, now colonel of the Upper Ninety Six Regiment, commanded on the South Carolina frontier. As such, on February 14, 1779, he successfully pursued and defeated at Kettle Creek, Georgia, 600 North and South Carolina Loyalists and bandits that were attempting to reach the British army. Although Kettle Creek was a badly needed American victory that won Pickens great praise, it was handled very badly and undoubtedly taught the young colonel valuable lessons about tactical battlefield operations.

Following the British evacuation of Augusta, Williamson's command was reunited, and Pickens served with distinction under Williamson at the Battle of Stono, South Carolina, and against the refugee Cherokee villages in what is now northwest Georgia. He also worked with the Georgia militia in stopping a large band of Creek Indians from reaching the British army at Savannah and, in 1780, led a raid against the British outposts near Savannah.

The surrender of Charleston, South Carolina, to the British on May 12, 1780, resulted in South Carolina being overrun by the British and their Loyalist allies. Complying with the wishes of almost all of their men, Williamson and Pickens surrendered to the British and became prisoners of war on parole. By December 1780, however, depredations by the Loyalists compelled Andrew Pickens to renounce his parole and rejoin the American cause. His command of the militia was decisive in the Battle of Cowpens, January 17, 1781, one of the great American victories of the Revolution. Congress awarded Pickens with a sword in honor of this victory.

As brigadier general of the South Carolina militia, Pickens actively recruited men from both Carolinas for the American cause while suppressing Loyalist resistance in the southern backcountry, remembered as some of the most merciless fighting by both sides during the war. Pickens took over the siege of the enemy garrison of Augusta, Georgia, in May 1781, which had been started sometime earlier by Georgia troops under James Jackson and Elijah Clarke. The Loyalist garrison of Augusta surrendered on June 5, after a very difficult struggle, to Pickens and Colonel Henry Lee. With the evacuation of Ninety Six, South Carolina, by the British shortly afterward, His Majesty's forces were steadily confined to Charleston and Savannah, until even those ports were finally evacuated in 1782. During these campaigns, Pickens participated in the siege of Ninety Six, and was wounded in the Battle of Eutaw Springs. In 1781 and 1782, General Andrew Pickens led desperate but successful campaigns against the Cherokees to end Loyalist-led Indian raids against the frontier settlements.

A popular hero of the American Revolution, Andrew Pickens served South Carolina in many capacities after the war, including as a congressman from 1793 to 1795. His most famous postwar work was as a federal Indian commissioner, during which he marked the boundary between the Indian and white settlements in 1797, a task he had basically done for the Cherokees at Long Swamp in 1782. Pickens declined consideration for governor in 1812 and died suddenly on August 11, 1817, at Tamasee in Pendleton District, South Carolina. However, his son Andrew and grandson Francis Wilkinson Pickens were governors of South Carolina. Counties in South Carolina, Georgia, and Alabama are named in honor of General Andrew Pickens. In character, the general was remembered as stern, a deeply religious Presbyterian, and a man of few, carefully chosen words.

Robert Scott Davis, Jr.

REFERENCE

Clyde R. Ferguson, "General Andrew Pickens," Ph.D. dissertation, Duke University (1960).

Pickering, Timothy (1745–1829)

Continental Army officer. Born on July 17, 1745, at Salem, Massachusetts, the eighth child of Timothy and Mary Wingate Pickering, Thomas Pickering belonged to the fifth generation of his New England family. The first Pickering, an English carpenter, had arrived in Salem in 1637, and the family developed a tradition of civic duty, both religious and political. Timothy Pickering filled many roles during the American Revolution, starting with his Revolutionary leadership in Salem.

At age 14, Pickering matriculated at Harvard College, graduating in 1763. He was a law apprentice, passing the bar in 1768, but he performed minimal and mediocre legal services. He worked in several civic positions, including as clerk and then register of deeds in Essex County, while in his twenties. In 1766 he was commissioned a lieutenant in the local militia.

Interested in military history and tactics, Pickering became reform oriented, stressing that military troops must be disciplined. Using pseudonyms, Pickering wrote letters and essays in the *Essex Gazette*, discussing corruption in the British ministry as well as supporting colonial rights and privileges and endorsing the strengthening of militia. He also composed pamphlets and speeches, joined committees, and dispersed petitions in support of the Revolutionary movement.

Although he practiced moderation in his resistance, Pickering was soon labeled by British leaders as a reactionary. In June 1774 the Massachusetts capital and Governor Thomas Gage had moved to Salem. In response to the Massachusetts Government Act, which severely restricted colonists' rights, citizens decided to hold a county convention. Despite laws prohibiting community gatherings, Pickering and other Revolutionaries arranged a town meeting to elect delegates to the convention. They were arrested, cementing Pickering's decision to be prowar even though this stance alienated his Tory father.

In 1775 Pickering published *An Easy Plan of Discipline For a Militia*, which was employed by Massachusetts and other colonies as guidelines for military operations. Pickering, who developed his ideas from English methods, stressed simplicity and maneuverability. Pickering asserted that intelligence in lieu of experience was useful against foes who seemed to have overwhelming advantages. He disliked elaborate weapons, advising militiamen to aim muskets precisely and with purpose, and he disdained flamboyant techniques, stressing that "*Americans* need them not: *their* eyes are not to be dazzled, nor their hearts awed into servility, by the splendor of equipage and dress: *their* minds are too much enlightened to be duped by a glittering outside."

Pickering advised officers to win their troops' respect and devotion; Pickering marched on foot with his men, wearing a heavy pack like them, in order to understand their experiences. He stressed that officers should demonstrate procedures by example and understand the enlisted men's situation. He disapproved of the use of fear to train troops, recommending that clear instructions would be more useful to instill discipline and stressing "that the men be clearly informed of the REASON of every action and movement—or the USES to which they can be applied."

He reminded officers that soldiers, serving for patriotic reasons, would endure "a just and necessary subordination and obedience . . . *only* to *defend* their *laws, liberties* and *country.*" Despite this sympathy for his troops, Pickering was against military egalitarianism, emphasizing that officers should always be respected by their troops. Pickering's basic ideas were acceptable for the militia; however, during the Revolution, Pickering's simplistic advice for discipline was insufficient. Experience, competence, endurance, and commitment to military service were decisive factors.

Pickering was promoted to colonel of his militia regiment and became involved in military operations in April 1775. A year later he married Rebecca White (the couple had ten chil-dren, several of whom were prominent during the nineteenth century). With his men Pickering helped defend the coast and joined George Washington's forces for winter maneuvers in New York and New Jersey.

Considering him talented and credible, Washington offered Pickering the position of adjutant general; initially Pickering refused, fearing that he would lose income from his civic job, but after insuring he could return to his civic position after the war, he accepted in May 1777. He desperately tried to secure necessary supplies but was frustrated when different supply departments refused to coordinate to get the available goods to camps and hospitals. By November he was elected to the Board of War, a less difficult position, and offered more money. He retained the position of adjutant general until January 1778 and also served as a judge in the courts of Suffolk, Essex, and Middlesex.

The Board of War faltered, becoming dysfunctional by the end of 1779. In August 1780 Congress appointed Pickering to replace resigning Nathanael Greene as quartermaster general. When he took the position, Pickering was well aware of the greed and corruption that hindered the Continental supply process. He proclaimed that "Americans can blame only their own negligence, avarice, and want of almost every public virtue." Although Pickering had personal administration problems, he confronted many obstacles that were out of his control. He was overwhelmed by the myriad details and duties—such as arranging transportation, ordering supplies, recording invoices—expected of the quartermaster general. Washington presumed Pickering would delegate authority and remain with the army, but Pickering, enjoying the political side of the supply process, often departed camp to travel to Philadelphia.

Pickering opposed corrupt personnel in the department who used their positions for profit and who never had enough money to run the Quartermaster Department properly. Wanting to reform the department, he endorsed the establishment of sound currency, the cutting of costs, curbing of abuses, and employment of personnel with integrity. He was upset that states did not fill their quotas and argued that private goods should be impressed by civilian, not military authorities. He was especially concerned for poor and common soldiers who most often went without supplies. He also protested military exemptions that allowed the wealthy to escape military duty. Shortages were severe, and Pickering was arrested for the public debt; financier Robert Morris helped bail Pickering out and provided necessary funds to dispense relief supplies.

Critical of Washington for being ungrateful, Pickering castigated the leader in correspondence to peers. Pickering himself endured heavy criticism from the unappreciative public and politicians for how he performed his responsibilities. Determined, Pickering surmounted many barriers, but he considered the quartermaster general as "an office so burdensome and a service so ungrateful." Afraid of the transition to civilian work, Pickering did not resign his position, even after the peace treaty was signed, acting irresponsibly by leaving camp and infuriating Washington. He criticized Washington's poor demobilization of troops without having funds to reward and reimburse the men. Pickering resigned in 1785 bitterly concluding that he had wasted his time serving the army.

After the war, Pickering worked as a merchant in Philadelphia, but depressed economic conditions caused him to move to the Wyoming Valley in 1787, where he farmed, speculated land, and criticized the American treatment of Loyalists. As a representative for Pennsylvania's government, he organized Luzerne County and resolved disputed land claims between Connecticut and Pennsylvania residents. Although many citizens disliked his negotiated settlements—even kidnapping Pickering—they responded positively to his sympathy and understanding of their situation and his benevolent manner. He represented the county at conventions to ratify both the United States and Pennsylvania constitutions.

Destitute because of his land speculation, Pickering decided that employment in a public office could offer him needed money. In September 1790 he applied to Washington for the position of postmaster general, but Washington instead sent him to persuade the Seneca Indians not to join warring western tribes. Pickering successfully completed the mission and became postmaster general in August 1791. He continued to negotiate with the Indians, having the necessary skills as well as sympathy for the native Americans and tried to protect them from encroaching settlers. Unfortunately, many of his ideas for Indian policy were—like his military tactics—too progressive for his superiors to accept. He

experienced problems in administration while postmaster general, mostly because of the department's recent creation and lack of precedents to follow. He recommended that a national military academy be established, aiding the founding of West Point.

In January 1795 Pickering began service as secretary of war, being responsible for military, Indian, and naval affairs (helping procure and equip the new fleet). During his work, he realized that Secretary of State Edmund Randolph had acted unethically in his relations with French diplomats, offering them bribes and fomenting internal strife, and he alerted Washington. As a result of this action, Randolph resigned, and Washington appointed Pickering secretary of state in August 1795. Pickering's service was warped by his fear of France subverting America, and his policies and actions were subsequently affected by this irrational anxiety.

Pickering, an ultraconservative, strongly abhorred President John Adams, who he also served as secretary of state, and countered him by reversing his orders, withholding crucial diplomatic correspondence, and communicating with Adams's political enemies. This opposition to Adams resulted in Pickering's forced resignation in May 1800. He returned to his Pennsylvania farm, but with the encouragement and prodding of political allies (who ensured that his land sold), returned to Massachusetts for a political career. Although he was defeated in his first election as a representative, Pickering won a seat in the Senate and served in that capacity from 1803 to 1811.

In the Senate he was regarded as a good debater, espousing ultra-Federal rhetoric and anti-Jefferson and Madison messages. He earned the wrath of opponents who burned him in effigy and printed satiric caricatures of the tall, bald Pickering. Certain that the accession of West Florida was illegal, Pickering was censured by Congress when he read a confidential letter from Talleyrand that claimed the United States had no legitimate claim to that territory. Convinced that the censure was the result of a conspiracy launched by his political enemies and realizing that he had lost public support, Pickering retired from his seat in 1811. Returning home, he was active in state and local politics. He served on the Executive Council in Massachusetts from 1812 to 1813. He won a seat and served in the House of Representatives from 1813 to 1817. He actively opposed the War of 1812, fearing the United States would be unable to survive the war intact and advocated the separation of a commercial northern confederacy. Pickering resigned his seat when he realized he would not be reelected because he was unpopular and unsympathetic to constituents' needs.

He returned to Salem, where he pursued his agricultural improvements with membership in the agriculture societies, correspondence with friends on various facets of agriculture, and participation in plowing competitions. In 1818 his friends tried to convince Pickering to return to the House of Representatives, but Pickering was uninterested. He labored on his farm, took long, healthy walks, and pursued abolitionist activities.

In his retirement Pickering planned to write books on American history—such as a biography of Alexander Hamilton, whom he greatly admired—but did not finish these works. He especially wanted to debunk myths of the prominent men of the Revolutionary age and publish truths such as that Hamilton and other talented men wrote Washington's speeches and letters. A prolific correspondent, Pickering penned slanderous political essays and letters that were published in newspapers and in three tomes: *Interesting Correspondence between His Excellency Governor Sullivan and Col. Pickering* (1808), *Political Essays. A Series of Letters Addressed to the People of the United States* (1811), and *A Review of the Correspondence between the Hon. John Adams . . . and the Late Wm. Cunningham, Esq.* (1824). These personal documents, although biased and somewhat raving accounts, are useful to portray the political scene of the Revolution and new republic, providing glimpses of people and scenes as varied as politicians, sailors, and Indians.

Described as being robust, Pickering was noted as having integrity and being industrious, able, ambitious, and frustrated by recurrent disappointments in his career. Some historians label him as being violent and even villainous toward those people whom he believed had restricted his opportunities or were fraudulent leaders. Pickering was outspoken, self-righteous, serious, and independently defended his beliefs, and his political character was extremely conservative and distrustful. The majority of his Federalist political peers regarded him as being reasonable. Throughout his life he protested abuses of individual rights, believing that egalitarianism was valid. Five months after his wife died in

1828, Pickering passed away after a sudden illness on January 29, 1829.

Elizabeth D. Schafer

REFERENCES

Henry Adams, *Documents Relating to New England Federalism* (1877); Gerard H. Clarfield, *Timothy Pickering and the American Republic* (1980); David McLean, *Timothy Pickering and the Age of the American Revolution* (1982); Octavius Pickering and Charles W. Upham, *The Life of Timothy Pickering*, 4 vols. (1867–1873); Harvey P. Prentiss, *Timothy Pickering as the Leader of New England Federalism, 1800–1815* (1934).

Pigot, Robert (1720–1796)

British army officer. The second son of Richard Pigot of Westminster and Frances Goode, Robert Pigot was born at Patshull, Staffordshire, in 1720. Referred to by General William Howe as "the little man," Pigot was a small, stocky officer who made up for what he lacked in height with courage in battle. Robert Pigot was also one of the oldest British officers to experience active duty in the War of Revolution, being 55 years old when he led the assault on the American redoubt at Bunker Hill.

Pigot began his army career with the 31st Regiment in Flanders and was present at the Battle of Fontenoy. Beginning in October 1745, Pigot's regiment was stationed near London and in 1749 was dispatched to Minorca for three years. Later the regiment was posted to Scotland.

Pigot was promoted to captain on October 31, 1751. In 1758, his battalion of the 31st Regiment was transferred to the 70th Regiment. Pigot was the senior captain in this battalion and soon rose to the rank of major. He joined his unit for service in the south of England and later in Ireland.

Pigot then served with the 38th Regiment and became its lieutenant colonel on October 1, 1764. The regiment was sent to the West Indies and then back to England. In July 1774 the 38th was dispatched to Boston as a part of the buildup of British troops to control the rebellious town.

The two flank companies of the 38th were engaged in the fighting at Lexington and Concord on April 19, 1775. Lieutenant Colonel Pigot led a detachment of his regiment to Charlestown that same evening to provide support for Lord

Hugh Percy and the demoralized troops returning from Concord.

When the Americans threw up a redoubt on Charlestown Heights on the night of June 16–17, 1775, to challenge British plans to break the American siege of Boston, Pigot was assigned as General William Howe's second in command with the local rank of brigadier general. While Howe attempted to turn the American left and get in behind the fortifications, Pigot led the left wing, composed of the 38th, 43rd, 47th regiments and the 1st Battalion of marines, in a direct assault on the redoubt. Howe's flanking maneuver failed to turn the Americans and resulted in great loss of British life.

Pigot's men, withstanding flanking fire from American pickets in burning Charlestown and galling fire from the redoubt to their front, repeatedly attacked the American position. Finally, through discipline and training on the British side and a lack of men, training, and ammunition on the American side, Pigot's men broke into the redoubt and cleared it of American resistance.

For the bravery he displayed that June afternoon in leading his men against stiff opposition, General Pigot was promoted by King George III on December 11, 1775, to the rank of colonel of the 38th Regiment. This was a fine tribute to the veteran officer.

When the British evacuated Boston on March 17, 1776, Pigot boarded the 50-gun ship HMS *Chatham* with General Howe for the voyage to Halifax to regroup. Within a few months, Pigot commanded the 2nd Brigade in Howe's army as the British moved to take New York City away from the Americans. Pigot's brigade, composed of the 5th, 28th, 35th, and 49th regiments of foot, formed of Lord Percy's Division.

At the Battle of Long Island in August 1776, Pigot's brigade was a part of Howe's 10,000-man column that flanked the American left and followed the Jamaica Road into the rear of the rebel army. Once the British had cleared Washington's army from the New York City area, Pigot's brigade was given to General Alexander Leslie. Pigot himself remained in New York as commandant of the city's garrison.

On July 15, 1777, Pigot was ordered by Howe to Newport, Rhode Island, to assume command of that important British post. Stationed in Rhode Island, Pigot missed the fighting that Howe's army experienced in Pennsylvania that summer and fall. On August 29, 1777, Pigot was promoted to major general. In 1778, Robert Pigot became the 2nd Baronet with the death of his older brother, George. At that point, Sir Robert Pigot, major general in His Majesty's service, also became a shareholder in the famous Pigot Diamond, weighing 188 grains.

Newport was not to Pigot's liking. He indicated that he missed the entertainment and excitement that could be found in New York. He knew that social life was also more active in Philadelphia, as long as Howe and the army occupied it. Pigot was an officer who enjoyed his merriment. He even plotted to tempt Admiral Richard Howe into enjoying himself during Howe's visit to Newport. The attempt failed. Howe was too strait-laced to enjoy the usual entertainment that so engaged other officers.

In March 1778 Pigot was considered for General Howe's second in command, but this move was never made. In a short time, Howe had resigned his position and returned to England. General Sir Henry Clinton became commander of British forces in North America and consolidated his forces in New York City. Pigot remained at Newport.

As a result of the French alliance of 1778, Pigot found the excitement he craved. From July 29 through August 31, 1778, he fought to hold Newport against a combined Franco-American force of land and sea power. Thanks to the timely arrival off Newport of Lord Howe, commander of the British fleet in North America, Pigot was saved from the Comte d'Estaing's French fleet and General John Sullivan's land force. He was able to hold out until reinforcements arrived under General Clinton from New York. Trapped between two enemy forces, Pigot had remained cool, calm, and in control. Ready for a last-ditch defense or a long siege, Pigot in the end had to face neither.

In October 1778 Pigot turned over his command of Newport to General Richard Prescott and returned to New York City. During the winter of 1778–1779, Pigot returned to England, one of several British generals to leave North America at this time. On November 20, 1782, Pigot was made lieutenant general. He died at Patshull on August 2, 1796. His younger brother, Hugh, was an admiral in the British navy who saw some fighting in the West Indies during the war in 1782.

Sir Robert Pigot married Anne Johnson of Kilternan County, Dublin, on February 18, 1765. They had a daughter, Anne, and three sons, George, Hugh and Robert. All three sons became military officers in the British service. *See also*: Newport, Rhode Island, Siege of; Rhode Island Campaign of 1778

Paul J. Sanborn

REFERENCES

Carl L. Baurmeister, *Revolution in America* (1957); *DAB*; Thomas J. Fleming, *The Story of Bunker Hill* (1960); Ira D. Gruber, *The Howe Brothers and the American Revolution* (1972); John Harris, *American Rebels* (1976); Richard K. Showman, ed., *The Nathanael Greene Papers*, 5 vols. (1978–   ), 2; Christopher Ward, *The War of the American Revolution*, 2 vols. (1952), 2; Charles P. Whittemore, *A General in the Revolution, John Sullivan* (1961); William B. Wilcox, *Portrait of a General, Sir Henry Clinton in the War of Independence* (1964).

Pinckney, Charles Cotesworth (1746–1825)

Continental Army officer, statesman. Born to a prominent family in South Carolina, Pinckney was educated as a gentleman; with his brother Thomas, he studied at three academies in England. After attending Oxford University and studying law at Middle Temple, Pinckney was admitted to the bar in 1769. He also attended classes in botany and military science in France. Pinckney began his law practice at home in 1770. By 1773 he was acting attorney general for three districts, and in 1775 he served on the committee of intelligence.

As captain in a South Carolina regiment by June 1775, Pinckney was involved in the seizure of Fort John on Charleston harbor and in the mounting of a gun battery at Haddrell's Point. He participated in the defense of Charleston during the British attack in 1776, but he saw little action. By September he became a colonel and an aide to Washington. Pinckney probably served at Brandywine and Germantown. Seeking glory, he returned to Charleston in order to participate in the expedition from Georgia that invaded West Florida (May–June 1778), but the campaign was aborted. Stationed at Fort Moultrie during Clinton's second attack on Charleston, Pinckney was captured in May 1780 and exchanged in January 1781. Thus, he had little opportunity to demonstrate military tal-

ent, and apparently he did not participate in a single victory in the war. Nevertheless, Pinckney was promoted to brigadier general in November 1783.

After the war Pinckney managed two plantations, was a director in two canal companies, and became one of the foremost lawyers in his state. Serving in the legislature, by 1782 he worked on educational matters, funding the debt, and budgetary problems. Elected to the Constitutional Convention, Pinckney defended slavery on economic grounds. After refusing five opportunities for presidential appointments, he became the successor to James Monroe as envoy to France. After arriving in Paris by December 1796, Pinckney encountered difficulties with the Directory. In October 1797, Pinckney was approached by a minister of the French government, who requested a bribe for his part in negotiating a treaty with the United States. Pinckney rejected the offer but apparently he did not state: "Millions for defense, but not one cent for tribute." In 1798 he was appointed major general and commanded troops in western Virginia and Kentucky to 1800. Pinckney was a candidate for vice president in 1800 and was the Federalist candidate for president in 1804 and 1808.

Richard L. Blanco

REFERENCES

DAB; George C. Rogers, *Charleston in the Age of the Pinckneys* (1965); Howard Swiggett, *The Forgotten Leaders in the American Revolution* (1955); Marvin R. Zahniser, *Charles Cotesworth Pinckney, Founding Father* (1967).

Pinckney, Thomas (1750–1828)

Continental Army officer, statesman. Educated in England with his brother Charles, Thomas studied law and was admitted to the bar in South Carolina in 1774. He became a lieutenant in the militia and then a captain in the 1st South Carolina Regiment. Pinckney served at Fort Johnson during the siege of Charleston in 1776. Thereafter, he was stationed at Fort Motte until May 1778. Promoted to major, Pinckney joined his brother on the aborted expedition to West Florida (May–June 1778). He fought at Stono Ferry, he was an aide to d'Estaing at the siege of Savannah, and he aided in the defense of Charleston (May 1780). At the Battle of Camden (August 16, 1780), Pinckney was wounded. Captured and then exchanged, he joined Lafayette for the campaign in Virginia (September 1781).

After the war Pinckney returned to Charleston to resume his legal career. From 1787 to 1788 he was governor of the state. Appointed minister to Great Britain in January 1792, he was handicapped in his mission because John Jay had been sent by Congress to London in order to negotiate a treaty. In April 1795 Pinckney accepted an assignment to Madrid. His diligence in Spain resulted in "Pinckney's Treaty" of October 27, 1795. This Treaty of San Lorenzo recognized the Mississippi and the 31st parallel as boundaries, gave the Americans free navigation of the Mississippi, and the right for three years to deposit goods at New Orleans.

Returning home in September 1796 Pinckney served in Congress (1797–1801). Made a major general to command the army in the lower South (March 1812), Pinckney saw no action. Thereafter, he engaged in scientific agriculture and published articles on the subject.

Richard L. Blanco

REFERENCES

DAB; Charles C. Pinckney, *Life of Thomas Pinckney* (1895); [Thomas Pinckney], "Letters of Thomas Pinckney, 1770–1780," ed. by John L. Cross, *South Carolina Historical Magazine, 58* (1957):12–23, 67–83, 145–162, 224–242. Charles C. Rogers, *Charleston in the Age of the Pinckneys* (1969).

Pistol

Handguns, aside from those of the few regular mounted troops that served during the war, were largely the personal property of officers and other private individuals who chose to carry them. There were several broad types of pistol, from holster pistols with barrels about 12 inches long, to belt pistols with 9- or 10-inch barrels, and pocket pistols with overall lengths from about 8 inches down to about 4 inches. Most pocket pistols were breechloading. The dueling pistol was only just emerging as a type distinct from the holster pistol at the time of the Revolution.

British light dragoons (the 16th and 17th) carried the regulation Light Dragoon pistol introduced in 1759, with a 0.65 caliber 9-inch round pin-fastened barrel, with brass furniture including a flat sideplate in the shape of opposed C-scrolls, and a heavy buttcap with short rounded

sidetangs. The Hessian mounted jagers (*jager zu Pferde*) carried pairs of Hussar pistols on their saddles. French officers carried two sorts of pistols, those made to regulation pattern for the officers dragoons and cavalry, Model 1763-66, and personal sidearms. American officers carried person arms, almost all of them of English manufacture.

The Royal Navy carried a fixed allowance of Sea Service pistols on each rating of ship. These have a 12-inch round 0.55 caliber barrel, pin-fastened to the stock, and the lock is flat with a faceted pan and no pan-bridle, with a flat ring-neck cock. The brass furniture is rounded, with a steel belt-hook on the left side, and the ramrod is wood. The French navy used arms made at the arsenal of Tulle. Ships carried muskets and the Model 1763-66 pistol for calvary and dragoons, second production from 1769, with a 9-inch 0.67 caliber round barrel, large double-strap band held by a round pin-spring, rounded brass furniture, and flat lock and cock with beveled edges, and an iron rammer. The Spanish navy carried pistols of their Model 1753 Navy pattern, with a $9^1/4$-inch half-octagon 0.70 caliber barrel held by one ornamental flat brass band, with a round pin-spring on the right side of the stock. The lockplate and cock are flat with beveled edges, but the plate is rounded across the tail; there is no pan-bridle, and the cock-screw had a large ring-head. Brass furniture included a long-spurred buttcap, a rounded L-shaped sideplate, a rounded trigger guard, and a collared tailpipe with a wood rammer.

De Witt Bailey

REFERENCES

Howard L. Blackman, *British Military Firearms, 1650–1850* (1961); Jean Boudriot, *Armes a Feu Francaises Modeles d'Ordonnance* (1961–63); Juan L. Calvo, *Armamento Reglamentario y Auxiliar de Ejercito Espanol*, Vol. 1 (1975).

Pitt, William, 1st Earl of Chatham. *Known as* the Elder Pitt (1708–1778)

British statesman. A British politician and opponent of British policy in America, William Pitt was the descendant of a landed family enriched by service in India. Pitt served a brief spell in the army before he was elected to Parliament in 1735, launching a political career that would last for more than 40 years. He early established a reputation as an able orator, usually in opposition, and made himself obnoxious to George II by frequent charges that the government's foreign policy sacrificed British interests to Hanoverian ones. Marrying into the Grenville family, by the mid-1750s he was one of the most formidable figures in British politics. After the Seven Years' War got off to a disastrous start, Pitt seemed to many to be indispensible. In 1757 he and the Duke of Newcastle formed a coalition government that proceeded to turn the direction of the war around. An unabashed imperialist, Pitt was convinced that Britain's future lay overseas, and the successful prosecution of the war outside of Europe from 1758 did much to secure Britain's position as the dominant colonial power. Pitt's apparent success as a war minister made him immensely popular with his countrymen and secured his reputation as one of the founding fathers of the British Empire. (More recently, historians have tended to see Pitt's role as a war leader as less dominant and the coalition's success as more the result of a well-coordinated team effort.)

Pitt resigned in 1761 when the cabinet and George III, the new king, would not support a preemptive strike against Spain (which shortly declared war on Britain anyway). For the rest of the 1760s, Pitt's career was characterized by inconsistency. This derived in part from Pitt's manic-depressive personality and his tendency toward ill health. Though refraining from "formed" opposition, he spoke against several measures of the administration of his brother-in-law, George Grenville. Approached in 1763 and 1765 about returning to office, Pitt declined. Cultivating an aloofness from the hurly-burly of politics, Pitt remained a wild card. Able to change positions more adeptly than any other major politician of the age, Pitt retained his popularity as "the Great Commoner" and displayed the knack of attracting the loyalty of able men. He disdained, however, the role of party leader.

Maintaining his independence, he supported the first Rockingham administration's repeal of Grenville's Stamp Act, while opposing the accompanying Declaratory Act. His speech in favor of repealing the Stamp Act was widely reported in Britain and America and outlined the basis from which his ideas on American policy developed: Pitt acknowledged the legislative supremacy of Parliament but argued that it did not extend to taxation. Colonial taxes, he maintained, should only be levied by colonial assemblies. (The revenue raised from the Navigation Acts Pitt considered legitimate because it was incidental to the legislation's main purpose, that of regulating trade within the empire).

Pitt's opposition to the Stamp Act and his support for its repeal were widely heralded in the colonies and cemented his heroic status there. Americans, in fact, tended to give Pitt much more credit for the Stamp Act's repeal than his parliamentary efforts deserved.

In the summer of 1766, Pitt agreed to form a new ministry that, it was hoped, would end the chronic ministerial instability that had plagued British politics since George III's accession. His ministry, he declared, would not be based on party distinctions but rather would end them. Pitt, at the same time, was surprisingly raised to the peerage as Earl of Chatham and took the honorific post of Lord Privy Seal.

Launched with high hopes, the Chatham administration proved to be a fiasco. After briefly appearing in the House of Lords in the fall of 1766, Chatham soon fell ill and absented himself from Parliament and politics. His condition seems to have been at least partly psychogenic. It placed on the unwilling shoulders of the Duke of Grafton the burden of holding together a government that lacked its central focus. It was in this context that Charles Townshend seized the initiative in colonial policy and pushed through the revenue act that bears his name. Parliament's dispute with the American colonies immediately rekindled.

Chatham never returned to head the ministry he had formed, and in 1768 he resigned. In 1770 and 1771, he returned to active politics, this time in opposition, by joining the attack on the government's handling of the Wilkes-related Middlesex elections and a variety of other matters. Chatham's relations with the other groups in opposition were not close, however, and a united opposition failed to materialize. After 1771, Chatham's parliamentary appearances became less frequent. In the spring of 1774, he briefly reemerged in the midst of consideration of the Coercive Acts. Though condemning the Boston Tea Party, Chatham actively opposed the Quartering Act and the Quebec Act, and in general he arraigned the government's American policy. Chatham blamed the troubles in America on the attempt to tax the colonies and continued to criticize the 1766 Declaratory Act. This did little to endear him to the Rockinghamite portion of the opposition.

Chatham next appeared at the beginning of 1775 as the crisis in colonial affairs was nearing its climax. Purposely keeping his intentions secret, he made two dramatic appearances in the House of Lords: once to move for the withdrawal of British troops from Boston and again to introduce a reconciliation bill. The latter, which may have been influenced by contact with Franklin, recognized the sovereignty of Parliament within the empire but stipulated that no tax could be levied in America without the consent of the appropriate colonial assemblies. It also called for recognition of the Second Continental Congress as a lawful assembly with responsibility for providing a colonial contribution to imperial finances. Finally, the Coercive Acts would be suspended. Whether or not the bill might have proved acceptable to the colonists is moot; there was too little support in Parliament for such a measure, and the lords quickly rejected it by 68 votes to 32.

The outbreak of war coincided with another collapse in Chatham's health, mental and physical. It was almost two years before he attended Parliament again. He made known his continued opposition to the war, however, and often coupled his condemnations with ominous warnings that the Bourbon powers would take advantage of the situation. He continued to believe that if something like his earlier reconciliation bill were adopted by Parliament that all would be well.

Chatham may also have believed that the lengthening war, with its prospect of foreign intervention, would lead to his return to office. In 1777 he returned to active politics, attacking the government's policies and predicting doom if America were lost. In March 1778, overtures from the king were made, exploring the possibility of Chatham's joining the North administration. Chatham refused to share power with ministers he blamed for leading the empire into civil war, nor would he come in without other elements of the opposition.

Chatham, however, also maintained his distance from the Rockingham Whigs, the largest of the opposition parties. To earlier differences over the Declaratory Act was now added a major disagreement about American independence.

With French intervention looming, both Chatham and Rockingham believed that Britain should stop fighting in America and concentrate its strength against the traditional enemy. Rockingham felt that this would be aided by recognition of American independence. Chatham, however, refused to agree to what he viewed as the dismemberment of the empire. He continued to believe that a way could be found, perhaps with himself as war minister, to maintain the unity of the empire *and* defeat France. It was somewhat ironic, though not uncharacteristic, that Chatham's last speech (on April 7, 1778) was in opposition to a motion from the Rockinghams for recognition of American independence. In a dramatic finish to an often dramatic career, Chatham collapsed in mid-speech on the floor of the House of Lords. He died five weeks later.

Of the leading British politicians of the Revolutionary era, Chatham was the one best known and most admired in America. (One historian has located almost 3,500 references in American newspapers to Chatham in the period 1756–1778, the vast majority of them favorable.) American opinion of the Great Commoner turned earl was often uncritical but nonetheless important. After the debacle of the Chatham administration, Chatham's role in British politics was reduced to that of part-time leader of the second largest group within the parliamentary opposition. In American eyes though, as in his own, he remained a mighty force, forever on the verge of a return to power. This contributed to the American tendency to overestimate the strength of those in the mother country who supported American resistance. Had Chatham's relative lack of influence been more accurately perceived by his American admirers, they might have acted differently. As it was, he unintentionally became another source of Anglo-American misunderstanding.

William C. Lowe

REFERENCES

Stanley Ayling, *The Elder Pitt, Earl of Chatham* (1976); Peter Brown, *The Chathamites. A Study of the Relationship between Personalities and Ideas* (1967); ———, *William Pitt, Earl of Chatham, the Great Commoner* (1978); Carol Lynn H. Knight, "A Certain Great Commoner: The Political Image of William Pitt, First Earl of Chatham, in the Colonial Press," *Proceedings of the American Philosophical Society*, 123 (1979):131–42; J. H. Plumb, *Chatham*

(1953); O. A. Sherrard, *Lord Chatham and America* (1958); W. S. Taylor and J. H. Pringle, eds. *The Correspondence of William Pitt, Earl of Chatham*, 4 vols. (1838–40); Basil Williams, *William Pitt, Earl of Chatham*, 2 vols. (1913).

Pollock, Oliver (c. 1737–1823)

American agent. A native of Ireland, he immigrated to Carlisle, Pennsylvania, in the 1750s. After associating with the Philadelphia trading firm of Willing and Morris, he became their corresponding representative at Havana, where he rose to prominence as a leader in the Irish–Roman Catholic merchant community tolerated by the Spanish government in that city. A personal friend of the Spanish general Alejandro O'Reilly, he accompanied this commander to New Orleans in 1769 when Spain reasserted control over Louisiana after the failed regime of former governor Antonio de Ulloa. Pollock established residence at New Orleans, and O'Reilly granted him lucrative trading rights, including contracts to supply the local military garrison with flour and foodstuffs. Continuing his mercantile relationship with Willing and Morris, he established numerous trading connections between the lower Mississippi Valley and various Atlantic coast merchants during the 1770s. In so doing, he earned great wealth and became associated with James Willing, younger brother of the Philadelphia merchant, who moved to the region and established a plantation on the river above Baton Rouge.

Pollock quickly sided with the rebel cause upon receiving news of Lexington and Concord, becoming a staunch supporter of independence. He wrote the Continental Congress, offering his assistance in securing military supplies and material from the Spanish government in Louisiana. In late 1775, Captain George Gibson and a small detachment of rebel troops floated down the Mississippi to request gunpowder and supplies from the Spanish governor, Luis de Unzaga. Pollock secured an audience for Gibson with this official, convinced Unzaga to furnish the needed items from local military stores, and arranged for their shipment up the inland river system to Fort Pitt. Pollock thereafter undertook a regular trade between New Orleans and rebel ports, both by way of the Mississippi and the sea. In 1777, the Congress appointed him its official commercial agent at New Orleans, and the fol-

lowing year, he provided safe refuge at New Orleans for the military expedition led against British West Florida by his former associate, James Willing. Starting in 1779, Pollock also provided large amounts of supplies for George Rogers Clark.

Pollock formed a close personal friendship with Bernardo de Galvez when this Spanish official became governor of Louisiana in 1777. Galvez loaned the Continental Congress almost 70,000 pesos on Pollock's personal guarantee, most of which was used to purchase supplies for Clark. Pollock also accompanied Galvez's army in the taking of Baton Rouge from the British and also participated in the Battle of Pensacola. In 1783, Pollock moved to Havana, where he served as commercial agent for the Congress. He was imprisoned at Morro Castle in that year because he failed to repay loans to various New Orleans merchants that he had earlier negotiated for the purchase of military supplies. Robert Morris, acting as Superintendent for Finance, was eventually able to secure Pollock's release and safe return to Pennsylvania. Pollock settled first in Carlisle, eventually moving to Baltimore. He returned to the lower Mississippi Valley after the War of 1812, spending his final years at his plantation, "Old Tunica," where he died in 1823.

Light Townsend Cummins

REFERENCES

Light T. Cummins, "Oliver Pollock and George Rogers Clark's Service of Supply: A Case Study in Financial Disaster," in *Selected Papers from the 1985 and 1986 George Rogers Clark Trans-Appalachian History Conferences* (1988); ———, "Oliver Pollock's Plantations: An Early Anglo Landowner on the Lower Mississippi, 1769–1824," *Louisiana History*, 29 (1988): 35–48; James A. James, *Life of George Rogers Clark* (1928); *Oliver Pollock: The Life and Times of an Unknown Patriot* (1937); William F. Mulloney, "Oliver Pollock: Catholic Patriot and Financier of the American Revolution," *Historical Records and Studies of the U.S. Catholic Historical Society*, 28 (1937): 164–236.

Pomeroy, Seth (1706–1776)

Massachusetts militia officer. A gunsmith from Northampton, Massachusetts, Pomeroy became a lieutenant colonel during the French and Indian War. In 1774 he served on a committee of safety and soon after represented his town in the First and Second Provincial congresses. Elected brigadier general in October 1774, Pomeroy helped to reorganize the militia. He was active in recruiting and in training troops from western Massachusetts.

At Bunker Hill, armed with a musket that he had made, the 69-year-old veteran was an inspiration to men inexperienced in combat. Named a brigadier general in the Continental Army (June 2, 1775), Pomeroy declined the appointment but accepted the rank of major general in the Massachusetts militia. While marching to join the army in New Jersey in February 1776 he died on the way.

Richard L. Blanco

REFERENCES

DAB; L. E. de Forest, *The Journals and Papers of Seth Pomeroy* (1926).

Poor, Enoch (1736-1780)

Continental Army officer. Enoch Poor was born to Thomas and Mary Poor on June 21, 1736 in North Andover, Massachusetts. In his youth, he received only a rudimentary education and served an apprenticeship to a cabinetmaker. Poor moved on to Exeter, New Hampshire, in 1760 and in time, became a shipbuilder, trader, merchant, and politician. He was extremely active in local government in New Hampshire. He was happily married to Martha Osgood of Andover, Massachusetts. Their marriage produced two daughters. He served two years of active duty with the colonial forces in the British army during the French and Indian War.

After the Battle of Lexington in 1775, Poor was appointed commander of the third company of the first three raised by new Hampshire. On May 24, 1775, he was commissioned colonel of the 2nd New Hampshire Regiment and led his regiment to Boston, where they served in the siege. In 1776, Poor was sent to help in the defense of New York City, and shortly thereafter his regiment was sent as reinforcement to assist in the American retreat from Canada along Lake Champlain. He was one of the many officers who objected to the evacuation by General Philip Schuyler of Crown Point without a fight.

Returning south to rejoin Washington's army, Poor led his regiment bravely and effectively in the Battles of Trenton and Princeton. On Feb-

ruary 21, 1777, Poor was promoted to the rank of brigadier general and was given command of the New Hampshire brigade. His rival for this honor, Colonel John Stark, resigned in anger at having been passed over by one he considered a junior officer.

As the campaign of 1777 opened, Poor and his brigade marched north to once again become a part of the Northern Department under the command of Schuyler, and later his replacement, General Horatio Gates. General John Burgoyne's powerful British/German army invaded New York State along the Lake Champlain–Hudson River waterway, and Poor's New Hampshire brigade was in the thick of the fighting to stop Burgoyne before he reached Albany.

Under the tactical leadership of General Benedict Arnold, Poor's regular line infantry formed the American center and fought Burgoyne's best to a stalemate in a heated, vicious contest at Freeman's Farm. A month later, Poor's men held the position of honor on the right of the American line that pushed a British reconnaissance in force back from the Barber wheat field. In the battle that would be known to history as Bemis Heights, Poor's brigade went on to attack both the Balcarres and Breymann redoubts. Once again following General Arnold's inspiring lead, Poor's men broke the British line at the Breymann redoubt, and only darkness prevented Poor from striking the British camp. Almost 60 percent of American casualties suffered in these two battles came from Enoch Poor's brigade.

With the defeat of Burgoyne, Poor was ordered to march his veteran force south to rejoin Washington's army in Pennsylvania. Poor arrived in time to encamp at Valley Forge. His men were assigned the center of the outer line that protected the camp from British attacks. By the time that spring arrived, Howe had resigned and the French had openly allied themselves with the Americans. It became clear that the British would evacuate Philadelphia. General the Marquis de Lafayette was given his first independent command when he was sent to Barren Hill to reconnoiter the British positions to discover their intentions. With him went Enoch Poor and his tough New Hampshire line brigade.

The British were alert and almost succeeded in capturing Lafayette at Barren Hill in a trap. But the discipline of Poor's soldiers and the cool, calm leadership of Lafayette prevailed. The

Americans walked out of the trap. When the British did leave Philadelphia and began their retreat across New Jersey, Poor's men were part of the van under the command of General Charles Lee. In the terrible heat of the Battle of Monmouth, they fought in the first, unsuccessful part of the battle and were still fighting at the end of the day in the more favorable actions directed by Washington himself, once Lee had been relieved of command.

After the Cherry Valley massacre of November 1778, it was determined to send a strong American force to invade the territory of the Iroquois nations and destroy their towns and crops. General John Sullivan commanded this expedition. Once again, Poor and his brigade played a crucial role in the campaign. At the Battle of Newtown on August 29, 1779, Poor detected Joseph Brant's ambush and smashed into it, along with Morgan's rangers and Parr's Pennsylvanians. Flanking Brant's Indians on their left, Poor forced the Indians to flee from the field.

The following year, General Enoch Poor was posted at West Point until General Arnold arrived. Then he was sent to New Jersey in August to become one of two generals honored with command of a brigade of the light infantry. The other brigadier was General Edward Hand of Pennsylvania. The two brigades of the light corps were commanded by Lafayette.

Poor was extremely popular with his men. They followed him with a strong devotion and never failed him in battle. He was a good leader of men and a trusted friend of Washington. Poor was one of the best liked and ablest commanders of the army. It was a terrible loss, therefore, when he became ill with the putrid fever and died at his camp in northern Jersey on September 8, 1780.

General Poor was honored with the largest and most elaborate military funeral in Continental Army history. Washington and his entire staff attended along with most of the other general officers of the army and many of Poor's soldiers. A long procession took the general's body to his grave in a church graveyard in Hackensack, New Jersey. Dead at 44 years of age, Poor was remembered by Washington as "an officer of distinguished merit, who, as a citizen and a soldier, had every claim to the esteem of his country."

There were rumors surrounding the relatively sudden death of General Poor. The most common of these puts Poor in a duel with a Lieutenant Porter, an American, the result of which was Poor's death. Another version had Poor fighting a duel with a French officer and being mortally wounded. The duel was hushed up to avoid an international incident. There was concern that the French would react negatively to this duel and punishment of the French officer, all of which might threaten the alliance. There is no documentary proof of any of these stories. Poor fell victim, as far as history is concerned, to a disease that killed all too many in the American army.

Paul J. Sanborn

REFERENCES

DAB, John Elting, *The Battle of Saratoga* (1977); Benson J. Lossing, *The Pictorial Field Book of the American Revolution*, 2 vols. (1851–52), rpr. 1972; Dorothea Thompson "Enoch Poor," in Peter E. Randall, *New Hampshire Years of Revolution* (1976); *Webster's American Military Biographies* (1978); Colonel John W. Wright, "The Corps of Light Infantry in the Continental Army," *American Historical Review*, 31 (1926):454–461.

Porto Praya, Cape Verde Islands, Battle of (April 16, 1781)

When the United Netherlands declared war on Britain in December 1780 it was essential that Britain capture the Dutch colony of the Cape of Good Hope. Table Bay at the Cape had one of the best harbors in the world that provided haven for East Indiamen sailing to and from the Indian Ocean. If the Dutch held it, their French allies, already positioned with warships at Mauritius and Reunion off the east coast of Africa, would be better prepared to wrest control of India from the English.

The task of capturing Capetown, and reinforcing Admiral Sir Edward Hughes in the Indian Ocean, was entrusted to Commodore George Johnstone. He sailed on the *Romney* from Spithead, England on March 13, 1781, with one 74-gun, one 64-gun, and three 50-gun vessels, plus three frigates, and troop transports. On April 16, the squadron arrived at the Portuguese Cape Verde Islands and anchored in Porto Praya Bay for water and provisions. Johnstone permitted his captains to anchor anywhere they chose; he made no plans if he were attacked, nor did he send a ship out to cruise.

In pursuit of Johnstone in the race for Capetown was Admiral Pierre de Suffren de Saint Tropey with five ships of the line (two with 74 guns, three with 64 guns, and eight troop transports). Like his British counterpart in other waters, Admiral George Bridges Rodney, Suffren represented a new breed of naval seamen. For decades, tactics at sea had been dominated by the *Fighting Instructions*, which, while revised frequently and amplified for local conditions, kept restrictions on the admirals' ability to maneuver and to devise fresh tactics. Sea fights heretofore in the eighteenth century had been basically a *querre de postes* in which opponents avoided pitched battles and fought generally inconclusive fights along parallel lines. The change in naval tactics was instituted by Rodney, Admiral Richard Kempenfelt, and Suffren, sometimes termed the "Apostle of Action."

On April 16 as Suffren neared the Cape Verde Islands, his squadron also needed water, and he aimed at Porto Praya. As soon as he spotted the enemy, Suffren left his convoy and sought battle. Without forming a line he pushed the attack in disdain of traditional French naval traditions of caution in an engagement. Aboard the *Heros*, (74 guns), Suffren sailed right into the harbor followed by the *Annibal*, (74 guns). Suffren anchored in position to fire at the British *Hero*. The French captain of the *Annibal* either misunderstood instructions or was not prepared for battle. He even anchored so close to the *Heros* that Suffren had to drop astern and out of position in order to engage the *Hero*. The captain of the third French ship rammed into an East Indiamen and both ships drifted to sea. The other two French warships did not enter the harbor and merely fired some rounds. After an hour of combat, Suffren slipped his cable and put to sea with the heavily damaged *Annibal* following.

When the *Annibal* cleared the harbor, Johnstone determined the condition of his ships. With the exception of the *Isis*, the ships were able to fight, so Johnstone proceeded to follow Suffren, for there was a good chance to capture the slow-moving *Annibal*. But the British vessels were slow to clear the channel, the captain of the *Isis* refused to obey Johnstone's signal be-cause of damaged masts and rigging, and Johnstone, in his haste to pursue, had neglected to arrange a rendezvous for his transports. The British suffered 166 casualties, the French 309. Nearly all the French casualties were on the *Heros* and *Annibal*. The British captains demonstrated little skill at Porto Praya, and only their gunnery was good. If Johnstone had been a capable commander he could have continued the fight, and he could have sent his frigates against the French convoy. But he was unable to form a line, and a chase would have been dangerous. Perhaps the fury of the unexpected French attack disconcerted him and his subordinates. Johnstone placed the captain of the *Isis* under arrest, and he spent two weeks more at Porto Praya repairing his ships.

By the time Johnstone arrived at the Cape the colony's defenses had been strengthened, and Suffren had already sailed to Mauritius. Sending the *Isis* and two other ships of the line to India, Johnstone returned to England. The captain of the *Isis* was tried, exonerated of all charges, and awarded 6,000 pounds sterling in a civil suit. He never collected the sum because the House of Lords decided that to uphold such a verdict would impair the discipline of the Royal Navy.

Suffren's error at Porto Praya was not to have prepared a battle plan beforehand and to assume that his captains could comprehend his signals and follow his unorthodox tactics. Suffren himself improvised brilliantly in this action, but he required his subordinates to demonstrate a high degree of initiative in the face of rigid training to conformity. Suffren sailed on to the Indian Ocean, where he would wage five bloody battles with his opponent Hughes, and where he would earn the reputation of being a master tactician. *See also*: Indian Ocean, the American Revolution in; South Sea Expedition

Richard L. Blanco

REFERENCES

Jonathan R. Dull, *The French Navy and American Independence* (1975); Raymond Cavaliero, "Admiral Suffren in the Indies," *History Today, 20* (1774):472–481; W.N. James, *The British Navy in Adversity* (1926); Charles Moran, "Suffren, the Apostle of Action," *United States Naval Institute Proceedings, 64*(1938):315–325; William P. Willcox, "The Battle of Porto Praya, 1781," *American Neptune, 5* (1945):64–78.

Potts, Jonathan (1745–1781)

Continental Army physician. Born at Popodickon, Colebrookdale, in the future Berks County, Pennsylvania, Jonathan Potts was the son of John Potts, a Quaker and a prominent ironmaster, and Ruth Savage Potts, also of an iron-making family. In 1752 John Potts moved his family to newly built Pottsgrove Manor. In addition to extensive mining and forging interests, John Potts owned sawmills, gristmills, breweries, and tracts of timber. As the leading entrepreneur for the area he virtually dominated the Manatawny region. The village of Pottsgrove (the future Pottstown) was "a company town."

Young Jonathan was educated at home by schoolmasters; he also attended an unknown boarding school nearby and the academy of the Seventh Day Baptists in Ephrata. In 1751 he continued his studies at the prestigious Academy in Philadelphia, where Quaker grandees enrolled their sons. Five of Jonathan's six brothers joined their father's business or mercantile firms; John, Jr., became a lawyer and Jonathan a doctor. At the age of sixteen, Jonathan began his four-year apprenticeship with Dr. Phineas Bond, one of the most famous physicians in the colony. Potts also attended the lectures on anatomy given by Dr. William Shippen, Jr., a remarkable surgeon and obstetrician whose courses constituted the first regularly organized teaching of medical subjects in the North American colonies. Jonathan pursued his studies at the Medical School linked to the College of Philadelphia, where he attended lectures by Shippen and by the equally reknowned Dr. William Morgan, who taught chemistry, materia medica, and pharmacology. Classroom education was supplemented by the demonstrations of Dr. Thomas Bard at the Pennsylvania Hospital, where Potts and friend Benjamin Rush enrolled in December 1765. By the summer of 1766 Potts had acquired a medical education far superior to most American practitioners. He now sought advanced training at the University of Edinburgh.

Medicine at Edinburgh was taught at a higher intellectual level than any other contemporary institution, and since 1749 it had attracted many of America's future medical doctors. The theoretical training at Edinburgh, which lasted three years, was preceeded by, or concluded with, short periods in London, where at the four hospitals of the metropolis, students could "walk the wards" under the guidance of a superior. Along with such teaching hospitals, students in London had opportunities to observe the demonstrations of William Hunter (the foremost anatomist of his day), to study the obstetrical techniques of Dr. Colin McKenzie, and to listen to Sir John Pringle expound upon the principles of military medicine.

Potts and Rush departed on August 31, 1766, from Philadelphia on the *Friendship*. Prior to his voyage, Potts became engaged to Grace Richardson of a wealthy Quaker family in Philadelphia. The young Pennsylvanian had a stormy voyage, and during one fierce gale Potts was so terrified that he prayed to God for aid. Apparently this awesome experience at sea and his "Deliverance" by a "Divine Hand," as Potts noted in his diary, left him with an invigorated religious fervor.

Landing at Liverpool on October 21, Potts soon ingratiated himself into the local meeting there that was part of the transatlantic network of the Society of Friends. With a certificate from the Philadelphia Yearly Meeting, Potts had an entree to Samuel Fothergill, a distinguished preacher, who provided the young student with letters of introduction to Quaker communities in London and Edinburgh. Arriving in London on November 6, Potts and Rush waited for letters from Benjamin Franklin, who regarded such young men from America as his protégés.

At Edinburgh Potts attended classes held by Joseph Black in chemistry, John Hope in materia medica, Alexander Munro II in surgery and anatomy, William Cullen on institutes of medicine (pathology and physiology), and James Gregory, who taught the practice of medicine. Potts found the intellectual milieu of the Scot city to be exciting. He found an outlet for his religious enthusiasm with the Edinburgh Meeting of Friends.

In late January 1767 he learned that his fiancée was pregnant, so he sought a homeward-bound ship from London. Sailing home on March 5 he anguished over the fact that the prized Edinburgh degree now seemed unobtainable. Potts probably arrived in Philadelphia too late for the birth of his daughter on April 4, 1767. Evidently encountering obstacles in their efforts to be married, the couple were joined in an unofficial but still recognized Quaker gathering in Berks on May 5, 1767. Hereafter Potts, who fathered another five children, maintained tenuous links with Quakerism, though he remained a deeply religious man. Although his prospects to advance in the profession were less promising without the Edinburgh degree, he had certain advantages (education, influence, ambition), and he was able to continue his studies at the College of Philadelphia.

Meanwhile Potts opened his office on May 28, 1767, and he soon had about 30 patients. In December 1767 he returned to Philadelphia to prepare for his examinations. Graduating with his bachelor's degree in medicine on January 21, 1768, Potts gave the valedictory address to commemorate the first graduation at a medical school in North America. Aided by a substantial bequest for the estate of his father (who died on June 6, 1768), Potts resumed his practice in Pottsgrove in July 1769. There he prepared his dissertation on intermittent fever (malaria). On June 18, 1771, Potts received his M.D. degree from the College of Philadelphia.

His prestige now enhanced and desirous of a more lucrative practice, Potts selected Reading, a bustling town and the seat of Berks County. Here Potts prospered, with 240 patients in 1772 and 330 in 1774. Among them were Edward Biddle, Daniel Brodhead, and Thomas Dundas, as well as the Boone and Lincoln families. Typical of many medical men of the era, Potts increased his income by maintaining an apothecary shop. And while in Reading, Potts was instrumental in notifying the public about the benefits of inoculation from smallpox. In 1771, in particular, he made a determined effort to halt the ravages of the disease by an appeal to the local German inhabitants to accept inoculation procedures, which had been well tested and with excellent results.

Thus, Potts typified the "new breed" of doctors emerging in the 1770s. Known and admired in their communities, they were frequently called upon for advice in local affairs. Many doctors served on committees of correspondence at the county and provincial level, and many helped to provide the growing tide of support for the Revolution. Twenty-one doctors were members of the First Provincial Congress of Massachusetts, five physicians were signers of the Declaration of Independence, 16 delegates with medical training served in the Continental Congress, and 1,400 medical men volunteered for the Continental Army or Navy.

When the fighting erupted at Lexington and Concord on April 19, 1775, Potts was already a dedicated Patriot who had already voiced his opposition to the Boston Port Act (1774). In Reading on July 2, 1774, Potts was elected to the local Committee of Correspondence. Soon after he was appointed to the Provincial Convention in Philadelphia. Though Potts played only a minor role in the proceedings there, because of his acquaintance with numerous German families he sought their support for the First Continental Congress. Potts also served on the local Committee of Observation, and he was also Reading's representative to Pennsylvania's Second Provincial Congress.

In July 1775 Potts joined a company under Captain George Nagle as a surgeon. Although the Berks County company was part of Colonel William Thompson's battalion, which arrived at Cambridge, Massachusetts, on July 5, apparently Potts did not serve at the siege of Boston. He remained in Reading involved with public duties. In November 1775 he informed the colony's Committee of Safety about the production of gunpowder in Berks; in December he reported on the manufacture of muskets by local gunsmiths. In February 1778 he supervised the handling of British prisoners of war (men, women, and children) captured at Fort Ticonderoga and who were confined in Reading and Lancaster. During March and April, Potts inspected the health of troops under Colonels Anthony Wayne and Arthur St. Clair.

On April 29, 1776, Potts petitioned Congress for a medical appointment. On June 6 he was designated "a Physician and Surgeon" to serve under Dr. Samuel Stringer, Director of the Hospital in the Northern Department (upper New York and Canada). Washington assigned Potts to the army hospital on Lake George, and in late June the young doctor sailed up the Hudson in the company of General Horatio Gates to assume his new post.

By the time Potts arrived at the Lake George Hospital in early July, stragglers were coming in from the aborted American invasion of Canada. Driven from Quebec up the St. Lawrence by a British army under General John Burgoyne, the Americans were defeated at Trois Rivieres on June 8. The beaten force began to disintegrate in its frenzied retreat up the Richelieu River to St. Johns. In early June when some 7,000 men embarked for Ticonderoga, about 2,000 had smallpox, another 2,000 had dysentery or "fevers," and only 3,000 were fit for duty.

Potts now faced the challenge of his life. He found severe shortages of beds, blankets, drugs, and surgical equipment at the hospital built for 300 patients. On July 12, hundreds of pox-ridden men stumbled out of their boats. Potts was inundated with sick men and he lacked the staff, facilities, and equipment to treat them. A hospital return dated July 12–26 indicates that 1,497 men were admitted, 439 were discharged 51 died, 3 deserted, and 1,003 remained for treatment. Exhausted by the toil of handling the sick, Potts did not realize that he was administering what would be the largest American military hospital of the war.

He was also involved in protecting the health of troops at Ticonderoga under Gates. There Potts not only provided the military with advice about hygiene and sanitation but he was instrumental in establishing preventive measures to check the spread of smallpox. With Gates's support, Potts formed several checkpoints on routes to Ticonderoga in order to inspect the health of reinforcements coming from New England. By September, smallpox was no longer a major problem in the area. By November 20, the hospital at Fort George was closed for the winter.

Granted a furlough on November 12, Potts headed for Reading. But he was soon back to duty. As a result of successive defeats inflicted upon Washington's troops by the British army in the autumn of 1776, the American forces had retreated from lower New York and through New Jersey. By December, hundreds of casualties under Potts's supervision were housed in Philadelphia or in villages of eastern Pennsylvania.

Then Potts volunteered to serve at Trenton with General Thomas Mifflin's Pennsylvania militia. Presumably, Potts treated the wounded after the fighting at Assunpink Creek. He trudged along with Washington's troops on the daring attack on Princeton, and he described the carnage that he witnessed on the battlefield. After Washington marched to Morristown in early January 1777, Potts remained in Princeton to treat the wounded, one of whom was the dying General Hugh Mercer.

Potts was then appointed Deputy Director General of the Northern Department on April 11, 1777. Leading a wagon train laden with medical supplies, he had already arrived in Albany on April 2. His drugs and equipment were adequate and his staff consisted of 22 (surgeons, mates, stewards, clerks). Potts established a major hospital at Albany and minors ones along the Mohawk and Hudson rivers. In May at Ticonderoga, Potts supervised the construction of a hospital at nearby Mount Independence.

As Burgoyne's large force descended from the north, the Americans questioned their ability to retain Ticonderoga. St Clair, the commander there, had only 2,500 effectives, and supposedly 10,000 men were needed to hold the extensive lines of the fort. Before the British attacked, General Philip Schuyler, in charge of the Northern Department, ordered Potts to evacuate the sick downstream. After the enemy captured Ticonderoga and moved down Lake George, Potts moved his patients to Albany or to villages along the Hudson.

Potts then joined Gates at Saratoga, supervising hospital arrangements at Bemis Heights. With 200 Americans wounded on September 16 and another 100 on October 6, in addition to several hundred British casualties, Potts and his surgeons were inundated with casualties. The most serious cases were hauled by wagons to Albany. Here the medical men (American, British, German) attended to 550 patients. Another 500 maimed soldiers poured in and Potts had to find additional housing for them in Schenectady, some 16 miles away.

The medical men under Potts at Saratoga performed well. This time there were no recorded complaints about shortages of staff and surgical instruments, and Potts may have stockpiled the largest amount of drugs and hospital stores for any campaign in the North with the exception of the siege of Boston. The relatively low incidence of sickness may be explained by the near eradication of smallpox there, the infrequency of typhus, the constant changes of campsites, and the generally favorable weather. From March 1 to December 16, 1777, only 207 men died in these hospitals, a relatively low figure in relation to the number of casualties on both sides. Potts received praise for his work from Major James Wilkinson, Dr. John Jones (a famous surgeon), and from Benjamin Rush. Due to Gates's request, on November 6, Congress declared its thanks to Potts and his staff for their accomplishments at Saratoga. This congressional praise of medical men was the only such testimonial to the skills of army doctors during the entire war.

At home by November 16, Potts was recalled to assist with casualties from the Battles of Brandywine and Germantown. In Reading, Potts found housing for some wounded in various buildings, and he tended the sick and maimed soldiers posted at nearby villages. In an overhaul of the much-criticized Medical Department led by Dr. Shippen, Potts was named Purveyor-General and Deputy Director General of the Middle Department.

Now Potts had almost purely administrative duties—procuring drugs and Peruvian bark, finding linens and blankets, acquiring wagons, and handling wages. Washington's army had been at Valley Forge since late December and Potts had to provide a steady flow of hospital supplies to the encampment. Potts also supervised the dispatch of drugs and equipment to the Yellow Springs Hospital. Praised for his efforts by Dr. John Warren of Boston, by Andrew Craigie the apothecary, and by General von Steuben, Potts contributed to the survival of the army at Valley Forge.

Yet Potts increasingly encountered more resistance from Congress over his requests for funds. His dilemma was typical of the problems of the Medical Department in 1778–1780. Staff morale was low, salaries remained unpaid. Shippen was under investigation for fraud and speculation, and Congress refused to grant medical men the same pension and land bounty privileges extended to line officers. Furthermore, the Department was wracked by bitter controversy as Dr. John Morgan, who had been ousted as the first medical director, feuded with his successor Shippen. Potts, however, had a knack for avoiding the many controversies among ranking military and medical men. Nevertheless, Potts was charged with enriching himself by selling medical supplies to the public. After acquitting himself, Potts asked to resign on the basis of poor health, and he left the service on October 7, 1780.

After he returned to private practice, he quickly faded from public life. On October 19, 1781, at the age of 36, Potts died in Reading and was buried in the family plot in Pottsgrove. How does one judge Potts? Although not a Rush, Morgan, or Shippen, Potts was a capable and popular medical administrator who displayed a deep humanitarian concern for sick and wounded troops. *See also:* Medicine, Military

Richard L. Blanco

REFERENCES

Richard L Blanco, *Physician of the American Revolution. Jonathan Potts* (1979); Larry L. Burkhart, *The Good Fight: Medicine in Colonial Pennsylvania* (1989); Louis C. Duncan, *Medical Men in the American Revolution, 1775–1783* (1931); John W. Jordan, "The Military Hospitals at Bethlehem and Lilitz During the Revolution," *Pennsylvania Magazine of History and Biography,* 12 (1888):385–406; Lester S. King, *The Medical World of the Eighteenth Century* (1958); William S. Middleton, "Medicine at Valley Forge," *Annals of Medical History,* 3 (1941):480–486; Howard H. Peckham, *The Toll of Independence* (1974).

Prescott, Richard, Capture of (July 9–10, 1777)

On December 12, 1776, General Charles Lee was captured by a party of British dragoons while at a tavern in Basking Ridge, New Jersey. The Americans could regain Lee's service only by exchanging him for a prisoner of equal rank. They had no such captive, and since the British held a large number of American prisoners, the British had no reason to exchange for several men of lesser rank.

A bold plan was effected not only to get an officer of equal rank, but to return the embarrassment that had been suffered from Lee's loss. The British garrison in Rhode Island was commanded by General Richard Prescott. Many Rhode Island inhabitants were sympathetic to the rebel cause, and so provided detailed information about the British troop dispositions. Prescott was quartered in the Overing house, located near the center of the island and therefore as close as possible to all parts of his command. His 5,000 soldiers were on the northern and eastern sides of the island, close to the mainland. To the west, a wide bay afforded protection, and several frigates guarded these approaches. To the south was the sea. Prescott's quarters were adequately situated.

On the night of July 9, 1777, a party of some 40 men in five whaleboats led by Lieutenant Colonel William Barton, left Warwick Neck on the mainland. Assisted by favorable tides, they rowed nearly ten miles down the bay and landed on Rhode Island. Oars muffled by wrapping them in cloth, they slipped unnoticed past the guard ships, even though they were close enough to hear the watch calling "All's well." A march of a mile brought them to the Overing house. The sentry there attempted to follow his orders by challenging the intruders three times before firing to raise the alarm, but he was overwhelmed after the second "Who comes there?"

Prescott and his aide-de-camp were removed from the house without time to change clothes and were brought to the boats. A British dragoon who was in the house remained silent to avoid capture. As soon as it was clear he rode with all speed to the nearest camp in the garrison. Rockets were fired to raise the alarm, the garrison was turned out and sent patrols along the shore, but it was too late. As the Providence newspaper reported soon after, "the bird had flown."

By dawn the daring raid known as "the capture of the bare-footed general" was complete. The Americans had their prisoner, and the British had suffered a severe embarrassment, laying them open to much deriding propaganda. Prescott's personal effects were sent to him under a flag of truce. The following year, after some negotiations between the two sides, Prescott and Lee were exchanged.

Don N. Hagist

REFERENCES

Frederick Mackenzie, *The Diary of Frederick Mackenzie* (1930); Florence Parker Simister, *The Fire's Center — Rhode Island in the Revolutionary Era* (1979).

Prescott, William (1726–1795)

Continental Army officer. William Prescott was born on February 20, 1726, in Groton, Massachusetts to Judge Benjamin Prescott and his wife, Abigail Oliver Prescott. Judge Prescott was a counselor of Massachusetts and his wife was the daughter of one. A man of position in Groton, Judge Prescott was a prosperous farmer and landowner.

William Prescott saw military service in the provincial forces of Massachusetts during both King George's War and the French and Indian War. As a lieutenant of provincials, Prescott was involved in the capture of Cape Breton Island and the fortress of Louisburg, Nova Scotia, in 1745. Prescott displayed such bravery and military ability in this campaign that the British offered the 19-year-old colonial officer a commission in the regular British army. Prescott turned down this high honor and returned home to pursue his farming.

Prescott settled down in Pepperell, Massachusetts. He married Abigail Hale of Sutton, Massachusetts, on April 13, 1758. Though a farmer by choice, Prescott was also an avid reader at a time when illiteracy was common and reading materials rare. He was thoroughly devoted to books; he read every one he could get his hands on; and he especially delighted in books on military science.

Politically, Prescott was a staunch supporter of the American cause. He remained active in the local militia, training them regularly. When Parliament shut down the port of Boston in 1774, Prescott collected food and shipped it overland into the beleaguered town. Prescott was chosen colonel of the militia regiment at Pepperell when tension increased between the colonists and British troops in Boston. He also agreed to store artillery in his town to protect it from being confiscated by the British.

On April 19, 1775, Prescott led the Minuteman detachment of his regiment to Concord as soon as news of the fighting at Lexington-Concord reached Pepperell. He and his men were too late to participate in the fighting. They continued east and arrived at Cambridge to join the American forces outside Boston. Prescott was appointed to the council of war that oversaw the operation of the New England militia surrounding Boston.

When spies informed the Massachusetts authorities that the British intended to go on the offensive and seize Dorchester and Charlestown Heights around Boston, the council of war determined that American troops must be sent to Charlestown Heights as quickly as possible in an attempt to disrupt British plans to break up the American siege lines.

General Artemus Ward, commander of the Massachusetts forces at Boston and nominal commander of all New England troops involved in the siege, selected his most aggressive, militarily experienced commander to go to Charlestown Heights and construct a fort. Already in favor of just such a move, Colonel William Prescott readily accepted the assignment and moved within hours to take control of the Heights.

A tall, muscularly trim man with simple, direct ways, Prescott disliked talk when action was called for. He had penetrating sky-blue eyes and a firm, fixed mouth. At all times and in all situations, Prescott considered himself a soldier and carried himself so. When talk was appropriate, he never hesitated to speak his mind. Some considered Prescott to be unconventional, yet he was fortified by the inner confidence of having given matters much thought.

Prescott was especially adept at leading men. He gained their respect and obedience through the force of his personality and strength of his convictions. In times of crisis, Prescott was habitually slow and unhurried in his movements. Calm and collected, his plans of action were well considered and methodical in their execution. Under fire, Prescott was cool, and always in control of himself in the most pressing of situations. He understood his men and knew how to get the most effectiveness out of militia.

The fortification of Charlestown Heights was an assignment that was particularly suited to Prescott's strengths as a military commander. He brought his regiment, along with men from other units, out onto the Charlestown Peninsula and determined that it would be necessary to place the proposed redoubt on that part of Charlestown Heights closer to Boston. The British could not afford to ignore the American position. The British would have to delay their plans to break the siege until the American fort was taken.

Through the night Prescott drove his men with the sheer force of his boundless energy and will to complete the redoubt on top of Charlestown Heights (now called Breed's Hill) before daylight caught them in the open. When day finally did break, the British were surprised to find an American redoubt on top of Charlestown Heights that threatened their hold on Boston. The British decided to attack that same day, June 17.

Prescott demonstrated courage, bravery, and outstanding leadership in keeping his untrained militia under control during the subsequent fighting for Charlestown Heights. His key innovation was to hold the initial American volley until the British were almost at point-blank range. Then the damage done by American fire sent the British reeling back twice before a third assault finally cleared the redoubt.

Shot through the coat, and fighting bayonets and muskets off with his sword, Prescott was one of the last Americans to leave the redoubt. Returning to Ward's headquarters in Cambridge, Prescott offered to retake the hills that night with fresh regiments. His offer was turned down.

Ward did not have any fresh troops to spare. In the fighting on Charlestown Heights, Prescott lost many friends from his home town. His regimental casualties were the highest in the American army that day: 42 killed and 28 wounded.

Prescott remained a part of the American army besieging Boston and became colonel of the 7th Continental Regiment on January 1, 1776. He accompanied Washington and the army to New York City after the British had evacuated Boston. Prescott was involved in helping the American army evacuate Long Island, and was present at the engagement at Kip's Bay. The effects of a farm injury and old age combined to prevent Prescott from further active service in the war. However, he assisted General Horatio Gates as a volunteer in beating back General John Burgoyne's invasion in 1777 at Saratoga, New York.

Prescott retired to Pepperell, where he farmed and became involved in politics. He served as a selectman for his community and as a representative for the general court. Prescott did not have sympathy for Daniel Shays's Rebellion in 1786 and was prepared to put it down himself if called upon. Fortunately for all parties concerned, the rebellion ended in Massachusetts without Prescott's active involvement.

A man of the hour, Colonel William Prescott was in the right place at the right time on June 17, 1775. Although he played no further major role in the war, and military leadership passed on to others, Prescott found ample use for his years of experience and study in military matters that June day. His contribution could be found in the rapidly constructed redoubt and the fierce determination displayed by his men to defend it against the best the British had.

Colonel William Prescott, the hero of Bunker Hill, died in Pepperell on October 13, 1795, and was buried there with full military honors. His grandson, William Hickling Prescott, was the noted American historian of the nineteenth century.

Paul J. Sanborn

REFERENCES

DAB; Thomas J. Fleming, *The Story of Bunker Hill* (1966); John Harris, *American Rebels* (1976); Benson J. Lossing, *The Pictorial Field Book of the American Revolution*, 2 vols. (1851–1852), rpr. 1972; *National Encyclopedia of American Biography* (1967); Christopher Ward, *The War of Revolution*, 2 vols. (1952), *1*.

Prevosts of the Royal Americans

The names of the various British regiments raised before and during the American Revolution were misleading. For example, Fraser's 71st Scots Highlander Regiment was enlisted mainly from Ireland and western England. Some regiments even had problems with being termed British. The Royal Americans (the 60th) Regiment, now the King's Royal Rifle Corps, did include some Americans, although it also included men from many European nations, and it was dominated by a Swiss family of officers.

The Prevosts can be traced to Poitou, France, although from at least as early as 1570, they were prominent in the affairs of Geneva, Switzerland. One branch of this family, the descendents of Augustin Prevost (1695–1740), came to so dominate the Royal Americans Regiment in America that this unit came to be known as the Prevost Regiment.

The oldest of the Prevost brothers, Jean Louis (b. 1718) is believed to have died in the British service in India in 1748. His younger brother, Augustin (1723–1786), served against the French at Fontenoy in 1745, apparently in the Dutch service. He was commissioned as major in the Royal Americans on January 9, 1756, and was wounded serving with James Wolfe at the British capture of Quebec in 1759. The scar from his wound earned him the nickname of "old bullet head" from his men. In 1761 he was promoted to lieutenant colonel and served in the sieges of Martinique and Havana before returning to England in 1763, where his battalion was disbanded. In 1774–1775, he was in Europe to raise a new battalion of the Royal "Americans" for service in British East Florida.

Augustin Prevost and his command arrived in East Florida when they were needed most. They were the largest part of the British Regulars that defended the province when Georgia joined the American Revolution and began to invade East Florida. Prevost's command was difficult. His troops had to work with Indians and undisciplined irregular and provincial soldiers. Relations between Prevost, Governor Patrick Tonyn of East Florida, and British Indian Commissioner John Stuart were always strained. In addition to defending East Florida, Prevost also had to direct offensive operations against Georgia and to provide support for cattle rustling operations by the irregulars, a necessity to keep the civilians and military in East Florida from starvation. His position would have been difficult even for a more astute and tactful commander. Augustin Prevost reportedly was not popular with his men, and Lieutenant Colonel Archibald Campbell regarded him as too old for much more than garrison duty.

When Savannah fell to a British invasion force from New York, Prevost and his Royal Americans Regiment marched to Savannah, where he then assumed command. He was promoted to major general on February 19, 1779. In the spring and summer of that year he directed a mismanaged raid against Charlestown, which left his command dangerously divided. In September 1779, a French fleet and army arrived in Georgia under the command of the Comte d'Estaing. The French count demanded surrender, which Prevost reportedly was ready to accept when the timely arrival of the forces he had left in South Carolina saved Savannah for the king. Prevost's command successfully repelled a joint French and American assault upon Savannah on October 9, 1779.

Augustin Prevost returned to England in 1780. He died in 1786 at his estate at Hertfordshire, England, reportedly from diseases he had acquired in the tropics. His son Augustin Prevost (1744–1821) was a major in the Royal Americans.

The next youngest of General Augustin Prevost's brothers was Jacques Marcus Prevost (1725–1778), another veteran of the British victory at Quebec. He was promoted to lieutenant general in 1772, made lieutenant general in 1772, and made lieutenant governor of Antigua.

The youngest and the most colorful of the four Prevost brothers was also named Jacques Marcus (or James Mark) Prevost (1736–1781). Despite his youth, he was commissioned as captain in the Royal Americans on January 17, 1756. Wounded in the British attack against Fort Ticonderoga in 1758, he survived to distinguish himself further in the French and Indian War. In the early 1770s, he served in Georgia, Florida and the West Indies. Under his brother Augustin, Jacques rose to the rank of lieutenant colonel and won a major British victory at the Battle of Briar Creek, Georgia, against the American troops of General John Ashe. Augustin was relentless in seeking favors for his brother, and Jacques did serve as royal civil governor of Georgia until the return of Governor James Wright in the summer of 1779. Jacques then traveled to Jamaica, where he was seriously wounded putting down a local uprising in 1779 and where he died from illness in 1781. Prevost's widow married the famous Aaron Burr, and their daughter, Theodosia Burr, married the grandson of Prevost's opponent at Briar Creek, General John Ashe. Prevost's two sons, although teenagers, were officers in the Royal Americans. They were, however, adopted by Aaron Burr and would become prominent United States citizens.

Robert Scott Davis, Jr.

REFERENCES

Alexander A. Lawrence, *Storm over Savannah* (1951); Milton Lomask, *Aaron Burr: The Years from Princeton to the Vice President, 1756–1805* (1979); Edward G. Williams, "The Prevosts of the Royal Americans," *Western Pennsylvania Historical Magazine,* 56 (1973):1–37.

Prince of Wales Loyal American Volunteers

This Loyalist regiment, sometimes known as "Browne's Corps," should not be confused with Thomas Brown's South Carolina Rangers, or with the Prince of Wales' Regiment of the regular army, which never served in America. Montfort Browne, royal governor of New Providence, was captured in command in Essek Hopkins's raid on Nassau (March 3–4, 1776). When exchanged in September, he went to New York and raised a regiment there. In August 1777 the Volunteers were stationed at Kings Bridge and numbered about 450 members. In 1778 they were on Staten Island. In 1780 the regiment sailed with other Loyalist units under Lord Francis Rawdon to Charleston. It served in the Carolinas until the end of the war. Part of the Volunteers was wiped out at the battle of Hanging Rock (August 6, 1780) during the Camden campaign. Two weeks later the Volunteers suffered further heavy losses at the hands of "Swamp Fox" Francis Marion in a skirmish at Nelson's Ferry. Major Andrew Maxwell, who surrendered Fort Granby on May 15, 1781, was a member of this regiment; and it is assumed that what was left of the regiment was part of the garrison.

Tom Martin

REFERENCE

Bernard A. Uhlendorf, ed. and trans., *Revolution in America: Baurmeister Journals: Confidential Letters and Journals 1776–1784 of Adjutant General Major Baurmeister of the Hessian Forces* (1957).

Princeton, New Jersey, Battle of (January 3, 1777)

By Friday, December 27, 1776, Washington and his entire army were back across the Delaware River at their Bucks County campsites in Pennsylvania, the day after their victory at Trenton. In four days, a majority of the army's enlistments would expire. At that point the men would probably go home. The cold weather had not abated and there was every possibility that the Delaware River would soon freeze. By the time Washington had refitted and resupplied his men, he would have one or two days at most to use his full force against the enemy. Trenton had brought no final solutions to the many problems that still faced the commander-in-chief.

It was also on December 27 that General John Cadwalader and his Pennsylvania militia finally succeeded in making it across the Delaware River from Bristol to capture an empty Burlington, New Jersey. The Germans and British had vanished. When the news of Trenton had reached Colonel Karl von Donop at Mount Holly, he immediately pulled his forces back to join with the British garrison at Princeton. Cadwalader occupied the town.

Washington soon received a report from Cadwalader detailing the situation in the Jerseys and suggesting that Washington recross the Delaware and join forces with the Pennsylvanians to continue the work accomplished at Trenton. Washington agreed, and on December 30, the American army came back across the Delaware. The weather remained frigid, with snow on the ground and ice floating in the river. Washington marched his men to Trenton, where he was forced to perform one of his most difficult duties of the entire war.

In one day his soldiers would be free to return to their homes. He addressed some of the New England troops on parade in Trenton and requested that they agree to sign on for another six weeks in the service of their country. In return, Washington guaranteed them ten dollars a piece as a bounty. He did this on his own authority without informing Congress beforehand, such was the crisis faced by the American cause that very day. At first no one came forward, and Washington was reduced to pleading with the soldiers to remember their homes and country in this terrible time of need. Many of the New Englanders had no particular fondness for this southerner who had criticized them and their leveling ways when he first assumed command of the American army outside Boston. But then one and finally another moved to the front to sign on for another six weeks, until perhaps half of the New Englanders agreed to take the bounty.

But half went home, including most of Colonel John Glover's Marblehead Seamen, who had saved Washington's army in the retreat from Long Island, had fought well at Kip's Bay and had ferried the army back and forth across the Delaware within the past week. The Massachusetts seamen wished to go home and sign on with privateers where good money and many a fortune could be made in a life at sea that was dangerous and hard, but not as bad as the wretched conditions they'd experienced in the past six months.

Mifflin has better success with Daniel Hitchcock's New Englanders who were camped with George Ewing's force at Bristol. Other general officers pleaded with the remaining units of the Continental Army with mixed results. In the end, about 1,100 men agreed to stay on. Washington quickly contacted Robert Morris in Philadelphia with a request that he bring as much money as he could raise, especially in hard currency, to the army. Washington noted that his spies liked to be paid in hard money and the army needed its bounty. Morris gathered $50,000 in paper dollars and 124 pounds, 7 shillings, and 6 pence in hard money and brought it to Washington, providing the vital financial backing to keep the army in the field. (Morris would perform this service again in 1781 when the army refused to march to Yorktown without being paid their just wages.)

The next day Washington received word from Congress that they had elected him dictator for six months in response to the present crisis. It was certainly a vote of confidence, and Washington was careful not to abuse his newly granted responsibilities, and felt pressure to perform under increased scrutiny from the more suspicious and distrustful congressmen.

On January 1, 1777, the weather changed. It grew warm and rain fell, turning the roads and fields into seas of mud. Washington concentrated his remaining forces just outside and to the south of Trenton. Unlike Colonel Johann Schann Rall,

Washington's men fortified their position, which ran for three miles along the south bank of the Assunpink Creek from the Delaware River to Phillip's Ford. The position chosen was a strong one, made more so with the entrenchments. By the end of the day, Washington had been joined by Thomas Mifflin and Cadwalader, bringing his strength to 5,000 men, most of them untested militia, and 40 cannon under General Henry Knox.

Washington knew that the British were distressed over the affair at Trenton. Cornwallis had his leave canceled and was ordered back into New Jersey by Howe to finish Washington and his army off as quickly as possible. If nothing else, Cornwallis was to undo the damage of Trenton. Rushing to New Brunswick to join Grant, Cornwallis gathered more than 8,000 men and began his march toward Trenton, where Washington waited. This time there would be no delays. The pace was fast and unrelenting by eighteenth-century standards.

Washington placed his advance force just south of the village of Princeton. General Matthias Fermoy, the French adventurer who was a worthless drunk, was placed in command. Over a 1,000 men and two guns waited for the British to appear. They did not wait long. On January 2, Cornwallis sent his troops out of Princeton on the Post Road (today's Route 206) toward Trenton. Fermoy, spotting the British advance, left his command and returned to Trenton without explanation. (Later in 1777 at Fort Ticonderoga in the northern campaign, Fermoy behaved disgracefully and almost single-handedly caused an American disaster in the evacuation of Ticonderoga. He resigned in 1778, claiming the Americans did not appreciate his abilities. He was an excellent example of why many Americans did not trust foreign officers in command positions.)

The leadership of the American advance was left to Colonel Edward Hand of Pennsylvania, the Irish-born commander of the 1st Pennsylvania Continental Rifle Regiment. Hand had a vital role to play in this drama. and he did so effectively and with such élan that the British were unable to arrive in Trenton until dusk. Washington personally had visited with Hand during the day to provide him guidance and to encourage his men to perform their duty. Things worked out as planned. Hand's men and artillery delayed the British with constant harassment and hit-and-run attacks that forced Cornwallis to stop and deploy his men in line to resist what he felt might very well be Washington's entire army. These effective tactics consumed valuable time, all to the advantage of the Americans.

Cornwallis continued his disrupted approach to Trenton with his 7,000 men organized in three columns. The main column marched on the Post Road and the other two flanked it on both sides as they moved through the neighboring fields. Von Donop and the surviving Hessians of Rall's Brigade led the van. The revengeful Germans were instructed to take no American prisoners. At dusk the British force reached Trenton and arrived in front of the half-hearted attempts to force the bridge and to probe the American positions at the creek, but all three efforts were easily repulsed, particularly by Knox's artillery. Darkness fell on the field.

Cornwallis had decided to wait until January 3 to attack Washington. He told his officers he would bag the fox in the morning. Several of the officers, especially General William Erskine, felt Cornwallis should have attacked right then and there. In light of what happened, many historians since then have echoed these sentiments.

However, one must consider the following: the American artillery, uncovered in the skirmishes at the creek, was well placed and expertly handled. The Americans were found to be entrenched in strong positions along a creek that was running high with the recent rains. The British artillery was not ready to support a British assault. There was only one real weakness in the American position and that was three miles east at Phillip's Ford. To move large numbers of troops there when it would soon be pitch dark could have the makings of a disaster for the British. It would be more prudent to form the men in the next day's light. Cornwallis camped his men, not in Trenton, but in the exact position north and east of town that would allow the British to attack Phillip's Ford in the morning. Only 1,000 of his 7,000 men were in the town itself to hold the attention of the American center.

When Cornwallis did arrive in Trenton late that afternoon of January 2, he found himself outnumbered. It would take until nightfall for his strung-out force to come up on line. Two brigades were back at Princeton and Maidenhead, respectively, with orders to march to join Cornwallis the next morning. Another Breed's

Hill had to be avoided. Professional soldiers in the eighteenth-century military culture were to be treated as valuable commodities, and were not to be expended frivolously. In addition, his men were fatigued after their march from Princeton, fighting both Colonel Hand's men and the mud along the way. It can be argued that Cornwallis was a prudent professional and not a fool given to rash attacks without proper support and preparation.

His only mistake, a crucial one in retrospect, was to ignore the suggestions of some of the German officers to put a British or German light force cross the Assunpink on Washington's open or right flank and hold him in place over night. That Cornwallis could have done, and normally should have done. But he did not. In that neglected move lies the tale of Princeton.

On the other hand, in the American camp, some historical interpretations would have one believe that Washington, the creative director of the brilliant attack on Trenton, had suddenly become the willing dupe of Cornwallis, a true professional soldier. Now that "the first string was on the field," Washington took his army to Trenton, away from their boats. Thus they could not across the Delaware. He then selected a position that put his army's back against the river with no place to run except south along the Jersey banks of the Delaware, until Cornwallis would have the Americans trapped at Cape May.

However, there is strong evidence to interpret these events otherwise. Washington chose Trenton to receive Cornwallis, perhaps in some sense of military irony. Washington's aide, Joseph Reed, was born in Trenton and raised there. He was quite familiar with the entire Trenton area. It is not unreasonable to assume he would have discussed the area with Washington as a part of the ten days' campaign and provided him with intelligence on the local road system. Washington's headquarters was located at this time in a tavern across the Assunpink from town. The tavernkeeper and his wife were also knowledgeable about the area, and local history credits Jinnie Waglum, a friend of the tavernkeeper's wife, as being Washington's guide to Princeton along the back roads the night of January 2–3. There is also every reason to believe that Washington's previously effective spy system was functioning efficiently, especially since Robert Morris had brought the necessary funds to provide for their services.

From Joseph Reed's papers, one does not get the impression that the council of war held by Washington the night of January 2–3 at Captain Alexander Douglas's house (still standing but moved) was a frantic meeting of generals seeking to devise a way to escape Cornwallis. Washington called the council in session at General Arthur St. Clair's headquarters in the Douglas home since his own, in the tavern, was now within range of British artillery. St. Clair, who later claimed he informed Washington of the hidden and little-used road that the Americans in fact did use to "escape" Cornwallis, probably was performing his duty by having had the road checked out by scouts and picketed to protect the line of march.

All along this vital route during the afternoon and evening of the march, American light horse were posted to provide the marching army directions. Considering all these points, it is reasonable to detect a planned pattern of events. This was Washington's way of slipping Cornwallis's noose and shaking the British a second time. The conclusive evidence that Washington was planning to lure Cornwallis into an American blind end at Trenton comes from the existence of a letter from John Cadwalader to Washington in Reed's papers that furnishes a map and description of the same road Washington was to take to Princeton early on January 3. This letter is dated December 31, 1776. Washington made brilliant use of this intelligence, brought to the Americans by an American gentleman who escaped the British at Princeton and followed the road he had described to Cadwalader right into the American right flank.

Washington met with Hand and ordered him to delay Cornwallis from reaching Trenton until dark. Hand fought brilliantly that day to provide Washington that needed time. Given the time and the road, Washington brilliantly took the responsibility for his daring flanking move.

Washington informed his generals of the plan. They agreed to it and left to prepare their respective commands. Left behind in the American lines that night was a force of 400 New Jersey militia to keep the campfires burning and to make noise to let the British think the Americans were still there in force. Then they could return to their homes. This is what happened. At the same time, the American baggage was sent south and placed under the protection of General Israel Putnam.

Washington waited until after midnight to be sure that Cornwallis was settled in camp and moving toward what both men realized was the only obvious choice for a British attack in the morning on the American line. If Cornwallis was moving at night, it would complicate the planned American flanking march. The two might even run into each other in the dark. In the event, some of the militia did take fright in the pitch dark along the line of march and feared they were surrounded by Hessians. It took a while to restore order and calm down the men. One piece of luck was that the weather turned frigid that very night. The cold returned and the muddy roads that would have sucked and pulled at the American artillery turned hard and passable.

At 1 A.M. on January 3, the great flanking march toward Princeton began. By 3 A.M. the van of the American army was approaching Princeton from the southeast along Washington's little-used road. Cornwallis and his men remained facing the now empty American works at Trenton. To make the march a secure one, the wheels of the guns had been wrapped with rags and the men had covered any tin, such as a canteen or weapons, so that no noise alerted the enemy. The march was an unqualified success, as the soldiers began crossing the Stony Brook Creek at Quaker Bridge just before dawn.

Princeton was a small town that hosted the College of New Jersey, although people were now beginning to call the college after the town. Founded in 1746 in Newark, Princeton was the fourth college founded in America, after Harvard, William and Mary, and Yale. It was the first to call its grounds a "campus" and was housed for 50 years, from 1756 until 1806, in just one building at Princeton, Nassau Hall. This building had 52 rooms and contained the library, dormitory, kitchen, chapel, classrooms, and offices of the college. The educational institution was named after the late king of England, William III, who was from the House of Nassau.

The president of the college in 1777 was John Witherspoon, who had signed the Declaration of Independence and was to suffer the loss of a son in the American cause at the Battle of Germantown. The British used the building as a barracks and hospital. Later, in 1783, Congress moved here for a time from Philadelphia, and Nassau Hall became the Capitol of the United States. News of the signing of the Treaty of Paris reached Congress while it sat here. Princeton graduates were leaders on the American military and political scenes. Aaron Burr, James Madison, and "Light Horse" Harry Lee were only three of many such graduates.

Lieutenant Colonel Charles Mawhood had 1,700 crack British troops at Princeton guarding the baggage train and holding the rear guard position while Cornwallis chased the Americans. His brigade was designated the 4th British Brigade. It was composed of three regiments: the 17th, the 40th, and the 55th Regiments of Foot. There were also other minor units and some dragoons at Princeton. At dawn on January 3, Mawhood led the 17th and 55th regiments and some dragoons south along the Post Road to join General Alexander Leslie and his 1,200 men at Maidenhead (Lawrenceville today). From there, both brigades were to march to join Cornwallis at Trenton for the assault on the American lines. Mawhood left the 40th Regiment behind in Princeton to guard the baggage train.

Followed by his pair of springer spaniels, Mawhood, the colonel of the 17th but commander of his brigade, had already crossed the Stony Brook Bridge on the Post Road with his regiment when at 8:00 A.M. he spotted some men moving off to the left in the distance. The men were armed. At first he thought they were Hessians. Then he thought they might be Americans retreating from Cornwallis's attack of the day before. In any case, they deserved to be investigated.

Soon it was clear from the reports of his dragoons that there were two groups of men marching, one along a back road into Princeton and the other up toward the Post Road itself. The reports also indicated they were not Hessians and not retreating Americans. Rather they seemed to be attacking Americans. Mawhood had only 246 men, two guns, and some dragoons immediately with him, but he quickly ordered a retreat across country to try to head off the American column trying to gain Princeton from the rear.

At the same time, General Hugh Mercer, Washington's old friend from Fredericksburg, Virginia, and an excellent general officer, was leading the remnants of his brigade, about 350 men, up a road from the Quaker Bridge over Stony Brook to the Post Road Bridge. This was the second American column. Mercer's orders were to destroy the bridge so that the Princeton garrison would be cut off from help once the Americans attacked. Mercer did not expect that Mawhood's troops would be on the road so early and in the exact position for which he was heading. As Mawhood led his men back toward Princeton across country, he passed in front of Mercer's men. Mercer followed the British lead and took his men along a parallel course.

Mawhood's men were quicker and managed to gain the fence of William Clark's orchard, where they hid. Mercer and 120 of his men in the van were passing through the fields of corn stubble and cleared ground when they came upon the orchard. They entered it and immediately found themselves fired upon by the British, who rose up from the fence and poured a volley into the American flank from 130 feet away. Both sides then exchanged rounds for two or three minutes. But the Americans were armed mainly with rifles and the British with muskets. The rifles were too slow to reload and carried no bayonets. Mawhood, realizing this, ordered a bayonet charge, and the Americans broke under pressure for the rear.

Colonel John Haslet of the Delaware Regiment, and Mercer's second in command, brought the rest of Mercer's detachment up to support the now retreating van. Haslet was shot in the head and died instantly. Mercer lost his horse, shot from under him. On foot, he was soon surrounded by the enemy who demanded his surrender. Mercer refused and was soon pinned to the ground with seven bayonet wounds. The Scottish physician was mortally wounded in the savage British attack. Mercer was left for dead under an oak tree that stills stands today on the field at Princeton. The William Clark farm is gone, but it stood by the oak, and the orchard used to be where Mercer Street runs today. Built in 1807, the street covers the scene of the heaviest fighting at Princeton.

Mercer's men were routed. Washington, positioned on the Back Road, which no longer exists, brought Cadwalader's men up to support the flight of Mercer's troops. One thousand Philadelphia militiamen came onto the field and charged the 17th Regiment. The British broke the charge and the militia joined the other fleeing Americans off the field. Captain Joseph Moulder of the Philadelphia militia literally saved the day for the Americans when he brought up his two 4-pounder guns and placed then at the right of the Thomas Clark House (still standing) and battered back the British attack.

This allowed Washington the opportunity to ride onto the field of battle and to rally his troops, assisted by General Nathanael Greene and Washington's staff. Cadwalader's men formed on the advancing forces of Daniel Hitchcock's brigade of New England Continental Line Regiments and Hand's Pennsylvanians. Major Israel Angell of Rhode Island led Hitchcock's men, since Hitchcock himself, after valuable service to the cause, was ill with pleurisy and would be dead in ten days.

Washington got his men into a line and advanced on the British. The two lines came to within thirty yards or so of each other, and Washington rode right in between the two lines as both cut loose with a volley. Colonel John Fitzgerald, Washington's aide, covered his face with his hat, expecting to see Washington dead on the field. The smoke cleared to find Washington still in the saddle and urging his men to attack the 17th Regiment and push it off the field.

The American line surged forward and the 17th broke for the rear, running as fast as possible. Washington called to Fitzgerald "to bring up the troops, for the day is ours!" The 17th ran south toward Cornwallis and away from Princeton. They did not stop until they reached General Leslie's force at Maidenhead. Mawhood and his spaniels followed quickly behind. Of the 246 men of the 17th, 66 were killed or wounded and 35 were captured. For eighteenth-century standards, this was a high loss indeed and reflected favorably on the valor of the regiment. Heavily outnumbered, the 17th fought with honor and were known ever after in England as "The Heroes of Prince Town." They were also called "tigers" for their actions in this battle, and this nickname was the one assumed by Princeton University as its mascot, which is still used at athletic events today.

Washington was excited and thrilled by his success in the Clark fields south of Princeton. He waved his hat and led the pursuit, crying out, "It's a fine fox chase, my boys!" Fortunately his aides caught up with him before he was captured by the dragoons still present along the Post Road.

Mawhood's second regiment, the 55th, had also gone off the road to the left following the 17th. The 55th, however, took position on what is today called Mercer's Heights. There they watched the destruction of the 17th Regiment without being able to help them. The reason for this was that Sullivan and St. Clair had their troops along the back road closer to Princeton. The Americans in this main column turned in the road to face the 55th on the Heights. If either side moved first, the other could fire into the flank of their opponent and cause great destruction. It was a standoff. When the 17th fell apart, the 55th fell back through the fields toward town. The 40th Regiment in town had heard the gunfire and marched out of Princeton, joining with the 55th south of town at a position on the edge of a ravine named Frog Hollow, where the Princeton Inn is today, along Alexander Road. The two remaining British regiments tried to establish a line of defense for the town at that point.

Quickly sizing up the situation, the Americans led by Sullivan began to flank the two British regiments at Frog Hollow and, without too much pressure, both regiments fled. The 55th Regiment went toward Rocky Hill with some of the baggage train, while part of the 40th Regiment took refuge in Nassau Hall. (This same regiment would pull the same trick later in 1777 at the Battle of Germantown when they holed up in the Chew Mansion, Cliveden.) Captain Alexander Hamilton brought his guns up and fired the first round right through the front doors of the college. Legend has it that the shot decapitated the portrait of King George II, who granted the college its charter. A second shot glanced off the stone walls of the building and almost killed Major Wilkinson's horse. A white flag soon appeared and 194 British walked out prisoners.

It was all over in less than 30 minutes. This time it was not a Hessian brigade that had tasted the bitterness of defeat. This was the British fourth brigade that had been mauled. For the second time in ten days, Washington had accomplished what his fellow countrymen and enemies considered impossible. With the exception of about 20 percent of the soldiers in the American force at Princeton, Washington had accomplished these deeds with essentially two completely different armies. The American army that won at Trenton was not the one that achieved victory at Princeton. In this campaign, it was the commanding general and a few of his

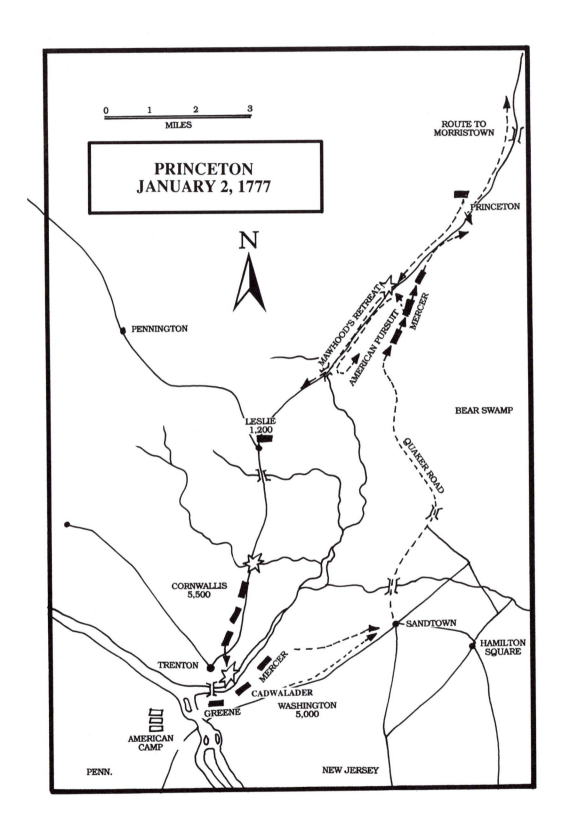

PRINCETON
JANUARY 2, 1777

0   1   2   3
MILES

N

ROUTE TO
MORRISTOWN

PRINCETON

PENNINGTON

MAWHOOD'S RETREAT

AMERICAN PURSUIT

MERCER

BEAR SWAMP

LESLIE
1,200

QUAKER ROAD

CORNWALLIS
5,500

SANDTOWN

HAMILTON
SQUARE

TRENTON

MERCER

CADWALADER

WASHINGTON
5,000

GREENE

AMERICAN
CAMP

PENN.

NEW JERSEY

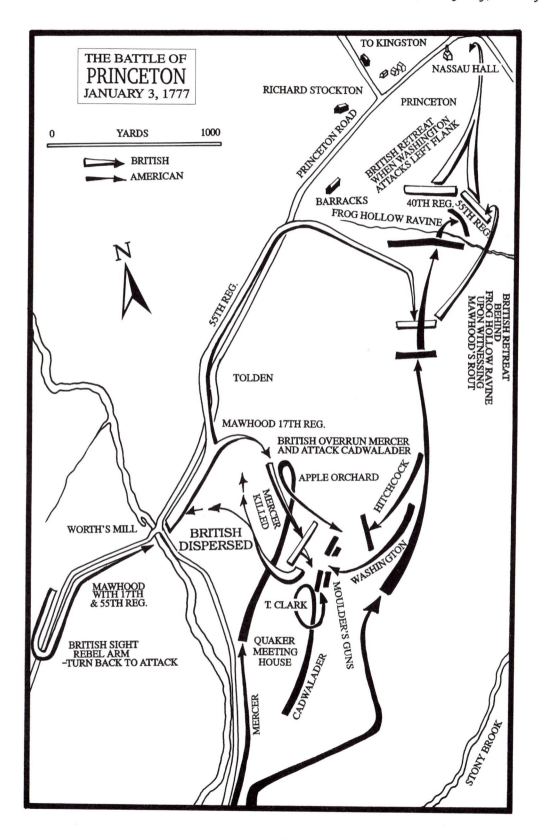

officers who provided the constant factor of quality.

Washington gave his men two hours to resupply themselves at the expense of the British and anyone else still living in Princeton. The wounded were taken care of, and Mercer was taken to the Thomas Clark house, where he would later die of his wounds. A group of militia destroyed the bridge along the Post Road over Stony Brook, just finishing as the van of the fast approaching British main army arrived on the other side.

Cornwallis was still in Trenton preparing his assault when he heard the gunfire to his rear. Instantly he realized what Washington had done and the general assembly was sounded throughout the British camp. In short order the British were marching back up the Post Road toward Princeton. Cornwallis picked up details of the affair at Princeton from survivors of the 17th at Maidenhead. Leslie's force joined the column, and the British pushed on to Princeton. When they reached the Stony Brook, they found the bridge out and the van had to wade through the water to cross. According to Knox, in a letter to his wife, Lucy, the British came on "in an infernal sweat, running, puffing, blowing and swearing at being so outwitted."

The last Americans were leaving Princeton as Cornwallis's men entered the town. The British did pursue Washington lightly beyond Princeton, but Captain Moulder kept them at bay with his two guns in the rear guard. The Americans, exhausted, could not go on to attack the main British base at Brunswick. Washington had no fresh troops and his men were exhausted. The Americans camped at Somerset Court House and then made their way to Morristown, where they went into winter cantonment. They had survived another campaign and turned what had been a series of bitter defeats into a glorious chapter in American military history.

The Americans had lost 40 men killed and wounded while the British suffered 28 killed, 58 wounded, and 187 missing. Many of the dead from both armies are buried yet on the field where they fell. There are memorial stones in the ground near the memorial columns standing on the State Battlefield Park grounds to designate the burial lots. The British were outfought, outgeneraled and outwitted. Howe now complained to Lord Germain that an additional 15,000 troops were needed to finish the job that

only 20 days before Howe declared virtually complete. New Jersey was freed from British control except for two minor areas near New York City. The line of posts was withdrawn. Once news of these successes reached Paris, the French permitted the Americans to purchase more weapons and equipment, an act of war that the British decided to ignore for the time being.

In conclusion, two significant points are presented for consideration. On January 12, 1777, Mercer died of his wounds. On January 15, his casket was carried across the Delaware in a hearse to Philadelphia from New Jersey on top of a solidly iced Delaware River. The British missed their chance to walk across the river by 12 days. Almost five years later, in a little town along the York River in Virginia, Charles, Lord Cornwallis, presented a toast to Washington after the surrender at a meal shared by officers of the French, American, and British armies in which he stated:

> When the illustrious part that your excellency has borne in this long and arduous contest becomes a matter of history, fame will gather your brightest laurels rather from the banks of the Delaware than from those of the Chesapeake.

From the vanquished at Yorktown and Princeton to the victory of both, a neat summary to put the ten crucial days into perspective. Washington may never have equaled what he accomplished at Trenton and Princeton in the remainder of the war. But in those crucial times of 1776 and with those few men, Washington met the test and persevered until that distant final victory was reached.

Paul J. Sanborn

REFERENCES

Alfred Hoyt Bill, *The Campaign of Princeton* (1948); Frederick English, *General Hugh Mercer, Forgotten Hero of the American Revolution* (1975); Thomas Fleming, *1776, The Year of Illusions* (1975); William B. Reed, *The Life and Correspondence of Joseph Reed*, 2 vols. (1847), *1*; Samuel Steele Smith, *The Battle of Princeton* (1967); Christopher Ward, *The War of the Revolution*, 2 vols. (1951), *1*; Franklin and Mary Wickwire, *Cornwallis. The American Adventure* (1970).

Prisoners of War

As the American Revolution got underway in 1775–1776, it soon became apparent that neither of the belligerents had given serious thought to the matter of how prisoners of war should be detained and treated. The British army entered the struggle confidently expecting it to be hastily terminated and, consequently gave little attention to the matter of captives as hostilities commenced. The first American captives, 27 in number, were taken by the British army at the Battle of Bunker Hill in June 1775. During the remainder of 1775 and into early 1776 more captives were taken by Lord Dunmore in Virginia and by General Sir Guy Carleton in Quebec when the ill-fated American invasion of that colony faltered. In those early months of the conflict, most of the Americans who were captured were either paroled, exchanged, or placed in hastily improvised local military prisons. Any such expedient seemed acceptable to the British. No one worried much about prisoners in the first encounters between the British army and the newly formed colonial forces.

Then, in the summer and autumn of 1776, the situation regarding American prisoners of war changed dramatically and the British could no longer ignore a growing problem. General William Howe's New York and New Jersey campaigns were conducted with an astonishing degree of success and yielded, by eighteenth-century standards, a host of prisoners. In a report to his superiors in London dated December 13, 1776, Howe declared that the army detained at least 4,430 American officers and enlisted men. It was at this point that the British army and the American forces had to begin to examine the prisoner of war issue with greater attention.

From the beginning of the war in America until the final evacuation of the British army in 1783, the New York City area became the site of the main detention centers for American captives captured while under arms against royal forces. American captives were first quartered in a prison the British called the Provost. The Provost was the city's Old Jail, which had been slightly renovated and renamed. In addition to the Provost, the British also used New Bridewell, the city's other jail, as a military prison. As the flood of captives swept into the city in late 1776, additional prisons had to be opened. The quickest answer to the dilemma the British faced was to employ some of the old sugar warehouses along the waterfront as the primary sites for holding the prisoners reaching the city. Three sugar houses, Van Courtland's, Rhinelander's, and Liberty Street, were converted to prisons and earned notorious reputations. The sugar warehouses were not equipped to be suitable prisons, and since Liberty Street remained in operation throughout the war, it acquired a particularly somber reputation. Van Courtland's and Rhinelander's were smaller versions of Liberty Street, and they functioned as prisons only into 1777, but they were equally undesirable in the environment they provided to the captives. In addition to the sugar houses, other sorts of structures were also pressed into service as prisons. King's College, City Hall, and several of the city's churches were temporarily employed as prison compounds as the British struggled to develop housing for all their captives. King's College, City Hall, and most of the city's municipal facilities used to house the captives were eventually returned to less unhappy tasks and the churches were eventually converted into hospitals once the numbers of captives held in the city declined in 1778.

American captives taken by the British army were also confined elsewhere. As the theaters of operations shifted during the war, new prisons were created. Since the British army rarely occupied any area, other than New York City, for an extended period of time, the prisons outside the New York system flourished and then disappeared when the army moved to new fields of operations. Prisons were established in Philadelphia, Pennsylvania, when that city was occupied briefly; prisons were created in Charleston, South Carolina, and Savannah, Georgia, when they fell to British forces late in the war, and other small temporary sites were opened and closed as the vagaries of the war dictated. In all the prisons established by the British on the North American continent, there was never a time when more than approximately 5,500 Americans were detained in them. At times during the war when there was a lull in military activity, such as in 1778–1779, the total number of Americans held in the British army's prisons declined to less than 1,000.

In 1776, in an effort to cope with a rising prison population, Howe created the post of Commissary General of Prisoners. The commissary general's tasks were to oversee the administration of existing prisons, the creation of new prisons, to establish rules for the treatment of prisoners, to issue rations and clothing, to provide medical care, and to see exchanges of captives if such opportunities arose. Joshua Loring, an American Loyalist from Massachusetts, was appointed to fill the post, and it was he who dealt with the prisoners on a daily basis. Loring became notorious among Americans and symbolic to them as the representative of a thoughtless enemy's policy toward its captives. Actually, Loring was the agent of a poorly conceived program that caused misery among the prisoners more through neglect and mismanagement than by any policy of premeditated cruelty. The British never solved their problems in prisoner care during the war; although they did, from time to time, seek to reform the system and to improve the conditions in the several prisons.

One means the British employed to reduce the congestion in the prisons and to provide better accommodations for some American captives was to parole them to live in the homes of local citizens. This policy of paroling Americans (nearly always commissioned officers) was first begun in the New York City area. In 1776, a number of American officers were paroled and allowed to live in the homes of carefully selected residents of New York City. Then, as the number of private dwellings in the city that were qualified to billet captive officers was exhausted, the British decided to continue the program and sought quarters elsewhere for the newly arriving American captives. Such villages on Long Island as Flatbush, Flatlands, New Eutrecht, Gravesend, Bedford, and New Lots were deemed suitable sites to house the parolees until they could be exchanged or until the war ended. Thus, in 1777, the British enlarged the policy of paroling American officers and soon scores of them were living on Long Island and impatiently awaiting an end to their captivity.

Captured American seamen also endured difficult conditions during the American Revolution. As hostilities formally commenced between Great Britain and her former colonies, privateering became a major portion of the wartime naval activities of the states and the Continental Congress. In addition to authorizing privateering forays against British shipping, both the Congress and the states attempted to create navies, and while all these endeavors met with varying degrees of success, one of the inevitable consequences was that a good many Americans were taken captive by the British navy.

The British navy was no better prepared to deal with captives than was the British army at the outset of the war. As many American sea-men were taken in 1776, the navy had to turn its attention to a growing problem already somewhat familiar to the army under Howe's command. The basic solution to the prisoner question was a simple one. Once the British were safely ensconced in New York City, the navy converted an old vessel, the *Whitby*, into a floating prison and anchored her near Remsen's Mill on the western end of Long Island. The *Whitby* was stripped of all her usable fittings, speedily modified to house prisoners, and pressed into service as the navy's first major effort at solving its shortage of space to detain captives. Using old and useless vessels as prisons proved so easy and simple a task that the navy quickly adopted this plan as its means to cope with its rising crisis of prisoner containment. Other ships were obtained and commissioned as prisons. Most of the prison ships were eventually located in Wallabout Bay (the site of the present-day New York Naval Shipyard) on the western end of Long Island just across the East River from New York City. Before the war finally ended, at least twenty-six ships at one time or another were anchored on Wallabout Bay, on the East River, or on the Hudson River, where they served as prisons. In addition to the prison hulks situated on the New York area waterways, three more vessels were converted to use as hospitals to provide medical attention to those captives who fell seriously ill. Prison ships were also in evidence in Charleston after the British occupied that city in 1780, and a prison ship was stationed at St. Lucia in the West Indies as a drop point for captured American seamen out of privateers taken by patrolling British warships as they tried to stem American raids on their shipping. American seamen were also confined in prisons in Halifax, Nova Scotia; St. Augustine, East Florida; and other places such as Philadelphia, while the city was occupied by the British army in late 1777 and early 1778. Sooner or later, however, surviving captured American seamen, taken in the Western Hemisphere, were transferred to the prison fleet at New York City, where the captives then awaited an exchange that might set them free, an end to hostilities, or some other turn of fate that would terminate their misery. Prison ships were notorious for their miserable living conditions, harsh discipline, high death rate among their inmates, and for their gloomy, foreboding environments and images.

American seamen who were captured outside American waters usually suffered a different fate than those seized near the North American mainland. Most of these men were transported to Great Britain, where they were incarcerated in one of two prisons. Forton Prison, near Portmouth, and Mill Prison, near Plymouth, became the focal points for detention of American seamen captured at locations too distant from New York to make it practical to send them there to sit out the war. Both sites became fairly notorious among Americans, as Mill and Forton (or "Fortune" as it was facetiously termed by its inmates) functioned as prisons for the duration of the war. Conditions for the captives in either prison were not ideal, but on the whole, the Americans were treated fairly well by their captors. For brief periods, Americans were also detained in Senegal in Africa, in ports in Portugal aboard British warships, and on the island of Guernsey before they were dispatched to Mill or Forton, where regular facilities had been established to control naval prisoners of war.

The actual number of captives detained by the British navy and its various adjuncts is difficult to determine. At the end of 1777, for example, the available sources of information would seem to indicate that about 2,500 Americans were situated in the British prison fleet in New York and the prisons in England. As the war dragged on and as the privateering efforts of the United States escalated, the numbers of captives steadily rose. By 1780, the number of American seamen held in the various prisons probably peaked at a high of about 5,300. A host of problems arises when trying to develop a census of the men captured and imprisoned by the Royal Navy. The greatest problem, other than the passing of time and the inevitable attrition of public records, is that the eighteenth century did not exhibit the modern-day penchant for record keeping, and what few efforts were undertaken have survived in fragmentary form. As a result, about all modern-day historians can do is to estimate how many captives the British made on the high seas.

Throughout the war, David Sproat, who was stationed in America, held the post of Commissary General of Naval Prisoners, and he, like his counterpart for the British army, Joshua Loring, was charged with the responsibility of handling all the affairs related to the welfare of naval prisoners. Sproat set the standards through which the captives were treated by their captors, conducted the negotiations to exchange American seamen for captured British sailors, and dealt with nearly every question that touched upon the day-to-day welfare of American naval captives. Sproat became a notorious figure in the eyes of many American Patriots, who believed he was a particularly vindictive man. Both Sproat and Loring, who were less than wholly desirable human beings, were principally handicapped by a poorly formed and poorly executed policy that often led to neglect of prisoners. Understandably enough, Americans were disposed to view British shortcomings in the treatment of their captives as clear-cut cases of wanton cruelty; in reality, many American captives did suffer, but they were not the objects of a savage policy of reprisal.

The questions of the treatment and exchanging of prisoners of war became an acrimonious quarrel between Great Britain and the United States and remained so throughout the conflict. In an effort to ameliorate the hardships Americans faced while languishing in enemy prisons, the Continental Congress decided to establish an agency to see to their needs. The office of a Commissary General of Prisoners was organized, and Elias Boudinot was nominated to serve as the first commissary general. Boudinot was commissioned a lieutenant colonel in the Continental Army and given the authority to attend the needs of Americans held in British prisons, effect exchanges of captives, and determine policy regarding British personnel held by American military agencies. Boudinot's powers were substantial and his responsibilities awesome; the well-being of a good many men was literally placed in his hands. One of the first steps Boudinot took was to persuade the British to let him send an agent into New York City to live there on a permanent basis and to function as a representative of the commissary general's department. Lewis Pintard, an American who had been engaged in commerce in the city prior to the war, agreed to accept the task of serving as Boudinot's agent in New York City and a relief program for American captives was inaugurated. Shipments of food, fuel, clothing, and money were authorized by Boudinot and supervised by Pintard. The standard British policy was to issue each American captive food rations equal to two-third's the daily allowance of a British soldier. Food allotments made to the British soldier were none too generous, and as a result, most Americans found their daily fare inadequate and monotonous. Clothing, bedding, and other necessary articles were always in short supply among the prisoners, and Boudinot sought to provide as many of these items as his meager means would permit. Boudinot's efforts to improve the lives of American captives did yield important results, although he and Pintard lamented the fact that they did not have the resources to effect a complete relief of all the prisoners' urgent needs. As the war dragged on, Boudinot was eventually succeeded by John Beatty, and Pintard was replaced by John Franklin as the New York agent for the commissary general's office.

Regardless of who the commissary general may have been, the American effort to relieve the captives' distress was an ongoing one that enjoyed only limited success. Nevertheless, many American captives found their lives in British prisons made somewhat easier by the sustenance they received from the American relief program. Efforts to aid American captives in Mill and Forton prisons in England were far less effective than those mounted to assist imprisoned American personnel in New York. Even so, Benjamin Franklin did the best that he could to aid American seamen who ended their voyages in the British prisons in England. Franklin's approach was to locate someone in England who would take a friendly interest in the captives and then provide as much aid as he could muster for them through a British intermediary. In October 1777, Franklin, who was at his diplomatic post in Paris, wrote to David Hartley, a member of Parliament, and asked Hartley to look into the conditions of the American captives and to provide them with whatever aid he could manage to deliver. Franklin promised to reimburse Hartley, which he did after Hartley visited the prisons and distributed a small amount of money among the prisoners he contacted. In addition to Hartley, Franklin also relied on Thomas Wren, a Presbyterian minister and resident of Portsmouth, England, and William Hodgson, a London merchant, to serve as his messengers to the English prisons. Whenever Franklin had funds available he sent them to either Wren or Hodgson, and they delivered them to the captives in either Mill or Forton prisons. Franklin constantly badgered Congress for appropriations for the captives, but, unfortunately, the sums of money set aside were small and only token relief was provided to the men. Congress, its representatives, and their agencies all did the best they could for the prisoners, but it was not enough.

Short of dying, a captive could expect to regain his freedom in one of four ways. First of all, a captive could attempt an escape from his captors. Escapes were dangerous, carried heavy penalties if the effort failed, and required a good deal of courage and some physical strength and endurance. Most prisoners, if they were to try an escape, normally had to resort to such an effort early in their captivity, since the loathsome conditions of the prisons usually sapped their strength to a level that they soon lacked the stamina to make good on an escape attempt. Many Americans did escape from British prisons, but such an action on the part of the captives was a truly desperate decision and usually taken when the captives believed there was no alternative. A second means open to Americans for release from the enemy's prisons was to enlist in either the British army or the British navy. It was common procedure for the British recruiters to visit the prisons and offer Americans the opportunity to enlist and to escape the threatening conditions the men faced in their new and intimidating environment. American authorities soon become convinced that the British deliberately kept the prisons as horrid pens in order to encourage the enlistment of frightened and dejected American captives. In reality, there was no conscious policy on the part of the British military command to use the prisons as a means to coerce Americans into enlisting in either the army or the navy. While some Americans did join the enemy's forces, the haphazard efforts to recruit American prisoners of war into the British military met with little success.

The quickest form of release from British prisons available to Americans was by a parole. A parole, if a prisoner was fortunate enough to obtain one, simply meant that the parolee was to take no further part in hostilities until he was formally exchanged as a prisoner of war. The terms of paroles varied. A British commander, usually the deputy of the commander-in-chief, set the conditions through which a prisoner was admitted to parole. Prisoners were often released and allowed to return to their homes and remain there so long as their conduct was neutral. A parolee also agreed to return to captivity any time the British revoked the privilege of parole. Another type of parole was to allow captives to live outside the prisons but to require them to reside in the immediate area where they had been imprisoned, similar to the policy inaugurated at New York City in 1776. The British used a policy of paroling American personnel rather freely. Paroling captives had, from the British viewpoint, several positive aspects. Paroling American captives, mostly officers, would, the British reasoned, encourage similar treatment of captured British officers. Additionally, paroling captives also reduced the congestion in the already overcrowded prisons and simultaneously conveyed the image of a forceful yet humane adversary to the Americans. Consequently, the British military forces resorted to paroling large numbers of Americans throughout the war.

The commonest path to freedom for a captive was through an exchange of prisoners. Exchanges of prisoners were made irregularly during the Revolution, but they often involved considerable numbers of men. At the outset of the war, American authorities attempted to establish a means for a routine exchange of captives, but the British proved reluctant to enter into a formal agreement. This reluctance was promoted by a belief by the British that any formal agreement for the exchange of prisoners might be interpreted by Britain's European enemies as a tacit recognition of American independence and encourage them to involve themselves openly on behalf of the colonies. As a consequence, the British would only accept a policy of partial exchange. A partial exchange was nothing more than a gentlemen's agreement between two military commanders for an exchange of a specified number of captives at a specified time and place. Then, once a partial exchange was transacted, another agreement would have to be negotiated for the next repatriation of captives. It was a cumbersome policy and subject to all manner of whims and political pressures, but the British felt that partial exchanges avoided the appearance of recognizing American sovereignty and thereby served diplomatic ends. Whether such a policy did in fact forestall action on the part of Britain's enemies is doubtful, but the British high command believed that it was performing an important diversion of more dangerous adversaries and remained inflexible on the exchange question.

Although the British proved reticent to enter into a formal commitment governing the exchange of captives, Washington, who was delegated broad powers by the Continental Congress on the question of prisoner exchanges, never relented in his quest for such an arrangement. A "cartel" was the term that Washington used for the desired general agreement that would promote an automatic exchange of prisoners, and he regularly pressed his British opponents for such an accord. In the early months of the war, numbers of American captives in British prisons exceeded the total of British personnel taken into American custody, and as a result, Washington's bargaining position to seek a cartel, or any exchange of prisoners, was a poor one. Nevertheless, he convened a meeting in March 1777 in Brunswick, New Jersey, between his representatives and those of Howe, the commander-in-chief of the British army, to develop the mechanics for a proposed cartel. Since few British soldiers had been lost to the Americans and since the Americans also sought to establish a cartel, the meeting quickly foundered and produced no agreement of any sort. While a comprehensive pact governing prisoner exchanges could not be developed at this juncture, partial exchanges negotiated by the appointed deputies of the two commanders-in-chief were effected. In 1777, American fortunes in the war changed somewhat with the capture of General John Burgoyne's army at Saratoga that autumn, and the whole issue of prisoners of war took on a different context. Now, for the first time, Washington appeared to have an improved bargaining position. In what proved to be a vain effort to establish a cartel, Washington again instructed his deputies to seek a meeting with the enemy and to arrange a comprehensive exchange of captives. During 1778, a total of three prisoner exchange conferences were held at Germantown (Pennsylvania), Newtown (Pennsylvania), and Amboy (New Jersey), successively. From the American point of view, each of the meetings proved a disappointment. The British remained reluctant to enter into any type of a formal agreement for the exchange of captives; but they eagerly sought to continue the policy of partial exchanges. So, for the balance of 1778 and into early 1779, captives were regularly repatriated in partial exchanges guaranteed by the personal word of honor of the commanding officers who authorized the agreements. Another prisoner exchange conference was held in April 1779 in Amboy, New Jersey, and it proved to be a reprise of the earlier conferences. The British continued to insist on partial exchanges and the

American negotiators again pressed for a cartel. Since they soon deadlocked, the conference dissolved, and, in effect, the British triumphed since for the remainder of the year several partial exchanges were transacted. In early 1780, Washington again applied pressure to his counterpart in the British army, General Henry Clinton, and sought to establish a formal understanding on how captives ought to be routinely exchanged. In March 1780 two conferences were held in Amboy, and each failed to achieve the results Washington desired. Eight prisoner-of-war conferences were convened between 1777 and 1783 and only the last of them witnessed a significant alteration in the British position regarding exchanges. From the beginning of the war through 1782, the American authorities were forced to content themselves with partial exchanges, and while a cartel would have been more satisfying to Washington, thousands of Americans regained their freedom as they were exchanged for British personnel through the informal policy that emerged during the war. Then, as the war came to its conclusion in 1782, another exchange conference was held at Tappan, New York, for the specific purpose of establishing guidelines for the final repatriation of all personnel. The Tappan meeting failed to produce the final exchange agreement. Nevertheless, partial exchanges on a broader scale were developed and the general cartel issue remained open to debate. Finally, on May 6, 1783, Washington and General Sir Guy Carleton met at Tappan, New York, and solved all the remaining questions that obstructed a general exchange of all captives. By July 1, 1783, Washington notified Benjamin Lincoln, the American secretary of war, that the general exchange of prisoners was finished except for a few German mercenaries who were about to be liberated. Later that month, Benjamin Franklin recorded that all Americans once detained in Great Britain had been set at liberty. After slightly more than eight years of wrestling with the complicated and emotional question of prisoners of war, all the captives were at last free of their captors.

Prisoners of war did suffer during the American Revolution. No other conclusion can be reached regarding the welfare of captives on both sides. Men were beaten, deprived of food by corrupt officials, denied bedding and clothing, and harassed in other ways but, fortunately, such incidents of outright cruelty were not routine events. Actually, most of the suffering of the men came from the more subtle torment usually brought on by neglect on the part of their captors. Neither the American nor the British authorities sought to induce suffering among the men in their prisons, yet the men did want for basic services. The shortcomings on both sides of the conflict in providing for the captives were evident, but the motivations behind the failures were not evil or vindictive in their origination. Neither party entered a program of deliberately tormenting prisoners. Rather, the failure to support the prisoners adequately stemmed from the complicated issues surrounding what was then a unique war. The limitations of the eighteenth century's technological and medical skills contributed to the dreadful care the captives received, and it can also be safely asserted that the contemporary military mind was not overly concerned with the welfare of those unfortunate men who became prisoners of war. The British response to the issue of American prisoners of war was poorly handled, and in many instances, it lacked direction and proper supervision, but the British policy could not be typified as deliberately cruel. *See also*: Asgill-Huddy-Lippincott Affair; British Prison Ships of New York City; Convention Army; Hayne, Isaac, Execution of

Larry G. Bowman

REFERENCES

Francis Abell, *Prisoners of War in Britain, 1756–1815* (1914); Larry G. Bowman, *Captive Americans: Prisoners During the American Revolution* (1976); Danske Dandridge, *American Prisoners of the Revolution* (1967); Charles Metzger, *The Prisoner in the American Revolution* (1971); Catherine M. Prelinger, "Benjamin Franklin and the American Prisoners of War in England During the American Revolution," *William and Mary Quarterly*, 32 (1975):261–94; Olive Anderson, "The Treatment of Prisoners of War During the American War of Independence," *Bulletin of the Institute of Historical Research*, 27 (1955):63–83.

Privateers

When on March 19, 1776, the Continental Congress authorized American ships to conduct privateering operations against British merchant ships, they only instituted a traditional form of naval warfare. Privateering had been practiced by Americans since the first French and Indian War (known in Europe as King William's War,

1689 to 1697). There were some individuals who continued the practice after the war was over, becoming pirates.

A merchant ship became a privateer when its owner obtained from the Continental Congress or one of the state provincial congresses a letter of marque and reprisal. This document authorized the holder to seize enemy merchant ships and then to sell them. Once the privateer arrived in a port with its "prize," an agent for the owner of the privateer brought a condemnation suit against the prize ship in a local admiralty court. If the court determined that the ship was an enemy vessel, it was condemned and sold at auction. The money received from the sale of the ship went to the owner or partners, the prize agent, the captain, and the crew. The amount that a crew member received was determined by his rank, while the prize agent and owners had determined the size of their shares before the privateer had left port.

Some privateer owners made huge fortunes during the war of the Revolution and some crews also did well, for a number of seamen had their yearly wages doubled by a good sale. However, the risks were great for Americans. Their letters of marque and reprisal had been issued by governments that had not been recognized by His Majesty's government. This meant that if a privateer was captured by a ship of the Royal Navy, its crew was considered a band of pirates and could be hanged as such. Execution was infrequent, but as prisoners their treatment was terrible and many died in the hulls of British prison ships and in infamous prisons in England.

Many privateers had obtained letters of marque and reprisal from Congress and the states, which makes an exact determination of the number of ships engaged in privateering difficult to estimate. A determination is even harder to make when one considers that many shipowners did not bother obtaining authorization from either Congress or the states. We know that Massachusetts issued 1,000 letters of marque and reprisal, while South Carolina, Maryland, Rhode Island, Connecticut, and New Hampshire issued letters as well. Congress itself issued another 1,697 letters. Taking into account that one ship may have had two or three letters, one can estimate that about 2,500 to 3,000 American ships were authorized to attack British shipping. It has been estimated by several scholars that approximately 70,000 men served on American priva-

teers. These men were lured to the ships by the possibility of making a fortune. This hampered the growth of the Continental Navy, where prize money was lower because Congress received half the value of the prize ship. There were even cases of soldiers deserting their units and farmhands leaving the land in order to make money at sea.

When the fighting first started, Americans put to sea in virtually any vessel they could find. As the war progressed American privateers became faster, more maneuverable, and more seaworthy in contests with the Royal Navy. By the war's end American privateers often carried about 15 to 20 guns. Privateers carried large crews because when an enemy merchantman was captured a prize crew was put on board to bring her into port. The prize crew consisted of enough men to bring the ship into port. If a privateer had captured many ships, its crew could be quite diminished as it returned to home port.

American privateers were bold. Many positioned themselves close to New York City, within sight of the watches in the crow's nest of British ships, where British seamen could see the Americans capture British merchantmen as they entered or left the harbor. Sometimes American privateers even took prizes that were escorted by the Royal Navy. Once during a foggy night in 1779 three American privateers came upon a British convoy. The Americans pretended to be British warships and within a few days they were able to capture and keep eight ships (three were recaptured). The American privateers' favorite hunting grounds were the Caribbean, and the coasts of Ireland and England. Prizes taken in the Caribbean were taken to Charleston, South Carolina, before that city fell in 1780. Philadelphia, Boston, and Providence were used by privateers operating in northern waters. In Europe, once France and Spain entered the fray, Americans brought their prizes to ports in these countries.

American privateers did well during the war. Lloyd's of London, who insured many British merchantmen and therefore had a reason to keep records on such matters, stated that American privateers captured about 3,100 ships, 900 of which were retaken or ransomed. By 1778 American privateers had taken about 2 million pounds' sterling worth of British ships and cargoes. Insurance rates rose throughout the war, and many British merchants took to shipping their goods in foreign ships, which was another blow to the

British merchant marine. It is not surprising that there was a strong antiwar sentiment in the British merchant community.

The American Patriots were not the only ones to engage in privateering. Their opposites, the American Loyalists, as well as the British, also had privateers. Once New York City was firmly in British hands (by September 1776) it became a major base of operations for Loyalist privateers (other bases were located in Jamaica and the British West Indies, where Loyalist privateers were constructed). Many Loyalist privateers operating from New York City received their letters of marque and reprisal from William Tryon, the last royal governor of New York. In one year (September 1778 to August 1779) Tryon issued about 120 letters. Most of these privateers operated from New York City, where they found a ready market for their prizes. New York City had difficulty in obtaining foodstuffs locally, so when a Loyalist privateer brought in a prize ship that had been carrying food, there were individuals waiting to pay high prices for the cargo.

In the spring of 1779, Tryon reported to his superior that for the period from September 1778 to March 1779 Loyalist British privateers hauled 150 prizes into New York City, where the ships brought 600,000 pounds' sterling of goods on the market. Loyalist privateers actively recruited the soldiers and sailors of His Majesty's army and Royal Navy to serve on their ships. British officers had to remind their men that they could be put to death for desertion.

Privateering operations were conducted right up to the end of the war in 1783. Militarily the privateers of each side were not important, but the American privateers did perform a particular service. As mentioned above they created a strong antiwar sentiment in the politically influential British mercantile community. This attitude helped bring the British to terms.

Anthony P. Inguanzo

REFERENCES

William B. Clark, *Ben Franklin's Privateers: A Naval Epic of the American Revolution* (1956); Nathan Miller, *Sea of Glory: The Continental Navy Fights for Independence, 1775–1783* (1974); Bertram M.H. Rogers, "The Privateering Voyages of the Tartar of Bristol," *Mariners Mirror,* 17 (1931):236–243; Page Smith, *A Now Age Now Begins: A People's History of the American Revolution,* 2 vols. (1976); Thomas Jefferson Wertenbacker, *Father*

Knickerbocker Rebels: New York City During the Revolution (1945).

Privateers of North Carolina

The North Carolina coast was the site of sporadic naval activity throughout the Revolution. The North Carolina coast is characterized by dangerous shoals and reefs, narrow and shallow inlets, shifting channels around numerous barrier islands, and the stormy weather that has given the Cape Hatteras region the unenviable nickname "The Graveyard of the Atlantic." These conditions severely hampered peacetime commerce but proved to be an asset during wartime. The British navy, stretched thin by its global obligations, never made a concerted, sustained effort to shut down oceanborne trade in the state.

In order to protect this shipping, the North Carolina government established a state navy. This five-ship navy consisted of three two-masted brigs and two galleys. The brigs, apparently converted merchantmen, were the 120-ton *Pennsylvania Farmer* (16 carriage guns, 10 swivels guns, 110 men), the *General Washington,* and the *King Tammany* (12 carriage guns). This navy was not particularly effective. It was poorly organized and underfinanced. On a few occasions the three brigs were sent privateering but came back empty-handed. The most notable action involving the navy occurred in 1778 when the *Pennsylvania Farmer* went trading in the West Indies. On its return the ship's captain, Joshua Hampstead, sold the cargo of arms, ammunition, and salt, pocketed the money, and fled the state. The ineffectual brigs became such a drain on the state's treasury that the *General Washington* was sold in 1778 and the *Pennsylvania Farmer* was scuttled in 1779. It is not certain what happened to the *King Tammany* except that it disappeared from the public records sometime during 1780.

A major reason for the failure of North Carolina's fledgling navy was its inability to obtain competent and reliable crews. For several reasons, experienced sailors preferred to crew with one of the privateers funded by merchants in New Bern, Edenton, and other North Carolina port cities. The privateers were relatively free of strict military discipline, spent the overwhelming majority of their time in pursuit of prizes, and offered the chance of great wealth.

It is not clear how often this opportunity for wealth was realized. Records for North Carolina privateers are sketchy. Because of this it is not possible to determine the exact number of privateers that operated from the state. Nonetheless, it is certain that several attained a measure of success against the British.

One of the most successful was the *Bellona*, owned by New Bern shipbuilder Richard Ellis. In 1778 the 16-gun brig captured at least four ships, including the brig *Elizabeth*, from St. Augustine, loaded with indigo and lumber, and the schooner *Actaeon*, bound from New York to New Providence with specie. In 1780 the *General Nash* seized two armed ships, one from Scotland with a cargo of tea, sugar, wine, dry goods, and hardware valued at 10,800 pounds and the other from St. Kitts, carrying sugar, rum, and fruits. Other privateers operating from North Carolina included the *Lydia*; the sloop *Betsey*; the 14-gun, 100-man *Sturdy Beggar*; the *Chatham*; the 120-ton *Fanny*; and the 100-ton *Rainbeau*.

Privateering in North Carolina, as elsewhere during the war, was efficient. Ships operated individually, with few attempts made to coordinate actions, while little captured cargo directly reached the American fighting forces. In addition, squabbling over the prizes was not uncommon. In one celebrated episode the privateers *Grand Turk* and *Dolphin* captured the British schooner *Three Friends* in Edenton in 1782 and then took the prize to Virginia. North Carolina and Virginia officials feuded over the ship for months, although it remained in the latter state before being sold. Yet in the absence of a strong state navy, privateering was the only available option for contesting the British at sea.

Jim Sumner

REFERENCES

Randolph B. Campbell, "An Incident in Maritime Regulation During the Revolutionary War," *Virginia Magazine of History and Biography*, 74 (1966); Walter Clark, ed., *The State Records of North Carolina* (1895–1905); Charles Christopher Crittenden, *The Commerce of North Carolina, 1763–1789* (1936); Norman C. Delaney, "The Outer Banks of North Carolina During the Revolutionary War," *North Carolina Historical Review*, 36 (1959); William N. Still, Jr., *North Carolina's Revolutionary War Navy* (1976).

Propaganda in the American Revolution

Propaganda issued by both colonists and Britons during the American Revolution played a significant role in manipulating public opinion on both sides of the ocean. In the colonies, especially in New England, Patriots organized propaganda through meetings and publications. Propaganda can be defined as an organized effort to disseminate ideas and policies such as the Revolutionary ideology of independence. Although propaganda was presented in a tangible form such as newspapers, pamphlets, and speeches, its concepts were often abstract and could be interpreted in a variety of ways.

Because its ultimate purpose was to control the actions of the populace's attitudes, propaganda was issued both indirectly and directly. It was also both intentional and unintentional, with some aspects of presentation proving more successful than the original plan. Propaganda was spread over an extensive area for the necessary task of uniting dissenters, such as the colonists, against British dominance.

In the American Revolution, the propaganda leadership was small but had a great influence. Many of the men came from wealthy families and had been distinguished in the decades before the Revolution in cultural and intellectual circles. There were many levels of propaganda: not only did propagandists use newspapers and pamphlets but they facilitated literary, political, and religious outlets. For the most part, in their propaganda, Whigs depended on attracting mobs who would pose a physical threat to the British. They tried to appeal to the working and lower classes by relying on tales of folk heroes as examples of Revolutionaries. For all classes they used the media of songs, theater, magazines, ceremonies, and almanacs—for a few examples—to convey their propaganda.

The propagandists for the most part were from the segment of colonial society that controlled politics internally; they were assemblymen who had protested against English abuses present in parliamentary acts that affected the structure of the colonies. At first the men subtly hinted that they disagreed with British policy, but as they became more angry and braver, their accusations were blatant, in the form of anonymous declarations, although most of the men publicly denied making the statements. The propagandists considered the issue of reconciliation versus independence, realizing that in order to secure the latter the support of the people would be crucial.

They also understood that the propagandists could have disagreements and that the resulting factions could prove detrimental in the attempt for propaganda to unify the colonists. The propagandists used the eighteenth-century natural rights philosophy as a rationalization for their action, claiming that they were innately good men versus evil institutions as represented by Britain and that they had natural rights to land, property, and freedom. Through this anti-Tory propaganda aimed to achieve freedom for all colonial citizens, the various classes were united by a common voice.

Propaganda was present for at least a decade before the Revolution in the form of speeches, sermons, articles, and resolutions. However, it was never centralized or unified. Local organizations and correspondence were the only means to synchronize efforts in towns. The propagandists were able to use government agencies because of their access to political assemblies. They printed commentary on their beliefs and activities in newspapers and announced them at town meetings, which became banned in many cities when they were viewed by royal officials as detrimental. Through committees of correspondence, such as the one organized in Boston by Samuel Adams, local agitation was unified through protests to arouse the people and, most importantly, to disseminate propaganda. Embellished newspaper accounts reinforced dissatisfaction. By canvassing the county, the propagandists were in touch with rural opinion, and by August 1774 the propaganda machine was in place throughout the colonies for the Revolution.

Merchants and mechanics were especially affected by British legislation and organized during the early period of propaganda. The Boston merchants were the first to assemble. They sent petitions to Parliament and had their colonial assembly send petitions too, but these efforts were not well received in London. They then tried coercive measures such as nonimportation and boycotts of British goods. These protests worked, but because most merchants did not want to pursue political goals, being influenced solely by economic motives, they stopped their agitation. Propagandists achieved some economic relief as a result of the boycotts, but the merchants did not greatly alter colonial opinion.

The Sons of Liberty emerged as a working-class group to protest unfair British regulations. They were especially incensed by the Stamp Act, forming in the summer of 1765 and spreading throughout the colonies. In semisecret meetings, the workmen met to discuss solutions; they communicated with committees of correspondence to link with other Sons of Liberty groups in a network. Their efforts, for the most part, were successful. However, the original character of the Sons of Liberty changed after the repeal of the Stamp Act. The groups' composition varied, including nonworkmen, and they lacked widespread support. The workers formed other organizations to seek solutions for their needs, which were no longer coercive, political appeals. The dissemination of propaganda formerly done by the Sons of Liberty was now performed by committees of inspection and safety.

Propagandists began enlisting the aid of churches in 1775 to influence church members. Preachers such as Charleston's William Tennent orated fiery religious sermons to arouse their congregations. The church was the most powerful institution the propagandists could use to effectively organize and disseminate propaganda. Through religious institutions, the propagandists emphasized the moral aspects of their crusade against Britain. With endorsement from a church, the propagandists were guaranteed to be supported by its membership.

In 1775, 3,200 churches representing 18 denominations existed in the colonies. Through the variety of religious beliefs and interests, the propagandists could attract a diverse group of supporters by using varied messages to unify them. Ministers served as agents of propaganda. The ministers would publicly declare their opinions regarding revolution, which the membership accepted as being valuable and credible, and also reemphasized propaganda points on religious days of prayer and holidays such as Thanksgiving. Although not religiously oriented, Masonic lodges also encouraged their membership, which represented much of the male citizenry, to pursue revolution.

The propagandists chose the most suitable and appealing methods of propaganda and presented them selectively. There were four groups that had to be dealt with: nationals (for whom the propagandists tried to cultivate a hatred of the enemy); allies (whose friendship had to be retained); neutrals (whose neutrality needed to be stabilized); and the enemy (which the propagandists tried to demoralize). Each targeted group necessitated different methodologies to foment revolution in the most unified manner possible. The propagandists pursued four basic aims: to justify the propaganda course they advocated, to demonstrate the advantage of a Patriot victory, to arouse hatred for the enemy, and to neutralize unfavorable portrayals of the colonists by the enemy.

The propagandists circulated in towns throughout the 13 colonies so that they could be in touch with the people's opinions, attitudes, and prejudices, and subsequently, link the diverse groups by implementing general and vague propaganda that each group could interpret differently for the ultimate goal of dissent. In the propaganda both rewards and warnings were used as incentives for acceptance. Two objectives included preventing enforcement of British legislation and ultimately acquiring independence. In order to do this, the propagandists attempted to justify their opposition and reiterated their legal rights, stressing that the British parliamentary acts violated colonial self-interest. The Patriot propagandists emphasized the future freedoms, both civil and religious, that could be acquired with victory. They noted that the colonists would win safety and security. To rationalize revolution, the propagandists commented that foreign aid would be issued only after the colonies declared their independence from Britain.

Revolutionary propagandists related their actions with the worldwide campaign for liberty. They depicted the colonists as being more honest and cultivating a higher civilization than Great Britain. The Mother Country was portrayed to be frenzied with hate, corruption, fraud, and immorality. Propagandists reveled in making personal attacks on the king and royal family. They also did not hesitate to construct embellished atrocity stories about true incidents such as the Boston Massacre.

The propagandists stressed that the colonists were not alone in their struggle because European nations would help and—in the best propaganda reasoning of all—because they believed that God sided with the colonies. Arguments that war was sinful were quickly overshadowed by

approval of and participation in revolutionary activities by ministers; propagandists bombarded the vulnerable populace with demonstrations, celebrations, and allegations. Propaganda was present in songs and plays (some craftily penned by Mercy Warren), which were available to both literate and illiterate residents. Effigies were hung, and revolutionary anniversaries were celebrated. Major propaganda events included leaders speaking or making symbolic gestures, the erection of liberty poles, dispersal of engraved caricatures, public addresses, and speaking tours. Some of these propaganda attempts backfired, with crowds becoming extremely hostile; speakers feared violent uprisings would emerge that might eventually defeat the propaganda's purpose. Written propaganda in the form of pamphlets, broadsides, almanacs, magazines, and newspapers reinforced oral statements and was viewed as being most important because people tended to believe and retain what they read. Newspapers symbolized their discontent and emotionally charged their rhetoric by printing coffins with names of martyred soldiers and civilians and publishing melancholic elegies.

Propagandists needed to counter enemy propaganda that suggested the English were stronger, confident of victory, and vital for colonial trade. The propagandists responded by reminding the common people—the easiest targets of the British—of the grievances they had and why the British should be blamed. British troops were pictured as being inferior. The propagandists ridiculed redcoats by printing alleged quotes by soldiers that expressed their discouragement. Propagandists were privy to captured letters when the British fled from some of the first engagements; these enemy retreats elated propagandists by giving them legitimate weapons to use.

Sam Adams was the best colonial propagandist, dispersing his work using at least 25 pseudonyms. He prolifically penned essays for the press, especially the *Boston Gazette*, for which he helped format and compile editorial content. He was on the Boston Committee of Correspondence, and although he was not regarded as a great orator, Adams used his literary skills to write consistently to colonial leaders in addition to producing various essays. He was especially significant for organizing propaganda in Massachusetts as well as throughout New England. His cousin, John Adams, was active in the Sons of Liberty and wrote, using his own name, in support of Samuel. Josiah Quincy, using the name "Hyperion," developed propaganda by touring the southern states and sailing to England, where he communicated ideas. Joseph Warren cleverly used emotional and strong language to convey his ideas. James Otis—who coined the infamous phrase "no taxation without representation"—helped inflame the lower classes in Boston to establish mob action.

Joseph Hawley, a lawyer outside Boston, organized dissent in the county and cooperated with Adams. Alexander Hamilton contributed polemical essays to the *New York Journal*. The Quaker John Dickinson penned in 1767 "Letters from a Farmer in Pennsylvania to the Inhabitants of the British Colonies," which denounced the Townshend Acts as well as composing the "American Liberty Song." Arthur, William, and Richard Henry Lee were prominent propagandists. Arthur and William were in England during much of the Revolution but were able to have access to leaders in America. In 1772 Arthur wrote Samuel Adams, "By bending all our attention to keeping alive in the People, a due sense of their wrongs, & by digesting a plan for their redress, we shall meet the first great occasion, perfectly prepared."

Sam Adams manipulated dissent by instigating the Boston Tea Party. Other events that did not directly result from the propagandists, such as the Boston Massacre, were in retrospect used to manipulate emotions. After the Boston Massacre, propagandists hired Henry Pelham to make engravings of dead martyrs, which were printed by Paul Revere to incite an emotional response in Boston's citizens.

At least 50 percent of colonial men and 25 percent of women were literate and could read written propaganda, which was circulated widely. The Patriots published justifications of their propaganda, emphasizing they were acting in national self-interest. They stressed the advantages of victory and the utter depravity of the enemy, categorizing George III as a tyrant and fool. They stressed patriotic anniversaries such as the 4th of July and the announcement of the French alliance. They spread rumors and falsehoods and accused the enemy of being evil through imagery in dreams, fables, and allegories, often caricaturing the British as the devil. Propaganda had created the Declaration of Independence, which in itself was a propaganda piece carefully crafted

by Thomas Jefferson, a master propagandist, to list grievances, each with a psychological impact aimed at persuading domestic and foreign readers. Many of the ideas expressed had been festering in the colonies for several decades. With the aid of Jefferson they were clearly expressed as common fears, hopes, and desires for the nation's future.

The Loyalists were unable to spread propaganda effectively until 1774. The British and Loyalists responded to Patriots' propaganda through defense of British actions. Anglican clergymen, such as Samuel Seabury, seemed to be credible sources of propaganda. Seabury as "A Westchester Farmer" wrote four pamphlets: in "Free Thoughts on the Proceedings of the Continental Congress" he appealed to farmers to remain loyal to the Crown; in "The Congress Canvassed" he appealed to merchants; in "A View of the Controversy Between Great Britain and her Colonies" he proposed that constitutional reforms should be sought to give colonists rights but to preserve the British Empire; "An Alarm to the Legislature of New York" asked that body to use its authority to settle the matter.

Loyalist and British propaganda had three goals: to uphold the authority of the king and Parliament but not any specific acts issued by them; to combat colonial riots instigated by Whig propaganda and to expose their methods as being illegal; and to offer alternative solutions to revolution. The Loyalist propaganda machine was never comparable to that created by the Whigs. Tory propaganda was limited to addresses to officials emphasizing their loyalty to the Crown and a few organizations; most Loyalist propaganda relied on the efforts of individuals, not groups.

The Tories countered Whig claims and defended that the British constitution could not be interpreted and thus the colonists had no grievances. The Loyalists also emphasized that the colonists were given the same rights as Englishmen and that the protested taxes were actually beneficial. The Tories stated that the colonists would only fail if they entered into a war against Britain, and promised a peaceful solution including trade protection and quality goods at low prices if the colonists quit their protests.

The British propaganda was based on alleged accounts of the Whigs' depravity and atrocities they had supposedly committed. The Tories wanted to maintain Loyalist morale and to demoralize the Patriots and colonists. The appealed to the colonists not to be deceived by Patriot promises because a revolution would only make their lives more insecure. The Tories stated that France would not help the colonies and that Congress would be unable to financially support a war. They emphasized that the colonists would never achieve victory. Relying on humor and satire, the Tories embellished statements, charging Patriots with mistreating British soldiers while trying to conceal stories that depicted the British and Loyalists unfavorably.

In May 1775 the first military propaganda broadside targeted the Royal Irish Regiment in New York by sympathizing with the men: "As the service on which you were sent here is dishonourable and injurious to your country, we have reason to think it is highly disagreeable to you." Realizing that the Irish had an inherent hate for the English, the Patriot propagandists promised that if they deserted, "You shall be protected against the Army and the military laws of Great Britain, which have no legal force in America."

The British also attempted to encourage desertion. Lieutenant General Thomas Gage called for Patriot withdrawal from Boston, and he distributed broadsides guaranteeing safety for deserters; two or three Patriots deserted with Gage, who ordered more propaganda sheets to be dispersed. They were discharged to Patriot camps at night by being wrapped around bullets and thrown into camp. Gage published his own broadsheet castigating rebel leaders and in turn was ridiculed in the Patriot press.

In the summer of 1776 the Howe brothers first coordinated the British military propaganda effort. Sir William Howe found abundant forage in Pennsylvania when he landed and realized that paying large bounties to residents for produce would be an excellent propagandistic device to gain their favor. He issued rules to his soldiers to be polite and to take only necessities because looting could destroy colonists' remaining loyalty to the British. He executed offenders to prove his intent to capitalize on good relations with colonial citizens.

Both Howes carried letters attesting to their good character and offering pardons to Patriots. They issued broadsheets to encourage desertion. By December 1776 the colonists were experiencing serial military defeats, and the British decided to take advantage of their low morale by encouraging further desertion and exacerbating their sense of frustration. Patriot propagandists responded by designing atrocity stories that embellished the looting and pillaging by British and Hessian soldiers. Tales of rape and crimes committed against young children were especially harmful to the British interests; sexual depravity of the British forces was a common theme utilized to lower the colonists' opinion of them.

Thomas Paine, a volunteer in the Conventional Army who had already published *Common Sense*, penned *The American Crisis*. He wrote: "Tyranny, like hell, is not easily conquered; yet we have this consolation with us, that the harder the conflict, the more glorious the triumph." General George Washington ordered officers to read Paine's document to troops in an attempt to encourage the demoralized troops. The victory at Trenton reversed the negative aspect of troops' morale, and patriotic propaganda proudly proclaimed the positive aspects of battle while denouncing the British.

A new propaganda phase began in January 1777. Washington issued a broadsheet especially targeted to those soldiers who had been persuaded by Howe's previous proclamation, telling them they should swear allegiance to America. Howe had encouraged them to retreat behind enemy lines. Desertion appeals were issued to both sides, and by March Howe offered full pardons and the value of weapons surrendered by any deserters. In May the Continental Congress prepared colonists for such propaganda, warning them not to be convinced.

They told them to beware of agents who:

> gain and transmit intelligence; they invent and propagate false and injurious reports; they create and foment jealousies between states and individuals; they magnify the power, numbers, and resources of the enemy; they undervalue yours. By these means, the timid are dismayed; and the honest but unsuspicious are misinformed and misled.

Washington told Congress that the British propaganda had "an unhappy influence on too many of the soldiers; in a particular manner on those who are not natives." He continued, "I could wish some means could be devised to cause more frequent desertions of their troops."

In Maryland, Howe distributed broadsheets to colonial soldiers, hoping "to disunite their army." Throughout 1777 the British continued issuing appealing rewards for desertion. During the winter of 1777 to 1778 the British especially tried to woo the soldiers suffering at Valley Forge. By March approximately 1,134 rebel soldiers and 354 sailors—mostly immigrants of Great Britain—had deserted and sworn an oath of allegiance to England at Howe's camp at Philadelphia. In April Congress offered to pardon Loyalist soldiers, printing the document in both German and English. The Loyalist *Evening Post* responded by stating that American troops would have to serve longer terms than they had been signed up for when volunteering, aspiring to demoralize the troops and encourage them to defect.

Washington responded to this lie:

> Our enemies, finding themselves unable to reduce us by force of their arms, are now practicing every insidious art to gain time and disunite us, but the General hopes that men who have struggled with every difficulty and encountered every danger are not to be conquered by artifices which are so easily exposed.

He dispatched secret agents to find information to use in future propaganda attacks; the British also had spies collecting intelligence to manipulate troops and public opinion.

In June 1778 the British peace commission, consisting of the Earl of Carlisle, William Eden, and George Johnstone, visited occupied Philadelphia to launch a propaganda campaign, which the Patriot propagandists labeled "a last dying speech." Their "Manifesto and Proclamation" was dispersed to the Continental Congress, governors, officers, and the citizenry, insisting that the colonists had originally only wanted grievances corrected, not revolution, and offering pardons if the rebellion concluded. The British carefully selected how to present their insinuations that the colonists lacked the authority to rebel and that war was more destructive than diplomatic attempts to resolve the conflict.

In October the Continental Congress advised colonists to prepare safe shelters outside battle vicinities and, if attacked, to seize, burn, and destroy any Loyalist property nearby to avenge the aggression. An October 30 manifesto countered British allegations and treaties, promising vengeance for wrongdoing in the colonies. The dissemination of propaganda and counter-propaganda multiplied rapidly, and by December the peace commission departed the colonies. In January 1779 propaganda in the southern colo-

nies became important as the battlefront shifted. Benedict Arnold's treason was used for propaganda; the British lamented that the colonists ignored two addresses written by Arnold ("What is America but a land of widows, beggars, and orphans?") that requested the colonists acquiesce to a peaceful solution to preserve the British Empire.

During the winter of 1779 and 1780 the British and Tories encouraged mutineers at the Morristown encampment. The camp experienced bitter winter weather, sickness, and a severe dearth of provisions—clothing, shelter, and food—as well as not being paid for several consecutive months. The British developed handbills with the aid of spies that sympathized with the men's distress and told them they should desert because their uncaring officers "can no longer conceal from you the misery of your situation. You are neither clothed, fed, nor paid. Your numbers are wasting away by sickness, famine, nakedness." In comparison, in January 1781 the Patriots had a British deserter, Henry Pumphrey, write appealing letters to his former military peers advising them "to escape from bondage and tyranny to liberty and happiness." In return, he promised that they would receive free land and rewards.

Propaganda was not confined to the colonies. In October 1774 the "Address to the Inhabitants of the Province of Quebec" was successful because of the French influence in Canada. Although Canadians resisted at first—primarily because many citizens were illiterate, could not read English, or resented the writers' criticisms of Quebec's administration and Catholic influence—some ultimately turned to embrace propaganda emitted from Boston. This acceptance was due largely to committee of correspondence agents who had traveled to Canada to communicate directly with residents. This personal attention was much more effective than written propaganda, and some French Canadians supported the Patriots' cause. The British capture of Ethan Allen in October 1775 proved to be a propaganda defeat, but when the Patriots captured St. Johns in November, the propaganda tide returned to the Patriots.

The British responded with psychological warfare techniques such as shooting letters into camps and cities on flaming arrows. They primarily aimed propaganda at citizens, believing that if they controlled civilian opinion they could also manipulate the military. The colonists used the French clergy to woo Canadians. General Sir Guy Carleton released Patriot prisoners so they could spread indoctrinated—and most often false or misleading—British propaganda. In October 1778 Admiral Comte d'Estaing released a broadside announcing the French alliance with the colonies to reassure friendly Indians as well as clergy. The Marquis de Lafayette also wrote propaganda to seal French–colonial relations.

The main role of propaganda designed for North American Indians was to assure their neutrality or to gain their allegiance. Beginning in 1775, the most effective propaganda to attract Indian attention was based on economic and military topics. The best mode of transmittal was verbal messages through agents or scouts because most Indians did not read English. In Indian propaganda the British had the advantage of prior alliances and trade relations; their argument that the colonists had encroached on Indian and British land was also convincing.

British propaganda attempts to win Indians' loyalty were countered by an incident that altered colonial opinion of Indians who supported English troops. Jane McCrea, a Loyalist soldier's fiancée, was kidnapped and killed by Indians who defended Major General John Burgoyne. Although Burgoyne had specifically forbidden Indians to murder civilians, the guards who secured McCrea disregarded his warning and publicly displayed her scalp. This blatant disregard for a woman's life horrified colonists, many of whom had not previously committed to the Revolutionary cause.

Major General Horatio Gates stated that Burgoyne had hired Indians to murder colonists; in fact, Gates asserted that Burgoyne received "a price for each scalp so barbarously taken," further enraging colonists. Now, believing the British incited Indians to murder, more colonists openly avowed revolution against the British. Indians fought on both sides during the Revolution, some aiding the rebels while others supported the British. The Continental Congress wanted the formal support of the Six Nations but finally decided that obtaining their neutrality was the best strategy.

Black slaves were used by the British as a weapon; they manipulated the colonists' fear of a slave insurrection. When the Earl of Dunmore issued a proclamation to free and arm blacks in Virginia, the colonists were astonished, reacting rashly. They planned for a regiment especially to combat any possible slave revolts. Meanwhile, the British organized a regiment of black soldiers by stealing slaves or enticing them to join the British in order to gain, as the British promised, their freedom. Henry Laurens suggested that the colonists also use blacks to fight for independence, but Washington discouraged him. The Continental Congress devised a plan for deploying black soldiers, but the ultimate decision rested with the states, who, with the exception of Rhode Island, strongly defeated the proposal.

The introduction of Hessian troops in the war provided another source for colonial propagandists. In August 1776 a committee consisting of Jefferson, James Wilson, and Richard Stockton sought inducements that would convince Hessians to quit fighting. Rewards to deserting Hessians included land, liberty, and protection. These were advertised in broadsides that were worded and distributed with the help of German immigrant and superintendent of bakers Christopher Ludwick. The sheets offered surrendering Hessians 50 acres and "they shall be protected in the free exercise of their respective religions, and be invested with the rights, privileges and immunities of natives, as established by the laws of these states."

A second broadside offered officers greater tracts of land; for example, a colonel would receive 1,000 acres, and the land amount decreased with each lower rank. Anthony Hasselaband, an early Hessian deserter, claimed that the Hessians were unhappy with their attachment to British troops because the British failed to pay them or provide ample provisions as promised when they were enlisted. Others Hessians were discontent because they had been forced to serve by being kidnapped or impressed through the use of alcohol, destruction of identification papers, or other deceptive methods.

The Patriots often released imprisoned Hessians, after indoctrinating them, to return to British troops and encourage more mercenaries to desert. British victories in the fall of 1776 resulted in German soldiers being less interested in defecting, but the Patriot victory at Trenton reversed this trend. At least 948 Hessian prisoners were captured; they were indoctrinated and taken to nearby German communities, where they were given employment and encouraged to become permanent settlers.

Franklin supposedly wrote *The Sale of the Hessians* in 1777, claiming that Great Britain and German princes had conspired for the sale of the mercenaries; in addition to being paid for every German soldier serving, the princes would receive "blood money" for every Hessian killed. Franklin wrote this propaganda in the form of a letter from fictional characters, Count de Schaumbergh to Baron Hohendorf, the supposed commander of Hessian troops, in order to convince the Hessians the document was valid. As the war continued, the Hessians become more discontent and vulnerable, and propagandists offered new inducements of land. The British meager response was to use captured Hessian agents as spies in the rebel camps. The Patriots' most successful propaganda campaign was the one targeted against Hessians, netting more than 5,000 defectors out of the 29,867 Germans deployed.

Other subversion propaganda included kidnapping leaders—or at least spreading rumors of possible attacks, especially on General Washington—and planting false rumors. Deceptive letters and bribes were valuable propaganda tools to encourage officers to defect. Major General Charles Lee was captured by the British in December 1776 and accused of treason because he had previously been commissioned in the British army and was considered a deserter. Congress attempted to arrange an exchange of five Hessians and an incarcerated British officer for Lee, but Lee was kept imprisoned for more than a year.

The Patriots captured the commander at Newport, Rhode Island, British Major General Richard Prescott, in July 1777. They discovered the general enjoying a tryst with a "nymph [who] thus spoil'd a General's mighty plan, and gave him to the foe—without his breeches." Washington exchanged Prescott for Lee.

The Loyalists performed much of the subversive activity for the benefit of British troops. Spreading rumors of possible schemes to poison leaders was a profitable method of chilling psychological warfare that kept officers and guards on edge. This nervousness and paranoia was harmful to military planning and implementation. Claims of germ warfare, such as colonists purposefully spreading smallpox, were generated by the British to denounce the Patriots and discredit them. Alarming rumors such as these were effective in manipulating citizens to spurn the Patriots and approve the British presence.

Propaganda designed for Europeans originated with the distribution of the Declaration of Independence. This document was carefully penned to appeal to France, who had suggested such a formal document needed to be prepared in order for the colonists to receive foreign financial aid. The Americans realized they had to make formal declarations of their intentions in order to attract the favor of European nations. Benjamin Franklin traveled to Europe, where he communicated Revolutionary concepts in both oral and written formats. He arranged for Common Sense and the Declaration of Independence to be published in French periodicals as well as other receptive European magazines.

These periodicals agreed to print colonial propaganda through excerpts from newspapers and pamphlets. Hoping to acquire foreign allies and cause England problems domestically, Franklin wrote "To the Good People of Ireland" in October 1778, focusing on that country because of its dissatisfaction with British rule. Foreigners received colonial propaganda both positively and negatively, but for the most part approved of the colonies rebellion. John Adams traveled to Holland and France during the Revolution as a congressional peace commissioner. In 1780 he contributed propaganda to Edmund Charles Genet's French newspapers as well as Dutch periodicals.

In 1782 Franklin wrote the "Supplement to the *Boston Independent Chronicle*" in an attempt to sway public opinion against Britain while the peace talks occurred so that the colonists might receive concessions. In a format similar to newspapers, Franklin printed propagandistic letters and essays, including an especially arousing piece describing numerous confiscated scalps that Indians had shipped to George III. The scalps were described grotesquely, explaining that bullet holes and knife marks were present. These gruesome details were designed to disgust colonists and cause them to demand retribution from Britain.

Colonial military leaders realized that the myth of colonial riflemen being strong and unconquerable was widely publicized. They decided to perpetuate this image and take advantage of British fears by dressing soldiers in buckskin garments designed to scare the enemy. Weaponry was another propaganda tool; the colonists promoted the rifle, although slow to reload, as being more reliable than the British bayonet.

In fact, Patriot soldiers were inexperienced and of poor quality. On all war theaters, most Revolutionary soldiers fought despite shortages of arms, supplies, food, clothes, blankets, shelter, medical care, and wages. As a result of deprivation, they became desperate and disillusioned and often expressed loyalty only to their colony and not the United States. Their hatred of other colonies created prejudices toward other troops and caused discipline problems and disunity. Many rebels were averse to service in regions other than near their home, only wanting to preserve independence for their colony.

In 1778 Inspector General Friedrich von Steuben attempted to instill in the troops respect for discipline, but mutinies and infractions resulted from the soldiers' sense of inferiority as compared to British forces. Poorly trained, the raw recruits exhibited panic and cowardice. Many had believed in 1775 that the war would be won quickly and were eager to quit when defeats occurred. Fewer recruits volunteered their services, and soldiers suffered from inactivity, boredom, and monotony during the winter lulls; desertion became prevalent with at least one-third of regular troops disappearing as fugitives as the war waned and they became homesick. The nonpayment of bounties demoralized troops, and hardships, including starvation and lack of proper clothing, lowered esteem and loyalty. These psychological factors were manipulated by the British in their propaganda against the colonies and troops.

Although sources of and physical equipment to produce propaganda were often inadequate, an effective outpouring of verbiage regulated morale at home, abroad, and in military circles. Even though delays and uncertainty about facts spawned rumors, or propagandists deliberately altered or ignored important factors, the resulting propaganda tended to persuade its audience as intended. Washington tried to establish centralized control over publicity. In 1777 Washington requested an allocation from Congress for a traveling press that would be located at headquarters "to give speedy and exact information of any Military transactions that take place with proper comments upon them."

Washington believed that these official reports would help correct falsehoods, be a centralized source of formal war reports, and help boost soldier morale by giving them access to factual news grounded on reports to headquarters that would be issued on a routine basis, but Congress delayed his efforts, and soldiers received Patriot propaganda only through public readings or limited dispersals of available materials. In contrast, British propaganda inundated camps, offering soldiers pardons and benefits unavailable from the Patriots.

Congress gave French printer Fleury Mesplet $200 in 1776 to put a press in Canada to distribute papers to the colonies and Canadians and to incite Hessians to desert, but the distribution was too slow for an overwhelming affect. In the southern colonies, Major General Nathanael Greene and Lafayette tried to establish presses to disseminate propaganda but failed to achieve a permanent organization. Military propaganda tended to be poorly organized and mostly created by officers and political propagandists who stressed the holy cause of the war, attempted to mislead enemy agents, tried to maintain good relations with the public, wanted to indoctrinate prisoners, and struggled to convert Tories to the Revolutionary cause; this propaganda was circulated in and near encampments.

The Revolutionaries fine-tuned their propaganda efforts, realizing that Washington was the most credible propaganda symbol for colonists, understanding the vulnerabilities of foreign powers, citizens, and mercenaries, and developing rhetoric that united the widespread opinions held by colonists. By using propaganda to control and manipulate opinion, the Revolutionary propagandists stimulated and sustained the colonists' desire for independence. Countering Tory and British propaganda that attempted to lower soldier and civilian loyalty, the Patriot propagandists maintained support and enhanced their cause. They realized that propaganda's suave rhetoric was not a substitute for military weapons and victories on the field but that it supplemented physical efforts through emotional and intellectual motivations. Propaganda served independence best by arousing and maintaining the Revolutionary fervor so that military forces were able to persevere on the battlefield.

Elizabeth D. Schafer

REFERENCES

Carl Berger, *Broadsides and Bayonets: The Propaganda War of the American Revolution* (1976); Allen Bowman, *The Morale of the American Revolutionary*

Army (1943); Dr. Lyman H. Butterfield, "Psychological Warfare in 1776: The Jefferson-Franklin Plan to Cause Hessian Desertions," *Proceedings of the American Philosophical Society* (June 1950); Philip Davidson, *Propaganda and the American Revolution, 1763–1783* (1941); John C. Miller, *Sam Adams: Pioneer in Propaganda*, (1936); Arthur M. Schlesinger, *Prelude to Independence: The Newspaper War on Britain, 1764–1776* (1958).

Pulaski, Count Kazimierz (1748–1779)

Polish military officer. Kazimierz (or Casimir) Pulaski was born the second of three sons of a wealthy noble family. His father, Jozef Pulaski, was a lawyer for the powerful Czartorski family. Although the Pulaskis belonged to the Szlachta class (the minor nobility), they were considerably richer than many Magnates (the high nobility). Jozef Pulaski, in fact, owned 14 cities and 108 villages.

Kazimierz's early years were typical for a young man of his social class. He spent a relatively carefree childhood on the family's rural estates. When he turned 12, his father took him to Warsaw and enrolled him in the school of the Teatyni Fathers, an institution known for producing well-disciplined and socially polished young noblemen rather than scholars. After completing the formal portion of his studies, the boy rounded off his education with a brief stint as a courtier at the court of Prince Karl of Courland at Mitau.

Despite the comfort and security Pulaski enjoyed during his youth, it was a troubled and turbulent time for Poland—turbulent even by Polish standards. A Saxon king sat on the Polish throne, and the country was dominated by Russia, and also by Prussia and Austria. Internally, the 25 or so Magnate families, who virtually owned Poland, were in a constant state of competition with one another. Alliances, confederations, and revolts sprang up and disappeared from week to week. When King Augustus III died in 1763, a massive internal power struggle to name his successor resulted. In the midst of all the infighting, Catherine the Great of Russia, with the help of her army, forced the election to the Polish throne of Stanislaw August Poniatowski, one of her former lovers.

Russian control of Polish internal affairs did not end there. In 1766 the Russian Ambassador, Prince Repnin, forced a measure through the Polish Sejm (Senate) conferring equal rights upon members of the Russian Orthodox Church in Poland. Most of staunchly Roman Catholic Poland was outraged, but something in Jozef Pulaski snapped. A prudent and politically expedient man all his life, he suddenly withdrew from the established political and social circles and made plans to form a military confederation to oust the Russians. He was 64 years old at the time, and neither he nor any of his three sons had any military experience, but he was ready to commit his considerable fortune to the cause. For the 18-year-old Kazimierz, it was the start of a continuous string of campaigning that would last the rest of his life.

Jozef Pulaski spent more than a year planning and organizing his revolt, while his sons launched into a crash self-study course of military matters. On February 29, 1768, he gathered a few hundred of his followers at the tiny village of Bar and proclaimed the insurrection. Four days later, in an elaborate religious ceremony, the Confederation of Bar inaugurated its military arm, the Knights of the Holy Cross. Jozef Pulaski was elected Grandmaster of the Order, and his three sons were among his immediate subordinate commanders. Only in Poland could something like that have happened in the middle of the eighteenth century, and been taken seriously.

The Knights of the Holy Cross was essentially a cavalry organization—no Polish nobleman would ever fight on foot. On April 20, 1768, the young Kazimierz got his first taste of combat when he successfully led a small mounted detachment against a larger Russian force near Podhorele. Nine days later the Russians turned the tables and ambushed Pulaski near Kaczanowka, killing close to 100 of his men. It was not the last time Kazimierz Pulaski would be caught in an ambush.

In late May, Kazimierz led the 1,400-strong main body of the Knights into the monastery at Berdyczow, where they made a stand against a larger Russian force. After a two-week siege, however, the Poles capitulated, and that marked the end of the Confederation of Bar. The Russians initially captured Pulaski, but he managed to escape to Turkey with his father and brothers.

Pulaski spent most of the next four years fighting Russians in association with the various confederations and insurrections that continually sprang up in Poland. During that period one of his brothers was killed and his other brother was captured by the Russians; his father died in a Turkish prison; and the Polish government confiscated the Pulaski estates on orders from Moscow. Although he was not a professionally trained soldier, Pulaski eventually earned a reputation as one of the most aggressive military commanders in Europe. His high-water mark came in early 1771 when he successfully beat back a 3,000-man Russian siege of the monastery of Czectochowa, Poland's holiest shrine and home of the famous "Black Madonna." Pulaski became an instant national hero, the first commander to lead a Polish military force in a significant victory in more than 100 years.

Hotheaded and flamboyant, Pulaski was never fully accepted or trusted by the leaders of the Generalcy, the very loose ruling political body of the various patriotic movements. They considered him a "loose cannon," albeit a militarily useful one. Pulaski, on the other hand, saw himself as the only true defender of Poland, while viewing the Generalcy as nothing but another self-serving special interest group. The situation developed into a crisis in late 1771 when one of the more radical revolutionary groups approached Pulaski with a plan to kidnap King Stanislaw August. Pulaski refused to participate. The conspirators tried to carry off the king anyway, but bungled the job. Pulaski got the blame, however, and the charge somehow shifted from kidnapping to attempted regicide. Russia then seized on the incident as one of the final justifications for the April 1772 First Partition of Poland.

Overnight Pulaski went from being the Hero of Czectochowa to an accused murderer. The leaders of the Generalcy hastily disowned him, and Moscow put additional pressure on Warsaw to bring him to bay. Finally, on May 31, 1772, convinced that his presence was now a major liability to his country, Pulaski left Poland by way of Silesia, never to return.

Pulaski spent the next five years of his life as a wandering exile. In September 1773 the Polish government tried him *in absentia* and sentenced him to death. He tried to secure a commission in the French army, but he was rejected as a convicted regicide. In 1774 a group of Polish exiles in France mounted a military expedition to Turkey, to enlist Turkish aid against the Russians. Pulaski commanded the force, but they landed in Turkey just in time to witness the final Russian victory over the Turks at Jeni Pazar. Pulaski and his staff barely managed to escape Turkey, losing everything they owned in the process. He eventually made his way back to France and landed in Marseilles, heavily in debt. A few months later the French authorities arrested him and threw him into a debtor's prison.

Friends managed to bail Pulaski out of prison after a few months, but the principal on his debts (incurred mostly from his military operations) was too large for them to pay off. Furthermore, his presence had become an acute embarrassment, both to the French government and to the Polish exile community in France. Everybody, it seemed, had an interest in finding a neat and clean way to get him out of France, or better still, out of Europe.

With the arrival of Silas Deane, the American commissioner in Paris, in the summer of 1776, Pulaski himself thought he had found a way out. On October 17 he wrote to Deane, describing his "zeal which I have to contribute in my particular way to the success of the cause of English America." But Deane never answered the letter. When Benjamin Franklin arrived in Paris, the French government, in the person of Claude Carloman de Rulhiere, took a direct hand. De Rulhiere first arranged a meeting between Pulaski and Franklin and then negotiated directly with Franklin on Pulaski's behalf. Franklin agreed to pay Pulaski's passage to America but not his previous debts. De Rulhiere then arranged for the French government to guarantee the debts, but he let Pulaski think the Americans were picking up the tab. Armed with a letter of introduction from Franklin to Washington, Pulaski finally set sail for America on June 13, 1777.

Pulaski arrived at Boston on July 23 and met Washington the following month. He immediately felt frustrated by the fact that Washington could not grant him a commission on the spot, but that he had to refer the matter to the Continental Congress. Pulaski asked for a cavalry command and was shocked to learn that up to that point there had been no permanent American cavalry. The recent reorganization of the army, however, included four regiments of dragoons, and Washington was still looking for an overall commander for the corps. On August 27, Washington wrote to John Hancock, president of the Congress, recommending Pulaski for the job.

The commander-in-chief noted, "The Count appears, by his recommendations, to have sustained no inconsiderable military character in his own country; and as the principal attention in Poland has been for some time past paid to the cavalry, it is to be presumed this gentleman is not unacquainted with it."

To Pulaski's further chagrin, the Congress took its time in considering the recommendation. By the Battle of Brandywine, on September 11, Pulaski still did not have an answer, so he volunteered to serve as an aide on Washington's staff. When the battle turned badly for the Americans and their right wing began to break, Pulaski asked Washington to give him temporary command of the 30-man headquarters cavalry detachment. He then led the small force in a violent counterattack that relieved some of the pressure on the withdrawing American army. If nothing else, Pulaski proved at Brandywine that he was in America to fight. Four days later the Congress voted to commission him a brigadier general and Commander of the Horse.

Pulaski's next combat action came during the unsuccessful attack on Germantown on October 4. His cavalry only conducted scouting missions during the operation, but 45 years later Pulaski's role in the battle became a matter of intense controversy. In 1822 a Judge William Johnson of Charleston wrote a book in which he claimed Washington found Pulaski asleep in a farmhouse during the battle. Captain Paul Bentalou, Pulaski's former aide, hotly denied the allegation, maintaining it was totally inconsistent with Pulaski's character. In 1824 Lafayette lent support to Bentalou's position. There was never a shred of evidence to back Johnson's claim, but for many years it was widely accepted.

Right from the start, Pulaski had serious command problems and in many ways he added to them himself. His four regiments of cavalry amounted to a mere 727 men, and none of them was really well trained. Because of his difficulties with the English language, he tended to surround himself with other foreign officers (he spoke both French and German), which in turn further increased the American resentment against the foreign volunteers. Colonel Stephen Moylan, one of his own regimental commanders, became one of his greatest adversaries. In late October, Pulaski preferred court-martial charges against Moylan for "disobedience to the orders of General Pulaski, a cowardly and un-

gentlemanly action in striking Lieutenant Zielinski, a gentleman and an officer in the Polish service when disarmed . . . and giving irritating language to General Pulaski." Moylan was acquitted and became a more embittered opponent.

Pulaski was also frustrated by the American concept of cavalry as an auxiliary arm, rather than one capable of independent action. Although cavalry reigned supreme on the open plains of central Europe, it enjoyed far less mobility on the heavily forested east coast of North America. Nonetheless, Pulaski felt the Americans never really appreciated its capabilities. In his conception of the cavalry's proper place in the scheme of things, he steadfastly insisted he was an independent commander, subject only to the orders of the commander-in-chief.

In December 1777 Washington took the main body of the army into winter quarters at Valley Forge. He sent Pulaski's cavalry to Trenton. By late February, Washington's troops were on the verge of starvation. Receiving no support from the Congress, he finally ordered General Anthony Wayne to take 500 troops into south New Jersey to collect cattle. General William Howe learned of the expedition and sent 2,000 British troops out to intercept Wayne at Haddonsfield. True to his own nature, Wayne decided to fight rather than run. He knew that the cavalry was close by in Trenton, and he sent orders to Pulaski to come to his assistance.

This put Pulaski on the horns of a dilemma. While strongly believing that Wayne had no authority to give him orders, he also did not want to avoid combat. So Pulaski wrote out his resignation and sent it off to Washington, and then went to Wayne's assistance, protesting his independence every step of the way. He linked up with Wayne on March 1, and the two generals immediately started bickering about who was to give orders to whom. Between arguments they managed to coordinate their efforts enough to beat off Howe's troops and send them packing back to Philadelphia. In his after-action report Wayne did give Pulaski a fair share of the battlefield laurels by noting: "General Pulaski behaved with his Usual Bravery . . . with a Spirit that would have done Honour to the Oldest Veteran."

Washington accepted Pulaski's resignation with mixed feelings of relief and regret. He believed the Pole was a valuable asset, if he could only find his proper niche. With Washington's support, Pulaski petitioned the Congress to let him raise an independent corps of mixed infantry and cavalry, organized and trained along European lines. He also asked for permission to recruit German deserters and prisoners, as they would have had European training. Congress referred his proposal to the Board of War under General Horatio Gates, who in turn referred it to General Charles Lee for his opinion. Lee, who had served in the Polish army as an aide-de-camp to King Stanislaw August during the period of the Confederation of Bar, was well acquainted with Pulaski's reputation. Lee enthusiastically recommended approval, and even suggested doubling the size of the proposed organization.

On March 28, 1778, Congress voted to create the Pulaski Legion of 68 horse and 200 foot. They permitted Pulaski to retain his rank as brigadier general and appropriated $50,000 for pay and equipment. Pulaski basically got everything he asked for, but Washington later vetoed the recruiting of prisoners of war. Pulaski picked Baltimore as the Legion's home base, and he selected his officers almost exclusively from among his European colleagues. In a few weeks he not only filled all his unit vacancies, he over-recruited by 62 men. In his enthusiasm, though, he ran afoul of Washington's prohibition against recruiting prisoners. Pulaski's practice of recruiting deserters would come back to haunt him.

In his rush to train and equip his new unit Pulaski was careless in accounting for his expenses and supplies. He was constantly in trouble with the Congress on this point, and his paymaster, Captain Jozef Baldeski, had a full-time job in trying to keep the books straight. No one ever suggested that Pulaski misused public funds or diverted them to his own use; he simply did not follow the proper administrative procedures. For Pulaski, it was a rerun of the same sort of relationship he had with the Generalcy in Poland, and he often regarded the Congress in the same contemptuous manner. All the while, the faithful Baldeski trailed along after his chief trying to pick up the pieces.

By mid-summer Pulaski reported the Legion fit for active service. On August 15 the unit marched to Philadelphia and passed in review before the Congress. Then they sat in place for a month waiting for orders. Pulaski finally complained to the Congress on September 17 and requested "permission to march against the enemy." In early October, the Legion finally got a mission. It was ordered to the south New Jersey coast, to protect the operating base of American privateers from a recent series of British raids from the sea.

The Legion moved into the area near Little Egg Harbor on October 6. Pulaski positioned the infantry on Mincock Island and started conducting local patrols with the cavalry. Shortly after their arrival, a former German deserter, Lieutenant Gustav Juliet, got into a bitter argument with the Legion's infantry commander, Colonel Baron de Botzen. Juliet defected back to the British. On the night of October 14 he guided a 250-man force from the 71st Regiment, under Captain Patrick Ferguson, back to the Legion's infantry positions. The British managed to kill about 50 Legion infantrymen, including de Botzen, before they were driven off by the arrival of Pulaski with the cavalry. The Legion's first time in combat had turned into a disaster.

Pulaski moved his Legion back to Trenton to reorganize his badly mauled infantry. In November Washington ordered him to take the Legion to the frontier village of Minisink, on the Delaware River, and provide security for the local settlements. Pulaski passed the winter there, but on November 26 he complained to Congress that he had "nothing but bears to fight." Pulaski became increasingly depressed. He considered resigning and returning to Poland somehow. But then the American situation abruptly changed with the British invasion of Georgia. On February 2, 1779, Pulaski received orders to move south in support of General Benjamin Lincoln.

The Legion reached Charleston on May 8, just as the British forces under General Augustine Prevost were moving against the city. Governor John Rutledge of South Carolina and the City Council seriously considered surrendering without a fight. On May 10, Pulaski and Colonel John Laurens forced their way into the council meeting, where Pulaski declared that as an officer of the Continental Army he would not permit Charleston to surrender. When General William Moultrie, the commander of troops in the city, sided with Pulaski and Laurens, they managed to sway the council temporarily. The next day Pulaski and the Legion moved out to attack Prevost's 900-man advance guard.

The Legion was vastly outnumbered and did

not have a chance in a head-to-head fight. Instead, Pulaski planned to use his cavalry to lure the British into an ambush set by his infantry. The Legion's well-trained cavalry performed according to the plan, but his only recently recruited infantry replacements rushed out of their positions prematurely and were cut to ribbons by the larger British force. Infantry commander Colonel Michael Kowacz and about 40 infantrymen were killed. For the second time the Pulaski Legion's infantry had been effectively annihilated. While it was a bitter tactical defeat for Pulaski, he did help Charleston, however, by delaying Prevost. On the night of May 12–13, the British commander withdrew his forces across the Ashly river after he learned Lincoln was moving toward the city with a 4,000-man relief column.

Throughout the summer of 1779 the inquiries into Pulaski's accounts dragged on. On August 19 he wrote to the Congress: "Is there any one act of mine, Ever since the battle of Brandywine down to the present period, the campaign of Charleston, that has not demonstrated the most disinterested zeal for the public cause? I believe the most profligate of my Enemies Cannot presume to deny it. Whence come it then, that I have so Little Credit among you Gentlemen?" The letter never reached the Congress in Pulaski's lifetime.

In October 1779 a combined force of 4,000 Americans under Lincoln and 3,000 French under Vice Admiral Count Hector d'Estaing attacked the British occupied city of Savannah. During the planning and coordination leading up to the attack Pulaski was the chief liaison officer between the Americans and the French. On October 9, the attack kicked off with Pulaski in command of the cavalry, following the left column of the French troops, and preceding the American light infantry. The allies had a sound tactical plan, but unfortunately, General Prevost knew it all thanks to a deserter. Things went badly for the allies, and the entire attack began to falter when Admiral d'Estaing fell wounded.

The accounts of Pulaski's death differ. According to one version he was cut down at the head of a "brave but stupid" cavalry charge. But Pulaski's aide, Captain Bentalou, gave a much different account. According to Bentalou, Pulaski saw d'Estaing go down and reasoned that next to the French commander he had the greatest knowledge of the overall plan and should there-

fore assume command. Pulaski turned control of the cavalry over to a Colonel Horry and started out for d'Estaing's command post, accompanied only by Bentalou. Almost as soon as they started, Pulaski was cut down by a blast of grapeshot and Bentalou was wounded by musket fire.

The British held their fire while Pulaski was evacuated from the field. He was mortally wounded in the groin and beyond the help of the surgeons from the French fleet. They transferred the dying Pole to the American ship *Wasp*, in the hope that it could reach Charleston in enough time to get him proper medical attention, but he died at sea early on October 11. Because the weather was hot, the corpse putrefied rapidly. They had to bury Pulaski at sea, somewhere off the Georgia coast.

On October 22 the city of Charleston held a public funeral for the Pole. On December 28 Congress voted to accept Pulaski's reports of his accounts. Baldeski, his faithful paymaster, was promoted to major and allowed to retire. When King Stanislaw August of Poland finally learned of Pulaski's death, he commented: "Pulaski has died as he lived—a hero—but an enemy of kings."

Still regarded as a major national hero in Poland, Brigadier General Kazimierz Pulaski is one of the more difficult characters in American military history to summarize. Considering only his period in the Continental Army, he is all too easy to dismiss as falling somewhere between George Custer and Don Quixote. When his earlier experiences in Poland are taken into account, however, a picture of a far more complex man emerges. On the one hand he identified strongly with the class-oriented traditions and values of the other European volunteers in America. On the other hand, he sympathized only too well with the largely self-taught American soldiers and their unorthodox tactics. A devout Roman Catholic who once fought against religious freedom in Poland, he fought equally hard for an America that espoused religious freedom, but which in fact had a fairly strong anti-Catholic streak.

Kazimierz Pulaski was incredibly brave, fanatically dedicated to the causes he fought for, and an inspirational combat leader. All of his battlefield successes stem from those qualities. He was not, however, a particularly clever tactician; nor was he a very thoughtful or analytical leader. His battlefield defeats, as well as his political problems, can be attributed squarely to those characteristics. His greatest significance today, perhaps, is the strong psychological bond between Poland and the United States that he and his fellow countryman, Tadeusz Kosciuszko, have come to symbolize.

David T. Zabecki

REFERENCES

Clarence A. Manning, *Soldier of Liberty: Casimir Pulaski* (1945); C.H. Metzger, "Casimir Pulaski," in *New Catholic Encyclopedia* (1967), XI: pp. 1021–1022; Helena Waniczek, "Casimir Pulaski," in *Great Men and Women of Poland*, ed. by Stephan P. Mizwa (1943): pp. 144–156.

Pulaski's Legion

Following his resignation as commander of the Continental Light Dragoons, Brigadier Kazimierz Pulaski petitioned Congress for authorization to raise an independent corps of mixed cavalry and infantry, to be organized and trained along European lines. The proposal was endorsed by Washington and approved by the Board of War under General Horatio Gates. On March 28, 1778, Congress authorized Pulaski's Legion, to consist of one troop of lancers, two troops of dragoons, one company of riflemen, and two companies of light infantry. Total strength was set at 68 troopers and 200 infantrymen.

Pulaski organized the corps between April 10 and July 29, 1778, at Baltimore. He recruited heavily among non-English-speaking groups, particularly deserters from the British German regiments. He also wanted to recruit prisoners of war. Washington vetoed that idea, but Pulaski, in his haste to fill the unit, enlisted some prisoners nonetheless. The officers were almost all foreigners: Colonel Michael Kowacz, colonel commandant; Lieutenant Colonel Baron de Botzen, infantry commander; Major Henry Bedkin, brigade major; Captain Paul Bentalou, adjutant; and Captain Jozef Baldeski, paymaster.

The uniform of the Pulaski Legion was the standard Continental blue coat with red facings, white waistcoats, and white breeches. Both the cavalry and the infantry wore the dragoon-type helmet. The cavalry also wore boots.

Pulaski's Legion, particularly its infantry, turned out to be a hard-luck unit. In its first engagement at Little Egg Harbor on October 14, 1778, a British raiding party from the 71st Highland Regiment caught the infantry by sur-

prise and killed about 50, including Colonel de Botzen. In their second major engagement at Charleston on May 11, 1779, the infantry was again drawn into a trap. About 40 soldiers, including Colonel Kowacz, were killed this time; but the Legion helped buy time for the city, which was relieved a few days later by General Benjamin Lincoln. Finally, Pulaski himself fell at Savannah on October 9, 1779.

After the death of their commander, Pulaski's Legion was consolidated with the Free and Independent Chasseurs to form Armand's Legion on February 23, 1780. Armand's Legion was later redesignated the First Partisan Corps. As members of that unit, the survivors of Pulaski's Legion fought their last engagement at Yorktown.

David T. Zabecki

REFERENCES

Donald W. Holst and Marko Zlatich, "Dress and Equipment of Pulaski's Independent Legion," *Military Collector and Historian,* 16 (1964): 97–103; Clarence A. Manning, *Soldier of Liberty: Casimir Pulaski* (1945); Robert K. Wright, *The Continental Army: Army Lineage Series* (1983).

Putnam, Israel (1718–1790)

Continental Army officer. Born in Salem, Massachusetts, Putnam moved to Connecticut's frontier (later Pomfret), where he farmed. During the French and Indian War he served in many campaigns and had many adventures, including being captured by Indians. Demonstrating ability in scouting and in unconventional warfare, Putnam became a militia colonel in 1762.

He joined the Sons of Liberty, was a town selectman, and a member of the general assembly. In 1773, Putnam explored part of the Mississippi River and surveyed tracts of land. Soon after Lexington and Concord he was named brigadier general by the Connecticut Assembly and then a major general. Considered a great military figure, Putnam supervised the defenses at Bunker Hill. During the first British assault, he reputedly said, "Don't one of you fire until you see the whites of their eyes."

Putnam was ordered in March 1776 to prepare the American encampment at New York. Putnam's real test as a commander came during the Battle of Long Island in which he was clearly outwitted by General William Howe. Putnam was partly responsible for the American defeat at Brooklyn Heights.

Washington then sent the elderly hero to prepare the defenses at Philadelphia in late 1776 and then to command in the Hudson Highlands in 1777–1778. But Putnam sometimes misunderstood Washington's orders and thereby angered the commander-in-chief. Furthermore, he was criticized for being too lenient with Loyalists and for delaying the fortifications at West Point. In October 1777 Putnam was again duped, for General Henry Clinton easily captured Forts Clinton and Montgomery on the Hudson. Putnam underwent a court-martial for negligence, but he was exonerated. Washington never again entrusted him with a field command and was anxious to replace him. While on leave in November 1779 Putnam suffered a stroke and became partially paralyzed. His military career was over.

Untrained in strategy and orthodox tactics, poorly educated "Old Put" was part of the contemporary folklore. His exploits during the French and Indian War about crawling into a wolf's den, about fighting Indians, and about saving an entire garrison at Fort Edward were probably embellished in the retelling of the tales. The story about how "Old Put" immediately quit his spring plowing at the news of Lexington and Concord in order to fight for his country became a legend enshrined in the patriotism of the era.

Richard L. Blanco

REFERENCES

Worthington C. Ford, ed. *General Orders Issued by Major-General Israel Putnam When In Command of the Highlands in the Summer and Fall of 1777* (1983); William F. Livingston, "The Homes and Haunts of Israel Putnam," *New England Magazine,* 17 (1897):193–212; F.S. Luther, "General Israel Putnam," *Worcester Historical Society Proceedings,* 20 (1904):204–214; Increase N. Tarbox, *Life of Israel Putnam* (1876).

Putnam, Rufus (1738–1824)

Continental Army officer. Born and raised in Massachusetts, Putnam was a millwright's apprentice. In 1759 he enlisted in the militia to fight in the French and Indian War. Putnam soon demonstrated his mechanical ability by aiding in the construction of fortresses near Lake Champlain. After his service he farmed, surveyed, and built mills.

As a lieutenant colonel in the Massachusetts militia he displayed engineering talent in helping to fortify Dorchester Heights near Boston in March 1776. Later that year he worked on the defenses of New York City, and he was promoted to colonel. Putnam served at Saratoga, West Point, and Stony Point. He was involved in the framing of the Newburgh Address (March 10–12, 1783) urging that officers be provided with substantial land grants in the Ohio country. Made a brigadier general in June 1783 Putnam retired from the army.

After the war Putnam became superintendent of the Ohio Company and he founded a colony at Adelphia (Marietta, Ohio) in 1788. He was appointed a judge of the Northwest Territory in 1790 and a brigadier general in 1792. Putnam helped to negotiate treaties with the Indians, and he was named the first surveyor general of the United States (1796–1803). However, Putnam was dismissed from this post by President Thomas Jefferson due to his deficiencies in mathematics. He remained a prominent figure in Ohio politics until his death.

Richard L. Blanco

REFERENCES

Rowena Buell, *The Memoirs of Rufus Putnam* (1903). Sidney Crawford, "Rufus Putnam and His Pioneer Life in the Northwest," *American Antiquarian Society Proceedings, 12* (1898):431–454; *DAB.*

Pyle's Massacre (North Carolina) (February 25, 1781) (Alternate names: Action at the Haw River, Pyle's Hacking Match, Altamahaw Ford Affair)

This action took place in modern Alamance County off Route 49 near Bellemont and Graham, North Carolina.

At 25 years of age, "Light Horse" Harry Lee of Virginia was Washington's outstanding cavalry commander. Lee had cold blue eyes and blond hair that he queued tightly against his head with an eelskin band. He had an engaging way with women that was balanced by a temper difficult to control. Dashingly handsome, he was impatient in the face of frustration and did not take criticism well. In his favor, though, he never stopped learning and expanding his understanding of war and became one of the leading players in the Revolution, especially in the southern campaign of General Nathanael Greene.

Lee was promoted to lieutenant colonel and placed in command of "Lee's Partisan Corps," or "Lee's Legion," which was created by Congress in November 1780. A legion was a military unit that combined infantry and cavalry, although the cavalry was trained to move on the enemy and, if necessary, be prepared to fight on foot. Lieutenant Colonel Banastre Tarleton and Count Casimir Pulaski also commanded legions during the war. Almost immediately, Lee and his newly created command were sent south to bolster Greene's small and tattered army.

Lee brought to Greene an enthusiasm and patriotism that was contagious. Medium in height, Lee was thin, thoughtful, and prudent. The key to understanding Lee in battle is that he was always mobile, using speed and activity to confuse and confound his enemy. Lee also admired and valued fine horses. His men were regularly mounted on only the best horses to be found in the country. To increase his mobility and thanks to his selection and care of the horses, Lee's infantry could often ride double behind his cavalry on their missions, covering more distance than any other similar unit in as short a time.

When reporting to Greene in North Carolina on January 13, 1781, Lee had 180 infantry divided into three companies and 100 horse in three troops. His cavalry wore short green coats similar to those worn by the enemy in Tarleton's Legion. Commanding the best disciplined and trained men in Greene's army, Lee and his men were often the rear guard and he was one of the first American officers to lead his men back across the Dan River to renew the campaign against Lord Cornwallis when the time came.

After a highly successful career in the North, Lee was anxious to run up against Tarleton once more. They had met during the encampment at Valley Forge in a skirmish in Tredyffrin Township in 1778. Both men were looking forward to their next contact. In comparison, Lee had the better education, graduating from Princeton in 1773. He was never satisfied with himself but was always seeking to know more and thus developed as a better military leader as the war progressed, something Tarleton never seemed to do. Lee was expert at gathering intelligence and putting that knowledge to good use, excelling even Tarleton, who was past master at the military skill. Lee was a true professional soldier. His strength lay in carrying out the care-

fully calculated surprise blow that did its damage before the enemy knew what hit them. By that time, Lee was gone.

In the preceding months, Cornwallis had chased Greene's army north through North Carolina until Greene had reached safety by crossing the Dan River into Virginia. Without boats, Cornwallis could not follow. Moving back into the interior of the state, Cornwallis seized the state capital at Hillsboro. Having burned his supply wagons in the race to catch Greene, Cornwallis needed to resupply and refit his men. In addition, the British army needed the support of the thousands of Loyalists who were supposedly living in North Carolina. On February 22, Cornwallis raised the royal standard and issued a proclamation that called upon all Loyalists in the state to come to Hillsboro with their weapons and ten days' rations.

Greene sent Lee back across the Dan toward Cornwallis on February 18. Along with his Legion came two companies of Maryland infantry. Lee's force joined with that of General Andrew Pickens who assumed overall command of the force. Pickens' men were militia from North and South Carolina and numbered about 700. Their combined task was to observe Cornwallis and report his moves to Greene. They were also to harass and delay the British and discourage any Loyalists that might be tempted to flock into the British camp. And, if they could, Lee and Pickens were to bag Tarleton and his men to complete the work Morgan had begun two months earlier at Cowpens.

Tarleton needed men to replace those lost at Cowpens. Cornwallis needed infantry and scouts to supplement his depleted ranks. Cornwallis was therefore overjoyed when he received word that Doctor John Pyle, a colonel in the Loyalist militia, was prepared to lead his 300 to 400 men into Cornwallis's camp. Pyle was a longtime Loyalist who had participated in the Battle of Moore's Creek Bridge in 1776 and was captured there with his son. Taking the oath of loyalty, Pyle managed to stay alive playing two against the middle, mainly through his medical efforts on behalf of both sides during the civil war that was the Revolution raging in the South. Pyle himself was from Chatham County, North Carolina, and raised his men from the countryside between the Broad and Haw rivers.

Tarleton was sent out to bring Pyle's men into camp in safety. Pyle and his men were in no hurry, however. They took their time, visiting friends, drinking farewell toasts, and enjoying their newly assumed military roles. Tarleton never succeeded in making contact with them.

Hot on Tarleton's trail, intent on destroying his force before it could rejoin Cornwallis to the east, Lee and Pickens attacked a plantation on the "Great Road" to Hillsboro at noon on February 25. Intelligence had placed Tarleton and his men there, but the Americans found only two British staff officers who had stayed behind to place their papers in order. Tarleton had moved ahead to another location. Lee and Pickens continued their pursuit and found Pyle's men ahead in the road. Pyle and his several hundred militia were wandering about North Carolina trying to link up with Tarleton. At this time they were pointed in the right direction but had no idea where Tarleton was, or what he looked like. Pyle had word he was to meet Tarleton at General John Butler's plantation. Pyle was taking his men in that general direction. It was late afternoon on Sunday, February 25, 1781.

As Lee's van pursued Tarleton's route in the growing dusk, two of Pyle's militia came out of the woods and identified themselves as Loyalists, thinking the green coats that Lee's men were wearing meant Tarleton. The two were brought before Lee, who was happy to play Tarleton for them, sending one of them ahead to Colonel Pyle to request that Pyle move his men off the road so that "Colonel Tarleton" and "his men" could move past the militia on their way to camp without delay. Pyle saw no problem in this. His militia cavalry would follow right along behind their protection. Pyle moved his men off to the right of the road, where they stood with their weapons on their shoulders pointed to the rear. Pyle waited at the far end of his line of men. (If Pyle had moved them to the left, then Lee would have had to change whatever plan he had in mind because Lee would have met Pyle first and the Americans would not have been able to line up right beside the Loyalists along the road.)

Helping in the deception, the two captured British officers were placed up front with "Tarleton" as the American force moved toward Pyle's position. Pickens, whose men wore green twigs in their hats to designate their rebel leanings, went into the woods out of sight of Pyle's men on the road and attempted to pass the Loyalists on the flank unseen.

Lee claimed later, in writing his history of the war in the South, that his intention was to ride up to Pyle and identify himself as Colonel Lee and present Pyle with a choice. The Loyalists could disband and go home or they could join with Lee and fight the British. Lee and his men approached Pyle's force on the road locally referred to as the "race paths." Lee rode past the Loyalists, smiling and waving to them, with his Legion right behind him until he finally came to Pyle. Some of Pickens's men were on horseback in the rear of Lee's column. Lee's men had their swords drawn in salute as they rode past the unsuspecting Loyalists, who were cheering "Tarleton's men."

As Lee came abreast of Pyle, he reached out and shook Pyle's hand and was exchanging compliments with him when the fighting suddenly began. Due to conflicting accounts, no one knows to this day what really happened. There are those who say that some of Pyle's men in the rear of his column, which Lee passed first on his way to greet Pyle, spotted some of Pickens's men in the woods and fired at them. Another story is that some of Lee's militia officers, unaware of Lee's plan, suddenly realized by the red ribbons in the hats of Pyle's men that these cavalry on the side of the road were the enemy, thought Lee had made a serious mistake and tried to save him by attacking the Loyalists. Whichever version is true, it was Captain Eggleston of Lee's Legion, commanding the mounted militia, who led the attack. (His grandson would be General Joseph Eggleston Johnston of Confederate Army fame.)

Lee and Pickens also claimed that they wanted to bypass Pyle's relatively harmless band of militia and get at Tarleton on the road straight ahead of them. That rings true. But soon it all went out of anyone's control. The Loyalists never knew what hit them. It was a complete surprise. Worse, the Loyalists believed, even after the action ended, that Tarleton had attacked them by mistake. The Loyalists cried out "Hurrah for King George!" and "You're attacking your own men!" Lee's men slashed out with their sabers and inflicted serious damage on Pyle's command. In ten minutes the affair was over. Ninety-three Loyalists lay dead on the field. Most of the rest were wounded in one manner or another. Legend has it that Pyle, seriously injured himself, crawled to a nearby pond and dove in. He remained there with only his nose showing until nightfall allowed him to get back home. He survived his wounds and survived the war, too, by medically treating Americans on both sides, without again participating in active service for either army.

There was no mercy shown to the Loyalists. The Legion remembered "Tarleton's quarter" that the British had shown to Abraham Buford's Americans at the Waxhaws in 1780. The civil war was too bloody and too many evils had taken place for mercy to be rendered. Lee insisted that once the action began, no one could afford to offer mercy. The two lines of cavalry were next to each other, a few feet apart. If Lee's men were to survive, they had to strike out quickly and effectively. They did. Pyle's men were hacked to death. There was little gunfire, except by a few of the Loyalists. The American casualties were one horse killed.

Lee denied that this action was a massacre. There was no pursuit, and every Loyalist could have been killed if one had been ordered. It was the nature of the fight that resulted in so many dead for the Loyalists. Lee knew that Tarleton and his force were about one or two miles off and could not afford to order a pursuit in case Tarleton were to suddenly appear. There was every chance he would. To add to the horror of this scene, shortly after the action was finished, a group of Catawba Indians under Captain Oldham, serving the American cause, came on the field and began spearing the Loyalist wounded lying about. At least seven or eight were dispatched in this manner before control was restored.

Sitting in his camp at Colonel O'Neal's plantation, a short distance away, Tarleton learned of Pyle's massacre when some of the wounded and scared Loyalist survivors rode up, bitterly complaining that Tarleton and his men had just attacked them. Tarleton summoned his Legion to action but called off his offensive when a message arrived from Cornwallis, requesting that he fall back on Hillsboro. Greene had crossed the Dan into North Carolina. Tarleton and his men packed up and moved to join Cornwallis. Pyle's militia rode home. Evidently neither Pyle nor Tarleton ever made it to Butler's plantation.

Pickens and Lee did not pursue the Loyalists, who were riding for their lives. They instead went after Tarleton. They found him as the captured British officers said they would. To their delight, Tarleton had posted no videttes around his camp. Just as Tarleton was learning of Pyle's massacre and receiving Cornwallis's message, Pickens and Lee brought their men to within striking distance of Tarleton's camp. The hour being so late and darkness falling, the Americans felt it best to wait until morning to attack. In the morning, Tarleton had vanished.

This bloody, ferocious action prevented an encounter between Pickens, Lee, and Tarleton. But it did disrupt the Loyalist concentration around Cornwallis. With Greene's return to North Carolina, Cornwallis's departure from Hillsboro shortly thereafter, and Pyle's massacre, the Loyalists in North Carolina could not afford the risk of coming out in open support of the British.

Cornwallis complained to Lord Germain, the secretary of state for the American colonies, that Pyle's men were "inhumanely butchered, when begging for quarter, with making the least resistance." Green wrote to Lee that his success was "so happily timed, and in all probability will be productive of such happy consequences, that I cannot help congratulating you."

Three weeks of maneuvering followed until the two armies closed in Battle of Guilford Court House on March 15, 1781. Cornwallis went into that major action without the services of Loyalist troops. Why? There were three reasons. Cornwallis insisted that the militia serve for a term of 18 months. That was too long a period for any militia to serve on either side in 1781. On March 4, Tarleton and his men actually did attack Loyalist militia coming to join Cornwallis near the Deep River. The British were jumpy and it was all a misunderstanding, but it did not help to bring in Loyalist support. The final reason and most significant of all was Pyle's massacre.

One of Lee's militia troopers, Moses Hall, of Rowan County, North Carolina, deposed in 1835 to qualify for a pension, that he was present at Pyle's massacre and he believed Lee knew what he was doing. Lee had his bugler give the signal of the attack and Hall witnessed brutality and atrocities committed on both sides in the events then and to follow. Lee was applauded at the time. Revenge had been taken for the actions of the British earlier in the war. And Lee accomplished a major feat. If the Loyalists were ever coming out to support Cornwallis, they never did after February 25. There would be time for Lee and Tarleton to clash later. The Loyalists were taken care of first. This burdened Cornwallis with one more reason to leave the Carolinas and move to his destiny in Virginia.

Paul J. Sanborn

REFERENCES

John C. Dann, *The Revolution Remembered* (1980); Noel B. Gerson, *Light Horse Harry* (1966); Henry Lee, *The American Revolution in the South* (1989); Hugh Rankin, *Greene and Cornwallis: The Campaign in the Carolinas* (1976); Charles Royster, *Light Horse Harry Lee* (1981); George Troxler, *Pyle's Massacre* (1973) Christopher Ward, *The War of the Revolution*, 2 vols., (1952) 2; Franklin and Mary Wickwire, *Cornwallis, The American Adventure* (1970).

Quakers in the American Revolution

In the middle of the eighteenth century, the Quakers constituted one of the leading religious bodies in the American colonies. Although a significant presence in most of the colonies, their fame derived from the founding and governance of Pennsylvania, which by the Revolutionary period had become the largest and wealthiest of the North American colonies. Pennsylvania was widely known for the principles of religious liberty enunciated in William Penn's Charter of Liberties.

The Quakers were mostly agrarian, except in the Newport area of Rhode Island and in Pennsylvania, where large numbers were concentrated in and around Philadelphia. Many Philadelphia Friends were prominent merchants and traders and thus deeply involved in the mercantile life of the British Empire. At the same time, many leading British Friends were prominent London merchants, controlling much of the colonial American trade, and a number of them were members of the London Meeting for Sufferings, the permanent executive body of the Society of Friends in Britain. Naturally, Philadelphia and London Quaker merchants had close ties and mutual economic interests.

Moreover, many Friends in Pennsylvania were descendants of those who had migrated from Great Britain after the founding of the colony, and consequently there was a familial as well as a close religious bond between English and Pennsylvania Quakers. Friends in the colonies and in Britain considered themselves members of an all-embracing religious community, which, despite the distance separating them, was enhanced by frequent transatlantic religious visitation and correspondence.

English Friends felt a certain responsibility for the problems of the colonial Quakers vis-à-vis the British government, especially in the case of Pennsylvania, and often acted as a go-between for them. Conversely, they were to a certain extent held responsible by the British government for the conduct of affairs in that province. Thus the Quakers were directly involved, both economically and governmentally, in the imperial system.

Friends' pacifist testimony, according to which human life was sacred and the taking of human life was wrong, barred them from supporting or participating in any military activity. They owed allegiance to any government under which they lived, but they would peacefully protest unjust and oppressive laws and government actions, and they would refuse to conform with laws that they considered wrongful, despite the cost to themselves. The peaceful resolution of conflicts, they maintained, would be more productive than a resort to violence with its inevitable destructive results.

For this reason, two decades before the Revolutionary War, most Friends in the Pennsylvania Assembly, where they held a majority, resigned their seats there because they could not support military action in the French and Indian War. With the return of peace in 1763, however, many Quakers resumed their activities in government and politics, although there was pressure from Quaker spiritual reformers to abstain from participation in political affairs. They thus continued to be strongly influential in the province until 1775.

It was also a positive aspect of their peace testimony that during the decade preceding the Revolution the Friends both in England and America did their utmost to persuade the British government to adopt a less autocratic and a more flexible approach to colonial problems, and at the same time to persuade the colonists to avoid violent manifestations that would prejudice the British authorities against them.

The constitutional controversy between the Mother Country and the colonies began when Parliament passed the Stamp Act in 1765, requiring a revenue stamp be attached to all official documents and printed matter issued in the colonies. Although the colonists accepted the power of Parliament to enact imperial legislation affecting all parts of the Empire alike, they rejected its right to enact laws affecting them only, since they were not represented. The English Quakers understood and supported the colonial position, since they themselves were calling for the reform of a corrupt and unrepresentative parliamentary system in which the new merchant and industrial classes in England had no voice in public affairs.

Both the American and English Quakers joined in the debate over the constitutional powers of Parliament. Stephen Hopkins, Quaker governor of Rhode Island, in his *Rights of the Colonies Examined*, rejected the right of Parliament to tax the colonies. The London Quaker merchant Thomas Crowley published his *Controversy Between Great Britain and Her Colonies Briefly Examined*, calling for colonial representation in Parliament. Dr. John Fothergill, a prominent Quaker physician in London who counted among his patients members of Parliament and various government ministries, declared in his *Considerations Relative to the North American Colonies* that "A British Parliament has certainly power to do many things which it has no right to do." He subsequently intervened on behalf of the colonial cause with Lord Dartmouth, head of the Board of Trade, to whom he presented a copy of his statement.

On the economic side, both the American and the British merchants entered the fray. When the Stamp Act went into effect, 80 Philadelphia Quaker merchants joined a nonimportation agreement. A Quaker-dominated committee of the merchants addressed a memorial to the London merchants asking them to interpose with Parliament for the repeal of the Stamp Act. In response, two leading Quaker London merchants obtained the support of the British merchant community on behalf of the Americans. The Quaker merchants David Barclay and Capel Hanbury appeared before Parliament to plead the American cause, and other Quakers interceded with members of Parliament and the government ministries.

The Stamp Act was soon repealed, but on the appointment of a new ministry, Parliament passed the Townshend Acts, levying duties on certain goods imported into the colonies rather than levying a tax within the colonies. The Quakers in both America and Britain immediately joined in protesting this action and in calling for the repeal of the Acts. In Philadelphia, Quaker merchants actively supported the colonial protest, and John Reynell, treasurer of Philadelphia Yearly Meeting, the central body of Friends in Pennsylvania, New Jersey, and Delaware, chaired the Philadelphia merchant's committee. Many Quakers also joined the nonconsumption movement, which was launched at this time.

The merchants' committee addressed a memorial to the British merchants and manufacturers, stressing the unconstitutionality and the harmful economic effects of the Acts. In reply, the London merchants promised to solicit Parliament "for Relief from the late Revenue Act." British Quakers lobbied Parliament on behalf of the colonies. Benjamin Franklin arranged a meeting between the Speaker of the House of Commons and Abel James, a Philadelphia Quaker merchant then in England, to provide the speaker with good arguments for adopting a different policy toward America.

When Parliament refused to repeal the Acts, the Philadelphia merchants joined the intercolonial nonimportation agreement. A few months later, John Reynell wrote his English correspondents that the Americans would never agree to being taxed by a Parliament in which they were not represented.

Despite their strong support for the colonial cause, the Quakers wanted to avoid a show of belligerence against the Mother Country, fearing such action would destroy any hope for reconciliation. Philadelphia Meeting for Sufferings, acting for the Yearly Meeting, issued an epistle to members of the Society, calling upon them to preserve a peaceful demeanor in the current controversy, which under "the influence of that Spirit (of the Gospel) will most effectually tend to our relief . . . and would add a convincing force to the reasonings necessary to be used in support of our civil liberty and rights.

During the period 1770–1774, many of the Pennsylvania Quaker leaders, especially the more conservative ones, came to fear that uncontrolled activities by the more radical elements might result in illegal and even violent actions, which would not only acerbate relations with Britain, but would also ultimately lead to political changes within the colony, thereby threatening the liberties guaranteed by their Charter. Those apprehensions were given credence following the passage of the Tea Act of 1773, when the two Philadelphia tea assignees, both Quaker merchants, resigned their commissions after threats made by a mass meeting of citizens at the Philadelphia State House, now Independence Hall. The meeting, in which a number of Quakers participated, resolved that since the Tea Act provided for taxation without representation, those involved in its execution were "enemies of their country."

Thereupon, a meeting of all Friends in the Philadelphia area was called, at which was read an advice of George Fox to avoid "bustling and Troubles or tumults," and cautioning epistles of London and Philadelphia Yearly Meetings.

Those present were advised to maintain "a due consideration of the nature of our religious profession . . . (which) requires us to keep quiet and still both in respect to conversation and conduct." From this point on, Friends in Pennsylvania and New Jersey, as well as in the other colonies, largely withdrew from the agitations that were taking place.

When Philadelphia Yearly Meeting held its annual sessions in the fall of 1774, the First Continental Congress met in Philadelphia. Although the Quakers supported the idea of a petition to the king, and doubtlessly would cooperate with nonimportation, nonexportation, and nonconsumption proposals that the Congress adopted, they objected to the extralegal and extragovernmental association that was set up to oversee and enforce the agreements. Accordingly, the Yearly Meeting issued a general epistle to all Friends in America, pointing out that their ancestors had always remonstrated against unjust laws, but at the same time they had avoided plots and conspiracies. The Friends in America were indebted to the king for the enjoyment of their liberties and should manifest their loyalty and allegiance.

This statement was widely published in the American and British presses. Outside the Society the conservatives applauded, while the radicals denounced the epistle. British Friends feared its effects, and Dr. John Fothergill expressed to an American Friend the desire that "Friends would studiously avoid everything adverse either to administration here on the one side—or Congress on the other. Submission to the prevailing power must be your duty. The prevailing power is the voice of America."

During the interval between the First Continental Congress and the outbreak of hostilities between the Mother Country and the colonies in 1775, the English Quakers bestirred themselves as individuals and as a society to persuade the British government to adopt more conciliatory measures regarding the colonies. Two English Quakers acted as mediators between Benjamin Franklin, representing the colonial cause, and those in the British government who were inclined to listen to and to consider conciliatory proposals. The negotiations extended over a period of several weeks, but because of the inability of either side to make sufficient concessions, the effort fell through. Franklin then left for

America, where he soon became one of the leaders in the independence movement.

British Quakers also attempted to prevent the passage of the Massachusetts Restraining Act. On the introduction of this bill in Parliament, David Barclay and Dr. Fothergill pleaded with Lord North for two hours not to support it. Shortly afterward, they served with several other Friends on a committee of the Meeting for Sufferings to draft an address to the king, which was subsequently presented at a public levee. The petition declared that the Friends were convinced of the loyalty of the colonists, and it urged that some way be found to prevent war with the colonies. Individual Friends also wrote to and had personal audiences with the king. As one correspondent wrote to an American Friend: "The Quakers in England have petitioned the king themselves as a people, and now attend the city petition; all join in one voice against the Ministry, and are all faithful to the people of America. The Quakers are the most hearty in the cause, and see the dreadful consequences of a civil war."

Before the end of 1775, the military phase of the struggle for independence was well under way. In October, the Pennsylvania Assembly passed an act providing for enlistment in the Continental Army, allowing exemptions for conscientious objectors for a stipulated payment. The Second Continental Congress advised the various colonies to abolish their present governments, thus cutting their imperial ties, and to establish new and independent governments. This action filled the Quakers with foreboding, for they feared the loss of their Charter of Liberties, and they opposed independence if achieved by war.

At the Yearly Meeting sessions held that fall, a committee, including visiting Friends from other Yearly Meetings, adopted a statement urging the local Monthly Meetings to act against all members guilty of military deviations, and exhorting them to avoid any acts, even of being spectators at training grounds, that might compromise their religious principles. By the end of the year, Monthly Meetings had begun to disown members who entered military service.

As a final attempt to stem the tide for dissolving the ties with Britain, in January 1776 the Philadelphia Meeting for Sufferings issued "The Ancient Testimony and Principles of the People called Quakers renewed with respect to the King and Government, and touching the Commotions now prevailing in these parts of America, addressed to the People in General." The Testimony contended that the current difficulties resulted from a departure from true religion and righteousness. It declared that the benefits enjoyed under the king's government in the past called for "constant endeavors, to guard against every attempt to alter, or subvert that interdependence and connection." It was not the business of the Quakers to join in plots and contrivances, since the setting up and pulling down of kings and governments was God's special prerogative.

The publication of this statement aroused much negative comment in the colonies and profoundly affected the attitude of many toward the Friends who were now seen as enemies of the Revolution. Even the New England Friend Moses Brown declared it would have been better if the statement had been issued as usual, that is, to the members of the Society and not to the general public.

Within a few months independence was declared, and the old charter of Pennsylvania was swept away. In this crisis the Pennsylvania Friends urged all the other American Yearly Meetings, New England, New York, Maryland, Virginia, and the one for North and South Carolina and Georgia, to send representatives to the sessions of Philadelphia Yearly Meeting to be held in the fall. At that time a committee consisting of representatives from all the Yearly Meetings drew up a set of advices governing the position and conduct of Friends in the prevailing situation. The recommendations as adopted by the Yearly Meeting enjoined all Friends from participating in any way in civil government, since the new authorities were established through "the Spirit of Wars, & Fighting." Friends were forbidden to pay any fines, penalty, or tax in lieu of personal military service, nor were they to engage in any business likely to promote the war, nor were they to buy or vend prize goods of any kind, as they were spoils of war. At the same time the Friends were reminded of the distress and suffering existing throughout the continent, and they were urged to cut their own expenses and contribute liberally to the relief of the distress of those of all societies and denominations.

The trials and tribulation that beset the Friends during the conflict reflected the tides of war. The contending armies seized all types of supplies and sequestrated Quaker homes and meetinghouses for which, of course, the Friends would accept no compensation. In August 1777, shortly after the British army had arrived in the Philadelphia area, the American forces discovered a spurious document, supposedly issued by the nonexistent Spanktown Yearly Meeting, which seemingly implicated the Quakers in passing important military information to the British. Naturally, this discovery alarmed the Pennsylvania authorities, who proceeded to round up a number of prominent Friends and send them off to exile in Virginia. No evidence was ever found to prove the authenticity of the documents or in any way to implicate the exiles. Therefore, the following spring, after the death of two of the exiles, the Continental Congress ordered their return to Pennsylvania, and they were soon set at liberty. This affair, despite the unfounded nature of the charges, greatly prejudiced the situation of the Quakers throughout the country, but especially in Pennsylvania.

All the new state governments soon passed laws requiring military service and tests of allegiance, as well as levying taxes to support the war. Colonial militia laws had generally provided various types of exemption for Quakers and other pacifist groups. During the Revolution these laws were supplanted by more stringent ones, although the provision allowing conscientious objectors to hire a substitute or pay a fine in lieu of military service was retained. In some cases a special annual tax was levied for granting a permanent status of exemption. Failure to pay such taxes or fines incurred distraint of the offender's property to the designated amount owed, although in some cases penalties included varying periods of imprisonment.

As the war progressed and the need for recruits became more pressing, primarily during the years 1777 through 1779, the laws became more severe. At that time Pennsylvania enforced its conscription laws with great severity, with penalties ranging up to multiples of ten times the basic amount. In most of the other colonies, however, both the laws and their enforcement were comparatively moderate, as was the case especially in Massachusetts.

Another type of legislation, causing even greater suffering to the Friends, required an oath or affirmation of allegiance known as the Test. These laws were passed as soon as independence was declared and required an abjuration of loyalty to the Crown. Their purpose was to weed out the Loyalists, but the Quakers, of course, fell afoul of them. Some laws levied heavy fines and taxes as penalties for those who refused to subscribe, and some even prescribed exile. In 1778, reflecting the immediate British military threat, Pennsylvania legislation reached its harshest, requiring all males 18 years and over to take the Test. It barred all those refusing the Test from engaging in most professions, including the maintaining of schools and teaching, and it subjected offenders to certain civil disabilities. As a consequence, all the Quaker schools closed for a time, and some Friends were imprisoned for teaching without subscribing the Test.

In New York, a few Friends who refused the Test were exiled from the mainland to British-occupied Long Island. In North Carolina, at one point, the authorities confiscated the estates of practically all the Friends in Perquimans County for their refusal to take the Test. On appeal to the state authorities, the legislature provided for the restitution of the estates to the original owners. Intercession of higher authorities on behalf of the Quakers was not uncommon in other states also.

The payment of taxes was another problem that the Quakers had to face. As already indicated, the official policy of the Society was that war taxes could not be paid. As to mixed taxes, war and civil, it was agreed that the decision to pay should be left to the individual's conscience, with strong support given to those who felt they could not pay them. There was no bar to paying taxes levied solely for the normal conduct of government, although there were some Friends in Pennsylvania who questioned even the payment of such taxes, since they were for the support of an authority established by means of war. Consequently, many Friends suffered extensive distraint of property for refusal to pay war and mixed taxes.

In New England, a controversy arose over the payment of taxes, which led to the formation of a small dissident group whose members believed that all taxes should be paid. This group, led by Timothy Davis of Sandwich Monthly Meeting in Massachusetts, never became large enough to establish an independent meeting. After the war, when the reason for the controversy had faded away, most of those involved returned to the fold of their former meetings.

Finally, the Friends were faced with the question of whether or not they could accept the paper money issued by the Continental Congress and the new state governments. In this case also, the decision was left up to the individual Friends, although some of the Pennsylvania Quakers contended that accepting such currency was tantamount to paying war taxes, since much of the money issued supported the costs of the war. In New England, the Friends accepted such currency, with the exception of a Massachusetts issue bearing the effigy of a soldier.

Because of the Friends' refusal to accept alternatives to military service or to provide any support for the war, they incurred varying degrees of hardship denoted as "sufferings," the severity depending on local conditions and attitudes. Total penal exactions amounted to approximately 103,195, taken largely through distraint of property. The Pennsylvania Quakers were the heaviest sufferers because of the prevailing political climate.

The Society did not hesitate to employ disciplinary measures against those failing to observe the pacifist testimony, which barred participation in or support of war in any way. The most frequent offense was military service, followed by paying fines and taxes, taking the Test, and various other actions such as hiring substitutes, joining a Patriot organization, and so on. A total of 1,724 members, according to available records, were disowned for the above indicated reasons. Military service accounted for 63 percent of the disownments, paying war fines and taxes for 14 percent, taking the Test for 11 percent, and miscellaneous types of assistance to the war effort for 12 percent.

In some quarters the refusal of the Quakers to cooperate aroused the suspicion that they were Loyalist sympathizers or outright Loyalists. This was especially so in Pennsylvania, where their outspoken opposition to the activities of the colonial radicals and to separation from Britain brought upon them virulent attacks. Elsewhere, the Quakers had no political interests to prompt them to issue quasi-political statements that would arouse animosity. In New England they were treated with a surprising degree of tolerance and understanding. The Friends there, as well as in other states, accorded what amounted to a de facto recognition of legitimacy to the new authorities and freely dealt with them, although they withheld official recognition until the war was over.

The consistency of the Quaker position in abstaining from any participation whatsoever in the war on behalf of either side is seen in the Friends' refusal to comply with British requisitions as strictly as with American military demands, as evidenced when the British controlled northern New Jersey in early 1777 and occupied Philadelphia later that year. Throughout the seven years when New York City was the focal point of British military and naval power in America, the Quaker inhabitants persistently refused to cooperate with them in any way. Moreover, Friends Meetings in Pennsylvania, New Jersey, and Maryland disowned the few Quakers who joined the British forces.

Before July 1776, the Quakers preferred to retain the imperial relationship rather than undergo military confrontation and the type of upheaval that occurred in Pennsylvania. But when the war broke out, they followed a policy of strict neutrality in withholding support from either side. At the conclusion of the war, those Quakers who had taken the Loyalist side either migrated to Canada or sailed for England with the returning British forces. The absence of confiscation of Quaker property because of Loyalist preference and participation shows that state and local authorities conceded the genuinely pacifist, neutral position of the Friends.

A considerable number of Friends obviously supported the war against Britain, for which they were disowned. One of these Friends was the Quaker minister Samuel Wetherill, Jr. Around him gathered a number of other disowned Friends such as Clement Biddle, quartermaster under General Horatio Gates at Valley Forge; Owen Biddle, Deputy Commissioner for Forage for the Continental Army; William Crispin, commissary general in Washington's army; the physician Benjamin Say; and two women, famous for their role in the Revolution, Lydia Darragh and Elizabeth Griscom Ross, known as Betsy Ross. Wetherill and his followers believed that the principle of guidance by the "Light Within," a cardinal Quaker tenet, should allow members of the Society, if they felt so led, to support the Revolution. Many of them also believed that they were supporting the creation of a divinely ordained new order of society on the American continent.

During and following the war, many others with similar ideas joined the group. In 1781 they organized the Society of Free Quakers, with a discipline resembling that of the Society of Friends, but without disciplinary procedures or provision for disownment. In 1783 they built a meetinghouse in Philadelphia on the lintel of whose doorway was the inscription: "Built in the Year of the Empire Eight." By 1800 there were well over 100 members, but as the impulse for the founding of the meeting receded into the past, the numbers dwindled, and the last meeting for worship was held in 1836.

Despite their noncooperative position during the war, the Quakers did adhere to the advice of 1776, urging them to cut their expenses and contribute liberally to the distressed of all denominations and societies. When the British occupied Boston in the winter of 1775–1776, and Newport, Rhode Island, in 1776–1777, the Friends in Pennsylvania, Delaware, and Maryland raised over £5,000 for the relief of the inhabitants of the beleaguered cities.

On the British occupation of Philadelphia in the winter of 1777–1778, the Pennsylvania Quakers undertook to relieve the distress of those affected by the requisitions and depredations of the contending armies. Quantities of food, clothing, other supplies, and money were gathered and distributed. According to the French diplomat Crevecoeur, the Friends sent "the necessitous all they had and shed tears over the fate of those they were unable to help."

When the war shifted to the South and the British occupied Charleston, the Quakers offered their country estates for the accommodation of those who had to flee the city. A year later, at the Battle of Guilford Court House in North Carolina, Friends, who were caring for over 100 persons in their meetinghouse, promised General Nathanael Greene, himself a former Quaker, that they would do what they could to succor the wounded.

In England, a committee of London Quaker merchants appealed to Lord Sandwich at the Lords of Admiralty in January 1778 on behalf of American prisoners of war housed in unsanitary conditions. Accordingly, Lord Sandwich ordered the construction of temporary buildings in which to lodge the prisoners. The merchants also raised over £8,000 for assistance to the prisoners through solicitations in Bristol, Nottingham, and Yorkshire. Bristol Friends sent a shipload of flour, peas, grits, and barley for the relief of the war sufferers in America, and London Friends likewise sent a cargo of food to Philadelphia for such purposes. Subsequently, Irish and English Friends raised substantial sums for war victims' relief in America.

Although the Friends could not join their countrymen in achieving independence from Great Britain because of their pacifist principles, they did their utmost to succor them in their time of need.

In the decades following the war, the impact of the Quakers' experience became obvious in their complete withdrawal from any political or governmental activity. However, when the bitterness of the war years had passed, the Friends soon acquired a reputation as exemplary citizens and as a positive force in their respective communities. On the establishment of the new national government in 1789, Philadelphia Yearly Meeting took the occasion to present an address to President Washington, assuring him of the firm loyalty of the Friends and pledging to contribute freely to the necessary support of civil government and to the exigencies of the poor. Washington replied with a gracious statement of his high regard for the Quakers and the constructive role they played in society. *See also*: Mennonites in the American Revolution; Wrightsborough, Georgia, Quaker Settlement

Arthur J. McKeel

REFERENCES

Richard Bauman, *For the Reputation of Truth* (1971); Margaret E. Hirst, *The Quakers in Peace and War* (1923); Arthur J. McKeel, *The Relation of the Quakers to the American Revolution* (1979); Isaac Sharpless, *A History of Quaker Government in Pennsylvania*, 2 vols., (1899) 2.

Quartermaster General

In June 1775 the Continental Congress, in addition to state and military representatives, planned to create a central authority to supply the Continental Army. The Quartermaster Department was designed to help in troop movements and armament. Congress gave General George Washington the power to appoint the quartermaster general; Washington stated the individual he named would have to meet strict qualifications and be a "man of great resource and activity, and worthy of the *highest* confidence."

Although the quartermaster general had no authority over the troops, he was the conduit for orders, passing them from the commander-in-chief to general officers. He was aware of all movements, including those that were secret. He was also responsible for collecting information, planning marches, examining possible theaters of battle, repairing roads that would be used for both advance and retreat movements, erecting and repairing bridges, setting up camps, and assigning quarters. A man wearing many hats, the quartermaster general was also expected to procure a vast array of supplies such as shelter, livestock, forage, wagons, and boats. Ultimately, he had to be clever, forceful, charismatic, and diplomatic, exhibiting military, administrative, and business skills.

Washington named Thomas Mifflin, a prominent Pennsylvanian, to the position on August 14, 1775. He received $80 monthly; his assistants earned $40 per month plus rations. His department was divided into three units, similar to the military troops, with a headquarters staffed with clerks and assistants and two field groups. His purchasing agents, usually local merchants, earned commissions. The quartermaster's primary responsibility was transportation, providing wagons and drivers to transfer supplies as well as boats for water movements; the department also was responsible for providing forage and shelter and assembling a group of talented artificers to build and repair structures and vehicles.

Mifflin's first priority was the purchase of arms and ammunition. Colonial industry was immature, and most saltpeter was made by citizens in homes or purchased from local merchants. A congressional committee agreed to buy the most critical supplies—especially weaponry—from foreign allies, and officers were also required and expected to outfit their troops with aid from state and local governments; however, many troops were armed with minimal supplies, if any.

In addition to locating weapons, the quartermaster general was supposed to procure and distribute nonfood items such as tools, chains, paper, and lead as well as to serve as the principal staff officer in arranging for troop movements, determining the route, and assigning reconnaissance missions.

Between 1775 and 1780 the Quartermaster Department experienced expansion with a diverse group of several thousand employees serving as wagon masters, storekeepers, clerks, weighers, collectors, and a variety of other positions. Problems in the department were myriad: employees received low wages, and delays slowed deliveries. Mifflin was promoted to the rank of brigadier general because of his help in recruiting militiamen, but the office of quartermaster general was limited to colonels. Mifflin resigned, and Assistant Quartermaster General Hugh Hughes served temporarily in the position until Stephen Moylan replaced Mifflin as quartermaster general. He proved incompetent, and an inspection committee asked Mifflin to reconsider, agreeing that he could keep his advanced title; in November Mifflin returned to the position. He stayed in Philadelphia, where he prevented the British from capturing stores and also helped raise troops. He was rewarded with the rank of major general for these actions.

May 1777 was the first time Congress regulated the Quartermaster Department, requiring all personnel to send in monthly reports using standardized forms as well as creating specialized subdepartments. At this time the quartermaster general was rarely at headquarters, and three assistants performed his duties: Joseph Thornsbury was wagonmaster general; Clement Biddle was commissioner general of forage; and Colonel Henry Emanuel Lutterloh, who had been quartermaster for the army of Brunswick, served as Mifflin's deputy.

In July 1777 Lutterloh was in charge while Mifflin was absent, protecting supplies in the East; because of the decentralized structure, the quartermaster general's services were disorganized and ineffective. Congressional indecision and neglect contributed to the disintegration of the Quartermaster Department: Congress detained Mifflin, who was eager to return to his staff, in Philadelphia to discuss reorganization of the department, preventing him from performing his administrative duties at headquarters. The army underwent a series of defeats, and by October 1777, an unhealthy and frustrated Mifflin resigned, but Congress did not accept his resignation until one month later, naming him to the Board of War so that he could get his commission as a major general. Mifflin advised that Congress choose Lutterloh as his successor, and Lutterloh assumed the quartermaster general's responsibilities. Unfortunately, his inexperience and lack of knowledge of potential resources and how the entire department functioned triggered various problems for supply.

As a direct result of this personnel change and ineffective regulation by Congress, the supply system faltered, sparking the catastrophic winter at Valley Forge. Remaining suppliers had little experience, and the systems slowly ceased in the autumn. As a result of the Valley Forge disaster, Washington, extremely concerned, requested that a congressional committee meet at his headquarters. They decided to centralize supply by finding a prominent, reliable, and competent individual to serve as quartermaster. Nathanael Greene was considered the best choice. Greene served as quartermaster general from March 1778 to August 1780 with assistants John Cox, purchaser and examiner, and Charles Pettit, accountant, who were allowed to retain a 1 percent commission, an amount which the three men decided to divide equally.

Greene followed Mifflin's example, utilizing a plan Mifflin suggested in February 1778 that the department should be separated into a military section supervised by the quartermaster general and a civilian branch, procuring forage, wagons, and supplies as directed by a hierarchy of deputies and purchasing agents. Greene kept Mifflin's competent deputies and increased personnel as offices duplicated in each locale. At this time the military complained that too many individuals employed by the quartermaster general received high ranks, especially that of colonel, causing friction between military authorities and supply leaders.

Although supplies were often delayed, the army was satisfactorily stocked for 1778 campaigns. But prices skyrocketed and rumors of abuses in the Quartermaster Department circulated. An inquiry was held in the fall of 1778 because some congressmen thought Greene was "making a fortune too rapidly." His reputation questioned, Greene threatened to resign, but the investigators in 1779 expressed their confidence and support of him, and Greene agreed to remain in the office. The states agreed to locate and fire corrupt officials, agents, and employees, and by 1780 Congress was eliminating excess positions in the department.

States were still relied on for basic supplies. Military defeats were especially damaging in the South, instigating a search for optional supply solutions. Both Greene and Washington thought it was necessary to seek alternatives to state supply.

The Quartermaster Department was reorganized on July 15, 1780, by reducing unneeded staff and having the Board of War and state governors appoint assistants in order to cut expenses. Personnel was drastically decreased, and salaries, not commissions, were allocated. According to the renovated directives, the quartermaster general's sole concern was supply.

With this reorganization Greene resigned as soon as he received the plans, acerbically sniping that "Systems without Agents are useless things. . . . Administrators seem to think it far less important to the public interest to have this department well filled, and properly managed, than it really is, and as they will find it by future experience." Timothy Pickering, who had helped write the regulations, succeeded Greene as quartermaster general and was given the rank of colonel but paid at the rate of brigadier general.

Although he was not very interested in the position, he attempted to perform his duties and prevent superfluous purchases. Pettit served as his assistant, but Pickering had trouble hiring sufficient personnel because the positions offered inadequate salaries. He placed as many states under the jurisdiction of one deputy as possible for economic reasons. Unfortunately, he lacked ample money to make the system work and was unable to buy food or clothing or arrange for transportation of an adequate amount of supplies. Delays and obstacles such as these induced the supply system's death throes. Washington reacted to the quartermaster's predicament by acting as his own supplier because he did not have faith that Pickering and his staff could successfully outfit the troops.

Financier Robert Morris began to secure supplies by a system of contracts, and Congress reduced the salaries of Quartermaster Department personnel. An upset Pickering was ready to resign but was obliged to continue in his position, even though the departmental supply system had dissolved, to finalize accounts and disperse government property after the war, until July 25, 1785, when the Quartermaster Department was liquidated.

Elizabeth D. Schafer

REFERENCES

E. Wayne Carp, *To Starve the Army at Pleasure: Continental Army Administration and American Political Culture, 1775 –1783* (1984); John C. Dann, ed., *The Revolution Remembered: Eyewitness Accounts of the War for Independence* (1980); John C. Fitzpatrick, ed., *The Writings of George Washington*, 30 vols. (1931–1939); Erna Risch, *Quartermaster Support of the Army: A History of the Corps, 1775–1939* (1966); Kenneth R. Rossman, *Thomas Mifflin and the Politics of the American Revolution* (1952); Orlando W. Stephenson, "The Supply of Gunpowder in 1776," *American Historical Review*, 30 (1925):271–81; Theodore Thayer, *Nathanael Greene: Strategist of the American Revolution* (1960).

Quebec Act

See Carleton, Guy, 1st Baron Dorcester.

Queen's Loyal Rangers

A loyalist regiment organized in 1775 by John Peters of Moortown in the New Hampshire Grants. Compelled to flee to Canada by his Patriot neighbors, John Peters was granted a commission by General Sir Guy Carleton and returned to upper New York with General John Burgoyne, where he recruited his followers. The regiment fought at the Battle of Bennington and later at Saratoga, suffering heavily in both encounters. The Queen's Loyal Rangers are not to be confused with the Queen's Rangers, who also originated in New York but were a unit of the regular British army.

Tom Martin

REFERENCES

Robert McCluer Calhoon, *The Loyalists in Revolutionary America, 1760–1781* (1973); Philip Ranlet, *The New York Loyalists* (1986).

Queen's Rangers

Robert Rogers, of French and Indian War fame, received a commission as a provincial lieutenant colonel from Sir William Howe on August 6, 1776. He was to raise and lead a unit originally designated the Queen's American Rangers, and later the Queen's Rangers.

Rogers gathered recruits mainly from New York and Connecticut. Toward the end of the month the Rangers absorbed the remains of Lord Dunmore's Queen's Own Loyal Virginia Regiment, recently arrived in New York from the Old Dominion.

During the Battle of Long Island the Rangers remained on Staten Island. While a detachment served with the artillery, the Rangers, some apparently still unarmed, landed at Throgs Neck late in October and occupied Mamaroneck. Here on October 21 the unit was surprised by the rebels and absorbed about 58 casualties.

Rogers remained in effective command until March 1777, but the state of the regiment was not very satisfactory. Major Christopher French of the 22nd Foot was brought in at that time to reform the Rangers. He dismissed 23 unsuitable officers, confirmed the 10-company organization, and began to rebuild the unit's strength.

Rogers was finally discharged in May, at which time Major James Wemyss of the 40th Foot took command of the Rangers. They numbered about 400 during this period, but by the time they embarked for the Philadelphia campaign on July 8 they were down to 278. In order to help rebuild the regiment, it received permission to enlist rebel deserters, something that no other provincial unit had received authority to do.

The Rangers were with Howe when he landed at Elk Ferry, Maryland, on August 25. They performed well at Brandywine on September 11 and at Germantown on October 4, where Wemyss was wounded. He was succeeded as commandant of the Rangers on October 15 by Captain John Graves Simcoe of the 40th Foot. Given the provincial rank of major, Simcoe at once formed an eleventh company composed of Highlanders in their native dress. He also received permission to mount 12 men, and they grew into a full troop of Hussars by December.

While in Philadelphia the Rangers were engaged in almost constant outpost duty, and two larger, rather bloody engagements in March 1778 against rebel militia at Quintan's Bridge and Hancock's Bridge. Simcoe was promoted to lieutenant colonel on May 25, and was given permission to enlist Irish recruits. His was one of only three Loyalist organizations permitted to do so during the war. In June the Queen's Rangers were in combat at Monmouth, at which time they numbered about 300.

Back in New York, the Rangers resumed outpost duty at Kingsbridge and then went into winter quarters on Long Island. On May 2, 1779, Simcoe's unit was honored by being named the

1st American Regiment on the newly created American establishment.

After a brief return to Westchester, the Rangers were back at Oyster Bay, Long Island, in August. At that time the commander-in-chief placed Diemar's Hussars and Sandford's Bucks County Light Dragoons under Simcoe's direction.

In September, the infantry of the Rangers received orders to join the expedition of Lord Cornwallis being sent to reinforce Jamaica in the West Indies. However, the fleet was at sea for only one day when it received a warning of the approach of a French fleet, and immediately returned to New York.

The infantry landed on Staten Island, where it was joined by the cavalry units from Long Island. Simcoe was soon leading a raid into New Jersey at the end of October, where he was captured. After about a month of imprisonment, Simcoe was exchanged and was present when his Rangers helped defend Staten Island against Lord Stirling's raid in January 1780.

Early in April the Queen's Rangers infantry, about 400 in number, was embarked as part of Lord Francis Rawdon's force bound for Charleston to reinforce Clinton's army besieging that southern city. Upon the successful conclusion of the siege, the Rangers returned to Staten Island late in June rejoining their cavalry contingent and attached units.

While in the New York area, the unit participated in various minor operations. In August the Rangers were expanded to include two new troops of light dragoons. One of these troops was sent on General Alexander Leslie's expedition to Virginia in mid-October to complete its recruiting in the South. The troop was with Leslie when he went to Charleston toward the end of the year.

Upon being reinforced by Althause's New York Volunteers rifle company and Thomas's Bucks County Volunteers, the Queen's Rangers joined Benedict Arnold's expedition to Virginia. Sailing from New York on December 21, 1780, they reached the Chesapeake nine days later and moved up the James River. The British force faced little or no opposition as it destroyed part of Richmond and carried off numerous stores. By early January 1781 Arnold's troops had withdrawn to Portsmouth, which they occupied for the winter.

When General William Phillips reinforced Arnold from New York on March 27, further operations up the James were begun. The Queen's Rangers, now numbering 455, were engaged at Petersburg and Osborne's Landing, and were the first unit to make contact with the army of Cornwallis moving north from Wilmington, North Carolina. Cornwallis reached Petersburg on May 20 and the Rangers came under his command.

In June, elements of the Rangers accompanied Banastre Tarleton on his raid to Charlottesville, and they were at Spencer's Ordinary on June 26th. Missing the Battle of Green Spring, the unit reached Portsmouth on July 14 and moved to Yorktown on August 2. As part of the garrison of Gloucester Point opposite Yorktown, the Rangers, by then down to about 360, surrendered with Cornwallis on October 19, 1781.

All but two troops of Rangers light dragoons had become prisoners of war. On December 19, Simcoe became a lieutenant colonel in the regular army, and Captain John Saunders assumed command of the Rangers when he arrived in New York from Charleston.

After spending a year in the New York garrison, the Rangers were taken onto the British establishment on December 25, 1782, making them regulars and recognizing their useful services. They had rebuilt their strength to 276 by August 1783, but were finally ordered to Nova Scotia in October to be disbanded.

Various uniform descriptions exist for the Queen's Rangers. One indicates for cavalry, "Short Green round Jacketts—black Cuff & Collar—with Plain Black Cloth Hussar Capt—Memento Front," and the infantry as, "Green Short Coats, Lappel Same, Black Cuffs & Collar." Another shows green coat and facings with silver metal. Buttons exist showing either "QR" or "1" surrounded by "American" with a crown on top.

Walter T. Dornfest

REFERENCES

John R. Cuneo, "The Early Days of the Queen's Rangers August 1776–February 1777," *Military Affairs*, 22 (1958):65–74; H.M. Jackson, "The Queen's Rangers, 1st American Regiment," *Journal of the Society for Army Historical Research*, 14 (1935):143–154; George H. Locke, *Queen's Rangers* (1923); H. Charles McBarron and Rutledge F. Smith, "The Queen's Rangers (1st American Regiment), 1778-1783," *Military Collector and Historian, 24* (1972):20–21; John G. Simcoe, *History of the Operations of a Partisan Corps, called the Queen's Rangers . . .* (1844), Arno rpr. 1968.

Quintin's Bridge, New Jersey, Engagement at (March 18, 1778) (Alternate spellings: Quinton's, Quintan's)

To counter General Anthony Wayne's February cattle drive in New Jersey (securing beef for the American army at Valley Forge) and to conduct their own foraging operations, a large detachment of British troops was dispatched in March 1778 from Philadelphia to explore the Salem County region of south Jersey. This force had two engagements of note with the Jersey militia forces. The first of these took place at Quintin's Bridge.

In 1778, Quintin's Bridge was the middle of three bridges in Salem County that crossed Alloways (Aloes) Creek, on a road that ran from Salem to the Maurice River and Millville. The bridge took its name from the first English settler along Alloways Creek, Tobias Quintin (Quinton, Quintan), and was at that time a wooden drawbridge made of rough-hewn planks.

Colonel Charles Mawhood, the British brigade commander at the battle of Princeton, led the 17th, 27th and 46th Regiments of Foot on the expedition. His force was augmented by the Queen's Rangers under Major John Graves Simcoe and the Loyalist New Jersey Volunteers. Total British strength was approximately 1,200 to 1,300 men. Mawhood also brought along four cannon, two howitzers, and provisions for two weeks. Anchored in the Delaware River close to Salem were six transports for Mawhood to fill with cattle, horses, and forage. The frigate *Camilla* under Captain Charles Phipps provided security for the ships.

Mawhood's men embarked on March 12, 1778, and fell down the Delaware River until a landing was effected on March 17 near Salem, New Jersey. Colonel Elijah Hand hastily assembled local Jersey militia units to meet the British threat. One group of 300 militia was positioned three miles southeast of Salem at Quintin's Bridge to block a British advance into the interior.

The militia lightly fortified the east side of the creek and took up the planks of the bridge as an added safeguard. Mawhood sent 70 men from the 17th Regiment to the west bank of Alloways Creek to screen the bridge and Americans from the foraging British work parties. When the British infantry became too closely engaged with the Americans to safely withdraw, Mawhood was called upon to come to the rescue.

While Mawhood and Simcoe approached the troops of the 17th Regiment in the open, other British units secretly took positions to create a trap for the Americans. A detachment of Queen's Rangers under Captain Stephenson hid in the brick, two-storied Wetherby's Tavern, which stood on the British side of the creek along the Bridge Road. Another group of rangers under Captain John Saunders were hidden beyond the tavern in the field behind a fence bordering the road. Simcoe and the remainder of the rangers waited in the woods off the road.

Mawhood then ordered the 17th to withdraw from their exposed position. The Americans discharged their muskets at the departing British. Quickly the planks were replaced on the bridge. At the urging of Lieutenant Duclos, a French officer present with the militia, the Americans crossed the creek. Unaware that the Rangers lay in wait, the militia split into two groups. While 100 men remained on the high ground close to the western bank of the creek, Captain William Smith led the other 200 militiamen in pursuit of the British.

The militiamen passed Wetherby's Tavern and moved up the road from the bridge. Suddenly the Americans heard someone laugh behind the fence. In an instant, the Rangers were up and at the Americans. The militiamen began running back up the road toward the creek. Just then Stephenson's company came out of Wetherby's Tavern to block the American escape. Flustered and confused by the trap, the Americans fled south off the road and across the fields in panic. In the confusion, Captain Smith was wounded twice and had his horse shot from under him.

Simcoe sent the 30 mounted Hussars of the Rangers to harass the American retreat. Mawhood turned the 17th around and joined the pursuit, accompanied by Simcoe's main body of rangers coming out of the woods. The rout was on.

Some militia were shot as they fled. Others were cut down by the Hussars before they reached the creek. Some drowned in the creek as they attempted to swim to safety. The 100 American militiamen who had remained by the bridge were able to recross before the trap was shut. An American named Andrew Bacon grabbed an axe and cut away the drawbridge section of the bridge under fire to keep the British from crossing. Bacon was severely wounded in this action and was crippled for life.

At the same time, a company of Cumberland County militia under Colonel Elijah Hand arrived at the eastern bank of the creek with two cannon. They provided cover for the American survivors and stopped the British advance.

An official count of American casualties was never taken. The Americans left behind 30 to 40 dead. No one knows how many drowned. Participants considered the American death toll to be a heavy one. The British admitted to having one Hussar killed. The Americans called Quintin's Bridge a massacre. The action inflamed Loyalist-American passions in New Jersey. Tactically, it was a well-planned and professionally executed trap perpetrated by the British on the unsuspecting and militarily naive Americans. Two days later, Simcoe struck the Jersey militia again, this time at Hancock's Bridge.

Paul J. Sanborn

REFERENCES

John W. Jackson, *With the British Army in Philadelphia, 1777–1778* (1979); Benson J. Lossing. *The Pictorial Field Book of the Revolution*, 2 vols. (1851–2), rpr. 1972; William McMahon, *South Jersey Towns* (1973); Adeline Pepper, *Tours of Historic New Jersey* (1973); John F. Reed, *Valley Forge, Crucible of Victory* (1969); John G. Simcoe, *A History of the Operations of a Partisan Corps called the Queen's Rangers* (1844), rpr. 1968; Sol Stember, *The Bicentennial Guide to the American Revolution*, 2 vols. (1974), *1*.

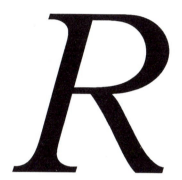

Raleigh

A frigate of 32 guns, the *Raleigh* was one of the 13 ships authorized by the Continental Congress in December 1775 and was probably the first to be launched. Her keel was laid in Portsmouth, New Hampshire, on March 21, 1776, and she was launched only 60 days later on May 21, 1776. She was built by the renowned James K. Hackett. Under her first captain, Thomas Thompson, *Raleigh* fought in engagements with the British warships *Druid* (14 guns), *Ariadne* (20 guns), and *Ceres* (16 guns), while on a mission to obtain supplies from France during the fall and winter of 1777–1778. In May 1778, Captain John Barry replaced Thompson as commanding officer. On September 25, 1778, within hours of leaving Boston harbor on her first voyage under Barry, *Raleigh* was sighted by two British warships, *Experiment* (50 guns) and *Unicorn* (22 guns). *Raleigh* survived pursuit by the British for some 60 hours, but was finally crippled in Penobscot Bay, near present-day Bangor, Maine, by damage to her masts. After a fierce seven-hour battle, *Raleigh* was run aground on a rocky island, and Barry attempted to burn her. His plan did not succeed, and *Raleigh* was salvaged by the British, although Barry and many of his crew were able to escape to the mainland. *Raleigh* was taken to England, repaired, and entered into service with the Royal Navy under the same name. She was later involved in battle off Charleston, South Carolina, and helped destroy the American sloop *Ranger*. The dimensions of *Raleigh* were: length on berth deck, 131 feet, five inches; beam, 34 feet, 5 inches; depth in hold, 11 feet; height of mainmast, 86 feet; burden, 697 tons. *See also:* Continental Navy

Mark E. Furber

REFERENCES

Howard I. Chapelle, *The History of American Sailing Ships* (1935); ———,*The History of the American Sailing Navy: The Ships and Their Development* (1949); Department of the Navy, Naval History Division, *Dictionary of American Fighting Ships*, Vols. 1–3 (1959–1968); William James Morgan, "John Barry: A Most Fervent Patriot," in *Command Under Sail: Makers of the American Naval Tradition: 1775–1850,* James C. Bradford, ed. (1985); William G. Saltonstall, *Ports of Piscataqua* (1941).

Ramsay, David (1749–1815)

American physician, historian. A physician by training, a Patriot and Federalist by conviction, and historian by avocation, David Ramsay was born in Lancaster County, Pennsylvania. He graduated from the College of New Jersey in 1765, worked briefly as a tutor, and studied medicine at the College of Pennsylvania. He practiced for a year in Maryland before moving to Charleston, South Carolina, in 1773.

Ramsay promptly joined the Patriot faction in that southern city to oppose British policies and champion American independence. From 1776 to 1780 he was a prominent member of the state legislature. When British forces captured Charleston, Ramsay was among 33 Patriot leaders who were arrested and exiled to St. Augustine. He was imprisoned for a year before he was allowed to return to Charleston, where he resumed his seat in the assembly. From 1782 to 1785 Ramsay was a delegate to the Continental Congress, where he supported efforts to amend the Articles of Confederation. He returned to South Carolina, where he held a seat in the state house of representatives and later the state senate until he retired from public service in 1798.

David Ramsay is best known not as a Patriot but as a historian of the Revolution. In 1785 he published a two-volume *History of the Revolution in South Carolina*. Although Ramsay copied extensively from the *Annual Register* in this study, he also provided an eyewitness account of many events. Four years later, Ramsay produced a broader, less provincial summary entitled *History of the American Revolution*. Although it was praised as "a prototype for scholars of his generation," Ramsay again incorporated materials extracted from the *Register* and from contemporary historians. Ramsay pursued his literary interests with a biography of George Washington published in 1807 and a *Universal History*, which appeared posthumously.

David Ramsay was a skilled physician who promoted the use of vaccination against smallpox, a Patriot who contributed to the struggle for independence, a moderate Federalist who advocated an effective central government, a humanitarian who opposed the slave trade, and a scholar who sought to record his country's early history. He died in 1815, murdered by a mentally unbalanced assailant.

Marvin L. Cann

REFERENCES

Orin Grant Libby, "Ramsay as a Plagiarist," *American Historical Review*, 7 (1902):697–703; David Duncan Wallace, *South Carolina: A Short History* (1951).

Ramsay, Nathaniel (1741–1817)

Continental Army officer. Noted for bravery at the Battle of Monmouth for helping to check the American retreat, Nathaniel Ramsay was a colonel in the Continental Army and was the brother of David Ramsay, South Carolina political leader, physician, and historian.

Ramsay was born on May 1, 1741, in Lancaster County, Pennsylvania, to James and Jane (Montgomery) Ramsay. He studied law at the College of New Jersey, where he graduated in 1767, and practiced in Maryland for several years. He served as a delegate to the Maryland Convention of 1775 and as a delegate to the Continental Congress. In January 1776 he was commissioned captain of William Smallwood's Maryland Regiment, which was incorporated into the Continental Army in July 1776 as the 3rd Maryland. Ramsay was commissioned lieutenant colonel of the regiment.

He was noted for bravery at Long Island and at Monmouth, where, on the orders of Washington, he helped to check the retreat by men under General Charles Lee. At Monmouth, he was wounded, left for dead, and captured by the British. He was paroled in December 1780 and retired from service the next month.

After the war he served in the Continental Congress from 1785 to 1787 and then as a naval officer for the Baltimore District until his death.

Harold Campbell

REFERENCES

DAB; W.S. Stryker, *The Battle of Monmouth* (1927); Theodore George Thayer, *The Making of a Scapegoat: Washington and Lee at Monmouth* (1976); Christopher Ward, *The War of the Revolution*, 2 vols. (1952), 2.

Ramsour's Mill, North Carolina, Battle of (June 20, 1780) (Alternate spellings: Ramsauer's, Ramseur's)

After the fall of Charleston in May 1780, with the surrender of the major Continental Army in the South and the subsequent establishment of

British bases in Camden, Cheraw, and Ninety Six, the war prepared to move into North Carolina. Both Whigs and Loyalists organized and recruited with a purpose in the weeks immediately following the devastating American defeat. For North Carolina Loyalists the new situation promised deliverance by General Lord Cornwallis, a chance to avenge their rout at the Battle of Moore's Creek in February 1776, and an opportunity to settle up years of grievances. For the desperate Whigs, only the militia stood in the way of the British troops, at least until a new Continental Army arrived.

Cornwallis would have preferred that the Loyalists not take up arms too soon. He needed time to consolidate his new positions and believed the best immediate service the Tories could offer him would be to harvest the wheat that he would eventually need to feed his troops. The restless Loyalists jumped the gun, however. In early June, Colonel John Moore, who lived near Ramsour's Mill in Lincoln County, returned to his home county after serving with Cornwallis in South Carolina. Moore called for a meeting to be held at his father's house on June 10. Some 40 men responded. Moore detailed Cornwallis's plan to invade and to secure North Carolina and called for Loyalists to flock to the King's standards at Ramsour's Mill beginning June 13. About 200 showed up that day, and more continued to pour in during the following days. Within a week, Moore's forces numbered between 1,100 and 1,300, about 300 of whom were unarmed.

While Moore and his men were organizing, the nearby Whigs were doing likewise. By mid-June approximately 800 Whigs had assembled near Charlotte under the command of General Griffith Rutherford, while 400 had gathered under Colonel Francis Locke at Mountain Creek. Another group had encamped under the command of Major Joseph McDowell. Rutherford wished to remain in place as he did not want to leave Charlotte undefended. Since Locke was closer to Moore's troops than any other Patriot group, Rutherford ordered him to disperse the large Tory force.

As Locke's militia approached Ramsour's Mill on June 20, Moore's forces appeared to be in a fairly secure position. Not only did Moore outnumber his pursuers but he also occupied a sound defensive position. His troops were encamped along the crest of a long ridge about 300 yards

from the mill, just north of the present town of Lincolnton. A long slope, free of brush, lay in their front, giving the defenders a good field of fire. Moore, who was aware that hostile forces were in operation in the area, stationed about a dozen men as pickets some 600 yards in front of the encampment.

These pickets turned out to be more of a hindrance than a help to Moore, however. Locke's men, approaching quietly through nearby woods, surprised the pickets, who loosed a few ill-aimed volleys and then fled to the camp, which they threw into a state of panic. The appearance on the hill of the few mounted troops that Locke possessed threw Moore's forces into further confusion, causing some of the Loyalists to flee the battle without firing a single shot.

The remainder of Moore's forces held firm, however, and drove the Patriot horsemen back down the hill. A brief counterattack by Moore's force was repulsed, and the Loyalists withdrew back to the crest of the hill. Gradually, Locke's militia surrounded the hill and closed with their opponents. By this point the battle had become unusually chaotic. Neither side was particularly well-trained or organized nor did any leader have a coherent battle plan. The Tories wore green leaves in their hats as identification, while their adversaries wore corresponding white scraps of paper. These quickly fell off in the heat of combat, however. As the two sides grappled in hand-to-hand combat, it became increasingly difficult to tell friend from foe. Neither side had bayonets, while many Tories were unarmed. Rifles were used as clubs, while some combatants were reduced to using rocks or fists. Yet, many of these men bore a deep and lasting animosity toward their neighbors, and the infighting was especially vicious, despite the lack of training and equipment.

The outcome of the battle was still in doubt when Tory captain Warlick was shot. Captain Warlick had been particularly effective in directing resistance during the struggle. With his death Tory efforts collapsed, and Moore's forces retreated in disarray. Locke's troops, in almost equal disarray, were unable to reorganize for effective pursuit.

Each side suffered about 70 dead and 100 wounded. About 50 Loyalists were captured. Most of the captured were quickly paroled, although a few were held prisoner in the Salisbury jail. Moore escaped capture and eventually made his way to a furious Cornwallis with only 30 troops.

Despite its almost comic-opera aspects, the fight had serious consequences for the British. After waiting four years for British deliverance the defeated Loyalists were again discouraged, disheartened, and weary. Later that year when Major Patrick Ferguson came through the area they were not again so eager to run off to war. Thus Moore's premature and ill-advised adventure may have deprived Ferguson of 1,000 troops who might possibly have changed his rendezvous with disaster on King's Mountain.

Jim Sumner

REFERENCES

Robert O. Demond, *The Loyalists in North Carolina During the Revolution* (1940); William Graham, "The Battle of Ramsour's Mill, June 20, 1780," *The North Carolina Booklet*, 4 (1904); Hugh F. Rankin, *North Carolina in the American Revolution* (1959); Blackwell P. Robinson, *The Revolutionary War Sketches of William R. Davie* (1976); Christopher Ward, *The War of the Revolution*, 2 vols. (1952), 2.

Ranger

An American ship-rigged sloop of war, 18 guns, the *Ranger* was launched in May 1777 at Portsmouth, New Hampshire. During April and May 1778, under her first captain, John Paul Jones, the *Ranger* operated off the British coast, carrying out raids on coastal towns and capturing several merchantmen and a British man-of-war, the *Drake* (20 guns). In April 1780, the *Ranger* fought at Charleston, South Carolina, as part of a squadron under the command of Commodore Abraham Whipple, where she was destroyed in battle with a British squadron. The dimensions of the *Ranger* were: length on gun deck, 116 feet; beam, 34 feet; depth in hold, 13 feet, 6 inches; burden, 308 tons; complement, approximately 140 men; nominal battery, 18 9-pounders.

Mark E. Furber

REFERENCES

Howard I. Chapelle, *The History of American Sailing Ships* (1935); ———, *The History of the American Sailing Navy: The Ships and Their Development* (1949); Department of the Navy, Naval History Division, *Dictionary of American Fighting Ships*, Vols. 1–3 (1959–68); Lincoln Lorenz, *John Paul Jones: Fighter for Freedom and Glory* (1943); William G. Saltonstall, *Ports of Piscataqua* (1941); Christopher Ward, *The War of the Revolution*, ed. by John R. Alden (1952).

Rangers

See Rogers, Robert

Raven of Echota

Raven was a Cherokee war title given to a leader who scouted ahead of a raiding party in search of the enemy. Every Cherokee town had "Ravens," but the Raven of Echota was perhaps the most famous. The Raven was the nephew of the famous Oconostota (Great Warrior), who, along with his uncle and other leading chiefs such as Old Hop and Attacullaculla, attended the Saluda treaty conference in 1755. Here the Cherokees ceded over 5½ million acres to South Carolina. In return, that state agreed, among other things, to build Fort Loudoun.

At the beginning of the Cherokee war of 1760–1761, the Raven of Echota, along with two other great Cherokee chiefs, Little Carpenter and Oconostota, sought the release of the Cherokee chiefs held at Fort Prince George. After the war he was one of the chiefs who searched for permanent peace.

When the Cherokees sided with the British in the American Revolution, the Raven led one of three attacks on the North Carolina–Virginia frontier settlements. The Raven of Echota struck Carters Valley, but only succeeded in burning a few abandoned cabins before returning to Echota.

The Americans retaliated brutally. After North Carolina and South Carolina troops devastated the Lower, Middle, and Valley Towns, Colonel William Christian and 1,800 Virginians began marching toward the Overhill Towns, where Echota was located. Seeking peace, the Raven met Christian before he crossed into Cherokee territory. Christian demanded the surrender of Alexander Cameron, British agent among the Cherokees, but Raven refused. Consequently, Christian destroyed the Cherokee towns of Tellico, Settico, and Chilhowee before the Cherokees agreed to peace.

In July 1777, the Overhill Cherokees met at Long Island of the Holston, where Raven and Old Tassel were speakers. The Raven expressed hope that the new boundary line drawn after ceding more land would be "as a wall to the skies, so that no one could pass it."

Shortly after this treaty, the Raven realized that the Virginians would not willingly supply food and ammunition to the Cherokees, so he began corresponding with British officials to acquire supplies for his people. Meanwhile, North Carolinians began crossing the 1777 boundary. The Raven protested to North Carolina governor Richard Caswell and received assurances that the violations would not continue, but they did. Still, the Raven and most Cherokees desired peace. In 1782, the Raven and Old Tassel headed a delegation that traveled to the Delaware Indian village at Coshocton, in Ohio, where the two tribes agreed to remain neutral in the continuing conflict between the English and the Americans. The pledge of neutrality amounted to little since the Chickamauga Cherokees and white Tennesseans made it impossible for any Indian to remain neutral. Old Tassel was killed by Tennessean John Kirk under a flag of truce in 1788.

William L. Anderson

REFERENCES

John Brown, *Old Frontiers: The Story of the Cherokee Indians from Earliest Times to the Date of Their Removal West, 1838* (1938); Archibald Henderson, "Treaty of Long Island of Holston, July 1777, *"North Carolina Historical Review, 8* (1931):55–116; James H. O'Donnell, *Southern Indians in the American Revolution* (1973); ———, "Virginia's Expedition Against the Overhill Cherokee, 1776," *East Tennessee Historical Society Publication, 39* (1967):13–25; Grace Steele Woodward, *The Cherokee* (1963).

Rawdon, Francis Lord (1754–1826)

British army officer. The eldest son of the Irish Earl of Moira, Francis Rawdon was known as Lord Rawdon until succeeding to his father's earldom in 1783. Educated at Harrow and Oxford, Rawdon entered active service in the army in 1773 as a lieutenant in the 5th Foot. Athletic and high spirited, Rawdon was popular among his fellow officers and played the role of dashing young aristocrat well. At the end of 1773, he was posted to Boston and spent most of the next eight years in America.

Rawdon saw more action in America than did many British officers. Though not involved in the opening hostilities at Lexington and Concord, Rawdon distinguished himself in combat at Bunker Hill and was thereafter appointed to a captaincy in the 63rd Foot. In early 1776, he was seconded for staff duty as an aide-de-camp to Sir Henry Clinton, and he accompanied Clinton on the unsuccessful expedition that was dispatched against Charleston. Clinton and Rawdon returned north in time to see action again at the Battle of Long Island, and Rawdon was subsequently involved in other fighting around New York. He continued on Clinton's staff in New York (where his chief gained a reputation for excellence among British officers) and sometimes acted as a go-between, carrying dispatches to Sir William Howe after the latter's capture of Philadelphia. In June 1778, he was promoted to lieutenant colonel and named adjutant general of the army at Philadelphia, now under Clinton's command.

While in Philadelphia, Rawdon was encouraged by Clinton to raise a regiment of Loyalists. He complied, recruiting the Volunteers of Ireland, as the regiment was called, mainly from Scots-Irish deserters from the Continental Army. Rawdon himself received the provincial rank of colonel as commander of the regiment. He soon worked them into shape, and the Volunteers of Ireland proved to be one of the most effective provincial units in the British service. Rawdon and the Volunteers took part in the Battle of Monmouth (June 28, 1778) during the British retreat across New Jersey. Back in New York, Rawdon became estranged from Clinton; in September 1779 he resigned his position as adjutant general. He was left behind when Clinton embarked for his second expedition to Charleston at the end of the year.

It was in South Carolina, however, that Rawdon was destined to establish his military reputation. In March 1780, the Volunteers of Ireland were ordered to join the army besieging Charleston as part of a sizable reinforcement. After the city's fall, Clinton prepared to return to New York with the majority of British troops. Rawdon joined the army to remain in the South under Lord Cornwallis. He proved himself a useful subordinate in the events leading up to the Battle of Camden (August 16, 1780). There Rawdon efficiently commanded the British left wing. Afterward, he played his part in Cornwallis's attempt to pacify the Carolinas.

When Cornwallis moved into North Carolina in early 1781, he left Rawdon behind to hold South Carolina and Georgia. At the age of 26, Rawdon had his first independent command, and he acquitted himself well against an able opponent. After the Battle of Guilford Court House, Nathanael Greene moved south into South Carolina rather than following Cornwallis eastward. As Greene approached Camden, where Rawdon had established his base, Rawdon seized the initiative and successfully attacked Greene just north of Camden at Hobkirk's Hill (April 25, 1781). Cornwallis, upon hearing of Rawdon's victory, assumed him to have the situation in hand and marched north from Wilmington into Virginia (and eventually to Yorktown). Rawdon, however, realized that he was overextended. Camden and other outlying British posts were threatened by Greene and various partisan groups. Rawdon began to pull British troops back closer to Charleston. In the process, he relieved the siege that Greene had laid to Ninety Six, though that post too had to be abandoned in favor of a more central position.

While in South Carolina, Rawdon was often perplexed by the unreliability of the Loyalist militia and by the lack of support the British received from the local population. He warned his superiors against placing too much faith in the prospect of widespread popular support. Rawdon himself gained something of a reputation for severity. When the Volunteers of Ireland moved into the Waxhaws district of South Carolina after the Battle of Camden, Rawdon made public a letter in which he threatened severe reprisals against South Carolinians who aided the rebels or who assisted deserters from the regiment. He further added a bounty for those bringing in deserters: five guineas for each deserter brought in alive, ten if only the head! Called to account by Cornwallis, Rawdon passed his action off as a joke designed to inspire fear among the locals. Coming as it did on the heels of Clinton's proclamation requiring those captured at Charleston to take the oath of allegiance or to be considered as rebels, Rawdon's pronouncement did little to endear the British to the local population. Also controversial was Rawdon's role in the execution of Colonel Isaac Hayne in August 1781.

By this time Rawdon was suffering from fatigue and ill health and had asked to be relieved. In July 1781, he turned his command over to Lieutenant Colonel Alexander Stewart and prepared to return to England. His ship, however, was captured by the French, and Rawdon was taken prisoner. Ironically, Rawdon was able to witness, from the decks of a French man-of-war, the naval battle off the Chesapeake Capes that sealed the fate of Cornwallis at Yorktown. Arriving in France, Rawdon was exchanged in the spring of 1782 and returned to England. He was made an aide-de-camp to the King and, in March 1783, was granted a British peerage (as Lord Rawdon) in his own right.

Still in his twenties when he returned from America, Rawdon's experience in the American War of Independence matured him and provided the foundation for what would be a long, active, and distinguished career. He eventually reached the rank of full general, seeing further action against the French in the 1790s and later in India (where he was a governor general from 1813 to 1822). Known as the Earl of Moira after succeeding his father in 1783, in 1817 he was created Marquess of Hastings.

William C. Lowe

REFERENCES

Sir Henry Clinton, *The American Rebellion; Sir Henry Clinton's Narrative of His Campaigns, 1775–1782, with an Appendix of Original Documents*, ed. by William B. Willcox (1954); *Correspondence of Charles, First Marquess Cornwallis*, ed. by Charles Ross, 3 vols. (1859); Historical Manuscripts Commission, *Report on the Manuscripts of the Late Reginald Rawdon Hastings*, Vol. III (1934); Henry Lumpkin, *From Savannah to Yorktown. The American Revolution in the South* (1981); Oliver Snoody, "The Volunteers of Ireland," *Irish Sword*, 7(1965):147–159; Walter H. Wilkin, *Some British Soldiers in America* (1914).

Reed, Joseph (1741–1785)

Continental Army officer, war governor. Born in Trenton, New Jersey, to a wealthy family, Reed was educated at the Academy of Philadelphia and earned his B.A. at the College of New Jersey (1757). After studying law he began his practice in 1763. Reed held several political offices on the eve of war—he served on the Philadelphia Committee of Correspondence, the Pennsylvania Committee of Observation and Committee of Safety, and he was president of the Second Provincial Congress of Pennsylvania.

Reed became a lieutenant colonel in the Pennsylvania militia in April 1775. In June 1775 he was on Washington's staff as an aide and at the rank of colonel in the Continental Army. Yet he quit this post within three months in order to handle his legal cases. Washington, who held Reed in high regard, had him appointed adjutant general. Reed served at Trenton and Princeton. Dubious of Washington's military ability, Reed resigned his commission on January 23, 1777; yet he served as a volunteer at Brandywine, Germantown, and Monmouth.

In 1777, he served in Congress. In 1778 he was on the peace commission that dealt with Lord George Carlisle. By December that year he was elected President of the Supreme Executive Council of Pennsylvania.

During his tenure as the state's chief executive (to November 1781), Pennsylvania was free of British troops. But it was wracked by inflation, shortages of commodities, and by political strife. By January 1781 the state's currency had virtually collapsed as a medium of exchange. Reed was also confronted with the mutiny of the Pennsylvania Line. He returned to his legal practice in late 1781. Considering the circumstances under which he had to govern in a war-torn state, Reed did a commendable job as chief executive.

Richard L. Blanco

REFERENCES

Ellsworth Elliot, Jr., *The Patriotism of Joseph Reed* (1943); Richard M. Ketchum, "Joseph Reed," *American Heritage*, 27 (4) (1976):65, 93; John T. Roche, *Joseph Reed: A Moderate in Politics* (1957).

Refugees, Loyalist, in East Florida

From the beginning of the Revolution, Loyalists in the South sought refuge in the British colony of East Florida. Free land was available to them there, and the garrison at St. Augustine, although small, provided protection from which they could organize resistance against the Revolutionaries. From late in 1775, Loyalists in St. Augustine proposed schemes by which like-minded settlers and Indians in the backcountry would join a British invasion of the South. Governor Patrick Tonyn recommended such proposals to British officials, believing that a southern campaign would bring his colony greater protection. Such plans as those initiated in 1775–1776 by Superintendent of Indian Affairs John Stuart, Moses Kirkland from South Carolina's Ninety Six District, and Thomas Brown, promoter of a recent settlement in the Georgia backcountry, eventually influenced General Sir Henry Clinton's 1778 decision to order the capture of Savannah, thus beginning the southward shift of British policy. Thereafter, most of the Loyalist refugees left East Florida to return to their homes or to the British-held areas near their homes. Then at the end of the war, East Florida received the largest concentration of Loyalist exiles from the Carolinas and Georgia. Their familiarity with East Florida, as well as its proximity to their former homes, facilitated their start toward rebuilding their lives, but Britain's 1783 cession of East and West Florida to Spain forced the Loyalists to disperse again. They relinquished East Florida reluctantly, resenting what they considered British betrayal of their loyalism.

Loyalists fled to East Florida from the Carolinas following their unsuccessful initiatives there in the autumn and winter of 1775–1776. In November the success of an attack on a fortified Revolutionary camp at the village of Ninety Six was reversed by a dragnet after local Revolutionaries were reinforced by their North Carolina allies. The following February, a similar roundup of opponents of the Revolutionaries occurred in eastern North Carolina following the defeat at Moore's Creek Bridge of government supporters, largely Highland Scots from the Cape Fear Valley, on their way to meet a supposed British landing at Wilmington. Such men generally left their families behind and went to East Florida in small groups that reflected their prewar militia organization. Whole families of Georgians more commonly went to East Florida early in the war. During 1778 the influx of refugees from Georgia and the Carolinas swelled as the new state assemblies defined treason, tightened militia service, and required oaths of allegiance, which specifically abjured allegiance to the Crown.

In East Florida, the refugees from the Revolutionary South organized themselves for resistance, most notably as the South Carolina Royalists and the East Florida Rangers. In 1778 men who held commissions from South Carolina's last royal governor asked the British commander to East Florida to embody them and others from the upcountry as a South Carolina unit. The commander, Brigadier General Augustine Prevost, recognized their value as a magnet for other backcountry Loyalists and so embodied them as the South Carolina Royalists and assigned his brother, Major James Mark Prevost, to train them. They chose as their commander one of the leaders of the 1775 attack at Ninety Six, Joseph Robinson. He worked closely with Evan MacLaurin, a storekeeper in the "Dutch Fork" between the Broad and Saluda rivers who had received Tonyn's emissaries since the beginning of the war. In East Florida the South Carolina Royalists made four infantry companies of 45 men each and 2 companies of rifle dragoons with 40 men each.

The East Florida Rangers, or Tonyn's Rangers, on the other hand, were authorized and promoted by the governor. Initially planned in 1775 by Thomas Brown, James McGirtt, and Daniel McGirtt, three vengeful Georgians, the Rangers were organized in 1776 as Tonyn's response to raids on plantations along the St. Marys River, the border with Georgia. By early 1777 the Rangers consisted of about 130 men in four companies. Brown recruited and organized the corps, and his leadership reflected his perception that the war as it related to Georgia was fundamentally an Indian war. The Rangers were a source of contention between Tonyn and Prevost, with the governor maintaining that they were an organ of the colony and not of the army. Tonyn acknowledged that the Rangers and their Indian comrades were under the control of the garrison commander when they worked occasionally with the regular troops. One such fragile collaboration was the February 1777 attack on Fort McIntosh, a new stockade fort on Georgia's Satilla River. Perhaps as many as 120 Rangers and 60 Creeks defeated about 70 defenders from the South Carolina Horse and the Georgia 1st Battalion in a seven-hour exchange of fire, but Brown initiated the surrender only after the regulars arrived and their commander called a truce. The object of the attack was to obtain meat for the garrison, and the Rangers drove some 2,000 cattle from the area to St. Augustine.

Both the South Carolina Royalists and the East Florida Rangers went to Georgia after the British established a beachhead at Savannah. There a second battalion of the South Carolina Royalists was formed in 1779, and approximately 400 of them helped defend Savannah during the Franco-American siege. In June 1781 they numbered 415 men in 9 companies. Meanwhile, the East Florida Rangers were discharged in Georgia, but some of them formed the nucleus of a new provincial corps under Brown's leadership, known variously as the Georgia Rangers, the King's Rangers, the Florida Rangers, and finally as the King's Carolina Rangers. Other groups raised in Georgia were added to Brown's corps so that it eventually numbered 847 men.

Late in 1782, when the British evacuated Savannah and Charleston, their last installations south of New York, a majority of departing refugees chose East Florida over the alternatives, primarily Britain, Nova Scotia, the Bahamas, Jamaica, and other West Indian islands. For both coastal planters and backcountry farmers, individuals as well as families, East Florida was the most familiar option and the one nearest their former homes. Its nearness could be convenient for men who had been unable to bring their families with them. It could facilitate return to their homes in the event of a British cession of East Florida to Spain, as rumor already was suggesting, and if the Revolutionaries should allow the exiles to return. Along with civilian refugees, many of whom had been Loyalist militiamen, approximately 700 men in the 3 provincial corps raised in the South (the King's Carolina Rangers, the South Carolina Royalists, and the Royal North Carolina Regiment) went to East Florida. A total of 8,279 people were enumerated in the sailings from Savannah and Charleston to East Florida. Perhaps 5,000 people entered in other ways. A total of approximately 17,000 refugees, slaves, and prewar residents were in East Florida by April 1783, with a racial proportion of roughly 5 Blacks to 3 whites.

Records for the evacuations of Savannah and Charleston show that 12 men held more than 35 percent of the slaves and that 68 percent of the white households included no slaves. White men leaving Charleston had proportionally fewer slaves and families than did white men leaving Savannah. Moreover, backcountrymen had proportionally fewer families and slaves than did Charleston and Savannah evacuees in general. Only those backcountrymen who lived near the interior British installations had brought their families inside the forts prior to the British departure from the vicinity.

Land was an immediate concern for the new East Floridians. During the war, Tonyn had received permission from the Board of Trade to escheat the grants of absentee landowners in order to grant land to Loyalists. The influx of Loyalists at the war's end overwhelmed his land-granting apparatus, so that newcomers were more likely to settle with a warrant to survey or simply squat on the land they wanted than they were to obtain a grant. Even so, some of them got grants and others bought or rented land. With the arrival of the refugees, St. Augustine underwent a real estate and building boom. Outside St. Augustine, Loyalists concentrated in the northeastern section of the province along the St. Johns, the Matanzas, and the St. Marys rivers. Early in the autumn of 1782, Thomas Brown helped the first arrivals find land at the mouth of the St. Johns River and got what tools he could from Tonyn and the British commanders at Charleston and New York. Farming methods and crops were a hasty adaptation of the subsistence farming prevalent in the southern backcountry.

Civil order and personal security were precarious north of the St. Johns River. Marauders, including Daniel McGirth, formerly of the East Florida Rangers, operated far from Tonyn's reach. Two cavalry units, authorized by the governor, composed of Loyalists and commanded by a militia leader from Ninety Six District, made some headway against the robbers, but the gangs remained active and complicated the transition to Spanish rule.

Politically, the Loyalists' impact on East Florida was to make it more like the other Continental colonies, now states, than it had been before the war. Prior to the Revolution, East Florida had no elected assembly; Loyalists' clamor for one resulted in elections in March 1781. Thereafter, the Loyalist lower house pressured the governor and positioned itself against him and the Council, which served as the upper house. The chief controversy was over a slave code. The proposal arose in the lower house and was modeled on the slave codes in Georgia and South Carolina. The governor and Council considered a detail of the proposed slave code oppressive. Thereupon, the lower house refused to consider a declaratory act which Secretary of State Thomas Townshend had requested until its slave code should be accepted by the Council and the governor. Moreover, the Loyalists in the lower house insisted that any declaratory act serve as an elections act, regulating the calling of a General Assembly and granting it certain privileges. The Board of Trade upheld the South

Carolina and Georgia models on grounds of consistency of British law, so the lower house got its slave code in the final legislative compromise.

Such adaptation of East Florida's legal and political structure to meet the expectations of the Loyalists was rendered futile by Britain's cession of the colony to Spain. News of the completed treaty arrived in April 1783 and sparked plans for a May Day mutiny among the provincial corpsmen. The would-be mutineers intended to take control of the British colony and oppose by arms any Spanish effort to occupy it. It was even rumored that the provincials intended to arm the Blacks in St. Augustine and promote a slave insurrection. The senior officer among the provincials, Lieutenant Colonel John Hamilton of the Royal North Carolina Regiment, stymied the projected mutiny when he refused an offer to head the project and vowed to oppose it. Plans to resist the Spanish rumbled on, even after the provincials were discharged or removed to Nova Scotia in October 1783. After evacuation orders arrived in the spring of 1784, plots to prevent the Spanish from assuming control were a threat to a peaceful transfer of power. The most elaborate plans surfaced in the northern part of the province under the leadership of John Cruden. Formerly a merchant in North Carolina, Cruden had enjoyed some brief prominence as General Lord Charles Cornwallis's supervisor of confiscated property, largely slaves in coastal South Carolina. Apparently Cruden wanted to organize a military unit with which to oppose the Spanish when they arrived, and he intended recruiting for it in the Carolinas and Georgia. Cruden's associates were even more reckless than he, and some of the robber gangs forced their way into the enterprise. At that point the earnest Cruden abandoned the project and probably was the means by which Tonyn learned of it. Cruden later headed a futile petition to Carlos III asking that the northern area be allowed autonomy under Spanish sovereignty.

Spain, in the person of Governor and Captain General Vicente Manuel de Zespedes y Velasco, took possession of East Florida and West Florida in July 1784. He extended Britain's evacuation period until July 1785, but the last British ship was not ready to sail until September 1785. (Governor Tonyn's frigate, delayed by wind damage, did not leave until November.) There were several reasons for the slow evacuation. The few Spanish in the colony were an insufficient market for houses and lands put to sale. Loyalists named in confiscation and banishment acts in the nearby states lingered in hopes of reversals or exceptions. Some hazarded a return to their homes and then came back to East Florida. Moreover, the conspiracies and rumors briefly halted emigration in May and June 1784, almost as soon as it began. With a few exceptions, the Spanish considered the British undesirable residents and wanted them to leave. Even so, they did not press civilians without criminal records to go. Tonyn did urge the British to evacuate, but he was in no position to force them. In 1786 he estimated that 5,000 backcountry people had returned overland to the United States during the evacuation period.

Evacuation figures show about 3,400 whites and 6,500 Blacks leaving East Florida, largely for the Bahamas, Nova Scotia, the United States, Jamaica, Dominica, and Britain. They show more than 70 percent of the evacuating Blacks being taken to the United States and the Bahamas. These returns, kept by Tonyn's assistant, indicate that 450 whites and 200 Blacks remained with the Spanish.

When the reality of the cession and the evacuation became clear, several Loyalists in St. Augustine produced a pamphlet, "The Case of the Inhabitants of East Florida" (St. Augustine, 1784) in which they argued that the British government should compensate East Floridians for property they lost because of the cession. The anonymous writers acknowledged the right of the King in Parliament to deprive persons of their property for the good of the entire British community. They maintained, however, that the nation must pay the individual for such property, appealing to the feudal contract to support their contention that the Crown was obligated to protect the subject's real property in return for the subject's allegiance. The pamphlet was published by John Wells, whose family had published the *South Carolina Gazette* and who later would publish the *Bahama Gazette*. In 1785 and 1787 Parliament provided for compensation to persons who had lost East Florida property because of the cession. Memorials and evidences for extant East Florida claims are in Audit Office Papers, classes 12 and 13. *See also*: Florida in the American Revolution

Carole Watterson Troxler

REFERENCES

Joseph Byrne Lockey, *East Florida, 1783–1785: A File of Documents*, ed. by John Walton Caughey (1949); Charles Loch Mowat, *East Florida as a British Province, 1763–1784* (1943), rpr. 1964; Carole Watterson Troxler, "Loyalist Refugees and the British Evacuation of East Florida, 1783–1785," *Florida Historical Quarterly*, 60 (1981):1–28; ———, "Refuge, Resistance, and Reward: The Southern Loyalist Claim on East Florida," *Journal of Southern History*, 55 (1989):563–596.

Regulators

See North Carolina in the American Revolution; Tryon, William.

Revere, Paul (1735–1818)

American Patriot. This man gained his reputation during the War of Revolution for playing a number of unsung but critical roles for the patriotic cause, particularly in his hometown of Boston. Later his noted ride to Lexington was publicized across the country by Longfellow's poem in 1863, a fact that insured his immortality.

Paul Revere was born January 1, 1735, in Boston to Apollos Rivoire (the name was changed to its present spelling so that the people of Boston could pronounce it) and Deborah Hitchbourne. Of French Huguenot descent, he was the third of 13 children. Paul was given a basic education in the Boston schools and then learned his father's trade of silversmithing. In 1756, Revere had his introduction to military life when he took part in the British attack on Crown Point as a lieutenant of Continental Artillery.

Returning to Boston, he married Sarah Orne on August 17, 1757, and would later have eight children from their marriage. Setting up his shop as a silversmith, he soon found the competition in Boston and demands of the trade such that he began to branch out into other fields. He became a mason, and he joined the Long Room Club. Politically active, he was one of the leaders of the Tradesmen and Mechanics in Boston and associated with the likes of Samuel Adams, John Adams, Joseph Warren, and the other American leaders of opposition to British rule in the colonies. From 1761 until Lexington in 1775, not much happened in Boston that Paul Revere did not know about, even if he was not personally involved.

A skilled propagandist, his services were always in demand. One of his most famous engravings was the one depicting the Boston Massacre of March 1770. He did other types of engraving, silver work, printing, and even dental work. Paul Revere was one of Boston's most active and political figures. He was a leader of the Sons of Liberty and was dressed as an Indian as he and his fellow protesters dumped the East India Company tea into Boston harbor in December 1773.

After the death of his first wife, Paul remarried October 10, 1773, only a few months before the tea party. He took Rachel Walker as his wife and their marriage produced another eight children. As an express rider for the Massachusetts Committee of Safety, he took the Suffolk resolves (Suffolk is the county in which Boston is located) to the First Continental Congress meeting in Philadelphia. He also rode regularly between Boston and other locations of importance such as Providence and New York in order to keep the Revolutionary spirit alive. Shortly before the fighting began at Lexington and Concord, Revere brought word to New Hampshire that General Thomas Gage, British military commander in North America, planned to seize their store of arms and powder. The colonials safely hid the materials. Two days before his famous ride to Lexington, he rode to Concord to encourage the Patriot leaders there to hide the military stores present in the small Massachusetts town.

On the night of April 18, 1775, Paul Revere made his most famous ride as a courier when he left Boston, was rowed across the Charles River, and from Charlestown, rode to Lexington to alert Samuel Adams and John Hancock of the danger from the British force that had left Boston that night. William Dawes, a shoemaker, was also sent to spread the warning. Neither Dawes nor Revere ever made it to Concord, but Dr. Samuel Prescott did. Others, such as Joseph Hall, Solomon Brown, Richard Devens, and Ebenezer Dorr also got involved informally in spreading the word throughout the countryside. But in the end, it was Paul Revere who made it to Lexington first with the news.

During the war, Revere engraved the seal still used by the commonwealth of Massachusetts; managed a powder mill in Canton, Massachusetts, to provide that critical element for the American war effort; and commanded Castle William from 1778–1779. This fortification guarded Boston harbor. Revere also served for a time on the local Committee of Safety, responsible for maintaining order in Boston.

In 1778, Revere participated in the Rhode Island expedition of General John Sullivan and then took part in the ill-fated Penobscot Bay affair of July–August 1779 under General Solomon Lovell. The British had come out of Canada to establish a base in Penobscot Bay of the province of Maine. Without waiting for Continental assistance, Massachusetts organized a force and sent it to take Maine back from the British. Paul Revere went along as a lieutenant colonel in the artillery. The Americans delayed too long. British reinforcements arrived and blocked the Americans in the bay, and those that could had to make their way back home through the wilds of Maine. Due to his actions in this expedition, Revere was accused of cowardice, disobedience to orders, and unmilitary behavior. The disaster tarnished his reputation. He was relieved of command and sent back to Boston under house arrest.

It took another several years before a court-martial could be formed to examine the charges against Revere. In the end, on February 19, 1782, Revere was cleared of all charges. With the war ending, Revere returned to his business in Boston. He made silver, some of the best quality found in the United States. He also made gunpowder, copper bells, cannons, and molded much of the hardware for the frigate *Constitution*, including the copper sheathing of the hull of the ship. He also put the copper leaf on the dome of the new Massachusetts State House. Politically he was a Federalist and supported the adoption of the new form of government under the United States Constitution.

Revere served as Boston coroner in 1796, and in 1798 he began the successful Massachusetts Mutual Fire Insurance Company. In 1799, he was Boston's health officer. He lost his second wife in 1813. He continued to wear the old "revolutionary" style of clothing until his end. Paul Revere was treated as a respected and honored member of the Boston community until he died on May 10, 1818, at 83 years of age. He was buried in the family vault in the Granary Burial Ground, Boston.

Paul J. Sanborn

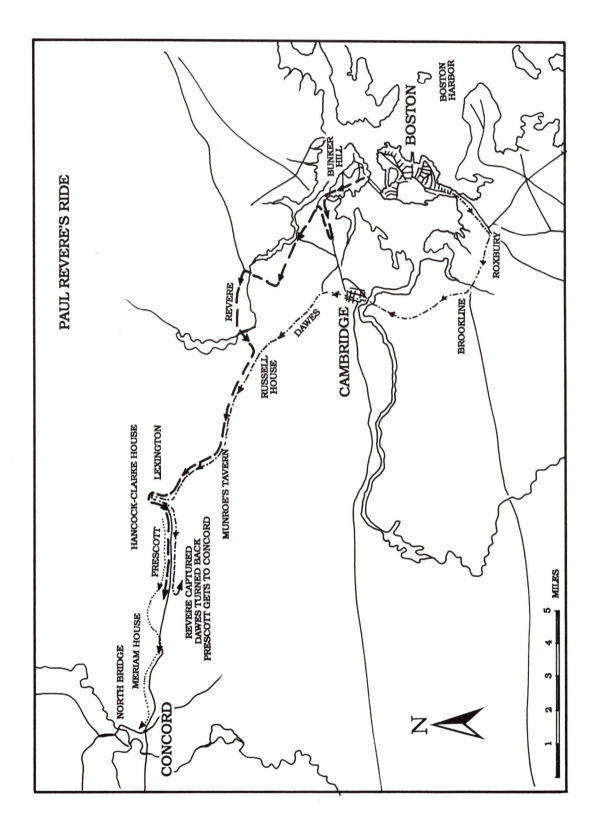

PAUL REVERE'S RIDE

BOSTON

BOSTON HARBOR

BUNKER HILL

REVERE

DAWES

RUSSELL HOUSE

CAMBRIDGE

ROXBURY

BROOKLINE

HANCOCK-CLARKE HOUSE

LEXINGTON

PRESCOTT

MUNROE'S TAVERN

REVERE CAPTURED
DAWES TURNED BACK
PRESCOTT GETS TO CONCORD

NORTH BRIDGE

MERIAM HOUSE

CONCORD

N

1 2 3 4 5 MILES

REFERENCES

DAB; Elbridge H. Goss, *The Life of Colonel Paul Revere*, 2 vols. (1891); Charles B. Flood, *Rise and Fight Again* (1976); Esther Forbes, *Paul Revere and the World He Lived In* (1942); John Harris, *American Rebels* (1976); Henry J. Kaufman, *The Colonial Silversmith* (1969); [Paul Revere], *Paul Revere's Three Accounts of His Famous Ride* (1976); *Webster's Dictionary of American Military Biography* (1978).

Rhode Island, British Occupation of (December 1776–October 1779)

Soon after consolidating their victories in the New York City area, the British armed forces fitted out an expedition to seize Rhode Island and the port city of Newport. This area had great strategic value because it was the only harbor in the northern part of America that could be entered directly from the sea by large vessels, without having to cross sandbars or wait for specific wind conditions. It would make an excellent anchorage for the British fleet, and it was well situated to interdict shipping out of Boston and other New England ports. Furthermore, any port held by the British was one that could not be used for privateering by the American Patriots.

On December 7, 1776, a large fleet under the command of Admiral Sir Peter Parker entered Narragansett Bay. The next day an army of 7,000 men—10 British battalions and 7 German—landed on Rhode Island (the largest island in the bay, known as Aquidneck, was referred to typically as Rhode Island; the mainland was regarded as a separate entity). The army and navy was prepared for resistance but met none. The few defenses that had been prepared in the area would have been easily overwhelmed, and so the rebel forces abandoned the island. The British quickly seized Conanicut, the next largest island. The remaining 12 islands in the bay were uninhabited and remained so throughout the war.

In the years before the war, Newport had prospered as a shipping center. Much of the trade through the city was of questionable legality, and so Newporters had long disdained British commerce laws. There had been many violent encounters with British revenue cutters, and when it was learned that an army of occupation was on the way, it was feared that trade would be completely stifled. Largely for this reason, about half of the population of the island fled north, more

in pursuit of free enterprise than in support of the American Revolution.

The British army immediately set about two major tasks: securing the area from any risk of counterattack and sheltering the soldiers from the windy winter weather on the islands. The latter need was accommodated by the many abandoned houses and buildings in the city. For defense, a series of earthen redoubts was built at strategic points around the island. By March, it was clear that there was no imminent danger of attack. The fleet returned to New York, leaving behind one British brigade of three regiments and a German brigade of five regiments, and several frigates, as a long-term garrison for the islands.

The long, narrow island lies close to the mainland at its northern tip and along its eastern shore. The soldiers were concentrated in these areas, in redoubts and barrack rooms set back from the shore on rising ground to command a good view. Sentries were posted along the shoreline, with frequent patrols from post to post. Every soldier knew a set of alarm signals and procedures governing which body of troops would go where in the event of an alarm. The western approaches, where the bay is much wider, were covered by several frigates, which were particularly vigilant for shipping trying to slip down the bay from Providence to the open sea.

In spite of these precautions, rebel activity was high. Almost every night, particularly in the summer, men would make their way to Rhode Island in boats with muffled oars. Sometimes they would spar with the sentries, attempting to capture one or encourage desertion. Other objectives included plundering, both of military and civilian objectives, distribution of pamphlets and similar propaganda material, spying, and simple harassment. The King's soldiers were well trained and diligent, but the Americans knew the land, water, and weather well because many of them were displaced Rhode Island residents.

By day, things were generally calmer, the routine activities of the garrison being punctuated only by occasional cannon shots fired at extreme range from the mainland; one such shot entered a guardroom window and smashed an officer's chair moments after he had left it. The garrison was kept busy training and maintaining the state of the island's defenses. Parties of a few hundred men made frequent excursions to Long Island and Shelter Island to cut firewood, a commodity that the garrison consumed at a rate of some 300 cords per week in the winter. Expeditions to Martha's Vineyard and neighboring islands siezed sheep and cattle. Soldiers were placed as safeguards at buildings requiring protection and to quell an occasional public disturbance. Raiding parties, sometimes entire regiments, sallied to the mainland to seize stores, to spike cannon, and to disrupt operations.

The frigates and their tenders frequently left their stations to pursue vessels trying to slip out of the bay at night. A number of American privateers were trapped in the upper bay and made frequent attempts to escape. The frigates were fast and, with 28 to 32 guns, much better armed than any American vessel, but they were also relatively large and therefore unable to use all of the waters in the bay. The British were superb seamen, but they were opposed by sailors who had lived their entire lives in Narragansett Bay. Small American vessels would sail from Providence in the daytime and tempt a frigate into giving chase, then escape through shallows in an effort to run the larger ship aground. In early January 1777, they were successful when the frigate *Diamond* grounded on Warwick Neck at high tide. When the tide lowered, the ship careened to one side, making her guns ineffective. The Americans failed to send boats to attack the *Diamond*, however, and she was refloated the next day. In November of that year the frigate *Syren* grounded on Point Judith. Her crew was captured, but sailors from other British ships managed to scuttle the *Syren* to prevent her capture.

A great many American privateering vessels were captured or driven ashore and burned, but an equal number escaped on foggy nights when intimacy with the waters afforded them every advantage. They relocated to ports in Massachusetts and Connecticut, some operating successfully throughout the war.

Many skirmishes occurred on and around the small uninhabited islands in the bay. Parties from the British ships that were sent ashore to get water, make beer, or to train were attacked by boatloads of Americans. Horses sent to graze on the islands were captured and recaptured. While the major actions of the war were being fought elsewhere, soldiers and sailors on both sides were involved in intensive small-scale fighting.

The Americans planned several times to attack and dislodge the garrison in Rhode Island, but they were never successful. Soon after the island was taken, Benedict Arnold concocted a plan to retake it, but no attempt was made. In October 1777, a large force was assembled under the command of General Joseph Spencer. A fleet of boats was carefully numbered, and each of several thousand men was assigned to a boat. Three separate simultaneous landings would be made in order to split up the defenders. But the preparations were bedeviled by delays, and by the end of the month only a few days were available before enlistments ran out. On the night of October 20, the troops were actually embarked and boats began to move toward the island, but British sentries raised the alarm immediately. On succeeding nights, troops were brought to the boats, but again preparations were inept and poor weather intervened. Each time, the British gained a few more hints of the impending assault. When an attempt on October 25 was stopped due to inclement weather, the dispirited invasion army could no longer be kept together. The attack was aborted.

The following summer, a more elaborate attempt was made, this time with the support of the French navy. For the entire month of August 1778, the garrison was besieged in the town of Newport while a large army under General John Sullivan occupied the remainder of the island. A damaging storm and an aggressive British fleet forced the withdrawal of the French Navy to Boston. Once again, the attacking force fell into disillusionment and withdrew, fighting an intense battle on August 29, now called Battle of Rhode Island. This was the last American attempt to seize the island.

The American troops on the mainland were composed of local militias, independent companies of infantry, militias from neighboring states, and some Continental Line regiments. Men from surrounding areas would come to serve three-month enlistment obligations, and Rhode Island Line regiments were sent to the area to regroup and recruit between campaigns. Vigilance was required against raiding, but there was little threat of a large-scale assault from the British. The Americans found amusement in trying to toss cannonballs onto the island and made great sport of their nightly forays to harass the garrison.

The most successful raid of all occurred on the night of July 9–10, 1777, when a small American force slipped past the guardships, landed near the middle of the island, and captured General Richard Prescott, commander of the garrison. A prisoner of Prescott's rank was needed to exchange for the captured American general Charles Lee. The expedition was a complete success; by the time the garrison was alarmed, their commander was well in the hands of the Americans. While this action had no effect on the operational course of the war, it was a demoralizing embarrassment for the British and a coup for the Americans.

Although a large number of inhabitants had fled the town, they were replaced socially by the numerous officers of the British army and navy and their families. These people generally took quarters in the homes of residents, while the rank and file of the army stayed in designated barracks. Those merchants who remained kept a flourishing business, providing all manner of goods from Europe to "gentlemen of the army and navy" as well as to citizens. Fine fabrics, books, jewelry, gold and silver fittings for uniforms, telescopes, the latest medications, wines and foodstuffs all could be purchased in Newport. Even necessary items for the soldiers—shirts, shoes, stockings, and regimental buttons—were offered for sale. Lotteries were held to benefit the poor. There were cockfights, cricket matches, concerts, and theater shows. Balls were held on special occasions such as when prominent military officers visited, including General John Burgoyne after being paroled from capture. The army and navy provided ample business for all trades, from the tailor making fine new officers' uniforms, to the schoolmaster teaching the soldiers' children.

The garrison of some 5,000 soldiers and sailors did put a strain on the resources of the island. The army typically got most of its food from England, by way of New York, a tenuous and sporadic supply line. When stores of flour went bad, they could not be readily replaced. Fresh vegetables were grown by soldiers in the summer, but supplies dwindled during the long winters. All food that was grown on the island was put in the care of the military commissary, regardless of the producer, and it was apportioned to the garrison and the civilian populace. Hay was so plentiful that it was sent to New

York. The winter of 1778–1779 saw the near starvation of the garrison when the provisions fleet from New York was several weeks late. Firewood was always in short supply. The island had no forests, and so each winter shortages were stemmed by breaking up abandoned houses and wharves, old ships, fences, and finally by cutting down orchards. Some fuel was obtained by mining coal and cutting peat, both available on the island, but never enough to relieve shortages. What fuel was available, like the food, had to be allotted to both the inhabitants and the garrison. Prices of staple goods were regulated by the military, a necessary but disliked practice.

A small corps of soldiers was formed of loyal and able-bodied inhabitants. Armed with weapons from the British army stores, they were very active in raiding the mainland. Similar to the American raids, they were harassing but accomplished little of importance. On a few occasions, navy press gangs took men from the town. This despised practice was legal and well known to Englishmen, but it did not invoke sympathy for the British cause.

Both sides observed their political holidays with vigor. The Americans fired salutes, lit beacons, and flew "the thirteen stripes" on Independence Day, pointing their revery toward the garrison. The British fired salutes on their monarchs' birthdays and coronation day, the navy firing at noon and the army at one o'clock. On the Queen's birthday in January 1777, the frigate *Diamond* accidentally fired two shots into a nearby transport during the salute.

Periodically, citizens were allowed to leave the island, and loyal inhabitants of the mainland were allowed to come to the garrison. Many of Rhode Island's residents were sympathetic to the rebel cause, and these "disaffected" inhabitants were arrested if they became overzealous in expressing their sentiments. Both sides employed prison ships to ease the burden of guarding their prisoners, both military and civilian. Deserters from both sides found their way across the bay, the American deserters usually in stolen boats. A British or German soldier had only to wait for a dark night to be picked up by a waiting American boat, secretly arranged by locals who managed to keep in constant contact with the mainland. One British regiment, the 22nd, lost 26 men to desertion in the three years that it spent on Rhode Island, a rate not unusually high for any campaign. By comparison, this same regiment lost about 20 men killed in battle, and 35 died of other causes during the same period.

Numerous instances of theft, rape, vandalism, and malicious drunkenness by soldiers occurred, but again, no more than was typical in any place where a large army was present. Military and civilian lawbreakers were arrested by authority of the town major, an officer of the garrison, and charged by court-martial. Restrictions were necessarily put on the use of boats to insure the security of the garrison. This put a strain on fishermen, who were required to have permits and were subject to scrutiny and were often arrested for suspicious behavior.

Several British officers, and presumably many soldiers, married Rhode Islanders. Generally, the women were from loyal families and would go with their husbands when the army departed, but not always. The lieutenant colonel of the 54th Regiment abandoned his Rhode Island bride and later denied the marriage when she sent complaints to the British commander-in-chief in New York, where the regiment was later stationed. The major of the same regiment, on the other hand, married a local woman, resigned from the army, and remained a Newport resident.

A weekly newspaper, the *Newport Gazette*, was published by John Howe. A Loyalist, Howe had published the *Boston Gazette* before the war, and he followed the army when that city was evacuated in 1776. After the war, he began yet another newspaper, in Halifax, Nova Scotia. His newspaper was typical of the day, carrying political commentary and news from abroad, based on letters, other newspapers, and even rumor. Nearly half of each four-page paper was filled with advertising of merchants and tradesmen.

The year 1779 saw a winding down of military campaigning in the North. The military situation in Rhode Island, as in New York, had become static. The need to send troops to the West Indies, and the accelerating campaigns in the southern colonies, placed a strain on British manpower. The decision was made to withdraw from Rhode Island and use the soldiers there to strengthen the New York garrison. In early October, orders were received to begin packing heavy baggage and equipment. Throughout the month works were dismantled, artillery loaded onto ordnance transports, and stores removed. Provision was made for friends of the government to leave with the army; those inhabitants who had been actively supportive of the British cause chose this option.

On October 25, 1779, the last barracks and guardrooms were set afire to prevent their capture, and the regiments of the garrison boarded transports and sailed away. Ironically, a ship carrying orders from New York countermanding the evacuation met the transports in Long Island Sound, too late to stop the withdrawal. American soldiers entered the town, followed the next year by a large French fleet and army. In 1780 and again in 1781 the British laid plans to retake the island, but contrary circumstances intervened, and Rhode Island saw no more fighting for the remainder of the war.

Don N. Hagist

REFERENCES

Israel Angell, *The Diary of Israel Angell* (1899); William Bell Clark, *Naval Documents of the American Revolution* (1964–1988); Paul F. Dearden, *The Rhode Island Campaign of 1778—Inauspicious Dawn of an Alliance* (1980); Fleet S. Greene, "Newport in the Hands of the British: "A Diary of the Revolution," *The Historical Magazine*, Vol. IV (1860); Frederick MacKenzie, *The Diary of Frederick MacKenzie* (1930); *The Newport Gazette* (1777–1779).

Rhode Island Campaign of 1778 (July 29–August 31, 1778) (Alternate name: Battle of Newport)

The campaign to regain control of Rhode Island and its major harbor at Newport began with the arrival of a French fleet in North American waters in the summer of 1778. In what was to be the first major Franco-American initiative of the war, an American land force attempted to coordinate its approaches to Newport with the French fleet. The results of this operation frustrated both France and America, but it did not poison the relationship between the two allies. The mission's lack of success can be attributed to the weather, the British fleet, the geography of the site, a gap in communications between allied commanders, and poor luck.

When confirmation reached Washington that the French had signed a Treaty of Alliance with the United States, he wrote to Congress, "I believe no event was ever received with more heartfelt joy." This was a commonly held American view at the time. France was seen as a key to an ultimate American victory. News of the alliance bolstered American confidence, prompting its leaders to look east for the first fruits of this union. They were not long in coming.

In April 1778 French foreign minister Vergennes dispatched Charles Hector Theodat, the Comte d'Estaing, with the Toulon fleet to North American waters to cooperate with the American army under Washington. A favorite of Marie Antoinette and a distant relative of Lafayette, d'Estaing had begun his military career in the army and later transferred to the navy. Now an admiral, he commanded 12 ships of the line, 6 frigates, smaller vessels, and 4,000 troops for a total of 834 guns. In his flagship, the 90-gun *Languedoc*, d'Estaing carried the first minister from France to the United States, Conrad Gerard.

D'Estaing took his time crossing the Atlantic, drilling his men and preparing for the upcoming campaign. Having left Toulon in mid-May, d'Estaing arrived off the Chesapeake on July 5. Finding nothing of value there and having missed Admiral Richard Howe's British fleet coming out of the Delaware River by ten days, d'Estaing sailed on to Sandy Hook outside New York harbor to join forces with Washington's main army.

Arriving July 11, d'Estaing found the mouth of New York harbor too shallow and narrow for his deep-draft vessels. His pilots cautioned against crossing over the bar at Sandy Hook, a place passable only at high tide and with the right wind. Admiral Howe, British naval commander in North America, positioned his outnumbered ships in a line inside Sandy Hook so that each French ship passing into the harbor would encounter a broadside from each British ship in turn. Such a maneuver was too risky for Admiral d'Estaing. He looked elsewhere for a more suitable theater of operations.

After consultation with Congress, Washington recommended that d'Estaing take his fleet to Newport, the only logical target remaining for the French fleet. On July 22, d'Estaing accepted this advice and made sail for Rhode Island. There he would join with an American land force under the command of John Sullivan of New Hampshire to reduce the British garrison occupying Newport, Rhode Island's leading port city.

General John Sullivan, a New Hampshire lawyer, was 38 years old, vain, and ambitious. A delegate to both the First and Second Conti-

nental Congresses for New Hampshire, he was elected brigadier general by Congress. He served with Washington at Boston and was sent to command the American army in Canada as it retreated from Sorel. Foolishly brave but outmaneuvered in the Battle of Long Island, Major General Sullivan was captured by the British. He was exchanged in time to fight at Trenton and Princeton.

Washington described Sullivan as "active, spirited and zealously attached to the cause" but warned that Sullivan had "a little tincture of vanity . . . an over desire to be popular, which now and then leads him into some embarrassments." Sullivan failed in an attempt to capture Staten Island in August 1777 and commanded the turned right wing of the American army in the defeat at Brandywine. He participated in another American disaster at Germantown before going into winter quarters at Valley Forge.

The Americans were confident that a combination of French sea power and American troops would make short work of General Sir Robert Pigot's command at Newport. As d'Estaing left New York, Washington felt the "balance of power now shifting." America now had "the fairest hopes that were ever conceived." There was a "moral certainty of success."

The French fleet permitted the Americans to attack Newport by neutralizing British sea power off the Atlantic coast for the first time in the war. The French fleet also kept the lines of communication open for coordinating such a move and provided a fail-safe opportunity for the Americans if retreat became necessary.

A center for commerce, refinement, fashion, and taste, Newport was the leading town and capital of Rhode Island when the Revolution began in 1775. Located on Aquidneck Island (also known as Rhode Island), Newport boasted of having one of the finest harbors in North America. Prosperous from its sea trade, Newport contained many fine homes and gardens located beyond the many wharves that lined the harbor. Before the war, some 5,000 individuals resided in the town.

The British had captured Newport in December 1776 when a 6,000-man force under General Henry Clinton occupied the town. Command was passed to Lord Hugh Percy and then in turn to General Richard Prescott, an overbearing, tyrannical officer who generated much animosity in Newport by his actions. General Sir Robert Pigot replaced Prescott after Lieutenant Colonel William Barton successfully kidnapped Prescott in July 1777. (Prescott was exchanged for General Charles Lee in the spring of 1778 and returned to Newport to command a brigade under Pigot. When the British evacuated Newport October 25, 1779, Prescott was once again in command.)

Pigot had been warned by Clinton, the British North American commander, of an impending Franco-American attack on Newport and had begun digging fortifications in mid-July. Later Pigot had his troops disarm all civilians on Aquidneck Island, fill the wells with stones, fell trees, and bring all the livestock within British lines. Pigot's reinforced garrison of 6,700 men prepared itself for an allied attack.

In his first independent command since the retreat from Canada in early 1776, General Sullivan had been in command of American forces in Providence, Rhode Island, since mid-March 1778. Replacing General Joseph Spencer, Sullivan had 1,000 Continentals and some militia watching the British garrison at Newport from the north. Washington sent word of the French move on Rhode Island to Sullivan on July 22. Sullivan immediately called for 5,000 militia to turn out from the New England states and prepared to work in cooperation with the French fleet.

Washington dispatched the two veteran brigades of James Varnum and John Glover to augment Sullivan's force. These Friedrich von Steuben–trained troops provided the backbone for Sullivan's militia in campaign. General Marquis de Lafayette was sent to command the troops of Sullivan's left wing, while General Nathanael Greene came to command Sullivan's right. Washington could not resist Greene's entreaties, since Rhode Island was Green's home state and his talents as quartermaster general could be used to Sullivan's advantage in generating supplies. In Lafayette's case, he had to be involved in the first French campaign on American soil in the war. Marching overland from the main American army in Westchester County, New York, these regulars and their commanders did not arrive in Providence until the first week of August.

However, Comte d'Estaing arrived off Point Judith, near Newport, on July 29, 1778. Joseph Champlain, a 16-year-old, and his brother had been fishing off the coast when the French fleet sailed in from Sandy Hook. The two boys were taken on board the flagship as pilots, guided the fleet to anchorage, and then were released with many thanks and gifts. The Americans under Sullivan were not yet ready. This delay, while obviously unavoidable, was inimical to the project. Sullivan, with only five days' notice, needed until August 5 to have enough troops to begin the offensive against Newport.

Washington had sent his secretary and translator, John Laurens, with d'Estaing to coordinate American and French movements. Laurens explained Sullivan's plan to d'Estaing on July 29. Sullivan proposed that the French land their troops on the western shore of Aquidneck Island, above Newport a bit south of the northern British line of fortifications. Once this threat forced the British to retreat into Newport, the Americans would cross from the mainland in the east to the northern part of Aquidneck Island, take the vacant British lines, move south, and join with the French. Both forces would then attack the Newport lines in conjunction with the French fleet's bombardment of the harbor. D'Estaing agreed to the feint and combined assault.

But the French admiral was impatient to begin. He needed fresh provisions and water. He wanted to get his troops on land for the first time in four months. Before formal operations began, d'Estaing sent two frigates up the east passage and two ships of the line up the west passage to bracket the British forces on Aquidneck Island and a smaller island to the west, Conanicut. One of the most effective French admirals of the time, Admiral Pierre Andre de Suffern de Saint-Tropez, led this preliminary expedition.

The British responded by withdrawing their troops from Conanicut Island and burning their ships to protect the Newport garrison. The *Cerebus* (32 guns), a frigate in Narragansett Bay, attempted to return to Newport, ran aground, was set afire, and exploded. The frigates *Juno*, *Orpheus*, and *Lark* (all 32 guns), the *Kingfisher* (16 guns), and *Pigot* galley met the same fate. The *Flora* (32 guns) and *Falcon* (18 guns) and several transports were scuttled and sunk in front of Newport to block the French from coming in close. The net result gave control of the sea and channels around Aquidneck Island to the French.

Sullivan met d'Estaing on the flagship July 30 for the first time. The French expressed their concern for speed. Supplies were needed, and the British fleet in New York under Admiral Howe would surely do something to help Pigot. Sullivan needed more time to bring in the militia and organize his force. In the end, the conference ended amicably with an agreed delay for the Americans until August 9–10 when both allied forces would move in unison.

On August 4, Lafayette arrived and went to visit d'Estaing. Lafayette's dream was to command a mixed Franco-American force that would attack the British as one. He persuaded both Sullivan and d'Estaing of the symbolic importance of this plan. The original concept was changed so that there would be no French feint. Both allies would land on Aquidneck together and would attack together.

By the first week of August, the militia from the New England states had arrived in force in Sullivan's camp, along with their famous leaders, such as the speaker of the New Hampshire Assembly, John Langdon, and the former president of the Second Continental Congress, John Hancock. Added to the 2,000 Continental Line already present, Sullivan felt his army ready to open the campaign.

On Friday, August 7, Sullivan marched his 10,000 troops out of Providence for Tiverton and the ferry to the northern tip of Aquidneck Island. The Continental Line and the militia had arrived in enough force for Sullivan to move. The Americans arrived at Tiverton on Saturday, August 8. That same day the French fleet forced the middle passage and anchored off Conanicut Island, bombarding Newport as they sailed past. D'Estaing allowed his sick to land on Conanicut to help restore their health while waiting for the scheduled allied attack set for August 10. Sullivan sent Lafayette with 1,000 men to join the French in preparation for this assault.

With the allied approach, Pigot withdrew his units from the northern lines ten miles above Newport to fortifications just outside town. The British planned a last-ditch defense, which Pigot hoped would turn into a siege. That in turn would permit Howe time to relieve the garrison. Informed of this, Sullivan decided to move unilaterally onto Aquidneck without telling the French, in order to seize the vacated high ground. This move was completed on Sunday, August 9.

Sullivan's maneuver disrupted allied relations. D'Estaing was distressed that Sullivan had taken precedence over the French by landing first without prior consultation. The French approved of the American move tactically, however, as it was the only smart thing to do. The problem soon became academic. Just as the Americans and French were closing in on the British position and the situation seemed hopeless for Pigot, Howe and his fleet arrived at Point Judith from New York on August 9.

The French admiral withdrew all his land forces and prepared his fleet to meet the British off the coast of Rhode Island, despite Sullivan's entreaties to the contrary. D'Estaing did not wish to be trapped in the channels of Newport by Howe, nor could the French allow the West Indies to lie unprotected from British attack. In any case, Howe's fleet had to be driven off if Newport was to surrender.

The British troops would not lose hope if their fleet was readily available. D'Estaing saw Howe as the principal target of the French fleet. With British sea power engaged in battle, Sullivan's American force would be safe on the island and could continue the operation alone.

Howe's fleet was not as powerful as the French, but he was reinforced at the end of July with four ships of the line. One came from the West Indies, two from Halifax, and one from Admiral John Byron's fleet (the *Cornwall*, 74 guns). Howe put together a fleet of 8 ships of the line, 4 ships of 50 guns each, 2 of 44 guns, and 6 frigates. He had 914 guns to the French total of 834. Sighting the British fleet greatly uplifted the morale of the garrison in Newport. Yet Howe did not attack. He waited off the coast to see what the French would do.

D'Estaing slipped his cables and came out with a northeast wind on Monday, August 10, leaving the Americans standing their ground on the northern tip of Aquidneck Island. With the weather gauge behind them, the French pursued the British. Howe stood off and maneuvered all day without closing in an attempt to take the wind away from the French. Howe's principal goal was to protect Newport, not to engage the French under unfavorable circumstances. After a full day of cat and mouse, Howe finally gained the weather gauge from the French. It was then that a great gale arrived to batter both fleets for the better part of two days. The hurricane ended all chances of battle and placed every ship from both fleets in grave danger.

By the morning of August 14, the great storm had finally passed, leaving five of d'Estaing's ships of the line damaged. Howe's fleet was not much better off. Both fleets were scattered over hundreds of miles off the American coast. In the end there were only a few individual actions between a few of the British and French ships before both sides withdrew to recover. For example, the French flagship *Languedoc* (90 guns) was dismasted by the storm and lost her rudder. She was then attacked by the British *Renown* (50 guns). Unable to maneuver, d'Estaing was so sure he would have to surrender the ship that he destroyed all his confidential papers. But other French ships came to the rescue, and the *Languedoc* limped back to the channels of Newport while Howe's fleet returned to New York.

Back on Aquidneck Island, Sullivan decided to continue the move against the British lines without the help of the French fleet. Sullivan had shown great initiative in getting his troops and supplies organized (with Greene's help), in planning the attack, and in moving with dispatch. A general with a thirst for fame and military success, he was brave and daring but had suffered from bad luck. Now, outside Newport, Sullivan wished to seize the glory, with or without the assistance of the French fleet.

On Tuesday, August 11, Sullivan opted to move his army south. Set to move at 6 A.M., the Americans were forced to cancel their march as the hurricane struck Aquidneck Island. Unable to take shelter, the American army was soon reduced to defending itself with only the bayonet. All cartridges were ruined in the rain. It took several days to bring up fresh rounds. Fortunately, the British found it impossible to capitalize on the storm. Neither side could move in the mud, flooding, and wind.

Finally, on Saturday, August 15, Sullivan was able to move his men toward the lines that protected Newport in an arc from Tonomy Hill in the west to Easton's Pond in the east. The British had strengthened their lines with extra abatis and stronger breastworks, but the Americans were confident of victory. Sullivan advanced in four columns with Greene and Varnum anchoring the right along the West Road. Lafayette and Glover commanded the American left on the East Road.

At 2 P.M., the American troops were within two miles of the British lines. Sullivan began his siege of Newport. While Glover was pulled to the rear to train the Salem volunteers and Boston independent company in the use of boats for future amphibious operations, the Americans entrenched before the British lines. Artillery batteries were established and parallels dug, with a concentration on the eastern side of the island close to the pond. This permitted the French to return and take up their station on the western side.

For five days the siege proceeded as the British attempted unsuccessfully to disrupt American progress with artillery fire. But poor British marksmanship and ground fog combined to insure American progress. By August 19, some American artillery was within musket range of the British lines, all accomplished without American loss. American artillery opened fire on the British lines on the afternoon of August 19. The Americans brought additional cannon on line the next day. Both sides then cannonaded but without much effect.

On Thursday, August 20, the first French ships returned from their maneuvering with the British and their battle with the storm. At first it appeared as if the British fate in Newport was sealed. The next day, however, d'Estaing informed Sullivan that the fleet would sail to Boston to refit. Sullivan was totally stunned. Lafayette, Green, Laurens, and Langdon were quickly sent aboard the *Languedoc* to request that the French delay their departure for at least 48 hours.

Greene and the others pointed out to d'Estaing that the project was only undertaken in the first place with the guarantee that the French fleet would work with the Americans. Now everything was ready for the final assault. The British were sure to surrender within a very short time if they were trapped between the French fleet and American land force. The French fleet could also refit at Providence and take refuge there if necessary since it was a better, safer harbor than Boston. From Newport, the French and Americans would have a base to attack British lines of communication and supply. The victory would surely strengthen the alliance and demoralize the British.

D'Estaing had Greene write out the American reasons for continuing the joint attack, and the admiral presented the document to his captains in conference. The French officers were not impressed and voted to go to Boston. D'Estaing upheld the vote.

D'Estaing's orders directed him to repair to Boston if the fleet suffered damage in North American waters. Again, although the French admiral had done well enough in his engagement with Howe, he may not have had the full confidence of his officers. They had not forgotten that d'Estaing was a general who had turned admiral. It was their advice to make sail for Boston.

D'Estaing also had received word from his sources that Admiral John Byron's ships had arrived in American waters to reinforce Howe. The French orders indicated that, in the event that a powerful British force formed against him, d'Estaing should refit and sail to protect the West Indies. The West Indies were far more important, and d'Estaing decided to be prudent.

Reacting to this decision with frustration and disappointment, Sullivan and his general officers sent a letter to d'Estaing repeating the American arguments for staying. In addition to what has already been stated, they believed that the damaged French ships would be at risk sailing around Nantucket shoals to Boston. French honor would be injured by the move. There was no sign of Byron's fleet, and the original orders could not apply to this situation, where only a few ships were damaged and the British were ready to surrender.

Lafayette refused to sign this document and took offense to it and to Sullivan's statement in his general orders of August 24. Sullivan, out of sorts and a victim once again of a campaign doomed by forces beyond his control, reacted with more candor than was wise. When confronted by Lafayette, Sullivan agreed to change the orders, but the damage was already done. Many American officers agreed with Sullivan and saw the French departure as desertion. Sullivan blamed the French and never apologized for his views.

The French fleet sailed for Boston on August 22. The militia, supportive and involved up to this point, lost interest now that the French were gone. Over the next few days, several thousand men returned home, greatly diminishing Sullivan's effective strength.

Sullivan called for a council of war to discuss the alternatives. The American officers were dismayed over the French departure. Greene felt it folly to continue the siege, on the other hand, he believed it dangerous to retreat. With approximately 7,000 men left in the army, Sullivan faced 6,000 British entrenched around Newport. In the east, where the American troops were entrenched, the British were the strongest. An attack could be made in the west against weaker British lines, but Sullivan decided not to risk the losses; he would withdraw and wait to see if the French fleet would reappear.

For a few days, Sullivan attempted to bluff Pigot by remaining in line and continuing the siege. It had no effect. On August 24, Sullivan received word from Washington that General Henry Howe was coming to Newport's relief. It was at that point he decided to pull back to the northern tip of Aquidneck Island and await the French return. Lafayette left for Boston on August 26 to speak with d'Estaing and attempt to persuade him to return to Newport. Concerned about missing a possible battle during the withdrawal, Lafayette rode the 70 miles to Boston in 7 hours. He failed to persuade his fellow Frenchman. Riding back faster than he went, Lafayette covered the 70 miles to Tiverton in 6 1/2 hours. In spite of these efforts, Lafayette missed the Battle of Rhode Island.

On the evening of August 28, Greene began pulling his troops out of line and moving northward on the West Road. The rest of the American army followed. By 3 A.M. on August 29, Sullivan had between 5,000 and 6,000 men digging south of Butt's Hill. Sullivan positioned his army near the Bristol Ferry, in the northwest corner of Aquidneck Island, 12 miles north of Newport. The American line stretched for two miles from the east passage to the Narragansett Bay. John Glover's men formed the left flank near the East Road, facing Quaker Hill. Tyler's Connecticut militia protected Glover's left.

Colonel Christopher Greene's brigade guarded the American center with Butt's Hill directly behind. Ezekiel Cornell's Rhode Island brigade protected Greene's right flank up to the West Road. Varnum's continentals and Colonel James Livingston's regiment were on the American left, across the West Road and facing Turkey Hill to the south. Major Samuel Ward commanded Christopher Greene's Black Rhode Island regiment in a redoubt, which strengthened the American far left flank, facing out toward Narragansett Bay. Nathanael Greene commanded the American left flank. Sullivan had overall command and directed the American center and right.

A second American line, 800 yards in the rear, was composed of Jonathan Titcomb, Solomon Lovell, and West's militia battalions. Three miles in front of the American position Sullivan placed the light infantry, with Colonel Lauren's men on the West Road and Colonel Livingston's men guarding the East Road.

Pigot discovered the American retreat early in the morning of August 29 and promptly pursued in two columns. General Francis Smith, of Lexington and Concord fame, took to the East Road with his British regiments. General Von Lossberg marched up the West Road with Hessian jaegers and two Ansbach battalions. His force was later augmented with Edmund Fanning's provincials and another Hessian battalion.

As the sun rose in the sky, Saturday, August 29 grew hot, humid, and hazy. It soon became a typical late summer's day in Rhode Island. Pigot wasted no time in attacking the American positions. Sullivan found himself for the first time in his military career in overall command of a battle.

At 7 A.M., the American light infantry began skirmishing with the British advance along both the East and the West roads. Giving way gradually under pressure, the Americans took advantage of stone walls and trees to disrupt the British advance. Eventually the British pushed the light infantry back. The British were soon in possession of Quaker and Turkey hills, just over a mile south of the main American line. Between the two armies were meadowland and fields bordered by stone fences.

At 9 A.M., with artillery support, General Smith led his men from the Quaker Hill across fields toward Sullivan's left flank. Smith's goal was to push the American flank back, opening the road to Howland's Ferry (Tiverton) and exposing the American escape route. Glover's Continental brigade and other American units held their ground, repelled the assault, and pushed Smith's men back to Quaker Hill in much confusion. Subsequent British artillery fire was ineffective, and the American left flank was not threatened again.

Meanwhile, on the other end of the American line, the British left flank under Von Lossberg advanced on the American right. In the vanguard, the jaegers succeeded in capturing several small outworks in front of the American line. These sites provided the British with a clear field of fire into the American flank. Artillery was quickly brought forward and began firing on the Americans.

In addition, the *Sphynx*, the *Vigilant* (sloops of war), the galley *Spitfire*, and the brig *Privateer* sailed up the middle passage from Newport. With this increased firepower, Pigot decided to make his main effort an attack to crush the American right and cut them off from the Bristol Ferry. With luck, Pigot could turn the tables on Sullivan and force him to surrender.

Cannon fire from land and water soon pounded on American entrenchments. The Americans held. General Greene turned heavy American artillery on the British ships and forced their retirement. Then Pigot unleashed Von Lossberg and his battalions. Twice Von Lossberg attempted to take the redoubt commanded by Major Ward. The Black troops fought valiantly against Von Lossberg's Germans in hand-to-hand fighting, repulsing two "furious onsets" of Hessians. This was the first instance in American history in which Black troops fought as a unit; the 130 men fought extremely well.

Between 2 and 3 P.M., a reinforced Von Lossberg made his final attack on the American right. Passing by Ward's redoubts, Von Lossberg's men pushed the American line back briefly. General Greene then counterattacked with Varnum's Continental brigade, Solomon Lovell's Massachusetts militia, and Livingston's light infantry. With the bayonet and musketry, Greene's men pushed Von Lossberg back in severe confusion, leaving the German dead and wounded behind.

Sullivan, the victor, wished to chase the British, pushing them off Turkey and Quaker hills. He discovered that his troops had had no food or rest for 36 hours. No one was fresh. Sullivan called off the pursuit. In the end, artillery fire was exchanged by both sides for another hour or so without much effect. Sporadic musketry continued thereafter until dark.

The American army had fought well. Both Continentals and militia had performed with spirit and discipline. Casualties for the Americans were 30 killed, 137 wounded, and 44 missing. The British lost 38 killed, 210 wounded, and 44 missing. Although the siege had failed its purpose, the Battle of Rhode Island was an American victory. Lafayette believed the battle to be "the best fought action of the war."

Both sides maintained their respective positions throughout the next day, August 30. Pigot sent for additional cannon and troops from Newport while Sullivan boldly faced him in the entrenchments. Word then reached Sullivan that the British fleet was near and that the French fleet would not return. It was agreed in a council of war to retreat to Tiverton.

That night, August 30, Sullivan withdrew his men across Howland's Ferry to Tiverton, and from Bristol Ferry to Bristol. Every gun and all the baggage was safely ferried across. No one was left behind. By 3 A.M., the last of the Americans were on the mainland. The ferry work was accomplished by the Salem boatmen under Glover's direction. (Glover's original unit of Marblehead fishermen, the Marblehead Mariners, who did the ferrying at Long Island and Trenton, had disbanded by this time.) Sullivan dismissed his militia and returned to Providence with the regular line troops. The last major operation of the 1778 campaign had ended.

The British were aware of the American withdrawal. But Pigot became ill, and his second in command, General Richard Prescott, did not dare risk an attack without orders. General Clinton arrived at Newport by sea the next day, September 1, with eight fresh British regiments, a battalion of grenadiers, and one of light infantry. Clinton was annoyed that Pigot had not waited until these 5,000 troops had arrived before starting his pursuit. With the fleet and fresh troops surrounding the Americans, Sullivan's fate probably would have been sealed.

D'Estaing and the French fleet reached Boston, but their troubles were not over. Admiral Howe, finally augmented by Byron's fleet, had chased the French to Boston but decided not to attack. Now the French had to deal with the American discouragement over the Rhode Island campaign. The people of Boston were so irritated over the turn of events that the fleet was almost not repaired. It took the political talents of Horatio Gates, John Hancock, and Lafayette, the latter two recently returned from Rhode Island, to smooth things over.

Even though the French were on their best behavior in Boston, several riots broke out. Four or five Frenchmen were killed in the confusion. Finally, the French ships were repaired, supplies taken on, and d'Estaing sailed with his fleet and 4,000 infantry for Martinique on November 4.

The first attempt at collaboration had ended in failure. Both sides recriminated against each other. Washington handled matters from afar.

He warned Sullivan about French pride, their ability in warfare, and a strict code of military etiquette, which Sullivan had virtually ignored. Americans had to learn to work in harmony with the French, despite cultural differences. Washington also wrote to Greene, Lafayette, and William Heath, among others, to smooth ruffled feathers on both sides of the alliance.

Congress passed two resolutions on October 17, 1778, praising the bravery, wisdom, and zeal of d'Estaing and his command, and thanking him for the services rendered to the American cause. Congress also thanked Sullivan on September 19 for his services in the siege of Newport and Battle of Rhode Island.

Both France and the United States realized that failure at Rhode Island should not be allowed to ruin the alliance. After Newport, the Americans developed a more realistic view of the French. No longer did the Americans expect a quick, decisive victory brought about by their allies. The war would go on.

Josiah Bartlett, New Hampshire delegate of the Continental Congress, expressed a commonly held opinion when he wrote "the Rhode Island expedition, though not successful, yet brought no disgrace to our arms, nor have the enemy any great cause for boasting." Washington informed Heath that the public explanation for the French retirement would be the storm damage done to the fleet. The matter was officially put to rest.

Many Americans wondered what would have happened if d'Estaing had made a quick passage across the Atlantic. Would the strong French fleet have trapped Howe and Clinton in the Delaware River, stopping the British evacuation of Philadelphia? At New York, would it have helped to push aggressively into the harbor while the British fleet still was at a numerical disadvantage? Finally, at Newport, should d'Estaing have held his ground and forced Pigot to surrender first before coming out against Howe? No one knows.

The British maintained their martial law rule over Newport until October 25, 1779, when Prescott's troops were withdrawn to New York in preparation for the British southern campaign of 1780. Newport was left in ruins.

Paul J. Sanborn

REFERENCES

George A. Billias, *General John Glover and His Marblehead Marines* (1960); Paul F. Dearden, *The*

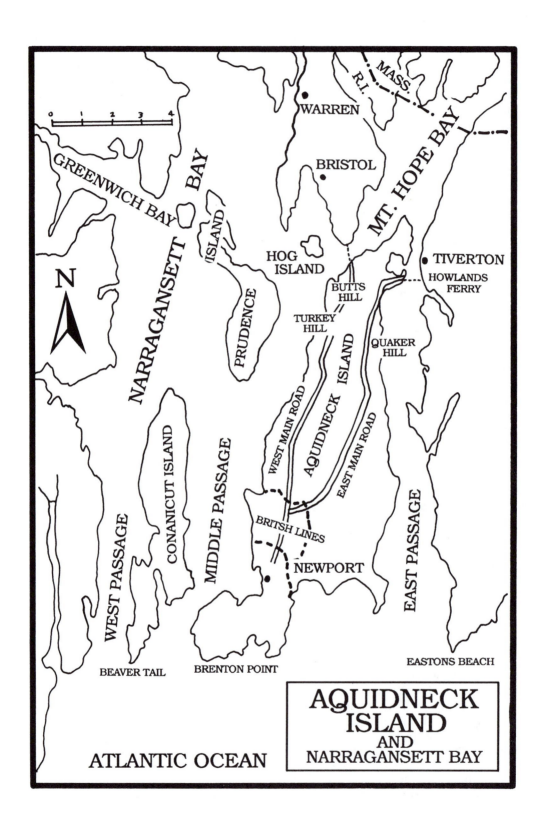

WARREN

BRISTOL

GREENWICH BAY

NARRAGANSETT BAY

MT. HOPE BAY

R.I.

MASS.

HOG ISLAND

ISLAND

PRUDENCE

BUTTS HILL

TURKEY HILL

TIVERTON

HOWLANDS FERRY

QUAKER HILL

N

AQUIDNECK ISLAND

WEST MAIN ROAD

EAST MAIN ROAD

CONANICUT ISLAND

MIDDLE PASSAGE

WEST PASSAGE

BRITSH LINES

NEWPORT

EAST PASSAGE

BEAVER TAIL

BRENTON POINT

EASTONS BEACH

ATLANTIC OCEAN

AQUIDNECK ISLAND
AND
NARRAGANSETT BAY

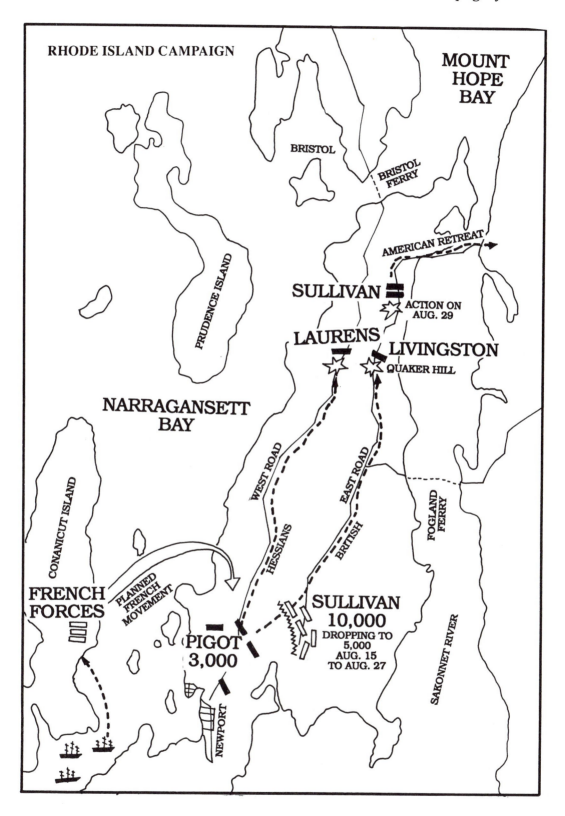

Rhode Island Campaigns of 1778 (1980); Douglas S. Freeman, *George Washington*, 7 vols. (1957); Louis Gottschalk, *Lafayette in America*, 5 vols. (1935–56), 2; Ira D. Gruber, *The Howe Brothers and the American Revolution* (1972); Stanley J. Idzerda, ed., *Lafayette in the Age of the American Revolution*, 4 vols. (1977–), 2; Lt. Frederick Mackenzie, *Diary of Frederick Mackenzie*, 2 vols. (1930); Nathan Miller, *Sear of Glory* (1974); Richard K. Showman, ed., *The Papers of General Nathanael Greene*, Vol. 2 (1980); Florence P. Simister, *The Fire's Center* (1979); William C. Stinchcomb, *The American Revolution and the French Alliance* (1969); Christopher Ward, *The War of Revolution*, 2 vols. (1952); Charles P. Whittemore, *A General of the Revolution; John Sullivan of New Hampshire* (1961); William B. Willcox, *Portrait of a General: Sir Henry Clinton* (1964).

Rhode Island in the American Revolution

As a colony singularly dependent on international trade, the British imperial crisis had a particular impact on Rhode Island. Parliamentary efforts to extract revenues from it especially threatened its livelihood, while nonimportation, the usual method of resistance to such a measure likewise threatened the provincial economy. While comparatively little fighting occurred there, British troops threatened or occupied much of Rhode Island for most of the war, and the destruction and hardship that the province faced required extraordinary measures to avoid destruction and economic collapse. The method upon which the new state fell back, the printing of paper money, renewed and increased the longstanding hostility between Rhode Island and the other states and prevented Rhode Islanders from ratifying the Constitution until 1790.

Two factors contributed to Rhode Island's response to the imperial crisis beginning in 1763—its terrain and its original charter. Rhode Island had received one of the most liberal colonial charters from the Crown. It named and compensated all its own officials, including governor, council, and judges, and the charter did not even require the colony to follow London's directive more than was reasonably possible. The frequency with which the Rhode Island General Assembly had restored to emissions of paper money ensured that many people would have enough personal assets to register to vote; typically, more than 60 percent were eligible.

Preservation of charter liberties took an over-riding importance to Rhode Island Whigs and even to many Loyalists. They did not use political theory or constitutional doctrine in their rhetoric, for the charter did not expressly protect personal liberty or republican forms of government. Rather, the charter protected the self-government that allowed pursuit of trade and promotion of manufactures. Whig rhetoric always discussed threats to the charter as attacks on Rhode Island's prosperity.

The colony's small size and extensive coastline required it to rely on commerce. It had little hinterland that could develop sufficient agriculture to support its ports. Ever since a group of religious dissenters left Anne Hutchinson at Portsmouth and moved farther down Aquidneck Island to form Newport, maritime commerce provided the most important economic activity for Rhode Islanders. Rhode Island shippers thus developed extensive trading networks along the coast of North America and to the British West Indian islands, carrying the cattle products, timber, and fish collected within the colony itself and developing an extensive carrying trade throughout the western Atlantic.

Carrying food products to Caribbean slaves provided Newport merchant captains with regular income, but the slave trade made them wealthy. They traded extensively in the Atlantic triangle that carried slaves to the sugar islands, molasses to New England, and finished goods to Africa. The use of molasses provided employment for hundreds of people in the manufacture of rum in Newport and Providence alone; that and other manufactures depended on imported raw materials. The slave trade also gave Newport the largest proportional population of Blacks and of slaves in the North.

Even before 1763, the dependence on the sugar trade gave Rhode Island merchants expertise in evading imperial restrictions on American trade. Although they were required to buy molasses from the English islands in the Caribbean, captains developed various methods of buying and shipping cheaper French molasses. They also knew how to smuggle it into Rhode Island to avoid the six-penny duty that the Navigation Act of 1733 had placed on it, including the bribing of the Newport collector of the customs. Under the charter, the colonial general assembly appointed the collector, so generally he was apt to be more sympathetic to local merchants than to London. As conflicts between

Parliament and the American merchant marine escalated, Rhode Island's lawbreaking quickly went beyond evasion of the Navigation Acts to violent challenges to British authority.

The Revenue Act (or Sugar Act) of 1764, by halving the duty on molasses, threatened the entire economy of Rhode Island by ensuring collection. Word of the legislation came while Rhode Island was entering a postwar depression that would last most of the decade, aggravated by increasing numbers of slaves who competed with free labor. Governor Stephen Hopkins began a pamphlet war over the impost when he persuaded the general assembly to endorse a remonstrance that he wrote to Parliament and to Minister of the Treasury George Grenville and that he later published as *The Rights of the Colonies Examined*. Hopkins argued that inhibitions on the molasses trade would damage both the Empire and Rhode Island. Rhode Island's decreased trade with the Caribbean islands would harm both economies. Because Rhode Island was so dependent on goods imported from the rest of the Empire, moreover, any diminution in colonial wealth would diminish metropolitan income.

Hopkins's pamphlet presented a sound economic argument, but its attempts to find constitutional limitations on Parliament's right to tax its colonies vacillated. On the one hand, Parliament did need to regulate the whole Empire, yet a body that represented only one part of the Empire, he asserted, could not make laws that taxed the whole. Newport lawyer Martin Howard, Jr., writing as "a Gentleman at Halifax," answered Hopkins by asserting that Parliament retained authority over British subjects no matter where they traveled; the sovereignty of King in Parliament was as much a part of the rights of Englishmen as "life, liberty, and estate." Hopkins and others wrote furious replies to Howard, but James Otis, Jr., of Massachusetts, who heard the debate, ended it by engaging Howard and those like him in a remarkably vituperative *ad hominem* attack.

More than Howard's support of the Sugar Act upset Otis and other Whigs. Rhode Island's charter was being threatened simultaneously with its trade. Rhode Island had developed a party system that many found inconsistent with contemporary political thought. Two factions developed in the state: Hopkins's group received most of its support around Providence, although many in the southern part of the colony, especially Joseph Wanton of Newport, supported him, while most Newporters supported Samuel Ward of Westerly. A dispute over finance at the end of the French and Indian War was the only ideological difference between the factions; merchants led both groups, and they both had their share of people who became Loyalists and Patriots. The stakes in colonial elections—patronage, internal improvements, and tax assessment—were sufficiently high to cause resort to slander and fraud.

While none of the party leaders liked the system, Howard and other recent immigrants from England to Newport took particular offense, especially because the parties sought to appeal to the lower ranks of the colony's large enfranchised population. They approved of Benjamin Franklin's attempts to acquire a royal charter for Philadelphia and asked him for advise on revoking Rhode Island's corporate charter. Publication of their letter earned them the name of the Newport Junto, and they became targets of crowds who blamed British imperial policy for Newport's declining economy. English mercantile policy had been popularly blamed for the chronic shortage of specie that necessitated periodic emissions of paper money but that became worse after the French and Indian War. Newporters also resented the presence of English troops, because they were obnoxious, competed for scarce jobs, and often impressed local sailors. Besides its threat to sailor's liberty, the impressment policy tended to drive away coasting vessels from Rhode Island ports while inflating seaman's wages.

News of the Stamp Act of 1765 solidified opposition to the Newport Junto. Rather than repeating the pamphlet war over the Sugar Act, Newporters took to the streets to demonstrate opposition. On August 29, a crowd directed by William Ellery and the prominent merchants hung in effigy Howard, physician and Junto member Thomas Moffatt, and Augustus Johnson, Rhode Island attorney general and appointive stamp commissioner. Moffatt quickly retired to his farm, while the other two along with customs collector John Robinson retreated to the British warship *Cygnet*.

The following morning, after Robinson and Howard returned to Newport, they became embroiled in a dispute perhaps instigated by the merchants. The crowd, having heard about the

Boston Stamp Act riots, responded by pulling down Howard's and Moffat's houses. It spared Johnson's but carted off many goods. Moffatt and Howard took the next ship back to England, while Johnson, still a popular figure in town, promised to resign his commission.

Resisting merchants who instigated the riots soon regretted their actions, for the sailor whom they had hired to lead the riots turned against them. Twice his arrest led to threats to pull down the houses of leading Sons of Liberty. Never again did the Sons of Liberty instigate a riot in Rhode Island.

Providence faced the challenge more calmly. Its town meeting voted to recommend a convention of delegates from all the colonies; the general assembly endorsed this recommendation and adopted resolutions that expanded the Virginia Resolves. The Rhode Island version included three extra articles, including one that maintained that the population was bound to pay only those internal taxes that the general assembly imposed and one that promised to indemnify any state official who disregarded the Act. The general assembly also sent two delegates to the Stamp Act Congress. While the Rhode Island delegates endorsed the report of the Congress, the colony never joined the nonintercourse agreements that finally brought sufficient pressure on British merchants to effect repeal.

By late October 1765, Newporters knew that the stamps were aboard the *Cygnet*, ready when the Act was to take effect on November 1. Ships cleared the port for other American ports to avoid buying stamps after that date. Robinson's move back to the *Cygnet* prevented him from issuing any papers to ships engaged in foreign trade, virtually closing down the port to that trade. He refused to deliver the stamps from the *Cygnet*; Johnson certified the impossibility of their use, and Newport shipping resumed as Newport effectively nullified the Act.

Rhode Islanders' reaction to the imposition of the Townshend Duties in 1767 demonstrated the insecurity that their reliance on maritime commerce brought. While the duties themselves would fall especially hard on Rhode Island, the colony could no more afford to end all commerce than it could two years earlier. Merchants there did not join those in other ports who entered into nonimportation agreements. In fact, Rhode Island merchants at first welcomed vessels that other ports turned away and agreed to stop foreign trade only when other ports threatened to end all commerce with the colony.

After having been coerced into starting nonintercourse, Rhode Island merchants ended it at the first opportunity. In 1770, upon the duties' partial repeal, Newport merchants voted to end nonimportation. Although Providence merchants, like those in Newport, never stopped the illegal trade, they joined those in other colonial ports in heaping vituperation on Newport. But few colonial ports could maintain adherence to the nonimportation agreements, and the plan collapsed.

Rhode Islanders throughout the period maintained their own active method of resisting unfavorable British imperial policy. Newport and Providence mobs repeatedly liberated seized contraband and merchant vessels. They also attacked British vessels themselves. In July 1754, a crowd seized the battery on Goat Island and fired on the frigate *St. John* as it pursued a merchant vessel. In June 1765, a larger crowd in Newport seized and burned a long boat of the warship *Maidstone*, which was engaged in impressment duty. In 1769, the officers of the HMS *Liberty* seized two vessels, shooting the captain of one, and impressed three sailors. When the *Liberty*'s captain conducted his prizes to Newport, a crowd siezed him, ransacked his quarters, and scuttled the ship. In 1770, a mob in the same city drove customs officers off the wharf.

Providence merchants engaged in the most important of such incidents. In 1764, the *Gaspee* under Captain William Dudsington was ordered to Rhode Island to patrol Narragansett Bay. Instead, Dudsington searched every vessel that he could that crossed the bay, seizing vessels under every possible pretext. Because he knew that he could not win condemnation of contraband in the vice-admiralty court in Newport, he sent ships found with contraband to the one in Boston for trial. Both Dudsington and Admiral Montague in Boston curtly refused Wanton's formal complaints.

In 1772, Dudsington pursued a smaller vessel upwind and against an ebb tide. The pursued vessel tacked in front of a point, and the *Gaspee* ran aground. When the news reached Providence, prominent merchant John Brown organized a party to end the troubles with the *Gaspee*. Led by Captain Abraham Whipple, 60 people in 3 long boats rowed down upon its bow, so that it could not fire upon them. When Dudsington ordered them to stop, Abraham told him he was under arrest, and someone shot Dudsington in the groin. The *Gaspee* was boarded and Dudsington taken to his quarters, where his wounds were dressed. Several boarders examined his records while ransacking his office, and the ship was burned after its evacuation.

Governor Wanton expressed horror at the act, posted a £100 reward for the arrest of its perpetrators, and did nothing more in public, although privately he unsuccessfully tried to convince the ministry that the attack was not the result of a conspiracy. The Admiralty ordered a commission to investigate the burning and find sufficient evidence to transport any suspects to England for trial. American papers raged about the latest threat to traditional British liberties, and Rhode Islanders created committees of correspondence to communicate with leaders of the resistance in other colonies. The threat of distant prosecutions, foreshadowed in Dudsington's Boston prosecutions and enumerated in the First Continental Congress' petition to the King and in the Declaration of Independence, became a central Whig grievance.

Meanwhile, the investigating commission wallowed in impotence. All its members but one were native-born Americans, and Massachusetts chief justice Andrew Oliver faced strong political distrust at home for his participation on it. Lord Dartmouth actually feared that publicizing the incident would only encourage more violent resistance. Whether the commission had any subpoena power was unclear. Samuel Adams urged members of the general assembly to ignore the commission, and many merchants and lawyers called to testify refused on the grounds that they were preoccupied. Only a mental incompetent and an obvious perjurer actually testified, and the only person ever punished was Dudsington, who faced a corurt-martial in London. Neither attempts to enforce the Navigation Acts nor resistance to them ended.

Rhode Island's economy improved during the late 1760s, greatly on the strength of manufacturing, and from 1772 to 1774, its foreign commerce increased dramatically. The two years between the attack on the *Gaspee* and the imposition of the Coercive Acts were thus quiet, although private military companies formed throughout the colony. The news of the Boston Tea Party and of Parliament's reaction to it

quickly recreated the old divisions between Rhode Island merchants and the Crown and between differing people in Rhode Island. Especially disconcerting was the Massachusetts Government Act, by which Parliament attempted to override that colony's charter. Fear for its own charter as much as sympathy for Boston motivated the Rhode Island reply.

In May 1774, the Providence town meeting first called for a continental congress that would establish "the firmest union" between the various colonies, and the Newport meeting objected to the "injuries done to . . . Boston." In June, the general assembly endorsed Providence's recommendation, and the governor proclaimed a day of prayer and fasting. Despite the apparent rapidity with which Rhode Island responded, divisions arose. The vicar at Newport's Trinity Anglican Church criticized the hypocrisy of the fast, and Newport argued over aid to Boston until the following March, when it granted its rival port less than 80 pounds sterling.

The Coercive Acts ended the Ward-Hopkins rivalry. The Rhode Island General Assembly sent Samuel Ward and Stephen Hopkins as its delegates to the Continental Congress. While Hopkins became one of the more cautious delegates, unwilling to repudiate parliamentary power over trade and taxation completely and favoring a new American house of Parliament, Ward became one of the most radical delegates.

Others back in Rhode Island supported Ward's views. As early as 1768, Silas Downer had celebrated the planting of the liberty tree in Newport by calling for independence. Now, Newport newspapers wrote that the King merited allegiance only insofar as he served the people and that royal and parliamentary disregard of colonial grievances eliminated American obligations to England. Ezra Stiles, the pastor at Newport's Second Congregational Church, believed that only independence would prevent the slavery and loss of liberties that the English Crown and Anglican church were, he feared, plotting for America. Stiles feared a plan to name an American bishop, whom he feared would garner sufficient influence to eliminate the liberties of American religious dissenters.

No matter how much support resistance to Britain had in theory in Rhode Island, the way in which Congress sought to secure those liberties was still unacceptable there. The Continental Association's revival of nonintercourse put

Newport into a dilemma. The town depended on both coastal and foreign trade, and no other ports would trade with Newport if it traded with Great Britain. The town's merchants finally created a committee of inspection of 37 merchants, some of whom would later become Loyalists. Trade with Britain continued, which many local merchants again blamed on the town's Jewish merchants.

Rhode Island began to prepare for war in 1775. The general assembly responded to the news of Lexington and Concord by voting to raise 1,500 men into a colonial military force. Recently reelected Governor Wanton and Deputy Governor Darius Sessions opposed the measure, Wanton citing his oath of allegiance to the King. In May, the legislature tried again, this time calling it an "Army of Observation" and proclaiming that it was in the King's service for the protection of American liberties. Wanton, not swayed, refused to take his oath of office so that he could not sign the orders raising the force. The general assembly then passed legislation permitting the colonial secretary to sign. Rhode Island troops, led by Nathanael Greene, were among the last to arrive in Boston, too late for the powder alarm and seeing only minor action on Bunker Hill. In October 1775 the general assembly declared the office of governor vacant, and Sessions quit. The legislature declared Joseph Cooke the acting governor and William Bradford of Bristol the acting deputy governor. In January 1776, Cooke was elected governor in his own right.

In July 1775, Providence built a string of forts and trenches around the town, and Captain James Wallace, commanding the HMS *Rose*, started a reign of terror within the state. He captured only one ship, noting that he could not permit commerce by a people in open rebellion. That same month he bombarded Newport for the first time and threatened to burn down the city. In October 1775, Wallace positioned the *Rose* off Bristol and demanded that the town's leading men or magistrates come out to the ship. When they failed to do so after an hour, he shelled that town as well. Wallace demanded several hundred sheep and several dozen head of cattle; he later left with 40 sheep. Actually, most of the shells went over the town, and the raid injured no one.

Wallace's raids created a new dilemma for Newport. Beginning in July 1775, Wallace caused further division between Newport and the rest of the colony by demanding supplies from Newport. The town agreed to furnish him supplies if he did not destroy it, causing other towns to doubt Newport's commitment. Wallace effectively kept Newport in fear throughout 1775; on December 11 he shelled the town again, later announcing that he would burn it down to celebrate Christmas. That same month a British force landed on Conanicut Island, destroying 12 houses, while a rebel raid on Goat Island captured the King's artillery. In January 1776, Wallace attacked Prudence and Patience islands in Narragansett Bay, destroying all of the houses on one and one house on the other and carrying away one hundred sheep. The next day, the militia, including forces from Bristol and Warren, engaged the British on Prudence in a three-hour battle.

In August 1775, the general assembly responded to the King's declaration of the colonies' rebellion by declaring "treasonous conversation" with British troops a capital crime, although it specifically exempted Newport's deal with Wallace. In December 1775, Stephen Hopkins, and a month later, Governor Greene, agreed that only independence would preserve charter liberties. In May 1776, the General Assembly, fearing an invasion of Newport by British troops, moved its meeting place to Providence and created a council of war to meet during its own adjournment. During June, the assembly ordered the confiscation of all money in the customs house. Customs Collector Charles Dudley, who had earlier alienated Newport's merchants by refusing their gratuities, resisted until Esek Hopkins threatened his life, compelling him to flee to the *Rose*. That same month, General Charles Lee came on behalf of the Continental Army to take loyalty oaths; those who refused were imprisoned.

Despite the mission granted to the Army of Observation, the deputies saw the contradiction of rebelling against the King to whom they had sworn obedience. On May 4, the general assembly renounced its allegiance to the King. It did not declare independence; the sole effect of the resolution was to repeal a law criminalizing questioning the authority of the King and of Parliament. Until July 18, Rhode Island continued to refer to itself as an English colony.

In December 1776, 6,000 troops finally began the British occupation of Newport. British attention to Rhode Island was not accidental.

During the earlier imperial wars, Narragansett Bay had been a center for privateering, and by occupying Aquidneck Island, the British intended to prevent it. The British were not the only ones who feared Rhode Island's privateers; many in Philadelphia feared that privateering's high remuneration would discourage enlistment in the Continental Army. The British move was effective; by 1777, privateering had virtually ceased in the area.

The British occupation of Newport was the central event of Rhode Island's participation in the war. In 1776, many of the town's wealthiest citizens evacuated, and the general assembly sought to provide for the relocation of poorer refugees. Later, it accepted the commitment of providing for poorer refugees who came from other parts of the colony. By 1777, around 300 Newport refugees lived in Providence, and poor relief formed the town council's primary business until 1780.

In Providence from 1776 through 1777 were about 1,000 Continentals. This force increased to 10,000 troops when General John Sullivan prepared for an assault on Aquidneck Island. Rhode Island College, later Brown University, became a barracks and hospital for the Continental Army, and the locals welcomed the troops that increased their security during the war. The relationship between the town and the soldiers was not always happy, for even American troops were at times compelled to requisition goods and destroy fields. After 1780, the town treated French troops under the Comte de Rochambeau, who replaced the Continentals, more diffidently, deciding that their educational needs outweighed the French use of the college by refusing to permit the French to use the campus buildings or hospitals.

The general assembly responded to the occupation of Newport by raising two state regiments in March 1777, for two years, with reenlistment for each following year until the crisis in Newport had passed. Continental officials feared that recruitment for the new force would compete with recruitment for the two Continental Army regiments assigned to Rhode Island. Washington opposed its creation until the legislature assured him that the two regiments would become integrated into the Continental Army once the state was out of danger. These troops joined the various local militias and independent companies in the defense of the state.

After the British left, the state kept its word by sending them to the South, where they fought at Yorktown.

Before the occupation, British troops under Lieutenant General Hugh, Earl Percy, emphasized fair treatment toward the rebellious residents, and he experienced some success in winning over some of the population. The commander of the occupation forces, however, Major General Richard Prescott, replaced paternalism with abuse. On July 9, 1777, Lieutenant Colonel William Barton led 40 Continental troops onto the west shore of Aquidneck Island above Newport and captured Prescott in bed at a local farmhouse. Prescott was later exchanged for General Charles Lee.

British troops stationed on Aquidneck raided several towns on the mainland, including East Greenwich, Warwick, and the Kingston for food and supplies. As Sullivan prepared his troops to invade Aquidneck, the attacks increased to keep the Americans on the defensive. On May 25, 1778, 500 British and Hessian troops landed west of Bristol. The troops burned several dozen flatboats collected there along with the row galley *Washington* and a gristmill. The local militia misjudged the size of the force, and it could not drive the British from town until the enemy had burned around 30 houses, including that belonging to Deputy Governor Bradford. The British attacked Warren the same day and Tiverton six days later. The siege of Newport did not begin until July; the British finally left in 1779.

Rhode Island played an important role in the development of a navy. In 1775, the state had ordered 2 row galleys, each with a crew of 60, and officers. The colony's delegates to the Continental Congress had earlier prompted the adoption of a Continental Navy, and in 1775 Congress authorized several states to build and outfit ships. Rhode Island's assignment of two ships became a source of patronage until the general assembly instituted centralized direction of their construction. These vessels were completed in 1776 but could not sneak past the British vessels at Newport until 1778. The 28-gun *Providence*, commanded by Abraham Whipple, who had led the attack on the *Gaspee*, captured 8 enemy vessels before its capture at the siege of Charleston in 1780; John Hopkins commanded the 32-gun *Warren*, which participated in 1 or 2 missions before its destruction on the Penobscot expedition in 1779.

In 1779, the British troops left Aquidneck, but the state's economic condition did not improve rapidly. The siege devastated Newport, and the rest of the state also suffered. Lack of access to fuel on the mainland meant that many houses on the island had been stripped or razed for fuel. The winter of 1778 and 1779 had been especially harsh, and Narragansett Bay had frozen over. After much effort and negotiation, Providence merchants acquired grain from Connecticut, but some merchants, including Nicholas Brown of the town's most famous merchant family, withheld it from market to drive the price up. The British continued to blockade Narragansett Bay even after they had left Newport. The result was a large increase in poverty in Newport and in other towns during the war.

The state's economy greatly concerned the Rhode Island General Assembly. Raising money for the state's Continental and provincial regiments and trying to control the economic dislocation that the war caused, filled the legislature's agenda. The legislature mainly sought to finance the war the way it had repeatedly raised money throughout the Colonial period—by issuing paper money. By the end of the war, the more than £400,000 in circulation caused severe inflation and drove specie from circulation. The state also borrowed over £150,000, which later proved a burden during the postwar depression.

Partly due to its own financial acts, the state faced tremendous shortages during the war. A December 1776 meeting of New England states produced a commitment to curb monopolies and regulate prices, and Rhode Island passed the necessary laws the following month. The state's enactments proved ineffectual, however, and on July 30, 1777, those states along with New York recommended the repeal of all such laws. Later that same year the four states, this time with New York, met again in Springfield and agreed to repeal antimonopoly legislation. In 1779, the general assembly called for a convention of towns in East Greenwich, which sought ways to halt the rapid depreciation of the currency and impose a schedule of prices.

War and relief for the poor severely taxed the state's resources. It became unable to pay its obligation to Congress. In November 1779, South Carolina agreed to pay $50,000 for Rhode Island's portion, and Connecticut donated grain. The state's self-imposed obligation to reimburse the towns for the funds spent for the relief of Newport's poor still required increasing taxes on the towns able to pay it. Between 1779 and 1782, the burden of taxes amounted to more than $8,500,000, and the tax rate rose to one-third of all taxable goods. The high taxes made citizens outside Newport question whether the charter that they had gone to war in order to save truly guaranteed their freedoms.

The Rhode Island charter had granted six deputies to the general assembly to Newport and four each to Providence, Warwick, and Portsmouth, the colony's four original towns, while granting only two to each other town, regardless of its size. The system caused no dissatisfaction before the war, even though by 1774, 15 towns had larger populations than Providence, so long as the original towns could pay taxes commensurate with it. With the Aquidneck towns first occupied and then blockaded and with Portsmouth's trade diminished, the burden of taxation fell most heavily on the southern agricultural towns, and the unequal representation appeared tyrannical.

In 1782, delegates from six towns met at South Kingstowns (now Kingstown) to demand charter revisions. The once-hallowed charter, the Charlestown meeting resolved, should be replaced with a new constitution. Throughout the Confederation period, liberty for rural Rhode Islanders meant equal representation for each town among the deputies. Their calls had no effect besides introducing principle to Rhode Island politics; the charter was not replaced until 1843.

Rhode Islanders did note the contradiction of rebelling in order to retain their liberties while the slave trade remained critical to their wealth. In 1774, the general assembly proactively freed any slave imported from that date, but the freed slaves only received the status of Indians, and Newport merchants ensured that significant loopholes remained in the law. In 1775, Moses Brown suggested that the general assembly emancipate all slaves. It refused, but it did prohibit exporting slaves without their consent.

In 1778, the legislature allowed slaves to gain their freedom by enlisting. Their masters, who would be compensated, need not agree to the enlistment. The Rhode Island Black recruits, unlike Black Patriot recruits elsewhere, would receive the same pay as whites. Unlike whites, they were required to enlist for the duration of the war. Over 200 Rhode Island Blacks enlisted;

the state was the only one to form separate Black units. The Rhode Island troops served ably in the siege of Rhode Island, Red Bank, Pointer Bridge, Yorktown, and Oswego. Rhode Island had Black Loyalists as well. As early as 1775 some Blacks escorted Wallace around Conanicut showing him which houses to burn, and others deserted to the British soon after enlisting in the Continental Army.

The general assembly's act responded to two conditions. During the winter at Valley Forge, many of the Rhode Island troops had died or deserted, and General James Varnum suggested to Washington that Black troops replace them. Meanwhile, the British were attempting to encourage slave enlistment in Newport and to incite rebellions elsewhere. The measure received opposition from some slaveholders, who feared the moral consequences of enlisting slaves to fight for their master's freedom and of demonstrating that insufficient whites would enlist.

The state's Black population fell significantly during the war. The general assembly removed a statute that required a £100 bond for manumission, which made the procedure much more common than before the war. In 1784, the legislature passed a gradual emancipation act that freed slaves born after the enactment once they reached the age of majority, and after 1787 Rhode Island ships were officially prohibited from engaging in the slave trade.

Rhode Island contained many Loyalists. Many like Governor Wanton feared that, without British supervision and the protection of the Royal Navy, the state could not maintain its liberties under its charter, and once out of the empire they could not maintain their trade privileges with the rest of the English empire. While Stephen Hopkins's argument against the Sugar Act depended on Rhode Island merchants' violation of the law, the growing resistance to imperial authority made merchants fear an inability to maintain order against mob depredations. Even former resistance leaders came to prefer Parliament over mob rule.

Loyalists actively aided the British effort in several ways. Some gathered intelligence, and in 1775 George Rome was imprisoned for selling more flour to the British than the agreement with Wallace called for. After the occupation began, the British organized Loyalist raiding parties and privateering crews.

Newport's many prominent Anglicans and its British occupation made Toryism there prominent. Quakers, who officially remained steadfastly neutral (although many joined the Revolutionaries) were suspected of disloyalty as well. The British occupation led wavering residents to proclaim their continued loyalty. Many left at the occupation's end, and a 1779 council of war in Hartford ordered the confiscation of property belonging to 47 identified Loyalists. Other Loyalists faced more subtle pressure: they found that their trade had evaporated and charged that Whig merchants and politicians had deprived them of the same liberties that rebellion was meant to save. In 1780, the general assembly banned leading Loyalists from Rhode Island, but by 1783, many had returned with their lands restored.

At war's end, Newport faced physical destruction, the loss of half its population, including many leading merchants, and the loss of trading routes. America's major economic expansion was to be to the West, and an island port without access to the West could not compete. Newport merchants continued to engage in the outlawed slave trade until 1800 and developed a trade in rum, tobacco, and rice with Baltic ports.

Providence, on the other hand, developed economically during the war. During 1775 and 1776, the port expanded with the relaxation of imperial trading restrictions until the British imposed a blockade in the latter year. Merchants then had to bring goods through other ports in Massachusetts and Connecticut. Merchant houses consolidated, and most remaining merchants profited by the war. Consumer goods were generally available, and the war spurred Providence's budding manufacturers, especially foundries for munitions. After the war, the port's access to mainland agriculture spurred its commerce as well.

The state was a major holder of congressional debt instruments. By 1781, however, it faced inflation and stagnation due to the paper money and debts that the government had issued. The general assembly looked to foreign commerce to rejuvenate the state's economy and produce revenue from duties on shipping. It thus opposed the impost that Congress proposed to finance Robert Morris's Bank of North America. Merchants again led the radicals who opposed the new revenue duty as a violation of the liberties for which they had fought the Revolution. As usual, their arguments directly applied republican ideas to their economic status. The impost threatened to diminish the state's authority under its charter, to introduce legions of corrupt placemen who had no obligation to the general assembly, to require a standing army for its enforcement, and to further impoverish the state besides. Not even the specially imported rhetorical skills of Thomas Paine could convince Rhode Islanders to approve the impost.

The struggle over the impost typified the longstanding effect of the war. From its founding, Rhode Island had been regarded as an outcast, and the war did nothing to change the perception. The state contributed heavily financially and militarily to the war effort and had been one of the instigators of both the stamp Act and First Continental Congress. Resistance to nonimportation and Newport's halfhearted response to the Coercive Acts rendered its commitment to the Continental cause suspect. The refusal to approve the impost, considered essential to American economic recovery, and later the refusal to ratify the Constitution reinforced the American perception of "Rogues' Island."

James Eschen-Pipes

REFERENCES

Samuel Greene Arnold, *History of the State of Rhode Island*, 2 vols. (1860); Benjamin Cowell, *Spirit of '76 in Rhode Island* (1850); Elaine Forman Crane, *A Dependent People* (1985); Sydney V. James, *Colonial Rhode Island* (1975); David S. Lovejoy, *Rhode Island Politics and the American Revolution, 1760–1776* (1958); Irwin H. Polishook, *Rhode Island and the Union 1771–1795* (1969); Lynn Withey, *Urban Growth in Colonial Rhode Island* (1984).

Riceboats, Battle of the (Savannah, Georgia) (March 2, 1776)

Georgia and particularly its ruling rebel leadership in Savannah was heavily criticized for tardiness in joining the other colonies in the gathering American Revolution. However, by January 1776, Georgia Whigs had taken over the colony's militia, arrested the royal governor and council, adopted the Continental Association, and replaced the colonial assembly with a provincial congress. These actions were put to the test in January 1776 when a British fleet from Boston under Commodore Andrew Barkley arrived off Savannah to buy provisions for the British army.

Technically, the Georgia rebels could have waited until March 1, when the Association would expire, and then they could have traded with the fleet. However, at the last minute, the Georgia Council of Safety chose not to sell to the British, with or without the support of the Continental Association. (The British army was required to buy provisions only from loyal citizens—only from enemies could food and provisions be seized.) The Council also ordered Savannah to be defended but destroyed, if necessary, to prevent supplies from being obtained by the enemy.

Georgia's rebels too readily believed the speculations of the royal governor, Sir James Wright, that Savannah would be attacked. On March 2, 1776, Barkley used his smaller vessels and marines to seize 10 ships, carrying 1,600 barrels of rice, from Savannah harbor. The mixed force of Georgia and South Carolina soldiers under Colonel Lachlan McIntosh were too busy defending the town to have stopped Barkley, although the rebels did succeed in burning some of the other merchant vessels and driving the British from Hutchinson Island, across from the harbor. British firing on a group of Creek Indians at Jonathan Bryan's house brought the aid of these Indians to McIntosh's command. Until Barkley's fleet left on March 31, the Indians helped McIntosh's soldiers in skirmishing with British shore parties, the only significant Indian support for the American Revolution in Georgia.

Although the importance of this "victory" at Savannah was greatly overblown by the rebels, it demonstrated that Georgia, despite many political, economic, and military problems, was firmly committed to the American cause.

Robert Scott Davis, Jr.

REFERENCES

Robert S. Davis, Jr., "The Battle of the Riceboats: British Views of Georgia's First Battle of the American Revolution," *Proceedings and Papers of the Georgia Association of Historians* (1983):111–22; Harvey H. Jackson, "The Battle of the Riceboats: Georgia Joins the American Revolution," *Georgia Historical Quarterly*, 58 (1974):229–43.

Riedesel, Fredericke von, Baroness (1746–1808)

German military officer's wife. As a child, Fredericke Charlotte Louise von Massow (nicknamed Fritschen) followed her father Hans Jurgen Detloff von Massow, commissary in chief for Frederick the Great, during military campaigns in Europe. During her travels, Fredericke met the Baron of Eisenbach, Friedrich Adolf von Riedesel, a Brunswick cavalry officer, and married him in 1762.

When her husband decided to fight in the American Revolution, the baroness demanded to travel with him. Waiting to depart until her third child was born, the baroness prepared for her journey. After her daughter was born, she traveled with her three children, two German maids and a servant, and a German nurse named Lena. The general insisted she travel with a "lady of quality."

Considering herself superior to other camp followers, the baroness was arrogant to the soldiers' common German wives. As she wrote in the journal that she penned during the Revolution, "They were *women*, not ladies." Unlike Martha Washington, who spent money freely while following her husband, the baroness carefully noted her expenditures in her journal. Although frugal in many aspects, the baroness wore fashionable clothes of silk and satin, in contrast to her lower-class counterparts who donned woolens and cotton rags.

Despite her rank, however, she attended the wounded during the Battle of Saratoga. Baroness Riedesel and the German camp followers sought shelter in the cellar of a house that was crowded with wounded soldiers. During a lull in fire, the baroness ordered the German women to utilize their cleaning skills to fumigate the house by sprinkling vinegar on burning coals. In another incident, she heroically saved the regimental flag at Saratoga, presenting it to the Brunswickers.

During the American Revolution, the baroness gave birth to two more daughters: they were named America and Canada. In Boston, local women spat at the baroness, expressing their contempt for the mercenaries. Baroness von Riedesel complained that the German camp followers were Americanized during the Revolution, becoming lazy, complacent, and materialistic. Needing them to work for the troops, she stated that "There was nothing like a good German woman" who was a "neat, industrious wife." By herself she prepared such delicacies as German cucumber pickles for the troops.

In 1783 the baroness left America with her husband, returning to Brunswick. The general died in 1800, the same year that the baroness's book was printed in a limited edition. Fredericke spent her widowhood reminiscing about her adventures in America. She died in Berlin and was interred in the family vault at Lauterbach. *See also:* Camp Followers (German)

Elizabeth D. Schafer

REFERENCES

Marvin L. Brown, Jr., ed. *Baroness von Riedesel and the American Revolution: Journal and Correspondence of a Tour of Duty, 1776–1783* (1965); Elizabeth F. Ellet, *The Women of the American Revolution*, 4th ed., 3 vols. (1969); Fredericke C.L. Riedesel, *Letters and Journals*, trans. by William L. Stone (1867); Friedrich A. Riedesel, *Memoirs, Letters, and Journals of Major General Riedesel* (1969); Louise H. Tharp, *The Baroness and the General* (1962).

Rifle

A longarm on which the internal surface of the barrel (the bore) is cut with grooves in order (at first) to collect fouling and ease the loading of the ball (and subsequently) to impart a spinning motion to the ball, giving it much greater accuracy at increased distances. Rifling is probably a German invention, which may have appeared as early as 1476, but its use can be firmly ascribed to the first quarter of the sixteenth century; the earliest known dated rifle barrel is 1547. Although spirally grooved rifling became the most popular form, straight rifling, which offered a compromise with more accurate shooting than a smoothbore and easier loading than spiral rifling, remained in use well into the nineteenth century in Europe and America

America

The significance of the rifle as a "truly American weapon" has been grossly overstated by American writers in the past. Its use was confined to the frontiers of the colonies south of New Jersey, and even there it was popular only with a tiny percentage of the frontier population, who used them as tools to earn a parlous living by hunting for the settlements and for personal protection while exploring for land agents or personal gain. Most frontier settlers favored a more robust, practical, and less demanding all-purpose weapon, the musket or fowling piece, which could effectively use ball or shot for food gathering and defense. Rifles were brought to America before the end of the seventeenth century, but appear to have been made in Pennsylvania from the early 1740s, and in Virginia and the Carolinas from about the same time. They were carried by some of the provincial troops raised in America during the French and Indian War and were also used by a few Indians (particularly the Shawnee and Delaware) from the mid-1750s (either stolen from the settlers or obtained in trade; rifles were sometimes given as gifts to important warriors in the English interest).

In design, American "Pennsylvania" or "Kentucky" long rifles of the early and Revolutionary periods are characterized by octagonal barrels in excess of 40 inches in length, and calibers of 0.52 to 0.65 (very occasionally smaller and larger), and full-length stocks of maple with brass furniture and a wooden ramrod and patchbox cover. The plain single trigger was usual, but very occasionally double-set triggers were fitted, as were simple two- or four-piece brass patchbox covers. These features would have increased the cost considerably. They were designed as hunting weapons often intended to be carried for long distances on foot and were not as heavy as many rifles made after the Revolution, and were not equipped with either bayonets or slings.

They were loaded with a loose powder from a horn with a separate powder measure, and a lead ball wrapped in a greased cloth patch, and usually took a little less than a minute to load. In good hands they could be relied upon to hit a man at 200 yards, although propaganda and tradition as well as rare "lucky shots" have doubled this distance. Their use as military weapons was decried by most high-ranking American officers, since they were extremely delicate in construction and very slow to load with their wooden ramrods and tight-fitting patched ball; they did not take a standard size of ammunition that could be supplied in bulk, and they were not designed to take a bayonet.

Germany

The German rifle of the eighteenth century was a combination of proportions worked out in the seventeenth century expressed in terms of current French styles in lock mechanism and stock design as modified by the German gunmakers. Although most rifles were short, with

octagon barrels of about 30 inches, by the 1730s barrels in excess of 36 inches had appeared, particularly in the Rhineland area, producing an overall appearance very similar to the so-called American "transitional long-rifle." The transition appears to have taken place in Germany rather than America. The Germans had used rifles for military purposes as early as 1631, but always in temporarily raised units. In 1740 Frederick II (The Great) of Prussia raised the first permanent jaeger corps outside of Scandinavia, where the Norwegians had armed their ski troops with rifles in 1712. It was from their experiences with German rifle-armed troops during the War of the Austrian Succession (1740–1748) that the British first took an interest in the use of the rifle.

Very few examples of rifles used by the German auxiliary troops in America during the Revolution have been identified. Those that can be reasonably attributed to such use are signed by T.W. Pistor of Schmalkalden and Schmalenback of Hanau. Both of these towns are known to have supplied the troops of Hesse-Kassel and Hesse-Hanau with small arms. These rifles have octagonal barrels of about 28¾ inches, of 0.62 caliber with 7-groove rifling. The full-length stocks are of walnut with brass furniture including a large grip-guard and an oval escutcheon at the wrist, and sling swivels fitted with a cheekpiece and a wooden patchbox cover. They have a plain single trigger, and the block rearsight has a single-hinged leaf. The rammer is steel. With one exception there was no standard fitting for a bayonet. The Hesse-Hanau Freikorps that went to New York City in 1781 was the only unit that had bayonets on their rifles. A proportion of the carbines carried by the Brunswick dismounted dragoons in Burgoyne's army were very short-barrelled (approximately 12 to 14 inches) rifles on the Prussian hussar carbine pattern, which were different from the rifles carried by the Brunswick jaegers. German military rifles (known at the time as *jagerbuchse*, the civilian hunting rifle being known as the *pirschbuchse* or stalking rifle) were much shorter than American rifles, were fitted with a steel ramrod and sling swivels, and took a standard size of ammunition. The marksmanship of the jaeger recruits was of a high standard, and modern trials indicate that the German rifles were as accurate as their American counterparts.

Great Britain

British eighteenth-century rifles follow either the French (that is, the contemporary English sporting arm style) or very rarely the German pattern. Most British rifles of the first half of the century were made on one or other form of screwplug breech-loading mechanism, muzzle-loading rifles being comparatively scarce. The British first obtained rifles for military use in 1746, but they probably saw no service until the Braddock expedition of 1755, when they were carried by the engineers. Late in 1756, 300 rifled carbines with steel rammers and bayonets were purchased in Germany by Colonel James Prevost of the Royal American Regiment, and these rifles were scattered throughout the British regular troops during the campaigns from 1757 onward. Several breech-loading rifles were purchased in 1762 for experiments, and ten were used by the engineers during the siege of Havana that year.

During the Revolution the British forces used two types of rifles: 1,000 muzzle-loading rifles (200 from Hanover and 800 from Birmingham) and 100 breech-loading rifles on Patrick Ferguson's design. The English muzzle-loading rifles have octagon barrels of about 29 inches' length of carbine-bore, about 0.62 caliber, with full-length walnut stocks very similar to the conventional musket stock in design, and brass furniture with several variations from the usual Land Pattern furniture, including a grip-guard. Originally they were fitted with a steel swivel ramrod, with a special mounting at the muzzle, but these have all been removed on existing examples. They have flat-surface carbine-size locks with conventional Ordnance markings, and were made by four Birmingham gunmakers who also made the Ferguson rifles: Barker & Whatley, Galton, Grice, and Willetts. The one known example of the enlisted man's Ferguson rifle has a 30-inch round barrel with 8-groove rifling of 1 turn in 60 inches, military pattern full stock, wooden cleaning rod and brass furniture, and takes the British carbine-bore ball (.615").

France

Although rifles were in use in the French cavalry from the 1680s, there is no evidence that any were used by French forces in America during the Revolution.

De Witt Bailey

REFERENCES

De Witt Bailey, *British Military Longarms 1715–1865* (1986); George Shumway, *Rifles in Colonial America*, 2 vols. (1980).

Riflemen

America

On June 14, 1775, the Second Continental Congress voted to raise ten rifle companies: two from Maryland, six from Pennsylvania, and two from Virginia. Each company establishment consisted of 1 captain, 3 lieutenants, 4 sergeants, 4 corporals, 1 drummer, and 68 privates, for a total of 810 men. These included the Maryland companies of Michael Cresap and Price, and the Virginia company of Stephenson. Daniel Morgan's Independent Company was also raised under this authorization, and six Pennsylvania companies. Initially 1,400 men volunteered, but they soon dwindled with the tedium and discipline of siege life around Boston.

Under a unified command, and renamed the Maryland & Virginia Rifle Regiment of nine companies in June 1776, the unit was almost entirely captured at Fort Washington, and officially disbanded in November 1776. The Virginia remnant was transferred to the 11th Virginia Regiment in February 1777, and the Maryland remnant was attached as a single company to the 4th Maryland. In March 1779 it was finally reorganized as Rawlings Independent Corps and disbanded in January 1781. Morgan's company was captured at Quebec December 31, 1776, but reorganized in February 1777 under Captain Porterfield. The six Pennsylvania companies authorized in June 1775 became the Pennsylvania Rifle Regiment of nine companies and was twice renamed: 1st Continental Regiment (January 1776) and 1st Pennsylvania Regiment (January 1777). Pennsylvania companies raised by John Doyle and John Nelson during 1776 were of short duration; Nelson's was joined to the 5th Pennsylvania Regiment (March 1777) and Doyle's was disbanded (July 1778). The Pennsylvania State Rifle Regiment organized between March and May 1776 consisted initially of two battalions of six companies each; in April 1777 it was amalgamated with the Pennsylvania State Musketry Regiment and renamed the Pennsylvania State Regiment of Foot with eight musketry and two rifle companies. In November 1777 it was renamed the 13th Pennsylvania Regiment.

Many state and local militia troops in the southern colonies also carried rifles, but the nature of both the weapon and the people who habitually carried them rendered them of only limited military use. They were basically a weapon of the backwoods, and the war was not basically a backwoods war. As early as the 1740s it was recognized that it was the lawless and most "uncivilized" segment of frontier society who carried rifle-barrel guns, and this characteristic was retained by the majority of men who volunteered for the various rifle companies raised for Continental, state, and militia service. They were singularly unwilling to conform to military behavior and mutinied or deserted (often to the British) rather than accept conventional military discipline. Most officers, including Greene, Lincoln, Muhlenberg, Wayne, and Washington himself lamented the large number of rifle-equipped troops who could not be made into useful line infantry until muskets could be found for them. There were probably fewer men in the organized rifle companies who could be used in conjunction with Continental troops, than their equivalent in the British army (the German Jaegers), since most riflemen were in one of the several types of militia units.

In June 1776 Congress authorized another group of six rifle companies, two from Maryland and four from Virginia, to serve for three years. These were to be regimented with three others already in service giving a total of 500 men and were, from April 1777, commanded by Daniel Morgan. This unit served through the Saratoga campaign, where the American rifle probably achieved its most important psychological effect of the war by adding to the insecurity already felt by the British forces due to their overextended supply lines. While encamped at Valley Forge it was reorganized as part of a line regiment, the 11th Virginia. It was the last regimental-sized rifle unit of the American army. From the conclusion of the Saratoga campaign, the use of riflemen was reduced to companies and detachments, which were, in fact, far more suitable for their type of service.

Unlike the units of their opponents, the American rifle companies were individually of short duration and ad hoc organization; there was no fixed rifle establishment present in the rebel army for the entire duration of the war.

Riflemen were present on both sides at virtually all the major and most of the minor battles of the war, but they never made a decisive contribution to the outcome of any major engagement. Possibly the mortal wounding of General Simon Fraser at the battle of Bemis Heights (October 7, 1777) was the single most important achievement of a rifleman during the war, perhaps equally effectively countered by the serious wounding of Benedict Arnold by a German jaeger at Breymann's Redoubt on the same day. Riflemen were more common during the southern campaigns on both sides (as Loyalist and rebel militia), but their effect was no greater than earlier in the war in the North. Major Patrick Ferguson's tactical position at King's Mountain was the cause of his defeat rather than the rifles of his opponents: it was like shooting fish in a barrel, and the weapons used were irrelevant. At the Cowpens, it was Morgan's leadership, tactical position, and Washington's cavalry versus the cock-sure but exhausted Legion dragoons that decided the hard-fought battle, not the militia riflemen.

Germany
See Feld Jaeger Corps.

Great Britain
The Hessian and Ansbach jaegers formed the most significant part of the rifle-armed forces used by the British during the Revolutionary War, but there were also at least 1,000 British regulars and some Loyalist troops making use of the muzzle-loading flintlock rifles made for the Board of Ordnance in 1776 in Hanover and Birmingham. Too little is known about the precise issue of these rifles, although 50 were sent to Burgoyne before his force departed from Canada in 1777, and another 50 went to General William Howe in New York at the same time. The remainder appear to have gone to New York during 1778 and were distributed at the discretion of the commander-in-chief, based on regimental requests. When the idea of arming some troops with rifles was first discussed by the Master General of the Ordnance and Lord George Germain, the secretary of state for the colonies, in December 1775, the suggestion was to equip a certain number of known marksmen in each regiment with rifles, particularly in the Highland Regiments, and this is probably what was done. We know that Andrew Emmerich's

Chasseurs carried rifles, either of Ordnance manufacture or brought with the volunteers from Germany, and it seems probable that Captain John Althouse's New York Volunteer Rifle Company had Ordnance-made rifles. We know that the Rifle Company of the Queen's Rangers received 33 rifles from Ordnance Stores in 1779. Loyalist militia, where they had not been disarmed by their rebel counterparts, would have carried their own American-made rifles, but it is clear that most of these troops had been robbed of their arms and were re-equipped with muskets from British stores. At Moore's Creek Bridge in February 1776, no less than 1,500 rifles were taken from the Scots Loyalists. Indians in the British interest were also equipped with rifles, a total of 1,750 being sent from England through Quebec and Pensacola, in addition to those taken by the Indians.

The use of the rifle was incorporated into the light infantry tactics developed in the British army prior to the Revolution. Apart from the 100 Ferguson rifles that were an experimental effort, British rifles like American ones and almost all the German ones did not carry bayonets. The riflemen were designed to be backed by light infantry with bayonetted muskets. Because this backing was part of their training, all involved understood this need and no lack of it is recorded in British deployments. If the number of jaegers and British riflemen are taken together, there were probably around 2,000 rifles in use by the British forces during each campaign of the war from 1777. But because they formed an integral part of light infantry and skirmishing tactics, they were not commented on by contemporary writers to the extent that American riflemen were, largely, it would appear in retrospect, because contemporary American writers needed something positive to say about their forces, and because of the bizarre character of their riflemen rather than the effects of their weapons.

De Witt Bailey

REFERENCES

De Witt Bailey, *British Military Smallarms 1689–1815*, forthcoming; ———, "The Rifle in the American War, 1775–1783," *Guns Review* (1969):8–12; Joe D. Huddleston, *Colonial Riflemen in the American Revolution* (1978).

Rittenhouse, David (1732–1796)

American scientist. A select few individuals in the American colonies were as accomplished in such a wide variety of technical, scientific, and political areas as David Rittenhouse. Thomas Jefferson wrote, "The world has but one Rittenhouse, and it never had one before." He mastered skills in the fields of astronomy, instrument making, surveying, clockmaking, and mathematics. Briefly, his major peacetime accomplishments and achievements included the surveying of the Pennsylvania–Maryland border, which was accepted both by Mason and Dixon; the development of the first American-made telescope later improved by him with spider webs for cross hairs; the design of his famous orrery, the calculations for and the observations of the 1769 transit of Venus; the presidency of the American Philosophical Society after the death of Benjamin Franklin; and his appointment as the United States Mint's first director.

He was born on April 8, 1732, outside of Philadelphia near the small village of Germantown in America's first paper industrial community, later known as Rittenhouse Town. David was the great-grandson of America's first papermaker, William Rittenhouse, and the third of ten children of Matthias and Elizabeth Rittenhouse. The family moved to their farm near Norristown, approximately 20 miles from Philadelphia, when he was in his infancy. It was here that he developed his extraordinary mathematical and mechanical abilities including the famous clockmaking skills. Clearly, his later acclamation by Jefferson was justified at even an early age.

By the time of the American Revolution, his name was widely known and respected throughout the colonies and also in Europe. Countless commissions and offices were granted to him on all levels. With the outbreak of warfare, Rittenhouse quickly offered his services to the Patriot cause and became a member of the Pennsylvania Committee of Safety in 1775. He supervised the casting of cannon and the manufacture of saltpeter, selected a site for a powdermill and a magazine for military stores, experimented on rifling artillery and musket shot, and substituted iron for the lead clockweights throughout Philadelphia to obtain this necessary metal for making bullets. He was also instructed to prepare an inventory of all of the cannon shot available in Pennsylvania and to award contracts for munitions to qualified shotmakers.

To defend the city against British naval attack, he designed a plan for a chain stretched across the shipping channel of the Delaware River; however, it was never implemented. In addition, he was directed by the Committee of Safety to survey sites for suitable fortifications. Based on Rittenhouse's recommendations, the site later known as Fort Mifflin would be expanded to control the river approach to Philadelphia along with Fort Mercer.

By 1776, Rittenhouse became the newly designated Council of Safety's vice president and later its president in 1777. He was appointed to a committee that defined high treason and recommended the punishment, as well as the penalty, for counterfeiting bills of credit. Individuals who knew Rittenhouse often increased his overwhelming workload by requesting his personal assistance in resolving matters rather than approaching the rather slow-moving Council.

Politically, he was an active member of the Pennsylvania General Assembly and supported the radical element during the state's constitutional convention of 1776 along with his close friends Charles Willson Peale and Thomas Paine. As one of this governing document's authors, he was called upon repeatedly to defend it especially concerning the dominant position and power it gave to the Pennsylvania Assembly over the other branches of government. In addition, he served as one of the original members on the Board of War and as Pennsylvania's state treasurer. With the British occupation of Philadelphia following the Battle of Brandywine, Rittenhouse accompanied the state's government into temporary exile to Lancaster. He returned to Philadelphia after the British evacuated it the following June 1778.

Following the war, Rittenhouse continued to lead a full and active life. He remained a close friend and confidant of such notable individuals as Benjamin Franklin and Thomas Jefferson. Portraits of him were painted by two former famous Revolutionary War officers, Charles Willson Peale and John Trumbull, which further attests to Rittenhouse's importance in the development of the Republic. In addition to his prominence in the scientific community as the president of the American Philosophical Society, he received the ultimate honor by being made a foreign member of London's Royal Society in 1795.

Rittenhouse continued to serve the new nation in other official capacities. His work on the commission to organize the Bank of the United States led President Washington to appoint him as the first director of the United States mint from 1792–1795.

It was said his character was irreproachable. He demonstrated a kindness and almost universal good will. If he possessed any major faults or weaknesses, it was a large amount of modesty. Although Rittenhouse was physically frail and often in ill health, he could display great endurance under periods of stress and activity. David Rittenhouse parted from this world on June 26, 1796. To many his legacy was that of a man without rivals, an excellent clockmaker, and a surveyor of states' boundaries, routes for canals, and turnpike roads. Others remembered him as a great Patriot who had tirelessly served America and had brought Pennsylvania back to financial stability following the war. Many felt he was the ideal man of science who, after self-learning the fields of astronomy, optics, mechanics, electricity, and natural history, continued to seek knowledge for its own sake in order that man could have a better understanding of the world around him. Truly, the world had but one Rittenhouse, and it has never had another.

Andrew A. Zellers-Frederick

REFERENCES

John M. Faragler, ed., *The Encyclopedia of Colonial and Revolutionary America* (1990); Edward J. Ford, *David Rittenhouse* (1946); Dumas Malone, *Jefferson and His Times*, 4 vols. (1948–63), *1*.

Rivington, James (1724–1802)

Loyalist. Born in London, Rivington and a brother operated a printing firm they had inherited from their father. He succeeded at first in the competitive publishing world of London, but eventually neglected his business for social pursuits. Still, Rivington was able to sell his interest in the family farm at a profit, and he immigrated to America in 1760. He became involved in several money-making schemes, including land speculation in Maryland, but he was soon bankrupt. Rivington established successful bookstores in Philadelphia, New York, and Boston, but he lost those as well. He then returned to New York and established the printing firm of J. Rivington and Company, located first in Hanover Square and later (1768) on Wall Street. Rivington's fortunes improved with his publication of the popular poetry of Charles Churchill and with his marriage in 1769 to Elizabeth Van Horne, daughter of a prominent family. After 1773 he accepted a job printing pamphlets and handbills as well as books. Finally, on March 18, 1773, he published the first issue of his newspaper, known in full as *Rivington's New-York Gazetteer, or the Connecticut, New-Jersey, Hudson's River, and Quebec Weekly Advertiser*. It underwent several changes of name, and during the Revolution the Patriots called it "Rivington's Lying Gazette."

The *Gazetteer* was an immediate success; in typography and editing it was probably the best newspaper in the colonies. It was generally objective and gave wide coverage to European news. Its circulation in 1774 was about 3,600, and in 1775 Rivington had 16 employees. When Revolutionary fervor struck New York, he attempted to print both sides of the story, and for this he was condemned by the Sons of Liberty and other radical groups. In November 1775 his press was destroyed by a mob, incited by Patriot leaders whom Rivington had criticized. Prior to the mob action the provincial and Continental congresses had investigated the *Gazetteer* and found it innocent of wrongdoing, though Rivington had signed with the Association out of fear. He wrote to the Congress, speaking of himself in the third person, declaring that "as a man of honor and veracity, he can and does solemnly declare that however wrong and mistaken he may have been in his opinions, he has always meant honestly and openly to do his duty as a servant of the public. . . . He declares that his press has always been open and free to all parties." Nevertheless, he was driven out of business, and according to legend his type was melted down to make bullets for the militia.

In January 1776 Rivington fled to England. But within a year he was back, appointed King's Printer in New York City, which was now occupied by the British. The *Gazetteer* soon resumed publication as *Rivington's New-York Loyal Gazette*, and later, *The Royal Gazette*. Between May 1778 and July 1783, with the help of other printers and in the face of wartime shortages, he published America's first daily newspaper. He also published a host of Loyalist pamphlets and broadsides.

Throughout this same period he was acting as a double agent, sending secret military information to Washington's besieging army. When the British evacuated New York, not only did the victors allow Rivington to remain, but he was protected from the Patriots' vengeance by American troops, and George Washington even called on him. Historians long assumed, from fragmentary data, that Rivington had a secret life; but final proof was not adduced until 1959. (See Catherine S. Crary, "The Tory and the Spy: The Double Life of James Rivington," *William and Mary Quarterly*, 16 (1959):61–72). The newspaper, now called *Rivington's New-York Gazette and Universal Advertiser*, limped along until the last day of 1783, when New Yorkers again put him out of business. On July 10, 1782, he pleaded in the *Gazette*: "He begs them [the patriots] to look over past errors and depend on future correctness." The plea fell on deaf ears. Rivington remained in business as a bookseller and stationer, but he died in poverty in 1802. *See also:* Journalism in the American Revolution

Tom Martin

REFERENCES

Catherine S. Crary, *The Price of Loyalty: Tory Writings from the Revolutionary Era* (1973); Lorenzo Sabine, *Biographical Sketches of Loyalists of the American Revolution*, 2 vols. (1864), II.

Robertson, James (1717–1788)

British army officer. James Robertson was born to George Robertson and Christian Dundas at Newbigging, Scotland, on June 29, 1717. His father was a laird in their district, that is, a "heritor" or a freeholding landowner. The Robertsons were a family of moderate influence. It appears that James received a sufficient education since he could write well, read French, and often quoted classical Latin writers in his letters. In time, James would grow into an intelligent, politically cunning man with a great capacity for hard work. He had cultivated tastes and a lively interest in women and good food.

Choosing the military as a career, James joined a marine regiment in Scotland as a private soldier before 1739. James lacked the wealth to purchase a commission in a British line regiment. Therefore, he placed his hopes on advancement from his personal merit and bravery.

His father died in 1740. The inheritance was too small to purchase a commission. He accompanied his regiment to the West Indies, where sickness and military bungling against the Spanish in the war of Jenkins Ear cost the regiment over half its strength. Yet Robertson survived the campaign. He was promoted to sergeant on merit and returned to Scotland with his regiment. Further meritorious conduct brought Robertson a promotion to captain on September 12, 1745. Attaching his star to a man of great influence, John Campbell, the Earl of Loudoun, Robertson may have participated in the Battles of Inverness and Culloden. He did stay with his marine regiment until it was disbanded in 1748. Loudoun then used his influence to help James purchase a captaincy in the 30th Regiment of Foot, the earl's personal regiment.

In 1747, James married Ann White, an Englishwoman from Southwick, Southampton. They moved to Ireland as a part of the Irish establishment under the command of his protector and sponsor, Earl Loudoun. For five years, James served along with the 12,000-man army in Ireland. In 1755, he was successful in purchasing a majority in the 38th Regiment of Foot, but it was based in the West Indies and James desired to avoid service in that area of the world. At the same time, war broke out in North America with the French, and his mentor, Loudoun, was chosen as commander of British forces. Loudoun was permitted to raise a new regiment in the colonies, the Royal Americans (6th) with Loudoun as colonel. Robertson was brought into the regiment as regimental supply officer and as acting major.

This was Robertson's first position as a staff officer. After organizing and dispatching the supply and materials necessary to conduct war from England across the ocean, James followed his leader and arrived in North America in 1756, where he was appointed deputy quartermaster general on Loudoun's staff. In this capacity, he served as operations officer to the general. He was responsible for supply, transport, logistical plans, troop movements, intelligence operations, and any other duty the commander placed upon him. He was the chief aide to the commander-in-chief in North America. His staff service became a career that kept him in America for the next 27 years.

When Earl Loudoun was replaced by General Robert Abercrombie and then in turn by General Jeffrey Amherst, James Robertson stayed on as the deputy quartermaster general to all three. As difficulties arose, it was Robertson who was dispatched to settle them. He was the one who smoothed over the rough edges of frustrations and frictions that developed between the colonial governments, colonial troops, the British royal government, and the British military establishment in the war against the French.

In the midst of the war, James and his wife had their only child, Anne Loudoun, born December 7, 1758. She had Earl Loudoun as her godfather and was called "Loudoun" by her father who doted on her. He felt she was a true "beauty." Unfortunately, she died in childbirth when she was 23 years old, on February 6, 1782. The news of her death devastated him. Her child, his granddaughter, Ann Isabelle survived.

Colonel James Robertson became the indispensable staff officer, the one who runs the institution by the force of his personality and energy. He had his hand in everything that went on in the British army in the colonies. The time between the end of the French and Indian War and the beginning of the War of Revolution saw Robertson become barrackmaster for the colonies. He lived in New York City, associating with the rich and powerful. Eventually he gained the rank of brigadier general although it was only titular for the colonies. He was always an ambitious man, beginning as a private and becoming a general.

He was viewed as an American expert and counted as friends such people as the Earl of Bute, Cadwallader Colden, William Tryon, and William Smith, Jr. Personally he advocated the use of force against the rebels, especially in Boston. He warned against the use of leniency and spoke out for strong action to limit the power of people like Samuel Adams. Once the war began, however, he changed his philosophy.

James Robertson was there at the beginning. He accompanied general Thomas Gage as one of his chief aides to Boston and was in Boston during Lexington, Concord, and Bunker Hill. It was Robertson who arranged the details for the evacuation of Boston under General William Howe in March 1776. When Howe invaded New York City, it was Robertson who advised landing first on Staten Island instead of Long Island until the British fleet could fully gather to support the army's moves. Robertson commanded the 4th, 15th, 27th, and 45th regiments during the Long Island and Manhattan campaigns, his only battlefield command in his long career. His brigade mostly followed behind the front lines, mopping up resistance.

Following the capture of New York City, Robertson was made military commandant of the city. He turned out to be a wise and well-respected leader. During the fire that arsonists set off to burn down New York City, Robertson organized the firefighting such that only 10 percent of the city was lost instead of the over 50 percent that many feared would be destroyed. In mid-1777, he returned to London to report to Lord Germain on Howe's New York campaign, including a smoothing over of the affairs of Trenton and Princeton. He carried Howe's personal dispatches.

Howe had picked the wrong man to send home. Robertson felt that Howe had been too easy on the rebels and was too lenient to his army. Many Loyalists throughout New York and the Jersies found themselves as much the victims of the British and German troops as the rebels. When Howe returned to England in 1778, turning command over to General Henry Clinton, in order to defend his record in the war, Robertson testified for three days before the House of Commons on his view of Howe's conduct.

Robertson felt that persuasion was the only way to regain control of the colonies. Washington and his army should be pushed back into the Hudson Highlands and sealed in. Up until 1778, the British had conducted a leisurely war, keeping the costs down to the British taxpayer by using mercenaries and blocking the coast with the Royal Navy. Now that Howe was gone and his policy had not worked, and now that the French were openly in the war, the English had to change their approach if they were ever to succeed in regaining their former colonies.

Once Washington was contained, Robertson believed that the Loyalists could take over the civil government and regain control of the countryside. People who were naturally loyal but afraid to openly show their feelings could flock back to the royal standards. Robertson felt that as many as 75 percent of all Americans felt this way. The idea was to quickly get the army out of the colonies, repeal all outside taxes, allow assemblies to be elected, and reestablish civil control loosely under the King and Parliament.

Germain approved this idea and returned Robertson to the colonies as military commandant of New York City and also as civil governor of New York. New York would be used as the "pilot project" for the other colonies.

One major benefit of this plan was that it freed the army to fight against the French in other theaters. It left the fighting and struggle for control to the Loyalists in the colonies. It was the Americanization of the war. The problem began with General Clinton, who did not agree with this proposal and felt that New York would never reach that stage of pacification where Robertson could proceed with the creation of his civil government. Clinton wanted the army involved.

Robertson tried to raise revenues to support the civil government from commercial duties. He convened a council to advise the governor. He tried to cooperate with Clinton. Through 1780 and on to 1782, Robertson remained military commandant of New York City, but at no time did Clinton turn the province over to him. Many Loyalists were unsatisfied with the British effort and complained. Robertson furnished them with much to criticize. He maintained a mistress. He lived high, ate well, and associated with the better sort regularly. He was also accused of irregularities in his accounts while barrackmaster in North America. The government claimed he owed them £10,000. The issue over misuse of funds was not settled until years after his death.

Eventually, Robertson was promoted lieutenant general, and Clinton assigned him the province of New York but did not allow him the power or capacity to achieve the goals Germain had set. Robertson made the best of a bad situation and even stayed on as a member of Clinton's staff. But the Loyalists never came in, Washington's army remained in the field, Cornwallis surrendered at Yorktown, and the British war effort gradually wore down. As Cornwallis was being trapped in Virginia, it was Robertson who urged and fought to have reinforcements and supplies sent to relive Cornwallis's besieged force.

When Clinton himself resigned and returned to England, Robertson could not get along with his successor, General Sir Guy Carleton. Carleton was an enemy of Germain and any friend of Germain was considered an enemy of the new commander. On April 16, 1783, Robertson left America for the last time to live in retirement on Wimpole Street at Cavendish Square until his death five years later of jaundice, March 4, 1788.

Robertson is little known to Americans today. Even so, he played a vital role in the British conduct of the war and represents a class of officers and men who exist to perform the essential staff work necessary to keep an army in the field. He who carries the ledgers and pens also serves as those who carry the musket. Robertson was the premier example of such an effective staff officer who could get things done, support what operations were going on, and develop new plans to achieve what the commanders wished to achieve. What distinguishes Robertson was his climb from private to lieutenant general in the army, his proposal to win the war without fire and sword, and his experience for so many years in America that made him an extremely influential expert to those in London. *See also:* New York City, British Occupation of

Paul J. Sanborn

REFERENCES

Bruce Bliven, *Under the Guns* (1972); R. Arthur Bowler, *Logistics and the Failure of the British Army in America* (1975); Sir Henry Clinton, *The American Rebellion* (1954); Milton M. Klein and Ronald W. Joward, eds., *The Twilight of British Rule in Revolutionary America* (1988); Douglas Edward Leach, *Roots of Conflict* (1988); John Shy, *Toward Lexington* (1965).

Robinson, Beverley (1721–1792)

Loyalist. The Robinsons were a prominent Virginia family. Robinson's father John was acting governor of Virginia following the retirement of Governor William Gooch. Migrating to New York, Beverly Robinson married Susanna, daughter of the wealthy patroon Frederick Philipse, and through careful management he increased the fortune that she brought to the marriage. He saw himself as a country gentleman and landowner, and he hoped to avoid taking sides in the Revolution, though he cooperated with the Association. When forced by John Jay to make a choice, he left his estate and took refuge with the British in New York City. The mansion was confiscated and used as a Patriot military headquarters and a hospital.

In New York, Robinson raised the Loyal Americans and was made the regiment's colonel; he also commanded a unit called the Guides and Pioneers. Though without military experience, he acquitted himself well in the siege of Fort Montgomery (October 6, 1777) and participated in other actions. More important, he was a key figure in the secret service. He had traveled widely and was acquainted with or related to many of the American aristocracy, and so he was especially suited to this task. On one famous occasion he visited his former estate under flag or truce, ostensibly to check on its condition. In fact, he was carrying a secret message offering reconciliation to General Israel Putnam, then headquartered at the house. He gave the message to the invalid Mrs. Putnam, but a few days later she died. It is not known whether she had an opportunity to pass the message along. There is some evidence that Putnam agreed to meet with Robinson, but we do not know whether the meeting took place, or whether Putnam knew its purpose.

Robinson was also in communication with Benedict Arnold before the latter's treason, and he arranged the initial meeting with Colonel John André. According to Lorenzo Sabine, Robinson warned André not to trust himself to "a man who was seeking to betray his country." André was captured and was held for a time at Robinson's mansion before his trial and execution. Robinson wrote to George Washington, whose friend he had been before the war, asking that André's life be spared.

In October 1779 Robinson, his wife, and son were formally banished from New York and all their property was seized. Robinson remained in New York City until August 1782, and then he was appointed to the New Brunswick Council, but went on to England without taking his seat. The British government granted him £17,000 compensation, and he settled near Bath, where he lived quietly and unhappily until his death. Two of his sons made careers in the British army and were knighted; two others settled in Canada.

Tom Martin

REFERENCE

Lorenzo Sabine, *Biographical Sketches of Loyalists of the American Revolution*, 2 vols. (1864), II.

Rochambeau, Comte de (Jean-Baptiste-Donatien de Vimeur) (1725–1807)

French army officer. Born in Vendôme on July 1, 1725, the younger son of an old aristocratic family from the region, Rochambeau was originally destined for an ecclesiastical career. The death of his older brother, however, allowed him to enter the profession of arms; on May 24, 1742, he was commissioned a coronet in the regiment of Saint-Simon Cavalry. During the War of the Austrian Succession he campaigned in Bohemia, was promoted to captain in July 1743, served as aide-de-camp of the Duke of Orleans, became colonel of the regiment of La Marche Infantry, and was seriously wounded at the Battle of Laufeldt in 1747. After the war ended, Rochambeau married Jeanne Thérèse d'Acosta, the daughter of a wealthy bourgeois family of Portuguese origin, on December 29, 1749.

Thereafter, Rochambeau devoted his attention to peacetime military duties until the outbreak of the next round of hostilities between France and England, the Seven Years' (or French and Indian) War. He participated in the capture of Minorca and was promoted to brigadier in 1756. The following year he began a series of campaigns in Germany; he took command of the Regiment of Auvergne Infantry in 1759; and in February 1761 he was promoted to major general (*maréchal de camp*) for his conduct at the battle of Clostercamp, during which his regiment lost 58 (of 80) officers and more than 800 men in helping to turn a near defeat into victory. Despite such efforts, the war ended in humiliating failure for France in 1763. Rochambeau emerged as a battle-worn, cautious commander.

Ironically, France's defeat removed the greatest threat to the British colonists in North America and thereby contributed to their growing spirit of independence. When this resulted in open rebellion a dozen years after the Treaty of Paris that ended the Seven Years' War, many French leaders saw it as an opportunity to avenge the humiliation of 1763 and to adjust the balance of power that had swung too far in England's favor. Early French aid to the Americans, however, was unofficial, surreptitious, and restricted. As French naval and military preparations advanced, as the possibility of American success improved, and as confrontations with Britain intensified, French intervention increased and culminated in the Franco-American treaty of alliance in February 1778.

The immediate impact of France's entry into the war was limited, even discouraging. Efforts by the Comte d'Estaing to cooperate with American forces in attacks upon British garrisons at Newport, Rhode Island, in the summer of 1778 and at Savannah, Georgia, in the autumn of 1779 were disillusioning failures that strained the recent alliance. Meanwhile, Franco-Spanish plans for an invasion of England in the summer of 1779 had to be canceled, although not before a large French army had been gathered in Normandy and Brittany, the advance guard of which was under the orders of Rochambeau. When King Louis XVI decided to send a special expedition to the United States he drew its personnel from these units and on March 1, 1780, named Rochambeau to command them; simultaneously, he promoted Rochambeau to lieutenant general.

Rochambeau turned out to be an excellent choice for such a mission. His small army, some 5,500 officers and men, would be the only significant force of foreign allies ever to serve on American soil. Generations of hostility and conflict had resulted in strong American prejudices against the French that still lingered. Rochambeau would be operating hundreds of miles from the nearest French base and would go months without receiving funds, supplies, reinforcements, or even instructions. On top of everything, after five years of inconclusive fighting, Americans were increasingly weary and disheartened. In these circumstances Rochambeau's patience and discretion would be as essential as his considerable military experience.

From his appointment, Rochambeau had to deal with daunting difficulties. He had to select the staff officers and combat units that would accompany him. He had to supervise the logistical preparations required for their trans-atlantic voyage and to insure their self-sufficiency for an indeterminate period after their arrival in America. He had to cope with bureaucratic inertia and the limitations imposed by available resources (e.g., he had to leave behind 2,500 troops assigned to him for lack of sufficient transports). Despite the problems, on May 2, 1780, his corps sailed from Brest for Newport, Rhode Island, where it arrived exactly ten weeks later, on July 11.

Although American civil and military authorities warmly welcomed the French, the local populace was more reserved. Rochambeau faced more pressing problems, however. Thirty of his men had died from disease during the crossing and some 700 were ill, scores of whom would perish in the coming weeks. In addition, within a week and a half of their arrival, a British fleet had appeared to blockade Newport. Frantic efforts were made to provide adequate defenses. In the midst of this, the Marquis de Lafayette arrived. He had been sent by Washington personally to coordinate American and French military action. Lafayette, who had earlier used his influence to try to get command of the French expedition, now urged an immediate attack on New York. Rochambeau, who had been promoted to brigadier general the year before Lafayette was born, declined, pointing out the serious problems that he faced and the dire consequences that could follow a failure at this stage of the war and the alliance. He remained firm but friendly in the face of persistent nagging by his young countryman, whose unrealistic optimism was matched only by his sense of self-importance.

Instead of precipitous action, Rochambeau methodically went about restoring his men to health and establishing cordial relations with the local inhabitants. The latter he achieved primarily by imposing an exemplary discipline on his troops, although the purchase of large quantities of supplies with hard cash also helped to warm Yankee hearts. While relations between French soldiers and American civilians improved, differences in language, religion, customs, even food generally kept the two groups from becoming close. Furthermore, many French felt that they were being "fleeced" for poor quality goods and services. From time to time during the winter of 1780–1781 suppressed tensions surfaced and resulted in conflicts, which both Rochambeau and American officials were quick to "hush up."

During the same period American military fortunes reached their lowest point. Benedict Arnold's treason in September was not only an individual betrayal but it reflected more widespread disillusionment with the American cause. Further evidence of this sentiment was the mutiny of line units from New Jersey and Pennsylvania in January 1781, after months without adequate pay or supplies. By early 1781 British forces had established control over most of the South and were threatening Virginia. Meanwhile, the French remained inactive at Newport.

When Rochambeau finally did take some action, it was on a limited scale and did not achieve significant success. In February and again in March he dispatched two small expeditions to the Chesapeake; both inflicted damage on British shipping; neither seriously affected the military situation. American frustration deepened; even the long-suffering Washington was reaching the limit of his patience. On May 22, 1781, the French and American commanders met at Wethersfield, Connecticut. Unlike their inconclusive meeting at Hartford the previous September, this conference resulted in decisive action; Rochambeau felt ready to join Washington in a combined attack on New York, the most important British position in North America.

The French began leaving Newport on June 9 and reached the American army at Philipsburg, New York, by July 6. They were in the middle of preparations for the siege of New York City when a courier arrived with dispatches for Rochambeau on August 14. The most important news was a message from Admiral François Joseph Paul de Grasse indicating his plans to leave the Caribbean with a fleet of nearly 30 ships of the line and an army of over 3,000 men and sail to Chesapeake Bay, where he would remain available for assistance, until the middle of October. This situation offered a unique opportunity to crush the British in Virginia and convinced Washington to give up his cherished New York project. Within four days he and Rochambeau had their armies on the march south.

Meanwhile Lafayette's American corps had been harassing the British under Lord Cornwallis in Virginia since early summer. In early August the British commander took up positions on the York River, which he assumed would allow him ready access to supplies, reinforcements, or, in an emergency, evacuation by sea. At the beginning of September, de Grasse's ships anchored in nearby waters, and the army aboard them began to disembark under the orders of the Marquis de Saint-Simon. After linking up with Lafayette's forces they tightened the lines around the British at Yorktown and awaited reinforcements from the North. On September 5 began the most important engagement of the campaign—perhaps of the entire war. De Grasse encountered an English fleet under Admiral Samuel Graves off the Virginia Capes; although the fighting ended in essentially a draw, the Chesapeake remained in French hands. The arrival of more French ships from Newport on September 10 confirmed their control.

On September 14 Washington and Rochambeau, who had gone on ahead of their main forces, reached Williamsburg, a dozen miles from Yorktown, and set up headquarters. Within two weeks the bulk of their armies arrived and the siege commenced. Although he does not appear in the accounts of daring actions or individual bravery during the battle, this victory was very much the personal achievement of Rochambeau, the expert but uncharismatic professional. The siege was carried out in classical eighteenth-century fashion, and no one was better fit to supervise it than this veteran of more than a dozen European campaigns. His skills in handling people enabled him to dissuade the impulsive de Grasse from sailing off to engage an English naval squadron in the area and to convince the French admiral to detach 800 of his marines to assist in the land operations. As before, Rochambeau managed to minimize Franco-American friction and to assure a continuous supply of essential goods and materials to his men. The steady, inexorable advance of the allied lines reflected Rocahmbeau's expertise and personality. When the inevitable capitulation took place, Cornwallis's representative, General Charles O'Hara, tried to surrender the English commander's sword to Rochambeau, who, in characteristic fashion, referred him to Washington.

Celebrations and congratulations greeted this decisive victory in America and Europe; Rochambeau was honored for his essential, but unspectacular, contributions to it. The French then settled into winter quarters in Virginia. Rochambeau won the good will of Virginians by the same policies that had succeeded in Rhode Island, although some tensions inevitably arose. In the absence of instructions from home, Rochambeau began moving his army northward at the beginning of July 1782. By mid-September the French were once more encamped in New York, next to Washington's main army. As the British cause in North America now seemed lost, Rochambeau directed his troops toward Boston, where they would board French ships for the Caribbean, while he transferred his command to Baron de Vioménil and sailed for France, where he arrived on February 20, 1783.

In France, Rochambeau soon resumed routine duties, while Lafayette received most of the glory for the defeat of England. More importantly, domestic developments were rapidly propelling France to the brink of its own revolution. Rochambeau, the professional soldier, was largely apolitical, but he did sympathize with a number of the demands for political and financial reform. Disorder and popular violence, however, appalled him; even worse was the disintegration of military discipline that he witnessed in his command in Alsace during the second half of 1789. After a leave for reasons of health, the 65-year-old general took command of the army of the North in September 1790. The following year he was promoted to the highest military grade, marshal of France. Despite growing reservations about the revolutionary changes being introduced, Rochambeau felt obliged to remain at his post, unlike thousands of other officers who emigrated. However, one month after the outbreak of war in April 1792, totally opposed to the offensive strategy proposed by the French Revolutionary government and in failing health, Rochambeau resigned.

From his retirement in Vendôme, he was disturbed by the further radicalization of the revolution, yet proud of the army's achievements against foreign enemies. On April 6, 1794, like so many fellow nobles, Rochambeau was arrested as a "suspect"; he remained in prison until October 27. He then resumed his retirement on the family estates and rarely returned to Paris. A notable exception came when Napoleon Bonaparte received Rochambeau amid some of his generals, including Louis-Alexandre Berthier who had served on Rochambeau's staff in America. The First Consul introduced the officers as Rochambeau's "pupils." With his typical graciousness and humility, the last marshal of the ancien régime replied, "The pupils have far surpassed their master." He continued to enjoy official honor and respect until his death on May 12, 1807.

Sam Scott

REFERENCES

Lee Kennett, *The French Forces in America, 1780–1783* (1977); Howard C. Rice, Jr., and Anne S.K. Brown, eds., *The American Campaigns of Rochambeau's Army, 1780, 1781, 1782, 1783,* 2 vols. (1972); Jean Edmond

Weelen, *Rochambeau, Father and Son: A Life of the Maréchal de Rochambeau and the Journal of the Vicomte de Rochambeau* (1936); Arnold Whitbridge, *Rochambeau* (1965); M.W.E. Wright, ed., *Memoirs of the Marshal Count de Rochambeau, Relative to the War of Independence of the United States* (1838), rpr. 1971.

Rochefermoy (LaRochefermoy), Mathieu Alexis de (1725–1782)

French army officer. One of the first French officers to volunteer his services for the American cause, a nobleman, Rochefermoy was born in Bordeaux on November 7, 1725. He began his military career in 1743 as a lieutenant of militia in his native Guyenne. He served subsequently in Martinique, in the West Indies, where he was captain of grenadiers of a "French regiment." Details of his military career are murky, but it appears that captain was the highest grade he attained in the French army.

He made his way to America in 1776 and was awarded a commission as brigadier general in the Continental Army on November 5, 1776. He commanded a brigade, consisting of the regiments of Edward Hand and Nicholas Haussegger, at Trenton (December 26, 1776) but thereafter his fortunes fell. He was absent from his post as commander of the delaying force opposed to the British advance on Trenton on January 3, 1777 (the day Washington won the Battle of Princeton), and he was soon (March) bundled northward to serve under General Arthur St. Clair.

As one of St. Clair's principal subordinates at Fort Ticonderoga during John Burgoyne's brief siege (July 3–8, 1777), Rochefermoy voted with the majority in council of war to abandon the fort to the British and to evacuate the garrison to the Vermont side of Lake Champlain during the night of July 5–6. As the withdrawal got underway, Rochefermoy's incompetence was once again manifest: he fell asleep at a crucial hour and neglected to inform all of his troops of the withdrawal order and then ordered his headquarters burned to the ground—an act that illuminated the withdrawal and alerted the British, who initiated a pursuit at once. The pursuit was checked at Hubbardton (July 7) by Seth Warner, and St. Clair's army was saved from destruction.

Thereafter, Rochefermoy languished without a command. He resigned his commission on January 31, 1778, and returned to the West Indies. Andre Lasseray states that he served as a volunteer with local French forces at Dominica and St. Lucia (September–November 1778) prior to his death in 1782.

Rochefermoy's name has been rendered in various ways. Both Thomas Balch and Capt. Gilbert Bodinier list him as Rochefermoy, although Balch gives his Christian name as Mathieu Alexandre. Lasseray lists him as de La Rochefermoy, while Mark Mayo Boatner prefers Fermoy, a shortened version that appears rather frequently and was contemporary, the chevalier Dubuysson complaining about a "M. de Fermoix."

His son, Mathieu Alexandre de Rochefermoy (1755–1782), served in Rochambeau's expedition.

Curt C. Johnson

REFERENCES

Thomas Balch, *The French in America During the War of Independence of the United States,* Vol. II (1895); Mark Mayo Boatner III, *Encyclopedia of the American Revolution* (1969); Capt. Gilbert Bodinier, *Dictionnaire des officiers de l'armee royale qui ont combattu aux Etats-Unis pendant la guerre d'Independence, 1776–1783* (1982); Andre Lasseray, *Les francais sous les treize etoiles (1775–1783),* Vol. I (1935).

Rockingham (2nd Marquis of Charles Watson-Wentworth) (1730–1782)

British statesman. The Marquis of Rockingham was a prominent leader of the Whig opposition in British politics during the period of the American Revolution. He led the ministry that repealed the Stamp Act and passed the Declaratory Act in 1766. He was the leader of the Rockingham Whigs in opposition from 1766 to 1781. In March 1782 he again became first minister of the British government determined to end the war in America based upon recognition of the independence of the United States. Throughout his political career he worked for conciliation with the American colonies and for reduction of the power of the British monarchy.

Charles Watson-Wentworth was the only surviving son of Thomas Watson-Wentworth, Marquis of Rockingham, and great-great-grandson of Thomas Wentworth, first Earl of Strafford. He was styled Viscount Higham from 1734, became Earl of Malton in 1746, and acceded to the marquisate in 1750. He attended Westminster School. His parents decided not to send him to Cambridge but, instead, in 1746 on a tour of Europe. His parents arranged a marriage with the heiress Mary Bright, daughter of the Earl of Nottingham. They married when he returned to England upon the death of his father in 1750. The basis of his wealth and status was immense landholdings in Yorkshire, Northhamptonshire, and Ireland. He was interested in the business of his estates and devoted much of his time to such activities as coal mining, iron mining, coke and iron production, brick making, devising agricultural implements, and draining and fertilizing his lands. He was also well known for his stables and racing successes.

It was natural that as a landed magnate of an Old Whig family, Rockingham would enter politics when he inherited the title. He began his political career in 1753 by nominating members for the House of Commons from his territorial base in Yorkshire. At first his interest in politics was limited, and he preferred involving himself in his estates and attending racing meets. His health was poor and he believed that this precluded a sustained, active political career. He found much in politics that was boring and sordid. However, his wealth, position, and interests brought him into close contact with the leaders of the Whig party, especially the Duke of Cumberland and the Duke of Newcastle. By 1761 the Marquis was an active figure in Whig politics. Few expected him to become a leader of the Whig party because of his unassuming nature and because of his known preference for the racecourse over the House of Lords. A major drawback to emergence as a political leader was his inability to speak in Parliament, a handicap that limited his effectiveness throughout his career. In 1760 he seemed destined for a conventional life of officeholding without the responsibilities of political decision and government business. But his even-tempered personality, his reputation for honesty and integrity, his adherence to Whig principles, and his connections to both the older and younger generations combined to place him in a leadership position. In 1765 George III was forced to turn to the Whig opposition to form a government to replace that of Grenville.

The King was not enthusiastic about Rockingham as a choice to lead his government. Rockingham was inexperienced and had clearly shown animosity to Lord Bute and other "king's friends." Rockingham had supported the Duke of Devonshire when he was dismissed from the Privy Council, had opposed the peace treaty of 1763, had paid for publication of pamphlets criticizing the Cider Tax, and had attacked the use of general warrants in the Wilkes case. But George had no alternative to Rockingham, because William Pitt had refused to form a ministry. Therefore the King accepted the advice of his uncle the Duke of Cumberland and, on July 10, 1765, named Rockingham First Lord of the Treasury and First Minister to the King.

During Rockingham's first ministry, his wife and Edmund Burke, his private secretary, became two of his most important political advisers. The marchioness gave Rockingham detailed political advice. She often made detailed suggestions on policy and political management, particularly on how to handle the King. She occasionally functioned as a personal emissary for her husband to other political leaders such as Pitt. Edmund Burke became Rockingham's private secretary shortly before his first ministry. Burke advised on policy and spoke for the Marquis in the House of Commons, where he took his seat in December 1765, through Rockingham's influence. Burke was loyal to Rockingham's party throughout the Marquis's lifetime.

When his ministry began, Rockingham's agenda was headed by a desire to establish a dominance of the Old Whigs in British government. To this end he used political patronage at his disposal and attempted to rally public opinion behind his government. He used techniques of political management to pass popular legislation, such as modification of the Cider Tax and condemnation of general warrants. Unfortunately for Rockingham's ministry, the Stamp Act crisis overshadowed its legislative successes. Rockingham found most of his time as premier devoted to solution of the colonial problem.

When Rockingham's government came to power, it had no American policy. When news of American rejection of the Stamp Act reached London the cabinet was unsure as to whether to follow a policy of enforcement, to recommend modification of the Act, or to favor repeal. After consultation and reflection Rockingham decided that his ministry should advocate repeal. Rockingham favored repeal of the Stamp Act primarily because he was convinced that the British economy would suffer further depression if

Grenville's colonial policy continued. Likewise, Rockingham was convinced that the Act could not be enforced, and he feared that British authority would be undermined throughout the Empire. In addition, Rockingham hoped repeal would restore good relations with the American colonies. By January, the ministry had endorsed a policy of repeal of the Stamp Act.

It was clear that neither the King nor Parliament would back down on their constitutional right to tax the colonies, a right that Rockingham endorsed. Rockingham's problem was to repeal the Stamp Act on the basis of conciliation and economic necessity and, at the same time, deal with American defiance of parliamentary authority. Charles Yorke suggested, and Rockingham accepted, the idea of passing a Declaratory Act along with repeal. When Parliament met in January, Rockingham's ministry proposed a plan embodying both relief of America and acceptance of parliamentary authority throughout the Empire.

Rockingham's strategy for passage of repeal was to approach the issue from a practical economic position, emphasizing the damage being inflicted upon the Empire through Grenville's misguided American policy. Such an argument appealed to him because he had been a strong supporter of commercial development since the 1750s, before he became active in national politics. Rockingham's belief that an economic argument would be effective in convincing members of Parliament to support repeal of the Stamp Act led him to marshal mercantile forces throughout England to publicize the need for repeal. Burke arranged meetings between Rockingham and various merchants and manufacturers, notably Barlow Trecothick of London. The merchants, with the Marquis's support, organized into a committee to produce a national commercial agitation. They contacted mercantile friends throughout England who flooded Parliament with petitions in January 1766. Some members of Parliament were shocked that Rockingham's ministry had turned to such men to help the cause of repeal, but the campaign was effective.

Rockingham had some difficulty with the King. George was emotionally opposed to repeal and hesitated to support his ministry. George only withdrew his objections when Rockingham threatened to resign, but the King allowed his supporters in Parliament to vote against repeal without any retribution. Rockingham believed that the King, under the influence of Bute, had betrayed his government. Rockingham also had difficulty with Pitt, who supported repeal but opposed the Declaratory Act. During the Stamp Act crisis, personal animosity developed between Pitt and Rockingham that would last the rest of their lives. Though they periodically supported each others' policies, they were never able to trust each other enough to form a united Whig opposition.

In March 1766 Rockingham's strategy and the work of his supporters resulted in passage of the Declaratory Bill and repeal of the Stamp Act. George III signed both bills on March 18. Repeal legislation was completed in June with passage of a bill indemnifying those who had disobeyed the Stamp Act and validating all legal documents executed while the Stamp Act was in effect. Rockingham's first ministry was responsible for other changes in colonial policy, including resumption of bullion trade with Spain and establishment of a free port in the West Indies. The molasses tax was lowered to one pence but now was applied to all imported molasses, validating that Rockingham and his cabinet accepted Parliament's right to tax the colonies for revenue purposes.

Further plans for alterations in colonial policy were never implemented because the ministry fell in July 1766. In May the King had made known his dissatisfaction with Rockingham's government partly because of failure to get adequate allowances for the King's brothers. George began negotiations with Pitt, who agreed to form a coalition government. Pitt even offered to work with some of Bute's supporters, convincing Rockingham that Pitt had abandoned Whig principles. Rockingham left office believing that the party he led was the only true descendant of the Whigs of the Glorious Revolution and that it was now his duty to lead the opposition against the growth of Crown prerogative and influence. Thus began Rockingham's 16 years out of office.

When Rockingham was dismissed, commercial and manufacturing interests lauded him with outpourings of accolades and appreciation. They encouraged their friends in the colonies to write letters stating American thanks for repeal of the Stamp Act. The colonists demonstrated appropriate gratitude, but they ignored the Declaratory Act. Their emotional ties were clear to Pitt, who had accepted American constitutional arguments and ably defended America in the House of Commons. Rockingham did not endorse American constitutional arguments, because he never doubted the supremacy of Parliament within the Empire. He hoped to nullify the effects of sovereignty through practical and voluntary conciliation. In 1766 he believed England had everything to lose through a rigid application of principle and everything to gain through conciliation, and he maintained this position throughout his years of opposition. He frequently disapproved of American violence and rioting, but he never advocated the use of force against the colonies. He preferred a "sleeping sovereignty." In part this was because he wanted to strengthen the economic position of England. It was also because he saw the American cause as closely linked with the Whig struggle against the growth of Crown influence in British government.

Rockingham was in the Country Whig tradition and saw himself working to maintain the constitution as amended in 1689. His political principles included personal rectitude, preservation of the rights of individuals and corporate bodies under the law, opposition to corruption and gross forms of sinecures and bribery, opposition to extremes of parliamentary reform, and preservation of the political system dominated by the landed aristocracy and gentry. By 1766 he believed that the greatest threat to his political principles came from a secret junto of the King's friends. He thought that a ring of obscure men had gained supreme direction of policy with the goal of subverting the constitution and destroying the power of Parliament. He viewed the government's policy toward the American colonies as part of a plan to increase royal power and to free the Crown from parliamentary supply by acquiring revenue from both the American colonies and India. He believed his political mission was destruction of the King's cabal. As conflict between government and colonies deepened and widened in the 1770s, Rockingham came to view the Americans as fighting the same secret junto the Whigs were opposing in Parliament. He never condoned American violence or American rejection of parliamentary supremacy, but by 1776 he regarded Washington's armies as allies against "secret influence." Not all Whigs followed Rockingham's lead because many wanted radical parliamentary reform that would

limit the power of great magnates like the marquis. But most Whigs accepted his view that the fight for American liberties was part of the Whig program to preserve the constitution against encroachment by the Crown.

Between 1767 and 1774 American policy was of secondary concern to Rockingham. He and his party were primarily concerned with matters like the civil list debt and the Middlesex election, barely protesting against the Townshend Duties and other ministerial actions that were driving a wedge between England and her American colonies. But when Parliament began debate over the Coercive Acts, Rockingham and his followers took on the mantle of champions of the American cause. Rockingham even made one of his rare parliamentary speeches against the Massachusetts Government Act. The marquis condemned the perpetrators of the Boston Tea Party but objected to the punishment of Boston and Massachusetts without giving them a chance to defend themselves or to make reparations. He viewed the Massachusetts Government Act as a violation of charter rights and a threat to American and English liberties. He argued that conciliation was the only way that the American colonies and England could continue to enjoy economic benefit and maintain their relationship. He did not disavow the Declaratory Act, but over the next several months proposed that the supreme legislative authority confer on the American colonies the privilege of exemption from parliamentary taxation. He opposed the Quebec Act as enhancing monarchical power and spoke twice against the New England Restraining Act. He supported Pitt's motion in 1775 to withdraw troops from the American colonies. He formally registered his protest against the declaration of war in the *Lords' Journal* in October 1776 and then seceded from Parliament as a symbol of his opposition to the ministry's war against America.

He actively returned to the House of Lords after announcement of the Franco-American alliance in 1778. He was one of the first to advocate recognition of American independence, though in 1778 he may still have contemplated some form of federal alliance. However, he believed that recognition of independence would allow reestablishment of economic ties so essential to English economic growth and would deter the United States from entering the diplomatic and economic orbit of France. Rockingham's arguments were strengthened by the American victory at Saratoga and by the ineffective war policy of North's ministry. However, throughout the war he was accused of unpatriotic behavior because his support of America caused him to hope for American military victories over British forces.

In 1780, North's ministry was in serious trouble and Lord North proposed to save his government by entering into an alliance with Rockingham and his party. This seemed possible because of the support Rockingham had given the government during the Gordon Riots and because the Whig opposition had split over radical parliamentary reform. Rockingham had refused to accept reforms that would undermine the political power of the landed aristocracy and gentry. But Rockingham refused to enter the government unless American independence would be immediately recognized and only if he would be given a free hand in negotiating peace. He also demanded support for his program to curb royal influence in Parliament, reform of the Exchequer, and appointment of his friends to office. George III angrily rejected demands that would result in a diminution of Crown authority in government, and North withdrew his offer.

In 1780 Rockingham's position on the American war was a key factor keeping him out of government; in 1782, American victory in war vindicated his position and forced George III to dismiss North and bring Rockingham in as first Lord of the Treasury to head his second ministry. As in 1780, Rockingham demanded that the King support American independence, as well as reduction of the household, disfranchisement of revenue officers, and exclusion of government contractors from the House of Commons. George was both furious and disheartened; he actually contemplated abdication. He finally accepted Rockingham's terms but undermined the marquis's position by creating Shelburne as virtual co-premier. Immediately conflict arose over patronage, foreign policy, and the status of the United States, with Shelburne opposing recognition of independence before negotiations began. Because Rockingham controlled a majority of votes in the cabinet and in Parliament, in May 1782 the ministry voted to recognize American independence and to begin negotiating peace. Shelburne and the King began working against Rockingham's program, and the ministry was in disarray when the marquis fell ill with influenza.

At first his physicians believed he would recover, but Rockingham died July 1, 1782. There was mourning only in Yorkshire; the political nation's attention was drawn to Shelburne's new ministry and to negotiations with America. The Marquis of Rockingham was buried in York Minster. He died without issue and his honors became extinct. His political supporters would retain their identity as the Rockingham Whigs, but under the leadership of Charles James Fox. The Marquis of Rockingham spent most of his political career as a leader of the Whig opposition. Though the nineteenth-century Whig party admired him, his accomplishments were few. He was not particularly intelligent nor was he politically astute. His career rested on his integrity, the charm of his personality, and his commitment to the Whig constitution. The consistency with which he maintained the principles of the Glorious Revolution was the major element in his political legacy. These principles made him a leading English supporter of the struggle for American rights.

Allida McKinley

REFERENCES

G.H. Guttridge, *English Whiggism and the American Revolution* (1942); Ross J.S. Hoffman, *The Marquis: A Study of Lord Rockingham 1730–1782* (1973); Christie Ian, *Myth and Reality in Late-Eighteenth-Century British Politics* (1970); Ian Christie, *Wars and Revolutions: Britain 1760–1815* (1982); Paul Langford, *The First Rockingham Administration, 1765–1766* (1973).

Rodney, George Brydges (1718–1792)

British navy officer. Born in January 1718 and christened on February 3, 1718, George Brydges Rodney was the fourth child of Henry Rodney and Mary Newton. His mother was a Brydges, a family that had produced statesmen and soldiers in England for 500 years. The Rodneys were also an old family, although not as distinguished. Henry Rodney was a retired captain of marines and commanded the King's private yacht. He obtained this position through friends at court. In the eighteenth century, gentlemen often obtained financial rewards from the prerequisites of office that were available to men with the right connections. At the christening of George Rodney, King George I stood as one godfather, the other was George Brydges, Duke of Chandus, a distant cousin. When George's father suffered financial losses through bad investments, George Brydges became young Rodney's guardian. He attended Harrow School until he was 12. In 1732 he entered the navy on the muster list of the HMS *Sunderland* as a King's letter boy.

Since there was no formal training for aspiring officers of the Royal Navy, ships' captains took aboard young sons of relatives and friends so that they could become midshipmen. Advancement to lieutenant depended largely on the whim or patronage of the captain or other senior officer. A lad who came aboard with a King's letter, while not assured of making lieutenant, usually made that rank if he had normal aptitude and applied himself to his duties.

Rodney went to sea in the HMS *Dreadnaught* (60 guns) at the age of 16. He was of slight build with a patrician bearing and outlook. He stood apart from most midshipmen, sons of middle-class officials and businessmen who had finagled a midshipman's berth for their sons. The *Dreadnaught* spent most of her time in Lisbon, Portugal, to deter Spain from attacking this British ally. The Honorable Charles Compton, who had four daughters, was the British minister in Lisbon. Their circle of friends included the Klies family who had a daughter named Henrietta. Rodney frequently visited the Comptons and spent many happy liberty hours in subtropical Lisbon.

Duty on the *Dreadnaught* was followed by duty in a series of other ships: the *Romney* (50 guns); the *Dolphin* (24 guns), where he was appointed lieutenant in 1739; the *Essex* (70 guns); and in 1742 he reported aboard the *Namur* (90 guns) in Lisbon. This was the flagship of Vice Admiral Mathews, a crusty old sea dog who brooked no slackness and was cold and distant. He readily chastised or removed officers who displeased him. When the captain of the *Plymouth* (50 guns) was transferred to a larger ship, Mathews appointed the 24-year-old Rodney to captain the *Plymouth*. Handsome, suave, and well spoken, he was an imposing figure and enjoyed Lisbon and the Compton daughters even more than he had the previous eight years.

The *Plymouth*, in very poor condition, was ordered back to England. She escorted a 300-ship convoy home without incident. Rodney was too junior to retain his command. He was confirmed post captain in 1742.

From then on he commanded a series of ships of increasing size: the *Shearness* (24 guns), the *Ludlow Castle* (40 guns), and the *Eagle* (60 guns). In 1745 Rodney carried specie from Portugal to England and received his first freight money, £441, for its safe delivery. In 1748 he was presented to King George II who remarked that he did not realize how young and handsome his naval captains were. Lord Anson, First Sea Lord, who made the presentation, stated that he wished he had a hundred young officers of the stamp of Rodney. Anson was not noted for praising his officers.

In 1749 Rodney was appointed to command the *Rainbow* (60 guns) and to be military governor of Newfoundland. This required that he make an annual cruise to Newfoundland escorting the British fishing fleet to and from the fishing grounds. These cruises lasted four to six months. Therefore, Rodney had plenty of time to pursue his own interests. His most important goal was to get elected to the House of Commons. Influential noblemen and government officials "owned" seats in Parliament, that is, they owned large tracts of land in a district and managed to get their nominees elected. Rodney cultivated John Cleveland who had inherited the Saltash district. He was elected to the House of Commons from Saltash in 1751 and took his seat in 1752 when the *Rainbow* was paid off.

In 1752 Rodney went from the *Rainbow* to commander of the port of Portsmouth. He was headquartered in the guardship *Kent* in Portsmouth. This was an undermanned ship that needed only a full crew to go to sea. In 1753 he married Jane Compton, whom he had first met in Lisbon as a young officer. She was the daughter of the Seventh Earl of North Hampton, who had been the British minister to Portugal. Jane gave birth to two sons.

One of Rodney's duties as commander of the port and the guardship was to organize press gangs. These gangs roamed Portsmouth streets and the surrounding area to impress men into the navy. Any man who did not have a bonafide exception was forcibly taken and put aboard ship to serve at the pleasure of the crown. These men had no opportunity to say goodbye to their families nor put their affairs in order for an absence from home that could last years. Press gangs also manned boats to meet and board all incoming merchant ships. Crew members without official exceptions were immediately taken and placed on a King's ship. Numerous merchant seamen were pressed within sight of England when they were returning from a two- or three-year foreign cruise. More than 50 percent of the seamen on most British men-of-war were pressed men.

On the other hand, France resorted to the age-old European tradition of conscription to raise men for His Most Christian Majesty's ships. The maritime provinces of France were divided into six departments, which were further divided into quarters to facilitate administration. Every man, apprentice, and boy was required to register and indicate his marine skill or trade. When men were needed for the fleet, the commissaries in the various quarters picked the required number of names from the conscription lists and these men were sent to a shipyard to man the ships. Everyone hated conscription, but at least the conscript had a chance to plan his absence and provide for his family. The French system of raising crews for warships was not as cruel as the British method.

When the *Kent* was required for active duty, Rodney shifted to the undermanned *Prince George* and so it went. He commanded four ships in five years. In 1757 he had just transferred from the *Monarch* when Admiral Byng was executed on that ship. Byng had been convicted of cowardice in failing to relieve the French siege of Minorca in 1756. Also in 1757, Rodney's wife died giving birth to a daughter.

The Seven Years' War had begun in 1756, but Rodney did not go to sea until 1758, when he took command of the unlucky ship the *Dublin* (74 guns). While escorting a convoy to Nova Scotia the crew was struck down by a typhoid epidemic. The *Dublin* was forced to remain in port in Nova Scotia during the successful siege of Louisbourg, Nova Scotia. The ship returned to England in 1759 and Rodney was promoted to rear admiral of the Blue. He obtained a leave of absence for reasons of health, but this did not keep him from attending Parliament. (The successive steps of admiral were: Rear Admiral of the Blue, White, then Red; Vice Admiral of the Blue, White, then Red; Admiral of the Blue, then White. The regulations provided that there should be one admiral of the fleet who flew the union flag at the main. With few exceptions this was an honorary and not an active post.)

The same year he was elected to Parliament from Okehampton with the Earl of Newcastle as his patron. Rodney loved Parliament and

claimed it was the only club worth belonging to. He was elected to Parliament five times. The following year, 1760, King George II died and Parliament was dissolved. To get reelected Rodney offered command of his flagship the *Marlborough* (74 guns) to a Captain Peard in return for a seat in Parliament. He was reelected in 1761, but Captain Peard did not become his flag captain.

In 1760 he commanded a naval task force that destroyed French landing craft at Le Harve. In this campaign he flew his flag from the frigate *Vestal* commanded by Captain Samuel Hood. They had been shipmates in the *Dreadnaught* when they were midshipmen. Their friendship continued, although later, in 1781, when Hood was his second in command in the Caribbean, he was frequently critical of Rodney.

Rodney was appointed commander-in-chief of the Leeward Islands in 1761 and arrived in Barbados on December 24, 1761, in the *Marlborough*. He captured Martinique in February 1762. This was followed by the capture of St. Vincent, St. Lucia, and the Grenadines without a fight. After the capture of Martinique he wrote his patron, the Earl of Newcastle, about the lucrative possibilities existing there. On his own initiative he decided to join Admiral Sir George Peacock in an attack on Jamaica. The vision of Spanish treasure ships and potential prize money that a raid on Havana might bring undoubtedly affected his decision. At the last moment he received orders to remain in the Leeward Islands. His only prize money was 3,000 acres on a captured island that he never claimed. Peacock's prize money obtained as a result of the sack of Havana provided him a handsome fortune. In October 1762 Rodney was promoted to Vice Admiral of the Blue. The following year the Treaty of Paris ended the war and 15 years of peace followed.

George III had ascended to the throne in 1760. The fortunes of the Earl of Newcastle went into decline. The Earl of Sandwich had the power. It was a time of corruption and bribery in England. Patronage and chicanery were a way of life to those who had no scruples on how to reach the top. Rodney was no different from many of his contemporaries. He was a gambler and loved women. Good looking and urbane, he was at home in the highest circles of the court.

In 1764 the King awarded Rodney a barony. The same year he married Henrietta Klies. She was the daughter of a wealthy Lisbon merchant. Her family was friends of the Comptons when the Earl was minister to Portugal. Rodney had met her in Lisbon, where he also met his first wife. The fact that she was a commoner meant that she brought with her a sizable dowry. She bore him six children. In 1765 he was appointed governor of the Greenwich Hospital for indigent seamen. This hospital was noted for its corruption, as vendors and administrators stole goods and equipment to the detriment of indigent patients. Even the Earl of Sandwich was guilty of this fraud.

In 1768 Rodney was still ill but continued to be a member of Parliament from Penryn, and his sponsor was the Earl of Sandwich. Sandwich refused to sponsor him for the elections of 1768 even though Rodney wrote him humbling and beseeching letters. Finally the Earl of Northampton sponsored him in a race marked by blatant bribery. The election results were so close that the issue was decided in favor of Rodney on the toss of a coin. This election cost him £30,000 and left him heavily in debt.

In 1771 he was offered command of the British squadron in Jamaica. He accepted this position but desired to remain as governor of Greenwich Hospital. Sandwich, the naval minister, turned him down. In order to get aboard his flagship, he had to slip out the back door at night to avoid his creditors. In Jamaica he was Vice Admiral of the Red. He was in Jamaica when the governor, Sir William Trelawney, died. Rodney asked that he be appointed governor to succeed Trelawney, but Sandwich appointed Sir Basil Keith to that position. Rodney returned to England in 1774 a bitter man. He held the permanent rank of rear admiral of England with an annual stipend of £232, hardly adequate for a gambler heavily in debt and accustomed to life in court circles. He took the only course open to him and fled to Paris in 1775.

He was still in France when England and France went to war in 1778. The Earl of Sandwich ignored his letters asking for active duty assignment. Finally the Merchel Charles de Guntaut-Biron, a French noblemen, advanced him £2,000 to pay off his French gambling debts and return to England. Later Guntaut-Biron was roundly criticized by the French for providing funds to the Englishman who was responsible for Admiral de Grasse's final defeat.

He returned to England on May 6, 1778, and took up residence across the street from St. James Palace. His residence was inside the King's verge, which meant that while there he could not be arrested for his debts. He appointed his eldest son George by his first wife as his lawyer with power to settle his debts. He sought active duty. Finally on October 1, 1779, he was appointed to command the British fleet in the Leeward Islands of the Caribbean. His fleet was not ready to sail. The British were still suffering the pangs of General John Burgoyne's defeat at Saratoga and the Ministry demanded action. In early December Sandwich wrote, "For God's sake go to sea without delay."

He sailed on December 24, 1779, with 22 ships, 8 frigates, 66 stores ships, and a 300-ship convoy. He was directed to first join the Channel fleet and raise the blockade of Gibraltar whose garrison was reduced to eating wild onions and other food they could scrounge on the Rock. On January 8, 1780, he sighted a Spanish convoy of 16 ships with a small escort, which he captured in very rough seas. The seas were still very rough when he sighted a Spanish fleet off Cape St. Vincent, Portugal, on January 16, 1780. At 2:30 P.M., he hoisted the signal, "General chase and engage to leeward." If he had followed the standard procedure of engaging to windward, the guns would have fired into the seas as the ships were well heeled over. Firing from leeward the guns would fire higher into the enemy ships. Being to leeward would also prevent the Spanish from escaping into port. He told his flag captain, Walter Young, "Put me alongside the biggest ship or an admiral's ship if one can be found." Finally at 2 A.M. that night the *Marlborough* fired a salvo into the *Femix* (80 guns), flagship of Don Juan de Langara, which was engaged with a British frigate. The *Femix* surrendered. In the meantime, his ships had engaged all 17 of the Spanish ships. Only two ships and two frigates escaped. Heavy seas and strong winds drove several of the damaged Spanish ships on the lee shore, where they foundered with heavy loss of life. Superb ship handling on the part of the British prevented them from suffering a similar fate. The convoy of supplies that Rodney escorted began arriving at Gibraltar on January 16, 1780. Rodney arrived on January 21, 1780.

England was jubilant when news of this victory arrived. It helped to dispel the gloom that Burgoyne's defeat at Saratoga had produced.

Rodney sailed for Barbados, where he found 17 ships awaiting him, although two of them were in deplorable condition. There he was opposed by Admiral Luc Urbain de Bouexic de Guichen with 21 ships based at Martinique. De Guichen was a master tactician. He and Rodney sparred on three separate occasions in the spring of 1780 without either side being victorious. On one occasion with victory within his grasp de Guichen escaped because his subordinates were slow in obeying his signals. After the engagement Rodney told Rear Admiral Joshua Rawley, "The painful task of thinking is for the Commander-in-Chief. The rear admiral has but to obey signals and orders." Rodney's actions at this time lacked the spark that had given him the earlier victory over the Spanish. Rodney was frequently plagued with prostate problems and gout, particularly after a stretch of sea duty. On occasion he remained in his cabin during battle giving orders from his bunk. After one of his skirmishes with de Guichen, he was so weak that he had to be carried ashore at Barbados.

In the late summer of 1780, Rodney received intelligence that Admiral d'Arzac de Ternay with eight ships had arrived in Newport, Rhode Island. Believing that de Guichen might sail north to rendezvous with de Ternay, Rodney, on his own initiative, sailed for New York. There he became involved in an argument with Admiral Marriot Arbuthnot over the division of prize money. De Guichen did not sail north. Rodney returned to the Leeward Islands on December 6, 1780.

On January 27, 1781, Rodney received word from the Admiralty that England had declared war on the Netherlands and directed him to capture Dutch islands in the Caribbean, including St. Eustatius known as the "Golden Rock," so named because of the immense quantities of supplies that the Dutch maintained there. This was an important island from which the American colonies received much of their munitions and stores.

Sir Samuel Hood, a former shipmate of Rodney, arrived in the Leeward Islands with seven ships in January 1781 to be Rodney's second in command. Hood had not been the Admiralty's first choice for this position, but no one wanted to be the irascible Rodney's second in command. Rodney ordered Hood to take 17 ships and cruise to leeward of Port Royal, Martinique, to blockade the four French ships

in that port. Hood protested and wanted to cruise to windward, but Rodney overruled him. On March 21, 1781, Sandwich sent intelligence to Rodney via the cutter *Swallow* that a French fleet had sailed from Brest with the probable destination of America. Rodney did not receive this intelligence until one week after de Grasse was safely in Port Royal.

Rodney remained in St. Eustatius, enthralled with the island's loot. He was later severely criticized for not capturing the other Dutch colonies of Curaçao and Surinam. His portion and that of General John Vaughan, who commanded the army that captured this island, was said to be worth £300,000 and took 34 ships to transport it to England. This convoy was attacked by the French off the Scilly Islands just southwest of England, and the French captured 20 ships. Rodney first learned of de Grasse's arrival in the West Indies when the severely damaged *Russell* limped into St. Eustatius after a battle between Hood and de Grasse off Port Royal on April 29, 1781. Rodney immediately sent a message to Sir Thomas Graves, the fleet commander in New York, notifying him of de Grasse's arrival and warned him that de Grasse might visit North America. Hood and Rodney made their way to Antigua, where Rodney gave the ships only two days to make repairs and take on provisions and water. He then sailed to defend Barbados, the chief British base in the eastern Caribbean. Since there were 2,000 French prisoners on this island it seemed a likely target for a French attack.

De Grasse wasted no time in taking the war to the British. On May 10, 1781, he was repulsed in an attack on St. Lucia. He sailed south and attacked Tobago on May 23, 1781, the same day that Rodney arrived in Barbados. Rodney sent Rear Admiral Sir Francis S. Drake, a descendent of the famous English sea dog, with six ships to carry reinforcements to Tobago. Vastly outnumbered, Drake managed to escape de Grasse and rejoin Rodney. Tobago fell to the French on May 29, 1781. After Drake's return, Rodney put to sea with his entire fleet and sighted the French off the Grenadines. Although Rodney had the wind, he did not attack and was criticized for this inaction. The French sailed back to Port Royal unchallenged.

On July 5, 1781, de Grasse sailed from Martinique with his entire fleet of 25 ships and a large convoy bound for Cap François, Hispaniola. When Rodney received this news he surmised that the ultimate destination of the French was North America. He would not believe that de Grasse would take his entire fleet to North America. The French would require some ships to escort the annual convoy to France. Other ships would be required to defend French islands. Rodney estimated that de Grasse would not take more than 10 to 12 ships to North America. This faulty reasoning was a major reason for the British defeat at Yorktown. On July 7, 1781, Rodney sent a message to Graves in New York indicating that a part of the French fleet was reported to be destined for North America.

Rodney still had severe medical problems, so Sandwich gave him permission to return to England for treatment. After turning over his command to Hood he sailed for England on August 1, 1781, after transferring from the *Sandwich* (90 guns) to the *Gibraltar* (80 guns). He feared that the *Sandwich* could not safely make the voyage home. The *Gibraltar* had been the Spanish flagship *Femix* captured off Cape St. Vincent on January 16, 1781.

When Rodney reached England on September 11, 1781, the laurels he had gained by his actions in raising the siege of Gibraltar were already tarnished. He had not been successful against de Grasse, and the storm over the scandal of St. Eustatius was gathering. There was a flood of legal actions before the High Court brought by merchants and traders who felt that Rodney had stolen their merchandise at St. Eustatius. They claimed that Parliament had authorized them to trade with the Dutch. The Whigs in Parliament took up their cause.

Rodney went to Bath, where he was treated by Sir Caesar Hawkins, a prominent physician. In December the King ordered Rodney to return to the West Indies as soon as possible, since de Grasse and the entire French fleet had returned there after the French-American victory at Yorktown. Although his reputation was in a shambles, Sandwich wrote him, "The fate of the Empire is in your hands, and I have no reason to wish that it should be in any other's."

On January 8, 1782, Rodney sailed from Plymouth in the *Formidable* with 12 ships. Fortuitously, he appointed Sir Charles Douglas as his flag captain. Douglas was a gunnery expert with vision and daring. He was not welded to the age-old methods of fleet tactics and combat. Rodney with 12 ships arrived in Barbados on February 19, 1782. This was the same day that Hood escaped from de Grasse at St. Kitts after the French reduced the fort on Brimstone Hill. Rodney and Hood rendezvoused at St. Lucia. Rodney now had 37 ships. De Grasse was at Port Royal in nearby Martinique with 36 ships.

The French prepared to sail to Hispaniola, join the Spanish fleet, and attack Jamaica. Sixty-five hundred troops were loaded on the warships, and a 260-ship convoy carried supplies and munitions, including artillery. The French sortied from Port Royal early in the morning of April 8, 1782. The frigate *Endymon* patroled the nine-league-wide channel that separated the British anchorage at Gros Islet, St. Lucia, from Port Royal Martinique. (Leagues are used here since one league equals three nautical miles or three minutes of longitude at the equator. In the eighteenth century the term "mile" was ambiguous. For example, one German mile equaled 4.5 English miles. Both were used in charts and maps.) It immediately spotted the ships under sail. The *Endymon* flew back to St. Lucia, and the captain personally delivered his sighting report to Rodney. Rodney violently abused and harangued the captain for leaving his station. The British fleet got underway, and by that evening it had the mastheads of the French fleet in sight.

The winds were very light on April 9; however, eight ships of Hood's squadron engaged fifteen of the French. The British suffered heavy damage but all ships were able to maintain station. The *Caton* was so badly damaged that de Grasse ordered her to nearby Guadeloupe for repairs. This action lasted five hours.

The following night and day were spent in maneuvering in almost calm seas. During this time the *Zele* rammed the *Jason*, which also had to be sent to Guadeloupe for repairs. During the stormy night of April 11, the *Zele* rammed the *Ville de Paris*. This was her thirteenth collision in 14 months. The next morning the frigate *Astree* took her in tow and headed for Guadeloupe. De Grasse had previously ordered the convoy to anchor at Guadeloupe.

On the morning of April 12, the two fleets were but a few miles apart in very light breezes. Rodney ordered Hood to take four ships to capture the laggard *Zele* and *Astree*. De Grasse moved immediately to protect the unlucky ship. The two fleets converged sailing on opposite courses. They passed each other so close that burning wadding from enemy guns set fire on the decks.

The smoke was very dense and due to the light breeze it hung over the ships, greatly reducing visibility. De Grasse was headed for calm waters. To avoid this calm de Grasse twice ordered his ships to pivot 180 degrees. To execute this signal the French ships had to turn toward the enemy. Some French ships ignored the signal, others had their sails taken aback, and the French line became disorganized. The wind shifted further adding to the confusion. The *Glorieux* bore down on the *Formidable*, Rodney's flagship. The *Canada* and the *Namur* also closed the French ship, which was soon disabled and out of line.

What happened next is not clear. Sir Charles Douglas, Rodney's flag captain, pressed Rodney to break the French line in the break made by the *Glorieux*. Rodney refused. The Fighting Instructions, which covered British fleet actions, was very specific that each ship should engage the enemy opposite. Douglas kept insisting that Rodney break the line. Finally, Rodney acquiesced. He then retired to his cabin. The *Formidable's* wheel was put over, and she started through the line firing at ships on both sides. There was no signal to cover this situation, but fortunately the other ships astern followed the flagship. Shortly thereafter, Commodore Edmund Affleck in the *Bedford* cut the French line astern of the *Cesar*.

The battle deteriorated into a series of skirmishes as the British attacked the French ships. At 5:30 P.M., the *Cesar* struck, or surrendered, to the *Centaur*, and the *Hector* at 6 P.M. struck to the *Canada*. Later, the *Ardent* struck after only five minutes of combat. By 8 P.M., de Grasse was deserted by his ships, although the Comte de Bouganville's squadron was almost intact. Seven British ships concentrated on the *Ville de Paris*, and she surrendered to the *Barfleur* at 8:15 P.M. The battle was over. The French lost five ships, and the rest scattered to Curacao and Hispaniola. Rather than order a "General Chase," Rodney ordered his ships to hove to, or to cease sailing, in order to effect repairs. He dispatched a fast frigate to England carrying the following message: "It has pleased God, out of his Divine Providence to grant His Majesty's arms a most complete victory." Hood was outraged that Rodney did not pursue the French, but he was the second in command. After four days of lying to, or taking time out for repairs, the British fleet got underway for Jamaica, where they arrived on April 29, 1782.

De Grasse was in ill health and asked to be sent home. He sailed from Jamaica on May 19, 1782, for England. The *Ville de Paris*, now a prize, was also sent back to England under tow. In a wild North Atlantic storm some of the huge guns broke loose, and by rolling back and forth across the deck they punched holes in the side and the ship sank. Rodney remained in Jamaica overseeing the repairs to his fleet. He was at this time very ill and at one point had to turn over his command to his second. His chief concern was his stature in England. Finally on July 9 he wrote London complaining that he had not heard from the government since he left St. Lucia. There were no orders for the fleet, and he was preparing to take it to North America for the hurricane season. The next day Admiral Sir Hugh Pigot arrived in Jamaica on board the *Jupiter* with orders to relieve Rodney.

Unbeknownst to Rodney, the Lord North government had resigned in March. The British, weary of the war and the defeat of Yorktown, elected a Whig government. It was inevitable that a Whig government would replace Rodney, who had served in Parliament for five terms as a staunch Tory. They chose Sir Hugh Pigot, a senior admiral who had never commanded a fleet, to replace Rodney. Pigot sailed in the *Jupiter* on May 17, 1782. Later that same day news of Rodney's victory at the Saintes arrived in London. Frantic efforts were made to recall Pigot, but he had already disappeared over the horizon. The government hurried to make amends. On May 22 they voted thanks to Rodney, his officers, and his men. They also voted Rodney a pension of £2,000 and a barony. The Whigs defeated a Tory motion to make him an earl.

Unaware of these political actions, Rodney sailed for home on July 23, 1782. A storm forced him to land at Bristol on September 22. When the public, who was very critical of Parliament's actions, learned that he was in port, they began a celebration matching that which celebrated the victory of Admiral Hawke at Quiberon Bay, which ended the naval phase of the Seven Years' War. The celebration spread from Bristol to London and throughout England. Rodney did not care for this popular acclaim; he was only concerned with what the King and Parliament thought of him.

Painfully ill with gout, he took up residence with his son George and his family at Alresford, Hampshire. George also had a residence on

Hanover Square in London. By mutual agreement he and his wife lived apart. The reason for this arrangement is unknown. In spite of this situation his sixth child named Edward was born in 1783 and was even younger than some of his grandchildren. George became his mainstay and handled all of his affairs. In 1783 the merchants who thought Rodney had unlawfully seized their supplies at St. Eustatius again filed charges in the Whig Parliament. Sixty-four of them were awarded compensation. In 1784 and 1785 Rodney traveled in Europe as far as Florence, Italy. He was still plagued by poor health, particularly gout. He died of that disease on May 24, 1792. He was buried in the plain Georgian church at Alresford. Shortly after his death the Council of Jamaica ordered a marble monument of Rodney done in the Roman style. The city of London placed a statue of him in full uniform in St. Pauls Cathedral. Streets and pubs were named after him.

Rodney remains one of England's greatest naval heroes. The Royal Navy named ships after him, the latest being two battleships. The first *Rodney* laid down in 1884, the second in 1923. This was a sister ship of the *Nelson*, and these were the first British battleships to carry 16-inch guns.

Rodney was a complex man. One of his biographers, David Hannay, wrote that "Rodney was a very complete example of the aristocracy that governed England through the eighteenth century—with much selfishness and much corruption, no doubt, yet in the main with a high spirit, with foresight, with statesmanship and with glory."

In his later years Rodney stated that his victory at the Saintes was an accident. He preferred to rest his reputation on his clash with de Guichen off Martinique. There he had raised the efficiency and discipline from a very low level and had outfoxed the master French tactician.

Accident or not, the Battle of the Saintes marked the end of one era of naval warfare and the beginning of another. Prior to this battle the Royal Navy rigidly adhered to the Fighting Instructions. In fleet actions this meant that each ship would remain opposite the corresponding ship in the enemy line and fight until the enemy was sunk, or boarded and captured. To break through the enemy line was unthinkable.

Break through the enemy battle line is exactly what Rodney did when the *Glorieux* fell

out of position. There is still controversy about whose idea it was to break the French line. Regardless of whether it was Rodney's idea or that of his flag captain Douglas, the fact remains that it was Rodney's responsibility. At the time no tactical signal existed by which he could order the ships astern to follow the *Formidable*. Had the other British ships not followed through the gap he could have been surrounded and the British fleet deprived of its admiral. Fortunately, the British ships followed and insured victory. From then on breaking the enemy's line became a standard tactic that was perfected by Nelson. Planned or accidental this was Rodney's chief contribution to naval warfare of the eighteenth century.

George Hagerman

REFERENCES

Jonathan R. Dull, *The French Navy and the American Revolution* (1975); David Hannay, *Rodney* (1891); Charles Lee Lewis, *Admiral de Grasse and the American Revolution* (1945); David G. MacIntyre, *Admiral Rodney* (1963); Alfred Thayer Mahan, *Influence of Seapower on History* (1918), rpr. 1949; Nathan Miller, *Sea of Glory* (1974); David Spinnay, *Rodney* (1969); Charles W. Toth, *The American Revolution in the West Indies* (1975); Karl Gustaf Tournquist, *Naval Campaigns of Comte de Grasse* (1942); Barbara Tuchman, *The First Salute* (1988); Russell F. Weigley, *The Age of Battles* (1991); A.B.C. Whipple, *Fighting Sail* (1978).

Rogers, Robert (1731–1795)

British army officer. When Robert Rogers was still a young boy in Methuen, Massachusetts, his family moved to Great Meadow, on the New Hampshire frontier close to what is now Concord. He spent his formative years on the fringe of the vast northeastern forests and developed into a skillful woodsman. He was still only a teenager when he got his first taste of wilderness fighting as part of a local defense force, during King George's War (1744–1748).

All of his life, Rogers had trouble fitting into civilized society. In 1755 he was implicated in a counterfeiting ring and had to enlist in the provincial New Hampshire Regiment to avoid prosecution. He found his niche in the military. His talents as a woodsman and his natural leadership skills quickly gained him a commission as a captain of an independent ranger company. Rangers were then a new military concept, unique to the wilds of North America. They consisted mostly of provincial troops, skilled in the ways of the forest, with a primary mission of scouting and other special purpose operations.

Operating in the area of Lake George and Lake Champlain during the French and Indian War (1756–1763), Rogers's company achieved some notable successes and drew the attention of high-ranking British officers. Regular British officers soon started going out with the unit to learn his techniques. At the request of General John Campbell Loudon, Rogers drew up a set of some 19 standing orders for ranger operations. Starting with "Don't forget nothing," his orders may appear today as mere common sense, such as, "Don't never take a chance you don't have to." Some of his concepts, however, were original for their time and are still strictly practiced in small unit operations to this day, for example, "Every night you'll be told where to meet if surrounded by a superior force."

Always distrustful of provincial troops, the British army attempted to develop ranger capabilities in its regular force. In 1757, Loudoun authorized Lieutenant Colonel Thomas Gage to form such a regiment. Gage raised the 80th Regiment (today the British army's Staffordshire Regiment), which was the true beginning of light infantry in the British army. Gage, however, could not quite duplicate Rogers's success and quickly developed a grudge that continually haunted Rogers when Gage became British commander-in-chief in North America.

Rogers was not always successful. In January 1757 the French ambushed his company near Fort Ticonderoga, inflicting almost 40 percent casualties and wounding Rogers twice. On March 13, 1758, Rogers's force suffered 8 officers and over 300 Rangers killed in the "Battle on Snowshoes," also near Ticonderoga. Rogers's successes, however, far outnumbered his setbacks, and in 1758 General James Abercromby promoted him to major and gave him the command of nine ranger companies. Rogers continued to operate with notable successes, and in October 1759 he led the raid that destroyed the Indian town of St. Francis. In 1760 he took part in the final operations against Montreal and was then sent to Detroit to accept the surrender of the French garrison there.

After the French surrender, General Jeffrey Amherst rewarded Rogers with a regular commission. Although he had been a superb fighter and leader, Rogers had always been a poor ad-

ministrator. From the very start of his commissioned service, he was in constant trouble over payroll and supply accounts, and his inability to keep the required records. As a result, he spent most of his life deeply in debt.

After serving in Pontiac's War, Rogers went to England in 1765 in an attempt to gain reimbursement for his accounts claims. While in England he succeeded in having two books published, *The Journals of Major Robert Rogers* and *A Concise Account of North America*. Both books were well received, and his widespread fame as a ranger leader eventually got him some partial financial relief as well as an audience with King George III. He was also awarded the command of Fort Michilimackinac, a British outpost at the western end of Lake Huron.

Unfortunately for Rogers, Gage was now the British commander-in-chief in North America. After two years at Fort Michilimackinac, Rogers was charged with embezzlement and treasonable conspiracy with the French. He was arrested and transported to Montreal for trial. Rogers was eventually acquitted for lack of evidence, but his reputation was irreparably damaged, and his life went downhill from there. His modern biographer, John R. Cuneo, presents strong arguments to suggest Gage knew all along that the charges against Rogers were trumped-up. Even though Rogers was cleared of the embezzlement charge, Gage still rejected his accounts claims, plunging the ranger leader deeper into debt.

With nowhere else to turn, Rogers went back to London in 1769. This time, however, he returned as a suspected traitor and embezzler, rather than as a ranger hero. He got a cold reception and wound up spending 22 months as a debtor in London's Fleet Prison. In 1774, when Gage was in England, Rogers filed a damage suit against him, effectively preventing the general from returning to America. On the advice of several government officials, however, Rogers quickly dropped the suit.

When Rogers finally returned to America in mid-1775, he was a stranger in his native land. He knew little about the current fighting around Boston and cared even less. On his way north through Philadelphia that September, he was arrested on the grounds he was a half-pay British officer. The Continental Congress later authorized his release on the condition he not take up arms against the Americans.

In February 1776, Sir Henry Clinton offered Rogers an active British commission, but the ranger leader turned it down because of his oath to the Congress. Later that year Rogers secretly went to Philadelphia and applied to the Congress for a commission; but the wary Congress wanted no part of him. In June, Rogers came under suspicion of being involved in a plot to assassinate Washington, and the American commander ordered Rogers's arrest.

Rogers attested to his innocence and requested to be allowed to return to England by way of the West Indies. Congress rejected his request and ordered him returned to his native New Hampshire for confinement. With this prospect staring him in the face, Rogers concluded he was no longer bound by his parole. On the night of July 8, 1776, he escaped from his jail cell, and a few days later he was received by the British high command.

General Howe gave Rogers a lieutenant colonel's commission and the authority to raise a Loyalist battalion of rangers. Right from the start, however, Rogers once more ran afoul of the British army's administration. In recruiting, Rogers carried on the old colonial practice of rewarding commissions to anyone who could bring in the necessary number of men. This upset most of the British officer corps, because commissions were not going to "gentlemen."

The early combat record of the new "Rogers' Rangers" was spotty at best. On the night of October 22, 1776, General William Alexander (Lord Stirling) attacked Rogers's force at Mamaroneck, near White Plains. The Americans initially overran a Loyalist outpost, but were eventually driven back when they hit Rogers's main body. The Americans later claimed, however, they had decisively routed Rogers' Rangers.

In January 1777 Alexander Innes became inspector general of provincial forces in the British army. One of his first acts was to force Rogers out of the command. After Rogers left, his ranger unit eventually went on to become one of the most effective Tory units. It later became the 1st American Regiment of the Regular establishment, and it is today the Canadian army's Queen's York Rangers of Toronto.

Rogers remained in North America on half-pay status and continued as a recruiter for Loyalist units. Always a heavy drinker, he began drinking even more heavily and his health suffered. In January 1781 the Americans captured him at sea while he was en route to New York. Paroled in May 1782 he eventually returned to England with the evacuating British army. He spent his last years in South London in a drunken fog and died in Southwark.

Despite his character flaws, his personal problems, and his dismal end, Robert Rogers had a significant impact on both the modern British and American armies. Ranger units today are an important part of both armies; and while they are used for quite different purposes in each army, they both trace their origins to Rogers's Rangers. In today's British army, ranger units are light infantry, while in the American army, they have become special purpose forces equivalent to the British Commandos. In the days of the colonial wars, Rogers' Rangers actually served both roles.

Rogers today generally is considered a deeply flawed personality with a streak of military brilliance. Although Cuneo (1959) staunchly defends his character and blames his administrative ineptitude as the primary source of Rogers's problems, other historians are less charitable. It does seem, however, that Rogers had one standard for the military and quite another for the rest of the world. An indication of this can be found in his own words. In his Standing Order No. 4 he said: "Tell the truth about what you see and what you do. There is an army depending on us for information. You can lie all you please when you tell other folks about the Rangers, but don't lie to a Ranger or Officer."

David T. Zabecki

REFERENCES

John R. Cuneo, *Robert Rogers of the Rangers* (1959); Robert Rogers, *Journals of Major Robert Rogers*, introduced by Howard R. Peckham (1961).

Roman Catholic Volunteers

On October 7, 1777, General Sir William Howe granted authorization to Alfred Clifton to raise the Roman Catholic Volunteers in Philadelphia. Seven days later Howe approved the selection of officers, with Clifton as lieutenant colonel.

During the British occupation of the city, the Volunteers participated in a number of minor operations. Their numbers reached 212 organized into four companies in November, but by March 1778 they had declined to 173.

When General Henry Clinton evacuated Philadelphia in June, the Roman Catholic Volunteers were assigned to help guard the baggage and heavy artillery of the army. They took no part in the Battle of Monmouth.

Clifton tried to build the unit in New York and met with some early success. However, between growing desertions and the conviction of two officers for plundering during the march from Philadelphia, the regiment rapidly declined.

Clinton finally decided to disband the Volunteers on October 25, 1778. The remaining men, about 80 in number, were then transferred to the Volunteers of Ireland.

Buttons marked "RCV" have been found, but no other uniform details are known to exist.

Walter T. Dornfest

REFERENCES

Martin I.J. Griffin, *Catholics and the American Revolution* (1907–1911); Albert W. Haarmann, "Roman Catholic Volunteers, 1777–1778," *Journal of the Society for Army Historical Research, 49* (1971):184–185; John W. Jackson, *With the British Army in Philadelphia* (1979); Charles H. Metzger, *Catholics and the American Revolution* (1962).

Romans, Bernard (1720–1784)

American cartographer. Born in Holland, Bernard Romans, noted cartographer of the American Revolution, trained as a botanist, mathematician, and civil engineer in England. He moved to the colonies in 1757, serving as surveyor in British North America. In the 1760s William Gerard De Brahm hired Romans to survey parts of Florida and Georgia, a task that led to the publication of *A Concise Natural History of East and West Florida* (1775). This treatise contained novel botanical and geographical observations. British officials were so impressed with Romans's cartography and botanical skills that they provided him a pension.

This pension was denied Romans when he joined the colonists in the Revolution. Living in Hartford, Connecticut, where he wrote his natural history of Florida and articles on botany, Romans was recruited by the Patriots because of his engineering skills. Romans's contributions to the American Revolution were colored by his difficult personality. Romans was often involved in arguments concerning his ability as an engineer and military leader.

He was selected to lead the Connecticut Committee's expedition to Fort Ticonderoga, but his leadership was usurped by Colonels Benedict Arnold and Ethan Allen. Romans decided to attack Fort George instead, arresting the fort's only occupant, a semi-invalid, Captain John Norberg. After this event, Romans returned and helped to take inventory of cannon at Ticonderoga. He then moved to Connecticut to create more maps. The British, who had copies of Romans's maps, used them during the war.

The Committee of Safety of New York assigned Romans to build a fort on Martelear's Rock, across the Hudson River from West Point. This project, known as Fort Constitution, was supposed to protect American forces there. However, Romans was criticized by the Committee because the site was vulnerable, for working too slow and at great expense. He was removed from this position.

Romans was then named captain of the Independent Pennsylvania Artillery Company (who were matrosses) to support the proposed second Canadian invasion. While traveling to Fort Ticon-deroga, Romans denied his men the opportunity to drink at local taverns. The men became unruly and some deserted. Because his men destroyed civilian property, Romans went on trial as a result of his soldiers' behavior. However, he was acquitted.

Romans spent the remainder of the Revolution inspecting defense works at lumber mills and producing maps. He retired from the army in 1778 and moved to Wethersfield, Connecticut; in 1779 he married Elizabeth Whiting and published *Annals of the Troubles of the Netherlands*.

About 1780 Romans was ordered to join the army in South Carolina, but the British captured him en route and imprisoned him at Montego Bay, Jamaica. Romans's death is surrounded by mystery. His wife stated that he was kept in Jamaica until 1784 and was probably murdered on the return passage. British historians claim Romans lived in England until 1784 and that he died while sailing to New York. *See also:* Cartography in the American Revolution

Elizabeth D. Schafer

REFERENCES

Lincoln Diamant, *Bernard Romans: Forgotten Patriot of the American Revolution: Military Engineer and Cartographer of West Point and the Hudson Valley* (1985);

John B. Harley, Barbara B. Petchenik, and Lawrence W. Towner, *Mapping the American Revolutionary War* (1978); Philip L. Phillips, *Notes on the Life and Works of Bernard Romans* (1924); Bernard Romans, *A Concise Natural History of East and West Florida* (1775).

Ross, Betsy (1752–1836)

American Patriot. In her own right, Betsy Ross was a woman of personal fortitude, intelligence, and courage who faced a long life of adversity with a strong, positive attitude. By legend, she is credited with the honor of sewing together the first version of the Stars and Stripes, the national flag of the United States.

Elizabeth Griscom was born on January 1, 1752, to Quaker parents, Samuel and Rebecca, in Philadelphia. Samuel Griscom was a skilled and renowned builder who helped to construct Carpenters' Hall, which still stands on Chestnut Street in Philadelphia, and he assisted in the erection of the Pennsylvania State House, a building now known as Independence Hall. Today Samuel Griscom's name is listed on a document hanging on a wall inside Carpenters' Hall as having been a member in good standing of the Carpenters' Company. Her mother, Rebecca, was the sister of Able James, who, with the Drinker family, formed the prominent Quaker mercantile firm of James and Drinker.

Eighth of the seventeen Griscom children, Elizabeth, or Betsy, attended the Friends School on South Fourth Street and learned to do fine needlework, a valuable skill in colonial times. She was later apprenticed to the William Webster Upholstery Shop to learn the upholstery trade.

Webster's was the leading upholstery shop in the city. Webster himself made a small fortune on the side by developing a special lotion that colonials could rub on their bodies, especially any exposed portions, to protect themselves from the numerous flies and other insects that pestered and plagued Philadelphians. There were no screens for doors or windows in those days. Tradition had it that Webster's potion was so effective that all living creatures avoided those who fearlessly sprinkled themselves with it.

In any event, it was at Webster's that Betsy first met another apprentice, John Ross. An attraction developed, although John Ross's father was the Reverend Aeneas Ross of New Castle, Delaware, who was then serving as the assistant rector at Christ Episcopal Church in Philadelphia. The romance did not please the Griscoms, who were staunch Quakers, nor did it please the Friends Meeting that Betsy and her family attended.

In the end, love won out over all obstacles. After a wait of more than three years, until both were of proper age (21), Betsy and John took the ferry across the Delaware River and were married by the justice of peace, James Bowman, at Gloucester, New Jersey, on November 4, 1773, against the wishes of the Griscoms. At this time in Philadelphia, young people wishing to elope used the convenient services of this Jersey justice, who willingly obliged them with the power of his office. Returning to Philadelphia, John and Betsy Ross opened an upholstery shop somewhere along Arch Street between Second and Third streets. In May 1774, the Quakers formally read Betsy Griscom (Ross) out of the Meeting for her marriage outside the faith.

Following the religious beliefs of her husband, Betsy began attending Christ Church close to their home. Her pew was number 12 on the far left by the windows and a pillar (as one faces the altar). The Ross couple, without children, operated their business for three years, and they enjoyed a growing mutual love and respect for each other as time passed. But the world then intruded upon their personal young lives. The War of Revolution began and John was called to service with the Philadelphia Associators, the city militia.

As part of his military duties, one cold night in January 1776, John Ross was walking guard on a wharf, which contained a storehouse for munitions, along the Delaware River, when some accident caused a quantity of gunpowder to explode, mortally wounding Betsy's husband. John was brought back to his Arch Street home, but Betsy could do nothing to save his life. He died that night, January 21, 1776. Betsy at 24 years of age was a widow. Whatever the sorrow she bore, she did, however, possess the courage to continue on alone in conducting her upholstery business.

During this time, in 1776 and 1777, she made flags for the Pennsylvania navy, for there is documentary evidence to support that activity. So her business included upholstery and sewing contracts in her attempt to support herself. For example, on May 29, 1777, Betsy Ross was paid 14 pounds, 12 shillings and 2 pence for the flags she made for the state navy. She was one of at least three women to perform this service for Pennsylvania.

On June 14, 1777, the Continental Congress adopted a resolution that created the new national flag by stating that "the flag of the United States be thirteen stripes alternate red and white; that the union be thirteen stars white in a blue field, representing a new constellation." The very next day, Betsy Ross married her second husband, Joseph Ashburn, at Old Swedes Church in Wicaco in the Southwark District of Philadelphia. Ashburn was a sea officer and served on the brigantine *Patty*. This marriage resulted in the birth of two daughters. Betsy continued her business and lived on Arch Street as before with her husband.

Three years into their marriage, Joseph Ashburn sailed out of Philadelphia on the *Patty* and was never heard from again. After two long years of waiting, a mutual friend who had known both Betsy and her husband for years, arrived in Philadelphia to inform Betsy that the British had captured her husband's ship on the high seas. According to this friend, Ashburn had been put into the Old Mill Prison, Plymouth, England, where the friend, John Claypoole, had also been a prisoner. After two years of captivity, Ashburn died in British hands on March 3, 1782.

John Claypoole had been a soldier in Washington's army and had somehow managed to get himself imprisoned in England. Back in Philadelphia, he wasted little time in courting Betsy and eventually married her on May 8, 1783, little more than a year after Ashburn's death. Married for the third time in seven years, Betsy and John Claypoole had five daughters before Claypoole's health failed.

For the last 17 years of his life, John was bedridden, with Betsy left caring for him, along with her children and her business. Claypoole had been wounded in the Battle of Germantown in 1777 and had suffered in prison under the British. In the end, his constitution faltered under this collective strain. He lingered on until he died on August 3, 1817.

Betsy never did close her business. For over 50 years she offered her upholstery and sewing services to the residents of Philadelphia. Some of her customers included Benjamin Franklin, the Society of Free Quakers, and the state government as it refurnished the state house. She moved her business from Arch Street to Front Street. She raised her daughters who helped her in the business and later cared for her when she became too old to work.

John Claypoole and Betsy Ross had both been Quakers who had been read out of their Meetings. Betsy had married out of her faith, and John had served in the American army and broke the Quakers' belief in the peaceful life. When the Society of Free Quakers was formed toward the end of the war, both Betsy and John joined. This group wished to retain many of the Quaker teachings but had decided to support the American war effort in violation of traditional Quaker philosophy.

A meetinghouse was built in 1783 at Fifth and Market streets. The building still stands today, although it was moved west 55 feet when Fifth Street was widened in the twentieth century. The Meeting grew to about 200 members and used the building from 1783 until 1834. As Mrs. Claypoole, Betsy worshipped here, but after the war, the division between the different factions of Quakers ended, and gradually, the Free Quakers disappeared. Betsy was one of the last two members to leave, the other being the founder, Samuel Wetherill, a local chemist and druggist.

Betsy finally retired from her work in 1827 at 75 years of age due mainly to failing eyesight. She lived out the rest of her life with one or another of her daughters until January 30, 1836, when she died in peace at 84 years of age at the Canby House on Cherry Street.

She was buried in the Free Quaker Graveyard on South Fifth Street. In 1857, city officials dug up the casket and moved it to Mount Moriah Cemetery, where she rested until the bicentennial. At that point the casket was unearthed again. She was brought to Arch Street and buried with John Claypoole in the Garden Court of the Betsy Ross House at 239 Arch Street. This is where she rests today.

The legend of Betsy Ross making the first flag did not begin until 1870, when Betsy Ross's grandson, William J. Canby, read a paper at the Historical Society of Pennsylvania in which he claimed that 35 years before, his grandmother, Betsy Ross, on her deathbed, stated that she had made the first flag. He was eleven years old at the time. But to support the claim, Canby brought affidavits from three family members who all testified that they had heard Betsy make the statement. During that time of celebration over the country's one hundredth anniversary, the Betsy Ross story quickly became a popular one that many people believed, with or without proof. There is no documentary evidence to support the tradition that Betsy's family held secret until 1870.

Today historians generally agree that the Betsy Ross story is more legendary than historic. However, over the years there has been much heat generated as to whether the poor seamstress really did sew the first flag. Both sides come well prepared to argue their case. The debate still continues.

Briefly, Betsy did make flags and continued to do so for years. It was claimed that a secret committee of Congress came to her in May or June 1776 at her house. It was composed of Robert Morris, George Washington, and George Ross. Washington drew out the pattern for the flag in her back room, and Betsy showed Washington how to make a neater and better looking star with five instead of six points with the folding of a piece of cloth and one snip of the scissors. She then proceeded to make the flag with five-pointed stars. The story as told does not mention Francis Hopkinson, who had some role in designing the first flag, although how much no one can tell at this point. He billed Congress for his work. They refused to pay because they claimed too many people had a hand in the evolution of the final product.

George Ross was the uncle of John Ross. So he knew his nephew, recently killed, and perhaps took pity on his widowed in-law and wished to bring some business her way. Betsy and George Ross certainly knew each other. If George was on the original secret committee, he could surely have turned to a relative by marriage rather than someone else to do the sewing. Robert Morris and George Washington were good friends, even in 1776. It is possible they could have served together on the flag committee. Once again, there are no records or documents to support these suppositions.

Congress on June 14, 1777, created the flag by resolution. Why would a committee come to her one year earlier? Washington was in Philadelphia in the spring of 1776. It was the first time he had left his army since his appointment to command. He was in the capital to meet with Congress on military matters. Did he meet with Betsy Ross at that time? Did Congress argue over the flag design for a year? The answers to these questions depend upon evidence not everyone could agree upon.

After the war, Betsy supposedly did meet Washington and explained the five-point star trick, the results of which she gave to Samuel Wetherill, who put it into his safe, which was not opened until 1922 when the object was found. Is it possible that Betsy did sew the prototype for Congress sometime in 1777 and got the years mixed up in her old age as death approached? It is possible but no one knows for sure.

Even the house was not spared argument and bitter debate. Some people claim Betsy never lived at 239 Arch Street. Others claim she did. A taproom operator owned a tavern at 239 Arch Street during the 1870s. At the height of the centennial celebrations, he began claiming his establishment was the Betsy Ross House. The sign out front said "the old flag house" and many people believed it so. We only know she lived nearby, but in which house, no one is certain.

In any event, the Betsy Ross Memorial Association was formed to preserve both the memory and the house. Two million memberships were sold including many to school children at 10 cents apiece to purchase the house that was in danger of being torn down. In 1892, the association raised 1,040,270 dimes to help buy the house. But there were charges of graft leveled against the association, and in the end, the house was purchased by the city. Opened as a tourist site, it ranks second only to the Liberty Bell in total number of visitors annually. The house has been faithfully restored by Atwater Kent as a colonial home similar to the one that Betsy would have owned.

Someone sewed the first flag for Congress. One appeared at the Battle of Bennington in August 1777 but with a different configuration of stars. Some historians believe that the circular configuration of stars did appear for the first time at the Battle of Cooche's Bridge in Delaware during the Pennsylvania campaign of 1777. No one has come forward to claim the honor nor has any conclusive evidence appeared to clarify the mystery. Until the final verdict comes in, it seems a harmless enough story to accept, and it does draw attention to a very real woman who lived a long and full life, possessing a personal style we can all respect. *See also:* Flag, the American

Paul J. Sanborn

REFERENCES

Sally Smith Booth, *The Women of '76* (1976); *DAB*; Kenneth Finkel, "The Myth of Betsy Ross Grows and Grows," *The Philadelphia Inquirer*, December 2, 1985, editorial page; Theodore Gottlieb, *The Origin and the Evolution of the Betsy Ross Flag Legend or Tradition* (1938); John W. Jackson, *The Pennsylvania Navy, 1775–1781*; William C. Miller, "The Betsy Ross Legend," *The Social Studies*, 37 (1946); Robert Wilson, *Philadelphia Quakers, 1681–1981* (1981); Edwin S. Parry, *Betsy Ross, Quaker Rebel* (1930).

Ross, George (1730–1779)

American statesman. A noted Pennsylvania jurist and signer of the Declaration of Independence, George Ross was born on May 10, 1730, in New Castle, Delaware. After receiving a classical education, Ross established a law practice in Lancaster, Pennsylvania, in 1750. During the next year, he married one of his clients, Ann Lawler. Ross developed a reputation as an effective attorney, an expert on Indian affairs, and an advocate for the Pennsylvania Assembly in its frequent conflicts with the colony's governors. In 1768 Ross was elected to the Assembly.

In 1774, while recognized as a Tory, Ross was elected to the First Continental Congress. During the next year Ross became affiliated with the Patriot cause; in 1775, Ross was elected to the Second Continental Congress and became a relentless contributor to the independence movement. In 1776, Ross signed the Declaration of Independence, negotiated a treaty with the Indians who occupied northwestern Pennsylvania, and served as vice president of the Pennsylvania Constitutional Convention. Shortly thereafter, Ross became ill and had to withdraw from political activities. In 1779, while serving as a jurist on the Pennsylvania Admirality Court, Ross heard the case of the *Active* sloop and the entitlements associated with its cargo. Ross determined that those who seized it were entitled only to one-fourth of the yield; Ross based his decision on the primacy of law. A congressional committee reversed his decision; Ross responded that Congress did not possess the authority to intervene in a state court decision. For the next three decades, this issue was a point of contention between the Congress and Pennsylvania. Ross died suddenly on July 19, 1779, in Philadelphia.

William T. Walker

REFERENCES

H.P. Read, *Rossiana* (1908); *Historical Papers and Addresses of the Lancaster County Historical Society*, I (1897); *Minutes of the Provincial Council of Pennsylvania* (1852–53).

Ross, John (1762–1789)

British army officer. Ross was a lieutenant in the 34th Foot. During the French and Indian War he served at Havana, West Florida, and on the lower Mississippi, where he mapped a route. Made a captain in 1772, Ross was stationed with his regiment in Canada. The scope of his duty for the next eight years is uncertain.

In 1780 Ross recruited a battalion for the King's Royal Regiment. The unit built a fortress near Montreal and then in November 1780 occupied Carleton Island (New York). In 1781 Ross led regulars and Indians from Fort Niagara to raid the Mohawk Valley. Encountering a superior American force at Johnstown, Ross retreated. By April 15, 1782, Ross was engaged in fortifying Oswego, where he was promoted to major.

His next major task came in July 1783, when he was ordered to Ontario to assist Loyalist refugees. The founder of Kingston, Ontario, Ross built shelters, mills, a fortress, and a naval yard. In July 1784 he was appointed a magistrate so that he could adjudicate land claims of the settlers. Ross visited England in 1784 and in 1787.

Richard L. Blanco

REFERENCES

E.A. Cruikshank, "The King's Royal Regiment of New York," *Ontario History*, 27 (1931):193–324; *DCB*; Barbara Graymont, *The Iroquois in the American Revolution* (1974).

Royal-Deux-Ponts

The origins of the Regiments Royal-Deux-Ponts date back to the year 1751, when on March 30, Duke Christian IV of Zweibrucken (1722/35–1775), ruler of over approximately 2,477 square kilometers in southwestern Germany, including 495 square kilometers in the Alsace, and some 80,000 subjects, concluded a treaty with Louis XV of France (1710/1715–1774). Zweibrucken promised to raise and field a battalion of 1,000 infantrymen when and if needed by France in return for about 40,000 guilders annually in subsidies. The cost for the establishment and maintenance of this battalion, which was not to be used against the Holy Roman Empire and its allies on the part of France or against France and her allies when employed by the Duke of Zweibrucken, was to be covered by France.

Just before the outbreak of the Seven Years' War, Duke Christian IV bound himself in a treaty of April 7, 1756, to raise a complete regiment of infantry. Recruiting started in October 1756, when, in a patent of October 5, 1756, Christian advertised for soldiers willing to serve for a period of 4 years or 8 years. They had to have a minimum height of 167 centimeters and be between 17 and 30 years old. Originally only volunteers were accepted, but by the fall of 1758, all (in the language of the times) superfluous, useless, or unemployed subjects were put in the regiment, as well as vagrants and petty criminals sentenced to military service.

The agreement establishing the regiment as a "Royal" regiment, thus denoting it as a regiment composed of foreigners, with Duke Christian as *Colonel Proprietaire*, was signed on February 19, 1757. The practice of hiring foreign troops was common in the French army: the establishment of Royal-Deux-Ponts brought the French line to 112 regiments of infantry, 9 of which were Swiss, 8 German, 3 Irish, and 2 Italian. In wartime, Royal-Deux-Ponts was to consist of 3 battalions of 6 companies each, 4 companies of fusiliers at 116 men each, 1 company of grenadiers (with the first battalion), and one company of chasseurs (with the second battalion) with 101 men each, for a total of 1,998 men. Each company was divided into two platoons or four sections. Noncommissioned officers, line officers, staff, and supply personnel brought the strength of the regiment to 2,430 men.

On April 1, 1757, Royal-Deux-Ponts entered French pay, and on May 15 it left Strassburg under its colonel Baron Christian Karl Wilhelm von Closen (1717–1764) to join forces with the French and Imperial armies in Bohemia. On November 5, 1757, it participated rather ingloriously in the Battle of Rossbach. The rest of the Seven Years' War was spent in Hesse, where the regiment took part in the Battles of Bergen in 1759 and Billingshausen in 1760. Briefly augmented to 4 battalions between May 25, 1758, and January 18, 1760, it was reduced to two battalions on December 21, 1762, and returned to

Zweibrucken in the spring of 1763, where it remained until the end of 1765.

The next years were spent in the garrisons of Strassburg, Schlettstadt, Sedan, Metz, and Compiegne. After the death of Christian IV in November 1775, but also as a consequence of the French army reforms of 1776, which assigned Royal-Deux-Ponts the number 104 in the French line, Christian's successor Charles II (1775–1795) negotiated a new agreement with France concerning his regiment. Signed on March 31, 1776, this treaty is noteworthy for the fact that it clearly outlined the composition of the regiment: three-quarters of all soldiers and officers were to be recruited from the territories of the duke and one-quarter from those territories of the King of France where German was spoken.

When, in the fall of 1779, France decided to send an expeditionary force of 5,500 men under the command of General Rochambeau to aid the United States, one of the regiments chosen to go with him was the Regiment Royal-Deux-Ponts. On April 4, 1780, orders to embark were given in the harbor of Brest, and on April 6, the expeditionary force, some 5,088 men strong, left port in a convoy of 12 men-of-war and 33 transports.

The company of grenadiers (von Fuerstenwarther) was quartered on the *Eveille*, half of the company von Sundahl and the companies von Flad and von Flock (chasseurs) crossed the Atlantic on the *Comtesse de Noailles*, the companies von Wisch, Thuilliere, and von Stack on the *Venus*, the companies Hainault, Cabannes, and the other half of the company von Sundahl on the *Loire*, and the company Ruehle von Lilienstern on the *Eureil*. At departure, the regiment numbered some 63 officers, 1,150 men, with 6 wives and 3 children. Newly recruited personnel as well as a number of noncommissioned officers and officers, altogether some 200 men, were left behind in Europe. Brothers Graf Christian (1752–1817) and Wilhelm von Forbach (1754–1807), illegitimate children of Duke Christian IV and the dancer Marie Anna Fontevieux, served as colonel and lieutenant colonel, respectively.

After a trans-Atlantic crossing of 70 days, the fleet arrived at Newport on July 11. Given the crowded lodgings and the abominable food, it is surprising that the regiment lost only 9 men during the crossing, but some 450 men were stricken with scurvy and were rather weak at their arrival. Between July 12 and July 15, 1780, the French debarked and took up positions around Newport. The months of August to October 1780 were spent in fortifying the French camp and in mock battles and training exercises, and on November 1, the troops went into winter quarters, where they stayed until May 1781.

The only action worth mentioning between July 1780 and the summer of 1781 occurred in March 1781. On March 6, 1781, the chasseurs of Royal-Deux-Ponts and Saintogne, the grenadiers of Bourbonnais and Soissonais, as well as 150 select men of each regiment, some 1,000 men under the Baron de Viomenil, received orders to embark for Virginia. Their orders were to capture the traitor Benedict Arnold and his troops in Richmond and to relieve the pressure on General Nathanael Greene in the Carolinas. To achieve this goal, the French forces were to join up with an American corps of 1,200 men under the Marquis de Lafayette near Hampton Road, Virginia. The plan came to naught when an English fleet engaged the French forces on March 16 and forced Viomenil to withdraw. On March 26, the French were back in Newport, while Lafayette marched on to Annapolis, from where he later joined the forces of Generals Nathanael Green and Friedrich von Steuben in Virginia.

In June 1781, the decisive campaign of the Revolutionary War got under way, when on June 10, 1781, Royal-Deux-Ponts as the 2nd brigade and Bourbonnais as the 1st brigade, forming the 1st division of the French army under the command of Baron de Viomenil, left Newport for Providence. Soissonais and Saintogne as the 3rd and 4th brigade formed the 2nd division. The march took place in parallel lines or columns for an average of 12 to 15 miles per day. While marching through Pennsylvania with its large German population, many of which had emigrated from the recruiting area of the Royal-Deux-Ponts regiment, strong efforts to prevent desertions were of prime importance. By June 25, three men of Royal-Deux-Ponts had deserted, by July 6, three more were gone. They were brought back, tried, and executed. These draconian measures kept desertions down.

On July 4, 1781, the French joined Washington's army near White Plains, New York, and went into camp. On July 21, however, camp was broken and the march to Virginia began. On September 7, the regiment reached Head of Elk.

Here the elite grenadiers and chasseurs embarked for Williamsburg on September 9, where they arrived on September 23. The rest of the army marched on to Baltimore, where it embarked and reached Williamsburg on September 26. During the ensuing siege of Yorktown the regiment had its hour of glory on October 14, when the grenadier and chasseur companies of Royal-Deux-Ponts and Gatinais, some 400 men under the command of Colonel William von Forbach, stormed Redoubt #9. After the surrender of Lord Cornwallis, Wilhelm von Forbach was chosen to bring the news of the victory to France. He left the United States for France on the *Andromaque* on November 1, 1781, with the articles of capitulation.

The regiment itself spent the winter of 1781–1782 in Virginia and marched back to New England in July 1782. On December 21, 1782, the French forces embarked at Boston for the West Indies; the grenadiers, chasseurs and the first company of fusiliers sailed on the *Le Brave*, the rest of Royal-Deux-Ponts on the *L'Isle de France*. On February 1, 1783, the regiment reached Portò Caballo, from there it went on to Curacao and back to Cuba. Having lost only some 50 officers and men in casualties, Royal-Deux-Ponts finally left for Europe in April 1783 and arrived in Brest on June 17, 1783. On June 21, 1783, Royal-Deux-Ponts began its march back to Landau in the Palatinate, where it was stationed from 1783 to October 1785. From there it went to Pfalzburg, Metz, and Huningen. In March 1788, while stationed in Neubreisach, the regiment was assigned the number 102 in the French line.

Still in Neubreisach, it became entangled in the events of the French Revolution. On January 1, 1791, the regiment, stationed in Verdun by now, was renamed the 99th Regiment of Infantry. When Christian von Forbach, in response to this decision, laid down his command on March 16, 1791, most of the officers and men of the regiment followed his example and left the service of France. In June 1791, Royal-Deux-Ponts was one of the six regiments, four German and two Swiss, chosen to cover the ill-fated flight of Louis XVI to Varennes. Subsequently, on July 21, 1791, the French National Assembly abolished all differences within the military between regiments foreign and French, and integrated Royal-Deux-Ponts into the new army. The history of the regiment as a regiment of Germans in the service of France officially came to an end with the decree of Emperor Francis II of December 19, 1792, in which he ordered all Germans serving in France to leave the services of the republic or be considered enemies of the empire.

Robert A. Selig

REFERENCES

William de Deux-Ponts, *My Campaigns in America,* ed. by Samuel Abbott Green (1868); Ernst Drumm, "Das Regiment Royal-Deux-Ponts," *Mitteilungen des historischen Vereins fur die Westpfalz in Zweibrucken,* 8 (1936):1–35; Howard C. Rice, Jr., and Ann S.K. Brown, eds., *The American Campaigns of Rochambeau's Army 1780, 1781, 1782, 1783,* 2 vols. (1972); Rudolf Karl Tross, *Das Regiment Royal-Deux-Ponts* (1983); Pfalzgalerie Kaiserslautern, *Die Beteiligung des Regiment Royal-Deux-Ponts am Amerikanischen Unabhangigkeitskrieg* (1976).

Royal Dockyards

The six dockyards in England constituted the largest industrial organization in the land. The oldest established were Deptford and Woolwich on the Thames. Chatham was founded in Elizabethan times and grew to meet the seventeenth-century Dutch threat; a subsidiary yard at the mouth of the Medway, Sheerness, was built at this time. The most important, however, were the "Western" Yards of Portsmouth and Plymouth. There had been a King's dock at Portsmouth in medieval times, but the rise of the French navy of Louis XIV and the Anglo-French wars of the eighteenth century meant that the center of effort shifted to these two yards. Portsmouth was the largest in size and number of personnel, but it was soon to be overtaken by Plymouth (Plymouth Dock was renamed Devonport in 1824). In addition, there were three foreign yards, Jamaica and Antigua in the West Indies and Halifax in Nova Scotia, which were of importance in this war.

Each of the larger yards had a Resident Commissioner, who was a member of the Navy Board in London. All were naval captains who had come ashore, though in this war two went to sea again, James Gambier at Portsmouth (September 1773–January 1778) and Samuel Hood (January 1778–November 1780). They were respectively the least and most effective commissioners of the period.

Each of the home yards had five principal officers. Of greatest importance was the Master Shipwright, responsible for building and repairing, who controlled most of the work force. He had to work very closely with the Master Attendant (at the large yards there were two), who was responsible for ships afloat and for docking and undocking. The Storekeeper, the Clerk of the Cheque, and the Clerk of the Survey were the accounting officers. They oversaw a varied work force. The shipwrights were the most important and numerous workers (maximum was reached in early 1782 for all the yards at 3,359), but there were also caulkers, joiners, sailmakers, blockmakers, sawyers, smiths, riggers, as well as more spinners and hatchellors. The maximum number in the six dockyards, again reached in early 1782, was 9,477.

Once war had started, the dockyards built very few ships. Only 190 gunships were built exclusively in royal yards. Most of the 74 gunships and other rates were built at private yards based mainly on the Thames, Medway, the Essex rivers, and the Solent. This administration spread the building farther away from the southeast. Portsmouth and Plymouth undertook most of the refitting and maintenance, while the less well placed yards concentrated on the longer tasks of repairs. A major part of the work of Deptford and Woolwich was the inspection and fitting out of transports.

Twice during the American war did the dockyards spring into prominence. The first was during the strike of 1775. Lord Sandwich attempted to increase efficiency by the introduction of task work (payment by results) rather than the traditional day pay. Although some trades adapted successfully, the shipwrights would not accept the new way of working. All the yards, except Deptford, went on strike and the administration backed down. It was not finally introduced into all the yards until 1788. The other major incident was the successful burning of the Portsmouth ropery in December 1776 by John Aitken, or Jack the Painter, for which he was hung.

In spite of these difficulties, the dockyards constituted a formidable part of the war machine. As with other parts of naval administration, they have long been labeled as corrupt. Nevertheless, judged in eighteenth-century terms, they worked well. The buildings and docks constantly expanded through war and peace. Sandwich's efforts to build up naval stores in the early 1770s paid off, and there were no shortages of consequence, in spite of the hostility of the Baltic powers and the cutting off of American timber for masts. The fleet was very rapidly given copper sheathing between 1779 and 1781. It reached a peak in 1782, a factor that, more than any other, led to partial recovery in the West Indies and India and brought France to the peace table.

R.J.B. Knight

REFERENCES

Jonathan G. Goad, *The Royal Dockyards, 1690–1850; Architecture and Engineering Works of the Sailing Navy* (1989); R.J.B. Knight, "New England Forests and British Seapower: Albion revised," *The American Neptune* (1986):221–229; ———, "Pilfering and Theft from the Dockyards at the Time of the American War of Independence, *Mariner's Mirror*, 61 (1975):215–225; ———, *Portsmouth Dockyard Papers, 1774–1783: The American War* (1986); Piers Mackesy, *The War for America, 1775–1783* (1984); David Syrett, *Shipping and the American War 1775–83; a Study of the British Transport Organization* (1970).

Royal Greens

The Royal Greens was one of the three major Loyalist forces involved in the border warfare in upper New York (the others being Butler's Rangers and Joseph Brant's Iroquois). Sir John Johnson, son and heir of the "Mohawk baronet" William Johnson, raised this regiment from among the Loyalist refugees in Canada during the summer of 1777. Many had been his tenants and neighbors in the Mohawk Valley. However, Johnson was often occupied with the resettlement of the Iroquois in Canada, and so he rarely took part in his regiment's actions. The Greens were often under Colonel John Butler's command.

The Greens (then numbering 133 men in two battalions) participated in Colonel Barry St. Leger's expedition, and one battalion was at Oriskany (August 6, 1777). The regiment accompanied Butler on the Wyoming Valley raid in July 1778, and it aided in his attempts to halt the Sullivan-Clinton expedition in the summer of 1779. The Greens fought bravely at Newtown on August 29. In 1780, Johnson personally led the Greens on two successful raids into the Mohawk Valley in May and August. Their last action was the October 1780 expedition through the Schoharie Valley, which ended in the rout at Klock's Field. It is not known when the regiment was formally disbanded.

Tom Martin

REFERENCES

Isabel Thompson Kelsay, *Joseph Brant, 1743–1807: Man of Two Worlds* (1984); Howard Swiggett, *War Out of Niagara: Walter Butler and the Tory Rangers* (1933).

Royal Highland Emigrants

Lieutenant Colonel Allen MacLean arrived in New York from England about May 1775 with government permission to raise a provincial corps composed of Highland emigrants settled in America. He reported to General Thomas Gage in Boston, who issued an order dated June 12, 1775, authorizing the formation of the unit. The regiment was to consist of two battalions of ten companies each based on the British model of eight battalion companies, and one each of grenadiers and light infantry per battalion.

MacLean returned to New York, gathered men from that state, and moved them north to Canada. Meanwhile, Major John Small remained in Boston to coordinate recruiting efforts in the Maritime Provinces and the Carolinas. By late 1776, nine companies of the 1st Battalion had been formed and were operating in Canada under MacLean. Meanwhile, seven companies of the 2nd Battalion were in Halifax and officers for the other three were in the Carolinas recruiting. By January 1777, the 2nd Battalion was together in Halifax.

After General Howe had assumed command of the army late in 1775, he had separated the 2nd Battalion, also known as the Young Royal Highland Emigrants, from the Canadian command. From that time forward the battalion functioned as a separate entity with Major Small coming under Howe's orders.

On December 25, 1778, the regiment was added to the regular British establishment as the 84th Foot, retaining its two-battalion organization. Sir Henry Clinton became colonel of the regiment, and he was followed in 1783 by Sir Guy Carleton. MacLean became lieutenant colonel commandant of the 1st Battalion, while Small was named major commandant of the 2nd. Later, on December 6, 1780, both battalions were put on the same footing when Small was raised to lieutenant colonel commandant of the 2nd Battalion.

The most prominent service of the 1st Battalion occurred during the American invasion of Canada in 1775–1776. At that time, MacLean and about 200 of his men distinguished themselves at the defense of Quebec City during the rebel siege. Throughout the remainder of the war the 1st Battalion maintained a fairly constant strength of approximately 500 men. However, they saw little active service aside from garrison duty at various Canadian posts from Sorel to Michilimackinac. Two exceptions were Major Christopher Carleton's expedition to destroy rebel outposts in New York, in September–October 1780, to which 57 Emigrants were assigned; and Ross's expedition to the Mohawk Valley in October 1781, in which 36 Highlanders participated. Although ordered disbanded on August 9, 1783, the 1st Battalion was not reduced until June 1784.

Being under the orders of Sir William Howe and his successors, the services of the 2nd Battalion were far different from those of the 1st. When it became known that the Emigrants were being established, the light company was ordered from Halifax to join the main army in New York. It reached Colonel Henry Clinton's army north of New York City and was attached to the 2nd Light Infantry Battalion about the time that Wayne captured Stony Point, July 16, 1779.

The remaining companies of the battalion did garrison duty in the Maritime Provinces, maintaining a strength of between 400 and 500 men. Meanwhile, Major Small had gone to New York to recruit, and by February 1780 had raised 188 men. He also attempted to have the nine companies in the Halifax area reduced to five so that he could form four new ones locally. Small was seemingly unsuccessful with his efforts in regard to the Halifax companies, but went ahead and formed one additional company with some supernumeraries in New York.

Small and his men, including the light company, were sent with General Alexander Leslie's expedition, which sailed for Portsmouth, Virginia, on October 16, 1780. From there they were ordered to Charleston, South Carolina, which they reached on December 16. The 84th went on to take part in field operations in the Charleston area and had a detachment of 87 men participate in the Battle of Eutaw Springs on September 8, 1781.

By the time of the evacuation of Charleston in December 1782, Small's men numbered 110

formed into 2 companies. They were sent to Jamaica in the West Indies and did not return to Halifax until October 5, 1783. The entire 2nd Battalion was disbanded there five days later.

Much is known of the dress of this regiment. In the early days the 1st Battalion wore green coats with scarlet facings, collar, and cuffs, buff vests and breeches, and tri-corner hats. In 1777 it finally received its Highland dress of red coats with blue facings, collar and cuffs, bonnets, hose, and "the half plaid" to make a kilt. The 2nd Battalion had received its Highland clothing in 1776. Uniform buttons had designations for both the Royal Highland Emigrants and the 84th Foot.

Walter T. Dornfest

REFERENCES

Rene Chartrand, "Notes on the Dress of the Royal Highland Emigrants, 1775–1784," *Military Collector & Historian*, 38 (1986):76–77; Mary B. Fryer, *King's Men* (1980); Alexander McDonald, "Letter-Book of Captain Alexander McDonald of the Royal Highland Emigrants, 1775–1779," *Collections of the New-York Historical Society for the Year 1882* (1883):203–498; Christopher Ward, *War of the Revolution*, 2 vols. (1952), ed. by John R. Alden.

Royal Navy Board

The Navy Board, or "the Principal Officers and Commissioners of the Navy" was the core of the administration of the Royal Navy; it was subordinate to the Board of Admiralty, but in practice could exercise a good deal of independence. It was responsible for the building, equipping, fitting out, and repairing of the King's ships; to do this it administered the Royal Dockyards at home and abroad and supervised the contracts let to the shipbuilders of the Thames, Medway, and the South Coast, who built the majority of ships for the navy in this war. Civilian officials at ports such as Deal and Harwich who issued stores to King's ships at ports where there was no dockyard also worked for the Board. It governed the vessels employed in the Impress service and appointed pursers, gunners, and carpenters. It contracted for all naval stores and equipment, except ordnance, food, and medicines. The Board also hired, fitted out, and administered all shipping required to carry troops, naval stores, camp equipage, and certain other forms of army equipment and, after 1779, army provisions. It also prepared the naval estimates, directed the expenditure of most naval monies, audited and certified all naval accounts, and supervised the payment of ships' crews at Deptford and Woolwich dockyards and the payment of half-pay at the Navy Pay Office.

This substantial load was supported by the biggest office of state, the Navy Office; at its peak in this war the clerks in the office numbered over 100. It was situated in Crutched Friars in London some two miles from the Admiralty in Whitehall. This distance gave it its independence, as well as its seniority (its roots went back to the thirteenth century), but mainly because the Board consisted of naval officers, shipwrights, and professional bureaucrats, while the Board of Admiralty were politicians.

At its head was the Comptroller, which was filled first by Captain Maurice Suckling (April 1775–July 1778) and then Captain Charles Middleton (August 1778–March 1790, created Baronet October 1781). There were two Surveyors of the Navy during this period, Sir John Williams (June 1765–December 1784) and Edward Hunt (April 1778–December 1786). They had come up through the dockyards and were responsible for the design, building, refitting, and repair of all naval ships as well as buildings and slips. The other key figure was the Clerk of the Acts, George Marsh (July 1773–August 1796), who ran the paperwork and communications of the Board. In addition, there were those who "comptrolled" or balanced accounts; the Comptroller of Treasurers' Accounts, the Comptroller of Victualling Accounts, and the Comptroller of Storekeepers' Accounts. Three Extra Commissioners, with miscellaneous duties, were appointed during the period. Outside London the Resident Commissioners of Chatham, Portsmouth, and Plymouth dockyards were also members of the Board, as were the Commissioners of the dockyards of Jamaica, Antigua, and Halifax, Nova Scotia.

Until recently the historical reputation of the Navy Board has been poor, but reevaluations of the last 25 years have put its efforts in perspective. There is no doubt that Middleton galvanized the administration when the navy was under intense pressure and later laid the groundwork for a system that took the strain of a navy, which doubled in size during the Revolutionary and Napoleonic wars. The Board also achieved the remarkable feat of transporting and supporting the British army in North America.

Middleton also was at the center of the decision to equip the fleet with copper sheathing, and it was his board that masterminded the effort that gave Britain the hugely increased fleet, which reached its peak by 1782. His drive and ambition led to difficulties, in particular when he challenged the First Lord of the Admiralty, Lord Sandwich, over the right to make dockyard appointments. Nevertheless, in spite of the inefficiencies and slowness of communication that were endemic in the eighteenth century, and in spite of an office that its personnel had long outgrown (it moved to Somerset House in 1786), the Navy Board and its bureaucracy worked hard and improved its systems, during the long struggle between 1775 and 1783.

R.J.B. Knight

REFERENCES

J.M. Collinge, *Office-holders in Modern Britain, VII; Navy Board Officials, 1800–1832* (1978); R.J.B. Knight, *Portsmouth Dockyard in the American War of Independence: the Dockyard Records, 1774–1783* (1986); ———, "Sandwich, Middleton and Dockyard Appointments," *Mariner's Mirror*, 57 (1971):175–192; Piers Mackesy, *The War for America, 1775–1783* (1964); David Syrett, *Shipping and the American War, 1775–83; a Study of British Transport Organization* (1970).

Royal Provincial Troops

The American Loyalists and others in the ranks of the provincial forces supporting the Crown during the Revolution served in many types of military organizations. These units varied in the authority from which they emanated—their size, classification, and the duration of their service, with all factors usually governed by local circumstances. Loyalist militia units and associations, some of which made sacrifices equal to those of the Royal Provincial regulars, can be only briefly mentioned.

In order to understand the background for the authorization of the many diverse military bodies that were formed during the course of the war, the division of British command responsibility in the Americas must be briefly touched upon.

When General Thomas Gage became commander-in-chief of the British army in America after the French and Indian War, his responsibility stretched from Canada and Newfoundland to West Florida. The British West Indies did not come under Gage's authority, and during the Revolution, it consisted of two separate military commands based on Jamaica and the Lesser Antilles. Canada, renamed Quebec, also became a separate command under General Guy Carleton when Gage was officially replaced by General William Howe in April 1776.

While commander-in-chief in North America, Gage had to contend with various colonial governors who sometimes tried to impinge upon his military authority. While no serious problems arose in areas of close proximity to Gage's headquarters in New York, there were instances of conflicts between military and civilian authorities in the more distant areas. In the example of West Florida, Governor George Johnstone thought that he should control the regulars in his colony, but the senior military commander present felt obliged to obey Gage. The onset of the Revolution ended such debates and confirmed the Royal Warrant of 1760, which stated that in military matters the commander-in-chief came first and the royal governors second when in their own provinces.

During the Revolutionary War provincial military units were usually created by the area commander-in-chief, who could issue an order forming a corps to be counted on the provincial establishment within the boundaries of his authority. There were a few early instances of individuals receiving permission directly from the home government to raise units, such as Allen MacLean for the Royal Highland Emigrants, Francis Legge for the Loyal Nova Scotia Volunteers, and Joseph Gorham for the Royal Fencible Americans. But when these regiments had been formed, they too came under the control of the military commander in the area in which they operated.

Provincial governors exercised control over the militia in their jurisdictions and might also raise separate local corps under their own authority. This was the course followed by Governor Lord Dunmore of Virginia when rebellion broke out in his colony in 1775. He formed two units, which he called the Queen's Own Loyal Virginia Regiment and the Royal Ethiopian Regiment, consisting of about 300 Blacks. However, no governor had any guarantee that if he formed a unit and issued commissions, his organization would be recognized as being on the same establishment as those originating with the commander-in-chief. Dunmore's troops were, in fact, so decimated when they reached New York with him in July 1776 that they were absorbed into other corps or disbursed.

The earliest attempt to organize an armed force of Loyalists to curtail Patriot fervor had taken place in Massachusetts in the fall of 1774. Under the authority of Gage, Colonel Thomas Gilbert formed 300 armed men in Freetown to protect the King's friends. However, this association was of short duration as Gilbert was forced to flee due to rebel neighbors in April 1775. He ended up in Boston with his corps dissolved.

With the departure of Gage, Howe assumed what was supposed to be temporary command of the army on October 10, 1775. In an attempt to utilize the small group of militant Loyalists in Boston for some police and patrol duties, Howe approved three associated organizations late in 1775. These were the Royal North British Volunteers (one company) of Captain James Anderson in October, the Loyal American Associators (three companies) commanded by Brigadier General Timothy Ruggles in November, and the Loyal Irish Volunteers (one company) under Captain James Forrest in December. None lasted much past the evacuation of Boston.

When the British army returned to New York City in mid-1776, the only organized provincial troops to accompany Howe were the two New York Provincial companies he had organized at Halifax, the core of the soon to be formed New York Volunteers. However, once in New York, Howe was contacted by Robert Rogers, the famous ranger of the French and Indian War. He proposed to raise a provincial corps to carry out the same scouting tasks that his earlier unit had done so well for the British. Howe approved, and Rogers began recruiting for what was to become the most famous provincial regiment of the war, the Queen's Rangers.

At the beginning of the American conflict, Howe had very definite ideas about how the Loyalists should be utilized. Basing his opinion upon the army's experiences with the use of provincials during previous colonial conflicts, he was convinced that provincials were no substitute for British regulars. Howe was sure that their most useful functions would be as irregular raiders or as militia organized for interior defense. Any Loyalists who wanted to stand in the line of battle opposite the rebels could serve most usefully by enlisting in one of the regular regiments.

However, the government of London reached a different conclusion. Considering the number of leading Loyalists in the colonies and the fact that many had personal followings who might provide a pool of recruits, the Crown decided to create regular provincial regiments by a method known as "raising for rank." This practice was not favored by either the army or the King because of potential conflicts involving officers and benefits, but this course would move most of the costs of organizing the new units from the government to the individual raising the new corps. It was an attractive feature of the plan.

After receiving a warrant from the commander-in-chief, the potential colonel commandant of a new regular provincial regiment was expected to raise a unit consisting of 30 sergeants, 30 corporals, 10 drummers, and 500 privates divided into 10 companies. Each company was to consist of one captain, one lieutenant, one ensign, three sergeants, three corporals, one drummer, and fifty privates. The unit was to serve for two years or the duration of the war, and it was understood by the men that they would not be sent to the West Indies.

The granting of a commission by the commander-in-chief to an individual depended upon the success of that person in recruiting for the regiment. To become a captain, it was necessary to raise 30 men—a lieutenant, 15 recruits, an ensign, and 12 enlistees. The provincial officers were to receive the same pay as that of the regulars, but it would not commence until half of the required number of recruits had been enlisted. A major would not be commissioned until half of the regiment had been raised, a lieutenant colonel until 400 men had been recruited, and the colonel did not receive his commission until the entire unit was complete. Regarding the pay of the colonel commandant, he received compensation as a major from the date of the warrant until a major was appointed, then as a lieutenant colonel until all requirements had been met for the new unit.

To assist in the enlistment of noncommissioned officers and men, it was permitted to offer an official allowance of forty shillings or five dollars per man. However, this did not prevent abuses from creeping into the process in the sometimes cut-throat methods used by recruiters. Various tactics were tried by those raising regiments to keep other recruiters out of their supposed jurisdictions. And while some enlistees were later legitimately offered land for signing up, some of the new officers were given the promise of eventual half-pay and extensive tracts of land when it was simply not true.

After the British army captured Philadelphia at the end of 1777, Howe and his successor, General Sir Henry Clinton, were presented with the opportunity of raising additional regular provincial units. With new incentives enacted by the government late in 1778 and early 1779 to attract additional Loyalists to the colors, it was hoped that the ranks of the provincial regiments would grow. The revised benefits included a bounty of three guineas for each new recruit; a reward of one guinea for the capture of each deserter; and an annual allowance of forty pounds for each provincial regiment for hospital expenses, nurses, and an orderly room. These motivations were followed by an additional bounty of twenty-two shillings sixpence for each recruit; a special effort to attract the Europeans in the rebel army; and the offer of pardons to fugitives from justice wanted for crimes less serious than capital offenses.

It is difficult to classify many of the men attracted to the provincial service by the above benefits as Loyalists. Certainly many of them were favorably inclined toward the Crown, but others enlisted in the army that offered the most advantageous terms. The British were also in the habit of using the Provincial establishment as a catchall for units not easily assignable to the regular forces, for example, the Garrison Battalion composed of disabled British regulars and the Duke of Cumberlands's Regiment recruited from Continental army prisoners for service in the West Indies. A number of regular officers also served in provincial units to increase their efficiency and stiffen their resolve. It is estimated by one authority that, of the approximately 21,199 men who saw service in the provincial line, 19,000 were probably Loyalists.

A major problem and the source of much controversy was the seniority of provincial officers when serving with regulars. From the beginning of the war Howe had employed a policy that had functioned in a fairly satisfactory manner. Prior to 1779, when provincial officers were on the same service as regulars, the provincial officers were ranked as junior in the next grade below, as well as junior in their own rank. Thus a major of the regulars would command any provincial lieutenant colonel, and so forth through all ranks.

For their part, regular officers objected to the entire arrangement, arguing that in some circumstances it made them liable to the orders of possibly untrained provincial officers.

The situation grew more intolerable for the regular officers at the beginning of 1779. In order to make the provincial service more attractive, the King agreed to allow provincial officers to command as the youngest of their respective rank when on the same service as regular officers. A regular major would now command all provincial majors, but no longer the provincial lieutenant colonels. Again, this increased the possibility of provincial officers not sufficiently trained in military science commanding professional British officers. It also raised the possibility of regular officers in lower grades, transferred to the provincial line with senior provincial commissions, commanding regular officers to whom they would normally be junior. This condition was alleviated late in 1779 when the King ruled that no officer could hold both a regular commission and a provincial one simultaneously. Officers in this situation had to choose one and resign the other, but this regulation does not seem to have been strictly enforced.

In a final effort to improve the appeal of the provincial service, the King provided for the organization of an American Establishment. To be eligible for inclusion a provincial regiment had to be complete to the same number and proportion of officers and men as the current establishment of the regular regiments, and be recommended by the commander-in-chief as being properly officered and fit for service. The officers of such regiments received permanent rank in America, which allowed them half-pay upon the reduction of their regiments. This was the equivalent of what British officers were entitled to when their regiments were reduced.

When the British army departed from Nova Scotia for the attempted recovery of New York in 1776, four corps of provincial regulars were left behind by Howe to help secure that province. Unlike the majority of the provincial organizations yet to be formed in North America, these units were in large measure composed of men recruited in colonies not considered to be in rebellion against the Crown. They were the following:

- Hierlyhy's Independent Companies (five), raised by Major Timothy Hierlyhy, 1776–1782, maximum strength 212.

- Loyal Nova Scotia Volunteers, raised by Governor Francis Legge, 1775–1783, maximum strength 486.
- Royal Fencible Americans, raised by Lieutenant Colonel Joseph Gorham, 1775–1783, maximum strength 289.
- Royal Highland Emigrants, 2nd Battalion (84th Foot, December 28, 1778), raised by Colonel John Small, 1775–1784, maximum strength 500.

Upon the successful conclusion of the British campaign to capture New York, a number of prominent Loyalists came forward and expressed their desire to raise corps to aid in suppressing the rebellion. As a result, the following major units of provincial regulars approved by General Howe came into being in New York in the latter half of 1776 and of 1777.

- De Lancey's Brigade (three battalions) raised by Brigadier General Oliver De Lancey, 1776–1783, maximum strength 1,218.
- Emmerich's Chasseurs raised by Lieutenant Colonel Andreas Emmerich, 1776–1779, maximum strength 215.
- Guides & Pioneers, raised by Major Simon Frazer, 1776–1783, maximum strength 199.
- King's American Regiment (4th American Regiment), raised by Colonel Edmund Fanning, 1776–1783, maximum strength 588.
- King's Orange Rangers, raised by Lieutenant Colonel John Bayard, 1776–1783, maximum strength 362.
- Loyal American Regiment, raised by Colonel Beverley Robinson, 1776–1783, maximum strength 392.
- New Jersey Volunteers (six battalions), raised by Brigadier General Cortland Skinner, 1776–1783, maximum strength 1,972.
- New York Volunteers (3rd American Regiment), completed by Lieutenant Colonel George Turnbull, 1777–1783, maximum strength 364.
- Prince of Wales American Regiment, raised by Brigadier General Monteforte Brown, 1777–1783, maximum strength 499.
- Queen's Rangers (1st American Regiment), completed by Lieutenant Colonel John Graves Simcoe, 1775–1783, maximum strength 616.
- West Chester Refugees, completed by Lieutenant Colonel James Delancey, 1776–1783, maximum strength 500.

During the sojourn of the British army in Philadelphia, three troops of light dragoons were formed in addition to the following larger regular provincial corps:

- Caledonian Volunteers, raised by Colonel William Lord Cathcart, 1777–1778, maximum strength 151.
- Maryland Loyalists, raised by Lieutenant Colonel James Chalmers, 1777–1783, maximum strength 355.
- Pennsylvania Loyalists, raised by Lieutenant Colonel William Allen, 1777–1783, maximum strength 188.
- Roman Catholic Volunteers, raised by Lieutenant Colonel Alfred Clifton, 1777–1778, maximum strength 213.
- Volunteers of Ireland (2nd American Regiment; 105th Foot, March 21, 1782), raised by Colonel Francis Lord Rawdon, 1777–1783, maximum strength 632.
- West Jersey Volunteers, raise by Major John Vandyke, 1778, maximum strength 184.

The return of General Clinton's army to New York saw the creation in the North of several more important regiments of royal provincials between 1778 and the end of the war. These included the following:

- American Legion, raised by Brigadier General Benedict Arnold, 1780–1783, maximum strength 201.
- American Volunteers, raised by Major Patrick Ferguson, 1779–1780, maximum strength 200.
- British Legion (5th American Regiment), completed by Lieutenant Colonel Banastre Tarleton, 1778–1783, maximum strength 500.
- Corps of Foot in Newfoundland, raised by Lieutenant Colonel Robert Pringle, 1780–1783, maximum strength 300.
- Garrison Battalion (Royal Garrison Battalion), completed by Lieutenant Colonel Robert Donkin, 1778–1783, maximum strength 769.
- King's American Dragoons, raised by Lieutenant Colonel Benjamin Thompson, 1781–1783, maximum strength 290.
- Provincial Light Infantry Battalion, raised by Lieutenant Colonel John W.T. Watson, 1780–1781(?), maximum strength 194.

Major units of royal provincials raised in the South during the same period consisted of the following:

- Georgia Loyalists, raised by Major James Wright, 1779–1783; maximum strength 170.
- King's Rangers (a.k.a. Carolina Rangers, East Florida Rangers, or Florida Rangers), raised by Lieutenant Colonel Thomas Brown, 1779–1782, maximum strength 547.
- North Carolina Highlanders, raised by Governor Josiah Martin, 1780–1783, maximum strength 86.

- Royal North Carolina Regiment, raised by Lieutenant Colonel John Hamilton, 1780–1783, maximum strength 471.
- South Carolina Royalists, raised by Colonel Alexander Innes, 1778–1783, maximum strength 452.

During the course of the war, a number of corps were formed under the jurisdiction of Guy Carleton and his successor Frederick Haldimand in Quebec. The King's Rangers were authorized by Sir Henry Clinton in New York, but ended up recruiting in and operating from Quebec.

- Butler's Rangers, raised by Lieutenant Colonel John Butler, 1777–1784, maximum strength 500.
- King's Loyal Americans, raised by Lieutenant Colonel Ebenezer Jessup, 1777–1781, maximum strength 270.
- King's Rangers (three companies), raised by Lieutenant Colonel Robert Rogers under authority of Sir Henry Clinton, 1779–1783, maximum strength 213.
- King's Royal Regiment of New York (two battalions), raised by Lieutenant Colonel Sir John Johnson, 1st Battalion, 1777–1783, maximum strength 563; 2nd Battalion, 1780–1784, maximum strength 468.
- Loyal Rangers, raised by Major Edward Jessup, 1781–1783, maximum strength 543.
- Queen's Loyal Rangers, raised by Lieutenant Colonel John Peters, 1777–1781, maximum strength 311.
- Royal Highland Emigrants, 1st Battalion (84th Foot, December 28, 1778), raised by Colonel Allen MacLean, 1775–1784, maximum strength 500.

Several regiments of provincial regulars were raised for the defense of Jamaica and to help in offensive operations against the Spanish in the West Indies. Major units authorized by General John Dalling, Governor of Jamaica were the following:

- Duke of Cumberland's Regiment (two battalions), raised by Lieutenant Colonel Charles A. Lord Montague, 1st Battalion, 1781–1783, maximum strength 550; 2nd Battalion, 1782–1783, maximum strength 300 (composition: Continental Army prisoners recruited from prison ships at Charleston, South Carolina, to serve only in the West Indies).
- Jamaica Legion, raised by Major John Dalrymple, 1779–1780, maximum strength 213.

- Jamaica Rangers (three battalions), raised by Majors William H. Ricketts, William Lewis, and Nathaniel Beckford, 1782–1783(?), maximum strength unknown (composition: free people of color).
- Jamaica Volunteers, raised by Major John Macdonald, 1779–1781, maximum strength 258.
- Loyal American Rangers, raised by Major William Odell, 1780–1783, maximum strength 300 (composition: similar to the Duke of Cumberland's Regiment).
- Royal Batteaux Men, raised by Lieutenant Colonel Alexander Leith, 1779–1780(?), maximum strength 125.

While Sir William Howe commanded the army, his theory for the utilization of provincial regulars was generally practiced. The units were employed for ranging, skirmishing, and garrison duties, with little opportunity to stand beside regular regiments in pitched battles with the rebels. The same can be said for army operations under Burgoyne and the entire war conducted from the Northern Department and the West Indies.

The first real chance given provincial troops to perform in concert with regulars in a classic action was provided by Sir Henry Clinton during the assault on Forts Montgomery and Clinton in the Hudson Highlands on October 6, 1777. In the attack on Fort Montgomery, Emmerich's Chasseurs, the Loyal American Regiment, and the New York Volunteers formed in line with two regular British regiments and overwhelmed the rebel garrison.

Provincial regulars again stood in a line of battle against the rebels at the Battle of Rhode Island on August 29, 1778. That day, the King's American Regiment and the Prince of Wales American Regiment moved forward with British and Hessian regulars in an attempt to push the American army into Narragansett Bay. But the rebels successfully escaped to the mainland on the night of August 30–31.

However, it was when the focus of military operations moved to the southern colonies that provincial regulars were truly able to show their mettle when standing against veteran Continentals in open battle. The following chronology illustrates the increased utilization of provincial troops by the British in formal battle situations.

- *Savannah, Georgia*, December 29, 1778: De Lancey's Brigade, 1st and 2nd Battalions; New Jersey Volunteers, 3rd Battalion; New York Volunteers.
- *Camden, South Carolina*, August 16, 1780; British Legion; North Carolina Highlanders; Royal North Carolina Regiment; Volunteers of Ireland.
- *Cowpens, South Carolina*, January 17, 1781: British Legion.
- *Guilford Court House*, North Carolina, March 15, 1781: British Legion.
- *Hobkirk's Hill, South Carolina*, April 25, 1781: King's American Regiment; New York Volunteers; South Carolina Royalists; Volunteers of Ireland.
- *Green Spring, Virginia*, July 6, 1781; British Legion.
- *Eutaw Springs, South Carolina*, September 8, 1781: De Lancey's Brigade, 2nd Battalion; New Jersey Volunteers, 3rd Battalion; New York Volunteers; Provincial Light Infantry Battalion.

With the war in North America winding down after the surrender of Cornwallis in October 1781, the British government began to give some thought to the fate of the Americans who had remained loyal to the Crown. The military, in particular, was concerned with the disposition of those men who served in the regular provincial regiments, some since 1775.

Following the evacuation of Savannah on July 11, and Charleston on December 14, 1782, the provincial troops from the southern colonies were sent either to St. Augustine, Florida, or to the Bahamas. The regiments from the North were carried back to New York, where there was a large garrison of provincial troops.

The American Establishment effectively came to an end on December 25, 1782, when the King's American Regiment, the Queen's Rangers, and the cavalry portion of the British Legion were taken onto regular British Establishment along with the Corps of Foot in Newfoundland and the Royal Garrison Battalion. Of the other regiments that had made up the balance of the American Establishment, the Volunteers of Ireland had become the 105th Foot in March 1782, and the New York Volunteers and the infantry portion of the British Legion apparently reverted to the Provincial Establishment. It is also possible that the officers of the last two units received half-pay, but without rank in the British army.

Early in 1783 the provincial regiments were notified to expect to be reduced at any time.

They were instructed to compile complete muster rolls indicating the officers and men who wanted to escape the reduction, those who desired to be transported to Nova Scotia, and the soldiers who wanted to return to their original homes.

For the officers and men desiring to remain in the military service, it appears that their only option was to enlist as privates in one of the regular British regiments not scheduled to be disbanded. The soldiers choosing to go to Nova Scotia were to be provided with transportation to that province without personal expense. Once there they would receive a distribution of land in their new locale based on their military rank. Some of the veterans decided to try to return to their former homes, and they received three months' pay and two weeks' provisions. None were offered passage to England.

Walter T. Dornfest

REFERENCES

Mary B. Fryer, *King's Men* (1980); Philip R.N. Katcher, *Encyclopedia of British, Provincial, and German Army Units 1775–1783* (1973); John Shy, *Toward Lexington* (1965); Paul H. Smith, "The American Loyalists: Notes on Their Organization and Numerical Strength," *William and Mary Quarterly*, 3rd ser., *25* (1968):259–277; ———, *Loyalists and Redcoats* (1964).

Ruddle's and Martin's Stations, Raids on (June 24–26 1780)

The capture of Ruddle's and Martin's stations marked the only surrender of Kentucky forts in the Revolution. This episode illustrates the characteristics of war in the wilderness.

By June 1780 the forts of Captains Isaac Ruddle and John Martin, and nearby stockades and houses, were endangered. About 350 settlers lived in or near the two forts on the Licking River. Indian raids had decreased in the area since George Rogers Clark's capture in February 1779 of Vincennes, a major British-Indian base in the Illinois country. Due to the wet weather of early summer, Ruddle and Martin failed to send out the usual hunting and scouting parties. But the enemy was more diligent. Threatened by American expansion, the British and Indians vigorously pressed a wide-ranging offensive against the rebels. St. Louis, Cahokia, New Orleans, and Kentucky were targets. But only the raid on Kentucky achieved even partial success.

On May 25, British captain Henry Bird (8th Regiment of Foot) led a force from Detroit to attack Clark's garrisons at the Falls of the Ohio (Louisville). Bird had about 100 Lake Indians, 150 French Canadian militia, some American renegades like Simon Girty, Indian Department employees, bombardiers (Royal Regiment of Artillery), and two fieldpieces.

Bird expected that his artillery (never before used against a Kentucky fort) and the addition of 700 Indians who joined the expedition en route would insure victory. But when the little army reached the Ohio on June 9, the Indians refused to descend the river and assault Clark's fort. News that Clark was temporarily absent from his garrison encouraged the raiders, but rumors of his return frightened the Indians (Clark had artillery himself, and his reputation had grown awesome since Vincennes). Two days of argument by Bird failed to dissuade the Indians from ascending the nearby Licking River to ravage less heavily defended forts.

In May, some American prisoners who had escaped from Detroit warned the Kentuckians of a coming raid. Yet not until the Indians surrounded the forts by dawn June 24 did Ruddle learn of the enemy's presence. Bird's three-pounders were in place by noon and fired two shots, which only damaged the fort's walls. When a six-pounder was used, however, Ruddle seemingly had the choice of surrendering or being massacred. Negotiations with Bird and a debate among the settlers who advocated resistance took place. But Ruddle accepted capitulation to Bird.

Bird had proposed to take the prisoners safely to Detroit. Suddenly, Indians broke into the fort and seized captives and booty. Clothes were stripped from the inhabitants. White families were randomly divided as prisoners among various tribes. All cattle, a hated symbol of the whites, were slaughtered. In the melee, unknown numbers of settlers were butchered.

Two days later, Martin's Station, which surrendered at the sight of the artillery, was similarly plundered. Bird's white troops protected the prisoners, but the Indians burned the fort, outlying stockades, and houses. Some Indians clamored for retreat when they heard more rumors of Clark's approach. Others pressed for more assaults. But because Bird was unable to control the Indians and because he was fearful of Clark's presence in the area, he decided to return northward.

Reaching the Ohio in four days (approaching the forts, Bird had traveled the same route in twelve days), the march was difficult. Without any meat available, a handful of flour became the usual ration. Those prisoners who could not keep pace fell prey to Indians. On August 4, Bird and 150 prisoners reached Detroit. Later, Indians brought additional captives and sold them to the British.

The grim story of Ruddle's and Martin's abounded in irony. Apparently, many prisoners were Loyalists. Upon their release, many found employment in Detroit and Montreal. Thirteen even volunteered for service in the British Rangers. Other prisoners, however, escaped and some returned to Kentucky after 1782. Furthermore, Bird's raid produced not relief but a further setback for the Indians. In August 1780 the Kentuckians, incensed by the fate of Ruddle's and Martin's, crossed the Ohio in force and attacked Shawnee towns. In the ultimate irony, the flood of immigration into Kentucky continued for years with hardly a check—as if the Ruddle's–Martin's disaster had never occurred.

James Russell Harris

REFERENCES

J. Winston Coleman, Jr., *The British Invasion of Kentucky: With an Account of the Capture of Ruddle's and Martin's Stations, June 1780* (1951); "Haldimand Papers, 1780," *Michigan Pioneer and Historical Collections, 19* (1982):492–591; Maude Ward Lafferty, "Destruction of Ruddle's and Martin's Stations in the Revolutionary War," *Register of the Kentucky Historical Society, 54* (1956):295–318; Milo M. Quaife, "When Detroit Invaded Kentucky," *Filson Club History Quarterly* (1927):53–67; Charles G. Talbert, "Kentucky Invades Ohio, 1780," *Register of the Kentucky Historical Society, 52* (1954):291–300.

Rush, Benjamin (1746–1813)

Continental Army physician. Born in Byberry, Pennsylvania, in 1746, Benjamin Rush graduated from the College of New Jersey (later Princeton University) in 1760. At first he leaned toward a career in law but soon decided on medicine instead. He was apprenticed to John Redman, a prominent Philadelphia physician, from 1760 to 1766. He attended medical courses at the College of Philadelphia (later the University of Pennsylvania) in 1765 and 1766.

Rush first became interested in political affairs at the time of the passage of the Revenue Act of 1764. He sided immediately with the outraged colonists and spoke out vehemently against those, particularly Benjamin Franklin and the Quakers, who initially supported the new tax.

It was at this time, in 1765 and 1766, that Rush enrolled in courses at the College of Philadelphia. He took the courses offered by John Morgan and William Shippen, who were at odds with each other over professional matters. Rush hoped to remain neutral in their squabble, a position he rarely held throughout his life. He joined a medical society organized by Morgan and permitted Morgan to plan his own course of study at Edinburgh, where he had determined to go to further his medical education. In 1766 Rush enrolled in the medical school at Edinburgh University, considered at that time to be one of the best medical schools in the world. William Cullen, who taught the course in the institutes of medicine, influenced Rush more than any other man, either then or for the rest of his life. Rush wholly subscribed to Cullen's theory and practice of medicine. Cullen taught that illness was caused by stimuli to the brain that in turn caused spasms in the vascular system. Disease was due to either too much or too little stimulation. Treatment of disease therefore should consist of increasing stimulation by purges or decreasing stimulation by bloodletting. In his own practice of medicine, Rush was to carry purging and bloodletting to extremes. He always considered the two years he spent in Edinburgh the happiest of his life.

In September 1768 Rush left Edinburgh for London, where for several months he attended lectures in anatomy given by Dr. William Hunter, and he accompanied Dr. Richard Huck on his hospital rounds. Benjamin Franklin was in London at the same time, and he took Rush under his wing, entertaining him at home and introducing him into his own circles in the city. Relations between the colonies and England were growing worse, and Rush threw himself into political discussions with increasing fervor, always championing the American cause. He visited Paris for several months before returning to Philadelphia in July 1769.

Immediately upon his return, Rush set himself up in medical practice, opened an apothecary shop, and took in young men as apprentice physicians. His practice grew quickly, at first mostly among the poor, many of whom he treated without charge. Epidemics of scarlet fever, influenza, and smallpox, as well as the usual diseases and accidents of life afforded him ample opportunities to experiment with the theories and booklearning he had acquired in Edinburgh and London. In August 1769 he was chosen to be the first professor of chemistry at the College of Philadelphia, a post he had been hoping and maneuvering for even before he had gone abroad.

Soon after his return to Philadelphia, Rush began to publish papers on topics of medical interest. None of these early works was of any lasting value, but they kept his name in the public eye, enhanced his practice, and aroused envy in his colleagues. He also plunged into the works of reform for which he is justly remembered today. He became a physician to the almshouse, joined a group dedicated to inoculating the poor against smallpox, was a member of a volunteer fire-fighting company, and, most importantly, began to speak out against slavery. He owned a young male slave himself but excused this by stating that slavery had rendered the Blacks unfit for immediate freedom. Before they were set free, Rush believed that they should be taught to read and write and to be educated in religion, and that laws should be passed to limit their servitude and entitle them to the privileges of freeborn subjects. In 1773 he anonymously published a pamphlet, *An Address to the Inhabitants of British Settlements in America upon Slave-Keeping*. In it, he called for the end of slavery not only because it was itself evil and unjust but because it belied the very foundations of freedom on which the new country was based. In a short time, this path of reasoning led Rush to believe that slavery corrupted society and that freedom enlightened society. It was not difficult for him to take this philosophy and apply it to the relations between the American colonies and the Mother Country.

From the day he heard of the Battle of Lexington, Rush dedicated himself to American Independence. In the fall of 1774, he had met and come to like and admire many of the delegates to the First Continental Congress. When the Second Continental Congress met in 1775, he welcomed the members back to Philadelphia and served as something of a go-between and host to several delegations. He met Thomas Paine in 1775 and formed a long-lasting acquaintance with the author of *Common Sense*, although the two men did not become close friends. It was also in 1775 that Rush courted his future wife,

Julia Stockton, daughter of Richard Stockton of Princeton, New Jersey. They married in January 1776. Thirteen children were born to them. Rush adored his wife and counted his marriage a very happy one.

Early in 1776, Rush was elected to the Committee of Inspection and Observation in Philadelphia, his formal debut into politics. In June, he was elected to the Provincial Conference and in July to the Continental Congress. He, of course, voted for independence and signed the Declaration. In September, he was made chairman of a committee of five that was to try to provide the northern army with hospital supplies and medicines, no easy task as such items had not been stored up in anticipation of war, and transportation of what few supplies there were was difficult. He also sat on five other congressional committees including the Committee on Intelligence, of which he was chairman, and the Committee on Prisoners, in which capacity he attended those captured and held in the city's jails. All the while, he kept up his private practice of medicine.

When General William Howe's troops threatened Philadelphia in December 1776, Rush saw his family to safety outside the city; he then accompanied a regiment of Pennsylvania militia under General John Cadwalader to join Washington on the Delaware. He treated the wounded, including General Hugh Mercer, from the actions around Trenton and Princeton. Meanwhile, he kept alert for political gossip and made suggestions for the better ordering of army life on everything from haircuts to the treatment of prisoners of war and the organization of the Medical Department. In January 1777 Rush left the regiment to travel to Baltimore, where the Continental Congress was in session. Probably because of his opposition to the new Pennsylvania state constitution, he was not reappointed to the Congress at the conclusion of this session in February 1777.

In April 1777, Rush was appointed surgeon general of the Middle Department in the newly reorganized Medical Department, now headed by Dr. William Shippen, Jr. It was at this time that Rush made his most important contribution to military medicine. He wrote *Directions for Preserving the Health of Soldiers . . .* , published first in the *Pennsylvania Packet* and later in pamphlet form. Addressed to the officers of the army, the few short pages of this work gave what we would now call common-sense advice on keeping soldiers healthy and fit to fight. The camp, equipment, clothing, and body were to be kept clean. The diet should consist mainly of vegetables and grain. No liquor was to be drunk. Flannel shirts were to be preferred over linen. Soldiers were to be kept active and in good physical condition. Rush placed the responsibility for discipline and compliance with his rules of hygiene on the officers of the line. He also urged them to see to it that their men did not become too exhausted, wet, cold, or hungry because these conditions fostered sickness. Rush's pamphlet continued in use until the War of 1812, and most of it remains valid today. Although its contents were not particularly original, most having been published by John Pringle in England, the pamphlet is an early milestone in American military medicine.

In July 1777 Rush was appointed physician general of the Middle Department, second only to Shippen and Thomas Bond, Jr. He quickly became disillusioned and then outspokenly critical not only of the medical services for the American troops but with Washington's conduct of the war itself. He found headquarters officers variously drunk, lazy, cowardly, and stupid. The only officers he admired were Brigadier General Thomas Conway, and after his victory at Saratoga, General Horatio Gates. Rush began in earnest to attack Washington, his generals, and the Medical Department. But he literally authored his own downfall when, on January 12, 1778, he wrote an unsigned but scarcely anonymous letter to Patrick Henry severely criticizing the Medical Department leadership and Washington himself, calling for the replacement of the commander-in-chief. Henry passed the letter along to Washington, who recognized the handwriting at once. An uproar followed these attacks, and Congress appointed a committee to investigate Rush's charges against Shippen and the Medical Department. The committee did agree with Rush's criticisms, and on January 30, 1778, he resigned his commission and returned to private practice in Philadelphia.

Rush spent the rest of his life in medical practice, in teaching, and in working for reform in several fields, among them the education of women, temperance, medical services for the poor, and the abolition of slavery. During the yellow fever epidemic in Philadelphia in 1793, he remained in the city, caring for patients when many other physicians left for the relative safety of the countryside. Rush's practice of profusely bleeding his patients came under attack during this epidemic when it was shown that his patients died at a greater rate than those who were bled less or not at all. Rush's reputation was so damaged by this revelation that he considered leaving Philadelphia for New York. Eventually, the furor died down. But he never changed his mind about the value of bloodletting because he never changed his mind about the cause of disease, although there was a growing body of clinical and pathological evidence to refute the spasmatony theory he had learned from Cullen. His medical opinions were cast in stone.

Rush's work in psychiatry was much more in keeping with the newest theories being developed in England and Europe. He felt that the workings of the mind—intellect, emotions, and behavior—affected the body and in turn that the state of the body could affect the mind. He advocated humane treatment for the insane. In 1787 he was appointed the physician in charge of the insane at the Pennsylvania Hospital. His enlightened treatment of the insane and his published works on psychiatry have rightfully earned him the title of "Father of American Psychiatry" and it is upon this that his reputation as a physician rests.

Janet Brady Joy

REFERENCES

Carl Alfred Lanning Binger, *Revolutionary Doctor: Benjamin Rush, 1746–1813* (1966); Nathan G. Goodman, *Benjamin Rush, Physician and Citizen, 1746–1813* (1934); David Freeman Hawke, *Benjamin Rush, Revolutionary Gadfly* (1971); Benjamin Rush, *The Autobiography of Benjamin Rush . . .*, ed. by George W. Corner (1948); ———, *Directions for Preserving the Health of Soldiers: Recommended to the Consideration of the Officers of the Army of the United States* (1778); Richard Harrison Shryock, "The Medical Reputation of Benjamin Rush: Contrasts Over Two Centuries," *Bulletin of the History of Medicine*, 45 (1971):507–52.

Rutherford, Griffith (1721–1805)

North Carolina militia officer. Born in Ireland, Griffith Rutherford settled in the North Carolina backcountry west of Salisbury in the Locke settlement. He represented Rowan County in the North Carolina House of Commons in 1775. In April 1776, he was appointed brigadier general for the Salisbury military district by the North Carolina Provincial Congress.

Rutherford commanded an expedition against the Cherokees in the summer of 1776, which destroyed many villages and crops and effectively ended any threat from those Indians. Rutherford called out the Mecklenburg and Rowan militia to resist the threat of British invasion in the spring of 1780 and moved against Tory threats at Ramsour's Mill and the forks of the Yadkin River. In August 1780, Rutherford was captured by the British at Camden, South Carolina. After being exchanged, he took command at Wilmington, North Carolina, when the British evacuated that town.

In 1786, Rutherford served as the state senator from Rowan County. He moved soon thereafter to Tennessee, where he was appointed president of the Legislative Council of the General Assembly of that state in 1794. Counties in both North Carolina and Tennessee have been named in his honor.

W. Hugh Harkey, Jr.

REFERENCES

Minnie Rutherford Harsh Long, *General Griffith Rutherford and Allied Families; Harsh, Graham, Cathey, Locke, Holeman, Johnson, Chambers* (1942); John Hill Wheeler, *Historical Sketches of North Carolina*, 2 vols. (1851), I:79, II:383–384.

Rutledge, John (1739–1800)

War governor. Born near Charleston, South Carolina, Rutledge was the son of an Anglican minister. He attended Middle Temple in London and was admitted to the bar in 1760. Soon after, he returned to Charleston, where he began a political career. He served in the House of Assembly, and he was attorney general (1764–65). Rutledge represented the colony at the Stamp Act Congress in New York (1765) and in the First and Second Continental Congresses (1775). He was a member of the colony's council of safety and the second provincial congress, and he helped to draft the South Carolina Constitution of 1776. That year he was elected president of the state, was reelected in December 1778, and again in January 1779 to serve until 1782.

Through most of the war Rutledge was the state's chief executive. Fortunately for South Carolina, the first invasion under General Henry Clinton at Charleston was repulsed in July 1776. For the next two years the area was safe from British incursions. But in early 1779 the enemy invaded again, and in May 1780 Charleston fell to Clinton. For the next 18 months the seaboard of the interior towns were under British occupation, and Rutledge's government barely survived. Rutledge was nearly captured by Colonel Banastre Tarleton, and he had to flee to North Carolina. Rutledge encouraged partisan leaders like Thomas Sumter and Francis Marion to continue the fight, and he urged Washington to commit more troops to the South. Not until November 1781 could an election for the legislature be held. Rutledge, who did a remarkable job of maintaining a semblance of government under arduous circumstances, continued his political career by representing his state in Congress (1782–83).

Richard L. Blanco

REFERENCES

Robert W. Barnwell, Jr., "Rutledge, The Dictator," *Journal of Southern History*, 7 (1941):215–224; Richard H. Barry, *Mr. Rutledge of South Carolina* (1946).

Sag Harbor, New York, Raid on

See Meigs, Return Jonathan.

Saint-Aubin, Ambroise (?–1780)

Malecite Indian chief. From the St. John River (New Brunswick), Saint-Aubin's name has appeared as Ambroise Bear, Pier, or Var. He was one of the most powerful Malecite chiefs in the period leading up to the American Revolution. In 1768 Saint-Aubin and Pierre Toma negotiated for lands that became the first Malecite Indian reserve. The lands were very important to them. On several occasions English attempted to settle on the Indian lands. Conflicts resulted. On May 15, 1775, the provincial congress in Boston addressed a letter to all the "Eastern Indians" warning that the British were planning to take away land and liberty from colonists and Indians. The Nova Scotia Assembly passed a law that required a license for the trade of ammunition with the Indians. The Indians depended upon this ammunition from coastal traders for their winter hunting. They interpreted this law as a means to starve them to death. However, Massachusetts-Bay promised the needed ammu-nition and supplies in return for the Indians' support of the rebel cause.

The majority of the settlers in southern Nova Scotia, especially Cumberland County, and on the St. John River sympathized with Massachusetts. The Indians in the area, who had supported the French during the colonial wars, now wanted to be on the winning side.

In September 1775, Pierre Toma accompanied Saint-Aubin to the Penobscot trading post (now Bangor, Maine) and negotiated a "treaty" for both Malecite and Micmac to trade furs for arms and provisions.

Washington was in no hurry to accept these Indians as allies and delayed his decision for almost a year. Early in 1776, a delegation of Penobscot, Malecite, and Caughnawagha Indians visited Washington at his camp in Watertown, Massachusetts, to again offer their support. By summer Washington decided to accept their offer to serve with the army at full Continental pay for two to three years. Washington's decision coincided with a visit of three Malecite and seven Micmac chiefs to the Massachusetts-Bay Council, which culminated in a Treaty of Alliance and Friendship entered into and concluded by and between the governors of the state of Massachusetts-Bay and the delegates of the St. John River and Micmac tribes of Indians on July 19, 1776. Ambroise was accompanied to Boston by Newell Wallis and Francis Xavier, two other Malecite chiefs, to sign the treaty.

In the fall of 1776, Ambroise was the leader of 15 Malecites who joined in Captain Jonathan Eddy's unsuccessful attack on Fort Cumberland, Nova Scotia. The Malecites had expected a victory and were dismayed over their defeat. They returned to their village at Fort Meductic on the St. John River. Soon afterward Colonel John Allan, Superintendent of Indian Affairs in eastern Maine, led the 500 Meductic Malecite, including women and children, in a long journey over old Indian canoe trails from their St. John River village through eastern Maine to Machias. In a letter to the Malecite dated July 10, 1778, Allan named Ambroise Chief Councillor and commanded that all British prisoners be sent to him for exchange. Ambroise continued to be spokesman for his tribes by making many trips to Nova Scotia. As a courier and spy, he served the Americans faithfully.

Nicholas N. Smith

REFERENCES

DCB; Frederic Kidder, *Military Operations in Eastern Maine and Nova Scotia During the Revolution* (1971); William O. Raymond, *The River St. John; Its Physical Features. Legends and History from 1604 to 1784* (1950); L.F.S. Upton, *Micmacs and Colonists: Indian-White Relations in the Maritimes, 1713–1867* (1979); William Walker, "A Chronological Account of the Wabanaki Confederacy," *Political Organization of Native North Americans*, ed. by Ernest L. Schusky (1980).

St. Clair, Arthur (1736–1818)

Continental Army officer. Born in Thurso, on the northern coast of Scotland, Arthur St. Clair purchased a commission as ensign in the Royal American Regiment (the 60th Foot) in 1757. He served in the siege of Louisbourg and at the capture of Quebec. He married Phoebe Bayard, a Boston heiress, resigned from the army, and eventually settled at Ligonier on the Pennsylvania frontier. St. Clair held several local offices but took no part in the opposition to proprietary or imperial authority. Soon after the beginning of the war he was elected colonel of the Westmoreland County militia, and on January 3, 1776, Congress appointed him to the rank of colonel in the Continental Army. He recruited the 2nd Pennsylvania in six weeks and led it northward toward Quebec in May, just in time to help cover Benedict Arnold's retreat from Canada. Near Trois Rivières, St. Clair took command after Brigadier General William Thompson was wounded, and successfully extricated some 1,800 troops from a very difficult position. On August 9 he was promoted by Congress to the rank of brigadier general, and in November he was ordered to lead his brigade from Albany to join Washington's army in its retreat across New Jersey.

General St. Clair commanded his brigade for the crossing of the Delaware River and the surprise assault against the Hessians at Trenton on December 26. At Princeton on January 3, St. Clair was credited by some of his friends with suggesting the flanking movement that led to Washington's victory, and he certainly led his brigade through heavy fighting to the capture of the college buildings. In recognition of his services at Trenton and Princeton, St. Clair was promoted by Congress to the rank of major general, the only Pennsylvanian to reach that rank. In winter quarters at Morristown, St. Clair served briefly as Washington's adjutant general.

Late in April, St. Clair was ordered back to Albany to assist Major General Horatio Gates in resisting the British advance along Lake Champlain. When Major General Philip Schuyler was restored to the command of the Northern Department he ordered St. Clair to take charge of Fort Ticonderoga. St. Clair found the garrison under strength and poorly supplied when he reached the fort on June 12. Repairs ordered months earlier were unfinished, and St. Clair had some 2,200 troops to defend a position that required, by his estimate, at least 10,000 men. In addition to the old French fort at Ticonderoga the Americans had erected extensive outer works and a smaller fort called Mount Independence on the eastern shore of Lake Champlain. American scouts had only a vague idea of the British position until the enemy appeared within four miles of Ticonderoga on June 30.

By July 3 the British troops under Lieutenant General John Burgoyne had closed around Ticonderoga on the western shore of the lake and had begun to haul four 12-pounder cannon up the slopes of Sugar Loaf Mountain less than a mile away. Earlier, French engineers had considered its 758-foot elevation too steep for artillery, but the British rapidly proved them wrong and prepared to bring both Ticonderoga and Mount Independence across the lake under a devastating plunging fire from the height they renamed Mount Defiance. St. Clair realized that his position was an impossible one and decided to try to save his troops, although he surely would be accused of giving up the famed fort without a fight. The Ticonderoga garrison crossed to the eastern shore of the lake by way of a floating bridge on the night of July 5–6 and joined the troops at Mount Independence in a hasty but successful withdrawal. The entire force reached Fort Edward safely a week later and fought through the remainder of the Saratoga campaign, although no longer under St. Clair's command. "I may yet have the satisfaction," St. Clair wrote to Congress, "that by abandoning a post, I have eventually saved a state."

Time proved St. Clair right about evacuating Ticonderoga, but he would never again hold an independent command as a Continental general. He was condemned by some in the army and by many in Congress, and early in August he was relieved of command and ordered to report to Washington's headquarters. St. Clair's conduct was investigated by a committee of Congress without result except to delay the court-martial that he demanded in order to clear his name. He was unanimously acquitted in September 1778, "with the highest honor" and returned to active duty as a division commander with the main army under Washington. He served on the staff at Brandywine and had a horse killed under him, but he escaped unharmed. When General Benedict Arnold attempted to betray West Point, Washington ordered St. Clair to take command there. In 1781 he was ordered to recruiting duty in Pennsylvania and managed to reach Yorktown only a few days before the British surrendered. St. Clair's final field command was to lead six regiments to join General Nathanael Greene in South Carolina, and he remained with Greene until mid-summer as the fighting came to an end. In June 1783, St. Clair helped to dissuade the mutinous troops of the Pennsylvania Line from marching on the Continental Congress and so ended his eight years of active service with the army. He was a loyal and dutiful officer, skilled in military administration but lacking both flair and good luck as a combat leader. Washington could always trust him with routine duties, but never after surrendering Ticonderoga was St. Clair seriously considered for an independent command.

After the war. St. Clair settled in Philadelphia and attempted a mercantile career. In November 1785, he was elected as a delegate to the Continental Congress, and in February 1787, he was elected president of Congress. In October of that year he was chosen as governor of the new Northwest Territory and remained in that office until 1802. In 1791 he returned briefly to active military service, but suffered a severe loss to the Indians. St. Clair was a founding member of the Society of the Cincinnati and served as president of the Pennsylvania chapter from 1783 until 1789. In retirement St. Clair returned to his home at Ligonier, Pennsylvania, and died in poverty after a long struggle to secure payment from Congress for expenses incurred in his public service.

Patrick J. Furlong

REFERENCES

Martin H. Bush, *Revolutionary Enigma: A Re-appraisal of General Philip Schuyler of New York* (1969); Don R. Gerlach, *Proud Patriot: Philip Schuyler and the War of Independence, 1775–1783* (1987); Douglas Southall Freeman, *George Washington*, 7 vols. (1948–57), 3–4; William H. Smith, ed., *The St. Clair Papers*, 2 vols. (1882), rpr. 1970–71.

St. Eustatius, West Indies

A Dutch island in the West Indies, St. Eustatius played a significant role in the American Revolution. In a purely symbolic role, its governor was the first foreign official to recognize the sovereignty of a vessel of the United States. The island also provided the focus for extensive military operations in 1781, being captured by first the British and later the French. The attention paid to Eustatius stemmed from its role as a vital trading center, particularly as a conduit of gunpowder from Holland to the American colonies and the French West Indies. The supplies that Eustatius funneled to the rebellious colonists in 1775 and 1776 helped prevent the fledgling Revolution from perishing by "starvation of firepower."

Fortune triply blessed the island with respect to climate, location, and configuration. St.

Eustatius proved perfectly suited to the cultivation of sugar, the white gold of the eighteenth century. Located at the intersection of the Leeward and Windward isles at the midpoint of the West Indies, the island—locally known as Statia—attracted considerable commerce from Europe, North America, Africa, and the West Indian holdings of Denmark, England, France, and Spain. Its splendid harbor could hold up to 200 vessels at a time. In the decades before the American Revolution, the island proved so profitable for the Dutch that it became known as the "Golden Rock," one of the richest territories per acre on the face of the globe.

The profits of Statia resulted from the policies of the Dutch as well as the blessings of Providence. After the debilitating wars with France under Louis XIV, the Netherlands strove to maintain neutrality during the struggles of the great powers. While eager to avoid participating in the frequent fighting in the West Indies, the Dutch islanders were quite willing to sell their goods to any ship that stopped at Statia. Furthermore, they effectively undercut the competition because, contrary to the mercantile doctrines of the eighteenth century, they charged no customs duties. Thus, St. Eustatius made colossal wealth as a neutral entrepôt supplying all combatants.

After receiving word of the conflict between Britain and her colonies in America, the States General of Holland declared their neutrality. The sentiments of the pro-British nobility were somewhat counterbalanced by the mass of public opinion, sympathetic with the rebels; the weight of the merchant class in favor of neutrality and its attendant profits carried the day. Dutch traders soon established a booming traffic with the American colonists. The proximity of Statia to the American coastline and the inability of the British to patrol the waters of the West Indies as thoroughly as they did the trading lanes of Europe meant that the majority of the trade would be funneled through St. Eustatius.

The traffic with the Dutch meant a great deal to the American Revolutionaries. Between 1775 and 1778, when the French openly joined the war, the Revolutionaries suffered a shortage of gunpowder, for which they lacked the raw materials to produce in quantity. At the Battle of Bunker Hill in 1775, for example, with their powder almost exhausted, the colonial militia had to fight the British with clubbed muskets. The rebels gladly sent their tobacco, indigo, rice, timber, and horses to Statia in exchange for Dutch gunpowder. Small coasting vessels normally brought the gunpowder back in loads of 1,000 to 4,000 pounds.

The growth of this trade led Statia to assume a symbolic role in the American Revolution. On November 16, 1776, island governor Johannes de Graff ordered the guns of Fort Orange to return the salute of the American brigantine *Andrea Doria*. Those rounds constituted the first foreign acknowledgment of the sovereignty of the Continental Congress.

The British, naturally, resented the Dutch sale of munitions to the colonists. The British ambassador to Holland, Sir Joseph Yorke, conveyed London's requests that the Dutch stop selling military contraband to the rebels and instead provide Britain certain aids and subsidies specified under the Treaty of Alliance of 1678. The Dutch decision on November 20, 1780, to enter the League of Armed Neutrality rather than fulfill British demands for assistance led Britain to declare war on Holland. The British then decided to interdict the colonists' trade with St. Eustatius by capturing the island before its defenders became aware of the onset of hostilities.

Admiral George Brydges Rodney received orders to take St. Eustatius in January 1781. Rodney, one of Britain's best fighting admirals, commanded the Leeward Isles station in the Caribbean. He wholeheartedly threw himself into the task of capturing Statia and its treasure-trove. Sailing from Barbados with fifteen ships a mere three days after receiving his orders, he reached the harbor of St. Eustatius on February 3, 1781. The defenders of ancient Fort Orange, recognizing the hopelessness of their position, capitulated after a single forlorn volley. Rodney then seized the entire island.

The capture of St. Eustatius proved a mixed blessing for the British. At virtually no cost, they captured an immense quantity of material, including extensive naval stores and munitions, valued at some £3,000,000. They also seized some 130 merchant ships, 50 of which were American. On the other hand, they lost the services of a valuable naval officer. Rodney, who spent much of his life in fear of creditors, focused on the plunder of Statia rather than the defeat of the French forces in the vicinity. His subsequent attacks on Dutch shipping left his lieutenant, Rear Admiral Samuel Hood, with insufficient force to prevent a French naval concentration under Admiral Francois de Grasse at Port Royal, Martinique. Thus, Rodney's preoccupation with the booty to end his financial worries facilitated de Grasse's departure for American waters, a visit that had such a fateful effect at Yorktown.

At the conclusion of the war, St. Eustatius belonged, as it had at the beginning, to the Dutch. The French took the island from the British shortly after their victory at Yorktown. In November 1781, de Grasse sailed for the Caribbean. The British, fearful for the loss of Jamaica, detailed Rodney to defend that strategic island. Rodney left the defenses of Eustatius in good order. The French governor of Martinique then launched an expedition against Statia. His corps, which featured a division of French troops wearing red coats with yellow facings, confused the defenders and captured the island. In 1784, the French restored St. Eustatius to Dutch sovereignty. The island flies the Dutch flag today. *See also*: Gunpowder, Supply of

Raymond C. Gamble

REFERENCES

George Billias, ed., *George Washington's Opponents* (1969); William James, *The British Navy in Adversity: A Study of the War of Independence* (1926); Alfred Thayer, *The Influence of Sea Power upon History, 1660–1783* (1890); E.B. Potter and Chester Nimitz, eds., *Sea Power: A Naval History* (1960); Barbara Tuchman, *The First Salute* (1988).

St. Francis Abenaki Indians

The Abenaki village at St. Francis (Odanak) in Quebec originated as a French mission village. During the French and Indian War, large numbers of Abenaki Indians from northern New England withdrew from the cutting edge of the English frontier, taking up permanent or temporary residence at St. Francis. Warriors from St. Francis were among the staunchest allies of the French, and the English came to refer to virtually all Abenakis from Vermont and Quebec as "St. Francis Indians." In 1759 Robert Rogers' Rangers burned St. Francis but the community persisted.

Although not directly involved in the fighting, St. Francis felt the reverberations of the Revolution in the presence and threat of British force, in the migration of many of its inhabitants, and in the political dissensions within the community.

A handful of Abenakis joined Washington's army at Cambridge in 1775. Others appear to have served with the British, especially in repelling American invasions of Canada early in the war. For most St. Francis Abenakis the choice of allegiance was extremely difficult. The British dispatched troops to keep an eye on St. Francis, and Governor Sir Guy Carleton threatened to destroy the village if the inhabitants displayed American sympathies or harbored American spies. The Abenakis were reluctant to take up arms for the British or for the Americans, and most remained neutral throughout the conflict. Some however, served as couriers, carrying intelligence back and forth between Canada and the American colonies despite the British efforts to curtail such activities.

As in many other Indian communities, the Revolution generated serious divisions. About 45 families—perhaps as much as one-third of the population—left St. Francis and moved south to the upper Connecticut Valley, taking up residence around the American settlements at Newbury, Vermont, and Haverhill, New Hampshire. Colonel Timothy Bedel, commanding the militia in the area, made every effort to attract them and worked hard to secure supplies for them while they were there. Despite suffering from acute shortages of food, clothing, and shelter, the Abenakis served as a buffer protecting the American settlements. They acted as scouts and messengers for Bedel and some enlisted in a company of rangers.

Joseph Louis Gill, an influential chief at St. Francis who was the son of English captives who was adopted and raised by the Abenakis, added to the confusion. Gill appears to have acted as a spy for the Americans, and recognizing his influence, Congress agreed to the recommendation of Colonel Moses Hazen and Washington that he be granted a commission. Gill was closely watched by the British, however, and he may even have played both sides of the fence. In 1780 he took an oath of allegiance to George III and the British offered to make him "grand chief" as a way of securing his allegiance. St. Francis became divided between the faction supporting Gill and those who supported the Crown.

St. Francis remained a hotbed of factionalism and a center for the spread of intelligence, and British and Americans alike viewed the St. Francis Abenakis with suspicion until the end of the Revolution.

Colin G. Calloway

REFERENCES

Colin G. Calloway, *The Western Abenakis of Vermont; 1600–1800; War Migration and the Survival of an Indian People* (1990); Gordon M. Day, *The Identity of the St. Francis Indians* (1981); John C. Huden, "The White Chief of the St. Francis Abenakis: Some Aspects of Border Warfare, 1690–1790," *Vermont History*, 24 (1956).

St. Johns, Quebec

Located on the west bank of the Richelieu River, approximately 20 miles southeast of Montreal, Fort St. Johns stands at that point on the Richelieu where ship transit to the south, into Lake Champlain, becomes possible. The strategically significant site was first fortified by the French in 1666 and refortified by General Montcalm for the British in 1758. During the American invasion of Canada the British stopped the American advance at St. Johns for 55 days, and thereby forced the Americans into a disastrous winter campaign in front of Quebec.

After the American seizure of Fort Ticonderoga on May 10, 1775, Benedict Arnold staged a raid on St. Johns. On May 17 he surprised the small British garrison of 15 men and, before withdrawing, captured a 16-gun sloop. When a full-scale American invasion appeared probable, Canada's governor general, Guy Carleton, strengthened St. Johns' fortifications, which had been allowed to fall into disrepair. To link the barracks block and stone house, which formed the fort's inner core, Carleton built a system of communications trenches, and he constructed a line of projecting pickets along the outer base of the fort's walls. Into the fort he placed 700 troops, most of them British regulars, under the command of Major Charles Preston. Carleton's intention was to block the American advance at St. Johns, before the invaders could reach the St. Lawrence River. If the Americans tried to bypass St. Johns and move directly on to Montreal, they would face a devastating attack from the rear by the St. Johns' garrison.

From a base of operations established downriver at Ile aux Noix, the Americans under Philip Schuyler twice tried to land troops by boat and to seize Fort St. Johns. These attacks occurred on the nights of September 5 and September 10. In neither case did the Americans actually stage an assault. The first attack failed when the Americans, on their approach to the fort, were ambushed by a screening party of Indians in the British employ. The second attack failed when the main American contingent retreated in confusion after clashing mistakenly with a small American advance unit.

On September 16, after illness forced Schuyler to the rear, Richard Montgomery took command of the American invaders. Montgomery moved the main body of his army, now numbering about 2,000 troops, from Ile aux Noix into the St. Johns environs, and the Americans laid direct siege to the fort. But the subsequent American bombardment of St. Johns, which escalated as more cannon were brought up from Fort Ticonderoga, had little effect on the well-entrenched and highly professional British soldiers. Meanwhile, pelted by cold rains and running short of supplies, American morale began to decline. Faced with insubordination among both his officers and his men, Montgomery found it increasingly difficult to maintain the siege. In early October 1775 it seemed as though Carleton's plan to stop the Americans at St. Johns might prove successful.

In the end, the resolute British defense of St. Johns was undermined by two events that took place away from the fort. On October 18 an American advance party captured Chambly, a well-stocked British supply post 12 miles north of St. Johns. By seizing Chambly the Americans not only prevented the British from resupplying Preston and his men, they also obtained the ammunition and other materials they needed to continue their siege of St. Johns. Then, on October 30 at Longuevil, on the south shore of the St. Lawrence, another American advance party turned back Carleton and a force of 1,000 troops, mostly Canadian militiamen, as Carleton departed Montreal in hopes of relieving Preston at St. Johns. With no chance of relief, with less than a week's supply of food remaining, and with his garrison suffering fearful artillery barrages from new gun emplacements that Montgomery had established, Major Preston surrendered St. Johns to the Americans on November 2. Impressed with the determined British conduct during the siege, Montgomery permitted the British to march out of the fort under their colors, and he allowed Preston and his officers to keep their swords.

During the American retreat from Quebec in the late spring of 1776, Fort St. Johns almost became the site of more American-British combat. Fleeing the huge British army that had relieved Carleton at Quebec, the Americans reached St. Johns in mid-June, on their way to the relative safety of Fort Ticonderoga. On June 17 the main American force under General John Sullivan was joined at St. Johns by the retreating Montreal garrison under Benedict Arnold. As the Americans continued their withdrawal, Arnold and a small party stayed behind to burn the fort. After setting the fort on fire, Arnold and his men escaped by boat just as the British advance guard arrived.

With St. Johns once again in British hands, Carleton began rebuilding the fort in the summer of 1776, and the British subsequently used it as a base for both land and naval operations. It was at St. Johns that Carleton assembled much of the fleet that he employed at the Battle of Valcour Island. The fort also was used as a staging position for General John Burgoyne's ill-fated incursion into New York in 1777.

John Kramer

REFERENCES

Harrison Bird, *Attack on Quebec: The American Invasion of Canada, 1775* (1968); Robert McConnell Hatch, *Thrust for Canada: The American Attempt on Quebec in 1775–1776* (1979); Justin H. Smith, *Our Struggle for a Fourteenth Colony: Canada and the American Revolution*, 2 vols. (1907); George F.C. Stanley, *Canada Invaded, 1775–1776* (1967); Benjamin Trumbull, "A Concise Journal or Minutes of the Principal Movements Toward St. John in 1775," *Connecticut Historical Society Collections*, 7 (1899):139–173.

St. Leger's Expedition (June–September 1777)

Lieutenant Colonel Barry St. Leger commanded General John Burgoyne's diversionary effort along the Mohawk River during the summer of 1777. He was to lead a small army down the Mohawk Valley to meet Burgoyne's main force at Albany. St. Leger's expedition would tie down American troops in the valley, thereby easing pressure on Buygoyne's southern thrust along the river-lakes route. It was also designed to enlist support for the British war effort among Loyalists and the Six Nations Indians in the region. Burgoyne specifically tabbed St. Leger for this mission and elevated him to the temporary rank of brigadier general.

On June 23, 1777, St. Leger left Montreal and began working his way up the St. Lawrence River into Lake Ontario. He arrived at Oswego, New York, on July 25 in command of a variegated force of redcoats, Canadians, Tories, and Indians. One hundred–man detachments from the British 8th and 34th regiments and the German Hanau Jaegers were joined by Tories in Sir John Johnson's "Royal Greens," Tory Rangers under Colonel John Butler, and Canadian militiamen. Forty artillerymen, two 6-pounders, two 3-pounders, and four 4.4-inch mortars also accompanied the expedition. In addition to some 875 whites, St. Leger enlisted the services of 800 to 1,000 Indians, loosely under the direction of Joseph Brant.

St. Leger moved inland toward Fort Stanwix on July 26. His force advanced cautiously through the wilderness east of Oswego, averaging nearly ten miles a day. St. Leger had been led to believe that Fort Stanwix had fallen into disrepair and was held by only 60 men. Although this information had been correct earlier in the year, the Americans had taken steps to rebuild and garrison the fort. Colonel Peter Gansevoort and the 550-man 33rd New York Continental Regiment occupied the fort in April 1777 and immediately set about renovating the decayed fort. Gansevoort and his second in command, Lieutenant Colonel Marinus Willett, labored through the summer and restored Fort Stanwix to a formidable position by the time St. Leger's vanguard appeared before the fort on August 2. Advance British units arrived moments too late to prevent 200 reinforcements and large quantities of supplies from entering the fort. St. Leger thus confronted a well-constructed, well-supplied fort manned by approximately 750 Americans.

The British commander first sought to intimidate the defenders by parading his entire command back and forth in full view of the besieged. The colorful uniforms of the varied force must have been impressive; however, the sight of almost 1,000 Indians is what most deeply impressed the Americans. The presence of such a large number of Indians stiffened the Americans' resolve as they imagined the fate that awaited them and their families should they capitulate. Gansevoort met in silence St. Leger's demand for surrender of the fort. Convinced that Stanwix could not be stormed successfully, the British commander reluctantly undertook siege operations.

St. Leger's lines of investment formed a triangle with camps at each of the three points. A little over a quarter of a mile upstream (north) from Fort Stanwix, St. Leger established his main camp, where he posted most of the regulars. Also on the west bank of the Mohawk, about a half a mile south of the fort, at a place called the Lower Landing, the remaining regulars, most of the Canadians, Tories, and the Indians were placed. A third post, a half a mile west of the fort and manned by Tories, was erected on Wood Creek. Groups of Indians formed crude picket lines between the posts, thus surrounding the fort; the investment, however, was far from complete, particularly in light of St. Leger's subsequent moves. In order to bring up his artillery and to secure his line of communication, he needed to cut a 16-mile road through the forest. He also had to put men to work clearing Wood Creek of the trees felled by the Americans. Compelled to detach many of his white troops for these work projects, St. Leger found himself hard pressed several days later to organize a force to oppose an approaching American relief column. On August 5 when he learned that American reinforcements under General Nicholas Herkimer were only 10 miles from Fort Stanwix, St. Leger could muster fewer than 250 whites to send against Herkimer's column. Consequently, at Oriskany the following day, St. Leger had to rely heavily on his Indian allies.

While the bloody fight at Oriskany raged in the morning and afternoon of August 6, the defenders of Fort Stanwix were also active. Herkimer had sent runners ahead to inform the fort of the approach of his relief column. They did not reach the fort until late in the morning, probably not until the trap at Oriskany had been sprung. Three signal guns were fired, but it is likely that the din of the Oriskany battle drowned them out. Gansevoort nevertheless acceded to Herkimer's request for a sortie from the fort to try and divert the enemy's attention. Marinus Willett, 250 men, and one cannon were about to sally forth, but the same rainstorm that halted action at Oriskany forced the delay of their advance. When they could finally keep their priming powder dry, Willett's men advanced on the enemy's camps at and around the Lower Landing. With most of St. Leger's men engaged at Oriskany or dispersed on work details, Willett's

men easily brushed aside the camps' few defenders, thoroughly plundered the encampments, and carried away everything they did not destroy. They captured Sir John Johnson's papers and baggage, 5 British flags, and 21 wagonloads of material. Although St. Leger and troops from the main British camp moved to cut Willett off from the fort, the Americans moved rapidly enough to return to the fort with booty in hand and without losing a man.

This August 6 sortie, though limited in nature, had a significant impact on the subsequent campaign. The looting of the enemy's camps undoubtedly cheered the defenders of Fort Stanwix, but more importantly, it dealt a severe blow to Indian morale. When they returned and found their camps stripped of blankets and personal possessions, the Indians exploded with rage. The torture and murder of several of the American prisoners taken at Oriskany momentarily alleviated their anger, but the sting of the loss of all they had left behind surely grew more acute in the days that followed. St. Leger's failure to protect the Indian camps heightened their disappointment with this expedition on which they had yet to enjoy any looting and had done much of the heavy fighting at Oriskany. Never known for their perseverance on long campaigns and/or sieges, the Indians' commitment to St. Leger began to wane.

Following the actions on August 6, St. Leger again tried to bluff the fort's defenders into surrender. On the evening of the battle, he sent Gansevoort a letter from two American prisoners that reported Oriskany as a great British victory and urged capitulation of the fort. The next day, a British delegation delivered a second missive, this one containing a thinly veiled threat from the British commander. He claimed that he had destroyed Herkimer, that Burgoyne had reached Albany, and that there was no hope of relief. Unless surrender was immediate, he intimated it might be impossible for him to control his Indians. In other words, if the fort had to be taken by force, St. Leger professed that he would be unable to restrain the Indians not only from massacring the fort's occupants but also from ravaging all of the American settlements in the Mohawk Valley.

According to Marinus Willett, the following scene transpired. Willett, speaking for Gansevoort and Stanwix's defenders, indignantly responded to the British officers present: "Do I understand you, Sir? I think you say, that you come from a British colonel . . . to the commandant of this garrison, to tell him, that if he does not deliver up the garrison into the hands of your Colonel, he will send his Indians to murder our women and children." Scornfully, Willett refused to surrender and added, "I consider the message you have brought a degrading one for a British officer to send and by no means reputable for a British officer to carry." The British delegation, seeing that the fort would continue to resist, withdrew after receiving permission for a three-day armistice.

In the days that followed, St. Leger realized that his artillery was too light to batter down the walls of the American fort so he tightened his encirclement of Fort Stanwix by employing traditional siege tactics to push his lines steadily forward. His efforts convinced the garrison to seek outside relief, and on August 9, Willett and a companion slipped away from the fort. They carefully worked their way through their besiegers' lines, then hurried on to Fort Dayton. There they learned that a second relief column was already making its way up the valley. General Philip Schuyler, commander of American forces in New York, upon learning of the Battle of Oriskany and Stanwix's investment, determined to relieve the fort. He appointed Benedict Arnold to command the expedition. Leading a force of about 950 men, Arnold struggled westward over horrible roads, finally reaching Fort Dayton on August 21. Informed that St. Leger had some 1,700 men at Stanwix, even the aggressive Arnold paused; however, when he learned the following day that St. Leger had pushed his lines to within 150 yards of the fort, Arnold decided to press on. After marching ten miles on August 23, he received word from Gansevoort that St. Leger had abandoned the siege and was retreating. A ruse that Arnold had initiated while on the march had achieved greater results than Arnold ever envisioned.

Hon Yost Schuyler, a half-witted resident of the Mohawk Valley, had been sentenced to death for involvement in an earlier Tory plot. Arnold offered to pardon Hon Yost if he would enter St. Leger's camp and spread exaggerated tales about the size of the approaching American relief force. The demented Dutchman played his role to the hilt (perhaps in part because Arnold held his brother as hostage). He had lived much of his life among the Indians and, like most men-

tally handicapped people, was regarded with awe and respect. He passed himself off as an escaped prisoner—a fact made more convincing by the bullet holes he had shot through his coat. To reinforce Hon Yost's stories, several Oneida Indians followed him into the Indian camps and repeated similar stories of the awesome size of Arnold's force. St. Leger's Indians, already smarting from their losses at Oriskany and bored with the siege, were ripe for these rumors. Seeing the holes in Hon Yost's coat, terrified by his pointing to the leaves on the trees when they asked about Arnold's numbers, and further alarmed by the corroborating stories of the Oneidas, the Indians hastily began leaving their camps. Efforts by the British to reassure their Indian allies and stay their departure proved fruitless. With half of his army disintegrating, St. Leger had no option but to raise the siege and retreat immediately. His movement back toward Oswego was so precipitous that artillery, ammunition, and large quantities of supplies were abandoned. On the retreat, St. Leger's Indians turned on their white allies, stealing liquor and clothes from the officers and attacking and massacring stragglers.

After learning of St. Leger's withdrawal on August 23 while on the march to Stanwix, Arnold rapidly pushed on the 20 miles to the fort. The following day, he pursued St. Leger to Lake Oneida, but arrived just as the last of the British boats sailed away. Arnold left about 700 men at Fort Stanwix and at several other Mohawk Valley posts, then hurried with 1,200 men to reunite with the main American army falling back before Burgoyne. As St. Leger retraced his path back to Canada, he wrote of plans to rejoin Burgoyne; however, time and distance prevented such a timely redeployment. St. Leger's invasion was over. The failure of his diversionary effort assured Burgoyne's isolation and thus contributed to the debacle at Saratoga.

Ralph L. Eckert

REFERENCES

John Burgoyne, *A State of the Expedition From Canada* . . . (1780); Henry B. Dawson, *Battles of the United States by Sea and Land* . . . , 2 vols. (1858); Hoffman Nickerson, *The Turning Point of the Revolution or Burgoyne in America* (1928); John Albert Scott, *Fort Stanwix (Fort Schuyler) and Oriskany* . . . (1927); William L. Stone, *The Campaign of Lieut. Gen. John Burgoyne and the Expedition of Lieut. Col. Barry St. Leger* (1877); Howard Swiggett, *War Out of Niagara: Walter Butler and the Tory Rangers* (1933); Christopher Ward, *The*

War of the Revolution, 2 vols. (1952); William M. Willett, ed., *A Narrative of the Military Actions of Colonel Marinus Willett* 1831).

St. Louis, Louisiana, Assault on (May 26, 1780)

Soon after its founding in 1764, St. Louis grew into the leading trade center for the Spanish possessions in upper Louisiana. Most of St. Louis's commerce consisted of the Indian fur trade with tribes as far away as the Kansas River, the upper Mississippi, and the Great Lakes. Because of its importance, St. Louis became a critical location for the American Revolution in the West.

Although Spain did not officially enter the Revolution until 1779, the Spanish had supported the Americans before then. From his headquarters in St. Louis, capital of what was known as "Spanish Illinois," Lieutenant Governor Fernando de Leyba assisted American efforts in the Mississippi Valley. A lasting friendship developed between him and George Rogers Clark after Clark's western campaign, and Spanish participation in the war complicated British efforts to gain control of the Mississippi Valley. In the South, Bernardo de Galvez, governor general of Louisiana, drove the British from lower Louisiana and the Floridas.

When Leyba arrived in St. Louis in 1778, he found it without defensive works. Rather than building fortifications here, Spanish policy was to maintain friendship and control over the Indians by annual presents and by cutting off trade when problems developed. No Indians lived near St. Louis, and no fort was regarded as necessary, although there was a small post at the mouth of the Missouri River.

Despite the increasing threat of war, lack of funds meant there would be little change in St. Louis's defenses early in Leyba's tenure. Fighting at Vincennes in late 1778 and early 1779 brought the war closer to St. Louis, and when Spain broke off diplomatic relations with England in June 1779, the British government ordered its forces in Canada to attack American and Spanish posts on the Mississippi.

The only regular forces at Leyba's disposal were 15 men and a drummer at St. Louis, a corporal and 5 men at the small fort at the mouth of the Missouri, and a lieutenant and 12 men at the settlement of Ste. Genevieve down the Missis-sippi. Thus, Leyba would have to depend on his militia, which in July 1779 consisted of 175 infantrymen and slightly more than 50 cavalrymen. By December 1780 there were 220 men divided into two companies. However, many of the cavalrymen were cavalry in name only, since they had no horses. The militia were undisciplined, and rivalry and jealousy developed among some of the officers.

After St. Louisans heard rumors of an Indian attack from the north in early 1780, Leyba began to construct fortifications for St. Louis. He wanted to build four towers at the four corners of the town, but he could raise only enough money through public donations to build one. In addition to the tower, he brought five cannon from an abandoned fort down the Mississippi.

A British force of 750 men, including a number of Menominee and Sac and Fox Indians, under Emanuel Hesse, left Prairie du Chien for St. Louis on May 2, 1780. A short time later, Leyba learned of the attacking army and ordered the Ste. Genevieve militia unit to St. Louis as reinforcements. He also ordered two lines of entrenchments dug, one on the north side of town and the other on the south side.

The attack came on May 26. According to Leyba's report, the attackers killed a number of civilians, both whites and slaves, and killed or stole all the livestock and horses they could find. The Spanish artillery slowed the attack, but Leyba decided against a counterattack because his force was greatly outnumbered. Hesse quickly withdrew to the Illinois River, destroying farms and taking prisoners on the way.

St. Louis remained on alert for about two weeks after the attack. Leyba feared another attack from a British force coming down the Illinois from Chicago. When this did not occur, in mid-June a 200-man Spanish and American expedition left St. Louis to meet the British and Indians on the Illinois. Finding the Indian villages along the Illinois abandoned, the force burned them and destroyed their crops. Leyba, who had become ill before the British attack, died shortly after the expedition left.

Harold Campbell

REFERENCES

Louis Houck, *The History of Missouri*, 2 vols. (1908), *II;*
——, *The Spanish Regime in Missouri*, (1909);
Lawrence Kinnaird, "Clark-Leyba Papers," *American Historical Review*, 41 (1935):92–112; ——,

Spain in the Mississippi Valley, 1765–1794 (1946–1949); John Francis McDermott, "Captain Leyba and the Defense of St. Louis in 1780," in *The Spanish in the Mississippi Valley, 1762–1804,* (1974); James B. Musick, *St. Louis as a Fortified Town* (1941); Abraham P. Nasatir, "The Anglo-Spanish Frontier in the Illinois Country during the American Revolution, 1779–1783," *Illinois State Historical Society Journal,* 21 (1928):310–322.

Saintes, Battle of the (West Indies), April 12, 1782

Also known as the Battle of Dominica, the Battle of the Saintes was the greatest British naval victory of the War of the American Revolution. It was also the most controversial. The battle took place on April 12, 1782; it was named for the Iles des Saintes, a little archipelago in the channel midway between Dominica and Guadeloupe in the West Indies. The battle was fought between a French fleet commanded by Admiral Count Francois de Grasse and a British fleet commanded by Admiral Sir George Brydges Rodney.

In September 1781 de Grasse had won the Battle of the Chesapeake against an English fleet commanded by Admiral Thomas Graves (Admiral Sir Samuel Hood commanded the van in the action). One of the most decisive victories in the age of fighting sail, it made possible the Franco-American land victory at Yorktown. General George Washington then proposed an attack on Charleston, but de Grasse demurred. He had promised the Spaniards he would take his fleet to the West Indies at the end of the hurricane season for a joint attack on Jamaica. Washington then proposed a less ambitious attack on Wilmington, but it was finally shelved because of the press of time. Washington's repeated efforts to persuade de Grasse to maintain a decisive naval concentration in North American waters were unsuccessful; in early November de Grasse's fleet of 33 ships of the line sailed for the West Indies. The Caribbean sugar islands were vital to the economies of both France and Britain; the presence of substantial naval units in the West Indies showed that they played a much more important role in the naval strategies of both nations than did North America.

For Britain the situation at the end of 1781 appeared desperate. Gibraltar was besieged, Minorca was about to fall, and the French were victorious at sea off India. With the surrender at Yorktown, the American colonies appeared lost; Spain had retaken West Florida; in the West Indies the island of Tobago had fallen, and Jamaica appeared especially vulnerable.

In these circumstances London turned to Admiral Rodney. Although he was racked with gout and recovering from a bladder operation, Rodney agreed to return to the West Indies. He hoped to set out from England in early December in the *Formidable* (90 guns) along with 11 other ships of the line. When he arrived at Portsmouth, however, only four ships were ready, and there were problems in finding seamen. He also was prevented from sailing by three weeks of Atlantic storms.

In the interim, Sir Charles Douglas was able to accomplish a great deal. Rodney's appointment of Douglas as flag captain had been an excellent choice, for he was probably the top gunnery expert in the Royal Navy. He used the delay to improve the effectiveness of the cannon. While in command of the *Duke* (98 guns), in 1778, Douglas had recommended the application of flintlocks in place of match for firing cannon at sea. The Admiralty had rejected this proposal, but Douglas had, at his own expense, fitted the guns of the *Duke* with musket locks. He had also carried out innovations in the use of tackle to widen traverse of the guns, improved the composition of powder cartridges, and introduced quill tubes as part of the ignition system. All these greatly increased rate and accuracy of fire. The introduction of the flintlocks was particularly important; they were much more reliable than match and gave the gun captain more control over timing, especially important at sea where the rolling action of a ship affected the elevation of its guns. The subsequent Battle of the Saintes clearly demonstrated the value of gunlocks for cannon at sea. Both the *Duke* and the *Formidable* (to which Douglas transferred in November 1781) played key roles in the Battle of the Saintes, and Douglas had equipped both with locks. Before sailing for the West Indies, most of the British ships were also armed for the first time with carronades. These new short weapons, not yet adopted by the French, were very light for their caliber but had great smashing power at short range. The light weight of the carronades allowed the placement of 32-pounders on forecastles and quarterdecks. The carronades added greatly to weight of broadsides at the short ranges preferred by the Royal Navy.

The same storms that delayed Rodney also kept French naval units destined for the West Indies in their Atlantic ports. When French merchantmen and warships finally sailed, they encountered not only a bad storm but also a British squadron. The result was that only two ships of the line and five transports made it to the West Indies to reinforce de Grasse, while the rest were forced to put back into Brest. These French reinforcements were part of an ambitious plan to conquer all of the British West Indian islands.

Rodney's fleet of 12 ships of the line finally cleared Spithead for the West Indies on January 14, 1782, and arrived at Barbados on February 19. The situation in the British West Indies was precarious. The French recently had recaptured the island of St. Eustatius, and many British vessels were in poor repair. Only adverse weather had prevented de Grasse from striking at the main British base at Barbados.

On January 9, de Grasse arrived off St. Kitts and landed an 8,000-man invasion force. As soon as he was informed of this move, Admiral Hood set out with his entire fleet of 22 ships of the line; after embarking about 1,000 troops at St. Johns, they set sail for St. Kitts. Hood had planned a surprise daybreak attack on de Grasse's ships as they lay at anchor. It was an excellent plan, for the French vessels were in some disorder in the roadstead. It failed because of a collision during the night between the leading ship of the line, the *Alfred*, and a frigate, the *Nymphe*. Repairs to the *Alfred* threw off the timing of the attack, for the British did not arrive until the early morning of January 24, enabling the French to spot them and get to sea. Inconclusive maneuvering followed. On January 25, while he had the weather gauge, Hood tricked de Grasse into believing that he intended an attack. The British fleet then suddenly made for the roadstead. By the time de Grasse realized what had happened it was too late. Hood's captains succeeded in gaining the roadstead, although some of the rear vessels were damaged by fire from the French van as they approached the anchorage. De Grasse and the French fleet then sailed away, and Hood arranged his vessels in line with springs on the anchor cables to enable them to bring full broadside fire to bear on the French if they returned.

De Grasse returned on the morning of January 26 and sailed his warships in file past the British line. Both fleets exchanged broadsides without significant result. The French repeated the tactic in the afternoon, then withdrew to a position in sight of the island.

Hood hoped the greatly outnumbered British defenders on land would be able to hold out until Rodney arrived with reinforcements, but the French forced a British surrender on February 12. They also captured heavy guns on the island, including 13-inch mortars, and began positioning them to attack the British vessels at anchor. Hood resorted to a ruse to save his fleet from de Grasse's force, by then grown to 30 ships of the line, two 50-gun ships, and 7 frigates. During the night of February 23, the British crews cut the cables of their vessels and silently sailed away, leaving only lanterns on buoys to make it appear that the fleet was still there. The maneuver was executed perfectly, and the next morning de Grasse and the French saw only an empty anchorage. De Grasse then ordered his fleet to Nevis to take on stores.

Rodney and Hood finally joined forces off Antigua on February 25, and their joint fleet, now under Rodney's command, outnumbered the French. The British had 36 ships of the line; the French had 33, but these included 2 of just 50 guns each.

Rodney ordered the British fleet to Martinique, hoping to cut de Grasse off from his main base. He was disappointed, on his arrival there, to find de Grasse's fleet safely at anchor in Port Royal Bay. Rodney then set sail for St. Lucia to refit, leaving a few frigates to watch the French at Port Royal. Rodney had no doubts about French intentions. Intelligence information indicated that de Grasse would attempt to join the Spanish fleet at either Havana or Cap Francois for an attack on Jamaica. Realizing what was at stake, Rodney prophetically wrote to his wife, "I am of opinion that the great events which must decide the Empire of the ocean will be either off Jamaica or St. Domingo."

De Grasse awaited reinforcements and supplies from France. Rodney and Hood knew that the enemy was short of supplies and that the French would make an effort to reinforce. Indeed, both French and Spanish reinforcements were already en route. Rodney and Hood agreed that they must intercept and destroy the French convoy, but they disagreed over how to accomplish it. Hood wanted to divide the British fleet into two squadrons in order to guard the northern approach to Martinique as well as the traditional southern route. Rodney refused because dividing the fleet might have allowed de Grasse to escape his anchorage. He insisted that the French convoy would come in from the south. As a result of Rodney's mistaken decision, the British failed to intercept the French convoy that anchored in Port Royal Bay on March 20. It came into Martinique via the northern route, escorted by two ships of the line. It was fortunate for Rodney that only 2 additional heavy warships had been added to the French force, but they gave de Grasse 35 ships of the line. He also had the supplies and troops necessary for a land campaign against Jamaica.

Late on April 5, the British received word via French deserters on a ship arriving at St. Lucia that de Grasse had embarked a substantial ground force in transports and intended to join the Spanish for an attack on Jamaica. This proved accurate. On the morning of April 8 the signal that the enemy was coming out and standing to the northwest was passed through a chain of British frigates to Rodney. The British fleet at once weighed anchor at St. Lucia and cleared the harbor by noon.

De Grasse sailed with a force of 35 ships of the line, 6 frigates, and 150 unarmed ships. The latter included both store ships for the operation against Jamaica and merchantmen bound for France. His plan was for the merchantmen to sail for France as soon as they were out of range of British cruisers. De Grasse thus hoped to avoid battle until he was free of the convoy and united with the Spanish fleet. He sailed close to the islands on his westward passage so that the convoy could take refuge in case of attack. He believed that his advance start would enable him to outdistance his enemy, but the slow-moving merchant vessels foiled this.

On April 8, the British fleet of 36 ships of the line and accompanying frigates caught up with the French. By 2:30 P.M the leading British frigate had the French in sight, and by 6 P.M the main fleets had sighted each other from the mastheads.

By the morning of April 9 the distance between the two fleets had decreased to the point that the men on the ships in the British van could see the entire French fleet. Cohesion on both sides had been lost. During the night the French

had sailed close to Dominica, and by morning about 15 ships of the line had worked clear of the island; catching the trade wind, they had separated from the rest. The British underwent a like experience, with the result that about 7 A.M. Hood's van drew away from the center, his eight ships well in front of the others.

As the British fleet closed, it became clear to de Grasse that he had to change his plans. He ordered the convoy, escorted by the two 50-gun ships *Expériment* and *Sagittaire*, to put in to the nearby harbor of Basse-Terre on the island of Guadalupe; at the same time, he ordered the fleet to work to windward through the channel between Dominica and Guadeloupe. De Grasse hoped to draw Rodney away, and then, trusting to the superior sailing qualities of the French vessels, throw off the pursuit, rejoin the convoy, and run west to the rendezvous with the Spanish.

Hood's small division was, however, a great temptation, and the Battle of the Saintes opened in a fight between the two vans. Most of the centers and vans of both fleets were caught in variable winds under the lee of the island of Dominica. De Grasse ordered his van and part of his center, commanded by the Marquis de Vaudreuil and amounting to 15 ships of the line, to come about and attack Hood's van of 8 ships. De Vaudreuil's ships ran north and sailed alongside Hood's division, exchanging long-range broadsides. The British ships were almost stationary, with their topsails backed to slow progress. De Vaudreuil ordered his ships to tack in succession when the leading vessel was clear of the British. He then led the vessels around again for another exchange of long-range broadsides. The French did not close for fear of the British carronades. As de Vaudreuil later put it, "If we had put ourselves in close [à porte] to their carronades we would have been promptly unrigged and we would have been defeated." These two actions lasted from about 9:48 A.M. to 1:45 P.M. The imminent arrival of the rest of the British fleet caused the French warships to haul off. Some long-range fire took place between the British center and part of the French fleet, but it was of little consequence; indeed, Rodney ordered some of his ships not to return fire so as to save ammunition.

A number of the British ships in the van sustained damage in the fighting, and that night the British fleet lay to in order to repair damage in

Hood's van. The damaged ships were able to remain in the line, although Rodney did shift the van and rear. One 64-gun French ship, the *Caton*, badly damaged in the fighting, was forced to retire to Guadeloupe for repairs.

De Grasse had failed to capitalize on a splendid opportunity. Had he ordered all his ships, instead of merely half, against the British van he could have won a great victory. As Hood put it, "he might have cut us up by pouring a succession of fresh ships upon us as long as he pleased."

The next morning the British began the pursuit of de Grasse. At daylight on April 10 the French fleet was some 14 miles to windward. A British signaling error that evening might have enabled de Grasse to escape had it not been for a collision in the French fleet during the night. The *Zélé* (74 guns) damaged the *Jason* (64 guns) so badly that she was also ordered to Basse-Terre. De Grasse's fleet had now been reduced by a total of 4 ships of the line, to 31. The ships damaged in the engagement on April 9 also slowed the French fleet to the point that the British were able to keep it in sight. But the French lead had, if anything, increased by the morning of April 11. It looked as if de Grasse would escape.

But two of the French ships, the *Zélé* and the *Magnanime* (74 guns) had dropped off to leeward of the French fleet. Rodney ordered a general chase in the hope of catching these stragglers. By the late afternoon a number of British vessels had closed to the point that de Grasse, determined not to abandon any of his ships, turned back to protect them. There was no fighting, however; Rodney saw that his leading ships faced overwhelming odds and recalled them, but the French had lost much of their earlier advantage.

At 2 A.M. on April 12 the hapless *Zélé* rammed the French flagship, the *Ville de Paris* (110 guns), said to be the finest warship then afloat. The *Zélé* lost her foremast and bowsprit in the collision, and a frigate, the *Astrée*, was ordered to take her in tow and head for Guadeloupe.

All that night the British fleet had carried a press of sail. With the dawn the British sailors could see the *Zélé* and *Astrée* about 6 miles to leeward, while the main French fleet was spread out between 12 and 15 miles off the port bow. Rodney was delighted. He wrote, "I had the happiness at daylight to find my most sanguine desire was near being accomplished by my having it in my power to force the enemy to battle."

The two fleets were now between the northern tip of Dominica and the islets known as the Saintes. Rodney had the advantage in numbers—36 ships of the line to only 30 for de Grasse. At 5:45 A.M. Rodney signaled to van commander Drake in the *Princessa* to make more sail in order to gain the windward position. At 5:50 Rodney signaled the fleet for line ahead, two cables apart. Six minutes later he ordered Hood to detail ships to chase the *Zélé* and her consort. Hood ordered the *Monarch*, *Valiant*, *Centaur*, and *Belliqueux* to quit the line and chase to the north. If de Grasse took the bait and came to their rescue, he would have had to abandon his position to windward, and with it the weather gauge. De Grasse was determined not to abandon the crippled *Zélé*, but in his effort to rescue her, he came so far to leeward that a battle became inevitable.

About 7 A.M. Rodney recalled the four ships sent after the *Zélé* and ordered the fleet to form in line of battle one cable length apart. The British ships cleared for action.

In an effort to try to maintain the weather gauge, de Grasse ran to the south, close to Dominica. The two fleets were now heading for one another. De Grasse hoped to pass along the British line at a safe distance and avoid a close action, while Rodney ordered his van to cross the head of the French line and gain the wind. The British were in a well-ordered line, while the French had sizable gaps in their formation. Some of the French ships were as far as ten miles from the main body.

At about 7:30 A.M., still holding the weather gauge, the leading French ships, firing ineffectively at long range, passed across the bows of the British van. The battle began when the leading British ship, the *Marlborough* (74 guns), reached the sixth or seventh French ship in line, the 74-gun *Brave*; turning toward her but running on opposite course, at 7:58 the *Marlborough* fired the first broadside of the battle. The rest of Drake's division followed in succession. The center came next, with Rodney's flagship, the *Formidable*, firing her first broadside at 8:08. The intensity of the battle increased as each ship came into range. The two fleets moved slowly along on opposite tacks, broadsides crashing and the ships obscured in clouds of smoke.

De Grasse realized that if he continued on this course his rear ships would have to sustain the broadsides of each successive British ship while his own van was out of the fight. He altered course to starboard, and the firing became general along the entire line. To prevent the battle from being indecisive, Rodney kept the signal for close action flying, reinforcing it with an order to alter course to starboard, closer to the French.

The French suffered more than the English during this exchange, as their vessels were crammed not only with seamen but with soldiers for the invasion of Jamaica. The fire from the carronades was devastating at short range, and the rate of fire from the British ships was several times that of the French. Although the French were taking greater punishment, as long as they held the weather gauge the engagement would not be decisive, and within an hour or so they would be free of the British. De Grasse saw, however, that his course was taking his vessels into still waters in the lee of Dominica, where he could thwart Rodney's efforts at close engagement. De Grasse twice made the signal to wear, to pivot his ships so they would be able to steer back in the direction from which they had come, but his ships were at musket range from the British vessels. With no room to carry out the maneuver, his captains ignored the signal.

Just after 9 A.M., de Grasse's luck failed. There was a sudden shift in wind to the southward, forcing the French fleet to steer more to starboard. This created confusion among the French. Vessels were forced to turn or were pushed astern, and ships fouled each other and fell away to leeward. Rodney was now presented with the opportunity of his life, an opening in the French battle line.

He quickly ordered the *Formidable* through the hole in the French line. One of the two principal controversies of the Battle of the Saintes is whether Rodney previously had decided to attempt to pierce the enemy line in certain circumstances. Some sources even credit Douglas with suggesting it. All that matters is that Rodney gave the order and it was carried out. As naval historian Michael Lewis has noted, "As the blame, had it failed, would certainly have had to be borne by Rodney, so must the credit, when it succeeded, go to the same man."

The *Glorieux*, nineteenth ship in the French battle line, was raked by the *Formidable* as she pierced the line. Other British ships that followed the *Formidable* also pounded the *Glorieux*. One observer wrote of this point in the action:

> We passed within pistol-shot of the *Glorieux* of seventy-four guns, which was so roughly handled that being shorn of all her masts, bowsprit and ensign staff but with the whole flag nailed to the stump of one of her masts breathing defiance as it were in her last moments, became a motionless hulk.

Although Rodney gave no signal to break the line, five other British ships followed the *Formidable*, each raking the ships to either side as they crossed the "T" of the French line. In fact, there was no such signal in the Fighting Instructions, and this type of maneuver was hardly standard battle practice.

As soon as he had penetrated the French line and had the weather gauge, Rodney took stock. He must have been pleased by what he saw. Captain Alan Gardner of the *Duke*, the ship immediately ahead of the *Formidable*, noting Rodney's example, ordered his ship to cut through the French line at another point, and in the process inflicted heavy damage on four enemy ships. Commodore Sir Edmund Affleck in the *Bedford*, the sixth ship in line behind the *Formidable*, showed the same initiative in cutting the French line, passing close to the *César* and also making it to windward. He was followed through the French line by Hood's entire division of 12 ships. They inflicted terrible damage on both the *César* and the *Hector*. The French formation was completely shattered; cut into three separate divisions, the French never succeeded in reestablishing their line.

Those British ships ahead of the *Duke* had continued on a northerly course. In order to concentrate his ships, at 11:15 A.M. Rodney signaled them to tack. This signal was repeated 15 minutes later, and at 12:30, it was followed by the signal to close. De Grasse also tried to concentrate his fleet, but the fighting was now between individual ships, a situation favoring the British because of their superior seamanship and gunnery. The French vessels took a frightful number of hull shots but were less cut up above than the British, and thus better able to take advantage of the light winds.

For the next few hours both fleets were largely becalmed, and their crews spent the time repairing rigging and other damage to their vessels. By 1 P.M. the smoke had cleared sufficiently to reveal the French making off to leeward in several unorganized groups. The British captains were no longer bound by the signal of "line of battle," and on their own initiative, the three divisions of the fleet were soon running to westward trying to chase down the French ships.

The crippled French ships were taken first. The *Glorieux*, which had taken frightful punishment from the *Formidable* as the latter pierced the line, had lost all her masts and was under tow by a frigate. She was the first French ship taken. Her captain had ordered the line from the frigate cut so the smaller warship could escape. Next to be taken were the *César* and the *Hector*, both 74-gun ships that, along with the *Glorieux*, had borne the brunt of the British attack.

Throughout the afternoon the British pursued the French. With Rodney not signaling "chase," and his own ship under easy sail, the pursuit soon slackened. Hood was incensed. He ordered his ships to make more sail and even put out boats to draw the *Barfleur* into the wind. But the majority of the vessels in the British fleet followed the example of Rodney rather than Hood.

Later in the afternoon, the British took the *Ardent* (64 guns), a former British vessel. She was a particularly valuable prize as she carried the French siege artillery for the invasion of Jamaica.

The greatest prize was yet to be taken. The *Ville de Paris* had been badly cut up and was limping along at the rear of the French fleet, under only a few ragged sails. De Grasse tried to fight his way out of an encircling ring of British ships, but the flagship no longer answered her helm. Shortly after sunset, at about 6:30 P.M., de Grasse, one of only three men left standing on the upper deck, ordered her surrender to Hood in the *Barfleur*. This was the first time that a French commander-in-chief had been captured at sea (ironically, de Grasse, victor off Yorktown, had now fallen prisoner to the admiral he had beaten there). The battle was over. At 6:45, Rodney signaled to the fleet to bring it on the port tack, thus calling off the pursuit. The English vessels then lay to in the gathering darkness.

Hood was appalled. Not only would he have pursued the French more aggressively during the afternoon but he wanted to continue the chase that night and finish off the French in the morning. This was the second great controversy to arise from the battle. Hood later claimed that had he commanded the fleet, he would have taken upward of 20 enemy ships of the line rather than the 5 that had been captured by nightfall. Rodney later admitted that he might have been too cautious; but his ships had sustained considerable damage aloft. They were also short of ammunition, and it would have been dangerous to fight a night action. Moreover, the French ships had shown themselves faster than their British counterparts. At the very least, however, Rodney should have sent frigates to keep track of the French fleet, as he had done before.

At sunrise on April 13, Hood asked Rodney to resume the pursuit. Although Rodney agreed, he changed his mind after Hood left. Although many French ships had sustained heavy damage, under the command of de Vaudreuil they succeeded in reaching safety at Cap Francois.

The French had suffered appalling casualties in the battle. The *Ville de Paris* alone sustained 300 killed or wounded. The *Glorieux* also suffered heavy casualties. Aboard the *César* the survivors broke into the stores of spirits and got drunk. Someone upset a candle and the ship was soon engulfed in flames. Her magazine exploded and 460 men died—400 French and 60 members of a British prize crew—from the battle, the explosion, or from sharks in the water. Total French casualties were estimated at over 3,000; the British lost 243 dead and another 816 wounded. They spent the next four days repairing damage to their vessels.

De Grasse was quick to lay blame for his defeat on the "base desertion of his officers." Later he wrote a series of pamphlets in his own defense and attacking his officers. He also made much of the "superior discipline, neatness and order" in the British ships, an opinion echoed by John Paul Jones, who had sailed aboard the French fleet as an observer. Superior British seamanship was a major factor in the outcome of the battle, but de Grasse also must take major responsibility. His strategic plan was unsound. The British had taken St. Lucia early in the war, and so were in close proximity to the main French base at Port Royal and able to keep the enemy fleet under surveillance. Under constant observation, and with the main British fleet only 40 miles away, de Grasse's strategic plan to sail with a large convoy was hardly wise. The same could be said of his subsequent plan to double back, for it would have been better to send the convoy off to the west and decide the issue by battle. His fleet was equal in numbers to that of the British and he would have had a good chance of

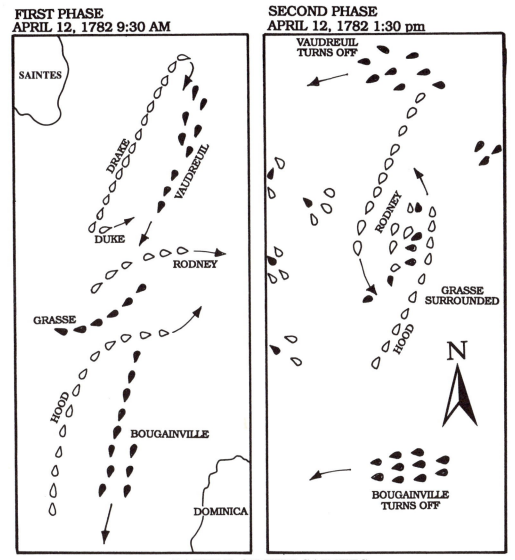

BATTLE OF THE SAINTES

inflicting significant damage on the enemy. But that would have meant keeping the fleet in tight formation and maneuvering to bring the British to battle. De Grasse had communicated no such instructions to his captains beforehand, and he went into battle with his fleet disorganized and widely separated.

By April 17, Rodney was ready to take the fleet to Jamaica. On that day he also authorized Hood, impatient as always, to take ten ships of the line and patrol in advance of the rest of the fleet. Two days later, in the Mona Passage between Puerto Rico and Santo Domingo, Hood's force sighted five French vessels. The British pursued and captured the 64-gun ships of the line *Caton* and *Jason*, the frigate *l'Aimable* (32 guns) and the sloop *Cérès* (18 guns). The two ships of the line were those damaged in the engagement of April 9 and sent to Guadeloupe for repairs. Hood was quick to inform Rodney: "It is a very mortifying circumstance to relate to you, Sir, that the French fleet which you put to flight on the 12th went through the Mona Channel on the 18th, only the day before I was in it." Without the self-imposed British delay, the French fleet of 26 sail, including frigates, would not have reached safety at Cap Francois.

On April 29, Rodney arrived at Port Royal, Jamaica, with the prizes and the British ships most in need of repair. He had sent Hood with 25 ships of the line to cruise for the enemy off Cap Francois. The combined Franco-Spanish West Indian force was still stronger than that of the Royal Navy in those waters, but Rodney correctly predicted that they would not dare to confront the British again. Any Franco-Spanish initiative was hampered by quarreling among the two allies, the damage inflicted on the French fleet, and the spread of disease among troops ashore. On the British side, the battle did have the effect of altering tactics. The advantage of piercing the enemy battle line was now clearly recognized and was written into the Fighting Instructions. No move was made on the part of the Admiralty to adopt flintlocks, however; perhaps this was because of the end of the war, but flintlocks did not become standard in the Royal Navy until 1790.

The Battle of the Saintes was the last major battle of the war in the Caribbean. Its restoration of British command of the seas came too late to affect the outcome of the American Revolution. But it was a sufficient victory for the British to retain all of their West Indian islands in the resulting Treaty of Paris that ended the war, and it placed Hood and Rodney in the ranks of Britain's naval heroes.

Ironically, Rodney was not long able to savor his victory. On July 10, the frigate *Jupiter* arrived at Port Royal with Admiral Sir Hugh Pigot, Rodney's replacement as commander of the Leeward Islands Squadron. The British defeat at Yorktown had ended Rodney's career. It also brought down the Tory ministry in London, and the new Whig government immediately ordered replacements for many of the Earl of Sandwich's appointees. News of the victory of the Saintes had reached London after the *Jupiter* had sailed, and efforts to overtake the frigate were unsuccessful. Rodney was rewarded on his return to England, however, with an English peerage, an additional pension of 2,000 pounds a year, and the thanks of the Parliament. Hood got an Irish peerage, and Drake and Affleck were made baronets.

Spencer Tucker

REFERENCES

William M. James, *The British Navy in Adversity. A Study of the War of American Independence* (1926); Alfred Thayer Mahan, *The Major Operations of the Navies in the War of American Independence* (1913); Nathan Miller, *Sea of Glory. The Continental Navy Fights for Independence, 1775–1783* (1974).

Salomon, Haym (1740–1785)

American Patriot, financier. Born in Lissa, Poland, little is known of Haym Salomon's early life because of a fire that destroyed much of the Jewish section of Lissa. It is believed, however, that he left his home at an early age and traveled widely, learning to speak Spanish, French, and Russian.

In about 1770, Salomon returned to Poland and joined the movement for independence. However, when Poland was partitioned in 1771 by Russia, Prussia, and Austria, Salomon was forced to flee the country, first to England and then to New York. There he went into business as a broker and merchant.

In the colonial struggle against England, Salomon became an ardent Whig and worked as a sutler selling provisions to the troops on the Canadian border. When he returned to New York, Salomon was one of a group of men who formed a plan to send fire ships up the Narrows of New York harbor to destroy the British fleet. Unfortunately, the scheme was discovered, and Haym Salomon was arrested and imprisoned as a spy during the British occupation of New York.

Salomon might have died in prison had it not been for his knowledge of foreign languages. He was rescued by Hessian mercenaries who needed competent personnel who spoke English and other languages and who could act as purveyors of commissary supplies. In this position, Salomon worked quietly, performing his tasks for the British, while at the same time helping French and American prisoners with money and with plans for their escape to the American lines.

After he was paroled, Salomon resumed his business as merchant, ship's chandler, distiller, and interpreter. He also continued to act as an undercover desertion agent among the Hessians. On January 2, 1777, he married Rachel Franks, daughter of Moses B. Franks, an influential Jewish merchant.

After his marriage, Salomon continued to induce Hessians to desert and helped imprisoned French and American officers to escape. When someone betrayed Salomon, he fled New York on August 11, 1778, leaving behind his wife, an infant child, and the estate he had amassed. Soon after, he established himself in Philadelphia as a shopkeeper and bill broker and brought his family there. As his business prospered, Salomon became one of the largest depositors in the Bank of North America, to which he was a subscriber.

Salomon was almost sole broker for the Continental Office of Finance in the sale of bills of exchange, and he contributed much to maintain the bankrupt government's credit. Robert Morris, who recently had assumed the post of Superintendent of the Office of Finance, depended on Salomon to sell bills of the French, Spanish, and Dutch governments, and to handle all types of government paper and currencies, both Continental and state.

After the British were defeated at Yorktown, Salomon became even more valuable to Morris. The two men worked diligently to maintain the credit of the new nation. So successful was Salomon, that Morris allowed him to advertise himself as the "Broker to the Office of Finance, to the Consul General of France, and to the Treasurer of the French Army."

By 1782, Salomon's reputation as a responsible bill broker was well established. Many notables in need of cash turned to him, including members of the Continental Congress, especially Edmund Randolph and James Madison.

While Salomon lived in Philadelphia, he also served the community as a merchant in the traditional sense. He had a shop and a storage room where he stocked, stored, and sold dry goods, liquor, groceries, tobacco, hemp, and indigo.

In 1784, Salomon decided to move back to New York, his first American home. Salomon probably suspected that there would be a brighter future for him as a broker, merchant, and as a Jew in New York. He purchased a house on Wall Street and announced that he would conduct a brokerage and auction business. Although the Wall Street house was opened, Salomon, who had been ill for some time, died before leaving Philadelphia and taking charge.

Haym Salomon was an observant and devoted Jew who conducted no business on the Sabbath or the Holy Days. While he was not active in congregational life, Salomon was known as a generous man and was highly respected for his concern for others. He served as treasurer of the short-lived Ezrat Orchim (Travelers Aid Society), the first recorded Jewish charity organization in the United States. It was an integral part of Mikveh Israel, in Philadelphia, one of the nation's oldest Sephardic congregations. By 1782, Salomon had become the largest contributor to Mikveh Israel's building fund, and as its most liberal donor, he was accorded the honor of opening the doors of the sanctuary in the formal dedication ceremony.

Salomon died on January 6, 1785, at the age of 45. The letters of administration indicate that Salomon died insolvent. He left a substantial estate, but most of it was in Continental currency and depreciated securities. Nothing was left for his family, although his widow was allowed to keep her household furnishings. After Salomon's burial, no money was left for a headstone; he lies today in an unmarked grave in Philadelphia's Spruce Street Cemetery.

Toward the end of the nineteenth and the beginning of the twentieth century, a myth began to develop that exaggerated Salomon's services to the American Revolution. What is not myth, however, is the fact that Haym Salomon , a Jew, was devoted to his people and to his family. He was generous in helping to build his Philadelphia congregation; he had risked his life in New York as an American secret agent; and he lent money to notables to help them carry on their work, in some instances asking no interest.

When Salomon passed away, a Philadelphia newspaper paid him this tribute, "He was remarkable for his skill and integrity in his profession and for his generous and humane deportment."

Burton A. Boxerman

REFERENCES

Stephen Birmingham, *The Grandees* (1971); Max Kohler, *Haym Salomon* (1931); Jacob R. Marcus, *United States Jewry 1776–1985 Volume I* (1989); Charles Edward Russell, *Haym Salomon* (1930); Edwin Wolf 2nd and Maxwell Whiteman, *The History of the Jews of Philadelphia* (1956).

Salt, Importance of

Always indispensable for colonial America's fishing and fur industries, an adequate supply of salt became even more vital during the Revolution. Without salt, meat could not be preserved. By 1775, most of America's salt came from Portugal or the West Indies, sources largely cut off by the British blockade. The Continental Army was desperately short of salt, especially in the first years of the war. Commissary General Joseph Trumbull warned Washington, "I must first know what salt I can be sure of, before I purchase provisions." In Virginia (1775) the commodity became so scarce that an armed mob commandeered a supply of salt from a neighboring town; it was still scarce seven years later when a group from another Virginia town stole the cargo of salt from a docked ship.

The problem of obtaining salt was compounded when the price of salt skyrocketed. Whereas in New Jersey salt sold for 20 pence a bushel in 1771, by 1777, John Adams reported, it was going for $27 a bushel. Salt had become an item for profiteering and price gouging.

Congress dealt with the salt supply problem by urging the states either to make their own or to find ways to import it. To encourage its manufacture Congress republished in 1775 *The Art of Making Common Salt*, by William Brownrigg, originally published in 1748. The pamphlet contained diagrams and instructions for making salt by the solar method. This method, which basically produced salt through evaporation, was a slow, painstaking process that resulted in coarse salt. Most of those who built saltworks in America during the war years probably used the alternative method of boiling sea water. Making salt this way was faster and produced a finer salt, but it required a large supply of firewood and steady workers, both hard to obtain.

Encouraged by Congress, the various states quickly enacted their own legislation concerning salt. During the war years most state legislatures subsidized or provided compensation for the construction of saltworks. They also provided bounties for its manufacture, attempted to fix its prices, prohibited its export to other states, and tried to distribute it fairly. New Jersey, Massachusetts, and Maryland had the most successful saltworks. By August 1777 New Jersey had so many saltworks that John Adams could write, "All the old women and young children are gone down to the Jersey shore to make salt. Salt water is boiling all round the coast." A Massachusets resident wrote John Adams about the same time that "great quantitys of Salt are made here," including 200 bushels a day at Sandwich, on Cape Cod. And a Baltimore merchant bragged in 1778, "Our People are running so fast on Salt Making, that there can be no doubt that they will . . . next Summer be able to supply the whole wants of that essential Article of Life."

Other states, like Virginia, did not do so well. Virginia invested thousands of pounds in an ambitious state-owned saltworks that, plagued by mosquitoes, labor and fuel shortages, and technical problems, produced only 50 bushels of salt. States unable to produce their own salt increasingly turned to other means, such as capturing British ships and by eluding the British blockade. In 1777 Connecticut's Council of Safety, responding to the "cry and want of the necessary article of salt," sent a convoy of ships out to obtain it. Other states, including Virginia, depended on ships from the Caribbean and Bermuda, especially, to bring salt to them; the going exchange rate varied between two or three bushels of corn for every one of salt.

The British also realized the importance of salt to the Americans. Intermittent British sea raids of the New Jersey shore between 1778 and 1782 destroyed a number of saltworks, several of which were rebuilt. And some British ships reportedly did a thriving business along the American coast, trading salt for fresh food. By about 1780, however, American efforts to obtain enough salt, though hampered by the British raids and American inexperience, had largely succeeded.

Jean F. Hankins

REFERENCES

Larry G. Bowman, "The Scarcity of Salt in Virginia during the American Revolution," *Virginia Magazine of History and Biography*, 77 (1969):464–472; John C. Miller, *Triumph of Freedom, 1775–83* (1948); Robert P. Multhauf, *Neptune's Gift: A History of Common Salt* (1978); C.C. Smith, "Scarcity of Salt in the Revolutionary War," *Massachusetts Historical Society Proceedings*, 15 (1856–57):221–227; E.B. Tustin, Jr., "The Story of Salt in New England," *Essex Institute Historical Collections*, 85 (1949):259–271; Harry B. Weiss and Grace M. Weiss, *The Revolutionary Saltworks of the New Jersey Coast* (1959)

Saltonstall, Dudley

See Penobscot Expedition.

Salvador, Francis (1746–1776)

American Patriot. Born in London to a prominent Spanish Jewish (Sephardic) family, Francis Salvador was educated by a tutor, studied in France for seven years, and returned to England to marry his first cousin Sarah. As a result of this marriage, Francis was both the son-in-law and nephew of Joseph Salvador. Adventure and business misfortunes evidently explained why Francis decided to leave England in December 1773.

Francis obtained approximately 7,000 acres from his father-in-law, who owned vast land tracts in South Carolina, and he became a successful plantation owner in the district of Ninety Six. Salvador grew indigo on his plantation manned by 30 slaves, but he encountered attacks from Indians who were backed by the English. Consequently, he supported the cause of the American Patriots.

Between 1775 and 1776 Salvador was selected to serve in the first and second South Carolina Provincial Congresses. During the first congress, he was appointed to two committees—the first committee being authorized responsibilities for determining electoral districts and procedures for the newly proclaimed state and the second one being delegated the power of executing the Continental Association. As a deputy of the second congress, meeting in early 1776, Salvador was assigned to a committee to ascertain ways to maintain security in the state and was named to a committee to draft a report about the newly proposed constitution. There is great significance attached to Salvador's participation in these two legislative bodies, for he was the first unconverted Jew to serve in an American assembly.

The energetic Salvador, too, served in the South Carolina militia. As a result of Indian raids in the Ninety Six District, Salvador, who was assigned to the detachment of Major Andrew Williamson, sought revenge. On August 1, 1776, Williamson and his men were ambushed by Cherokees in the village of Essenecca. Shot three times, Salvador fell from his horse, was scalped while still alive, and died of wounds within the hour. Salvador, then age 30, was the first Jew to die for the cause of the Patriots and has been

rightly perceived as a "British aristocrat who became an American democrat."

William Weisberger

REFERENCES

Barnett A. Elzas, *The Jews of South Carolina* (1905); Jacob R. Marcus, *Early American Jewry*, 2 vols. (1955), 2; Charles Reznikoff, *The Jews of Charleston* (1950).

Sampson, Deborah (1760–1827)

Continental Army soldier. In 1786 Colonel Henry Jackson, who had been a Revolutionary regimental commander, commented on the three-year service of a Revolutionary soldier he knew as Robert Shurtleff: "he had the confidence of his officers, did his duty as a faithful and good soldier, and was honorably discharged the army of the United States."

Shurtleff, better known as Deborah Sampson, symbolized the active participation of women in the American Revolution. Although Sampson is the only woman noted in historical records who disguised herself as a man to fight, other women traveled with their husbands to military encampments, helped load and fire weapons, or penned fiery Revolutionary rhetoric to intensify the conflict.

Born on December 17, 1760, in Plympton, Massachusetts, to a poor family that boasted hardy, influential colonial ancestors— such as Pilgrims Miles Standish, William Bradford, and John Alden—Sampson experienced deprivation at an early age. Her father, a sailor who was described by his peers as a roustabout who frequented taverns, was lost at sea. Deborah's mother, unable to provide for her six children, sent five-year-old Deborah to stay with an elderly family member. Three years later, the relative died, and a pastor's widow tended to Deborah.

Next, Deborah became an indentured servant to the family of farmer Jeremiah Thomas in Middleborough. Unlike many young women, Deborah toiled in the fields and became exceptionally strong from physical exertions. Unhappy that she could not attend school, Deborah borrowed books from the Thomas children and studied at night, teaching herself to read. With an enormous desire to learn, Deborah soon became well-read and able to discuss intellectual topics with ease. As soon as her indenture ended when she turned 18 years old, Deborah arranged to work for the Thomas family while attending school. Eventually she began to teach classes, earning money with which she bought cloth to sew masculine clothes.

Craving adventures and travel normally denied to women, Deborah donned her masculine attire and wrapped her chest with cloth, so as to prevent unwanted attention, and began frequenting taverns in order to learn more about the war. Her curiosity and feelings of patriotism, as well as her sense that she had no personal ties to sever, encouraged her to enlist in the Continental Army. As she explained years later during a lecture tour,

> My Mind became agitated with the enquiry—why a nation, separated from us by an ocean more than three thousand miles in extent, should endeavor to enforce on us plans of subjugation, the most unnatural in themselves, unjust, inhuman in their operations, and unpractised even by the uncivilized savages of the wilderness?

Deborah explained that "For several years I looked on these scenes of havoc, rapacity and devastation, as one looks on a drowning man, . . . without being able to extend [a] rescuing hand." By the 1780s recruits were needed desperately to fill the thinning ranks, as soldiers deserted because of lack of food, shelter, and clothing. Deborah considered these factors, as well as the fact that she was a woman, but "Wrought upon at length by an enthusiasm and frenzy that could brook no control, I burst the tyrant bonds which held my sex in awe, and clandestinely, or by stealth, grasped an opportunity, which custom and the world seemed to deny, as a natural privilege." She continued that, "I threw off the soft habiliment of my sex, and assumed those of the warrior, already prepared for battle."

In 1782 Deborah attempted to enlist at Middleborough, using the name Timothy Thayer, but her true identity became known when she spent her bounty money at a tavern and became inebriated. Townspeople, aware of her gender, alerted authorities who demanded Deborah return the money; the citizens also ostracized Deborah, canceling her church membership. In May 1782 Deborah tried again to enlist at Uxbridge, using her brother's name, Robert Shurtleff. With the aid of an agent, who pocketed a portion of Deborah's bounty, she registered successfully as a private, agreeing to serve for three years in the 4th Massachusetts Regiment, commanded first by Colonel William Shepard then Colonel Henry Jackson; Captain George Webb led her company.

Deborah's disappearance caused little alarm among those who knew her. A few rumors circulated that she had eloped with a British soldier or died. Deborah—disguised as Shurtleff—was regarded as a good soldier; her officers expressed confidence in her abilities, and the enlisted men nicknamed her "Molly" because she was cleanshaven. The handsome Shurtleff, who had several girls develop crushes and confess being in love with "him," acted like a regular soldier, flirting with local women, assuming camp duties, and participating in battles. However, Deborah had to plan carefully when and how to bathe and tend to personal matters.

In the summer of 1782, Sampson traveled to West Point; she also participated in spy missions and in raids against Tories at Tappan Bay, where she suffered a sword wound; in another skirmish against Tories at East Chester, she was shot in the thigh. Afraid that her gender would be discovered, Sampson treated her own wound, dislodging the musket ball with tools stolen from the hospital and praying that she would die instead of having medical personnel realize that she was a woman. She soon returned to the front, and as a result, the wound never healed properly, causing her pain for the remainder of her life. She continued her military duty on the frontier in skirmishes with Indians.

In 1783 Sampson developed a fever; the medical staff treating her removed her clothing and realized that she was a woman. A Dr. Barnabas Binney invited Deborah to live in his home, where his family helped her recover. Feeling obligated to her military commitment, Deborah joined a land surveying expedition with the 11th Massachusetts Regiment and traveled to the Ohio River valley. When her regiment was dismissed after the signing of the peace treaty, Deborah received a letter from Binney addressed to Major General John Paterson that described Deborah's valor and sincerity as well as revealed her gender. Her fellow soldiers, disbelieving Sampson was a woman, were convinced only when she changed clothes and paraded in front of them in a dress. General Henry Knox honorably discharged Sampson in October 1783, and she moved to Boston to work with an uncle on his farm while borrowing the name of another brother, Ephraim Sampson.

After the Revolution, Deborah enjoyed wearing men's clothing and her uniform while performing physical labor on the farm. She met Benjamin Gannett and married him in 1784, moving to his farm in Sharon. The Gannetts had two daughters and a son. Desperately needing money in the 1790s, Deborah petitioned for military service wages never paid during the war. The General Court of Massachusetts recognized that Deborah had "exhibited an extraordinary instance of female heroism by discharging the duties of a faithful gallant soldier, and at the same time preserving the virtue and chastity of her sex unsuspected and unblemished" and gave her 34 pounds. In order to justify her enlistment and earn additional income, Deborah became one of the first female lecturers in North America.

Traveling throughout New England in 1802, she presented speeches, wearing her uniform and discussing her life as a Continental soldier and her experiences in battle. Paul Revere, in an 1804 petition to Congress for additional funding to Deborah, stated that Deborah was "small, effeminate, and conversable" and possessed great intellect and ability to understand military tactics. As a result of his efforts, Deborah was placed on the Massachusetts Invalid Pension Roll, with a four dollar per month allotment retroactive to 1803. With this money, the Gannett family built a house and landscaped their yard with trees and shrubbery. She also received eight dollars monthly after Congress passed additional legislation in 1818.

Deborah Sampson Gannett died on April 29, 1827, and was interred in Rockridge Cemetery near her home. Her husband requested financial aid from Congress because he was a war widower. In 1836 Congress passed "an act granting half pay to widows or orphans where their husbands or fathers have died of wounds received in the military service of the United States." The act also stipulated that the widow had to be married to the soldier during the Revolution but would grant "pensions to widows in certain cases."

Benjamin, an unusual case because no other men designated that their wives had enlisted as Continental soldiers, claimed that Deborah died as a result of her war wounds, indicating her furtive self-surgery had chronically damaged her health. Congress permitted Gannett to receive a pension, but he died before he ever received any money. Deborah's heirs were provided a full military pension of $466.66, representing retroactive payments, on July 4, 1838, specially approved to recognize Sampson's unique contributions to the Revolution. *See also*: Women Soldiers

Elizabeth D. Schafer

REFERENCES

Elizabeth F. Ellet, *The Women of the American Revolution*, 2 vols. (1848–1850); Elizabeth Evans, *Weathering the Storm: Women of the American Revolution* (1975); Linda K. Kerber, *Women of the Republic: Intellect and Ideology in Revolutionary America* (1980); Herman Mann, *The Female Review; or, Memoirs of an American Young Lady* (1797); Mary Beth Norton, *Liberty's Daughters: The Revolutionary Experience of American Women* (1980); Deborah Sampson, "An Address Delivered in 1802 in Various Towns in Massachusetts, Rhode Island and New York," *Publications of the Sharon Historical Society* (April 1905); Julia Ward Stickley, "The Records of Deborah Sampson Gannett, Woman Soldier of the Revolution," *Prologue*, 4 (1972):233–241.

Sandwich, 4th Earl of (John Montagu) (1718–1792)

British statesman. The Fourth Earl of Sandwich, First Lord of the Admiralty during the American Revolution, was one of the most controversial public figures of the eighteenth century. For years afterward his alleged incompetence and scandalous behavior were regarded as prime contributors to Britain's defeat. Recent scholarship, however, has shown Sandwich to have been a more complex figure than his critics acknowledged.

He succeeded to the family title at the age of 11 and received the typical upbringing and education of an English aristocrat, including the traditional grand tour of the Continent. In 1739 he took his seat in the House of Lords and seems to have impressed his Tory colleagues immediately with his intelligent interest in affairs of state. On several occasions Sandwich was chosen to represent Britain in international conferences. He became particularly fascinated with the Admiralty (one of his ancestors was a famous admiral), and in 1748 he was appointed to the first of three terms as First Lord.

The intricacies of British politics thrust Sandwich into and out of the limelight at frequent intervals. In addition to his terms at the Admiralty he served as Secretary of State and as Postmaster General. He played the games of high society with a zest that even eighteenth-century London occasionally found excessive. Tiring of his wife, he packed her off to live with an entourage of servants and a handsome annuity on an estate in the country while he took up residence with an actress and harpsichordist named Martha Ray. Sandwich and some of his friends formed a club called the Medmenham Fraternity; the newspapers, labeling them the "Order of the Medmenham Monks," claimed they had purchased an abandoned monastery on the Thames and had stocked it with high-priced prostitutes. In 1763 Sandwich took the lead in the machinations that got another club member, John Wilkes, expelled from the House of Commons.

Yet Georgian society perceived no incongruity in the proposition that a middle-aged rake could be a competent public servant. The Admiralty had seen more knowledgeable First Lords, but none more conscientious. Sandwich's correspondence, much of which was published in the 1930s, testifies to the time he spent at his desk. He involved himself in every phase of Admiralty business, which encompassed such diverse subjects as the disposition of the fleets, the need to ensure that the sons of prominent Tories were promoted with sufficient rapidity, and the metallurgists' latest opinions on the virtues of the copper-sheathed hull. Far into the night Sandwich would remain in his office, passing freshly written letters to the copyists and sustaining himself on his own culinary innovation, a slab of meat between two pieces of bread.

At the start of the American Revolution the Royal Navy was in woeful condition. That state of affairs probably was due at least as much to the budgetary policies of the North administration as to any incompetence on Sandwich's part. In the years of peace following the treaty that ended the Seven Years' War in 1763, the British government had no desire to provoke a naval arms race with the French. Sandwich's defenders claim that he ran the navy as efficiently as he could with the funds available during that period, and made considerable progress in cleaning up the corruption that previously had infested the Royal Dockyards.

When the American Revolution started, Sandwich and the rest of the Admiralty Board failed utterly to develop a naval strategy that would deal with it. Instead they let a series of hapless admirals prove how irrelevant traditional naval strategy was to the situation. Samuel Graves, commanding in North America when the fighting broke out, was promised a vast armada of warships and was relieved of his command before they left England. The next admiral sent out to take the command, Lord Richard Howe, was given, in partnership with his brother the general, the authority to act as a diplomat as well as a naval officer. Sandwich, who apparently was barely on speaking terms with the Howes in the political arena, generally was content to let them run the war effort as they thought fit.

When France entered the conflict in March 1778, the Admiralty recognized that the character of the naval war had to undergo a fundamental change. Admiral Howe was informed that "the object of the War being now changed, and the contest in America being a secondary consideration, the principal object must be the distressing France and defending and securing his Majesty's own possessions against Hostile Attempts." That dispatch had the ring of shrewd strategy, but the government failed to realize that such decisions could not be taken unilaterally. The French, having entered into an alliance with the United States, made North America a center of their military effort because that was the only theater where the alliance could benefit them.

Instead of developing a coherent naval strategy for North America, Sandwich's Admiralty relied on what may be called the "detachment theory." When the French sent a fleet across the Atlantic a British squadron followed, the Admiralty having assumed that as long as the two belligerents had about the same number of ships of the line in the same hemisphere the problem would solve itself. Such thinking ignored the basic realities of naval warfare. A battle fleet moved fast and communications were slow; once the enemy had been handed the opportunity to take the offensive, the only effective way to frustrate his design was to defend every point at which he might strike—and that, obviously, was impracticable. Merely to chase him in the hope of catching him before he struck anywhere was to invite calamity.

Lord Howe was a skilled enough tactician, and his French adversary, the Comte d'Estaing, was a sufficiently mediocre one, to keep the North American theater in a stalemate through 1778. Sandwich's attention was occupied by a vicious combination of threats from the French and Spanish navies and the Whigs. By this time admirals of opposition tendencies were refusing to serve in North America. Sandwich found it expedient to appoint one of the navy's most prominent Whigs, the Viscount Augustus Keppel, to command a fleet in the English Channel—with a reliable Tory, Sir Hugh Palliser, a member of the Admiralty Board, as his second in command. When Keppel and Palliser failed to defeat the Comte d'Orvilliers at the Battle of Ushant (July 23, 1778), one of the grandest scandals of the war ensued. Each admiral demanded that the other be court-martialed; when Keppel was acquitted a mob broke the windows of Sandwich's house. Palliser received a gentle slap on the wrist and resigned his seat at the Admiralty.

Charles James Fox, the leader of the Whigs in the House of Commons, seized upon the Keppel-Palliser feud as an opportunity to launch a political assault on Sandwich's Admiralty. In March 1779, Fox introduced a series of resolutions that were designed to blame Sandwich for the Ushant debacle and force him from office. Lord North, the First Minister, chose the moment to make a stand. Resolutely declaring that the government as a whole must bear the responsibility for all the decisions that had led to the battle, he made it clear that if Sandwich were driven out the rest of the government would resign as well. All Fox's motions failed.

A similar anti-Sandwich movement was orchestrated in the House of Lords by the Earl of Bristol, a former naval officer. While Sandwich was preparing his defense his household was struck by tragedy: his mistress, Martha Ray, was murdered by a jealous suitor as she stepped from her carriage in front of the opera house at Covent Garden. Bristol chivalrously postponed the debate for a week. Sandwich thereupon delivered a virtuosic speech that led the Lords to defeat Bristol's motion by a vote of 78 to 39.

Sandwich's greatest professional weakness may have been his tendency to play the game of political patronage to excess. Patronage was supposed to ensure that men of ability were recognized, and that their talents were used as constructively as possible. During the War of American Independence it rewarded mediocrity. In February 1779, Sandwich engineered the appointment of Rear Admiral Marriot Arbuthnot as commander-in-chief of the North American squadron. Arbuthnot was a decent man and a good seaman, but he was 68 years old, he had never commanded a fleet before, and his tactical and strategic skills were negligible. Though he shared in the biggest British victory of the war, the capture of Charleston, South Carolina, Arbuthnot's tenure in North America was chiefly distinguished by his feud with his army counterpart, General Sir Henry Clinton. Sandwich resolutely ignored the mountainous evidence that the Clinton-Arbuthnot feud was undermining the British war effort. The First Lord insisted on defending his protégé until Arbuthnot, his health exhausted in a forlorn effort to do his duty, resigned. He left behind him in North America the seeds of the Yorktown disaster.

The fall of the North ministry in March 1782 sent Sandwich into retirement. He lived out the rest of his life in comfortable obscurity.

John A. Tilley

REFERENCES

G.R. Barnes and J.H. Owen, eds., *The Private Papers of John, Fourth Earl of Sandwich*, 4 vols. (1931–1938); *DNB*; Piers Mackesy, *The War for America, 1775–1783* (1964); George Martelli, *Jemmy Twitcher: A Life of the Fourth Earl of Sandwich* (1962); John A. Tilley, *The British Navy and the American Revolution* (1987).

Saratoga, New York, Battles of (September 17 and October 7, 1777)

Saratoga consisted of two distinct clashes that are often referred to separately as the Battles of First Freeman's Farm and Bemis Heights (Second Freeman's Farm), respectively. Alternately both battles together, or occasionally the last one alone, are called Stillwater, named after the village located south of where the fighting occurred.

Saratoga was the most important battle of the American Revolution, rivaled only by Yorktown. It resulted in the capitulation of an entire British army, leaving the British strategy of 1776–1777 in ruins and initiating the second phase of the Revolutionary War in which British efforts in North America shifted to the southern colonies. After 1777, the war took on a global nature that forced the British to mobilize more strenuously their military resources and detach considerable forces to face the new French threat. The Patriot victory at Saratoga resulted in French recognition of the United States and the concluding of the Franco-American military alliance (February 6, 1778), which made ultimate American victory possible, though not a certainty. Saratoga has therefore been called "the turning point" of the Revolutionary War.

Lieutenant General John Burgoyne, commander-in-chief of "The Canada Army," left Montreal, Quebec, in early June 1777 and by June 13 had concentrated 8,000 troops at St. Johns (presently St.-Jean). The army was initially very successful in its invasion of New York: Ticonderoga, "the Gibraltar of the North," fell July 6, and on July 7, the British defeated the Patriots at Hubbardton and Fort Ann. By July 10 Burgoyne had reached the north end of Wood Creek, but thereafter his progress slowed. As the British marched south of Skenesborough they were impeded by the swampy terrain and the delaying tactics of the American commander, Major General Philip Schuyler. Fort Edward, on the upper Hudson River, was finally occupied on July 30, but in the following weeks events were to turn against Burgoyne.

Supply problems forced Burgoyne to organize the Bennington expedition, which was decisively defeated August 16, costing the British almost 800 casualties. Burgoyne's western diversionary force under Brigadier General Barry St. Leger, which had halted to besiege Fort Stanwix on the Mohawk River, turned back the desperate relief attempt of Brigadier General Nicholas Herkimer at Oriskany (August 6), but retreated on August 23 in the face of Major General Benedict Arnold's subsequent bold advance. So by late August, Burgoyne was finding himself increasingly isolated in the American wilderness.

While the British floundered, the Americans organized to block the enemy advance down the Hudson. The Patriot army had contained only 4,000 troops when Major General Horatio Gates replaced Schuyler on August 19. But by early September Gates had over 7,000 men under his command, although less than half of these troops were of the Continental Line and equal to the caliber of Burgoyne's regulars. The Americans were reinforced by the Continental brigades of John Nixon and John Glover from Major General Israel Putnam's New York Highlanders command; Colonel Daniel Morgan's "Rifle Corps"; Major Henry Dearborn's Light Infantry and

Brigadier General Benjamin Lincoln, from George Washington's main army; and the aforementioned Arnold, who quickly proved his worth against the St. Leger expedition. Of equal importance were the literally dozens of militia regiments from New York and New England that arrived in Gate's camp, often poorly trained and indifferently uniformed but eager to fight invading British.

Despite the growing odds against him, Burgoyne decided to push on to his main objective, Albany, New York. On September 13–14, the British army crossed to the west side of the Hudson, using a pontoon bridge, and made camp two miles north of Saratoga (presently Schuylerville). Burgoyne's situation was not enviable. The entire force under his immediate command now numbered only about 6,000 men (roughly 4,500 regulars, including 2,500 British and 2,000 German troops; and 1,500 irregulars). After Bennington, many of Burgoyne's Indians, Loyalists, and Canadians had deserted, leaving the army short of scouts and light troops. Before crossing the Hudson, Burgoyne had stockpiled 30 days of supplies that had been, with great effort, transported the almost 180 miles from Montreal. As the army advanced toward Gates, Burgoyne's pontoon bridge was dismantled and the boats used to transport this cargo proceeded slowly down the Hudson, in the direction of Albany.

On September 10, Gates moved his army from just north of the village of Stillwater to Bemis Heights, about 10 miles south of Saratoga and 24 miles north of Albany. In the following days the American army entrenched itself in positions laid out by Gates's chief engineer, the Polish, colonel Thaddeus Kosciuszko. Redoubts and fortified lines, protected by an abatis, were constructed at strategic points on a range of hills (100 to 300 feet above the river) that stood at right angles to the Hudson. Below these hills ran the road from Saratoga that followed the river to Albany. Gates's position was a strong one, and Burgoyne would have to overcome it in order to proceed farther south.

Burgoyne crossed the stream, Fish Kill, on September 15, and camped four miles south of Saratoga. The British army was now only five or six miles from Gates's troops and able to hear the reveille drums in the American camp. Slowed by rain and the need to repair bridges and remove felled trees, Burgoyne advanced another three miles and then halted and formed his troops in a line a mile and a half long, stretching west from Sword's House on the bank of the Hudson. As Burgoyne advanced, the Americans remained largely inactive. Gates's scout had informed him that the enemy had crossed the Hudson, and although small patrols were sent to harass the British, the American army remained in its entrenchments. On September 18, one of these patrols killed ten British soldiers and captured twenty others as they foraged in a potato field. Burgoyne, now only three miles from the Patriot earthworks, realized that any further movement forward would result in contact with Gates. He made the decision to conduct a reconnaissance-in-force and to probe the American lines for weakness before a full-fledged attack was attempted. While testing Patriot strength and mettle, Burgoyne also intended to seize a hill on the American left that Gates had failed to fortify. It is thought that Burgoyne hoped to repeat his successful Ticonderoga maneuver and place guns on the hilltop to outflank the Americans; Gates would then be forced to leave his prepared position without a bloody assault.

Burgoyne organized in three columns the roughly 4,000 soldiers he had available. On the British right (west) Brigadier General Simon Fraser had approximately 1,500 regulars and 300 irregulars and 12 guns. The regulars included a composite grenadier battalion commanded by Major John Dyke-Acland; a composite light infantry battalion under the Earl of Balcarres; eight battalion companies of the 24th Foot; the Brunswick light infantry battalion; and the Brunswick grenadier battalion, Heinrich Breymann. On the extreme right Captain Alexander Fraser led the Indians, Canadians, and Tories, along with his own body of marksmen, "Fraser's Rangers." Burgoyne personally accompanied the center column, nominally commanded by Brigadier General James Hamilton. It contained the main attack strength of the army's 1,100 British regulars from 4 regiments, the 20th, 21st, and 62nd Foot, with the 9th Foot in reserve, and was supported by 6 fieldpieces under Captain Thomas Jones. To the left (east) of Burgoyne, closest to the Hudson, was deployed the column of Major General Friedrich von Riedesel, who commanded the predominately Brunswick force of 1,100 German mercenaries, hired by Britain for use in North America. The regiments of Rhetz, Specht, and Riedesel were accompanied by six field guns, a poorly mounted contingent of Brunswick dragoons, and a company of light infantry. Behind these, along the river road, Major General William Phillips brought up 7 additional field guns and 200 bateaux, escorted by the 47th Foot. Even farther to the rear came the park artillery, wheeled carriages, baggage, stores, and wounded soldiers guarded by a Hesse-Hanau regiment and some Tories.

First Freeman's Farm

As the day began, foggy and cold, on September 19, Burgoyne issued orders to his troops from Sword's House that the three columns were to advance simultaneously, but separately, toward the American lines. Before launching the main attack, Burgoyne intended to unite two of the columns (Fraser's and his own) at a rendezvous point just north of the Americans. Riedesel would move along the river road until he met the enemy. The British advance was to be seriously impeded by the wooded and hilly terrain, making Burgoyne's division of his forces all the more dangerous. Burgoyne and Fraser were forced to cross two large gorges, the "Middle" and "Great Ravines," in front of the American entrenchments, leaving Gates an excellent opportunity to counterattack if he wished. The local terrain made communication between the columns more difficult than normal, so Burgoyne improvised a signal system with three "minute" guns. However, the sound of musketry remained the most reliable indicator of a force's location. Burgoyne's plan was an ill-advised one, as it risked the "defeat in detail" of each column. It also seems to have assumed that Gates would sortie out of his entrenchments since the British made no preparations to assault the American earthworks.

By 11 A.M., the weather had cleared and the three guns were fired to start the advance. First Fraser crossed the "Great Ravine" at its widest point, and then followed a track that led east and south. He ultimately took up a position one mile north of the American lines on high ground west of the Freeman Farm, a clearing of some 15 acres and a cabin, owned by one Issac Freeman. The center column originally followed the right but crossed the "Great Ravine" at the south end, on an intact bridge, and then halted at noon, to allow Fraser, following a more circuitous route, time to get in position. In the meantime,

Riedesel, wary of ambush and stopping to repair dismantled bridges, was moving slowly, one and a half miles east. At 12:30 P.M., Burgoyne decided he had given Fraser ample time, again fired the "minute" guns, and then proceeded to advance toward the Freeman's Farm clearing.

American scouts reported these movements to Gates in the American camp, but he preferred to await further developments rather than attack the British while they were the most vulnerable. He eventually ordered Morgan and Dearborn to take the riflemen and light infantry and shadow the British advance. At 12:45 P.M., "Morgan"s Riflemen" met the "pickets" of the British center column and delivered a volley that devastated that body, killing or wounding every officer. Intoxicated with victory, the riflemen foolishly pursued the survivors of the "picket" and were in turn decimated by a detachment of 100 light infantry that sallied out from Fraser's position, under Major Gordon Forbes. The Americans were driven back and scattered through the woods, leaving Morgan alone and almost in tears. Blowing a turkey call, normally used to decoy wild gobblers, he rallied most of his men and, with Dearborn, took up a position along the southern edge of the clearing.

Burgoyne's brigade was at the same time, approximately 1 P.M., deploying along the northern edge of the clearing, and in the process they unwittingly fired on Forbe's victorious company. Burgoyne's four battalions formed up from left to right—the 20th, 62nd, and 21st Foot in a slightly concave semicircle, 300 yards long, with the 9th Foot behind and the artillery in support. Within the space of half an hour, Burgoyne was heavily engaged by the Patriots. Gates first released two Continental regiments of Brigadier General Poor's Brigade (Cilley's and Scammel's) and these were successively joined by the other three regiments under Poor (Cortlandt's, Livingston's, and Hale's, the latter now under Lieutenant Colonel Winborn Adams), and the two Connecticut militia regiments of Cook and Latimer. These bodies were all part of Arnold's division, but whether that infamous general was actually on the field and in command of them remains a point of debate. The evidence suggests that the Americans fought an uncoordinated battle with little higher direction.

By 2 P.M., the fighting in the center was raging furiously and was to continue that way for over three hours. British discipline and artillery were pitted in a see-saw struggle against American numbers and markmanship. Six times the Continentals attacked the red-coated regulars only to be driven back each time by fierce British bayonet charges. But the British in their turn were unable to hold the clearing and were forced to seek the shelter of the woods to try and escape the American musketry. Some of Morgan's men climbed trees for vantage and shot to kill British officers, distinctive targets in their bright uniforms.

While Burgoyne's column fought against Poor, Fraser continued to hold the rise to the west. He did little to support Burgoyne directly, although late in the day some of the battalion companies of the 24th Foot and some light infantry from Major von Bärner's battalion aided the center in a counterattack. Fraser's relative inaction left the outnumbered Burgoyne in an increasingly desperate situation by mid-afternoon. The British, thinned by accurate American fire, were forced to spread out to prevent from being outflanked. Phillips, on the river road, heard the "sound of the guns" to the west and came to the aid of the center with four cannon. Taking personal command of the 20th Foot he led them in a counterattack that saved the exposed 62nd from possible annihilation. The regiment had been raked by Patriot fire from the front and both flanks, but Phillips was able to withdraw it to a more protected spot to re-form. He set up his four guns, armed with grape shot, at the edge of the forest to the east. These then commenced to fire into the American flank, but their effect proved only temporary as Phillips's cannon soon ran out of ammunition.

Late in the afternoon, Gates finally decided "to weaken his lines" and release more forces for the battle in the center. He sent the four Continental regiments of Brigadier General Ebenezer Learned's Brigade (Bailey's, Jackson's, Wesson's, and Livingston's) and one regiment from Patterson's Brigade (Marshall's) to aid Poor. Learned, unfamiliar with the ground, first blundered into Fraser on the hilltop, and was repulsed, but his regiments eventually joined Poor and Morgan giving the American force close to 3,000 soldiers against fewer than 1,000 British regulars. By 5 P.M., the exhausted British could no longer advance into the clearing.

One division of the British army remained completely unengaged. At 1 P.M., when the battle at Freeman's Farm began in earnest, Riedesel, progressing down the river road, heard the sound of musket fire at 2 P.M. and shortly after received a message sent by Burgoyne. In reply, Riedesel sent his own officer west. He eventually returned to the column around 5 P.M., with orders from Burgoyne to leave defensive forces with the bateaux and march to the aid of the center. Riedesel took his own regiment, two companies of the Rhetz Regiment and two 6-pounder guns of the Hesse-Hanau artillery. He detailed only weak forces, principally the Hesse-Hanau infantry, to guard the bateaux and supplies, thus leaving them easy targets for Gates should he decide to attack. Riedesel marched quickly toward the American right wing. With the British center on the verge of collapse, Riedesel, having negotiated an intervening swamp, arrived at 5:30 P.M., and immediately began to attack the American troops southeast of Freeman's Farm. In a fashion similar to their attack at Hubbardton, the Germans came on cheering, with drums beating. They were committed piecemeal, but their effect on the Patriot right flank, resting on the North Branch Ravine but otherwise unprotected, was dramatic. The Germans fired into this flank and then climbed the ravine to join their British comrades at the edge of the clearing. The American right fell back into the safety of the woods after the initial volley of the Germans, but they were able to halt the first British and German attack. With considerable effort the two Hesse-Hanau cannon were hauled up the west slope of the ravine by the Germans, aided by some redcoats, and then proceeded to fire at Patriots, who were unable to reply in kind.

Even with the arrival of the Germans, the Americans held a two to one manpower advantage, but psychologically unbalanced by the sudden appearance of fresh troops on their flank and lacking firm leadership, they could not hold the field. Low on ammunition, the Continentals returned to the refuge of Gates's fortified lines, as night fell. Burgoyne considered it too dangerous to pursue them in the dark, so the battle came to a halt. The final fighting of the day occurred between Breymann's Grenadier Battalion and the 8th Massachusetts Continentals. Occasional musket fire was heard throughout the night. Burgoyne's exhausted army camped on the field they had purchased so dearly.

The British suffered badly in the battle. There were about 600 men killed, wounded, taken prisoner, or missing. Three hundred fifty of these

were from the four regiments of the center column: the 62nd Foot was left with only 60 men available for duty and it and the 20th Foot were, for the moment, destroyed as effective battalions. Captain Thomas Jones of the artillery lost his own life and 36 of his battery's 48 personnel were killed or wounded. American losses were lighter but still considerable: 300 Patriots were counted as casualties—80 killed, 200 wounded, and 36 missing. Both sides had achieved a victory of a sort but only the Americans could count an advantage. In the narrowest sense First Freeman's Farm was a British victory. Burgoyne had gained the honor of the day by holding the field, a victory by standard eighteenth-century convention, though he was still a mile north of the American lines and he had little to show for 600 men lost, not even the unoccupied hill on Gates's left. The Patriots, on the other hand, remained secure in their entrenchments and had halted the advance of and inflicted more casualties on one of the best armies that Britain had ever sent to America. There was, however, a negative side of the victory for the Americans. They had heavily outnumbered the British in the center but still failed to defeat them, proving the Continentals were not yet the equal of British regulars. Gates had shown little initiative or leadership and had allowed the fight to become an uncontrolled "soldiers battle." With a little imagination he might have crushed the center column or the detachment that guarded the bateaux. If Burgoyne had been decisively defeated in the first battle there may not have been a second. But to his credit, Gates's caution had minimized the chances that his army, the majority of which was raw militia, could suffer a catastrophic defeat. To win Gates need only keep the army intact; it was Burgoyne who needed a decisive triumph.

In his report to the Continental Congress, Gates failed to include the name of Benedict Arnold. It is unclear if this was because Arnold was not actively involved in the battle, or if the omission was part of the bitter factionalism that divided Gates's army. Gates, a New Englander, owed his command of the Northern Department to his New England friends in Congress, who had removed Schuyler the "Yorker" they distrusted. Arnold, despite being from Connecticut, had made himself champion of the New York faction in Gates's camp. After Freeman's Farm, the quarreling between the two factions became open and Arnold was relieved of his command of the army's left wing, by Gates. Arnold, however, remained in camp, idle, but waiting for the next battle that was surely imminent.

Burgoyne planned to assault the American entrenchments the next day, September 20, but Brigadier General Fraser claimed his grenadiers and light infantry, the troops who would have spearheaded the attack, needed a rest, and so a reprieve of a day was given. By not attacking, Burgoyne lost perhaps the best chance he would ever have to defeat Gates, for inexperienced Americans were disorganized and low on food and ammunition. On the morning of September 21, Burgoyne again prepared to attack when unforeseen events intervened to cancel these plans. Burgoyne received a message sent September 12 by Lieutenant General Sir Henry Clinton, the British commander in New York. Clinton, who had just been reinforced, now had 7,000 men and proposed to create a diversion for Burgoyne in the Highlands of the Hudson. Clinton, who was able to detach about 2,000 men (British, Germans, and some Tories) for the enterprise, intended to force Gates to send forces south, but not to link up with Burgoyne. Burgoyne, who seems to have believed that Clinton would actually try and reach his army, quickly returned a message that urged Sir Henry to haste, telling him that his army could not hold out later than October 20. Burgoyne then began digging in on the ground occupied on September 19 to wait for Clinton's diversionary force.

The British constructed a series of fortified lines and three major redoubts, which anchored the position. The largest, a log citadel built in the rear, was dubbed the "Great Redoubt." Here, overlooking Wilbur's Basin (the base of the "Great Ravine") were collected the bateaux and here was the point Burgoyne's engineers chose to bridge the Hudson. The position was guarded by the Hesse-Hanau infantry regiment, the 47th Foot, and some Loyalists. South of the "Great Redoubt" were the troops facing Gates: Riedesel's Germans were on the left; then came Hamilton's Brigade of four regiments, with outposts for the two brigades a few hundred yards in front; to their right was Fraser's Advanced Corp (the grenadiers and the 24th Foot); west and a little farther the light troops of the Corps held a fortification called the "Balcarres' Redoubt"; farther west and north stood "Breymann's Redoubt," containing the solders of the

German Advanced Corps; and the gap between "Balcarres' Redoubt" was held by the Canadians in two stockaded cabins.

Burgoyne's position was well constructed and secure, perhaps too secure for it, and the hope of help from Clinton lulled him into inactivity for three weeks. American harassment of the British camp increased and included an attack on the boats holding provisions. Food stockpiled for the advance in early September was almost exhausted, and on October 3 the standard ration was reduced by a third and the soldiers were forced to exist on a pound of flour and salt pork. Armed foraging parties had to be organized to bring in additional food; and desertion, especially by the Indians, Canadians, and Loyalists, continued.

While Burgoyne's army weakened, Gates's grew in strength. On September 20, Gates occupied and fortified the hill that had been Burgoyne's objective the day before, thus making the American position almost invulnerable from a northern attack. Two days later, Brigadier General Lincoln brought in a group of militia from the Bennington area and more arrived in the following week. Other fresh militia appeared in camp almost daily from New England and New York, and by October 7 Gates's army numbered 10,000 to 11,000 men. At the same time in Albany, Schuyler collected lead to melt down for musket balls and sent it north, easing the army's ammunition problems.

As the two armies faced each other in their respective entrenchments two smaller forces operated to the north and south of them. Before First Freeman's Farm, Gates, wanting to attack Burgoyne's supply system and communications with Canada, had sent Colonels John Brown, Samuel Johnson and Russell Woolbridge north. On September 18, directed by Brigadier General Lincoln, Brown attacked the Lake George landing site and captured a group of British seamen. The same day he occupied Mount Defiance and Mount Hope, outside Ticonderoga, and drove the garrison into the fortress. This bold attack netted Brown 3 companies of the 53rd Foot as prisoners, 200 bateaux, a sloop, and some gunboats. Brown was then joined by Johnson (Woolbridge went to Skenesborough), but still finding the main works of Ticonderoga too tough for an assault, they returned to Lake George. There the Americans tried, but failed, to surprise the 47th Foot on Diamond Island, and the

British recaptured some of their earlier losses. Although this minor battle forced the Americans to abandon their short-lived siege of Ticonderoga, the damage had been done. Brown's Ticonderoga raid had a considerable negative effect on British morale and a conversely positive one on Gates's army. The British heard the shouts of rejoicing in the American camp on September 21, and learned their cause on September 28. It was obvious Burgoyne's army was becoming increasingly isolated from its base in Quebec.

To the south, forces began operating in support of Burgoyne. Clinton started his move into the Hudson Highlands on October 3 and, only three days later, in a skillfully conducted operation, took Forts Clinton and Montgomery. Clinton, believing he had done all he had promised, garrisoned the forts and returned to New York with the majority of his force. However, before leaving he ordered General Sir John Vaughan to sail farther up the Hudson. Vaughan never made contact with Burgoyne's army, but he burnt Aesopus (presently Kingston) and reached to within 45 miles of Albany before halting because of the shallowness of the channel.

Burgoyne's situation was rapidly deteriorating, with no aid from Clinton in sight. As a result, on October 4 he called together a council of his generals to discuss the situation. Retreat was now clearly a reasonable option, but Burgoyne claimed he feared retreating north through forests thick with rebels and that he still wished to attempt a breakout to the south. He proposed leaving 800 men to guard the camp, hospital, and stores and to attempt to execute a turning movement against Gates's left flank, but Fraser and Riedesel, both in favor of a withdrawal to north of the stream, Batten Kill, were able to dissuade him from this desperate scheme. The next day, Riedesel suggested retreating to Fort Edward and reestablishing contact with Canada, but Burgoyne, always the gambler, decided on one more attack.

Bemis Heights

On October 7, Burgoyne selected 1,400 to 1,500 of his best regulars (with 600 auxiliaries), out of his less than 5,000 remaining troops, in order to conduct a reconnaissance of the American right flank. His intention was to determine if it was best to attempt another attack on Gates, stand firm in the fortified camp, or retreat across the Batten Kill. A secondary goal of the operation was to cover a major foraging operation, so desperate was the state of Burgoyne's provisions. Burgoyne deployed his regulars in three columns, supported by 10 guns: on the right was S. Fraser and the Earl of Balcarres with the light battalion; in the center deployed the 24th Foot, followed by the Germans under Riedesel (the Regiments Riedesel, Specht, Erb-Prinz, and Rhetz) and the German light troops; the left was held by Major Dyke-Acland's grenadier battalion. On the extreme west, Captain A. Fraser led 600 Indians, Canadians, Tories, and his own "Rangers." Their mission was to make a wide circuit to the right "on secret paths" and disrupt any American rear areas.

The British left their entrenchments between 10 and 11 a.m., marched three quarters of a mile southwest to a wheat field (the Barber farm), and halted at noon, on slightly rising ground. The British deployment was not easily defendable. With 1,500 men in a line 1,000 yards long the British were overextended, and their formations's flanks resting on woods, leaving any attackers a covered approach. While the troops rested and the camp followers cut wheat in the fields to the rear, Captain A. Fraser took the irregulars into the wooded hills to the right. Some of the senior British officers climbed to the roof of a log cabin to observe the American position (one and a half miles away) but could see nothing.

Major James Wilkinson, Gates's young adjutant general, returning from checking the outposts, reported to Gates that the British had emerged from their entrenchments and were foraging in a field to the northwest. Around 2:00 or 2:30 p.m., Gates decided to take action and with the dramatic words, "Order Morgan to begin the game," sent "Morgan's Riflemen" and Dearborn's light infantry to attack the left of Burgoyne's line. Poor's Brigade (five Continental regiments with Cook and Latimer's militia, 800 men in all) was ordered to the right (eastern side) of the British. Morgan and Poor were to work around the British flanks and strike simultaneously through the woods. When the enemy's flanks were defeated a third body, Learned's Brigade, was to smash the center.

Poor reached the British first, Morgan being delayed by the long circular march needed to get into position. Poor's men reached the base of the rise, below Major Dyke-Acland's grenadiers, and coolly deployed despite British cannon fire. When Poor's troops advanced, the grenadiers loosed a volley that, aimed too high, did little damage to the Patriots. Dyke-Acland, in defiance of the two-to-one odds against him, ordered an attack with the bayonet. The charge was shattered by a volley from Colonel Joseph Cilley's 1st New Hampshire Continentals and the hapless grenadiers fell in heaps. Dyke-Acland, shot in both legs, was captured, helpless as he lay propped up in one of the angles of a zig-zag fence. Any survivors in the grenadiers battalion were quickly swept over by the ecstatic Continentals. Shortly after, Morgan, routing the irregulars under Captain Fraser along the way, came into action against Balcarres. Attacking the right flank and rear of the light troops, Morgan forced Balcarres to face him and as a result the unfortunate British were driven back by Dearborn, who had followed behind the "Riflemen." Unlike the grenadiers though, Balcarres was able to retreat to the rear of the position and rally his men.

With both British flanks faltering, Learned's Brigade (four Continental regiments) went over to the attack against the Germans in the center. At this juncture, Burgoyne realized his line of battle was lost and ordered a retreat. He sent his aide-de-camp, Sir Francis Clerke, to deliver the message, but Lieutenant Clerke was mortally wounded before he could reach the Germans, and later died a prisoner in the American camp. As Learned advanced, Arnold suddenly appeared on the field. The New Yorkers of Livingston's Regiment cheered Arnold on and followed him into the Germans, ably commanded by Lieutenant Colonel Ernst von Speth. The Brunswickers repulsed the first Patriot attack but were soon in a hopeless situation, surrounded on three sides. Under great pressure, Riedesel managed to withdraw into the "Balcarres' Redoubt." As the British and German troops streamed back to their fortified lines, Brigadier General S. Fraser attempted to form a rear guard. Using the yet untouched 24th Foot and some of the light infantry battalion, Fraser rode back and forth forming his men. This activity did not go unobserved by Arnold who, fearing Fraser might yet halt the victorious Americans, turned to Morgan and told him to have his best sharpshooters bring Fraser down. Among those whom Morgan ordered to fire was Timothy Murphy, a legendary frontiersman and crack shot who is credited with putting the fatal bullet into Fraser. As the mortally wounded was escorted to the rear, Brigadier General Peter Ten Broeck arrived on the field, with his fresh New York militia, and the last British position on the field collapsed.

The first phase of the Battle of Bemis Heights was over. The British reconnaissance had been completely unsuccessful; it not only failed to gather intelligence but also lost 400 British soldiers and 8 guns for slight loss to the Americans. Fraser and Clerke were mortally wounded; Dyke-Acland, Captain John Money, the quartermaster general, and Captain Edward Williams, commander of the park artillery, were captured, and the list of high-ranking officer casualties was not yet complete.

Most of the survivors of the sortie retreated into the closest of the fortified positions, the "Balcarres' Redoubt." Arnold, in a state of high excitement, led the assault on this fortification. Lacking artillery, he could only penetrate the abatis and even when reinforced was unable to penetrate the breastwork. Leaving these regiments behind, Arnold galloped between the lines to "Breymann's Redoubt," ignoring the crossfire. Here he found Learned's Brigade advancing on the 200 men who were commanded by von Breymann. At Wilkinson's suggestion, Learned attacked the weakly held cabins between von Breymann and Balcarres, and led by Arnold, the Continentals quickly cleared them of the enemy, leaving von Breymann's flank exposed. With the regiments of Wesson, Brooks, and Livingston of Learned's Brigade, and Morgan, Arnold joined the already progressing attack on the redoubt, which overwhelmed the Germans. The brave, but brutal, von Breymann killed four of his own men, "to keep them to their work," before he himself was killed by a fifth potential victim. As the Americans entered the redoubt, a last volley by the fleeing Brunswickers killed Arnold's horse and wounded him in his "Quebec leg." If the ball had killed him then and there no Revolutionary general's name would have shone more brightly in posterity than Benedict Arnold's. As darkness fell the last hopeless action of the battle occurred. Speth, his honor wounded by the capture of "Breymann's Redoubt," tried to retake the position with a force of 54 men, but succeeded only in being taken prisoner. The capture of "Breymann's Redoubt" made the British position untenable, and Burgoyne was forced to fall back to the "Great Redoubt." Only night saved the British from further disaster.

Total British losses in the entire battle were close to 600 men (176 killed, 200 wounded, and 200 prisoners) and 10 guns lost. The final American assault added three German officers to the tally of casualties: Breymann, Speth, and Captain Carl von Geyso. American losses were comparatively light—30 to 50 killed and 150 wounded. In the two battles of Saratoga combined about 1,200 British were lost, compared to roughly 500 Patriots.

The dawn of October 8 found the British army concentrated around the "Great Redoubt," but not yet in retreat. At 6 P.M. that evening, Burgoyne, Phillips, and Riedesel buried Fraser at the top of the "Great Redoubt," for a time being accidentally cannonaded by Gates's artillery. Burgoyne waited for darkness to retreat, and with campfires burning to deceive the enemy and leaving 300 to 400 sick and wounded in the hospital, to be taken by the Americans. Carrying only a few days' rations, he slipped away to the north, his army struggling through the rain and mud. Burgoyne sent Lieutenant Colonel Nicholas Sutherland of the 47th Foot to reconnoiter the route ahead. Before the battle of October 7, Gates had ordered Brigadier General John Fellows, with 1,300 Berkshire County militia, to the east side of the Hudson. Fellows was instructed to get to a point north of Burgoyne and then recross to the west bank and entrench to block the British escape route. Sutherland found the unguarded camp of Fellows at Saratoga on October 8 and returned to Burgoyne that night to ask the commander's permission to attack with 250 men. Burgoyne, believing the risk was too great, refused to approve the request. The final chance for a British triumph in the face of defeat was lost.

The British continued to retreat slowly north, bringing the bateaux up the river as they went, and at 2 A.M. they camped on the high ground above the Hudson. On October 9, the army did not move until late afternoon and were now actively harassed by Americans who captured some of the bateaux. Late that evening, Burgoyne finally reached the vicinity of Saratoga. Fellows, heavily outnumbered, abandoned his fortified position and forded the river back to the east bank of the Hudson. The following day, the British and Germans, wet and exhausted, settled into their old works of September 13–14 and those recently abandoned by Fellows. Burgoyne once

again sent Sutherland north, this time with six companies of the 47th Foot, part of the 9th Foot, some Canadians, and Lieutenant William Twiss with a group of artificers. He ordered them to bridge the Hudson in the area of Fort Edward. Sutherland found the fort held by just 200 men, and he began to build the bridge only to be recalled by Burgoyne.

On the day after Bemis Heights, the Americans had followed the British to the "Great Redoubt," but were slow to pursue the retreat farther north. In order to draw and prepare rations Gates was forced, because of the primitive American supply system, to pull the whole army back to camp, the next day. He finally occupied Burgoyne's old position at noon on October 10, capturing the British hospital and some baggage. Suddenly acting more quickly, Gates marched the army north and reached Burgoyne's main force south of Saratoga by late afternoon of the same day. As the Americans approached, Hamilton pulled his three regiments north of the Fish Kill and burned the Schuyler mansion. Gates observed this activity and concluded Hamilton's Brigade was Burgoyne's rear guard withdrawing. During the night Gates planned an attack on the British army, which he now believed to be in full retreat. At dawn on October 11, the Americans advanced across the Fish Kill, with Morgan in the lead, but then prudently retreated when the fog lifted to reveal the strongly entrenched British deployed and ready for battle. The American army had, by a narrow margin, escaped potential disaster. However, Gates did succeed in capturing or destroying more bateaux and baggage.

That evening Burgoyne conferred with Riedesel, Phillips, and Fraser to decide on a new course of action. Riedesel was in favor of abandoning the baggage and guns and retreating north of Fort Edward, crossing the bend of the Hudson, and then continuing on to Fort George. Remaining undecided, Burgoyne again called together his generals, this time including Hamilton and Brigadier General Wilhem von Gall, the next day. The British officers were in favor of forcing a way to Albany if Gates shifted east, but Riedesel reiterated the proposal for a retreat to Fort Edward, at night, and this suggestion was accepted by those present. At 10 P.M., Riedesel was ready to move when Burgoyne canceled the operation. During the night of October 11–12, the victor of Bennington, Brigadier

General John Stark, crossed the Hudson with 1,100 New Hampshire militia and took up a position to block a British retreat north. Burgoyne, with only 3,500 effective troops, did not believe he was strong enough to force his way past Stark. To the south, Gates, with now close to 18,000 men, had set up gun batteries in Fellows post on the east side of the river. By October 13, Burgoyne was almost entirely surrounded and exposed to constant sniping and cannon fire. Dead bodies and horse and cattle carcasses gradually made the camp environment almost unbearable for Burgoyne's soldiers.

The Surrender

The morning of October 13, Burgoyne called a third "council of war," attended by all field officers and captains of corps. All now agreed that it was honorable to seek a capitulation agreement. Burgoyne sent a letter to the American camp requesting a meeting with Gates "to negotiate matters of high importance to both armies." At 10 A.M. October 14 a blindfolded Major Robert Kingston was escorted to the enemy camp. Kingston suggested to Gates a cessation of hostilities to consider terms. To the adjutant general's astonishment the American commander handed him a list of terms that amounted to unconditional surrender. Burgoyne and his officers were stung by this presumption and rejected the terms outright. In response, Burgoyne wrote out his own set of proposals, to be used as a basis for bargaining, which allowed the British to surrender on the most favorable terms. The British were to be granted full "honours of war" and they were not to be considered prisoners, but were to be marched to Boston, with all expenses incurred along the way to be paid by Congress. From Boston they were to be allowed to return to Great Britain "upon the condition of not serving in North America during the present contest." Other generous provisions included allowing the Canadians to return to Quebec, again at American expense. In addition, Burgoyne wished the armistice to continue until 10 A.M., October 15. Kingston returned to Gates with this document.

To Burgoyne's complete surprise Gates accepted these preliminary proposals, adding only the condition that they be signed by 2 P.M. that afternoon. Burgoyne correctly divined that Gates's haste was due to Clinton's activities lower down the Hudson. Gates had been alarmed by reports that British forces, in this case Vaughan's, were moving to join the army trapped at Saratoga. Burgoyne agreed to Gate's acceptance in "principle" but, in order to stall for time, claimed he needed to consider the agreement further before giving his final ratification. That evening, Colonel Wilkinson and Brigadier General William Whipple for the Americans, and Sutherland and Captain James Henry Craig, Burgoyne's judge advocate general, for the British, used Burgoyne's proposals to draw up the "Articles of capitulation" in detail, which was now even more favorable to the British. All four signed, and Burgoyne agreed to everything stated in the document, insisting on only one change— that "capitulation" be changed to "convention." Gates did not object to the change and the surrender appeared to be complete.

Late at night on October 15, a Tory entered the British camp and informed Burgoyne that Clinton had taken the forts of the Highlands, which was true, but also that Clinton had reached Esopus and was probably in Albany, which was false. Burgoyne was also told that Gates was shifting troops south to face Clinton, troops that were actually New York militia whose enlistments had expired. Burgoyne took this inaccurate information to his "council of war" and attempted to revoke the treaty. Saner heads prevailed and they voted 14 to 18 against such a move. In a last desperate delaying tactic, Burgoyne sent a message to Gates on the morning of October 16 accusing the American commander of detaching forces from his encircling army and he requested that two officers be sent into Gate's camp to confirm this. To his credit Gates refused and Burgoyne, persuaded by Sutherland, finally signed the capitulation document. Burgoyne and his staff, wearing their best uniforms, met with Gates in his camp and later that night dined with the victor of Saratoga in a simple log cabin.

The official surrender ceremony took place at 10 A.M., October 17. The British and German soldiers marched out of camp and piled their arms in the presence of two American officers, who watched as witnesses. The defeated troops forded the Fish Kill and marched between two silent rows of Americans as they headed on the road south toward Albany. As they passed, Patriot musicians played "Yankee Doodle," a song written by a British surgeon during the Seven Years' War to lampoon the motley Yankee militiamen of that conflict. When the British approached Gates's tent, Burgoyne emerged and offered his sword to Gates, who politely returned it.

Over 5,200 men surrendered that day, with their 5,000 muskets and 37 cannons. The army was marched first to Albany and then to Cambridge, Massachusetts, to await embarkation on British ships. The troops, however, were never returned to England during the course of the war and most were eventually taken to Virginia, as prisoners of war. Their numbers were gradually reduced by attrition and many in Burgoyne's army never saw Europe again. The Continental Congress, rightly believing that the British intended simply to shift Burgoyne's troops to areas outside North America and redeploy others to the war zone, never ratified Burgoyne's "convention."

Saratoga's influence on the war was both immediate and long-term. Once Clinton abandoned the forts of the Highlands and Sir Guy Carleton evacuated Ticonderoga in November, only New York City remained British, and the independent state of New York ceased to be a major theater of war, although the savage "frontier war" of northwestern New York was just beginning. The same was true for New England, an area that, except for Rhode Island, was to henceforth become relatively free of conflict. Patriot morale, which reached a low point after the fall of Philadelphia and the defeats suffered by Washington's main army, received an instant boost from the news of the victory. The British had clearly been beaten in two major battles and an entire army forced into surrender. It now seemed possible that the war could actually be won. The political benefits of Saratoga soon followed in the new year and by the spring of 1778 the French were in alliance with the United States to be followed, in lesser degrees of involvement, by Spain and Holland. In Britain, Burgoyne's surrender was greeted by howls of joy by the opposition in Parliament but to the rest of the nation it was a call to arms to face the old enemy of France. New regiments were raised, for the first time in the war, and a new spirit of determination appeared in the army and the navy.

Saratoga also had a dramatic effect on the careers of its high-ranking participants. It ended the military career of John Burgoyne and the 1777 campaign resulted in the replacement of Sir William Howe by the rising star of Clinton. For Gates, Saratoga led to the intrigues of the Conway Cabal and later to appointment as savior of the South and eventual defeat at Camden. And for Arnold, though few could foresee it then, it was a last hurrah in the service of the new Republic.

Brian E. Hubner

REFERENCES

Harrison Bird, *March to Saratoga: General Burgoyne and the American Campaign* (1777); John Burgoyne, *A State of the Expedition from Canada as Laid Before the House of Commons . . .* (1780); ———, *Orderly Book of Gen. John Burgoyne From his Entry into the State of New York . . .* (1860); Rupert Furneaux, *The Battle of Saratoga* (1971); Michael Glover, *General Burgoyne in Canada and America: Scapegoat for a System* (1976); Richard J. Hargrove, *General John Burgoyne* (1983); Roger Lamb, *Memoir of His Own Life . . .* (1811); Max M. Mintz, *The Generals of Saratoga: John Burgoyne and Horatio Gates* (1990); Hoffman Nickerson, *The Turning Point of the Revolution: Burgoyne in America* (1928); Baron Friedrich von Riedesel, *Memoirs and Letters of Major General Riedesel During His Residence in America*, 2 vols., ed. by Max Eelking, trans. by W.L. Stone (1868); James Thacher, *The American Revolution . . .* (1827); Christopher Ward, *The War of the Revolution*, 2 vols., ed. by John R. Alden (1952); James Wilkinson, *Memoirs of my own Times*, 3 vols. (1816).

The British: Saratoga
The Burgoyne Expedition, 1777— "The Canada Army"

1. Burgoyne's Army, July 1
A. i. Commanding Officer, ii. Aides-de-Camp, iii. Staff
B. The Advanced Corps
C. The British Division
D. The German Division
E. The German Reserve
F. Artillery
G. i. Canadians, ii. Indians, iii. Loyalists
H. Numerical Totals

2. Burgoyne's Army, First Freeman's Farm, September 19

3. Burgoyne's Army, Bemis Heights, October 7

4. Burgoyne's Army, Signing of the "Convention," October 16

5. Casualty Figures
A. First Freeman's Farm
B. Bemis Heights

1. Burgoyne's Army, July 1
Below is a table of organization for Burgoyne's army as it appeared just before the siege of Ticonderoga (July 2–6).
A. i. *Commanding Officer*
Maj. Gen. (local Lieut. Gen.) John Burgoyne, M.P., Col.-Commandant 16th Lt. Dragoons, Gov. of Ft. William (promoted full Lieut. Gen., Aug. 29).

ii. *Aides-de-Camp*

Lieut. and Capt. Sir Francis Carr Clerke (Clarke), Baronet, 3rd Foot Gds. (also acted as military secretary; p.o.w., Oct. 7; died of wounds, Oct. 13).

Capt. Henry Gardner, 16th Lt. Dragoons (returned to England with dispatches, July 12).

Capt. Charles Stanhope, Lord Viscount Petersham, M.P., 29th Foot (aide-de-camp after July 12).

Lieut. Richard R. Wilford, 2nd Dragoon Gds.

iii. *Staff*

Adjutant and Quartermaster General

Lieut. Col. Thomas Carleton, 29th Foot (returned to Quebec in Aug.).

Deputy Adjutant General and Military Secretary

Maj. Robert Kingston, Irish Invalids (acting Adjt. Gen. after Aug.; Lieut. Col., Aug. 29).

Deputy Quartermaster General

Capt. John Money, 9th Foot (acting quartermaster general, Aug.; p.o.w., Oct. 7).

Assistant Quartermaster General

Lieut. George Preston Vallancay, 62nd Foot (Adjt., Oct. 12).

Judge Advocate General

Capt. James Henry Craig, 47th Foot.

Provost to the Army

Lieut. Atherton.

Commanding Engineer

Lieut. William Twiss, R.E.

Cartographer

Lieut. William C. Wilkinson, 62nd Foot.

Commissary General

Mr. Jonathan Clarke.

Commissary General in Canada

Mr. Nathaniel Day.

Commissary to the Staff

Mr. Rosseau.

Assistant Commissary of Beer

Mr. John Powell.

Assistant Paymaster General

Mr. David Geddes (acting).

Royal Artillery

Capt. Thomas Blomefield (Bloomfield), R.A.

Department of Civil Affairs

Lieut. Col. (ret.; also called "Maj." and "Gen.") Philip Skene (former Lieut. Gen. of Ticonderoga and Crown Point).

Fleet Commander

Capt. Skeffington Lutwidge (Lutridge), R.N.

Ships: Royal George (24 guns), *Inflexible* (24 guns), *Carleton, Lady Maria, Loyal Convert, Thunderer* (bombketch), *Washington* (cap.), *New Jersey* (cap.), *Lee* (cap.), 28 gunboats, and 500 *bateaux*.

Naval Engineering Advisor (for bridge building)

Lieut. John Schank, R.N.

Naval Personnel

Midshipman Edward Pellow (Pellew), R.N.

Captain of the Bateaux

Capt. Munroe, R.N. (appointed Aug. 13).

Captain of the Artificers

Capt. George Lawes.

The Company of Army Pioneers

Capt. Wilcox.

Waggon Master to the Army

Mr. Robert Hoaksley (July 12).

Acting Physician

Mr. Vincent Wood.

B. *The Advanced Corps*

Commanding Officer

Lieut. Col. (local Brig. Gen.) Simon Fraser, 24th Foot (Col. in the army, July 22; died of wounds, Oct. 8). After Oct. 8, the Earl of Balcarres.

Grenadier Battalion

(10 companies composed of the grenadier battalions of the 9th, 20th, 21st, 24th, 29th, 31st, 34th, 47th, 53rd, and 62nd Foot) Maj. John Dyke-Acland, M.P., 20th Foot (p.o.w., Oct. 7).

Light Infantry Battalion

(10 co.'s same composition as the gren. bat.) Maj. Alexander Lindsay, Earl of Balcarres, 53rd Foot.

24th Foot (8 co.'s).

Lieut. Col. S. Fraser, vice Major Robert Grant (killed in action, July 7). After July 7, Capt, William Agnew (Maj. July 14).

Company of Marksmen ("Fraser's Rangers")

(1 co., 50 marksmen) Capt. Alexander Fraser (Frazer), 34th Foot.

C. *The British Division*

(right division or wing).

Commanding Officer

Lieut. Col. (local Maj. Gen.) William Phillips, M.P., R.A. (second in command of the expedition; promoted full Maj. Gen., Aug. 29).

Aide-De-Camp

Capt. Charles Green, 31st Foot.

1st Brigade (Brit.)

Lieut. Col. Henry Watson Powell (Powel), 53rd Foot (commander at Ticonderoga, Aug. 15).

9th Foot (8 co.'s)

Lieut. Col. John Hill.

47th Foot (8 co.'s)

(2 co.'s detached first to Ft. Edward then in late Aug. to Diamond Island, Lake George). Lieut. Col. Nicholas Sutherland.

53rd Foot (8 co.'s)

(regt. at Ticonderoga from Aug. 10th) Lieut. Col. Powell, Earl of Balcarres, Vice Capt. William Hughes (Maj., Oct.8).

2nd Brigade (Brit.)

Lieut. Col. James Inglis Hamilton, 21st Foot (commander at Ticonderoga from July 6 to Aug. 14).

20th Foot (8 co.'s)

Lieut. Col. John Lind (Lynd).

21st Foot (Roy. N. Brit. Fuzileers; 8 co.'s)

Lieut. Col. Hamilton, Vice Maj. George Forester.

62nd Foot (8 co.'s)

(regt. at Ticonderoga from July 6 until replaced by the 53rd Foot) Lieut. Col. John Anstruther.

D. *The German Division*

(left division or wing).

Commanding Officer

Maj. Gen. Baron Friedrich Adolphus Riedesel, Freiherr von Riedsel-Eisenbach.

Aides-de-Camp

Lieut. Friederich Christian Cleve, Capt. Laurentius O'Connel.

Quartermaster General

Capt. Heinrich Daniel Gerlach.

Paymaster General

Mr. Johann Conrad Godeck.

Brigade Specht (1st German Brigade)

Col. (Brig. Gen.) Johann Friedrich Specht (Second in command of the German troops), Reg. Specht.

Reg. Rhetz (5 co.'s musketeers; Brunsw.)

Lieut. Col. Johann Gustavus von Ehrenkrock.

Reg. Specht (5 co.'s musketeers; Brunsw.)

Col. Specht, Vice Maj. Carl Friedrich von Ehrenkrock.

Reg. Riedesel (5 co.'s musketeers; Brunsw.)

Maj. Gen. Riedesel, Vice Lieut. Col. Ernst Ludwig W. von Speth (Späth).

Brigade von Gall (2nd German Brigade)

Col. (Brig. Gen.) Wilhem R. von Gall, Reg. of Erb-Prinz.

Reg. Prinz Freiderich (5 co.'s musketeers; Brunsw.)

(regiment at Ticonderoga from July 6) Lt. Col. Christian Julius Prätorius.

Reg. Erb-Prinz (5 co.'s grenadiers; Hesse-Hanau)

Brig. Gen. von Gall, Vice Lieut. Col. Johann Christophe Lentz.

E. *The German Reserve*

(Corps of Reserve and unbrigaded troops).

Commanding Officer

Lieut. Col. Heinrich Christoph von Breymann (k.i.a., Oct. 7).

Grenadier Battalion von Breymann

(composed of the grenadier co.'s from the 4 Brunsw. regs.) Lieut. Col. von Breymann, Vice Capt. Ernst August von I. Bärtling (p.o.w., Aug. 16).

Light Infantry Battalion von Bärner

(composed of 4 lt. inf. *chasseur* co.'s and 1 *jäger* co.) Maj. Ferdinand Albrecht von Bärner. *Jäger company*, Capt. Carl von Geyso (p.o.w., Oct 7).

Unbrigaded (employed as H.Q. guards).

Prinz Ludwig's Regiment of Dragoons (4 dismounted troops Brunsw.)

Lieut. Col. Friedrich Baum (Baume; p.o.w., Aug. 16, died of wounds Aug. 18). After Aug. 16, Capt. Adolph von Schlagenteuffel.

Aide-de-Camp

Capt. Laurentius O'Connel.

F. *Artillery*

The British had 4 co.'s of *Royal Artillery*, a detachment of the *Royal Irish Artillery* and 1 co. of *Hesse-Hanau Artillery*. The army took with them, from Quebec, a total of 140 pieces of artillery, many of these being siege guns. Most of the heavy guns were left on board ship after the capture of Ticonderoga. Artillery organization was very flexible and was altered as circumstances dictated. The following 46 guns accompanied Burgoyne south:

Commanding Officers

Lieut. Col. Phillips, and extra Maj. of Brig. (Capt.) Blomefield.

Field Brigades
  1st Brig.
  (attached to the Advanced Corps) Capt. Ellis Walker, R.A.
      Four lt. 6-pdrs.
      Four lt. 3-pdrs.
      Two 5 1/2 in. royal howitzers.
  2nd Brig. (attached to the British Division)
  Capt. Thomas Jones, R.A. (k.i.a., Sept. 19).
      Four lt. 1-pdrs. (attached to the 1st Brig).
      Four lt. 6-pdrs. (attached to the 2nd Brig.).
  3rd Brig.
  (1 co. Hesse-Hanau Art.; attached to the German troops) Capt. Georg Pausch.
      Four lt. 6-pdrs. (attached to the German Div.).
      Two lt. 6-pdrs. and 2 lt. 3-pdrs. (attached to the German Reserve).

Park Artillery

Commanding Officer

Extra Maj. of Brig. (Capt.) Edward Williams, R.A.
  Right Brigade
  Capt. Walter Mitchelson, R.A.
      Two med. 12-pdrs.
      Two lt. 6-pdrs.
      One 8 in. lt. howitzer.
      One 5 1/2 in. royal howitzer.
  Center Brigade
  Capt. John Carter, R.A.
      Two 24 pdrs.
  Left Brigade
  Capt. Thomas Hosmer, R.A.
      Two med. 12-pdrs.
      Two lt. 6-pdrs.
      One 8 in. howitzer.
      One 5¹/2 in. royal howitzer.
      An additional two 8 in. mortars and four 5 [1/2] in. royal mortars were allocated to the field artillery and proceeded south with baggage, via Lake George.

Infantry attached to the Royal Artillery

A detachment of infantry (intended as a reinforcement for the 33rd Foot in New York) of 150 men under Lieut. George Anson Nutt (Nott), 33rd Foot.

G. *Canadians, Indians, and Loyalists*

(not formally brigaded with, but usually employed alongside, the Advanced Corps to act in concert with "Fraser's Rangers")

i. *Canadians*

(nominally designated to cover the British Division)

Commanding Officer

Charles-Louis Tarieu de Lanaudière (de La Naudière); aide-de-camp to Gen. Sir Guy Carleton, Governor of Quebec) appears to have acted as commander.

Capt. Monin's Company

Capt. David Monin (k.i.a., Sept. 19) After Sept. 19, Lieut. Beaubien.

Capt. Boucherville's Company

Capt. René-Amble Boucher de Boucherville.

Numbers

The largest recorded number of Canadians was 148, July 1. This figure was gradually reduced due to battle losses and desertion.

ii. *Indians*

(nominally designated to cover the German Division)

Commanding Officers

Maj. (ret.; local Lieut. Col.) John Campbell, 27th Foot, Commandant of the Indians and Superintendent and Inspector of Indians Affairs for the Province of Quebec, was officially in charge of the Indians in Burgoyne's army (Capt. A. Fraser was deputy superintendent). Actual command, beginning in July, was exercised by Luc de La Corne (La Corne Saint Luc, returned to Quebec after Sept. 19) and his son-in-law Charles-Michel Mouet de Langlade (returned to Quebec in late Aug.).

Numbers

When he left Quebec in June, Burgoyne had about 400 "semi-civilized" Indians from the settlements of St. Regis, Caughnawaga, Lake of Two Mountains, St. Francis, and Huron. At Skenesboro the army was joined by La Corne and de Langlade with 100+ more "warlike" Ottawa and Western Indians. After Aug. 16, these numbers declined sharply, although a handful of Indians joined Burgoyne from St. Leger after he retreated. It was reported that there were 80 Indians in the army on Sept. 1, and by Sept. 19, but 50 remained. Following First Freeman's Farm most of these, too, vanished.

iii. *Loyalists*

(unattached; used as baggage guards).

Commanding Officer

Lieut. Col. Skene appears to have exerted a vague authority over the Loyalists, although his main task was recruiting. The following formations have been identified:

The Queen's Loyal Rangers
Lieut. Col. John Peters.
The King's Loyal Americans
Lieut. Col. Ebenezer Jessup.
The Loyal Volunteers
"Col." Francis Pfister (k.i.a., Aug. 16). After Aug. 16, Capt. Daniel McAlpine.
Unnamed Company
Capt. Samuel McKay (enlisted as a "volunteer").
Unnamed Company
Capt. (Dr.) Samuel Adams.

Numbers

On July 1, there were 83 Loyalists in the army. As Burgoyne moved south, this total increased to a high of 682 in late Aug., but thereafter the number steadily declined; there were 456 Loyalists recorded to be with the army on Oct. 1. Forty Loyalist officers and n.c.o.'s and 172 men surrendered on Oct. 16; 303 had previously been captured.

H. *Numerical Totals—July 1*

Regulars (rank and file)

British:	3,724
German:	3,016
Total:	6,740

Artillery (rank and file)

Brit. Art.:	245
Hessian Art.:	78
33rd Foot:	150
Total:	473

Irregulars (rank and file)

Canadians & Loyalists:	250
Indians:	400
Total:	650
Grand Total:	7,863*

*To this total must be added the officers, n.c.o.'s, musicians, servants, cooks, batmen, noncombatant staff, smiths, mechanics, sutlers, wagon drivers, conductors, female camp followers and their dependents, about 150 *corvée* laborers, and assorted others. It is difficult to establish a final figure for the army in July, but it was probably slightly over 10,000 persons. Including the Indians and Loyalists, who joined in July and Aug., Burgoyne's whole command reached a peak size of about 10,500 persons just before the Battle of Bennington.

2. *Burgoyne's Army, First Freeman's Farm. September 19*

By Sept. 1, the army had fought at Ticonderoga, Hubbardton, Ft. Anne, and several other minor skirmishes, but its major losses in battle had occurred at Bennington. The German forces suffered the heaviest casualties although the Canadians and Loyalists also suffered serious losses. Strength returns for that date indicated there were 2,635 British and 1,711 German rank and file present with the main army. Burgoyne received a reinforcement of 300 men from the "additional companies" left as cadres in Quebec, Sept. 3, and these men were distributed among the British regiments. This gave Burgoyne a total of about 6,000 troops under his immediate command. It has been recorded that 4,876 men were in the attack force Sept. 19, but it seems the actual number was closer to 4,000. Burgoyne reorganized his forces before First Freeman's Farm, and the British and German line troops were now formed into a single brigade each. Below is the deployment of the army Sept. 19, roughly right (west) to left (east);

Commander-in-Chief

Lieut. Gen. Burgoyne.

i. *Right Wing*

(Right Column; about 1,500 regulars and 300 irregulars) Lieut. Col. S. Fraser.

Advanced Corps

Lieut. Col. S. Fraser.
British Grenadier Battalion, Maj. Dyke-Acland.
British Light Battalion, Earl of Balcarres.
24th Foot, Capt. Agnew.

German Reserve

Lieut. Col. Breymann.

Grenadier Battalion von Breymann, Lieut. Col. von Breymann. Light Infantry Battalion von Bärner, Maj. von Bärner (3 light inf. co.'s and 1 *jäger* co.).

Irregulars

Capt. A. Fraser (intended to screen the Right Wing and the Center Column).

"Frasers Rangers." Capt. A. Fraser.

Canadians (2 co.'s, about 70–80 men total).

Indians (about 50 men).

Loyalists (about 150 men, some Loyalists were used as baggage guards alongside the Reg. Erb-Prinz, see below).

Attached Artillery

Capt. Walker.

Four lt. 6-pdrs.

Four lt. 3-pdrs.

Two 5 1/2 in. royal howitzers.

Two lt. 6-pdrs. (Hesse-Hanau; attached to the German Reserve).

ii. *Center Column*

(Center Division; about 1,100 men) Lieut. Col Hamilton (Burgoyne accompanied this column and effectively assumed command).

Hamilton's Brigade

Lieut. Col. Hamilton.

20th Foot, Lieut. Col. Lind.

21st Foot, Maj. Forrester.

62nd Foot, Lieut. Col. Anstruther.

In Reserve

9th Foot, Lieut. Col. Hill.

Attached Artillery

Capt. Jones.

Four lt. 6-pdrs.

Two lt. 3-pdrs.

iii. *Left Wing*

(Left Wing or Division; about 1,000 men) Maj. Gen. Riedesel.

Advanced Guard

Light Infantry (1 co.).

Prinz-Ludwig's Dragoons (50 or fewer troopers mounted on poor horses).

Brigade Specht

Col. Specht.

Reg. Rhetz, Lt. Col. von Ehrenkrock.

Reg. Specht, Maj. von Ehrenkrock.

Reg. Riedesel, Lt. Col. von Speth.

Attached Artillery

Hesse-Hanau, Capt. Pausch.

Four lt. 6-pdrs.

Two lt. 3-pdrs.

iv. *Baggage and Camp Guards*

Bateaux and Additional Artillery

Maj. Gen. Phillips.

47th Foot (6 co.'s), Lt. Col. Sutherland.

7 extra field guns, Capt. Williams.

Park Artillery, Heavy Baggage, Stores, and Hospital

Loyalists and the Reg. Erb-Prinz (Hesse-Hanau), Col. von Gall.

had few Indians, Canadians, or Loyalists left. His total force now numbered 6,204 persons (including the wounded), with 4,402 effective soldiers. On Oct. 7, Burgoyne sortied out with 1,400–1,500 of his best regulars and 600 irregulars. The other troops remained in the entrenched camp. Below is Burgoyne's attack force, deployed right to left:

Commander-in-Chief

Lt. Gen Burgoyne.

i. *Extreme Right Wing*

(about 600 men) Capt. A. Fraser led a force that consisted of "Fraser's Rangers" and the remaining Canadians, Indians, and some of the Loyalists (including the "Albanians").

ii. *Right Wing*

(about 400 men) Lt. Col. S. Fraser.

British Light Infantry Battalion, Earl of Balcarres.

iii. *Center Column*

(about 800 men). Maj. Gen. Riedesel.

Reg. Riedesel.

24th Foot, Capt. Agnew.

Reg. Specht.

Reg. Erb-Prinz (Hesse-Hanau).

Reg. Rhetz.

German Reserve

(200 grenadiers, light infantry, and *jägers*). Col. Speth commanded the 300 men drawn from the German line.

iv. *Left Wing*

(about 300 men) Maj. Gen. Phillips.

British Grenadier Battalion, Maj. Dyke-Acland

Attached Artillery

Two 5 1/2 in. royal mortars (attached to the right).

Two lt. 6-pdrs. (Hesse-Hanau: attached to the centre), Capt. Pausch.

Two med. 12 pdrs. (attached to the centre).

Four lt. 6 pdrs. (attached to the left), Capt. Williams

The British Camp

(also described left to right)

German Reserve (about 200 men), Lt. Gen von Breymann.

British Advanced Corps (including the 20th and 62nd Foot), Maj. Campbell.

Hamilton's Brigade (about 2, 400 men): The 9th and 21st Foot, and the remainder of Reg. Riedesel, Specht and Rhetz, Lt. Col. Hamilton.

Gall's Brigade (about 500 men): the 47th Foot, Reg. Erb-Prinz (Hesse-Hanau) and the Park Artillery, Col. von Gall.

3. Burgoyne's Army, Bemis Heights, October 7

Burgoyne's army suffered serious casualties Sept. 19, falling mainly on the regiments of Hamilton's Brigade. To make up for some of these losses Burgoyne incorporated 120 Loyalists into the 6 battalions of the battalions of the British line, Sept. 21, and on Sept. 22 a reinforcement of "Albanians" (Tories from the vicinity of Albany) appeared in camp. But any augmentation Burgoyne received could not compensate for losses caused by desertion and harassment from American patrols. By early Oct., Burgoyne

4. Burgoyne's Army, Signing of the "Convention," October 16

Burgoyne's army suffered over 600 casualties at Bemis Heights. After the battle British losses due to desertion became a flood, especially among the Loyalists and the German troops, and 300 sick and wounded soldiers were left behind during the retreat. On Oct. 16 Burgoyne claimed he had about 3,500 effective remaining, 2,000 of them British. Below is the army surrendered to Maj. Gen. Horatio Gates:

British under arms:	1,905	rank and file
German under arms:	1,594	rank and file
Total:	3,499	rank and file
Total Brit. prisoners:	2,442	
Total Ger. prisoners:	2,198	(1,812 Brunsw.)
Burgoyne and staff:	12	
Sick and wounded:	598	
Grand Total:	5,250	

Five thousand "Stand of Arms" and 37 guns were also surrendered.

By the time of the surrender Burgoyne's forces had been reduced to half their peak size. The above figures did not include "Indians, Teamsters and Sutlers." As stipulated by the 9th Article of the "convention," "All Canadians and Persons belonging to the Canadian Establishment, consisting of Sailors, Bateaux Men, Artificers, Drivers, Independent Companies, and many other Followers of the Army who came under no particular Description, are to be permitted to return there [Canada]." A total of 1,100 persons were allowed to return to Quebec. Five hundred sixty-two Loyalists were paroled or included in that figure.

5. Casualty Figures
A. *First Freeman's Farm*

About 600 killed, wounded, captured, or missing.

B. *Bemis Heights*

176 killed, 200 wounded, 200 missing—a total of about 600 casualties.

Brian E. Hubner

REFERENCES

John Burgoyne, *The Orderly Book of Lieut-Gen. John Burgoyne*. . . . ed. by E.B. Callaghan (1850); ———, *A State of the Expedition from Canada as Laid before the House of Commons*. . . . (1780); M.B. Fryer, *King's Men: The Soldier Founders of Ontario* (1980); Michael Glover, *General Burgoyne in Canada and America* (1976); Barbara Graymont, *The Iroquois in the American Revolution* (1972); A.L. Haarmann, "The Army of Brunswick and the Corps in North America, 1776–1777," *Military Collector and Historian*, *16* (1964): 76–77; Howard Peckham, *The Toll of Independence* (1974); Baron Friedrich Adolphus Riedesel, *Memoirs, Letters, and Journals of Major General Riedesel*, ed. by Max Elking, trans. by W.L. Stone, 2 vols. (1868); J.P. Wilhemy, *Les Mercenaries Allemands au Quebec* (1984).

The Americans: *Saratoga From First Freeman's Farm to Burgoyne's Surrender*

Considerably less is known about the organization of the American forces than of Burgoyne's, because of haphazard record keeping and peculiarities of the Patriot militia system. It is therefore more difficult to state the exact composition of Gates's army. The Americans were heavily reinforced by militia between Sept. 19 and the time of Burgoyne's surrender and fifty-three separate militia bodies have been identified as having been present with the army. Many did not actively participate in the two battles and some were in Gates's camp for only brief periods.

1. Command
A. Commanding Officer
B. Staff

2. Continental Brigades
A. Right Division
B. Left Division

3. Other Forces
A. "Warner's Vermont Brigade"
B. Unbrigaded
C. Artillery

4. Calvary

5. Militia Brigades

6. Militia Colonels

7. Numerical Totals

8. Casualty Figures
A. First Freeman's Farm
B. Bemis Heights

Legend:
*unit engaged at First Freeman's Farm.
†unit engaged at Bemis Heights.

1. Command
A. *Commanding Officer, Northern Department*
Maj. Gen. Horatio Gates (officially replaced Maj. Gen. Philip Schuyler, Aug. 4, and assumed command Aug. 19).
B. *Staff*
Adj. Gen.
Col. James Wilkinson.
Engineer
Col. Thaddeus (Tadeusz) Kosciuszko (Kosciunsko).
Surgeon
Dr. James Thacher.
Quartermaster General
Col. Udney Hay.
Deputy Quartermaster General
Col. Morgan Lewis.
Commissary
Joseph Trumbull, commissary general of purchases.
Jacob Cuyler, deputy commissary general of purchases.
Charles Stewart, commissary general of issues.
Elisha Avery (later replaced by James Beeker), deputy commissary general of purchases.
Deputy Muster Master
Col. Richard Varrick.

2. Continental Brigades

Gates's main fighting strength was contained in his five brigades of Continentals (Nixon's, Patterson's, Glover's, Poor's, and Learned's) plus "Warner's Vermont Brigade." They were organized and deployed at First Freeman's Farm as follows:

A. *Right Division*

(Right Wing; as deployed right to left).

Commanding Officer

Maj. Gen. Benjamin Lincoln (command assumed personally, Sept. 19, by Maj. Gen. Gates).

Nixon's Continental Brigade

(1st Mass. Brig).

Brig. Gen. John Nixon.

3rd Mass. Cont. Regt. (8 co.'s), Col. John Greaton.

5th Mass. Cont. Regt. (8 co.'s), Col. Rufus Putnam.

6th Mass. Cont. Regt. (8 co.'s), Col. Thomas Nixon.

7th Mass. Cont. Regt. (8 co.'s), Col. Ichabod Alden.

Patterson's Continental Brigade

(3rd Mass. Brig.)

Brig. Gen. John Patterson.

˙10th Mass. Cont. Regt. (8 co.'s), Col. Thomas Marshall.

11th Mass. Cont. Regt. (8 co.'s), (Col. Ebenezer Francis. k.i.a., July 7), Col. Benjamin Tupper.

12th Mass. Cont. Regt. (8 co.'s), Col. Samuel Brewer.

14th Mass. Cont. Regt. (8 co.'s), Col. Gamaliel (Gamiliel) Bradford.

Glover's Continental Brigade

(2nd Mass. Brig.).

Brig. Gen. John Glover.

1st Mass. Cont. Regt. (8 co.'s), Col. Joseph Vose.

4th Mass. Cont. Regt. (8 co.'s), Col. William Shepard.

13th Mass. Cont. Regt. (8 co.'s), Col. Edward Wigglesworth.

15th Mass. Cont. Regt. (8 co.'s), Col. Timothy Bigelow.

New York Militia Attached to Glover's Brigade

2nd New York Militia Regt. (Schenectady Co.), Col. Abraham Wemple.

17th New York Militia Regt. (Albany Co.), Col. William Bradford Whiting.

Dutchess and Ulster county militia regts. (levies), Col. Morris Graham.

B. *Left Division*

(Left wing: as deployed right to left).

Commanding Officer

Maj. Gen Benedict Arnold (relieved of command on Oct. 1 and replaced by Maj. Gen. Lincoln).

Supernumerary Aides to Brig. Gen. Arnold

Col. Richard Varrick (former secretary to Maj. Gen. Schuyler).

Col. Henry Brockholst Livingston (former aid to Maj. Gen. Schuyler).

˙˙Poor's Continental Brigade

(New Hampshire Brig.)

Brig. Gen. Enoch Poor.

2nd N.Y. Cont. Regt. (8 co.'s). Col. Philip van Cortlandt.

4th N.Y. Cont. Regt. (8 co.'s). Col. Henry Beekman Livingston.

1st N.H. Cont. Regt. (8 co.'s), Col. Joseph Cilley.

2nd N.H. Cont. Regt. (8 co.'s), (Col. Nathan Hale, p.o.w., July 7), After July 7, Lt. Col. Winborn Adams.

3rd N.H. Cont. Regt. (8 co.'s), Col. Alexander Scammel (Scammell).

Connecticut Militia Attached to Poor's Brigade

Cook's Conn. Militia Regt., Col. Thaddeus Cook.

Latimer's Conn. Militia Regt., Col. Johnathan Latimer.

˙˙Learned's Continental Brigade

(4th Mass. Brig.)

Brig. Gen Ebenezer Leaned (Larned).

2nd Mass. Cont. Regt. (8 Co.'s) John Bailey.

8th Mass. Cont. Regt. (8 co.'s), Col. Michael Jackson (replaced by Lt. Col. John Brooks for the battle of Oct. 7).

9th Mass. Cont. Regt. (8 co.'s) Col. James Wesson.

1st N.Y. Cont. Regt. (8 co.'s), Col. Goose van Schiak.

1st Can. Cont. Regt. (8 co.'s), Col. James Livingstone

3. Other Forces

A. *"Warner's Vermont Brigade"*

This unofficial brigade was composed of Warner's Regiment joined by several companies of irregular New Hampshire Grants militia. Its composition at Bennington, Aug. 16, was the following:

i. Warner's Extra Cont. Reg. (6 co.'s; "The Green Mountain Boys"), Col. Seth Warner.

ii. Herrick's Regt. of Rangers (6 co's), Col. Samuel Herrick. Herrick was operating near the Quebec border on Oct. 17.

iii. Col. Brush (2 co.'s. Bennington militia).

iv. Col. Moses Robinson (1 co., Bennington militia).

v. Col. William Williams (1 co., Cumberland Co. militia), Williams held a New York commission.

vi. Capt. Dewey (1 co., Bennington militia).

B. *Unbrigaded*

˙˙i. "Morgan's Regiment of Riflemen" or "The Corps of Riflemen" (331 men), Col. Daniel Morgan, 11th Virginia Cont. Reg. Morgan's provisional rifle corps was formed from soldiers in Washington's main army on June 13. It was first assigned to Arnold's Div. and then, after Sept. 22, attached to Gates's H.Q.

˙˙ii. Battalion of light infantry (5 co.'s; 200 men attached to "Morgan's Regiment of Riflemen"), Maj. Henry Dearborn. Dearborn's Battalion was formed out of men from regiments in the Northern Department.

iii. Whitcomb's Rangers (2 co.'s, N.H.), Col. Benjamin Whitcomb.

iv. Stockbridge Indians (1 co.), Capt. Ezra Whittley.

v. Baldwin's Detachment of Engineers and Artificers, Col. Jeduthan Baldwin.

C. *Artillery*

i. Capts. Ebenezer Stevens's and Stephan Bedlams co.'s of the Cont. Artillery Regt.

ii. Capt. Andrew Moodies's co. of Col. John Lamb's 2nd Cont. Artillery Regt.

Gates had a total of 22 guns on Sept. 19. These were organized into five batteries of four guns each, and one battery of two guns.

Ten 6-pdrs.

Twelve 3-pdrs.

4. *Cavalry*

2nd Conn. Regt. of light horse (150 troopers; Conn.), Maj. Elijah Hyde. Hyde arrived in Gates's camp on Sept. 1.

Lt. Col. Sheldon's 2nd Cont. Lt. Dragoon Regt. (200 troopers; Conn.), Capt. Thomas Young Seymour.

5. *Militia Brigades*

Any militia regiments not yet mentioned were organized into eight separate brigades (Ten Broeck's, Stark's, Fellow's, Bayley's, Whipple's, Woolcot's, Brickett's, and Wemer's each of greatly varying strength:

⁺A. *Ten Broeck's New York Militia Brig.* (about 3,000 men) Brig. Gen. Abraham Ten Broeck. The militia regiments in Ten Broeck's Brig. were the following:

i. County Militia Regts. (levies), Col. Robert van Rensselaer and Col. Stephen John Schuyler.

ii. Dutchess and Ulster county militia regts. (levies).

iii. 1st N.Y. Militia Regt. (Albany City), Col. Jacob Lansing.

iv. 3rd N.Y. Militia Regt. (Rensselaerwyck), Col. Francis Nicholl.

v. 5th N.Y. Militia Regt. (Rensselaerwyck), Col. Gerrit Vanden Bergh.

vi. 12th N.Y. Militia Regt. (Halfmoon), Col. Jacobus van Schoonhoven.

vii. 13th N.Y. Militia Regt. (Stillwater), Col. van Veghten.

viii. 14th N.Y. Militia Regt. (Schaghticoke), Col. Johannis Knickerbocker.

ix. 18th N.Y. Militia Regt. (Cambridge), Col. Lewis van Woert.

B. *Stark's New Hampshire Militia Brigade* (about 1,500 men). Brig. Gen. John Stark. Stark held a N.H. commission and he received a Continental commission on Oct. 4. When the enlistments for Stark's militiamen expired Sept. 18, these troops left Gates's camp, but Stark returned on Oct. 11-12, to block Burgoyne's escape route on the west side of the Hudson. His brigade was a mixture of New Hampshire, Massachusetts, and Vermont troops. At Bennington, Aug. 16, the brigade included the following:

i. Col. Ebenzer Webster (N.H. Militia).

ii. Col. Benjamin Bellows (N.H. Militia).

iii. Col. Issac(?) Hubbard (N.H. Militia).

iv. Col. Moses Nichols (N.H. Militia).

v. Lt. Col. William Gregg (N.H. Militia).

vi. Col. Joab Stafford (Berkshire Co., Mass. Militia).

vii. Col. Ashley (Berkshire Co., Mass. Militia).

viii. Col. Brown (Berkshire Co., Mass. Militia).

ix. Col. Benjamin Simonds (Symonds; Berkshire Co., Mass. Militia).

x. Col. Thomas Stickney (Mass. Militia).

xi Col. Hobart (Mass. Militia).

xii. Capt. Solomon (1 co., Stockbridge Indians).

C. *Fellows's Massachusetts Militia Brigade* (about 1,300, Mass. Militia).

Brig. Gen. John Fellows was deployed on the west bank of the Hudson north of Burgoyne on Oct. 7, by the surrender he had redeployed to the east bank.

D. *Bayley's (Bailey) New Hampshire Militia Brigade* (about 2,000 men).

Brig. Gen. Jacob Bayley. Bayley was operating on Burgoyne's lines of communication near Ft. Edward on Oct. 7.

E. *Whipple's New Hampshire Militia Brigade*

Col. William Whipple. Whipple was present, with Gates, at Burgoyne's surrender.

F. *Woolcot's (Woolcut) Connecticut Militia Brigade*

Col. Oliver Woolcot.

G. *Brickett's Militia Brigade*

Col. James Brickett.

H. *Wemer's Militia Brigade*

Col. Wemer.

6. *Militia Colonels*

The following militia regiments identified by their colonels, and not noted elsewhere, are thought to have been present at the surrender. They helped compose the last seven militia brigades.

A. *Massachusetts*

Colonels: Ezra May, Elisha Porter, John Ashley, Charles Smith, Asa Barnes, Jonas Wilder, Samuel Johnson, John Mosely, Samuel Denny, Phineas Wright, Ebenezer Bridge, Russell Woodbridge, Joshua Titcomb, Jonathan Breed, Samuel Bulard and Joshus Whitney.

B. *New Hampshire*

Colonels: Stephen Evans, Jonathan Chase, John Langdon, and William Gerish.

C. *Connecticut*

Col. Josian Porter.

7. *Numerical Totals*

On Sept. 19, Gates had 7,000–8,000 troops, less than half of them Continentals. This number swelled to an estimated 10,000–11,000 men (mostly militia) on Oct. 7. By Burgoyne's surrender Gates's army had 1,698 officers and 20,652 men (not including artificers, bateaux men, and 700 riflemen), with about 1,000 sick and 4,000 troops between Burgoyne and Canada. The breakdown of Continental troops was as follows: 52 company officers, 457 company officers, 72 staff, 526 sergeants, 262 drummers and fifers, 7,644 rank and file (about 5,000 effectives).

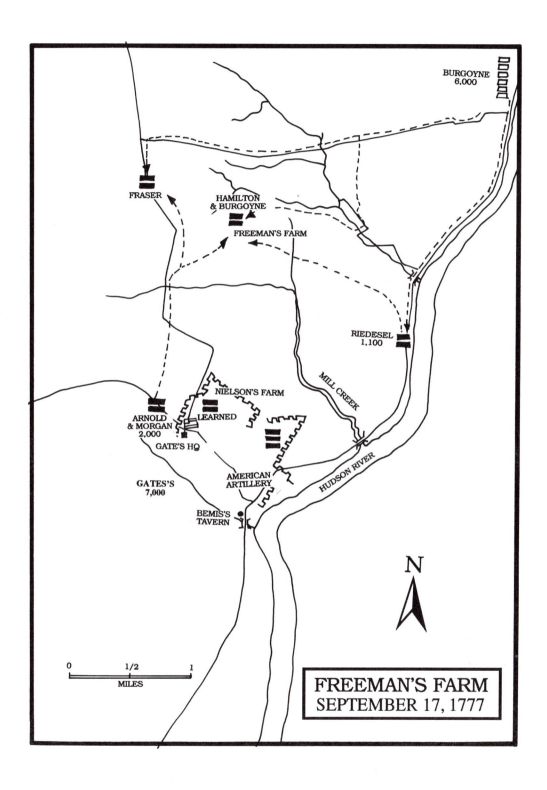

BURGOYNE
6,000

FRASER

HAMILTON
& BURGOYNE

FREEMAN'S FARM

RIEDESEL
1,100

MILL CREEK

NIELSON'S FARM

LEARNED

ARNOLD
& MORGAN
2,000

GATE'S HQ

AMERICAN
ARTILLERY

GATES'S
7,000

HUDSON RIVER

BEMIS'S
TAVERN

N

0   1/2   1
MILES

FREEMAN'S FARM
SEPTEMBER 17, 1777

1495

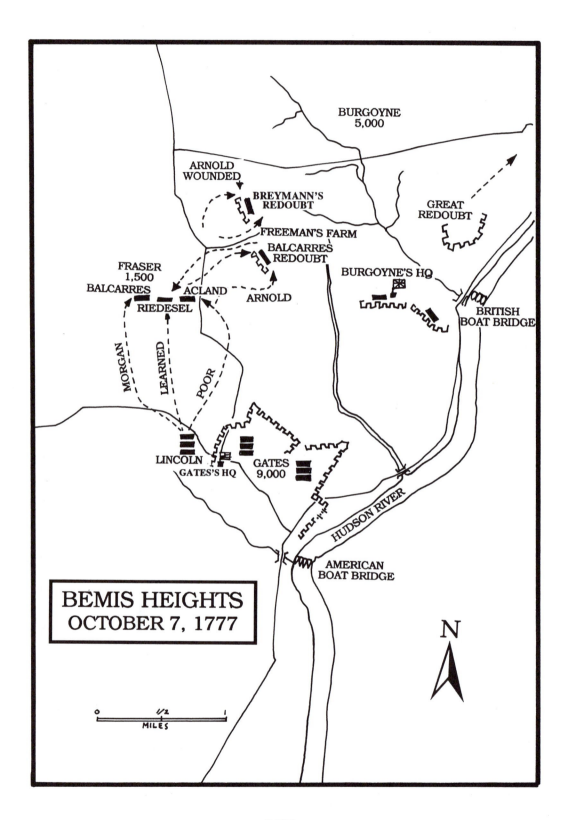

BEMIS HEIGHTS
OCTOBER 7, 1777

8. *Casualty Figures*

A. *First Freeman's Farm*

80 killed, 200 wounded, 36 missing—a total of about 300 casualties.

B. *Bemis Heights*

30–50 killed, 150 wounded—a total of about 200 casualties.

Brian E. Hubner

REFERENCES

John Burgoyne, *A State of the Expedition from Canada as Laid before the House of Commons.* . . . (1780); John H. Hayes, "The Connecticut Light Horse, 1776–1783," *Military Collector and Historian, 22* (1970):109–112; Borden H. Mills, "Albany County's Part in the Battle of Saratoga," *New York State Historical Society Proceedings, 15* (1916):204–224; Hoffman Nickerson, *The Turning Point of the Revolution: Burgoyne in America* (1928); Howard Peckham, *The Toll of Independence* (1974); Christopher Ward, *The War of the American Revolution,* ed. by John R. Alden, 2 vols. (1952); R.K. Wright, *The Continental Army* (1983).

Sauthier, Claude Joseph (1736–1802)

French cartographer. Born in Strasbourg, France, on November 10, 1736, the son of Joseph Philippe Sauthier, a saddler, and his wife Barbe Primat, Claude Joseph Sauthier studied architecture and surveying at the Grand Séminaire, where many of his sketches are preserved. During his adolescence, Sauthier witnessed the abundant cartographic activity in France, and as he pursued his career, the field was experimenting with novel methods, such as triangulation, to map all French provinces, requiring the services of numerous surveyors.

In addition to Sauthier's professional experiences and exposure to new methods, in 1759 De Luche, the superintendent of Alsace, requested an intricate survey of that province, incorporating agricultural facets—such as forests and pastures—in the final map. This project inspired Sauthier, who in 1763 completed a project examining civil and landscape architecture that contained a variety of blueprints, including a governor's mansion, revealing his ability to depict exquisitely and precisely a variety of structures and topographical regions.

One of the most prolific eighteenth-century cartographers, Sauthier published surveys and maps depicting both southern and northern colonies before the American Revolution. In 1767 he traveled to the colonies because Governor

William Tryon of North Carolina hired him to survey ten towns in North Carolina, asking him to depict both public and private buildings, transportation systems, and rural areas in great detail; as a result of Sauthier's surveys, the topography of colonial North Carolina is well recorded. Tryon also retained Sauthier to chart his property and design the governor's mansion at New Bern in addition to surveying that city.

In May 1771 Sauthier accompanied Tryon to Alamance, where he sketched four maps of a pre-Revolutionary skirmish where the Regulators—a group of provincial insurgents—were defeated. In late 1771 Tryon was appointed governor of New York, and Sauthier relocated with him to survey that colony and New York City. Tryon selected Sauthier to determine the boundary between New York and Quebec. He also granted him 5,000 acres in Norbury, Vermont. In 1774 Sauthier traveled with Tryon to England.

When they returned to New York in 1775, the colony had erupted with protests and dissension directed at British rule. Sauthier quickly adapted to the role of military cartographer when Sir William Howe landed troops on Staten Island in 1776 and asked him to draw a map of the island. Sauthier followed the British troops in New York, recording actions at Manhattan, then at White Plains. When Earl Hugh Percy attacked Fort Washington, Sauthier made engravings immediately after the battle, emphasizing Percy's tactical movements against the enemy.

He published his maps of New York, including several surveys by Bernard Ratzer, in 1776. Sauthier issued "A Plan of the Operations of the King's Army in New York" in 1777 in William Faden's *North American Atlas,* printed in London. He accompanied Percy on the Rhode Island campaign, where he drew a map of Newport, Percy's headquarters. Percy invited Sauthier to England, and he accepted a position as Percy's private secretary. He took maps of the colonies to Britain where military tacticians could study the colonial terrain and devise strategies.

Sauthier's "Chorographical Map of the Province of New York" was published by William Faden in 1779. Twentieth-century cartographer I.N.P. Stokes lauded it as "the most beautiful and probably the most accurate" map of Revolutionary New York, and the chart included territory which would later become part of Vermont and which at that time was disputed land between New York and New Hampshire, where

Sauthier continued to produce high-quality maps—including those published in William Faden's *Atlas of Battles of the American Revolution*—that were characterized by their clarity and preciseness as well as complexity and thoroughness. He drew estate maps for Percy, who became the second Duke of Northumberland, in England from 1785 to 1790. He then returned to Strasbourg, where he died on November 6, 1802. *See also:* Cartography in the American Revolution

Elizabeth D. Schafer

REFERENCES

William P. Cumming, *British Maps of Colonial America* (1974); Peter J. Guthorn, *American Maps and Map Makers of the Revolution* (1966); John B. Harley, Barbara B. Petchenik, and Lawrence W. Towner, *Mapping the American Revolutionary War* (1978).

Savannah, Georgia, British Capture of (December 29, 1778)

The American Revolution had stalled in the North by the winter of 1778–1779. Unable to defeat Washington's army but unwilling to give up, British political leaders in London sent General Sir Henry Clinton a long list of new directives. Among these orders was one for the British commander to renew the previously unsuccessful attempt to conquer the southern states. In late October 1778 with great reluctance, Clinton dispatched a grossly unprepared and unqualified Lieutenant Colonel Archibald Campbell with a fleet and 3,000 British, Hessian, and Loyalist troops to establish a foothold in the South. Campbell's objective was Savannah, Georgia, where American forces were believed to be weak and where an invasion force could be reinforced by troops from British East Florida, by Loyalists from the Carolina backcountry, and by Indians.

American authorities in the North learned of the coming campaign before Campbell did, but they were unable to do much more than send warnings to the South. Georgia's rebels were badly divided politically, and the state's military resources were weakened by Indian raids, invasions of East Florida, and counterinvasions from East Florida. Desertions and disease had also depleted the Continental forces in the South, and General Robert Howe, the highest-ranking officer there, was compelled to defend Savannah

while waiting to be relieved of his command. He constantly bickered with Georgia state officials.

The battle of Savannah was decided by the personalities of the opposing commanders. The British fleet fought off storms, privateers, and saboteurs to assemble off the Georgia coast on December 23, 1778. To meet his enemy, Howe had only 650 Continentals and 93 Georgia militiamen. The American general stationed his Continentals at Fair Lawn Plantation, immediately below Savannah, to wait for reinforcements or for the British attack, whichever came first. Colonel Samuel Elbert and other officers advised Howe to flood the nearby rice fields and to note that the British could be ambushed at John Giradeau's plantation. Howe made a personal inspection of the site and determined that it was too late to flood the fields and that there were many places available on the coast for a British landing. However, he did post a picket of 50 to 75 men at Giradeau's. Colonel George Walton of the Georgia militia warned Howe of trails through the woods on the American right that could be used by the British. Howe sent some cavalry to patrol that area, but Walton was unsatisfied and posted his militia there.

Meanwhile, the British commander, Archibald Campbell, had sent ashore a party that captured an overseer and a slave who directed him to Giradeau's plantation. A change in the weather allowed Campbell to land troops there on December 28 and they quickly overwhelmed Howe's small picket. Although he had no accurate knowledge of his opponents' positions, Campbell set out for Savannah with one-half of his army. Upon arriving at Fair Lawn, Campbell climbed a tree in order to see for himself the American troop placements.

On December 29, Campbell determined to charge the American line. However, a mulatto slave named Quamino Dolly offered, for a price, to guide the British troops through the woods around the American right, exactly as Walton had warned Howe. Sir James Baird and 200 British and Loyalist troops followed Dolly. When they reached the American right, a British officer in a tree signaled Campbell and the rest of his troops rushed Howe's Continentals.

Baird's 200 men collided with Howe's cavalry and Walton's Georgia militia. The American resistance was quickly crushed, and Walton was wounded and captured, but the delay gave Howe enough time to escape with most of his army. The Georgia Continentals under Samuel Elbert, however, were cut off. After having suffered many other times for the American cause, most of these men would not follow Elbert in swimming the river to escape. Instead they surrendered. Many of these men later died in British prison ships in Savannah.

That day, Campbell won the entire town for use as a British base for threatening Charleston and conducting campaigns against the South. He wrote that his men took

> [t]hirty-eight officers of different distinctions and four hundred fifteen non-commissioned officers, and privates, one stand of colours, forty eight pieces of cannon, twenty-three mortars, ninety-four barrels of powder, the fort with all of its stores . . . and in short the capital of Georgia, the shipping in the harbour, with a large quantity of provisions, fell into our possession before dark.

Campbell's loss was one officer and two privates killed and one sergeant and nine privates wounded. He claimed to have found 83 of the enemy dead in the field.

In January 1779, Campbell was reinforced and superseded in command by General Augustin Prevost from British East Florida. The British capture of Savannah began more than three years of campaigns that would devastate Georgia and South Carolina and lead to invasions of North Carolina and Virginia, cumulating in Cornwallis's surrender at Yorktown. Thousands of lives were lost, and an unestimated amount of damage was done in what is now seen as an eleventh hour effort by the British to win a war already lost.

An argument can be made that the British forces at Savannah would have won no matter who commanded the American troops there. However, Howe made tactical errors and thereby provided the British with a victory. Conversely, Campbell's gambles in the fight won him advantages that a more conservative British commander might well have lost. A court-martial brought about by George Walton in 1781 investigated Robert Howe's actions at Savannah in 1778. He was acquitted "with the highest honor."

Robert Scott Davis, Jr.

REFERENCES

Archibald Campbell, *Journal of an Expedition Against the Rebels of Georgia* (1983); Pierre Colomb, "Memoirs of a Revolutionary Soldier," *The Collector*, 53 (1950):198–201, 223–225, 247–249; Robert S. Davis, Jr., "The British Invasion of Georgia in 1778," *Atlanta Historical Journal*, 24 (1980):5–25; Alexander A. Lawrence, "General Robert Howe and the British Capture of Savannah in 1778," *Georgia Historical Quarterly*, 36 (1952):303–327.

Savannah, Georgia, Franco-American Siege of (September–October 1779)

After a successful campaign in the Caribbean in the course of which he captured the islands of Saint Vincent in June and Grenada the following month, Count d'Estaing, who held the ranks of both lieutenant general and vice admiral in the armed forces of His Most Christian Majesty, Louis XVI, sailed from Le Cap Francais in Haiti on August 16, 1779, headed for North American waters. There were nearly 3,900 troops in his expedition, drawn from European and colonial regiments and including a number of West Indian volunteers. By early September, the French fleet was off the coast of Georgia. A few days later a French officer was dispatched to inform the ranking American military commander in the area, General Benjamin Lincoln, that d'Estaing's forces were available to cooperate in regaining Savannah, which had fallen to the English at the end of the previous year. The French commander seemed determined to avenge his humiliating experience at Newport in August 1778.

Although d'Estaing put a few men ashore on Tybee Island on September 9, the main disembarkation, at Beaulieu plantation, a dozen or so miles south of Savannah, took place between September 12 and 14. Shortly after landing, some of the hungry French soldiers pillaged nearby farms, taking cattle, sheep, hogs, and poultry, along with some horses, wagons, and Jamaican rum. Thus refreshed, but increasingly resented by the local populace, the French advanced against Savannah. Before a junction with Lincoln's Americans could be achieved, on September 16 d'Estaing called upon the British commander, General Augustin Prevost, to surrender the town since any defense would be "absolutely impossible and useless, due to the Superiority of the forces attacking him by Land and by Sea." The shrewd Briton, exploiting this Gallic *noblesse oblige*, requested and was granted a brief truce to consider the demand, during which time

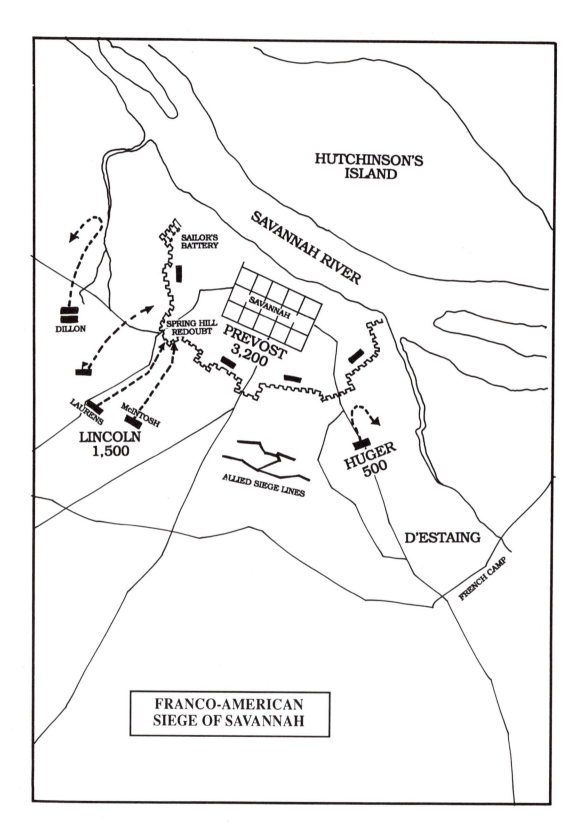

HUTCHINSON'S ISLAND

SAVANNAH RIVER

SAILOR'S BATTERY

DILLON

SPRING HILL REDOUBT

SAVANNAH

PREVOST 3,200

LAURENS

McINTOSH

LINCOLN 1,500

ALLIED SIEGE LINES

HUGER 500

D'ESTAING

FRENCH CAMP

FRANCO-AMERICAN SIEGE OF SAVANNAH

he received some 800 reinforcements under Lieutenant Colonel John Maitland, raising the number of defenders above 2,000 and thus making it possible to reject d'Estaing's summons.

On September 20–21 more French troops landed and shortly afterwards united with Lincoln's American forces, comprised of some 600 Continentals, 200 infantry and cavalry of Count Pulaski's Legion, and hundreds of local militiamen whose exact numbers varied substantially from day to day. By September 23, preparations for the allied siege were nearly complete, although the artillery bombardment of Savannah did not commence until the morning of October 4. Impatient with the slow progress of the siege, d'Estaing pressed for a direct attack. On October 9, some 3,500 French and between 800 and 1,000 Americans launched a vigorous assault against the British positions. Despite the courage exhibited by the allies (d'Estaing himself was twice wounded in three successive attacks), their offensive failed. French casualties exceeded 600 and Americans numbered more than, 200 while the British lost only about 150 men in all. Disillusioned by this failure, with his forces suffering from shortages of supplies and adverse weather, d'Estaing ordered a withdrawal. The French troops reembarked October 19 through 21, and the French ships sailed off between October 24 and 28. Meanwhile, the Americans pulled back to Charleston.

In spite of public statements lauding the gallantry displayed by both Americans and French, resentment festered. Lincoln had been slow in assembling his forces, and d'Estaing had been impetuous in pushing the attack. Americans were angered by the allegation that d'Estaing had called upon the British to surrender in the name of Louis XVI alone. French were embittered by a rumor that an American had betrayed the allied plan of attack to the enemy. Perhaps most importantly, in the 20 months since the signing of the Franco-American alliance, the American military situation had not improved and the French contribution to the war had been negligible—or so it appeared.

Although the obvious consequences of French entry into the American War for Independence were thus far unnotable, in fact, French participation had changed the conflict in a fundamental way; it had turned a colonial struggle into a worldwide war. When d'Estaing was getting ready to besiege Savannah, the French had taken the offensive in the West Indies, were threatening a cross-Channel invasion of England, and were supporting their Spanish allies in a blockade of Gibraltar. The French had regained control of Senegal, and they even posed a danger to British dominance in India. D'Estaing's voyage from the Caribbean had alarmed every British post in America between Jamaica and Halifax. Indeed, so concerned were British military and naval authorities that General Sir Henry Clinton ordered the evacuation of the 4,000 troops garrisoning Rhode Island; thus, d'Estaing achieved what he had failed to accomplish the previous year.

There can be little doubt that French intervention in the American Revolution put an immense strain on the resources of Britain and substantially affected its ability to repress the American rebellion. There can be equally little doubt that very few—if any—Americans appreciated the French role in global strategy. For most Americans, now into the fifth year of war, the only products of the French alliance had been failure and frustration.

Sam Scott

REFERENCES

Jonathan R. Dull, *The French Navy and American Independence: A Study of Arms and Diplomacy, 1774–1787* (1975); Charles C. Jones, ed., *The Siege of Savannah in 1779, As Described in Two Contemporaneous Journals of French Officers in the Fleet of Count D'Estaing* (1874), rpr. 1968; Harold A. Larrabee, *Decision at the Chesapeake* (1964); Alexander A. Lawrence, *Storm over Savannah: The Story of Count D'Estaing and the Siege of the Town in 1779* (1951); William Moultrie, *Memoirs of the American Revolution, So Far As It Related to the States of North and South Carolina, and Georgia*, 2 vols. (1802), 2, rpr. 1968.

Sayenqueraghta (?–1786)

Seneca Indian chief. Ever since the Revolution, Joseph Brant generally has been accepted as the most important Iroquois chief of his period. He himself was only too well aware that he was not. The Senecas were the largest and most powerful of the Six Nations, and their great war leader Sayenqueraghta had far more prestige than any Mohawk. Only in the desperate days leading up to the Battle of Newtown (August 29, 1779), when Sullivan's army defeated a weak and starving force of Iroquois, Butler's Rangers, and some regulars, did the two men, both brilliant commanders, come to an understanding. The great Seneca's name is spelled here as it is usually written, though, in fact, it is its Mohawk version. In Seneca it is Kaienkwaahton.

Sayenqueraghta was used to being courted by the British establishment in America, notably Sir William Johnson and his family. His home was at Ganundasaga (Geneva, New York). The Seneca Blacksnake recalled that Sayenqueraghta inflicted the devastating defeat on the British at the Niagara portage during the Pontiac uprising, but this is thought to be untrue. In 1777, he decided to fight as an ally of the British. He was so old that he rode regularly on horseback. From the Battle of Oriskany onward he was often in action and was one of the commanders at Wyoming (1778) along with Cornplanter and Colonel John Butler.

Sayenqueraghta's village was destroyed by the Sullivan-Clinton expedition in 1779, and he had to retreat to Niagara. The disaster forced Sayenquer-aghta to come to an understanding with Brant. His years of campaigning reached a final climax on Sir John Johnson's great raid on the Mohawk Valley in 1780.

After the war he elected to stay in New York rather than go to Canada. The admiring Blacksnake noted his commanding presence, his intellect and his eloquence, and stated that he fully enjoyed the confidence of his people.

Robin May

REFERENCES

E.A. Cruikshank, *Butler's Rangers* (1893); *DCB*; Barbara Graymont, *The Iroquois in the American Revolution* (1974); Isabel Thompson Kelsay, *Joseph Brant, 1743–1807, Man of Two Worlds* (1984); William L. Stone, *Life of Joseph Brant—Thayendanagea*, 2 vols. (1838).

Scammell, Alexander (1744–1781)

Continental Army officer. Born in Milford, Massachusetts, Alexander Scammell graduated from Harvard College in 1769 and taught school in Massachusetts and Maine, before moving to New Hampshire in 1772. There he worked as a "timber cruiser," marking mast trees for the Royal Navy, and as a surveyor, working with the mapmaker Samuel Holland. In 1774 he moved to Durham, New Hampshire, to read law in the office of John Sullivan, one of the leaders of the Patriot party in New Hampshire.

As one of Sullivan's law clerks, Scammell was part of the Patriot movement. When, on December 15, 1774, Sullivan led a raid on Fort William and Mary, at New Castle, New Hampshire, Scammell was with him, one of the crew that sailed a gondola carrying men from Durham down the Piscataqua River to New Castle. Sacking the fort, they carried off muskets, cannon, and about 100 barrels of gunpowder. Scammell, with Sullivan's two other law clerks and a hired man, worked for three days hiding these supplies in safe places in Durham and nearby towns.

When news of the fighting at Concord and Lexington reached New Hampshire, on April 20, 1775, Sullivan was in the Continental Congress in Philadelphia and Scammell was in Sullivan's law office in Durham. Needing firsthand news of the fighting, a committee of the New Hampshire Provincial Congress sent Scammell to Boston.

Scammell quickly returned to New Hampshire, made his report to the Provincial Congress, and wound up his work in Sullivan's office. He joined the army on June 12 as brigade major of the New Hampshire Brigade, commanded by General Nathaniel Folsom. When Sullivan replaced Folsom, Scammell remained as brigade major. He was with the brigade at the time of the siege of Boston, where he suffered an attack of dysentery, and in Canada, when Washington included the brigade among the reinforcements he sent to the northern army. When Sullivan left the northern army and rejoined Washington's forces on Long Island, Scammell went with him as aide-de-camp. After Sullivan was captured, Scammell served as aide-de-camp to Washington.

As the Continental Army retreated from Brooklyn to New York City Scammell made a mistake that could have turned into a disaster. On the night of August 29–30, 1776, Washington organized a retreat from Long Island across the East River to New York. As the first troops marched down to the boat landing, other regiments extended their front so that the lines continued to appear completely defended. The rear guard was to be General Thomas Mifflin's brigade.

About 2 A.M., Scammell—misunderstanding Washington's intentions—came to Mifflin and told him to pull his troops out of the line and march them down to the landing. As the troops were making their way to the ferry, Washington came up and demanded to know why they had abandoned their post. Mifflin replied that it was by Washington's orders as delivered by Scammell. Washington exclaimed that there had been a terrible mistake. He ordered Mifflin to return to his position before the British realized that the line was not defended. The retreat continued. By 7 A.M., all the troops with their baggage and supplies were safely in New York.

Scammell was with the army as a brigade major in General Charles Lee's division during the retreat from New York and across New Jersey. During the retreat Washington offered him command of one of the additional Continental Regiments then being raised. Scammell declined that appointment to accept command of the 3rd New Hampshire Continentals. In the winter campaign that followed, Scammell led his regiment through the Battles of Trenton and Princeton.

The enlistments of the men in the 3rd New Hampshire, along with those of much of the rest of the army, ran out with the end of the year. Scammell, as did most other regimental officers, returned home to recruit new troops for the coming year. By the spring of 1777, Scammell and his regiment were at Fort Ticonderoga, part of General Enoch Poor's brigade under General Arthur St. Clair.

The 3rd New Hampshire, even though it was at half-strength, was one of the strongest regiments at Ticonderoga. Scammell felt that he had a good set of officers but that the men, many of whom were sick, were undisciplined. Still, he was optimistic and thought they would behave well in battle.

Although he had been busy during the winter recruiting new soldiers and during the spring in training them, Scammell did not spend all his time on military affairs. That June, writing to Abigail Bishop, his fiancée, he hoped that

> ... early next Fall or Winter to do myself the pleasure of waiting upon you at Mistic unless you should forbid it. The tender moments which we have spent together still, and ever will, remain fresh in my memory—You are ever present in my enraptured heart—& a mutual return of affection from you I find more and more necessary to my happiness— cherish the love my dearest Nabby, which you have so generously professed for me.

Scammell never married. Abigail evidently broke off the engagement. Writing to Nathaniel Peabody not quite two years later, Scammell feared "that the war will doom me to old bachelorism . . . though this consideration don't fully correspond with my feelings on the opening of Spring.

"At present, the young women dread us as the picture of poverty; and the speculators, to our great mortification, are running away with the best of them."

Between the times of these two letters, Scammell had led his regiment in the retreat from Ticonderoga, fought the British grenadiers and light infantry at the Battle of Freeman's Farm, and fought the grenadiers again at the Battle of Bemis Heights, where he was wounded. After the British surrendered at Saratoga he marched with his regiment to join the main army at Valley Forge.

On January 15, 1778, Washington appointed Scammell adjutant general of the Continental Army. While adjutant general, Scammell not only worked closely with Washington, but also with Baron Friedrich von Steuben, the inspector general of the army. Together, Scammell and von Steuben worked to regularize the Continental Army's administrative methods. Von Steuben developed policies, together they developed printed forms for regular regimental and brigade reports, and Scammell handled the routine administrative work of Washington's headquarters. The success of this partnership led to the merging of the adjutant general's and the inspector general's departments under von Steuben.

As adjutant general, Scammell was part of Washington's military family. In Washington's mess, Scammell was a frequent source of humorous anecdotes. As the wine circulated after the meal, Scammell often took command of the conversation and amused everyone at the table, including Washington. Despite his good humor, Scammell often found his duties very heavy. He was ordered to arrest General Charles Lee after the Battle of Monmouth and to supervise the execution of Major John André, the captured British spy. Scammell, at the gallows, was the last person to whom André spoke. When Scammell resigned as adjutant general, September 30, 1780, to return to his regiment, Washington parted with him very reluctantly. Scammell had proved himself as an able officer performing his duty to Washington's entire satisfaction.

Scammell, as was the practice in the Continental Army, retained his position as colonel of the 3rd New Hampshire while he was adjutant general. As a result, the regiment was commanded by the lieutenant colonel, Henry Dearborn, or when Dearborn was absent, by the major, James Norris. (One of the organizational problems that plagued the Continental Army was that the company and field grade officers were part of some regiment so that when an officer was assigned to the staff or to some other duty his regiment had to carry on with his position vacant.)

At the end of 1780 the number of regiments authorized for the Continental Army was reduced. New Hampshire's quota went from three requirements to two. Scammell's regiment was disbanded, and the men whose enlistments had not expired were reassigned to the remaining two New Hampshire regiments. The junior colonel, Joseph Cilley, of the 1st New Hampshire was retired, and Scammell succeeded Cilley as colonel of the 1st New Hampshire.

Early in 1781, Washington took the light infantry companies from each Continental regiment and formed them into provisional light infantry battalions. He gave Scammell command of the battalion that included the New Hampshire companies. When Washington was assembling the troops that he would lead to Yorktown he included the light infantry. Scammell's light infantry battalion, raised to full strength, included the two New Hampshire light infantry companies, there Massachusetts companies, and three Connecticut companies, with a total strength of 384 officers and men. It was part of Moses Hazen's Brigade in Lafayette's Light Infantry Division.

At Yorktown, Scammell was the "Officer of the Day" on September 30, 1781. On that day as part of his duty, he was reconnoitering the British lines around Yorktown with an escort of American light horsemen. They were attacked by a detachment from Tarleton's Legion, and Scammell was wounded and captured.

Henry Dearborn claimed that after the British captured Scammell, "one of the horsemen came up in his rear, put his pistol near his back & shot him. The ball enter'd between his hip-bone and his ribs & lodg'd in him." Scammell was released on parole the next day. He died October 6, 1781, at 37 years old. Dearborn re-corded that Scammell was "universally lamented by all who knew him. The loss of so great & good an officer must be very severely felt in the Army at large; but in the New Hampshire line in particular." Eight days later the light infantry, led by Colonel Alexander Hamilton, attacked a British redoubt next to the York River. They charged through the abatis and over the parapet with fixed bayonets and in ten minutes the position was taken. As the prisoners were being secured. an anonymous New Hampshire captain tried to avenge Scammell by killing the British commander, a Major Campbell. Only quick action by Hamilton saved Campbell.

Scammell had proven himself a conspicuously able and gallant soldier. He had served as a staff officer to Sullivan and to Washington. He had worked closely with von Steuben, training the army. As a commander, his soldiers found him an inspiring leader. And he always enjoyed Washington's confidence.

Walter A. Ryan

REFERENCES

Henry Steele Commager and Richard B. Morris, *The Spirit of 'Seventy-Six* (1975); James Thomas Flexner, *George Washington in the American Revolution (1775—1783)* (1968); Gail Kelley, "Alexander Scammell," *New Hampshire, Years of Revolution, 1774–1783,* ed. by Peter E. Randall (1976); Charles P. Whittemore, *A General of the Revolution: John Sullivan of New Hampshire* (1961); Robert K. Wright, Jr., *The Continental Army* (1989).

Schuyler, Philip (1733–1804)

Continental Army officer. Born into a prominent New York family with Dutch antecedents, Philip Schuyler was raised in the aristocratic environment of the Hudson Valley squirearchy. Tutored at home and in Albany schools, young Schuyler received a classical education at a Huguenot academy in New Rochelle. As a youth, he joined trading expeditions into the Indian country, where he learned the Mohawk language and befriended chiefs of the Six Nations. His marriage in 1755 to Catherine van Rensselaer linked him to influential landlords, and his visits to England in 1761 and 1762 sharpened his business acumen.

He served as a militia captain during the French and Indian War under several British army officers—Colonels William Johnson, John

Bradstreet, James Abercrombie, and General Sir Jeffrey Amherst. Although Schuyler witnessed combat at Forts Oswego and Ticonderoga, he specialized in quartermaster duties. Ranked as colonel by 1759, Schuyler participated in four campaigns, and he mastered the techniques of feeding, housing, and transporting troops in the wilderness. He also understood the Indians and the strategy of defending the northern frontier.

As a business entrepreneur, Schuyler inherited a vast agricultural and commercial empire, which he expanded by speculating in land, by colonizing fertile tracts, and by developing a rudimentary manufacturing center at his Saratoga estate. Schuyler was also active politically. After a brief apprenticeship in local government, Schuyler was elected to the Provincial Assembly of New York in 1768. He was a cautious but consistent critic of British imperialistic policies toward the colonies, but he refrained from proclaiming the radical rhetoric of resistance to constitutional authority. Schuyler was, at first, a reluctant rebel, hoping for reconciliation with the Crown. In January 1775 Schuyler led the Assembly's opposition to coercive British legislation, and soon after, he was elected to the First Continental Congress. There he impressed Washington, who was almost his Virginia counterpart, defended the supposedly unauthorized seizure of Ticonderoga by Ethan Allen and Benedict Arnold, and he helped to procure supplies for the Patriot army during the siege of Boston.

As major general in June 1775, Schuyler, as commander of the Northern Department (New York), prepared for an invasion of Canada. He supervised the mobilization of troops, the acquisition of provisions, and the manufacture of weapons. He directed the construction of roads, docks, wharves, boats, foundries, fortresses, hospitals, as well as sawmills, grist mills, and powder mills. Schuyler likewise negotiated with the Iroquois in order to blunt Tory efforts to foment Indian warfare. Because of Schuyler, the Six Nations remained neutral until 1777.

Schuyler planned to lead the expedition northward by capturing St. John's on Lake Champlain, by advancing along the Sorel River that flowed to the St. Lawrence River, and by capturing Montreal. Then, in conjunction with a smaller force under Benedict Arnold advancing through Maine, Schuyler expected to capture Quebec before winter. But involved in Indian affairs at

Albany, Schuyler ordered Brigadier General Richard Montgomery in August to attack St. John's. Schuyler followed in September and directed the siege. Debilitated by chronic sickness, however, Schuyler returned to Ticonderoga, to direct the provisioning of Montgomery's force. St. John's fell to the Americans in October, and Montreal in November. In late December, Montgomery and Arnold led a valiant but aborted assault on Quebec. During the winter of 1775–1776 Schuyler remained in New York funneling supplies to the pathetic American army that invested Quebec. In early May 1776, plagued with smallpox and overwhelmed by newly arrived troops from Britain, the northern army, now under General John Thomas, retreated to Sorel. Reinforced with regiments led by General John Sullivan in late May, the Americans attempted but failed to halt the British offensive at Trois Rivières. Sullivan's battered army retreated to Lake Champlain to await evacuation. Toiling to extricate the nearly trapped American command, Schuyler acquired enough boats and canoes to convoy the troops to Ticonderoga

During the summer of 1776 Schuyler, assisted by General Horatio Gates, his rival for command in the North, supervised the defense of Ticonderoga and the construction of a navy at Skenesborough. Although the enemy fleet defeated the ramshackle squadron at Valcour Island in October, Sir Guy Carleton, the British commander, hesitated to attack sturdy Ticonderoga and to campaign in the winter. Consequently, his army retired to Canada for the season. Schuyler's delaying tactics thus provided the Patriots with another precious year to retain northern New York.

Schuyler was frequently castigated in Congress, particularly by New England delegates, for alleged failures in the Canadian operations. Sensitive to criticism, the haughty Schuyler bitterly contested the charges. So acerbic was the dispute that in March 1777 Congress reprimanded Schuyler for his intemperate remarks, and he was relieved of his position. Yet in May, when the nation needed him in the North to ward off another enemy offensive from Canada, Schuyler was reinstated in command.

Schuyler remained at Albany during the early summer of 1777 as General John Burgoyne's redcoats sailed unopposed to Ticonderoga. In July, Schuyler ordered General Arthur St. Clair to evacuate the fortress in order to save the army.

Unprepared for the loss of the so-called Gibraltar of the North, Congress was infuriated with the surrender of the bastion and the threat to the Hudson River. Plunged again into controversy, Schuyler meanwhile removed his troops to safety, lured Burgoyne down the waterways, and devised such tactics—wrecking roads and bridges, toppling trees over trails, destroying foodstuffs—that Burgoyne found his march from Skenesborough to the Hudson a logistical nightmare. Schuyler cannot be credited with the American victory under General John Stark over the British at Bennington, New York, in August, but he ordered a defense on the Mohawk that led to Arnold's victory at Fort Stanwix. Yet Schuyler hesitated to confront the British in pitched battle, he procrastinated about a defense north of Albany, and he increased the demoralization of his troops. In August, Schuyler was replaced by Gates. Hence, while Gates was properly praised for triumphs over Burgoyne at Bemis Heights in September and at Freeman's Farm in October, it was Schuyler who had prepared the northern army for the great victories.

The acrimonious debates about Schuyler continued. Accused of negligence that led to the fall of Ticonderoga, Schuyler was tried by a congressional court of inquiry in the autumn of 1778, but he was exonerated. Yet Schuyler's reputation was marred, he was intensely disliked by the troops, he bickered constantly with ranking officers and with prominent politicians, and he symbolized a string of disasters. After additional disputes, Schuyler resigned his commission in 1779.

Schuyler kept his interest in Indian and military affairs. Elected to Congress in 1779, he advised Washington about General John Sullivan's expedition to the Iroquois country, and he assisted in the reorganization of army staff departments. Still an influential figure in the postwar era, Schuyler, one of New York's first senators, championed the ratification of the federal Constitution. Due to ill health, he retired from public life in 1798 and lived out his remaining years in Albany.

Schuyler's military career was quite controversial. Although experienced in wilderness warfare, he never held an independent command before the Revolution. His qualifications for a generalship in 1775 were questionable, but the political necessity of placating his supporters determined his appointment.

Schuyler demonstrated energy and foresight in organizing the northern army. On his first field command at St. John's, however, he selected difficult terrain to initiate the siege, he overestimated British strength, and he left the fighting to Montgomery. It was Montgomery, ably assisted by Arnold, and not Schuyler—who remained at Ticonderoga—who nearly conquered Canada. Schuyler acted vigorously in the spring of 1776 to save the northern army from disaster during its retreat, but he was invariably blamed for the fiasco. Schuyler's arrogance, his indecisiveness, his contentious nature, and his intolerance of spirited New England soldiery increased his unpopularity and diminished his prestige with the military. In 1777 he neglected to appraise adequately the strength and movements of Burgoyne's army, and consequently, he justly shared in the blame for Ticonderoga's loss. Castigated for repeated failures, for the dismal state of army morale on the Hudson, and for irregularities in the commissary, Schuyler epitomized two years of frustration for the northern army.

Yet in fairness to Schuyler, it should be noted that he suffered acutely from gout and pleurisy and that these ailments may have hampered his efficiency. He correctly visualized his role as a pacifier of the Indians, and as the coordinator of equipment and provisions for his army. Schuyler grasped the strategic significance of Lake Champlain, and he undertook the construction of a fleet. Unfortunately for him, Congress failed to determine the scope of his authority, neglected to consult him about appointments to his staff, and delayed in forwarding him men and material. His decision to rescue Sullivan's army was sound, his plan to forestall Carleton at Ticonderoga was correct, and his advice to evacuate Ticonderoga in 1777 was likewise sensible. Yet, the haughty patroon had a stormy military career, and he symbolized failure, for he never had the luck, or the qualities, that could inspire troops. The congressional decision to replace him with Gates at Saratoga was necessary to regenerate a dispirited northern army.

Schuyler, one of the few high-ranking officers of the Revolution who never participated in a single major battle, merits attention for his knowledge of Indian affairs, for his strategic vision, and for his mastery of logistics. He made a distinct contribution to the war effort, not as a colorful leader on the battlefield, but as the tireless administrator behind the lines who prepared the northern army for eventual victory.

Richard L. Blanco

REFERENCES

Harrison Bird, *March to Saratoga* (1963); Martin A. Bush, *Revolutionary Enigma. A Re-appraisal of General Philip Schuyler of New York* (1967); Don R. Gerlach, *Philip Schuyler and the American Revolution in New York, 1733-1777* (1964); ——— *Proud Patriot: Philip Schuyler and the War of Independence, 1775-1783* (1987); Benson J. Lossing, *The Life and Times of Philip Schuyler*, 2 vols. (1860); Jonathan Gregory Rossie, *The Politics of Command in the American Revolution* (1975); Bayard Tuckerman, *Life of General Philip Schuyler, 1733-1804* (1903).

Scott, Charles (1739–1813)

Continental Army officer. As a sixteen-year-old orphan, fleeing a court-imposed apprenticeship, Charles Scott joined Washington's Virginia Regiment as a private after General Braddock's defeat in 1755. Scott rose through the ranks, being appointed captain at the end of the war, when he volunteered for the Virginia Cherokee expedition in 1760. Scott settled on a small farm he had inherited, located on Muddy Creek at the present Powhatan-Cumberland County line. He married Frances Sweeney in 1762.

In spring 1775, Scott commanded the Cumberland County independent company, and he took his troops to the encampment outside Williamsburg. In the summer he was elected by other officers as the commander-in-chief of all the Virginia troops, being later replaced in this position by General Andrew Lewis. On August 17, 1775, the Virginia Convention elected Scott lieutenant colonel of the 2nd Regiment. He had an important role in the defeat of Governor Lord Dunmore at Great Bridge on December 9, 1775. On February 13, 1776, Congress, in accepting the 2nd Regiment into the Continental Army elected Scott a colonel; in May 1776 Congress transferred Scott to the 5th Virginia Regiment.

With General Adam Stephen's brigade, Scott and his regiment joined Washington's army in New Jersey in late November 1776. Scott quickly won recognition in the field. Participating in the Battle of Trenton, he afterward commanded forward troops in contending the enemy's advance on the Princeton road, which became known as the Second Battle of Trenton.

With Washington's army encamped at Morristown during winter and spring 1777, Scott led infantry in checking British foraging parties. The Battle of Drake's Farm, February 1, 1777, was a heated engagement with British and Hessian troops. During this "second New Jersey campaign," Scott received attention for ordering his troops to fire at the legs of the enemy; one version has it: "Take care now and fire low bring down your pieces fire at their legs, one man Wounded in the leg is better [than] a dead one for it takes two more to carry him off and there is three gone leg them dam 'em I say leg them."

Scott's Virginians fought well at Brandywine, where his troops helped stay the thrust of Cornwallis's flank attack. At Germantown his troops, impeded by the hedges and the fog, soon veered away from the intended order of attack, and in the confusion joined other Virginians in retreat. Scott's Revolutionary War career came under the most criticism for his role at the Battle of Monmouth, at which time he retreated from the middle of the battle too far behind the lines. Scott, nevertheless, was a convincing witness at the court-martial of General Charles Lee, who was suspended from the army and later dismissed. Scott headed Washington's military intelligence during summer and fall 1778, and he also had charge of light infantry units that frequently engaged enemy units coming from New York City. He then went home, only to be soon assigned to recruitment of Continental troops in Virginia for the southern army.

Scott won praise for organizing a military force ready to contest the British invasion of lower Tidewater Virginia in May 1779—the Collier-Mathew expedition. The British force, however, stayed only two weeks. To show its gratitude, the Virginia Assembly, nevertheless, gave Scott a fine horse as a token of their appreciation.

In late 1779 Scott was ordered to bring his Virginia Continental Army recruits to join General Benjamin Lincoln's army in the South. Taking his time, receiving censure from both Congress and Washington, he arrived at Charleston just before the British closed off all access to the city and essentially just in time to join in the capitulation and to be made a prisoner of war. Scott and the other officers were confined at Haddrell's Point across from the city. He assumed responsibility for the Virginia Line in captivity. In March 1781 he was paroled and went back to the Virginia farm, unable to join American forces, even as Cornwallis's army passed down the James across from his home. Scott's parole status ended when he was exchanged for Colonel Lord Francis Rawdon in July 1782.

Scott moved with his family to Kentucky in 1787. On the frontier the Scott family had a precarious existence at a little farm on the Kentucky River near Vincennes. Indians scalped his 19-year-old son Samuel, before Scott's own eyes. Scott lost another son, Merritt, to the Indians in the Harmar campaign disaster of 1790.

Scott bided his time in Kentucky, letting his sons and slaves run the farm; he dabbled in politics, styling himself a Jeffersonian Republican, and several times was named a presidential elector. Scott won renewed recognition as major general of Kentucky mounted volunteers, leading two uneventful Indian expeditions—one along the Scioto River and the other into what is now north central Indiana, routing the Indians at Quiatanon and other places. Scott commanded the Kentucky militia at the Battle of Fallen Timbers, August 20, 1794. He assisted in laying out a new fort at Covington, replacing the federal fort at Cincinnati (Fort Washington). He continued to serve as major general in the militia. After his wife died in 1804 Scott briefly led a forlorn existence, but then married Judith Cary Bell Gist, the wealthy widow of Colonel Nathaniel Gist (who had served with Scott during the Revolution and was the reputed father of the famous Cherokee chief, Sequoya). The newlyweds lived at the ample Gist estate, Canewood, in Clark County.

Scott, as one of the last surviving Revolutionary War generals and the highest-ranking officer of the war in Kentucky, became a focal point in the war fever leading up to the War of 1812. Toasts, especially at the Fourth of July celebrations, honored Scott and the "Spirit of '76." In 1808 he was a candidate for governor and won handsomely over two well-known opponents. The election was as much a conferral of gratitude upon the Revolutionary War generation as it was a personal victory. Scott, as governor, was ably assisted by his secretary of state, Jesse Bledsoe, who undoubtedly kept Scott on an even course. Scott's administration exhibited firmness and was quite effective in upholding the public interest.

As governor, Scott actually tried to defuse the war fever and insisted upon blame for both France and England. In his last state of the commonwealth message (December 3, 1811), he declared: "We should ever bear in mind, that we have nothing so much to fear as from ourselves." Some of Scott's aphorisms and anecdotes told about him have became legendary. He has achieved a status as a folk hero, much like the better-known Daniel Boone.

When the War of 1812 came, Scott was energetic in promoting recruitment and getting Kentucky troops into the field. By making William Henry Harrison a major general in the Kentucky militia, he contributed to the elevation of Harrison's military career. Scott, for several years infirm and on crutches, died October 22, 1813, probably only shortly after learning of the victory of Kentuckians at the Battle of the Thames, October 5, 1813. Scott's own military career was rather undistinguished, but he showed energy and ability when called upon for particular assignments. Barely educated himself, he was an officer with whom common soldiers could identify. His addiction to the bottle was only evident during his later years. Scott was a man of action and few words; when called upon by Washington for an opinion, his response was always the most brief in comparison to those of other generals and to the point.

Harry M. Ward

REFERENCES

Col. Orlando Brown, "The Governors of Kentucky," *Filson Club Publication #6* (1889):93–112; Jared C. Lobdell, "Two Forgotten Battles in the Revolutionary War," *New Jersey History*, 85 (1967);225–34; Harry M. Ward, *Charles Scott and the "Spirit of '76"* (1988); J.W. Wickcar, "General Charles Scott on His March to Quiatanon, *Indiana Magazine of History*, 21 (1925):90–99.

Secret Committees of the Continental Congress

A form of legislative body employed on both the state and national levels during the early years of the American Revolution, secret committees or committees of secrecy were a form of select committee developed in the British Parliament and adapted to American circumstances. In Britain a secret committee was a relatively small committee that conducted its meetings with greater secrecy than usual. It was used generally for investigative purposes (that is, for digesting information and presenting conclusions to Parliament for its consideration). The best-known example was the secret committee that investigated the East India Company.

However, in Revolutionary America, where executive power was viewed with suspicion, select committees often had an administrative role. Until the evolution of administrative boards and executive departments, select committees served as more efficient administrative units than legislative assemblies as a whole could be. They were the first step toward the creation of a separate executive authority. Secret committees had a special place within this system.

The term "secret committee" invariably denoted a select committee with at least partially administrative functions that dealt with matters that were to be kept secret from the public and, at least in matters of detail, from the legislature itself. Secret committees thus dealt primarily with military procurement, foreign affairs, and intelligence issues. In other respects, a long-term or permanent chairman, small size, relative secrecy in its operations until called on the report, and separate meetings usually held in the evenings, American secret committees coincided with British practice.

Secret committees existed in such states as South Carolina, North Carolina, and New York in 1775 and 1776, where they were similar in function to committees of safety or inspection committees in other states. In the Continental Congress the term was applied primarily to the Secret Committee of Trade or Commerce, which is the one most commonly referred to as "The Secret Committee," to the Committee of Secret Correspondence, and occasionally to certain early naval and marine committees. Later in the Revolution the term ceased to be used. The name of the Committee of Secret Correspondence was changed to the Foreign Affairs Committee in April 1777, while the Secret Committee of Trade was replaced by the Committee of Commerce in July 1777.

The Secret Committee of Trade was created on September 18, 1775, as an administrative expedient to meet military supply needs while Congress developed its commercial policies during the course of fierce debates on trade issues that raged from September 1775 when nonexportation took effect until March 1776

when the decision was made to throw open American ports to foreign nations. Its first chairman was Samuel Ward of Rhode Island; after his death in March 1776, Ward was succeeded by Robert Morris of Philadelphia, who soon became the dominant force in its affairs. Other prominent members serving at various times included Benjamin Franklin, Silas Deane, Richard Henry Lee, Philip Livingston, Francis Lewis, Joseph Hewes, John Langdon, William Whipple, and Josiah Bartlett.

At first the Secret Committee contracted with various merchants in the different states to ship commodities or bills of exchange abroad and invest the proceeds in needed supplies. Contracts generally went to members of Congress or their associates, or to prominent merchants within their home states. Such awards were partly favoritism, partly a method of maintaining secrecy and security by working through those whose loyalty could be relied on. Later, the committee appointed agents, assigning them various supply roles on a commission basis as the need arose. Robert Morris, the second chairman of the Secret Committee, also became its chief domestic agent; often, for security reasons and to hold down prices charged the government, he disguised committee ventures as private operations of his firm, Willing and Morris. Such procedures naturally aroused suspicion that he juggled public and private operations to his own advantage. While no charges were proven, accounts did become confused, and several investigations occurred.

Other prominent agents of the Secret Committee were William Bingham and Stephen Ceronio in the West Indies, and in Europe, William Lee, John Ross, and Thomas Morris, Robert's dissolute half-brother who died in disgrace in 1777. Within the United States the Continental agents who handled marine affairs also acted for the Secret Committee, notably John Langdon of New Hampshire, John Bradford of Massachusetts, Nathaniel Shaw, Jr., of Connecticut, Joseph Hewes of North Carolina, John Dorsius in South Carolina, and John Wereat in Georgia. Agents conducted both public and private business. Their private affairs benefited from the additional scale of operations, prestige, and connections their public role gave them; the public gained the advantage of relying on the private credit of their agents when public funds became scarce, as was increasingly the case as the war progressed.

Although contracts and assignments to agents were widely distributed, the middle states benefited the most in 1775 and early 1776, especially through shipments of flour and other provisions abroad. Tobacco shipments from Virginia and North Carolina were also significant. However, as the blockade intensified, and the British occupied New York and Philadelphia, states on the northern and southern fringes dominated Secret Committee affairs. Rice, indigo, and other commodities were shipped from North Carolina, South Carolina, and Georgia to the West Indies, and sold there or transferred to neutral ships for transport to Europe. After 1776 munitions were primarily landed in Massachusetts or New Hampshire or in the southern states until the capture of Savannah and Charleston. Some munitions purchased abroad remained stranded in the West Indies or in Europe because of the problems of shipping them safely. However, in general the Secret Committee and its agents had greater success in procuring and shipping supplies abroad than they had in shipping remittances to pay for them, and the government was deeply in debt to its agents and their suppliers by the time the Secret Committee was replaced by the Commercial Committee in 1777. Thereafter, the supplies obtained through foreign aid programs became the mainstay of the Revolutionary effort.

The Committee of Secret Correspondence was also an executive committee created in 1775 (on November 29). Among its prominent members were Benjamin Franklin, John Jay, Benjamin Harrison, Robert Morris, Richard Henry Lee, William Hooper, William Whipple, and later James Lovell. Its chief function was to compose diplomatic letters to American overseas agents and correspondents and propagandistic tracts directed to foreign governments, foreign peoples, and potential American sympathizers. The committee also arranged for the transportation of such dispatches. It was not involved in making general foreign policy decisions. Rather Congress usually appointed special committees to consider major foreign policy issues, and decisions were made by Congress as a whole after extended congressional debate. Although there was some overlap in membership, there was little interaction between the two secret committees until after Congress agreed on independence and

sought foreign aid and trade. Silas Deane, Benjamin Franklin, Arthur Lee, and other diplomatic agents were appointed to seek aid abroad. When they succeeded, the primary responsibility for supervising supplies obtained from France and Spain fell into their hands. From that point on there were two sources of military supplies, one diplomatic, and one commercial, and therefore both secret committees became involved in the procurement and shipment of munitions. For awhile a valiant effort was made to keep each program clearly separate, but that proved impossible, and the two committees for a time converged in functions, personnel, accounts, and correspondence. The convergence created a short-term efficiency in the critical early days of the War of Independence but in the long run caused confusion, conflict, and scandal. Rivalries and jurisdictional conflicts broke out between agents of the two committees. Furthermore, as the commercial methods of obtaining and paying for supplies broke down, the diplomatic ones predominated. The French-backed shipments of Caron de Beaumarchais are the most famous example of this process. The power and importance of the Secret Committee of Trade fell while that of the Committee of Secret Correspondence, and especially of the American diplomatic agents under its auspices, rose. Consequently, the Commercial Committee, which replaced the Secret Committee in July 1777, was only a pale shadow of the Secret Committee of Trade in its heyday.

Both congressional supply programs became involved in a series of controversies, the most famous of which was the Deane-Lee affair. Settlement of accounts was difficult and protracted, with many Secret Committee accounts remaining unsettled until the mid-1790s, and the accounts of Silas Deane, Caron de Beaumarchais, and a few others remaining in dispute until well into the 19th century.

Elizabeth M. Nuxoll

REFERENCES

Helen Augur, *The Secret War of Independence* (1955); Robert A. East, *Business Enterprise in the American Revolutionary War Era* (1938); E. James Ferguson, *The Power of the Purse: A History of American Public Finance, 1776–1790* (1961); Elizabeth Miles Nuxoll, *Congress and the Munitions Merchants: The Secret Committee of Trade during the American Revolution 1775–1777* (1985); Jennings B. Sanders, *Evolution of the Executive Departments of the Continental Congress 1774–1789* (1935); Clarence L. Ver Steeg,

Robert Morris, Revolutionary Financier, With an Analysis of His Earlier Career (1954); George C. Wood, *Congressional Control of Foreign Relations during the American Revolution, 1774–1789* (1919).

Seminole Indians

Not yet fully separate from the Creek Confederacy during the era of the American Revolution, the nucleus of the emerging Seminole "tribe" was the Alachua Savannah (north central Florida), the site of Cowkeeper's village. The Alachua Seminoles initially sought neutrality. They refused British East Florida governor Patrick Tonyn's request in April 1776 for their aid in fending off American raids. But, soon after, still accepting nominal leadership from Lower Creeks, they acted on Creek urgings to ally with Tonyn. In May 1776, the Seminoles and British soldiers joined and together repulsed a Georgia force under Colonel John Baker and Colonel Samuel Elbert, which assaulted on St. Augustine. Two months later the Seminoles again allied with the British in East Florida when Americans raided British settlements along the St. Mary's River.

Although Cowkeeper's aid for the British was sporadic, the alliance with the British continued, because the Seminoles hoped an English victory would mean that white settlers would be kept out of the north central Florida region. In the summer of 1778, the Seminoles again came to Tonyn's aid, allowing the British to resist another American force led by General Robert Howe in East Florida.

While American rebels were fighting for independence, the Seminoles began to accept less and less Creek leadership. As the Revolution was entering its seventh year, the gulf between the Creeks and Seminoles was becoming irreversible. By the fall of 1782, however, the Creeks could foresee an American victory and sought to maintain the aid of the Seminoles. The Creeks believed that a united front of their combined people against the Americans could hold American settlers at bay. The Treaty of Paris (1783) called for British cession of Florida to Spain, so the Seminoles believed future enemy intruders on their lands would be Spanish settlers.

The Seminoles refused to rejoin their Muskogean relatives. The period from the Revolution's end to the end of the Creek (Red Stick) War (1813–1814) saw a dramatic increase in the Seminole population, as thousands of Creeks and members of smaller, allied tribes grew disillusioned with the Confederacy's leaders.

Cynthia R. Kasee

REFERENCES

Jesse Burt and Robert Ferguson, *Indians of the Southeast: Then and Now* (1973); John W. Caughey, *McGillivray of the Creeks* (1938); David A. Corkran, *The Creek Frontier, 1540–1783* (1967); R.S. Cotterill, *The Southern Indians* (1954); Charles Hudson, *The Southeastern Indians* (1976); Edwin C. McReynolds, *The Seminoles* (1957); James O'Donnell, *Southern Indians in the Revolution* (1973).

Sevier, John (1745–1815)

Frontiersman. A legend on the frontier in his own time, John "Nolichucky Jack" Sevier was a brave, resourceful fighter. He was equally adept in the practice of the arts of war, politics, and social graces. His greatest moment in the War of the Revolution was his participation in the great American militia victory over Major Patrick Ferguson's men at King's Mountain in October 1780. However, this was but one small chapter in a long succession of notable achievements Sevier accomplished in his 70 years of life.

Sevier's grandfather fled from Paris, France, to London, England, at the close of the seventeenth century to escape religious persecution. There the family name was Anglicized from Xavier to Sevier and was pronounced in the same manner as Paul Revere's name (suh-veer'). Sevier's grandfather had two sons, one of whom, Valentine, came from London to North America about 1740 to seek opportunity and fame.

John Sevier was born on September 23, 1745, to Valentine Sevier and his wife, Joanna Goade Sevier, a native of the Shenandoah Valley, at Augusta, approximately six miles southwest of where New Market, Virginia, would be located. John was the eldest of seven children. When John was ten, the French and Indian War broke out, and the family moved to Fredericksburg, Virginia, for safety. There John attended school for two years. When the danger had passed, the family returned to their homestead to find their home and outbuildings destroyed. Later John attended school for a time in Staunton, Virginia.

John began his career at an early age. He farmed for a time and then founded the village of New Market. Sevier laid out the village and sold town lots to immigrants coming up the valley from Pennsylvania. For a time, Sevier ran a public house in New Market, gaining the skills and polish necessary to become a leader in his community. In 1761, at age 16, he married Sara Hawkins, a local girl. Their marriage produced ten children before Sarah's death in early 1780.

Sevier was a wanderer by nature. Already he had gained experience fighting the Indians. Sevier moved west across the mountains to explore lands in what would later become the states of Tennessee and Kentucky. Sevier became a valued ally of James Robertson. He visited the Watauga and Holston settlements in 1771 and 1772 before moving his family there permanently in 1773. Sevier's father and a brother settled in the same region along the Nolichucky River in what is today eastern Tennessee.

Elected a commissioner of the Watauga Association, Sevier became the foremost defender of the Watauga and Nolichucky settlements from Indian attacks during the time he lived there, from 1773 through 1790. On July 21, 1776, Fort Watauga was attacked by the Cherokees under "Old Abraham." During the opening stage of the siege, tradition states that a girl who had been caught outside the walls when the attack began made a dash for safety and mounted the palisaded walls to jump into the arms of Captain John Sevier. Four years later this same girl and John Sevier married.

Shortly after the War of the Revolution began, Sevier helped draw up a petition sent to the North Carolina assembly asking for formal recognition of this Over-the-Mountains territory. It was the pioneers' hope to be annexed as a part of North Carolina. The new district would be called Washington County. North Carolina agreed, and Sevier served as a member of the North Carolina Provincial Congress at Halifax in November 1776, representing his district. In addition he was a member of the local Committee of Safety for Washington County, and in the fall of 1776, the provincial congress appointed Sevier lieutenant colonel of the Washington County Militia.

For the next four years, Sevier was busy protecting the frontiers of western North Carolina from attacks by the British-sponsored Cherokee Indians. Sevier matched the Indians in brutality and cunning, rarely ever losing in battle. Sevier also led the people of the western county of his state in their resistance to the British. There was little defection of frontier people to the British

cause. With his natural leadership qualities and demonstrated bravery, Sevier became the epitome of a frontier leader.

However, it was in September 1780 that John Sevier came east and played his vital role in the Revolution. Since their seizure of Savannah, the campaign had gone well for the British in the South. Charleston fell with the capture of 5,000 American troops. Waxhaws and any number of skirmishes went to Lieutenant Colonel Banastre Tarleton and his British Legion. General Horatio Gates had lost a second American army to Lord Charles Cornwallis at Camden, August 16, 1780. Now Cornwallis intended to invade North Carolina to reestablish English control in another southern colony.

Cornwallis's left wing was under the command of Major Patrick Ferguson. Ferguson was rolling up resistance to the British and approached the eastern fringes of the mountains that separated the eastern counties of North Carolina from Washington County and the frontier. Ferguson sent a captured American across the mountains to inform the Backwater Men, these Over-the-Mountain people, that they should return to their King or Ferguson would bring fire and sword to their communities.

The Indian danger was bad enough without this British threat added to it. John Sevier teamed up with Isaac Shelby, another American frontier leader, to strike at Ferguson before the Cherokees could mount an attack on what would be undefended American homes on the frontier. The attack would have to be swift. Leading 240 of their men, mounted and carrying their own provisions, Sevier and Shelby left from Sycamore Shoals in late September and crossed the Smokies to chase after Ferguson's force. This Over-the-Mountain force was joined by other American militia units from Virginia, South and North Carolina, and Georgia. The entire group was nominally commanded by Colonel William Campbell of Virginia.

Learning of the American approach, Ferguson began withdrawing back toward Cornwallis's army seeking support. Ferguson finally took position on top of King's Mountain, South Carolina. Ferguson's force had been run down 35 miles short of Cornwallis.

The Americans by this time numbered about 1,300 men. They arrived at Cowpens and picked the best 900 mounted men to continue riding toward Ferguson. Spies had pinpointed Ferguson's location and the disposition of his troops. On a rainy, gray, dark Saturday afternoon, October 7, 1780, the American militia succeeded in surrounding and attacking Ferguson's force on King's Mountain.

Sevier led the approximately 120 men directly under his command up King's Mountain at the "heel" of the hill, which is configured at its summit like the sole of a shoe. Campbell's Virginians, Shelby's backwater men, and Sevier's men, including his two sons, Joseph and James, managed to overcome the British defense, and together came up on the heel to force the British back on their camp. It was over within an hour. The British force was destroyed. Ferguson was dead. Sevier's men immediately set off for home. In spite of this success, the frontier was still unguarded.

The victory at King's Mountain set Cornwallis back in his conquest of North Carolina and gave General Nathanael Greene and his American army the chance to seize the initiative in the war in the South. It was the solitary victory of the war for the Over-the-Mountain Boys, but it was enough. The victory became the first in a series of events that led to the eventual surrender of Cornwallis at Yorktown in October 1781.

Sevier led his men back to their homes and then assembled his men once more to go against the Cherokees. Sevier defeated the Cherokees on December 16, 1780, at the Battle of Boyd's Creek. Sevier continued to fight the Cherokees on the frontier for the remainder of the war.

On a happier note, on August 14, 1780, Sevier married Catherine "Bonny Kate" Sherrill, the girl he reportedly caught in his arms at the attack on Fort Watauga in 1776. "Bonnie Kate" had her work cut out for her, being a frontier woman and taking responsibility for Sevier's ten children from his first marriage. Sevier would have an additional eight children with Catherine Sherrill. By all accounts, the Indian fighter was a considerate and patient father to his family.

In the fall of 1781, Sevier recrossed the mountains with 200 men to help Francis Marion fight against the British presence in the Carolinas. Sevier had been promoted to full colonel on February 3, 1781.

After the war, Sevier was appointed brigadier general of the militia in November 1784, but he turned down his commission in order to be elected governor of the new state of Franklin, a

position he held from 1784 to 1788. Franklin did not last as a state as it declined, so did the fortunes of John Sevier.

It was during this period that Sevier became involved in a Spanish conspiracy. He was in contact with the Spaniards, who wished to make the territory of what is today Tennessee a part of the Spanish Empire. Georgia also claimed the land and called it Bourbon County. Sevier was closely tied up in land speculation his entire life. He was now selling lots at Muscle Shoals on the Tennessee River west of Washington County. He was communicating with officials from Georgia and Spain at the same time.

Because of his dealings with the Spanish and Georgians, North Carolina declared him to be an outlaw and ordered his arrest on the charge of rebellion against the state. Sevier was arrested but was freed from jail by a group of his friends. When things looked darkest for Sevier, he developed a strategy to reestablish himself with the government.

North Carolina had refused at first to ratify the new constitution. Sevier made himself a Federalist and campaigned for the Constitution. Sevier's actions worked. He was reinstated by North Carolina and served in the North Carolina Senate in 1789. He was appointed once more as brigadier general of the militia. He voted for the ratification of the Constitution. From 1789 to 1791, Sevier served as a congressman to the new Congress representing North Carolina's western district, but not before defeating John Watts and his Cherokees at Flint Creek on January 9, 1789. "Nolichucky Jack" had not lost any of his fighting ability.

When North Carolina ceded the territory that became Tennessee, Sevier was made brigadier general of the militia in 1791 in the new territory and became the first governor of Tennessee, serving three successive terms from 1796 to 1801. Then he withdrew from office as state law required and returned to the governorship for three more terms from 1803 to 1809.

At the same time, he had moved to the Knoxville area and had resumed the life of a plantation owner, who also owned an ironworks, operated a general store, owned slaves, and was surrounded by a wife and most of his 18 children. He speculated in land, as always, and became associated with the Presbyterian church in his community. Sevier was a pillar of society. A military hero, a dashing figure, well mannered, and a great companion, Sevier was cordial, effective as a public official, and a wealthy man. Tall, thin, fair complexioned and blue-eyed, Sevier was considered by many to be the most handsome man in Tennessee.

In 1796, Sevier began a feud with Andrew Jackson over power in Tennessee that lasted until Sevier's death. Sevier lost military control to Jackson in 1801 when Jackson was appointed to the military leadership of the state. Sevier's career was far from over though. He served in the state senate of Tennessee from 1809 to 1811 and went back to Congress until death ended his service. His interests rested in military matters, and his congressional service involved the years in which the War of 1812 was fought.

John Sevier died "on service" settling the boundary of the Creek Indian nation cession obtained by Jackson's military victories in 1814 in Alabama. Sevier died in camp on the east side of the Tallapoosa River near Fort Decatur, Alabama, on September 24, 1815. His remains were buried with full military honors in Knoxville, Tennessee, at a later date.

Sevier had fought the Indians for most of his life, yet had made so many treaties with them they called him "Treaty-Maker." Sevier had speculated in land most of his life, yet was never involved in any major land scandals. He never evidenced fear in any of his many battles. He was a military, political, and community leader. Sevier was also a fine family man. It was Nolichucky Jack's service at King's Mountain, however, that helped keep the South in the United States.

Paul J. Sanborn

REFERENCES

John Richard Alden, *The South in the Revolution* (1957); *DAB*; Lyman C. Draper, *King's Mountain* (1978); Carl S. Driver, *John Sevier, Pioneer of the Old Southwest* (1932); Benson J. Lossing, *The Pictorial Field Book of the American Revolution*, 2 vols. (1851–1852), rpr. 1972; Henry Lumkin, *From Savannah to Yorktown* (1981); Hank Messick, *King's Mountain* (1976); *Readers' Encyclopedia of the American West*, ed. by Howard R. Lamar (1977).

Shawnee Indians

An Algonquian tribe with a complex history of early migration, the Shawnees had reassembled in Ohio by the mid-eighteenth century. Shawnee resistance against white encroachments on their lands continued, however, and in 1768 Iroquois delegates at the Treaty of Fort Stanwix ceded to the British large amounts of lands claimed by the Shawnees. As tension grew and the Shawnees prepared to fight, the British Indian Department worked to isolate the tribe and prevent a general Indian war. In Dunmore's War (1774), Shawnee warriors under their chief Cornstalk, fought a day-long battle against the Virginians at Point Pleasant and then were obliged to accept the terms of the Treaty of Camp Charlotte, whereby they agreed with Governor Lord Dunmore to accept the Ohio River as the boundary between Indian and white lands. This was essentially the line established at the Treaty of Fort Stanwix, and the Shawnees led the fight to defend this boundary for the next 20 years.

At the beginning of the Revolution, some Shawnees simply continued their war against the Virginians, and Shawnee delegates carried a nine-foot war belt to the Cherokees, helping to ignite the Cherokee war of 1776. The Mingoes and other tribes already at war with the United States pressured young Shawnee warriors to join them, and the Shawnees' geographic location ensured that they would become caught up in the fighting. Many other Shawnee headmen tried to remain neutral, however, and even provided the Americans with news of developments in Indian country. The Revolution produced serious divisions within the tribe. Some Shawnees migrated rather than continue what seemed an endless war against white expansion. One group journeyed south and took up residence in Creek country, and a large part of the tribe migrated west of the Mississippi, taking up lands under Spanish auspices near Cape Girardeau in Missouri.

Those who remained in Ohio became increasingly embroiled in the frontier warfare of the Revolution. In 1777, Cornstalk and several other Shawnees were murdered by American militia at Fort Randolph, an act that shocked American leaders and Shawnees alike. Cornstalk's division, the Maquachakes, continued to work for peace and some moved to the Delaware capital of Coshocton to better preserve neutrality. But most other Shawnees joined the British. The British Indian agents Alexander McKee and Matthew Elliott both had Shawnee wives and exerted their influence to win the Shawnees over to the Crown. Shawnee commitment to the British was never unanimous and their participation in the fighting was never total. But for the rest of the war,

Shawnee warriors waged guerrilla warfare against American settlers in Kentucky (on one occasion capturing Daniel Boone) and inflicting serious damage on the Americans in numerous skirmishes and in major engagements like the Battle of Blue Licks in 1782.

The Revolution also brought devastation in Shawnee country, however. Thomas Jefferson identified the Shawnees as a principal enemy who must be exterminated or driven from their lands, and the Shawnees witnessed a steady stream of American armies march against their towns. In 1779 Colonel John Bowman led an expedition from Kentucky against the principal Shawnee town of Chillicothe. The Shawnees held off the invaders and harassed them on their retreat, but Bowman's men burned the town and crops and inflicted a mortal wound on the chief, Black Fish. The following year, the Shawnees burned Chillicothe themselves rather than let it fall to George Rogers Clark. Luring Clark's army on to ground of their own choosing, they fought a major engagement at the neighboring town of Piqua until Clark's artillery dispersed them. Clark's men destroyed their houses, burned extensive crops, and dug open Shawnee graves for scalps and plunder. Two years later Clark returned, burning crops and villages in retaliation for the American defeat at Blue Licks. With each invasion of their country, the Shawnees shifted their villages to the north and west, from the Scioto River to the Mad and Miami rivers and eventually to the Maumee River. They rebuilt their towns in new locations but frequently these new towns retained the original names. Shawnee warriors traveled far afield to join other tribes in their fight against the Americans, and warriors from other tribes took up residence and made common cause with the Shawnees.

The Shawnees felt betrayed by their British allies at the Peace of Paris (1783), and after the Revolution many accepted terms from the Americans, ceding most of their Ohio lands at the Treaty of Fort Finney in 1786. One of the leading advocates of accommodation was the Shawnee chief, Moluntha. That same year, Colonel Benjamin Logan led another expedition against the Shawnees in which Moluntha was taken prisoner and murdered. For the Shawnees, the war to preserve their lands and culture did not stop simply because the Revolution ended. The winning of independence unleashed a flood of American settlers into Shawnee country, and the Shawnees remained on the front line of the struggle to preserve the Ohio River boundary. In the postwar years, the Shawnees played a leading role in the fight for Ohio until the Treaty of Greenville in 1795, and in later years a new generation under Tecumseh continued the struggle in Indiana.

Colin G. Calloway

REFERENCES

Randolph C. Downes, *Council Fires on the Upper Ohio* (1940); James H. Howard, *Shawnee: The Ceremonialism of a Native Indian Tribe and Its Cultural Background* (1981); William Albert Galloway, *Old Chillicothe: Shawnee and Pioneer History* (1934); Reuben G. Thwaites and Louise P. Kellogg, eds., *Frontier Defense on the Upper Ohio, 1777–1778* (1912); ———, *The Revolution on the Upper Ohio, 1775–1777* (1908).

Shelburne, 2nd Earl of (William Petty Fitzmaurice) (1737–1805)

British statesman. Descended from an Anglo-Irish family, Shelburne originally sought a military career and distinguished himself in several actions during the Seven Years' War. He entered politics as a follower of Lord Bute early in George III's reign. Through his handling of the resignation of Charles James Fox, Shelburne acquired a reputation for political duplicity that would dog his entire career.

Shelburne's involvement with American affairs began with a brief stint as president of the Board of Trade in 1763, during which he laid the groundwork for the royal Proclamation of 1763 that sought to limit settlement east of the Appalachians. He resigned after differing with the Grenville administration's treatment of John Wilkes and gravitated toward William Pitt. He refused to join the first Rockingham administration in 1765 but did support its repeal of the Stamp Act the following year. He was, however, one of only five peers to oppose passage of the accompanying Declaratory Act in the House of Lords.

When Pitt became Earl of Chatham and formed a new administration in the summer of 1766, Shelburne took office as Secretary of State for the Southern Department, which at that time included the colonies. Shelburne faced the problem of raising a revenue from the colonies in the wake of the Stamp Act's failure. His inclination was to do so through the collection of quit rents.

His scheme, however, required much preparation, and during Chatham's virtual abdication of ministerial leadership, initiative in colonial revenue matters was wrested away by Charles Townshend, the Chancellor of the Exchequer, resulting in the provocative Townshend Duties of 1767. Increasingly isolated from the rest of the cabinet, Shelburne was forced out of office in 1768. By this time colonial affairs had been taken from his department and assigned to a new (third) secretary of state.

Shelburne spent the next 14 years in opposition. Generally considered the chief lieutenant of Chatham (though the two men were not close personally), the latter's frequent illnesses and absences from the political world meant that it was Shelburne who usually bore the burden of leading Chatham's followers in Parliament, and the fact that the Chathamites persisted as a coherent opposition group owes much to his leadership. Though few in number, the party included effective speakers—Shelburne and Camden in the Lords and Isaac Barré and John Dunning in the Commons. Shelburne retained strong interest in American affairs. He opposed the Coercive Acts of 1774 as well as subsequent measures of compulsion. In general, he espoused Chatham's argument that harmonious relations with the colonies had been disrupted by the attempt to impose taxes, an action that exceeded Parliament's proper legislative powers.

Once war broke out in 1775, Shelburne opposed the resort to force and attempted to coordinate activities with the Rockingham Whigs and other segments of the opposition. Such cooperation was handicapped by mutual distrust between Shelburne and the Rockinghams and by differences over a variety of policy matters, especially American independence. Unlike the Rockingham Whigs, Shelburne and Chatham refused to recognize American independence, hoping instead that some way could be found to end the war with the colonies still part of the Empire. After Chatham's death in May 1778, Shelburne became the acknowledged leader of the Chathamites. The pattern of alternating periods of cooperation with the Rockinghams and alienation from them continued. Shelburne remained one of the most forceful parliamentary critics of the war and also emerged as an advocate of fiscal and parliamentary reform.

By early 1782 the failures of the American war were changing the face of British politics.

Lord North, having lost his majority in the Commons, resigned and advised the King to send for the leaders of the opposition. George III was reluctant to do so, though if forced he much preferred Shelburne to Rockingham. Shelburne refused to come into office alone but did agree to act as go-between in negotiations between the King and the rest of the opposition. The result was the second Rockingham administration, which drew support from most of those formerly in opposition. Shelburne took the post of Home Secretary, one of the two newly reorganized secretaryships of state. Though his followers were a minority in the cabinet, Shelburne continued to enjoy the good will of the King. When Rockingham died at the beginning of July 1782, the King chose Shelburne to succeed him. Most of the Rockingham Whigs followed Charles James Fox, the Foreign Secretary, and resigned.

Shelburne's ministry lasted from July 1782 through February 1783. It was hampered by uncertain parliamentary support and dominated by the pressing need to bring the war to an end. Negotiating the preliminary peace settlement was to be its major legacy. Shelburne has already gained a say in the peace negotiations as Home Secretary, the latter office having inherited the responsibilities of the now-defunct colonial secretary. He now became the dominant British influence on the discussions underway in Paris. He had brought himself (and the King) to acknowledge the necessity of recognizing an independent United States, but he intended that this should be a concession made as part of the settlement, rather than an action made preliminary to it, as Fox had wished. Historians have interpreted Shelburne's conduct during the peace negotiations differently, some seeing his generosity toward the Americans as a visionary attempt at creating an Anglo-American free trade zone, while others have viewed it as the result of a poor bargaining position coupled with a desire to ensure that the new United States did not become a satellite of France.

In February 1783 the peace preliminaries met a lively reception in Parliament: an address approving them barely passed the Lords while a similar measure went down to defeat in the Commons before the coalition of Fox and North. (The defeat, however, did little to alter the content of the definitive treaty.) Shelburne resigned and never held ministerial office again. In 1784 George III created him Marquess of Lansdowne.

Shelburne was one of the most brilliant politicians of the age, and his circle of friends included such luminaries as Richard Price, Joseph Priestley, and Jeremy Bentham. He was always something of an outsider in politics, however, and his career was plagued by a remarkably persistent ability to inspire distrust. These factors did much to limit his ministerial career.

William C. Lowe

REFERENCES

Clarence A. Alvord, *Lord Shelburne and the Founding of British-American Goodwill* (1935); Peter Brown, *The Chathamites. A Study of the Relationship between Personalities and Ideas* (1967); Lord Edmond Fitzmaurice, *Life of William, Earl of Shelburne*, 2nd ed., 2 vols. (1912); Vincent T. Harlow, *The Founding of the Second British Empire*, 2 vols. (1952); Ronald Hoffman and Peter J. Albert, eds., *Peace and the Peacemakers: the Treaty of 1783* (1986); John Norris, *Shelburne and Reform* (1963); C.R. Ritcheson, "The Earl of Shelburne and Peace with America, 1782–1783: Vision and Reality," *International History Review*, 5 (1983): 322–45.

Shelby, Isaac (1750–1826)

North Carolina militia officer. Of Welsh descent, Isaac Shelby was born in Maryland on December 11, 1750. His father, Evan Shelby, was a major landholder, trader, settler, and local military leader who well-prepared four sons for the rigors and dangers of frontier life. From earliest memory Isaac was presented with the usual backcountry challenges and an endless succession of skirmishes and wars with the Indians. He learned the military craft from his father through hard practice, and more than any of his brothers, he imitated and surpassed his father's record of distinguished military service. Although brought up in a family that expected leadership in all areas of public and private endeavor, it was military service, most notably during the Revolutionary War years, that established Isaac Shelby as a politician, landowner, and community leader in his adopted state of Kentucky.

When Isaac was in his twenties his father removed the family to the Holston region of southwestern Virginia (now east Tennessee). Once again on the edge of the wilderness, the family prospered, establishing Shelby's Fort and a general store. Here Isaac met Daniel Boone, passing through on his way to Kentucky, and many other noteworthy frontier figures.

Indian hostilities in 1774 led to service under his father as a lieutenant in Lord Dunmore's War. It is related that when receiving his commission from Colonel William Preston the youthful Isaac thoughtlessly sat down in his presence, to which his father angrily commanded: "Get up, you young dog, and make your obeisance to the Colonel!"

Along with public lessons in etiquette, military service was filled with dangers and rewards. Like his father, Isaac Shelby was large framed, formidable in appearance, and a natural Indian fighter and military leader. When he was 23 he took part in his first major battle, the fiercely fought day-long Indian attack upon an assembly of militia at Point Pleasant, Virginia, October 10, 1774. After a senior officer had fallen, Evan Shelby moved into that command. Isaac then led his father's company and was one of several young officers entrusted with a flanking attack that broke the will of the Shawnee and won the battle. He was rewarded with appointment as second in command of the fort established on the site.

The action at Point Pleasant, generally considered the most hard-fought Indian battle of the era, not only ended Dunmore's War, but it opened Kentucky up to further exploration in 1775. When the militia disbanded in July, Isaac journeyed to Kentucky as a surveyor for the Transylvania Company. He was also busily engaged in staking land claims for both his father and himself. In 1776, during his absence, he was appointed captain of a militia company by Virginia governor Patrick Henry. During the first few years of the Revolutionary War Shelby was designated commissary officer for a series of outposts on the Virginia frontier threatened by the British and their Indian allies. He served until 1779, when he was elected to the Virginia legislature.

In 1779 Shelby, now a major, commanded the militia providing protection from the Indians for the boundary commission created to extend the North Carolina–Virginia line westward past the Shelby homestead. When the survey was completed, Shelby found that he was actually a citizen of North Carolina. He was immediately appointed a colonel of militia in that state.

Shelby was back in Kentucky when Charleston fell to the British in May 1780, taking with it the largest American force in the South. The British were advancing and were consolidating their control. As a result, militia colonel Charles McDowell was urgently calling for men and supplies. Shelby returned home and raised 200 mounted riflemen on 30-day enlistments, bringing McDowell's force up to 1,000 militia, although many of the men were poorly armed. Against them were 1,500 to 1,800 Loyalists under the command of a single British officer, Major Patrick Ferguson. While many American soldiers fought against British regulars or the Hessians, Isaac Shelby's war in the Carolinas was a civil war, with Loyalists on one side and Patriots on the other.

Shelby's first duty of the campaign was to take a Loyalist outpost on the headwaters of the Pacolet River in South Carolina called Thicketty Fort, which he accomplished July 31, 1780. Surrounded by Shelby's 600 men, the fort surrendered without a shot, yielding 94 prisoners and a good stand of arms. Ferguson was furious, and in early August, at an unanticipated engagement at Cedar Spring, he was keen to destroy the American force and to avenge his earlier loss. Although vastly outnumbered, the Americans were able to escape to a hill some four or five miles distant. From their position they taunted Ferguson, readily distinguishable by his fine uniform and sword. Shelby fought, like his men, in hunting clothes.

In common with most militia commanders, Shelby was plagued by the knowledge that his soldiers had agreed to serve for only a short period of time. As their enlistments were almost up, it was decided to mount a last offensive. Shelby and Lieutenant Colonel Elijah Clarke chose 200 men and rode all night in order to surprise a Loyalist force at Musgrove's Mill, South Carolina. Arriving on the morning of August 18, 1780, they found the enemy prepared to meet them and numbering around 500. Retreat was impossible, since their horses were exhausted. Quickly the Americans prepared a breastwork to blunt the Loyalist attack. It was a short, severe engagement. Shelby saw his flank give way under a bayonet charge but was able to rally his frontiersmen. When the fighting ended, the Americans were left on the field.

Any thought of pursuit was ended by news of the rout of the American army under General Horatio Gates at Camden on August 16. Now Ferguson was free to pursue them, and the small American force retreated rapidly back into North Carolina. There McDowell's militia army melted away. Shelby took his men over the mountains, to the "western waters," to await further call.

Overconfident, Ferguson sent a personal message to Shelby and his men to lay down their arms or he would personally come over the mountains, hang their leaders, and subject the countryside to fire and sword. The insulting tone of this challenge guaranteed that it would fail to have the desired effect. Incensed, Shelby immediately rode to his friend John Sevier and together they began to raise a striking force. By October 4, 1780, five North Carolina counties and one Virginia county had raised 1,500 men, and they expected to be joined by 1,000 more from Georgia and South Carolina. For Isaac Shelby the pursuit and destruction of Ferguson was now a personal affair.

Ferguson fell back upon their advance, and the Americans chose from among their best men, horses, and weapons to give pursuit. The weather turned against them and only Shelby's determination kept them in the saddle through a driving rain. As they approached King's Mountain, just over the border in South Carolina, the Americans learned that Ferguson was camped on the plateau, protected on all sides by steep hillsides, with a force of 150 Provincial Rangers and 800 to 900 Loyalist militia. The American force numbered about 1,000.

Before dawn on October 7, 1780, the Americans completely surrounded the Loyalists and advanced up the slope taking advantage of natural cover. Ferguson had neglected to fortify his perimeter, a fatal mistake. Attacking from all sides at once, the Americans fought stubbornly. If driven back they retreated only as far as pushed, then advanced again to the summit, where the Loyalists were consumed by enfilading fire. Ferguson was killed and the surviving loyalists surrendered to a man.

To Isaac Shelby has gone much of the credit for the King's Mountain victory. Although Virginian William Campbell was in command, Shelby was the motivating force behind the raising of the Patriot force, the pursuit, and by some accounts, the plan of attack. He was conspicuous in his bravery and effective in command. King's Mountain was a personal victory, and a decisive blow to the hopes of the British. The crushing defeat ended ebbing Patriot support in the Carolinas and halted the British advance. In his Kentucky years Shelby was known as "Old King's Mountain" in honor of his achievement.

Isaac Shelby and his men participated in only one other campaign. Called out before but arriving in the theater of war after the surrender of Cornwallis at Yorktown, Shelby and his men were placed at the disposal of Francis Marion, the "Swamp Fox," who used them to good effect through Shelby's ability to intimidate the commander of a strong British fort near Monck's Corner, South Carolina, into surrender. The war was over in the South, and Shelby went home.

Shelby wound up his affairs in North Carolina, including service in the legislature, and crossed the mountains into Kentucky, where he quickly established himself. In 1783 he married Susannah Hart at Fort Boonesborough and made his home at "Traveller's Rest." Shelby was active in the statehood movement and was elected Kentucky's first governor in 1792. The term was devoted to defending Kentucky against the Indians and putting the government of the state in order. He was not disappointed to return to his farm in 1796, and there he remained, although involved in a variety of civic duties, until elected governor a second time (1812–1816). He effectively governed his adopted state during the emergency conditions of the War of 1812 and in 1813 personally led 4,000 Kentuckians in the American invasion of Canada, which culminated in the defeat of the British and Indians in the Battle of the Thames. After the war he returned to Traveller's Rest. In 1817 he was offered the post of Secretary of War by President Monroe, but declined. He remained active in local and even military affairs until his death on July 18, 1826.

John Gillig

REFERENCES

Lyman C. Draper, *King's Mountain and Its Heroes* (1881), rpr. 1971; G.W. Griffin, "Memoir of Governor Shelby," in *Memoir of Col. Chas. S. Todd* (1873); J.G. deRoulhac Hamilton, ed., "King's Mountain: Letters of Colonel Isaac Shelby," *Journal of Southern History*, 4 (1938):367–383; Archibald Henderson, "Isaac Shelby: Revolutionary Patriot and Border Hero," *North Carolina Booklet*, 16 (1917) and 17; Sylvia Wrobel and George Grider, *Isaac Shelby: Kentucky's First Governor and Hero of Three Wars* (1974).

Shell's Bush, New York, Raid on (August 6, 1781)

During the American Revolution, Tory-Indian raiders, particularly under Joseph Brant and John and Walter Butler, who were directed from British-held Fort Niagara, struck at settlements in Tryon County that spread across southern New York. This border warfare for several years consisted of major engagements like Cherry Valley and minor skirmishes, as, for example, the heroic stand of the outnumbered Shell (probably spelled Schell) family.

When Donald McDonald and more than 60 Indians and Tories attacked Shell's Bush on August 6, 1781, most inhabitants fled to Fort Dayton, several miles away. However, John Christian Shell and his family, who were working in the fields, decided to stay and fight. After two young sons were captured, Shell, his wife, and four other sons were able to reach their two-story blockhouse. Firing through its gun holes this small garrison kept the raiders (who even attempted to burn the building) at bay for several hours. When McDonald tried to force the door with a crowbar, he was shot in the leg and captured. Shell's wife loaded weapons and at one point stopped an assault when she used an ax to bend the barrels of the muskets thrust through the gun holes. By tricking the raiders into believing that reinforcements had arrived, the Shell family was able to withdraw and to reach the safety of Fort Dayton.

The attackers left eleven dead and six wounded on the scene, with nine more dying before they reached Canada. McDonald did not survive the amputation of his leg, and on a subsequent date, Indians killed John Shell and one son and wounded another son while they were working in the fields. The ordeal of the Shell family had come to an end.

Harold J. Weiss, Jr.

REFERENCES

William Brewster, *The Pennsylvania and New York Frontier: History of from 1720 to the Close of the Revolution* (1954); William L. Stone, *Life of Joseph Brant—Thayendanegea: Including the Border Wars of the American Revolution . . .*, 2 vols. (1878), 2, rpr. 1969.

Sherman, Roger (1722–1793)

American statesman. Perhaps Connecticut's greatest Revolutionary figure, Sherman was the only person to sign all of the principal documents of the Revolutionary and early national period, including the "Declarations and Resolves" of the First Continental Congress, the Articles of Association of 1774, the Declaration of Independence, the Articles of Confederation, and the U.S. Constitution. In addition he was one of those voting to ratify the 1783 Treaty of Paris. All told, Sherman served in national Congresses for about six months in each of the 16 years from 1774 to 1793, a record unequaled by anyone. If it is true that there was a bit of luck in the fact that Sherman was able to participate in such extraordinary events, it is also true that Sherman was an extraordinary man.

The third of the seven children of William Sherman, a farmer and cobbler, and his second wife, Mehetabel (Wellington), Sherman was born in Newton, Massachusetts, and probably attended common school in that part of Stoughton, now Canton, to which his family moved a few years after his birth. His first trade was that of his father, shoemaking. Although he received no formal education beyond the primary level, Sherman early in life developed a habit of reading voraciously and widely in subjects ranging from politics to theology. He became particularly proficient in mathematics. At the age of 20 he joined the Congregational Church in Stoughton. Sherman remained a devout and active Congregationalist throughout his life. In 1743, two years after his father's death, Sherman followed an older brother to New Milford, Connecticut. According to one tradition he walked the distance of 150 miles from Stoughton to New Milford, carrying his cobbler's tools on his back. There Sherman, having borrowed money with his and his siblings' patrimony as collateral, purchased a house and farm, the first of several successful real estate transactions.

Once settled in Connecticut, Sherman turned to other ventures. Continuing to read and study on his own time, Sherman gave up shoemaking by 1745, when he was named surveyor for New Haven, later Litchfield, County. He also took an active role in church and town affairs, becoming a New Milford selectman in 1753. In 1750, shortly after his first marriage, Sherman opened a general store in partnership with his brother William; Sherman became sole proprietor in 1756. In 1750 Sherman also published the first of a series of successful almanacs, which included some of his own astronomical calculations. Two years later he published a pamphlet titled *A Caveat Against Injustice*, an argument condemning the practice of permitting the unsound money of other colonies to circulate in Connecticut.

Sherman's latest biographer, Christopher Collier, points to his ability to accomplish what now seems impossible, to combine honesty with political success. Sherman did so despite the fact that his lack of education and social prominence placed him outside Connecticut's political establishment. In 1755 Sherman moved up from town politician to Connecticut officeholder, serving as New Milford's deputy to the Connecticut General Assembly (1755–1761) and justice of the peace.

Less than a year after the death of his wife Elizabeth in 1760, Sherman moved with his four children to New Haven, a larger and more dynamic community. Here, too, Sherman plunged into the social and political mainstream. In New Haven he opened a store, practiced law, continued to speculate in real estate, remarried, shifted his religious (and political) affiliation from Old to New Light Congregationalist, became treasurer of Yale College, and served again as deputy to the General Assembly, now as a delegate from New Haven (1764–1766). In 1766 he became a member of the governor's council. Sherman also was named justice of the peace in 1765 and the following year became judge of the colony's superior court, a post he held until 1789.

Sherman's long political apprenticeship in Connecticut served him well, when in 1774, he became one of the colony's delegates to the Continental Congress. He served in Congress from 1774 to 1781 and again from 1783 to 1784. As early as 1765 Sherman maintained that Parliament had no "authority to make laws for America." At the same time he was, like others in central Connecticut, a political moderate opposed to radicals like the Sons of Liberty, whose excesses he believed weakened governmental authority.

Sherman's friends and opponents alike all commented on his awkwardness, his humorlessness, his rustic manners, and what a Georgia congressman called his "strange New England cant." But most commented as well on his honesty, reasonableness, and tenaciousness. Historian Clinton Rossiter has called him "the complete Yankee," one who represented all the virtues and limitations of the Yankee way of life. John Adams called him "one of the most sensible men in the world . . . one of the soundest and strongest pillars of the Revolution."

One of the longest-serving members of the Continental Congress, he was also considered one of the hardest-working members. According to one observer, "Sherman rose at 5 A.M., worked in committee from 7 to 10 A.M., then in sessions of the Congress from 10 A.M. to 4 P.M., and then in committee session again until 10 P.M." By the end of the Revolution he was considered one of the most powerful figures in Congress. With some exaggeration, Thomas Sedgwick, a Massachusetts delegate, wrote that Sherman's influence was such that "no measure or part of a measure which he advocated, ever failed to pass."

As a member of the First Continental Congress, Sherman signed both its "Declarations and Resolves" and the 1774 Association, which established a boycott of British goods. During the two Congresses, Sherman served on committees concerned with military supplies, Indian affairs, army contracts, and army enlistments. He was also one of the five-member committee that drafted the Declaration of Independence, which he himself signed. In 1778 and 1779 he was instrumental in formulating the compromise whereby several states, including Connecticut, Virginia, and New York, would eventually cede their western land claims to the federal government. This compromise ended the claims by Connecticut's Susquehannah Land Company (in which Sherman was not a stockholder) to lands in Pennsylvania but provided that Connecticut would retain ownership of three million acres of land in Ohio called the Western Reserve.

In addition to working hard at the national level, Sherman was involved on the state and local levels during the Revolutionary period. He was a member of Connecticut's Council of Safety (1777–1779 and 1782) and was one of the two lawyers who wrote Connecticut's first law code after statehood. In 1784 he became New Haven's first mayor.

As one of Connecticut's delegates to the Constitutional Convention of 1787, Sherman is best remembered for introducing and spearheading the adoption of the Great Compromise, known also as the Connecticut Compromise and even

as the Sherman Compromise. This compromise provided that the representation in the lower house of Congress should be based on population; in the Senate each state should have an equal vote. Sherman's compromise, which he had first proposed several years earlier, was a rejection of the Virginia Plan, favored by the larger states but opposed by the smaller ones, in which both houses would have proportional representation. During the debate over representation, which lasted several weeks, Sherman argued that the smaller states would never support Virginia's plan. He maintained that "Each state had its particular habits, usages and manners, which constituted its happiness."

Thanks perhaps to his long experience on committees, Sherman was adept at forging and agreeing to compromises. He himself was no democrat and regarded the Constitution as a compact made by the states. Thus, representatives of the state governments, rather than the people at large, should choose the President. He assumed that the electoral college facilitated this method. In this same context, Sherman moved successfully that when no majority was obtained in the electoral college and the vote was thrown into the House of Representatives, each state should have only one vote, rather than having a number equal to its representatives. Sherman also engineered the constitutional compromise that forbade export duties. He also urged that the President not be given an absolute veto, lest he "overrule the decided and cool opinions of the legislature."

Satisfied that the Constitution finally produced was the best possible document under the circumstances, Sherman actively lobbied in Connecticut for ratification. Subsequently Sherman became one of Connecticut's five representatives to the First U.S. Congress. There he showed his fiscal conservatism by backing Hamilton's economic policies. He also supported a federal tariff in order to pay off the federal debt as quickly as possible. Sherman's last contribution to the constitutional debate was his argument that, if amendments must be made to the Constitution, they should be appended rather than integrated into the original document. In 1791 Sherman moved from the U.S. House to the Senate when he was appointed to serve out the unexpired term of Connecticut's William Samuel Johnson, who had resigned. Sherman died only a month after attending a Senate session in 1793.

At his death the ambitious Sherman had not become wealthy. His long years of service for state and nation gave him little chance to pursue private interests, and his large family (15 children, some of whom died young, by 2 wives) kept him financially strapped. Sherman's success was wholly in the political realm. The Reverend Jonathan Edwards, Jr., preaching at his funeral, summarized the style of this Puritanical Yankee:

> His abilities were remarkable, not brilliant, but solid, penetrating, and capable of deep and long investigation. . . . He had a happy talent of judging what was feasible and what was not feasible, or what men would bear, and what they would not bear in government. And he had a rare talent of prudence, or of timing and adapting his measures to the attainment of his end.

Jean F. Hankins

REFERENCES

Roger S. Boardman, *Roger Sherman, Signer and Statesman* (1938); Lewis H. Boutell, *The Life of Roger Sherman* (1896); Christopher Collier, *Roger Sherman: Puritan Politician* (1976); ———, *Roger Sherman's Connecticut: Yankee Politics and the American Revolution* (1971); John G. Rommel, *Connecticut's Yankee Patriot: Roger Sherman* (1980); Clinton Rossiter, *1787: The Grand Convention* (1966).

Shippen, William, Jr., (1738–1808)

Continental Army physician. With medical training in Edinburgh and London, the imaginative Shippen of Philadelphia was one of North America's outstanding physicians. As Director of Hospitals for the Flying Camp in July 1776 he demonstrated administrative ability in caring for sick and wounded soldiers during the campaigns in lower New York and in New Jersey. After Dr. John Morgan, his arch rival and Director General of the Medical Department was dismissed by Congress (January 9, 1777), Shippen assumed the post on April 11, 1777. He was highly effective in establishing hospitals in Pennsylvania for casualties after the Battles of Brandywine and Germantown.

However, because of high mortality rates of troops stricken by typhus and dysentery and the shortages of drugs, surgical instruments, and medical supplies, Shippen was castigated for incompetence. Due mainly to the complaints of Dr. Benjamin Rush, a congressional committee investigated Shippen's administration in January 1778. Trimmed of authority over regional hospital staffs, the arrogant Shippen antagonized doctors, generals, and politicians. By mid-1779, Morgan charged Shippen with misconduct and malpractice, and Washington ordered Shippen to stand trial (January 15, 1780) at Morristown. On August 10, 1780, Congress acquitted the Director General of the charges, censuring him only for peculation.

The disgraced Shippen resigned his post (January 3, 1781) and returned to private practice, where he resumed his vitriolic feud with Morgan. What may have been a brilliant career was wrecked by circumstances beyond his control—the lack of nurses, surgeons, equipment, and especially the ravages of disease in Washington's army.

Richard L. Blanco

REFERENCES

Richard L. Blanco, *Physician of the American Revolution. Jonathan Potts* (1979); Larry L. Burkhardt, *The Good Fight: Medicine in Colonial Pennsylvania* (1989); Betsy Corner, *William Shippen Jr., Pioneer in American Medical Education* (1951); Thomas Herbert, "The Great Pioneer of American Obstetrics," *Annals of Obstetrics and Gynecology,* 57 (1939):512–517; John Morgan, *Vindication of His Public Character in the Station of Director-General of the Military Hospital* (1777); William P. Williams, *America's First Hospital: The Pennsylvania Hospital, 1745–1841* (1976).

Shuldham, Molyneux (c. 1717–1798)

British navy officer. Having entered the Royal Navy in 1732 as a captain's servant, Shuldham passed his lieutenant's examination seven years later, and by 1746 he had attained the rank of captain. During the Seven Years' War he commanded several ships of the line and spent two years as a prisoner of war. From 1772 to 1775 Shuldham served as commander-in-chief on the Newfoundland station, with the title of commodore. He was promoted to rear admiral in March 1775.

A few months later the British government learned that the commander of its North American Squadron, Vice Admiral Samuel Graves, was under siege in Boston harbor. The Admiralty decided to send Graves substantial reinforcements. The expanded fleet in North America would be too large a command for one admiral, so Shuldham was appointed Graves's second in command.

Getting the reinforcing armada ready consumed several months, during which the government was inundated by complaints that Graves was mishandling the naval war effort. In September the administration decided that Graves must be removed from the command and that Shuldham must relieve him.

Shuldham, flying his flag in the HMS *Chatham*, arrived at Boston on December 30, 1775. By that time the curtain was lowering on the first act of the Revolution. He presided over the evacuation of Boston the following March, convoying General William Howe's army and a throng of Loyalist vessels to Halifax.

In the meantime the statesmen in London were laying plans for the great offensive of 1776. It was determined that the campaign should be directed jointly by Howe and his brother, Vice Admiral Richard Howe, one of the navy's most distinguished officers. Shuldham was offered the option of serving as Howe's second in command or coming home. He chose the latter.

While Admiral Howe was crossing the Atlantic, Shuldham, having been informed of the plans for the new campaign, convoyed General Howe's troops from Halifax to New York harbor. Admiral Howe arrived there on July 12, 1776, and assumed the command of the North American Squadron. Shuldham remained on the station for the rest of the year; he found his situation disagreeable, but while the campaign was in progress no warship could be spared to take him home. He finally left New York early in 1777.

During his six-month tenure Shuldham had made no noticeable mistakes, and the Admiralty went out of its way to emphasize that fact. The Earl of Sandwich had him promoted to vice admiral and arranged that he receive an Irish peerage, with the title Baron Shuldham. He was awarded those honors before the Admiralty received his first dispatch from North America. Shuldham, ironically, thereby became the only British admiral of the war to receive a peerage, or any other substantive commendation, for his service in North America. In 1778 he was appointed port admiral at Plymouth; he held that post for the remainder of the war.

John A. Tilley

REFERENCES

William Bell Clark and William James Morgan, eds., *Naval Documents of the American Revolution*, 9 vols. to date, (1964–); *DAB*; Robert W. Neeser, ed., *The Despatches of Molyneux Shuldham* (1913); William M. James, *The British Navy in Adversity: A Study of the War of American Independence* (1926); John A. Tilley, *The British Navy and the American Revolution* (1987).

Simcoe, John Graves (1752–1806)

British army officer. A respected British expert in partisan warfare, John Graves Simcoe was the eldest of two sons of Captain John Simcoe and Katherine Stamford. He was born at Cotterstock, Northamptonshire, on February 25, 1752. Simcoe's father was the captain of the HMS *Pembroke*. He was killed serving at Quebec in 1759. (Simcoe's younger brother died in childhood from drowning.) Receiving his education at Exeter, Eton, and Merton College, Oxford, John Simcoe entered the army in 1771 as an ensign of the 35th Regiment of Foot.

Sent to New England with his regiment, Simcoe arrived in Boston the same day as the Battle of Breed's Hill (June 1775), serving as regimental adjutant. Simcoe's offer to raise a special battalion of Blacks for service at Boston was not accepted by British authorities. Before leaving Boston in March 1776, Simcoe procured a commission as captain in the 40th Regiment.

John Simcoe was severely wounded leading the Grenadier Company of 40th Foot at the Battle of Brandywine in September 1777. On October 15, 1777, General William Howe nominated Simcoe to major commandant of the provincial corps known as the Queen's Rangers. His genius at leading men, mastering the tactics and techniques of partisan warfare, maintaining discipline without overwhelming initiative, and applying lessons learned from military history now came to the fore.

The Queen's Rangers were originally formed by Major Robert Rogers during the French and Indian War. The second incarnation of the Queen's Rangers (to become the 1st American Regiment in May 1779) was again raised by the same Robert Rogers in Connecticut and New York in the late summer of 1776. Organized as a provincial light infantry unit, it had three commanders and had its first major action at Brandywine before Simcoe assumed command.

With its ranks originally filled by American Loyalists, the Rangers fielded 11 companies in 1777, including a light infantry, Grenadier, and Highlander companies. Thirty mounted Hussars completed the roster. The unit grew from 300 rank and file to 600 by 1780, but the numbers always fluctuated. Simcoe permitted unrestricted recruiting, which increased the proportion of Continental Army deserters, Englishmen, Scots, Irish, and Germans in the unit.

The Rangers had uniforms of green coats without facings and concealed (nonwhite belts) accouterments. Under Simcoe's direction the Rangers soon became one of the most proficient units in the British army. Personally brave and tactically astute, Simcoe instituted a strict system of discipline for the Rangers. Simcoe did not permit plundering or marauding. Marching everywhere at quick-time, the Rangers were trained to fire with precision at specific targets. After lengthy and repeated drills, they became masters at the bayonet. When appropriate, the Rangers learned how to disperse and then rapidly rally together at some predetermined site. Thanks to Simcoe's continuing attention, the Rangers never gave a false alarm while on duty nor had a sentinel surprised during the entire war after 1777.

The Rangers formed the vanguard of the British approach to Whitemarsh in December 1777. In March 1778, at Quintin's and Hancock's bridges in New Jersey, Simcoe led the Rangers in the mauling of two American militia units. Shortly afterward, on May 1, 1778, the Rangers cooperated with the light infantry in savaging a small group of Pennsylvania militia at Crooked Billet, northeast of Philadelphia. The Rangers led General James Grant's column in an attempt to trap General Lafayette at Barren Hill on May 10. However, Simcoe could not persuade Grant to increase the speed of march, and Lafayette escaped with his men. In the withdrawal of the British army from Philadelphia across the Jersies to New York, Simcoe and the Rangers once again distinguished themselves by protecting the British rear and disrupting American threats to General Henry Clinton's exposed line of march.

Once the main British army returned to New York City, Simcoe's men were engaged in a number of skirmishes, small unit operations, foraging and defensive posturing in and around Staten Island, Long Island, North Jersey, and Westchester County, New York. Recognizing the value of Simcoe's military talents, Clinton promoted Simcoe to lieutenant colonel (local rank) of the Rangers in June 1778.

The Rangers were present but not engaged in the massacre at Tappan in September 1778. Simcoe and the Rangers formed the vanguard in Clinton's capture of Stony Point and Verplanck's Point on the Hudson River in June 1, 1779. In October 1779, Simcoe and several of his Hussars were ambushed while returning from a raid to Somerset Court House in New Jersey. Simcoe's horse was shot five times and Simcoe himself was knocked senseless as he fell from the dying horse. Captured along with four of his men, Simcoe was paroled to Bordentown, New Jersey. He was exchanged on December 31, 1779, and returned to his command.

In March 1780, Simcoe and the Queen's Rangers were sent to the Carolinas to participate in General Clinton's southern expedition, which led to the capture of Charleston, South Carolina. Simcoe was present through the siege and at the surrender of General Benjamin Lincoln's American army. Then, on May 31, 1780, Simcoe returned to New York with his men. Arriving June 21, Simcoe was just in time to join General Wilhelm von Knyphausen and the British forces raiding New Jersey at Connecticut Farms and Springfield. He performed brilliantly during the raids, repeatedly outmaneuvering his American opponents.

Clinton entrusted Simcoe with the responsibility of taking the necessary steps to coordinate with Major John André in Benedict Arnold's betrayal at West Point. Frustrated and angry, Simcoe could do nothing, as Andre was captured by the Americans, tried, and hanged as a spy.

On December 21, 1780, Simcoe took his Rangers to Virginia as part of Arnold's raid, which sought to rally the Loyalists, seize supplies, and cut general Nathanael Greene off from his Virginia base. Simcoe directed his unit through a series of successful encounters with the Americans at Richmond (January 5, 1781), Charles County Court House (January 8), Petersburg (April 25), Point of Fork on the James (June 5), and Spencer's Ordinary (June 26). During this time, overall command of the raiding force passed from Arnold to General Phillips (died May 13) to Lord Cornwallis.

When Cornwallis's army made its final stand at Yorktown, Simcoe positioned his Rangers on the left of the British lines across the York River at Gloucester Point. When Cornwallis surrendered, the Rangers numbered approximately 320 officers and men. By the end of the campaign, Simcoe and most of his men were in ill health, worn out by the months of rigorous marching, fighting, and the strain of surrender. Simcoe and most of the Rangers were permitted to board the *Bonetta*, a sloop of war, and pass through Franco-American lines to New York City without hindrance. The Rangers never took the field again during the War of Revolution and were disbanded officially in New Brunswick, Canada, on October 13, 1783.

John Graves Simcoe's style of leadership was that of a military scholar who successfully applied what he learned. He was regularly seen reading the works of renowned military experts such as Tacitus and Xenophon in camp. He seemed familiar with the military history of all countries in Europe. His character was thought to be mild and obliging in nature. Simcoe possessed an enlightened mind, which usually concentrated on military projects. He was an excellent conversationalist. Most importantly, Simcoe never stopped his intellectual growth.

Simcoe placed his stamp on the Queen's Rangers. Through the years of campaigning, the Rangers typically displayed self-restraint in victory, were always combat ready, used light infantry tactics with good effect, and compiled an illustrious record in the face of the enemy. General Clinton wrote to Lord Germain that the "History of the corps under Simcoe's command was a series of gallant, skillful and successful enterprises against the enemy without a single reverse. The Rangers have killed or taken twice their own numbers."

John Simcoe returned to England in December 1781. Clinton promoted him to colonel in the army at the same time. Simcoe was presented to King George III on January 2, 1782, at a levee at St. James Palace and then withdrew to live the life of a country gentleman on his estates. Simcoe married Elizabeth Posthume on December 30, 1782. The couple had two sons and seven daughters. In 1790, Simcoe was elected to Parliament representing St. Maw's, Cornwall.

In 1791, Simcoe was appointed lieutenant governor of Upper Canada under the governor, Lord Dorchester (General Guy Carleton). Simcoe arrived at Newark (now Niagara), Canada, on July 8, 1792, to assume his duties. He oversaw the management and settlement of a new country. Simcoe's interests lay mainly in the military defense of Canada and its agricultural development. Many Loyalists, formerly of the United States, came to join Simcoe. A new corps of Queen's Rangers was established, with Simcoe as colonel, to help protect and develop Upper Canada. In 1793, Simcoe transferred the capital city from Newark to Toronto, a city he practically founded.

While there are conflicting evaluations on the quality of Simcoe's term as lieutenant governor, he appears to have been an able administrator. He maintained a jaundiced view of the United States. Evidently he left a favorable impression on the Canadians since a lake, town, and county in Ontario are named after him.

Simcoe was promoted to major general on October 3, 1794, and appointed commandant of Santo Domingo with the local rank of lieutenant general. In July 1797, Simcoe returned to England and was promoted to lieutenant general in the army on October 3, 1798. When the French threatened to invade England in 1801, Simcoe was appointed commander at Plymouth. In 1806 Simcoe was taken ill on a voyage to the Tagus River to meet with the Admiral Earl St. Vincent to protect Portugal from France. Simcoe returned home at once and died in Devonshire on October 26, 1806.

Before his death, Simcoe had been appointed commander-in-chief of British forces in India, but he was never able to assume command. John Graves Simcoe died at 54 years of age, a knowledgeable professional who had earned military and personal respect by the valor of his achievements.

Paul J. Sanborn

REFERENCES

Sir Henry Clinton, *The American Rebellion* (1954); *DAB*; Captain Johann Ewald, *Diary of the American War* (1979); John Graves Simcoe, *A History of the Operations of a Partisan Corps Called the Queen's Rangers* (1844), rpr. 1968.

Simsbury Mines, Connecticut

This site where Loyalist prisoners were confined has been termed "the Black Hole of Connecticut." The abandoned copper mines at Simsbury (ten miles northwest of Hartford) were used as a prison from 1773 until 1782 and again from 1786 to 1827. During the Revolution, the Connecticut Assembly built defenses at the mines and sent the most "atrocious villains" of the Loyalists there. A blockhouse was constructed over the entrance to the mines, and prisoners were conducted down through a labyrinth of trapdoors and ladders to hot and poorly ventilated tunnels. Across the road from the blockhouse stood a tavern, which prepared food for the inmates and which served as a residence for the warden, Captain John Viets. Conditions in this subterranean "woeful mansion" were intolerable, and on several occasions prisoners tried to escape by setting the blockhouse on fire. One of these blazes got out of hand in 1782 and left the mines unfit for use as a prison. However, they were restored and used again by the state of Connecticut until closed down by popular outrage in 1827.

Tom Martin

REFERENCE

Catherine S. Crary, *The Price of Loyalty: Tory Writings from the Revolutionary Era* (1973).

Sinclair, Patrick (1736–1820)

British army officer. Born in Lybster, Scotland, Patrick Sinclair enlisted in the British army about 1754 and fought in the Caribbean and New York in the 42nd Regiment. In 1761 he exchanged his commission for one in the 15th Foot and joined the British marine forces on the recently captured Great Lakes. In 1764 he went to the upper lakes and was the first British captain to sail on Lake Huron.

In 1769, he returned to Great Britain to recruit, and in April 1775 he was appointed lieutenant governor of Michilimackinac (Mackinaw City, Michigan). He took ship immediately, but two attempts to reach his post via the thirteen colonies failed because of the Revolutionary turmoil. Eventually in 1778 he arrived in Halifax, Nova Scotia, but not until October 1779 did he finally reach Michilimackinac. There at the most important British post in the upper lakes he replaced Arent Schuyler DePeyster. Almost immediately he decided to move the fort and community from its defenseless location on the mainland to the cliffs of nearby Mackinac Island. There he erected a limestone fort.

In 1780, since the Spanish had recently joined the conflict, Sinclair organized an expedition to capture the Spanish garrison at St. Louis, Missouri. The force of 1,000 traders and Indians advanced to the city walls, but it was repulsed.

Despite the disaster, Sinclair was able to keep the Indians in the British interest through lavish outlays of presents. Unfortunately, many of his bills were protested by his superiors, and upon his return to England in 1785 he was thrown into Newgate Prison for debt. Eventually freed he retired on half-pay to his home town of Lybster. Until the end of his life in 1820 he drew his salary as lieutenant governor of Michilimackinac. *See also:* St. Louis, Louisiana, Assault on

David A. Armour

REFERENCES

David Arthur Armour and Keith R. Widder, *At the Crossroads: Michilimackinac during the American Revolution* (1978): *DCB*; Brian L. Dunnigan, *King's Men at Mackinac: The British Garrison, 1780–1796* (1973); Hamish B. Eaton, "Lieutenant-General Patrick Sinclair, An Account of his Military Career, *Journal of the Society for Army Historical Research*, 56 (1978):128–142, 215–232, 57 (1979):45–55; ———, *Patrick Sinclair, Builder of Mackinac and Founder of Lybster: An Account of His Life and Times* (1979).

Skene, Philip (1725–1780)

British army officer. Born in England, Skene entered the British army in 1739. He was promoted to lieutenant in 1750 and to captain in 1757. Skene was wounded while fighting at Ticonderoga during the French and Indian War. In 1758 as a major he commanded at Crown Point. Attracted by the economic potential of the Lake Champlain area, Skene retired from the army on December 4, 1759. Seeking his fortune in landholdings, he and 24 associates petitioned the government on November 12, 1763, for a grant of 25,000 acres at Wood Creek Bay. By March 13, 1765, he received the patent and his grant was incorporated into a township called Skenesborough (now Whitehall, New York). Later he obtained a grant of an additional 9,000 acres adjoining the north side of the original patent. Skene established what became an important commercial center in the wilderness featured by the construction of a sawmill, docks, stores, houses, a forge, and a shipyard. Skenesborough was strategically important because it formed a link with Fort Ticonderoga, thereby providing the British with control of Lake Champlain. By 1775, Skene, a Loyalist, had been appointed lieutenant governor of Ticonderoga and Crown Point and surveyor of the nearby forests.

During the planning by Americans to capture Fort Ticonderoga, Ethan Allen ordered Captain Samuel Herrick of Connecticut and 30 men to capture Skenesborough. Herrick seized the village on May 9, 1775. At that time, Skene was in Philadelphia, where he was imprisoned by Patriots and then paroled. Soon after he exceeded the boundaries of his parole; he was recaptured and remanded to jail. Exchanged in September 1776, Skene went to New York City, where he served under General Sir William Howe. In 1777 Skene went to Canada, where he served as an advisor to General John Burgoyne in the British invasion of upper New York. Captured at Saratoga, Skene was penalized for his loyalism by the confiscation of his estate under the New York Act of Attainder (October 22, 1779). Unable to recover his property, Skene returned to England at the war's end, where he lived in retirement at Adersey Lodge, near Stoke Goldington, Buckinghamshire.

Skenesborough is significant in American naval history. Using the ships and dockyard facilities there, Benedict Arnold built a fleet of small vessels that fought the British at Valcour Island in October 1776. Therefore, Skenesborough, or Whitehall, has been termed the birthplace of the American navy.

Horace S. Mazet

REFERENCES

Appleton's Cyclopedia of American Biography, 6 vols. (1886–89), *3*; Carl Van Doren, *Secret History of the American Revolution* (1941); John Luzader, *Decision on the Hudson* (1970); Doris P. Morton, *Philip Skene of Skenesborough* (1959); Joseph W.P. Parker, *The Battle of Bennington* (1970); John Pell, "Philip Skene of Skene of Skenesborough," *New York State Historical Association Quarterly*, 9 (1928):27–44.

Skinner, Cortlandt (1728–1799)

Loyalist. A first cousin of Oliver De Lancey and related to many of the leading families of New York and New Jersey, Skinner was speaker of the New Jersey Assembly when the war began, and shortly after became the colony's last attorney general. In March 1776 a Patriot committee arrested him and confined him to prison because of his Tory sympathies. His wife and 13 children were permitted to stay in Perth Amboy. In September he was exchanged, along with

Montfort Browne, for the Patriot General William Alexander (Lord Stirling), and he was commissioned by British authorities to raise a Loyalist regiment (the West Jersey Volunteers). Holding the rank of brigadier general, he was active throughout the war. The Skinner family was in New York City at the time of the peace. Mrs. Skinner and the children embarked for England, but she was forced by bad weather to land in Halifax. Skinner joined them there when the last royal troops were evacuated from New York. The Loyalist Claims Commission granted him some money, and he received the half-pay of a brigadier general for the rest of his life. Two of his daughters married British generals, and his son achieved the rank of lieutenant general in 1825. Skinner died at Bristol; his wife died in 1810 in Ireland.

Tom Martin

REFERENCES

Catherine S. Crary, *The Price of Loyalty: Tory Writings from the Revolutionary Era* (1973); Lorenzo Sabine, *Biographical Sketches of Loyalists of the American Revolution*, 2 vols. (1864), *II*.

Slavery and the American Revolution

On the night in June 1776 when Thomas Jefferson sat at his desk in Philadelphia, dipped his quill into his ink bottle, and wrote that "all men are created equal" and are "endowed" with the "inalienable rights" of "life, liberty, and the pursuit of happiness," he was not alone. Somewhere nearby, in the same or an adjacent room, Jefferson's slave and body servant, Richard, awaited his master's next command. Fourteen months earlier, when the "embattled farmers" of Lexington stood their ground against British redcoats "and fired the shot heard round the world," their ranks included Prince Estabrook, a local slave. The silent (and largely forgotten) presence of slaves both at the moment when the Revolution began, and when its highest ideals were first articulated, offers a symbolic reminder of the very ordinariness of slaves in the world in which the Revolution took place, and an example, in miniature, of the complex interrelationship between the institution of slavery and the ideals and progress of the Revolution itself.

In 1776, Black Americans comprised approximately 20 percent of the country's population, a proportion larger than they would have in any subsequent census. All but a small percentage of these half-million Black Americans were slaves. Slaves were a common sight throughout all of the American colonies. Their numbers in the local population ranged from less than 5 percent in New England and Pennsylvania, to 10 percent in New York and New Jersey, to a third of the population in the Chesapeake, North Carolina, and Georgia. In South Carolina, alone among the North American colonies, slaves formed a majority of the inhabitants.

A half-million people, whatever their condition, could not have passed through the massive disruptions of the Revolution without effect. Likewise, the actions (and very existence) of so many slaves had an important influence on the ideas and actions of the American Revolutionaries and their British and Loyalist opponents. The nature and degree of this interrelationship differed from region to region according to the number of slaves and the importance of slavery in the local society as well as the changing tides of the war. By 1783, however, slavery had helped shape the course of the Revolution throughout America, and in turn, the events and ideals of the Revolution had transformed the institution of slavery in the new United States.

The roots of slavery in America lay in the very origins of colonial settlement. The first slaves were brought to Virginia in 1619, a year before the Pilgrims established Plymouth. From the start, the relatively easy access to land in the colonial environment rendered any large-scale or long-term reliance upon free wage labor impractical. Those in pursuit of workers were therefore driven toward the utilization of various forms of bound labor. In the seventeenth century, although some thousands of slaves were imported, the need for bound laborers was largely met through the employment of white indentured servants from the British Isles. In the decades after 1700, however, Black slaves replaced white servants as the predominant form of unfree labor in the colonies. By mid-century, when North American involvement in the trans-Atlantic slave trade was at its peak, as many as 10,000 slaves a year were being brought to the colonies from Africa. In all, almost 400,000 slaves were imported into North America before the outbreak of the Revolution.

The legitimacy or morality of slavery was seldom questioned in the Colonial period. The right to keep, to buy, and to sell slaves was defended by law and custom in every colony. Colonial justifications of slavery were based at bottom upon appeals to the past and to tradition. First, Africans were often depicted as un-English, un-Christian, "strangers," who were therefore excluded from participating as equals in the body politic. As more and more slaves adopted Christianity, the idea that all slaves were necessarily "heathen" was abandoned, but the notion that slaves were excluded from inheriting "the rights of Englishmen" remained. Second, John Locke had argued in his 1690 *Second Treatise of Government* that the condition of slavery was justifiable if it resulted from capture in a "just war." Indian war captives were commonly sold into slavery in the Caribbean under this pretext, and the same theory could be extended to Africans who were supposedly captured in "just wars" in Africa. Finally, in an age in which hierarchy and inequality were taken for granted, and the dutiful submission of children to fathers, wives to husbands, servants to masters, and all before the King was seen as the basis of all forms of authority, most Americans accepted without much thought the subordination of slaves as an ordinary part of the existing social order.

Nonetheless, although white Americans in the Colonial period lived amidst and condoned slavery, they exalted liberty and considered themselves a part of the most free society in the world. Although this paradox seems striking to the modern mind, the contradiction was not so readily apparent to the minds of the mid-eighteenth century. Colonial Americans drew their concept of liberty largely from English political culture. The Americans' favorite source of political philosophy were the writings of English "Whig" or "Country" party advocates. According to Whig ideology, the origins of "English liberty" lay in the "Ancient Constitution" of England, which, since Anglo-Saxon times, had been carefully maintained and preserved. Whigs saw this inherited liberty (which, according to Americans, the first settlers had brought to America) as a birthright of every Englishman. Each new generation was charged with keeping the lamp of "English Liberty" lit and with defending it against the forces of tyranny and corruption, which constantly threatened to extinguish it.

Whig ideology, therefore, portrayed liberty as belonging almost uniquely to the English people, and also as a vulnerable and passive "goddess" perpetually at risk even among those who already possessed it. Eighteenth-century Whigs could not conceive of an aggressive and conquering liberty that might expand to include the freedom of slaves. Instead, they accepted slavery as the unfortunate but natural fate of those who failed to defend their own freedom. Consequently, the sight of slaves might actually have furthered the white colonists' zeal for their own liberty, providing as it did a vivid example of what might befall them if they did not steadfastly protect their inherited rights.

Along with Whig ideology, colonial Americans also were very familiar with the political theories of John Locke and used them to condone and even to support the existence of slavery in a land of "liberty." Locke argued that liberty was not inherited via an ancient constitution but was rather the product of historical developments, the most important of which was the creation of private property. For Locke, private property not only predated government, but its preservation was the sole purpose of civil authority. Colonial Americans, following Locke, firmly believed that the possession and sanctity of private property was the fundamental precondition of personal as well as civil liberty. Propertyless men, whether servants, tenants, or sons awaiting their inheritances, necessarily lived under the authority of another, whether master, landlord, or father, and were therefore less than free. As only men who governed themselves were regarded as fit to have a part in the governing of others, propertyless men were commonly denied the right to vote or sit on juries. The conflation of liberty and property in Lockean thought meant that slaves, as private property, could actually be thought to convey personal independence and therefore civil liberty to their owners. Likewise, a man who freed his slaves at the cost of his propertied independence, in effect, enslaved himself. By the same logic, any encroachments by outside forces upon private property (including slaves) threatened individual liberty and had to be resisted.

The tenets of Lockean political thought and Whig ideology were in many ways complementary. Both ideas shared a conservative vision of a fragile liberty that was liable to be menaced by governmental intrusions upon individual rights. The prevalence of such views in the half-century prior to 1776 explains why the vast majority

of colonial Americans saw no contradiction between the liberty they enjoyed and the presence of Black slaves. The little anti-slavery sentiment that existed in the Colonial period was based on moral rather than political considerations. Such views were confined to the relatively few Americans who belonged to religious groups (such as Quakers, Methodists, or "New Light" Baptists) that were outside of the dominant social order. In large part, their criticism of slavery was part of their critique of society in general. Consequently, as the Methodists and Baptists became "mainstream" churches in the later eighteenth century, they gradually abandoned their advocacy of antislavery

When Americans first protested against parliamentary taxation in the years between 1765 and 1775, they operated within these existing modes of political thought. Americans claimed to be defending their traditional English liberty and property right against parliamentary encroachment. African slavery was not an issue. The Sons of Liberty, who led American protest in this decade, claimed, as their name suggests, to be protecting their own inherited liberty and not promoting the liberty of all. The presence in America of a half-million slaves was not thought relevant in what was essentially seen as a "family quarrel" among Englishmen.

The political crisis following the outbreak of the war in 1775 caused many Americans to question or reject these traditional assumptions. Independence, for some, severed all ties with England and freed Americans from the need to rely upon the past. To defend and explain independence, and to describe the social foundations of their new governments, many Americans began to think in new ways. One product of this intellectual emancipation was a new definition of liberty that demanded freedom for all men, including slaves.

Such ideas made slavery a vital political as well as a moral question for the first time in American history. During the decade after 1776, interest in antislavery reached unprecedented levels and achieved remarkable successes. Yet, advocates of antislavery did not have the field completely to themselves. Old and ingrained ideas of thinking could not be swept away with the stroke of John Hancock's pen on the Declaration of Independence. The traditional idea of a passive and exclusive liberty that was inherited, based on property, and threatened by government, continued to exist alongside the new revolutionary vision of a liberty that was natural, expansive, and inclusive. The varying fortunes of antislavery sentiment and activity in America in the ensuing decade were both indicators and products of the clash of these two conflicting definitions of liberty.

Black Americans were not merely the helpless and passive subjects of this struggle. They themselves played an important role in transforming the meaning of liberty in a way that would allow them to also claim a share of it. The actions of slaves in the Revolutionary War caused all Americans to consider anew the relationship of slaves and slavery to the idea of liberty and to the ideals of the Revolution.

From Prince Estabrook at Lexington in April 1775 to the final demobilization of the army in 1784, Black Americans actively participated in the American cause. In doing so, they sought not only to defend American liberty but also to obtain their own personal independence. In most cases, slaves who agreed to serve in the American army were manumitted upon enlistment or were promised their freedom after the war. Estabrook, for example, after being wounded at Lexington, joined Washington's army, served in almost every campaign, and was eventually freed.

By the war's end, an estimated 5,000 Black Americans had served in the Continental Army. Moreover, because Black soldiers were usually enlisted for the duration of the war, they were disproportionately represented among the veterans of long service. In the summer before Yorktown a visitor to Washington's army noted that "a quarter of them were negroes, merry, confident, and sturdy."

Most Black soldiers fought in the ranks of predominantly white regiments recruited from the area in which they lived. One battalion, the 1st Rhode Island Regiment, which served with distinction in the Continental Army for five years, was entirely comprised of Black volunteers, both free and slave. Although south of Pennsylvania the policy was never officially condoned, in every state at least some slaves were accepted into the army as substitutes for their drafted masters. Although most Black soldiers were destined to serve out the war as privates, they otherwise shared equally in the scant fare and hard life of the common Continental.

Ironically, Black soldiers were most common in the brigades of the New England states where Blacks were proportionately fewest in number. In that region, Black Americans were most assimilated into the surrounding culture. By 1775, the vast majority of New England Blacks were native born. In many ways, they were Black Yankees whose own identity was closely tied with their native region. Prince Estabrook probably thought it only natural that he should stand with his neighbors against the invading English army. By supporting the American cause in the war, such Black Patriots not only stood by their local community against a common foe, but also sought to gain their freedom in a way that would enable them to return to the place they called home to enjoy it.

From the perspective of many other slaves, the relationship of their personal liberty to the causes and parties in conflict necessitated a different decision. Many slaves, particularly in the South, retained a close cultural affinity to Africa or were imbedded in large-scale slave communities where a distinct Afro-American culture had developed separate from the surrounding white population. Members of such communities were less likely to see the interests and concerns of the surrounding society as their own. In fact, for these groups, opposition to their masters and to the dominant culture was a part of their cultural identity and distinctiveness.

Such slaves, following the logic that "the enemy of my enemy is my friend," saw the invading British army as a possible ally in their ongoing struggle against their masters. The belief that the Union Jack was the banner of liberty was apparently widespread among the slave population. "Upon the approach of any detachment of the King's troops," a British officer in South Carolina wrote, "all negroes, men, women, and children . . . thought themselves absolved from all respect to their American masters, and entirely released from servitude. Influenced by this idea, they quitted the plantations and followed the [royal] army."

However, slaves who came to the British lines in hopes of gaining their freedom were acting under a false presumption. British policy toward the slaves was never so clear-cut. While the British were often tempted and occasionally willing to employ slaves in their effort to conquer rebellious slaveholders, they were not interested in ending slavery or in securing permanent liberty for their slave allies.

From the start, the British treated slaves and

slavery from motives of convenience rather than conviction. The most famous episode of British-slave collusion occurred on November 7, 1775, when Lord Dunmore, royal governor of Virginia, offered freedom to all slaves of rebel masters who would bear arms for the King. Within a week, over 500 Virginia slaves, risking death if captured, had made their way to Dunmore's camp at Norfolk. In a gesture intended to inspire slaves, frighten rebels, and ridicule the hypocrisy of slaveholder Patriots, the governor outfitted his Black recruits with a uniform that included a knit cap bearing the motto: "Liberty to Slaves."

However, Dunmore's campaign ended with his defeat at the Battle of Great Bridge on December 9, 1775, and the governor abandoned most of his Black recruits when he afterward left Virginia. Many of Dunmore's Black recruits may even have been sold back into slavery in the Caribbean. All in all, the episode was not a promising one for those slaves who wanted Britain and the British army to assume the role of liberator to the slaves. Like their American opponents, the British military balked at the principle of recruiting slaves as soldiers but widely condoned it in practice. Often, as in Dunmore's case, slaves were given arms only when sufficient regular or white Loyalist forces were not at hand. Some slaves were accepted as soldiers in "irregular" Loyalist guerrilla bands or went into battle alongside their masters in Loyalist militias. Even before the Revolution, many British regiments had employed Black recruits as drummers and musicians. This custom continued throughout the war and spread to include the regimental bands of the German, or "Hessian," units that fought alongside the redcoats. As the war dragged on, the British reluctance to employ slaves in arms gradually diminished. By the 1780s many of the battalions of British and German "regulars" that had come to America at the start of the war were reduced to a fraction of their original strength and willingly put escaped slaves into uniform in order to bolster their numbers.

In the last years of the war the British became more willing to embody separate units comprised entirely of escaped slaves. For example, when the small British garrison of Savannah was besieged by a much larger Franco-American army in 1779, a body of 200 "armed Negroes" was raised from the thousands of local slaves who had fled to the British lines and played an im-

portant role in the city's successful defense. After the British evacuation of Georgia in 1782, some of these Black troops, calling themselves "the King of England's soldiers," continued to wage a guerrilla war on their ex-masters from a camp in the Savannah river swamps.

Likewise, during the British occupation of Charleston in 1781–1782, cavalry units consisting entirely of fugitive slaves and commanded by Black officers patrolled the countryside outside of the city. The activities of these "Black Dragoons" terrified white Carolinians both rebel and Tory. On several occasions, the "Black Dragoons" clashed with Patriot (and white) horsemen. From his camp outside of Charleston, the American general Nathanael Greene estimated that the British army in South Carolina contained over 700 Black soldiers. Some of these ex-slaves turned soldiers secured their freedom by remaining in uniform. Before the final evacuation of Charleston at the end of 1782, the governor of Jamaica recruited a battalion from among these Black redcoats to form a "Black Carolina Corps," which was then posted to the permanent defense of that island and later became the Royal West Indies Regiment.

Although the thought of British-armed slaves frightened slaveholder Patriots, the vast majority of Black Americans who escaped to the British were armed not with muskets but with spades, axes, and other tools of common labor. They were put to work cutting wood, building forts, or washing the clothes of the white soldiers. For most of the British and Loyalists, the question was not so much whether slaves should be made to work, only for whom. The response of British commanders to the hundreds of fugitive slaves who flocked to their camps was left to their individual discretion. Most of them recognized the utility of employing slave labor and receiving the information slaves provided of rebel numbers and movements and therefore willingly sheltered the refugees, but most were not concerned with the long-term prospects of the Black Loyalists. Often, when the British forces retreated or withdrew from a given area, they left any fugitive slaves to the mercy of their enraged and vengeful masters.

The closest that the British came to establishing an official policy regarding the status and treatment of fugitive slaves was General Henry Clinton's "Philipsburg Proclamation" of June 30, 1779. In this statement, Clinton, the commander of all royal forces in America, offered refuge to "every NEGRO who shall desert the Rebel Standard" and promised fugitives that while they were within territory under royal control, they would be allowed "to follow . . . any occupation which . . . [they] shall think proper." While Clinton granted slaves protection from their masters and permitted them a de facto freedom behind British lines during the duration of the war, he carefully limited this offer of the slaves of rebels and made no mention of the condition of refugee slaves after the cessation of hostilities.

Of course, it was impossible to distinguish whether fugitive slaves had escaped from loyal or rebel slaveholders, so, in practice, one result of the Philipsburg Proclamation was that any runaway slave who reached British lines and wanted refuge was able to secure it. But the freedom slaves gained in this way was tenuous. British policy alternated between treating the Black Loyalists as subjects deserving protection or as confiscated property that could be confiscated to punish rebel and reward loyal white subjects.

Despite the obvious risks and the uncertainty of freedom once behind the British lines, thousands of slaves abandoned their plantations and asserted their personal independence under the flag of the King. Exactly how many slaves escaped to the British during the course of the war cannot be known with any certainty. Jefferson later asserted that over 30,000 slaves were "lost" to the enemy in Virginia alone, and as many as 25,000 South Carolina slaves (a quarter of all the slaves in the state) were thought to have found refuge with the British. Whatever the true figure, the number of slaves who escaped to the British in the war was doubtless in excess of 50,000, or over one-tenth of the entire Black American population of the nation.

For most of the Black Loyalists, the hope of finding freedom behind British lines proved to be a tragic illusion. Many thousands died from starvation and exposure, abandoned by their erstwhile British allies and afraid of the violent and often deadly retribution that awaited them if they returned to their home plantations. Other fugitives perished from the diseases that ravaged their makeshift camps. Still others secured passage on a British ship departing America only to be betrayed and sold into renewed slavery in the Caribbean. In the end, the British recognized and protected the liberty of only about 5,000 of the escaped slaves who had aided their cause in the war. These fortunate few were evacuated with the Royal Army and taken to Nova Scotia and, in 1792, to West Africa, where they established the British colony (and later nation) of Sierra Leone.

The actions of so many people whether in arms for or against the American cause, or in flight from the plantations to the British army, had a powerful impact on American attitudes toward slavery. Colonial attitudes depicting Black Americans as either insensible of liberty or incapable of acting to secure or defend it, were decisively weakened. After independence, Americans looking for the origins of their liberty outside of the now discredited notion that it was inherited from England turned to Enlightenment theories of the existence of "natural rights" shared by all mankind. The efforts of the thousands of slaves who were, at that moment, struggling violently to procure liberty for themselves served to prove that Black Americans also possessed these "natural rights."

In the Revolutionary years, many white Americans began to recognize and question the contradiction of proclaiming their own rights to liberty while keeping slaves. "Would we enjoy liberty?" a New England minister asked his congregation in 1774, "Then we must grant it to others." Similarly, many Loyalist opponents of the Revolution doubtless echoed the British writer Samuel Johnson's famous jibe: "How is it that we hear the loudest *yelps* for liberty among the drivers of negroes?" Such accusations moved Patriots to amend this glaring and embarrassing inconsistency.

Constrained as Black Americans were by their condition, their voices were nonetheless heard on this issue, which was of such crucial importance to them. In 1774, an anonymous writer who called himself "A Son of Africa" asked the readers of a New England newspaper if it were just to "hold men in slavery who are entitled to liberty by the law of nature, equal as yourselves?" Three years later, a group of slaves petitioned the Massachusetts Legislature that "they may be Restored to the Enjoyments of that which is the Natural Right of all men." Other Black Americans sent numerous similar petitions to the legislatures of their respective states or to the Continental Congress.

Motivated by such entreaties, and by the ongoing efforts of Black Americans to secure liberty for themselves with the British or American armies, and also by the new idea of a liberty that was based on "natural rights," the Revolution spawned a widespread and powerful current of antislavery. The American Revolutionaries were among the first to see slavery and liberty as principles that were irreconcilable and indeed implacably opposed. The ideology embodied in both the Declaration of Independence of 1776 and the new state constitutions, proclaimed a liberty that was both unbounded and expansive. This concept of liberty differed significantly from the passive and fragile liberty of the Colonial era.

"Revolutionary republicanism" sought to create a new social order based on liberty alone, and whose survival depended upon equal parts of freedom, civil equality, and "public virtue." The latter was defined as the willingness (and ability) of each individual to take part in the governing of the society and to place the good of the entire community before private interest. The institution of slavery was thought to be antithetical to the basic principles of a successful republic. Writing in 1781, Jefferson, in his *Notes on the State of Virginia*, asserted that slavery taught masters to be despots and rendered them incapable of the selflessness of "public virtue." From this point of view, slavery, if it were allowed to continue, could corrupt the virtue of the young republic and ultimately threaten the liberty of all Americans.

By 1776 and in the ensuing decade, many Americans increasingly came to see slavery and liberty as institutions which were not only incompatible but which could not safely coexist within one government. For liberty to be secure, slavery would have to be destroyed, or at least placed on the road to eventual extinction. Everywhere throughout the country in the years from 1776 to 1786, Americans considered the question of how slavery could be abolished. The character and result of this process varied widely from state to state and from region to region, according to the relative importance of slavery as an economic and social institution.

In those areas where slaves were few in number, the forces of antislavery were able to gain quick and decisive victories. In northern New England abolition was achieved through the new state constitutions. Vermont, where virtually no slaves lived at all, became the first polity in the Western world to abolish slavery by law. In 1777,

Vermonters declared in their state constitution that since "All men are born equally free," none could be held as a slave. Four years later, slavery was likewise ended in Massachusetts via an appeal to the state constitution of 1780. In this case abolition was the result of judicial action rather than explicit legislative intent. In 1781, Quock Walker, a Massachusetts slave, sued his master for his freedom. In his decision granting Walker his liberty, Chief Justice William Cushing interpreted the clause in the state constitution which asserted that "all men are born free and equal" to mean that slavery was abolished in the Bay State. Without the support of the courts, the institution soon crumbled. A similar court challenge accomplished the same end in New Hampshire in 1783.

In Pennsylvania, where slaves comprised between 2 percent to 3 percent of the population, emancipation was gained through legislation rather than appeals to the state constitution. The debates held in the Pennsylvania Assembly revealed what was a central problem for antislavery advocates in the Revolutionary age. In freeing the slave as a person, abolition also necessarily annihilated the slave as property. Outright emancipation, therefore, threatened to strip slaveholding citizens of their private property and, according to Lockean ideology, threatened their liberty.

To escape this dilemma, the Pennsylvania emancipation act of 1780 freed only slaves born after the law went into effect and even they only after they had worked for their masters for 28 years. This concession to the property rights of slaveholders was a triumph of concrete politics over abstract principle. It was a necessary compromise that accepted continued slavery in the short term to secure its abolition in the long run. Similar clauses were included in the emancipation acts that were passed by Connecticut and Rhode Island in 1784 and that eventually were enacted in New York in 1799 and in New Jersey five years later.

The *post-nati* principle, in which only slaves not yet born were to be freed, circumvented the dilemma posed by considering slaves as property. *Post-nati* laws conceded to slaveowners their private property rights to any slaves they already possessed, while barring any future "acquisitions," whether through birth or purchase, of this "very troublesome species of property," as Washington described slaves in this period.

While slaveholders were only a small percentage of the population of northern states, they were drawn disproportionately from the wealthiest sector of the community and wielded considerable influence. Therefore, political expediency, and the need for unity in the Revolutionary cause, required that some concessions to the slaveholding interest be made if emancipation was to be achieved at all.

With the passage of *post-nati* emancipation laws in lower New England, the wave of emancipation acts that were concurrent with the Revolutionary War was ended. By 1784, slavery had been abolished outright only in Massachusetts, New Hampshire, and in the unconfederated and as yet unrecognized republic of Vermont. Slavery was still lawful, although placed upon the road of gradual destruction through *post-nati* laws, in Pennsylvania, Connecticut, and Rhode Island. In the remainder of the 13 states of the newly independent Confederation, the institution of slavery was still unhindered by antislavery legislation. The states where the Revolutionary War had not resulted in any concrete acts to abolish slavery differed from those where it had in one important characteristic. In the eight states where no progress toward emancipation was achieved, slaves comprised between 10 percent and 50 percent of the local population. Even at the lower end of this spectrum, in New York and New Jersey, the power and influence of the slaveholding interest was proportionately much stronger than in neighboring Connecticut or Pennsylvania, where only one in forty residents had been enslaved. In New York and New Jersey, and even more so in those states to the south where slaves were far more numerous, the Lockean dilemma of liberty and property that had confronted antislavery advocates in Pennsylvania was a far more formidable obstacle to emancipation

For southern planters, slavery was the mainspring of their economy and the natural increase in the slave population was itself an important source of wealth. In Virginia, slaves formed a third of the population and were by far the most valuable form of property in the state. Moreover, many planters, including Thomas Jefferson, lived in a constant state of indebtedness to British merchants. For Jefferson, and others in his condition, the loss of their slave property through abolition would leave them unable to pay what they owed. In the eighteenth-century mind, a bankrupt was considered little better than a slave, because he was both property less and completely in the power of his creditors.

Yet, despite these difficulties, there is little doubt that many Virginians were sincerely opposed to slavery in the Revolutionary era. In their writings, Jefferson, Washington, Patrick Henry, and other members of Virginia's Revolutionary leadership proclaimed their belief that slavery was incompatible with the ideals of the new Republic. The problem was to devise a means of ending the bondage of the slave without imperiling the freedom of the slaveholder. For most Virginians, the enactment of outright or even *post-nati* emancipation legislation was an unacceptable expansion of government's power to infringe on property, and therefore liberty.

The moral struggle over slavery that took place in Virginia in the Revolutionary years reveals the possibilities and limitations of Revolutionary antislavery. For the most part, this struggle centered on two conflicting ideas of liberty—the older, Lockean view of a liberty that was passive and derived from property, and the newer, Revolutionary view of an expansive and natural liberty. The mainspring of liberty and government in Lockean ideology was self-interest and private property. Revolutionary republicanism, by contrast, depended upon self-sacrifice and the good of the entire community. According to the Lockean view, slaves, as property, had to be protected from any governmental intrusion, while the ideology of Revolutionary republicanism proclaimed that for liberty to survive slavery must be destroyed or at least its eventual extinction secured.

Historians have long debated which side of this struggle Thomas Jefferson himself was on. Those who would place him in the camp of the advocates of Revolutionary liberty point to the Declaration of Independence. When Jefferson sought to list the "inalienable rights" that all men were possessed of, he initially borrowed from John Locke. But, where Locke had written, "Life, Liberty, and Property," Jefferson penned, "Life, Liberty, and the Pursuit of Happiness." The change was a subtle but significant one. By removing property from the Lockean trinity, Jefferson opened the door to the Revolutionary republican idea that "happiness," or the public good, took precedence over private property rights, including slaves.

However, other barriers existed to emancipation in Virginia and the states to the south beside the sanctity of property. Jefferson, and many of his fellow Virginians, held prejudices and fears that made them doubt whether whites could live alongside Blacks in the new nation in a relationship of liberty and equality. In his *Notes on the State of Virginia*, written during the Revolution in answer to a series of queries posed by a French correspondent, Jefferson posited the notion that Blacks might be innately inferior to whites in terms of their intellect and imagination and even suggested the possibility that they might be a distinct (and lower) species. Such speculations indicate that one solution to the dilemma of slavery in a republic would be to assert that slaves did not contradict the doctrine that "all men are created equal" because Black Americans were not "men." Although Jefferson considered these questions, he stopped well short of any such declaration or easy escape from his dilemma. The idea that Blacks were a separate species ran counter to the Enlightenment belief that racial differences were caused by climate and had few strong supporters in the eighteenth century

Yet, the presumption of Black inferiority did not have to be based upon biological reasoning to have a devastating impact upon the prospects for emancipation and equality. In a cruel irony, many Virginia whites feared that generations of slavery might have rendered Black Americans unable to enjoy their freedom. The ideology of Revolutionary republicanism held that the preservation of liberty depended upon a large measure of personal self-control, independence, and "public spirit." Never having governed themselves, Jefferson, and other whites, thought that Black Americans, once freed, might prove incapable of such self-government. If slavery was a school of tyranny for masters, it was likewise a school of servility for slaves. Both attributes were equally inimicable to liberty. Uneducated and propertyless as a result of their servitude, freedmen might easily fall under the sway of a demagogue and so menace the Republic's survival.

Moreover, the ideal of Revolutionary republicanism depended upon a shared sense of community, amity, and purpose among the population. Virginia whites feared that Virginia Blacks, enslaved and viciously oppressed for more than a century, would naturally harbor a large degree of hatred and suspicion toward their white neighbors and toward American society as a whole. Consequently their inclusion as free citizens might well divide the community and destroy the unity of the Republic. Deprived of unity, "public spirit" would wither, and with it, republican liberty itself.

These prejudices and fears were not unknown in New England and Pennsylvania, where slavery had nonetheless been abolished or the emancipation process begun. But in these areas slaves were such a small proportion of the population that the danger they posed to the Republic once freed was small. Time and the experience of freedom, New England whites felt, would teach New England's freedmen how to be free men. Virginia and the other states where slaves formed a much larger part of the population could not afford such a complacent approach. For republicans in these states, where the number of slaves was equivalent to a third or more of the total population, to add thousands of ex-slaves into the body politic, all of whom were ill-prepared for the responsibilities of republican citizenship, seemed to doom the experiment in liberty before it had fairly begun.

However much Jefferson might have sincerely wished for the abolition of slavery, the survival of his own liberty and that of the new American republic was, in his view, always the foremost priority. In the long term, Jefferson believed that there was no conflict between these two goals. In fact, he felt that they were mutually dependent. If liberty were to survive in America, slavery would eventually have to perish. But, in the immediate context Jefferson felt that the vulnerability of the American experiment in liberty required that emancipation proceed with great caution and circumspection.

These beliefs and perceived necessities shaped the one piece of antislavery legislation achieved in Virginia in the Revolutionary years. In 1782, the Virginia Legislature passed a law that removed all restrictions on private manumissions. Hitherto, any masters who sought to manumit a slave had first to secure the consent of the governor and council. This limitation had the effect (as was intended) of greatly restricting manumissions. The 1782 law, however, left manumission completely at the master's discretion. Previously manumission had been discouraged and regarded at best as a public nuisance; now, in contrast, it was publicly encouraged and commended.

The Virginia manumission law of 1782 embodied much of the idealism and many of the inherent limitations of Revolutionary republicanism. Based upon the voluntary acts of slaveholders, and not legislative compulsion, it avoided the dangers to liberty posed by a government that encroached on slave property via emancipation acts. Similarly, because no one anticipated a unanimous and instantaneous decision by Virginia's slaveowners to manumit their slaves, abolition through voluntary manumission would be a very gradual process. As they were freed, each new group of Black citizens could be slowly absorbed and assimilated into the body politic. Virginia would thereby escape the problems that the sudden creation of a vast unprepared and propertyless class posed to the republican experiment.

Like republican government itself, the manumission act relied for its success upon the "public virtue" of Virginia's citizens. Just as Virginians were asked to place the good of the community before self-interest in politics, so they were now asked to sacrifice their slave property for the welfare of the commonwealth. Those who believed in, or hoped for, the triumph of Revolutionary liberty could see the manumission act as a test of republican virtue. If Virginians were truly virtuous, they would willingly and voluntarily act to rid themselves of slavery; if they were not, the continuance of slavery was little more than a symptom of the Republic's inevitable demise.

It would be easy to decry the Virginia manumission act of 1782 as a measure that was at best naive and at worst an exercise in rationalizing the continued coexistence of slavery in a land of liberty. Certainly most Virginians, including Jefferson himself, never felt able or willing to part with their property in slaves for the sake of the public good. But the Revolutionary idealism and hope for a better future that the act represented should not be dismissed without giving credit for what it accomplished. Although the vast majority of Virginia slaveholders were not moved by a sense of their "civic duty" to manumit their slaves, hundreds of slaveholders did comply. During the 22-year tenure of the act, over 10,000 Virginia slaves, including those manumitted by George Washington in his will, were freed under its auspices.

Following Virginia's lead, similar laws lifting the restrictions on manumissions were passed by the legislatures of New York, New Jersey, Delaware, and Maryland between 1785 and 1789. While they directly affected only a small minority of Black Americans, the Revolution-inspired manumission acts freed as many slaves as were liberated by the combined results of abolition in northern New England and emancipation in Pennsylvania, Connecticut, and Rhode Island. Moreover, the creation of a large class of free Blacks forever changed the character of slavery in the states of the upper South.

If, in New England, the small demographic weight of slavery in the region meant that the scales of liberty and property were tipped decidedly in favor of the former, in South Carolina, where slaves were a majority of the population, the situation was quite the reverse. South Carolina saw little debate on the possible abolition of slavery during the years from 1776 to 1783. In South Carolina the Revolution and the resulting state constitution retained a very conservative cast. The leaders of the new state of South Carolina were drawn from the same men who had governed the colony. In declaring independence from Britain, they had explained that necessity and not any "love of innovation" guided their actions. As a result, the older, Lockean idea of a passive liberty that was based on property still held sway in the state.

The only chance for any emancipation legislation in South Carolina occurred when the state was faced with occupation and defeat and driven to consider desperate measures. In May 1780, a large British army besieged and captured Charleston and with it almost the entire American military force in the state. Preoccupied at the best of times with the need to maintain control over their 100,000 slaves, South Carolina's 50,000 whites were able to mount only a weak defense. Faced with bankruptcy, conquest, and occupation, the state authorities urgently appealed to the Continental Congress for assistance.

Into this breach stepped 25-year-old Colonel John Laurens. No wild-eyed radical, Laurens was an aide to Washington, and son of Henry Laurens, a prominent South Carolinian and president of the Continental Congress. With the encouragement of Congress, Laurens came to South Carolina to urge the state's leaders to tap an as yet neglected resource of manpower. Laurens proposed that the state create a brigade of Black soldiers by giving arms to 3,000 of the state's slaves and offering them freedom after the war in exchange for their good behavior.

Young Laurens, as is apparent from his letters, was fired with a mixture of Revolutionary fervor, antislavery zeal, and a desire for martial glory (he was to command the slave soldiers). Sharing many of Jefferson's reservations about the corrupting effects of slavery and of the freedmen's suitability for citizenship, Laurens saw his proposed slave brigade as a test in miniature of emancipation. If his Black troops demonstrated their bravery and virtue in battle, Laurens wrote, they deserved their freedom and also proved that slaves could be made into worthy citizens. South Carolina legislators, however, with few exceptions, greeted the proposal to resort to arming slaves to defend the state with fear and derision and the idea died when Laurens was killed in a skirmish with a British raiding party in August 1782.

Rather than expand the meaning of liberty by offering it to slaves, the South Carolina Legislature indicated that it still saw liberty not as a result of "natural rights" but as a creation of property, including property in slaves. Instead of adopting Laurens's proposal, the bankrupt assembly voted to raise white recruits by offering payment in slaves confiscated from Loyalist plantations. The promised bounties increased with rank. Privates were offered "one grown negro" in return for one year's service, while majors were to receive "two large and one small negro." Enticed by these inducements, men traveled from as far away as Virginia and North Carolina to enlist and secure for themselves a Loyalist's slave. Using slave property as its currency, South Carolina was able to raise several thousand fresh troops and to renew the fight with the royal forces that occupied the state.

That men might fight for their own liberty and yet accept payment in slaves, reveals the persistence of older, Lockean concepts of liberty and property in the midst of the Revolution. For small farmers or for propertyless men, the ownership of a slave might make the difference between economic self-sufficiency and indebtedness. Many of South Carolina's new soldiers probably saw no contradiction in their actions. In fact, many may have felt that they were fighting for their independence in two ways. If they hoped to secure their political independence by defeating the British, they also hoped to gain economic independence by acquiring a slave. The

difficulty that the state had in enlisting soldiers before it offered payment in slaves suggests which was the more important priority in the eyes of many of the recruits.

The dual character of slaves as both persons and property had a powerful influence on the outcome of the struggle between the Revolutionary conception that liberty was universal, expansive, and based on "natural rights," and the older pre-Revolutionary idea that liberty was fragile, passive, and based on property. Where slaves were relatively unimportant as property, the triumph of the Revolutionary idea of liberty led to the acceptance of the principle that the slave was first and foremost a person possessed of natural rights. This view, in turn, led to the subsequent abolition, or gradual emancipation, of slavery. In the South, however, where slavery was the foundation of the local economy, the dominant character of the slave was as property. The result was that the Revolutionary concept that liberty was based on personal and not property rights made little headway, and antislavery sentiment consequently also was weakened or deterred.

The states that lay between northern New England, where slavery was abolished, and South Carolina, where slavery was actually enlisted in the Revolutionary cause, formed a spectrum based on the importance and numerical significance of slavery in the local society. In each of them the struggle over the meaning of liberty took place with differing results. Virginia, in this view, represents the fulcrum of this struggle. Here, both ideas of liberty, one based on natural rights, or one based on property, wielded powerful influence. Virginians, like Jefferson sought to respond to the dictates of both. They sought to embrace the new without forsaking the old. The Virginia manumission act of 1782 represents their efforts to somehow reconcile these two contradictory impulses.

Whether individual Black Americans secured their liberty in the Revolutionary era depended in part on their own actions and in part on which part of the country they happened to live in. Prince Estabrook of Lexington, for example, won his freedom fighting with Washington's army, but the other slaves in Massachusetts were freed in 1781 by the court's interpretation of the state constitution. By contrast, the only opportunity that Richard, Thomas Jefferson's servant, would have had for freedom came when a British raiding party visited Monticello in 1781. Thirty Monticello slaves escaped to the British on this occasion. Their ultimate fate is unknown. But this dichotomy between choice and chance is too simple. By refusing to remain silent, Black Americans of the Revolutionary era played a key part in the creation of a new concept of liberty that could include themselves. Their actions insured that the Revolution could not take place without acknowledging and addressing their existence. For Black Americans, the work of the American Revolution was left unfinished. But in helping to redefine the meaning of liberty, Black Americans had at least insured that the work was begun.

Robert Olwell

REFERENCES

David Brian Davis, *The Problem of Slavery in the Age of Revolution, 1770–1823* (1975); Philip Foner, *Blacks in the American Revolution* (1975); Sylvia Frey, *Water From the Rock: Black Resistance in a Revolutionary Age* (1991); Sidney Kaplan, *The Black Presence in the Era of the American Revolution, 1770–1800* (1973); Benjamin Quarles, *The Negro in the American Revolution*, (1961).

Smallwood, William (1732–1792)

Continental Army officer. A planter, merchant, and member of the Maryland Assembly, William Smallwood was the son of Bayne and Priscilla Heaberd Smallwood. He was born in Charles County, Maryland, and is reputed to have been educated in England. An Episcopalian, Smallwood was a member of the landed gentry of his colony.

William Smallwood saw action in the French and Indian War and returned home to serve in the Maryland Assembly, beginning in 1761. Active in politics, Smallwood tended toward the radicals and allied himself with Thomas Johnson and William Paca. In 1775 Smallwood became a member of the Association of the Freemen of Maryland. This group pledged itself, among other things, to armed resistance to Parliament's arbitrary acts against the colonies.

In January 1776 Smallwood raised a regiment of Marylanders, which he trained into an effective unit. In early July 1776, Colonel Smallwood marched nine companies of his regiment from Annapolis northward to join Washington's army in New York City. Major Mordecai Gist was Smallwood's second in command.

The Marylanders soon gained a reputation for bravery and excellence in the American army. At the Battle of Long Island in August 1776, Smallwood was absent from his regiment, doing court-martial duty in New York City. Major Mordecai Gist led in his place. The regiment fought on the American right wing under the command of Lord Stirling (William Alexander) at the Gowanus Creek.

In the resulting American retreat, Gist and the Marylanders served as the rear guard for Stirling's troops. The Marylanders' direct attacks against overwhelming numbers gave Stirling time to withdraw his men. In the end, only Gist and nine men escaped.

Smallwood, newly appointed brigadier general by Congress, commanded his men at the Battle of White Plains on October 28, 1776. His men were involved in the fighting for control of Chatterton's Hill. Wounded in this affair, Smallwood was not present for the remainder of the Jersey campaign of 1776. In December, Smallwood returned to Maryland to raise fresh troops. His Marylanders, however, continued their participation in the campaign, serving with honor at Fort Washington, Trenton, and Princeton.

In the Pennsylvania campaign of 1777, Smallwood commanded approximately 1,100 Maryland militia. His men played a distant, indirect role in the Paoli Massacre by not reaching the field in time to assist General Anthony Wayne hold off the attack of General Charles Grey. Had Smallwood arrived in time, it is possible his men could have been a factor in the event.

At Germantown, Smallwood's men formed an outside column on the far American left. In effect they were General Nathanael Greene's left flank. In the confusion of forming in the misty fog and marching over uncertain roads, Smallwood's men never made it into the battle. For the winter of 1777–1778, Smallwood commanded most of Sullivan's former division at Wilmington, Delaware, located not too far from the main American encampment at Valley Forge. Smallwood protected Washington's supplies at Head of Elk, suppressed a Loyalist uprising along the eastern shore of Maryland, and kept a close eye on the Chesapeake Bay.

After several years of inconclusive campaigning in the North, Smallwood and his men were ordered south to help protect the Carolinas from

British attack. Leaving Morristown in the spring of 1780, under the command of the Baron Johann de Kalb, Smallwood commanded the 1st Maryland Brigade of the 1st, 3rd, 5th, and 7th regiments.

De Kalb's troops did not arrive in time to reinforce General Benjamin Lincoln in Charleston. Charleston surrendered in May 1780, resulting in the loss of the southern American army. Congress soon appointed General Horatio Gates as commander of a newly formed American southern army centered around De Kalb's men. Gates led his men south to find Cornwallis.

The American and British forces collided at Camden, South Carolina, on August 16, 1780. The battle turned into an American disaster that mauled Gates's army. The Baron De Kalb was killed in the fighting. Smallwood's Maryland brigade formed as the American reserve and were then swept from the field when Cornwallis routed the other American units. Smallwood was forced to the rear with his men. While the Marylanders did provide some cover for the fleeing Americans, the Battle of Camden was not their greatest hour.

Three days after Camden, Gates placed Smallwood in command of De Kalb's division. Congress voted Smallwood their "Thanks" for his actions at Camden and appointed him major general on September 15, 1780. At this point, Smallwood sought to gain Gates's position in command of the remnants of the American troops. Instead the Baron Friedrich von Steuben arrived to assume control.

Angry and distressed, Smallwood protested to Congress at this treatment. He threatened to resign his commission rather than serve under a foreigner. When General Nathanael Greene arrived in December to assume command of the American army, he diplomatically sent Smallwood north to Maryland to raise troops and supplies for the southern army. Both Congress and Washington held firm and refused to give in to Smallwood's demands.

Smallwood continued his service in the American army until November 15, 1783, when he resigned at the end of the war. He later served as governor of Maryland for three terms. William Smallwood died on February 14, 1792, at Mattawoman in Charles County, Maryland, and was buried at "Smallwood's retreat."

His military career was that of an able administrator and an experienced drillmaster. He fought in one major action, at White Plains, in 1776, where he was wounded. Otherwise, Smallwood was either present but not involved, or absent, in the major actions of the American army during the war. Smallwood excelled at raising men. He also was adept at gathering supplies to support the American armies.

On the other side, Smallwood did not think that Congress recognized his talents nor did they promote him fast enough. Smallwood did not like foreigners and had difficulty working with them or serving under their commands. Smallwood never married.

Paul J. Sanborn

REFERENCES

Appleton's Cyclopedia of American Biography (1932); *DAB*; Francis B. Heitman, *Historical Register of Officers of the American Revolution* (1982); Henry Lee, *The American Revolution in the South* (1969); John W. Raimo, *Biographical Directory of American Colonial and Revolutionary Governors, 1607–1787*(1980).

Smith, Claudius (?–1779)

Loyalist. Leader of a band of ruthless marauders in the hills of Orange County, New York, during the first half of the war Claudius Smith was "a terror to the country" according to author Lorenzo Sabine. Little is known about Smith himself, but his gang was notorious for its depredations against Patriot families, and for its arsons and murders. The Smith gang seems to have operated with the blessing of British authorities, to whom it turned over part of their loot. Governor George Clinton offered a $500 bounty for Smith's capture. Smith went into hiding on Long Island, but he was captured by a raiding party from Connecticut. He was tried and hanged at Goshen. His son Richard took over the gang and led it on to new depths of depravity. His men killed John Clark, a Patriot, and pinned to his coat a warning: "You are hereby warned, at your peril, to desist from hanging any more friends to Government as you did Claudius Smith." The note demanded the release of Tory prisoners, reminded the Patriots that they had started the troubles, and warned that the gang would continue to pursue rebels "till the whole of you are murdered." Richard's fate is unknown, but the gang seems to have disbanded sometime during 1779.

Tom Martin

REFERENCES

Catherine S. Crary, *The Price of Loyalty: Tory Writings from the Revolutionary Era* (1973); Lorenzo Sabine, *Biographical Sketches of Loyalists of the American Revolution*, 2 vols. (1864), I.

"Snow Campaign" (South Carolina) (December 1775)

The "Snow Campaign" in late 1775 successfully concluded the effort by the South Carolina Provincial Congress and Council of Safety to control and ultimately to crush the backcountry resistance to its plan to unite the province against the policies of the Lord North administration in England.

William Henry Drayton, the Council's emissary, had met strong resistance in the backcountry to his efforts to organize associations of men who would support the Council and to purge the militia of men friendly to the Crown. The King's supporters, led by the Cunningham brothers, Joseph Robinson, and Thomas Brown of Georgia, formed counter-associations. When Drayton threatened to use force, these Loyalists assembled about 1,200 men and marched to Ninety Six, where they exchanged shots with his followers. Both sides agreed to a parley, which resulted in a treaty highly favorable to the Council of Safety. When the treaty was repudiated by the Cunninghams and other leaders of the King's supporters, another confrontation took place near Ninety Six in which the Crown's supporters gained the upper hand.

Meanwhile, the Council of Safety had authorized Colonel Richard Richardson to lead an expedition to crush the resistance in the backcountry. As Richardson moved into the interior, his force was augmented by local militia units, which enabled him late in December to overwhelm the last of the Loyalists at the Great Cane Brake on Reedy River. Many of those captured by Richardson were sent to Charleston, where a few of the ringleaders were jailed, while others were released to their homes upon agreeing not to take up arms against the Congress again. The last days of the campaign were featured by unusually heavy snow and sleet, followed by steady rain. Thus the name "Snow Campaign" was affixed to describe the action that broke the resistance in the backcountry and left the provincial congress triumphant throughout South Carolina.

Robert S. Lambert

REFERENCES

Marvin L. Cann, "Prelude to War: The First Battle of Ninety Six, November 19–21, 1775," *South Carolina Historical Magazine*, 76 (1975):197–214; John Drayton, *Memoirs of the American Revolution as Relating to the State of South Carolina* (1821); Robert Wilson Gibbes, ed., *Documentary History of the American Revolution*, 3 vols. (1972), I; Lewis P. Jones, *The South Carolina Civil War of 1775* (1975); Edward McCrady, *The History of South Carolina in the Revolution, 1775–1780* (1902).

Sons of Liberty

Known also as the Liberty Boys, the Sons of Liberty were generally secret and relatively informal colonial societies that sprang into existence during the widespread opposition to the Stamp Tax in 1765. They took their name from a phrase used by Colonel Issac Barre in his reply to a speech made by Charles Townshend, Chancellor of the Exchequer, during the debate over passage of the Stamp Tax in the House of Commons.

Townshend had portrayed the colonies as portions of England transplanted to the New World, cared for and nurtured by the King and Parliament. All colonials, he claimed, owed their allegiance to Britain. Barre, who had served under General James Wolfe during the French and Indian War, sarcastically answered Townshend that most Americans fled from England to escape oppression, had been left to their own devices to survive in a wilderness, and had been sent a long line of corrupt officials who spied on them, repressed them, and preyed upon them causing the blood of "these sons of liberty" to recoil within them.

At first the Sons of Liberty lacked consistent goals. Gradually, they joined in defiance against British power. Composed mainly of artisans, craftsmen, shopkeepers, and mechanics, they shared a common anger against the taxation policies of Parliament placed upon themselves and their fellow Americans.

Symbolically, many Sons wore medallions about their necks. One side displayed a liberty cap on the top of a liberty pole, while the image of a liberty tree was stamped on the reverse. In Boston, the Liberty Tree, which stood at the corner of Washington Street and Essex Street, became the Sons of Liberty rallying point. It was there that important meetings were held within full public view. Liberty poles were erected throughout the colonies.

Some of the Sons wore the number "45" on their hats in sympathy for the struggles of John Wilkes, the British statesman who stood on the side of liberty at home and for the colonies abroad. The "45" stood for the notorious issue Number 45 of *The North Briton* of April 1763 in which Wilkes criticized King George III himself on the proper conduct of the government concerning the rights of Englishmen.

Although each colony approached the matter differently, all shared an emotional indignation over the unlawful parliamentary taxation measures and took actions to rectify the situation. The Sons of Liberty were willing to use either violent or peaceful means to achieve their ends. They tarred and feathered opponents, burnt public records, whipped and beat outspoken individuals, ransacked homes, and intimidated Loyalists on a regular basis.

During the period from 1765 to the outbreak of the War of the Revolution, it was often the peaceful means, the ritualistic threats, that had the most effect on the people. In Boston, the Sons would often wake individuals up in the morning with the playing of violins. Burning certain officials and public figures in effigy also cast fear into many hearts. The Sons were seen by many Americans as dangerous, drunken men bent on violence; a reputation frequently gained by a judicious mixture of actual violence and the menace of violence symbolically displayed in parades, meetings, and other peaceful means.

Contrary to contemporary common opinion, membership in the Sons of Liberty (particularly in Boston) was limited to those of the better sort, who roused the lower orders or the rabble to a violent pitch whenever necessary to impress the government on some point. The Sons in Boston came from the Masons, the Caucus Club, and the Ancient and Honorable Artillery Company, among other groups.

Boston's steering committee for the Sons was known as the Loyal Nine, a secret group that met at Chase and Speakman's Distillery on Hanover Square. The committee was composed of a ship captain, two small–businessowners, two

braziers, a distiller, a painter, a jeweler, and a printer. The Loyal Nine and the Sons kept themselves distinct from, but in control of, the Boston mob. Samuel Adams, Paul Revere, John Avery, Henry Bass, John Hancock, Benjamin Edes, and Joseph Warren, among others, were all influential leaders.

Boston had a trained, disciplined mob, however contradictory that may sound. Its nominal leader was Ebenezer Mackintosh, a shoemaker and fireman, who led Boston's South End mob. The Loyal Nine succeeded in joining the mobs from both the North and South ends of Boston into one functioning faction, ready to carry out its orders. At times the mob became difficult to handle or outbid itself in its zeal to impress Loyalists. Generally speaking, however, the Boston mob was not a headless beast that sought to disrupt the town on whim by random violence.

The effectiveness of the Sons of Liberty was demonstrated when all the Stamp Tax agents in the colonies resigned before the November 1765 date when the Stamp Tax was to go into effect. Later, after the Stamp Tax crisis, the Sons continued to exert their influence on public opinion. They helped enforce the nonimportation measures so that colonial merchants would not deal in English goods while disputes over taxation remained with Britain. The Sons were also skilled in molding public opinion on the streets, gathering a crowd at a moment's notice, stifling opposing opinions, monitoring public officials and their actions, and other means of controlling a town.

When word reached Boston that the Stamp Tax had been repealed by Parliament, the Sons celebrated the victory by lighting 280 lamps in the shape of a pyramid for all of Boston to witness. Each August 14 was celebrated with a parade and banquet as the founding day of the Sons in Boston. On that date in 1765, the first public protest to the Stamp Tax was staged, forcing Governor Francis Bernard and Andrew Oliver, an appointed stamp tax collector in Boston, to flee to Castle Island for safety.

Another very active and powerful Sons of Liberty group was established in New York City by John Lamb, a maker of mathematical instruments; Isaac Sears, a merchant; Marinus Willet, a cabinetmaker; and others. Several years later, future Revolutionary general Alexander McDougall also became a leader of the New York Sons. Since New York City was the center of

British military power in the colonies, the Sons in New York had to be careful in agitating as far as they could without forcing the British commander into too harsh a retaliatory action.

In Pennsylvania, William Bradford, publisher of the *Pennsylvania Journal* was an ardent and prominent Son. Christopher Gadsden was a Sons of Liberty leader in the Carolinas.

In the ten years from 1765 until 1775, the Sons of Liberty remained a radical vanguard, leading the American people into revolt against the British. The Sons' membership went on to form other groups, such as committees of correspondence and committees of safety, to meet different circumstances as the relations between the colonies and Britain continued to deteriorate and war drew near.

Paul J. Sanborn

REFERENCES

Catherine Drinker Bowen, *John Adams and the American Revolution* (1949); Esther Forbes, *Paul Revere and the World He Lived In* (1942); Laurence Gipson, *The Triumphant Empire* (1965); John Harris, *America Rebels* (1974); Merrill Jenson, *The Founding of a Nation* (1968); Robert Middlekauff, *This Glorious Cause* (1982); William Pencak, *War, Politics, and Revolution in Provincial Massachusetts* (1981); Peter Shaw, *American Patriots and the Rituals of Revolution* (1981).

South Carolina in the American Revolution

One of Great Britain's wealthiest colonies, South Carolina, though primarily agricultural, was economically quite diverse. The wealthy planter elite who grew rice and indigo in the low country, or Tidewater region, of the colony dominated the government in Charleston, but by the 1760s their hegemony was being challenged by a growing number of yeoman farmers and stock growers in the backcountry.

In many ways South Carolinians disapproved of the taxation measures of the British government in the 1760s as strongly as other colonies, but they were somewhat distracted during that decade by the power struggle within their own colony. The farmers of the backcountry appeared far more concerned about their small number of representatives in the South Carolina Assembly and the absence of courts outside of Charleston than measures passed in London.

The planters, whose lifeblood was the markets for their rice and indigo and who purchased most of their luxuries and necessities abroad, found parliamentary taxation much more disturbing. Their distress increased even though rice and indigo planters had always been and still were treated quite well by the British government. Rice planters enjoyed consistently high prices for their product throughout the Colonial period. Indigo planters were also fortunate because the British government subsidized them with a bounty on their crop.

Though certainly not unanimous in their sentiments, most low-country planters became increasingly agitated during the 1760s as Parliament sought to tighten its economic grip on the American colonies. Like other colonial legislatures, the South Carolina Commons was concerned that its legislative power was being usurped by Parliament. Furthermore, the Commons engaged in a number of struggles with several colonial governors in the 1760s and early 1770s over legislative power in South Carolina.

When Parliament passed the Stamp Act in 1765, South Carolina, like a number of other colonies, sent a petition of protest to Parliament. When the stamps were actually landed, the royal government under Lieutenant Governor William Bull thought it best to place them under guard in Fort Johnson. An expedition by the Sons of Liberty to intimidate stamp officials ended with the looting of Henry Laurens's wine cellar. Bull was able to save the stamps by placing them on a ship in Charleston harbor. They were never distributed in South Carolina. The less violent opponents of the act chose to send Christoper Gadsden, Thomas Lynch, and John Rutledge to the Stamp Act Congress in New York, when they concurred with the majority of delegates in deciding to send petitions of protest to the King and Parliament.

Meanwhile, the backcountry took little notice of these events. Far more concerned with the growing lawlessness, exacerbated by the lack of courts on the frontier (or anywhere outside of Charleston), many residents took matters into their own hands and formed vigilante groups, which became known as the Regulation or Regulators. Though Governor Charles Greville Montagu tried to stamp out this movement in the late 1760s, it did not disappear until courts were created in the backcountry in 1769.

The low country–dominated Commons took relatively little interest in the problems of the backcountry as they continued to protest the measures of the British government. When the Townshend Duties were passed in 1767, South Carolina agreed with the other colonies to boycott British goods. In 1769 the Commons voted £1,500 to the "Wilkes Fund" in Great Britain, which had been established to aid John Wilkes, a member of Parliament who had been jailed for libel when he criticized the King's policies. Though the governor and his council refused to sanction the sending of the money, the Commons had made a clear statement of its sentiments regarding the King's policies. Its insistence on the right to originate any money legislation brought the government to a virtual standstill for the next several years.

South Carolina radicals were ready for action when the British Parliament passed the Tea Act in 1773. Charleston radicals threatened to destroy the tea when it arrived; therefore, Lieutenant Governor Bull secretly unloaded the tea and placed it in the cellar of the Exchange Building. When word arrived in Charleston of the Boston Tea Party and the Coercive Acts subsequently passed by Parliament, South Carolinians for the most part seemed sympathetic to the Bostonians, although somewhat disturbed by the destruction of private property. In fact, many feared that similar measures might be enacted against any colony that had opposed the landing of the tea.

Representatives from all over the colony met in July 1774. Though the meeting split between moderates and radicals over the best course to take toward the British, it agreed to send representatives to the First Continental Congress to be held in September 1774. The convention also decided to allow the delegates to be popularly elected and to give the delegates authority to join with other colonies on actions Congress deemed necessary.

The voters of South Carolina elected Christopher Gadsden, Henry Middleton, John Rutledge, Edward Rutledge, and Thomas Lynch to represent them at the First Continental Congress. Though the most radical member of the delegation, Christopher Gadsden, urged immediate war on the British in Boston, most of the delegation preferred a more cautious stance. The delegates agreed to all of the resolutions of the Congress. However, all but Gadsden wanted exceptions made for rice and indigo in the embargo of exports to Great Britain. Congress eventually agreed to a compromise in which only indigo and not rice would be withheld from export. The compromise so angered indigo planters in South Carolina that the government there decided to insist that one-third of the profits from rice exports go to compensate other farmers.

By the end of 1774 South Carolina began establishing a new government. This government consisted only of a provincial congress, which assembled in January 1775. This body immediately began establishing committees to oversee enforcement of the embargo in British trade and to prepare the defense of the colony. A committee of 39 men was also appointed to conduct business while the congress was not in session. The congress sent the same five delegates who attended the First Continental Congress to the Second Continental Congress in May 1775.

Lieutenant Governor Bull, awaiting the arrival of the new royal governor, Lord William Campbell, had become little more than a figurehead. Charlestonians eyed him with increasing suspicion as rumors abounded that the British government intended to encourage Indian and slave rebellions to distract the South Carolinians. Such rumors undoubtedly sparked a group of men to seize the arms and ammunition from the Charleston powder magazine in April 1775.

When news of the hostilities at Lexington and Concord arrived, the South Carolina Provincial Congress was called back into session. Henry Laurens was chosen president as this body increased measures to raise a military force and to vigorously enforce the Continental Congress' embargo.

While the provincial congress began its deliberations, Governor Campbell's arrival on June 18 lacked the usual celebrations accompanying the appearance of a new royal governor. In fact, Governor Campbell was all but ignored. The new provincial government busily promoted unity to deal with the apathy and occasional hostility exhibited by the backcountry.

In July, backcountry Loyalist militia thwarted an attempt to remove government powder to Ninety Six. The congress tried persuasion rather than force when it sent emissaries under William Henry Drayton to argue congress' case to the backcountry. The best Drayton could do was to arrange a truce in September 1775 between

Loyalists and supporters of the Revolution. Drayton also met with Cherokee leaders in hopes of assuring them that the new South Carolina government meant them no harm.

Drayton's truce between the militias did not last long. The first military engagement of the war in South Carolina occurred at Ninety Six on November 19, 1775 and, after three days, ended in a draw. Shortly thereafter, the provincial congress dispatched a large force under Colonel Richard Richardson, which over the next few months subdued the Tories. In fact, Richardson so reduced the Loyalist partisans that they would not be a threat in the backcountry for over three years.

In the meantime, in September 1775 South Carolina troops seized Fort Johnson on James Island, which guarded the south entrance to Charleston harbor, and Lord Campbell fled to a British ship in the harbor. A new provincial congress elected in the fall would be in name as well as in fact the government of South Carolina.

After electing William Henry Drayton as its president, the new provincial congress spent the early months of 1776 drawing up a formal constitution for South Carolina. The document the delegates finally agreed upon created an executive position called president. Unlike many of the executives of the other newly formed colonial governments, the president of South Carolina had a veto power and could be reelected. The lower house of the legislature, called the general assembly, was also strengthened with specific authority to initiate all money bills and the power to choose the upper house, called the legislative council. Proportionment for the legislature was still heavily weighted toward the low country, though the backcountry had more representatives than under the royal government. John Rutledge was chosen the first president of South Carolina under this new constitution.

South Carolina hardly had time to adjust to its new government or to take notice of the growing sentiment for independence in the Continental Congress before a British assault threatened Charleston. In order to take advantage of the apparent Loyalist strength in North Carolina, an expedition commanded by Admiral Sir Peter Parker was outfitted in Ireland in early 1776. General Sir Henry Clinton, coming from New York, was to rendezvous with Parker and, in cooperation with an expected Loyalist uprising, subdue the colony of North Carolina. How-

ever, before the arrival of the British, the uprising of Loyalist Scot Highlanders had been crushed at Moore's Creek Bridge in North Carolina on February 27, 1776.

This defeat disheartened Loyalists in both the Carolinas and threatened the success of the British invasion. Clinton and Parker, however, decided to proceed but to change their target to Charleston, South Carolina. They arrived in early June.

To meet this new threat to the southern colonies, George Washington had dispatched General Charles Lee to organize the defense of Charleston. Lee arrived almost simultaneously with the British and was distressed by the pitiful state of Charleston's defenses. While Lee pressed hard to complete defensive works, Parker began probing to secure passage for his ships over the bar into Charleston harbor.

Approaches by water to the town were guarded by Fort Johnson on James Island and the yet to be completed Fort Sullivan on Sullivan's Island, guarding the northern entrance to the harbor. Fort Sullivan, appearing the more vulnerable of the fortifications, became the focus of British military action on June 28, 1776. An unsuccessful British attempt to land infantry on the northern end of the island prevented Parker from securing the envelopment of the still incompleted fort. Therefore, General William Moultrie, commanding the fort, was able to turn all of his guns on the British ships while absorbing in the fort's spongy palmetto logs their return fire. After two of his ships ran aground and one had to be destroyed before it fell into rebel hands, Parker withdrew. After discussing other options for several days, Parker and Clinton decided to join General William Howe's attack on New York City.

While Charlestonians celebrated their miraculous victory over the British, war erupted on the frontier. The British government had encouraged its agents among the Indians to recruit the Indians as auxiliaries to help put down the rebellion. John Stuart, Superintendent of Indian Affairs for the Southern Department, feared that without military support from the British, the Indians would be defeated. Therefore, he encouraged the southern Indians, especially the Creeks and Cherokees, to remain vigilant in case such an opportunity for cooperation arose, but to otherwise remain at peace with the colonists.

Stuart was too ill to argue his case before the Cherokees, so in the summer of 1776 a faction of Cherokees led by Dragging Canoe began raids on outlying settlements in the Carolinas and Virginia. Militias from Virginia to Georgia were called out to meet this threat to the frontier. In South Carolina Major Andrew Williamson led about 1,200 militiamen against Lower Cherokee towns, destroying most of those east of the Blue Ridge Mountains by the end of summer. He then joined with a force of North Carolinians in attacking more remote towns.

Though the fighting was over within a few months, peace was not officially made between South Carolina and the Cherokees until May 1777. In a treaty signed at De Witt's Corner the seriousness of the Cherokee defeat was made clear when they were forced to cede to South Carolina much of what is now the western part of the state.

While the militia fought the Cherokees on the frontier, the newly established government in Charleston adjusted to its new status as the government of an independent state. All four of South Carolina's delegates to Congress—Edward Rutledge, Thomas Lynch, Jr., Arthur Middleton, and Thomas Heyward, Jr.—had signed the Declaration of Independence. When word reached South Carolina about this event, August 5 was set aside to proclaim officially all of the colonies' independence. A large ceremony, including a military procession down Broad Street, began the event, which culminated with parties and balls around the city.

These celebrations temporarily masked a great deal of discontent in the new state of South Carolina. While the Loyalists were still temporarily cowed into submission, many supporters of the Revolution, especially in the backcountry, were openly hostile to the low country–dominated government. To answer some of these grievances, the general assembly appointed a committee chaired by Christopher Gadsden in September 1776. The main recommendation of the committee was that the legislature should be more representative. The assembly seemed to concur when it suggested that the legislative councilors be elected from specified voting districts. However, no changes were effected until a new constitution was adopted in March 1778.

The constitution of 1778 brought a number of significant governmental changes to South Carolina. The executive's power diminished with the loss of the power of the veto. He also could not be elected again for four years after completion of his two-year term. The legislative council was replaced by a senate chosen by the voters of the individual election districts; it was a change, given the fairly wide suffrage, which weakened the voting power of the Charleston area. John Rutledge objected to the adoption of the new constitution. However, because he faced such overwhelming opposition from the general assembly, he resigned, leading to the selection as governor of Rawlins Lowndes who approved the changes.

Ever vigilant against threats from within the state, the new legislature required that all adult males swear an oath of loyalty to South Carolina. Though some citizens felt such precautions to be unnecessary, many were persuaded by the end of 1778 when the threat of a British invasion, possibly aided by Loyalists within South Carolina, seemed inevitable.

Loyalists had continued to press for a major British invasion of the South since the failure of the Charleston expedition in 1776. By 1777 Lord George Germain was convinced that such a strategy would succeed, but his commander in America, William Howe, was not interested. When Henry Clinton replaced Howe, Germain suggested the strategy to him. Clinton agreed to test the idea with an expedition commanded by Lieutenant Colonel Archibald Campbell to Savannah, Georgia, at the end of 1778. By the end of January, Campbell had control of most of Georgia.

The success of the British in Georgia seriously threatened South Carolina's security not only because of the British presence there, but also because of the encouragement it gave to Loyalists throughout the Southeast. Loyalists from North and South Carolina traversed the South Carolina backcountry heading to Georgia to join the British. In response to this threat, the South Carolina legislature chose John Rutledge as governor in early 1779, hoping his experience would help to meet the crisis.

In the meantime, Colonel Andrew Pickens, leading South Carolina militiamen, sought to stop Loyalist reinforcements from reaching the British in Georgia. On February 14, 1779, he attacked a party of North Carolina Tories at Kettle Creek, killing their commander and dispersing most of the men.

Major General Augustin Prevost joined Campbell from St. Augustine by the end of January 1779. Prevost immediately attempted to establish an advanced base in South Carolina on Port Royal Island. Generals William Moultrie and Stephen Bull with 300 South Carolina militia forced him out of the state on February 2, 1779. This action did not deter the British from establishing bases all along the Savannah River.

Congress had appointed General Benjamin Lincoln to assume command of the defense of the southern states. Rather than simply defending the remaining states, he decided to attempt to recover Georgia from the British. To aid Lincoln's movement against the British and to prepare the defense of South Carolina, the state government called out all of the state's militia, poorly armed, organized, and disciplined as they were. Very anxious over the readiness and near mutinous attitude of much of the militia, Lincoln determined to leave as many as possible behind to man the posts in South Carolina while he used the bulk of his regulars to invade Georgia.

Lincoln intended to march most of his army from his headquarters at Purrysburg to join General John Ashe's North Carolina militia and Continentals on Briar Creek in Georgia. Before this rendezvous could occur, Lieutenant Colonel Mark Prevost attacked and decimated Ashe's force on March 3, 1779. The American defeat at Briar Creek demoralized South Carolinians, who now displayed little enthusiasm for Lincoln's plan to move into Georgia. However, in April 1779 Lincoln, with about 2,000 men, began the invasion.

Lieutenant Colonel Prevost, realizing the vulnerability of South Carolina, invaded the state on April 28, 1779. General Moultrie, charged with protecting the state in Lincoln's absence, frantically sent appeals to Lincoln for reinforcements. While he awaited word from Lincoln, Moultrie watched as his militiamen slowly melted away to protect hearth and home. Retreating ahead of Prevost, Moultrie arrived at Charleston on May 9.

By that time, unknown to Charlestonians, Lincoln was rushing to the rescue. Governor Rutledge and his council grew nervous when Prevost was joined by his brother, Major General Augustin Prevost, with reinforcements. The council suggested to Moultrie that talks with the British be opened and that Charleston perhaps should declare its neutrality. The Prevosts would accept no terms that did not include the surrender of Moultrie's army, a demand that Moultrie flatly refused. Much to the relief of Moultrie and Charleston, the British withdrew on the night of May 12, the approach of Lincoln having put them in a precarious position.

Charleston once again had been spared, but South Carolina had felt the full effects of the British invasion. Plantations and farms had been looted, and Loyalists had been emboldened. By the summer of 1779 a full-blown civil war had erupted in the backcountry that would last for the next two years.

While the partisan war raged on the frontier, Lincoln still hoped to force the British from Georgia. He attempted, in cooperation with a French fleet under Admiral Charles Comte d'Estaing, to retake Savannah in the fall of 1779 but he was forced to withdraw when the French gave up the siege.

The success of the British in holding Georgia convinced Clinton of the wisdom of a southern strategy. After an abortive start due to bad weather, Clinton and a fleet commanded by Admiral Marriot Arbuthnot left New York City for Charleston on December 26, 1779. A difficult passage ended with the expedition regrouping outside of Savannah at the end of January 1780.

Congress suggested that South Carolina arm slaves to meet the impending threat. This practice had been used in earlier colonial wars, but now South Carolinians were unwilling to implement it. They were willing to use slaves to build fortifications, though Charleston actually had taken few such precautions since the last invasion.

By the second week in February, Clinton was loading his troops back on the ships and moving toward Charleston. He landed his men south of the city and began moving slowly toward his objective, taking care to maintain his lines of supply.

Lincoln, with about 1,500 Continentals and 2,000 militiamen, worked frantically to complete the defenses of the city. He was expecting the primary attack to come from the sea, so he expended most of his efforts on harbor defenses.

While Clinton moved overland, Arbuthnot crossed the bar into Charleston harbor on March 20. A little over a week later, Clinton crossed the Ashley River and began siege operations against the city. Lincoln still had a chance to escape across the Cooper River but remained in the city at the urging of the civilian government. He also feared that in his absence the government would conclude a separate peace with the British that would probably declare the neutrality of the entire state.

By April 14, Lincoln was trapped. Lieutenant Colonel Banastre Tarleton captured Moncks Corner cutting off Lincoln's forces from areas north of Charleston. Knowing he could not escape, Lincoln asked Clinton on April 21 if he and his men could leave should he surrender the city. When Clinton refused, Lincoln surrendered on May 12, 1780, to spare the city the devastation of a full-scale bombardment. The militiamen under his command were paroled, and his Continentals, now numbering 2,500 were taken prisoner. The fall of Charleston was not just a blow to South Carolina and the Southeast but to the entire American war effort. The loss of 2,500 soldiers, their weapons, and supplies could never be replaced.

Clinton initially hoped to subdue the remainder of the state with a show of leniency. He issued a proclamation on June 1 urging citizens to take oaths of allegiance in return for pardons. While many citizens, including some who had been prominent in the Revolutionary government, rushed to take the oaths, Clinton tried to insure their loyalty by establishing garrisons throughout the state. Clinton soon undid a lot of the good done by his earlier proclamation by issuing another on June 3 requiring active support for the British cause in order to receive a full pardon. Shortly afterward, Clinton returned to New York, leaving his second in command, General Lord Charles Cornwallis, to deal with the unrest this proclamation created.

As Loyalists were emboldened by the British success at Charleston, rebels and neutrals were angered by Clinton's second proclamation. The result was an intensification of the civil war in the backcountry. A number of battles between partisan groups occurred through the summer of 1780. Tory raids on farms and plantations brought erstwhile rebels like Thomas Sumter and Andrew Pickens, who had taken the oath, back into the fray. The actions of people like Banastre Tarleton, who had the body of partisan leader General Richard Richardson exhumed, and Major James Wemyss, noted for destroying

hundreds of homes, garnered many previously neutral South Carolinians for the rebel cause.

Rebel partisans retaliated for even rumors of Loyalist raids, and so made more violent the already chaotic civil war raging over much of South Carolina. Thomas Sumter led rebel forces near Camden, Andrew Pickens operated near Ninety Six, and Francis Marion in the area of Georgetown. Hoping to bring an end to this partisan warfare, Cornwallis continued Clinton's stategy of establishing military posts throughout South Carolina.

In the meantime, Congress responded to the loss of Charleston by appointing General Horatio Gates (against George Washington's advice) to command the Southern Department. He was to join Major General Johann de Kalb in North Carolina as soon as possible and then attempt to liberate South Carolina. Gates arrived at de Kalb's camp on July 25, 1780, and within two days set out for South Carolina.

Against the advice of his officers, Gates determined to make straight for the British outpost at Camden, South Carolina, even though a less direct route promised to yield more forage for his men. Cornwallis, alerted to Gates's approach, personally led reinforcements to Camden on August 10. He instructed other outposts also to send men to Camden. Not only was Gates completely ignorant of these movements, but he also seriously overestimated the strength of his own force.

On the morning of August 16, 1780, the two armies faced each other in an open field outside of Camden. Gates lined up his men with the militia on the left and Continentals on the right, a move that would cost him dearly. The first British assault on the American left routed the militia and exposed the Continentals' left flank. As his shattered army collapsed, Gates led the retreat on horseback, traveling almost 200 miles in 3 days. In just a little over three months two southern armies had been destroyed. The hope of reclaiming Georgia and South Carolina from the British now seemed dim. However, even though the Battle of Camden seriously hurt organized resistance in the state, the civil war continued.

Shortly after Camden, Cornwallis temporarily moved into North Carolina. Because his baggage train and stragglers were subject to repeated attacks by partisan rebel bands, he stopped at Charlotte and sent Major Patrick Ferguson to deal with the rebel irregulars. Ferguson was one of the few British officers able to command the loyalty of Tory partisans. As he marched his Loyalist partisans into South Carolina in September 1780, he issued a proclamation threatening dire consequences to anyone who continued to resist. This proclamation, as Clinton's June 3 edict had done, only angered many in the Carolinas. By the end of September over 1,000 South Carolina and North Carolina partisans were chasing Ferguson. He stopped to fight just over the North Carolina line at King's Mountain on October 7. His force suffered a massive defeat, and he was killed.

The defeat of the Tories at King's Mountain and Cornwallis's absence from the state brought rebels rushing to the colors. Partisan warfare became so vicious that South Carolina gained the reputation for being the most ferocious theater of the war. The biggest problems Cornwallis had during November and December 1780 were Francis Marion and Thomas Sumter. While cutting communication lines between British posts, Marion managed to elude a determined pursuit by Banastre Tarleton. Thomas Sumter, the new overall commander of the South Carolina militia, also proved annoying. In early November Major James Wemyss chased Sumter to Fishdam Ford on the Broad River, where Sumter dealt him a severe defeat on November 9. Tarleton then took up the pursuit, chasing Sumter to Blackstock's Ford, where Tarleton won the field but allowed Sumter to escape.

The economy of the state suffered during this partisan warfare. Farmers with little time to plant or harvest often saw what was produced requisitioned by British, Tory, or rebel soldiers. Slaves disappeared, many taking advantage of the chaos to escape to freedom. Others were taken by British or Loyalist troops.

Because his campaign into North Carolina had been unsuccessful and due to the threat to some of his military posts, Cornwallis began moving back into South Carolina by the middle of October. His return did not end the partisan raids, but for the time being the British hold on their military posts seemed secure.

In the fall Congress finally accepted George Washington's advice and named Nathanael Greene to command a new southern army. At Hillsboro, North Carolina, on November 27, 1780, he found a very small, demoralized force. He immediately moved this army to join an-

other small force at Charlotte, where he made his headquarters. He worked to improve the supply system but soon realized it would be necessary to divide his force to find forage for the winter.

Greene sent his second in command, General Daniel Morgan, to western South Carolina while Greene moved the remainder east toward Cheraw. When Cornwallis learned of these movements, he sent Tarleton and his Legion after Morgan. Cornwallis moved in pursuit of Greene. Eluding Tarleton as long as possible, Morgan made a stand at Hannah's Cowpens on January 16, 1781. In one of the better uses of militia and regulars of the war, Morgan virtually destroyed Tarleton's force on January 17, 1781.

Morgan immediately set out to join Greene. Cornwallis, learning of Tarleton's defeat, tried to catch Morgan before he could rejoin Greene. Cornwallis was so anxious to keep Morgan and Greene apart that he dumped much of his baggage to speed his pursuit. Morgan delayed Cornwallis at the fords over the Catawba River and so joined Greene in North Carolina.

Greene eagerly searched for a place to do battle before Cornwallis could replace Tarleton's cavalry. However, Greene's men were exhausted, and he realized that they were in no condition to fight. With Cornwallis in hot pursuit, Greene retreated into Virginia.

Returning two weeks later to North Carolina with supplies and reinforcements, Greene's army met Cornwallis outside of Guilford Court House on March 15, 1781. Though the battle was fought to a draw, Greene retreated, leaving the field to the British. Because his army was short of supplies and quite weary, Cornwallis chose to move to the coast at Wilmington to receive supplies rather than pursue Greene into South Carolina. Cornwallis ultimately moved into Virginia, leaving a much reduced British force under General Lord Francis Rawdon to hold South Carolina.

Greene saw his opportunity and moved his army back into South Carolina in April 1781. He made much use of militia and partisan bands in his campaign to retake South Carolina. Though he would not be successful in open battle with Rawdon's main force, South Carolina militia with Continentals under Henry Lee gradually took most of the British outposts in the state.

The campaign began on April 23 when Francis Marion and Lee took Fort Watson south of Camden. At the same time Andrew Pickens threatened Ninety Six. Greene's first encounter with Rawdon came two days later on April 25 at Hobkirk's Hill just north of Camden. Even though Greene was forced from the field in this engagement, partisan bands with the help of Greene's Continentals were making life miserable for the British in the interior of South Carolina.

In May 1781 Thomas Sumter liberated Orangeburg, and Francis Marion took Fort Motte. By July the isolation of the British force at Ninety Six forced its retreat. In fact, the interior of South Carolina had become so hostile to the British that Rawdon decided to withdraw toward Charleston. By the end of July the British in South Carolina were limited to the Charleston area.

Weary of these rear guard actions, Rawdon had asked to be relieved and left his command to Lieutenant Colonel Alexander Stewart. The new British commander, not satisfied to sit quietly in Charleston, moved part of his force northwest of the city. Greene anxiously sought to bring the British to battle. On September 8, 1781, Greene's men surprised a British foraging party near Eutaw Springs. Panic spread to the main British camp, and the Americans forced most of the British force to retreat. Because the Americans stopped to plunder the British camp, the pursuit disintegrated, and the British were able to regroup and reclaim the field. However, the attack so unnerved the British that Stewart kept his men close to Charleston for the remainder of the war.

Greene, determined to maintain pressure on the British in Charleston, had to wait until November before his force was strong enough for offensive action. By that time General Alexander Leslie had assumed command in Charleston, and he was reluctant to test his strength against Greene. British forces were pulled closer into Charleston.

Except for the Charleston vicinity, supporters of the Revolution controlled all of South Carolina. The civilian government was restored, and in an attempt to return order as quickly as possible, Governor Rutledge extended a pardon to most Tories in the state. Many Loyalists happily accepted the offer.

However, many who had supported the Revolution throughout the conflict or who had suffered at the hands of Loyalist partisans were not able to forget so easily the savage fighting of the previous year. When Governor Rutledge called for elections at the end of 1781, the voters elected a large number of militia and army officers to the new legislature. The legislature convened at Jacksonboro, 30 miles outside of Charleston, on January 18, 1782. After electing John Mathews governor, the men passed legislation confiscating or heavily taxing the property of specified Loyalists. The money raised was to be used to help rebuild the state.

Though revenge pleased some people, it did not distract the backcountry from realizing that politically very little had changed in the state. The low-country planters were easing back into their positions of political dominance. They saw the government's primary responsibility as restoring their lost property, particularly slaves. Governor Mathews worked hard to persuade the British in Charleston not to steal slaves and to return those they had taken. In October 1782, he negotiated an agreement to that effect with the British in return for a promise that confiscations would stop. The backcountry, where many citizens expected to profit from the confiscations of Tory property, saw the agreement as one designed to protect the interests of the rich, low-country planters. The argument eventually proved to be a mute one when the agreement was violated by the British.

With the signing of a preliminary peace in Europe, the British left Charleston on December 13, 1782, bringing all of South Carolina under the control of the state government. Some British merchants were allowed to remain for six months to sell their goods. Many saw this agreement as only working to the advantage of the planters around Charleston. Planters would be able to purchase goods at distress sale prices from the British merchants, and Charleston merchants would suffer.

With the war behind them, South Carolinians gradually forgot their animosity toward the Loyalists and turned their attention to many of the same concerns they had had in the 1760s and 1770s. Though some low-country planters like Christopher Gadsden realized that the Revolution had been fought for more than the rights of the low country, others resisted relinquishing the privileges they had enjoyed for decades. However, the backcountry (at least 50 percent of the population of the state) was hopeful that the departure of the British would now bring equitable representation in the government. A new, less violent struggle had begun.

Jeanne T. Heidler

REFERENCES

Edward McCrady, *The History of South Carolina in the Revolution, 1775–1780* (1901); Jerome J. Nadelhaft, *The Disorders of War; the Revolution in South Carolina*; John S. Pancake, *This Destructive War; the British Campaign in the Carolinas, 1780–1782*; Russell F. Weigley, *The Partisan War: The South Carolina Campaign of 1780–82* (1970); Robert M. Weir, *"A Most Important Epocha"; the Coming of the Revolution in South Carolina.*

South Sea Expedition

Great Britain throughout her history has tried to detach the weaker enemies allied with her main enemy; a strategy manifested as recently as World War II with her Mediterranean strategy against Italy. In the American Revolution, prior to the Dutch entry into the war, she attempted to detach Spain from the alliance, going so far as to consider trading Gibraltar for peace, which, most likely, would have been the price Spain would have demanded to forsake her French ally. Further, as early as December 1779 Britain was in contact with the Spanish government through the offices of Father Hussey.

With Gibraltar appearing to be an impossible price for Great Britain to pay, for maintaining civic peace at home in that event was considered doubtful, she turned to the alternative of forcing Spain out of the war by attacking her South American possessions. This, in part, is the reason for the expedition to Nicaragua. But the most daring idea was to mount a seaborne raid that might reap vast sums of booty, like Anson's voyage in the War of Austrian Succession. A base might soon exist for it on the Central American coast, if the expedition in Nicaragua reached the Pacific. It might, as well, help the revolts in Colombia, which was crushed by June 1781; and, in Peru, the larger of the two revolts, Tupac Amaru and his followers, which had broken out in November 1780. This latter one would become so grave as to threaten the foundations of Spanish rule in Peru and news about it was deliberately kept from King Charles III.

So Lord Germain seriously advanced the proposal in 1780, formally approving it on August 3, 1780. The expedition would consist of two regiments, with 2,000 East India Company sepoys under Commodore Johnstone, with a ship of the line and some smaller warships. What was unique about this expedition was that it was to proceed east via the Cape of Good Hope and the East Indies, instead of around Cape Horn, which is best passed in December or January due to the storms there. It would follow the route pioneered by Captain James Cook. The expedition initially would seize a Spanish base in the Celebes and Mindanao in the Philippines. From there it would proceed to South America, and then proceed up the coast to Central America. Facing it in South America would be a Spanish squadron of three small uncoppered Spanish ships of the line (only one Spanish ship of the line was coppered in the course of the war).

The expedition was slated to leave in December 1780, and at Johnstone's suggestion, would first call at the River Plata to try to seize a Spanish treasure fleet thought to be there. The Spanish learned of the expedition to the Plata and told their French allies that they might have to detach part of their main European fleet to proceed to Argentina.

But then everything began to fall apart. The war was not going well and with the Dutch entry into it, the British government believed that it must turn and deal with this threat, especially with the Dutch bases at the Cape of Good Hope and Ceylon. So, on December 27, 1780, the expedition was canceled, the reason given being the withdrawal of the sepoy troops from India, which would weaken the British position there. Great Britain was about to pass from the initiative to the defensive and part of that change would be the cancellation of the South Sea expedition.

Jack Greene

REFERENCES

Jonathan R. Dull, *The French Navy and American Independence* (1975); Howard Ray Killion, "The Suffren Expedition: French Operations in India During the War of American Independence." Unpublished Ph.D. dissertation. Duke University (1972); Piers Mackesy, *The War for America, 1775–1783* (1765).

Southern Indians in the American Revolution

In 1773, approximately 70,000 Indians lived south of the Ohio River. The four largest tribal groups were the Creek, Cherokee, Choctaw, and Chickasaw. The Creeks were the most numerous with some 20,000 individuals living in two geographic divisions, the Upper and Lower Towns. Together, the Creek towns claimed most of the present states of Georgia, Alabama, and Florida. Cherokee settlements lay to the north, with a combined population of about 15,000. The Cherokee were divided among four regional divisions, the Lower, Middle, Valley, and Overhill Towns. Cherokee territory extended from northwestern Georgia and South Carolina through parts of modern Tennessee, North Carolina, and Virginia. The Choctaw villages were situated west of the Creek towns in what is now western Alabama and eastern Mississippi. Three distinct geopolitical divisions, the Western Division, the Eastern Division, and the Six Towns, contained at most 12,500 individuals. Remote from the major settlements along the eastern seaboard, the Choctaw were more closely linked to British West Florida, as were the Chickasaw. The Chickasaw towns lay to the north of the Choctaw and west of the Creeks and had a population of approximately 2,250 people.

British-Indian relations revolved around two related issues—land and trade. For the southern Indians, their economic and military survival depended on foreign imports, particularly guns and ammunition, tools and cloth. The southeastern Indians paid for these imports with deerskins, which were a valuable commodity in the European leather markets. They also traded a variety of other items, including honey, venison, handmade baskets, medicinal herbs, and horses. A huge trade imbalance existed, due largely to the high cost of imported goods in relation to the prices paid for deerskins and other Indian produce. Excessive consumption of rum heightened this trade deficit, as did conflicts between the tribes, which escalated military spending and reduced hunting time. Merchants involved in the trade provided liberal credit arrangements and the southern Indians quickly chalked up enormous debts, particularly the Creeks and the Cherokees.

In 1773, due to heavy pressure from their traders, leading Creeks and Cherokees jointly ceded over two million acres of land to Georgia in order to pay off their debts. Even though the cession eradicated the national debts of both tribes, substantial segments of the population in both Creek and Cherokee towns were dismayed as the area had been prime hunting land. Many Indians believed the traders had cheated them out of their lands by the overextension of credit and sale of illegal rum. Even with the additional land opened for settlement, settlers and their cattle continued to push onto unceded tribal lands, which resulted in numerous incidents along the Anglo-Indian boundary.

In December 1773, Creek warriors raided settlements on the Ceded Lands, killing 16 Georgians. Though there was some prowar sentiment among those who opposed the cession, the majority of Creek headmen moved swiftly to avoid open conflict. In the face of growing colonial unrest, Georgia Governor James Wright also favored a quick solution. Rather than take military action, Georgia levied a trade embargo against the Creek towns, and the affair was quickly settled by a compromise agreement.

Even with the end of trade embargo, goods remained scarce in Creek towns due to nonimportation agreements by Patriot merchants and a general shortage of gunpowder in the colonies due to the trouble around Boston. Other southeastern tribes were also affected by the meager supplies of goods. To many of the tribesmen, it seemed their supplies of weapons were deliberately being withheld. Some believed that the white people wished to deprive them of weapons and other goods in order to take more of their land. Thus, the attitudes and actions of the southeastern Indians toward the American Revolution were shaped by their need to secure adequate arms, ammunition, and other trade goods, and their need to defend their lands against white encroachment.

The man responsible for directing British relations with the southern Indians was John Stuart, who had served as Superintendent of Indian Affairs for the Southern Department since 1762. Stuart's headquarters were in Charleston, South Carolina. He was a fair and honest man, and was widely respected by the Indian leaders, and many headmen supported Britain during the American Revolution because they knew and trusted John Stuart. Stuart relied heavily on his deputy agents and commissaries for information and to implement British policy. During the war years, Alexander Cameron served as the deputy superintendent and acted as principal agent to the Cherokee while Charles Stuart served in the same capacity at Mobile, West Florida, where he administered Choctaw and Chickasaw relations. David Taitt served as deputy to the Upper Creeks, William McIntosh to the Lower Creeks, James Colbert to the Chickasaw, and Farquhar Bethune to the Choctaw. With the outbreak of hostilities, Stuart and his deputies initially advised the tribes to remain neutral in the conflict. Stuart realized that unsupported Indian action against the frontier would unify the backcountry settlers against the tribes and probably hurt the British cause as well.

Meanwhile, John Stuart was forced from his headquarters in South Carolina by irate Patriots who spread false rumors that the superintendent had urged the Cherokee to attack the frontier settlements. Stuart sought safety in Georgia, and from there traveled to St. Augustine, East Florida. He made his new base of operations Pensacola, West Florida. Throughout the war, Stuart's main concern became the procurement of adequate supplies of arms and equipment for the tribes in order to maintain their loyalty to Britain. He also hoped to alienate pro-American tribesmen by pointing out that it was the frontiersmen who coveted Indian land, not the British government.

American use of local Indians in fighting around Boston in 1775 led the British government to approve the use of Indian troops against the colonials. In September 1775, General Thomas Gage informed Stuart that he should work diligently to keep native warriors firmly in the British interest. Accordingly, Stuart took steps to prepare the way for the time when Indian forces could be employed effectively. He instructed David Taitt and Alexander Cameron to begin preparing Indian warriors to act in concert with British forces in the near future and to continue reassuring the Indians that the British would supply them. He also took steps to negotiate an end to the Creek-Choctaw War, which had raged under British auspices since 1765. Now in need of allies, it became expedient for Stuart to free the warriors from the intertribal struggle in order that they might better serve Britain. Peace was concluded between the tribes in October 1776.

In 1775, the Second Continental Congress created an Indian Department to deal with the Indian issue. Responsibility for the southern tribes was to be divided among five commissioners. The Congress named Willie Jones of North Carolina and John Walker of South Carolina. The task of filling the other three appointments fell to the South Carolina Council of Safety, which named three prominent Indian traders to the vacant posts—Creek traders George Galphin and Robert Rae, and Edward Wilkinson, a well-known Cherokee trader. The commissioners were given the authority to negotiate with the southern tribes and were charged with securing the neutrality of the tribes during the war.

The first real test of influence in the Indian towns came in 1776. The Cherokee people were angered over the loss of hunting land by previous treaties and the continuing encroachment on their lands, particularly the settlements along the Holston and Watauga rivers in modern western North Carolina and eastern Tennessee. During long and troubled deliberations in the towns, the majority of the headmen had supported the idea of punitive raids against these white settlements on Cherokee lands. War fervor was heightened by the arrival of northern Indian delegates who encouraged the Cherokee to strike out against those who took their lands. Henry Stuart, brother of the superintendent and special envoy to the tribe, joined with Cameron in urging the headmen to remain peaceful until Cherokee strength could be augmented by British and Loyalist forces and used against Patriot armies rather than the civilian frontier. The two even attempted to negotiate with the illegal settlers. The attempt was a dismal failure and despite Cameron's pleas for restraint, Cherokee headmen launched a series of punitive raids against the white settlements beginning in late June 1776. Warriors from the Lower Towns struck along the South Carolina frontier. Overhill forces concentrated on settlements along the Tennessee River near North Carolina and Virginia and the isolated Kentucky settlements while Middle and Valley warriors swept into North Carolina.

Stuart and Cameron were blamed for inciting the raids, but the Cherokee were not acting as British pawns. Though the Cherokee sought and expected British arms and support for the raids, they were not fighting for Britain. They were fighting for their land and against those who ignored established boundaries and who encroached on tribal hunting lands.

But frontier inhabitants did not perceive the attacks as defensive and the response to the Cherokee action was immediate and harsh. Patriot governments in Virginia, North Carolina, and South Carolina organized retaliatory strikes against the Cherokee towns. As a result, over three dozen Cherokee towns and granaries were burned. Though the raids left relatively few immediate fatalities, many Cherokees ultimately perished due to starvation. Such devastation and hardship instilled a legacy of bitterness that outlasted the conflict. Still fearing Cherokee raids, North Carolina offered bounties on Indian prisoners and scalps. By 1777, the distressed Cherokees had no choice but to petition for peace. The American negotiators refused to recognize that the initial Cherokee raids had been defensive acts against illegal settlers. Instead, the treaties signed in 1777 between the Cherokee towns and their neighboring state governments resulted in the forfeiture of considerable territory.

Cherokee refugees flooded into Creek towns. The Creeks were shocked by their descriptions of the destruction and pillage by the American armies. American Indian Commissioner George Galphin warned the Creeks that if they joined the Cherokee, their towns might be invaded too. This fear led the majority of Creeks to opt for neutrality in the Cherokee-American war and in the larger conflict between Britain and the colonies. Still, a strong pro-British element, led by Emisteseguo of the Little Tallahassee, existed in the Upper Towns. The main Cherokee offensives had occurred when leading Upper Creeks were formalizing the peace treaty with the Choctaw in Pensacola. As a result, the pro-British Creeks did not participate in the Cherokee debacle. Division over the proper course of action in regard to the Cherokee caused tremendous strains in Creek councils, and civil war threatened as neutralist factions feared that support of the British might mean an American invasion with a concomitant loss of land. Alexander McGillivray, mixed-blood warrior of Little Tallahassee, emerged as the leader of the pro-British faction among the Upper Creeks and was named as British deputy to the Creeks by John Stuart. It was logical that the Lower Creeks seemed more inclined to favor a neutral position, as they were closest to Georgia and stood to suffer the most in the event of an American invasion. Even so, neutralist and pro-British factions existed in both Upper and Lower Towns throughout the war.

Factionalism also divided the Cherokees. Chincohacina (Tsu-gun-Sini), chief and leading warrior of the Big Island Town (Overhill Division), better known to the Americans as Dragging Canoe, opposed the 1777 peace accords, since they had resulted in the loss of more Cherokee territory. He and his radical faction opposed any peace treaty that alienated even more Cherokee land and failed to address the problem of white encroachment. His faction migrated away from the older Cherokee settlements and established new towns south along the Tennessee River. They later became known as the Chickamaugas.

With the British invasion of the South in 1778, the focus of the fighting shifted to Georgia. Indian fighting was primarily directed against boundary violators as was the case in August 1778, when Creek warriors killed between 20 and 30 inhabitants on the Ceded Lands. Other white settlements were also raided. Warriors destroyed property and livestock, and carried off captured Black slaves and horses. Some Creek parties attacked American positions, inflicting casualties and damaging fortifications. Encroachments continued on Cherokee land as well. While the British establishment actively sought the assistance of the tribes along the Georgia–East Florida frontier and in West Florida, American agent Galphin had repeatedly cautioned the Creeks to remain neutral in the conflict lest the Americans use their aid of the British as an excuse to launch an expedition against the Creek towns and take their lands. No American army retaliated for the strikes along the Georgia frontier, but in the Creek towns neutralist and pro-American Creeks disavowed the British-supported raids and threatened action against those who continued hostile action along the Anglo-Creek frontier.

Meanwhile, British agents had been urging the tribes to action. British forces now held Savannah, and raids were undertaken against the American-controlled backcountry. Some 300 Creek warriors, led by Alexander McGillivray and David Taitt, presented themselves for service at Savannah in the spring of 1779. The Creek warriors were used in foraging raids in South Carolina and to round up deserters. Creeks also participated in various action along the Georgia–East Florida frontier.

On March 21, 1779, John Stuart died in Pensacola, and the British government used the occasion to reorganize the Southern Indian Department and divide it into two departments. Thomas Brown, commander of the East Florida Rangers, became the superintendent of the Atlantic District, comprised of the Cherokees and the Creeks. Alexander Cameron, longtime Cherokee deputy, was reassigned as superintendent of the Mississippi District in charge of Choctaw/Chickasaw relations.

Shortly after Stuart's death, and at the urging of Alexander Cameron, Dragging Canoe and about 200 of his warriors set out with a Loyalist force for British-held Savannah. While the warriors were absent, Patriot forces from North Carolina and Virginia raided and destroyed the Chickamauga towns. Despite the burning of the towns again several weeks later, the Chickamauga remained steadfast in their opposition to peace with the Americans.

Major action in 1780 centered in West Florida, where Mobile and Pensacola were under threat from America's cobelligerent, Spain. In 1780, Mobile was taken by the Spanish. British-armed Choctaw war parties harassed the new Spanish possession, but to no avail. Chickasaw warriors, led by British commissary James Colbert, waged sporadic warfare against American posts along the Mississippi. Meanwhile, the British commander at Pensacola, John Campbell, did not want the expense of maintaining a large Indian defense force. Instead, he hoped to call them down to Pensacola from the Indian towns when the city was threatened with attack. After several false alarms, Campbell faced a Spanish invasion force led by Bernardo de Galvez. Tired of Campbell's vacillation, many Indian warriors failed to heed his final call for help. In all, about 1,000 Indians actually participated in the siege of Pensacola. The Indians were primarily Choctaw, but a small body of Creeks and an even smaller number of Chickasaw warriors also took part in the action. Native troops were primarily used to harass enemy lines and were credited with inflicting one-third of Spain's casualties during the protracted siege.

Meanwhile, Creek participation in the war peaked in late summer 1780 in fighting around Augusta, Georgia. With the help of 250 Creeks and a group of Loyalists, Thomas Brown captured Augusta and later repulsed an American attempt to retake the town. Creek warriors pursued fleeing rebels and tortured those they captured. Cherokee warriors, encouraged by the British success in South Carolina and Georgia, planned more raids against the frontier. However, before they could act, the Americans learned of their plans. In December 1780, Lieutenant Colonel John Sevier and a force of 300 North Carolina volunteers and 400 Virginians under the command of Colonel Arthur Campbell invaded the Cherokee country for the second time, burning towns and laying waste to the countryside. Other punitive raids followed in 1781.

The British experienced several major reversals along the southern backcountry during 1781. Pensacola fell in May, and Britain's native auxiliaries, along with Superintendent Cameron, fled to the Indian country. Slowly, American forces regained control of the eastern frontier, including Augusta. Creek involvement in fighting ended in May 1782 when Emisteseguo and a force of Upper Creek warriors were badly defeated by General Anthony Wayne in combat around Savannah. Emisteseguo was killed during the fighting.

Dispirited and defeated, the tribes faced bitter negotiations with the victorious Americans. Frontiersmen and speculators used the Cherokee raids as an excuse for pillage, destruction, and dispossession. Peace negotiations completely ignored the issue of encroachment on Indian land. Instead, the Cherokee forfeited considerable territory to the Americans by right of conquest. The loss of so much territory and manpower accelerated Cherokee acceptance of commercial farming as a replacement to their hunting economy.

While the Creeks grasped the magnitude of the Cherokee error in openly challenging the Americans on the battlefield, they failed to profit from their foresight. As the British evacuation of the Southeast proceeded, some Lower Creek chiefs feared that earlier Creek involvement in the fighting around Augusta and along the East Florida boundary might result in retaliatory raids by Georgia. To prevent this, they signed the Treaty of Augusta in 1783, which guaranteed peace, called for the establishment of trade between the Creeks and Georgia, and turned over 800 square miles of Creek hunting land to the new state in order to atone for Creek actions during the war.

Meanwhile, Upper Creek headmen, led by Alexander McGillivray, sought Spanish aid in stopping American expansion. McGillivray's primary goal was securing a dependable supply of arms and ammunition free of American control. Both goals were achieved by the 1784 Treaty of Pensacola between the Upper Creeks and Spain. Creek American relations remained unstable until 1790, when Alexander McGillivray headed a successful treaty delegation to New York to negotiate with the Washington administration. The years following the Revolutionary War saw Pensacola replace Augusta as the center for the Creek trade. There, former Loyalist William Panton and his partners operated what eventually became the largest and most successful of all the southern Indian trading concerns, Panton, Leslie and Company. The Choctaw survived the war without loss of territory, but the Chickasaw lost land to North Carolina at war's end. Both ultimately gained a measure of independence from American traders by establishing a Spanish alliance and trade partnership.

Kathryn Braund

REFERENCES

Edward J. Cashin, "'But Brothers, It Is Our Land We Are Talking About': Winners and Losers in the Georgia Backcountry," in *An Uncivil War: The Southern Backcountry During the American Revolution,* ed. by Ronald Hoffman, Thad W. Tate, and Peter J. Albert (1985); ———, *The King's Ranger, Thomas Brown and the American Revolution on the Southern Frontier* (1989); William S. Coker and Robert R. Rea, eds., *Anglo-Spanish Confrontation on the Gulf Coast during the American Revolution* (1982); David H. Corkran, *The Creek Frontier, 1540–1783* (1967); R.S. Cotterill, *The Southern Indians* (1954); Robert L. Ganyard, "Threat from the West: North Carolina and the Cherokee, 1776–1778," *North Carolina Historical Review* 45 (1986):47–66; James H. O'Donnell III, *The Cherokees of North Carolina in the American Revolution* (1976); ———, *The Georgia Indian Frontier, 1773–1783* (1975); ———, *Southern Indians in the American Revolution* (1973).

Spain in the American Revolution

Spanish participation in the American Revolution must be seen as a continuation of Spain's longstanding foreign policy regarding Great Britain, her international rival for much of the European Colonial period in the Americas. These two nations, with Spain usually allied with France, had been military and diplomatic adversaries for several centuries, with the years from the late seventeenth century to the American Revolution being a period of intermittent warfare. Spain's role in the American Revolution should thus be viewed as the culmination of international forces set in motion during this latter period of intercolonial warfare, which lasted from 1689 to 1763.

Spain and France fought Great Britain in four major international conflicts during the period of intercolonial warfare in the seventeenth and eighteenth centuries. Although the causes of these wars rested firmly on European considerations of empire and national rivalry, the American possessions of these powers sometimes witnessed conflict and combat with neighboring enemy colonies. These wars were the War of the League of Augsburg (known in British America as King William's War) (1689–1697); the War of the Spanish Succession (known in British America as Queen Anne's War) (1701–1713); the War of the Austrian Succession (known in British America as King George's War) (1744–1748); and the Seven Years' War (known in British America as the French and Indian War) (1756–1763).

Spanish and British colonies in North America engaged in open fighting during these wars. For example, in October 1702 approximately 500 South Carolina militiamen and 300 Indian allies under the command of Governor James Moore attacked Spanish St. Augustine, sacking the town and forcing most of its inhabitants to take refuge behind the walls of Fort San Marcos. Unable to breach the fort, Moore and his British army returned to Charleston and, the following year, marched back to Florida and destroyed 13 Spanish missions in the panhandle region near Tallahassee. The year 1740 saw renewed fighting in the area when General James Oglethorpe and a British army again laid siege to Fort San Marcos in St. Augustine after it took several lesser Spanish outposts along the Georgia-Florida border. This offensive failed, however, and the British withdrew back to Georgia, only to be attacked in retaliation by the Spanish. Oglethorpe and his British forces defeated their Spanish attackers at the Battle of Bloody Swamp in 1742. By the 1750s, Spain and Great Britain had therefore established a long tradition of diplomatic rivalry and military confrontation in North America.

The Seven Years' War, as the great conflict for European empire in the Americas, brought the final resolution of these intercolonial rivalries on the part of Great Britain, France, and Spain. The Spanish were late entering this conflict, having remained neutral during its early stages. Finally, the French King prevailed upon his Spanish cousin, Charles III, to declare war against Great Britain in 1762. The war did not go well for Spain: within a few short months she lost Havana and Manila to invading British forces. Meanwhile, French Canada had fallen to British troops. By early 1763, both allied Bourbon kings were ready to sue for peace, signing the Peace of Paris (1763) with the British. This international accord was nothing short of a resounding humiliation for France and Spain. By its provisions, France transferred Canada to British sovereignty, while Spain gave Florida to Great Britain. In addition, French Louisiana became Spanish, primarily because the British did not want France to retain this province but did not desire it for themselves. British diplomats instead felt that the administration and military defense of Louisiana would further debilitate an already weakened Spanish colonial presence in North America.

The Spanish King and his ministers smarted badly from the indignities that the Peace of Paris thrust upon them, and they sought international revenge. The British colonial crisis of the 1760s and 1770s, followed by the American Revolution, provided a ready-made and unsolicited weapon by which they could assist in humbling Great Britain. Spanish assistance to the Patriot cause would set in motion a series of events that would surely weaken the underpinnings of the British Empire. At the same time, Spain had to guard against provoking the wrath of the British, who might retaliate and attack Spanish possessions in repayment for assisting the rebels. Given this need for maintaining such a balance, Spanish involvement in the events of the Revolutionary era fell into three distinct chronological periods—the years of Spanish observation in British America, 1763 to 1775; the era of Spanish neutrality, 1775 to 1779; and the period of open warfare, 1779 to 1783.

In the 15 years before the American Revolution, Spain employed a variety of methods to observe events in British North America. Her motivation in so doing was to provide advance notice of any surprise attack against her New World dominions, especially Cuba and her Caribbean possessions. The captain general of Cuba,

and his military subordinate, the governor of Louisiana, directed this surveillance from their bases in Havana and New Orleans, respectively. The captain general used the commercial fishing fleet based in Cuba to monitor English shipping in the region, while he employed a Catholic priest in Florida, Father Pedro Camps, to furnish information about events there. The captain general also enlisted merchants from the *Asiento de Negroes*, Spain's slave-trading monopoly, to solicit information when they visited British ports. In addition, a Spanish subject named Luciano de Herrera remained behind in St. Augustine when Spain vacated that city to the British. Herrera became an important spy for the captain general, furnishing much information before and during the Revolution.

The governor of Louisiana, especially Luis de Unzaga in the period from 1770 until 1776, also served as an important Spanish spy master whose employees and agents observed events in British America. Unzaga closely monitored the settlement of West Florida, especially the Mississippi River districts around Baton Rouge and Natchez. He often visited with Englishmen passing New Orleans on the river and, upon occasion, sent confidants to Pensacola and Mobile in order to gather covertly news about events in the British colonies. In 1772, the Louisiana governor dispatched a spy to New York and Philadelphia. This individual, Juan de Surriret, reported on problems in those colonies stemming from colonial dissatisfaction with the New Colonial Policy. He also noted the state of military preparedness in British areas, especially West Florida.

By 1775, Spain had long been following the growing political disorders in British North America. Her policymakers at court, based on information developed by the captain general of Cuba's espionage network, had decided upon a course of action well before Lexington and Concord. Spain would remain neutral. At the same time, she would give secret and subtle encouragement to the rebel Americans. This would encourage them to resist British authority, thereby weakening Great Britain internationally. At the same time, however, Spain would avoid taking any action in support of the Patriots that might offend the British. This would provide the Spanish military ample time to prepare for war, with Spain's actual entry into the conflict occurring at the most opportune time possible should she eventually choose to become a belligerent.

In the process, the Spanish King and his ministers formulated their particular goals for the war with Great Britain that the Revolutionary crisis might bring. First, they wanted a return of Gibraltar in the Mediterranean from British control, a possession they had lost at the Peace of Utrecht in 1713. Second, Spain wanted to regain the Floridas and clear the British from the lower Mississippi Valley and the coasts of the Gulf of Mexico. Third, they hoped to clear the eastern coast of Central America of the British logwood-cutting establishments that had been located there. Fourth, they desired to end the special trading privileges granted to British merchants operating in Spanish America by earlier treaties ending previous intercolonial wars. Fifth, they hoped after 1776 that the American Revolutionaries would successfully win their independence, thereby diminishing the size of the British Empire. In this latter category, however, Spain clearly did not support the concept of rebellion against the authority of monarchy, something that as the largest colonial power in the Americas she found repugnant. Her policy of secret help to the rebels came not from solidarity with the American cause (something that Spain never embraced), but out of powerful hatred for Great Britain.

The outbreak of fighting in Massachusetts in 1775 created much debate at the Spanish court regarding the policy Spain should follow in responding to the revolt. Two schools of thought emerged: the Marquis de Grimaldi, the foreign minister, favored neutrality, while the Conde de Aranda, the ambassador to France, advised joining the French in declaring war against Great Britain. Grimaldi and his followers prevailed, especially since Spain was then fighting Portugal over a territorial dispute in South America and this consumed her military resources. Nonetheless, the Aranda faction was successful in convincing the Spanish King to join with France in providing secret funds and supplies for the rebels. The American envoy Arthur Lee unofficially visited Spain and secured from the Spanish government a million *livre* loan along with an agreement to ship military supplies to the Americans via Havana and New Orleans. In all, approximately $200,000 in war material and supplies reached the rebel armies by this means.

During this time, Spanish observation of North America continued. Spanish colonial minister Jose de Galvez superintended from his office in Spain an active espionage operation directed in the Americas by the captain general of Cuba in Havana. Agents gathering information about the course of the Revolution secretly visited Jamaica, West and East Florida, Virginia, and Philadelphia in their successful efforts to ascertain the nature of the rebellion and gauge the ability of the rebels to gain victory. Luciano de Herrera, Juan Eligio de la Puente, Miguel Eduardo, Bartolome Beauregard, Juan de Miralles, and Antonio Raffelin all served as important agents in this intelligence service. The information that they provided convinced Jose de Galvez to increase secret assistance to the American rebels. The minister's nephew, Louisiana governor Bernardo de Galvez, became an important ally for the American cause as New Orleans emerged as a significant supply base for the Americans during 1777 and 1778. In that latter year, the Continental Congress appointed New Orleans merchant and Patriot Oliver Pollock as its official commercial agent. He worked closely with Bernardo de Galvez in finding ways to support the rebel cause without openly compromising Spain's official neutrality in the conflict.

During late 1777, the captain general of Cuba dispatched Havana merchant Juan de Miralles to Philadelphia as an agent in the secret intelligence-gathering network. Miralles had the task of providing regular reports on events at the Continental Congress while he ostensibly occupied himself with a mercantile business that shipped flour and foodstuffs to the Caribbean and Spain from colonial markets. This agent, a vocal partisan of the rebel cause, quickly forged firm friendships with important Patriot leaders, including Henry Laurens, John Jay, George Washington, and Robert Morris. Within a year of residence in Pennsylvania, Miralles became Spain's unofficial spokesperson and, although he carefully refrained from implying that he had any official standing with the Spanish government, most Americans treated him as an unaccredited envoy co-equal with the French ambassador. The Spaniard accordingly articulated a wide variety of foreign policy positions that would eventually determine the initial issues of early diplomatic relations between the United States and Spain. For example, he advocated that the Floridas be returned to Spain, that the United States be denied "full and free" navigation of the Mississippi River, and that the eastern boundary of Louisiana extend well into the trans-Appalachian interior of the Ohio, Cumberland, and Tennessee River valleys. Upon his death in 1780, Miralles was replaced by Francisco Rendon, who served as Spain's unofficial observer in Philadelphia until the end of the Revolution.

Meanwhile, the Marquis de Floridablanca had replaced Grimaldi as Spanish foreign minister in 1777. This new advisor at court, like his predecessor, also favored neutrality, but he demanded a more aggressive foreign policy for Spain regarding her potential involvement in the Revolution. France's entry into the war in early 1778 placed additional pressures on Spain since King Charles and his ministers refused to join with the French in either allying with the rebels or declaring war against the British. Floridablanca instead preferred to increase his nation's military preparedness in the Americas and continue to press for diplomatic advantage in Europe. He saw the Revolution as a chance to increase Spanish influence and prestige internationally to a far greater extent than had Grimaldi. In the fall of 1778, Floridablanca presided over a special meeting of the Spanish council of ministers, a group that composed the King's important advisors. This group agreed to play a dangerous diplomatic game with Great Britain. Spain offered to mediate with France to bring an end to the war in return for an agreement resolving possession of Gibraltar, Minorca, and Florida, along with trade concessions and an end to British commercial intrusions in Central America. The British refused this offer, and Spain had little choice but to ally herself formally with France, which she did in April 1779. These two traditional British rivals signed the Treaty of Aranjuez, by which they agreed to fight Great Britain as a common foe without making a separate peace until Gibraltar was returned to Spain. This agreement began a deteriorating diplomatic crisis in Europe that resulted in Spain declaring war on Great Britain on June 21, 1779. Spain did not, however, make an alliance with the United States because the Spanish court had a basic distrust of the rebel Americans. Floridablanca was especially convinced that the threatening implications of revolution being advanced by the Patriots might eventually spread to the Hispanic colonies of Latin America. As well, he was convinced that an independent United States would simply replace Great Britain as a North American rival, especially in the Mississippi Valley, along the Gulf Coast, and in Caribbean trade. Hence, there would be no alliance with the United States, and Spain did not recognize the young Republic until after the Revolution.

Jose de Galvez had given his nephew in Louisiana advance word during the summer of 1779 that Spain would be declaring war against Great Britain. Bernardo de Galvez was therefore very well prepared to embark on immediate military attacks against British West Florida once word of belligerency formally arrived at New Orleans. In late August, he began a series of military campaigns that would give Spain control of the entire lower Mississippi Valley and all of the northern coast of the Gulf of Mexico. During the fall, his army successfully took the British settlements at Manchac, Baton Rouge, and Natchez, thus clearing the British from the Mississippi. The following year, Galvez commanded a victorious army at Mobile, and after his forces recovered from the destruction of a hurricane, he conquered Pensacola in the spring of 1781. Enobled by the King for these victories, Bernardo de Galvez achieved for Spain some of her important North American war goals. Additional skirmishes occurred in the Mississippi Valley, but without major significance. For example, a British force attacked St. Louis in 1780 without taking the post while the Spanish captured Fort St. Joseph near Detroit in January 1781. None of these engagements, however, detracted or added to the net success of Bernardo de Galvez.

The American Revolution saw more limited military successes for Spain in Central America, where British logwood cutters had long dominated the Mosquito Coast. In 1779, Spanish armies commanded by Matias de Galvez, father of the Louisiana governor, successfully drove the English occupiers from Belize and Rotan, although his forces were unable to clear the Mosquito Coast itself of British interlopers. The British thereafter launched a counterattack against Spain's holdings in the interior of present-day Nicaragua while they also captured the stronghold at Omoa. By 1782, Matias de Galvez was able to dislodge his British adversaries from these locations, but they remained in possession of various coastal settlements for the remainder of the Revolution.

Spain's military campaigns in the West Indies also achieved mixed results in terms of fulfilling her war goals. For example, the capture of Jamaica was an important Spanish priority that was never realized. Bernardo de Galvez, fresh from his victory at Pensacola, spent much of 1781 and 1782 organizing a major expedition against Kingston. This attack, however, never took place because of various complications. Field Marshal Juan Maria de Cagigal did enjoy a bloodless success with his invasion of New Providence Island in the Bahamas. On April 22, 1782, he and his force arrived off the island and requested that the British commander surrender. This the British officer did in the face of superior numbers. In early May, Cagigal signed a capitulation by which the British turned over to Spain all of the Bahama Islands.

Foreign Minister Floridablanca continued to press for Spanish diplomatic advantages during the years of Spain's military participation in conflict with Great Britain. Even as Spain entered the conflict, he was engaged in discussions on this matter with Richard Cumberland, Great Britain's envoy at Madrid. King George III, however, consistently refused to consider returning Gibraltar, and it thus became Spain's primary military goal in Europe. The joint Spanish-French siege of Gibraltar from 1779 to 1783 became the longest and one of the largest military campaigns of the War of the Revolution. This "Great Siege," as it is still known in Mediterranean history, began on June 21, 1779, when Spanish army and navy forces blockaded the British garrison. General George Elliot commanded a force of approximately 5,400 English troops, along with 1,300 German mercenaries. Since they were so well ensconced behind impregnable bastions on the rock itself, Spanish strategy called for a slow starvation of the British defenders. The emperor of Morocco, however, was neutral in this conflict and, because of the proximity of Tangier and Ceuta, the Spanish and French were accordingly never able to maintain a secure blockage of Gibraltar from the sea. Supplies and reinforcements were often able to slip across the straits from Morocco for General Elliot's forces. Most notable among these relief expeditions was that led by Admiral Sir George Rodney in January 1780. Rodney landed several new regiments along with over a year's worth of supplies and material. The month of September 1782 witnessed the most concentrated and prolonged bombardment of the Revolutionary era. The attackers had 186 artillery pieces on land, augmented by 142 floating batteries, all of which went into action on September 13. The Spanish hills around Gibraltar were crowded with spectators who had come to see the spectacle, including the King of France's brother, the Comte d'Artois. Both sides fired red-hot shot, and casualties were very heavy. By the end of the month, the attackers had spent all of their energies without success. The arrival of Admiral Lord Richard Howe's fleet early in the following month ended this bombardment of the British positions. Floridablanca, however, decided to continue the siege of Gibraltar into 1783 in an effort to gain a bargaining position at the peace talks of that year and, hence, peace did not come to the rock until the formal treaties ending the war were signed.

Most of Floridablanca's activities during the 1780s concentrated on diplomacy rather than concern with military affairs. The Continental Congress had appointed John Jay as its official envoy to Spain September 27, 1779. Jay and his family arrived in Spain early the following year and remained until the spring of 1782. His instructions charged him with negotiating a formal alliance with Spain, something King Charles and his ministers (especially Floridablanca) refused to consider. For that reason, Floridablanca and Jay engaged in a series of meetings that were frustrating and unsatisfactory to the American diplomat. The Spanish minister steadfastly refused to consider any action that could be interpreted as a formal diplomatic recognition of the United States, let alone consider an alliance. Jay did secure loans in the amount of almost $200,000, so his mission was not a complete failure although he never achieved his diplomatic goals.

Floridablanca was more interested in Spain's role in postwar European diplomacy than in allying with the United States, a nation whose republican values he found repugnant. For that reason, Spain joined the League of Armed Neutrality in 1781, and by the following year, Floridablanca spent most of his energies anticipating the peace negotiations. Spain's approach to the treaty discussions in Paris clearly showed that she viewed the United States as simply a new territorial rival, replacing Great Britain in that role after 1783. The signing of separate treaties frustrated some of Spain's desires to work maximum advantage from the negotiations, but this development also insured postwar boundary problems between the United States and Spanish Louisiana. The Anglo-American treaty set the southern boundary of the new Republic as the 31st parallel, while Spain contended the northern boundary of her Florida territory ran almost 100 miles northward along the line 32° 22'. This guaranteed that the 1780s would be a time of territorial dispute between the United States and Spain. Indeed it was.

In 1785, Spain sent Diego de Gardogui to the United States as her first accredited diplomat envoy to the young nation. The Spanish diplomat's primary purpose was the negotiation of a treaty resolving this territorial dispute. During the year following, he negotiated with John Jay on this question and the matter of free American navigation on the Mississippi as it passed through Spanish territory. These discussions failed to produce an accord. It would not be until the Treaty of San Lorenzo (Pinckney's Treaty) in 1795 that Spain would recognize the legitimacy of the 31st parallel as the southern boundary of the United States, permit free American navigation on the Mississippi River, and give United States citizens the duty-free "right of deposit" at New Orleans for their goods in transshipment to Atlantic ports from the trans-Appalachian river system. *See also*: Charles III; Convention of Aranjuez

Light Townsend Cummins

REFERENCES

Jose A. Armillas Vicente, *El Mississippi: frontera de Espana: Espana y los Estados Unidos ante el tratdo de San Lorenzo* (1977); Manual Conrotte, *La intervencion de Espana en la independencia de los Estados Unidos de la America del Norte* (1920); Manuel Davila y Collado, *Reinado de Carlos III*, 6 vols. (1891–96); Miguel Gomez Campillo, ed., *Relaciones diplomaticas entre Espana y los Estados Unidos segun los documentos del archivo historico nacional*, 2 vols. (1944); Juan J.F. Yela Utrilla, *Espana ante la independencia de los Estados Unidos*, 2 vols. (1925).

Spencer's Ordinary, Virginia, Engagement at (June 28, 1781)

This little known engagement is of significance to the War of Revolution for the following reasons:

1. This was the first actual encounter between a main portion of the Marquis de Lafayette's American army and a major part of General Lord Cornwallis's force in the Virginia campaign of 1781.

2. This action involved some of the more famous light infantry officers and troops on both sides. Lieutenant Colonel John Graves Simcoe and his Queen's Rangers played a major role as did their allies, the Hessian Jaegers, under the command of Captain Johann Ewald. Colonel Richard Butler, the American commander, had won glory in the storming of Stony Point and was Daniel Morgan's second in command during the battles against Burgoyne. Lafayette believed that the American light infantry under Butler was the best infantry of its kind. The dragoons and grenadiers and riflemen also had their part to play. Spencer's Ordinary pitted the elite from both armies against each other.

3. While both sides claimed victory, the results of the American surprise attack gave Cornwallis notice that the rebel force facing him in Virginia was no longer the makeshift militia that he had so easily brushed aside in the recent weeks of raiding. Once again, the possibilities of additional disaster such as Cowpens and King's Mountain faced Cornwallis. His concern may also explain his hesitation to close his trap on Lafayette at Green Spring several days later. Whatever the strength of Lafayette's force, and no matter how he mocked "the boy," Cornwallis acted carefully with the Americans as if he respected their potential.

4. A combination of General Sir Henry Clinton's meddling interference in the campaign and the growing threat from Lafayette gradually robbed Cornwallis of the initiative and eventually led the British into a passive defense of a post along the banks of the York River, while forces beyond Cornwallis's control massed to determine his destiny in America.

By the middle of June, Cornwallis had ended his raiding. He concentrated his army, destroyed the Elk Hill Plantation, and marched through Richmond. The British continued eastward to the former capital of Virginia at Williamsburg, where Cornwallis hoped to receive additional instructions from Clinton, the British commander in North America, as to what action the southern British army should now take in its pursuit of the war. Clinton's communications had been confusing and contradictory. Cornwallis hoped the new orders would soon become clearer.

Lafayette and his force, numbering about 4,500 men, followed along behind, keeping about 20 miles' distance between the 2 forces as the British moved toward Williamsburg. Lafayette had every hope of luring Cornwallis into battle on favorable terms. But the British general declined an action and ignored Lafayette. Banastre Tarleton and his Green Horse Dragoons served as an effective rear guard.

Once Cornwallis received his orders from Clinton, then he could act. If Clinton permitted a concentrated Virginia campaign, then Cornwallis could turn and destroy Lafayette. If Clinton ordered Cornwallis to send troops back to New York, then other measures would have to be considered.

Lafayette did his best to create the impression that his force was larger and more powerful than it was in order to fool Cornwallis. But there were too many spies operating in the Virginia countryside representing both sides to fool either general. Cornwallis and Lafayette knew each other's strengths.

Cornwallis reached Williamsburg with the main portion of his army on June 25. A large detachment under the command of Simcoe had been sent on a burning and foraging mission to the Chickahominy River area on June 23. These troops had collected a large number of cattle that they were driving into Williamsburg, and they had burned tobacco and other crops along the way. In the early morning of June 26, Simcoe's force was only six miles out of Williamsburg when they arrived at Spencer's Ordinary.

Captain Ewald had halted the men to rest the horses and eat breakfast along the road in front of Spencer's (an ordinary was a type of tavern that served common people plain fare at reasonable prices). Simcoe was in the rear watching for American raiding parties and joined up with Ewald's men while they were still resting at Spencer's. It was a peaceful but hot summer morning, and Ewald was asleep when the Americans struck the unsuspecting British.

Lafayette had moved his army to Bird's Tavern, ten miles out of Williamsburg, and was headquartered at Tyre's Plantation. Spencer's Ordinary was just about halfway between the two

armies. Hearing of Simcoe's mission from scouts, Lafayette decided to send out a large force to trap Simcoe and destroy him. Tarleton, guarding the rear, had his men north of Simcoe's men at Spencer's, and he never detected the American detachment under Colonel Richard Butler. Thus Simcoe received no warning. The Americans marched all night and came to within an hour of the British in the final darkness before daybreak. When Simcoe and Ewald halted for breakfast, the delay provided Butler's men with enough time to catch up.

There were two American divisions under the overall command of General Anthony Wayne out hunting Simcoe's column. But the summer heat (even at night) and the fast-paced pursuit were too much for one column. It did not move quickly enough to cooperate with Butler's men, who arrived on the scene first. Guided by a local resident who had been sent out by Simcoe to find the Americans, Butler came upon the resting British force at Spencer's

Lafayette's original plan was to cut the road between Cornwallis and Simcoe, attack on the flank, get into Simcoe's rear, and destroy his elite force. Butler, noting his advantage and afraid of losing it, decided to move in without waiting for the other American column. He attacked.

Fortunately for Simcoe, the Americans had been too fast in their pursuit. Major William McPherson had mounted 50 light infantry and, along with 50 of his dragoons, had ridden hard after the British. The American horsemen suddenly came upon the British outposts and charged. McPherson did not wait until Colonel Butler could bring the rest of his command up into position. This premature and excited cavalry charge saved the British column from being overwhelmed.

The British outposts came riding into camp crying out the alarm. As the Americans charged down the Jamestown Road after the pickets, they failed to note the unmounted British horsemen resting in a field to the right of the road. Seeing the pickets retreating and spreading the alarm, the British cavalry (mounted rangers) saddled up and charged unexpectedly into the Americans with such force that Major McPherson was knocked from his horse by the shock of the British charge. Vicious saber-to-saber fighting took place, which allowed McPherson to escape unwounded. The fighting also saved the British left flank from being turned. Simcoe took command here, rallied his men, and soon had the American horsemen in retreat. At the same time, Simcoe sent a rider to Cornwallis in Williamsburg for assistance.

The gunfire and shouting awakened Ewald from his sleep. He immediately formed companies of the rangers, the light infantry, the grenadiers, and his Jaegers in line in the fields by the road at Spencer's and moved them north toward the Ordinary's orchard. It was here that fast approaching American riflemen of Majors Call and Willis ran into Ewald's line. Noting that his line overlapped the Americans on their left, he ordered his Jaegers to flank the Americans and strike their rear. Captain Ewald then turned to the British light infantry and grenadiers and ordered a bayonet charge to shock the Americans.

Flanked on their left and attacked in the front with the bayonet, the American riflemen still took their toll of the attacking enemy. They waited until the British line was but 40 yards off when they unleashed their volley into the line. Nearly half the grenadiers went down, but the British held to their advance. However, without bayonets, the riflemen were unable to withstand the charge. They fell back into the cover of the woods, closely followed by Ewald's force.

Ewald believed in the use of the offensive whenever possible. He now seized the initiative away from the attacking Americans. Before the American riflemen and their support were ready to open their attack, the American cavalry had ruined the American plan. Once alerted, Ewald immediately ordered the advance, and threw the Americans into confusion. Ewald felt that most of Lafayette's army was there. He felt that when an issue such as this one was in doubt, it was vital to take the offensive. Had he not attacked that morning, his men would have run in panic.

As the American riflemen fell back, Ewald felt vindicated and confident. With Simcoe taking care of the left and his troops handling the right, Ewald pressed home his advantage. Yet his flanking force of Jaegers became dispersed in the woods, losing their cohesion and firepower. The smoke of the musketry hung low in the woods and visibility was quite limited. Lack of intelligence and the confusion of battle now began to hinder the British advance. Ewald's men began to lose their momentum.

On both flanks the Americans had been driven back in a hot fight characterized by hand-to-

hand fighting. The riflemen and cavalry had retreated, but they were soon in contact with Colonel Butler's Continental light infantry line that advanced to the support of the retreating men. Ewald now realized that his opponents now outnumbered him and were of a different caliber of soldier than heretofore engaged. He called his men back and requested that Simcoe order a retreat.

Simcoe agreed and ordered his command to retire along the Williamsburg Road. They made it two miles down the road when they met Cornwallis coming out of Williamsburg to their support. This was not the Cornwallis who risked much in the "race to the Dan" earlier that year. The British general could have ordered a full advance with Simcoe's men leading the way and fought a pitched battle with the Americans then and there. He decided against that choice. Simcoe's men had been handled roughly and there was no reliable intelligence on the Americans. He could not afford to lose men when Clinton was expecting them in New York.

The Americans had not pursued Simcoe in his retreat because Butler knew the Americans on the field were not equal to Cornwallis's strength. Butler did not want to bring on a general engagement at this point. Wayne was not up in support just yet, and Lafayette would have had to sacrifice his advanced corps. This was not the time or place for a full-scale battle. The Americans claimed a victory and returned to Tyre's Plantation and Bird's Tavern to observe what Cornwallis would do next.

Cornwallis led the army back to Spencer's. Simcoe also claimed that he had won a sizable victory. But he had retreated, leaving his dead and wounded behind. He also specifically had avoided giving battle to the American light infantry. Being outnumbered was not usually a British excuse for a retreat unless they had more respect for the American regular line than they cared to admit. They may have believed they were fighting against Lafayette's entire army but that only reflects well on Butler's handling of his men and their conduct in battle. While Cornwallis shielded the area, the British dead and wounded were removed.

Cornwallis commended both Simcoe and Ewald for their actions at Spencer's Ordinary in his dispatches. Simcoe admitted to 10 killed and 23 wounded. Lafayette claimed there were 60

British killed and over 100 wounded. The British claimed they captured 3 officers and 28 privates. The Americans admitted to 9 killed, 14 wounded, and 14 missing. It is difficult to determine what the real figures were.

Cornwallis returned to Williamsburg. Instead of gaining a free hand, he received orders to ship some of his best troops to New York City to reinforce Clinton who felt himself surrounded by the French and American armies and the French fleet. New York and not Virginia would be the center of British power as long as Clinton commanded.

These orders only added to the conflict between Clinton and Cornwallis over the conduct of the war. Cornwallis took his time in Williamsburg making preparations to move to the coast while Lafayette moved his camp almost daily to avoid being caught by surprise and keep the British under observation. Spencer's Ordinary became the opening act in the drama that would play itself out less than four months later at Yorktown.

Paul J. Sanborn

REFERENCES

Robert D. Bass, *The Green Dragoon* (1957); *Captain Johann Ewald, Diary of the American War*, trans. by Joseph P. Tustin (1979); Henry P. Johnson, *The Yorktown Campaign* (1881); Benson J. Lossing, *The Pictorial Field Book of the Revolution*, 2 vols. (1851–52), rpr. 1972; Christopher Ward, *The War of the Revolution*, 2 vols. (1952); Franklin and Mary Wickwire, *Cornwallis, the American Adventure* (1970).

Sports and Games (Continental Army)

"I went a chesnuting with a number of respectable gentlemen that belonged to the army and we had a rifle frolick." So wrote Massachusetts minuteman Samuel Haws on October 13, 1775. He and his fellow soldiers had spent the afternoon boasting of their talents with muskets and substantiating their claims by shooting at a target, risking winning or losing bets of liquor. Revolutionary soldiers relied on recreation such as this to relieve them from the stresses of combat.

Ironically, at the time of the Revolution, Continental Army officers did not realize the impact that recreation had on enhancing morale. In fact, many officers viewed summer sports such as ball played in the tepid weather as unhealthy and attempted to limit such activity. Haws remarked that a "Lieutenant Foster had Likt [*sic*] to have been put under guard for playing ball." Officers expected soldiers to refrain from recreation on Sundays and to attend religious services, and at all times gambling was prohibited. This ban included such favorite pursuits as billiards, cards, and pitch penny; however, the soldiers continued to hold secret matches away from the surveillance of their superiors.

Revolutionary recreation was basically informal and unorganized. Spontaneously, men participated in spur-of-the-moment activities that relieved tension, provided fraternal companionship, and represented their selection of preferred behavior, allowing them control over a fraction of their lives in a system that strictly regulated soldiers' actions. General George Washington expressed that he preferred his officers study tactics during their spare time and that enlisted men should train during any leisure hours they had. Yet, Washington regarded some outdoor recreation as invigorating and useful for the Revolutionary cause because open-air, team sports improved physical health as well as uplifted emotions and strengthened morale.

Continental soldiers enjoyed both communal and solitary recreational pursuits. Some games required mental skill, such as backgammon, chess, checkers, dominoes, and cards. Darts demanded a good eye and agility, and other sports entailed muscular strength and speed. Soldiers played shinny, a game resembling hockey using curved sticks and blocks of wood, and football and baseball. Tug-of-war was a popular year-round pastime.

Horse and foot races provided opportunities to exercise, to exhibit athletic prowess, and to bet and drink. Boxing and wrestling were another form of diversion. Soldiers would strip off their clothing and pummel each other in a designated area. Often in the winter, the frozen slush absorbed blood from the wounded participants.

Recreation was seasonal. Joseph Wood, a Rhode Island soldier, recalled a snowball fight held in his camp. "The snow was wet and would pack very hard. Many of the soldiers got hurt, and the blood ran freely, and the battle became so warm and so much in earnest that the officers interposed and stopped it." In the winters, soldiers enjoyed skating on ponds and rivers, riding in sleighs, sledding, ice fishing, and hunting for game.

Spring and summer offered opportunities for swimming, fishing, boating, and hunting. New Jersey soldier William Lloyd stated his company enjoyed "diverting ourselves by riding horses in the millpond there [Tinton Falls] and sliding off of them and taking them by the tails, and they would draw us after them." Autumn ushered in cooler weather and chances to hunt for migrating game.

Holidays, such as Christmas, Thanksgiving, and May Day, and anniversaries of significant Revolutionary dates were either celebrated with ceremonies, balls, and feasts or ignored depending on the military situation of each camp. Most soldiers were relieved of full-duties on holidays if possible. The Fourth of July was recognized with speeches and 13 shots from muskets and cannon to symbolize each rebelling colony. Soldiers partook in games and imbibed rum provided by commanding officers. The anniversary of Burgoyne's surrender was noted with fireworks and games as was the announcement of the French alliance. The release of a prisoner or stay of execution sparked jubilant celebration, representing the stresses and relief each soldier felt vicariously in the experience.

Rank often determined the level of recreation. Officers received more privileges than enlisted personnel. Officers' wives were also frequently present in camp, arranging parties and social events. Officers tended to play sports like cricket and had permission to embark on hunting expeditions, but enlisted men who could pursue their chosen but forbidden activities without arousing attention or being caught did so.

Some soldiers found that watching other men being punished was entertaining. They also enjoyed arranging pranks and practical jokes on their peers and ridiculing, taunting, and obscenely gesturing toward both Continental and British soldiers. Soldiers competed with local Indians in contests of bow and arrow shooting.

Unusual diversions included shooting into clusters of bats, watching the aurora borealis, collecting oysters, and pigeon hunting, depending on the geographic region in which each soldier was stationed. Many soldiers kept pets for companionship and amusement. Pets also became food when rations were unavailable or meager. Races between cockroaches and lice were held, with soldiers eagerly betting on the out-

come. Men enjoyed gathering war mementoes such as enemy cannonballs and artillery shells after battles.

Storytelling was another form of entertainment. Tall tales, ghost stories (many of the ghosts had been seen in camp or while the narrator was on guard duty), and humorous stories were popular. Speeches, debates, and spelling bees also passed time, and food was a source of diversion when barbecues and banquets were scheduled to provide both recess and nourishment for the men.

Soldiers spent their leisure time whittling and working with their hands, producing various arts and crafts. They amused themselves by etching designs in their powder horns, procured from bovines. This handiwork had been practiced in the French and Indian War; soldiers carved designs, using their knives to scratch the keratin, such as landscapes, buildings, or personal names. One horn warned: "Steel not this Horn For Fear of Shame, For on it is the Oners [*sic*] name."

Some soldiers, bored away from battle, enjoyed firing their muskets and flintlocks for fun in mock battles. Drummer boys and fife players, who did not engage directly in real battles, particularly relished playing war. Washington lamented in 1776 on the men's careless behavior, "Seldom a day passes but some persons are shot by their friends." Duels between Continental officers became frequent during the Valley Forge winter as they felt obligated to defend the honor of friends or themselves.

Other recreations encompassed the intellectual sector. Soldiers voraciously read novels and plays, often sharing these works with others, but as Major John Singer Dexter complained, "I have seen the Soldier who owns the letters of Eloisa and Abelard and no arguments or offers of Satisfaction could prevail on him to part with them." Camp newspapers as well as tabloids from nearby cities provided news, parodies, and resources for camp discussions.

Music was another outlet. Soldiers sang ballads, usually hymns or patriotic or love songs, and played instruments, violins, flutes, and fifes being the most common. One British prisoner complained about "the noise of the American soldiers who vociferate their songs so loud that the whole house rings with War and Washington, a favourite ballad." Alone, soldiers jotted letters home to wives, parents, children, and friends, or composed narratives of their interpretations of the war and their individual adventures in journals and diaries.

Dramatic productions provided an outlet for soldiers to adopt temporarily another identity and act out aggressions or other emotions they might feel. Soldiers presented plays to entertain local audiences as well as attending local productions.

Drinking was the most popular recreation, with drinking games and visits to taverns often being noted in soldiers' journals. Haws remembered after one drinking bout "we came home and there was a high go of Drinking Brandy and several of the company were taken not well prety [sic] soon after." Toasts, usually poking fun at others in camp, were another favored diversion. The men also savored smoking and dancing.

Soldiers delighted in flirting, teasing, and pursuing women. A blushing Haws, alluding to a personal encounter, penned this journal entry on October 26, 1775: "This morning early their [sic] was several Laidies [sic] came down from wrentham and they went to cambridg [sic] and the rest of their acts are they not written in the Lamentations of Samuel Haws, finis."

Veterans' organizations, such as the Saint Tammany Society, named for an Indian sachem, were organized before the war concluded, with active membership in many regiments. These groups were created in order to provide for soldiers and their families during and after the war. Soldiers eagerly participated in such organized merrymaking as parading at Valley Forge around a Maypole.

Games and recreation provided camouflage for both colonists and British soldiers. Haws remembered standing guard for his camp near a creek where "their [sic] was 3 Boston men came out under pretence of fishing but they made their escape to Dorchester point." Spies pretended to be fishermen, swam across bodies of water, or secured information while enthusiastically participating in drinking and tavern games. The allusion of having fun often clouded the judgment of men, permitting a prisoner or deserter to escape.

Recreation was an escape mechanism for Continental soldiers, providing them opportunities to release frustration, anger, and belligerence off the battlefield. Sport also encouraged fraternal ties, pulling soldiers together into a bonded fighting force. Without recreation, Continental morale would have seriously declined.

The variety of games and sport pursued by Revolutionary soldiers indicates their desire to seek normality and comfort by familiar activity during war, as well as the right to control a portion of their time by selecting their mode of recreation, while the extremes of drinking and aggression indicate the raw stresses, tedium, and boredom of war that plagued the common soldier.

Elizabeth D. Schafer

REFERENCES

Charles K. Bolton, *The Private Soldier Under Washington* (1902); Allen Bowman, *The Morale of the American Revolutionary Army* (1943); John C. Dann, ed., *The Revolution Remembered: Eyewitness Accounts of the War for Independence* (1980); Joseph Plumb Martin, *Private Yankee Doodle: Being a Narrative of Some of the Adventures, Dangers and Sufferings of a Revolutionary Soldier*, ed. by George F. Scheer (1962); Charles Royster, *A Revolutionary People at War: The Continental Army and American Character, 1775–1783* (1979); Abraham Tomlinson, *The Military Journals of Two Private Soldiers 1758–1775* (1971).

Springfield and Connecticut Farms, New Jersey, Raids at (June 1780)

These two strong British raiding expeditions sought to destroy both Washington's main army and also the valuable supplies and arms at the American base at Morristown, New Jersey. Their response to these attacks was the New Jersey militia's finest hour.

The origin of these raids lay with the Loyalist informers in Jersey who reported that the American cause was on the verge of collapse in the spring of 1780. Soaring inflation had ruined the currency, along with some very active British counterfeiting. The countryside was coming out of the most severe winter in the century. The American army at Morristown had almost starved to death. In any event, desertion and the expiration of enlistments had reduced Washington's force to less than 4,000 able-bodied men. Recruitment could not replace the missing men, and the pay for the soldiers was months behind. The 4th and 8th Connecticut regiments had mutinied in May over the lack of food and pay. If the British would only move, then the Loyalists of New Jersey, hiding all these years, would appear and flock to the King's banners. The same old siren song heard so many times throughout the war was being sung once more.

This time though it was different. There were many in the British camp who wanted to believe these things. In fact, the Loyalists were right. All the problems besetting the Americans were generally true. Former New York governor William Tryon and William Smith, a well-connected New York Loyalist, all advocated a violent, destructive war against the small number of rebels in Jersey. Then the rest of America would come back into the fold. They cried for a "no quarter" war. General Henry Clinton had difficulties in trying to control them.

Joining this group in New York City was General James Robertson, an elderly, shrewd veteran of many military conflicts, who supported the Loyalists in their demands. He had helped to ease General William Howe's departure from the war, and now he was after General Henry Clinton, whom he hated. He opposed Clinton's style of warfare, vicious as it was, and wanted a change in policy. When General Clinton sailed south on December 25, 1779, with a large portion of his British army to lay siege to Charleston, South Carolina, this group of Loyalists became even more active.

Left in command at New York City was the Hessian general Wilhelm von Knyphausen. General Tryon was second in command. Pressure was immediately brought to bear on the German general. The militia was useless and could easily be dispersed, it was claimed. There were too few Continentals with Washington. The people would welcome the royal standards. Knyphausen conducted several raids along the Jersey coast but planned no major operations. Then word arrived that Clinton had successfully captured Charleston. The Loyalists cried that "The Knight," as they called Clinton, was winning the war all by himself in the South. Something in the North must also be accomplished.

Pressure was increased on Knyphausen to do something significant in the Jersies. With the intelligence he had, Knyphausen realized that the picture the Loyalists had painted of the rebels was not far from the truth. But the German was in a difficult position. He was not English. It was the English who controlled all operations in the war.

There was a distinct pecking order among the officers of both armies, German and English. This was one of the few times in the war when a German general had been left in command of a major garrison. He had no orders from Clinton. The indirect news was that Clinton had done well in the South, but no news had come directly from his excellency. In the end, Knyphausen decided to act. He would attack Jersey.

Just as these plans were being formulated, Clinton's aide, Major William Crosbie, arrived from the South. He carried no orders from Sir Henry. Clinton did not like to write out orders that later could come back to haunt him. He had a plan and Crosbie knew it. But Clinton was also secretive and wished to keep the plan hidden until he was ready to set it in motion. Crosbie felt he had to keep quiet and not inform Knyphausen as to what Clinton was planning. Crosbie believed that Knyphausen and the officers who surrounded him were not trustworthy. He would, however, accompany the British column into Jersey.

Knyphausen on the other hand assumed that Clinton would attack Virginia on the way north and that a strong New Jersey raid would aid in this action by pinning Washington down and creating a diversion. Crosbie arrived on June 5, and Knyphausen was ready to move the next day with 6,000 men. From Staten Island the British were ferried across Arthur Kill to Elizabeth's Point and began their march toward the Short Hills and Hobart Gap on June 7. Eleven miles past this gap lay Morristown, Knyphausen's goal. In the middle between Hobart Gap and Elizabethtown lay Connecticut Farms.

Washington did not have the troops to stop this expedition, to cover all of Jersey, and to protect the Hudson Highlands too. But he did call out the militia and sent what troops he could to delay the British advance. Even Washington's Life Guard was dispatched. At Elizabethtown, the van of the British army under the command of General Thomas Sterling, the 47-year-old commandant of Staten Island, came under American fire. Sterling was a prudent officer who had been opposed to the raid. Sterling's goal, with Colonel Friedrich von Wurmb and his jaegers in the lead, was to march seven miles to Springfield, arriving there at sunrise. The van was then to continue on to Hobart Gap. This force numbered 1,300 men. In Elizabethtown, one of Washington's guard succeeded in mortally wounding Sterling in the leg, thus depriving the British of the services of a good officer.

As more and more of Knyphausen's force landed on the mainland and moved into Elizabethtown, the British van moved out along the road to Springfield, harassed the whole way by the Jersey militia, coming out to repel this invasion of their state, and Colonel Elias Dayton's 3rd New Jersey Regiment. The British had to repair two bridges that had been torn apart to retard their progress and eventually reached Connecticut Farms (which became Union, New Jersey, in 1880).

At this time, it was a small village of twenty-five houses on the banks of the Elizabeth River, resting two miles along the Galloping Hill Road, only two and a half miles southwest of Springfield. The militia fought house to house to defend the site and then withdrew in the face of overwhelming British pressure. The militia had even used the bayonet on the advancing enemy in some violent street fighting.

By now General William Maxwell and his New Jersey brigade had come up to support the militia. Knyphausen and his 6,000 troops were marching into Connecticut Farms when a British soldier, seeing movement in a house window, fired a double-shotted load into the house and killed Mrs. Hannah Ogden Caldwell. The mother of nine children, two of whom were with her at the time, had been hiding in the kitchen with a neighbor. Mrs. Caldwell was mortally wounded in the breast and stomach. Her body was removed from the house when the building was burned by the British, but not before her house was looted by the light infantry.

Mrs. Caldwell was the wife of the Reverend James Caldwell, known as "the High Priest" of the Revolution. He was the pastor of Elizabethtown's Presbyterian church, which the British had burned earlier in the war. The Caldwells had moved to safer ground, but this day's events rendered their efforts useless. Some 40 American regular line officers had been members of his church, and he was both chaplain and quartermaster for Jersey troops during the war. During the battle this day, he rode the roads encouraging the men, little realizing his love had departed this earth at the rough hands of the enemy.

In the confusion of the fighting that day, it is possible that the British claim of an American shooting Mrs. Caldwell was true, but the commonly believed story was that the British deliberately killed her. Her husband would live only a year longer before being killed by an American sentry who in turn was executed. Mystery clouds the whole issue, but her killing appears to have been only a tragic accident. Another version of the story was that one of the children went to the window and that brought the British fire.

As the fighting died down in the village of Connecticut Farms, the British went to work systematically looting and pillaging the houses and then setting them on fire. The smoke of the burning buildings including the rebuilt Presbyterian church increased the rage of the American militia and regulars alike. Knyphausen had started something this day that could not be easily controlled. The Americans began striking back. Little quarter was granted on either side.

The alarms spread on the Watchung Mountains using smoking tar buckets and the booming of "old sow," a huge mortar, at Turkey Hill. The Jersey militia continued to flock in. Washington brought the Pennsylvania and Connecticut brigades down from the Short Hills to the opening of Hobart Gap in support of William Maxwell's men. Finally Knyphausen's troops were stopped at the Rahway River Bridge, where the Americans were making a determined stand. The invincible guards, Jaegers, and other crack troops failed in carrying the bridge against the Jersey regular line and their supporting units.

Now the Americans counterattacked across the river and bridge, driving the British before them. Hand-to-hand fighting, bayoneting, and close discharges characterized this portion of the action. Knyphausen began to suspect his intelligence had been wrong. These peasants may have had problems but they had forgotten them to join in their evident hatred of invaders. As the afternoon passed, Knyphausen realized he would not pass the bridge that day and had his men dig in to camp the night.

In the American camp it was clear that Knyphausen would not have made this invasion without the express orders of General Clinton. Where was Clinton? In ships off the coastline? Waiting at the Amboys? Floating up the Hudson to threaten the Highlands? Hiding beyond Knyphausen's screen? Where would he strike? Washington came to one conclusion. He would attack Knyphausen where he lay that night at midnight. The Americans would carry the offensive to the enemy. The plans were set. Sterling, Greene, Steuben, Lafayette, and the others all prepared for the attack.

It was at this point in the operation that Major Crosbie, aide to General Clinton, had a change of mind. Perhaps he should let Knyphausen in on the plans after all. He informed the general that Clinton was not invading the Virginias. He was coming to Jersey to take that state or the Hudson Highlands. The southern army would soon be in the New York area. Probably the 4,000 men would land at the Amboys and make for Mordecai Gap. From there, Morristown was a close target.

The army Knyphausen commanded would march straight across Jersey through Hobart Gap and trap Washington between the two forces. The success of this plan rested on a peaceful countryside with the Americans lulled into a sense of security. What would Clinton now think? Knyphausen had the whole country in an uproar. A village was destroyed. People were mad as hornets. The American army was in the field, operating with élan and purpose in attacking the British openly. What was going on? Knyphausen could see no further easy gains on the morrow. The American army faced his with militia on both flanks. He was in trouble.

Knyphausen and Crosbie could both see their careers ending right then and there at the Rahway River. Speechless at first, Knyphausen then gave quick orders to get out and back to Staten Island. In the dark, the British left and retreated back to Elizabethtown. As they moved along the Galloping Hill Road a severe thunderstorm broke out, lighting the dead bodies and burnt buildings along the way back in a ghostly fashion. The British reached Elizabethtown and settled into camp there, wet, tired, and beaten. But, to keep people from thinking that the British army had retreated, they camped on the mainland in a swampy area for the next 13 days and fought with American skirmishers daily.

With the rain, Washington was forced to cancel the battle. The water wet the powder and made fighting impossible. The Americans were discouraged but when morning arrived, their feelings turned to disgust when it was discovered the British army had ignominiously retreated in the night. The Jersey brigade of Maxwell and some militia units followed down the road, picking up stragglers and blocking the British in at Elizabethtown. The Americans even tried to attack the British in their positions around Elizabethtown, but all such efforts failed to dislodge them.

On June 18, 1780, Clinton arrived back in New York City to find his troops roughly handled, the element of surprise for his plans lost, and confusion everywhere in the British command system. Tryon and Robertson and the others were notably silent. Clinton refused to speak to Robertson and Knyphausen. He also had serious trouble with Admiral Marriot Arbuthnot, commander of the British navy in North America.

On June 16, a bridge of boats was constructed between Staten Island and the mainland to facilitate a retreat if necessary or to move the southern army across to Elizabethtown if Clinton moved in the opposite direction. It stretched some 228 yards long across Arthur Kill. Clinton was receiving letters from a Mr. Moore, a spy in the American army highly placed, whom we now know as Benedict Arnold. Arnold would play a major role in the following drama at Springfield. He sent Clinton word that the French were coming to Rhode Island. Washington was in a weakened state, and the sad condition of West Point left it open for the taking.

Clinton now formulated his plans, based on the intelligence he had at the time. Only now do his actions make sense with the release of his papers. During June 1780, much of what Clinton did puzzled Washington and many others involved in stopping the British. What was Clinton after? Washington feared for the Hudson Highlands. He began moving his army toward West Point to cover that position. Behind in Springfield, he left Nathanael Greene in his first independent command. Camping around Pompton, Washington was leaving Greene on his own with about 1,500 regulars and the militia.

The country was worked up over the wanton killing of Mrs. Caldwell. The militia was out. Constant skirmishing went on at Elizabethtown. After some days of tense waiting, Knyphausen began his march for Springfield with 5,000 men. On Thursday, June 23, at 5 A.M., his force moved out in two columns. Under General Edward Mathews marched John Simcoe's Rangers, the Guards, Cortlandt Skinner's Greens, the German regiments, and other units, numbering 2,400 men. In the second column under General Tryon, came the 37th, 38th, and 42nd regiment, the jaegers, the 57th Regiment, and some German regiments, numbering 2,500 men. Immediately, they ran into Maxwell's men and the Battle of Springfield was on.

A running fire fight once again proceeded up the Galloping Hill Road toward Connecticut Farms, past that destroyed village, and then on toward Springfield. The British had the Rangers and Skinner's Greens in front. The fighting was vicious and emotional. The weather was hot and sultry.

Clinton wanted to keep Washington busy so that the Americans could not attack New York. He was not worried about West Point since there was every hope that Benedict Arnold would turn over the post without a fight. If Washington came back to help Greene, then he could be trapped. Washington did not come back, and it was just as well, since Clinton could not have attacked the Americans from the rear anyway. It seems that the British admiral had taken off all the boats and shipping needed to move Clinton's army from Staten Island to Bergen County without telling Clinton.

There were two roads that Greene had to worry about. The Galloping Hill Road ran directly into Springfield with two branches of the Rahway River crossed by two bridges. The other road, the Vauxhall Road, crossed the Rahway River north of the first road. The planks were taken up from all the bridges.

Colonel Dayton and his 160 men of the 3rd New Jersey fell back, fighting the whole way, with Colonel Israel Angell's 2nd Rhode Island veterans. Assisted by one cannon, the Americans waited at the bridge at the Galloping Hill Road. Knyphausen divided his force into two columns. General Mathews and his men were sent to take the Vauxhall Road bridge and come in behind Greene to trap him. Knyphausen would take the rest of his men and come straight ahead toward the village of Springfield.

The inhabitants of Springfield fled, taking what valuables they could with them. The American troops moved into position and prepared to resist the British attacks. Soon the British pushed out against the American lines. Outnumbered five to one, Greene could only hope for luck.

The Americans fought hard, forcing the British to retreat three times before being forced to retire. The Rhode Islanders held on for 40 minutes before falling back. The British crossed the river by fording it and pushing the Rhode Islanders back on the 2nd New Jersey Regiment under Colonel Israel Shreeve. Along with militia units, these Americans did what they could in hard fighting to hold the masses of British back,

but eventually the Americans evacuated the town. The British used six cannon to overwhelm Colonel Henry Thompson's single gun. Thompson was mortally wounded in his vain attempt to halt the British.

Henry Lee and his legion along with Matthias Ogden's New Jersey men and other militia units, numbering less than 600 men, held off the Rangers, the Greens, the Guards, and other British units who attacked the Bridge on the Vauxhall Road at the same time Knyphausen hit the other bridges. Greene sent Henry Jackson's Massachusetts regiment and Samuel Webb's Connecticut regiments to strengthen Lee's line. These additional forces came just as Lee's men were being forced back from their original positions along the river. Hard fighting was also commonplace on this part of the field.

The main attack had begun at 11 A.M., and by noon, the British had control of Springfield. Greene recalled his men to the safety of the Short Hills and kept watch on the British in town.

Knyphausen, with the town in his grip, now hesitated to attack Greene in such an advantageous position. He also feared Washington might show up with the strength of the militia. He decided therefore to abandon his quest, ate lunch for several hours in full view of the Americans, burned most of the homes in the town of Springfield, and then began the return to Elizabethtown. This time, the militia could not be restrained, and they pursued the British the seven miles back along the road, inflicting and taking casualties the whole way. General John Stark and his brigade were also sent in pursuit by General Greene, but the British had too much of a lead for Stark to catch up.

Both British columns retreated. Another Concord was in the making but for the efforts of Simcoe and his rangers along with the Jaegers who made a combined effort to protect the British rear. However, it was noted that the British column was moving at an undignified trot as they entered Elizabethtown and kept going across Arthur Kill to Staten Island by 5 P.M. that evening.

The British losses in both actions during that terrible June are unknown. One Hessian soldier, Joseph Popp, claimed he saw wagons filled with 400 to 500 casualties. The Americans lost 13 killed, 61 wounded, and 9 missing. Some figures place British losses at 307 casualties in the second action alone, at Springfield. The Germans

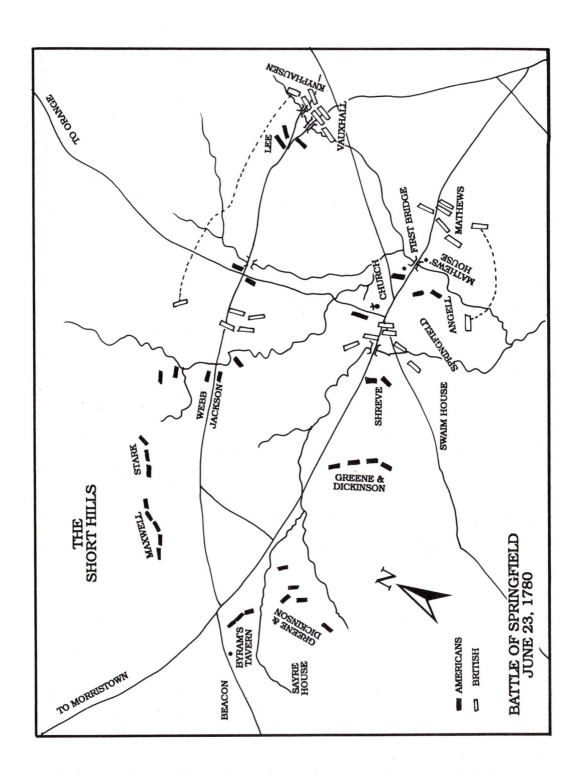

TO ORANGE

KNYPHAUSEN

LEE

VAUXHALL

FIRST BRIDGE

MATHEWS

MATHEWS'
HOUSE

CHURCH

ANGELL

SPRINGFIELD

SHREVE

SWAIM HOUSE

WEBB

JACKSON

STARK

THE
SHORT HILLS

MAXWELL

GREENE &
DICKINSON

GREENE &
DICKINSON

N

BYRAM'S
TAVERN

SAYRE
HOUSE

TO MORRISTOWN

BEACON

AMERICANS

BRITISH

BATTLE OF SPRINGFIELD
JUNE 23, 1780

lost 25 killed, 234 wounded, and 48 missing in the combined missions.

According to ensign Thomas Hughes, it was a 2-week failure in which 6,000 men penetrated the country 12 miles, burnt a village, and returned. The British were then placed on ships and sailed north on the Hudson to Philipsburg to join Clinton's southern army waiting to take West Point with Arnold's help. This was also another Clinton attempt to maneuver between Washington and the Highlands. It was all for nothing.

The internal battles between the Loyalist leaders, some of the British officers, the navy, and Clinton all helped to insure a disorganized and disjointed approach to the British operations. There must be unity of command with men of high statute willing to divert their personal egos for the common benefit. The British severely lacked this quality during this campaign.

The Battle of Springfield was a creditable success for Greene and Philemon Dickinson, the commander of the Jersey militia. Approximately 1,000 men held off 5,000 successfully with the use of a defense in depth. The Americans gave as good as they got. The British showed an obvious respect for the American regular line and were constantly looking over their shoulders for the Pennsylvanians, the light infantry, and the other state lines in Washington's army.

Mrs. Caldwell's death, in its tragic aspects, helped the American cause and brought the people of New Jersey together. So too did the burning of Connecticut Farms and Springfield. Elizabethtown was also ruined. The Americans won the propaganda war over these actions and the war no longer touched the Jersies. The major campaigns of the war in the North were over. The British for the most part would remain in their lines around New York another three years. The "cockpit" of the Revolution was finally at peace, although no one knew that at the time.

The final irony of this campaign was that Arnold's aborted treason actually helped save New Jersey and Washington's army. By promising Clinton West Point and warning him of the French approach, he changed the British plans in their two invasions of New Jersey. The British never achieved the concentration of power and coordination of forces that could have ended the war in 1780 in the King's favor.

Paul J. Sanborn

REFERENCES

Rodney Atwood, *The Hessians* (1980); M.C. Diedrich, *The Battle of Springfield* (1955); Thomas Fleming, *The Battle of Springfield* (1975); ———, *The Forgotten Victory* (1973); Douglas Southall Freeman, *George Washington*, 7 vols. (1948–57); Leonard Lundin, *Cockpit of the Revolution: The War for Independence in New Jersey* (1940); Samuel S. Smith, *Winter at Morristown* (1979); Christopher Ward, *The War of Revolution*, 2 vols. (1952), 2; William Willcox, *Portrait of a General, Sir Henry Clinton* (1964).

Stark, John (1728–1822)

Continental Army officer. Of Scots-Irish descent, John Stark was born in Londonderry, New Hampshire, on August 28, 1728. When he was eight years old, his family moved to Derryfield, New Hampshire (now Manchester), where they farmed on the frontier. Stark grew up skilled as both a farmer and a woodsman.

In 1755, as the French and Indian War broke out, Stark joined Rogers's Rangers and rose to the rank of lieutenant, serving in the Battle of Crown Point (1755), James Abercrombie's disaster at Ticonderoga (1758), and Jeffrey Amherst's successful attempt in capturing Ticonderoga the next year. He was praised by colonials and British officers alike for his demonstrated leadership ability and soldierly qualities. He left the Rangers with the rank of captain, a respected Ranger officer.

He married Elizabeth Page of Dunbarton, New Hampshire, on August 20, 1758, and called her Molly Stark for the rest of their lives together. They had eleven children—five boys, five girls, and one daughter who died as an infant. After his service in the French and Indian War, he returned to Derryfield with his wife and resumed farming.

When news of Lexington and Concord reached him, Stark organized his fellow New Hampshire men and led some 2,000 of them to Boston. At the time, he was already a veteran military leader. Stark was of medium height, thin but erect, with light blue eyes and a cold, piercing stare. His lips were usually compressed. He was appointed colonel of the 1st New Hampshire Militia and served with great honor and valor at the Battle of Breed's Hill in June 1775. His men held the left of the American line along the beach, stopping the British from turning the flank of the main American redoubt on top of the hill.

One of Stark's subordinate officers in this battle, who later in life would become a general himself, Captain Henry Dearborn, related a story that revealed much of Stark's character in battle. As Stark led his men to their position, the regiment came under fire. Start did not increase his precise pace. Captain Dearborn asked if it would not be better to quicken the pace somewhat, and Stark turned to him, regarding the captain with that particular expression peculiar to Stark, and replied calmly "Dearborn, one fresh man in action is worth ten fatigued ones." They then continued their march at the same cadence until they reached the beach and began fortifying it.

After the siege of Boston, Stark was sent to New York City to help improve the defenses of that city. He and his men were in New York a short time before they were sent north to help support the American retreat from Canada along Lake Champlain. He was appointed colonel of the 1st New Hampshire Regiment of the regular line on November 8, 1776, and fought with his regiment at Trenton and Princeton.

Sent to raise more troops to fill out the Continental ranks, he soon learned that Enoch Poor of the 2nd New Hampshire Regiment had been promoted to brigadier general by Congress in the spring of 1777 and placed in command of the New Hampshire brigade. Believing Poor to be his junior, Stark resigned his commission in March 1777 and returned to his home. Poor's promotion was the result of his social graces, tactful tongue, and connections with the right people. By comparison, Stark was lacking in these areas.

Stark was not a politically polished man, especially with his superiors. While immensely popular with his men, he was headstrong in the extreme and difficult to control as a subordinate. Many times this was due to his excellent military foresight and an inability to tolerate incompetents, especially when they occupied positions of responsibility where men's lives depended upon their decisions.

From the beginning, Stark attempted to understand his military opponents, study their weaknesses and strengths, and predict their moves. He understood Indians, the British, and the Loyalists. However, he rarely seemed to use this ability to good advantage with his own superiors.

When Burgoyne's army invaded New York in the summer of 1777 and threatened New Hampshire, Stark placed himself at the disposal of the New Hampshire Legislature. They commissioned him a brigadier general in the state militia. Stark immediately raised a large group of men and led them to victory over the Germans at the Battle of Bennington. Then he returned home to raise even more men to replace the first group whose enlistment period had expired. With these troops Stark helped surround Burgoyne as the British retreated northward after the Battle of Bemis Heights. For his actions, he received the commendations of Congress and a promotion to brigadier general, which he did accept.

From 1777 to 1780, Stark was commander of the Northern Department twice and served in Rhode Island with Horatio Gates. During Wilhelm von Knyphausen's invasion of New Jersey in 1780, Stark commanded troops at the Battle of Springfield and helped push back the German attack. Later that same year, he sat on the board that tried Major John André for spying in the Arnold treason case.

In September 1783, Stark was breveted major general and resigned in November to return home to his family and his farm. He operated his farm and involved himself in his family until he died in Manchester on May 8, 1822, at 93 years of age. According to tradition, he was the last of the general officers of the War of Revolution to die.

Paul J. Sanborn

REFERENCES

DAB; John Elting, *The Battles of Saratoga* (1977); Thomas J. Fleming, *The Story of Bunker Hill* (1962); John Harris, *American Rebels* (1974); Frederic Kidder, *The First New Hampshire Regiment* (1973); Benson J. Lossing, *The Pictorial Field Book of the American Revolution*, 2 vols. (1851–1852), rpr. 1972; Isabel Tarrant, "General John Stark," in Peter E. Randall, ed., *New Hampshire, Years of Revolution* (1976); *Webster's American Military Biographies* (1978).

Staten Island, New York, Raid on (August 21–22, 1777)

As Washington moved his army to defend Philadelphia in August 1777, he directed General John Sullivan to encamp at Hanover, New Jersey, in order to perplex General Sir Henry

Clinton in New York about the movements of the American forces. On August 21, without receiving specific authorization, Sullivan marched 1,000 men to Elizabethtown for a raid on Staten Island. The plan was to capture enemy troops and to dislocate British positions on Manhattan. Sullivan's men disembarked in boats to Staten Island in two units, each landing at a different point. One column went to the upper end of the island in order to seize General Cortlandt Skinner, a prominent Loyalist. The second column moved inland some two miles. Neither column was successful in its undertaking. Due to the long marches without rest, many of the troops became fatigued and fell behind. To Sullivan's surprise, the British had been warned, and the 52nd Regiment was prepared to repel the attack. When the two American columns joined at Old Blazing Star Ferry to return to the Jersey shore, there were insufficient boats to convey them. Sullivan detailed 200 men to cover his escape in the few boats that he could find.

The raid was a fiasco. Sullivan returned with few prisoners, and his mission did not modify Clinton's strategy to defend New York. Moreover, Sullivan had casualties of some 28 killed and wounded, and 172 of his troops were captured. Criticized in Congress by Thomas Burke of North Carolina and by the Maryland delegates (for Marylanders had participated in the raid), Sullivan demanded a court of inquiry. After the Battle of Germantown (October 4), when again Sullivan's military competence was questioned, a court of officers under General William Alexander (Lord Stirling) investigated the matter and exonerated Sullivan. The officers held that the raid was carefully planned and well executed but that it failed due to unforeseen circumstances.

Richard L. Blanco

REFERENCES

Francis B. Culver, "General Sullivan's Descent Upon the British on Staten Island—The Escape of William Wilmot," *Maryland Historical Magazine*, 6 (1911):138–144; Steward Pearce, "Sullivan's Expedition to Staten Island in 1777," *Pennsylvania Magazine of History and Biography*, 3 (1879):167–173; [John Sullivan], *Letters and Papers of Major-General John Sullivan*, ed. by Otis G. Hammond, 3 vols. (1930–39), *1*; Charles P. Whittemore, *A General of the Revolution. John Sullivan of New Hampshire* (1961).

Staten Island, New York, Raid on (January 15–16, 1780)

This operation was Washington's only offensive operation during the bitter-cold winter of 1779–80 while at Morristown. The idea of hitting the isolated 1,000-man British outpost in a surprise attack had been suggested to Washington by General Nathanael Greene and General William Alexander (Lord Stirling). Washington assigned the task to Stirling because of his reputed familiarity with the terrain. Originally scheduled for January 11, from Elizabeth, New Jersey, the raid was postponed because of uncertainty about the weather and about enemy dispositions on the island. Stirling determined that a surprise was virtually impossible. When the attack was launched with 2,700 troops, the temperature was so cold that ice provided a natural bridge from the mainland to Staten Island. Stirling attempted the assault in daylight because he believed that the outpost was short of provisions and that it could not be reinforced from Manhattan. The British withdrew to a main defense—an abatis of 10 feet high covered with ice-glazed snow—and repulsed the American attack. To Stirling's dismay, the route between Staten Island and New York was open and soon reinforcements were ferried across. After a frigid night in the open, the American troops retired on January 16.

The incident had no significant military consequences, yet it contributed to the viciousness of hit-and-run warfare along the coast of New Jersey. New Jersey militia on the expedition plundered homes on the island and returned with sleighs laden with loot. In retaliation the British and Loyalists conducted several raids along the New Jersey coast. If the raid had been a surprise it might have succeeded. But once the element of surprise was over, it should have been obvious that a brief siege, conducted in cold weather, was necessary to capture the garrison. Washington and Stirling gambled on this operation. They were fortunate that only three men were killed and a dozen frostbitten. Both Washington and Stirling were negligent in considering the danger of the weather and for having insufficient knowledge about enemy positions. The examples of the successes of Anthony Wayne at Stony Point and Henry Lee at Paulus Hook the previous summer were obviously unmatched by this fiasco.

Richard L. Blanco

REFERENCES

Douglas S. Freeman, *George Washington: A Biography*, 7 vols. (1948–57), 5; David M. Ludlum, *Early American Winters*, 2 vols. (1966); Paul David Nelson, *William Alexander, Lord Stirling* (1987); George F. Scheer, ed., *Private Yankee Doodle Dandy . . .* (1962); Richard K. Showman, ed., *The Papers of Nathanael Greene*, 5 vols (1978–), 5; Samuel S. Smith, *Winter at Morristown, 1779–1780: The Darkest Hour* (1979).

States' Navies

In the rush to create means of defense in the months following Lexington and Concord, 11 of the 13 rebelling colonies formed their own naval forces. They were encouraged to do so by a resolution from the Continental Congress passed July 10, 1775. Their aggregate strength was greater than that achieved by the Continental Navy, but because they generally remained solely under local government control, they served to dissipate rather than enhance the American naval effort. Massachusetts, Connecticut, Pennsylvania, Maryland, Virginia, and South Carolina had the largest forces. Rhode Island, New York, and North Carolina had small squadrons, while New Hampshire with one vessel and Georgia with four row galleys barely ranked above New Jersey and Delaware, which did not have state navies.

The state navies generally were composed of units smaller and less heavily armed than their Continental Navy counterparts. Their main purpose was to defend their own seaports and coastal trade, not to seek battle on the high seas. Row galleys and armed small craft of many types were popular, so floating batteries, barges, and fire ships were among the most common craft in service. The only state whose navy had more seagoing vessels than inshore craft was Massachusetts.

Formation of a navy in Massachusetts already had been under consideration for over a month prior to the congressional resolution. Talk gave way to action when a petition from citizens of Machias (Maine) reported in August that they had taken two small armed British craft and wished them formally commissioned. Sloop *Machias Liberty* and schooner *Diligent* were placed in service that month with Jeremiah O'Brien commissioned as commander-in-chief. By February 1776 Massachusetts legislators decided that the Bay State should build ten sloops of war, each of 14 to 16 light guns. This decision shortly

was modified to build five and modify five existing vessels. Sloop *Tyrannicide* and brigantines *Rising Empire* and *Independence* were completed by July, and sloops *Republic, Freedom,* and *Massachusetts* three months later. Brigantine *Hazard* was added in October 1777, brigantine *Active* in the spring of 1779, and later that year the 28-gun frigate *Protector,* the largest unit in the fleet. Altogether, Massachusetts had some 32 vessels owned outright or chartered for service. Many of these were employed almost exclusively in voyages to France for military supplies.

Units of the Massachusetts Navy operated singly and in small groups mainly in the waters off New England, although some conducted raids against British shipping both in European waters and in the Caribbean. In June 1779 the British, after a very active season of attacks on American shipping off New England, set about establishing a lodgement in the vicinity of what is today Castine, Maine, near the mount of the Penobscot River. The American response was a large amphibious expedition combining units of both the Continental and Massachusetts navies, the lone New Hampshire unit, frigate *Hampden,* 32 guns, 13 hired privateers, and 20 transports carrying 1,000 militia troops. The force arrived at its objective on the last day of July and found the British defenses still incomplete. Excessive caution on the parts of the American naval and militia commanders found them still trying to agree on a plan of attack two weeks later, when a superior British naval force appeared on the scene and panicked the Americans. Disaster followed as ships, including New Hampshire's only warship, were driven ashore and were left afire as the colonials fled into the covering forests. Only two or three of the craft were captured by the British; 37 vessels were destroyed.

The Penobscot disaster nearly eradicated the Massachusetts Navy. Commodore Dudley Saltonstall, the naval commander, was cashiered. Steps were taken to restore some naval strength. Two armed vessels of 10 to 14 guns were ordered in March 1780, 2 more in 1781, 1 in 1782, and another in 1783.

The *Protector,* which was not yet ready for service in the summer of 1779, in June 1780 had a memorable, and victorious, encounter with the 32-gun British privateer frigate *Admiral Duff.* The battle raged for an hour and a half before the Britisher caught fire and blew up. Only 55 survivors were picked up by the *Protector,* which had lost 6 men. About 11 months later, the *Protector* had the misfortune to meet the HMS *Roebuck*, 44 guns, and the HMS *Medea*, 28. The flagship of the Massachusetts Navy became the HMS *Hussar*. The final cruise by a unit of the Massachusetts Navy was made by sloop *Winthrop*, one of the post-Penobscot acquisitions, to the West Indies in the winter of 1782–1783. She was sold upon her return in June.

The Rhode Island Navy in June 1775 consisted of chartered sloops *Washington* and *Katy*. The former was soon returned to her owner, but the latter became the USS *Providence* in the nascent Continental Navy in December of that year. As such, she had a rather memorable career, including a very successful period under the command of John Paul Jones. Rhode Island built two galleys in 1776, added a galley and a sloop in 1779, and another sloop in 1781, by which time the first two galleys had been lost.

Connecticut created a small navy—ten units total during the war—primarily to defend coastal traffic in Long Island Sound from British blockaders. The largest unit was the 18-gun ship *Oliver Cromwell*. The first unit, the *Minerva*, went into service in October 1775, but it was returned to her owner two months later. Most units commissioned in 1776 and all but two were lost by the end of 1777. The *Oliver Cromwell* and the next largest unit, brigantine *Defense*, 14 guns, survived until 1779, when the former was captured and the latter wrecked.

New York had little opportunity to form a navy because the state's sole major port was occupied by the British for most of the Revolution. Schooner *General Putnam* and sloops *General Schuyler* and *Montgomery* served briefly, together with several armed boats, in a vain attempt to prevent the British advance up the Hudson River. The state also contributed to the formation of Benedict Arnold's squadron on Lake Champlain, which fought the Battle of Valcour Island, which delayed the British advance south from Canada for a year.

Pennsylvania's navy was a local defense force, composed primarily of galleys, armed boats, floating batteries, and fire rafts intended to defend against British incursions of the Delaware River. The row galleys eventually numbered 13, each in the neighborhood of 40 feet long and mounting 1 long gun from 18- to 32-pounder size. The more than 20 armed boats were of smaller dimension, and their single long gun

usually was a 4-pounder. Ten fire rafts were loaded with hogsheads full of combustibles, surrounded with pine kindling, and dusted with powdered rosin. In 1776, the floating batteries *Arnold* and *Putnam* were added, each square-ended scow armed with a number of 24- and 32-pounders. On May 6, 1776, the Pennsylvanians rowed out against British frigates *Roebuck* and *Liverpool* at the mouth of the Delaware. Neither side did much damage to the other, but the enemy withdrew to New Castle, Delaware, leaving the enthused Patriots still masters of those waters. The state navy had grown by 15 sailing ships up to schooner size in 1777, but the British operation against Philadelphia in August drove those not destroyed upriver above the city when they occupied the city. All but three galleys and armed boats were destroyed on General Washington's orders in April 1778 and the excess crews discharged. In March 1779, the state commissioned the ship *General Greene*, which took five prizes later in the year. Ordered sold on November 1, 1779, the *General Greene* lingered at a pier until February 13, 1781, when she was finally purchased.

Like the Pennsylvania Navy, that of Maryland largely consisted of one-gun galleys, armed boats, and barges designed to work in the shallows and restricted waters of Chesapeake Bay. At least 18 of these saw service in 1777 and 1778, on occasion providing useful escort for American troops and supplies traveling that waterway. In addition, Maryland commissioned the 22-gun ship *Defense*, schooners *Resolution* and *Dolphin*, and sloop *Amelia*. The *Defense* bore the flag of the Old Dominion State as far afield as the West Indies, where she took a number of prizes in support of the cause.

It was the actions of Royal Provincial Governor of Virginia Lord Dunmore that led directly to the formation of the Virginia Navy. Dunmore had taken up residence in the British frigate *Fowey* at Yorktown in June 1775, when news of events farther north became known in Virginia. He gradually assembled a flotilla of small craft and, in October of that year, began a series of attacks against rebel coastal enclaves. Repulsed at Hampton and Great Bridge in October and December, on January 1, he burned Norfolk. By that time, the Virginia Provincial Convention had authorized the formation of a navy, which gradually took shape over the following six months. A schooner, two brigs, and two boats initially were purchased and armed, and construction was begun on a number of galleys. Over time, the Virginia Navy acquired a total of ten ships, eight brigs, a sloop, nine galleys, and six armed boats. Virginia's navy was supported by the largest shore establishment of any of the state navies, but it was more shape than substance. The navy was perennially short of men, guns, supplies, and leadership. In devastating raids in 1779 and 1781, the British wreaked havoc on this force. The latter incursion, led by Major General Benedict Arnold, resulted in the loss of more than 20 vessels. The brig *Liberty*, the sole survivor, is singular in that, coming as she did from a service largely obliterated by the British, she survived in service until 1787—longer than any unit in any of the Revolutionary squadrons, including the Continental Navy.

North Carolina, although having an "inland sea" equal to Virginia's Chesapeake Bay, lacked any ports of the importance compared to her sister state. Her naval effort was limited to the acquisition of three brigantines to defend Ocracoke Inlet near the Virginia border. These later were supplemented by two ships built in Virginia but jointly financed by the two states. One, the *Caswell*, sank on station in 1779. As the British showed little interest in the North Carolina coast, these units had little to do.

Farther south, South Carolina had a small but active navy, although it was hampered by a shortage of seamen. (Early in 1776, the state was permitted to recruit 300 Yankees from Massachusetts to ease the problem.) As early as July 1775, two armed South Carolina barges made a major contribution to the war effort by capturing a British supply ship carrying eight tons of gunpowder, and the following month another unit captured six tons more. Principal operating areas for the "Palmetto navy" were off the Carolina and Florida coasts. Between 1776 and 1779, it managed to take about 35 prizes.

Unique among the states' navies, South Carolina's included two frigates built with French money: the *South Carolina*, 40 guns, and the *Bricole*, 44 guns. The former has a particularly interesting history in that she had a French design and was built in a Dutch yard for the Continental Navy. Her name while building was the *L'Indien*, and she was intended for the command of John Paul Jones after his victory over the HMS *Serapis*, September 23, 1779. British intelligence, however, got wind of the plan and pressured the Dutch into stalling the delivery. After many months, the ship was delivered to the French, who, in turn, delivered it to South Carolina while the British were busy making sure that Benjamin Franklin and his fellow commissioners did not get it for the Continental Navy. This deal soon was followed by those involving the *Bricole* and the light frigate or corvette the *Truite*, 26 guns, to the same state. The latter two, together with nine other vessels, were sacrificed as block ships at the mouth of the Cooper River in a vain attempt to prevent the British from taking Charleston in April and May 1780. The *South Carolina* was one of a number of American units that participated with Spanish forces in the capture of the Bahamas in May 1782. She was taken at sea by three British frigates off the mouth of the Delaware River on December 19 that same year.

Georgia assembled a navy that consisted of a 10-gun schooner for a few months in 1775 and 4 galleys built in 1777. All four were lost in 1779, two by stranding and the other pair captured.

The states' navies suffered from the same problem as the Continental Navy—shortages of funds, men, weapons, and stores. Furthermore, by their very existence, they, as well as the myriad of privateers commissioned during the war, inhibited the development of that navy into a more potent force.

Tyrone G. Martin

REFERENCES

Erio Beerman, "The 1782 American-Spanish Expedition," *United States Naval Institute Proceedings, 104* (1978):86–87; M.V. Brewington, "The Battle of Delaware Bay, 1782," *United States Naval Institute Proceedings, 65* (1939):231–237; Howard I. Chappelle, *The History of the American Sailing Navy* (1949); Jack Coggin, *Ships and Seamen of the American Revolution* (1969); Vincent J. Dowdell, "Captain Mugford and the Power Ship," *United States Naval Institute Proceedings, 82* (1956); 1358–1359; Lt. Cdr. M.D. Giambattista, "Captain Jeremiah O'Brien and the Machias Liberty," *United States Naval Institute Proceedings, 96* (1970):85–87; Edgar S. Maclay, *History of the Navy,* 2 vols. (1895); Nathan Miller, *Sea of Glory* (1974); Navy Department, *Naval Documents of the American Revolution,* 9 vols. to date (1964–1986); Charles Oscar Paullin, *Paullin's History of Naval Administration, 1775–1911* (1968); James M. Perry, "Disaster on the Delaware," *United States Naval Institute Proceedings, 88* (1962): 84–92; Hope S. Rider, *Valour Fore & Aft* (1976).

Stephen, Adam (c. 1721–1791)

Continental Army Officer. Adam Stephen's long association with Washington throughout the French and Indian War, in Virginia politics, and during the early part of the Revolutionary War led to increasingly strained relations between the two men, abetted by Stephen's proneness to act independently in command (verging on insubordination), criticisms of the ability of Washington, his own easy credulity, and his tendency to exaggerate. Stephen, a wealthy landowner in the northern Shenandoah Valley, frequently used his army connections as means of disposing commodities from his plantation. Stephen was one of the most controversial of Washington's generals, and no one gave Washington a more difficult time than did Stephen. Stephen was at a disadvantage in his service for high command for several reasons: he was better educated than his peers and also more intellectually inclined; he was much older than others in the officer corps (55 years old when entering the Continental Army); and he was overfond of drinking.

Stephen grew up in Aberdeenshire (along the Highland-Lowland line), Scotland. His father was probably a farmer and stockman. Attending parish schools, he entered the University of Aberdeen in 1736 and received the M.A. four years later; subsequently, he fulfilled all the requirements for a medical degree at the University of Edinburgh. He served as a naval surgeon in the British navy, even manning guns against enemy vessels off the coast of northern France. Unhappy with ship duty, Stephen came to America in 1748, settling at Fredericksburg, Virginia, where he briefly had a medical practice. Moving to the Valley, he established his Bower plantation (now located in Jefferson County, West Virginia), where, and at other sites he owned, he was successful as a farmer and cattleman.

Entering military service as a captain in the Virginia Regiment in 1754, Stephen fought with Washington at Little Meadows and at Fort Necessity. He saw action at Braddock's defeat in 1755. Much of the time, with Washington frequently absent, Stephen was de facto commander of the Virginia Regiment. As commandant at Fort Cumberland he had the prime responsibility for administrative affairs and training of the troops. In 1757 he led a Virginia contingent to South Carolina in anticipation of a French invasion of that colony, which never materialized. Stephen was in charge of much of the road building in western Pennsylvania in preparation for Forbes campaign of 1758. Stephen commanded British and American troops at the last battle with the French in western Pennsylvania, the siege of Fort Ligonier, July 1759. In 1760–1761 he commanded the Virginia expedition against the Cherokees, avoiding bloodshed by making peace with them. During the French and Indian War, Washington acquired a distrust of Stephen's actions as well as a dislike of Stephen himself.

Between wars, Stephen, as county lieutenant and colonel of militia, aided in defending Virginia's frontier against the Indians. In 1774, he commanded troops in Lord Dunmore's Indian expedition and was a principal author of the Fort Gower Resolutions, an early statement indicating the willingness of the soldiers to fight against British tyranny. He found time, as a general medical practitioner, to tend to his neighbors' ills. Stephen served as sheriff, justice of the peace, and in other local offices. His campaign for burgess from Frederick County (1761) pitted him against George Washington in a bitter contest, marked by charges of low tactics from both sides. Stephen never married, and presumably his housekeeper was the mother of his sole child, Ann, who married Alexander Spotswood Dandridge (brother-in-law of Patrick Henry) and, afterward, Moses Hunter; there are numerous Adam Stephen descendants from both the Dandridge and Hunter families.

In 1775, Stephen was chairman of the Berkeley County Committee of Safety and a delegate to the Virginia Convention, from which he was ousted because of election irregularities; he also served as an Indian commissioner, appointed by the House of Burgesses, and participated in the treaty of Fort Pitt. Appointed colonel of the 4th Virginia Regiment in January 1776, Stephen did not get into the field until May, whereupon he commanded troops in the lower Tidewater; his supervision of fortifications at Portsmouth and elsewhere was a deterrent factor in Lord Dunmore's calling off his "invasion" of Virginia. On September 4, 1776, Stephen was elected brigadier general in the Continental Army by Congress. Throughout his Revolutionary War career, Stephen had the important backing of the Virginia delegation in Congress, especially Richard Henry Lee, and also support from

Benjamin Rush and Governor Patrick Henry of Virginia.

Leading troops northward in late 1776, Stephen's brigade joined Washington's army during its retreat in New Jersey. Stephen almost ruined Washington's attack on Trenton, having the day before sent troops on his own near the town, which resulted in a skirmish with Hessian pickets. The affair could have made the enemy troops at Trenton alert; as it was, the Hessian commander at Trenton considered the intelligence that the Americans were going to attack to be that referring to Stephen's action, and hence the troops in Trenton were unprepared for the assault by Washington's forces. Stephen distinguished himself at Trenton, helping to prevent the escape of some of the enemy at the lower part of the town.

Stephen became a division commander, upon election by Congress, February 19, 1777, to the rank of major general. During winter–spring 1777, he had the important responsibility of deploying light infantry to harass enemy detachments and foraging parties, gaining, however, criticism from Washington for acting too precipitously, especially at the Battle of Piscataway. Accused of exaggerating the effectiveness of this action, Stephen responded by accusing some of the officers of cowardice. On several occasions, he blamed General Nathanael Greene as being the source of poor advice to Washington. Stephen insisted that Washington keep up the piecemeal attacks in New Jersey, at a time when the commander-in-chief had decided to seek only major engagements.

From the marches in New Jersey and New York in the summer of 1777 Stephen drew criticism for being inebriated and generally was perceived as tippling too much. At the Battles of Brandywine and Germantown he showed courage and bold leadership, yet his judgment and personal behavior drew strong censure, especially for the Germantown engagement, where his troops became involved in exchange of fire with those commanded by General Anthony Wayne. Stephen allegedly was responsible for giving orders for an early retreat. Most damaging, however, was the accusation that he left his troops during the retreat, failing to collect his men to stand against the British pursuers. Several other generals would face charges and court martials, as Stephen would, but were acquitted. Largely due to accusations leveled by Virginia generals Charles Scott and William Woodford, Stephen was answerable to a court of inquiry on charges of being drunk, negligence at Brandywine and Germantown, and frivolously taking "snuff" with "strumpets" in camp. Tried by court-martial, which had some irregularities in composition, Stephen was found guilty of "unofficerlike behaviour, in the retreat from Germantown, owing to inattention" and having been "frequently intoxicated since in the service, to the prejudice of good order and military discipline." Dismissed from the service, his division was taken over by Lafayette, who had for a long time been pestering Washington for such a command. Stephen planned to mount a strong protest to his dismissal, but found little support in Congress or among his former backers.

Returning home to his plantation, Stephen found that he could commiserate with two neighbors, Generals Horatio Gates and Charles Lee, over their mutual misfortunes in the army. Further enhancing his wealth, Stephen was active in community affairs, including helping to promote the town of Martinsburg, which he had founded on his property. Stephen served in the Virginia House of Delegates (1780–1785), though not often attending the majority of the time of each session. He seemed to encounter no opprobrium in western Virginia for his having been dismissed from the army.

Stephen was a delegate to the Virginia Convention for ratifying the Constitution, which met in Richmond during June 1788. He had a visible and key role in winning acceptance for the Constitution; he gave two speeches denouncing Patrick Henry's views. Stephen died July 16, 1791. Though subtracting from his overall competence and dedication as an officer, Stephen's flamboyance, probative instincts, and recklessness offer a freshness and a high degree of individuality among the officers of the French and Indian War and the Revolution. Stephen's home in Martinsburg is preserved as a landmark and is open to the public.

Harry M. Ward

REFERENCES

Douglas S. Freeman, *George Washington*, 5 vols. (1949–51), *1–4*; Mary V. Mish, "General Adam Stephen, Founder of Martinsburg, West Virginia," *West Virginia History*, 22 (1961):63–75; Harry M. Ward, *Major General Adam Stephen and the Cause of American Liberty* (1989); Don C. Wood, "The General Adam Stephen House . . . Copy of His Will," *Berkeley Journal*, 7 (1978):30–43.

Steuben, Friedrich Wilhelm von (1730–1794)

Prussian military officer. Friedrich Wilhelm Ludolf Gerhard Augustin von Steuben was born on September 17, 1730, in Magdeburg, the eldest of nine children of Wilhelm Augustin von Steuben, a captain in the corps of engineers, and his wife Maria Justina Dorothea von Jagow. At the christening, one of the godparents was Frederick William, King of Prussia. A few decades earlier, such an honor would have been unthinkable. Steuben's ancestors originated from Heldra in the Landgraviate Hesse-Cassel, where Steuben's great-great-grandfather Klaus Steube (the original spelling of the family name) had owned a mill in 1595. Steuben's grandfather Augustin Steube, a Protestant minister, married a genuine Grafin, Charlotte von Effern, in 1688. This favorable marriage later helped him falsify the family tree, and around 1708, he boldly assumed the noble title "von." This meant upward social mobility for his descendants, especially since it opened the way into the ranks of the Prussian officer corps for them. It is unknown whether Friedrich Wilhelm von Steuben knew the details of the fraudulent connection from the miller to an extinct branch of the noble family von Steuben, but the ruse, not uncommon in the eighteenth century, served Augustin and his descendants well.

Steuben's childhood was spent in Russia, where his father served from 1731 to 1739 with the consent of King Frederick William. After his return from Russia and the First Silesian War, Steuben spent the rest of his childhood in Breslau, until he joined the Regiment Lestwitz as a lance-corporal (Gefreiten-Korporal) in September 1746. At the outbreak of the Seven Years' War, Steuben was an ambitious second lieutenant, who hoped to make his fortunes after the boring garrison life.

Yet Steuben's regiment spent the campaign of 1756 rather inactively in the Silesian mountains. In 1757, Steuben and his regiment took part in the Battles of Prag and Leuthen, where the regiment suffered extremely high losses. Ordered to defend the city of Breslau at all cost, the regiment dissolved rather ignominiously in late 1757, when the rank and file deserted by the hundreds to the Austrians. After the capitulation of Breslau in November, its commander, Colonel von Lestwitz, was sentenced to death but this sentence was commuted to two years in jail. These events hurt the pride of Steuben so much that throughout his lifetime he pretended to have taken part in the victory of Rossbach rather than the debacles of Breslau and Leuthen. Steuben decided it was time to escape the wrath of the King, which was affecting the whole regiment, and to look for new opportunities.

He found these opportunities in a rather unlikely place. By the spring of 1758, Steuben had joined the *Freibataillon* of Colonel Mayr, even though he was still listed in the regimental lists of Lestwitz. In peacetime, such a move from a line regiment to a *Freibataillon* would have been considered punishment and a loss of status. An indispensable part of warfare by the middle of the eighteenth century, the troops of this unit were nevertheless poorly paid and often forced to live off the land. Composed mostly of deserters, foreigners, prisoners of war, and other undesirables, they were considered a necessary evil at best; at worst they were cannon fodder and expendable. Officers did not have to be of noble ancestry, but on the other hand, promotions did not follow the principle of seniority either. This aspect, combined with the opportunity for independent, spectacular actions in partisan warfare, the opportunity of making a name for himself (and for plunder, which was acceptable even for officers), and the appointment as adjutant to Colonel Mayr, convinced Steuben to try his fortune with the irregular troops. During the American Revolution, Steuben's experiences with irregular warfare from his time in the Freikorps Mayr would prove to be invaluable.

The service with Mayr lasted barely one year, but it served its purpose. During Mayr's raids into Franconia, Steuben proved his abilities as a staff officer and gained the attention of his superiors, notably Prince Henry of Prussia, brother to the King and a lifelong friend of Steuben's. Consequently, Steuben's return to his old regiment after the death of Mayr in January 1759 was brief. By June 1759 he was serving on the staff of General Hulsen. Wounded slightly in the Battle of Kunersdorf, Steuben's fortunes nevertheless started to improve. Three years of warfare had thinned out the ranks of the officer corps, and by December 1759 Steuben was a first lieutenant, albeit in his old regiment Lestwitz. During the campaign of 1760 Steuben took part in the siege of Breslau and the Battle of Torgau. The decisive event of Steuben's career came in the spring of 1761, when he was able to move out of the anonymity of a line officer into the top of the military hierarchy. Through his acquaintance with Major Wilhelm von Anhalt, whom he knew from his time in the staff of General Hulsen but who was now *general-quartiermeister*, Steuben was appointed adjutant and one of only four deputy quartermasters (*quartiermeisterlieutenant*) in the staff of Frederick the Great on June 19, 1761. Since the Quartiermeister Corps was essentially the forerunner of the modern general staff, Steuben was now one of the few general staff officers of the Prussian army. His duties included the planning of marching routes and marching schedules, the location and fortification of resting places, and the coordination of supplies. If these staff duties did not achieve the level of strategic planning as in a modern general staff, they were of paramount importance in the eighteenth century. This was especially true in the years after 1761, when the primary goal of Frederick had to be the avoidance of a major engagement. Steuben performed his duties well while gaining administrative experience for his tasks during the Revolutionary War.

In October 1761, Steuben was taken prisoner by the Russians, and his tenure in the Quartiermeisterstab as well as his chances for advancement seemed to have come to a rapid end. But again fate interceded for the young lieutenant. Unlike most of his fellow officers, who went to St. Petersburg, Steuben chose Konigsberg, occupied by Russian troops since January 1758, as his abode. It was here that he heard the news of the death of the Tsarina Elizabeth (December 25/January 5, 1761/1762) and the accession of Peter III, an ardent admirer of the Prussian King, to the throne of Russia. Steuben immediately informed Frederick of this event and of his acquaintance with Prince Georg Ludwig von Holstein-Gottorp, one of the closest relatives of the new Tsar, who was also in Konigsberg at the time. Suddenly Steuben had become a player in international diplomacy, an intermediary between Frederick II and the new Russian government, as the "Miracle of the House of Brandenburg" unwound. Frederick himself corresponded repeatedly with Steuben, who had become so important that he even accompanied the official Prussian envoy Graf Goltz to St. Petersburg in February 1762. By the time the reign

of Peter III came to an early end in May 1762, Russia had left the alliance against Prussia, and Steuben was back at the court of Frederick the Great. Promoted to captain, Steuben spent the rest of the war in Saxony rebuilding the Regiment Salmuth. With Russia out of the war, Austria and France sued for peace in 1762.

That the end of the war in the spring of 1763 also meant the end of Steuben's career in the Prussian army was as much his fault as anyone else's. Steuben had hoped to be recalled to the *Generalquartiermeisterstab* and thus to remain in the vicinity of the King. A royal order of March 1, 1763, however, appointed him only a *Stabskapitan* in the Regiment Salmuth, a demotion from his previous rank as captain. When Steuben became more and more urgent in his appeals to *Generalquartiermeister* Moritz von Anhalt, who had sponsored his original appointment in 1761, for transfer back into the *Generalquartiermeisterstab*, this rather quarrelsome but highly influential officer refused any further help. His pride deeply hurt, Steuben retired from the army on April 29, 1763, after almost 17 years of service without having joined the Regiment Salmuth.

Unlike many other discharged officers, Steuben was fortunate enough to find a new position rather quickly. Probably through the intercession of Prince Henry and the Princess of Wurttemberg, a Prussian princess by birth, Steuben was appointed *Hofmarschall* (chamberlain) to the Prince of Hohenzollern-Hechingen, the Catholic branch of the family, in the summer of 1764. His tenure in this position of routine administrative work and annual visits to local spas, which he kept until the spring of 1777, was only briefly interrupted by his introduction into the Order of Fidelity in March 1769. Required to submit proof of his noble ancestry, Steuben seems to have used this opportunity to polish his family tree even more by adding the title of "Baron" to his name. As financial matters went from bad to worse in Hechingen, the prince decided in 1771 to disband his court and to move to Montpellier for a few years. Steuben accompanied him to southern France, where he stayed for more than three years. Back in Hechingen in the summer of 1775, Steuben started to make serious inquiries for a new position.

After attempts at entering the service of Great Britain and France had failed by the summer of 1776, and his efforts to join imperial services of the Hapsburgs in the spring of 1777 had come to naught, Steuben set his eyes on the rebellious American colonies. His contact in this endeavor was P. Burdett, an Englishman at the court in Stuttgart, who contacted Benjamin Franklin in a letter of June 1, 1777, concerning the recruitment of the baron. Interrupted only by a brief return visit to Germany to defend himself against accusations of homosexuality, Steuben negotiated in Paris from June 10 to September 10, 1777, with the French Secretary of War, the Comte St. Germain, Pierre de Beaumarchais, Silas Deane, and Benjamin Franklin. Eventually he received a recommendation from Franklin and Deane, addressed to General Washington. In it he was described as a former lieutenant general and quartermaster general in the service of the King of Prussia, who wanted to serve as a volunteer in the American army. After he had received an additional recommendation from Beaumarchais and the promise of employment in the French service after three years in the United States, Steuben left Europe on the *L'Heureux* on September 26. Sailing from Marseilles, he was accompanied by his servants Karl Vogel, Thevenaud de Francy, and Pierre Etienne Du Ponceau, who remained Steuben's adjutant until 1779. After a lengthy passage, Steuben stepped ashore in Portsmouth, New Hampshire, on December 1, 1777.

Immediately after his arrival in Portsmouth, Steuben wrote a letter to Congress, in which he simply asked for his orders without mentioning rank or pay, a brilliant political gesture to soothe the anger in Congress over the recent promotions of Baron Johann DeKalb, Marquis de Lafayette, and other foreigners. Six days later, on January 12, Congress asked Steuben to repair to Valley Forge as soon as convenient and to contact Washington. Via Boston, Hartford, Reading, and York, where he met with Congress, he proceeded to Valley Forge, where he arrived on February 23, 1778. Both Steuben as well as Franklin and Washington knew that Steuben's military record and exalted rank in the Prussian army were not quite true, yet in the situation of 1778, this deceptive practice proved both psychologically clever and extremely successful. Steuben's supposed apprenticeship with the world-famous King of Prussia "created a favourable predisposition enabling Steuben to develop his talents for the benefit and welfare of

the Americans who were fighting for their liberty."

Steuben, and the Continental Army, sorely needed the nimbus of the general of the great Frederick who had come to aid the fledgling colonies—an important reason why neither Congress nor Washington, or Steuben himself, ever tried to set the record straight. The troops that he found at Valley Forge were cold and hungry, wearing tattered uniforms, sick and barefoot, their weapons rusty and almost useless. The army, some 11,000 strong in the fall of 1777, was losing men by the thousands to typhus, dysentery, smallpox, tuberculosis, not to mention desertions, and was on the verge of dissolution. Building on the devotion of the soldiers to the cause of freedom, Steuben immediately set out to create an organizational framework through which this dedication to the common cause could be channeled into military strength. This proved to be extremely difficult: there was no unified code of army regulations, no training manual, no firmly established fighting units, petty fights over prerogatives between the troops of the various states and within the officer corps, and only a rudimentary command structure. Despite the prevalent myth of the invincible people in arms, many military and civilian Revolutionary War leaders, including George Washington, had come to realize that without at least a core of professional soldiers, a centralized support and supply system, and the ability to meet the enemy on its own ground and defeat him in an open battle, the war would not be won. Washington was proven right by the events of the war—Yorktown was just such a traditional battle. By January 1778, however, such a military complex did not exist even on paper. Steuben was chosen to conceive such a structure and to make it become a reality.

Steuben had to start from scratch. Within days he formed model platoons of ten to twelve men who went through basic training under the guidance of the baron himself, even though he spoke no English and had to use a translator. His experiences in the Freikorps Mayr proved invaluable: the arms drill and movement in formations were cut down to the absolutely necessary elements and adapted to the new environment. Steuben was no ordinary Prussian drillmaster. His goal was not the creation of European-style automatons but the integration of emotions, for example, love of freedom, into the science and art of warfare. Beyond teaching them the use of their arms and the basics of deployment, he immediately realized that the American soldier fought because he wanted to fight and not out of fear of punishment. Consequently, he treated them with respect, tried to make them understand the reasons for his orders, and led them by his own example. As he gained the respect of the Continental Army, the ragtag soldiers responded both in appearance, discipline, and improved weapons skills. When the Continental Army celebrated the entrance of France into the war with a parade in April 1778, a new army had emerged. Even before this new army had proven itself on the battlefield at Monmouth, Congress appointed Steuben a major general and inspector general of the United States Army in May 1778. This, however, meant that the exact status of the inspector general within the U.S. Army also had to be defined.

When Steuben found out that his position did not involve the actual command of combat troops on the battlefield, he was sorely disappointed. He saw his opportunity of gaining fame disappearing behind administrative paperwork. He briefly thought of retiring, and it took an encouraging letter by Washington to make him stay on. Resigned to his fate, Steuben decided to make the best of it. Almost immediately he set out to write a drill manual based on the experiences of Valley Forge. His famous "Blue Book," the official military manual until the War of 1812, was published in the spring of 1779.

Throughout 1779 Steuben was busy inspecting troops and expanding and organizing his new department, while the war seemed to have entered a stalemate. The winter of 1779–1780 was spent in fruitless negotiations with Congress concerning the reorganization of the Continental Army, but in June 1780 General Rochambeau arrived with the French expeditionary force in Newport, and spirits rose in the American camp. The French had been awaited anxiously; in the South the war was not going well, and the arrival of the French provided a much-needed boost for American morale. Much to the surprise of the colonists, the French spent the summer of 1780 rather inactively in New England and went into winter quarters without having engaged the enemy.

After the loss of Charleston, the situation in the South had become desperate for the Americans. In October 1780, Washington appointed General Nathanael Greene new commander of the Southern Department to replace General Horatio Gates. Steuben was ordered to accompany Greene to Virginia to organize, train, and equip the new southern army. With the arrival of Steuben in Virginia in November 1780, the most difficult year in his military career began, and only the victory of Yorktown saved him from a possible court-martial by the state of Virginia.

In Virginia, the two diametrically opposed concepts of Thomas Jefferson and Baron Steuben on the role of government within society in general and of the military within the state in particular clashed very early on. For Steuben as an officer in the Continental Army the interests of the federal government always came first. National defense policy took precedence over Virginia's war aims. Jefferson, as governor of Virginia and a Virginian Patriot always, placed the interests of his home state first. This added a political dimension to Steuben's task: a proponent of a strong federal government met an ardent fighter for states' rights and a weak government. With the invasion of Virginia by Generals Benedict Arnold and William Phillips in the spring of 1781, matters quickly came to a head. Steuben saw ample resources for the defense of Virginia, but was unable to use them. Following months of struggle with the governor and the Virginia Legislature, Steuben lost his temper. After he had been refused help toward the construction of a small fort, because, Jefferson thought he had no power "to call a freeman to labor without his consent, nor a slave without that of his master," he concluded that Jefferson either could not, or did not want, to help in the common cause. While he was begging desperately, but in vain, for some help against the British invaders, the Virginia Legislature was busy equipping an expedition against the Indians in the west to stake new territorial claims for the state. Even Greene, dependent upon support from Virginia, had to admit that he knew of no case in history when a state was escalating a war with a neighbor while another enemy was within its borders.

On March 9, Steuben finally informed Jefferson that "if the powers of the State are inadequate to furnishing what is indispensably necessary," then he would "suspend giving any orders" until the situation was remedied. Jefferson, mistrustful as ever of the military, mailed a very blunt response to Steuben the next day. "We can only be answerable for the orders we give and not for their execution. If they are disobeyed from obstinacy of spirit or want of coercion in the laws, it is not our fault. . . . We did not think it proper to resign ourselves & our Country implicitly to the demands of a Quartermaster, but thought we had some right of judgement left to us." If this position was incomprehensible to the former Prussian officer, the personal slight deeply hurt his pride. From now on, relations between Steuben and the Virginia government were confined to the bare minimum, and Steuben wanted nothing more than to leave the state. Steuben was not the only one with problems in Virginia: all officers including Gates and Greene had reason to complain about the refusal of Virginia to support the war effort, and even Lafayette had to inform Jefferson in late April 1781 that his task would be considerably easier if the population would support him and would not hide horses, carts, and other supplies at his approach.

As relations between Steuben and the governor deteriorated, so did the military situation. When large supplies stored at Point of Fork were destroyed in early June, Steuben became the scapegoat for the lackluster war efforts of the state. On June 22 the legislature formally asked Lafayette for an investigation of Steuben's behavior surrounding the loss of the stores at Point of Fork. Steuben, who fell ill a few weeks later, spent the summer months working on his own defense. After the victory of Yorktown the Virginia legislature had no interest in pursuing the matter and quietly dropped the investigation. Governor Benjamin Harrison told Steuben, who had inquired twice about his status, in December 1781 to let matters rest the way they were. Military developments had "turned the world upside down" and quenched all thirst for revenge on both sides. If the command in Virginia represents one of the low points in Steuben's career, greatly damaging his reputation, it would also be in Virginia that Steuben experienced one of the happiest moments in his life.

By late summer, Lord Cornwallis had retreated to Yorktown, where he planned to wait for supplies from the North and to spend the winter months. At the same time, the combined French and American armies were closing in on him. By September 9, Steuben was in Williamsburg; on September 14 Rochambeau and Washington arrived; and by September 28, the combined armies were on their march to Yorktown.

Washington divided his troops into three divisions, one of which was commanded by Steuben, the other two by Lafayette and Benjamin Lincoln. On October 6, the first parallel was opened, on October 9, Steuben's division opened the second parallel some 300 yards from the enemy. When Cornwallis sent out a flag of truce, requesting a 24-hour cease-fire and the appointment of two officers to negotiate the surrender of Yorktown around 10 A.M. on the morning of October 17, 1781, Lafayette's division occupied the trenches. Yet it was through Steuben's division that the British had to march to lay down their arms. This has led so distinguished a historian as Julian Boyd to claim that "the honors that should technically have gone to LaFayette's troops (he had been on duty when negotiations were begun and had been relieved by Steuben) went instead to the general who had spent several months [e.g., his command in Virginia] trying desperately to keep away from Cornwallis. But these were empty honors." Such accusations, however, are not supported by the facts.

After Cornwallis's first message of 10 A.M. had been received, Washington changed the time request to a two-hour period from the delivery of his reply and transmitted the new terms to Lord Cornwallis around 2 P.M. Except for a brief moment to let the emissaries pass back and forth, firing was kept up until at least 2 P.M. Between 3 and 4 P.M. Cornwallis agreed to the new terms and rushed back preliminary proposals. Even though Washington found at least some of them unacceptable, hostilities were suspended for the night around 5 P.M. on October 17, and the four peace commissioners met the next day to work out the details of the surrender. By then, Steuben had relieved Lafayette at noon on October 17 as specified in general orders of October 7, 1781, for the siege. In accordance with European practice, which accorded this place of honor and the right to plant the regimental flags over the conquered town to the troops occupying the trenches when negotiations for surrender began, Steuben refused to leave the trenches for Lafayette when the latter wanted back in again.

If this schedule of events, especially the resumption of firing, shows that the place of honor was rightfully Steuben's, there is other evidence to support his claims. In the French camp too, regiments relieved each other around noon on October 17 as scheduled in their orders for the siege, with the consequence that Royal-Deux-

Ponts and Bourbonnais, and not Gatinais and Saintonge, which had been relieved, occupied the trenches for the time span between the beginning of negotiations and the surrender of the British forces at 2 P.M. on October 19. When Washington was asked to decide the matter as to who would occupy the trenches, he decided for the baron. And why did Lafayette allow Steuben to relieve him at noon on October 17? Either because even Lafayette did not consider the overtures of Cornwallis around 10 A.M. on October 17 as the beginnings of surrender negotiations, or because he did not know about the initial contact by Cornwallis. Yet that would mean Lafayette grossly neglected his duties as commander of the trenches at the time. Instead of accusing Steuben of taking "the honors that properly belonged to LaFayette," it seems as if Lafayette tried to wiggle his way back into a position of honor which rightfully belonged to Steuben and his men.

With the war as good as over, Steuben went to Philadelphia to settle his affairs, or in the words of the anti-Steuben Boyd: "Thereafter his chief goals were lands and money." But again, this only part of the truth, Steuben himself admitted that he never was able to live within his means—he was always in need of money. But at the same time he was convinced that he was entitled to some compensation for his services to the new United States, which had been promised him in 1777. From early 1782 on he repeatedly asked the government for funds, petitioning either himself or through one of his friends, notably Alexander Hamilton. He was very proud of the gold-hilted sword that he received in April 1784 in recognition of his services, but this did not solve his financial problems either. Neither did the financial rewards from the Continental Congress, tens of thousands of dollars in specie during the 1780s alone. Most of the money disappeared in dubious land schemes and high living, and by the spring of 1789 he was virtually bankrupt and in receivership. If he had hoped that the first Congress, which met in March 1789, would solve his financial problems, he was sorely disappointed. On March 10, 1790, Congress awarded him a pension of $2,500 per year, beginning January 1, 1790. This sum was not enough to pay his debts of almost $7,000. Only through the help of his friends, notably Hamilton and William North, and by mortgaging the 16,000 acres of land he had been granted by the state of New York in June 1786 as security was he able to avoid outright bankruptcy.

The rest of Steuben's life was spent improving his estate in upstate New York. Due to Steuben's lifelong inability to match income with expenses and his tendency to build castles in the air, his life did not go as well as he had planned. By the spring of 1794, Steuben Manor was still only a two-room log house with a lean-to in the rear, situated on the fringes of civilization that had been settled by some two dozen families. Still heavily in debt but as enthusiastic as ever about some new colonization scheme, Steuben died of a stroke on November 28, 1794. He left his estate to his two best friends, Benjamin Walker and William North. In 1870, a large monument was erected over his grave, and in 1915, some German-Americans erected a monument to him next to the large drill field at Valley Forge.

As is the case with most historical figures, Steuben and his role in the American Revolution are constantly being reevaluated. Steuben has had both his apologists as well as his enemies. At some point or other, Steuben has been labelled "one of the most effective professional soldiers in all history" by some as well as a "Prussian drillmaster . . . turned loose upon the soldiery to try and turn them into the automatons of the classic eighteenth century battlefield," by others. He has been called a bankrupt German mercenary looking for employment, "quite conscious of his own insubstantial claims either to nobility or to the distinguished service under Frederick the Great" as well as "indispensable to the achievement of American independence." Steuben was all of this, and more. He was a colorful figure, both likable in his folksy manners as well as annoying in the careless way in which he spent his money. He took liberties with his past, but there can be no doubt that he knew his profession when he rode into the camp at Valley Forge. "Valley Forge on 23 February 1778" was, to quote Gunther Rothenberg, "one of the rare moments in history when circumstances and the individual come together to exert decisive influence." If his contributions to the Revolutionary War cannot seriously be questioned, his influence on the American military establishment outlived him. Not only was he one of the founders of the Society of the Cincinnati in 1783, but his plan for a military academy became reality in 1802 with the foundation of West Point.

His "Blue-Book" remained the official training manual for the U.S. Army for decades, and his proposals for the establishment of a national defense system based on the militia system formed the basis for the military reforms of the 1920s.

Robert A. Selig

REFERENCES

Werner Giesebrecht, ed., *Friedrich Wilhelm von Steuben. Leben Zeit und Zeitgenossen* (1980); John McAuley Palmer, *General von Steuben* (1937); Gunther E. Rothenberg, "Steuben, Washington, and the Question of 'Revolutionary' War," *Indiana Military History Journal*, 3 (1978):5–11; Horst Ueberhorst, *Friedrich Wilhelm von Steuben, 1730–1794* (1988); Edith von Zemenszky, *The Papers of General Friedrich Wilhelm von Steuben, 1777–1794* (1984).

Stevens, Ebenezer (1751–1823)

Continental Army officer. Prior to the outbreak of hostilities, Ebenezer Stevens was a member of a provincial artillery unit in Boston and a member of the Sons of Liberty. He participated in the Boston Tea Party in December 1773. After the Boston Port Act in 1774, Stevens moved to Providence, at about the same time as John Crane. Both Crane and Stevens became commanders of artillery companies in Rhode Island, but Crane later became the overall commander of the Rhode Island Train of Artillery. When the Rhode Island Train was merged with Colonel Henry Knox's Regiment on January 1, 1776, Crane was designated the regiment's first major, and Stevens a company commander.

After the British evacuated Boston, Knox's Regiment moved to New York with the main army. Knox then sent Stevens's unit and one other artillery company to support the Northern Department, where they took part in the Lake Champlain battles. When the enlistments of those companies expired in late 1776, General Philip Schuyler sent Stevens back to Massachusetts to recruit some more. Stevens raised a provisional battalion of three artillery companies (Buckland's, Donnell's, and Winslow's) and one artificer company (Nichols').

"Stevens' Corps of Artillery," as it became known, was one of the more confusing elements in the Continental Army's seemingly never-ending organizational jumble. Stevens was recruiting in Massachusetts and Rhode Island at the same time that Crane was supposed to be forming the new 3rd Continental Artillery Regiment from the same area. Knox and the Congress considered Stevens' Provisional Battalion part of Crane's Regiment, and therefore authorized Crane to raise only 9 companies instead of the 12 companies that the other regiments were to have. Stevens, on the other hand, insisted he had an "independent corps," subject only to the orders of the commander of the Northern Department. Successive Northern Department commanders supported Stevens's claim. The situation was further complicated in May 1778 when General Horatio Gates apparently exceeded his authority and appointed Stevens over the head of John Lamb as artillery commander of the Northern Department. Lamb had been named to that post by the Congress in January 1776, when he was still a prisoner of war in Canada. Lamb protested directly to Gates. He also protested to Knox, to Washington, and to the Congress, all of whom sided with Lamb. The incident resulted in some poor relationships between Lamb and Stevens.

By early 1777 Stevens had his new battalion formed and marched it to Ticonderoga. The unit and it's commander served with distinction at Saratoga. In May 1778 Stevens' Battalion was transferred from the Northern Department to the Highland Department, partly as a counter to Gates's moves to support the unit's claims to independence. In July the battalion was transferred to the main army; and on December 22, 1778, Stevens' Battalion was finally broken up and fully integrated (minus its former commander) into Crane's Regiment.

Regardless of the political and organizational disputes, Stevens was one of America's best artillerymen. He was one of only five officers to receive two brevet promotions from Congress during the course of the war. In May 1777 he was promoted to brevet major, and the following April he was promoted to brevet lieutenant colonel for his services at Saratoga as Gates's artillery commander. Oddly enough, his second brevet promotion was into the infantry. The reason for that was Stevens's refusal to serve under his old arch rival, Crane. A few months later, the resignation of Eleazer Oswald created a vacancy for an artillery lieutenant colonel, but it was in Lamb's Regiment. Neither Lamb nor Stevens were happy about that, but they made the best of the situation.

Stevens and Lamb eventually "buried the

hatchet" and actually worked quite well together. They were a very effective team at Yorktown, and Knox cited them both in his brigade order of October 21, 1781. After the Revolution, Stevens became a successful merchant in New York City and remained active in the New York militia. During the War of 1812 he served as a major general of state troops. *See also:* Artillery (Continental)

David T. Zabecki

REFERENCES

Lieutenant William E. Birkhimer, *Historical Sketch of the Organization, Administration, Materiel, and Tactics of the Artillery, United States Army* (1884); Colonel William H. Powell, *List of Officers of the Army of the United States from 1779 to 1900* (1900); James G. Wilson and John Fiske, *Appletons' Cyclopedia of American Biography*, 6 vols. (1886–90), 5; Robert K. Wright, Jr., *The Continental Army: Army Lineage Series* (1983).

Stewart, Walter (c. 1756–1796)

Continental Army officer. Known as the "The Irish Beauty" by the women of Philadelphia, Walter Stewart was considered to be the most handsome man in the American army. He was also its youngest colonel. A respected and able officer, he was known for his care of his men. In the field he shared the same fare as the men. He was, in short, a brave, concerned, and high-minded field officer. He clearly had the respect of his men and fellow officers.

Of Irish descent, he was born in Philadelphia, but there is little known of his early life. His subsequent military and final civilian years demonstrated that he was adept socially and an expert politician.

Stewart began his military career in the 3rd Pennsylvania Battalion as the captain of Company F on January 5, 1776. Stewart evidently came from at least a moderately well off background in order to gain this rank. The men in his regiment were drawn from all over the state, but the officers mainly came from Philadelphia. From this position, he was appointed aide to General Horatio Gates on May 26, 1776.

Gates found him an excellent aide, able to handle many of the details of the general's business with aplomb. Stewart served under Gates in the northern theater in the campaign that included the Battle of Valcour Island and the preparation to meet Guy Carleton's invasion. On Gates's staff, he was promoted to major on June 7, 1776, and to lieutenant colonel on November 19, 1776. Three days earlier, Stewart's former regiment was captured at Fort Washington.

The Pennsylvania Committee of Safety created the Pennsylvania State Regiment (also known as the 13th Pennsylvania Regiment) on March 1, 1777, with two rifle companies and eight line companies. Colonel John Bull was appointed colonel of this unit. His appointment prompted a revolt of the officers, who refused to serve under him.

Lieutenant Colonel Stewart was in Philadelphia with Gates at the time. Using his influence and desiring a line command, Stewart met with the officers of this troubled regiment in the City Tavern on June 17 to discuss the situation over a few gallons of Madeira wine. The officers were won over to the newly proposed regimental commander, and the possible mutiny was avoided. Bull had resigned, and Stewart became the commander. On June 18, the very next day after Stewart left Gates's service, Gates made a spectacle of himself in Congress, attempting to gain command of the Northern Department.

With a strength of over 500 men, Stewart's regiment was assigned to George Weedon's brigade in Nathanael Greene's division. At the Battle of Brandywine, it was Weedon's men, with Stewart's regiment present, who were rushed four miles in 45 minutes to cover the retreat of the American right wing and thus prevented a complete collapse of the American army. Stewart's men fought against the pursuing British at a distance of 50 yards in the sandy hollow and held. The British were stopped long enough for Washington to make his escape. Stewart and his men then followed the American army to Chester that night.

At Germantown, Stewart again fought with Weedon's brigade in the left wing under Nathanael Greene. Stewart later wrote to Gates: "When I first engaged we were a mile and a half from German-town, and before we ended, I got to the Market House at Germantown." After fighting through a buckwheat field, Stewart's men had penetrated to Market Square in the center of the British lines when they came up against two British regiments and "They both ran lustily and I [Stewart] took a little flush redoubt with three pieces of cannon from them; I had cursed hot work for it before they left them." Stewart then received orders from General Adam

Stephen to withdraw. In this action, the regiment had marched 45 miles in 24 hours, fought a major battle, and remained intact.

As the 13th Pennsylvania Regiment, Stewart's men served at Whitemarsh and then marched to Valley Forge. During the encampment, Stewart instituted "tactical walks" for his officers. They would walk about camp, discussing answers to questions of "What if the British did this?" or "What could we do to improve this or that position?" Stewart was one of the first to train and improve the skills of his officers in such a manner. He also initiated a system of rotating dinners that his officers were to conduct in order to improve esprit and morale within the regiment. There is also some evidence that Stewart played a significant part in patching up the difficulties between his former general, Gates, and Colonel James Wilkinson over matters that related to the Conway Cabal.

In its last action as a unit, the 13th under Stewart's leadership formed part of General Charles Lee's van in the Battle of Monmouth. Stewart formed the right of the first American line to meet the first British counterattack and helped defend Freehold from attack under General Anthony Wayne's command. During the retreat, Washington held the 13th along with a Maryland regiment, holding the British pursuit until the main army could form. At the hedgerow by the causeway, Stewart fought with Wayne. It was here that Stewart was wounded in action, evidently his regiment's only casualty in the battle. Stewart was warmly admired by Wayne, a fighting general, who looked for good officers to lead his regiments. Monmouth marked the end of the 13th Pennsylvania Regiment. On July 1, 1778, it was combined with the 2nd Pennsylvania Regiment. Stewart became the colonel, since he was senior to Colonel Henry Bicker, who then left the army. Stewart commanded this unit for the rest of the war.

Perhaps due to his wounds suffered at Monmouth or perhaps due to his bravery on the field of battle or even due to his charm and ability to persuade, Stewart was sent by Wayne to Philadelphia with Colonel William Irvine to inform the Pennsylvania Assembly of the pay, clothing, and food problems suffered by the Pennsylvania troops. Stewart wrote back that the first class of leaders of the Revolution were now gone and their places taken by a real set of "Caitiffs." Stewart went on to explain that society

had gone on to forget the army and now enjoyed the pleasures of civilization with much splendor. The people had lost their native innocence. Things surely had changed since the earlier days, before the war, he reported.

Returning to the army, Stewart operated on the New York–New Jersey border during the remainder of 1778 and wintered at Middlebrook, New Jersey. The following summer, Stewart was chosen to be in the light infantry and in that capacity was a part of Wayne's force that captured Stony Point from the British on July 16, 1779. Congress voted Wayne a gold medal for his gallantry, and Stewart a silver one. (Colonel Louis de Fleury gained the third of three congressional medals issued for this feat.) With 452 men in his command, Stewart formed part of the garrison at West Point as a part of Wayne's brigade in October 1779 and marched to winter quarters at Morristown for the horrible winter of 1779–1780.

While in camp at Morristown, Stewart was instrumental in helping to end peacefully the mutiny of the Connecticut Line, caused by poor food, lack of pay and uniforms, and other sundry grievances. The following spring and summer, Stewart fought at Paramus on May 18, Connecticut Farms on June 7, and Bergen Heights on July 21. On September 21, he formed part of the detachment that marched with Washington to Hartford, Connecticut, to meet General Rochambeau and then was rushed to West Point after the discovery of Benedict Arnold's treason, to guard that post.

In December 1780, Stewart led his men back to Morristown to go into winter encampment. It was there that the Pennsylvania Line mutinied over their poor conditions and a lack of response from the politicians. It was a dangerous time but Stewart and Colonel Richard Butler assisted Wayne in handling the men in a cool and sympathetic manner that avoided excessive bloodshed and rioting, although there were some casualties. Stewart stayed with Wayne at Princeton, where the men were headed off and were met by a delegation of political leaders from Philadelphia. Stewart also sat on the board that tried and executed the two British spies caught trying to persuade the Pennsylvanians during the mutiny to come over to the British.

After the mutiny, the Pennsylvania Line was reorganized, and Stewart served as one brigade commander along with Richard Butler as commander of the other, with Wayne in command of the whole. Stewart marched south with Wayne and fought at Green Spring and participated in the siege of Yorktown in General Steuben's division along with the rest of Wayne's command. (*Appleton's Cyclopedia* identifies Stewart as the first full-length portrait on the left of standing American officers in John Trumbull's painting of the surrender at Yorktown.)

After Yorktown, the army returned north, except for Wayne's command, which was sent south to help Greene in reconquering the South. Retiring January 1, 1783, eventually Colonel Stewart made it to New Windsor, where the American army waited out the last months of the war. Washington persuaded Stewart to accept the position of inspector general for the Northern Department, and Stewart left retirement to serve.

Stewart may have been one of the officers involved in the Newburgh conspiracy. Some authorities have Stewart carrying the petition from the officers to Congress for a redress of their complaints and then returning with Congress' answer of "no" on March 8, 1783. Congress intended to disband the army without providing the officers with any recompense for their services. Stewart fought and received General Horatio Gates's help in organizing a protest against this treatment. There are others who place Stewart sick in bed in Philadelphia during the time he was supposedly riding back and forth from Congress. His role in this affair may have been confused with that of Major John Armstrong, who wrote a pamphlet in the spring of 1783 that encouraged the officers to rise up and gain their just rewards.

In any event, the war finally ended, and Stewart was breveted brigadier general on September 30, 1783, by Congress, at the end of a long and distinguished career in the American army. His military life over, Stewart established himself in business in his native Philadelphia, where he became a prominent civic leader and major general of the militia.

Paul J. Sanborn

REFERENCES

Appleton's Cyclopedia of American Biography, 6 vols. (1886–1889), 5; Francis B. Heitman, *Historical Register of Officers of the Continental Army during the War of Revolution* (1973); Joseph Plumb Martin, *Private Yankee Doodle* (1961); Lynn Montross, *Ragtail and Bobtail* (1932); Paul David Nelson, *General Horatio Gates* (1976); ———, *Anthony Wayne* (1985); John B.B. Trussell, Jr., *The Pennsylvania Line* (1977); Glenn Tucker, *Mad Anthony Wayne and the New Nation* (1973); Carl van Doren, *Mutiny in January* (1943); Russell F. Weigley, ed., *Philadelphia; A 300 Year History* (1982).

Stirling, Lord

See Alexander, William.

Stockbridge Indians

The English established a mission at Stockbridge, Massachusetts, in the 1730s to cater to the Indians of western Massachusetts. The Indian converts were primarily Mahicans and Housatonics but came to be known simply as Stockbridge Indians.

The Stockbridge Indians were among the first of the tribes to join the Americans in the Revolution. At the outbreak of the Revolution a company of Stockbridge Indians enlisted in the American service under Captain Daniel Nimham. They served as scouts and suffered heavy losses at the Battle of White Plains in October 1776. Nimham was among the dead.

At the end of the Revolution, the Stockbridges petitioned Massachusetts and Vermont for land, but with pressures on their own land increasing, most of them accepted an invitation from the Oneidas to settle in New York. Subsequent migrations took them to Ohio, Wisconsin, and Oklahoma.

Colin G. Calloway

REFERENCE

Deirdre Almeida, "The Stockbridge Indians in the American Revolution," *Historical Journal of Western Massachusetts*, 4 (1975):34–39.

Stono Ferry, South Carolina, Battle of (June 20, 1779)

Unable to take Charleston in May 1779, British General Augustin Prevost withdrew his army across the Ashley River to James Island. He then crossed the Stono River to John Island and marched overland to the banks of the Stono River (two miles southeast of modern Rantowles). There the British troops boarded boats and followed the Stono River around the northern end of Johns Island to Stono Ferry (modern Church

Flats). Using the boats to form a bridge across the river, Prevost began to fortify the site. The dual purpose of the post was to provide a haven for British foraging parties roaming the countryside, and also to guard and protect the river retreat through Wadmalaw Sound to the North Edisto River and to the sea.

Upon his return from his foray into Georgia, Major General Benjamin Lincoln made plans to attack the British works on Stono on May 31. When American scouting parties reported the strength of the fortification, the attack was canceled.

Leaving a force to occupy Johns Island, Prevost returned to Savannah leaving his brother Colonel J.M. Prevost in command of 1,500 men at Stono Ferry.

Lincoln and Governor John Rutledge of South Carolina planned an attack against the British post on June 15. In the meantime, Colonel Prevost almost invited an attack by leaving for Savannah and taking with him virtually all the boats and the bulk of the British troops, and leaving behind only 500 men commanded by Lieutenant Colonel John Maitland. Maitland spent June 17 to 19 ferrying the sick and wounded, Indian allies, liberated slaves, horses, and baggage to the southwestern tip of Johns Island, intending to abandon the post and then "island-hop" his way down the coast to Beaufort.

Informed of the evacuation underway and the now weakened defenses of the post, Lincoln ordered General William Moultrie to prepare for an attack. But Moultrie had few boats to ferry his troops across the Ashley River, and he had only half his force on James Island when the battle opened on June 20. In fact, by the time Moultrie reached the Stono end of Wapoo Creek with his 700-man army, the battle was over.

At midnight on June 19, Lincoln left his encampment with 1,400 men and arrived at Stono Ferry just after dawn on June 20. The Continentals were positioned on the left. There they faced the 71st Highlanders, a seasoned British unit. On the American right were the North and South Carolina militia. In the rear was a reserve of Virginia militia and cavalry. Light infantry were positioned to protect the left flank.

Within the fortifications were the 2nd Battalion of the 71st Regiment of Highlanders, one battalion of Hessians and a contingent of Loyalist troops. About 40 men of the Highlanders occupied a circular redoubt on the British right, the remainder of the regiment was between the circular and central redoubts. The central redoubt itself was manned by Loyalists. A Hessian regiment held the left flank. At 7 A.M. on June 20, the American attack began.

Maitland sent two companies of Highlanders to locate the Americans. The Highlanders ran into the advancing Continentals and were badly mauled. Refusing to surrender or retreat until all their officers were killed or wounded, only 11 men of the 2 companies sent out returned.

Lincoln ordered his Continentals to attack with bayonets, and they pressed forward toward the abatis. There they encountered a marsh and creek, which barred their way. Disobeying Lincoln's order not to fire their muskets, the troops fired anyway. On the British left, the American militia units had also pressed forward and had engaged the Hessians in another fire fight. Maitland then withdrew a number of Highlanders from the redoubts to reinforce the Germans, who were fighting stubbornly against overwhelming odds.

Lincoln ordered the Continentals to stop firing and again ordered a bayonet charge. But the men refused to charge, and the firing resumed. British reinforcements were then spotted running for the ferry. Realizing that he could not capture the work, Lincoln ordered a retreat. The retreat became disorganized, and taking full advantage of the American confusion Maitland ordered a counterattack. The American reserve of cavalry was ordered forward to check the British advance, and to give Lincoln time to extricate his troops. The British, however, knew how to stop a cavalry charge. They formed two parallel lines and closed ranks. The first rank dropped to one knee, set the butts of their muskets on the ground, and presented a solid row of bayonets to the enemy. The second line still standing, fired a volley. The front rank rose and gave another while the second line reloaded. Thus the American cavalry charge stopped in the face of bullets and bayonets and began to retreat. The reserve of Virginians was called in next, and it managed to hold off the British until Lincoln's force left the field. The Battle of Stono Ferry was over.

The battle lasted 56 minutes. In that time, the British had 126 casualties. The Americans lost 165, of which 50 were dead, and 115 were wounded. It was a British victory in the face of superior numbers.

Completing his withdrawal from Johns Island on the night of June 24, Maitland moved by way of creeks and islands to Beaufort on the coast. There he established another strong British post.

Gary M. Cope

REFERENCES

Warren Ripely, *Battleground, South Carolina in the Revolution* (1983); David Duncan Wallace, *South Carolina. A Short History, 1520–1840* (1966).

Stony Point, New York, Assault on (July 16, 1779)

Stony Point was a British fortified position dominating the western landing of King's Ferry and a major crossing place of the Hudson (North) River just north of Haverstraw Bay in New York State. On the night of July 15–16, 1779, 1,350 American light infantry assaulted this post. The British garrison was captured. Along with valuable stores and artillery, in the War of Revolution, the capture of Stony Point was an exceptional American military achievement.

Stony Point was a high, rocky eminence of difficult ascent, and it possessed strong natural defenses. It jutted out into the Hudson River more than a half mile. A forbidding place, it rose 150 feet above the water, which surrounded it on three sides. Together with Verplanck's Point, which was less than 1,000 yards away on the other bank, Stony Point formed a narrows for the Hudson River at the southern limits of the Hudson Highlands. The critical American post of West Point was only 12 miles to the north.

The western landing for King's Ferry stood at the foot of a depression on the northern side of the point. A causeway and bridge leading from the ferry to the mainland ran over a morass, which was especially deep and wide in 1779. This swampland made all approaches difficult, particularly at high tide when the morass flooded.

Before May 1779, there was only an unfinished blockhouse with a small American detachment guarding Stony Point. Across the river, Captain Thomas Armstrong commanded 70 North Carolinians at Fort Lafayette, a small work on Verplanck's Point. Washington's main army was still camped in their winter cantonments in New Jersey.

General Henry Clinton opened the northern campaign of 1779 in late May by threatening the Hudson Highlands. The British massed some 6,000 men on 70 vessels and 150 flat-bottomed boats and moved north up the Hudson to take control of King's Ferry. Protected by Commodore George Collier's British fleet, this force easily chased off the Americans at Stony Point. Fort Lafayette was easily taken after a short bombardment. By June 1, King's Ferry was secure in British hands, forcing American dispatch riders and supply convoys to use more northern crossings involving detours of more than 30 miles.

The British immediately expanded the fortifications on both banks of the Hudson. Clinton had two sets of works constructed on Stony Point. On the summit they erected a series of earthen and stone batteries, some 7 in number, where most of the 15 ordnance pieces were positioned. The trenches that were to connect these batteries were never completed. On the high ground within the batteries, a stronghold was created from a natural rock formation. The British soldiers camped in tents nearby. A curved abatis running from shore to shore was erected 50 feet down the slope to protect the works on the summit.

Farther down the hill were three flèches, each built to take advantage of the terrain. These earthenworks were guarded by grenadiers and also sheltered artillery. A second line of abatis fronted this forward position. All trees were cleared away from the British lines to afford clear fields of fire. Commodore Collier left behind the *Vulture* to protect the rear of Stony Point. Pickets were placed across the morass on the mainland to provide advance warning if it would ever become necessary. The British considered the place impregnable, however, and named it "Little Gibraltar."

General Clinton chose Lieutenant Colonel Henry Johnson of the 17th Regiment, a young and brave officer, as commander at Stony Point. The garrison included the 17th Regiment, along with the grenadiers of the 71st Regiment, some provincial troops, and artillerymen for the guns. There were approximately 625 British soldiers at Stony Point by the end of June 1779. To the east, Lieutenant Colonel James Webster of the 33rd Regiment commanded at Verplanck's Point.

A major goal of Clinton's campaign was to lure Washington from the protection afforded by the New Jersey hills to open ground, which was thought to be a more advantageous arena for the British. If Washington moved into the Hudson Highlands and away from New Jersey, then Clinton could attack Washington's exposed supply bases at Trenton, New Jersey, and Easton, Pennsylvania. As Clinton moved up the Hudson, Washington responded by moving the American army across New Jersey to the Highlands.

These proposed British maneuvers were based on the assumption that 6,600 troops would soon arrive from England, giving Clinton the necessary force to accomplish his goals. As events unfolded, these additional soldiers did not reach New York City until August.

With the narrows of the Hudson in his possession and King's Ferry cut, Clinton fell back down the Hudson to Philipsburg, near present-day Yonkers, where he waited for Washington to react. In July, Clinton sent General William Tryon on an expedition also aimed at luring Washington out into the open. Tryon raided the towns of New Haven, Fairfield, Norwalk, and the coast of Connecticut. Washington did not move. Clinton was forced to wait impatiently for the promised reinforcements.

In order to protect the vital Highlands, Washington positioned his men in a line running from east to west approximately 12 miles north of Stony Point. The American left under General Alexander Heath camped above Continental Village on the east bank of the Hudson. General Alexander McDougall commanded the American center at West Point. General Israel Putnam and the American right were located near the Forest of Dean in Smith's Clove, 14 miles west of the Hudson River near Tuxedo Lake. Washington made his headquarters at New Windsor.

Washington refused to be duped by Clinton by moving the American army away from its defensive positions. Yet Washington needed some measure of success to maintain American morale and insure the continuation of the war effort. The British garrison at Stony Point was an "affront" to the Americans, but Washington at first considered the position too strong to attack. He was soon to change his mind.

In June, Washington sent orders to Major Henry Lee to reconnoiter the British works at Stony Point. Allen McLane, an American partisan officer and part of Lee's Corps, made several trips to the neighborhood of the Point. On July 2, 1779, McLane, disguised as a country bumpkin, entered the fortifications under a flag of truce, along with a Mrs. Smith who had wished to see her sons (who were evidently provincial soldiers at Stony Point). McLane noted the incomplete trenches between batteries. He felt the place could be taken by a *coup de main*.

McLane's report gained Washington's full attention. Here was an opportunity to reply to Clinton's maneuvers by capturing this British "affront." Such a victory would rally the entire country and dismay America's enemies. Washington had just the troops to attempt the task.

In June, the Baron Friedrich von Steuben had begun assembling an elite body of light infantry, the members of which were drafted from each brigade in the army. Composed of hardened veterans and experienced soldiers, this corps of light infantry had been placed under the command of the popular brigadier from Pennsylvania, General Anthony Wayne.

Wayne assumed leadership of the light infantry at Sandy Beach on the Hudson near Fort Montgomery, five miles south of West Point, on July 1, 1779. He immediately increased the pace of training and drill for his men in order to sharpen their military skills. Washington sent Wayne orders to reconniter Stony Point.

Wayne and two of his officers, Colonel Richard Butler and Major John Stewart, scouted the Point from the safety of nearby high ground. The three agreed that the British had turned Stony Point into a very strong post. Their opinions were not as favorable as McLane's had been.

Washington, receiving varying reports, decided to see for himself. On July 6, Washington personally examined Stony Point, covered by McLane's men. The British took notice of the American party, and the visit was reported in the New York newspapers. The element of surprise now seemed to be lost. Yet Washington believed a successful plan could be devised.

For two weeks Lee and McLane haunted the fort. From deserters, and from local farmers who brought their produce into the British camp, McLane was able to forward very accurate intelligence to Washington. For example, scouts from Lee's Corps picked up a British deserter who informed them that Sandy Beach on the southern side of Stony Point was virtually clear, with only slight obstructions.

Colonel Rufus Putnam, Major Lee, and Major Thomas Posey also made reconnaissances. Putnam, an engineer, spent three days surveying the place and inspecting British lines from a distance. He, too, thought an attack could succeed but that it should not be postponed too long. The British would continue to develop the post, and eventually they would finish their trenches.

Based on the intelligence he had received, Washington gave Wayne a detailed plan of attack on Stony Point on July 10. While allowing Wayne some latitude, the basic elements of the assault were set down by the commander-in-chief. Wayne was to attack with between 1,000 and 2,000 men. The vanguards were to use only the bayonet. Midnight was the time suggested, since everyone was prepared for a dawn assault. The men were to wear white feathers or cockades in their hats as a distinguishing mark. All officers were to be instructed and to know their responsibilities. Secrecy was essential.

The next day Wayne went back to study Stony Point. This time he was accompanied by Lieutenant Colonel Christian Febiger and Colonel Butler. From his reconnaissance, Wayne was able to draw up a plan, which was based on Washington's, but which included a variation that called for an attack with two columns and one feinting movement. Wayne submitted this plan to the commander-in-chief early in the morning of July 15.

Washington immediately gave Wayne permission. That same morning Wayne paraded his men for an inspection at Sandy Beach. Each man appeared freshly shaved with his hair powdered. Wayne always connected a good military appearance with fighting ability. Without warning, Wayne led his light infantry from the parade ground west and then south on a 14-mile march toward Stony Point. The men were forced to move mostly by single file through morasses, over mountains, and down difficult defiles.

Security was a primary concern. Wayne had concentrated his force away from the objective and then proceeded to move the light infantry there quickly. Major Lee's men had gone ahead to seal off the British strong point from any warning. Every dog within three miles of the fort was taken by Lee's detachment. People going to the fort with provisions were stopped. Along the line of march, any civilians encountered were detained. While few if any men straggled, orders were given that no one would leave the line of march unless escorted by an officer.

By 8:00 that evening, the column had reached the farm of David Springsteel, about one and a half miles to the west of Stony Point. The Americans kept out of sight. Wayne formed his men into two columns for the attack. Febiger, a Danish veteran of Benedict Arnold's march on Quebec, commanded Virginia and Pennsylvania light infantry in the first unit of the right column. Febiger's men were followed by the Connecticut troops of Colonel Return Jonathan Meigs, also a veteran of the march on Quebec. Twenty-four-year-old Major William Hull's Marylanders completed this column. Leading the advanced guard of 150 men on the right was Lieutenant Colonel François Louis de Fleury, who had collaborated with the Baron von Steuben on the American drill regulations.

In the left column, Colonel Richard Butler commanded the first unit of Pennsylvania, Maryland, and Delaware light infantry. Major Hardy Murfree of North Carolina, and the founder of Murfreesboro, Tennessee, followed Butler's men with his North Carolinians. The 150 men of the advanced guard for the left column was led by Major John Stewart of Maryland.

A "forlorn hope" detachment (i.e., soldiers with a particularly difficult mission) of 20 volunteers and one officer, armed with axes, preceeded each column. They were ordered to clear a path in any line of obstructions. Lieutenant George Knox of the 9th Pennsylvania led the forlorn hope on the right, while Lieutenant James Gibbons of the 6th Pennsylvania took the left. Artillerymen attached to Wayne's light infantry came along without their guns to service any captured British pieces.

Only Hardy Murfree's men were permitted to load their muskets. All other light infantry had use of just the bayonet. There would be no premature explosions to alert the British. The whole force wore pieces of white paper in the front of their hats, a common custom in night attacks of the time that helped differentiate friend from foe.

Wayne was confident that the attack was still a surprise. At 11:30 P.M. the two columns silently moved out along the forest paths that took them toward Stony Point. Wayne had told the light infantry that the death penalty would be imposed on any soldier who attempted to fire his musket, cry out ahead of time, retreat, or disobey an officer in the coming operation. The men were also told of Washington's bounties of $500, $400, $300, $200, and $100 for the first five men into the British post. Once the light infantry crossed into British lines, the cry "The fort's our own!" was to be yelled out by every American until the fort fell.

Wayne marched with the right column, since this was to be the main American thrust and had the most men. The right column was to move across the morass, along the south beach of Stony Point, and then up on to the summit through the lines of obstructions. The left column was to take the northerly route and climb from the ferry landing road to the summit of Stony Point. Murfree's men were to detach themselves from the left and feint at the British center, firing off their muskets once the American right had engaged. It was hoped Murfree's diversion would mislead the British.

Just after midnight on the moonless, pitch black night of July 16, Wayne's columns, moving in tandem, crossed from the mainland to Stony Point and began circling the British post before the British realized the danger. The British had pulled their pickets back to the inner edge of the marsh at night and had no other patrols beyond. As the right column under Wayne's personal command moved through a wider and deeper morass than expected, the general alarm sounded in the British camp.

Ignoring the British musketry and artillery fire, the Americans raced through the water, along the beach and then around the end of the first line of abatis. At the second abatis, Wayne was knocked down by a musket ball that grazed his head. The ball created a bloody but nonlethal two-inch gash and momentarily stunned the general. But he was helped up by his aides, Captains Benjamin Fishbourn and Henry Archer, shook off the effects of the wound, and resumed his place in directing the attack.

At this point, as the right column engaged, Major Murfree with his two companies of North Carolina light infantry unleashed a feint on the British center. Abreast the main road to the fort and outside the lower abatis, Murfree's men created such an effect that Colonel Henry Johnson, the British commander, was fooled. In the darkness, Johnson brought six companies of the 17th Regiment off the summit to counter what was perceived as the main attack. Almost half the British strength was committed to stopping this American feint.

On the left, Lieutenant James Gibbons and his men of the forlorn hope mounted an attack on the abatis. British fire hit 17 of the 20 men.

Despite losses, the left column continued its advance, pushing the British before them.

Men from Wayne's column were the first to enter the British main fortified position. The British batteries were not fully enclosed, and the Americans easily rushed through the gaps. Fleury's advanced guard was through the sally port and over the parapet into the flag bastion of the main redoubt before the British knew it. In the dark many of the defenders mistakenly thought the Americans were part of the garrison. Confusion reigned throughout British lines.

Lieutenant Colonel Fleury was the first American into the fort, tearing down the British flag as he arrived. Fleury was followed closely by Lieutenant George Knox of the forlorn hope, Sergeant Baker of Virginia, who was wounded four times, Sergeant Spencer of Virginia, and finally Sergeant Donlop of Pennsylvania. These men earned the bounties Washington had promised.

The Americans repeatedly shouted "The fort's our own!" at the top of their lungs as they raced through the fort. In the uproar, the British were unable to form an effective defense. The American left forced the British back against the American right. Soon the British were crying for quarter. Colonel Johnson was taken prisoner by Febiger's men, who had cut the British commander and his six companies off from the main redoubt. Within 30 minutes, the action at Stony Point was over. With just the bayonet, the American light infantry had taken the British strong point.

The rules of warfare of the time permitted the slaughter of any soldiers taken in a night attack. With restraint and discipline, the American light infantry granted quarter. The British reported 20 killed, 74 wounded, 58 missing, and 472 captured. The Americans claimed 63 killed, 70 wounded, and 543 captured British casualties. The American losses were placed at 15 killed and 83 wounded. Along with military stores and supplies, the Americans captured 15 artillery pieces. Most of these guns were later lost when British naval gunfire sank the barge carrying them north to West Point. British prisoners were marched off to Easton, Pennsylvania.

Lieutenant Roberts of the artillery was one of the few British to escape from Stony Point. He swam the Hudson to the *Vulture* and reported the fall of the fort. His story was soon

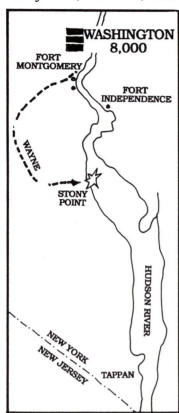

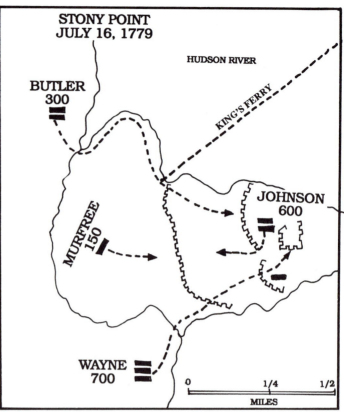

confirmed as the Americans turned the captured guns and opened fire on the *Vulture* and Fort Lafayette at Verplanck's Point. The sloop of war dropped downstream out of range. There was no visible effect from the American bombardment, nor did the British return the fire.

Washington's initial plans had also called for the capture of Fort Lafayette. A demonstration by a small force under the command of Colonel Rufus Putnam was made on Fort Lafayette during the Stony Point attack. This was to be followed up with a full assault by two brigades under General Robert Howe if Stony Point was captured. Delays in bringing up the heavy guns and securing the necessary equipment held up Howe's progress. Clinton reinforced Fort Lafayette before the Americans could attack. Howe withdrew the troops.

Washington came to Stony Point to examine the position for himself. He had no intention of holding it. The works were destroyed and the stores removed. The light infantry were paraded, and Washington gladly shook the hand of every man who had made the assault. Wayne hosted a dinner party for Washington, von Steuben, and others. Shortly thereafter, the Americans withdrew from Stony Point.

The British reoccupied Stony Point once it was clear of Americans. The fortification on the summit was rebuilt, but this time it was completely enclosed. A larger garrison was stationed there. However, by November, the troops were withdrawn and the Americans returned to fortify the place once more.

The principal result of this successful night bayonet assault was the uplifting of American morale. Wayne was voted a Gold Medal by Congress. Fleury and Stewart were awarded silver medals. Gibbons and Knox were breveted captains. The $500 Fleury won for being first to enter the British fort he distributed to the men in his advanced guard. The value of the captured military stores and ordnance was put at $158,640. This sum was divided up among the 1,350 officers and men who had made the attack.

The action brought praise for Wayne and his light infantry. There had been no atrocities. Quarter had been granted. It was a thoroughly professional exercise, worthy of troops of the highest caliber. The Americans had displayed bravery. American intelligence was superior. Security had been maintained. Coordination of the two attacking columns was outstanding, even in the dark and under difficult conditions. The speed, skill, and daring of the light infantry's assault directly contributed to their success. Had the Americans stopped to fire and reload their muskets, the British might have easily located their opponents in the dark and had the time to defend themselves.

It should be noted that the British withdrawal of their pickets from the mainland, along with a lack of patrols, allowed the Americans to approach the fort without giving alarm. The British garrison was relatively small in number for the size of the fortifications. In addition, the lack of British naval support from the river permitted the Americans to move along the southerly beach, past the obstructions, and into the works before the British could react effectively. When the Americans reached the main works, they were able to penetrate them with ease because the connecting trenches were incomplete.

General James Pattison, Clinton's chief of artillery, reported that "no instance of inhumanity was shown to any of the unhappy captives; no one was unnecessarily put to the sword." Clinton felt the attack was "a very great affront to us, the more mortifying since it was unexpected and possibly avoidable." The disaster at Stony Point ended any future campaign plans Clinton had for the North during the rest of 1779. From the British base in New York City, Clinton would now turn his attention to the South to recapture the Carolinas and Virginia for the Crown.

Stony Point had been no lucky victory. A planned and carefully calculated gamble, it was in fact a gallant and brave assault. The operation was summed up by Wayne when he said the American light infantry had "behaved like men who are determined to be free."

Paul J. Sanborn

REFERENCES

Sir Henry Clinton, *The American Rebellion* (1954); James Flexner, *George Washington in the American Revolution* (1967); Douglas S. Freeman, *George Washington*, 7 vols. (1948–57), 5; Henry P. Johnston, *The Storming of Stony Point on the Hudson* (1971); David H. Murdock, *Rebellion in America: A Contemporary British Viewpoint* (1979); Paul D. Nelson, *Anthony Wayne* (1985); Charles J. Stille, *Major General Anthony Wayne and the Pennsylvania Line* (1968); Christopher Ward, *The War of Revolution* (1952); William B. Willcox, *Portrait of a General: Henry Clinton* (1962).

Stormont, 7th Viscount (David Murray) (1727–1796)

British Statesman. From an aristocratic Scottish family and the nephew and heir of the eminent jurist Lord Mansfield, in the 1750s, Stormont entered the diplomatic service and held a variety of posts before being named ambassador to Vienna in 1763. Regarded as an able and energetic diplomat, Stormont came to influence British foreign policy beyond the confines of Austria. In 1772 he became ambassador to France, arguably the most prestigious post in the diplomatic corps.

It was in Paris that Stormont encountered the American Revolution. After the outbreak of hostilities, Stormont anticipated that the Americans would seek French assistance and did his tenacious best to make such aid difficult. He kept close tabs on the Americans that appeared in France, assisted by a highly effective network of spies and informers (including Edward Bancroft, the secretary to the American mission). Stormont continually barraged the French government with complaints that its various covert efforts at aiding the Americans were violations of its neutrality, while at the same time trying to convince them that Britain was winning the war in America. Though unable to prevent Benjamin Franklin (whom he labeled "a dangerous engine") and the other American commissioners from maintaining contact with the French government and eventually negotiating treaties of alliance and friendship, Stormont undoubtedly complicated their job, and his vigilance may have limited some forms of French aid before 1778. In a humorous effort to counteract Stormont's effectiveness, Franklin amused Parisian society by punning on Stormont's name: the French verb *mentir* (to lie) became *stormontir*. It was in part to secure Stormont's immediate recall that the French government made public in March 1778 (three months before the declaration of war) its treaty of amity and commerce with the United States.

After the break in relations with France, Stormont returned to Britain, where he became a favorite of George III and was often sought out by the cabinet for advice on diplomatic matters. In October 1779 he became Secretary of State for the Northern Department. In this capacity he assumed responsibility for handling relations with northern Europe, though he quickly established himself as the cabinet's most knowledgeable authority on foreign affairs in general. One of the most important events of his secretaryship was Britain's declaration of war against the Dutch in December 1780, a decision taken by the King and cabinet at Stormont's urging. Stormont was anxious to prevent the Dutch, who had been carrying on an annoying trade with the Americans for some years, from joining the Russian-led Armed Neutrality. He had also become convinced that war would strengthen the hand of the supposedly pro-British Prince of Orange in Dutch politics. Russia itself was also an object of Stormont's attention. In 1780 and 1781, he attempted to end Britain's diplomatic isolation by securing an alliance with Russia, holding out to Catherine the Great the possibility of gaining Minorca as a Mediterranean foothold. In the event, the plan misfired, as did a complicated maneuver aimed at organizing a joint Russian-Austrian mediation of the war.

As Secretary of State, Stormont also led the Lord Frederick North administration's forces in the House of Lords. A Scottish representative peer since 1754, Stormont's diplomatic career had minimized his actual parliamentary experience. He nonetheless made an effective leader of the house and came to be one of the primary parliamentary apologists for the war effort. In 1780 he orchestrated the election of solid slate of government supporters in the elections for the 16 Scottish representative peers.

When North resigned in March 1781, Stormont followed suit. Thereafter, he opposed the Rockingham and Shelburne administrations, speaking and voting against the peace preliminaries in February 1783. He supported the Fox-North coalition. After its dismissal, he spent most of the rest of his life in opposition before coming over to Pitt with the Portland Whigs in 1794. Professional and competent, both as ambassador and as Secretary of State, Stormont provided a needed element of stability to British foreign policy during the American Revolution.

William C. Lowe

REFERENCES

Jonathan R. Dull, *A Diplomatic History of the American Revolution* (1985); Isabel de Madariaga, *Britain, Russia and the Armed Neutrality of 1780* (1962); David Schoenbrun, *Triumph in Paris: the Exploits of Benjamin Franklin* (1976); H.M. Scott, "Sir Joseph Yorke, Dutch Politics and the Origins of the Fourth Anglo-Dutch War," *Historical Journal*, 31 (1988):571–89; Marion Ward, *Forth* (1982).

Stuart, Gilbert (1785–1825)

American painter. Gilbert Stuart was born in Rhode Island, the son of Gilbert Stuart, a native of Scotland who was a snuff maker. In 1761, the snuff manufacturing having failed, the family moved to Newport, Rhode Island. Young Stuart early showed a predilection for drawing and copying pictures, and at age 13 he began drawing portraits with graphite. When the Scots artist Cosmos Alexander came to Newport in 1769, Stuart became his pupil and returned with Alexander to Edinburgh, Scotland. Upon Alexander's death in 1772, Stuart, unable to support himself there by his work, returned to Rhode Island. The country, on the eve of the Revolution, was not the place for a portrait painter to prosper, and Stuart sailed for London, where he resided from November 1775 until 1787. Consequently, he took no active part in the Revolution. His inclusion here is made because later in his career so many Revolutionary figures sat for him later in their lives.

After struggling to make a living by painting on his own, he was accepted as a pupil by Benjamin West, with whom he studied for five years. His painting of "The Skater" caused a sensation when shown at the Royal Academy in 1782, and after that he had much fashionable patronage and could command high prices. His personal finances, always a problem during his life, were such that he left London to avoid debt in 1787 and went to Ireland. There he was again successful as a portrait painter but again ran into debt. In 1793 he returned to the United States working in New York until 1794, when he moved to Philadelphia, the capital at the time.

Stuart's first portrait of President Washington brought him instant success and his commissions exceeded his capacity to complete them. Such Revolutionary figures as Generals Henry Dearborn, Henry Knox, Matthew Clarkson, as well as Robert Morris and John Jay were his subjects. Stuart remained in Philadelphia until 1803, when he spent a brief two years in Washington. In 1805 he moved to Boston, where he spent the rest of his life. Ever improvident, his financial problems continued to plague him until his end. His portraits of the first five Presidents of the United States are familiar to all today. His portrait of Washington, unquestionably the best known, was at one time hung in reproduction in every schoolroom in the country. There is no question that Stuart himself is one of the very best as well as best known of America's portrait painters. *See also*: Trumbull, John

Robert G. Stewart

REFERENCES

Richard McLanathan, *Gilbert Stuart* (1986); Lawrence Park, *Gilbert Stuart: An Illustrative Descriptive List of His Works*, 4 vols. (1926).

Stuart, John (1718–1779)

British Indian agent. Born at Inverness, Scotland, September 25, 1718, as a young man, John Stuart found employment in Scottish mercantile firms, first in London and then Spain. He left Spain due to the War of Jenkins Ear, and in 1740, signed into the Royal Navy as a clerk. He sailed with the famous George Anson expedition, which circumnavigated the globe attacking Spanish possessions in the Far East and the Americas. The young clerk earned a promotion as a result of his conduct during the voyage. In early 1748, Stuart sailed for South Carolina and established himself as a Charleston merchant. His various mercantile endeavors were not particularly successful, but Stuart did acquire sizable landholdings and became a prominent member of Charleston society. He also served in the Charleston militia.

As the Seven Years' War opened, South Carolina agreed to build a fort among the Overhill Cherokee in order to help protect them from French-inspired Indian attacks. In July 1756, South Carolina governor William Henry Lyttelton appointed John Stuart as one of two captains instructed to raise two companies of provincial militia to be stationed at the new garrison, dubbed Fort Loudoun, located at the junction of the Little Tennessee and Tellico rivers.

While stationed at Fort Loudoun, Stuart excelled at Indian relations with the Cherokee and became a friend of the great Cherokee chief Attakullakulla, or Little Carpenter. Trade problems, encroachments, and other frontier troubles erupted into open warfare between the Cherokee and South Carolina in 1760. Fort Loudoun, isolated and unsupported, was besieged. Stuart met with the leading hostiles and arranged the capitulation of the garrison in August 1760. During the long retreat, the Carolinians suffered heavy casualties, including most of Stuart's fellow officers. Stuart was captured and later ran-

somed by Attakullakulla. Ultimately, Stuart was instrumental in the reestablishment of an Anglo-Cherokee peace.

Stuart's leadership abilities and expertise in Cherokee affairs led to his appointment as the successor of Edmund Atkin, the first Superintendent of Indian Affairs, on January 5, 1762. Stuart's superintendency was marked by two related aims—securing an Indian boundary line and the establishment of fair trading regulations. Stuart believed that a secure boundary and regulation of the Indian trade were essential for peaceful Indian relations. Stuart failed at both, but his fairness and moderation earned the respect and confidence of leading headmen from all the southern tribes. Though he was able to establish and demarcate boundary lines with all the major southern tribes, the boundaries were widely ignored by white settlers. The vacillation of the home government regarding the regulation of the deerskin trade and squabbling among colonial officials thwarted Stuart's efforts to bring order to the troubled commerce.

As the rebellion escalated in the colonies, rumors were spread by disaffected South Carolinians that Stuart had ordered his deputies to prepare the Indians in their districts for an assault on the frontier. Other rumors claimed that he had sacrificed the garrison at Fort Loudoun during the Cherokee War. Stuart's denials fell upon deaf ears, and in late May 1775, he fled Charleston for Savannah, leaving his wife and property behind. Patriots there also accosted the superintendent. In order to quiet the mob, Stuart allowed its leaders to review his correspondence with his deputies. Unfortunately for Stuart, the exercise had the opposite effect, and Stuart proceeded to St. Augustine. He arrived there on June 21, 1775.

Though he was able to meet with groups of Lower Creeks and Seminoles, East Florida was isolated from the major southeastern tribes, and Stuart decided to relocate to Pensacola, West Florida. He arrived in Pensacola in late spring 1776. In the fall of 1775, General Thomas Gage had instructed the superintendent to win the support of the Indians in his department and prepare them to take up arms against the rebels. Stuart urged caution regarding the employment of Indian warriors, fearing that indiscriminate use of Indians would result in casualties to all ages, races, sexes, and political persuasions. He hoped to use Indian warriors only in conjunction with a British offensive in the South and under the direction of his deputies and commissaries. To secure Indian loyalty, Stuart worked vigorously to maintain adequate supplies of trade goods and provide generous presents to those headmen who supported the British viewpoint and pledged their readiness to act on his order. In 1776, the Cherokee ignored the pleas of Stuart and his agents and went to war unsupported by British troops, with disastrous results. The success of American armies in chastising the belligerents made other tribes, particularly the Creeks, reconsider vigorous aid for the British effort. In October 1776, Stuart oversaw the establishment of peace between the Choctaws and Creeks, who had been warring since 1763. With the devastation of the Cherokee, it was these two tribes, particularly the Creeks, who contributed the most to Britain's war efforts in the South.

Though he never traveled into the Indian country after his appointment as superintendent, Stuart maintained close contact with the southern tribes by use of a corps of deputies, commissaries, and loyal traders. Sentiment for the British cause vacillated and Indian aid was sporadic, unpredictable, and expensive. Stuart and his deputies were occasionally criticized by royal governors, military commanders, and British officials who did not fully appreciate the difficulties they encountered, including poor lines of communication, the decentralized nature of native political structure, the economic and social forces at work on the tribes, the natural reluctance of the Indians to provoke an attack from the American states, and the efforts of American agents who consistently urged the natives to remain neutral during the conflict.

In December 1778, British forces captured Savannah, Georgia. Stuart's Creek deputies were immediately sent forth, resulting in the most important Indian participation in the Revolutionary struggle during Stuart's superintendency. The Indian action during the early part of 1779 was, for the most part, directed by his deputies, with significant effect. Stuart, who remained in Pensacola, had been ill for some time and did not live to see the results of his cautious and costly policy of securing ready allies by providing necessary trade goods. He died in Pensacola on March 21, 1779. Following his death, the Southern Indian Department was thoroughly reorganized and its budget was sharply cut. Stuart was succeeded by Alexander Cameron and Thomas Brown.

Kathryn Braund

REFERENCES

John R. Alden, *John Stuart and the Southern Colonial Frontier* (1944); David H. Corkran, *The Creek Frontier*, 1540–1783 (1967); Philip M. Hamer, "Fort Loudoun in the Cherokee War 1758–1761," *North Carolina Historical Review*, 2(1925):442–458; ———, "John Stuart's Indian Policy during the Early Months of the American Revolution," *Mississippi Valley Historical Review*, 17 (1930):351–66; James H. O'Donnell III, *Southern Indians in the American Revolution* (1973).

Suffren de Saint-Tropez, Pierre-André de (1729–1788)

French navy officer. Born on July 17, 1729, to a noble family at Saint-Cannat near Aix, Suffren began his naval career at a young age. The Parliament of Aix encouraged the development of a strong navy in order to deter Spanish and Barbary pirates, and because Suffren was a younger son, he, like several of his siblings, entered the *Gardes de la Marine* in 1743. His first battle experience was on the *Solide* at the Battle of Toulon in February 1744. Suffren carefully observed tactics used by both sides and revealed his innate ability as a strategist in his insightful criticisms—commenting on both leaders' failures—in correspondence to his father.

Suffren also sailed on the *Pauline* in the West Indies and in the 1746 attempt by D'Anville to take Cape Breton. He continued naval duties until 1747 when he was captured by the British at the Bay of Biscay. As a prisoner he performed galley duty with the Order of Malta; after his release, he served as a lieutenant at Minorca, where the British surrendered, and from which incident Admiral John Byng was court-martialed. However, Suffren was captured again in 1757 by Admiral Boscawen near Lagos. Upon expatriation Suffren served as captain of the xebec *Cameleon*, fighting against Barbary pirates before serving the Order of Malta from 1767 to 1771 as a commander, training officers of the French navy until the American Revolution began.

Suffren's Revolutionary activity is overshadowed by his later performances in India. Between 1778 to 1779 he sailed under Admiral d'Estaing's command. In August 1778, military actions at

Newport, Rhode Island, were hindered by d'Estaing's unwillingness to cooperate fully with allied ground forces by coordinating his naval forces. Despite this poor performance by d'Estaing, Suffren performed well but became leery of his commanding officer's abilities.

At the Battle at Grenada on July 6, 1779, Suffren outlasted Admiral John Byron's forces but lost 62 men on the *Fantastique*. Critical of d'Estaing's talents as a naval commander, Suffren commented afterward that "had the admiral's seamanship equalled his courage, we would not have suffered four dismasted vessels to escape." D'Estaing, who had recently been transferred from the French army to the navy, was not well prepared for his position, and Suffren, complaining to his superiors, disapproved of his timidity. As a result of this action, Suffren was given command of five ships of the line to defend the Dutch colony at the Cape of Good Hope against the British.

Suffren sailed from Brest, France, on March 22, 1781, for the West Indies with his new commander Admiral de Grasse; at the Azores he detoured his five ships of the line on March 29 toward the Cape Verde Islands because he received news that the British were approaching the Cape. Suffren learned that the British—under the command of Admiral George Johnstone—were near the Cape Verde Islands, a Portuguese possession whose surrounding waters were neutral. Known for his "inborn military genius," Suffren realized that Portugal would not enforce the island's neutrality rules and decided to pursue the British instead of waiting for them to reach the Cape.

In a series of maneuvers, Suffren inflicted damage on the British and secured the Cape Colony, but he was unable to acquire a total victory due to the lack of his captain's cooperation and commitment. Despite this hindrance, Suffren's attack on the British at the Cape Verde Islands saved the colony and impressed the British that the French navy—especially with an analytical strategist like Suffren in command—should be respected.

Suffren's offensive sea-power policy countered traditional French defensive measures but won French naval forces recognition and respect as a powerful figure in global matters. Suffren returned to the Isle of France in the autumn of 1781, but he was relocated to the Indian theater in December 1781.

Although Suffren had no clear-cut victories in the India campaigns, mostly due to inept and pathetic captains, his style became more aggressive. He joined the command of Comte d'Orves, until the commander died. At that time, Suffren became commander, and his new nemesis was Sir Edward Hughes, who had blocked the Indian port of Trincomalee.

In a series of four military actions during 1782, Suffren executed offensive moves against Hughes. Along the coasts of India and Ceylon, he attacked the British, ultimately provoking a surrender. He captured the Port of Trincomalee, which was returned to Holland in the peace negotiations in 1783. Because he did not consider the victory complete, Suffren revised his strategy for a new offensive, but the declaration of peace interrupted his plans, and he returned to France as a hero and was appointed a vice admiral by the King.

Suffren, who was labeled by contemporaries as a glutton who often raged in violent temper fits, experienced declining health due to his poor eating habits and stress. He suffered from erysipelas and was unable to sail with his newly assigned fleet; when a local doctor bled him, Suffren lost too much blood and died on December 8, 1788. He was buried in the Knights Templar's sanctuary at Sainte-Marie-Madeleine de la Ville-cveque, but his remains were vandalized by an angry mob. In tribute to the novel naval strategist who innovated French naval methods and secured global respect for the French navy, Napoleon commented that if Suffren had lived during the French Revolution, "he would have been my Nelson." *See also*: Indian Ocean, the American Revolution in the; Porto Praya, Cape Verde Islands, Battle of

Elizabeth D. Schafer

REFERENCES

G.A. Ballard, "Hughes and Suffren," *The Mariner's Mirror*, 13 (October 1927):348–356; ——, "The Last Battlefleet Struggle in the Bay of Bengal," *The Mariner's Mirror*, 13 (April 1927):125–144; Roderick Cavaliero, "Admiral Suffren in the Indies," *History Today*, 20 (1970):472–80; Alfred Thayer Mahan, *The Influence of Sea Power Upon History 1660–1783* (1890); Charles Moran, "Suffren, The Apostle of Action," *United States Naval Institute Proceedings*, 64 (1938):315–325; Sir Herbert W. Richmond, "The Hughes-Suffren Campaigns," *The Mariner's Mirror*, 13 (July 1927):219–237.

Sullivan, John (1740–1795)

Continental Army officer. An early leader of the Patriot party in New Hampshire, John Sullivan was born February 14, 1740, in Somersworth, New Hampshire. He read law under Samuel Livermore in Portsmouth, and after being admitted to the bar, he first practiced in Berwick, Maine, before moving to Durham, New Hampshire, in 1763. Sullivan was the first lawyer in Durham and very early exhibited the ambition and vanity that were to mark him throughout his career. His neighbors accused him of encouraging suits and extorting unreasonable fees. By 1766, some of them were so incensed that they attacked him at the house of Joseph Cilley, in nearby Nottingham, New Hampshire.

By 1774, however, much of the animosity between Sullivan and his neighbors was past. They elected Sullivan to the First New Hampshire Provincial Congress in 1774. The provincial congress later elected him as one of New Hampshire's delegates to the First Continental Congress. In Philadelphia, Sullivan quickly joined the radicals. When the Congress dissolved, Sullivan returned to New Hampshire and continued to help lead the Patriot party.

On the afternoon of December 14, 1774, the Patriots, fearing that Governor John Wentworth had sent for British troops, attacked the fort at the mouth of Portsmouth harbor. Led by John Langdon, they overpowered the 6-man garrison and took some 100 barrels of gunpowder. The next day Sullivan appeared in Portsmouth. After an interview with the governor, in which he promised to disperse his followers, Sullivan led a second raid on the fort. The raiders carried away about 60 muskets and 15 cannon.

The following spring New Hampshire once again sent Sullivan to the Continental Congress. He continued as part of the radical party there, working closely with John Adams. When news of the fighting at Concord and Lexington reached Congress Sullivan welcomed it.

Congress moved ahead, adopting the army that had gathered outside of Boston, and selecting Washington and the other generals who would lead it. John Sullivan of New Hampshire was the seventh of eight brigadier generals that it appointed.

Sullivan joined the army in Cambridge on July 10, 1775. Washington gave him command of a brigade in Major General Charles Lee's division, which was camped at Winter Hill. Sullivan's introduction to battle occurred a few weeks later when Washington decided to establish an advanced post on Plowed Hill. Sullivan, with 1,200 men, seized the hill on the night of August 26. By dawn the troops were dug in. When the British saw the American trenches, which were within cannon shot of the British lines in front of Bunker Hill, they opened fire. Soon, a ship and two floating batteries in the harbor were cannonading Sullivan's trenches. Sullivan maintained his position and gave better than he got, driving away the ship, and sinking one of the floating batteries.

Although there was a stalemate around Boston, the British were aggressive elsewhere. They burned Falmouth (now Portland, Maine) on October 17, and Washington feared that Portsmouth, New Hampshire, might be next. Accordingly, he sent Sullivan north to take charge of the defense of the town. Arriving in Portsmouth, Sullivan energetically set to work. As it turned out the British did not attack Portsmouth, and Sullivan returned to the army once the alarm was over.

During this time Sullivan was busy not only as a general but also as a politician. He corresponded steadily with Revolutionary leaders in New Hampshire and with friends in Congress. Sullivan was an early supporter of independence, and for some time he had been urging that New Hampshire form a government. By December 1775, his thoughts had advanced to the point that he wrote Meshech Weare, chairman of New Hampshire's Committee of Safety, with an outline for a government having a governor and a two-house legislature.

Early in March 1776, Washington fortified Dorchester Heights and the British were forced to evacuate Boston. Soon after the British left Boston, Washington marched the army to New York. Shortly after reaching New York, Washington ordered Sullivan to lead six regiments north as reinforcements for the army in Canada. When Sullivan arrived at St. John's he found himself in command of an army ravaged by smallpox and threatened by the British. Sullivan made a rash attempt to attack the British at Trois Rivières but soon accepted the fact that only a retreat could save his army. By June 10 the army reached Isle-aux-Noix, carrying with it over 780 sick men. Stubbornly, Sullivan wanted to hold Isle-aux-Noix, the last post in Canada, but sounder advice prevailed and the retreat continued. The remnants of the northern army reached Crown Point on July 1.

At Crown Point, Sullivan learned that Congress had appointed Major General Horatio Gates to relieve him. Outraged by what he saw as a slight by Congress, Sullivan headed to Philadelphia to resign from the army. John Hancock convinced him not to resign but to accept Congress' order to report to Washington in New York. Sullivan's hurt feelings must have been soothed when, in August, Congress promoted him to major general.

Washington ordered Sullivan to Long Island on August 20 to replace Nathanael Greene, who was sick. Two days later the British landed on Long Island, and along with reinforcements, Washington sent General Israel Putnam to assume overall command there. Sullivan remained on Long Island, commanding the troops outside of the Brooklyn fortifications, under Putnam. There was some skirmishing between the Continentals and the British on August 23, which Sullivan reported to Washington as a repulsed attack, and additional reinforcements were ferried over the East River to Brooklyn.

Washington went to Long Island the next day to inspect the lines. He ordered Putnam to make some changes in the disposition of his troops but either he did not notice or did not think it important that Sullivan's left flank was "in the air" (i.e., without protective terrain).

There were about 7,000 American soldiers on Long Island. Sullivan commanded about 2,800 of them spread along the heights blocking the approaches to the Brooklyn defenses. There were four major approaches to the Brooklyn fortifications, and Sullivan had stationed most of his troops blocking the three roads that led most directly from the British camp to Brooklyn. The fourth road, on the American left, went through Jamaica Pass. It was guarded by a mounted patrol of five militiamen.

Early in the morning of August 27 the British attacked the American right and center. While these attacks developed, 10,000 British troops under General Henry Clinton were marching through Jamaica Pass and behind the American front line. When the British reached Bedford they fired two signal guns and all of the British then attacked in earnest. Surprised and almost surrounded, Sullivan's troops soon retreated in confusion. Sullivan, with some 400 men, was trapped in a cornfield near the Flatbush Road. There, a pistol in each hand, he faced the attacking Hessians, but by noon he was their prisoner.

This was probably the darkest day of Sullivan's military career. Many writers, both among Sullivan's contemporaries and later historians, have blamed Sullivan for the defeat on Long Island, but if there was much blame there were many to blame, including Washington and Putnam.

Sullivan was taken aboard Admiral Lord Richard Howe's flagship. There he dined with the admiral and listened to his proposals. Howe, who was both an admiral fighting the rebels and a commissioner hoping to make peace with them, convinced Sullivan to serve as an intermediary between himself and the Congress. Sullivan was gulled by Howe. He accepted a parole to present Howe's proposals, which conceded neither independence nor the renunciation of the right of taxation by Parliament, to the Congress. John Adams called Sullivan "Howe's decoy duck" and wished he had been killed in battle rather than present such a potentially divisive proposal to Congress.

Sullivan was back with Washington's army by the end of September, having been exchanged for the captured British general Richard Prescott. In command of his division, Sullivan joined the retreat of the American army from New York City, north to White Plains. There, Washington ordered him to join General Charles Lee's command at North Castle. When, on December 13, Lee was captured, Sullivan, as his second in command, promptly marched to join Washington.

Sullivan reached Washington by December 20. When Washington crossed the Delaware River to attack Trenton on December 26, Sullivan was with him at the head of a division made up of New Hampshire, Massachusetts, Connecticut, and New York Continentals. Some of those troops, marching from Ticonderoga, did not reach Washington until after December 22.

At Trenton, Sullivan's division formed Washington's right wing. When Sullivan reported to Washington that the sleet had so wet his men's muskets that they could not be fired Washington sent back telling Sullivan to use the bayonet. Sullivan did so. The division, with Colonel John Stark in the lead, charged the Hessians, cutting off their retreat to the south. Washington captured Colonel Wilhelm Von Knyphausen's regiment and one battalion of Lossberg's. Washington, and Sullivan, finally had a victory.

Four days after his victory at Trenton, Washington returned to New Jersey. The New England Continentals' enlistments had expired at the end of the year. Many of them agreed to reenlist for a six-week winter campaign upon Washington's promise of a ten dollar bounty and a continuation of their pay. These, with the militia that had been joining, gave Washington the force that he needed. Slipping away from the British in front of Trenton, Washington headed toward Princeton with Sullivan's Division toward his front.

Sullivan, with his division, entered Princeton from the east early on the morning of January 3, 1777. After a stiff fight the British broke. Sullivan's men chased them into the college yard, where some surrendered immediately. Others, who had sheltered in Nassau Hall, surrendered after artillery was brought up and opened fire.

The army went into winter quarters at Morristown, but Sullivan, suffering from stomach problems, took leave and returned home for the winter. While there, he corresponded with Washington, complaining, among other things, that he had not been given command of Fort Ticonderoga. Washington told Sullivan that no other officer in the army had thought himself so slighted with less cause. Rebuked, Sullivan returned to camp in the spring. In May he was in command of his division garrisoning Princeton.

The summer of 1777 found Washington waiting to see where Howe would strike. As Howe maneuvered, Washington responded. He stationed Sullivan first at Rocky Hill and then at Flemington, New Jersey.

In July, hearing that General John Burgoyne was approaching Fort Ticonderoga, Washington shifted north. He ordered Sullivan first to Pompton, New Jersey, then farther north into the Ramapo Mountains, and then to Peekskill, New York. Later that month, when it became clear that Howe had left New York and sailed south, Washington hurried Sullivan, along with the rest of his army, toward Philadelphia. Unsure of Howe's intentions, Washington halted Sullivan at Morristown and then ordered him a few miles east to Hanover.

British troops on Staten Island were in the habit of foraging along the New Jersey shore.

While Sullivan was at Hanover, he led some of his troops in a counterraid on Staten Island. He was at first successful but as the day wore on his men began to straggle. The crossing back to New Jersey was chaotic. Although there was a shortage of boats, loot was still being ferried across as British reinforcements came up and overwhelmed Sullivan's rear guard.

While Sullivan was raiding Staten Island, Washington received firm news that Howe was on the Chesapeake. He started to concentrate his army and sent orders to Sullivan to march at once. Sullivan reached Washington early in September and commanded the army's right wing at the Battle of Brandywine on September 11, 1777.

Sullivan's role at Brandywine was almost a replay of Long Island. There was inadequate reconnaissance, the American right was turned, and the army was driven from the field. Sullivan was criticized for his conduct both at Staten Island and at Brandywine, and Congress voted to recall him from the army to face an inquiry.

At Washington's request the recall was delayed. Washington continued Sullivan in command and was with him as Sullivan led his division into battle at Germantown.

On the morning of October 4, 1777, Sullivan led his troops down the Germantown Road against the British. On a foggy battlefield he drove the British back; his troops charging with the bayonet, stopping British countercharges, and advancing again. Sullivan advanced into the center of the town but Anthony Wayne, who had been on his left flank, had withdrawn. Sullivan was unsupported and his men were low on ammunition. The attack was spent and the troops started to retreat. Although the attack failed and the retreat was rapid and disorganized, the army was not discouraged. Both officers and men felt that a victory had been almost won and that only the fog had deprived them of it.

Washington led the army back to Pennybacker's Mill, where they camped and rested. As the army rested, Sullivan's court of inquiry met. After hearing the evidence the court voted unanimously to acquit him. Congress later passed a resolution endorsing the verdict.

Sullivan was with the army when it camped at Valley Forge. Until February he was involved in building a bridge over the Schuylkill River. When that task was completed he applied for leave to go home and see to his financial affairs.

Washington refused him, remarking that he needed all of his generals. When Sullivan continued to push his request, Washington offered instead the command in Rhode Island, which had recently become vacant. That would station Sullivan nearer his home and give him the independent command that he so clearly wanted.

Sullivan set out for Rhode Island late in March 1778, but first he went to New Hampshire to see his family and arrange his finances. He arrived in Rhode Island on April 17, and the next day the Rhode Island Council of War placed all the troops in Rhode Island under his command.

When Sullivan arrived in Rhode Island he found few troops actually there for him to command, and few supplies for the troops that he did have. Sullivan set to work with his usual energy to remedy the situation. Although as late as May 8 he had only 360 soldiers, more were coming. The remainder of a New Hampshire regiment of state troops was on the road, and he was writing to Governors Jonathan Trumbull of Connecticut, James Bowdoin of Massachusetts, William Greene of Rhode Island, and Meshech Weare of New Hampshire urging them to hurry on the troops that had been requested from their states.

At the same time that he was searching for troops, Sullivan was looking for supplies. He wrote letters to Major General William Heath, commanding at Boston, to Henry Laurens, president of the Congress, and to Jeremiah Wadsworth, commissary general, requesting supplies and munitions. Sullivan needed artillery, muskets, slow match, uniforms, and much else to supply his army. In many cases the militia that were joining him had no supplies, not even muskets.

In July, Sullivan learned that he would not have to spend the summer on the defensive. Washington wrote him on July 17, warning that it was probable that the French fleet and army would be sent to join him in Rhode Island. Sullivan was ordered to call out 5,000 militia from New England, collect provisions, assemble boats, and hire pilots familiar with the waters around Newport. To form a core for the militia, Washington sent Lafayette's division of Continentals to Sullivan.

The Comte d'Estaing, with a French Fleet, arrived off Rhode Island on July 29. Meanwhile, Lafayette, with his two brigades, John Glover's and James Varnum's, was marching to join Sullivan. Although not all of the militia that he called for joined him, Sullivan's force grew to over 6,000 men, about half of whom were Continentals. Some of the militia were still on the march when d'Estaing arrived. The plan was that on July 10 the French would land their 4,000 troops on the west side of the island. At the same time the Americans would cross at the Tiverton Ferry and land on the island's northeast corner.

The British realized that an assault was coming, and on the evening of August 8–9, they abandoned their positions at the northern end of the island and withdrew to the fortified lines about Newport. Sullivan, quick to seize an advantage, crossed his force immediately and notified d'Estaing. Before d'Estaing landed all of his troops, a British fleet under Admiral Richard Howe from New York appeared. Quickly reembarking his soldiers d'Estaing set sail to meet the British.

While d'Estaing was chasing Howe, Sullivan moved toward the British lines outside of Newport. He started to dig entrenchments and to approach the British lines with a series of parallels. As soon as cannon were emplaced Sullivan opened a heavy bombardment to which the British replied in kind.

Meanwhile, the two fleets had fought a confused running battle in the midst of a storm, and the British returned to New York to refit. D'Estaing returned to Rhode Island on August 20, but only long enough to tell Sullivan that he was sailing immediately for Boston to make repairs. Although Sullivan protested, d'Estaing was adamant, and the French fleet sailed for Boston immediately.

Sullivan estimated that the British had about 6,500 men on Rhode Island. His own strength he gave as 8,174 infantry rank and file of which about 7,000 were militia. (Other sources indicate that Sullivan had over 1,800 rank-and-file Continental infantry in addition to his militia and state troops.) Faced with the departure of his ally, Sullivan had no choice but to withdraw. He was not strong enough to risk an assault on the British lines and without a fleet of his own he risked being cut off on the island.

Sullivan started to withdraw his troops on the night of August 28. The British followed him and attacked both his flanks. Sullivan maneuvered his troops with skill, inflicting heavy casualties while beating back each of the British attacks. He withdrew from the island on the night of August 29–30, taking with him all of his artillery and supplies.

Sullivan was both disappointed and angered by d'Estaing's actions. He and his generals sent a protest to d'Estaing in which they called the admiral's actions "derogatory to the honor of France . . . and highly injurious to the alliance formed between the two nations." Both Congress and Washington had to act quickly to head off a confrontation between Sullivan and d'Estaing. Congress resolved to prohibit the publication of Sullivan's protest, and Washington pointed out to Sullivan the importance of the French alliance. Still, there was a great deal of discontent with the French in New England, and Sullivan never seemed to realize the bad effect that his dispute with d'Estaing could have on the French alliance.

By early September Sullivan and his remaining troops were back at Providence. Sullivan sent the remaining militia home and settled down to watch the British. That winter, short of forage and flour, he entered into a protracted dispute with the Commissary Department that called out his most contentious characteristics. Even his friend Nathanael Greene thought that Sullivan had "turned Lawyer again." Sullivan remained in command at Rhode Island until March 1779, when Washington offered him the command of an expedition against the Indians of the Six Nations.

Sullivan's expedition against the Six Nations was made up of three brigades, William Maxwell's, Enoch Poor's, and Edward Hand's, as well as several guns manned by a detachment of Continental artillery. The division, just over 3,000 officers and men, assembled at Easton, Pennsylvania, and marched first to Wyoming, then to Pennsylvania, and finally to Tioga. Two days later, Sullivan burned the Indian village of Chemung after a brief skirmish. The expedition then marched up the Chemung River and into the Finger Lakes district of New York.

The Indians and their British and Tory allies did not make a stand until Sullivan approached the village of Newtown. There they attempted to ambush Sullivan's Division, but the trap was spotted before it could be closed. Sullivan made a full-scale attack, and after a sharp action the enemy gave way. After Newtown, the army marched as far as Genesee Castle, burning villages and destroying crops as they went. By the middle of October the expedition was back at Easton, Pennsylvania.

Although the campaign was called a success, it did not destroy the ability of the Indians to raid the frontier. Many people, in and out of the army, ridiculed both the campaign and Sullivan. Congress, irritated by Sullivan's many complaints, decided to appoint an investigating committee. While the committee was conducting its investigation, Sullivan, complaining of poor health, tendered his resignation. Washington tried to dissuade him, but Sullivan persisted, and on November 30, 1779, Congress voted to accept his resignation.

As a general, Sullivan had had an undeservedly bad reputation. Although no analysis would place him among the first rank of Washington's generals, a careful look at his military activities, as opposed to his military correspondence, should place him in a more favorable light. Sullivan's bravery and energy were never questioned. He was an efficient administrator but perhaps too solicitous of the welfare of his troops. He was at his worst at Long Island and Brandywine, seemingly only able to look straight ahead. He showed to best advantage at Trenton and Princeton, where he demonstrated ability if not brilliance. Although he has been called unlucky and was intemperate in his correspondence, he was always loyal to Washington, and Washington valued his services. It may be best to let Washington have the last word. In a letter to Sullivan shortly after his resignation, Washington wrote, "The confidence you have experienced, and the manner in which you have been employed on several important occasions, testify the value I set upon your military qualifications, and the regret I must feel that circumstances have deprived the army of your services."

After resigning from the army, Sullivan returned home to New Hampshire. He got his mills back into operation and reopened his law practice. Soon he was back in public life. The New Hampshire Legislature appointed him its agent to settle the dispute with New York over the territory that is now Vermont. They also elected him as a delegate to Congress, and on September 11, 1780, he once again took a seat in that body. As a member of Congress, Sullivan usually supported measures that promoted a stronger central government and more efficient finances. Sullivan left Congress for the last time on August 11, 1781, to return to New Hampshire.

In New Hampshire, Sullivan was active in state politics. At various times he served as legislator, attorney general, judge, militia general, and president of the state. When the United States Constitution was sent to the states for ratification, Sullivan was elected president of the New Hampshire ratifying convention. A strong Federalist, Sullivan was active in securing New Hampshire's vote for the Constitution.

In 1789, after the new federal government had been organized, Washington appointed Sullivan federal district judge for New Hampshire. Sullivan was President of the State of New Hampshire at the time. When the New Hampshire Legislature objected to his holding offices, Sullivan resigned the presidency a few days before the end of his term.

Although Sullivan was only 50 years old he was deteriorating quickly. In the early 1790s he was financially strapped. At the same time he was involved in numerous disputes with his neighbors. Drinking heavily and rapidly becoming senile, John Sullivan died January 23, 1795. Sullivan was a complex and flawed man. He was intemperate and pompous. He was also an active leader, a skillful politician, and a strong nationalist.

Walter A. Ryan

REFERENCES

Steve Adams, "John Sullivan," *New Hampshire, Years of Revolution, 1774–1783*, ed. by Peter E. Randall (1976); James Thomas Flexner, *George Washington in the American Revolution (1775–1783)* (1968); Otis G. Hammond, ed., *Letters and Papers of John Sullivan, Continental Army*, 3 vols. (1930–1939); Richard F. Upton, "John Langdon and John Sullivan, A Biographical Essay," *New Hampshire, The State That Made Us A Nation*, ed. by William M. Gardner II, Franc C. Mevers III, and Richard F. Upton (1989); Charles P. Whittemore, *A General of the Revolution: John Sullivan of New Hampshire* (1961).

Sullivan-Clinton Expedition to Iroquois Country (June–October 1779)

On September 30, 1779, Major General John Sullivan and his force of nearly 4,000 Continental soldiers marched in triumph onto the grassy river plain near Fort Sullivan (present-day Athens, Pennsylvania) to be greeted by the sounds of cheering soldiers and a 13-gun salute fired from the small fort's cannon. Behind him lay the ruins of the once powerful Iroquois nation. In the two months that his forces had operated in the Indian country, they had reaped a whirlwind's worth of destruction on their Tory and Indian adversaries. His soldiers had torched 40 Iroquois towns and villages. In the fields near the villages lay the remains of an estimated 160,000 bushels of corn that had been burned or cut down to rot in the frost-touched autumn mornings. Thousands of fruit trees hanged withered and dying, their trunks girdled by Sullivan's men. The Iroquois had been turned out of their homeland and forced to take refuge with their British allies at Fort Niagara throughout the snowbound winter of 1779. Both the Continental Congress and George Washington congratulated Sullivan and his men on a job well done, though later historians would differ on the degree to which accolades were due.

Three clear themes have arisen in the histories written of this campaign. A. Tiffany Norton and David Craft wrote the first accounts of the operation in the late nineteenth century and argued that it was a tremendous success given the destruction that Sullivan's men wrought upon the Iroquois. These historians saw the expedition as a purely punitive campaign launched to rid the white frontier settlements of the Indian threat. Twentieth-century historians such as Alexander Flick expanded on the Norton-Craft thesis claiming that the campaign was critical in supporting United States claims to western lands south of the Great Lakes given Iroquois influence there. Donald McAdams's works represented the campaign's final school of thought and stood in opposition to opinions of earlier historians. McAdams saw Sullivan's expedition as a failure since Indian raiding parties returned to raid the frontier regions of Pennsylvania and New York during the following summer.

The truth may lie someplace in the middle, for though Sullivan did force the dislocation of the Iroquois, he nonetheless failed in his mission to destroy their military power, since he was unable to bring about a classic battle of annihilation. In addition, he failed to meet Washington's instructions to capture as many Indian women and children as possible. American military and civilian leaders hoped to hold these as hostages and thereby neutralize the threat posed by Iroquois warriors. However, these failures cannot overshadow the fact that Sullivan's actions did force Iroquois raiding parties to operate from closer to Fort Niagara in western New York throughout the following years. The distances involved complicated Iroquois operations and limited the size of their raiding parties. Though Indian raids remained numerous, none matched the death and destruction of earlier raids launched in 1778 against Pennsylvania's Wyoming Valley or the New York settlements of German Flats and Cherry Valley. In addition, Sullivan's campaign drove an immovable wedge into the Iroquois Confederacy, splitting the allegiance of the tribes between the British and their rebellious colonists. This division made it far easier for whites to push their claims into the old lands of the Iroquois in the years after the war.

Though the Iroquois question had plagued the Continental Congress from the start of the war, the before mentioned Iroquois raids on the Wyoming Valley, German Flats, and Cherry Valley finally forced Congress to push Washington for a punitive expedition against the Iroquois. Though some congressional and military officers hoped for a winter campaign to be conducted before the close of 1778, Washington resisted the pressure, taking a broader view of the strategic circumstances facing his army. Congress' desires for a campaign against the Iroquois had to be matched against the capabilities of the Continental Army and the probable courses of action open to the British. As 1778 drew to a close, the British fleet patrolled the Atlantic coast, but British land forces largely had been confined to the ports of New York and Newport, Rhode Island. A combined French-American operation against the latter had been planned for the summer of 1778, but it had to be cancelled when the French withdrew their fleet. Washington saw 1779 as a year of promise for the rebel cause. His British foes seemed preoccupied with the threat posed to their worldwide Empire by France and were unreluctant for the time being to resume the offensive in North America. This passivity left the Virginian a window of opportunity for taking the offensive.

Washington found himself facing several options as the new year approached. He could attempt to expel British forces from New York. This, he estimated, would require over 20,000 soldiers, and the presence of the British fleet would severely complicate the operation. A second possibility would be to try once again to attack the British in Newport should the French fleet become available. A third proposal envisioned another attempt to invade Canada along the Hudson River–Lake Champlain route. A fourth option would be to keep the British bottled up in their seaport towns while launching an offensive against the British stronghold of Fort Niagara. Such an operation would cut the flow of arms and ammunition of the Iroquois while presenting the British with a viable threat to their position along the Great Lakes and in Canada. This alternative would require fewer troops than the others but would demand the construction of a rebel naval fleet on Lake Ontario for a successful siege. A final possibility envisioned the invasion of the Iroquois homelands with the intent of eliminating the Indian threat to the frontier regions of western Pennsylvania and New York.

Weighing the options at hand against his own combat strength and that of his enemy, Washington opted for the campaign against the Iroquois. He was enough of an opportunist to take advantage of any opening the British might allow him at Niagara, but a siege of the British stronghold was not a prime consideration. The logistics problems involved simply precluded it as a possibility. Soldiers would need to drag siege artillery over long distances through a nearly unbroken wilderness of steep heavily wooded mountains, a back-breaking, time-consuming labor. Washington could ill afford such a siege in the wilderness of New York.

Given Washington's desire to complete the expedition in the shortest possible time, his choice of commanders seems on the surface to have been peculiar. The Virginian originally offered the command to General Horatio Gates. When Gates refused the assignment, the command fell to the next in line, General John Sullivan. Sullivan had not enjoyed a particularly successful military career during the war and was never known for his speed in executing orders. The New Hampshire lawyer did have a reputation for being a detailed planner and had demonstrated marked courage in previous battles. Perhaps Washington intended to capitalize on Sullivan's attributes while assuming that Sullivan could be goaded into executing the operation at an accelerated pace.

Even before the commander-in-chief had

settled on a commander, Washington had been busy gathering information of the proposed area of operations. One of the biggest problems facing any force operating against the Iroquois was the lack of anything approaching an adequate map of the region north of Tioga (now known as Athens), Pennsylvania. Guides with firsthand knowledge of the region were just as difficult to find. Washington worked to overcome this deficiency by sending inquiries to officers he felt might have knowledge of the area. Included in the questionnaire were inquiries as to the depth and navigability of the North Branch of the Susquehanna River from Fort Augusta (present-day Sunbury, Pennsylvania) to Tioga, and the trafficability of trails north along the Susquehanna and west connecting the Susquehanna and the Allegheny River. His interest in trails connecting the Susquehanna with the Allegheny clearly indicated that he was at least considering the possibility of a flanking movement in support of Sullivan from the vicinity of Fort Pitt.

As intelligence concerning the Iroquois homelands trickled into Continental Army headquarters in New Jersey, Washington settled on a two-pronged attack with the main force moving from Easton, Pennsylvania, to the Wyoming Valley and then north along the Susquehanna into the Finger Lakes. A second wing of Sullivan's army under the command of Brigadier General James Clinton would stage out of Canajoharie, New York, and either move up the Mohawk River or down the Susquehanna from Lake Otsego. Washington left the choice as to Clinton's route to Sullivan, though the commander-in-chief clearly favored the latter route because it concentrated the two wings of the army faster. As to the possibility of a supporting attack up the Allegheny, Washington counted this out as too difficult to execute but later changed his mind at the suggestion of Colonel Daniel Brodhead, Fort Pitt's commander. Washington never insisted on a coordinated effort but permitted Brodhead to organize an attack against Indian settlements on the upper Allegheny and instructed him to open a correspondence with Sullivan so that the two commanders could be kept informed as to each other's plans and progress. In light of the supply problems plaguing the Americans at Fort Pitt, the commander-in-chief must have known that he could not guarantee Brodhead the supplies necessary to make the American drive up the

Allegheny an integral part of the operation. Washington may have been hoping that Sullivan's presence at the southern door to the Iroquois settlements would force the Indians and their Tory allies to shift their forces to the east in order to meet this threat. This would strip the western Iroquois settlements along the Allegheny of their braves and open the region to destruction at the hands of Brodhead's small force.

To assist Sullivan in gaining the element of surprise, Washington ordered Sullivan to leak rumors that another expedition would soon be launched against Canada. Lending credence to the rumors, Washington ordered Colonel Moses Hazen to begin gathering supplies in Newbury, Connecticut, and start construction of a road up the Connecticut River toward the St. Lawrence River and Montreal. The feint worked as Philip Schuyler later reported to Sullivan that his sources had counted only four companies of enemy reinforcements passing up the St. Lawrence during the spring. In addition, Washington had ordered his quartermaster general, Nathanael Greene, to construct bateaux for a possible move up the Hudson River toward Lake Champlain. Both strategies fed British fears that Canada or Fort Niagara was the real objective of Patriot endeavors.

Washington's feint had succeeded in isolating his adversaries. British intelligence sources had done an admirable job in identifying Continental troop movements in Pennsylvania along the Delaware River and in New York along the Hudson. The British correctly but belatedly guessed that Washington would launch these units into New York, but the American commander had succeeded in keeping the final objective of the operation a secret. The British believed that Sullivan's ultimate aim was Fort Niagara, which explains why so few British regulars were sent to the aid of the Iroquois. On the British list of priorities, Quebec, Montreal, Fort Oswego, and Fort Niagara all ranked higher than the security of the Iroquois buffer states.

Washington was quite clear in the goals he set for Sullivan. To Sullivan, he wrote:

> The expedition you are appointed to command is to be directed against the hostile tribes of the Six Nations of Indians, with their associated and adherents. The immediate objects are the total destruction and devastation of their settlements and the

capture of as many prisoners of every age and sex as possible. It will be essential to ruin their crops now in the ground and prevent their planting more.

The commander-in-chief made no mention in either the initial or subsequent guidance of a requirement to conduct a linkup with Brodhead. Neither did Washington specify that Fort Niagara be included as one of the primary objectives. He did caution Sullivan that "should Niagara fall into your hands . . . you will do everything in your power for preserving and maintaining it."

Despite the limitations facing Sullivan, Washington was clearly intent on supporting his subordinate to the best of his ability. To underscore this, Washington eventually assigned over 4,000 Continental regulars, the cream of his army, to Sullivan for the expedition. Sullivan would guard this asset carefully, politely but firmly refusing every request from Pennsylvania's politicians for the use of part of his force for guard duty on the frontier.

While Greene began the process of gathering boats and supplies to provision the campaign, Sullivan and Clinton began assembling the two elements of the expedition in Easton and Canajoharie. In far off Fort Pitt, Brodhead started to garner his meager assets in preparation for his own campaign along the northernmost reaches of the Allegheny.

The first task facing Sullivan and his men in the spring of 1779 was that of cutting a road through the wilderness that stretched between Easton and Wyoming. While the road was under construction through the virgin forests of the Pocono Mountains, an advanced party under the command of Lieutenant Colonel Adam Hubley worked on the Susquehanna River to move the supplies that had been purchased by Greene's agents upriver, first to Fort Augusta, (present-day Sunbury, Pennsylvania) and then on to the Wyoming Valley. Sullivan hoped to have his supplies stockpiled and waiting for him when he moved the main body of his soldiers to Wyoming. In a day when roads were poor and water navigation dependent on water levels in the naturally shallow rivers of Pennsylvania and New York, the question of when to concentrate men and provisions required intricate timing. The trick was to stage the movement so that supplies and provisions arrived in the proper quantities at designated depots only slightly in advance of troops. Commanders were to move their troops out of the depots in the shortest time possible after securing their supplies and provisions so as to minimize the amount of provisions consumed prior to resuming their mission. Numerous problems plagued the officers and men who labored to build Sullivan's stockpile of supplies. When Sullivan and the main body arrived at Wyoming on June 23, 1779, stockage levels were insufficient to permit an immediate offensive. Sullivan and his army waited until July 31 before the logistics problem could be marginally met by Greene's officers.

Sullivan's delay gave the British sufficient time to attempt to divert the Americans from their task. Though unable to provide any substantial numbers of regulars, General Sir Frederick Haldimand, Britain's governor-in-chief in Canada, made use of Tory commander John Butler and his small band of rangers as well as Iroquois warriors under Iroquois chiefs such as Joseph Brant to harass the frontier regions. Lacking sufficient ammunition and food for a concerted campaign, the best the British and their allies could do was to raid colonial settlements at Minisink on the Delaware River and Fort Freeland 15 miles north of Fort Augusta. Neither effort turned Sullivan's eyes from his objective.

While Sullivan grappled with his supply problems in the Wyoming Valley, Clinton more easily gathered his resources in New York. By mid-June, he was ready to portage his bateaux to Lake Otsego on the headwaters of the Susquehanna. Once at Otsego, he moved his boats through the lake's narrow 15-yard-wide outlet to the river and grounded them along the stream's banks. Next he had his men dam the lake to raise the water level above the boats. When Clinton finally received his orders to move to his linkup with Sullivan, he simply had his men blow up the dam with several kegs of gun powder. The ensuing flood floated his boats across the shallows existing in the upper reaches of the Susquehanna and on toward the rendezvous point at Tioga.

Sullivan began his march from Wyoming on July 31 and proceeded almost without opposition to Tioga arriving on August 11. Indian raiding parties occasionally succeeded in lifting the scalp of a lone sentry but found themselves impotent to slow the progress of the small army. Credit for the move's success belongs to Sullivan.

The commander organized his expedition with a keen eye toward maintaining its security. Light infantry led the march as point security at least a mile in advance of the main body. Flank security elements marched on each side of the main body and also on the opposite side of the Susquehanna River. The task of opposite shore security was supported by small artillery pieces mounted on some of the supply bateaux moving in the river. Sullivan dedicated several boats to the task of extracting this company should they meet a superior force along the far shore. If Hand's lead elements made contact with the enemy, Sullivan's order of battle called for those elements to fix the enemy in place while his flank brigades under Brigadier Generals Enoch Poor and William Maxwell maneuvered to an open flank to envelop the enemy.

No such intricate maneuvers proved necessary on the march to Tioga. At Tioga, Sullivan halted his men to await the arrival of Clinton. Making good use of the time, the Americans built a small stockade fort on the river plain and named it Fort Sullivan in honor of their commander. The crude fort would serve as Sullivan's most advanced supply depot for the critical final thrust into the Iroquois homelands.

While Sullivan waited for Clinton to float downriver to rendezvous at Tioga, Brodhead and his ragged band of 600 soldiers began their trek up the Allegheny on August 11. As hoped, the Iroquois had their eyes focused on the threat posed by the Americans to the southern entrance to their lands. Brodhead's men met inconsequential opposition, burning 8 villages and over 500 acres of crops before turning back to Fort Pitt as their supply situation became critical with the approach of colder weather. No attempt was ever made to linkup with Sullivan.

Sullivan's first skirmish with his Tory and Indian foes occurred at the Indian village of Chemung the day after Brodhead began his move up the Allegheny. The engagement was brief and Sullivan's men easily carried the day. After burning the village, the Americans returned to Tioga to await the arrival of Clinton.

Clinton and his men along with many badly needed supplies arrived at Tioga on August 22. With this linkup, Butler and Brant's final chance to defeat the Americans while the two wings of Sullivan's army were split vanished. Unknown to Sullivan as he started his army on its march northward toward the Indian settlements nestled along the shores of the Finger Lakes, his Continentals now enjoyed better than a three-to-one superiority over their foes.

Both Butler and Brant realized that time was no longer on their side. Facing dwindling morale among their ranks, the two men managed to convince the other chiefs present that Sullivan had to be stopped and hopefully destroyed before he penetrated into the Finger Lakes. The question became one of where to engage the Americans. After considerable disagreement, the chiefs finally decided to ambush Sullivan's army just below Newtown (near present-day Elmira, New York), the site of a Delaware village. They hoped that the element of surprise would compensate for their deficiency in numbers. Neither Butler nor Brant liked the choice of Newtown, but it was Indian custom that the warriors from the village most directly threatened should select the spot for combat. Though the Delawares were little more than conquered wards of the Iroquois, they were nonetheless given the deciding vote on where to fight.

The site that the Delawares selected for the ambush was adequate with Chemung Creek on the west and high ground on the east. Working side by side, Tory rangers and Iroquois braves built a barricade of brush and timber a half-mile long to the west of the trail along a narrow 10- to 15-foot-high ridge of glacial rocks. The barricade was within musket range and at an oblique angle to the trail that Butler and Brant expected the Americans to take. Perpendicular to the path and forward of the barricade, Iroquois braves constructed a few well-camouflaged positions along a small stream bed designed to allow the braves to fall upon either the American rear elements or the pack train that carried Sullivan's critical supplies. To the east of the trail, Butler and Brant placed additional warriors and soldiers. Essentially, the ambush was laid out as a "U." Sullivan's men were to enter the ambush along the bottom curved portion of the "U." Once the ambush was executed, the well-hidden braves along the bottom of the "U" near the stream bed would seal the escape routes out of the ambush and deal with Sullivan's rear guard using the confusion and panic created by the ambush to compensate for their numerical inferiority. The Tories and their Indian allies no doubt hoped to recreate for Sullivan the same fate that had befallen General Edward Braddock during the French and Indian War.

Fortunately for Sullivan, the ambush site was completed too early. Rather than worry about the construction of additional ambush positions north of the main site, both Tories and Indians settled in to await the arrival of the Americans. Boredom soon overtook the defenders and with the boredom came carelessness. Some braves talked among themselves as they hid in the bushes of the ambush. One Indian fired his musket at a deer that wandered within range. Another brave, painted in bright red war paint, decided to shift his position. His was the move that saved Sullivan and his men.

One of Sullivan's light infantry men spotted the brave's movement among the bushes to his front and signaled his unit to halt. Silently, the signal was passed to trailing regiments. The American light infantrymen dressed in their buckskin hunting shirts faded into the brush to await orders while word of the ambush site was passed back to Sullivan.

The two opposing forces became aware of each other's presence at about the same time. Frustrated in their attempt to have the Americans walk unknowingly into their trap, the Indians now tried to entice their foes into a frontal attack that would perform the same function. For three hours small bands of Indians ventured forward to skirmish with their buckskin-clad foes then retreated in mock panic back along the trail toward their own positions. Sullivan recognized the ruse and refused to allow his men to follow. While the two sides skirmished among the trees, Sullivan put his own plan into operation.

Much as originally envisioned, Sullivan attempted to execute a double envelopment of his foes. Two brigades under Enoch Poor and Clinton maneuvered to the east with the intention of falling on the enemy flank while another regiment under Matthias Ogden attempted to flank the ambush along Chemung Creek. Hand's light infantry, who had been engaged in the three-hour-long skirmish, were to permit Poor and Clinton one hour to conduct their flank movement then begin a frontal attack on the enemy positions. Thomas Proctor's artillery were to move forward behind Edward Hand's men and provide fire support.

The plan did not work as Sullivan desired. One hour proved to be too short a period for Poor and Clinton to move into position due to the difficulty they encountered moving through a swamp located along their route of maneuver.

As a result, the fury of Hand's assault coupled with the rain of shot and shell from Proctor's artillery that pelted the ambush began to break Indian morale. It was quite clear to both Brant and Butler that they could not stand up to the Continentals in any pitched battle in which Sullivan could bring the full weight of his numbers and firepower to bear. Both Indians and Tories began to run to the rear just as the American right flank units arrived in position on the high ground east of the ambush. These flank elements were unable to envelop the ambush before most of its defenders had deserted it. Sullivan and his men easily carried the field but failed to destroy their opponents.

After Newtown, Sullivan pressed his men forward into the Indian heartlands located around the Finger Lakes. The terrain leading into the Finger Lakes was well suited for the same kind of delaying operations that Patriot militia had used so effectively to cripple the progress of General Sir John Burgoyne's forces on their march southward to Saratoga two years before, but the Indians lacked the heart and discipline necessary to return the favor on Sullivan's Continentals. Though Butler and Brant both understood that a delaying operation, effectively executed, might well buy them enough time to allow the approach of winter to curtail Sullivan's efforts, neither could garner enough forces to make such a defense work. Instead, both Indian and Tory watched helplessly as Sullivan's army emerged from the forest and fell upon the Indian villages located along the shores of Seneca Lake. The army marked its route northward that September with the charred ruins of one Indian village after another as Sullivan's men began the process of burning the Iroquois heartlands.

Newtown proved to be a tremendous psychological victory for the Americans. Neither Butler nor Brant were able to piece together by further attempts to stop Sullivan until the Americans stood at the gateway to Chenesse, the Seneca capital located on the Genesee River. Even this attempt proved unsuccessful when an American reconnaissance patrol of 23 men under Lieutenant Thomas Boyd stumbled into an ambush Butler had set for Sullivan. The mistake cost Thomas his life along with the lives of most of the rest of his patrol but forced Butler and his Indian allies to beat a hasty retreat to the safety of Fort Niagara. Butler knew that he no longer had the combat power necessary to stand up to

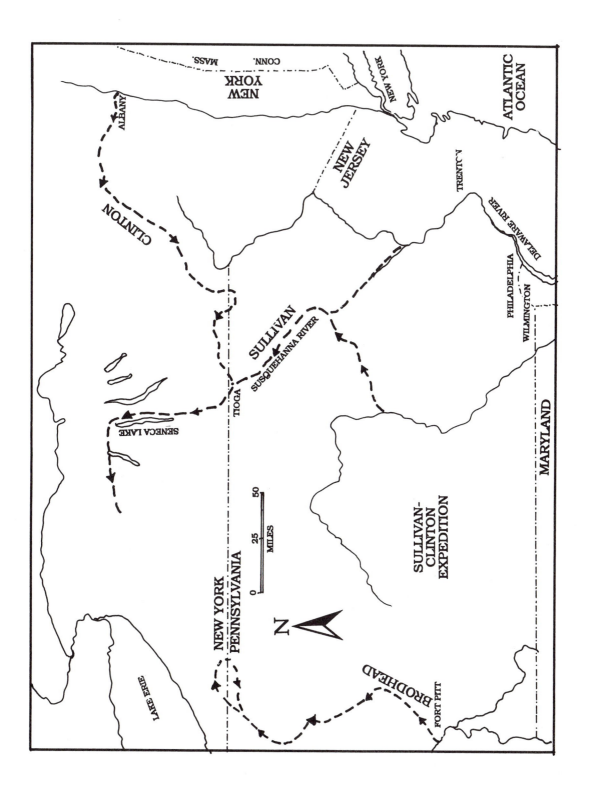

the Americans, and Boyd's patrol had cost the Tory leader the element of surprise that Butler felt was necessary to compensate for his numerical inferiority. In addition, Butler had interrogated Boyd before the American lieutenant's death at the hands of Butler's Iroquois allies. As a result of the interrogation, Butler knew that Sullivan had neither the supplies nor the time to continue on to Niagara.

After burning Chenesse, Sullivan and his men began the trek back to Easton by way of Tioga and Wyoming. On the return trip, the Americans continued ravaging villages that had been missed on the approach march. Sullivan arrived in Wyoming on October 7 to the praise of both Washington and the Continental Congress. Both the commander-in-chief and the Congress hoped that the Indian threat had finally been removed. The truth was that, though Sullivan and his men had crippled the Iroquois, the Americans had not destroyed their foes. Iroquois raiding parties would be back the following year, though without the sting they had once possessed. That their new attacks would lack the fury of their past exploits was not hard to understand. The charred remains of their old villages stood as stark testimony to the power of the Americans. Four thousand Continental soldiers under the command of a New Hampshire lawyer had marched into the center of their lands and burned them to ashes. More than just their homes and fields had been destroyed. Gone was the unity of the Iroquois Confederation, for one of the Six Nations, the Oneidas, had actively helped Sullivan. Gone too was the image of Iroquois power, particularly as it applied to the land-hungry colonists of New York.

The flames that Sullivan's men touched to life finally flickered and died with the passing of autumn. The remnants of the Iroquois nation lay shivering in the first snows of winter outside Fort Niagara. Those that survived the bitter cold winter of 1780 would return to some of their villages in the spring, but things would never be the same again. The Americans had taken the measure of the Iroquois and found them wanting. As Britain's emphasis shifted to the South, it became apparent that the Iroquois could neither repair the damage themselves nor count on their allies substantially to assist them.

Joseph R. Fischer

REFERENCES

Frederick Cook, ed., *Journals of the Military Expedition of Major General John Sullivan Against the Six Nations of the Indians in 1779* (1972); David Craft, *The Centennial Celebration of General Sullivan's Campaign Against the Iroquois in 1779* (1879); Alexander C. Flick, "New Sources on the Sullivan-Clinton Campaign in 1779," *New York Historical Association Quarterly Journal*, 10 (1929):185–224, 265–317; Donald R. McAdams, "The Sullivan Expedition: Success or Failure," *New York Historical Society Quarterly*, 54 (1970):53–81; A. Tiffany Norton, *History of Sullivan's Campaign Against the Iroquois: Being a Full Account of That Epoch of the Revolution* (1879).

Sumner, Jethro (1735–1785)

Continental Army officer. Born in Virginia, Sumner served as a militia lieutenant in the French and Indian War. In 1764 he moved to But (now Warren) County, North Carolina. Active in local politics, Sumner was elected to the provincial congress in August 1775 and was appointed major in the Halifax County militia.

He served in Virginia during the campaign near Norfolk in late 1775 and at the defense of Charleston in June 1776, becoming a colonel in the North Carolina Line. In 1777 he led his 3rd North Carolina Regiment northward to fight at Brandywine and Germantown, and to winter at Valley Forge. After recuperating at home from illness in 1778 Sumner recruited for the army. A brigadier general by January 1779 he helped to repulse the British at Stono Ferry, South Carolina. After another recruiting effort, Sumner joined in the American effort to harass the British advance under Cornwallis to Charlotte, North Carolina. Because General William Smallwood was given command of North Carolina troops in October 1780, Sumner refused to serve until General Nathanael Greene urged him back (February 1781). Sumner ably commanded three North Carolina regiments at Eutaw Springs, and for the rest of the war he led North Carolina's troops.

Richard L. Blanco

REFERENCES

Kemp P. Battle, "Career of Brig. General Jethro Sumner," *Magazine of American History*, 20 (1891):415–433; *Dictionary of North Carolina Biography* (1985).

Sumter, Thomas (1734–1832)

American militia officer. Born to Welsh parents in a frontier settlement of Virginia, Sumter was a strong-willed youngster who enjoyed cockfighting and bear hunting. Sumter had little formal education, and after his father's death he became a plow boy for a local farmer.

In 1755 Sumter joined a militia regiment as a private and fought the French at Fort Duquesne. He also served in the war against the Cherokee of the Lower Towns in 1760. After this campaign Sumter and a companion journeyed with a peace treaty to the Cherokee Over the Hill tribes in the Great Smoky Mountains. There he won the friendship of three tribal chiefs. In 1762 the colony of Virginia sent him to London in order to present these Indian leaders to George III.

Returning to Virginia, Sumter was thrown into jail for nonpayment of debts. He escaped from prison and fled to North Carolina. Awarded £700 for his services with the Cherokee, Sumter paid off his loans and then moved to Eutaw Springs, South Carolina, where he opened a trading post. After marrying a wealthy widow in 1764, Sumter acquired more property and local influence. In 1766 he heard the fiery speeches of Christopher Gadsden about the injustices of the imperial system, and consequently, he became an ardent Whig. In 1773 he was appointed a justice of the peace, and in 1775 he served in the provincial congresses.

In 1776 Sumter resumed his military career as a captain in Colonel William Thompson's Rangers. Promoted to lieutenant colonel of the 2nd Rifle Regiment, Sumter helped to defend Charleston against a British attack from General Sir Henry Clinton. That year Sumter also joined the border war being waged against the Cherokee, and he performed with distinction. Ordered to join General Robert Howe at Sunbury, Georgia, he then fought in a campaign to repell an invasion by Loyalists from East Florida to 1778. Ill with malaria, Sumter returned home.

Remaining on his plantation for the next two years, Sumter was brought back into action in 1780. The British pacification of South Carolina was underway, and Banastre Tarleton's Legion burned his home. Sumter recruited volunteers to begin guerrilla warfare against the enemy. He demonstrated how to wage partisan warfare as he raided British departments and supply lines. His first significant victory was at Williamson's Plantation (July 12, 1780). Because of his blue uniform with a hat decorated by a cock's feather Sumter was termed "The Gamecock."

In late July Sumter's campaign became part of a larger war in the South. Washington had sent General Johann de Kalb with troops to assist at Charleston's defense. But the city fell to the British while de Kalb was still in North Carolina. While the Continentals, now under General Horatio Gates, were defeated at Camden (August 16, 1780), Sumter mounted his own offensive. In August he lost at Rocky Mount, but he won at Hanging Rock. Then he lost again at Fishing Creek. Sumter, now a brigadier general, had a minor victory at Fish Dam Ford in November, but at Blackstock's Ford, Tarleton fought him to a bloody draw. Sumter resumed his own war on February 19, 1781, by attacking Fort Granby. But a large contingent under Lord Rawdon marched to the relief of the fort and Sumter had to retire. Pursued down the Santee River, Sumter lashed back at Bellville and at Fort Watson.

Desperate for recruits who would serve more than 60 days, and in the absence of a legislature for the state, Sumter devised his own wartime decree. In March 1781 on his own authority he proclaimed what became known as "Sumter's Law." All property, including slaves, that was confiscated from Loyalists would be sold to cover the cost of wages for Sumter's men. Furthermore, volunteers enlisting for ten months were promised horses, clothing, and equipment. "Sumter's Law" was not endorsed by the exiled Governor John Rutledge. It's main result was to intensify the brutal level of partisan warfare. Even with the promised rewards, however, Sumter only recruited a few hundred men by August 1781.

By 1781 the main contest in the South was being waged by General Nathanael Greene as he challenged Cornwallis for dominance in North Carolina. For partisans like Sumter, Francis Marion, and Andrew Pickens, this was the opportunity to conduct more raids on British outposts. Marion and Pickens usually coordinated their efforts with Greene, but Sumter regarded himself as an independent commander. He struck at isolated enemy bases—Fort Granby, Bellville, Fort Watson, Fort Motte, and Orangeburg. Though Sumter did not join Greene for the fight at Hobkirk's Hill in April 1781, he did assist Greene at the siege of Ninety Six (May–June 1781).

In a military career filled with remarkable exploits Sumter committed a famous error. In his haste to defeat 700 British troops at Monck's Corner on July 17, 1781, Sumter, without proper reconnaissance, ordered his horsemen to charge over nearby Quimby Bridge. The Americans suffered many casualties in this defeat.

As the British clung to Charleston, by late 1781 Greene began to reestablish civil government in the state. "Sumter's Law" was abrogated. Tired from campaigning and stung by bitter criticism, Sumter resigned his commission in January 1782.

Sumter served several terms in the assembly. He was plagued by the threat of lawsuits due to his policy of confiscation. However, both the legislatures of South Carolina and North Carolina enacted statutes, which exonerated him from court action. Sumter speculated in land. He served in Congress for many years and was a senator in 1810. But hounded by creditors over his debts, he led an unhappy life. In 1827 the South Carolina Assembly enacted a moratorium on his debt to the state banks.

As a partisan leader, Sumter was capable in minor engagements. But Sumter was a poor tactician; he often neglected to scout the terrain for a battle, and he seemed unable to coordinate his men in a fight. Sumter had a weak sense of strategy, and he seemed more concerned with waging his own private war than cooperating with the Continental Army.

Richard L. Blanco

REFERENCE

Robert D. Bass, *The Life and Campaigns of General Thomas Sumter* (1961).

Supplying the Continental Army

Initially, when Revolutionary conflicts began, soldiers relied on equipment procured from home or their community. There were no central sources for basic supplies for the military such as weapons and ammunition, tents, or equipment. As long as the military actions and the troops remained near Boston, food supplies were available, although salt was scarce, limiting preservation of staples such as meat and fish.

Thus, supplying the Continental Army was a complex task.

Throughout the American Revolution, the Continental Congress was unable to organize effectively a method of supply. On the other hand, the British were better organized and prepared because they already had a supply system that had served reliably during the eighteenth-century military conflicts with France. The British had a command structure and cabinet policy that regulated supply. Four departments were responsible for locating supplies—War Office (ordered supplies), Treasury Department (contracted and purchased goods), Board of War and Ordnance (bought weapons and ammunition), and Navy Board (transported items)—while five units worked directly with the army: Quartermaster Department, Commissary Department, Medical Department, Barrackmaster Department, and Engineer Department.

Colonial leaders tried to prepare a supply system for the conflict, but they had little prior administrative or practical experience with supply. Another limiting factor was that the rebels believed the war would be short, and officials reacted to crises and events, not planning for long-term procedures or supply needs. This erratic method proved ineffective and uncoordinated. In the preindustrial era, colonial manufacturing was immature when the American Revolution began, and cottage industries were never able to develop enough goods to provide adequate supplies. Because few indigenous sources were available, supplies were secured from foreign merchants (French companies such as Roderique Hortalez and Company contracted to send weapons), captures of enemy supplies, or purchases by agents abroad using credit, which quickly became worthless as the war advanced. A Secret Committee was established to import crucial supplies in exchange for payments of tobacco and other American products that appealed to foreign nations.

In an attempt to centralize and regulate supply, the Continental Congress, state, and military authorities decided to create and operate supply departments. On June 16, 1775, Continental Congress delegates organized two supply offices accountable to Congress—the Quartermaster General and Commissary General of Stores and Purchases. Joseph Trumbull became commissary general on July 19 and had the role of feeding the army.

Congress gave General George Washington the power to appoint the quartermaster general, and he named Thomas Mifflin on August 14, 1775. Lieutenant Colonel Edward Carrington served as quartermaster general in the Southern Department. Mifflin's first priority was the purchase of arms and ammunition. Despite attempts at centralization of production, saltpeter was made in home industries or purchased from local merchants. A committee was formed and decided to buy the most critical supplies from foreign allies. Officers were required and expected to outfit their troops with help from the state and local governments, a task that was often difficult to fulfill.

In addition to locating weaponry as varied as bayonets, cannonballs, and muskets, the quartermaster general's purpose was to procure and distribute nonfood items such as clothing, boats, tools, chains, paper, and lead. The quartermaster general was also the principal staff officer in arranging for troop movements, including determining the route, contracting for road and bridge repair and maintenance, constructing camps, building wagons, bridges, roads, and storehouses, and assigning reconnaissance missions.

Between 1775 and 1780 the Quartermaster Department experienced expansion. A diverse group of approximately 3,000 employees (wagon masters, storekeepers, clerks, weighers, collectors, and a variety of other laborers) worked in subbranches, such as the forage branch, wagon branch, and boat department. A staff officer composite depicted the average supervisor as native born, from the middle colonies, between 30 to 39 years in age, a merchant, and college educated. The average annual congressional expenditure on the war was staggering, ranging from $20 million in the early years to over $150 million at the climax of the crisis.

The Ordnance Department was organized in July 1775, and Washington appointed Ezekiel Cheever as Commissary of Military Stores to receive and issue weapons. Colonel Henry Knox, interested in the arming of the Revolutionary army, proffered advice, suggesting that laboratories be built near camps in order to produce ammunition. Knox traveled throughout New England to locate precious metals needed for weapons and powder manufacture. In 1777 Benjamin Flower became the Commissary of Military Stores. The position came under the super-

vision of the Board of War in 1778, and Knox served as Chief of Artillery, recruiting artificers to produce high-quality weapons. Flower died in 1781, and his replacement was Samuel Hodgdon. Throughout the war weapons and ammunition were in short supply, and Washington blamed careless soldiers for irreversibly damaging weapons. Foreign merchants shipped both weapons and powder to the Continental Army.

By June 1776 the Board of War and Ordnance was overwhelmed with too many duties. Problems were myriad: employees received low wages, and delays slowed deliveries. Stephen Moylan replaced Mifflin as quartermaster general, but he proved incompetent, and in November Mifflin returned to the position. The Commissary Department was able to feed the army adequately until it departed Boston. When troops retreated from New York City through New Jersey in 1776, Congress realized that reform of the Commissary Department was necessary in order to keep the army fed.

The Board of War and Washington decided that Trumbull's position should be divided into a Commissary General of Purchases and a Commissary General of Issues. Trumbull approved the division but wanted to earn a commission of 1 1/2 percent of all money spent—not a fixed wage. His request was denied, but his deputies, however, were permitted to retain 2 1/2 percent of purchases.

After the evacuation of New York City in October 1776, Congress established the office of Commissary of Clothing, which had the role of distributing regimental clothing to the states that would pay for their delivery to regimental paymasters who would issue clothing to troops, deducting costs from soldiers' wages. George Measam took this position in the northern army, but Washington did not fill the position for his army, explaining in December to Congress that the clothier general should be one man, not two, who provided for the entire Continental Army, but Congress ignored his suggestion.

A Philadelphia merchant named James Mease, who had served as commissary to Pennsylvania troops since January 1776 and filled supply orders for Congress, asked Washington for the position and was given it in January 1777. Despite his experience, Mease performed poorly, and the army suffered from a shoe shortage that was so extreme that soldiers became incapacitated, leaving bloody footprints as they marched, and many were incapable of duty. Like the British soldiers, men were expected to provide their uniform—which had to be standard with those of their peers—and other comforts such as blankets, which were often procured from citizens and charity groups.

The Hide Department was organized in November 1776 to acquire cattle skins so that the Commissary of Hides could trade them for tanned leather or shoes. The department also was to establish tanyards to make shoes and clothing or to contract for manufacture of these products with independent craftsmen or industries. George Ewing was in charge of this department as of August 1777 but resigned in April 1779. Next, the Board of War commanded these operations under five commissioners: William Henry (representing Pennsylvania, Maryland, and Delaware), John Mehelm (New Jersey), Moses Hatfield (New York), Lamb (Massachusetts), and George Starr (Connecticut).

The Hospital Department had been organized in 1775 and suffered a shortage of personnel—primarily because the colonies had few educated physicians—as well as a lack of hospitals, medicines, and surgical equipment. Hospitals were poorly ventilated, unsanitary, overcrowded, and undersupplied. Soldiers built temporary hospitals near battle sites, but Brigadier General Anthony Wayne described one of these shelters as being a typical "house of carnage." Smallpox became prevalent under these conditions, killing a vast number of men, and amputation was the most common operational procedure, resulting in unnecessary deaths. Medicinal supplies were imported from abroad or purchased or seized from local drug stores or supplies abandoned by Loyalists or the British. Clothing and bedding for patients was scarce, often being stolen or captured from the British, washed, and reused. Food was also in low supply for the hospitals, being procured from a variety of sources.

In April 1777 the Hospital Department was reorganized to represent four geographic areas with deputies in each of the war theaters. Dr. William Shippen served as director general, overseeing all hospitals. Critics complained that the Hospital Department was under the control of one man, the director general, and as a result, the department was reorganized in February 1778 to decentralize the power of the director general and implement strict bookkeeping and

use of forms for all purchases. Employees were threatened with suspension if they did not comply with the new directives. Tensions erupted at the department's higher levels, and feuds between the Hospital Department's first Director General Dr. John Morgan and Shippen resulted in a court-martial that cleared Shippen. Although he was reappointed, Shippen resigned and was replaced by Dr. John Cochran. Even though the hospital system proved inefficient and divided at the executive level, local doctors reliably provided services to troops camped near their villages.

Leaders tried to improve the supply system in order to win the war, and the period between 1777 to 1778 was one of reform and reorganization. Despite attempts to change, the supply still acted momentarily and relied on officers, civilians, and committees, especially state and local, to supply troops. Congress did not respond immediately to complaints and criticism, and as a result, a sense of low morale loomed in many supply departments.

In May 1777 Mifflin was appointed both Commissary of Forage and Wagonmaster General until June 1777, when the position of Commissary of Forage was divided into two jobs—Commissary of Purchase and Commissary of Issues—in order to make the duties more manageable. A system of checks and balances was implemented to prevent graft: Congress appointed deputy commissaries who then named their assistants, thus decentralizing authority. Problems also stemmed from the vast number of positions; many were duplicated for every military district.

Congress issued guidelines on June 10, 1777, and elected new officers, including Trumbull as Commissary General of Purchases and his deputies William Aylett, William Buchanan, Jacob Cuyler, and Jeremiah Wadsworth; and Charles Stewart as Commissary General of Issues with his deputies William Mumford, Matthew Irwin, and Elisha Avery. Because they were denied the privilege of earning commissions, most of the recently elected personnel resigned. Trumbull's deputies quit, and Trumbull resigned, being replaced by Buchanan in August 1777. (Buchanan was replaced by Jeremiah Wadsworth in April 1778, who was followed by Ephraim Blaine in January 1780, who served as Commissary General of Purchases until after Yorktown in October 1781.)

Congress published directives that demanded records be kept, especially purchase receipts, in great detail to prevent fraud. Monthly reports traveled through complex channels, in order to prevent falsification or forgery, to Congress, and were recorded on preprinted forms and books, in an effort to make supply more systematic. Supply areas were defined so that purchasing agents would not unnecessarily bid against each other and drive prices to exorbitant levels.

In 1777 the quartermaster general was rarely at headquarters, and three assistants performed his duties: Joseph Thornsbury was Wagonmaster General; Clement Biddle was Commissioner General of Forage; and Colonel Henry Emanuel Lutterloh, who had been quartermaster for the army of Brunswick, served as Mifflin's deputy.

Because of the decentralized structure, the quartermaster general's services were disorganized and ineffective. Congressional indecision and neglect contributed to the disintegration of the Quartermaster Department; Congress detained Mifflin, who was eager to return to his staff, in Philadelphia to discuss reorganization of the department, preventing him from performing his administrative duties at headquarters. By October 1777, an unhealthy and frustrated Mifflin resigned, but Congress did not accept his resignation until one month later. Mifflin then joined the Board of War at the rank of major general, and Lutterloh assumed the quartermaster general's responsibilities.

Trumbull also resigned, claiming that he did so because he received no commissions nor had the authority to appoint his assistants. As a direct result of this personnel change and ineffective regulation by Congress, the supply system faltered sparking the catastrophic winter at Valley Forge. Remaining suppliers had little experience, and the systems slowly ceased in autumn. In October 1777 Deputy Commissioner Peter Colt lamented, "no person knows how to act or what to do. Every kind of Commissary Business is here entirely stopped."

As officials realized that the war would last longer than expected, new committees were arranged and reforms sought to curb abuses. The major reforms were in the Commissary, Quartermaster, and Hospital departments to separate specialized responsibilities into subdepartments. Other measures included eradicating internal corruption, for example, fraudulent increase of prices and embezzlement. Seeking public ac-

countability, leaders made one of the first reforms the establishment of a revised Board of War, consisting of three non-congressmen, named in November 1777—Thomas Mifflin, Adjutant General Timothy Pickering, and Robert H. Harrison.

A lack of transportation was the major supply failure. Contrary to many depictions of Revolutionary conditions, food and supplies were actually abundant but unavailable to troops because few wagons were available and few drivers were willing to transport goods to the camps. Taking advantage of the situation, drivers requested high wages to transport goods, refusing to move them unless their expensive demands were met. The Continental Army suffered during the winter at Valley Forge because of Lutterloh's incompetence and Congress' mismanagement.

In order to mitigate shortages, states were asked to send food to the troops. Washington ordered local farmers to thresh grain for the army, threatening that they would risk seizure of all their grain if they did not give a portion of it to the army. Revolutionary camps did not have an organized kitchen or food supply. Men were provided raw provisions and camp kettles to cook with. Livestock herds followed troops and were slaughtered for meals. Other meat was cured when salt was available, but it rarely was, and salt became as valuable as money and was imported when possible.

By February 1778 the Continental Congress provided for several companies of bakers. One under the command of a captain named John Torrey discovered that military maneuvers prevented him from building adequate ovens, but other baker companies were able to construct brick kilns and bake abundant loaves of bread. Alternative sources of food included rice shipped from the South.

A forage branch in the Quartermaster Department was to provide forage for cavalry, artillery, and wagon horses, but adequate sources of hay were minimal. Often, horses died of starvation, like the soldiers. When lush pastures were located, the horses were turned loose to graze freely. Alcohol (rum and whiskey) was also needed, but in short supply, to enhance troop morale or deaden pain in hospitals.

As a result of the Valley Forge disaster, Congress decided to centralize supply and to place prominent and reliable individuals in charge such as Nathanael Greene who served as quartermaster general from March 1778 to August 1780 with assistants John Cox, purchaser and examiner, and Charles Pettit, accountant, who were allowed to retain a 1 percent commission, an amount that the three men decided to divide equally. Jeremiah Wadsworth was named Commissary General of Purchases and given the power to appoint or remove his personnel. Eliphalet Dyer, a Connecticut Congressman, explaining his peers' willingness to transfer this control of the supply procedure, rationalized: "They Wish to have the Army supplied at any rate."

Meanwhile, Washington became suspicious of Mease's operations and, in April 1778, requested a congressional investigation, claiming that Mease was not capable of performing the department's duties. At this time more clothing was procured from France, the states became more involved in supplying their own regiments, and the Board of War began purchasing items for the Continental Army. Washington still insisted that a reorganization of the Clothing Department was necessary, and in March 1779 the Continental Congress contemplated action to pursue. Mease, who suffered from poor health, had officially resigned in December 1777 but continued in the position until his successor could be selected. In July 1779 James Wilkinson was hired to take orders from both Washington and the Board of War, with each state appointing a clothier to handle local distribution.

Between 1778 and 1780 prices increased dramatically, and subsequently, currency depreciated because Congress printed more paper money than precious metals held in reserve. A financial crisis ensued, and agents and soldiers were given certificates to exchange for goods. Greene even asked his friends and relatives to provide supplies for the troops, and other supply officers created factories to make needed items. Supplies were also procured by theft and capture, and some soldiers were able to receive supplies from home or have clothing and other goods mended by their wives, mothers, or children. Camp followers, mostly wives and children, performed valuable services, maintaining supplies, arranging meals, and foraging for food. Winter became a period—usually free of conflict—for suppliers to locate, import, and stockpile goods for upcoming campaigns in the spring and summer.

Another method to secure supplies was im-

pressment (the seizure of civilian property by soldiers), and representatives were sent to work with local officials to prevent strife between military and civilians. Quotas were set for each community, and inspectors, accompanied by a justice of the peace as the primary magistrate official, traveled door to door to appraise goods and reimburse citizens. Emphasis was placed on consideration for citizens, and state laws to control military impressment were passed. Washington warned that impressment officials were to act without violence, obey laws, keep records, consult local officials, and to impress Tories' property first. They were also to attempt to balance impressed goods with available supply sources.

Washington, who disliked impressment, ordered the officials to act "with as much tenderness as possible to the Inhabitants, having regard to the Stock of each Individual, that no family may be deprived of its necessary subsistence." Livestock, especially cavalry horses, were impressed, depriving citizens of transportation and farm animals. Many civilians resisted seizures, and several disputes even went to trial. Other disputes were settled on the spot with vigilante justice. The greatest resistance and refusal occurred in the South, where citizens often sabotaged impressed goods and transport wagons. During the southern campaigns, armies were forced to live off the countryside because no organized authority or system provided them goods. However, the British inflicted great damage to the countryside, depriving both citizens and soldiers from needed food and supplies. Colonists also had to encounter and resist British impressment of men and supplies.

From 1778 until the end of the war, embargoes, antimonopoly laws, and wage/price control measures became necessary. As the money situation declined, many agents were denied credit, which was a humiliating situation for officers. Merchant who felt threatened economically sued. In addition, the international economy was damaged by recurrent plagues, poor weather, and the British blockade. The French continued to import supplies, and supply officers hired merchants to search for needed goods. Competition from a proliferation of officials resulted in even higher prices. Informal supply systems based on citizens and families providing goods in exchange for defense were implemented.

Corruption, which was linked to the high cost of war, was a term often applied to the supply system. The public viewed the system as over-staffed with officials they considered to be idle, greedy, rich, and corrupt, believing that officers purposefully raised prices to make profits. In reality, officers attempted to lower prices as much as possible, applying punishments to those corrupt individuals who paid exorbitantly high prices. Punishments for infractions included court-martial, forfeiting bonds, and suspension. Congress also believed that the supply officers were corrupt and had states investigate alleged crimes. Congress conducted an inquiry into supply conduct and insisted that no private trading occur and that superfluous activities be suspended. However, few investigations found supply personnel guilty of corruption.

Paper shortages prevented officials from keeping accurate records, and record keepers sometimes died in battles, were captured, or failed to comply with orders. As a result, inaccurate or missing records meant that not all soldiers and creditors were compensated for their service, debt, or credit. Ironically, many men had to pay fines to the government because they were falsely accused of corruption in audits based on inaccurate documents or absent information.

Many officers complained about this abusive treatment because they had joined the service for patriotic reasons—to serve their country and to gain prestige for their family. They felt they had a personal responsibility to Washington and the rest of the country as well as defending their honor and personal reputation.

Rumors spread suspicions that the commission system lined the pockets of purchasing agents, and as a result of these false charges, Greene and Wadsworth threatened to resign. They were reassured when Congress made a public statement expressing confidence in them, remaining in their positions until the fall of 1779.

While Greene and Wadsworth were in charge, a temporary period of relief was experienced, but in 1779 shortages again became a problem. Congress never could understand the true problems, such as external factors as weather, and placed the blame on officers. Meanwhile, from the staff's point of view, the Congress was not entirely sympathetic nor helpful.

The terrain proved an almost insurmountable obstacle to transporting supplies. Poor roads, lack of bridges, bad weather, and poor crops also hindered transport. Conflicts between the states and the army developed in which they became competitive in their efforts to provide for soldiers, often resulting in overpriced goods or goods never reaching the intended recipients. There were few incentives for laborers to perform efficiently: wages were low, and many employees, especially wagoners, succumbed to self-interest, embezzling money, stealing goods to sell at higher-priced markets, using food and supplies for personal needs, or purposefully damaging goods at the army's expense. Few punishments were meted out to these employees, as they were in low supply in contrast to the large demand for labor.

Other problems included civilians who stole from camps or supply stores, contractors who did not always deliver high-quality goods, and troops that were negligent of their supplies, wasting them, throwing them away, selling them to civilians, or deliberately destroying them. Soldiers also stole supplies to sell for liquor and/or cash. Others innovated new uses for supplies such as making blankets into clothes. Supply distribution lacked supervision, resulting in erratic and inappropriate dispersement; for example, socks were given to soldiers without shoes.

In order to curb these abuses, Washington appointed Baron von Steuben as Inspector General in March 1778 to discipline infractions. Unfortunately, von Steuben was unable to devote himself to enforcement until October 1780 and by then the system had deteriorated because he had been absent from headquarters to oversee administrative matters. Another abuse was that many soldiers retained their weapons after they left the service, depleting remaining troops of functioning arms.

The winter of 1779–1780 was extreme, and Congress failed to provide relief. In December 1779 Congress decided to shift responsibility for supply to the states but provided no central direction. This system failed to meet supply needs mostly due to poor leadership. Congress continued to request the states to enact legislation and investigate officers suspected of corruption.

In 1780, food became a state responsibility, and the Commissary Department was overhauled in January 1780, providing a fixed salary to chief Commissary General Ephraim Blaine and commissions to his assistants on their purchases. Their goals included reducing public expenditures and setting quality standards and price ceilings.

In the spring, currency reform destroyed old bills and issued new ones, which the states were required to use to buy supplies and pay military personnel. The states rejected these actions because they wanted more compensation but agreed to name commissary agents to supply the army. In April 1780 most congressmen and the public believed that fraud and corruption was a major problem in supply even though factually this was not so. Some reformers wanted to grant state suppliers dictatorial powers for impressment, but congressional delegates did not support this concept.

The Quartermaster Department was reorganized on July 15, 1780, by reducing unneeded staff and having the Board of War and state governors appoint assistants in order to cut expenses. States were still relied on for supplies. Military defeats were especially damaging in the South, instigating a search for solutions. Both Greene and Washington thought it necessary to seek alternatives to state supply. Reformers sought three goals. The first was to upgrade Congress, but this seemed a long-range possibility. Next, they wanted to replace departmental officials with a single administrator. Finally, they thought Congress should be given sovereignty. Army officers and state government officials, who had firsthand experience with military supply needs, were especially trying to strengthen Congress. This effort to bolster congressional representation was known as the Nationalist movement.

In March 1780 Thomas Burke, governor of North Carolina, proposed that states give Congress the right to tax exports and imports, but this suggestion was disliked, although a committee was formed to consider its merits. Drastic measures were sought: the New England states met in conventions, drafting 13 resolutions asking that Congress be given the power to make states perform their duty for the army. The November Hartford Convention requested that Washington be made military dictator and that one man assume management of finances. Although these radical suggestions were not implemented, other provisions were successful, such as states sending better qualified men, including some with military experience in the Revolution, to Congress to speak for improvements such as centralizing authority.

Timothy Pickering succeeded Greene as quartermaster general and operated under a new congressional plan installed in July 1780 that stated the quartermaster general's only concern was supply. Pickering's duties included trying to prevent superfluous purchases. Unfortunately, he lacked ample money to make the system work and was unable to buy food or clothing or arrange for transportation of an adequate amount of supplies. As a direct result, Washington told the troops to leave their camps because there were not enough supplies during the winter of 1780.

The winter of 1780 was devastating to the troops with not much food available at all due to poor transportation. Washington wrote Gouverneur Morris that "it would be well for the Troops, if like Chameleons, they could live upon Air, or like the Bear, suck their paws for sustenance during the rigour of the approaching season." The military was not confident in the states' ability to provide food: starvation racked the camps, and in January 1781, two mutinies occurred because threadbare troops in Pennsylvania and New Jersey were discontented due to a lack of money, food, and clothing.

Fortunately, Robert Morris, a clever financial expert, provisioned the army in campaigns through Yorktown, which was crucial in attaining victory. Congress ordered a Committee at Headquarters to discuss with Washington the possibility of limiting regiment size and to curb alleged abuses, especially those in the Quartermaster, Hide, and Hospital departments as well as eliminating superfluous offices, improper issue of rations, and unnecessary medical services.

Washington sent General William Heath in the spring of 1781 to New England for aid; Congress implemented a new system using private contractors to find, deliver, and issue rations, with financial support and arrangements made by Morris. In 1781 Morris was in charge of purchasing clothes and providing money to pay for its manufacture. Wilkinson quit in March 1781, and John Moylan succeeded him in that position. By the end of 1781, Morris assumed the duties of Commissary General of Purchases and Issues from Blaine and Stewart. Morris performed efficiently and well, eliminating the Commissary Departments and consolidating supply functions to reduce superfluous expenses such as administrative ones.

Morris wanted to raise revenues and frugally expend them. He thought financial ruin was due to waste, extravagance, and lack of a systematic method. He tried to make a financial plan in order to win the war. Morris implemented a system of contracts, with the lowest bidder winning. He worked closely with agents, arranged for transportation, and demanded that the states fulfill expectations. He used French loans, his own money, and credit to finance the latter stages of the war.

Morris, however, was unable to meet the demands of contractors, refusing to acknowledge their demands for the immediate payment of contracts. He canceled his contract with Comfort Sands and Company, who would not provide him additional credit, and contracted with Wadsworth and Carter, who gave him credit, which cost one-third more per ration. Morris rationalized that, although this was not a good deal, he was "In a situation where only bad things can be done, to adopt the least pernicious is all which can be expected." The army and navy were adequately provisioned to win the paralyzing battle at Yorktown; the British continued to fight, crippling the French in maritime skirmishes, who sought negotiations to conclude the war. The Americans, afraid of losing French military support—including supplies—arranged for diplomatic talks to finalize the peace.

Ironically, now that armistice discussions were being pursued, Washington wrote: "I have . . . the satisfaction of seeing the troops better covered, better clothed, and better fed than they have ever been in any former Winter Quarters." The peace treaty, signed in September, ended the need for military supply, with the departments being phased out during the next several years.

Historians label the Continental supply system as a disaster citing several examples of failure: Congress' poor planning, the lack of funds and equipment to transport goods, Congress' inefficient attempts at reform, and delays that resulted in goods never being received or spoiled. They also claim that Congress overestimated the states' abilities to meet quotas and that it was unaware of and unsympathetic to specific circumstances, such as natural disasters and problems—some of international proportions such as the economy—that hindered supply.

Poor communication existed between Congress and the states, and military leaders. Provincialism resulted in states acting contrary to congressional orders, and no provisions permitted the national government to punish states for disobeying. Financial problems and worthless currency plagued purchases of available supplies because agents lacked specie or credit to purchase them, and sellers would not accept certificates unless they were redeemable. Lack of supplies resulted in desertions (for example, approximately 11,000 men deserted during the worst war winter because of low supplies), mutinies, and military defeats.

The Continental supply system was weakened by leaders' inexperience and the false assumption that the war would be short. Authority was decentralized and overrelied on the states. Perpetual rumors of corruption harmed the morale of supply leaders. As a direct result of problems encountered in Revolutionary supply, men sought to increase congressional power and improve the caliber of individuals sent as their representatives, hoping this effort would create a body of knowledgeable representatives who could understand, sympathize with, and provide for the needs of the new American nation.

Elizabeth D. Schafer

REFERENCES

E. Wayne Carp, *To Starve the Army at Pleasure: Continental Army Administration and American Political Culture, 1775–1783* (1984); Louis Clinton Hatch, *The Administration of the American Revolutionary Army* (1904); Victor L. Johnson, *The Administration of the American Commissariat During the Revolutionary War* (1941); Erna Risch, *Quartermaster Support of the Army: A History of the Corps, 1775–1939* (1966); Jacob Weiss, *The Letterbook of Jacob Weiss, Deputy Quartermaster General of the Revolution* (1952).

Swedish Diplomacy

From 1771 to 1792, Sweden was ruled by King Gustav III, who had regained royal supremacy from the Riksdag in 1772. This shift in the internal Swedish balance of power was financed through French loans passed through the Comte de Vergennes, the French ambassador to Stockholm, who later served as the French foreign minister during the American Revolutionary War. Gustav III, a Francophile, wanted to restore Sweden to great power status, and for this difficult task he needed French support. Throughout his reign the Swedish king felt threatened by his giant Russian neighbor, who coveted Swedish Finland, and mighty Prussia, who desired Swedish Pomerania. Sweden's archrival in the Baltic was Denmark, who felt that Gustav III wanted to take Norway away from her. This fear drove Denmark into an uneasy alliance with Russia, directed against the revived Sweden. Such was the Swedish international situation on the eve of the American Revolution.

When the American colonies revolted against England in 1775, Swedish opinion was divided. Numerous newspapers and individuals supported the rebels, but the king and most nobles were anti-republicans who tended to sympathize with George III of Britain. In a letter to his French minister in 1778, Gustav III summarized his views when he wrote, "I cannot admit that it is right to support rebels against their king. The example will find too many imitators in an age when it is fashionable to overthrow every bulwark of authority."

Although he was adverse to the rebel cause, Gustav III was able to separate his private opinions from matters of state. Opportunities for Swedish trade to grow at the expense of Great Britain were too tempting to be resisted. By 1777 American ships freely entered Swedish ports, and Swedish exports to the New World increased from 6,107 to 153,005 rixdalers between 1777 and 1783. Trade with other nations also increased, and Swedish exports, primarily naval stores and timber, nearly doubled during this period.

With the French declaration of war upon Britain in June 1778, Gustav III's skill at maintaining Swedish neutrality while concurrently rebuilding her strength was continuously tested. France, quite naturally, expected increased Swedish assistance in return for her financial largesse. Sweden responded through two means—exporting Swedish military volunteers and vigorously defending neutral rights at sea.

France's war was largely fought at sea, and she needed experienced seamen to help man her warships. Gustav III encouraged his citizens to fight in the French navy, and over 100 Swedish volunteers served on French vessels. The Netherlands also declared war upon Britain, and 116 Swedes enlisted in the Dutch navy. A further 32 Swedes served on Continental warships or American privateers.

In addition to providing the French and allied forces with military volunteers, Sweden also assisted the French war effort through a vigorous defense of neutral trading rights. When France entered the war, Britain, which had the world's foremost navy, took an expansive view of war contraband in an attempt to drive France out of the conflict. Goods such as naval stores, which were the primary exports of Sweden and Russia and critical for the success of the French naval effort, were now classified by Britain as contraband goods. As such, they were subject to seizure by her warships. While Denmark accepted the British definition of naval stores as contraband and the Netherlands went to war with Britain over conflicting views of neutral rights, Sweden looked for a middle path.

In 1778 France, Sweden, Denmark, and Russia discussed various means to reinforce neutral rights at the expense of Great Britain, but traditional rivalries broke up these talks. By March 1779, 32 Swedish merchant ships had been confiscated by British Admiralty courts, and with each seizure the Swedes grew more outraged. In December 1778, Gustav III instructed his minister in London to protest "in such sharp terms that Lord Suffolk expressed himself unable to distinguish it from a formal declaration of war." By February 1779, an exasperated Sweden became the first Baltic nation during the Revolution to escort her merchant ships and forcibly defend Sweden's narrow definition of contraband, which excluded naval stores. Russia, confronted by similar British outrages, finally adopted this narrow interpretation. In March 1780, Catherine II issued a proclamation on neutral rights and invited other nations to join her in the League of Armed Neutrality, which was directed against both Britain and Spain. Russia's ally Denmark joined in July, her foe Sweden followed in September, and eventually Prussia, Austria, Portugal, and the Kingdom of the Two Sicilies also entered this neutral alliance. Britain already faced numerous enemies and did not wish to add any more, so the British gradually reduced privateering raids upon neutral shipping. This enabled Swedish and other neutrals' exports to rapidly expand, and France and her allies received increased shipments of naval stores and other "contraband" items.

Sweden wanted both to support her French patron as well as to maintain her own lucrative trade with America. In May 1782, Count Gustav Creutz, the Swedish ambassador to France, approached Benjamin Franklin, America's representative in Paris, about a commercial treaty between the two countries. Franklin refused to sign a treaty before America had treaties with her French and Dutch allies. Once these two solicited treaties were concluded, on April 3, 1788, Franklin and Creutz signed the United States' first treaty with a neutral nation. Count Creutz put this agreement into perspective when he remarked to Franklin, "I hope it will be remembered that Sweden was the first power in Europe which, without being solicited, offered its friendship to the United States." This treaty was signed five months before the Treaty of Paris and served as a model for future American agreements with other European powers. The 27 provisions of the document included most favored nation status for both nations; the principle of free ships, free goods; a narrow definition of contraband; and the end of privateering by one signatory on the other.

Sweden had supported France during the American Revolution through all means short of war. In return, France continued paying subsidies to Sweden. After the Treaty of Paris, France further rewarded her ally by granting Sweden the undeveloped West Indian island of St. Bartholomew. This sole Swedish colony in the New World was the only territorial gain for the Swedes during the Revolutionary War, and its acquisition further strengthened Gustav III's attempts to make Sweden into a great power.

Although Gustav III was surrounded by enemies, he had played a shrewd diplomatic game during the American Revolution. First, he stayed loyal to France while avoiding war with Britain. Second, he set the example for the future League of Armed Neutrality. Third, Sweden was the first neutral nation to sign a treaty with the United States. Fourth, Sweden gained land without going to war. All these events elevated the status of Sweden in European affairs and led an overconfident Gustav III to war with Denmark and Russia a few years after the Treaty of Paris. *See also:* Catherine the Great

David C. Farner

REFERENCES

H. Arnold Barton, *Scandinavia in the Revolutionary Era* (1986); ———, "Sweden and the War of American Independence," *William and Mary Quarterly*, 23 (1966):408–430; Samuel Flagg Bemis, *The Diplomacy of the American Revolution* (1957); Adolph Burnett Benson, "Our First Unsolicited Treaty," *American-Scandinavian Review* (1919):43–49; ———, *Sweden and the American Revolution* (1926).

Swedish Navy

Sweden, the mistress of the Baltic in the seventeenth century, was a declining power in the eighteenth century. King Gustav III was determined to revive both Sweden's military might and her prestige. Therefore, Sweden, although it had only Europe's seventh largest navy with ten ships of the line and six frigates, led the Northern powers in combating British privateering during the early years of the American Revolutionary War. In 1779, Sweden dispatched six ships of the line and six frigates to escort her convoyed merchantmen, while the numerically superior Russian and Danish fleets sent out a combined total of only 13 vessels to protect their own shipping. Continued British privateering and violation of neutral rights led to the formation of the League of Armed Neutrality in 1780. Defended by her navy and her new allies, Sweden's trade reached new heights between 1780 and 1782. Although her merchantmen were still preyed upon by British privateers, such incidents gradually grew less frequent. The relative effectiveness of the league resulted in a dramatic shift in Swedish naval deployment. Whereas Sweden defended her convoys more vigorously than the other northern powers in 1779, by 1782 Sweden's escorts were numerically inferior to both Russia and Denmark. Sweden's first aggressive and then cost-effective naval strategy was highly successful during the war, and the Swedish navy's sole loss was the *Sophia Albertina*, a ship of the line, which ran aground on the Dutch coast.

David C. Farner

REFERENCES

R.C. Anderson, *Naval Wars in the Baltic (1522–1850)* (1910); H. Arnold Barton, *Scandinavia in the Revolutionary Era* (1986); Samuel Flagg Bemis, *The Diplomacy of the American Revolution* (1957); Knute Emil Carlson, *Relations of the United States with Sweden* (1921); Jonathan R. Dull, *A Diplomatic Review of the American Revolution* (1985).

Swords in the American Revolution

From time immemorial, the sword in the Western world has represented the embodiment of the warrior's soul. Because of the antiquity of the sword, and the role it had in the Revolution, it is interesting to learn how a Revolutionary era sword was created. First, a cast steel bar was cut into two equal lengths. Each half of the bar was destined to become a sword. The half a bar was fed through a rolling mill. The mill pressed the bar of steel into the desired size and shape. Then the bar, as George C. Neuman explains, was "ground by large stone wheels, tempered by warm oil or water, and struck by hardwood blocks for testing. Before being finished by the polisher, the blade had a soft iron tang welded to its upper end." The tang was the tip of the sword blade that was fitted into the hilt or grip of the sword. The cast steel bar was the product of forging and hammering in a furnace.

Like contemporary Revolutionary firearms, there were infinite gradations in the quality of the swords. The swords, as with the firearms, fell into two categories—the regular "government issue" swords for the enlisted men, and special swords that officers would often purchase for themselves, or that were presented to them by friends. Indeed, this division in American swords endured until our Civil War. The swords that the officers possessed, along with their scabbards or sheaths, were invariably of a finer quality and workmanship than the "GI" issue carried by their men. This extended to the blades, hilts, and the scabbards themselves. Sometimes gold and even silver were utilized to decorate them. This was especially true of the ultimate type of privately purchased sword, the presentation sword, which was awarded to an officer by Congress or by influential friends for an act of gallantry on the field of battle. Washington wore just such an elaborate, privately purchased sword, with a silver hilt when he resigned his commission as Commander of the Continental Army in 1783 and when he was inaugurated as the first President of the United States in 1789. Washington also carried another, less ornate, sword during the war.

An interesting facet of the study of Revolutionary War swords, and an aid to their identification, is the markings that appear on the blade. These markings help to identify not only the country of origin but sometimes even the craftsman who created it. A common British sword marking was the running fox; another British mark might be the arrowhead, which would probably denote government manufacture, perhaps at the Tower of London. The royal fleur-de-lys appeared on many French swords. Sometimes, the royal cypher, or initials, of a sover-

eign would be etched on the blade, such as "GR" for Georgius Rex, King George III of England, or "FR" for Fredericus Rex, or Frederick II (the Great) of Prussia. Occasionally, the name of the craftsman has come down to us on the blade he made with his own hands. Samuel Harvey was one such British sword maker (or cutler). Andrea Ferrara was an Italian sword cutler making weapons for the British; his name is found in a variety of spellings, such as "Andria Ferara" and "Andre Ferara." An American named Potter in New York City was a sword maker, while a Spaniard named Ayzivilla crafted swords that may have been carried by the soldiers of Bernardo de Galvez.

Undoubtedly the most interesting marking one can find on a Revolutionary War sword is a motto, whether a national one, or a martial one. *"Vive le roi"* ("Long live the king") was a common French national battle cry, while *"Por el rey"* ("For the king") is found on Spanish blades, as in *"Por el rey Carlos III."* A traditional Spanish *lema*, or motto, that appeared on many blades was *"No me saques sin razon; no me embaines sin honor,"* meaning "Do not draw me without reason; do not sheath me without honor." Coincidentally, a French sword bore the same expression put into the French tongue: *Ne me tirez pas sans raisons; ne me remettez point sans hommeur [sic: honneur]."*

It is even possible to identify the city where some swords were made. The names of famous sword manufacturing cities, such as Solingen in Germany and Toledo in Spain sometimes were etched upon a blade, occasionally with the actual year of creation.

Another distinction to note is that swords for the infantry, engineers, and artillery were always referred to as swords, but the swords for mounted troops were known as "sabers." So much did the term "saber" come to typify the sword for mounted troops that the cavalrymen themselves, whether regular cavalry or dragoons, became known as "sabers."

To the horseman, the saber was far more important than the sword to the infantryman. Indeed, by the time of the Revolution, many foot soldiers had already discarded their swords. For the man on horseback fighting in the American Revolution, the saber was the chief weapon for offense and for defense. Consequently, much care was given to insure that sabers of premium quality be provided both officers and men. In the

British cavalry, for instance, a colonel of a regiment might purchase privately sabers for his entire unit to insure quality control over his troopers' primary weapon. Looking backward to his military days, a Massachusetts cavalry veteran of the War for Independence, Epaphras Hoyt, recalled the power of the saber:

> It is by the right use of the [saber that cavalry] are to expect victory. This is indisputably the most formidable and essentially useful weapon of cavalry. Nothing decides an engagement sooner than charging briskly with this weapon in hand.

Cavalry sabers, whose blades usually measured some 32 to 37 inches long, were designed to be used primarily for cutting (more accurately, chopping) or for thrusting with the point of the blade, the origin of the romantic term "at sword's point." Some officers carried a lighter saber, with a blade a few inches shorter than usual. The difference in the uses of the saber was critical, for it led to the evolution of two types of sabers: a single-edged, slightly-curved, saber for cutting and chopping, and a broadsword saber, with a straighter, double-edged blade for cutting (chopping) and thrusting. A main requirement leading to a specialized saber for cutting and chopping was that a principal use of calvary was to charge scattered enemy infantry on the battlefield. In this tactical use, the horseman would chop at the foot soldier on the ground afoot, aiming if possible for the infantryman's head (in the Napoleonic Wars, this particular sword cut was called in a British cavalry manual "the St. George cut"). A curved blade was much better for this grim business than a straight broadsword. In cavalry clashes where the opposing riders would be on the same level of weaponry, both cutting or thrusting blows would be used, thus either straight-edged broadswords or curved sabers could be equally lethal.

In a situation where two cavalry troops were hacking and hewing away at each other, the most vulnerable part of a horseman's anatomy was not his head but his hand. Consequently, a protection for the hand sometimes figured prominently in the design of a horseman's saber hilt. A common type found in infantry swords, the D-shaped hilt (so-called because it was shaped like the letter D), provided precious little armor for the trooper's hand, let alone the thumb. Therefore, many cavalry sabers, both straight-edged broad-swords and curved-sabers, were armored with a broad metal covering for the entire hand, giving rise to the term "basket hilt." It was these "basket hilts" that demonstrated the sword cutler's work at its highest level of artistry. Most hilts, it should be noted, were made of brass, while some were of iron. Some German and French horse sabers actually had a brass seashell worked into their brass hilts, giving rise to the term a "shell-guard." A Spanish cavalry saber known as a *bilbo* had, although not a basket hilt, a cupped guard for the hand making it look much like the rapiers of D'Artagnan and the Three Musketeers. With its straight-edged blade, the *bilbo* resembles a rapier, although its blade is much wider.

After the Seven Years' War, an innovation was underway in the development of cavalry sabers. During this era, the influence of the Ottoman Turks in the military world was high, as the "Jingling Johnnies" (staffs with bells) and the turbans of the drummers of the Brunswick Dragoon regiment demonstrate. At the same time, the nations of eastern Europe, such as the Hapsburg Empire, also exerted an influence on military life. Emblematic of this was the rise of the hussars, a type of light cavalry first seen in the Hungarian forces of the Austrian Empire, which was originally raised to match the light Turkish cavalry. By 1775 most European armies had extravagantly dressed hussar contingents.

Central to the armament of the hussars was a sharply curved and single-edged cavalry saber. This was the sword introduced into the American Revolution by the hussars of the Lauzun Legion. This saber was directly based on the Turkish scimitar, itself part of a class of Asiatic sabers that dominated warfare in Asia for centuries. It is interesting to observe that for many years the dress saber of a British general was a saber patterned directly on the scimitar, symbolic of British India.

Unfortunately for the Americans, of all the belligerents in the Revolution, their cavalrymen had the least protection for their hands. A great number of the known American sabers had the simple and inadequate D-shaped guard on the hilt, which offered minimum safety to its user. This in itself demonstrates the backward condition of domestic American arms manufacture during the war, and the haste with which it was necessary to mass produce sabers of the four American light dragoon regiments. The pattern for this lightly armored weapon seems to have been that of the British light dragoon saber. The Rappahannock Forge, according to American cavalry historian Randy Steffen, "supplied 1,000 sabers patterned after the British light cavalry saber to the American forces." With many Continental swords and sabers, however, the hilt was made in America, perhaps by the extremely versatile blacksmith, and the blade was an overseas import.

A unique American armament came directly from the hands of the enemy. After the Brunswick Dragoon Regiment von Riedesel was interned after its defeat at Bennington, its sabers (broadsword type) were used by the American 2nd Light Dragoons. The Brunswick saber had an elaborate basket hilt featuring the letter C, which stood for the name of Brunswick's Duke Karl in Latin—Carolus. A pattern of two C's intertwined also appeared in the four cantons or corners of the Brunswick flags. The C on the saber bore an ornate crown.

It was among the infantry that the greatest variety of sword types arose. The most common type of officer's sword was the small sword, because its blade was considered shorter than the usual military sword, having a blade around 30 inches long. This name is actually a misnomer, since its blade was about average in length for infantry usage. What actually characterized the short sword was the fact that its blade was thinner than most other swords, and it was designed almost exclusively for thrusting cuts. Consequently, its use required certain skill and dexterity. (Some small swords were designed for both cutting and thrusting.) The thin-bladed small swords, as a matter of fact, bear a close kinship to the rapiers of D'Artagnan's time.

Small swords, indeed, represent the acme of the sword cutler's art in the Revolutionary period. The hilt and often the blade of a small sword gave the cutler a chance to show off his skill. Some French small swords, of a style originating in the reign of King Louis XV, employed the decoration of the hilt in gold. Some American small swords had a brass hilt overlaid with a coating of silver.

A unique hybrid type of the small sword was known as the colichemarde. The colichemarde featured a thick blade near the hilt that tapered to the tip in a sharp point. It made an excellent blade for thrusting because the thickness of the blade near the hilt gave it enhanced strength. In this sense, the colichemarde was a functional marriage of the thick-bladed broadsword and the thin-bladed rapier—both thrusting weapons.

Officers also carried the "short saber." This weapon may have been carried by officers on foot and on horse. It had a slightly curved saber blade and sometimes a type of hilt that was increasingly becoming popular, the stirrup hilt, because it was shaped something like the cavalry stirrup. American general Israel Putnam, who led troops in both the French and Indian War and the Revolution, favored a short saber with a wooden grip (hilt) and a guard of bronze.

In commenting on officers' swords, it would be worth describing here a little-known type of sword, the spadroon. According to George C. Neumann, the spadroon "was employed in the last half of the 18th century to designate a slender sword having a light hilt and a long single-edged blade."

Perhaps the least usable of officer's swords was the so-called hunting sword, which was carried by officers of all European armies. Another term for the hunting sword is the cuttoe, which comes from the French term the *couteaux de chasse*, literally, the "hunting sword (or knife)." The blade was usually under 26 inches long, and too light for combat. Moreover, the hunting sword often lacked a guard.

Another universal sword, for infantrymen, was known as the hanger. This sword, with a characteristically shortened infantry blade (some 25 or so inches), had a long history. It represented a tradition that infantry be armed with swords for their protection. However, with the perfection of the bayonet as the wars of the eighteenth century wore on, the hanger was being supplanted by the bayonet.

In the British Royal Warrant of 1768 infantry hangers were restricted to sergeants of regiments, drummers and fifers, Highlanders, and grenadiers. The hanger was kept for Britain's best offensive troops, those best schooled and conditioned for hand-to-hand killing—grenadiers and the Scot Highlanders.

A number of British infantry hangers had variations on the D-shaped or stirrup guards, especially those issued out to the battalion or "hat" companies, so-called by their wearing the classic three-cornered "tricorn" hat. Grenadiers, on the other hand, were issued hangers with a full basket hilt for the best protection for their sword hands. (One British saber bore the regimental insignia of the 23rd Foot, the Royal

Welsh Fusiliers, the three feathers with a crown above them, with the Prince of Wales' motto, "Ich Dien," "I serve.")

However, even among these shock troops, the day of the sword was passing. The 42nd Highlanders of the Black Watch tended to discard their swords in combat for the use of bayonets and clubbed muskets for close combat. In 1783 Highlanders were given permission to return their broadswords to the regimental quartermaster. A year later, an investigation by a Board of General Officers learned that the grenadiers themselves had forsaken the blade for the bayonet. Consequently, the sword was dropped for use in the grenadier companies. Only regimental drummers continued to wear them.

Paradoxically, in both the British and Continental armies, the sword was fast becoming the best personal defense of the officer at the same time it was disappearing from the belts of the rank and file. Like Washington, the British army had attempted to get British infantry officers to fight with the pikelike spontoon. But, like their American foes, the redcoats found the spontoon unwieldy and relied on the sword. Of the 63rd Foot, an inspection return noted in 1784: "Just arrived from America, where the officers never made use of espontoons; saluted with swords." Two years afterward, spontoons were abandoned by the British officer corps.

In the French army, the sword—*l'arme blanche*—was also experiencing its decline. In 1764, infantry hangers were officially restricted in use for all but sergeants and grenadiers. There is reason to infer that the hangers were still carried by French sergeants and grenadiers throughout the American Revolution.

French infantry hangers had the so-called stirrup-shaped hilts, which were uniformly made from brass. The hanger had a slightly curved blade with a length that varied roughly from 27 to 30 inches. (By the time of Napoleon, the infantry hanger would be known as the *sabre-briquet*.) Sometimes, the grip or hilt would be covered in leather.

In all of the armies mentioned here, the main armament of the artilleryman was the blade, virtually identical to that of the infantry. In many instances, however, gunners also used their ramrods as defensive weapons. The German artillerist's sword, known as the *pallasch*, was almost a complete reproduction of the cavalry broadsword, such as carried by the Brunswick dragoons, with a half-basket hilt manufactured from brass.

German sword cutlers exerted a significant influence on the French and British arms industries. English authorities had tried repeatedly to entice German sword makers to immigrate to Britain but with little success. France, however, was more successful in this respect, perhaps because of the tradition of Germans serving French kings, like the Royal-Deux-Ponts regiment. German swordsmiths were lured to Klingenthal in Alsace from Solingen in 1729. Most of the German regiments in the French army recruited heavily among the German Alsatian population.

Regarding the Spanish who fought the British under Bernardo de Galvez, the same distinction in quality between the infantry swords of officer and enlisted man prevailed. Since the Bourbon Phillip V became king in 1700, Spanish military usage had become increasingly influenced by the more advanced French army practices. An interesting custom among Spanish colonial regiments was to change the blades of seventeenth-century rapiers by shortening them and adapting them with eighteenth-century sword hilts.

By a Spanish royal decree of 1768, infantry hangers were restricted to grenadiers and to infantry sergeants in the regular army. Yet among the colonial troops, most foot soldiers retained their hangers until the close of the eighteenth century.

The Spanish hanger had a solid brass hilt and guard, which was called the multibranch guard because several strips of brass made up the grip to defend the user's hand.

In the war at sea, swords were essential. In the Age of Fighting Sail, if an enemy ship did not surrender after a devastating bombardment virtually the only way to capture the vessel was to board her in murderous, hand-to-hand fighting. In this melee, the naval cutlass was the weapon par excellence.

The typical cutlass was a simple weapon well designed for its work. The blade, usually single-edged and designed supremely for a chopping blow, had a length that varied widely, measuring from 30 inches to less than 20 inches. All of them, nevertheless, shared the characteristic of being wide, the better to deliver a forceful blow without breaking. Cutlass blades were either slightly curved or straight.

Cutlasses usually had heavy guards to protect a sailor's hand. Some American cutlasses showed a cruder manufactured quality than those of European nations, which reflected the hard-pressed conditions of the Yankee arms industry. As with many infantry swords or sabers for the horsemen, naval cutlasses were sometimes turned out by village blacksmiths.

Keeping with the "no frills" nature of these cutlasses, their grips were inexpensive and were often crude, sometimes being simply made of wood. Instead of the finer brass grips found on infantry hangers, cutlasses had a cheaper iron grip, or a grip made of bone.

The knife was widely used as a weapon in the war. Here was a weapon designed for a wide variety of uses, from skinning squirrels to cutting off a gangrenous limb. But, above all, it was a blade designed for killing.

The basic type of knife known to the Revolutionary soldiers was the belt knife or dagger, the main difference being that the dagger had a crossguard to give some protection to the hand, while the belt knife was devoid of any safety measures for its user. Most daggers seem to have been double edged rather than single edged. Another differentiation between the knife and the dagger is that the degree of craftsmanship was uniformly higher with the dagger, a fact partly explained by the fact that the dagger was the small blade that officers used most. As with swords, the quality of officers' weapons was always superior. The blades of some daggers as well as knives were actually cut from older swords. Many knife and dagger blades used by the Americans were also imported.

Insofar as the hilts were concerned, a wide variety is found among Revolutionary War examples. Sometimes the grip or hilt would be made of antler or bone; others show hilts of wood. One has an exquisite ivory hilt, obviously made for a man of substance.

The greatest variety in knives and daggers came from Europe. The European knife that has generated the most interest has been the Scottish dirk. Carried by the Highlanders, it had a long-edged blade averaging a potent 12 to 17 inches in length. The grips often have beauti-fully carved Celtic designs. Wooden grips carved from ivy or heather were frequently seen, as were those with grips of ivory, horn, or even pewter. Sometimes smaller knives were carried in the same scabbard with the dirks which were used at table. Occasionally, dirks were made, too, from old swords: one bears on its blade the inscription of the famed swordsmith Andrea Ferrara.

However, the Highlanders were not content to trust their lives to only one knife. Each Scot carried a second, shorter, knife called the *sgian dhu*, or "black knife," either up his sleeve or in the top of his stocking. Today, the black knife and dirk are still carried by most Highland pipe and drum regimental bands in parade dress. Most Revolutionary *sgian dhus* had a straight blade and a wooden grip, often crafted from heather root. Both weapons were routinely carried on the right side.

Although swords and knives have long been replaced by firearms as basic weapons, one solitary testament remains of the enduring lethality of these edged weapons. While there is no resemblance whatsoever between the flintlock musket of the Revolution and the MAT-10 submachine gun of today, swords, knives, and daggers have changed little over the span of 200 years. This fact demonstrates the efficiency of the edged weapon.

John F. Murphy, Jr.

REFERENCES

Sidney B. Brinckenhoff and Pierce A. Chamberlain, *Spanish Military Weapons in Colonial America, 1720–1821* (1972); Donald F. Graves, *French Military Terminology, 1670–1815* (1979); Major James A. Hicks, *French Military Weapons, 1717–1938* (1964); Major J.K. Money, *The Uniforms and History of the Scottish Regiments* (1960); Warren Moore, *Weapons of the American Revolution and Accouterments* (1967); George C. Neumann, *The History of Weapons of the American Revolution* (1967); ———, *Swords and Blades of the American Revolution* (1973); Harold L. Peterson, *Arms and Armor in Colonial America, 1526–1783* (1956); ———, *The Book of the Continental Soldier* (1968); Colonel H.C.B. Rogers, *The Mounted Troops of the British Army* (1967); ———, *Weapons of the British Soldier* (1968); Edwin Tunis, *Weapons: A Pictorial History* (1972).

T

Taitt, David (c. 1740–1834)

British Indian agent. A native of Scotland, David Taitt arrived in the new colony of British West Florida in 1764 and served as assistant surveyor from 1764 until 1767. In January 1772, Taitt was employed as a commissary by John Stuart, Superintendent of Indian Affairs for the Southern Department, to travel through the Creek towns in order to report on conditions regarding the deerskin trade and the disposition of the Indians toward land cessions to West Florida and Georgia. He was also instructed to make detailed observations on the Indian country and to produce a map. Taitt's thoroughness and deft handling of the assignment resulted in one of the most valuable accounts of the Creek Indians during the 1770s and earned him a permanent position in Stuart's department as commissary to the Upper Creek Towns. His counterpart in the Lower Towns was William McIntosh. Taitt was eventually made Deputy Superintendent of Indian Affairs.

During the early phases of the Revolution, Taitt worked diligently in both Upper and Lower Creek Towns to maintain support for Britain's position in the conflict. In September 1777, Taitt and Alexander Cameron, another of Stuart's deputies, were forced to flee the Creek towns due to machinations of American Indian Commissioner George Galphin when a group of pro-American Lower Creeks attempted to assassinate the British agents. Alexander McGillivray, a leading Upper Creek chief and newly named member of the British Indian Department, warned the pair, aided in their escape, and eventually smoothed the way for Taitt's return.

During the heated action along the southern seaboard in 1779, Taitt and McGillivray led groups of Creek warriors from the Upper Creek Towns into Georgia and South Carolina on raids and foraging expeditions. Taitt remained in Georgia through the fall of 1779, and he commanded two pieces of artillery during the siege of Savannah in October 1779.

Taitt's activities among the Indians was questioned by East Florida governor Patrick Tonyn, who charged that Taitt, acting on Stuart's orders, had failed to support properly the British cause in East Florida. The charges were unfounded, but they cast an unflattering light on the deputy. Following John Stuart's death in

March 1779, a West Florida commission appointed to direct Indian affairs declined to retain Taitt, primarily due to budget restraints, but Tonyn's complaints may have played a role. Following his release from the Indian Department, Taitt returned to West Florida by December 1779. On June 1, 1780, he was captured about 30 miles north of Spanish-held Mobile. The arresting Spaniards had been specifically dispatched to capture Taitt due to his influence among the Indians. He was paroled and allowed to travel to British Pensacola after he vowed he would not use his influence among the Creeks to incite them against the Spanish.

Taitt suffered much from his government service. The administrators who followed Stuart at first refused to honor Taitt's expenses, and he was threatened with lawsuits by his creditors. With the fall of Savannah and Pensacola, he lost considerable property, including land, horses, slaves, and equipment. He returned to London in 1782 and lodged claims with the Loyalist Claims Commission for back wages and compensation for the various losses he suffered in both Georgia and Florida. He hoped to put his experience in the Indian Department to use and applied for a number of positions relating to the Indian trade. In the end, his training as a surveyor proved his only means of advancement. He was dispatched to the newly formed colony of Cape Breton in 1784. He surveyed and laid out the city of Sydney, served as the colony's first provost marshall, and served in the colony's executive council on two occasions. He died on August 4, 1834, at the age of 94, and is buried in Halifax, Nova Scotia.

Due to the erroneous memory of the nineteenth-century historian Thomas Woodward, Taitt generally is believed to have died during the late phases of the American Revolution and to have been buried at the Lower Creek town of Coweta. This story is given credibility due to the fact that his mixed-blood Creek son, by the sister of Alexander McGillivray, accepted this view. Apparently, Taitt never contacted his Creek family after leaving Pensacola and is likely he never knew of the boy's existence. The child, Davy Tate, was educated in Philadelphia and later Scotland at the direction of Alexander McGillivray. Tate later inherited the majority of McGillivray's property, as was his right under matrilineal traditions of the Creeks, since he was McGillivray's nephew. Davy Tate sided with the Americans during the Creek War of 1813, and his descendants were prominent in Alabama history during the antebellum period.

Kathryn Braund

REFERENCES

John R. Alden, *John Stuart and the Southern Colonial Frontier* (1944); David H. Corkran, *Creek Frontier, 1540–1783*; K.G. Davies, ed., "David Taitt's Journal to and through the Upper Creek Nation" and "David Taitt's Journal to and through the Lower Creek Nation," *Document 4 of the American Revolution, 1770–1783*, 20 Vols. 5:251–282; Robert J. Morgan, "Orphan Outpost: Cape Breton Colony, 1784–1820," Ph.D. dissertation, University of Ottawa, Ontario (1972); James H. O'Donnell III, "Hamstrung by Penury: Alexander Cameron's Failure at Pensacola," in *Anglo-Spanish Confrontation on the Gulf Coast During the American Revolution* (1982); ———, *Southern Indians in the American Revolution* (1973); Thomas S. Woodward, *Reminiscences of the Creek or Muscogee Indians, Contained in Letters to Friends in Georgia and Alabama* (1859).

Tar and Feathers

Tarring and feathering was one of the triad of techniques of social violence—the other two being vigilante justice and the lynch law—found in Revolutionary America. To support their belief in the sovereignty of the people, rebel mobs stripped, tarred, and feathered British officials and their Loyalist sympathizers from the 1760s through the period after the signing of the Declaration of Independence. The use of hot tar (even molasses), tar brushes, and feathers (or "Hogs Dung" in the case of Loyalist Abner Beebe) was a terrible sight to behold and became a common practice in mob rule in the century after the Revolutionary War.

Harold J. Weiss, Jr.

REFERENCES

Richard M. Brown, *Strain of Violence: Historical Studies of American Violence and Vigilantism* (1975); ———, "Violence and the American Revolution," in *Essays on the American Revolution*, ed. by Stephen G. Kurtz and James H. Hutson (1973); Wallace Brown, *The Good Americans: The Loyalists in the American Revolution* (1969); Don Higginbotham, *The War of American Independence: Military Attitudes, Policies, and Practice, 1763–1789* (1971); Philip Ranlet, *The New York Loyalists* (1986).

Tarleton, Banastre (1754–1833)

British army officer. Dashing and brutal, a born cavalry leader, Banastre Tarleton commanded the British Legion during Lord Charles Cornwallis's southern campaign of 1780–1781. An excellent horseman, courageous, and full of spirit, Tarleton was of less than medium height, muscular, energetic, and quite handsome, despite a hawk nose.

His manners were elegant; his speech, glib and intelligent, yet in battle he was ruthless and arrogant toward his enemies. He possessed boundless endurance, was continually active, and was uncommonly strong. Vain and self-assured, he considered women to have been created for his amusement and entertainment. During the War of the Revolution, he gained the respect of his superiors and the hatred of his foes. He was one of Cornwallis's favorite officers.

Tarleton was born on August 21, 1754, in his parents' house on Water Street in Liverpool, England. His father, John Tarleton, was a successful merchant who had made his fortune in shipping. The family owned plantations on Jamaica and on several other West Indian islands. Much of the family wealth was derived from the slave trade. John Tarleton was elected mayor of Liverpool in 1764. Banastre's mother was Jane Parker Tarleton.

One of seven children, Tarleton was named for his maternal grandfather, Banastre Parker of Curedon, Lancashire. Tarleton was educated locally in Liverpool and then enrolled in the University College at Oxford in 1771. He turned out to be an outstanding cricket player, but somewhat less of a student. He excelled at riding, boxing, tennis, cricket, and any type of gambling, while at Oxford.

In 1773, Tarleton's father died. Left with an inheritance of £5,000, Tarleton decided to study law at the Middle Temple in London. Within two years, his wealth was gone, a victim of gambling and the high life of a rake out on a continual spree. Not surprisingly, Tarleton's law studies had not progressed. Rather than to books, it was to the theater, clubs such as the Cocoa Tree, and gaming tables that Tarleton was drawn.

In dire financial straits, Tarleton was saved by his mother on April 20, 1775, when she purchased a cornet's commission for him in the King's Dragoon Guards. Tarleton entered the army and endured a short period of training before requesting permission from the King to accompany Cornwallis's force to North America. Permission was granted, and Tarleton set out from Portsmouth on December 26, 1775, to help put down the rebellion in the colonies.

Cornwallis joined General Henry Clinton at Cape Fear, North Carolina, on May 3, 1776. This combined British force failed in its attempt to take the city of Charleston, South Carolina, on June 28–29, 1776. Discouraged, the British sailed north to join General William Howe's main army camped outside New York City on Staten Island.

During the New York campaign, Tarleton was attached to the British cavalry under the command of Sir William Erskine. Tarleton was present at the Battle of Long Island and through the long campaign to push Washington out of lower New York. In the subsequent British pursuit of the Americans across the Jersies, Cornet Tarleton led the advanced patrol that successfully captured the second in command in the American army, General Charles Lee, at Basking Ridge on December 13, 1776.

Following this bit of glory, Tarleton took part in the operations under Cornwallis in the Jersies that centered around Princeton, Trenton, and Brunswick. By now Tarleton was gaining the attention and recognition of his superiors for the aggressive military talents he so daringly displayed. Colonel William Harcourt, commander of the cavalry unit to which Tarleton was attached, promoted him to acting captain for his courageous acts in the face of the enemy.

In July 1777, Tarleton accompanied General William Howe's army as it fought the Pennsylvania campaign to capture the rebel capital at Philadelphia. Tarleton participated in the Battle of Brandywine and was on the field at the Paoli Massacre. On September 26, 1777, Tarleton rode in the vanguard with the 16th Dragoons as the British entered Philadelphia. Tarleton was a minor participant in the Battle of Germantown and also in the capture of Forts Mifflin and Mercer, two American fortifications that blocked the British supply line to the sea along the Delaware River.

In 1777, following the fall of General John Burgoyne's army at Saratoga, the British government decided to expand the army by creating additional regiments. On January 8, 1778, the citizens of Liverpool elected Tarleton captain of the 1st Company of Liverpool Royal Volunteers, a company in the newly organized 79th Regiment of Foot.

Tarleton and his men rode out of Philadelphia to skirmish with the Americans on a regular basis. It was Tarleton's mission to keep open the roads for farmers and others to bring much needed produce and goods to market in Philadelphia in order to supply the British army. At the same time, he gathered intelligence and gained valuable fighting experience.

On January 20, the British cavalry surprised Captain Henry Lee and his men inside the Spread Eagle Tavern, about six miles from the American encampment of Valley Forge.

Recklessly charging Lee's horses to stampede them, Tarleton had his own mount shot three times, lost his helmet, and had his coat holed several times.

But Captain Lee held his post and evaded capture by pretending that American reinforcements were arriving to aid the cavalrymen pinned in the tavern. The British withdrew without taking "Light-Horse Harry." This was not the last time the two dashing cavalry opponents would meet during the war.

Back in Philadelphia, when not on patrol, Tarleton lived his typical rakish life-style to the limits, wenching, drinking, gaming, and playing various roles in theatrical performances presented by the British officers under the lead of Captain John André. Tarleton narrowly avoided a duel when he was caught in bed with the mistress of Major Richard Crewe of the 17th Dragoons, reportedly just one of his numerous conquests that winter. Intermediaries were able to mollify Major Crewe, and the affair was settled without further difficulty.

In May, Tarleton played the Sixth Knight of the Burning Mountain during the Meschianza, the stunning tribute performed by loyal British officers in honor of Sir William Howe on the occasion of his departure for England. As the British prepared to evacuate Philadelphia for New York City under their new commander, General Henry Clinton, Tarleton was appointed brigade major for the cavalry by General Henry Erskine. On June 13, 1778, Tarleton was promoted to captain in the Dragoon Guards for his bravery in action.

Tarleton directed the cavalry as a screen for Clinton's army as it marched across the Jerseys. Tarleton's cavalry fought at the Battle of Monmouth, particularly against General Charles Lee's advanced division. On August 1, 1778, General Clinton appointed Tarleton Lieutenant Colonel (local rank) of the newly formed British Legion.

While Lord William Cathcart was to serve as colonel, Tarleton became the tactical leader of the Legion. Only 24 years old and in the army but 3 years, Tarleton now commanded a mixed force of Loyalist cavalry and light infantry. Like the Queen's Rangers, the British Legion wore green uniform coats. This provincial force soon became a unit of highly skilled partisan fighters, well suited to the tactical demands of campaigning against the rebels in America.

Stationed first at King's Bridge and later on Long Island, Tarleton kept his men constantly on the move, drilling them incessantly to improve the coordination in battle between cavalry and the light infantry of the Legion. Tarleton worked well with Lieutenant Colonel John Graves Simcoe of the Queen's Rangers. Both units harassed Americans in the Jersies in the territory north of British lines in New York. The Legion soon became known as "Tarleton's Green Horse."

Whenever Clinton moved outside his New York lines to probe American defenses, the Legion and the Rangers always formed the vanguard. With little loss of men, Tarleton repeatedly proved himself in many actions and skirmishes against the Americans. For his actions, Clinton made Tarleton commandant of the Legion in the fall of 1779, following Tarleton's promotion to brevet major in the British service on August 11, 1779.

On December 26, 1779, Lieutenant Colonel Tarleton, commandant of the Legion and commander of cavalry for the southern army, sailed with General Clinton's army for the beginning of the southern campaign. The voyage to the South was a rough one with violent weather. Many of the Legion's horses died.

Tarleton was able to procure replacement mounts from various southern plantations and then led his men off to their most famous exploits of the war. After a minor setback or two, Tarleton surprised three American regiments of cavalry at Biggin Church and Bridge near Monck's Corner on April 14. Tarleton granted the completely surprised Americans no quarter. His men captured 83 American horses.

On May 6, Tarleton hit the American cavalry again, this time at Lenud's Ferry across the

Santee River. The Legion succeeded in capturing all the baggage and 400 horses and dispersed the survivors in a total rout. Already Tarleton's tactical plan had developed. He used Loyalists to gain intelligence about his enemies. Using great mobility, Tarleton sought to surprise his opposition, always attempting to destroy the baggage and military stores.

Charleston surrendered on May 12, 1780. Tarleton was highly praised by General Clinton in his dispatches. General Cornwallis then marched out of Charleston into the countryside to quell the rebellion throughout South Carolina. Tarleton led the way. When the British were alerted to the approach of a small American force under Colonel Abraham Buford, Cornwallis sent Tarleton off in pursuit.

Colonel Buford was bringing reinforcements to Charleston. When he learned of the surrender, he turned and retreated north. Tarleton caught up to Buford at the Waxhaws on May 29 by riding 105 miles in 54 hours. Tarleton hurled his Legion directly at Buford without hesitation as soon as the Americans were in sight. Buford's force was destroyed, all the baggage and military stores taken, and no quarter given. "Tarleton's Quarter" became a rallying cry for the Americans in the South. The Legion had gone far in developing a reputation as butchers and as stern avengers of rebellion against the King. Since the vast majority of the Legion were Loyalists and not British regulars this brand of civil war was the more vicious.

In July Tarleton came down with severe malarial fever. It incapacitated him for a time but the natural strength of his constitution prevailed. By the time Cornwallis was preparing to meet General Horatio Gates's offensive in August, Tarleton was back in the saddle leading his men. Major George Hanger, a man after Tarleton's heart, commanded the cavalry while Major Charles Cochrane led the Legion infantry.

On August 16, 1780, the two armies of Cornwallis and Gates met in battle near the town of Camden, South Carolina. The battle turned into another British rout. Tarleton led his Legion in the final charge that cleared the fields of Americans. He then conducted a pursuit 20 miles to Hanging Rock, capturing much of the American baggage and artillery along the way.

By now Cornwallis had complete confidence in his young Legion commander. In England, Tarleton had become a hero. In American eyes,

he was a savage, cruel butcher known as "Bloody Ban." Tarleton continued his successes by defeating General Thomas Sumter and an American militia force twice his strength at Catawba Falls near Fishing Creek on August 18.

Shortly thereafter Tarleton came down with the yellow fever and was indisposed as Cornwallis began his first invasion of North Carolina. The Legion under Major Hanger did not perform well as under Tarleton. An unexpected defeat of Major Patrick Ferguson's detachment at King's Mountain sent Cornwallis back to Winnsboro to regroup.

Once Tarleton had regained his health, he led his men against General Sumter at Blackstock's Ford on the Tyger River. It was a bloody fight in which Sumter was severely wounded and the Americans were forced to withdraw at the end of the battle. With this event, Cornwallis changed his mind and decided to invade North Carolina during the winter before the new American commander, General Nathanael Greene, could become a dangerous opponent.

Cornwallis sent Tarleton out on the British left flank to cover Cornwallis's sweep north, to protect the garrison at Ninety Six, and to catch General Daniel Morgan's force and destroy it. Greene had split his army in the face of Cornwallis's invasion, and Morgan commanded one of the two American divisions. Morgan was somewhere near Ninety Six and had to be dealt with.

Tarleton took his Legion, the 7th Regiment, the 1st Battalion of the 71st Regiment, 350 additional cavalry, and 2 field guns. Tarleton commanded about 1,000 men total, his largest independent command of the war. Tarleton caught up with Daniel Morgan's men at the Cowpens on the morning of January 17, 1781.

Morgan was waiting for him. Tarleton attacked head-on, as was his custom, without delay. The battle took one hour. In that time, Tarleton's force was destroyed and Tarleton sent running, along with the surviving Legion's cavalry. Morgan's men captured the colors of the 7th Regiment, the baggage train, and the artillery, along with 600 of Tarleton's men. Tarleton joined Cornwallis with the dismal news at Turkey Creek.

In spite of the defeat at Cowpens, Cornwallis entered North Carolina and chased after Greene on the famous "Race to the Dan" River. Burning his baggage, Cornwallis gambled and lost the race by a short margin. Tarleton and the survivors of his Legion totally routed several American militia units on the way but could not penetrate "Light-Horse Harry" Lee's cavalry screen protecting Greene's army.

After a brief pause, Greene recrossed the Dan River from Virginia and came back into North Carolina to offer battle to Cornwallis at Guilford Court House. On March 15, the two armies collided. Cornwallis eventually won the field after hard fighting but suffered the loss of one-quarter of his army. Tarleton performed bravely but was wounded in the right hand twice in the Guilford campaign, resulting in the amputation of his fore and middle fingers.

Tarleton accompanied Cornwallis to the coast at Wilmington, following Guilford Court House, to regroup and resupply the army. When Cornwallis invaded Virginia several weeks later, Tarleton's men formed the van of the British army. On June 4, Tarleton led a quick-moving but unsuccessful raid to capture Governor Thomas Jefferson and members of the Virginia Assembly at Charlottesville. Warned by a local militia officer, Jefferson escaped ten minutes before Tarleton's men arrived at Monticello.

On June 15, 1781, Tarleton was promoted to lieutenant colonel of the 79th Regiment in the British army. Tarleton's men formed the decoy at the Battle of Green Spring, Virginia, almost luring Lafayette's small army into a lethal trap. At the last moment the British plot was uncovered, and Lafayette's men escaped Cornwallis's grasp. Tarleton followed this up with an extended raid into the heart of Virginia, riding 400 miles between July 9 and 24. He rejoined Cornwallis in Suffolk.

When Cornwallis went into camp at Yorktown, Tarleton and his men formed part of the 600-man British force at Gloucester, across the York River. His last action was fought on October 3 against the French Hussars of the Duke of Lauzun. Tarleton was unhorsed but succeeded in getting away, shaken up but otherwise unharmed.

After Cornwallis's surrender, Tarleton was afraid that the Americans would try to kill him for his past deeds in the southern campaign. He requested the protection of Count Rochambeau. Rochambeau gave it, but expressed the belief that Tarleton was without merit as an officer, being

merely the usual butcher and barbarian some cavalrymen tended to be.

The period after the surrender was a difficult one for Tarleton. The American officers did not offer him invitations to dinner as they did to Cornwallis, Charles O'Hara, and other British officers. Tarleton complained to the Marquis de Lafayette, but it did no good. The French officers, on the other hand, were more tolerant and did invite Tarleton to dinner.

Four days after the surrender, Tarleton was riding to eat just such a meal with some French officers when the steward for Sir Peyton Skipwith stopped Tarleton right in the main street in Yorktown and demanded that Tarleton surrender his master's horse. It appears Tarleton had confiscated the animal and now the tables were turned. A French officer came to Tarleton's aid and loaned him a horse so that the British officer would not have to walk to dinner.

Tarleton sailed to New York, unharmed, with Cornwallis and left there for London on parole on December 15, 1781. On the return voyage, the fleet was scattered by the weather. Tarleton's ship, an ancient merchantman called the *London*, had the misfortune of being captured by a French privateer. Tarleton paid 400 guineas ransom and was set free to arrive in London on January 18, 1782.

Tarleton was treated as a hero upon his return and was granted a private audience with the King. He met the famous "Perdita," Mary Robinson, at the studio of Sir Joshua Reynolds while they were having their portraits painted. Mary was a beautiful woman, with great charm, red hair, blue eyes, and usually attired in the most up-to-date London style. Tarleton and Mary Robinson, a noted playwright, poetess, and writer, became lovers for 15 stormy years. Mary had been the mistress to the Prince of Wales, later George IV, before taking up with Tarleton. Mary died alone at 43 years of age on December 26, 1800.

Tarleton was appointed lieutenant colonel of the Light Dragoons on December 25, 1782, and the British Legion was placed on the British Establishment the same day, a situation that provided some financial security for its officers once the war ended. Tarleton could not afford to live the high life of excitement and gaming he desired on the half-pay of an army field officer. However, he and a Captain Hardy of the Guards eventually opened a faro bank at Daubigney's

Tavern, becoming in effect professional gamblers.

Tarleton also became interested in politics and ran for a seat in Parliament from Liverpool. After an initial failure, he succeeded in winning a seat in the House of Commons in 1790. He ran for reelection in 1796 against his own brother, John, and won. Tarleton managed to hold his seat until he was defeated in 1806 for his lack of interest in commercial affairs and little understanding of trade matters while representing a commercial port, Liverpool.

With the help of Mary Robinson, Tarleton wrote his account of the southern campaign, which was published in 1787. Not particularly objective, Tarleton wrote it to protect his reputation from the effects of the defeat at Cowpens. He was fast friends with the two royal heirs to the throne and led a merry life in London and throughout Europe, the effects of which were not fully felt until old age set in.

Tarleton was promoted to colonel in the army on November 18, 1790, and to major general on October 3, 1794. On December 17, 1798, he married the 23-year-old natural daughter of the Duke of Lancaster, Susan Priscilla Bertie, a wealthy, educated, attractive individual who was woman enough to match the demands of General Tarleton, the womanizing gamester. Shortly after their marriage, Tarleton was placed on active duty and sent to Portugal. His wife went along. In a short time, Tarleton managed to get recalled. There was no action there, and he had developed a painful case of the gout, which hindered his military capacities.

On January 1, 1801, Tarleton was promoted to lieutenant general and was shifted first from colonel of the Durham Fencible Cavalry, then to colonel of the 22nd Light Dragoons, and finally to the 21st Light Dragoons. On September 25, 1803, Tarleton was sent to take command of the Cork Military District in Ireland. However, he was transferred within a brief time to the Seventh Military District in western England. At a time when Napoleon was making moves to invade England, Tarleton had his hands full preparing to repel the French. His district included, among others, the counties of Radnor, Gloucester, Monmouth, and Pembroke. Tarleton held command there for six years.

During these years a noticeable change came over Tarleton. No longer the hell-raiser he had been in earlier times, he was now a polite, quiet, and dignified elder officer. His wife, Susan, had become a major civilizing influence on the general.

On February 23, 1808, Tarleton was made governor of Berwick and Holy Island, an office that required little work but did much financially to raise the style of living of the Tarleton household when coupled with his pension and his wife's money. Tarleton was promoted to full general on January 21, 1812, and was created a Baronet on November 6, 1815. He was transferred as colonel from the 21st to the 8th Light Dragoons on January 15, 1818. On May 20, 1820, Tarleton was made a Knight Grand Cross of the Order of the Bath by George IV, his old drinking partner and friend.

In his later years, Tarleton spent most of his time with his wife at Leintwardine House, Leintwardine, Shropshire. He suffered from rheumatism, arthritis, the gout, and a number of other ailments brought on by his many years of rich living. He died on January 25, 1833, and was buried in the churchyard nearby. His marriage with Susan Priscilla Bertie produced no children, but they did share a special love. Susan erected a monument over his grave as a sign of her affection. She lived until 1864.

At the end of their relationship, in 1799, Mary Robinson wrote a novel called *The False Friend* in which she described a character called Treville that everyone knew to be Tarleton. Of him, she said, he was "too polite to be religious; too witty to be learned; too youthful to be serious; and too handsome to be discrete." Perhaps since this is the Tarleton many knew, he is not readily remembered in England today. During the War of the Revolution, it was quite another Tarleton that Americans came to know. The reputation of the brutal, dashing cavalryman known as "Benny or "Bloody Ben" is still talked about in the United States to this day.

Paul J. Sanborn

REFERENCES

Robert D. Bass, *The Green Dragoon* (1973); Sir Henry Clinton, *The American Rebellion* (1954); *DAB*; Thomas J. Fleming, *Downright Fighting* (1988); Henry Lee, *The American Revolution in the South* (1969); Benson J. Lossing, *The Pictorial Field Book of the American Revolution* (1972); Banastre Tarleton, *A History of the Campaign of 1780 and 1781 in the Southern Province* (1787), rpr. 1968; Franklin and Mary Wickwire, *Cornwallis: The American Adventure* (1970).

Tarleton's Monticello Raid (June 3–4, 1781)

General Charles Cornwallis, commander of the southern British army in North America, decided the only way to pacify the Carolinas and Georgia was to attack the source of southern supplies, material, and manpower at its base, the commonwealth of Virginia. For months Cornwallis had battled General Nathanael Greene to a standstill in the Carolinas. Almost no matter what losses Cornwallis inflicted upon Greene's force, the Americans were able to draw upon Virginia to replenish their needs. From Wilmington, North Carolina, against the direct orders of General Henry Clinton, supreme British commander in North America, Cornwallis and his army marched into Virginia in late May 1781.

General Benedict Arnold, now in the service of King George III, had terrorized Richmond, burning and destroying buildings and supplies all along the rich James River corridor. To reinforce Arnold, Clinton dispatched Major General William Phillips with a force of an additional 2,000 men. Phillips assumed overall command and continued the gradual destruction of Virginia. The Patriot tide was at low ebb already when Cornwallis marched his men into the Commonwealth on May 20.

General Friedrich von Steuben and local Virginia militia generals such as Thomas Nelson had had only mixed success in raising a force to counter the British invasions. Washington was so intent on capturing Arnold that the first American-French plot to cooperate in a Virginia joint operation to trap Arnold and bring him to justice developed. General Marquis de Lafayette and the better part of the crack corps of light infantry was sent south from Washington's main army to work in tandem with French sea power and troops. It was all for nothing, but it did bring a Continental force into Virginia at the exact time that Cornwallis entered the state. It also established a prototype plan that might be used later.

Cornwallis immediately took advantage of Virginia's river systems and British sea power to ferry bodies of troops up the many rivers quickly, before the Americans could react, and spread desolation throughout the Tidewater region. Besides burning and disrupting the supply network, Cornwallis accomplished two other significant goals. He gathered a large number of well-bred horses with which he mounted his infantry and made them even more mobile. And he liberated the slaves. In a short time, in spite of Lafayette's force, it seemed the British could do what they wished and Virginia was ready to cave in and capitulate.

Thus, when Cornwallis learned from a captured dispatch on June 1 that the Virginia Assembly was in Charlottesville and the governor, Thomas Jefferson, was at his home, Monticello, the British general saw a way of destroying the government of Virginia with one swoop. If that could be accomplished, Virginia would certainly have fallen. For this mission, Cornwallis selected his Green Dragoon, Lieutenant Colonel Tarleton.

As a second prong of this same mission, Cornwallis sent Lieutenant Colonel John Graves Simcoe, his rangers, and other forces to Point of Fork, today's Columbia, to destroy rebel supplies and capture von Steuben and his men. Lafayette and von Steuben had been powerless to stop Cornwallis. Once again, this would be the case.

Cornwallis had sent Tarleton with 180 of his mounted dragoons, wearing their short green jackets, and he originally ordered a detachment from the 2nd Battalion of the 71st Highlanders Regiment to accompany the dragoons. The 71st, however, had not forgotten Tarleton's abandonment of their first battalion at Cowpens several months before and requested that they serve elsewhere. Cornwallis mounted 70 men from the 23rd Royal Welsh Fusiliers under the command of Captain Champaigne to go with Tarleton, and the 71st was assigned to Simcoe.

Jefferson and the government had originally fled to Charlottesville to escape the raid of Benedict Arnold. Tarleton was sent to bag the whole group if possible. Tarleton, the "Hunting Leopard," moved at once. It was a 60-mile ride from Cornwallis's camp on the North Anna River to Charlottesville. Tarleton was a ruthless, daring, stocky, and dashing officer who had failed only at Cowpens. If he could capture Patrick Henry, Richard Henry Lee, Thomas Nelson, Thomas Jefferson, Benjamin Harrison, and others, then it would be disastrous for American morale.

Tarleton's force, well mounted for once on Virginia livestock, moved with speed and covered the 60 miles in 24 hours. Tarleton left camp early on Sunday, June 3 and stopped at midday to rest the horses. Then he moved to the Cuckoo Tavern in Louisa County between nine and ten o'clock at night. The day had been a hot one. The horses and men were tired, but there was no time to lose.

The Cuckoo Tavern took its name from a cuckoo clock possessed by the owner of the establishment. Such an item was quite a tourist attraction in those days and a novelty that people enjoyed listening to. The tavern's former name was the King's Ordinary. Obviously it was politic to change the name. Today the tavern is gone but the site is marked on the map on the highway between Louisa County Court House and Goochland.

As Tarleton's men rode up to the tavern and halted for a brief rest, they were seen by Captain John "Jack" Jouett, Jr., of the 16th Virginia State Regiment. Jack was 6 feet, 4 inches tall, weighed over 200 pounds, was an expert horseman, and knew the countryside as well as the inside of his own home. At the time of the raid, he was 27 years old. Jouett was home on leave recovering from wounds received in the Carolinas fighting the British. He knew exactly what the British were after. He knew what had to be done. Jefferson and the assembly had to be warned in time.

Jouett's father was a Patriot who served as a commissary in the Virginia militia and owned the Swan Tavern in Charlottesville. He used to own the Cuckoo Tavern before he sold it. Jumping on one of the best thoroughbred horses the Jouett family owned, Jack was off riding as fast as he could for Monticello. Fortunately there was a nearly full moon that night. Using back roads and then just plunging through the woods with branches whipping him across the face and body, Jack was able to maintain his speed as he moved toward Charlottesville. The light of the moon guided his horse's steps.

In a short time, Tarleton was back on the road with his men moving at a fast pace in the night's cool air. Within an hour, Tarleton stopped again for a longer but necessary rest at a plantation near Louisa County Court House. For three hours the British relaxed. Then it was back on the road at a canter for Charlottesville. Suddenly a wagon train appeared in the road. The British captured the 12 wagons, which were filled with military supplies and equipment for General Greene. Tarleton's men burned the wagons. There was no time for delay.

At the break of day, Tarleton split his force, one group riding to Castle Hill, a Walker family home six miles from Charlottesville, and the second group going to Belvoir, another Walker estate. At these plantation houses, the British managed to catch some of the assemblymen in bed and took them as prisoners, including two of Thomas Nelson's brothers, William and Robert. A half-hour rest was allowed the horses. Tarleton paroled some of his prisoners and others he kept with the column.

There is a legend that Dr. Thomas Walker arranged for a large breakfast for the British in order to delay Tarleton, which it supposedly did. Tarleton never mentioned it later in his account of the raid. It is possible that the British did eat there, perhaps spending too much time in that activity.

At the same time, Captain Jack Jouett was nearing Monticello. He crossed the Rivanna River at Milton Ford and rode up the mountain at 4:30 A.M. to the mansion, where he found Jefferson and his house guests, including the speaker of the assembly, asleep in bed. He woke everyone up and warned them of the British approach. No panic, no problem. Jefferson refreshed Jack with some of Monticello's best Madeira and then sat down to breakfast with his guests. Jack drank his wine and then rode quickly to town to warn the citizens of Charlottesville of the danger.

The group at Monticello ate breakfast at their leisure and then the politicians excused themselves and went to Charlottesville to join the rest of the assembly. Jefferson went to his study and spent the next two hours securing his papers while his family packed and prepared to escape.

Tarleton's men brushed aside a detachment of American cavalry at the river outside of Charlottesville and moved into town. Tarleton sent a group to climb the mountain and secure Jefferson at his home. Just as the British detachment from the main column was climbing the hill to the mansion, Jefferson sent his wife and children off on a 14-mile journey to the Coles estate. A Continental officer, Captain Chris Hudson, arrived to warn Jefferson that the British were on top of him. Jefferson had sent his horse to be shoed and waited patiently until the horse was ready.

While waiting for his horse, he used his spyglass to pick out the British troops riding through Charlottesville. He rode off just as the British arrived at Monticello from the other side. Jefferson quickly dashed into the woods and was swallowed up by the trees. He rode to the Carter's plantation at Blendheim, where he caught up with his family. The Jeffersons dined with the Carters and then moved on to stay with the Coles at a safer distance from Monticello.

Captain Kenneth McLeod led the detachment to Monticello with the orders that no damage was to be done to the estate. The British obeyed those orders with the exception of a few of the troopers, who managed to sneak into the wine cellar to take a few bottles of wine. The Jeffersons had hidden their silver and valuables under the wooden floor of the portico. One of Monticello's slaves, Caesar, hid as the British arrived and remained there for the 18 hours that the British stayed at Monticello.

The assembly fled for Staunton, 40 miles west, where they set up Virginia's government in some safety several days later. Although, during their stay in that town, a group of American dragoons, dressed like the British, rode into town and scared the assembly into fleeing out of town as fast as possible until they were assured it was a friendly force.

As of June 2, 1781, Jefferson's term as governor had expired. One act of the assembly in Staunton was to elect Thomas Nelson as governor and grant him dictatorial powers to handle the crisis that Cornwallis had brought to the Commonwealth. Nelson became both the political and military leader of Virginia.

Remaining in town to direct his men, Tarleton had captured seven of the assembly including Daniel Boone, the representative from what is today Kentucky. The prisoners spent the night in a coal cellar and were paroled the next day. The main leaders all managed to escape. Tarleton did destroy or take over 1,000 muskets, powder, tobacco, and clothing, all meant to help Greene's southern army. Jouett attracted British attention and was chased, allowing the plainly dressed General Edward Stevens, wounded at Guilford Court House, to escape unmolested.

The British slept overnight in Charlottesville and then began to move back toward Colonel Simcoe's force. Simcoe and his 500 men went to Point of Forks, where von Steuben had several hundred Continental recruits guarding one of the main supply bases in Virginia. Point of Fork is where the Fluvanna and Rivanna rivers join to form the James River. Von Steuben got his men away safely, but some of the British crossed the river and brought back canoes and rafts that Simcoe used to ferry his men across the river to take most of the Continental supplies intact, including several guns that Cornwallis would use with effect at Yorktown.

Tarleton and Simcoe joined forces. They in turn were joined by Cornwallis and his army on June 7. The British force moved to Elk Hill near Columbia, Virginia, 30 miles southeast of Monticello. This was one of Jefferson's plantations, and Cornwallis had it destroyed. The crops were burned, as were the barns and outbuildings. The horses and cattle were taken off, and 30 slaves were freed. Cornwallis hoped his army from the Elk Hill position could cut off von Steuben from Lafayette and destroy him. But von Steuben and his men eluded the British once again.

Cornwallis then moved his army toward Richmond with Tarleton's men at the rear guard. From Richmond, the British moved to Williamsburg and then, eventually, to Yorktown. When General Anthony Wayne brought his brigade of three Pennsylvania regiments to join Lafayette, the American force began to grow in strength. Cornwallis then received word from Clinton that New York was under pressure, and Clinton needed many of Cornwallis's best troops sent back to help hold New York. Cornwallis was ordered to find a port. That ended the very effective offensive operations that Cornwallis had initiated in Virginia. These measures had nearly worked. But time had run out for Cornwallis.

The assembly voted Jack Jouett a sword, which he received in 1783, and a pair of pistols, which he received early in the next century for his 40-mile ride in the night to warn the American leaders of Tarleton's approach. His ride, more dangerous and certainly harder than Revere's, is much less known.

In 1782, Jack moved to Kentucky and in 1784 married Sallie Robards, the sister of Lewis Robards. By coincidence, Lewis Robards was the first husband of Rachel Donelson who later married Andrew Jackson in the mistaken impression she had been divorced from Robards. Jack Jouett was the one who introduced the bill in the assembly to investigate the Robards-Donelson marriage for possible divorce, but Andrew Jackson and Rachel had mistakenly thought the divorce had gone through. Everything was worked out in the end, and this did not affect Jack's lasting friendship with Jackson. He visited him at the hermitage often. Jack also became good friends with Henry Clay. He died in 1822.

Jefferson finally wound up living at Poplar Frest, 90 miles from Monticello, where he promptly broke his arm riding his favorite horse, Caractacus. He was confined to bed for six weeks. From there, Jefferson would go on to serve the United States in a number of vital roles, including that of the President, for the next several decades. Criticized for fleeing Monticello as the British approached, Jefferson defended his honor, and it is hard to see what he could have done beyond what he did. He did not panic, he saved his papers and his family, and he left only as the British were approaching his house.

Had Tarleton been able to capture the assembly and Jefferson, there probably would have been no capture of Yorktown. But he failed, thanks to a young man who rode through the woods to spread the word. The plan of trapping Arnold on the coast of Virginia with a French fleet and an American-French land force was stored for the time, but when Cornwallis entered the same trap, the plan was taken out, dusted off, and used with great effect. It all began with the efforts of Jack Jouett, a little-known but important figure in the War of Revolution.

Paul J. Sanborn

REFERENCES

Robert D. Bass, *The Green Dragoon* (1957); Virginius Dabney, *From Cuckoo Tavern to Monticello* (1966); Benson J. Lossing, *The Pictorial Field Book of the American Revolution*, 2 vols. (1851–52), rpr. 1972; Dumas Malone, *Thomas Jefferson, The Virginian* (1948); Alf J. Mapp, Jr., *Thomas Jefferson* (1987); Christopher Ward, *The War of Revolution*, 2 vols. (1952); Franklin and Mary Wickwire, *Cornwallis, The American Adventure* (1970).

Tarleton's Virginia Raid (July 9–24, 1781)

Shortly after the Battle of Green Spring and once the entire British army had been ferried across the James River to the southern bank, Cornwallis detached Tarleton's Green Horse troops for an extended raid into the heartland of Virginia. The purpose of this raid was to burn and destroy American supplies, gunpowder, weapons, uniforms, and all public stores across the southern tier of Virginia's counties, heretofore untouched by the war. It was also designed to keep Tarleton and his men busy.

With three supply wagons and his mounted legion, Tarleton left Cobham, across the river from Jamestown Island, on July 9 and rode south of Petersburg and on to Prince Edward Court House. From there, the Green Horse rode on to New London in Bedford County at the foot of the Blue Ridge Mountains. The raiders burned and destroyed a path through south-central Virginia, but most of what was destroyed was the tobacco crop and not military stores.

When they reached the turnaround point in their raid, Tarleton's men had come approximately 180 miles. They covered at least 20 and sometimes as much as 40 miles a day. Their horses were badly worn by the hard ride. Fortunately, this section of Virginia, along the Blue Ridge Mountains, was, and still is, one of the best horse-breeding regions in North America. The British were able to remount themselves and rest in preparation for the return ride. They camped in Bedford County for two days.

The Marquis de Lafayette moved his army to Malvern Hill. Word soon arrived describing Tarleton's raid. Washington even heard of the raid and mentioned it in his papers. Lafayette sent General Anthony Wayne to Amelia Court House and General Daniel Morgan, who had returned to active service and joined Lafayette, to Petersburg to cut off Tarleton's return. Cornwallis learned of these moves and sent warning to Tarleton, reaching him before he left Bedford County.

In Bedford County, Tarleton heard of General Nathanael Greene's siege at Ninety Six and was informed that Greene was gradually recapturing the Carolinas. Once he received Cornwallis's message, he burned the three supply wagons and led his men in a southerly route to avoid contact with Wayne and Morgan. Riding through Lunenburg County, Tarleton's men averaged 40 miles a day as they raced back to rejoin Cornwallis. The Green Horse moved so quickly that they passed by the Americans before anyone realized they had been there.

On July 24, Tarleton returned to Cornwallis's camp at Suffolk. In his review of the campaign in his papers, Tarleton observed that the mission was not destructive enough for the damage sustained in skirmishes en route and the loss of men and horses by the excessive heat of the climate. His men had ridden almost 400 miles in

15 days during the heat of the summer. Both men and horses were exhausted and worn.

Once Tarleton had completed the raid, and his army was intact again, Cornwallis marched to Portsmouth to begin the transfer of troops to General Henry Clinton in New York. Tarleton's was the last great raid in Virginia that the British would make.

Paul J. Sanborn

REFERENCES

Robert D. Bass, *The Green Dragoon* (1957); Henry P. Johnston, *The Yorktown Campaign* (1881); Benson J. Lossing, *The Pictorial Field Book of the Revolution*, 2 vols. (1851–1852), rpr. 1972; Christopher Ward, *The War of Revolution* (1952); Franklin and Mary Wickwire, *Cornwallis: The American Adventure* (1970).

Ternant, Jean Baptiste, Charles de (1751–1816)

French army officer. Born in Damvillers, Meuse, France, Ternant became a lieutenant in the French corps of engineers (1771). He either resigned in order to join the American cause or he may have been sent to North America in an official capacity to gather information. At Valley Forge by February 6, 1778, he requested a commission. Hesitant to employ still another French engineer after Congress had indicated its displeasure at the number of Frenchmen with commissions in the American forces, Washington found employment for Ternant. He became one of General Friedrich von Steuben's sub-inspectors, and he assisted von Steuben in training troops as a lieutenant colonel (March 1778).

Ordered to join General Robert Howe in the Southern Department, Ternant noted the weaknesses of the Charleston defenses (November 21, 1778). He fought under Robert Howe at Savannah. Ternant next served under General Benjamin Lincoln at the Perrysburg encampment as inspector. He fought at Stono Ferry and at the siege of Charleston. Ternant was sent to Havana in order to get Spanish naval assistance against the British blockade of Charleston, but he was unsuccessful. Captured at Charleston, he was soon after paroled. Ternant, holding the title of Inspector of the Southern Army, then joined Colonel Charles Armand's Legion in North Carolina. He was highly regarded by Washington, and he was praised by Thomas Mifflin, president of Congress.

Richard L. Blanco

REFERENCES

Douglas N. Adams, "Jean Baptiste Ternant," *South Carolina Historical Magazine*, 86 (1985):221–240.

Thacher, James (1754–1844)

Continental Army physician. Born in Barnstable, Massachusetts, James Thacher studied medicine as an apprentice to Dr. Abner Hersey in Barnstable. At the outbreak of hostilities in July 1775, Thacher became a surgeon's mate under Dr. John Warren at the Cambridge, Massachusetts, provincial hospital. He cared for the wounded from Bunker Hill. In February 1776, Thacher was appointed surgeon's mate to Dr. David Townsend in Colonel Asa Whitcomb's regiment stationed at Prospect Hill. In July of that year, Thacher and Townsend received orders to inoculate all the soldiers in their regiment against smallpox. They completed this work by August 5, 1776, with only one fatality.

Thacher joined his regiment at Ticonderoga in late summer of 1776. They saw no action against the British that following winter although Indian raiding parties often attacked, and Thacher cared for the wounded from these skirmishes. In April 1777 Thacher asked for a transfer to a general hospital as a surgeon's mate. He was posted to the general hospital at Ticonderoga and again served under his friend Townsend.

On July 6, 1777, General John Burgoyne moved against Ticonderoga. The Continental forces abandoned their position, piled their supplies, hospital, and patients into boats and, pursued by the British, sailed south to Fort Anne. On July 25, Thacher was ordered to move his remaining patients to Albany. Once arrived in Albany, he went to work in the 500-patient general hospital there. In September the hospital began receiving large numbers of patients from the Battle of Saratoga. Thacher treated General Benedict Arnold, whose leg had been broken by a musket ball. British and Hessian prisoners were also lodged in the Albany hospital, often cared for by their own surgeons. Thacher thought well of the British doctors but felt that the German doctors had but callous regard for their patients.

On June 1, 1778, the hospital moved by river from Albany to Highlands of the Hudson, across the river from West Point. Thacher met George Washington there and escorted him on a tour of the wards.

In September 1778, Generals William Woodford and John Peter Muhlenburg and a division each of troops from Maryland and Virginia made their quarters at the Highlands. Thacher was so impressed by the southern troops that he requested and was granted a transfer to the Virginia regiment under Colonel George Gibson. Thacher also met the Marquis de Lafayette while at the Highlands.

In July 1779, Thacher left the Virginians to join the Massachusetts troops at Providence, Rhode Island. He became surgeon there to Colonel Henry Jackson's regiment. He accompanied them in August on their unsuccessful assault against the British post on the Penobscot River. In the fall of 1779, the Massachusetts regiment marched to New Jersey. Throughout the following terrible winter, the troops suffered greatly from severe weather and shortages of food, clothing, and shelter. By July 1780, Thacher noted that these troops had recovered their physical health but were restless and unhappy at being so long away from home. In the fall of 1780, Thacher returned to the West Point area in time to see Major John André executed. He remained there and at Crompond over the winter of 1780–1781, caring for the men wounded in the many small engagements and raids taking place so close to the British lines. In the spring of 1781, he carried out another smallpox inoculation campaign among his troops. In the summer of 1781, Thacher was chosen to be surgeon to a corps of light infantry under Colonel Alexander Scammell, which was to move south in advance of the main army to the vicinity of Yorktown, Virginia. He stayed with them through the final battles of the war and was an eyewitness to the surrender of Cornwallis at Yorktown. After the surrender, Thacher returned with the troops to West Point. He stayed in the army for more than a year longer, finally mustering out on January 1, 1783.

After the war, Thacher set himself up in medical practice in Plymouth, Massachusetts, and lived there for the rest of his 90 years. He was much respected and highly productive as a physician, educator, and medical writer. He took many students into his own home as medical apprentices. His medical writings, chiefly *The American New Dispensatory*, first published in 1810, and *American Modern Practice*, first published in 1817, went through several editions, were well thought of in their time, and are still useful as sources on early nineteenth-century American medical practice. His diary, *Military Journal of the American Revolution* kept from the beginning to the end of his service in the Revolution and first published in 1823, makes fascinating reading and is an invaluable source of first person information on the war. Thacher died in Plymouth.

Janet Brady Joy

REFERENCES

Mary C. Gillett, *The Army Medical Department, 1775–1818* (1981); Martin Kaufman, Stuart Galishoff, and Todd L. Savitt, eds., *Dictionary of American Medical Biography* (1984); James Thacher, *Military Journal of the American Revolution* (1862); Henry R. Viets, "James Thacher and His Influence on American Medicine," *Virginia Medical Monthly*, 76 (1949):384–99.

Thomas, John (1724–1776)

Continental Army officer. Born in Marshfield, Massachusetts, Thomas studied medicine under Dr. Simon Tufts in Medford. In 1746 and 1747 he was a surgeon for the British army in Nova Scotia. He began his service in the French and Indian War as a captain; by the end of the struggle in which he engaged in eight campaigns, Thomas was a colonel. He settled in Kingston, Massachusetts, and became a justice of the peace by 1770.

Thomas was at the siege of Boston with a regiment that he had raised, and until Washington arrived to assume command, Thomas supervised the camp at Roxbury. On January 15, 1776, he was appointed brigadier general of Massachusetts militia. Thomas performed ably at Boston, and he was responsible for the defense of Dorchester Heights (March 1776).

Promoted to brigadier general in March 1776 in the Continental Army and then to major general, Thomas was ordered to the siege of Quebec. He had the difficult task of leading an army stricken with smallpox on a retreat up the St. Lawrence River (May 1776) while being pursued by a British force. Although Congressman Samuel Chase and Charles Carroll warned Thomas to be inoculated, he disregarded their advice and died of the disease at Sorel.

Richard L. Blanco

REFERENCES

Charles Coffin, *The Life and Service of Major General John Thomas* (1844); Edward Pierce Hamilton, "General John Thomas," *Massachusetts Historical Society Proceedings, 84* (1972):44–52; Arthur Lord, "Major-General John Thomas," *Massachusetts Historical Society Proceedings, 18* (1903):419–432.

Thompson, Benjamin (Count Rumford) (1753–1814)

American scientist, Loyalist. Born at Woburn near Boston, Massachusetts, March 26, 1753, Benjamin Thompson was the son of Ruth Simonds and Benjamin Thompson. His father died in November 1754, and his mother was remarried in March 1756 to Josiah Pierce, Jr. Benjamin attended village school in Woburn and schools in Byfield and Medford until age 13. The boy had little liking for farming or village life, and his young, scientific mind was probably considering devices and alternatives to reduce drudgery. In October 1766 he was apprenticed to John Appleton, a merchant in Salem. Benjamin found Salem quite different from the small farming community of Woburn, and he was impressed with the upper classes, their lifestyles, their stately homes, and the ships from foreign ports with goods that he had not seen before. Appleton was one of a number of merchants who signed a nonimportation agreement, in reaction to the Stamp Act. As a result, his business declined. In 1760 Benjamin was badly hurt while grinding ingredients for rockets and fireworks, and he returned to his mother's home to recuperate.

After his recovery, he was apprenticed to Hopestill Capen, a dry-goods merchant in Boston. Business in Boston was brisker, there was a great deal of political activity, and English soldiers and officers strolled the streets. The officers made a particular impression on 17-year-old Benjamin. The Boston Massacre, during which British soldiers fired into an angry mob, occurred March 5, 1770, a short distance from the place where Benjamin was staying. After two months in Boston, he returned to Woburn, and in December 1770 he became apprentice to Dr. John Hay, the town physician. Benjamin's heart was not in this apprenticeship, and he spent a great deal of time in other pursuits—scientific investigations, lectures in natural philosophy, learning French, and playing the fiddle. In order to pay for his apprenticeship he served brief periods as a schoolteacher at Wilmington and Bradford. At age 19 Benjamin was described as having bright blue eyes and dark auburn hair, being six feet tall, well built, handsome, and possessing charming manners.

In the summer of 1772 he traveled to Concord, New Hampshire (formerly known as Pennicook and as Rumford), to be a schoolteacher. That November he married Sarah Walker Rolfe, the 33-year-old widow of one of Concord's leading citizens. Benjamin now had a large estate, a fortune, and social contacts of which he made full benefit. A daughter, Sarah, was born in 1774. He became acquainted with Governor John Wentworth (New Hampshire), who appointed him, at age 19, a major in the 2nd Provincial Regiment of New Hampshire. Through Wentworth he was introduced, in November 1774, to General Thomas Gage, the newly appointed governor of Massachusetts. Thompson impressed these men with his plans for locating deserters and returning them to their units, and with regular reports on the status and activities of American forces. Thompson's activities had not escaped notice by his neighbors, and he was charged by the Committee of Correspondence of Concord with being a "Rebel to the State." On learning that a group of firebrand Patriots was on its way to his house to tar and feather him, he hurriedly fled to Boston. He never saw his wife again, and he did not see his daughter until many years later when he was living in Europe. In March 1776, General William Howe and his British troops abandoned Boston. Benjamin Thompson sailed with them to Halifax, Nova Scotia. Thompson left soon after for England.

Howe and others provided Thompson with letters of introduction to important men in London, especially to Lord George Germain, the Secretary of State for the Colonies. In December 1776 Thompson was appointed Secretary and Register of Records for the Province of Georgia. He pursued scientific interests, and in 1780, he was made a fellow of the Royal Society. When France declared war on Britain in June 1778, Thompson was an aide to Admiral Charles Hardy of the Channel Fleet. As aide his duties were to observe and recommend improvements in firepower, signaling, and ship design. Late in 1779 Thompson was Deputy to the Inspector General of Provincial Forces, in which capacity he was responsible for shipments of clothing and accouterments from England to armed forces in the colonies. During these years Thompson submitted many reports for Loyalists seeking support and favors from the government.

All the while, Thompson was establishing himself as an English gentleman and freeing himself from the taint of being a colonial, and he was always acting to improve his situation. When Lord Germain's political fortunes waned in 1780, because of high taxes and an unpopular war, Thompson was able to secure an appointment as lieutenant colonel and commandant of the King's American Dragoons. This appointment cost him £4,500. In October 1781 he sailed to assume his new command in New York. However, General Sir Henry Clinton, commander-in-chief, did not look favorably on Thompson's coming to America, and apparently orders were given to stop him before he reached New York.

The King's American Dragoons were stationed at Huntington, Long Island, and Thompson arranged for a review of his troops by Prince William Henry, future King William IV. Major Benjamin Tallmadge of the American army was delivering regular reports to General George Washington on the activities of Thompson's unit. The people of Huntington and vicinity had low regard for this unit, in that they "live upon the inhabitants as they please, and commit the greatest acts of violence." Following the signing of the articles of peace on November 30, 1782, British forces were withdrawn from Long Island, and Thompson returned to England. Thompson requested, and through the intervention of Lord North, was granted a promotion to full colonel and a retirement at half-pay. Later George III bestowed on him the honor of knighthood.

In September 1783, at age 30, Thompson embarked on a grand tour of Europe. He drew the attention of Prince Maximilian, who introduced him to the reigning Duke of Bavaria, Carl Theodor. Thompson saw an opportunity to enter the service of the Duke, but he needed permission from King George III to do so. The Court of St. James wanted closer relations with Bavaria, and hoping that Thompson would keep the British government informed of the Duke's political actions, permission was granted. Sir Benjamin Thompson was given the title of Count Rumford of the Holy Roman Empire in May 1792. When his patron and supporter died in February 1799, Theodor's successor, Maximilian

Joseph, stripped Rumford of his military command, but he let Rumford keep his pension. After 15 years at the Bavarian court, Rumford left Munich. Back in England, Rumford contemplated returning to America, and he proceeded to make appropriate contacts. These contacts included Rufus King, the American Minister in London; James McHenry, Secretary of War; and Vice President John Adams, President of the American Academy of Arts and Sciences. President George Washington had received a copy of Rumford's essays, and Alexander Hamilton had recommended to his military staff Rumford's essays on feeding armies. When John Adams was President, after some misgivings, he offered Rumford the position of Superintendent of the Military Academy. Rumford declined.

Throughout his life Rumford was an astute observer, and experimenter with scientific apparatus, and an inventor. As was the case with other prominent eighteenth-century scientists, Rumford had a wide variety of interests, and he made a number of significant contributions to science and technology. He may have been fired from his apprenticeship in Boston because he spent time "under the counter with gimlets, knife, and saw, constructing some little machine, or looking over some book of science, than behind it arranging clothes or waiting on customers." He and his boyhood friend, Loammi Baldwin, performed electrical experiments, and Benjamin Franklin is reported to have sent an electrical apparatus to them from London. Rumford's first recorded scientific observation was a description of a monstrous child delivered by his mentor Dr. John Hay. This description was presented to the American Philosophical Society of Philadelphia in 1773. Among his many inventions were a more efficient stove for cooking, improved pots and pans, thermometers, an oil lamp, and an improved design for fireplaces. Measurement was an important part of his investigations, and he devised a number of kinds of measurements for determining, for example, the force of gunpowder, the insulating value of fabrics for clothing (particularly for military uniforms), and the illumination of candles.

During his years in Bavaria, Rumford was responsible for reviewing and reforming the military establishment, including everything from recruiting to feeding troops to designing uniforms. Rumford developed an interest in solving problems associated with the poor—the hungry, the unemployed, the homeless—a major problem in Bavaria at the time. He organized a workhouse in Munich to which beggars and vagrants were brought. Here they were clothed, fed, housed, given training and work to do, and the children were provided with some schooling. His inventions were used to improve living conditions, to improve nutrition, and to reduce costs.

For years Rumford was interested in the nature of heat and its propagation. In the process of studying the insulating properties of clothing materials, he discovered that the insulating value depends on the air trapped among the fibers. This discovery was recognized as important, and in 1792, he was awarded the prestigious Copley Medal of the Royal Society of Great Britain. The dominant theory of heat was that heat is a fluid, contained by hot objects, which could be passed from one object to another. This fluid was called caloric or phlogiston. As the result of Rumford's cannon-boring experiments and related experiments, he demonstrated that heat is a form of energy and not a substance. This understanding, while not comprehended as completely as it is today, was similar to the results of similar experiments performed by Antoine Laurent Lavoisier, the noted French scientist, economist, and social reformer.

On May 9, 1802, Rumford left England for the last time and settled in Paris. Among the many women he knew was Mme. Marie Paulze Lavoisier, widow of Antoine Lavoisier, who had been executed during the French Revolution. Count Rumford and Mme. Lavoisier were married October 24, 1805, but their marriage did not go well and they were formally separated in 1809. Rumford retired to a villa at Auteuil at the edge of Paris. On August 21, 1814, he died suddenly and was buried in a cemetery at Auteuil, with few people in attendance and without relatives to lament his passing. His grave marker has his birthplace incorrect and the adjectives used to describe his life in the inscription—celebrated, renowned, illustrious, cherished—are not true. Rather than establish and nurture friendships, Rumford used people to attain his goals, and at this he was very successful. Even though his accomplishments are astonishing, few people today know of Sir Benjamin Thompson, Count Rumford.

David C. Blewett

REFERENCES

Duane Bradley, *Count Rumford* (1967); Sanborn C. Brown, *Benjamin Thompson, Count Rumford* (1979); ———, *Benjamin Thompson–Count Rumford, Count Rumford on the Nature of Heat* (1967); ———, *Count Rumford, Physicist Extraordinary* (1962); Douglas McKie, *Antoine Lavoisier: Scientist, Economist, Social Reformer* (1952); Vrest Orton, *The Forgotten Art of Building a Good Fireplace* (1974); Duane Roller, *The Early Development of the Concepts of Temperature and Heat: The Rise and Decline of the Caloric Theory* (1950); Charles Singer, *A Short History of Scientific Ideas to 1900* (1959).

Thompson, Thomas (1739–1809)

Continental Navy officer. Thompson was born in England and settled in Portsmouth, New Hampshire, in 1767, after service as a mate aboard British merchantmen. He became a friend and protégé of John Langdon, a leading citizen of New Hampshire, and soon established himself in the shipbuilding and trading businesses. In 1776, Langdon secured Thompson an appointment as superintendent of the frigate *Raleigh* (32 guns), then under construction at Portsmouth. On October 10, 1776, Thompson was commissioned by the Continental Congress as a captain in the Continental Navy, appearing sixth on the list of ten captains. He was given command of the *Raleigh* and sent to France in August 1777 to obtain supplies for the Continental Army. On this passage, Thompson intercepted and ravaged a British frigate, the *Druid*, that was escorting a convoy, but he was unable to take any prizes. On the return voyage, the *Raleigh* was accompanied by the ship *Alfred* (24 guns), commanded by a Captain Himan. The two ships, both laden with supplies, were set upon by two British warships, *Ariadne* (20 guns) and *Ceres* (16 guns). The *Alfred* was taken early in the battle, and Thompson decided to flee under full sail rather than fight the British alone. He returned to the United States in April 1778 and was relieved of his command. During his court-martial, Thompson was severely criticized for his failure to continue the action, although he stated that he fled in order to protect the supplies desperately needed by the Continental Army. After this experience, Thompson returned to his home and family. There is little evidence of any activities during the remaining years of the Revolution. After the war, he became prominent in building and construction work in New Hampshire and was appointed colonel of the artillery regiment of the state militia in 1785. He died in Portsmouth, New Hampshire, on February 22, 1809.

Mark E. Furber

REFERENCES

Jeremy Belknap, *History of New Hampshire*, 3 vols. (1784–1792); Howard I. Chapelle, *The History of the American Sailing Navy: The Ships and Their Development* (1949); William James Morgan, "John Barry: A Most Fervent Patriot," in *Command Under Sail: Makers of the American Naval Tradition: 1775–1850* (1985); William G. Saltonstall, *Ports of Piscataqua* (1941); Richard Upton, *Revolutionary New Hampshire* (1971).

Thompson, William (1736–1781)

Continental Army officer. A colonial and Revolutionary soldier, Thompson immigrated to the colonies from Ireland and settled near Carlisle, Pennsylvania, while still a young man. In 1756, during the French and Indian War, he was active in several campaigns against the Indians and emerged as a local military leader. After the war, he developed his business interests along the Pennsylvania frontier, and in 1774, Thompson surveyed large tracts of land in Kentucky for his fellow officers. His activities in the Revolution began with his election to a Committee of Correspondence in 1774 and to the Provincial Committee of Safety in 1775. The news of Bunker Hill prompted action, and Thompson was elected to command a regiment of riflemen from Pennsylvania. He was one of the first to be commissioned into the Continental Army, with the rank of colonel, and his riflemen were among the first colonial units to march to the relief of Boston. On March 1, 1776, Thompson was appointed brigadier general and was ordered to Canada, where the American army was in considerable disarray. The new commander, Brigadier General John Sullivan, ordered Thompson to take Trois Rivières (Three Rivers), midway between Montreal and Quebec on the north bank of the St. Lawrence River. Believing the town lightly defended, Thompson attacked. Actually the town was strongly held, and in the retreat Thompson and many of his officers were captured. He was placed on parole and returned to the colonies, where he moved freely but could take no part in the war. This status caused him much suffering and led him to accuse Congress-

man Thomas McKean and others of delaying his exchange. On November 23, 1778, Congress voted to censure Thompson for the remark. He was brought before Congress and apologized, which settled the matter. He was finally exchanged on October 25, 1780, but he took no further part in the war. He died in Carlisle on September 3, 1781.

John Gillig

REFERENCES

Allan G. Crist, *William Thompson . . . a Shooting Star* (1976); Justin H. Smith, *Our Struggle for the Fourteenth Colony: Canada and the American Revolution*, 2 vols. (1907), 2.

Throg's Neck, New York, Battle of (October 12, 1776)

On the night of October 11, 4,000 British and Hessian regulars were placed on 80 ships anchored in Kip's Bay on Manhattan Island. From there they were to sail to Throg's Neck in the Bronx with the goal of cutting off Washington's escape routes from Manhattan. It was a foggy night, and several of General Sir William Howe's subordinates advised against making the move under such conditions, since the convoy would have to pass through Hell's Gate with its dangerous currents. However, Howe could not be dissuaded from following his plan. The convoy made its way safely, and unobserved due to the fog, through the various dangers of the night to Throg's Neck, where on the morning of October 12 the first troops under the command of General Henry Clinton went ashore unopposed. Once his forces were ashore, Howe planned to march eight miles to Kingsbridge and to cut Washington's escape route.

Howe preferred this course of action to his other alternative—a direct assault against Washington's strong defenses on Harlem Heights. Howe, remembering the carnage of Bunker Hill, was probably repulsed by the thought of losing many of his men, especially since it would be difficult to replace such highly skilled soldiers. So Howe opted for the plan that seemed to promise minimal casualties.

The landing, which began in the morning, was over by the afternoon. Throg's Neck is separated by the mainland at low tide by a marshy creek and at high tide by deep water. At the time of the battle there were two ways to get to the mainland—by a bridge and causeway at one point and by a fording place at another point. Both places were easily defendable as Howe's men were to find out. They first tried the fording place, but heavy firing from 30 Americans of the 1st Pennsylvania Rifle Regiment of Colonel Edward Hand halted their advance. Hand's men were firing from concealed positions and were thus poor targets for the British and Hessian regulars. Howe's men next tried the causeway and the bridge. The Americans stationed here destroyed the bridge and kept up a heavy fire on Howe's men, who had to halt their advance again.

Meanwhile, Washington rushed two Continental regiments—one from Massachusetts and one from New York—numbering eighteen hundred men to the scene of the fighting. That evening additional reinforcements arrived and Howe's men were stuck on a small neck of land. Here they remained for six days, until Howe tried a similar move at Pell's Point and failed again. The Battle of Throg's Neck brought Washington precious time, allowing him to remove his army to safety.

Anthony P. Inguanzo

REFERENCES

Stephen Jenkins, *The Story of the Bronx: 1839–1912* (1912); Thomas Jefferson Wertenbaker, *Father Knickerbocker Rebels: New York City During the Revolution* (1948); William B. Willcox, *Portrait of a General* (1964).

Ticonderoga, New York

See Fort Ticonderoga, New York; Fort Ticonderoga, New York, Capture of.

Tilghman, Tench (1744–1786)

Continental Army officer. Born on his father's tobacco plantation near Easton, Maryland, Tilghman was tutored at home. From 1758 to 1761 he attended the Academy and Charitable School of Philadelphia. In 1763 he joined his uncle's business in Philadelphia, and in 1765 he signed the Non-Importation Agreements. By the summer of 1775 he was a lieutenant in the Ladies' Light Infantry in Philadelphia. In August 1775 he served as secretary for a congressional committee negotiating with the Iroquois at Albany.

In the spring of 1776 his unit joined the Flying Camp in New Jersey. Tilghman then sought duty on Washington's staff as an aide. Henceforth, he was at Washington's side at headquarters and in the field during the Manhattan campaign and at White Plains, Trenton, Princeton, and Germantown. Tilghman performed a variety of duties that an entire staff would perform in the twentieth century. He was discreet, exercised good judgment, and handled a mass of correspondence. Tilghman wrote dispatches for Washington, handled letters to Congress, translated letters in French, and he interrogated prisoners. Modest and loyal, Tilghman was less gifted than Alexander Hamilton, another of Washington's aides, but he had no political ambition and he did not seek to become the indispensable assistant to Washington.

Tilghman was with Washington at Monmouth, and he testified at the court-martial of General Charles Lee. He was also at the Morristown and New Windsor encampments. Holding only a courtesy rank of colonel, he did not receive the military appointment of lieutenant colonel until the spring of 1781. Tilghman rode 245 miles in 4 days to carry the news of Yorktown to Congress. Repeatedly refusing a field command in order to assist Washington, Tilghman served 7 years as his aide, the longest tenure of the 32 aides who served Washington.

After the war he formed a business partnership with Robert Morris (January 1, 1784). From Baltimore, Tilghman traded extensively overseas, particularly with France. In 1794 he was an investor in the ship *Empress of China*, and he was also Washington's business agent for Washington's estate at Mount Vernon, Virginia.

Richard L. Blanco

REFERENCES

DAB; Samuel A. Harrison, *Memoir of Lt. Colonel Tench Tilghman* (1870); W. Jackson Stenger, Jr., "Tench Tilghman. George Washington's Aide," *Maryland History Magazine*, 72 (1982):128–33.

Tilton, James (1745–1822)

Continental Army physician. Born in Kent County, Pennsylvania (now in Delaware), James Tilton studied medicine as an apprentice with a local physician before earning a Bachelor of Medicine degree at the College of Philadelphia in 1768. He practiced in Dover, Delaware, for a short time, and then returned to the College of Philadelphia to get an M.D. in 1771. Afterward, he again set up practice in Dover. When the Revolutionary War began, he was serving as lieutenant in the infantry of his local militia. He gave up his practice in 1776 to join the Delaware regiment commanded by Colonel John Haslet. He served as a surgeon to these troops when they were engaged in the Battles of Long Island and White Plains. Taking the sick and wounded with him, he went to Wilmington, Delaware, where he spent the remainder of the winter of 1776–1777 caring for them.

In the spring of 1777, Tilton was ordered to Dumfries, Virginia, where he took charge of the smallpox inoculation of the soldiers marching north from the Carolinas. Later in 1777, as the British moved toward Philadelphia, Tilton was put in charge of the hospital at Princeton, New Jersey. He complained bitterly about the filthy, overcrowded conditions he found at this hospital and was soon stricken himself with "hospital fever" (typhus). After a slow, nine-month recovery, during which he was given up for dead several times, he returned to active duty. In the campaigns of 1778 and 1779, he directed the hospitals at Trenton and New Windsor. In 1779, he was asked to take the chair of materia medica at his alma mater, now reorganized as the medical department of the University of Pennsylvania. However, he turned down this position to remain with the army. He accompanied the troops to Virginia and directed a hospital at Williamsburg. He was present at the surrender of Cornwallis at Yorktown and remained there afterward to take charge of the Yorktown hospitals. He was mustered out in 1782.

As early as 1777, Tilton was agitating for reform within the army's Medical Department. The abject state of the hospitals, the paucity of medicines and supplies, the poor food, the towering disease rates, and especially the needless human suffering goaded him into a ceaseless campaign for change. He designed a hospital hut that would keep the sick separated from the wounded, thereby lessening the spread of infection. The Tilton hut was a three-room building shaped like a fat letter H. As it was originally designed, each hut was to accommodate 28 patients. The walls were to have no windows, the floors were to be of beaten earth, and each room was to have a fireplace in it with a hole in the roof above to let the smoke out. The patients

were to be placed with their feet toward the fire. As designed, the Tilton hut was a distinct improvement over the haphazard facilities in which Continental soldiers usually found themselves. There is, however, little evidence that this design was utilized anywhere other than in one structure built at Basking Ridge, New Jersey, during the winter of 1779–1780.

Tilton was one of those most instrumental in bringing about the much-needed reorganization of the Medical Department in 1780. He spoke out against the abuse-ridden practice of combining the position of purveyor with that of director general of the Medical Department. In 1778 and 1779, he visited many camps and hospitals and was appalled not only by the misery they fostered but by the loss of manpower to the army due to excessive morbidity and mortality. His letters and reports on these conditions, couched in the strongest terms, and a plan he drew up for the reorganization of the Department carried much weight in the eventual passage of the 1780 congressional act of reorganization.

After the war, Tilton returned to medical practice, first in Dover, then near Wilmington, where he practiced horticulture as well. He was a member of the Continental Congress from 1783 to 1785 and served several terms in the Delaware House of Representatives. He was government commissioner of loans for Delaware from 1785 until 1801.

In 1813, when the country was again at war with Great Britain, Tilton published his best-known work, *Economical Observations on Military Hospitals and the Prevention and Cure of Diseases Incident to an Army*. This treatise, based on his experience as a Revolutionary War physician, set out in detail his recommendations for the construction of hospitals, the management of the sick and wounded, and the prevention of disease. As important as he felt it was for each individual soldier to follow the rules for preserving health, Tilton heavily emphasized that it was the responsibility of line officers to establish and maintain military hygiene, especially in an inexperienced army and among new recruits.

Shortly after the publication of this treatise and probably largely because of it, Tilton was appointed physician and surgeon general of the army. On inspecting the hospitals under his command, he found the sanitary conditions as bad as they had ever been during the Revolution and invested all his energy again in reform. The result of his efforts culminated in the issuing of general orders in December 1814 in the form of *Regulations for the Medical Department.* These regulations clearly set out for the first time the duties of medical officers and hospital and sanitary personnel. His term of service ended in 1815. He returned to his farm near Wilmington and eventually died there.

Janet Brady Joy

REFERENCES

Stanhope Bayne-Jones, *The Evolution of Preventive Medicine in the United States Army, 1607–1939* (1968); Mary C. Gillett, *The Army Medical Department, 1775–1818* (1981); Howard A. Kelly and Walter L. Burrage, *Dictionary of American Medical Biography* (1928), rpr. 1971; James M. Phalen, *Chiefs of the Medical Department, United States Army, 1775–1940: Biographical Sketches* (1940); James Thacher, *American Medical Biography* (1827), rpr. 1967.

Tonyn, Patrick

See Florida in the American Revolution; Florida, Invasions of.

Torrence's Tavern, North Carolina, Skirmish at (February 1, 1781) (Alternate names: Tarrant's, Torrance's)

After crossing the Catawba River at Cowan's Ford, Lord Cornwallis dispatched Colonel Banastre Tarleton's dragoons reinforced by the 23rd Regiment of Foot in pursuit of the fleeing Patriot militia. About ten miles from the river, Tarleton came upon a body of militia who had stopped to refresh themselves and were attempting to regroup at Torrence's Tavern. Tarleton exhorted his troops with the cry, "Remember the Cowpens." The British advanced and routed the militia.

Tarleton claims to have killed 50, wounded many, and dispersed more than 500 Patriot militia with a loss of only 7 men and 20 horses. Other sources number the Patriot militia strength at between 100 and 300 and their losses at only 10 dead.

The defeat of the militia at Cowan's Ford and Torrence's Tavern so thoroughly discouraged the local Patriots that Cornwallis's force was able to move through the area without meeting any further resistance.

W. Hugh Harkey, Jr.

REFERENCES

Major William Graham, *General Joseph Graham and His Papers on North Carolina Revolutionary History* (1904); David Schenck, *North Carolina, 1780–1781* (1889); Charles Stedman, *The History of the Origin, Progress and Termination of the American War,* 2 vols. (1794), *II*; Banastre Tarleton, *A History of the Campaigns of 1780 and 1781 in the Southern Provinces of North America* (1787).

Tousard, Anne Louis de (1749–1817)

French army officer. Louis de Tousard was a lieutenant in the French artillery, when Silas Deane recruited him for the American army, offering him the rank of captain. Tousard arrived in America on April 20, 1777, with the du Coudray expedition, only to learn that, in the controversy surrounding du Coudray's contract, neither of the others' contracts would be honored. Tousard then volunteered as an aide to Lafayette and served at Brandywine and Germantown.

Following du Coudray's death, Congress granted Tousard the commission in his original contract. On August 28, 1778, he captured a British gun during an engagement in Rhode Island, but his right arm was severely wounded in the action. He ordered the doctors to amputate his badly mangled arm, so he could return to duty faster. On October 27, Congress recognized his gallantry with a brevet promotion to lieutenant colonel and a lifetime pension of $30 a month.

When he returned to France in 1779, he was made a Chevalier of the Order of St. Louis and given a major's commission in the French army. In 1784 he became a member of the Society of the Cincinnati. That same year he went to Santo Domingo as the lieutenant colonel of the Regiment du Cap and further distinguished himself in operations against the native uprising there. In October 1792 he ran afoul of France's revolutionary government and was arrested and sent to prison in France. The following February, the American minister in France secured Tousard's release and arranged his return to the United States. On February 26, 1795, Tousard was reinstated in the American army with the rank of major in the Corps of Artillerists and

Engineers. For the next five years he planned and supervised the construction of fortifications at West Point and Newport, Rhode Island. On May 26, 1800, he was appointed Inspector of Artillery for the U.S. Army, and at the same time he became the lieutenant colonel-commandant of the 2nd Regiment of Artillerists. He held those positions until April 1, 1802, when he was forced into retirement by Secretary of War Henry Dearborne, who was out to purge the U.S. Army of foreign officers.

Tousard returned to France in 1802 and was welcomed by Napoleon's regime. In 1805 Tousard returned to the United States again, this time as a French consular officer. Over the next 11 years he served in New Orleans, Philadelphia, Baltimore, and New Orleans again. He returned to Paris and retired in 1816.

Tousard had his greatest impact on the American army during his 1795–1802 period. As an artillery officer who received his original training under France's great General de Gribeauval, Tousard was instrumental in implementing the final conversion of American artillery from the British system to France's Gribeauval System. When George Washington was still President in 1795, he asked Tousard to develop an artillery manual for the American army. Tousard had not finished the task when Dearborne forced him out in 1802, but he continued to work on it. The resulting two-volume *American Artillerist's Companion* was published in 1809 and 1813 and influenced American artillery thinking up through the dawn of the Civil War.

David T. Zabecki

REFERENCES

Lieutenant William E. Birkhimer, *Historical Sketch of the Organization, Administration, Material, and Tactics of the Artillery, United States Army* (1884); *DAB*; William H. Powell, *List of Officers of the Army of the United States from 1779 to 1900* (1900).

Treaty of Amity and Commerce (February 6, 1778)

At the outset of hostilities in 1775 there were some Americans who knew that in order for the rebellion to be a success French assistance and recognition were necessary. So in 1778 Congress sent Benjamin Franklin to Paris to obtain French diplomatic recognition of the United States and a formal treaty.

When Franklin arrived in France in December 1776, the French head been covertly sending aid to the Americans for the past several months. Franklin, who made friends wherever he went in Paris, was able to ensure continuation of this recent aid, and he was able to obtain a loan from the French government. But Franklin was unable to obtain a treaty or formal recognition of the American cause.

The French foreign minister, the Comte de Vergennes, was being cautious, and understandably so. Official recognition of the American rebels could mean war with England, and before Vergennes committed his nation to such a course of action he wanted to see if the Americans had a chance of defeating the British. The American military prowess at Germantown and their victory at Saratoga convinced Vergennes that the young Republic could win the war. After this victory the English began putting out peace feelers to see if the Americans would come to terms. The French learned of this activity and asked Franklin what would keep the Americans from coming to terms with the English. Franklin responded that French recognition of the American cause and treaties of commerce and alliance would satisfy Congress. In the meantime, Vergennes had been able to persuade Louis XVI that it would be in the best interest of France to aid the Americans openly, so on February 6, 1778, Franklin and Vergennes signed the Treaty of Amity and Commerce and the Treaty of Alliance.

The Treaty of Amity and Commerce had three principal provisions. The first was that both France and America received most favored nation status in each others' ports with regard to trade (Article Two). The French agreed that free ships make free goods. That is, if at some future date France was at war with a nation her enemy could ship goods on American ships and these items could not be seized, except contraband (Article Twenty-Five). The third provision was that the French accepted the narrow American definition of contraband (Article Twenty-Six), which included only weapons, ammunition, and other military equipment. The immediate result of this treaty was that France and England were at war shortly after the treaty was proclaimed. In fact, the United States could not have won the war without French naval and military assistance.

Anthony P. Inguanzo

REFERENCES

Samuel Flagg Bemis, *The Diplomacy of the American Revolution* (1957); Gilbert Chinard, ed., *The Treaties of 1778 and Allied Documents* (1928); Lawrence C. Kaplan, *Colonies into Nation: American Diplomacy, 1763–1801* (1972); Thomas G. Paterson, J. Garry Clifford, and Kenneth J. Hagan, *American Foreign Policy: A History, to 1914* (1983).

Treaty of Long Island of the Holston (July 20, 1777)

Long Island of the Holston River, near modern Kingsport, Tennessee, was an ancient Cherokee treaty ground and the site of a peace treaty in July 1777, ending the Cherokee War of 1776. The Lower, Middle, and Valley Town Cherokees journeyed to DeWitt's Corner (now Due West, South Carolina) to negotiate peace, while the Overhill Cherokees traveled to Long Island of the Holston. The most important Cherokee, Oconostota, the Great Warrior, was to be the Cherokee spokesman, but because of his age he deferred to his nephew, the Raven of Chota, and Old Tassel of Toquo.

Three Virginia colonels, William Preston, William Christian, and Evan Shelby, represented the Virginians, and Waighstill Avery, William Sharpe, Robert Lanier, and Joseph Winston represented the North Carolinians. The Chickamauga Cherokees, who refused to accept the peace and the land cessions, had withdrawn from the Cherokee Nation. As punishment for starting the war, the American commissioners demanded that the Cherokee cede all land north of the Little Tennessee River. Old Tassel eloquently objected, pointing out that the 1776 conflict began over the white man's constant cry for more land. He stated that "Although the Great Spirit has given you many advantages, he has not created us to be your slaves." During the negotiations, Big Bullet, the mixed-blood son of interpreter John McCormack, was killed. Fearing a possible trap and massacre, the Cherokees withdrew, and it was several days before negotiations were renewed. The white commissioners slightly moderated their demands, and peace was signed on July 20. According to the treaty, the Overhill Cherokees ceded all of their land north of the Nolichucky River (3,951,960 acres). Together with the Treaty at DeWitt's Corner (involving 1,312,640 acres) in which the other Cherokees gave away most of their remaining land in South Carolina, the cessions amounted to over 5,000,000 acres consisting of 8,000 square miles. The policy of the spoils belonging to the victor, which was followed at these two treaties, continued in later federal Indian policy.

The treaty also contained other stipulations. The Cherokees demanded that Long Island itself not be part of the negotiations but be given to Nathaniel Gist, Sequoyah's father. The Cherokees agreed to return any prisoners and proopery that they had taken. Also, North Carolina and Virginia assumed responsibility to appoint agents to reside in the Overhill towns. Virginia subsequently sent Joseph Martin, who lived for some years with Betsy and Nancy Ward. Gist's claim to the island was ultimately not recognized and the Cherokee sold it to the United States in 1806. In 1976 Kingsport, Tennessee, in cooperation with the Mead Corporation, returned a portion of the island to the Eastern Band of Cherokees.

William L. Anderson

REFERENCES

John P. Brown, *Old Frontiers: The Story of the Cherokee Indian from Earliest Times to the Date of Their Removal to the West, 1838* (1938); Archibald Henderson, "The Treaty of the Long Island of the Holston, July, 1777," *North Carolina Historical Review, 8* (1931):55–116; Duane H. King, "Long Island of the Holston's Sacred Cherokee Ground," *Journal of Cherokee Studies, 1* (1967):113–127; James H. O'Donnell, *Southern Indians in the American Revolution* (1973); Charles C. Royce, *The Cherokee Nation of Indians* (1975); Muriel Spoden, *The Long Island of the Holston: Sacred Island to the Cherokee Nation* (1977).

Treaty of Paris (September 3, 1783)

See Diplomacy of the American Revolution.

Trenton, New Jersey, Battle of (December 26, 1776)

Named after Justice William Trent, who had built his home there in 1719, Trent's Town (or Trenton) was a small place in 1776, situated on land that sloped gradually toward the Delaware River and the Assunpink Creek. Surrounded by open fields cleared of woods, there were several taverns and churches, a meetinghouse, a jail, and a hundred houses grouped along two main streets. Until December 1776, its eighteenth-century significance had been geographic. Trenton was the last navigable river port along the Delaware River. By the first day of 1777, Trenton would mean something entirely different.

The year 1776 had turned bitter for Washington and his American army. After initial successes at Boston, Charleston, and Moore's Creek Bridge, among others, the American cause was staggered by General William Howe's relatively effortless string of victories that captured New York City with its vital harbor and transformed an American army of over 20,000 men in July into a straggling, ragged, and tattered band of less than 8,000 men, most of whom were fleeing into Pennsylvania by December. It was an unexpected turn of fortune that lowered American morale, caused Congress to flee Philadelphia for Baltimore, and sent thousands of citizens back under the protective umbrella of the British army, including most of those living in New Jersey. It was the first critical period in the War of Revolution for the Americans.

Once New York City and its surrounding territory were firmly under British control, Washington divided his army in order to protect remaining vital American positions. He left troops in the Hudson Highlands to guard the Hudson River. Units were stationed at Morristown and in Bergen County, New Jersey, to protect northern Jersey. Washington and the few soldiers left under his command fled across the Jersies, pursued by Howe's British army. Washington's purpose was to take sanctuary in Pennsylvania and shield the new nation's capital, Philadelphia, from British occupation. Washington's men reached Trenton on December 3 and finished crossing the Delaware River on December 7, taking with them every boat they could locate for 70 miles along the Jersey River bank. Cornwallis, leading the British van, reached Trenton two days later.

Howe's leisurely chase of the rebels had driven many Loyalists and several British officers to distraction. Joseph Galloway, the former speaker of the Pennsylvania Assembly, who had come north to join Howe in the vain assumption that Howe would soon enter Philadelphia, charged that Howe had calculated perfectly the exact time it would take for Washington's men to escape and moved his army accordingly. After reaching the Delaware River, Howe discovered the lack of boats. Taking into account the lateness of the season, he decided it was time to go into winter

quarters, and on December 13 he declared the campaign for that season at an end.

Several of the British and German officers requested permission to cross the Delaware and to do two things. One was to destroy what remained of Washington's army and the second was to capture Philadelphia. The lack of boats was no problem. There was enough wood available to build rafts and boats quickly for a crossing. Barns and houses, fences and wagons could be made at any number of places above the head of navigation at Trenton, protecting the troops from American ships of the Pennsylvania Navy.

Howe was not interested. Cornwallis was instructed to establish a line of posts across New Jersey to keep Washington in Pennsylvania and to protect the citizens of New Jersey from rebel harassment for the winter. A series of strong points that stretched from Bordentown through Trenton and northward to Princeton and New Brunswick was garrisoned by German and British troops and placed under the overall command of General James Grant. In the end, the line would run 100 miles from the Delaware to the Hudson River and involve 14,000 British and German troops. Cornwallis was given leave to return to England to visit his sick wife. Howe returned to New York City and to his mistress, but not before having breakfast with Colonel Johann Rall in Trenton.

Colonel Karl von Donop was the German field officer in command of the southern tip of the British line. Von Donop did not want Rall to exercise independent command and suggested to Howe that Rall bring his troops to join von Donop's force and leave Trenton unoccupied. Howe initially agreed but changed his mind after having a talk with Rall on December 14. Rall and his brigade were permitted to stay at Trenton. That same day, Howe and Cornwallis left for New York City, where the main British army would go into winter quarters.

Washington faced three major problems. The winter was severe enough that the Delaware River might freeze over, allowing the British to march across the ice to capture Philadelphia. Secondly, on December 31, 1776, the enlistments of most of his army would expire. The men would then be free to return to their homes. Many did leave, such were the rigors of the past campaign. Washington would be without an army in less than three weeks. Finally, the recent American reverses were so great and the losses in personnel and equipment so staggering that Washington had to make some sort of statement and take some action soon in order to keep the fires of the Revolution burning.

Washington's answer was the brilliant winter offensive that resulted in his victory at Trenton, followed by that of Princeton, within the space of ten days. By the creative use of luck and calculation, Washington reversed American fortunes and gained worldwide respect for the Patriot cause and for his military leadership.

Although it may not have seemed so at the time, the first lucky break for the Americans came with the British capture of General Charles Lee at Basking Ridge, New Jersey, on Friday, December 13. Lee was a former British officer who was now second in command in the American army and believed himself to be Washington's superior in military ability. He was fast becoming an uncooperative thorn in Washington's side. His removal at this critical point freed Washington to be himself and use his natural military instincts to develop his plan of attack without Lee's nagging and second-guessing.

Washington needed men. He called upon General Horatio Gates to bring men from the North. General John Sullivan arrived with what was left of Lee's force. The Pennsylvania militia was called into service under the command of Thomas Mifflin and John Cadwalader. By December 25, Washington had concentrated 6,000 men in Pennsylvania at several points facing the enemy across the Delaware.

The author of *Common Sense*, Thomas Paine, arrived in camp to visit the army. Washington approached Paine and requested that he write something that would give heart to the men and restore faith in their cause. Paine began:

> These are the times that try men's souls. The summer soldier and sunshine patriot will, in this crisis, shrink from the service of his country; but he that stands it now, deserves the love and thanks of men and women. Tyranny, like hell, is not easily conquered; yet we have this consolation with us, that the harder the conflict, the more glorious the easy triumph.

Paine and Thomas Jefferson met in Philadelphia and found a printer who would print quickly. Published December 19, Paine personally brought copies back to Washington, and this first in a series of essays collectively called *The Crisis* was read to the troops in camp on December 22. It had a pronounced effect on the men and officers.

Washington was tempted to attack Trenton. It was garrisoned by Colonel Johann Rall's brigade of Hessian troops. Washington's intelligence network spread throughout the Jersies. He soon learned that Trenton was an isolated post, lacking in defensive features. Rall was known as the "Hessian Lion" by the British for his brave assault on Fort Washington and his effective work at White Plains.

In 1776, Rall was 56 years old, a veteran of the European side of the French and Indian War, who had also seen service for the Russians against the Turks. Rall did not speak English. He was courageous in battle and, for the period, relatively considerate and kind to his men. On the other hand, he was also passionate and obstinate, set in his opinions. One such view that Rall believed was that the Americans were "Country Clowns." He liked to drink, play cards, and attend social festivities. Rall was not a military genius by any standard. Yet he was faced with real problems that demanded creative solutions.

Under Rall's command were three Hessian regiments. Rall's total strength at Trenton was just under 1,600 men. Rall also had 50 jaegers and 20 troopers from the British 16th Light Dragoons. The Regiment Von Rall was unique in that all of its companies were grenadier companies, elite troops of the period. The Regiments Von Lossberg and Von Knyphausen were fusilier or regular line regiments. All three units had performed well in the New York campaign, but all three shared one critical weakness, which had something to do with Rall being in command of the brigade in the first place.

General Werner von Mirbich was the brigade's commanding officer, but he was ill and in New York City. Most of the experienced field officers of all three regiments were either wounded, sick, or dead. Rall was third junior colonel in the German army in America, but everyone outranking him in the brigade was absent by December 1776. Rall's second in command at Trenton was only a major, Friedrich von DeChow of Knyphausen's regiment, who had been wounded twice at Fort Washington but had to remain in the field because the colonel of the regiment had suffered worse wounds. Rall's brigade at Trenton suffered from a badly weakened field officer corps. German training and battle tactics presupposed strong leadership. This quality was definitely lacking at Trenton. Qualities the Germans did not excel in were military innovation and flexibility to change. Knowing this from the experiences of the recent New York campaign, Washington wished to catch the Germans in Trenton before they could form properly and fight in their normal order. It was imperative to hit them at dawn, before they were fully awake.

Colonel Karl Emil von Donop was 15 miles away from Trenton at Burlington with 1,800 men, including 3 grenadier battalions, the British 42nd Regiment, and additional jaegers. Von Donop was well aware of Rall's weaknesses, both in command and position. He sent his own engineering officer to Trenton to advise Rall where to fortify his position. On page 361 of the regulations for Hessian infantry, it clearly stated that when a regiment is close to the enemy and in position in a village, the commander must erect a redoubt in an advantageous spot large enough to provide protection for the regiment in the event of attack. Trenton was too open. Captain Georg Heinrich Pauli, von Donop's engineer, selected the height of land at the area known as Five Forks, or "The Gateway," where the two main Trenton streets, King and Queen streets, join with three roads leading out of town. Rall ignored the suggestion and cried, "Let them come! We want no trenches. We will go at them with the bayonet!" Pauli also suggested placing a second redoubt at the creek below town. This request was also ignored. The brigade at Trenton remained unfortified.

Rall sent out no systematic ranging patrols. He did post guards about the town but took little interest in them. His primary concern was for military parades, drill, and music. Each day he personally reviewed the troops on duty and frequently had them parade around in circles with the bands playing for his own enjoyment. There were endless drills. But the garrison was in a state of some readiness. One company was under arms at all times. One regiment was on duty each day and stayed in "Alarm Houses," where they had to remain dressed and prepared in case of attack. The posts were manned continually.

Once Washington began to turn his attention to Trenton, the sniping and harassment of Hessian troops by the Americans stepped up accordingly. The pressure was increased on the German garrison until finally the entire brigade had approximately 100 men fit for duty. The rest were worn out and sick from the fatigue of the rebel hit-and-run tactics. The cavalry had been so harried that it refused to ride out of town without infantry protection. The Americans continued their raids for two weeks until Christmas night. The chaos and uncertainty affected German morale. They were not used to such fighting. The winter cantonment season should be one of repose and recovery. The peasant rebels were not following the proper script.

On December 24, John Honeyman, a supplier of meat for the British army, visited Colonel Rall in Trenton. Honeyman, a former British soldier who had once served in General James Wolfe's bodyguard, had been captured by Washington's men in the Jersies and had had a private conference with the American commander before suspiciously escaping from American captivity and returning to Jersey. Honeyman immediately went to Rall to tell him about the sad condition of the American army. The men had no clothes. There was no food. The army was falling apart with many leaving and returning home. Rall listened and agreed. After the war, Honeyman received the personal thanks of Washington, who stopped by his Somerset County home on his way to New York.

The British also had their own spies and their system seems to have worked as well as the Americans'. Colonel James Grant warned Rall that Trenton would be attacked. The British knew the time, the place, and the hour. However, Rall had it on good authority, Honeyman's, that the Americans were incapable of crossing the icy river and attacking Trenton.

Grant himself is an interesting study. Both he and Washington served in the French and Indian War together. If possible, Grant held the Americans in even more contempt than Rall. Short and fat with an oval face marked with black, bushy eyebrows and several chins, Grant was forever surrounded by ducks and geese that eventually graced his table. Once fed, Grant was militarily inert. He refused to send Rall or von Donop aid or move a British force closer to Trenton to lessen its isolation. In any case, Rall evidently felt Grant was referring to the constant American raids and not to a full attack by Washington's main army. Disregarding Grant's warning, Rall issued no special orders for December 25 or 26.

The Germans were one group of Europeans who did celebrate the Christmas season, especially the first two days of the twelve-day season. Tannenbaums were set up in the troops' quarters, and the men were issued rum to celebrate the holiday. There is no indication that the entire brigade was drunk and indisposed beyond their normal condition when the American attack came. Rall himself may have been drunk, but not his men and especially not the regiment of the day. Such a charge of intoxication slanders the German regiments and cheapens the American success. However, Washington did select a good time to strike, as the Germans were celebrating the Christmas season. But there was little choice for Washington because the American army would go home in five days in any event.

Rall spent Christmas night at Abraham Hunt's, where cards were played and spirits freely imbibed all night and into the next morning. There had been an alarm earlier in the evening, and Rall had personally attended to it. When it appeared that it was just another hit-and-run affair, Rall had gone to Hunt's. It was while playing cards at Hunt's that a Loyalist appeared at the door and was refused admission by a servant. Unable to talk with Rall, the Loyalist left a message that was given to Rall, who placed it in his pocket unread. It warned of the coming American attack, but it was written in English. Rall probably would have had it translated in the morning.

Rall left Hunt's just before dawn and went to bed at 6 A.M. on December 26. It is interesting to note that Abraham Hunt was a wealthy Trenton merchant who managed to maintain his position throughout the war, bothered by neither side. Some historians believe Hunt may have been in Washington's employment as a part of his spy network. Since no records exist and Washington never revealed much about his sources during or after the war, this is only speculation. But by luck or design, Rall was shielded from the Loyalist and kept in a distracted state the entire night, as Washington's army closed in on Trenton.

For several days leading up to December 25, the American army had been paraded with 3 days' rations and 40 rounds of ammunition at 2 P.M. and then dismissed to return to their quarters. On December 25, they were not dismissed. Instead they marched down to McKonkey's Ferry and formed just out of sight along the river bank. Washington had developed his plan of attack on

Trenton. He would advance in three columns. General George Ewing would cross at Trenton Ferry with 1,000 militia and move to the Assunpink Creek, where he would cut off the German escape route south to von Donop. Colonel Cadwalader would take 2,000 Pennsylvania militia across the Delaware River at Bristol, 9 miles south of Trenton, to freeze von Donop in place and keep him from helping Rall. Washington would lead his main force of 2,400 men and 18 cannon in a frontal assault from the north on the garrison at Trenton. The password for the operation was "Victory or Death!" No more appropriate slogan could have been selected.

Christmas night, December 25, 1776, was a miserable night, cold with freezing sleet and falling snow. The flow of ice in the river had increased and made any crossing difficult if not impossible. Washington made Colonel Henry Knox responsible for the crossing. His stentorian voice could be heard booming everywhere on both banks as Knox organized the troops and sent them to the boats as planned. Washington was fortunate in having Colonel John Glover's Marblehead Fishermen present to ferry the army across the Delaware using unfamiliar boats, the Durham iron ore boats.

These boats ranged in length from 40 to 60 feet with an 8-foot beam. They could carry 20 tons of cargo with a draft of 5 to 30 inches. Four men with 16-foot oars poled the boats across the river by sticking their oars into the river bottom and walking the boat through the water by pushing on the poles as they used the two side walkways to move from front to back in the boat. The boat's captain used a 33-foot steering oar to guide the boat. The boats were named after Robert Durham of the Durham Iron Furnace, where the boats were originally developed to carry iron ore down the Delaware through shallow waters. In addition, the normal ferry was used to move the artillery and horses across the Delaware, since these items would not easily fit into the Durham boats. The ferry was of the typical "Pull on the Rope" variety.

General Ewing never crossed. Without the skilled boatmen that Washington had, the river ice stopped his men. Cadwalader got his men across but not his artillery, so his men recrossed to the Pennsylvania side and played no further role in the battle. That left Washington alone with his 2,400 men in attacking the Germans. There would be no turning back. Fortunately, another group of Jersey militia was able to distract von Donop and draw him into the Mount Holly area away from Rall.

Washington had planned to be completely across by midnight so that he could hit Trenton at dawn. At 3 A.M., the last of his men reached the Jersey side of the river. After an hour's rest, mainly for the boatmen of Glover's brigade, the army began moving south for Trenton, eight miles off and four hours late.

The first units across belonged to General Adam Stephen's brigade. His men guarded the landing area. From this brigade, 2 companies of 40 men each under Captain William Washington (the general's second cousin) and John Flahaven went ahead to a crossroads, where the American army would split into two columns, with orders to stop anyone coming in or out of Trenton. As these forward guards took their position, they found themselves near the home of Dr. John Riker, who at first tried to chase them away but then, realizing they were Americans and not the hated Germans, welcomed them and brought them food. He also volunteered to accompany them in the attack, which turned out to be fortunate for William Washington's 18-year-old lieutenant, James Monroe.

Four miles from town at Birmingham, the Americans stopped to recover and prepare for their final approach. All officers' watches were set on Washington's timepiece. Then the army split. Generals Washington and Nathanael Greene with Mercer's, Sterling's, Stephen's and Fermoy's brigades took the Scotch Road to the Pennington Road and moved down on the Germans from the north. General Sullivan took the River Road with Glover's, Sargent's, and St. Clair's men and nine guns to hit the Hessians from the west. Moving toward Trenton, Washington's van was startled to meet with a group of soldiers approaching in the other direction. At first thought to be Germans, it was soon discovered that Captain Richard Anderson (the father of the Union officer in command of Fort Sumpter in 1861) and his company of the 5th Virginia had been sent without Washington's knowledge to attack the outposts at Trenton by General Adam Stephen in some affair of revenge. This was the party that hit Trenton on Christmas evening causing Rall to think it was the attack General Grant had warned him about. Another piece of American luck, although Washington did not realize it at the time. Angered,

the general roundly criticized Stephen for his stupidity in putting the Hessians on the alert.

Already it was growing light. Sunrise was at 7:20 a.m. but the weather was cooperating. Another storm came up, with snow, mist, and low clouds providing cover for the American columns. The storm not only covered the American advance but was severe enough that Major Friedrich von DeChow canceled the normal patrol for that morning, assuring everyone that no one would be foolish enough to be out in such weather.

The Hessian outer picket at Trenton had but a few minutes warning before the Americans from Green's column were on top of them along the Pennington Road. The Germans from the Lossberg regiment fell back toward town spreading the alarm and firing into the mist. The Americans would not be stopped. According to Alexander Hamilton, the Patriots were ready "to storm hell's battlements in the night" if necessary. Three minutes later, Washington heard the report of Sullivan's column striking the jaegers near the Hermitage estate, the home of General Philemon Dickinson, commander of the Jersey militia. Leading the way was John Stark and his New Hampshire men. The jaegers were soon joined by the dragoons, and both groups quickly disappeared across the Assunpink Creek bridge toward the safety of von Donop's command before Sullivan could close off the bridge.

Colonel Charles Scott of the Virginia troops called out to his men to aim low and "Leg 'em." That way it would take three men out of the battle—one wounded and two men to carry him off. The rush was on. Mercer's men charged in from the west to block off that side of town. The rest of Greene's division formed to the north and east of town, firing down on the Germans trying to form in the streets below them.

As the alarm rang in town, the Lossberg regiment formed in a graveyard, many seeing this as a bad omen. The von Rail regiment, the Battalion of the Day, formed in the street in front of Rall's headquarters at the Stacy Potts house on King Street (Warren Street today) and attempted to attack north, with Colonel Rall in the lead. With only two hours' sleep and recovering from his drinking bout, Rall rallied his men and called out for all of his grenadiers to move forward. They were hit by American artillery set up exactly in the same spot that Rall had been instructed to construct his redoubt, at the junction of King and Queen streets, where the battle monument sits today. Rall's men made 40 yards and broke, fleeing into the side streets away from the artillery's reach, only to run into Mercer's men firing into town from its western side.

Only four of the German guns replied to the American artillery, but they were quickly silenced by Captain Alexander Hamilton's New York artillery battery of two guns firing down King Street. Captain Thomas Forrest with six guns cleared the Germans off Queen Street (today named Broad Street). Captain William Washington and Lieutenant James Monroe led the charge to capture the Hessian three-pound guns and succeeded, though Monroe was shot in the shoulder and Washington was wounded in the both hands. A Dr. Riker, still following the Virginians, was present to tie off the artery cut in Monroe's shoulder so that he did not bleed to death at Trenton and live to be our fifth President.

Sullivan led his column into town from the river, past the barracks (still standing) where the jaegers had been quartered, and on to the Assunpink Creek, where the Americans cut the bridge, sealing off that escape route. The von Knyphausen regiment was pushed out of town by the force of Sullivan's assault and went to form with the other two regiments in fields to the east of town. In the confusion of battle, orders to close up and attack the town were mixed up and the von Knyphausen regiment about-faced and marched off alone toward the creek. They soon found themselves surrounded on all sides. General St. Clair called upon them to give up or be blown to pieces. Sargent's, Glover's, and St. Clair's men had them cornered against the Mill Pond. Their officers placed their hats on the tips of their swords and the men clubbed or inverted their muskets. The von Knyphausens surrendered.

The fighting in the town had been fierce. The Americans quickly got inside the houses and fired at the Germans from windows in the basements and upper floors. Forced outside, the Germans soon found that their muskets were soaked by the snow and rendered inoperable. The Americans inside were able to keep their muskets dry. However, there were reports of Americans using only the bayonet in attacking the enemy. The weather made swords, bayonets, and the cannon the only practical weapons of the day.

It is difficult to gain a clear picture of the battle. Everything happened quickly in a white haze. Visibility was short. Troops moved in confusion. The Germans, without proper leadership and unable to form in their regular closed order retreated out of town. In an open field to the east, the Hessians tried to reorganize and retake the town. Greene had kept Stephen's and Fermoy's brigades out of battle until this moment, when he unleashed them to swing in from the north and cut off any hope of a German escape.

The trap was closed. Knox brought up more guns to break up any German attempt to form. Rall then led his men to an orchard nearby, where he was soon wounded twice in the side. The Hessians struck their colors and surrendered. Major DeChow was also wounded in the fighting at this point as he led his Lossberg battalion beside Rall's men.

By 9:30 A.M., the battle was over. Several hundred Germans and British had escaped by routes that were left uncovered when the other columns did not cross the Delaware. The Americans took 918 prisoners. The Hessians suffered 106 killed and wounded. Rall was carried to a church and placed on a pew. Then he was carried back to the Pott's house, his headquarters, where Washington met with him. Rall requested mercy and care for his men. The next day, he would die from his wounds. Major DeChow would also die at the same time. The Americans captured all three regimental colors, six cannon, and the baggage of the brigade, including enough instruments for several bands. Over 1,000 muskets, sorely needed, were taken along with 40 hogsheads of rum, which Washington ordered destroyed, but not before many of the Americans had sampled it.

The Americans had lost two soldiers frozen along the line of march. Two officers in addition to William Washington and James Monroe were wounded. Only one or two private soldiers were wounded. None was killed in battle. Washington could not afford to stay at Trenton to celebrate his victory. In a few hours, by noon, his men were marching back to McKonkey's Ferry along with their 900 prisoners. Washington took the Germans into Bucks County and then had them marched through Philadelphia guarded by Virginia troops, whose enlistments were over and who were going home. In the

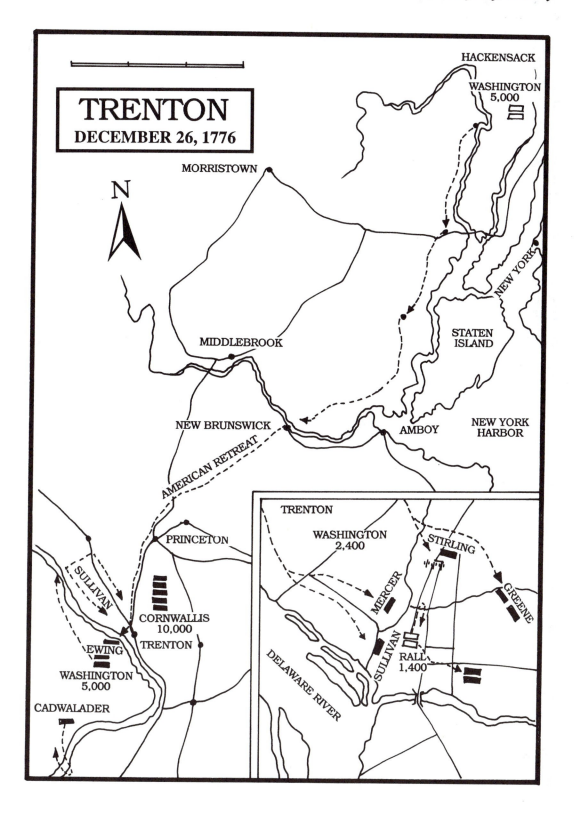

TRENTON
DECEMBER 26, 1776

N

HACKENSACK

WASHINGTON
5,000

MORRISTOWN

NEW YORK

STATEN
ISLAND

MIDDLEBROOK

NEW BRUNSWICK

AMBOY

NEW YORK
HARBOR

AMERICAN RETREAT

PRINCETON

TRENTON

WASHINGTON
2,400

STIRLING

SULLIVAN

MERCER

GREENE

CORNWALLIS
10,000

TRENTON

SULLIVAN

RALL
1,400

EWING

DELAWARE RIVER

WASHINGTON
5,000

CADWALADER

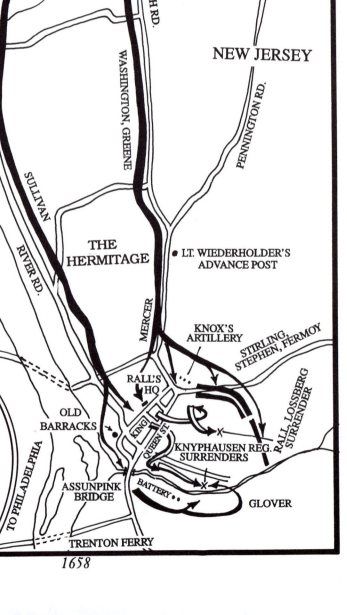

THE ATTACK ON
TRENTON
DECEMBER 26, 1776

BEAR TAVERN ROAD

BIRMINGHAM

HOWELL'S
FERRY

YARDLEY'S
FERRY

SCOTCH RD.

DELAWARE

NEW JERSEY

WASHINGTON, GREENE

PENNINGTON RD.

SULLIVAN

RIVER

RIVER RD.

PENNSYLVANIA

THE
HERMITAGE

• LT. WIEDERHOLDER'S
ADVANCE POST

MERCER

KNOX'S
ARTILLERY

STIRLING,
STEPHEN, FERMOY

RALL'S
HQ

RALL-LOSSBERG
SURRENDER

OLD
BARRACKS

KING

QUEEN ST.

KNYPHAUSEN REG.
SURRENDERS

⊳ BRITISH
▶ AMERICAN

ASSUNPINK
BRIDGE

BATTERY

GLOVER

TO PHILADELPHIA

0   ONE MILE   1

TRENTON FERRY

1658

end, the Germans wound up in Lancaster County, where many of them were lent out for work to the German farmers who inhabited that area of Pennsylvania. In time, they were exchanged and many returned to active service in the German army. Several, however, did decide to make their permanent homes in America.

Washington was deeply moved by his victory. He called it "A glorious day for our country." So it was. Washington had wanted to go on and attack Princeton, but his men were obviously worn and needed rest. Glover's men, for example, had rowed the army across the river with ice sticking to the boats for at least six hours. Then they had marched eight miles to Trenton and fought in a battle. Then they marched back to the ferry and rowed the American army and their 900 German prisoners back across the river! No rest or hot food in over 36 hours in the midst of two storms. Washington had no choice but to give his men relief.

This victory shattered the widely held and deeply felt American fear of Hessians. As they were paraded through Philadelphia, the citizens saw that these hirelings were men, well dressed and disciplined, but men just the same. The Americans both in and out of the army gained confidence and the news of the victory produced an electric effect throughout the country. American morale, at its lowest point yet, rose rapidly as the true brilliance of the victory became apparent. Here was a front line brigade of the hated mercenaries who had surrendered to a tattered and ragged band of rebels. Here was a turning point in American fortunes. Washington now turned to consider what else could be done to add to the value of Trenton. Princeton was his answer.

Paul J. Sanborn

REFERENCES

William M. Dwyer, *The Day Is Ours* (1983); Thomas Fleming, *1776, The Year of Illusions* (1975); James Thomas Flexner, *George Washington in the American Revolution* (1967); Richard M. Ketchum, *The Winter Soldiers* (1973); Samuel Steele Smith, *The Battle of Trenton* (1965); Christopher Ward, *The War of Revolution*, 2 vols. (1952), *1*; Kimble Widner, *The Christmas Campaign* (1975).

Trois Rivières, Quebec, Battle of (June 8, 1776)

The final attempt by American Revolutionary forces to seize the initiative during the failed invasion of Canada (1775–1776) was the effort to capture the fortified town of Trois Rivières (Three Rivers). Located on the north bank of the St. Lawrence River midway between Montreal and Quebec, the town was of obvious strategic importance. Its possession would limit British land and water communications between those cities as well as provide the Americans with a base from which to strike toward Quebec. It would also enable the Americans to consolidate Patriot influence among English Canadian sympathizers and French Canadians, whose loyalty to the King of England was questionable. The failure to capture Trois Rivières and a loss of a substantial portion of the forces sent to accomplish this task virtually ended the American attempts to conquer Canada during the Revolution.

The ill-fated Canadian invasion had begun with much promise. The British governor of Canada since 1766, General Sir Guy Carleton, had fewer than 1,000 regulars to hold the entire province. In August 1775 the Americans captured the valuable fort at St. Johns, on the Richelieu River just north of Lake Champlain. General Richard Montgomery pressed on to Montreal, which surrendered November 13. Montgomery then moved down the St. Lawrence. He captured Trois Rivières easily and left Colonel William Maxwell and the 2nd Jersey Regiment to guard the town. Montgomery continued to Quebec, already under siege by General Benedict Arnold's forces, which had come up from the South. The New Year's Eve assault on Quebec, however, was more valiant than realistic. In the darkness and confusion the attack stalled, and when Montgomery was killed, any hope of taking Quebec ended. Arnold, badly wounded in the assault, assumed command and remained with his men outside the city walls, although the defenders far outnumbered the besiegers. It was obvious that without strong reinforcements Quebec could not be taken nor the rest of Canada held. On May 1, 1776, American Major General John Thomas arrived before the city to take Montgomery's command. Additional American forces were on the way, but they were too late. The spring thaw freed British shipping on the St. Lawrence, and on May 2 word was received that a fleet was proceeding upriver (the ships were carrying the first of British general John Burgoyne's 13,000 regulars for the invasion of the American colonies). Thomas ordered a retreat, which soon disintegrated into headlong flight. Wearied by the harassment of the British, acute hunger, and the ravages of smallpox, the remnants of the American army retreated all the way to St. Johns. Trois Rivières was abandoned. Thomas, like many of his men, died of smallpox before St. Johns could be reached.

Despite the disastrous turn of events, the Americans were encouraged by the arrival of strong reinforcements. Brigadier General William Thompson, a tough Pennsylvanian whose Irish heritage insured distaste for all things British, was waiting at St. Johns with over 2,000 men. Another brigadier general, John Sullivan, who had been given overall command of the American Forces threatening Canada, arrived there with 3,300 men on June 1. Under firm instructions from Congress to take Quebec, Sullivan ordered Thompson to recapture Trois Rivières and gave him 2,000 of the best men to do it. Thompson, for his part, was confident that the Americans could retake the ground they recently had lost, but he was worried about the lack of military intelligence out of Canada. In order to prepare for every eventuality, he sent off his sick and heavy baggage. Now, if forced to retreat, he hoped he could so with little loss.

Based upon previous intelligence that British colonel Allen McLean held Trois Rivières with only about 800 regulars and Canadians, Thompson had anticipated an attack upon the town. In preparation he had ordered a detachment under command of Colonel Arthur St. Clair to Nicolet, a small settlement on the south bank of the St. Lawrence about ten miles upstream, or west, of Trois Rivières. Thompson organized his command into four divisions composed of Colonel William Maxwell and his 2nd New Jersey Regiment, Colonel Arthur St. Clair and the 2nd Pennsylvania Regiment, Colonel Anthony (later "Mad Anthony") Wayne and the 4th Pennsylvania Regiment rounded out by Colonel William Irvine and the 6th Pennsylvania Regiment. Lieutenant Colonel Thomas Hartley of the 6th Pennsylvania led the reserve. All four colonels were capable fighting men, as was Thompson. In addition, all except Maxwell were Pennsylvanians,

a factor that no doubt increased the unity of command.

With the bulk of his army in place at Sorel, on the south bank of Lac St. Pierre (where the St. Lawrence widens appreciably), Sullivan ordered Thompson on to Nicolet to join with St. Clair. On the evening of June 6, Thompson loaded his men into boats and, following the southern shore of the lake, dropped downstream. They arrived at Nicolet after midnight, and Thompson assumed overall command. The next day was devoted to resting the men and to making final preparations for the night crossing of the St. Lawrence.

Although surprise was considered an important asset on the American's side, Thompson reported to Sullivan on June 7 that his force might have been spotted by British ships the previous day. At this time, Thompson believed Trois Rivières to be occupied by between 500 and 1,500 of the enemy. He assured Sullivan that if he found the enemy in superior numbers or strongly entrenched he would decline battle and preserve his small force. What Thompson did not know was that Trois Rivières had been steadily reinforced with British regiments preparing for the invasion of the colonies, and that it contained several thousand regulars well supplied and eager for battle.

Blissfully unaware that he had no possibility of success, Thompson pushed ahead with his plans. The British had stationed several warships in the channel of the St. Lawrence five miles above Trois Rivières, so the crossing on June 7 took place at night. Beginning late that evening the Americans once more took to their boats, this time crossing the lower end of the Lac St. Pierre and landing at Pointe-du-Lac, some nine to ten miles above Trois Rivières. Leaving 250 men to guard his boats, Thompson and his striking force set out rapidly, under cover of darkness, for what they supposed was a lightly defended town. They planned to be in position to attack before daylight.

The misfortune that had plagued the expedition from the beginning continued unabated. Being unfamiliar with the country, Thompson was forced to rely upon a Canadian guide named Antoine Gautier. Whether by accident or design, Gautier led the Americans in circles. Thompson was outraged at this conduct, but helpless to repair the damage. Seeking to make up for lost time the Americans unwittingly attempted to cross a swamp, but were reduced to an exhausting struggle in mire up to their waists for several hours. Writing later, Wayne described it as "the most Horrid swamp that man ever set foot in." The small invasion force had also been spotted by a Pointe-du-Lac militiaman who hurried to Trois Rivières and gave the alarm at 4 A.M. British general Simon Fraser immediately ordered the disembarkation of additional troops from the warships in the river, supported by artillery, and arranged them for battle. When the Americans finally emerged along the river road leading to Trois Rivières it was daylight, and the British, already alerted to their presence, opened fire from three ships in the St. Lawrence. The Americans returned fire, but having no artillery, accomplished little. It was now fully daylight, Thompson and his men were several miles from their objective, and the enemy was most certainly alerted to their presence. A return to Sorel was probably the wisest choice, but everyone remembered that Thomas had retreated, with disastrous results, without even engaging the enemy. Irvine wrote in his diary: "Here we were at a loss what to do; had no intelligence of the strength of the garrison; to attack was hazardous, and to retreat without knowing the enemy's strength, we could not think of, therefore marched on." The Americans proceeded along the river for three-quarters of a mile under the British cannonade, when they were driven back from the shore by its ferocity and once again into the swamp. At this point the divisions separated. Thompson, with St. Clair and Irvine, pulled away from the river, while the forces under Wayne, Maxwell, and Hartley continued along it. Wayne arrived first at a clearing in front of the town, where he drove back the advance guard of the enemy. It was now around 8 A.M., and Wayne thought the Americans were winning until the small force received considerable fire from both flanks. This resulted in, as Wayne put it, "our Rear now becoming our front." It was, however, the first positive intelligence as to the numbers and disposition of the enemy. Thompson and the remaining Americans now burst from the woods before Trois Rivières and confronted what Wayne had already discovered. A newly reinforced line of entrenchments containing thousands of British regulars blocked the approach to the town. Nevertheless, the Americans attacked, Wayne's men leading. Under

murderous fire from the front the great superiority of the enemy became apparent. The Americans gave way and began to retreat in some confusion. Thompson, along with St. Clair and Irvine, sought to halt the retreat. Lieutenant Colonel Hartley brought up the reserves. The men rallied briefly and succeeded in stopping the advance of the British when word reached them that troops had been landed in the rear to cut the Americans off from the river and their boats. The road was now denied them, being occupied by large numbers of British troops (as well as being covered by men-of-war in the river), so the Americans were forced back into the swamps, where it was impossible to rally them or maintain any cohesion among units. Thompson and Irvine soon found themselves isolated and mired in the swamp with about 40 men. Under fire from Canadian irregulars and owing to the difficult conditions of the country, soon less than seven remained together. After 24 hours of exhausting struggle, surrounded on all sides by the enemy, Thompson, Irvine, and the rest of their party surrendered to the British.

Wayne fared better. St. Clair had been injured, so Wayne took command, and led the remnants of the latest American army to invade Canada as well as he could. He and his men retreated along the river toward the boats, but these had been removed upriver to prevent their capture. Nothing was left for the Americans but continuous retreat upriver until they could get safely across. The troops, exhausted by their struggle and defeat, were now pursued by a fresh and vigorous enemy as well as being devoured by "Musketoes of a Monstrous size and innumerable numbers." Many, however, did make it back to Sorel. Carleton, who still held hopes for reconciliation with the colonies and did not want to be burdened with numerous prisoners, called off the immediate pursuit and opened up the only remaining escape route, a bridge across the Riviere-du-Loup, by ordering the withdrawal of the British forces stationed there. Despite this, 236 of the American forces engaged were made prisoner, 50 killed, and about 400 lost overall. British casualties were about a dozen killed or wounded.

The disastrous outcome of Trois Rivières, followed by an eventual British pursuit toward the remaining American outposts, compelled the removal of all American forces from Canada. This completed the destruction of the second

American army that had set out to conquer that province and set the stage for the British invasion of the United States under General John Burgoyne.

John Gillig

REFERENCES

Allan C. Crist, *William Thompson . . . a Shooting Star* (1978); Charles Henry Jones, *History of the Campaign for the Conquest in Canada in 1778* (1882); Gustave Lanctot, *Canada and the American Revolution, 1774–1783* (1967); Justin H. Smith, *Our Struggle for the Fourteenth Colony: Canada and the American Revolution*, 2 vols. (1907).

Trumbull, John (1756–1843)

American painter. Born June 6, 1756, in Lebanon, Connecticut, John Trumbull was the first college-educated, professional artist in America. He was a fifth generation American. His mother, Faith Robinson Trumbull, was the great-great-granddaughter of John and Priscilla Alden. His father, Jonathan, was named governor of the colony of Connecticut in 1769 and was an active supporter of the American Revolution, establishing and supplying fighting units from Connecticut.

When John was a child, a fall down a flight of stairs caused permanent and serious damage to one eye. Even so, he was a good scholar, and it was assumed that he would attend Harvard to study law or religion.

Painting was his first love, and he began to study at an early age. He pleaded with his father to allow him to study with John Singleton Copley rather than attend college. Instead, he was sent to Harvard and graduated in 1773, the youngest in his class. He returned to Lebanon to teach and paint.

As war with England became imminent he served under General Joseph Spencer as an adjutant of the 1st Regiment of Connecticut and was subsequently stationed at Roxbury, Massachusetts, just south of Charlestown. Here he was able to "creep through the tall grass" after the battle of Bunker's Hill and to sketch the British position and fortifications.

He was at Dorchester Heights in March 1775 when, overnight, 1,200 men and 360 oxen and carts built an above-ground fortification, which eventually drove General William Howe and his British ships out of Boston harbor.

His talents as an artist were invaluable during the war, as he sketched fortifications and maps for Washington and other generals in Connecticut and New York. At Fort Ticonderoga he worked with Colonel Thaddeus Kosciuszko, the military engineer, planning and strengthening the fort.

John Trumbull's true value was not as an officer, soldier, or sketcher of fortifications, but as an accurate and vivid recorder on canvas of the events of the American Revolution. And although he painted all of his life, these paintings of the Revolution are considered to be his best work.

At Crown Point, in September 1776, General Horatio Gates appointed Trumbull as colonel. However, confirmation of this from Congress did not reach him until February 1777 while he was with General Benedict Arnold in Providence, Rhode Island. His anger over this delay resulted in his abrupt resignation.

He returned home to Lebanon to paint portraits and scenes from the Bible and mythology, and to engage in the family business. In 1790 while on family business in Paris, he obtained a letter from Benjamin Franklin to Benjamin West in London. Trumbull proceeded to London and to West's studio. Here he was accepted as a pupil, and he worked along with Gilbert Stuart, who was studying under West at the time.

This period ended abruptly when Trumbull was arrested for treason and sent to Bridewell Prison. It was thought that his arrest was in retaliation for the execution of Major John André by the Americans. Charles James Fox and Edmund Burke, two prominent Englishmen, interceded for him and a short time later he was released and returned to America, by way of Europe.

John Trumbull had seen enough of Europe to know that these professional artists were highly regarded, so when the war was over he returned to London, West's studio, and classes at the Royal Academy. He was encouraged by West to concentrate on his idea of painting scenes of battles of the American Revolution. His first subjects were the "Death of General Warren at the Battle of Bunker's Hill," begun in 1785, and the "Death of General Montgomery in the Attack on Quebec," begun in 1786. The "Death of General Mercer at the Battle of Princeton" and the "Capture of the Hessians at Trenton" were also painted in West's studio.

His paintings were accurate almost to every detail. He left the faces blank, then traveled around Europe and America painting from life the small portraits on the canvas whenever possible. Since most of the subjects were contemporaries of Trumbull's, most were painted from life. Jefferson, Washington, Adams, Lafayette, and Rochambeau were among those willing to sit for him. He traveled to the sites of the battles to study the terrain.

By the time he was 33 years old he had a good start on his most famous painting, "The Declaration of Independence." This work would take 8 years to complete and would include 48 portraits, 36 of which were painted from life. Trumbull was greatly encouraged by his good friend, Thomas Jefferson, who sketched the room arrangement at Independence Hall for him.

In 1793 while Congress was in session in New York he was able to paint many of the portraits needed for "The Declaration of Independence" and his "Surrender of Cornwallis at Yorktown." It was at this time that he also painted his famous full-length portrait of George Washington.

Between 1794 and 1800 he set aside his American series and became secretary to John Jay and again traveled to England and Europe. In those years he was closely involved with the Jay Treaty. He would never paint as well again.

While abroad he married an Englishwoman, Sarah Hope Harvey. They returned to America in 1804 and settled in New York. Here Trumbull exhibited his works and helped establish the American Academy of Fine Arts. He spent much time traveling through New York and Connecticut, painting landscapes and encouraging young painters such as Thomas Cole and Thomas Sully.

After the Capitol was burned by the British in 1814 Benjamin Latrobe was commissioned to restore the damaged areas. John Trumbull was then commissioned by Congress to reproduce, on a much larger scale, his Revolutionary War paintings. These were to decorate the Capitol Rotunda. Between 1817 and 1824 he worked on "Surrender of General Burgoyne at Saratoga," "Surrender of Cornwallis at Yorktown," "The Declaration of Independence," and "Resignation of Washington." President James Madison wished the paintings to be "as large as life," but Trumbull was used to painting "in the little." The paintings, 12 feet by 18 feet, were hung in 1826 and were criticized for not being of the same quality as the originals, which were only 2 feet by 3 feet in size.

His later years were beset with financial problems, and he had outlived his contemporaries of the Revolutionary era. He was an old, rather cantankerous man in the Jacksonian era. His financial state was eased when in 1831 Professor Benjamin Silliman of Yale University and Trumbull's nephew by marriage proposed the establishment of an art gallery at Yale to house Trumbull's paintings. In return he would receive an annuity of $1,000. He designed a neoclassical museum to house the collection and had his wife's body moved to beneath the building in 1832. He was buried beside her in 1843 when he died at age 87. His gravestone bears the inscription, "Patriot-Artist and Friend of Washington."

John Trumbull's works (numbering between 250 and 300), drawn from life of the principal figures and events of the American Revolution, make him the most accurate and prolific recorder of this most important era. *See also:* Stuart, Gilbert

Martha M. Reimers

REFERENCES

Irma B. Jaffe, *John Trumbull: Patriot-Artist of the American Revolution* (1975); Cuthbert Lee, *Early American Portrait Painters*; Theodore Sizer, *The Works of Colonel John Trumbull: Artist of the American Revolution* (1967); Theodore Sizer, ed., *Autobiography of Colonel John Trumbull: Portrait, Artist, 1756–1843* (1970); Christopher Weeks, "Revolutionary Village," *American Heritage, 40* (1989):80–91.

Trumbull, Jonathan (1710–1785)

War governor. Raised in Lebanon, Connecticut, Jonathan Trumbull was the son of Joseph Trumbull, a prominent cattleman and retailer. Sent to Harvard in 1723 to prepare for the Congregational ministry, Jonathan graduated in 1727, returning in 1730 for his M.A. in theology. The death of his brother Joseph brought Jonathan into the family business. He soon became head of the firm, specializing in livestock, packed meat, and the retail trade. In 1734 and 1736 he was elected to the Connecticut General Assembly. By 1735 Trumbull was a lieutenant in a horse troop and by 1735 a lieutenant colonel in the 12th Connecticut Regiment. He made a socially advantageous marriage in 1735; he had two daughters and four famous sons—Joseph,

Jonathan, Jr., David, and John. During the French and Indian War, Trumbull's firm contracted to arm and to provision Connecticut troops. He continued to be prominent in the general assembly, where he served as Speaker of the House (1740). Trumbull also tactfully handled religious disputes in the colony, and he served on a boundary commission that involved Massachusetts. Trumbull also served as a justice of the peace, as a court judge, and as a probate judge. Hence, he was respected for his diligence, his dependability, and for his adroitness in managing sensitive political issues. As deputy governor (1766–1769), as governor (1769), as champion of Connecticut's interests in the Susquehanna Company of Pennsylvania, and as a famous critic of British imperial policies toward the American colonies, Trumbull was prepared to lead his colony-state through the Revolution.

As war governor, Trumbull organized Connecticut's resources. By his policies of conscription, taxation, and trade controls he committed the state to a full prosecution of the war. In particular, Trumbull concentrated on supplying Washington's army with provisions, for Connecticut was uniquely crucial to the sustenance of the Continental Army. From the fertile river valleys of the Thames, Housatonic, and Connecticut came a variety of foodstuffs. Livestock throve on its grazing lands; and timber, minerals, and maple syrup were extracted from its forests. Because Connecticut was free from British attacks—except for coastal raids—the state provided a fine logistical organization by Trumbull and could funnel its products to the troops to such a degree that Connecticut became known as the "Provisions State."

There were other factors in Trumbull's success in supplying the army as well. He had a cooperative general assembly, the state's commissary staff seemed like a model of efficiency, and Connecticut towns were given quotas to provide clothing for the troops. At two crucial points in the war when the logistical system of the Continental Army virtually collapsed (at Valley Forge in 1777–78 and at Morristown in 1779–1780), Trumbull and Connecticut came to the rescue with cattle, flour, salt, and rum. The state manufactured gunpowder, muskets, cannon, and ammunition at its mills and foundries. Connecticut also had a state navy, under Trumbull's direction, of 13 vessels as well as 200 privateers licensed by the Connecticut Committee of Safety. Furthermore, Trumbull was effective in checking the danger of Loyalists (especially in Western Connecticut), and he maintained a strict embargo that forbade residents to trade with the enemy.

Yet as the struggle in the North became a stalemate, Trumbull's austerity measure earned him dissatisfaction from constituents. In 1780, 1781, and 1783, he failed to win a majority of votes cast for the governorship, and he only held office because the general assembly elected him. His diminishing support resulted from false charges that he had enriched himself by trading with the British, by his policy of taxation, and his support to national political centralization. In October 1783, tired of political turmoil and probably wracked by illness, Trumbull indicated that he would resign office in May 1784. In retirement he tried to pay off his debts, he wrote sermons, and he studied Hebrew. Trumbull won honorary degrees from Yale College and from the University of Edinburgh. He was elected to the American Academy of Arts and Sciences. And Washington remained grateful to Trumbull for being the most dependable war governor.

Richard L. Blanco

REFERENCES

Andrew M. Davis, "Trials of a Governor in the Revolution," *Massachusetts Historical Society Proceedings*, 47, 2nd Ser. (1914):131–141; Victor L. Johnson, *The Administration of the American Commissariat During the Revolutionary War* (1941); David M. Roth, *Connecticut's War Governor: Jonathan Trumbull* (1974); Glenn Weaver, *Connecticut's Merchant Magistrate* (1956); Oscar Zeichaer, *Connecticut's Years of Controversy* (1949).

Trumbull, Joseph (1738–1778)

Continental Army commissary general. A son of Jonathan Trumbull, Connecticut's governor during the Revolution, Joseph attended grammar school in Lebanon, Connecticut. At Harvard College, where students were "placed" according to status of their families, Trumbull ranked third in the class of 1759. After graduation, he worked in his father's retail and meatpacking business. From 1756 to 1763 he served in the Connecticut General Assembly, and in May 1773 Trumbull was a member of the Connecticut Committee of Correspondence. He represented Connecticut as an alternate delegate at the First Continental Congress.

Due to his public record, his mercantile experience, and his father's influence, Trumbull was appointed by the assembly in April 1775 to be commissary general for Connecticut troops. Successful in that office during the early stages of the siege of Boston, Trumbull was appointed by Congress (with Washington's endorsement) on July 19, 1775, to be commissary general of the Continental Army. He was authorized to receive a commission of $1^1/2$ percent on all supplies purchased.

Until Congress enacted regulations for his department, Trumbull, using the Connecticut commissary as his model, had to develop his own system of purchases and distributions of provisions. He gradually developed a centralized system to acquire and issue foodstuffs and equipment for the troops at Boston. In early 1776 Trumbull established four issuing stores at Medford, Cambridge, Roxbury, and Prospect Hill. At each site were storekeepers, clerks, coopers, and cooks. He also instituted a system of magazines where keepers supervised the flow of supplies like flour and livestock at depots some 20 miles from camp. This control, along with arrangements for purchasing agents (or deputies) to search for and to bid for commodities, functioned effectively at Boston, and Trumbull won Washington's praise.

But when the army moved to New York for the 1776 campaign, Trumbull encountered opposition to his system of centralized control by assemblies and committees in New York, New Jersey, and Pennsylvania. However, Congress upon Washington's urging, consolidated logistical functions of provisioning to Trumbull's benefit. A more complex issue arose that symbolized the sectional rivalries between New York and New England. General Philip Schuyler, the commander of the Northern Department, was so frustrated by the shortages and inefficiency of commissary personnel in Albany, that with the approval of Congress, he named Walter Livingston, his nephew, to be the local commissary general for the expedition to Canada. In July 1776, however, Congress resolved the issue by declaring that Trumbull had the authority in the Northern Department. By September, Livingston resigned, leaving the legacy of a bitter Schuyler-Trumbull feud.

Then Trumbull was criticized by some delegates for excessive expenditures in his budget. As a result, in September 1776 Congress enacted measures that decentralized his control over procurement and distribution. Then after further inquiry, Congress in December 1776 reversed itself and restored to Trumbull full powers over procurement and distribution. That month Trumbull went to Hartford, Connecticut, to oversee the salting and packing of meat destined for the troops. Trumbull appointed Carpenter Wharton as his deputy with Washington's army. But Wharton apparently was inept at his duty, and therefore, Washington in early 1777 had to develop his own procurement system in order to feed his men. As a result of higher prices of commodities due to competitive bidding between Continental commissary agents and state commissary agents in the Middle Department, Congress became increasingly critical. As a result, the newly formed Board of War in February 1777 (supported by Washington) recommended a separation of the purchasing and issues functions. Congress then began an investigation of Commissary Department procedures and uncovered fraud, shortages, and inefficiency, which were blamed on Trumbull's agents. Trumbull, who delayed too long in Connecticut, finally appeared in Philadelphia to dismiss Wharton and to clarify matters. Trumbull agreed that purchasing and issues be divided under separate officials.

While Congress considered the matter, Trumbull reported to Washington at Morristown, where he found his department in such disarray that he contemplated resigning. In the meantime, Congress enacted detailed regulations for a reformed commissary, splitting it into two units—purchasing and issues. Though the bureaucratic structure of the two departments appeared sensible on paper, the rules (record keeping, branding animals, tanning hides, etc.) were so complex that the administration of the two departments seemed inoperable to Trumbull. Trumbull was retained as Commissary General of Purchases with four deputies to assist him (with departments in the North, Middle, East, South), and Charles Stewart was appointed Commissary of Issues with three deputies.

By late spring, Trumbull was weary of the endless tinkering with the Commissary Department, by the criticisms of his staff, by charges that he had enriched himself, and by the trimming of his authority. He resigned on July 19, 1777. Yet, ever the patriot, Trumbull accepted an appointment to the Board of War in November 1777. But due to his arduous duties as commissary general, his health was impaired. By early 1778 he was suffering from jaundice and a partial paralysis of his hip. He resigned his post in April 1778 to die soon after. Considering the difficult circumstances under which he labored for the Patriot cause, Trumbull merits recognition for his achievements in feeding the troops.

Richard L. Blanco

REFERENCES

E. Wayne Carp, *To Starve the Army at Pleasure: Continental Army Administration and American Political Culture, 1775–1783* (1984); Victor J. Johnson, *The Administration of the American Commissariat during the Revolutionary War* (1941); Erne Risch, *Supplying Washington's Army* (1981); David M. Roth, *Connecticut's War Governor: Jonathan Trumbull* (1974); Jonathan Trumbull, "Joseph Trumbull, the First Commissary-General of the Continental Army," *Records and Papers of the New London County Historical Society*, Part III, Vol. II (1897).

Tryon, William (1729–1788)

Royal governor, British army officer. Born to a prosperous English shipping family of Dutch origins, William Tryon as a young man was financially and socially secure. His prestige increased when he married the socially prominent and wealthy Margaret Wake. Both his mother and his wife counted influential men among their relatives and friends, and it was probably through one of their connections that William Tryon, captain of the 1st Regiment of Foot Guards, was appointed lieutenant governor of North Carolina in 1764.

When Tryon arrived in North Carolina on October 10, 1764, he believed that Arthur Dobbs, the governor, would resign immediately, but Dobbs did not. In fact, he never did. Dobbs died at his post in March 1765, and it was not until then that Tryon was able to exercise authority when he became governor late in the summer of 1765 with his capitol at New Bern.

During Tryon's first year in office he was faced with difficulties arising from the Stamp Act, which Parliament had passed in order to raise some much needed revenue. Personally, Tryon was opposed to the act, because it required the tax to be paid in pounds sterling thus depleting his province of hard currency. However, Tryon was an obedient official, and he did his best to support the law. His support for the Stamp Act brought all business in the colony to a halt since legal documents, ships papers, and official documents had to be stamped. Tryon, in an attempt to win merchant support, stated that he would not collect certain fees that were due to him nor would he require wine licenses for taverns. But North Carolina merchants rejected this proposition, and Tryon was forced to cut short the meeting of the North Carolina Assembly in order to keep his province from sending delegates to the Stamp Act Congress, which was to meet in New York City in October 1765.

When Tryon adjourned the assembly, his troubles were not over. Crowds of North Carolinians, opposed to the Stamp Act, were intimidating royal officials into not enforcing the act. This intimidation was extended to Tryon when 400 members of the colony's militia surrounded his house and demanded the resignation of North Carolina's comptroller, who had taken refuge in Tryon's residence. Tryon refused to turn him over, but not wanting to endanger Tryon the official surrendered and had to apologize to the public for trying to enforce the act. The colony did not quiet down until news of the Stamp Act repeal arrived on June 25, 1766.

Tryon's next set of difficulties arose in the backcountry of North Carolina. The Regulators were a group of frontiersmen from North Carolina's western counties. They protested their lack of representation in the assembly and complained about government officials who practiced extortion in their dealings with the frontiersmen. Tryon, in an effort to keep the peace, ordered that government officials post in public places a list of the fees that they could charge. By this action it was hoped that extortion would be prevented. However, the Regulators were not satisfied, and so Tryon, leading the militia, went to Hillsborough, the scene of trouble.

The Regulators had gathered there, and the situation could have erupted into violence. A compromise was reached, however, and both the Regulators and the militia dispersed. Tryon promised to investigate the grievances, but he caused another confrontation when he asked the Regulator leadership to post bond as a guarantee of loyalty to the Crown during the trial of several Regulators. The Regulator leadership refused, and so Tryon assembled 1,400 men in Hillsborough to prevent rioting. The next crisis for Tryon was over the Townshend Acts.

Charles Townshend became the leader of the British government when William Pitt, now the Earl of Chatham, the prime minister, fell ill. In order to compensate for lost revenue that would occur when the British real estate tax would be reduced, Townshend proposed a set of import duties on tea, paint, paper, lead, and glass, as the items entered the American colonies. The revenue raised was to pay the salaries of the colonial governors, who heretofore had been paid by the assemblies. Thus, assembly influence over the governors would have been weakened. To ensure proper enforcement, new vice admiralty courts were created, a colonial board of customs commissioners was set up, and colonial supreme courts were authorized to issue writs of assistance so that customs officials could search warehouses. Parliament passed the Townshend Acts on June 29, 1767, specifying it would be effective on November 20 of that year. Many North Carolinians, like their fellow Americans, saw the Townshend Acts as another attempt by Parliament to confiscate their property and to destroy their liberty. Tryon experienced a great deal of difficulty with the North Carolina Assembly, which eventually sent a petition to the King denying the constitutionality of the Townshend Acts. There were the usual protests accompanied by the burning of the effigies of government officials. While the situation eventually simmered down, the potential for trouble remained until the news that some of the most controversial aspects of the act were rescinded arrived in 1770.

On September 24 and 25, 1770, the Regulators rioted in Hillsborough. Tryon made preparations for the calling up of the militia and ordered the construction of a redoubt in New Bern, the capital of North Carolina. In response to the riots of late September the assembly (dominated by coastal interests) passed what became known as the "Bloody Act" on January 15, 1771. The act stated that all rioters were guilty of treason, with the inference that they should be treated as traitors.

On March 18, 1771, Tryon decided to take the militia into Regulator country in order to serve warrants on the Regulator leadership. Tryon was able to raise 1,400 men, and on April 24, with Tryon in command, the North Carolina militia began its march. Tryon and the militia eventually caught up with the Regulators at Alamance Creek near Hillsborough. In a two-hour battle, Tryon's forces dispersed the Regulators and took several of their leaders as prisoners. One of them, James Few, was executed the next day, and 12 others were put on trial for treason. They were found guilty on June 17, but only 6 of the 12 were executed. The other six and their followers were forced to take an oath of allegiance to the North Carolina government.

While Tryon was suppressing the Regulators he learned that he had been appointed governor of New York. In July he left North Carolina to take up his new post in New York City. The inhabitants of the eastern sections of North Carolina were sad to see him leave. During his time in office he had clearly defined the colony's borders, and he had encouraged the growth of the Anglican Church. He also treated dissenters with a fairness that won their respect. Likewise, Tryon supported higher education in the colony by contributing to the support of Queen's College. He was so popular with the easterners that they named a county in the southwest portion of the colony for him. (During the Revolution, Tryon County was predominantly Loyalist.)

In New York, Tryon earned for himself a reputation as a fair and able administrator who was generally well liked. He assisted in the establishment of New York Hospital, and he contributed funds to King's College. New York City's links with other cities were improved as postal service between Quebec and New York City was instituted and a stagecoach line between New York and Boston was established. The provincial militia was strengthened, and Tryon tried to settle the New York–New Hampshire border dispute in New York's favor. In the winter of 1772–1773, Tryon won friends among the poor when he distributed firewood to them, paying for it out of his own pocket. Tryon became so popular that the New York Assembly, like its North Carolina counterpart, organized a new county and named it for him.

In the political controversies of the day, Tryon attempted to steer a middle course between the Patriot and Tory factions. His policy worked until the Tea Act forced him to side with the Tories. The Tea Act was passed by Parliament in May 1773 due to the vigorous lobbying efforts of the East India Company, which was near bankruptcy. The East India Company received a monopoly of the colonial tea trade with a duty of three pence kept on the tea. American Patriots regarded this legislation as another attempt to tax Americans without representation.

The New York Sons of Liberty organized mass meetings to condemn the act. Americans who imported English tea were considered traitors. Several merchants who had formerly agreed to handle the tea now refused to accept delivery. Tryon stated that when the tea arrived it would be stored at the battery. Tryon was bold because he had the support of the provincial council and a warship in the harbor. In the end, a confrontation did not take place because the ship carrying the tea was blown off course and never made it to the city.

Tryon sailed for England on April 2, 1774, to consult with his superiors, and he did not return until June 28, 1775. By then, the rebellion was underway. Tryon discovered that he had no actual authority in New York City. In fact, the situation was so bad that on October 19, 1775, he had to flee to a British man-of-war anchored in New York Harbor. From the ship Tryon was able to gather information on the American plans to attack Canada.

While Tryon was compiling data on American military activities he still attempted to bring about reconciliation. He wrote several letters to Lord Dartmouth and other government officials urging them to make at least one more attempt to resolve peacefully the problems that had led to rebellion. His pleas were ignored as the government was in no mood for reconciliation. Tryon also attempted to persuade New Yorkers that peace was the best course to follow. In an open letter to the people of New York City, that was published on March 16, 1776, Tryon urged the populace to maintain their allegiance to the Crown. But his plea was ignored by the majority of New Yorkers. By now Tryon must have realized that reconciliation was impossible.

Tryon remained on the ship until the fall of New York City to the British army. Tryon was able to return to his post, but the government of New York was now in the hands of the army, and Tryon was left without anything to do. It was at this time that Tryon turned his attention to military affairs. In 1772 Tryon had been promoted to the rank of colonel.

The unit that he was given to command was composed of Loyalists, and it was at this time that he became involved with a group known as the Associated Loyalists. The Associated Loyalists served as a pressure group whose purpose was to obtain compensation and relief from the English government for the losses of Loyalists. It was also a military organization that was responsible for the launching of many raids in the vicinity of New York City that resulted in the destruction of several American towns in New York, New Jersey, and Connecticut. Tryon personally led several of these raids. On April 28, 1777, Tryon led a raid against Danbury, Connecticut, where there was an American storage depot. Tryon not only destroyed the American supplies, but 39 private buildings as well. On October 9 Tryon led a Loyalist force that destroyed a village near Peekskill, New York. These raids and others like them prompted the Americans to respond in kind, and a destructive war of retaliation was the result. When General Sir Henry Clinton became commander of the British forces he expressed his disapproval of such raids because he felt they generated more opposition, but Lord George Germain, the American Secretary, approved of Tryon's actions.

For these efforts Tryon was made a colonel of the 70th Foot and was given the provincial rank of major general. The Associated Loyalists, acting independently of the army, continued to launch their assaults. From July 5 to July 11, 1779, Tryon led a raid against the Connecticut coast that was particularly destructive. Before this raid Tryon issued an "Address to the People of Connecticut" in which he criticized them for rebelling against good King George. Fairfield was hit first, and it suffered the destruction of over 200 commercial and residential buildings. Next came Norwalk, where Tryon burnt most of the town.

Due to his worsening health Tryon was relatively inactive for the remainder of 1779 and 1780. On September 4, 1780, Tryon sailed for England, and his American career came to an end. In 1782 the government, in appreciation for his efforts during the Revolution, promoted him to the rank of lieutenant general. Six years later he died, a very controversial figure.

Anthony P. Inguanzo

REFERENCES

Alonzo Dill, *Governor Tryon and His Palace* (1955); Marshall D. Haywood, *Governor William Tryon and His Administration in the Province of North Carolina, 1765–1771* (1901); Jonathan Trumbull, "The Conflicting Accounts of Tryon's Invasion of Norwalk, (1779), *Magazine of History, 3* (1900):18–

28; Thomas Jefferson Wertenbaker, *Father Knickerbocker Rebels: New York City During the Revolution* (1948).

Tucker, Samuel (1747–1833)

Continental Navy officer. Born in Marblehead, Massachusetts, Tucker went to sea as a youth, becoming a captain by 1768. Appointed commander of the schooner *Franklin* in Washington's navy (January 1776), he captured a British troopship. With the assistance of other naval vessels, Tucker went on to seize 30 prizes in 1776. After being commissioned a captain in the Continental Navy (March 1777), he sailed on the *Boston* to France, again capturing some enemy vessels. In 1779 Tucker sailed in a squadron led by Commodore Samuel Nicholson, which took eight prizes. Captured during the siege of Charleston, Tucker was imprisoned and then released. On his last voyage during the war as a privateer on the *Thorn*, Tucker was again captured and released.

After the war Tucker returned to the merchant marine for several years. Leaving Marblehead in 1792, he took up farming in Bristol (Maine). His last service was in the War of 1812, when he outfitted a schooner and captured a British privateer off the coast of Maine.

Richard L. Blanco

REFERENCES

John H. Sheppard, "Commander Samuel Tucker," *New England Historical and Genealogical Register, 26* (1872):105–115.

Turgot, Anne Robert Jacques, Baron de l'Aulne (1727–1781)

French statesman. Appointed Controller General of Finance by King Louis XVI in 1774, Turgot was an eminent physiocrat and reformer with a long career of public service. He had spent 14 years as intendant at Limoges (1761–1774) and had done much to improve the economy there. His appointment was a great surprise, but he wasted no time in unveiling a radical reform program for France based on his experiences at Limoges. Undoubtedly the most intelligent and prescient of Louis XVI's ministers, Turgot believed strongly that the Crown had to take a leading role in order for reform to be successful.

Turgot's program was a reflection of his physiocratic orientation. It stressed the removal of all restraints to freedom in trade, labor, and market pricing. It included suppression of the guilds, abolition of the forced labor service (*corvée*), religious toleration for Protestants, and most importantly, tax reform to abolish exemptions. It also included plans for subsidies to assist in modernization of certain industries.

The failure of Turgot's program has been attributed to his lack of tact (he was not above lecturing the King like a schoolboy), his determination to get things done in a hurry (he remarked "In our family we die at fifty"), and opposition from the privileged classes. He was also unlucky in timing. For example, when he freed trade in grain it came at a time of repeated poor harvests. As a result there were riots, and Turgot did not hesitate to call out troops and demand exemplary hangings in what has been known as the "flour war." Although Turgot regarded himself as the most liberal of the controllers general, he also made free use of *lettres de cachet* and imprisoned a number of his opponents in the Bastille.

In such circumstances, strong support from the Crown was essential if his program was to succeed. It was not forthcoming. The Queen disliked him, in part because he had acted against one of her favorites. Ultimately Louis XVI caved in to the pressure from his entourage and dismissed Turgot in May 1776. His reform program went with him. Supposedly Louis XVI remarked, "It is only Turgot and I who love the people."

Within the royal council, Turgot was the principal opponent of French aid for the American rebels. He believed that colonies in general were of negligible commercial value, and the loss of America would do little to cripple England economically. He had repeatedly told the King that governmental budget deficits could be handled only if there were no new wars and if the government practiced fiscal restraint. In this, he was putting the financial and internal conditions of France ahead of other considerations. He predicted that the costs of intervention would postpone, perhaps forever, any meaningful reform. He even went so far as to suggest that the fate of the monarchy rest on this one decision. Although his arguments were quite correct, the tactlessness with which he presented them did much to alienate others on the council. In any case, he failed to persuade the King, who decided to provide arms and money to the American rebels.

Turgot's departure meant not only the end of his reform program but also the removal of the chief obstacle to the Count de Vergennes's plans to involve France in war with England.

Spencer Tucker

REFERENCES

D. Dakin, *Turgot and the Ancient Regime in France* (1939); James B. Perkins, *France in the American Revolution* (1911); Simon Schama, *Citizens, A Chronicle of the French Revolution* (1989).

Uniforms of the American Revolution

In an age typified by its neoclassical style and simplicity, the military dress of the armies in the Revolution represents this era as much as a composition by Joseph Haydn or a painting by Joshua Reynolds. In a testimony to the orderliness of this period, the same general cut and style of uniform applied to all the armies involved in the war.

In 1775 the American army did not have a standardized uniform. Much literature had been devoted to the Minutemen, who turned out to meet the sartorially splendid British redcoats. The New England Minutemen did, in fact, face the British in Concord in their daily clothes. However, the concentration on these Minutemen has obscured the fact that there were well-clothed American troops in existence long before Lexington and Concord.

By the eighteenth century, in fact, the 13 colonies had regular colonial or provincial military regiments, which in some of the colonies reached a high level of sophistication in both their soldierly professionalism and in their martial uniforms. The New Jersey Regiment "The Jersey Blues" and the Virginia Regiment were especially noteworthy. "The Jersey Blues" distinguished themselves in General James Abercrombie's ill-starred attack on the French Fort Carillon, near today's Ticonderoga, New York, in July 1758. The *New York Mercury* in June of that year praised the "Blues" as "the likeliest well-set men for the purpose as has perhaps been turned out on any campaign . . . their uniforms blue, faced with red, grey stockings, and buckskin breeches."

The Virginia Regiment, under Colonel George Washington, also fought in the French and Indian War. Although first outfitted in red, the regiment changed its coat to blue in 1755; a general order of September 1775 stipulated "every officer of the Virginia Regiment to provide himself as soon as he can conveniently with a suit of regimentals of good blue cloth, the coat to be faced and cuffed with scarlet, and trimmed with silver."

Thus, by the time of the Revolution, the thirteen colonies already had a heritage of military costume to draw upon. Unfortunately, material for uniforms was in short supply. From the birth of the American army in June 1775 at Boston to the end of the war at Yorktown in October 1781, Congress would be constantly searching for clothing to outfit the troops.

Among the expedients that were tried was the purchase of military uniforms from the Netherlands, or from the Dutch Isle of St. Eustatius. Sometimes, uniforms and equipment were captured by American privateers from ships destined for the British. For part of the war Colonel Samuel Webb's Additional Continental Regiment wore British red. France was the most important foreign source of military uniforms for Washington's army. An example of the methods by which uniforms were altered for the Continentals is the habiliment of the 1st Pennsylvania Continental Regiment. Early in the war the Pennsylvanians were dressed in brown, while from roughly 1778, the regiment wore uniforms of blue.

Yet there was a drive for standardization in the Continental Army for a truly "national" uniform. This hope was realized by the passage in Congress of standardized uniform regulations for the Continental Army on October 2, 1779. This legislation was apparently due to Washington. The 1779 regulations divided the infantry of the Continental Army into four color-coordinated groups:

1. New Hampshire, Massachusetts, Rhode Island, and Connecticut—blue coats with white facings;

2. New York and New Jersey—blue coats with buff-colored facings;

3. Pennsylvania, Delaware, Maryland, and Virginia—blue coats with red facings; and

4. North Carolina, South Carolina, and Georgia—blue coats with deep-blue facings edged with white around the button-holes.

Henry Knox's artillery and artillery artificers were to have blue coats with scarlet facings, like the British Royal Artillery. The four regiments of Continental Light Dragoons were to receive coats of blue with white facings.

The typical outfit of the infantry and artillery was the three-cornered (or tricorn) hat, the familiar coat, shirt, waistcoat, and rather ill-fitting breeches, finished off with shoes and stockings. Washington, however, preferred a more practical pair of overalls for the soldiers that reached from the lower torso to cover the shoe.

Because of the demands of mounted service, the dragoons wore a shorter coat than did the infantrymen, known as a coatee, and leather jack-boots. As a rule, dragoons wore leather jockey-style caps, which may have been reinforced against saber chops by inner iron headguards. It is amusing to note that all American soldiers were issued square-toed footwear, with instructions to switch them continually so that no shoe or boot would pick up the shape of the left or right foot.

However, the Continentals rarely looked as good in actuality compared to European armies in the war. American fabrication and foreign aid (some 30,000 uniforms were imported from France alone) could not match the demand for army clothing. To allay the chronic shortage of military costume, Washington encouraged the wearing of long hunting shirts, because the hunting frocks were cheaper and easier to manufacture. There was also an element of psychological warfare in Washington's gambit. The British associated the hunting shirts with the Continental riflemen, whom they dreaded.

As for the light infantry, befitting their more mobile combat role they often were outfitted in the shorter-tailed coatee. They usually wore a jockey-style cap, adorned with a plume, and sometimes with the letters *LI* (light infantry) on the front plate.

The uniform history of the British army extended much farther back into military history than that of the United States. British units wore red doublets with the Tudor Rose emblem during the reign of King Henry VII. The Elizabethan Trained Bands, or militias, provided the model for the first organized colonial fighting forces in the English-speaking colonies. By the eighteenth century then, Great Britain had in force a longstanding policy of equipping a national army, and—unlike the Americans—an established industrial infrastructure to make such a uniformly accoutered force a reality. The British were clothed according to the Royal Warrant of 1768. The warrant provided for the clothing of the British troops with a minuteness and thoroughness that any modern military quartermaster department might envy. Literally everything from the material of a cavalry regimental standard (embroidered silk damask for a regiment of horse) to the colored loops around the buttonholes of a foot soldier's coat for the 21st Foot, was stipulated precisely.

In the infantry, a battalion might have 10 companies. Eight of the 10 companies were known as the "hat" companies, because the men in them wore the tricorn hat. The other two were the elite light infantry and the grenadier companies, which were sometimes combined for special tactical assignments. The grenadiers wore a bearskin cap with a metal front plate, to which was adhered the King's crest of silver-plated metal on a black ground, with the motto "Nec aspera terrent" ("Nothing frightens me"). A replica of a grenade was on the back part, with the number of the regiment on it. The light infantrymen wore the jockey-style helmet associated with light troops, either cavalry or infantry; the patterns of these helmets seem to have varied widely. Both light infantry and grenadiers wore "wings" on the shoulders of their coats, attesting to their status as elite troops. Light infantry, like their counterparts in the American army, often were issued the shorter-tailed coatee. The uniform of the infantryman was usually completed with a waistcoat, breeches, gaiters, and shoes.

An interesting type of unit was the fusilier regiment such as the 7th, or Royal Fusiliers; the 21st, or Royal North Fusiliers; and the 23rd, the Royal Welsh Fusiliers. These regiments were descended from special troops earlier assigned to guard the artillery. In recognition of their distinguished lineage, these regiments wore the elite bearskin cap, one slightly shorter than the foot-tall cap of the grenadiers. These regiments also had light infantry companies, of which the 23rd at least had its cap cut down from the regulation tricorn hat.

British infantry regiments also had other unique uniform designations—the "Six Old Corps" and the "royal regiments." The "Six Old Corps" were the first six British regiments of foot, a tradition of precedence adopted from the French army, which had its *six vieux corps*, its six oldest infantry units, the regiments of Picardie, Champagne, Navarre, Piémont, Normandie, and Bourbonnais. The British "Six Old Corps" were noted by distinctive additions to their uniforms: the 6th regiment, for instance, sported an antelope on its grenadier cap badge, while the 3rd, the Buffs, had the dragon, pointing to a Welsh heritage. Of the "Six Old Corps," the 3rd, 4th, 5th, and 6th served in America.

Regiments had royal status confirmed on them by virtue of long association with the Crown, or because of valorous service on the field. Royal regiments were noted by the deep blue color of the facings of their uniform coats. Facing colors of the older infantry regiments varied widely but were clearly enumerated according to the Royal Warrant. It should be mentioned that some other regiments had distinguishing features as well. The 18th, or Royal Irish, had "the harp and crown" on its grenadier cap.

The Highland regiments were unique. The most characteristic part of any Highlander's dress was the kilt, which has come to typify the Highland troops more than any other part of their uniform except for the bagpipe itself. Initially, the kilt was part of a much more capacious garment, sometimes called the plaid or tartan, which could act as a wrap-around shawl or blanket. This large-size plaid was worn by Scottish mercenaries in Europe in the seventeenth century and was still the garb of the gallant Highland clans who championed "Bonnie Prince Charlie" in the Jacobite Rising of 1745. By the time of the Revolution, the kilt had assumed its modern cut, wrapped around the Highlander's waist and usually secured by a handsome pin.

Design of the Highland regimental kilts, now called the tartan or plaid, has a rich and varied history. Although traditionally the Highlanders wore tartans associated with their own clans, such as the clans of Cameron, Forbes, and Grant, the British army had issued the "government tartan." The most famous regiment to wear this was the 42nd Foot, the fabled Black Watch, established in 1739. It appears that by 1775 some Highland units still clung to the old long plaid, the so-called *brecan-an-feilidh*, or "belted plaid." Others, however, had taken to the shorter kilt, or *philibeg*.

In place of pockets, which were (and are) lacking in the kilt, the Highlanders wore handsome purses called sporrans, which are still used today. Starting out as humble leather bags, by 1775 the sporrans had evolved into impressive decorative pieces. The sporran of the 84th, or Royal Highland Emigrants, was made of raccoon skin, while the Black Watch had sporrans made from the badger, each with ornate trim.

Another case of uniform evolution is exemplified by the striking feather bonnet, so much a part of contemporary "hieland" regalia. This distinctive headdress evolved over the nineteenth century and did not exist in Revolutionary times. By all evidence, it did not make its appearance until the Napoleonic Wars. During the War of Independence, Highlanders wore the flat-topped headdress that we would call a tam today, sometimes festooned with feathers. The only troops within a Highlander unit to wear something approaching the feather bonnet were the men of the grenadier company, issued a grenadier's cap.

The Highlanders wore a short jacket, in contrast to the long-tailed coats of the regular British and Lowland Scots infantry. Instead of gaiters, the clansmen were issued knee-length hose, into which many still put their ancient dirk, the *sgean dhu*. Like the infantry of the other regiments, they received the usual square-tipped shoes.

The classic music instrument of the Highlanders was the bagpipe, symbol of Scotland for all the world. At best as can be discerned, the piper had not yet achieved the high degree of sartorial finery that he would in the future. Drummers had been added to pipers by this time and, at least in the case of the Black Watch, there was also a regimental band. Presumably, pipers, drummers, and the other musicians received the regulation regimental uniform. Of all types of music played in the Revolution, no music probably best exemplified the culture and character of those who played it as the music of the Scottish Highlanders. Anyone who has heard the "pipes and drums" roar out "Highland Laddie," "All the Blue Bonnets Over the Border," or the "Piper of Drummond" can still feel what it must have been like to be in a Highland charge, broadsword or bayonet at the ready.

Of the British cavalry, only two regiments of light dragoons were in the American war, the 16th, the Queen's Light Dragoons, and 175th. The most arresting part of their uniform was the ornate helmet, described in June 1776 as "a leathern helmet, a good deal like that of the light infantry." However, in May 1772, the 17th was reported as receiving "a new set of helmets for the regiment, 140 brass helmets." Thus it appears that, as with many articles of clothing, there was some variation in the helmets from regiment to regiment. The 17th had a design of a death's head and the motto "or glory" on the front plate of its helmets. The 16th, the Queen's Regiment, had the Carter (the ancient symbol of the Order of the Garter) and the Queen's cipher, the letter *C*, for Queen Charlotte, on their helmet plates.

Unlike the four regiments of Continental Light Dragoons, the 16th and 17th seemed to have ridden in full-length coats, at least in the opening stage of the conflict. Later, when they became part of Banastre Tarleton's British Legion in the southern campaign, they adopted a more servicable outfit. Like the Continental Dragoons, they would have worn white boot hose underneath their heavy leather boots as protection for their legs.

Of the light dragoons, one of them wore a fundamentally different uniform—the farrier. The job of the farrier was to care for the horses. His uniform was blue, with facings of the regimental color; in a royal regiment, naturally, his facings would be blue. The farrier wore a bearskin cap. Of the two units of light dragoons serving in America, it should be noted that the 16th, being the Queen's Regiment, had blue facings, while those of the 17th had white.

The first troops from France to see service in America were uniformed according to the Royal Ordinance of 1776, which made a debacle of French uniform regulations. For instance, colonels and clothiers had to contend with two different shades of gray for regimental facings. According to noted French uniformologists Fred and Liliane Funcken, the 1776 Ordinance showed "contempt for the oldest established" uniform traditions in the army. For an army that honored its traditions from 1569, when the Picardie, Champagne, and Piémont regiments were first mustered, the 1776 Ordinance would not last long. On February 21, 1779, the minister of war, the Prince de Montbarrey, promulgated a simplified ordinance that restored tradition to French army dress.

With the exception of the royal regiments, like the *regiment du Roi* (the King's regiment), the Royal Regiment, and the Royal-Comtois, those of the princes, and the Picardie, the regiments of infantry were divided into 10 classes of six regiments each, according to their *rang d'anciennete*, or order of precedence. Each class of six regiments was further divided into two groups of three regiments each, using regimental facing color (*drap distinctive*) in such ways as edging for the lapels of the coats.

Since they took their position at the head of the army's order of precedence, something should be said about the royal regiments and the others that were exclusive of their regular infantry. One interesting point is that, as in the British army, the royal regiments were characterized by blue facings. Princely units like La Reine, the Queen's, Orleans, and Artois had scarlet facings and were organized into two groups, five in each.

The most fascinating group of French regiments were the *regiments strangers*, foreign units enlisted for the service of France which were the ancestors of today's French Foreign Legion. These foreign formations were uniformed in blue or red, with Irish regiments favoring red.

As befitting the logical spirit of the Age of Enlightenment, the French regiments were divided into grenadier, *fusilier* (the center or "hat" companies), and the *chasseur*, or light infantry companies. Each type of company was noted by a special uniform distinction on the "turn-backs" of their coattails. The grenadiers had a red grenade on their *retroussis* (turnbacks); *fusiliers*, a golden yellow fleur-de-lis; and the *chasseurs*, a *cor-de-chasse*, or hunting horn, a symbol of light troops made famous by Napoleon. (Ironically, until about 1812, there were really few basic changes in the French uniform coat, except for the change to a blue color during the French Revolution.)

No treatment of French uniforms of the Revolution could omit the dashing Lauzun Legion, of the Duc de Lauzun. The mounted troops of the legion wore a sky-blue tight jacket with yellow breeches, a typical hussar outfit, with some wearing a fur hussar cap or busby. The outer jacket was the same color as the tight shell jacket worn underneath. Trumpeters had the tricorn hat, with coats of the royal livery (blue with a read and white chain design). Infantrymen wore a blue coat with yellow facings, and white breeches and gaiters; shoes were black. The fusiliers wore the three-cornered hat, and the grenadiers were crowned with the august bearskin.

Like the French Maison du Roi (the royal household troops), the household guards of King Carlos III of Spain remained at home for the war. In 1766, large-scale riots in Madrid forced Carlos to flee the city for his country palace at Aranjuez. The King did not feel safe until his guards marched in. "Take my boots off," the relieved monarch said, "I am safe; my guards are here. I am going to have a rest."

Because none of the Spanish Guards came to American, they can only receive a cursory overview. Carlos had a mounted guard, the *Guardias de Cuerpo*, and basically two units of foot guards, the *Guardias Wallonnes* (the Walloon Guards) and the *Guardian Espanoles* (the Spanish Guards), each of about six battalions each. The Spanish kings kept an enormous Gard—there were some 600 *Guardias de Cuerpo* and 8,000 foot guards during the eighteenth century.

Of the Spanish troops who fought the British, mainly under Bernardo de Galvez, the Spanish governor general of Louisiana, the basic uniform coat of the infantry was white. This was the uniform, with blue facings, waistcoat, breeches, and white gaiters, that the provincial Louisiana Regiment wore at Galvez's investment of British-held Pensacola in 1780. The fusiliers, or regular infantry companies, wore the traditional tricorn hat, but the grenadiers, even in hot climates, still proudly clung to their fur bearskins. Spanish bearskin caps, for all infantry regiments, had beautifully ornate colored "bags" which hung down the backs of the cape, ending in a jaunty tassel. Spanish grenadiers would wear this unique headpiece into the Napoleonic Wars.

Spain actually had three armies in the Americas at this time. The first army was represented by the troops that were sent directly from Spain to serve in the Americas; the army was known as the *Ejercito de Refuerzo*, or the Army of Reinforcement, because its purpose was to augment or reinforce the troops Spain had already realized in the New World. The Irish Regiment of Hibernia, which fought at Pensacola, is an example of the *Ejercito de Refuerzo*, as are the Catalan Volunteers, who saw service fighting Indians farther west. The second Spanish army was that raised in the colonies, the colonial or provincial troops consisting of units like the Louisiana Regiment, the Habana Regiment in Cuba, or the Regiment of Puebla in Mexico. Spain's third type of troops belonged to the Provincias Internas, the "Internal Provinces" of Spain's Viceroyalty of New Spain. The Provincias Internas corresponded to the southwestern United States today and northern Mexico.

The uniform of the Army of Reinforcement was in many ways the same as that of the colonial troops. Drummers of the Louisiana Regiment, for instance, received uniforms in the royal livery, which bore an outstanding resemblance to that of the French troops. The military relationship between France and Spain was extraordinarily close: both Carlos III and Louis XVI belonged to different branches of the same Bourbon family. With its white coat, the Louisiana Regiment represented as good an example of the regular Spanish army as it did of the colonial troops.

An exception to the rule was the Irish troops, the regiments of Ultonia (Ulster), Hibernia, and Irlanda, descendants of Irish who had served Spain for decades. These units, regular army troops, were not kitted out in the traditional white. Instead, they were issued red uniforms like their Irish compatriots in the French forces. They did, however, wear Spanish blue waistcoats, breeches, and white gaiters, as the Irish in the French army wore the white waistcoats, breeches, and gaiters of the French uniform.

Spain's troops, including the Irish Brigade in the Service of Spain, wore the distinctive *escarapela roja*, or red cockade, in their tricorn hats, as the French were known by their white. When France and Spain became allies in the war against England in April 1779, Spain adopted a red and white cockade, much as George Washington adopted a black cockade with a white over it to symbolize the Franco-American alliance of 1778.

Of the Spanish army sent to fight the British, two other regiments should be listed on the role of honor: the Navarra Regiment, which saw service at Mobile, and the Mallarca, which took part in the action at Pensacola. They were two relatively "young" Spanish units, the Navarra being mustered in 1705, and the Mallorca, mustered in 1682. The Navarra Regiment was distinguished by dark blue cuffs, collars, and lapels, while the Mallorca was identified by facings of red.

The colonial or provincial regiments, like Nueva Espana (New Spain), Louisiana, Puebla, and Mexico, wore, as stated above, the traditional white uniform. However, the regiment in the provincial army donned the dark blue coat with red facings of the royal household troops of Carlos III. It should be noted that some depictions of these colonial troops, as well as Spanish regulars, show them at times in white waistcoat, breeches, and gaiters.

Of the Spanish cavalry, none of the regular regiments served in the war. The line or heavy cavalry (*caballeria de linea*) wore white uniforms, each regiment having its facing color, while all the dragoons (*dragones*) had uniforms of yellow,

also marked by facing colors. In 1805, the line cavalry would have blue coats, while the dragoons retained their yellow. Concerning the artillery, the uniform was identical to that found in the Royal Army. This was a blue coat faced in red and trimmed in gold lace. The waistcoat was red and the breeches were blue.

Among the British troops who were captured by Galvez at Pensacola, some were from the Waldeck Regiment, among the German Auxiliaries brought by George III to America. The Waldeckers were only one of many German units to wage war against the Americans. Regiments also came from German states as varied as Ansbach-Bayreuth, Brunswick, and Anhalt-Zerbst. Because so many of the Germans originated from the principalities of Hesse-Hanau and Hesse-Cassel, all the German soldiers have been referred to generically as "Hessians."

Due to the predominance of the Hessians, their uniforms merit attention. The basic Hessian uniform was a blue coat, with a white waistcoat and white breeches, finished off by knee-high gaiters. Hessian regiments were differentiated by the colors of their regimental facings, as were the French and the British. The Hessian Fusilier Regiment von Ditfurth, for instance, was identifiable by its yellow facings; throughout much of the war, the Hessian Erbprinz (Crown Prince) Fusiliers were distinguished by rose-red facings. When the Erbprinz became a musketeer regiment in 1780, facings were altered to a carmoisin red. The Grenadier Regiment von Rall, which was decimated at Trenton in 1776, had facings of scarlet.

As a way of clarification, no real difference existed between "musketeer" and "fusilier" regiments, although later fusiliers evolved into a form of light infantry. In the Revolution, the only real uniform difference is that the fusiliers wore a metal-fronted cap decorated with the Hessian lion and shield, and muskateers wore the tricorn hat. In these distinctions, German units were influenced by the army of Frederick the Great of Prussia. Each fusilier or musketeer regiment possessed its grenadier company, which was brigaded together with those of other fusilier or musketeer regiments for special missions. The Hessian artillerists coincidentally shared the same uniform coat with the British, French, and American gunners—a blue uniform coat, trimmed to red, and topped off with the ubiquitous tricorn hat.

The standard Brunswick soldier wore a blue coat, completed by a white waistcoat, breeches, and white or black gaiters. In common with much of the German infantry, Brunswickers during General John Burgoyne's campaign took to wearing long overalls of the type George Washington urged for his Continentals. Although the Brunswick overalls seem to have been essentially white, Hessians seemed to have preferred white overalls sometimes striped (or piped) in red. These overalls, which strapped under the instep of the wearer's foot, were often made of surplus army tents and ships' sails.

Grenadiers from Brunswick shared the same highly ornamental grenadier caps as did the Hessians, except that the Brunswickers wore the Horse of Brunswick rather than the Lion of Hesse, which identified both Hesse-Hanau and Hesse-Cassel contingents, even on their flags (the same red-and-white beast on a blue field of color). Other Brunswickers wore the tricorn hat. As with the Hessians, the Brunswick regiments were characterized by the color of their facings. The facings of the von Rhetz regiment wore white, while the Prinz Friedrich and von Riedesel regiments both bore yellow facings but were further differentiated by more minute uniform distinctions.

What made the German armies among the most colorful in the war were the outfits of *jaegers*, or hunters, who were recruited from the foresters or hunters on the princely estates. Bearing highly accurate rifles, they were the battlefield equivalent of Washington's riflemen. Both Brunswick and the Hessians had *jaeger* companies in America, both garbed in green uniforms, an early use of camouflage in an attempt to blend in with their forest environment, faced with red. There was one Brunswick *jaeger* company and two from Hesse-Cassel, one of which was mounted. (Brunswick also had a blue-coated light infantry battalion, also armed with rifles, which worked with the *jaegers*.) All rifles were usually privately purchased and were of a superior quality to the regulation-issue smoothbore muskets. Hesse-Hanau furnished a corps of *chausseurs*, or hunters, uniformed like the Hesse-Cassel *jaegers*. Most of the *jaegers* and *chasseurs* wore buff leather breeches, while the mounted company was issued boots. Their tricorns had feathers for full dress.

Brunswick also sent to the war the handsomely dressed Prinz Ludwig Dragoon Regiment, which was forced to fight much of the time on foot in their heavy cavalry boots. The dragoons wore the blue Brunswick coat, trimmed in yellow facings. A unique feature of this regiment was its Black drummer in his plumed white turban. In a contemporary journal, there is a good, concise description of the regiment's garb: "high and heavy jack boots with large long spurs, stout and stiff leather breeches, gauntlets reaching high up on his arms, and a high tuft of ornamental feathers."

Of the single Anhalt-Zerbst infantry regiment in America, an eyewitness sketch is provided by Frederick Mackenzie of the Royal Welch Fusilier, who wrote that they looked "more like dragoons than infantry. They are clothed in white, faced with red; felt caps a la hussar, boots and a red cloak." Their grenadiers still wore the distinctive caps, although of bearskin similar to the British. Waistcoats were white, and musketeers seemed to have adopted the tricorn. The boots apparently were abandoned in favor of more serviceable gaiters.

The Ansbach-Bayreuth contingent was a well-balanced infantry force, but without cavalry. Its first and second infantry regiments wore blue coats, the first with red facings, the second with black. The *jaegers* had the readily identifiable green coat faced red, also with a plume in full dress. The artillery company wore the classic blue coat with crimson facings. All wore white breeches and vests. The Ansbach *jaegers* were more specifically known as the *chasseur* company, like that of Hesse-Hanau.

One must mention the uniforms of the American-raised auxiliary troops for the Continental Army and for the British army. These were the state militias on the Patriot side and the Loyalist Provincial Corps on the British. On the British side, undoubtedly the most well known were Simcoe's Queen Rangers and Banastre Tarleton's British Legion. Simcoe's Rangers were mustered in 1776, originally led by Robert Rogers, famed chief of Rogers' Rangers in the French and Indian War. Under Simcoe's later command in 1777, the rangers were all dressed in green. The most colorful unit among the rangers was the troop of hussars. These wore a black hussar busby with a green bag, the front of the hussar cap trimmed with a white metal crescent with "Queen's Rangers" engraved on its surface. The hussar outfit was completed with a green jacket with pewter buttons and green overalls, although one authority mentions the wearing of green breeches and short boots. In 1780, three troops of light dragoons were raised, wearing green jackets, buckskin breeches, high jackboots, and the leather helmet with a fore-and-aft bearskin crest that would be named after Banastre Tarleton who fashioned it—the tarleton. Simcoe's men all wore plumes or feathers in their headdress.

Infantry elements of Simcoe's rangers were turned out somewhat differently. Those of the grenadier company wore tall cloth caps, white breeches, and brown cloth gaiters or black linen spatterdashes, completed with the *de rigeur* green jacket. The rest of the infantry, light infantry, and regular troops wore an identical uniform, save for a hat with a high front. A notable exception was the Highland or "Balmoral" bonnet and a kilt in the Back Watch's tartan, which was known as the "government sett [pattern]," because the Black Watch had been established by the royal government and thus it lacked any true clan identification or tarttan.

Tarleton's British Legion wore green jackets, white waistcoats and breeches, and most likely high jackboots. Its drummers wore green waistcoats and breeches. Possibly, as in a famed painting of Tarleton by Joshua Reynolds, short (Wellington) boots were the more likely footwear. Bernhard de Wiederhold, a Hessian officer, described the Legion cavalry as uniformed in "short round tight jackets, black collar and cuffs," while the foot soldiers wore a "short coat—green with same lapels, variety button hole (viz. laced) and black cuff and collar." In the hot south, there is some indication the Legion was garbed in white smocks, probably cotton or linsey-woolsey, which would have been considerably cooler than their regulation uniforms. Other Loyalist or Provincial formations, like the Prince of Wales's American Regiment or the King's American Dragoons, wore red uniforms faced with blue, like the royal regiments of the British regular army.

On the American side, one of the most colorful units was the legion formed by Charles-Armand Tuffin, le Marquis de La Rouerie, known to American history as Colonel Armand. The Legion, which Armand took over on his arrival from France in 1777, was first uniformed in an olive jacket with brown breeches, topped with a tricorn hat. In 1780, Armand's command donned blue coatees with white facings, the regulation uniform of the Continental light dragoons.

It was in 1780 that, on Washington's suggestion, the Legion entered the regular Continental Army, which would account for the appearance of the regulation uniform. The garb, according to research done by the French military artist Eugene Leliepvre, also included buckskin breeches, black boots, and a dragoon-style helmet. Leliepvre depicted buff facings on the uniform he reconstructed.

The other cavalry and infantry group recognized as partisans was that of "Light-Horse" Harry Lee of Virginia. Established in 1778, Lee's legion would mainly engage the enemy on foot. Lee's corps apparently was issued three successive uniforms. At first, the officers and men wore a bright green jacket with chamois or buff-colored breeches and a helmet with a horsehair crest. In 1780, they changed to a green jacket with white waistcoat and breeches, with a helmet with a fur turban. In 1781–1782, they finally were uniformed in a buff-colored uniform with green facings, and a tarleton-style dragoon helmet. (Charles Willson Peale, who painted many of the young Republic's cavalry chieftains, such as William Washington, also limned Lee.) About a third of Lee's Light Horse was mounted. The strength of the corps, like that of Armand's, varied from about 130 in 1778 to around 300 in 1780.

Other Continental auxiliaries wore little or nothing in the way of regular uniforms. The guerillas of Francis Marion, the "Swamp Fox," were primarily a true guerila outfit with no actual uniform, mustering together for a mission, then disappearing again to live among neighboring farmers. The Gloucester County militia, which played a part in Colonel Armand's raid on the Hessians near Gloucester, New Jersey, usually wore the hunting shirt and tricorn hat of the Continental riflemen. Like other militia units on both Patriot and Loyalist sides, the Gloucester Country men would most likely wear their own clothing, much like the minutemen at Lexington.

John F. Murphy, Jr.

REFERENCES

Christon I. Archer, *The Army in Bourbon Mexico, 1760–1810* (1977); Major R. Money Barnes, *A History of the Regiments and Uniforms of the British Army* (1960); ———, *The Soldiers of London* (1968); ———. *The Uniforms and History of Scottish Regiments* (1968); Michael Barthorp, *British Cavalry*

Uniforms Since 1660 (1984); ———, *British Infantry Uniforms Since 1660* (1984); Sidney B. Brinckenerhoff and Pierce A. Chamberlain, *Spanish Military Weapons in Colonial America, 1700–1821* (1972); Jose M. Bueno, *El Ejercito y La Armada en 1808* (1982); Rene Chartrand, "The Spanish Louisiana Regiment, 1769–1803," *Military Illustrated: Past and Present*, 12 (1988):32–38; Colonel John R. Elting, ed., *Military Uniforms in America: The Era of the American Revolution* (1974); Juan M. Fernandez, "El Ejercito de America: El Componente Humano," *Revista de Historia Militar*, 51 (1981):119–156; Fred Funcken and Liliane Funcken, *L'Uniforme et Les Armes des Soldats des Etat-Unis*, 2 vols. (1980); ———, *L'Uniforms et Les Armes des Soldats de la Guerre en Dentelle*, 2 vols. (1975); ———, *Le Costume et Les Armes des Soldats de Tous les Temps*, 2 vols. (1966, 1975); Donald E. Graves, *French Military Terminology, 1670–1815* (1970); Jack L.D. Holmes, "Military Uniforms in Spanish Louisiana, 1766–1804," *Military Collector and Historian*, 17 (4) (1965):115–117; Philip R.N. Katcher, *The American Provincial Corps, 1775–1784* (1973); ———, *Encyclopedia of British, Provincial, and German Army Units, 1775–1783* (1973); ———, *George Washington's Army* (1972); ———, *Uniforms of the Continental Army* (1981); Richard Knotel, Herbert Knotel, and Herbert Sieg, *Uniforms of the World: A Compendium of Army, Navy, and Air Force Uniforms, 1700–1937* (1980); Charles M. Lefferts, *Uniforms of the American, British, French, and German Armies of the War of the American Revolution, 1775–1783* (n.d.); Mark G. McLaughlin, *The Wild Geese: The Irish Brigade of France and Spain* (1980); John Mollo, *Uniforms of the American Revolution* (1975); Warren Moore, *Weapons of the American Revolution and Accouterments* (1967); George C. Neuman, *The History of Weapons of the American Revolution* (1967); Michael Petard, "L'Evolution du Costume Militaire [de France], 1775–1779," *Tradition*, 9 (1987):23–27; Harold L. Peterson, *Arms and Armor in Colonial America, 1526–1783* (1956); ———, *The Book of the Continental Soldier* (1968); Colonel H.C.B. Rogers, *The Mounted Troops of the British Army* (1967); Randy Steffe, *The [American] Horse Soldier 1776–1943; Vol. I: The Revolution, The War of 1812, the Early Frontier, 1776–1850* (1980); Hew Strachan, *British Military Uniform, 1768–96; The Dress of the British Army from Official Sources* (1975); Gregory J.W. Urwin, *The United States Cavalry: An Illustrated History* (1983); ———, *The United States Infantry: An Illustrated History* (1988); Robert and Christopher Wilkinson-Latham, *Cavalry Uniforms of British and the Commonwealth, Including Other Mounted Troops* (1969); ———, *Infantry Uniforms, Including Artillery and Other Supporting Corps of Britain and the Commonwealth, 1742–1855* (1969).

Ushant, France, Battle of (July 27, 1778)

The Battle of Ushant, which took place in the summer of 1778, may have represented Britain's last chance to win the American Revolution. Admiral Augustus Keppel hoped to emulate the decisive victories of his predecessors Edward Hawke and Edward Boscawen over the French during the Seven Years' War in order to isolate the French Bourbons from the struggle in America. Instead, Ushant ended in a draw, as three factors combined to prevent the customary British success—inflexible tactics imposed by the rigid character of the Permanent Fighting Instructions, a resurgent French fleet, and political division within the British command. The battle ultimately proved beneficial to the British, however, as the resulting courts-martial served to give more tactical flexibility to fighting admirals.

The Battle of Ushant revealed a long-standing flaw in the tactics of the Royal Navy. The Permanent Fighting Instructions, drawn up by Robert Blake during the seventeenth century and revised by Sir George Rooke in 1703, imposed the single line ahead as the correct formation for naval combat. Indeed, Admiral Matthews was court-martialed after the Battle of Toulon in 1744 for failure to maintain his squadron in line of battle. Yet the line ahead was limited by the speed of the slowest ship. Admiral John Byng was court-martialed after the Battle of Minorca in 1756 for "failing to do his utmost" when delays caused by the need to form line allowed the enemy to escape. The confining effects of the Fighting Instructions limited the ability of British admirals to catch opponents who refused to form opposing lines.

At the onset of the American Revolution, the Royal Navy faced the dual task of supporting military operations along the American coast and providing protection for British shipping against the depredations of colonial privateers. Admiral Lord Richard Howe handled these missions adequately. After the surrender of General John Burgoyne at Saratoga in 1777, however, the scope of the war widened. Within four months, colonial representative Benjamin Franklin concluded a secret treaty with the French minister of marine. On March 13, 1778, France announced to Britain the initiation of hostilities, and the naval conflict assumed the global nature of previous struggles.

France was better prepared in 1778 to contest command of the seas with Britain than in either previous or subsequent struggles. French ministers the Duke de Choiseul and Marquis de Castries had begun the work of rebuilding the Bourbon fleet even before the Peace of Paris had been signed in 1763. Receiving financial support on a scale that had been hitherto reserved for the army, they laid the foundation of a strong fleet of 63 ships of the line and 67,000 sailors in 1778. As the opening move in their campaign to gain control of the English Channel, the French in April dispatched Vice Admiral the Comte d'Estaing with 12 ships of the line from Toulon to American waters.

The Admiralty, under First Lord the Earl of Sandwich, recognized the necessity of reinforcing Admiral Lord Howe. Sandwich, in the face of a rejuvenated French fleet, abandoned Britain's customary strategy of close blockade in order to concentrate his forces in the Channel. Having allowed the French unfettered access to the Atlantic and hence America, the First Lord was constrained to send a fleet of 13 ships of the line under Vice Admiral John Byron to counter d'Estaing's squadron in American waters. This detachment weakened the strength of Admiral Augustus Keppel's Channel fleet, as the French had foreseen.

The Battle of Ushant resulted from a chance meeting of the forces remaining in European waters. On July 8, 1778, Admiral the Comte d'Orvilliers took the Brest fleet of 29 ships of the line to sea for a training cruise. The next day, Admiral Keppel put to sea with 30 ships of the line. His objective was to prevent a juncture of the Brest and Toulon squadrons; failing that, he was to attack if the odds were close and return for reinforcements if the French were "markedly superior." The two fleets sighted one another on July 23, 1778, approximately 100 miles west of Ushant, a small island off the tip of Normandy.

Keppel assumed Britain's customary role as pursuer, hoping to destroy the Brest fleet and thereby to reduce the chances of invasion or loss of the colonies. D'Orvilliers, interested primarily in returning safely to Brest, eluded the British for three days at the cost of losing two ships, which became separated during maneuvers. Keppel retained all of his vessels, thereby increasing his slight advantage to 30 ships against

27. On July 27, 1778, the British fleet drew near the French.

The Battle of Ushant was limited to a single indecisive pass. Keppel gave the order for a general chase. This maneuver sacrificed an orderly line of battle for the opportunity to mass on the rear of the French. D'Orvilliers, seeing the British break formation, turned his fleet together and headed for the British squadron, hoping to take advantage of the apparent disorder. Keppel rejected the option of falling off and reforming his line, perhaps remembering the example of Byng. He chose instead to engage without forming a line. As the French ships passed the British van and center, they fired on the upward roll dismasting several British vessels. The return fire, in the British custom, struck the French hulls. The British rear, nine ships under Sir Hugh Palliser, had time to form lines; as they bore up, these vessels were subject to the fire of the entire French fleet. The squadrons then passed out of range.

Both commanders tried fruitlessly to continue the action. D'Orvilliers sought to cut off the damaged British vessels, but Count Du Chaffault, the commander of the French van, either misunderstood or disregarded his orders. Keppel in turn came about and sought to continue the engagement. He tried to form his fleet into line, but Palliser refused to rejoin. Keppel tried both signals and a message sent by frigate to induce the rear division to close with the center, without success. Keppel finally bypassed Palliser and ordered the rear ships by individual signal to rejoin the British main body. By the time this was accomplished, night had fallen. D'Orvilliers took advantage of the darkness to break contact and run for Brest. Although his ships had suffered more casualties, they had inflicted greater material damage to the British fleet and had escaped the engagement without the loss of a single vessel.

Palliser's unwillingness to support Keppel reflected the sharp political division within the Royal Navy. Most of the senior officers, including Keppel, were Whigs who detested Sandwich, opposed the government's policy in America, and refused to serve against the colonists. Palliser, a protégé of Sandwich, staunchly supported the North ministry. He charged Keppel with throwing away a victory by his decision to try to form into line after the first pass. Keppel demanded a court-martial to clear his name and in turn charged Palliser with failing to obey orders to engage the enemy. Opposition leader Charles James Fox concurrently moved to dismiss Sandwich. The political tempest failed to shake the government, which enjoyed a safe majority, but the alienation of the Whig admirals squandered a resource Britain could ill afford.

For the British, the battle had one positive result. In a subsequent court-martial, Keppel was charged with (1) engaging without first forming a proper line of battle, and (2) failing to do his utmost to defeat the French by taking time after the first pass to form line. The verdict of not guilty, which met with popular acclaim, served to reduce the sacrosanct character of the Perma-nent Fighting Instructions. Thus, the Battle of Ushant helped prepare the Royal Navy for the victories of Howe, John Jervis, and Horatio Nelson against the navies of Revolutionary and Napoleonic France. *See also:* Keppel-Palliser affair.

Raymond C. Gamble

REFERENCES

Paul Kennedy, *The Rise and Fall of British Naval Mastery* (1983); Alfred Thayer Mahan, *The Influence of Sea Power Upon History 1660–1783* (1890); E.B. Potter and Chester Nimitz, eds., *Sea Power: A Naval History* (1960); James Stokesbury, *Navy and Empire* (1983); Barbara Tuchman, *The First Salute* (1988).

Valcour Island, New York, Battle of (October 11, 1776)

At first glance, the Battle of Valcour Island looks like a crushing defeat for the Americans. Nevertheless, many historians believe that Benedict Arnold's action on Lake Champlain was the key to success for the cause he later betrayed. The presence of an American fleet on the lake forced the British to delay their northern invasion, leading directly to the pivotal American victory at Saratoga in October 1777. William Fowler in his account of the American navy in the Revolution, *Rebels Under Sail*, notes that American naval operations on salt water "did not have any significant effect on the overall outcome of the Revolution," but the freshwater fleet on Lake Champlain "played a vital role in what was perhaps the most important campaign of the Revolution; in fact, this naval action among the mountains was the only battle fought by Americans that Alfred Thayer Mahan thought worthy of including in his *Major Operations of the Navies in the War of American Independence.*

Lake Champlain was recognized by both sides as the strategic key to the continent. It is the only feasible route between the Hudson and the St. Lawrence, and it is the line of demarcation between New England and the rest of the continent. Early in 1775 the Boston Committee of Correspondence sent an agent, John Brown, to seek support for the American cause in Canada. On March 29 Brown wrote from Montreal that "the Fort at Tyconderoga must be seised as soon as possible should hostilities be committed by the Kings Troops. The People on N Hampshire grants have ingaged to do this Business and in my opinion they are the most proper Persons for this Jobb." Both Benedict Arnold, under the authority of the Massachusetts Committee of Safety, and Ethan Allen, sponsored by Connecticut, rushed to seize Fort Ticonderoga, and the citadel fell to their joint expedition on May 10, only three weeks after the first shots at Lexington and Concord.

While Fort Ticonderoga was surrendering to representatives of "the Great Jehova and the Continental Congress," a detachment of 30 men under Captain Samuel Herrick captured Skenesborough. Skenesborough (now Whitehall, New York) is almost at the southern end of Lake

Champlain. There Major Philip Skene built a sawmill and boatyard. Herrick's prizes included Major Skene's yacht, the *Katherine*, a small schooner or ketch just over 40 feet long. This little vessel, which Captain Herrick renamed the *Liberty* and sent to Fort Ticonderoga, is arguably the American navy's first ship.

Colonel Benedict Arnold got her command as a consolation prize when Ethan Allen, whose Green Mountain Boys outnumbered Arnold's troops, claimed precedence at Ticonderoga. Arnold, an experienced merchant skipper, at once assembled a flotilla of the *Liberty* and two bateaux—large rowboats—full of soldiers and embarked for the British army post at St. Johns on the Richelieu River. Achieving complete surprise, the Americans overran the British garrison, taking 14 prisoners and, most important, the King's sloop *George*. John F. Miller has noted that "the date was 18 May 1775, and some enthusiasts claim that this was the first naval battle of the Revolution, even if there was no actual resistance by the British."

Now the American navy had two vessels, the *Liberty* and the *Enterprise* (nee the *George*), and complete control of Lake Champlain. It is true that the British had many soldiers in Canada—400 of them quickly reoccupied St. Johns. The world's biggest and best navy could put as many warships as it wished in the St. Lawrence, but the 12 miles of rapids between Chambly and St. Johns formed a more effective barricade than any number of forts. No army could venture much south of St. Johns if it did not control the lake. This had been true throughout the French and Indian War, and it would again be true in the War of 1812. Even had an army been able to march along the shore, its lines of communication would be at the mercy of whoever controlled the lake.

The rebellious colonies were, for the moment, secure against invasion from the north. At first the Continental Congress did not grasp this. It ordered that Forts Ticonderoga and Crown Point be abandoned, but protests from the New York and New England legislatures made Congress reconsider. On June 27, it resolved that St. Johns, Montreal, and any other part of Canada "which may have a tendency to promote the peace and security of these Colonies," should be captured.

In the meantime, Massachusetts decided to let Connecticut have the glory—and expense and headaches—of maintaining Fort Ticonderoga. It sent Colonel Joseph Henshaw to Hartford with an offer to bow out and, if Connecticut proved receptive, to order Benedict Arnold back to Cambridge. Henshaw succeeded in giving the fort to Connecticut, but he forgot to tell Arnold that he had been relieved. When Colonel Benjamin Hinman arrived in July with 1,000 Connecticut troops, Arnold refused to place himself under Hinman's command. He took the *Liberty* and the *Enterprise* out into the lake and sulked. When a committee rowed out to reason with Arnold, it was forced to state its case while standing before the fixed bayonets of Arnold's crew. After a day, however, Arnold cooled off enough to beat a surly retreat back to Massachusetts. Thus ended his first hitch as commander of the American fleet.

Congress had put the Northern Department, which had responsibility for carrying out the resolution to invade Canada, under Major General Philip Schuyler. Schuyler poured all his resources into building enough bateaux to ferry his troops and supplies north to attack St. Johns. His only armed vessels remained the *Liberty* and the *Enterprise*, although he knew the British at St. Johns were building two vessels to take back control of the lake. To make matters worse, Schuyler, while intelligent and industrious, was congenitally conservative and physically ill. Fortunately, his second in command, Brigadier General Richard Montgomery, took matters into his own hands. Montgomery's troops seized Fort Chambly and, after a six-week siege, on November 2 captured St. Johns and with it the third vessel to join the American fleet, the 100-ton schooner *Royal Savage*.

The winter of 1775–1776 saw Montgomery's and Arnold's ill-fated attempt to take Canada. Montgomery captured Montreal, then joined Arnold, who had marched his troops through Maine, in a siege of Quebec. But their assault on Quebec on New Year's Eve was repulsed, Montgomery was killed, and Arnold was wounded. As soon as the ice broke up in the St. Lawrence, the Royal Navy relieved Quebec, and the Americans, hotly pursued by General Sir Guy Carleton, made a retreat that turned into a rout. By mid-June the sick, exhausted, and demoralized remnants were back at St. Johns but found no safety there, for a "perfect sot" of an engineer officer had failed to prepare any fortifications. Salvaging only the timbers of a partly-built vessel (which would later be assembled as the *Cutter Lee*), Arnold and his men fell back to Crown Point. Now the only thing standing between them and Carleton's rested, well-supplied, and victorious army were the three little ships, *Liberty*, *Enterprise*, and *Royal Savage*.

Philip Schuyler's limited energy and resources were occupied with supplying the army in Canada. His carpenters in Skenesborough turned green timber into four bateaux every day. Bateaux were essential to ferry men and supplies north, but even 1,000 of the big rowboats would have been easy prey for a schooner with a couple of cannon. Neither Schuyler nor Congress grasped the necessity for bigger vessels until too late. In late January 1776 Schuyler finally asked Congress for a Champlain naval commander. He nominated Major William Douglass of Connecticut as commodore, with Jacobus Wynkoop of Albany, an old friend, to serve as deputy. Congress agreed but left the final appointment to the New York Provincial Congress. Douglass procrastinated for two months, hoping to be offered a better command, until the New York Provincial Congress in desperation turned the commodorship over to Wynkoop.

Commodore Wynkoop recruited a few experienced sailors from the Hudson River trade and got his three sailing ships into working condition by the end of May. But the old Dutchman was competent neither as a warship commander nor as a shipyard supervisor. He spent most of his time defending the prerogatives he imagined he had as commodore. He took the guns out of his schooners, reducing them, according to General Horatio Gates, to "Floating Waggons." Wynkoop was the despair of General Gates, a retired British army major whom the Continental Congress had designated as commander of American forces in Canada. By the time Gates arrived, the Americans had no forces in Canada, so Gates fumed under Philip Schuyler's seniority as a kind of spare wheel in the Northern Department. But in mid-July he asked Benedict Arnold, now promoted to brigadier general, to come down from Crown Point to see if he could bring any order to the shipyard in Skenesborough.

And order was certainly needed. Congress had told Schuyler that, in addition to keeping the troops supplied, building a wagon road from Fort Edward and constructing a lock at Skenesborough, he should build armed vessels to protect Lake Champlain. Philip Skene's sawmill and boatyard were the only available facilities. By now it was summer, and even if it had occurred to Schuyler to build a large ship that could carry heavy armament, he had neither the time nor the shipwrights to build it, nor the experienced sailors to take it into combat. He decided to build as many small, easily constructed vessels as he could—gundalows and galleys.

We know exactly what the gundalows looked like, because one of them, the *Philadelphia*, was raised in 1935 and is on display in the Smithsonian. Gundalows, also called "gondolas," were commonly used on American rivers to carry bulky cargoes like lumber and grain. Around 50 to 60 feet long and 16 feet broad, they had flat bottoms and drew only about a foot and a half of water. Gundalows look like—and in a way are—enormous rowboats. A square sail on a mast stepped amidships propelled the gundalow when the wind was just right, though the flat bottom and lack of keel must have made it extremely difficult to sail. The rest of the time, the gundalow was moved with sweeps—big oars pulled by the crew, which might number 45 men. Armament consisted of three cannon. Two ninepounders were mounted on carriages in the waist. A 12-pounder in the bow was mounted on fixed skids. It could be aimed only by turning the whole ship. Nine gundalows were built at Skenesborough, and eight of them saw action at the Battle of Valcour Island.

Galleys were much larger than gundalows—80 feet long and 20 feet broad—and carried crews of 80 to 100 men. With round bottoms and two masts, both lateen rigged, they were considerably better sailers and gundalows, but, like almost all inland sailing craft, they could also be moved with sweeps. A galley mounted 10 or 12 guns, but none of them bigger than an 18-pounder. They also drew six-and-a-half feet of water, nearly as much as the schooner *Royal Savage*. Skene's yard turned out four galleys, three of which, the *Washington*, the *Trumbull* and the *Congress*, served at Valcour Island.

The decision to build such vessels was not, as Kenneth Roberts would have it in *Rabble in Arms*, a brilliant improvisation by Benedict Arnold based on his Mediterranean experience, but rather a fairly standard approach, well within Philip Schuyler's limited imagination. There was plenty of precedent all over America, including the gundalow *Loyal Convert*, built by the American invaders in 1775, captured in the St. Lawrence by General Carleton in 1776, and shortly to see duty on the other side. As for row galleys, they had been used for harbor defense during the French and Indian War, and the American ports quickly turned to them again in the Revolution.

The wood that went into these vessels was cut from the forests of the Champlain valley and, still green, turned into ship timbers and planking. Vessels made from green wood do not last long, but longevity had the lowest possible priority in 1776. Wood alone, however, would not make a warship. Tons of materiel—nails, cordage, fittings, cannon, and a thousand other things—had to be boated, portaged, and manhandled from the Tidewater to Lake Champlain. Philip Schuyler's personal secretary, Captain Richard Varick, was adept at finding and securing such necessities. His letters in the *Naval Documents of the American Revolution* show that he is one of the unsung heroes of the American naval building race on Lake Champlain.

Even harder to find were shipwrights and carpenters who were skilled enough to build a navy. Such artisans already had plenty of lucrative work right at home in Portsmouth, Boston, New London, or Newport, building privateers and Continental Navy ships. Congress responded with the best incentive of all. Any shipwright who would go to Champlain would receive roughly 35 dollars per month—and be paid a month in advance. They all got one-and-a-half rations per day, including a half-pint of rum. Pay started as soon as they left home, and they received a day's pay for every 20 miles they traveled. Of all the officers and men in the Continental Navy, only Commodore Esek Hopkins was paid as much as a workman recruited for the erstwhile Skene's boatyard. Soon artisans from as far away as Philadelphia were headed for Skenesborough.

Finally, there was the problem of who would man this little navy. Benedict Arnold canvassed the whole northern army to find experienced seamen, but he got only 70 skilled volunteers, too few to man even one of the galleys. There were many more in the army, since most New England men were at least part-time sailors, but they did not come forward. The problem was that they were *too* knowledgable. They knew a fort would stand a great deal more punishment than a ship, and they also knew that the Royal Navy Jack Tars building and manning their own

freshwater navy were very good. There is a point at which patriotism and the thirst for glory and adventure give way to common sense. Attempts to recruit sailors from the seaports were even less successful, because of the lure of the privateers, with their promise of prize money. Lake Champlain offered no rich, vulnerable British merchant vessels. General Washington, fighting for his life, could spare no one from the main Continental Army. Thus it was that the Lake Champlain navy was manned mostly by the greenest sort of landsmen, and there was neither time, powder, nor an experienced cadre to turn them into anything else before they would go into battle.

Benedict Arnold received his second command of the Lake Champlain navy very late— far too late even to consider building a real fighting vessel, such as a frigate, which could have delayed the British advance indefinitely. On July 7, Schuyler and Gates left off feuding long enough to call a Council of War at Crown Point. They decided that Crown Point was indefensible and must be abandoned as soon as the British threatened it, leaving only a few little vessels to stand between the British army and the wretched, demoralized colonials in Fort Ticonderoga. The council resolved to beef up the water defenses by building more "Gundolas, Row Gallies [and] Armed Batteaus." Arnold paraded his knowledge of things maritime, and Gates urged that he be put in charge of the nascent navy. At that point, only a few vessels had been produced by Skene's boatyard under the lax supervision of Commodore Wynkoop, and those were neither rigged nor armed.

In spite of the urgency, Arnold did not leap immediately into the business of building a navy. Arnold's sponsor, Horatio Gates, quarreled with the theater commander, Philip Schuyler. Gates's authority was at best undefined, and he could not simply order a reform administration for the boatyard. But Gates did urge Arnold to come to Ticonderoga to see of he could do something about the vessels waiting to be rigged. It was almost two weeks before Arnold, as it is said, "blew into Ticonderoga like a gale," and he tarried there only long enough to stir up the men charged with putting the new vessels into fighting shape. Then he went on to Skenesborough, arriving on July 23. After giving directions on how he wanted more vessels—particularly galleys—built, Arnold rushed back to Ticonderoga.

Across the lake in Vermont, an outpost at Mount Independence stood on a bluff that rose straight up from the water. Arnold saw in this a natural dockyard, and from this bluff masts were lowered into the waiting gundalows and galleys. Arnold attended to everything imaginable—stepping masts, ballasting, rigging, placing guns, seeing to it that each vessel had a firebox and cooking and eating utensils, and many other tiny details. He searched diligently—though not very successfully—for experienced sailors. By early August, the three sailing vessels acquired in 1775 and four gundalows constructed in Skene's hot, swampy, mosquito-infested boatyard had all their gear. Arnold sent them and their green crews to Crown Point as an advance guard. By then, the Skenesborough yard, under the immediate command of Colonel Hermanus Schuyler (another unsung hero), had more vessels for Arnold to outfit.

On August 7, while General Schuyler was in Albany, General Gates ordered Brigadier General Arnold to go down to Crown Point and take command of all the American vessels on the lake. Jacobus Wynkoop, however, who had been appointed commodore by Philip Schuyler and the New York Provincial Congress, was damned if he would take orders from a mere brigade commander, especially on the say-so of that upstart Gates. On August 17, only two days after he returned to Crown Point, Arnold ordered two schooners to cover some workmen cutting wood for oars on a shore threatened by Carleton's Indian allies. Wynkoop, aboard the *Royal Savage*, fired a shot across their bows. After they came to, Wynkoop demanded to know under whose orders they were sailing. "General Arnold" was not, by Wynkoop's lights, an acceptable answer. Arnold complained to Gates, who angrily relieved Wynkoop of his command, ordered his arrest, and asked Schuyler to cashier him. Schuyler instead gave Wynkoop a shore job at Ticonderoga. Now Benedict Arnold was undisputed commander of the American vessels on Lake Champlain.

By August 24, Arnold's fleet at Crown Point had the schooners *Royal Savage* and *Revenge*, the sloop *Enterprise*, and the seven gundalows *Boston*, *New Haven*, *Providence*, *New York*, *Connecticut*, *Spitfire*, and *Philadelphia* (the Schooner *Liberty* was on the lake but not at Crown Point).

Arnold took these 10 vessels to the northern end of the lake and all the way to the Richelieu River, deep in enemy territory. On September 6, they were joined by the galley *Lee* and the gundalow *Jersey*. The sound of entrenching tools tipped Arnold off that the British were setting up an artillery battery, so on September 7 he prudently moved his fleet back to Isle la Motte. There he drilled his green crews, but he did not have enough powder to give them gunnery practice.

On September 23 Arnold finally moved his ships to the place where they would make their stand—Valcour Island, on the western side of the lake just below where Plattsburgh, New York, is today. There he received the remainder of the vessels built at Skenesborough—the galleys *Trumbull*, *Washington*, and *Congress*, each armed with an 18-pounder, a 12, 2 nines, and 6 sixes. (Arnold planned to arm the galleys with 8 24's and eight 18's, but he had to make do with what he was sent.)

Arnold positioned his ships near the south end of the channel, where they were protected on the left by the bluffs of Valcour Island, on the right by the New York shore, and in the rear by shallows that kept the big British vessels from attacking from the north. Unless a rare south wind came along, the British would have to tack their way into position under fire from anchored, stable guns. Drawn up in crescent-shaped battle array and resplendent in red barn paint, the American fleet now consisted of 15 vessels—two schooners, a sloop, four galleys, and eight gundalows. Manned by 800 men, their combined "weight of metal," that is, the weight of the cannon balls if all fired at once, was 703 pounds.

By contrast, the British fleet, commanded by Lieutenant Thomas Pringle, could throw over 1,300 pounds of metal. More important, Pringle's vessels were big enough to withstand a lot of punishment from cannonballs that weighed no more than 18 pounds—and Arnold's ships had only three cannon that large and only 12 12-pounders. Pringle's two largest ships, the *Inflexible* and the *Thunderer*, alone carried 6 24's and 24 12's. His smaller vessels by themselves would have been nearly a match in metal for the American fleet—and they were served by veterans of the Royal Navy.

The story of building the British Champlain navy is in its way as incredible as that of the American story. Granted that the British had unlimited supplies, shipwrights, and sailors, they were all on the wrong side of 12 miles of rapids.

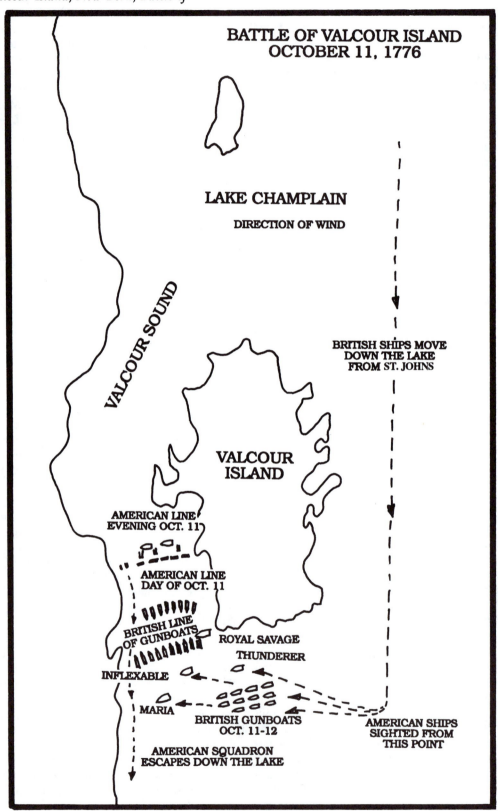

BATTLE OF VALCOUR ISLAND
OCTOBER 11, 1776

LAKE CHAMPLAIN

DIRECTION OF WIND

VALCOUR SOUND

BRITISH SHIPS MOVE
DOWN THE LAKE
FROM ST. JOHNS

VALCOUR
ISLAND

AMERICAN LINE
EVENING OCT. 11

AMERICAN LINE
DAY OF OCT. 11

BRITISH LINE
OF GUNBOATS

ROYAL SAVAGE

THUNDERER

INFLEXABLE

MARIA

BRITISH GUNBOATS
OCT. 11-12

AMERICAN SHIPS
SIGHTED FROM
THIS POINT

AMERICAN SQUADRON
ESCAPES DOWN THE LAKE

In less than 90 days they put together a fleet of 20 gunboats and 5 big sailing vessels. All but one had to be at least partially dissembled and their skeletons dragged on rollers over 12 miles of muddy road. The biggest of them, the 180-ton ship the *Inflexible*, got to St. Johns on September 7 and was assembled and in the water on October 4. The radeau *Thunderer*, at 423 tons by far the biggest ship Lake Champlain had ever seen, was entirely constructed at St. Johns. Essentially an enormous gundalow, *Thunderer*'s six 24's, six 12's, and two howitzers threw as much metal as all eight of Arnold's gundalows combined.

The British government's plan was conceived quite early, well before the American troops had been expelled from Canada. A Royal Navy squadron under Captain Charles Douglas was sent to the St. Lawrence in early April. It carried with it knocked-down gunboats, which were to be assembled at St. Johns. Once Lake Champlain was secured, two British armies were to seize the Champlain-Hudson line and cut New England off from the rest of the rebellious colonies. Douglas was one of the brightest stars in the Royal Navy, and he had under his command the brilliant naval engineer John Schank; midshipman Edward Pellew, whose long record of almost unbelievable heroics began at Valcour; and a host of other seasoned mariners. Douglas knew he could not seize control of the lake with the gunboats. Even the three little sailing ships the Americans had could make short work of them. Douglas did what he had to do. He built a fleet whose victory was assured, and he did it in record time.

The battle itself was an anticlimax. Douglas's subordinate, Lieutenant Thomas Pringle, did a thoroughly professional job in the Battle of Valcour Island. Beating against a north wind, Pringle's ships positioned themselves at the south end of the channel and pounded Arnold's vessels for six hours. Only one British vessel, the *Carleton* came under heavy fire, and she was saved by midshipman Pellew's heroics. The Americans lost both the *Royal Savage* and the *Philadelphia*, three others were heavily damaged (they were abandoned the next day), and they had used up three-quarters of their ammunition. They were in no condition to continue the fight. During the night, Arnold and his remaining 13 vessels managed to slip past the British and flee toward Ticonderoga, but at dawn the wind shifted to the south. Bending to their sweeps, the weary rebels kept ahead of the pursuing British for 24 hours, but then the wind shifted back to the northeast. The galley *Washington* struck to the enemy, while Arnold, under fire from six enemy ships, ran the *Congress* aground in Button Mold Bay, on the Vermont shore, where he set her and four gundalows afire. Arnold and the remnants of his men got to Crown Point on foot, just ahead of pursuing Indians.

The naval battle of Lake Champlain was a complete victory for the British. Its outcome could never have been in doubt and the Americans might simply have conceded to the British, as a chess player resigns a hopeless game, without changing history. But by mid-October it was too late for Sir Guy Carleton to start his army down the Champlain-Hudson line. The British cannot be faulted for the delay. They could hardly have brought Arnold's fleet to battle much sooner than October 11. But by then the first American navy had already bought a year, and that made all the difference. The Americans used the respite well, so that General John Burgoyne found himself trapped at Saratoga in October 1777. It was the building, not the fighting, of America's Champlain navy that changed history. In a very real sense, American independence was forged in Major Skene's boatyard.

Neil R. Stout

REFERENCES

John A. Barton, "The Battle of Valcour Island," *History Today*, 9 (1959):791–797; William Bell Clark, et al., *Naval Documents of the American Revolution*, 6 vols. (1964–), 1, 5, 6; William M. Fowler, Jr., *Rebels Under Sail: The American Navy during the Revolution* (1976); Philip K. Lundberg, *The Continental Gunboat Philadelphia and the Northern Campaign of 1776* (1966); John F. Miller, *American Ships of the Colonial and Revolutionary Periods* (1978).

Valley Forge, Pennsylvania, Encampment of (December 1777–June 19, 1778)

Valley Forge rests in the consciousness of every American as a symbol of suffering and trial for soldiers faithful to the cause of freedom in the Revolutionary War. This view of Valley Forge developed through the efforts of historians in the nineteenth century and has been perpetuated by teachers in the American classrooms ever since. What was Valley Forge? What part did it play in the War of Revolution?

Valley Forge was a cantonment or winter encampment of Washington's American army during the winter of 1777–1778. During the eighteenth century, the poor quality of the roads, along with the freezing of the waterways, inhibited the transport of the provisions and equipment from place to place. Without such support, an army could not conduct a full campaign in the field. It would literally starve long before any such action could take place. It was the custom for armies to go into winter encampment and to await the coming of the thaw and a new spring–summer season of campaigning.

However, there was some fighting during such encampment periods. In the winter of 1777–1778 there were constant skirmishes between detachments from both British and American armies in the no-man's land between Valley Forge and Philadelphia. Actions took place at such sites as Darby, Quintin's, and Hancock's bridges, the Crooked Billet Tavern, Marple, and Barren Hill, among others.

At the conclusion of the Pennsylvania campaign of 1777, the main British army under the command of General Sir William Howe had defeated Washington's American force in battle at Brandywine Creek and then outmaneuvered him and captured Philadelphia on September 26. Washington struck back against the British at Germantown in early October, but the attack fell short of accomplishing Washington's goals. There followed a period of stalemate lasting for several weeks, and finally it was necessary to go into winter camp.

Seven of Washington's generals recommended Reading as a camp, while five others suggested Wilmington, Delaware. Generals Anthony Wayne and John Peter Muhlenburg felt that Valley Forge was the most suitable campground. Located some 20 miles from Philadelphia and the British camp, it gave Washington enough room to maneuver, a fair defensive position against possible attack, and a placement to stop British moves against any American supply bases. It also provided cover for the towns of Lancaster and York, where the state government and the Continental Congress, respectively, had moved in the evacuation of Philadelphia. Reading and Wilmington were thought unsuitable for a number of reasons.

In a driving wind with snow falling, the American army broke camp at Gulph Mills on December 19, 1777, and began a six-mile march to the new campground in the fields surrounding Valley Forge. Such was their condition that the army moved one mile per hour, and the march consumed most of the day. Washington and his staff stopped at the King of Prussia Tavern for dinner while his army rested outside. At 4 P.M. the men resumed the march over the last three miles to camp. That night the men made fires and huddled around them. For once, no night guard was posted. Few had tents or shelter of any kind. It was a low point in a dismal season.

Washington's chief engineer, General Louis Duportail, a French officer, drew up a plan that placed Washington's best troops on a front line running on a soft ridge facing the enemy in the direction of Philadelphia. Then a second line, running behind the first and based on the hill known as Mount Joy, provided cover if an attack broke the first line. If there were a British attack and it succeeded, then Washington's army could retreat in either of two directions. They could cross a bridge that would be built at Fatland Ford across the Schuylkill River in the left rear of the second line, or they could cross Valley Creek and follow what is today Route 23 toward today's Phoenixville, Pennsylvania. The troops were to dig entrenchments and redoubts along both lines and were to construct their cabins in long lines along a street behind whichever line they were attached to defend. In any event, much of Duportail's plan was not followed, and the defensive positions remained unfinished in the spring. But the effort was made, in any case. It should also be noted that Duportail's plan was the "modern" type, which allowed for a series of interlocking works to be dug, thus supporting each other, rather than having just one major fortification constructed.

For most, Valley Forge is a place associated with great suffering in a terrible winter of snow and ice. In fact, there was great suffering. Thousands of soldiers became diseased, and many died. No one knows just how many, although estimates run as high as 2,000 or more. The troops were poorly clothed and had little food. Minor mutinies were constantly quelled, handled promptly by Washington's officers. The important point is to realize that much of this suffering could have been avoided.

It should be noted that the winter of 1777–1778 was not a particularly severe one. There were several snowstorms during the encampment period, six major ones of which we have records. The usual snowfall was measured at 4 inches, although 12 inches fell on January 11–12. According to many historians, this winter was one of the mildest of the century. It must be noted that records of weather are far from complete for this period of history. The winter was a typical Philadelphia one, with some snow, some clear and cold days, thaws spaced in between, and a regular fall of rain throughout the winter. The winter two years later, when the army was encamped at Morristown, New Jersey, was judged to be the worst of the century with over 20 major storms and drifts of a foot or more of snow. During that encampment, the records show only 83 deaths for the winter. What factors account for this difference in casualty rates in these two cantonments?

Washington's officers and men had learned the lessons of cantonment living. At Valley Forge we see for the first time in the war a large number of men camping in one place for several months. Never before had this happened, and Washington's officers and staff had never dealt with so many for so long in a difficult season before. Approximately 9,000 men had to be sheltered, fed, and clothed for six months. The logistical system at that time could not handle such a mass of men.

The weather, then, cannot be blamed for the deaths at Valley Forge, although standing without shoes and wrapped in a blanket without proper diet is not pleasant in any season, let alone during winter. The blame rests on two areas. First, the Quartermaster Department had completely broken down. General Thomas Mifflin had served as quartermaster general until November 1777, and then he resigned. He proved to be a poor administrator, and his resignation had only compounded the problems left to his assistants. The transport system failed. Wagons were not organized to bring food and clothing into the camp. Drivers and wagoners were not hired. The entire department was in a state of confusion. Along with the usual difficulty that Congress had in gaining the states' cooperation in supplying their men with clothing and equipment, there was no efficient means to transport goods to the army.

Another major problem lay with the officer corps. Inexperienced and unable to discipline their troops, the officers allowed certain practices to exist that guaranteed the suffering of the men. When the army first arrived at Valley Forge, it was cold and snowing. It made common sense to shelter the men as quickly as possible. The officers had been given orders directly from Washington to build cabins at certain dimensions, with proper fireplaces, doors, windows, roofs, and so forth added on. But it was cold, and the men could not be concerned with such details, so the huts went up any which way the men desired.

The commonwealth of Pennsylvania built ample cabins several decades ago that many tourists today assume represent the way the huts looked. The problem is that the state officials followed Washington's orders and built the huts 14 feet by 14 feet with proper roofs, fireplaces, and doors. Archaeology in recent years has shown a different story. Very few of the over 800 huts were constructed according to Washington's plans. They were dug into the earth. Their roofs were covered with sod. There were improperly constructed fireplaces stuck at any angle. Doors and windows were often missing. The officers did not maintain the discipline necessary to insure that their men would be hutted properly. The result was widespread sickness, due to a lack of supply and complicated by poor housing. At Morris-town, two years later, the orders were enforced by the officer corps and fewer deaths and less sickness resulted.

Today's visitors would surely be shocked to see the real Valley Forge of 1778. The soldiers did not take proper care of the latrines, or faults, as they were then called. Men seemed to relieve themselves at will, even though strict punishment for such action was threatened. Garbage and trash were thrown about the camp and living areas of the troops. The smell was terrible. Dead horses remained unburied. Offal covered the ground behind and between the cabins. The provisions that did arrive were usually spoiled or of poor quality from the start. The conditions were truly inhuman.

Washington's first concern was to shelter his men. He remained in his tents until the men were generally housed, and then he moved into the Potts House that he rented from the widow Deborah Hewes. The Potts home remained the headquarters for Washington at Valley Forge. Once the men were housed, in whatever condition, then Washington turned to the Quartermaster's Department. Working with a congressional committee, he eventually persuaded General Nathanael Greene, his best general, to assume the position of quartermaster general, which he did on March 2.

Greene, and later Anthony Wayne, led major foraging expeditions into the countryside to gather food and supplies for the army. These operations were successful. Wayne brought in so many cattle from the Jersies that he became know as "Drover" Wayne to the enemy. Greene had exceptional organization skills and a good eye for detail. With his assistants, Charles Pettit and John Cox, he was soon able to bring order out of chaos in his department, and the army began to receive supplies in such quantities that the spring saw an entirely different American army at Valley Forge.

Hospitals were established at Allentown, Bethlehem, Ephrata, Easton, Lancaster, Lititz, Princeton, Warwick, and Yellow Springs. The sick were initially treated at camp hospitals, and the more severe cases were removed to one of the main sites mentioned above. This may explain why archaeological investigations as yet have been unable to find any large numbers of bodies buried in the park grounds. Those who did die may very well have died out of camp. Those who did die in camp may have been buried secretly to keep the burials hidden from the enemy spies who moved through the camp.

Gradually things improved at Valley Forge. Martha Washington arrived at her husband's headquarters on February 10, and many of the other generals' wives also came to camp. The social life soon picked up. Congress sent a committee to visit the army at Valley Forge and worked with Washington for several months to assist in rectifying the problems faced by the soldiers in the areas of food, clothing, pay, recruiting, and training. They also had to deal with the officers' disputes over rank and seniority that remained a constant problem for Washington and resulted in many officers resigning their commissions.

When Americans think of the significance of Valley Forge today, they should not place the emphasis on the suffering and problems, severe as they were. Instead, they should realize that Valley Forge's real contribution to the American Revolution lay in the creation of the American army. On the fields of Valley Forge, the American army was formed and organized for the first time into an efficient and professional fighting force. The credit rests with many indi-

viduals, but the Baron Friedrich von Steuben played the central role in this accomplishment.

Arriving at camp on February 23, the newly appointed inspector general (replacing the resigned general Thomas Conway) covered the entire camp and began making the changes necessary to keep a professional army in the field. The first problem was that the army could not move or fight properly. Each regiment, each officer, had individual drills and systems of movement on the field of battle. Von Steuben changed all that. He took the Prussian drill and simplified it. On March 18, he took 120 men selected from the entire army and began teaching them his new drill in two sessions a day. Von Steuben himself took the musket in hand to demonstrate his drill, something new for American officers, who had copied the English tradition of leaving such matters for the noncommissioned officers. Von Steuben believed that an officer should know his men and be a model for them and that he should know the drill well enough to teach the men.

Since he spoke little English at this point, he used the help of American officers who spoke French and who translated his commands into English. He insisted that the entire army follow his 10-command drill, and the original 120 men, once taught, went out into the rest of the army to drill others so that the American army came together for the first time as an ordered and unified professional body, ready to face any other European trained force. Fighting in line, moving in compact bodies with enough firepower to break an enemy line, the American army would soon earn the respect of the enemy.

These, then, were the two results of Valley Forge for the War of Revolution. The Quartermaster Department was put on a firm foundation and organized to service the army. There would continue to be shortages and problems. That was natural. But there would be nor further breakdowns in the system, and for the rest of the war, Washington could count on his quartermaster to keep the army supplied, and General von Steuben brought his system of drill to the Americans so that there was a uniformity and professionalism to the army that it had lacked when it marched to Valley Forge in December 1777.

Of course, there were many events that occurred at Valley Forge that can only be mentioned. There was the famous Conway Cabal in which General Conway opened correspondence with General Horatio Gates, the hero of Saratoga and victor over John Burgoyne, with the idea, perhaps, of replacing Washington with Gates as commander-in-chief. Nothing ever came of it. Congress supported Washington, and Gates claimed he never had any intentions of seeking such a position. For awhile, it was the talk of the camp, and Conway became an outcast. In the end, he resigned as inspector general, was challenged to a duel, and was wounded in the face; he then returned to Europe.

On January 5, the famous "battle of the kegs" was fought by the British. Some Americans supposedly placed gunpowder in kegs and let them float down the Delaware River toward the British fleet. The British let loose with everything they had against these "kegs" for the better part of an entire day. No damage was done to any British ship, but great quantities of powder and shot were expended.

There was a constant battle between Washington's troops, under the command of men like Allen McLane, Dan Morgan, and General Israel Potter, and the residents of Pennsylvania, who insisted on bringing food and other goods into Philadelphia to sell to the British for hard currency.

On March 17, the German troops of the Pennsylvania Line erected a paddy to insult the Irish troops of the same line. The Irish Pennsylvanians were led to believe that the Massachusetts Yankees had done this perfidious act, and a brawl almost broke out. Washington himself stepped in to settle the matter and issued grog for all.

On April 23, 1778, General Charles Lee, second in command of the American forces, arrived at the King of Prussia Tavern to be greeted by Washington and his staff and general officers. Lee had recently been exchanged for a British general and was hailed gladly by all. Little did they realize the change in Lee that would cause confusion at the Battle of Monmouth and a resulting court-martial that would end Lee's military service to this country.

The soldiers celebrated May Day by erecting maypoles and drinking to the health of King Tammany, the famous Lenni-Lenape chief who was supposedly buried near Valley Forge. The officers held a dance that night to the same purpose.

That spring at Valley Forge, Congress passed a requirement that all general officers take an oath of loyalty to the United States and Congress. All did, including Benedict Arnold, who arrived in camp in April still limping on a cane from the wound he received in the Battle of Saratoga. British peace commissioners arrived in Philadelphia from London, offering to settle the rebellion by accepting many of the American complaints as long as the Americans returned to their former loyalty, the King and Parliament. No agreement could be reached.

But the spring also brought a cleaned-up camp at Valley Forge. The defensive positions as drawn up by Du Portail were as complete as they ever would be. The Americans wore better clothing, and food flowed in daily. Conditions improved with each day. The soldiers not only looked better, but they now had the drill and discipline to perform better in battle.

On Wednesday, May 6, a clear an sunny day, the newly trained American line demonstrated their improved drill and military ability by performing a grand parade and *feu de joie* in great order and discipline, much to the delight of Washington and his officers, in celebration of the French alliance. Word had reached camp just a few days before that the French had openly come out in alliance with the Americans. Hopes were running higher than ever before in the war. Washington ordered a grand parade to honor the French and display the effects that von Steuben had had on the army. Both goals were accomplished and more.

It was this alliance of the French and the Americans that caused the American departure from Valley Forge on June 19, 1778. General Sir William Howe had resigned his position as commander of British forces and had returned to London to defend his conduct in the war. His place was taken by General Henry Clinton, who had arrived in Philadelphia from New York, the main British garrison in North America. Hearing of the alliance, Clinton, realizing the peace commission was not successful and fearing the French fleet might block the entire British force in Philadelphia, decided to evacuate the rebel capital and return to New York.

Clinton and his army marched overland from Philadelphia through the Jersies to New York while the fleet took Loyalists, the sick, and much of the camp baggage and equipment back by sea.

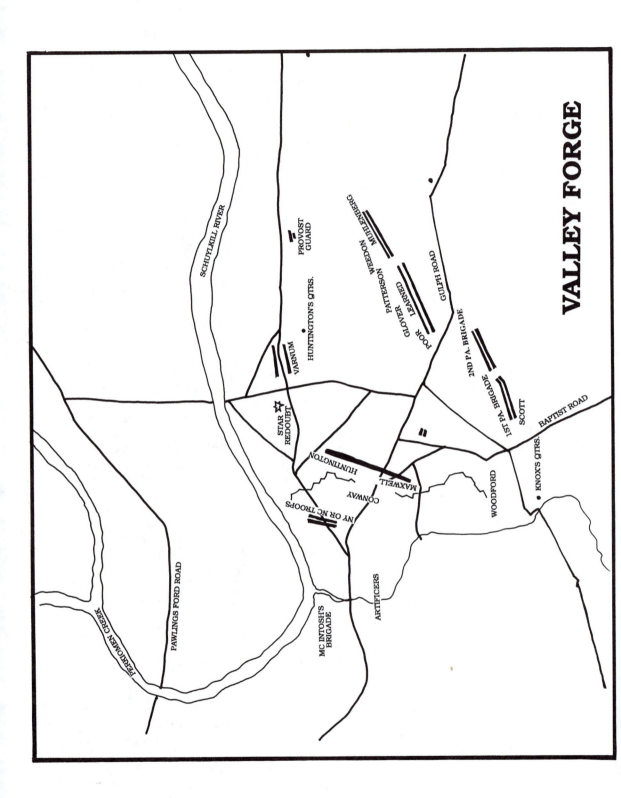

VALLEY FORGE

SCHUYLKILL RIVER

PROVOST GUARD

HUNTINGTON'S QTRS.

VARNUM

STAR REDOUBT

MUHLENBERG

WEEDON

PATTERSON

GLOVER

LEARNED

POOR

GULPH ROAD

2ND PA. BRIGADE

1ST PA. BRIGADE

SCOTT

BAPTIST ROAD

KNOX'S QTRS.

WOODFORD

MAXWELL

CONWAY

HUNTINGTON

VY OR NC TROOPS

ARTIFICERS

MC INTOSH'S BRIGADE

PAWLINGS FORD ROAD

PERKIOMEN CREEK

As soon as the British had left the city, American troops entered, and Washington put his army into motion to follow the British and try to catch them in marching order somewhere in New Jersey. By June 20, the campground was vacant, and Valley Forge became part of American history. It was a professional and better-clad body of men who left the Valley Forge encampment that June to face another five years of war. But the main American army had already faced its last major defeat. Never again would it lose on the field of battle. The British realized and came to accept eventually the quality and strength of this new army, forged and hardened during that terrible winter of trial. Much still lay ahead, and hardships would continue, but the American army now possessed a confidence they would never quite lose. Such was the legacy of Valley Forge.

Paul J. Sanborn

REFERENCES

Edward S. Gifford, Jr., *The American Revolution in the Delaware Valley* (1976); John F. Reed, *Valley Forge: Crucible of Victory* (1969); John T. Stoudt, *Ordeal at Valley Forge* (1963).

Vaughan, Sir John
(c. 1731–1795)

British army officer. Best remembered today as the British general who captured Fort Clinton in October 1777, Sir John Vaughan also figured prominently in several other Revolutionary War campaigns and, most importantly, was involved in the seizure of the Dutch Island of St. Eustatius in 1781.

Although the exact date of Vaughan's birth is uncertain, the year 1731 seems most likely, considering his military commissions. Vaughan was the second surviving son of Wilmot Vaughan, an Irish Peer (3rd Viscount Lisburne) and Lord Lieutenant of Cardigan, and Elizabeth Watson, eldest daughter of Thomas Watson of Berwick-on-Tweed. Vaughan entered the army at a young age, and, as is typical for many British officers of the period, little is known about his early life, except a list of his military commissions. He started his military career in 1746 as an ensign in Colonel Pawlett's 9th Regiment of Marines (the old 52nd Regiment of Foot), but two years later (April 9, 1748) he transferred to the 10th Dragoons as a cornet. Remaining in the 10th

Dragoons, Vaughan was commissioned a captain lieutenant on January 5, 1754, and a year later (January 38, 1755) was promoted to full captain. Vaughan's service had been restricted to the British Isles, but with the outbreak of the Seven Years' War the 10th Dragoons were ordered to Hanover, arriving in Germany in August 1758.

Vaughan left the 10th Dragoons on October 15, 1759, when he received a majority to raise a new regiment of light infantry, the 94th Light Armed Foot (the Royal Welsh Volunteers), intended for service in America. On January 12, 1760, Vaughan was named its lieutenant colonel commandant and, when the formation of the regiment was complete, its captain commandant (June 12, 1760). With the regiment, he proceeded overseas. Vaughan's first sojourn in North America ended after the fall of New France, when he and the 94th Foot were redeployed to the West Indies. Vaughan was part of the force under Brigadier General Robert Moncton and Admiral Sir George Rodney, which captured Martinique from the French in February 1762. Rodney was a naval officer with whom Vaughan would have extensive dealings in the future. Vaughan led the grenadier division, with distinction, and was favorably mentioned in Moncton's dispatches. On November 25, 1762, he was promoted lieutenant colonel of the 46th Regiment of Foot, and the 94th Light Armed Foot was disbanded shortly afterward. Vaughan and the 46th Foot remained in North America until 1767, when the regiment sailed to Ireland and he returned home to England.

Vaughan continued to be promoted during the period between the wars. He was commissioned a colonel in the army, May 25th, 1772, and colonel of the 46th Foot in 1775. Vaughan also began a political career, and he was elected to the House of Commons for Berwick-on-Tweed in 1774, holding the seat until his death. He sat in the Irish Parliament for Johnston from 1776 to 1783.

Vaughan resumed his active military service with the start of war with the American colonies. He sailed from Cork, Ireland, with Lord Charles Cornwallis and a convoy of reinforcements, in February 1776, having been promoted to the rank of local brigadier general in America on January 1. Sir Henry Clinton met the fleet at Cape Fear, North Carolina, and the whole force, now under his command, arrived on June 1, off

Charleston, South Carolina. Vaughan was to have commanded the two battalions that were landed to act in concert with Admiral Sir Peter Parker's naval bombardment of Fort Sullivan. Because of unfordable tidal shoals, the land attack never materialized. With the failure of the siege of Charleston, Clinton withdrew his forces and joined Sir William Howe's expedition to New York. Vaughan fought in the Battle of Long Island, where, under Clinton, he commanded the grenadiers of the right flank, who pushed their attack beyond the American fortified position of the "Brooklyn Lines." These forces were on the verge of a major triumph when they were ordered back by Howe. In Howe's battle against Washington at White Plains, Vaughan was wounded in the thigh. He returned disabled to England in the fall of 1776.

Vaughan was again in America for the campaign of 1777. He joined the garrison of New York City and was promoted to major general on the regular establishment of the army on August 29, 1777. Vaughan had a small role in Clinton's raid into New Jersey in mid-September, a foray that brought badly needed horses, sheep, and cattle into the garrison. After the departure of Howe for Pennsylvania, Clinton had been left in command of New York. In October he decided to conduct a raid on a much larger scale into the Hudson Highlands in support of Lieutenant General John Burgoyne's expedition, which was floundering north of Albany. Sailing up the Hudson River with approximately 3,500 men, Clinton descended on his two objectives, Forts Clinton and Montgomery. As Clinton's second in command, Vaughan led the main body of 1,200 British and Germans, who captured Fort Clinton. According to several secondary sources, on October 9 Clinton declared: "Fort Montgomery is henceforth to be distinguished by the name of Fort Vaughan in memory of the noble perseverance which Major-general Vaughan showed in the assault of it." It is unclear which of the two forts was renamed, as it was Lieutenant Colonel Mungo Campbell's column that captured Fort Montgomery, but on October 26th, Vaughan wrote two letters to Clinton from a fort he called "Vaughan.")

Vaughan's horse was killed beneath him as he dismounted to lead his soldiers forward on foot. Vaughan and 1,600 troops were sent by Clinton, with Commodore Sir James Wallace,

to continue the raid farther up the Hudson; Clinton gave Vaughan "orders to feel his way to General Burgoyne and do his utmost to assist his operations or even join him if required." On October 16 Vaughan and Wallace burnt Aesopus (presently Kingston, New York), which Vaughan called "a Nursery for almost every villain in the Country." For this act he was stigmatized with the sobriquet "General Aesopus" by the Patriots. Burning and destroying farms along the way, the expedition reached as far as Livingston Manor, within 46 miles of Albany, before Wallace's larger ships were halted by contrary winds and shallow water. The force was officially recalled on October 22 by Clinton, and after collecting the British garrisons along the river, Vaughan and Wallace returned to New York City.

Vaughan was part of Clinton's second expedition up the Hudson River that left King's Bridge in late May 1779. Its objectives were the American fortifications at Stony Point, five miles south of Forts Clinton and Montgomery. On June 1 as the main British force landed and advanced toward the works on the west bank, Vaughan landed on the east bank, eight miles below Verplanck's Point. Vaughan coordinated his assault on Fort Lafayette with the attack on Stony Point. In the latter stages of the attack, Vaughan was supported by British fire from captured Stony Point. Like Clinton's first foray to the Highlands, the operation was a great tactical success that yielded little; Stony Point was to be recaptured by Brigadier General Anthony Wayne the next month.

Vaughan left New York for the last time in December 1779. In the same month he was made land forces commander in the British "Leeward and Charibe Islands" (part of the Lesser Antilles), no doubt aided by his half-brother Wilmot Vaughan, now 4th Viscount Lisburne and a member of the Admiralty Board. It was an appointment that he had first been considered for in 1778, but at the time he professed no interest in the appointment, complaining of ill health. Vaughan was technically to hold the appointment for the rest of his life. He sailed from England with Rodney and two regiments intended as reinforcements and reached Barbados on February 11, 1780. Vaughan then proceeded to St. Lucia to oversee the scattered British garrisons, having orders to strike a blow at the French and

Spanish possessions in the West Indies. Vaughan's first taste of the war in the Caribbean came when, on March 23, Admiral Louis-Urbain du Bouexic, Count de Guichen, arrived from Martinique with 22 ships of the line. De Guichen intended to test St. Lucia's defenses, but he found Vaughan's fortifications too strong, and in the face of Admiral Sir Hyde Parker's 16 ships and Rodney's imminent arrival, the French admiral withdrew.

Vaughan first initiated offensive action against the French when Rodney returned from Barbados on December 6, after he had chased de Guichen back to Europe. Rodney reported that the hurricane, which had swept through the Caribbean in October and done great damage to the area, had devastated the defenses of French-held St. Vincent. On December 14 Rodney and Vaughan sailed from St. Louis and upon reaching their target, they put troops ashore. Vaughan personally investigated the fortifications and found the reports of damage greatly exaggerated. After only a day the troops were reembarked,and the expedition returned ignominiously to Gros Inlat Bay, St. Lucia.

On January 27, 1781, Rodney, stationed off Barbados, learned that Britain had declared war on the United Provinces the month before. He received orders to take the Dutch island of St. Eustatius, a geographically small and barren piece of rock. St. Eustatius was a hub of the West Indies trade not only for the Dutch, but also for American, French, and even British merchants, and it had been involved since the start of the Revolution in a lively trade of contraband goods with the American rebels. St. Eustatius was used as a shipping point for powder, arms, cordage, clothing, sugar, tobacco, coffee, cotton, and other goods, originating from many points, which were transported to the rebellious colonies. This flow of war materiel was especially important to the Americans in the first years of the revolt.

Rodney and Vaughan set to their task with relish, and taking 2,500 to 3,000 troops, surrounded the island on February 3, calling on the garrison to surrender. The totally unprepared Dutch governor, Johannes de Graaf, who did not even know his nation was at war, immediately complied and capitulated with his 50 soldiers. A group of 2,000 American sailors and merchants retreated into the interior of the island and attempted to resist, but they were hunted down and starved into submission by Vaughan's troops. The other enemy islands in the area, St. Martin, Saba, and the French island of St. Bartholomew, also quickly surrendered to Rodney. In March the British also took the Dutch colonies on the South America mainland.

The taking of St. Eustatius resulted in one of the largest hauls ever taken by the British in the West Indies, estimated to have been as high as three million pounds sterling, an astronomical sum for the time. Captured material included tons of goods piled in warehouses or in barrels on the beach, 130 or more merchant vessels, a Dutch frigate, and five other military warships. Not satisfied with this booty, Rodney instantly pursued and took a convoy of 27 merchant ships and a 60-gun ship of the line, which was 36 hours out of St. Eustatius. For several weeks the British left flying the flag of Holland to lure in 50 unsuspecting Dutch, French, and American vessels. Rodney and Vaughan seized everything of value on the island—Black slaves, horses, books, and both paper money and specie. Many of these goods belonged to British subjects, some residents of St. Kitts, whom Rodney labeled "traitors." Jewish merchants had their clothing searched for money and were then imprisoned and banished from the island without their families. Some of the captured goods were immediately used to supply depleted British garrisons, but the rest was auctioned off illegally as naval prizes to British as well as French and other enemy merchants, at prices as low as one-quarter of their actual value. Rodney and Vaughan packed up all the proceeds in a fleet of merchant ships (Vaughan's share was 9.2 percent or 150,000 pounds) and sent the ships to England. Vaughan's additional request for a land grant on St. Martin was refused by London.

The pair lingered on the island until May 4, at least two months too long, until the French again threatened St. Lucia. Vaughan then returned to his duties but was becoming increasingly frustrated by the trying conditions on the British Islands. He quarreled with his governors, could not obtain adequate supplies of medicine, had too few troops and lacked confidence in those he did have, and most importantly, by the spring of 1781 it was obvious Vaughan had failed in his primary mission to deal the French and Spanish colonies a serious blow. He had asked permission to leave the West Indies three times in 1780, and his request was finally granted in May 1781, officially for health reasons. He left the Caribbean in August.

The looting of St. Eustatius created a storm of protest in Britain from the merchants who had lost fortunes. This resulted in 64 civil claims against Rodney and Vaughan and a round of questions in Parliament in May. On December 4 Rodney and Vaughan defended themselves in the House of Commons against a motion for an inquiry into the St. Eustatius affair, tabled by Edmund Burke and supported by his parliamentary allies. Rodney denied any wrongdoing, and Vaughan defended himself. In the only time it was recorded that he spoke in the House, Vaughan declared that "he had not gained one shilling by the whole business." Burke's motion was defeated 163 to 89. Vaughan may have spoken close to the truth when he said he denied making any money in the enterprise. On May 22 a French force under Admiral La Motte-Piguet captured 22 of Rodney's and Vaughan's 32 treasure ships in European waters, and much of the rest of the booty was eaten up by lawsuits. By 1787 only 13 cases had been dealt with (nine with restitution) and the remainder continued in the courts until the deaths of the two alleged looters. Ironically, too, on November 25, St. Eustatius had fallen to the French admiral Marquis de Bouillé. It never recovered its former commercial prosperity. While Vaughan stayed in England, Rodney sailed again for the West Indies. His great victory in April 1782 at Les Saintes silenced any of his remaining critics in Parliament.

Vaughan was active in the House of Commons after his return to England. He voted in support of the Lord North ministry in the series of critical votes in February and March in which the government's majority hung on a thread. Vaughan voted against the Earl of Shelburne's Peace Plan of 1783, which eventually ended the war, and he voted for Charles James Fox's India Bill (November 1783). Vaughan opposed the new administration under William Pitt that took over after Fox's fall.

Because of his war service and political connections, Vaughan had acquired a number of posts, including that of governor of Fort William in 1778–1779, a post which, ironically, was previously held by Burgoyne, the man he was sent to aid in 1777. He was governor of Berwick Castle from 1780 to 1795, a sinecure worth 600 pounds a year. Honors continued to be bestowed

on Vaughan despite his reputation having been slightly blackened by the St. Eustatius affair. In 1782, he was made a major general and briefly considered as the new commander-in-chief in North America, to succeed his old superior, Clinton. In 1792 he was created a Knight of the Bath.

Vaughan's last military appointment was again to the West Indies. With the start of the French revolutionary wars, operations again resumed in the Caribbean. Vaughan sailed on October 26 1794, to replace Lieutenant General Sir Charles Grey as British land commander-in-chief in the Windward Islands. Vaughan spent the spring of 1795 occupied by attempts to suppress French-aided local Caribe revolts on the islands under his command. He had mixed success with these efforts. Vaughan died of disease on June 3, 1795, with the onset of the West Indies's "sickly season," although some sources indicate there was also a suspicion of poisoning. Vaughan had never married and had no known children.

Vaughan has been described as one of the ablest of the British generals to fight in the Revolutionary Wary, but his record of service is too brief to sustain such a claim. It appears he was not well liked by his subordinates. Vaughan was a competent general, and his activities of 1776 and 1782 do illustrate the sometimes devastating impact of British combined land and sea operations against an unprepared enemy and also the frequently ephemeral nature of those same operations.

Brian E. Hubner

REFERENCES

Sir Henry Clinton, *The American Rebellion: Sir Henry Clinton's Narrative of His Campaigns, 1775–1782, with an Appendix of Original Documents*, ed. by William B. Willcox (1954); *DAB*; M.I. Forsyth, "The Burning of Kingston by the British on October 16th, 1777," *New York State Historical Association Proceedings*, 7 (1911/12):62–70. J. Franklin Jameson, "St. Eustatius in the American Revolution," in *The American Revolution and the West Indies*, ed. by Charles W. Toth (1975):87–100. Orig. pub. in *American Historical Review*, 8 (1903):683–708; R.N. McLarty, "The Expedition of Major General John Vaughan to the Lesser Antilles, 1779–1781." Unpublished Ph.D. dissertation, University of Michigan (1951); *The Parliamentary History of England: From the Earliest Period to the Year 1803*. London: Printed by T.C. Hansard, 1814, pp. 770–786, Dec. 4th 1781; Alan Valentin, *The British Establishment, 1760–1784: An Eigh-*

teenth Century Biographical Dictionary, 2 vols. (1970),
2; Edna Vosper, *Report on the Sir John Vaughan
Papers in the William L. Clements Library* (1929).

Vergennes, Charles Gravier, Comte de (1717–1787)

French statesman. Charles Gravier, Comte de Vergennes, was a leading French statesman and architect of the policy of military involvement on the colonial side in the War of the American Revolution. When appointed foreign minister, Vergennes had already been a professional diplomat for almost a quarter-century and had served as ambassador to Turkey (1755–1768) and Sweden (1771–1774). Not popular at court, he owed his appointment in 1774 entirely to Louis XVI; he served as French foreign minister until his death in 1787.

Vergennes is often seen as animated by one goal: the humiliation of Britain for the disastrous losses inflicted on France in the Seven Years' War (1756–1763). He was, however, chiefly interested in preserving the balance of power. Vergennes became convinced, as a result of the Seven Years' War, that England's imperial appetites were insatiable. Acting in concert with the Spanish Bourbons and the Dutch Republic, he crafted a policy that painted Britain as the aggressor and the other states as seeking only to preserve the just goals of the Americans. Vergennes believed that the loss of her American colonies would prove fatal to British commercial power. This assumption proved to be fallacious, but it was widely believed at the time, even in Britain. French aid to America was thus pragmatic and not part of an ideological crusade. In 1782, after France had intervened to protect a successful democratically inclined revolt in the strategically important Republic of Geneva, Vergennes explained his approach both there and in America with these words: "The insurgents whom I am driving from Geneva are agents of England while the American insurgents are friends for years to come. I have dealt with both of them, not by reason of their political systems but by reasons of their attitudes towards France." Certainly, having Vergennes as foreign minister was extremely important for the Americans, given the great reluctance of King Louis XVI to get involved in their struggle with England.

In 1775, Vergennes repeatedly stated that France would take no part in the struggle in America. He also expressed concern over the effect that a successful revolt in America could have on French possessions in the New World, although he did not see any danger to France himself. He may not have been entirely sincere in his statements, but there was then no reason to doubt his word.

By the end of 1775, Vergennes had concluded that the uprising in America was doomed to failure without foreign assistance. Early the next year he presented Pierre Augustin Beaumarchais's plans for secret aid to King Louis XVI and also urged French (and Spanish) preparations for a future war with England. Since France was not at the time ready for war, her policy would be to deceive Britain until the right circumstances for war presented themselves. In the meantime, the American rebels would be armed and kept from reconciliation with Britain by vague promises of alliance. The revolt of the American colonials against the Mother Country was simply too great an opportunity to be missed.

Spain was at first cool to the project; Charles III was not interested in supporting an insurrection by a people against their sovereign. Louis XVI also wavered, finally supporting Vergennes over the objections of Controller General of Finance Anne Robert Jacques Turgot, Baron de l'Aulne.

On April 22, 1776, Louis XVI issued an order to rebuild the French navy and to supply new equipment to the army. This released a considerable stockpile of older military goods to be made available to the Americans through Beaumarchis's fictitious trading firm. On May 2, a million livres were ordered allocated for Beaumarchais. The Spanish reluctantly agreed to supply another million to Beaumarchis. All of this was to be kept secret. As Vergennes put it, "Everyone must shut his eyes to the exportation of munitions and implements of war, and the registers must not contain any item nor any indication of this connivance, entire liberty being left to the Americans to load and export as they please the articles in question."

On February 6, 1778, following the American victory at Saratoga, France concluded two pacts with the United States, thus formally recognizing the new republic. The first was the Treaty of Amity and Commerce, which contained a most-favored-nation clause; the second was the Franco-American Treaty of Alliance. In the latter, both parties pledged to continue the fight until American independence was "formally or tacitly assured." Neither power was to conclude a separate peace, and each guaranteed the possessions of the other forever.

On June 17, 1778, war broke out between France and England. Vergennes's American policy was immensely popular in France. He did not grant all American requests for aid, but France certainly liberally supported the American cause. Vergennes remained steadfast in his position that there could be no peace with England until American independence was assured.

The Americans, of course, negotiated with the British apart from France and even signed a preliminary arrangement with them. Vergennes was able to influence the composition of the American peace commission but did not make serious objection to the preliminary articles that the Americans signed with Britain. The reasons for this were that the cost of the war was steadily mounting and France had not been able to deliver Gibraltar to Spain. The American defection made it easier to bring Spain around to peace. Vergennes negotiated the Treaty of Paris signed on September 3, 1783, which formally ended the war.

The dangers inherent in Vergennes's American policy were not immediately apparent. Certainly as a foreign policy gambit alone, Vergennes's plan was immensely successful, but for both political and fiscal reasons it was also a great mistake.

The advantages of military alliance and trade arrangements with the Americans were lost soon after the war, but the chief result for France was increasing financial difficulties. While France aided the American rebels, she was also obliged to maintain a large army in Europe. One of the reasons Britain triumphed over France in their race for empire is that she did not have to sustain both a large army and a large navy; indeed, France was the only major power at the time that had to do so.

The costs of French intervention were immense, particularly in the naval sphere. In 1781 alone, 227 million livres were spent on the American campaign, 147 of that for the navy. This was nearly five times the cost of the peacetime navy. One estimate of the total cost of the American alliance in all its forms, from 1776 to 1783, is a staggering 13 billion livres, exclusive of interest payments of the new debt incurred. Of the funds needed to fight the American war, 91 percent came from loans that dramatically increased French budget deficits. The American intervention thus led directly to the need in France to raise new revenues through taxing the privileged classes. Threatened by the taxes, the nobles demanded the calling of the Estates-General, which they expected to control. In the process they unwittingly began the French Revolution.

Although Vergennes did not gain the notoriety of Lafayette among Americans as Perkins put it, "He did more than any other Frenchman to secure political independence for the American colonies."

Spencer Tucker

REFERENCES

Samuel F. Bemis, *The Diplomacy of the American Revolution* (1935); James B. Perkins, *France in the American Revolution* (1911); Orville T. Murphy, *Charles Gravier, Comte de Vergennes* (1982); Simon Schama, *Citizens. A Chronicle of the French Revolution* (1989).

Veterinary Medicine in the American Revolution

In a war that was fought primarily using livestock—horses, mules, cattle, and oxen—for transportation and food, an important figure was absent, the veterinarian. Professionalized veterinary medicine was nonexistent in the eighteenth century, but the need for veterinary services was great. The colonies experienced plagues of rabies, cattle distemper (affecting meat products), and sheep rot.

In 1777 George Washington ordered that slaughterhouses be maintained a mile away from the troops and that animal corpses be removed daily; six years later he issued orders requiring cattle that were killed for army meat products be inspected by Henry Wykoff. Soldiers had to care for their own mounts, locating forage and curing ailments. Washington ordered the officers of artillery to insure horses were properly shod.

On December 16, 1776, Washington accorded a farrier to the Connecticut Regiment of Horse. Farriers acted as veterinary surgeons, while smiths shoed horses. In the following year,

Washington formed a company of artificers attached to the artillery, which included 15 smiths and two farriers.

General Friedrich von Steuben brought a German veterinarian who served as farrier to the main staff of the army from 1778 to 1779. His nom *de querre* was Count Saxe, and he was noted as being very skilled. The British brought farriers in May 1775 with the 17th Light Dragoons to shoe their horses and to kill the maimed animals. However, the British easily requisitioned animals from locals and were not seriously concerned about veterinary care.

Washington complained that "there has been vile management of horses." He said that "could the poor Horses tell their tale, it would be in a strain still more lamentable" than the agony of the soldiers. In lieu of professional veterinary care and adequate military provisions, local farriers probably volunteered veterinary services to troops stationed nearby.

Elizabeth D. Schafer

REFERENCES

Bert W. Bierer, *History of Animal Plagues of North America* (1974); ———, *American Veterinary History* (1940); Louis A. Merillat and Delwin M. Campbell, *Veterinary Military History of the United States* (1935); J. Frederick Smithcors, *The Veterinarian in America, 1625–1975* (1975); *The American Veterinary Profession: Its Background and Development* (1963).

Vincennes, Quebec

Often called Post St. Vincent in British accounts, Vincennes, or Post Vincennes, was established in 1732 as a fortified trading post on the east bank of the Wabash River some 80 miles north of the Ohio River. It was named for its founder, Francois-Marie Bissot the younger, Sieur de Vincennes. The post passed to British jurisdiction with the Peace of Paris of 1763, but it was not occupied until 1765. By then, it had a population of perhaps 400, who successfully protested when the British ordered their village abandoned. In 1774 Vincennes passed under the jurisdiction of the expanded province of Quebec. A small British detachment from Detroit under the command of Lieutenant Governor Edward Abbott reached Vincennes on May 19, 1777, and erected a stockade, which he called Fort Sackville. Vincennes passed to American control in July 1778, when father Pierre Gibault traveled from Kaskaskia to tell the inhabitants that Colonel George Rogers Clark had captured the Illinois country. Vincennes immediately declared for the Americans, and Clark detached Captain Leonard Helm to assume command there.

Lieutenant Governor Henry Hamilton at Detroit reacted energetically and led a force of 170 regulars, militia, and Indians, who recaptured Vincennes on December 17 from its handful of American defendants. Hamilton settled down in winter quarters, built a barracks, and began to repair the fort. Most of his troops returned to Detroit, for he was confident that there would be no fighting before spring. Hamilton was completely surprised by George Rogers Clark's epic cross-country march. The fort was not yet prepared for combat, and Hamilton was forced to capitulate on February 25, 1779, after less than one day's resistance.

For the remainder of the war Vincennes remained an American outpost in the wilderness, held by only a small garrison and frequently threatened by Indian and British attack. Clark departed after a month, leaving Lieutenant Richard Brashers in command of 40 troops and the renamed Fort Patrick Henry, while Captain Helm took charge of civilian matters and Indian relations. Meanwhile, Virginia had established Virginia County with jurisdiction over all of the territory north and west of the Ohio River, with Vincennes as the county seat. John Todd arrived in May 1779, to set up the county government and assume command of the local militia. Virginia civil authority was never effective at Vincennes, but the post served as Clark's base for an expedition against the Indians in July 1779, as well as for his long-planned march against Detroit.

After the war Vincennes continued as the chief American outpost on the Wabash, but there was no secure authority until Lieutenant Colonel Josiah Harmar arrived on July 17, 1787, with a small force of regular soldiers. Harmar ordered the erection of a new stockade and left Major John Francis Hamtramck with two companies of infantry to carry out the construction of Fort Knox. Hamtramck also served as the unofficial civilian authority until June 20, 1790, when Knox County was established by officials of the new Northwest Territory.

Patrick J. Furlong

REFERENCES

John D. Barnhard and Dorothy L. Riker, *Indians to 1816: The Colonial Period* (1971); August Derleth, *Vincennes: Portal to the West* (1968); James A. James, *The Life of George Rogers Clark* (1928); George M. Waller, *The American Revolution in the West* (1976).

Virginia in the American Revolution

Perhaps the most important colony to engage in the Revolutionary conflict against Great Britain, Virginia was the most populous, with over a half-million inhabitants. She had the most potential for export commodity in tobacco, and she was by nature conservative. Her measured tones during previous conflicts led her to turn away from Oliver Cromwell's Protectorate and hence gained for her the designation "Old Dominion." During much of the 1760s only the most determined firebrands made menacing noises against Crown and Parliament. Men such as Patrick Henry could be discounted as habitual malcontents. The more staid of the Virginia gentry, represented by the likes of Peyton Randolph, were anxious about alienation from the only real authority they knew. The measured cadence of conservatives' voices restrained those who found Parliament insufficiently protective of English liberties in Virginia.

The influence of this small planter elite derived from extensive ownership of land. Forming only about 10 percent of the population, the wealthy planters owned nearly half the land in the colony. Small farmers owned the rest. Planters controlled the politics of the colony and involved themselves intimately in its royal governance. The unity of families like the Randolphs, Byrds, and Blands suffered from the Revolutionary turmoil. Yet in spite of an intrinsic conservatism, when the time came, the gentry families would put aside division within their ranks to oppose the British as resolutely as any yeomen.

The first glimmering of dissatisfaction with Britain occurred in Virginia the same time it did in other colonies. Changes in British policy required by the victory over the French in the Great War for Empire (1754–1763) caused American complaints. The Proclamation of 1763 marking the western limit of colonial expansion irritated many Virginians by interfering with their land speculations.

Also in 1763 a Virginia court case involving the Reverend James Maury in Hanover County revealed anticlerical and anti-British feelings. The case concerned the Two Penny Act of 1758, which assigned a value of two pence per pound of tobacco for the payment of public officials. Maury, a Church of England clergyman and hence under the act's stipulations, sued for the restitution of his full salary when Virginia's Privy Council nullified the act because it undervalued tobacco. Maury in essence lost his case when the jury awarded him only one penny. Patrick Henry, a vehement and flamboyant young attorney from Hanover County, argued that royal authority could not infringe upon the colony's right to enact laws for the benefit of the people.

The Revenue (or Sugar) Act of 1764 caused little stir in Virginia, but the Currency Act of that same year produced considerable concern. Virginia's principal export remained tobacco, a trade commodity that accounted for about 40 percent of all colonial exports for the 13 American colonies combined. Large wealth accrued from this, but there was also considerable debt. Currency scarcity plagued Virginia, as it did most of the colonies, reducing most financial transactions to a system of barter. Virginia's issuance of large amounts of paper currency to offset shortages was typical, but London considered it an irresponsible way to deal with the problem.

Yet in Virginia, as elsewhere, the Stamp Act caused the first serious eruption of hostility toward Parliament. Learning of a proposed stamp tax at the end of 1764, the Virginia General Assembly sent addresses to King George III and Parliament declaring that only the Virginia legislature could tax the colony. When the Stamp Act passed in March 1765 and word reached Virginia, the general assembly on May 22 passed Patrick Henry's resolutions against the act.

On the following day, Henry made the first of his famous speeches to the few Burgesses who had not left for their homes. Abandoning the accepted form of excluding the King from debate and exempting him from criticism, Henry concluded, "Caesar had his Brutus, Charles I his Cromwell, and George III would do well to profit by their example. The speaker of the house gavelled Henry to silence amid shouts of "Treason!" but not before he muttered, "If this be treason make the most of it."

On June 1 Lieutenant Governor Francis Fauquier dismissed the general assembly. Virginia had no way to respond to Massachusetts's call for a congress to meet in New York in October. Thus the colony did not send representatives to the Stamp Act Congress, but it did mount a protest as vehement as any seen elsewhere. Colonel George Mercer, Virginia's stamp agent, resigned without ever trying to distribute stamps, and courts ceased to operate.

As protests continued into 1767, county meetings showed a growing impatience with the conservatism of the planter elite. Further, revelations, following the death of John Robinson threatened the planter dominance of colonial politics. Robinson had been both the speaker of the House of Burgesses and the colony's treasurer. In the latter post he had used currency that he was charged in order to retire to make injudicious loans to his friends in the gentry. Only after Robinson's death did the colony realize the breadth of its financial embarrassment, scandalizing a generation of Virginians and tarnishing the luster of the Virginia aristocracy.

Wild celebrations greeted news of the Stamp Act's repeal. However, in June 1767, Parliament passed the Townshend Duties on lead, paint, paper, and tea, and Virginia was soon grumbling again. By the following March, Arthur Lee published "Monitor's Letters" recommending nonimportation to protest the duties. The general assembly, still reflecting conservative domination, merely sent petitions to the King and Parliament on April 16, 1767.

Governor Francis Fauquier died in March 1767. His replacement, Norborne Berkeley, the Baron de Botetourt, arrived in October 1768 to enthusiastic celebrations, in spite of the general assembly's continued objections about the Townshend Duties. The controversy briefly marred the otherwise excellent relationship Botetourt enjoyed with the colonial assembly. On May 17, 1769, he dissolved the assembly when it threatened to thwart Parliament. Many burgesses, however, gathered at Raleigh Tavern and agreed to form a nonimportation association. Peyton Randolph consented to preside at this extralegal gathering, indicating an important shift in the attitudes of the moderate gentry.

A new group of burgesses met officially in November. The intelligence that Parliament planned to repeal most of the Townshend Duties left the nonimportation association with little purpose. Its strictures fell into disuse, and the association itself was soon forgotten, but the burgesses persisted in declaring the principle that Parliament could legitimately tax the colonies.

Unhappily for everyone, the immensely popular Botetourt died in 1770. The new governor, John Murray, Earl of Dunmore, much maligned during the Revolution, has received more generous treatment from later observers. However, unlike his acclaimed predecessor, Dunmore had none of the polished civility that marked the charming and cordial Botetourt. A rough-hewn Scotsman, Dunmore liked the outdoors and lecturing his inferiors. The latter he classified as Virginians in general and the House of Burgesses in particular. Even the most equable personality would have found it difficult to cope with fractious colonists, but the royal administration of Virginia was singularly unfortunate to have at this critical time this man at this place.

Nevertheless, conditions remained calm until the spring of 1773. In March a few burgesses wanted to participate in setting up committees of correspondence in each of the colonial legislatures. And on May 10, 1773, Parliament passed the fateful Tea Act that gave a monopoly in North America to the financially ailing British East India Tea Company.

Virginia did not react immediately to the news of the Boston Tea Party. When that news arrived in January 1774, the colony was in the midst of a border dispute with Pennsylvania over possession of the area around Pittsburgh. Negotiations came to nothing, and the controversy almost deteriorated to armed conflict in January 1774. The issue remained in contention until August 1779 when commissioners from what by then were the states of Pennsylvania and Virginia settled the dispute. However, the line would not be surveyed until 1784.

Parliament passing the Coercive Acts in response to the Boston Tea Party roused the Virginia assembly to action. One of the so-called "Intolerable Acts" closed the port of Boston on June 1, 1774, until Massachusetts made restitution for the destroyed tea. On May 24, Dunmore dismissed the House of Burgesses for its proclamation, setting June 1 as a day of prayer and fasting to show sympathy with the plight of Boston. Replaying the events of five years before, 89 Burgesses met in Raleigh Tavern on May 27 to form a nonimportation association aimed at the East India Company. More significantly and reflecting the growing anger evinced in the half-decade since the earlier extralegal meeting, this Raleigh Tavern gathering agreed to send a call to other colonies for a Continental Congress. It was among the first of such proposals.

Most of the Burgesses had left Williamsburg when a circular letter arrived from the Boston Committee of Correspondence proposing nonintercourse with Britain. Those Burgesses who remained agreed that a convention of the colony should meet to discuss this radical and aggressive shift in strategy. Elections for the convention took place throughout the summer of 1774.

During the summer Virginia also waged a war against the Shawnee Indians, who had been attacking settlers in the Ohio Valley. Governor Dunmore himself led the Virginia militia in "Dunmore's War," which lasted well into the fall. Finally the Shawnee signed the Treaty of Camp Charlotte on October 19, admitting defeat and ceding to Virginia much of the upper Ohio Valley.

Meanwhile, Virginia county meetings throughout July called for a general congress and urged support for Massachusetts. George Washington presided at the Fairfax County meeting that proposed a boycott on British goods. The Fairfax gathering became the model for the Virginia convention that met on August 1 in Williamsburg. The convention established nonintercourse with Britain and elected a delegation to attend the First Continental Congress. The delegation consisted mostly of conservatives like Benjamin Harrison, Edmund Pendleton, George Washington, Peyton Randolph, and Richard Bland, but it also included the more radical Richard Henry Lee and the admitted firebrand Patrick Henry.

Virginia's importance in colonial protests became evident when the first Continental Congress chose Peyton Randolph as its president. This first congress met between September 5 and October 26, 1774, emulating Virginia's actions on nonintercourse. No imports would be allowed after December 1, 1774, and no exports after September 10, 1775. The most important action Congress took, however, was to agree to meet again the following spring.

In the interim Virginians acted vigorously to challenge British authority. On November 7 radicals dumped a cargo of tea into the York River from the *Virginia* anchored off Yorktown. Two days later some 500 merchants formed a Continental Association in Williamsburg. Such defiance invited attention from London, so in February and March 1775, Lord Dartmouth instructed Dunmore to disarm the Virginia resistance and to prohibit elections to the Second Continental Congress.

The Second Virginia Convention met even as Dunmore received these communications. Between March 20 and 27 the delegates in Richmond debated the theoretical and practical problems posed by the worsening political situation. The most memorable event of the gathering occurred on March 23 when Patrick Henry concluded his remarks with an inspiring declaration: "I know not what course others may take, but as for me, give me liberty or give me death!" The convention decided to organize military forces in each county.

Dunmore chose this unpropitious time to announce a new land policy. His management of westward settlement had been so far afield of British intelligence that London had reprimanded him for catering to Virginia's land hunger in western areas. The activities of speculators such as Richard Henderson and his Transylvania Company brought on the new policy. Dunmore declared that land would be sold at auction only after the government had declared it opened. The convention, already primed by other grievances, now had a fresh one. It appointed a committee to investigate the new land policy.

By April Dunmore, compelled to act on London's instructions to disarm the resistance, did so with characteristic bluntness. On April 1, Royal Marines removed the powder from the Williamsburg magazine, an act so aggressively impolitic that it brought heated protests from the staid Peyton Randolph and Robert Carter Nicholas. Patrick Henry tried to capture Receiver General Richard Corbin to force payment for the seized powder, and the population became so angry that Dunmore's family sought refuge aboard a British warship standing off Yorktown. Dunmore, surveying the unruly activities of the colony, broached the possibility of arming slaves to restore order.

That rash solution proved unnecessary for the moment. When word of the clash at Lexington and Concord reached Virginia, armed volunteers in Fredericksburg planned to march on Williamsburg. The persuasive appeals for calm by Randolph, George Washington, and others aborted the plan, but Patrick Henry so persisted in his call for armed resistance that Dunmore declared him an outlaw. Henry went into hiding.

Tempers calmed, Dunmore's family returned, and he called for a meeting of the general assembly to consider conciliation. In spite of rumors that the governor intended the session as a ruse so he could arrest leaders of the resistance, the burgesses met in Williamsburg on June 1. Peyton Randolph, who had been elected president of the Second Continental Congress, resigned his post to return for this important meeting of the burgesses. Williamsburg gave him a hero's welcome.

Dunmore hoped that an offer from Parliament for a measure of colonial autonomy would soothe Virginian anger. Years, perhaps even months, earlier, these men might have accepted the proposal of no taxes imposed by London if the colony would tax itself responsibly. However, by June 1775 too much had happened for such a simple solution to remain possible. The burgesses rejected it on June 10.

While the assembly debated this issue, another magazine crisis occurred. On June 3 a shotgun rigged with a tripwire injured three young men who were breaking into the Williamsburg powder magazine. Mobs gathered as bad feelings fueled a series of bitter disagreements between Dunmore and the burgesses. Finally on June 8 Dunmore and his family fled Williamsburg for the protection of the Royal Navy in the York River. Moderates now embraced the opinion that militants had been correct. They would have to help defend the colony.

Throughout the crucial month of June 1775, the situation continued to worsen in Williamsburg. News arrived that on June 15 the Second Continental Congress had appointed George Washington general-in-chief of the Continental Army. Soon Captains Daniel Morgan and High Stephenson led the first Continental forces from Virginia to join Washington outside of Boston.

On June 24, 1775, young radicals, including James Monroe and George Nicholas, broke into the Governor's Palace to steal some 200 firearms. They openly distributed them to the public at the powder magazine. It was only one example of many that marked the lawless activities of overeager and sometimes mischievous volunteers. Volunteer companies occupied the Governor's Palace and began menacing royal officials. The Third Virginia Convention, meeting in Richmond beginning July 17, tried to bring the volunteers to discipline, much to the relief of moderates in their ranks.

The Third Virginia Convention, beset by factionalism within and suspicion without, wrestled with the problems of defending the colony, erecting a provisional government, and paying for the whole. Finally shedding its spirit of self-recrimination, the convention regularized elections to make itself the colonial government. It appointed a committee of safety presided over by the venerable Edmund Pendleton. And by the time it adjourned on August 26 it had divided Virginia into 15 districts that would yield 68 men each for 1 year to defend the colony. Fifteen battalions of militia (or, as they were called, minutemen) would support the regular soldiery. Patrick Henry became commander-in-chief of the Virginia forces, although he had no military experience.

The convention had stood its ground, but the majority still hoped for reconciliation with the Crown. However, Virginians felt increasingly imperiled and began to think and act independently even before they were ready to declare independence. Militia forces occupied strategic points in the western part of the colony in the fall of 1775. Fears abounded that British ties with the Indians in the Ohio Valley would threaten the frontier with savagery. Representatives from Virginia, Pennsylvania, and New York, as well as delegates from the Continental Congress, finally secured an agreement on October 7 with the Indians. They promised to remain north of the Ohio River.

During the fall of 1775 Norfolk fell victim to a series of raids conducted from the sea by Lord Dunmore. In September the British tried to arrest John Hunter Holt, publisher of the *Virginia Gazette*. A detachment of soldiers confiscated Holt's press and seized some of his workers, but Holt successfully evaded the search. Norfolk's Loyalist sympathies in this and other incidents brought scorn from the rest of the colony.

By October almost 2,000 men had set up camps in and around Williamsburg. Enlistments under the terms stipulated by the Third Virginia Convention were filled by the end of the month. Meanwhile, Dunmore continued raids designed to seek and destroy arms and artillery colonists had stockpiled. Americans barely foiled a British attempt to burn Hampton.

On November 7 Dunmore issued a proclamation declaring a state of rebellion. In addition he sighed his infamous edict granting freedom to slaves and servants who joined him in putting down the rebellion. He waited over a week before making the proclamation public on November 16. By that time he had made Loyalist Norfolk his headquarters, raising the Royal Standard there as well as in Portsmouth. He crushed the meager militia in the area and within an additional week landed enough soldiers to claim complete dominion over the area.

The committee of safety responded by sending Colonel William Woodford's 2nd Virginia Regiment to Norfolk, thus manifesting a diminishing confidence in Henry's military ability. Woodford did not arrive at the land approach to Norfolk until late November to find Dunmore well ensconced in the town and allegedly preparing to threaten Suffolk. Woodford moved to Great Bridge on the Elizabeth River to prevent Dunmore's advance. After several days of maneuvering, Dunmore miscalculated his ability to surprise the Americans and thus suffered a stinging defeat on December 9 at Great Bridge.

Reinforced with Continental soldiers under Colonel Robert Howe and having received additional ordnance, the Americans retook Norfolk on December 14. The British consoled themselves by inflicting a naval bombardment on the town during the first three days of 1776. The damage caused by the Royal Navy, however, was as nothing when compared to that caused by rioting American soldiers. Fearful that the bombardment presaged a major assault by the British, Woodford and Howe allowed fires to burn unchecked and their army to run rampant. By the time American forces evacuated that unhappy city, soldiers had reduced Norfolk to a charred cinder in a shameful episode of the war.

Norfolk's Loyalist sentiments had incited much of the rage against her. Such sentiments that appeared in Norfolk, the western counties, and the Eastern Shore alarmed rebellious Virginians, who felt especially menaced by enemies in their midst. The Fourth Virginia Convention at the end of 1775 had occupied much of its time considering measures to assure loyalty to the rebellion. The western counties, filled with fiercely independent frontiersmen, exhibited alarming Loyalist tendencies. Dr. John Connolly,

celebrated and admired by Indians for tactful negotiations, was arrested in Maryland for plotting to lead an expedition from Detroit to isolate Virginia from northern colonies. Connolly had expected help from the frontier.

All was not well in the east either. Patrick Henry, incensed by open attempts to ease him out of military command, resigned on February 28, 1776. The men of Henry's 1st Virginia Regiment reacted violently to the news, and he was only barely able to dissuade them from mutiny. Military and civilian authorities clashed again when Major General Charles Lee arrived in Williamsburg. Washington had sent Lee south to prepare for an impending British assault led by Henry Clinton, an invasion that eventually occurred farther south in Charleston, South Carolina. Lee, of no relation to the Virginia Lees, alienated many Virginians, who regarded him as a meddlesome outsider. His attempts to improve Virginia forces met with resistance at nearly every turn, and his departure on May 13 relieved everyone, including Lee.

Amid such troublesome incidents, the Virginia Convention met for the fifth time on May 6 in Williamsburg. Everyone knew that independence would be the main topic of discussion. Earlier in the year Thomas Paine's *Common Sense* had convinced many Virginians of the inevitability of independence. The convention reflected this growing resolve. On May 15 it voted to instruct the Virginia delegation to the Continental Congress to make a motion for American independence. On June 7, 1776, Richard Henry Lee introduced the motion that passed as a resolution on July 2.

Thus, a Virginian instigated what was to be both the culminating and initiating pivot of the American Revolutionary experience. And another Virginian, young Thomas Jefferson, took the lead on the drafting committee to give the United States its first great state paper in the Declaration of Independence. The Second Continental Congress adopted the Declaration on July 4, 1776.

The same Virginia Convention that authorized the motion for American independence also drafted a state constitution. The convention first adopted a Declaration of Rights on June 13. Principally written by George Mason, the document would later provide the basis for the United States Bill of Rights.

The Virginia State Convention was adopted

on June 29, 1776. It provided for a governor chosen annually by the legislature for a maximum of three consecutive terms. Patrick Henry became the state's first executive. The governor was advised by an executive council, but the constitution granted him very few executive powers. For instance, he had no veto. A bicameral legislature called the General Assembly wielded most of the authority. The lower chamber, the House of Delegates, originated all money bills, while the upper chamber, the Senate, was elected by a complex procedure. The constitution also erected an independent judiciary.

This bold experiment proved more ideal than realistic, but Virginians were embarking on this challenging political journey in the middle of the war. Indeed, at one point the Virginia Convention had been forced to interrupt its deliberations for nearly a month because of the threatening military situation.

Virginia's forces finally dislodged Dunmore from his last stronghold at Gwynn's Island on July 7. Soon afterward, news of the Declaration of Independence arrived, and Governor Henry made the official pronouncement on July 25. Dunmore left Virginia waters for New York City in early August, so the state sent more soldiers to Washington's encampment outside that city.

Meanwhile, setting up a new state government preoccupied most of the Virginia establishment's attention in the fall of 1776. The General Assembly sat between October 7 and December 21, considering a wide variety of initiatives. At Thomas Jefferson's urging, the legislature abolished entail on November 1. It also passed measures to curb the activities of land speculators. However, Jefferson's efforts to disestablish the Anglican Church fell short in the legislature, which only exempted non-Anglicans from contributing to the Church's maintenance. The legislature also altered Jefferson's design for an expanded court system, providing for the addition only of a Court of Admiralty. Finally, demonstrating the persistent animus against Loyalists, the general assembly passed measures requiring people of British birth who still had economic interests in England to leave Virginia. Later the general assembly set up a process for confiscating Loyalist estates by putting them into a type of trusteeship under state control.

For some time after Dunmore left, the only military activity in the state occurred west of the Appalachian Mountains. The Cherokee War began during the summer of 1776 when a faction of Cherokees led by Dragging Canoe attacked American settlements. Virginia joined North and South Carolina militia in an efficient campaign that destroyed many Overhill Cherokee towns before forcing most of the Indians to a peace agreement on July 20, 1777. Virginians thus secured the neutrality of the Cherokees and gained vast tracts of land east of the Blue Ridge.

Other than prosecuting the Cherokee War, Virginians could only wait for news of military campaigns farther north. Washington's string of defeats in Pennsylvania, in which many Virginians fell, disheartened the state. However, John Burgoyne's surrender to Horatio Gates at Saratoga in October helped cheer the gloomy mood. Soon many of the British prisoners from Saratoga were interned near Charlottesville. British officers occasionally dined with Jefferson at Monticello.

In January 1778 Governor Henry authorized George Rogers Clark to lead an expedition into present-day Illinois to attack British posts there. Clark's intrepid drive and unflagging courage won a series of stunning victories limited only by his inadequate resources. His campaigns continued for the remainder of the war against the British and the Indians in the West. There was little in these magnificent exploits to foreshadow Clark's tragic decline into destitution and alcoholism after the Revolution. For the time his adventures in the West gave him first rank with Virginia's finest Patriot heroes.

On May 8, 1779, a destructive British raid on Portsmouth shattered the military calm in the east. The threat of future raids as well as a desire to placate the western population had much to do with the decision in early June to move the capital from Williamsburg to Richmond. However, the move did not occur until April 1780.

The general assembly that voted to move the capital also elected Thomas Jefferson governor on June 1, 1779, and commenced to deal with serious budget problems and the cryptic nuances of the Loyalist sequestration procedure. To cope with the financial crisis, the assembly levied new taxes. It also resolved to confiscate Loyalist property immediately, rather than through the earlier elaborate process.

The distress caused by the fall of Charleston in May 1780 was especially acute for Virginia. Almost all of the state's Continental Line and its commander, Brigadier General William Woodford, fell captive to Clinton's invading force. Woodford never saw Virginia again. He died a captive in New York City within a year.

Furthermore, gloomy predictions soon perceived an impending invasion of Virginia by this British force to the south, now under the command of Major General Charles Lord Cornwallis. The state government, increasingly concerned about necessary provisions leaving the state, had already made illegal the exportation of certain foodstuffs. In June 1780 the government set prices that producers had to accept for sale to the state.

As the government tried to prepare the homefront, the military news was mixed. Hundreds of Virginia militia were involved in the debacle at Camden, South Carolina, on August 10, 1780, but also many Virginians fought in the American victory at King's Mountain on October 7. One happy effect of King's Mountain was that Cornwallis afterward felt vulnerable enough to cancel Major General Alexander Leslie's invasion of Virginia.

Nathanael Greene, Horatio Gates's replacement as commander of the southern Continental Army, was en route to his shattered army in North Carolina when he stopped in Virginia to make the colorful Baron Friedrich von Steuben commander of Continental forces there. Nonetheless, virtually all Virginians, including Governor Jefferson, had lulled themselves into a false security when on December 20 a British invasion under Benedict Arnold, formerly of the Continental Army, shattered the tranquility. Rapidly penetrating the interior via the James River, Arnold's foray resulted in terrible destruction in Richmond and its environs during the first week of January 1781. By the time Arnold went into winter quarters at Portsmouth on January 19, he had shaken the state to its foundations.

The failure of efforts undertaken by the French to dislodge Arnold from Portsmouth took on a grimmer caste when it became obvious that following his costly victory at Guilford Court House, North Carolina, Cornwallis would move into Virginia. Von Steuben proposed a bold scheme to send 2,000 Virginia militia to Greene in North Carolina in hopes of tempting Cornwallis back the south. Fretful over the presence of Arnold, who had been recently reinforced and superseded by Major General William

Phillips at Portsmouth, Jefferson and his council rejected von Steuben's plan as too risky.

Keeping the militia in the state, however, proved of little value. Phillips and Arnold busied themselves pillaging the countryside. In late April the British destroyed supplies, warehouses, and at least one shipyard in raids that ranged from Williamsburg to Manchester. The only show of Virginia resistance occurred on April 24 when the British defeated militia under von Steuben at Blandford. Superseding von Steuben, the Marquis de Lafayette with 1,200 Continentals arrived in Richmond on April 29, but he did little more than momentarily surprise Phillips and Arnold. However, afterward, they directed their efforts toward joining Cornwallis, who was approaching from the south. On May 20 Cornwallis arrived in Petersburg, where Arnold (Phillips, afflicted by illness, had died the week before) was awaiting him.

Reinforcements from New York brought Cornwallis's strength to approximately 7,000 effectives. On May 24, he prepared to hurl this massive superiority against Lafayette. The young Frenchman, however, judiciously removed his meager force from Richmond toward Fredericksburg. Lafayette hoped to receive reinforcements from the north, and therefore he sought to protect approaches to him from that direction.

That necessity unfortunately left Virginia open to the destructive designs of the British. The most artful practitioner of such tactics was Lieutenant Colonel Banastre Tarleton, whose raiding exploits compelled the Virginia state government to resume its peripatetic existence. Already having moved from Richmond to Charlottesville, Jefferson and the general assembly had to evacuate Charlottesville for Staunton on June 4, with Tarleton's dragoons at their heels. Indeed, seven legislators fell into British hands.

This latest disaster so rattled the Virginia legislature that when it reconvened in Staunton on June 7, it considered giving autocratic powers to a new executive. Jefferson's term had expired on June 3, but not until nine days later did the General Assembly elect Thomas Nelson, Jr., not as an autocrat, but at least with significantly increased authority. Nelson was to have the power to rule virtually by edict in matters related to the military security of the state. The legislature also fell into the habit of ascribing blame for the calamities. It criticized von Steuben for his June 3 defeat at Point of Fork on the James River, and it impugned Jefferson's behavior as governor. Oddly enough, not only Jefferson, but Nelson as well, would eventually draw fire from the general assembly: Jefferson because he had been too weak a governor and Nelson because he wielded the increased powers the legislature gave him.

Months of ceaseless campaigning had wearied Cornwallis's force, so when he could not bring Lafayette to battle, he chose to withdraw toward the coast. By June 25 he had encamped around Williamsburg. Meanwhile, Brigadier General Anthony Wayne and nearly 800 Pennsylvanians joined Lafayette on the South Anna River. When von Steuben also joined Lafayette on June 19, the Frenchman could boast almost 3,000 effectives, of whom nearly 2,000 were soldiers of the Continental Line. Lafayette shadowed Cornwallis's move eastward so closely that skirmishes occasionally broke out between American advance parties and the British rear guard.

On July 4 Cornwallis pulled out of Williamsburg, apparently intending to cross the James River. Lafayette's plan to exploit the awkward disposition of the British army came to grief on July 6 when Anthony Wayne discovered that what everyone thought was Cornwallis's rear guard near Jamestown actually was the main body of the British force. After brushing aside this momentary distraction, Cornwallis moved to Portsmouth, encamping there by mid-July.

No one could have realized it in the summer of 1781, but Cornwallis was moving languidly to the military climax of the American Revolution. In the first week of August, he occupied the stage for the last scene of the drama by placing his army at Yorktown. From that place he expected to fulfill Clinton's orders to prepare a headquarters for Royal Navy activity on Chesapeake Bay. Instead, in two months he found himself trapped by a large Franco-American force to his front, while his back was pressed against waters that for once the Royal Navy could not command.

In late August, Washington formed the plan to catch the British in Virginia. It hinged upon the expected arrival in Chesapeake Bay of a French fleet under the Comte de Grasse, who had been operating in the West Indies. With an optimism entirely unjustified by experience, Washington initiated the complicated plan that called for the congregation of the Comte de Rochambeau's French army and siege guns from Rhode Island, the American army from New York, and the French fleet from the West Indies, all in the area of the New York Peninsula at roughly the same time.

Everything went right, beginning with de Grasse's besting Admiral Thomas Graves off the Virginia Capes and continuing with the virtually flawless combining of French and American forces at Williamsburg. By September 30, 1781, these forces had besieged Cornwallis. Just short of three weeks later, on October 19, he surrendered more than 7,000 men to the French and American allies, an act that signaled the end of the British effort to subdue the colonies.

While some minor military engagements would occur in 1782—principally against scattered Loyalists and Indians in the West—the Revolutionary War was all but over. Of more concern was the nearly three-year-old dispute between Virginia and Congress over tangled land claims north of the Ohio River. Virginia's cession, with qualifications, of these lands to Congress had cleared the way for the ratification of the Articles of Confederation in 1781. Yet pressure on Congress from land speculators had stalled the resolution of the matter. By the time the final terms of peace with England arrived in September 1783, Congress had decided to close the complicated matter by accepting Virginia's land cession without commenting on the state's claim to the area of Kentucky.

Thus with the settlement of this difficult issue, the state that would become known as the "Father of Presidents" emerged from the American Revolution ready to provide her considerable talents and resources for the advancement of the new republic.

David S. Heidler

REFERENCES

Hamilton J. Eckenrode, *The Revolution in Virginia* (1916); Ernest McNeill Eller, ed., *Chesapeake Bay in the American Revolution* (1981); Lucille Griffith, *The Virginia House of Burgesses, 1750–1774* (1968), Adele Hast, *Loyalism in Revolutionary Virginia: The Norfolk Area and the Eastern Shore* (1982); John E. Selby, *The Revolution in Virginia, 1775–1783* (1988); Charles S. Sydnor, *Gentlemen Freeholders: Political Practices in Washington's Virginia* (1952).

Volunteers of Ireland

The order of May 25, 1778, creating the Volunteers of Ireland was issued in Philadelphia by Sir Henry Clinton. Conceived by Clinton as a means of inducing some of the Irish emigrants in the service of the Americans to desert, he thought they might willingly join a regiment officered by their countrymen and headed by a well-known Irish captain, Francis Lord Rawdon-Hastings of the 63rd Foot.

Recruiting took place in Philadelphia and New York, where there was no hesitation in enlisting felons from prisons. When the unit under Rawdon, now a Colonel of Provincials, departed with the army for New York in mid-June, it totaled approximately 217 officers and men.

In New York, the Volunteers participated in several raids into New Jersey and up the Hudson River, and they were to be part of a canceled reinforcement for Halifax. On October 25, the regiment received drafts from Roman Catholic Volunteers, boosting their numbers to 362. The latter unit had had a breakdown in discipline resulting in plundering by some officers and men, and Clinton had disbanded it.

The Volunteers continued in the New York garrison, gaining an unenviable reputation as highway robbers and even as killers. Having grown to a strength of 427 officers and men, the regiment was sent in May 1779 as part of a raiding expedition to the area of Portsmouth, Virginia. Local towns and plantations were sacked, and the men returned to New York at the end of the month. Before landing, the unit was ordered up the Hudson again early in June to participate in the occupation of Stony Point.

Since its inception, there had been attempts by Clinton to have the Volunteers made a regular regiment of the British army. He was not successful in his early efforts, but when the government organized the American Establishment in orders dated May 25, 1779, the Volunteers were named the 2nd American Regiment. This made them a permanent regiment in America.

The Volunteers operated in Westchester and vicinity until late in September, when they boarded transports and sailed with a reinforcement under Cornwallis bound for Jamaica in the West Indies. However, after one day at sea, the fleet was warned of the approach of a large French fleet under Comte d'Estaing, and Cornwallis returned to new York.

Rawdon's men wintered in New York until April 1780, when, with their strength at 502, they were a part of a reinforcement sent to Clinton, who was conducting the siege of Charleston, South Carolina. The city fell on May 12, and the Volunteers remained with the southern army under Cornwallis.

The regiment was with Cornwallis when he defeated Gates at Camden, South Carolina, on August 16, 1780, remaining in the garrison of the town to help secure that area. During the battle the Volunteers fought very well and sustained 17 killed and 80 wounded, reducing their strength to 299.

When Green approached Camden in April 1781, the Volunteers once again formed for battle. As part of the force under Lord Rawdon they defeated the rebels on April 25 at Hobkirk's Hill, again sustaining heavy casualties numbering 13 killed, 75 wounded, and 17 missing.

Rawdon had been victorious, but he was still in a very insecure position. Short of supplies and surrounded by partisans, his men learned that several prisoners captured by Greene had been discovered to be deserters from the American army. On May 1 the rebel general hanged five of them. Since many of Rawdon's men fell into this category, there developed a growing wish in the garrison to leave the area and seek safety on the coast. With the situation rapidly deteriorating, Rawdon evacuated Camden on May 9 and succeeded in reaching Charleston with his men by the end of the month.

In September 1781 the Volunteers, then numbering 398, were still at Charleston. Continuing in that garrison, they participated in a raid up the Santee River in March 1782. That same month the regiment was finally taken into the British army as the 105th Foot on the Irish Establishment. However, in September the remaining men were ordered drafted into other units, and the officers were directed to sail for England. The regiment was disbanded in 1783.

Organizationally, the Volunteers resembled a regular British regiment with a grenadier and light infantry company and eight battalion companies. Regarding uniforms, buttons marked "2 American" are known, and an invoice dated 1782 notes "Red Coats, Green Brandenburg holes White Waistcoats & Breeches." It is also possible that after 1780 the entire unit wore some kind of cap instead of regulation hats.

Walter T. Dornfest

REFERENCES

Sir Henry Clinton, *American Rebellion* (1954); Albert W. Haarmann, "Some Notes on American Provincial Uniforms, 1776–1783," *Journal of the Society for Army Historical Research, 49* (1971):141–151; Richard J. Koke, "Britons Who Fought at Stony Point," *New-York Historical Society Quarterly, 44* (1960):42–71; Charles H. Metzger, *Catholics and the American Revolution* (1962).

Wadsworth, Jeremiah
(1743–1804)

Continental Army officer. Born in Hartford, Connecticut, Wadsworth was the son of a minister. Because his father died in 1747 Wadsworth was raised by Matthew Talbot, an uncle and ship owner. Young Wadsworth went to sea in 1761, and by 1771 he was a wealthy merchant captain.

Due to his uncle's influence, he was appointed commissary for the Connecticut militia in 1774. Because Wadsworth was a capable administrator, Commissary General Joseph Trumbull appointed him to be commissary general of the Eastern Department (1776). After Trumbull's resignation in August 1777, Wadsworth assumed the duties of deputy quartermaster general. By March 1778 he was appointed a colonel and commissary general.

Wadsworth toiled to provision the army, and he was praised by Washington for his efforts. Yet he was criticized for graft and inefficiency in his department and for offering high prices for foodstuffs on the market. Wadsworth worked harmoniously with General Nathanael Greene, and they were partners in Barnabas Deane and Company.

Tired of criticism and anxious to enhance his fortune, Wadsworth resigned his post in January 1780. As an entrepreneur he had holdings in several enterprises. Elected in 1788 to Congress, Wadsworth was a Federalist. He promoted scientific agriculture and was a patron of the arts. As an executor of Greene's estate, Wadsworth provided financial assistance to Greene's widow and family.

Richard L. Blanco

REFERENCES

DAB; Chester M. Destler, "Barnabas Deane and the Barnabas Deane and Co.," *Connecticut Historical Society Bulletin*, 35 (1970):7–19; ———, "The Gentlemen Farmer and the New Agriculture: Jeremiah Wadsworth," *Agricultural History*, 46 (1972):135–153; Robert A. Ernst, *Business Enterprise in the American Revolution Era* (1938); Erna Risch, *Supplying Washington's Army (1981);* Richard K. Showman, ed., *The Papers of Nathanael Greene*, 5 vols. (1978–), 2.

Wallpiece

The wallpiece was a long, large shoulderarm intended for long-range sniping (to about 300 yards) to defend the walls of fortifications against artillerymen and engineers. The caliber was generally under one inch in diameter. Often fitted with an oarlock-type support through the fore end of the stock to fit into a socket on the wall this firearm was a direct descendant of the early *hakenbusche*, on which the barrel had the support for fitting into the wall cast into it. Most were smoothbored and looked like enlarged muskets, with locks and furniture similar in design to the infantry musket. Some, particularly the German- and American-made examples, were rifled and looked like much enlarged rifles of the time.

British

Only 772 wallpieces were ordered by the Board of Ordnance between 1715 and 1783, of which 222 were set up between 1775 and 1783. These had 54-inch round 0.98 caliber smoothbore barrels firing a 0.89-inch ball, with an overall length of 73 inches and a weight of 37 pounds. They had either flat locks with ring-neck cocks and faceted pans, resembling the Sea Service musket, or rounded double-bridle locks of the Land Pattern, and the brass furniture was similar to the Long Land Pattern musket. They had steel rammers.

American

Probably the only wallpieces made by the Americans were the rifles made at Rapahannock Forge, Virginia, about 1776. These had 44¼-inch round barrels with a rifled bore of 1⅛-inch, brass furniture and a swivel similar to the British oarlock, and weighed 53½ pounds.

French

Known as the *fusil de rempart* and using the Model 1728 as its basis, these arms had 46¾-inch 0.70 caliber smoothbore barrels using a ball of 0.66 caliber, with an overall length of 62¾ inches. They were withdrawn from service prior to the Revolution, and any weapons of this type used by the French forces in America were of private manufacture and based on the Model 1763 design.

German

Although very popular in the many fortresses in the German states, it is thought that wallpieces *(wallbuchse)* were not used by the German troops serving in North America. The Amusette was much favored by them instead and was normally carried by their jagers.

De Witt Bailey

REFERENCES

De Witt Bailey, *British Military Smallarms 1689–1815* (forthcoming); Jean Boudriot, *Armes a Feu Francaises Modeles d'Ordonnance* (1961–63); Warren Moore, *Weapons of the American Revolution* (1967); George C. Neumann, *The History of Weapons of the American Revolution* (1967).

Walton, George (1750–1804)

Georgia statesman. Having lost his father shortly before or just after his birth in 1750 in Goochland County, Virginia, George Walton began what was remembered as a harsh childhood. He lost his mother too, while he was young, and was raised by relatives. At age 18, he was in Savannah, Georgia, where his brother John had apparently arranged for him to study law under Henry Yonge, Jr. In 1772, George Walton began practicing law and was by 1775 one of Georgia's most active attorneys and an officer in the colonial militia.

Despite his rise in the colonial establishment, Walton early became a leader in the Savannah faction of Georgia's Revolutionary War movement, serving as secretary and the president of the Georgia Provincial Congress before being elected a delegate to the Continental Congress. He arrived in Philadelphia just in time to hear John Adams's final arguments for independence, a speech he would remember all of his life. He became the youngest of the signers of the Declaration of Independence.

He returned to Savannah in 1777, where he married and attempted to retire from politics, at least until his finances were in better shape. Walton was colonel commandant of the Georgia militia in December 1778 when he was wounded and captured in the unsuccessful defense of Savannah from the British. He had the satisfaction of seeing that his unheeded warnings about the danger to the American right were correct. However, an investigation of the actions of the American commander, General Robert Howe, that Walton pressed for years later acquitted Howe.

When Walton was released late in 1779, he joined what was left of Georgia's rebel politicians in Augusta, which was at that time not under British occupation. Walton found that the remnants of the opposing Savannah and St. John Parish factions were fighting each other as fiercely as they had done before the British invasion. Apparently sensing the direction of the political winds, Walton abandoned the Savannah faction and joined his former political opponents. He was subsequently elected as their governor and soon after as a Georgia delegate to the Continental Congress. During this time, George Walton forged a letter to Congress allegedly from the Georgia Assembly calling for the removal from command of Walton's friend and former political ally, General Lachlan McIntosh. For the rest of his life, Walton would be hounded by the McIntosh family and their allies for this betrayal. Eventually Congress restored McIntosh to his rank, and in Georgia the general's allies succeeded in checking Walton's bid for another term in Congress.

Despite the unending storm of his actions in 1780, George Walton continued a successful political career upon his return to Georgia after the war, including three terms as chief justice and another term as governor. He became involved in fraudulent land grant schemes called the Pine Barren Frauds and later with the bribed sale by the Georgia legislature of the state's claims to western lands, known as the Yazoo Land Fraud. Because of his involvement with the latter, he lost his bid for election to the U.S. Senate. Despite his many political enemies, George Walton held on to his position as a superior court judge until his death on February 2, 1804. Whether he was an opportunist in a time and place where he should have instead stuck with party loyalty or was simply a victim of misunderstanding and a scapegoat is still debated.

George Walton is buried beneath the Signers Monument in Augusta. Meadow Garden, his home, is nearby and is maintained by the Daughters of the American Revolution, and Walton County, Georgia, is named in his honor.

Robert Scott Davis, Jr.

REFERENCE

Kenneth H. Thomas Jr., et al., *Georgia's Signers and the American Revolution* (1983).

War Widows

"Shall a widow that Lost her Husband Suffer and want?" Elizabeth Gaudin, whose husband was killed in Boston "defending the rights of america," asked in her 1787 petition for relief. Unfortunately, officials could not locate Gaudin's name on service rolls, and Elizabeth, who was denied her request, cynically commented, "I am sorry to say I think myself ill-used."

Eighteenth-century women had few property rights and usually were dependent totally on men—their father, guardian, or husband—for economic support, having no employable skills. When a woman married, any property associated with her—such as a dowry controlled by her family—transferred to her husband. Pre-Revolutionary laws concerning widows permitted them one-third of the husband's estate, unless the husband specified otherwise in a will, with children, especially the eldest son, being provided for first. Even after death, men were able to regulate their wives' lifestyles, indicating in their wills decisions for property dispersal, usually to individuals other than the spouse, such as business partners; many men, especially those from lower classes, did not leave wills, or soldiers were too hurried to record how they wished their belongings distributed in case of death. Often this property was seized by the community or creditors with minimal regard for the widow. Inheritances or the lack of them, especially if children receiving the majority of the estate refused to provide for their mother, often left women destitute, alone, and confused about their situation and how to survive.

When the Revolution began, women felt threatened. Some women tried to encourage their husbands not to fight, pleading for them to seek exemptions and expressing that their family did not need to participate and possibly suffer in the war effort. Most women privately feared becoming widows, losing companionship, and being denied support economically and emotionally. They did not want to suffer risks and losses that they considered unnecessary.

Despite these secret inner fears, women patriotically sent their husbands to war, shaming those men who did not wish to go. One New Jersey wife told her husband, "Remember to do your duty! I would rather hear that you were left a corpse on the field than that you had played the part of a coward!" In order to express their commitment, most women were publicly supportive of their husbands throughout the war, sending them supplies, repairing clothes, or following them to camps. Women who were already widows when the war began wished that they too could send a man to war. Eliza Wilkinson regretted, "I've no husband to fight against them."

Soldiers, in turn, worried about their families but trusted that states, towns, and charities would aid them. They also realized their wives' anxiety that their husbands would be killed, or even worse, that their husbands would be branded as cowards, traitors, deserters, or criminals, tainting the widow and family and eliminating possibilities of publicly supported assistance. John Hempstead recalled how his wife bravely embraced him as they said goodbye, then "After I got Under Way my wife Called to me prety loud. I Stopt my hors and ask'd her What she wanted. Her answer was Not to let me hear that you are Shot in the Back."

The absence of men resulted in broken homes and families. Juvenile delinquency became a problem, and many women complained that their husbands spent their salary on alcohol and frivolous items and did not support their family. Widows and orphans became a new group of war casualties. Alerted of their husbands' deaths in battles, widows succumbed to shock and felt a numbing sense of loss but had little time to recover. Widows were usually secluded, depressed, and unable to function. They were unfamiliar with their husbands' business procedures but had to cope with any commitments, contracts, or debts they owed. As a result, they were taken advantage of and ruined financially.

Widows were forced to accept employment in various jobs, many distasteful, in order to survive economically. Women worked as keepers and staff of inns, taverns, and lodging houses as well as performing services of sewing and cooking. The less fortunate—among them widows of foreign soldiers—turned to prostitution. Often widows did not believe that their husbands were dead and wasted time searching for clues that the men were alive; ghost stories and legends circulated, relating these women's quests to find their husbands. Religious beliefs helped comfort and soothe many widows, who had faith that they could be reunited with their husbands after death.

Many towns refused to let women live or board in the community unaccompanied by a husband or male guardian, with the male populace voting on whether or not to allow the women to stay. In a letter written to the *Connecticut Courant*, an angry citizen queried, "How is it that the poor soldiers' wives in many of our towns go from door to door, begging a supply of the necessaries of life at the stipulated prices, and are turned away, notwithstanding the solemn agreements of the towns to supply such?" These women, victimized by war, for whom towns and states had agreed to provide supplies, included war widows.

Widows of men executed or punished for crimes were penalized and disregarded, as if they had committed the offense. In 1779 Sergeant Samuel Glover was executed in North Carolina for sparking a mutiny because he had not been paid for 15 months. His widow apologized for his behavior but argued that she and her children should receive relief because her husband and his followers were "possessed of the same attachment and affection to their Families as those in command."

Many widows gave food and gifts to soldiers, improving their morale, but their actions were not rewarded. Rachel Wells had loaned money to New Jersey for the war, but the state refused to reimburse her interest earned on the principal. Rachel testified, in her archaic dialect, to the Continental Congress in 1786 that "I have Don as much to Carrey on the warr as maney that Sett Now at the healm of government." Demanding the interest owed her, Rachel painted this unselfish image of herself; "If She did not fight She threw in all her mite which bought the Sogers food & Clothing & Let them have Blankets." Rachel also noted that British soldiers had stolen her property and "This I can barr but to be Robd by my Contrey men is verey trying."

Initial pension legislation was for men only and was designed to inspire new soldiers to enlist for future monetary gain. In 1776 half-pay was awarded to officers and servicemen disabled in service; two years later officers who committed to serving for the entire war plus seven years of additional assignment were given half-pay, which was increased to five years of full pay in 1783. Widows and orphans of Continental officers who had signed up for the war and an extra seven years' service were permitted pensions in 1780, but this act only affected a minute portion of the population.

During the era of the American Revolution, war widows were not well provided for by the federal authorities. In many areas, local citizens confiscated Tory property, which was given to widows and orphans or sold for the benefit of widows and orphans. Veterans organizations such as the Saint Tammany Society cared for widows and orphans, as did states and towns, who tried to donate food and shelter to them.

Social rank and personal connections often determined the status of a war widow. The widow of Dr. Samuel Kennedy was given $5,000 for her husband's property for the Yellow Springs Hospital. Janet Livingston Montgomery, widow of Brigadier General Richard killed in 1775, was regaled with songs and poems depicting her life with her husband, esteemed as a martyr of the Revolution. Janet wore mourning clothes and a widow's cap, and because of her husband's lofty status, she maintained her social position and was kept busy with activities honoring her husband—a monument was erected, parades were held, and his biography was published. Janet, a wealthy widow, penned her memoirs and built a mansion by the Hudson River, where she received prominent visitors. Yet, as the war progressed, many officers' widows scrounged for necessities and were not given monetary rewards promised to their husbands for valor in the field.

Congress gave singular payments to individual women for various acts of bravery in the war. Margaret Corbin was wounded at Fort Washington. She had helped her husband load artillery until he was killed; Margaret then assumed his duties and was given a commission and clothes as compensation.

In the eighteenth century, widows of enlisted men were ignored by authorities. Because these women were dispersed throughout the nation and had no centralized location, imminent lobbyists, or supporters, pensions for widows of enlisted personnel were not distributed. Widows, believing they deserved monetary support, petitioned federal authorities for relief. Embarrassed because she had to beg and endure humiliation, Eleanor Healy stressed that she had "underwent the Severity of Cold and heat in the service of her Country—besides A Greater, which was the loss of her husband, who was killed." She demanded that she should be "Intitled to the priviledges, allowed the Widows

and Orphans belonging to the army." In response to her pleas, George Washington sent her a letter of introduction to General Henry Knox. When Healy presented her note, the general evaded her requests for relief.

Washington occasionally sent money to the widows who wrote him; he was especially generous to those women whose eloquent appeals touched him emotionally, but one man could not solely provide for enlisted war widows. The lack of a centralized, federal system to reimburse war widows for their loss and provide them sustenance resulted in these widows turning to the states for help as a last resort. The states could pass special bills of relief for certain cases, but war debts prevented the attainment of a general bill to fund all war widows in the states.

In 1795 the South Carolina Senate approved giving Phoebe Norwood five pounds annually because "Congress provides for the Soldiers wounded in the Continental Service, but not for the Widows of Soldiers who have died in the said service." Regrettably, the state's representatives lacked similar compassion and refused to approve the senate's generous offer. Other war widows petitioned for relief, with each request being judged singularly and being approved or denied based on provincial conditions and the degree of the widow's hardship. By the mid-nineteenth century, remaining war widows began to receive their due support.

The widows' acts, as a series of nineteenth-century legislation was labeled, provided yearly grants for the spouses of enlisted Revolutionary soldiers. The first widows' act in 1832 gave pensions to widows married at the time of the Revolution to men who had six months or more of service. Four years later Congress passed "an act granting half pay to widows or orphans where their husbands or fathers have died of wounds received in the military service of the United States," stipulating that the woman had to be married to the soldier at the time of the Revolution. In 1838 the pension was permitted to widows who had married the veteran before 1795. This limit was increased 10 years letter, stating that the widow had to be married to the veteran before January 2, 1800. In 1855 the pension was allocated to all widows regardless of when they married the veteran. By 1878 widows' pensions were given to any widow of any soldier who had fought in any one engagement or served for fourteen days.

Widows had to petition for the pension and often had difficulty securing proof of their status, as records were often inaccurate, incomplete, lost, destroyed, or damaged. Widows stressed in their depositions that they had been left destitute when their husbands died, emphasizing their economic needs (for themselves and children), lack of skills, powerlessness, desperation, and sacrifices made for the nation. They insisted that the United States owed them money for their anguish, due to their having lost their husbands as a result of the American Revolution.

Those who lost their spouses in the war were usually women, but one man received a pension because of his wife's service. Benjamin Gannett, widower of Deborah Sampson Gannett—who fought disguised as Robert Shurtleff—persuaded Congress to give him a pension under the 1836 act that stipulated "granting pensions to widows in certain cases."

The 1900 *World Almanac* named four Revolutionary War widows still listed on pension rolls, and in 1906 Esther Damon Vermont, the last surviving Revolutionary War widow, died at age 92. The failure of the new nation to implement a system of funding war widows with pensions until the mid-nineteenth century reveals the immature government's apathy toward women's issues and the absence of women—and their representatives—in politics of the new nation.

Elizabeth D. Schafer

REFERENCES

John C. Dann, ed., *The Revolution Remembered: Eyewitness Accounts of the War for Independence* (1980); Elizabeth Evans, *Weathering the Storm: Women of the American Revolution* (1975); Robert A Gross, *The Minutemen and Their World* (1976); Ronald Hoffman and Peter J. Albert, eds., *Women in the Age of the American Revolution* (1989); Linda K. Kerber, *Women of the Republic: Intellect and Ideology in Revolutionary America* (1980); Mary Beth Norton, *Liberty's Daughters: The Revolutionary Experience of American Women* (1980); Charles Royster, *A Revolutionary People at War: The Continental Army and American Character, 1775–1783* (1979); Gustavus A. Weber, *The Bureau of Pensions: Its History, Activities and Organization* (1923); Dixon Wecter, *When Johnny Comes Marching Home* (1944).

Ward, Artemus (1727–1800)

Continental Army officer. Artemus Ward was born at Shrewsbury, Massachusetts, a town located about 40 miles west of Boston, on November 26, 1727, to Colonel Nahum Ward, a local political leader and militia officer who also had the distinction of being one of the founders of Shrewsbury. His mother was Martha How. Artemus was next to the youngest of six children. Born to comfortable circumstances, Ward was schooled locally and then attended Harvard.

After achieving an excellent scholastic record in college, Ward graduated on July 6, 1748, and later received a master of arts degree from Harvard in 1751. Following graduation Ward taught school in the town of Groton, Massachusetts. While there, Ward boarded at the home of the Reverend Caleb Trowbridge. Artemus became engaged to the Reverend's oldest daughter, Mary Sarah, a "calm, self-possessed woman," who was three years his elder.

Ward returned to Shrewsbury to establish a general store, which he opened for business on April 21, 1750. He married Mary Sarah on July 31, 1750, at the Trowbridge house in Groton. Their marriage in time produced eight children, and Ward became devoted to his family.

On March 4, 1751, Ward was elected to his first public office, that of tax assessor, by his fellow townsmen. On June 22, 1751, Ward was elected justice of the peace. The following year, he became town clerk and a selectman, a particular office to which he would be reelected 20 times during his life.

Ward began his military career on January 28, 1755, when he was commissioned major of the 3rd Regiment of militia for the counties of Middlesex and Worcester and captain of the 1st Company of Shrewsbury militia; in August 1757, Ward was called west with his regiment after the fall of Fort William Henry to help defend Fort Edward against attack by the Marquis de Montcalm's army. His term of service was uneventful, for Montcalm returned north, and Fort Edward was considered safe by the time Ward's men arrived. Ward returned to preside over his business and continue his activities in politics.

Ward enlisted the following spring (1758) in Colonel William Williams's regiment as major and saw his first fighting during British general Sir Robert Abercromby's campaign to take Fort Ticonderoga from the French. Ward left with four companies from Worcester on May 30, 1758, for Lake George. On July 3, Ward was promoted to lieutenant colonel in the field.

In the bungled British operations, Williams's provincial regiment formed part of Abercromby's advanced force that unsuccessfully attacked the French outer lines around Ticonderoga. Weeks of inactivity in camp followed the failed assaulieutenant Finally, Williams's regiment was sent home on October 24. The rigors of active field service impaired Ward's health, causing him physical problems that he endured for life.

During Abercromby's campaign, however, Ward had the opportunity to meet individuals who would later play major roles in the War of the Revolution. He served with Charles Lee, Thomas Gage, Timothy Ruggles, John Whitcomb, Israel Putnam, and John Stark, among others.

Returning home with his men, Ward was soon promoted to colonel of the regiment. During the critical campaign of 1759–1760, Ward spent his time at home recruiting and forwarding men to the front. He was experiencing frequent and painful attacks of the calculus (the stone), an affliction that kept him from active service.

When the war ended, Artemus Ward resumed his public service. He became town moderator of Shrewsbury, and then church moderator for many years. Ward also served as a representative in the general court for his county until he entered the governor's council. On January 21, 1762, Ward became a judge of the Worcester County Court of Common Pleas. His service as judge characterized him as a law-and-order man who possessed a good legal mind and who made judicious decisions in his casework.

With the advent of the stamp tax crisis, Ward became an active and vocal Whig. His principled stand cost Ward a great deal. Governor Francis Bernard revoked his colonel's commission in 1766. Although elected in May 1770 to serve as a member of the governor's council, the acting governor, Thomas Hutchinson, refused to allow Ward to take his seat. Ward was eventually replaced in council in 1774 by one of the "Mandamus Councillors."

Ward worked alongside Samuel Adams, John Hancock, John Adams, James Otis, and many others to protest the loss of American liberties in Massachusetts Bay. He constantly supported the plans and was involved in the activities of the radical faction in Massachusetts, contesting the attempts of the royal government to extend its control over the colony.

When tension increased after the Boston Tea Party and resulted in the Boston Port Act of 1774, Ward was reelected colonel of his militia regiment on October 3, 1774, by the Worcester County Convention. Ward also served in the first Massachusetts Provincial Congress on October 11 at Concord, and then on October 17 at Cambridge.

The provincial congress appointed Ward one of three general officers on October 27, 1774. The senior general, Jedediah Preble, was too old to take an active hand in military preparations. The third and most junior general, Seth Pomeroy, was also advanced in years. Much of the burden of developing, organizing, and preparing the Massachusetts militia to meet a possible British threat fell on the 47-year-old Artemus Ward.

In February 1775, the second provincial congress reaffirmed the three original generals in their positions of command for another year. Ward also served as a delegate in this congress. The stresses and rigors of command once again led Ward to suffer from a severe attack of the calculus and forced him to bed, which is where he was when the express rider reached Shrewsbury with the news of the fighting at Lexington and Concord.

The very next day, Ward mounted his horse and rode east despite his pain to take command of the militia forces that were already besieging the British in Boston. Ward made his headquarters at the Jonathan Hastings house, which also became the meeting place for the Massachusetts Committee of Safety, the civilian board responsible for the conduct of the fighting.

As a vote of confidence and to formalize Ward's position, the provincial congress appointed him captain general of Massachusetts troops on April 22, 1775. On May 20, the provincial congress made Ward general and commander-in-chief of all Massachusetts troops. Due to his rank and the strength of his personality, Ward was also able to exert command over the troops from other states participating in the siege.

The difficulties that faced the committee of safety and General Ward in the conduct of this siege were considerable. Ward had to feed the men. The militia had not come prepared to remain in the field, particularly to take part in a siege. The troops had to be reorganized. Many were signed up right in the lines outside Boston.

Others went home and returned later. The men who agreed to stay were rotated home to attend to their personal business. New troops had to be enlisted and brought to the lines at Boston.

Little powder and few artillery pieces were available. American firing was limited to conserve ammunition. Ward had to cooperate with the politicians in the Massachusetts Provincial Congress, local leaders from each community that had sent men to the first day's fighting, officers and troops from other states who did not wish to place themselves under the command of a general from Massachusetts, and the local populace, who found their homes now located in a battleground.

Ward was also concerned with the military training and drill of his men. The New England army had to be prepared to fight to the British. Another problem to be faced was the proper positioning of the troops in the area surrounding Boston in order to maintain a proper siege.

In mid-June General Ward received word that the British had made plans to break the siege of Boston. To undercut the British move, the committee of safety ordered Ward to dispatch troops without delay to fortify Bunker Hill on Charlestown Peninsula. On the evening of June 16, Ward ordered Colonel William Prescott and his regiment, along with supporting troops, onto Charlestown Heights, where the Americans dug through the night to construct a redoubt on top of Breed's Hill.

The next day, June 17, the British were shocked to find an American fortification overlooking much of Boston. General William Howe led a large British force in an amphibious assault on the American position. After suffering severe casualties in three assaults, the British were successful in pushing the Americans out of their redoubt and off the field. Ward coordinated American troop movements supporting the force on Breed's Hill and took responsibility for the overall defense of the siege lines from his headquarters in Cambridge.

Through the fighting and all the difficulties, Ward earned the respect and regard of the men he commanded by his actions, his sense of tact, and his political ability. The force of his personality and his ability to command kept the New England army together until General George Washington arrived in early July to relieve Ward.

For valid political reasons, the Continental Congress appointed George Washington of Virginia as commander-in-chief of the American army on June 15, 1775. Ward was appointed as senior major general and second in command of the army. Washington came to Cambridge and assumed command from Ward on July 3.

On July 22, Ward was assigned to command the American right division while General Charles Lee commanded the left division. General Israel Putnam took the center at Cambridge. Ward's responsibility included Roxbury, Boston Neck, and Dorchester Heights. Ward made his headquarters at Brinley Place (Pierpoint Castle). Due to their very different heritages, one from the planter society of Virginia, the other from the Congregationalist society of Massachusetts, Generals Washington and Ward did not like each other. But throughout the siege Ward provided Washington with support and advice.

In 1775, Ward was clean-shaven, of medium height, and quite stout for his age. He was religious with definite convictions on God, society, and the truth of his beliefs. A quiet, reflective man, Ward was stern in appearance and spoke slowly, almost as if he were considering the full import of each word as he spoke it. His military background up to 1775 equaled that of Washington's. His health, however, was too delicate for him to serve actively in the field. Ward never saw himself as Washington's rival and served agreeably as second in command.

On October 17, 1775, the new Massachusetts government appointed Ward chief justice of the court of common pleas for Worcester County, but Ward continued his military service. On New Year's 1776, Ward worked hard to maintain an American presence in the lines as enlistments expired. Many of the American soldiers who had enlisted for eight months in the spring left for home. Order, discipline, and cleanliness also had to be enforced in camp. These were matters that Ward handled well.

Ward was one of the principal officers who persuaded Washington to make a rash attack with rowboats on the British in Boston during the winter months. In time, the value of Dorchester Heights became apparent to the American leaders. By March 1776, with chandeliers (wooden frames to stack fascines), barrels, and artillery that Colonel Henry Knox had brought from Ticonderoga, Washington's men were prepared to fortify Dorchester Heights, south of Boston.

Ward ordered his men out to begin their work on Dorchester Heights on March 4, 1776. This action sealed the fate of the British in Boston. On March 17, the British evacuated the town. Washington had little time to gloat, for he had to concentrate on the defense of New York.

Ward's health broke once again as the siege of Boston concluded. He submitted his resignation but agreed to stay in command of the defense of Boston until a replacement could be assigned. Congress accepted Ward's resignation on April 23 for reasons of health, although Washington hinted in correspondence to General Charles Lee that Ward would never serve beyond sight of his own chimney smoke.

Duties in Boston kept Ward in command there until he was relieved by General William Heath on March 20, 1777. In the meantime, Ward resumed his political career. He was a member and then president of the executive council of Massachusetts. In 1777, Ward served on an investigative committee to determine the possibilities of attacking the British in Rhode Island at Newport. Ward also served on the investigative board that examined the American fiasco in the Penobscot affair in 1779.

On November 18, 1779, the general court of Massachusetts elected Ward as a delegate to the Continental Congress. Ward took his seat in Congress in Philadelphia on June 14, 1780. It was a difficult time to be in Congress. The financial situation was deplorable. Troops were in mutiny. Benedict Arnold had defected to the British. Nothing militarily decisive had come as yet from the French alliance. Ward's term of service coincided with one of the lowest points in the War of the Revolution.

Ward was reelected for 1781 and served another full term. Due to reasons of health, Ward refused to serve a third term in Congress and returned to Shrewsbury. Ward had not been home long before he was chosen to be a state senator. He turned this honor down, preferring to serve as a representative. Ward served in the Massachusetts House for a total of 16 years, becoming the speaker of the house in 1785.

During Shay's Rebellion, Ward remained on the side of the state government and suffered a loss in popularity with the people because of his stand. He could be stubborn, especially when he was convinced his was the right view. In this case, he worked hard to solve the underlying problems that caused the rebellion, but he did not condone the violence and civil unrest caused by the rebels. Ward was highly esteemed for his political integrity, attention to duty, and independence of spirit. He was considered by most to be a fair judge and honest politician.

In 1791, Ward was elected to Congress and served for two terms, until 1795. He performed his greatest service in committees that dealt with military matters. He was a Federalist, but he did not befriend President Washington. The two men never liked each other.

Suffering continuously from the effects of the calculus and the gout in his feet, Artemus Ward returned home to spend the last years of his life with his family. After suffering two paralytic strokes, Ward died on October 28, 1800, at home. He was buried in Mountain View Cemetery in Shrewsbury.

A family man and a trusted politician who always concerned himself with the interests of Massachusetts, General Ward was a hard-working, dedicated individual who was steadfast in his convictions. The differences in personality and background made his relations with Washington, both during the war and later, strained but formal. Ward's health problems canceled his opportunities for military glory beyond that gained in the first days of the war, when Ward held together an unorganized collection of militia units until order could be established and victory at Boston ultimately won.

Paul J. Sanborn

REFERENCES

DAB; Thomas J. Fleming, *Now We Are Enemies* (1960); John Harris, *American Rebels* (1976); Richard Ketchum, *Decisive Day* (1974) Charles Martyn, *The Life of Artemus Ward* (1921); *National Cyclopedia of American Biography*; Christopher Ward, *The War of Revolution* (1952).

Warner, Seth (1743–1784)

Continental Army officer. Born in Woodbury (Roxbury), Connecticut, Warner moved in 1765 to Bennington in the New Hampshire Grants. There he became a leader of the "Green Mountain Boys." Along with Ethan Allen he agitated against the claims of New Yorkers for lands east of the Hudson River.

As captain of the Bennington company of militia, Warner, with his men, assisted Allen in the capture of Fort Ticonderoga (April 10, 1775). On May 12, Warner seized Crown Point. Soon after Warner testified in Congress about the need for a Continental regiment from the Grants. As a result, Warner's Regiment (Green Mountain Boys) was authorized June 23, 1775, in the Continental Army, and it was assigned to the Northern Department. On July 27, 1775, the regiment was organized to consist of seven companies from the New Hampshire Grants (portions of Albany and Charlotte counties, New York, later becoming Vermont) under the command of Lieutenant Colonel Warner. In the invasion of Canada in late 1775, Warner and his men served under General Richard Montgomery. During the spring of 1776 the regiment fought numerous rear-guard actions as the Americans retired to Fort Ticonderoga.

Made a colonel in June 1776, Warner was at Ticondergoa when General Arthur St. Clair ordered its evacuation. In the retreat from Ticonderoga to Skenesborough via Castleton before General John Burgoyne's force, St. Clair left Warner with some 1,200 men to protect the rear and to collect stragglers. St. Clair ordered Warner not to delay and to rejoin him at Castleton. However, Warner disobeyed and camped near Hubbardton, six miles away. There Warner's troops were surprised and attacked by a British-German force led by Brigadier General Simon Fraser and General Baron Friedrich von Reidesel. The Battle of Hubbardton (July 7, 1777) was one of the bloodiest fights—in terms of numbers of casualties related to the numbers of men engaged—in the entire war. Taking advantage of the wooded terrain, Warner managed to extricate his men, and he assisted St. Clair's northern army to escape the enemy.

Warner and his men arrived too late—after a long march from Manchester—to participate in the initial phases of the Battle of Bennington (August 16, 1777). But the Green Mountain Boys appeared in the last round of the fight, just in time to help General John Stark repulse German troops under Lieutenant Colonel Heinrich Breymann, and they harassed the enemy during their retreat to the Hudson. At Saratoga, Warner again led New Hampshire troops, but his men were not in the main battles. Serving again under Stark, on October 11–12, 1777, Warner's regiment and other New Hampshire units crossed the Hudson above Burgoyne's camp and proceeded to block the retreat northward from the battlefield.

Made a brigadier general on March 20, 1778, by the new Vermont legislature, Warner served in the army until June 1, 1783. Due to ill health, however, he saw little field duty after Saratoga.

Richard L. Blanco

REFERENCES

June Barron, "Seth Warner and the Battle of Bennington: Solving a Historical Puzzle," *Vermont History*, *39* (1971):101–106; David Chipman, *Memoir of Seth Warner* (1848); *DAB*; Simon Fraser, "Gen. Fraser's Account of Burgoyne's Campaign—Lake Champlain and the Battle of Hubbardton," *Vermont Historical Society Proceedings* (1899):139–147; Walter S. Fenton, "Seth Warner," *Vermont Historical Society Proceedings*, *8* (1940):325–350; John Luzader, *Decision on the Hudson* (1975); Joseph W.P. Parker, *The Battle of Bennington* (1970); John Williams, *The Battle of Hubbardton* (1988); Richard K. Wright, Jr., *The Continental Army* (1983).

Warren, John (1753–1815)

Continental Army Physician. A graduate of Harvard, John studied medicine under his brother Joseph Warren. In 1773 John Warren joined the Essex County militia, which marched to Cambridge in April 1775 after the Battles of Lexington and Concord. Warren tended the wounded after this fighting. He served as a volunteer at Bunker Hill. After the death of his brother in combat, Warren joined the Continental Army to become the senior surgeon of the army hospital at Cambridge. There he introduced the bark of the willow as a partially successful substitute for the scarce Jesuits' bark (from which quinine is obtained) in order to alleviate fevers.

After service at Long Island, Trenton, and Princeton, Warren returned to Boston as an army surgeon. In 1780 he supervised the Boston military hospital, and he practiced privately. He began the fourth series of lectures on anatomy and surgery in Boston, which led, in part, to the founding of the Harvard Medical Institute in 1782, where he was a professor of anatomy and surgery. Until his death, Warren was the dominant force in Boston medical circles.

Richard L. Blanco

REFERENCES

Philip Cash, et al., eds., *Medicine in Colonial Massachusetts* (1980); Howard L. Kelly and Walter L. Burrage, eds., *Dictionary of American Medical Biography* (1920); Edward Warren, *The Life of John Warren* (1874).

Warren, Joseph (1741–1775)

Physician, American Patriot. Born on June 11, 1741, at Roxbury, Massachusetts, Joseph was the oldest of the four sons of Joseph and Mary (Stevens) Warren and a brother of John Warren. After his 1759 graduation from Harvard, where he distinguished himself as a student, he served as master of the Roxbury Grammar School. He taught for one year, then decided to become a physician. He studied under Dr. James Lloyd and at the age of 23 established his practice in Boston, where he quickly earned a reputation as a scrupulously clean and talented doctor. Also in 1764, Warren married Elizabeth Hooten of Boston; they would have two daughters and two sons.

Even as his practice thrived and expanded, Warren was increasingly drawn into the political affairs of the day. In truth, in the years leading to the Revolution, he would virtually give up his practice as he devoted himself wholeheartedly to the Patriot cause. He soon became acquainted with the leading figures in Massachusetts like Jonathan Mayhew, James Otis, John Hancock, Paul Revere, and the Adamses. His friendship with John Adams began in 1764 when he inoculated the future president for smallpox—a unique procedure at the time. Warren's association with Samuel Adams would rapidly develop into one of the most significant relationships in his short life. First united in opposition to the Stamp Act, these kindred spirits grew steadily closer as troubles between the colonies and the Mother Country intensified.

Warren first rose to political prominence during the Townshend crisis when he took an active role in public meetings of opposition. From this point, he was constantly active, writing, speaking, and organizing the opposition movement in and around Boston. He demanded the removal of British troops before and after the Boston "massacre." His impassioned oration at the second commemoration of the March 5, 1770, "massacre" ushered him into the Patriot center stage. As a member of numerous committees, including the Committee of Correspondence, he worked tirelessly with Samuel Adams to promote colonial unity. In 1772, he wrote the second portion of *A State of the Rights of the Colonists* in which he chronicled "A List of the Infringements and Violations of Those Rights." Despite his wife's death in 1773, he protested loudly against the Tea Act and may have participated in the Boston Tea Party as a "Mohawk." In the wake of the British crackdown that followed and Samuel Adams's frequent absence from Massachusetts, Warren became the central directing figure of Patriot efforts in the colony in the second half of 1774. Among his multitude of services, he headed the committee of safety, organized opposition to the Regulating Act, and drafted the "Suffolk Resolves" that so influenced the First Continental Congress.

After the Continental Congress adopted the "Suffolk Resolves," Warren was selected as a member of the Massachusetts Provincial Congress. There he increased his involvement with countless local committees while writing almost daily letters to Adams in Philadelphia to keep him abreast of the colony's affairs. On March 6, 1775, at the Old South Meetinghouse, he delivered a second oration commemorating the Boston "massacre." His stirring address—though it stopped short of a call for independence and expressed hope for reconciliation—clearly warned England that unless it altered its course, serious trouble was inevitable. As the crisis heightened, he contributed to the military and defensive preparations that the Bay Colony was undertaking and, despite fears for his safety, remained in Boston observing British activity. On the evening of April 18, 1775, after detecting suspicious British movements, he sent William Dawes and Paul Revere to alert the countryside and to warn Samuel Adams and John Hancock in Lexington. When informed of the clashes at Lexington and Concord the following morning, he rode to Lexington, where he treated the wounded and later that afternoon directed troops as the colonists harassed the British on the long, bloody road back to Boston. Selected president *pro tempore* of the provincial congress on April 23 (and unanimously elected president at the end of May) Warren redoubled his activities and in essence headed the popular patriotic cause.

In the decisive propaganda battle that followed Lexington and Concord, Warren quickly and brilliantly moved to bolster the Patriot cause. He wrote and circulated the first account of the opening clashes less than one day after the shots were fired. In his circular, Warren employed language that could support any and all of the wild rumors flying about, and yet his masterful narrative forcefully called for the formation of a provincial army. To that end, he oversaw efforts to organize and retain the thousands of militiamen who had converged on Boston. He also wrote an April 26 letter to the British people, which, along with a packet of depositions and local newspaper accounts of April 19, reached England two weeks before Gage's official report. The fact that the colonial side of Lexington and Concord received wide circulation in England well before Gage's account was published undoubtedly contributed to the opposition within the Mother Country. Warren's adroit handling of the propaganda campaign, the organization of a provincial army around Boston, and the impact upon the British population may have been his greatest contributions.

On June 14, Warren was appointed major general of militia. He had declined the position as physician general, opting instead for more hazardous duty. Three days later, upon learning that the British were landing at Charlestown, he headed for the action on the peninsula and arrived on Bunker Hill as the battle was about to begin. He met with General Israel Putnam who supposedly offered to turn command over to him, but the physician refused, saying he was only a volunteer and would serve wherever he might help. (In fact, Warren, though he had been appointed major general, had not received his commission.) Putnam sent him to the redoubt on Breed's Hill, where, again supposedly, the officer in charge offered him command, but Warren similarly refused. Serving as he wished—as a volunteer—Warren fought coolly and gallantly at the redoubt, helping repulse two British assaults before a third finally carried the position after a brief hand-to-hand melee. Among the last of the defenders to leave the fort, he was attempting to rally the Americans when he was shot in the head by a British soldier. Only 34 years of age, he died instantly.

Great uncertainty concerning the fate of Warren persisted in the days that followed. It was unclear whether he had been killed, wounded, or captured. When his death was confirmed, tremendous grief greeted the announcement. He had been buried in an unmarked grave on the battlefield, so it was not until the following spring when the British evacuated Boston that positive identification could be made. It was his friend, Paul Revere, who supplied the definitive identification when he recognized the two artificial teeth he had personally fashioned for the physician. This may have been the first recorded case of using dental records to identify a corpse. After his body was exhumed, it was reinterred several times before finally resting at Forest Hills Cemetery in 1855. Although Warren was only 34 when he died, he ranked as one of the most active, popular, and influential Patriot leaders in Massachusetts in the years leading to the Revolution.

Ralph L. Eckert

REFERENCES

DAB; Esther Forbes, *Paul Revere and the World He Lived In* (1942); Richard Frothingham, *Life and Times of Joseph Warren* (1865); Arthur B. Tourtellot, *Lexington and Concord: The Beginning of the War of the American Revolution* (1959).

Warship Armament

Revolutionary War naval ordnance, for the most part, reflected tried and true technology. There were no great innovations introduced, with the exception of the carronade, a British invention that only began to be fielded in any great quantities after 1780. The emphasis in naval ordnance was more on improvements, especially of the British, who had recently become the first industrial nation and were taking advantage of various advances in metallurgy engendered by this new era. British naval ordnance was acknowledged to be the best of the time, and thus it is not surprising that the American rebels largely tried to copy British designs, rather than to design their own. Even though Britain had a high industrial capability, this was not transferred to the colonists in the prewar period, as the British wished to keep the colonies a captive market. Thus, the American cannon industry had to start from scratch at the beginning of the war, and only partially achieved the goals assigned to it. As it turned out, the colonists ended up by equipping their ships with a motley complement of domestically produced guns, cannon captured from the British, and what could be bought from the French, Spanish, Dutch, and Swedes.

The typical naval gun of the Revolution was made of iron, although there were still some made of brass. Cast iron was the preferable material because of its cost, with other materials being too expensive for mass production. The gun carriage was made of wood with two sidepieces (or cheeks) separated by heavy cross-pieces. The gun barrel was set on the carriage via trunnions extending from each side of the barrel, with caps securing the two trunnions to the carriage. The carriage itself sat on four small wooden wheels (or trucks), which moved freely. A set of ropes with block and tackle helped to secure the gun in place and kept it from rolling around.

Aiming the gun was accomplished by wedging handspikes under the breech end of the barrel and inserting quoins (or wedges) of a certain height to achieve a particular range, and using handspikes or side tackle for train adjustments (sideways or azimuth). The attached block and tackle allowed the gun to be run out for firing and restrained the gun upon firing. Since sights were at best a notch on the breech and another on the swell on the muzzle, precise aiming was difficult, and continuous aiming nearly impossible. In action, the first broadside was usually the only precise one, with succeeding ones being increasingly inaccurate. However, accuracy was not a high priority in most cases, since action tended to be at close quarters. Speed in loading was what counted, and the advent of the carronade, with its very short barrel, did much to speed the loading process. Accuracy was further diminished by the dense clouds of powder smoke that soon developed in any brisk action.

The gun's bore was determined by the size of the ball to be fired, with a little added on for windage. Windage allowed cannonballs slightly out of round (from rust or poor manufacturing) to be pushed down a sometimes not entirely true bore. Inaccuracies in casting made it vital that the ball did not jam on its way out of the tube. The accepted standard of the mid-1770s was about 1/20th of the cannonball diameter being added on to the bore for windage, although by the end of the century, windage was decreasing as boring became more accurate.

The most common—in fact, the preferred—projectile was the round shot, with the British being particularly fond of it. There were a number of reasons for this preference, including the fact that the round shot was the densest and heaviest projectile that could be fired, along with offering the greatest penetration at the farthest range. A good range in terms of reasonable accuracy was considered to be about a half-mile. Using the 32-pounder as an example, extreme range at a 10 degree elevation was 2,900 yards, while point-blank range (the point at which the

shot hits water when fired at a zero-degree elevation) was about 350 yards. The long gun was more accurate than the short-barrelled version of the same caliber. Most gun classes were cast in both long and short versions.

Other shot types included grapeshot, canister shot, langrange, chain and bar shot, shells, and carcasses. The first four types were all used for anti-rigging firing, in which one tried to bring down the opponent's sails or even masts, and for anti-personnel actions. The shell, because of its limited power, was mostly used by bomb vessels (which carried large sea mortars); the carcass (a hollow projectile filled with incendiary material) was used against forts or other suitable targets. The importance of the round shot to the Royal Navy can be seen in the typical magazine complement of a 78-gun ship in the 1780s. This included 2,800 round shot, 166 rounds of grapeshot, 84 rounds of double-headed shot, 115 of langrange, and 173 of canister.

Powder charges of the time were related to the shot size. For example, the powder charge for a 9-pounder was 66 percent of the ball's weight, that for an 18-pounder was 50 percent of the weight, and that of the 42-pounder was 40 percent of the weight. In the Revolution, flannel cartridges were common because the material was totally consumed in the explosion, although paper was still popular.

In discussing Revolutionary War naval ordnance, it is best to establish the foundation on British equipment, both because British naval forces were so dominant and because the colonists used so much captured British ordnance in equipping their ships. At the time of the Revolution the standard British naval gun classes ranged in size from 42-pounders to swivel guns. The pound figure refers to the weight of the cannonball fired by the gun. A class-by-class breakdown follows:

42-pounder. This was the heaviest gun and was fitted only to first-rates, the biggest warships. The usual length was 9 feet, 6 inches, and it weighed 6,500 pounds. However, by the time of the Revolution, the 42-pounder was in decline, being replaced after 1778 by the 32-pounder because the 42-pounder was perceived as having a lower rate of fire due to the very heavy ball weight.

32-pounder. This gun had by now been recognized as the ideal gun for the ship of the line (the heavy warship of the time), since it was the heaviest gun that could be handled efficiently in battle. By 1782 there were two basic types of 32-pounders, one of 5,800 pounds and 10 feet long, and the other of 5,500 pounds and 9 feet, 6 inches long. The 32-pounder was the main armament of the 70- and 74-gun ships of the line.

24-pounder. In the Revolution this gun class was in decline, although it was still in use as the main battery for the 64-gun ship, as well as being the second heaviest gun carried by the First Rate, the two-deck 80-gun ship, and the biggest of the 74-gun warships.

18-pounder. The evolving role for this gun class saw it entering a whole new application in 1780 as the main armament of the 38-gun frigate. This gun already formed the upper deck armament of most 74-gun ships. There already existed the 9 feet, 6 inches, 4,100 or 4,200 pounds variant and the 9 feet, 3,200 or 3,400 pounds variant, to which was added in 1780 a much smaller 3,700 to 3,800 pounds variant. The new version was issued for use on frigate gundecks.

12-pounder. This ubiquitous gun filled various roles such as forming the main armament of 32- and 36-gun frigates. There were two types, one 8 feet, 6 inches long for the upper decks of 50-gun ships, and another of 7 feet, 6 inches (2,850 pounds) for use on frigates.

9-pounder This class came in 7 different sizes by the end of the Revolution, ranging from the 7 feet (2,300 pounds) type for the main battery of Sixth Rates, to the 9 feet, 6 inches size used on bigger warships. These guns were used as the main armament for small frigates that carried 28 guns or less.

6-pounder. This type of gun was mostly carried on the quarterdeck or the forecastle and, as of 1782, came in 7 sizes, ranging from 6 feet (1,600 pounds) to 9 feet (2,400 pounds).

4-pounder. This gun had only very limited applications on 24- and 30-gun warships.

3-pounder. This gun was mainly used on sloops and cutters as well as on the quarterdeck of small frigates. The usual dimensions were 4 feet, 6 inches long with a weight of 7,000 pounds.

Swivel guns. This class of guns came in various sizes, but those using a half-pound ball were fairly standard. In the 1770s these were allotted to ships of the line and frigates for fitting to the ship's boats as well as the fighting tops (small platforms built across the trestletrees at the top of the fore and main masts).

Following are descriptions of the various British ship classes of the time in order to show typical deployments of the various gun types. Some of the guns such as the 42- and 32-pounders were fielded only on certain-sized warships. It should be pointed out that, after 1755 (under Admiral George Anson's able administration), the best warships were designed around a specific armament fit, in particular, the new 74-gun ships. Ships are listed by their rates and guns. The rate system was going out of fashion toward the end of the 1700s in favor of ships being designated by their gun complement (although carronades were never included in this number).

First-rate. The typical first-rate at the beginning of the Revolution carried 100 guns. Of these, 30 guns were 32-pounders, 28 were 24-pounders, 30 were 18-pounders or 12-pounders, and 12 were 12-pounders (these replaced 6-pounders on the quarterdeck and forecastle). After 1779, 10 carronades were added to the fit, although these never were figured in the gun total. In the Revolution, the 42-pounders for the most part had been replaced by 32-pounders. First-rates had three gun decks.

Second-rate. Second-rates mounted from 90 to 84 guns. Although they started out as 90-gun ships, the decision in 1778 to add 8 guns to the quarterdecks made them close to first-rates in firepower. Typical gun complements on these 3-gundeck ships included 32-pounders on the lower deck, 18-pounders on the middle deck, and 12-pounders on the upper deck.

Third-rate. Third-rates mounted from 64 to 80 guns with two basic classes, the 74-gun and 64-gun ships. The two-decker 74 was considered the workhorse of the fleet, since it was both cheaper to build and required a smaller crew than the ponderous three-deckers. Yet, the 74's typical armament of 32-pounders (28), 24-pounders (28), and 9-pounders (18) compared very favorably with that of the 3-deckers. The 64-gun ship was used during the Revolution, but its comparatively light hull and armament led to its subsequent decline. Typical gun complements for the 64-gun ship included 24-pounders (26), 18-pounders (26), and 9-pounders (12). Around the time of the Revolution it became evident that this class was too small for the line of battle.

Fourth-rate. This 50 to 60 gun class was revived in the 1770s, with the main task of acting as flagships for small squadrons or for convoy escort duty. Due to its fit of 22 24-pounders (as well as 12- and 9-pounders), this class was quite powerful, especially in comparison to frigates. The only problem with the 50-gun ship was its poor sea-keeping ability.

Fifth-rate. This rating included 44- and 31-gun ships and large frigates. The 44-gun ship, like the 50s, was another class revived in the 1770s, and mounted 18-pounders (22), 12-pounders (20) (these replaced 9-pounders around 1780), and 6-pounders (2). The 38- and 40-gun frigates were usually captured French ships, although the British built some copies in the 1780s. Some of the 40-gun ships carried 24-pounders, which made them exceedingly powerful for frigates (some called them frigates, some designated them as ships of the line). The 38-gun frigate was the largest frigate type in use in the late 1700s and were armed with 18-pounders and 9-pounders. The 36-gun frigate was not yet in common use.

Small Fifth-rate. This rating was somewhat hazy but seems to have included 28- and 32-gun frigates. The main armament of these ships was the 12-pounder, which made the 32-gun frigate one of the success stories of the mid-1700s. The 32s were the standard patrol and reconnaissance vessels by the time of the Revolution.

Sixth-rate. These included various small frigates, usually armed with 9-pounders for the main armament. They normally carried between 20 and 28 guns.

Below these ships were sloops (16 to 18 guns, with the 6-pounders as the main weapon), cutters (10 to 14 4-pounders) and bomb vessels, which were specialized ships used for shore bombardment. Besides one or two sea mortars, the latter sometimes carried as many as a dozen 9-pounders.

At the time of the Revolution, the ship of the line was considered to be a warship of 60 guns and over. In 1775 there were 131 ships of the line in the Royal Navy, and by 1783 there were 174. Of small two-deckers and frigates (20 to 56 guns), there were 98 in 1775 and 198 in 1783. The fifth- and sixth-rates made up the cruiser squadrons. The frigates were the most common ship size, with 32-gun frigates the most prevalent, followed by 28s, 44s, and 36s.

Ironically, the British warships of this general time period were inferior in design to French warships. One cause was the "establishments," that is, the Navy Board scales of ship dimen-

sions that set limits on class tonnage. As the 1700s advanced, British ship designers, having to use limits set in 1719, were forced to cram increasingly heavier gun complements into hulls that were ill-suited for additional or heavier gun fittings. The British began to copper-bottom their hulls in significant numbers during this era, which resulted in markedly enhanced speeds in many cases, yet this technology still had teething problems, and thus copper bottoms were not yet a standard fit.

Also, by 1778, when the French entered the war, the Royal Navy was dangerously overextended. One problem was the fact that almost one-third of British-flag merchants were American-built and manned by 1770. The rebellion of the colonies is estimated to have deprived the Royal Navy of an estimated 18,000 prime seamen. There was too much territory to protect with too few resources, aggravated by the addition to the fray of the French, Spanish, and Dutch navies.

As the single notable naval ordnance innovation of the Revolution, indeed, of the whole eighteenth century, the carronade bears more detailed study, even though, as far as is known, the British were the only users of the gun during the Revolution. There is a possibility that some may have been captured by the rebels, but no firm evidence of this exists. Also, American sea captains preferred the long gun, since it allowed them to engage the British at some distance, where the usual British broadside throw-weight advantage was not such a factor.

The term "carronade" has its origins in the name of the Scottish company, the Carron Ironworks. There were two people instrumental in developing and bringing to fruition the carronade concept. General Robert Melville is acknowledged as being the originator of the concept, although the general viewed his design as more of a howitzer firing shells, with the primary application being as a heavy fortress gun. The gun actually ended up firing solid shot on a horizontal trajectory, with the navy being the prime customer. Charles Gascoigne, one of the partners at Carron, supervised the experiments and is presumed to have had significant input along the way.

The carronade as used during the Revolution was a preliminary design in that modifications were being made fairly rapidly during the war years. The prototype was cast early in 1779 and was adopted by the Admiralty in July of the same year. There was a great deal of testing even as the gun was approved, with various sizes being tried out for performance. This included 68-, 24-, 18-, and 12-pounders being compared to 6-, 4-, and 3-pounder long guns. Further tests and modifications came during the war as, for example, it was found that the first generation of designs was too short, having the nasty tendency to set one's own rigging on fire. The original guns used trunnions to suspend the gun. This was changed sometime late in the war, or after the end, to a loop under the barrel. Also about this time came the use of a screw thread for elevation and depression. This method compared very favorably with the quoins and wedges that were traditionally used for the same purpose with long guns.

The carronade offered three particular features that made it a superior weapon. Its short length and low weight (half that of a comparable long gun) made it much easier to handle. A carronade of a particular weight could fire a cannonball that was four times as heavy as that of the equivalent long gun. Yet since the carronade was meant to be specifically a short-range weapon, the barrel could be shorter and the powder charge lighter (between one-fourth and one-third that of long a gun). Since the carronade was bored from the solid, it featured a reduced windage. Also, windage now could be made standard for all sizes, rather than proportional as required for long guns, thus making large guns more accurate than previously.

The prime advantage of the carronade was its smashing power. The smaller ball fired by the long gun tended to go right through the hull, leaving a hole that could be plugged fairly easily, although the heavier balls fired by the bigger long guns could leave huge holes when they exited the opposite side of the hull, along with a cloud of splinters (which killed more than the actual cannonball). In contrast, the large carronade ball tended to leave a large ragged entrance hole that was quite difficult, if not impossible, to plug. The carronade was particularly effective in close action, with a carronade broadside exacting a fearful toll. Due to the carronade's light weight and lower manpower requirements, merchantmen now could mount a respectable armament for beating off the ubiquitous American privateers.

Although the carronade offered a number of advantages, acceptance was slow by the generally conservative British sea captains, who expressed significant opposition. However, the Navy Board did what it could to accommodate itself to the captains, and by 1780 opposition was waning. The gun showed its mettle in a number of actions over the next several years, and by 1782 had been fully accepted, with 167 ships (over one-quarter of the fleet) carrying carronades, with the emphasis on equipping smaller ships.

The American colonies labored under a severe handicap in providing for their ordnance needs during the Revolution. The industrial level of the colonies at the beginning of the Revolution was quite low in many areas, mainly due to the British policy of mercantilism, which saw the colonies as nothing more than the provider of raw materials for the Mother Country. The making of finished goods was discouraged, especially in the years before the Revolution, although the colonists did set up a surprising number of small manufacturing facilities in contravention of the British dictates. The British had encouraged the development of an iron-smelting capability because British merchants needed the iron for their own products. Iron-smelting operations already existed in Connecticut, Massachusetts, Rhode Island, Pennsylvania, Maryland, and South Carolina. In fact, the American colonies accounted for 14 percent of the world's iron by 1775. However, the making of iron finished products was something in which the colonies had limited experience, and as far as cannon-making, there were not even any persons with any background in the area, let alone an industry.

Yet the lack of knowledge in cannon-making did not discourage the colonists, and the Continental Congress laid out ambitious plans for the fitment of all new American ships with domestically made cannon. An immediate problem was encountered in the form of a shortage of bronze, which was remedied by a requisition campaign of all available bronze objects, including doorknockers. By February 1776, successful experiments in casting cannon had been carried out in Maryland, New York, and Pennsylvania.

The most immediate major project of the colonial government involving naval ordnance was the equipping of a new class of 13 frigates. Authorized in 1775, the class was to consist of 5

32-gun frigates (26 12-pounders, 6 6-pounders), 5 28-gun frigates (26 12-pounders, 2 6-pounders), and 3 24-gun frigates (24 9-pounders). The task of casting the cannon was assigned to Pennsylvania foundries. However, they proved unequal to the task, and Salisbury Furnace in Connecticut was chosen to provide the cannon for two of the frigates. Salisbury, in turn, also proved incapable of meeting the full requirement, and John Brown of Rhode Island was given the remaining work. This chain of events was symptomatic of the poor grasp of reality that the Congress had as to the ability of the colonies to provide for all their own needs.

Furthermore, the guns for the frigates were supposed to be standard, yet the actual fit was rather haphazard. For instance, the frigate *Warren*, which was rated at 26 12-pounders and 6 6-pounders, actually carried 12 18-pounders, 14 12-pounders, and 8 9-pounders. The 18-pounder was the heaviest American naval gun to be built during the war, but the 12-pounder was the naval gun most commonly used.

American-built naval guns generally were thought to follow British designs and were made of iron. Only one book on artillery was available in the colonies during the war, the *Treatise of Artillery* by John Muller (originally published in 1757), and this was published in 1779 in an American pirated edition. This book is thought to have influenced the Americans more than did the British, and led to such innovations as placing trunnions on the centerline of the barrel. It would appear that some American cannon foundries made guns based on French designs, but there is no evidence of any actually being fielded. There were very wide variations in length and weight of American guns, largely a reflection of the designs of the foundry where the gun was builieutenant Variations in areas such as trunnion placement later led to problems when the barrels were delivered for fitting to their carriages (generally very similar in design to British gun carriages).

Characteristics of American-made guns included having a thicker wall at the muzzle, as well as longer lengths. Double-fortified guns were an American innovation and were considered equal to guns one step up in shot weight. Longer than standard guns, they exhibited a superior range and accuracy to their standard equivalents, and were popular as bow guns, especially on heavy gunboats.

Swivels were quite popular on American ships and were much easier to cast than the larger guns. The most common type was from 34 to 36 inches in maximum length, with a bore of from 1/2 to 3/4 inches, and throwing a shot of 1/2 to 3/4 of a pound in weight.

American powder quality during the war was generally quite poor, with very low reliability. There were problems with getting good quality ingredients, and proportions were generally uneven. The first American powder mill was established in 1775.

The Americans soon realized that their naval ordnance needs could not be satisfied domestically. Thus, purchase abroad and capture of pieces from the British became very important supply sources. The colonists were lucky in capturing significant quantities of cannon in several incidents early in the war. The seizing of Fort Ticonderoga in May 1775 provided 78 serviceable guns ranging from 4-pounders to 24-pounders, as well as thousands of cannonballs. In November of the same year, the colonists captured the British ordnance brig, the *Nancy*, which resulted in a haul of bronze and iron guns ranging in weight from 4-pounders to 24-pounders. The best haul came from the successful expedition to the Bahamas in March 1776 (possibly the most successful American naval operation of the war), where troops led by Commodore Esek Hopkins captured 88 cannon ranging from 9-pounders to 32-pounders, 15 bronze mortars, more than 16,500 roundshot and shells, as well as 24 barrels of powder.

As the war progressed, France became the chief source of arms. The colonists had already been making purchases abroad from the time the British embargoed the sale of munitions to the colonies in 1774. Since the French were in the midst of rebuilding their navy, considerable numbers of cannon became available (albeit aged, with some dating back to 1678). The early purchases came through a shell company named Hortalez et Cie, specially set up for deniability purposes by the French government and run by Pierre Augustin Caron de Beaumarchais. The British protested strenuously against this trade, but the French continued their sales, including the outfitting of many American ships in French harbors. The official entry of the French into the war after the Battle of Saratoga in 1777 resulted in the French navy dealing directly with

America. The colonists also bought cannon from Scandinavia, Spain, and Holland.

In contrast to the British ship "establishments," it is almost impossible to show any organized ordnance fits for American ships, whether naval or privateer. In the first year of the war, the availability of cannon was limited to those seized in the opening days of the war and whatever was captured at Ticonderoga and elsewhere. Both then and later in the war, ships were fitted out with whatever was available, resulting in very motley mixtures of guns that tended to be 12-pounders or smaller. The early years of the war saw a great proliferation of entities putting demands on the available supply. This included a navy established by the army, the Continental Navy, the navies established by 11 states (the largest ones fielded by Massachusetts, Connecticut, Pennsylvania, Maryland, Virginia, and South Carolina), a force of converted merchantmen, and a host of privateers issued commissions or letters of marque by both Congress and most of the states. Also fielded were such impromptu fleets as the Lake Champlain squadron commanded by Benedict Arnold. The numbers of platforms being fielded meant that it was not possible to satisfactorily equip all of them, and the situation was not helped by the high ship attrition rate, which meant that their guns were taken out of circulation.

The preponderance of British naval power in North American waters can be seen by the fact that the British had at least 71 large ships (average of 28 guns apiece) in the area in 1776. Against this number the colonists could only muster 27 ships that carried an average of 20 guns each (and smaller ones at that), with few of these ships actually at sea.

It was especially characteristic of the Continental Navy to be undermanned and undergunned throughout the whole war. Men were more interested in serving aboard privateers, with the possibility of prize money. Also, since privateers were usually fielded by merchants with a fair amount of capital, they could afford to pay for more extensive cannon fits than might be the case with the always penurious Continental Congress or state governments. The dichotomy can be seen in the disparate numbers between naval warships and privateers during the war. At its peak in 1776, the Continental Navy consisted of fewer than 5,000 men manning 34 ships. In contrast, in 1782 there were 405 privateers (6,700 guns) manned by 20,000 men. During the war, Congress issued letters of marque to 1,697 ships that carried at least 14,872 guns.

The privateers were largely equipped with ordnance from overseas sources, and usually carried small guns, with 4-pounders being the most common. The largest gun normally encountered was the 9-pounder. Continental Navy ships also tended to carry small guns, since few very large warships were fielded. The most powerful was the 74-gun *America*, which was launched only in 1782 and then given to France. The America's largest guns were only 18-pounders (30), backed up by 12-pounders (32). The renowned 42-gun *Bonhomme Richard* of John Paul Jones was the second most powerful ship fielded by the navy, and its largest guns were also 18-pounders, and only 6 of those at that. An exception to the 18-pounder limit was the 40-gun frigate *Indien*, which was equipped with 36-pounders (32) as well as 12-pounders (12). The army's navy of 1777 had no guns larger than 4-pounders. Arnold's Lake Champlain fleet consisted of 17 vessels equipped with 102 guns (ranging in size from 2- to 18-pounders), as well as 186 swivels. Many of Arnold's guns came from those captured at Fort Ticonderoga and Crown Point. Invariably, few ships that served in any of the various rebel navies survived the war.

Revolutionary War naval ordnance was woefully inefficient when one considers the destructive potential compared to the weight of the gun, its carriage and tackle, and the shot. The need to arm ships with many guns to achieve a decent broadside led to significant design compromises. The carronade was a breakthrough in cannon technology, yet its full potential was not to be fully realized until the Napoleonic Wars. The Revolution did help to establish in American minds the need to combine heavy firepower with long, swift hulls. These considerations were to bear fruit in the War of 1812, when American warships made a fine showing. Even during the Revolution, the American ships, although often very underarmed, were able to escape the clutches of heavily gunned British warships because of the former's superior ship design. The Royal Navy and American naval forces met mostly in small-scale actions, in which the overwhelming firepower of the British often was a hindrance in that the weight of British ships often made them poor maneuverers. Even the large-scale actions with the French in the war's later years did not reflect well on the British and their slower ships. All too often during the Revolution, it would seem that ship design was the decisive factor and not the weight of the broadside. *See also*: Continental Navy; Naval Ordnance; Warships, Classes of

Tom Baranauskas

REFERENCES

E.H.H. Archibald, *The Wooden Fighting Ship in the Royal Navy: AD 897–1860* (1970); Howard I. Chapelle, *The History of the American Sailing Navy* (1949); Jack Coggins, *Ships and Seamen of the American Revolution* (1969); Brian Lavery, *The Arming and Fitting of English Ships of War 1600–1815* (1987); Spencer Tucker, *Arming the Fleet: U.S. Navy Ordnance in the Muzzle-Loading Era* (1989).

Warships, Classes of

Eighteenth-century naval vessels were labeled with terms that have no modern equivalents. To understand the functions of the various ship types requires an understanding of how the eighteenth-century navy worked. The great moment in naval warfare was the sea battle, in which fleets of warships fired broadsides at each other by the hour in an effort to settle the issues of the war in an afternoon. By the end of the seventeenth century naval thinkers had developed a tactical doctrine that was to dominate European naval warfare for the next 100 years.

That doctrine had to accommodate a basic truth of nautical technology: a wooden warship's guns could only be mounted in rows along her sides. The naval architects had not developed a means of installing more than a few guns at the bow or the stern without introducing a dangerous strain on the ship's structure. The warship captain's nightmare was to have his T crossed — to find an enemy vessel firing broadsides the length of his ship, while he was denied the opportunity to reply.

The tacticians' answer to this problem was the "line of battle." When the opposing fleets sighted each other each admiral would form his ships into a long, straight line ahead, so close together that no enemy vessel would be able to pass between them. The opposing lines would bear down on each other until they were within firing range. Each ship would then engage her opposite number in the enemy line, and the battle

would continue (in theory at any rate) until one admiral or the other surrendered.

The vessel designed to participate in such a battle was the "line-of-battle-ship," or "ship of the line." She was an imposing creation; few manmade objects of the day were larger. She was about 200 feet long, and the tallest of her 3 masts stood almost that high above the water. Her guns fired shot weighing 18, 24, or 32, pounds; the standard field artillery piece, by contrast, was the 6-pounder.

The British navy classified its warships into six "rates." A first-rate ship was armed with 100 guns; a second-rate, 84 or 90; a third-rate, 64, 70, 74, or 80. Ships of the first three rates were considered powerful enough to fight in the line of battle. By the start of the American Revolution experience had established that the most effective ship of the line was the 74-gun ship, frequently referred to in contemporary documents simply as the "seventy-four." The first- and second-rates mounted their guns on three full-length gundecks; the third-rates mounted theirs on two. The guns projected through "gunports" in the ships' sides, looking from a distance like rows of square black dots. Ships of the line were sometimes referred to informally as "three-deckers" and "two-deckers."

A fourth-rate ship carried 50 or 60 guns, a fifth-rate 32, 36, or 44, and a sixth-rate 20, 22, 24, or 28. The 60-, 50-, and 44-gun ships were hybrids, the products of dubiously successful building programs. They resembled small ships of the line, with their guns mounted on two full-length gundecks, but were judged too weak to fight in the line of battle; they were clumsy sailers, unable to keep pace with lighter warships. During the American war such vessels saw considerable service as convoy escorts and in support of army operations. The HMS *Serapis*, which was captured by John Paul Jones's *Bonhomme Richard*, was a 44-gun ship.

The ship of 28, 32, or 36 guns was generally called a "frigate." The frigate's physical dimensions approached those of the ship of the line, but she was much lighter and faster; she was not designed to fight battles. Most of her guns were mounted on a single gundeck, augmented by a few light weapons on the forecastle and quarterdeck. Frigates were attached to the battle fleet to seek out and maintain contact with the enemy, to carry messages, and to repeat admirals' signals amid the smoke of a battle. They also attacked the enemy's commerce and escorted convoys. The young frigate captain's ultimate ambition was to encounter an enemy frigate on the high seas and capture her in a "single-ship action."

The generic term for most naval vessels of fewer than 20 guns was "sloop of war." That designation was used rather carelessly; in the British naval bureaucracy the most important distinction between a sloop of war and a larger warship seems to have been that the latter vessel was commanded by a captain and the former by a lieutenant or a commander. The largest sloop of war, carrying 18 guns, was built like a small frigate, with three square-rigged masts and a raised quarterdeck and forecastle. The "brig-rigged sloop," or "brig of war," had two masts, both square-rigged. (A square-rigged sail is suspended from a horizontal spar, or "yard." When the ship is running before the wind, the yards, viewed from above, are perpendicular—"square"—to the ship's centerline. A "fore-and-aft-rigged" sail is set roughly parallel to the ship's centerline. A "schooner" had two masts, each carrying a fore-and-aft-rigged sail suspended from a diagonal spar called a "gaff." (In the eighteenth century many schooners also set small square sails on one or both masts.) A "cutter," the smallest of seagoing warship types, had one square-rigged mast.

The word "sloop," in eighteenth-century usage, is confusing. In the naval context it usually referred to a small, three-masted warship with one gundeck, but it was also used as a rigging term. In that context a "sloop" was a vessel with one mast, square- or fore-and-aft rigged. The 1780 edition of Falconer's *Universal Dictionary of the Marine* compounds the ambiguity by defining a "cutter" as "a small vessel . . . . furnished with one mast, and rigged as a sloop."

Sloops of war, brigs, and cutters performed a wide variety of functions that were necessary to keep the navy operating. They carried dispatches and supplies, escorted merchant ships, and, in time of peace, enforced the customs regulations; the British "revenue cutters" were operated by the Customs Service. Small British warships saw extensive service in North America, becoming familiar sights in the colonial harbors, bays, and rivers.

The French navy did not have such a precise taxonomy of ship types, though its vessels generally were similar in appearance to their British counterparts. (Modern research has generally disproved the long-standing view that French naval architecture was categorically superior). French three-decked ships of the line were armed with 120, 110, or 90 guns; two-deckers had 80, 74, 64, or 50, the latter two classes being regarded as too small to lie in the line of battle. In the French navy the term "corvette" was coming into use to describe the equivalent of the British ship-rigged sloop-of-war. The "lugger" rig, with two or three masts carrying distinctive fore-and-aft "lugsails," was popular in small French warships.

The Continental Navy was a miscellany of warships, some built for the purpose and many purchased as they were needed. Only one American ship of the line, the *America*, was built during the Revolution; she was given to the French before she was launched. The American frigates of 32, 28, and 24 guns apparently were excellent ships; one of the 32s, the *Hancock*, was described by her British captors as "the finest and fastest frigate in the world." Several other frigates and smaller warships were purchased or borrowed from the French. The Continental Congress also commissioned numerous sloops of war, brigs, and schooners, as did the individual states. Many of the purchased ships were given casual and inconsistent designations. The *Alfred* and John Paul Jones's *Bonhomme Richard*, for example, are referred to in some contemporary documents as "Continental frigates"; both were actually converted merchantmen.

The small-scale naval race on Lake Champlain in 1776 produced a fleet of small warships designed for use in shallow water and unpredictable winds. Benedict Arnold's squadron at the Battle of Valcour Island included a sloop, three schooners, a cutter, three galleys, and three gondolas, or "gundalows." One of the latter, the *Philadelphia*, is on exhibit at the Smithsonian Institution. She is a shallow-draft, single-masted open boat about 53 feet long and 15 feet in beam, armed with one 12-pounder and two 9-pounders. She was fitted with long oars, or "sweeps," for rowing. The galleys in Arnold's fleet were larger (about 75 feet long), with two-masted fore-and-aft rigs and ports for 18 light guns. The British fleet on Lake Champlain included gunboats (open boats with carriage guns mounted in their bows) and one square-ended, barge-like craft called a "radeau."

Several other types of warship were devised to perform specific functions. A "fireship," usually an old vessel retired from some other use, was loaded with combustible materials, set on fire, and abandoned to drift into an enemy ship. Fireships were decisive in the defeat of the Spanish Armada of 1588; the Royal Navy elaborated on the concept for more than 200 years in the hope of repeating that success, but eighteenth-century fireships never achieved particularly impressive results. A "bomb vessel" was armed with a pair of huge mortars intended for shore bombardment. British bomb vessels of the 1770s were generally ship-rigged (i.e., with three square-rigged masts). The French clung to the older "bomb ketch," which had two masts—an enormous square-rigged mainmast in the center of the ship, aft of the mortars, and a small mizzenmast. The term "armed vessel" was applied to any warship that did not fit into any of the usual categories. An armed vessel was usually a converted merchantman.

John A. Tilley

REFERENCES

E.H.H. Archibald, *The Fighting Ship in the Royal Navy A.D. 897–1984* (1984); Jean Boudriot, "The French Fleet During the American War of Independence," *Nautical Research Journal*, 25 (1979); Howard I. Chapelle, *The History of the American Sailing Navy* (1949); William Falconer, *An Universal Dictionary of the Marine* (1780), rpr. 1970; Anthony Preston and David Lyon, *Navies of the American Revolution* (1975).

Washington, George (1732–1799)

Commander-in-chief, Continental Army; first President of the United States. By any measure an exceedingly ambitious youth, George Washington was the third son of a moderately prosperous planter and businessman, and he set his life's goals in early adolescence. They were to acquire considerable landed wealth and to establish a personal reputation for honorable action that would distinguish him among his peers. Both were essential elements for success in the aristocratic society that dominated colonial Virginia, a fact of which young Washington was acutely aware, and he pursued them with uncommon energy and determination. His ambition, as he said later regarding Alexander Hamilton, was "of that laudable kind, which prompts a man to excel in whatever he takes in

hand." Washington from first to last expected much of himself and of those about him. Whether claiming western lands or ordering household goods from London, cultivating wheat or breeding mules, organizing an army or establishing a new national government, Washington seldom was satisfied with anything less than the best.

Initially Washington's personal circumstances, while far from the worst, were noticeably less than the best. His father's death when George was 11 years old left the boy on the outer fringes of the landed aristocracy with few appreciable assets of his own. Because of the family's reduced finances, he could not expect to continue his education at the English preparatory school attended by his two older half-brothers, nor did he inherit a large productive plantation on the Potomac River as each of them did. Washington's principal legacy from his father was a small tract of mediocre land on the Rappahannock River across from the busy port town of Fredericksburg. Called "Ferry Farm" because of the free ferry to and from the town nearby (an inconvenience rather than an advantage to the Washingtons), the tract included a modest house that the boy was obliged to share with his strong-willed mother and four younger siblings—a sister and three brothers.

Washington was aided in his rise to prominence by the influence of powerful people and by fortuitous events, but from an early age he consciously prepared himself through various methods of self-improvement to gain the favor of such people and to take advantage of such events. If Washington was not an entirely "self-made" man, he was in the words of W.W. Abbot a "self-constructed" one, always at work on himself. With studious care, young Washington molded his dress, conduct, and speech to conform as closely as possible to the highest standards of the Virginia aristocracy at the middle of the eighteenth century. He did not want for role models. During his teens Washington often visited Mount Vernon, the Potomac River home of his eldest half-brother, Lawrence Washington, a rising young planter who served as adjutant general of the colony, and through Lawrence he became intimate with Lawrence's in-laws and nearby neighbors at Belvoir, the Fairfaxes, who, from their elegant mansion, controlled the vast Northern Neck proprietary stretching from the mouth of the Potomac to its headspring, nearly five million acres in all.

Washington's surviving school books do not reveal exactly when and where the boy learned the rudiments of grammar and mathematics, but it is certain that his education in the important matters of his life occurred at Mount Vernon and Belvoir, where he heard politics, military affairs, and land speculation discussed at length and where he gained a lasting appreciation for fashionable clothes, fine furnishings, swift horses, and useful books. Under the influence of his Fairfax mentors, young Washington also became adept at playing billiards and popular card games, took dancing and fencing lessons, and learned to savor good wines. "I should be glad to hear," Washington wrote his younger brother Jack in 1755, that "you live in Harmony and good fellowship with the family at Belvoir, as it is in their power to be very serviceable upon many occasion's to us as young beginner's; I would advise your visiting often" (GW to John Augustine Washington, May 28, 1755, in Abbot, *Papers of GW, Colonial Ser.*, 1:289–293).

The Fairfaxes were especially helpful to Washington in 1749 when they arranged for him to become surveyor of Culpeper County. Because surveyors controlled access to new lands, they were persons of some importance in colonial Virginia, and naming a 17-year-old boy to be a county surveyor was an unprecedented act. Washington's Culpeper appointment testifies not only to the power of the Fairfaxes but also to their confidence in his budding talents and remarkably mature judgment and character. "He seemed young when his elders looked at him, but not when they listened to him," biographer Douglas Southall Freeman says. At some undetermined time during his youth, Washington adopted a hard code of personal conduct that required him "to adhere absolutely to truth, to practice rigid honesty, to do his full duty, to put forth his largest effort, to maintain uniform courtesy and, above all, to deal justly." His earnest pursuit of those ideals, although inevitably falling short of perfection, impressed members of the older generation and, Freeman thinks, accounts in large part for his success in dealing with colonial leaders as a young man (Freeman, *Washington*, 2:383–384).

Character was not Washington's only qualification for the Culpeper surveyorship. At the age of 15, soon after his mother scuttled a plan proposed by Lawrence to send the boy to sea, Washington worked his way through a short course in the practicalities of Virginia surveying, apparently under the tutelage of a local surveyor. The apex of Washington's limited formal education, that course, and his subsequent experience as a professional surveyor reinforced his strong sense of order. "Every task," Freeman says, "was performed as if it were a land survey—step by step, with the closest possible approach to absolute precision" (Freeman, *Washington*, 1:385). Washington's mind was a methodical one, which means, as Thomas Jefferson observes in an often-quoted letter, that "it was slow in operation, being little aided by invention or imagination." It also means, as Jefferson says in the same letter, that Washington's mind, although not of "the very first order," was "great and powerful," strong in penetration and "sure in conclusion." Given time for study, Washington inevitably discerned fundamental factors underlying military and political events that many of his contemporaries missed. "As far as he saw," Jefferson says, "no judgment was ever sounder" (Jefferson to Walter Jones, Jan. 2, 1814, in Ford, *Writings of Jefferson*, 9:448).

Besides strengthening the methodical habits of his mind, surveying inured Washington to the rigors of wilderness living, gave him an eye for good land, and brought him financial rewards essential for his advancement. Most of Washington's surveying was done not in relatively well-settled Culpeper County, but west of the Blue Ridge, where an abundance of unclaimed lands assured energetic surveyors of many jobs and many fees. No one outworked Washington. In slightly more than three years of frontier surveying, he ran the boundaries of nearly 200 tracts and may have earned as much as 400 pounds in Virginia currency, an income exceeded only by the colony's best lawyers. More important, Washington used his money and opportunities to acquire about 2,300 acres of good Shenandoah Valley land, a holding that matched Lawrence Washington's Mount Vernon in size if not prestige.

Washington interrupted his surveying in the fall of 1751 to sail to Barbados with Lawrence, who was ill, apparently with tuberculosis. On the island Washington survived a case of smallpox, thereby becoming immune to that dreaded disease. Lawrence was less fortunate. The tropical air of the West Indies did not alleviate his persistent cough, and he died at home in July 1752, leaving Mount Vernon to his infant daughter. The child's death a short time later enabled Washington to gain control of the plantation in December 1754 by lease from Lawrence's widow, who held a life title to it. The widow's death seven years later gave him outright ownership of Mount Vernon as the residual heir. Although Washington continued to invest heavily in western lands after 1754, Mount Vernon became the center of his life from that time forward.

Land acquisition satisfied only one of Washington's animating ambitions, however. He continued to hunger for the sort of honorable reputation that neither surveying nor tobacco planting could provide. Seeing military service as his most likely path to personal distinction, Washington seized the first available opportunity to embark on it. In the spring of 1752 he learned that Lawrence Washington's adjutancy would be divided into districts, and he promptly mounted a campaign to persuade Governor Robert Dinwiddie to appoint him to one of them, despite his lack of the knowledge and experience necessary to train militiamen, the principal duty of Virginia's adjutants. "My best endeavours will not be wanting," he promised the governor, "and doubt not, but by a constant application to fit myself for the Office" (GW to Dinwiddie, June 10, 1752, in Abbot, *Papers of GW, Colonial Ser.*, 1:50–51). On December 13, 1752, Dinwiddie commissioned Washington adjutant of the southern district with the rank of major and an annual salary of 100 pounds. Sometime during the next several months Washington arranged to move to the adjutancy of the northern district, in which Mount Vernon was located.

Washington's military career truly began in October 1753 when he volunteered to investigate reports of French incursions in the Ohio Valley. Traveling through largely unbroken wilderness with a small party of backwoodsmen, Washington reached Fort Le Boeuf a few miles south of Lake Erie in mid-December and gave the French commandant a letter from Governor Dinwiddie requesting French withdrawal from the region. Washington returned to Virginia the following month with an unaccommodating reply and intelligence about French forces. His meticulous journal of the arduous trip was immediately published and widely distributed, affording him a first taste of the renown that he so ardently desired.

Washington did not aspire to command the provincial regiment that Virginia raised in the spring of 1754 to oppose the French, conceding that he lacked the necessary experience. What he asked for and received was the second rank as lieutenant colonel, but when at the end of May the designated colonel died in an accidental fall from a horse, Washington accepted that higher rank and took command of the regiment without second thoughts. Washington already had marched an advanced contingent across the Alleghenies, and on May 29 he ambushed a small French party, killing several men, including its commander, Joseph Coulon de Villiers, sieur de Jumonville. Washington viewed his aggressive action as a preemptive strike against a hostile force. The French charged that he had assassinated a peaceful envoy. In either case, the incident sparked open hostilities between Britain and France, marking the beginning of what was called the French and Indian War in North American and the Seven Years' War in Europe. A large French force led by Jumonville's brother soon retaliated against Washington. Retreating to a hastily built circular stockade appropriately named Fort Necessity, Washington surrendered to the French on July 4, 1754, after a brief resistance and marched his men home.

Washington accepted defeat with what his mentor William Fairfax called a "philosophic mind" (William Fairfax to GW, Sept. 5, 1754, in Abbot, *Papers of GW, Colonial Ser.*, 1:201–203) In spite of evident military shortcomings, he did not think himself disgraced, for he had acted with courage in defense of his "country"—Virginia. He had "heard Bulletts whistle," Washington told his brother Jack and had found "something charming in the sound" (GW to John Augustine Washington, May 31, 1754, in Abbot, *Papers of GW, Colonial Ser.* 1:118–119). Washington possessed what every soldier desires—coolness under fire. He could lead men in battle without being incapacitated by fear or distracted by the chaos about him. Faced with adverse circumstances, Washington strove to do his best, accepting what could not be helped without relaxing his efforts to influence events that he could control.

What Washington could not accept, however, was his removal from command in the fall of 1754. With the outbreak of war, British regulars were sent to America, and at the suggestion of Governor Dinwiddie, Virginia's provincial troops were reduced to the status of independent companies, leaving young Colonel Washington no regiment to lead in the next campaign. Faced with the prospect of being demoted to the captaincy of a company, Washington angrily resigned his commission in October 1754. The least likable aspect of Washington's youthful character was an acute sensitivity about his public reputation. Any perceived slight to his "honor" invariably occasioned much whining about injustices done to him and threats of resignation. Having been a provincial colonel, Washington believed that he could not serve honorably in a lesser rank, regular or provincial. At the same time, he recognized that he was a neophyte in the art of war and had much to learn about it.

Washington was given a way out of his dilemma by General Edward Braddock, who arrived in Virginia in February 1755 to lead an expedition against the French in the Ohio Valley. Braddock allowed Washington to serve him as a volunteer aide-de-camp, which avoided the question of rank while affording the young Virginian a rare chance to observe at close hand one of the best administrators in the British army. In an age when most professional military officers learned their craft, not by formal schooling, but by talking with veterans, observing field operations, reading standard works, and practicing on their own, Braddock's expedition was an educational opportunity not to be neglected, and Washington sought to take full advantage of it by systematically recording most of the general's daily orders in notebooks for future study. At Braddock's headquarters Washington also met and conversed with many bright young British officers, whom he consciously began to imitate in dress and conduct.

Braddock's disastrous defeat at the Monongahela River on July 9, 1755, did not invalidate the lessons that Washington learned from him, but rather added to them. On the march to the Monongahela, Washington witnessed for the first time the impressive discipline and organization of a professional army in the field, and at the river, where a ragged force of French and Indians struck a lucky blow at a rare moment of British carelessness, Washington saw for himself how uncertain the fortunes of war were. He did not join other colonials in disparaging Braddock's abilities and character after the defeat, but blamed the British rank and file for falling into a panic that prevented their officers from effectively deploying them against their less disciplined foes. His own escape from the killing field without harm, despite having two horses shot under him and four bullets pass through his coat, Washington attributed to the workings of a benevolent but impersonal "Providence, that protected me beyond all human expectation" (GW to John Augustine Washington, July 18, 1755, in Abbot, *Papers of GW, Colonial Ser.*, 1:343).

Although Washington was lauded throughout Virginia for the courage that he had again displayed while assisting the fatally wounded General Braddock on the field of battle, he was bitterly disappointed that he had nothing concrete to show for nearly two years of service to the colony in the Ohio country. Prior to the disaster at the Monongahela, Washington had harbored hopes that Braddock would reward him with a commission as an officer in the British army, a position of honor and profit that he had come to covet more than any other. With Braddock defeated and dead, Washington pursued another route toward that elusive goal. In late August 1755 he accepted command of the reconstituted Virginia Regiment with the rank of colonel and immediately set about molding it into a professional unit of such high quality that it would be incorporated in the British army as other provincial regiments had been in previous wars, enabling him and his subordinate officers to obtain commissions from the King in place of the ones that they held from the colony.

Washington's task proved to be a formidable one, because in the absence of British regulars in Virginia after 1755, he was obliged to try to defend 350 miles of western frontier by building and garrisoning a string of forts with the meager resources granted him by the colony's general assembly. "I am wandering in a wilderness of difficulties," he wrote to the speaker of the House of Burgesses a year after taking command of the regiment (GW to John Robinson, Aug. 5, 1756, in Abbot, *Papers of GW, Colonial Ser.*, 3:323–333). Chronic shortages of provisions, clothing, equipment, arms, ammunition, and men plagued Washington until British subsidies were pledged for the campaign of 1758, and recruits before that time generally had to be drawn from the lowest levels of society. Washington succeeded, nevertheless, not only in defending Virginia against Indian raids during 1756 and 1757, but in making his regiment equal in discipline and esprit de corps to any regular unit in North America. He did so largely by instilling a professional ethic in his subordinate officers, instituting efficient administrative procedures throughout the regiment, and setting high standards of personal conduct for both officers and enlisted men while assuring them that they would be treated with absolute fairness in all matters large and small.

Washington was not so tactful or effective in dealing with his military or political superiors during the French and Indian War. Focusing rather too narrowly on the needs and tasks of the Virginia Regiment, he showed little appreciation of the larger problems involved in fighting "a backwoods conflict marked by human and material shortages home-front discord, inadequate governmental machinery, and jurisdictional conflicts." Washington complained bitterly and at length to both executive and legislative authorities in Virginia about the colony's meager support of his regiment, and his open impatience with "Chimney Corner Politicians " reveals, as Don Higginbotham (1985) says, a "less-than-respectful attitude toward civil control." At the same time Washington roundly criticized British military commanders for their delay in sending a new expedition into the Ohio Valley to destroy Fort Duquesne, the French post chiefly responsible for Indian attacks on the Virginia frontier, and whenever he could, he pressed to have the Virginia Regiment put on the royal establishment. In 1756 Washington traveled to Boston to present the regiment's case to General William Shirley, the acting British commander-in-chief in America, and the next year he renewed his appeal to Shirley's successor, Lord Loudoun, in Philadelphia.

Loudoun's flat rejection of Washington's request meant that the young Virginian would never exchange his provincial blue coat for the red coat of a British regular. Disappointed and frustrated though he was by the arbitrary blocking of his military ambitions, Washington refused to be left out of the expedition against Fort Duquesne that finally was approved for the campaign of 1758. The expedition's commander, General John Forbes, had a low opinion of provincial troops and officers, but he found Washington to be a notable exception and allowed him to practice the art of military command on a larger scale than any he had yet encountered. In response to a request that Forbes made to

each of his colonels in October 1758, Washington submitted a detailed plan for marching a force of 4,000 men through wooded country and deploying it quickly in battle order (see GW to Forbes, Oct. 8, 1758, in Abbot, *Papers of GW, Colonial Ser.*, 6:66–70). Forbes used a nearly identical arrangement a few weeks later when he marched his army to Fort Duquesne, and in the advancing column Washington commanded a brigade consisting of about 700 provincial troops from four colonies. Despairing of resisting Forbes's force, the French abandoned and burned their fort shortly before the British arrived.

The destruction of Fort Duquesne was the climax of Washington's first military career. Having achieved what was essential to protect Virginia and all that was possible in terms of personal rank, Washington resigned as colonel of the Virginia Regiment at the end of 1758 to marry a wealthy widow and take a seat in the House of Burgesses. His early education as a soldier might have been better if he had commanded larger, more complex bodies of troops, including artillery and cavalry, and if he had fought in larger, more formalized engagements. Not having such opportunities, Washington characteristically made the best of the ones available and became by 1758 a first-class military administrator, a man who could organize, train, equip, supply, and march troops even under difficult conditions. Introduced to military administration by Braddock, Washington spent three years in what Freeman calls "the school of experience" as commander of the Virginia Regiment, taking "hard classes" in such subjects as "recruitment, discipline, and fort building," before attending what Higginbotham calls "the Forbes school of management techniques" (Freeman, *Washington*, 2:204; Higginbotham, *GW and the American Military Tradition*, p 29). Despite bitter arguments with Forbes about choosing a Pennsylvania route to Fort Duquesne rather than a Virginia one, Washington found him, like Braddock, an excellent role model as an administrator and studied his crisp, clear orders as carefully as he had those of the unfortunate Braddock—undoubtedly with greater benefit because of the more active role that he played in Forbes's expedition.

Washington also proved himself a good administrator in his private life after 1758. His marriage on Jan. 6, 1759, to Martha Dandridge

Custis (1731–1802), widow of Daniel Parke Custis, gave him use of a third of one of the greatest fortunes in Virginia but entailed management of a complex, troublesome estate. Over the next 16 years Washington devoted a considerable portion of his time to dealing with the multitude of legal and financial problems relating to the Custis estate and made sure that its vast tobacco lands and many investments in stocks and bonds continued to yield a high return, not only for the sake of himself and his wife, but also for Martha's two young children by her first marriage, John Parke ("Jacky") Custis and Martha Parke ("Patsy") Custis, for whom Washington was named legal guardian in 1761.

The fact that the Washingtons had no children of their own has been attributed by some scholars to the effects of the bad case of measles that Martha suffered soon after their marriage and by others to the alleged impotence of the man who, ironically, gained renown as the "father of his country." Whatever the reason for their childlessness and whatever the economic motivations for their marriage, George and Martha were clearly congenial from the start, and each of them was equally pained by the separations imposed on them by the events of the Revolutionary War, separations that they shortened as much as possible by having Mrs. Washington live at headquarters whenever she could safely do so. Washington's youthful infatuation with his neighbor's wife, Sally Fairfax, which had not been reciprocated, cast no shadow on his marriage When George wrote to Sally near the end of their lives and rather ambiguously recollected "those happy moments, the happiest in my life, which I have enjoyed in your company," Martha added a long friendly note full of news about family and mutual friends (Fitzpatrick, *Writings of GW*, 36:262–265).

The happiest years of Washington's life most probably were the ones that he spent with Martha at Mount Vernon during the decade and a half before the Revolution. Using his share of the proceeds from the Custis estate, he began remodeling the mansion house into a much larger and more elegant structure and filled its rooms with fine furnishings, many of them imported from England. Washington also greatly expanded the acreage of his plantation by purchasing neighboring tracts and used land grants based on service in the French and Indian War to acquire large wilderness holdings in the Ohio Valley. By the time of Washington's death he owned about 7,300 acres at Mount Vernon, more than three times the plantation's original size, and about 45,000 acres west of the mountains. In the early 1760s Washington took advantage of the financial independence that the Custis estate gave him to free himself of debt from the English tobacco merchants and soon began growing wheat in place of tobacco at Mount Vernon. In the early 1770s he built a large commercial gristmill on a nearby creek, and on the eve of the Revolution he was attempting not only to grind his own wheat but to export high-quality flour directly to markets in the West Indies aboard his own vessel. Much of the work at Mount Vernon, both skilled and unskilled, was done by the 200 or so Black slaves that Washington owned.

Washington's favorite recreation at Mount Vernon was foxhunting, which involved hours of hard riding over the fields, and at Williamsburg, where he usually went at least twice a year to discharge his obligations regarding the Custis estates and to sit in the House of Burgesses, he indulged his passion for the theater at every opportunity.

Washington was first elected to the House of Burgesses in 1758 from Frederick County in the Shenandoah Valley, where he had done much of his surveying, and not until seven years later did he become a burgess for his home county of Fairfax. Service in the house of Burgesses introduced Washington to the fine art of politics and augmented his practical education as a military leader in important ways. "From his burgess seat," Higginbotham says, "he had to study such matters as taxation and expenditures as well as public policies from an angle of vision different from that of a soldier, to be conscious of electoral behavior and political realities—subjects often foreign to men in uniform .... He came to appreciate the deliberative process that characterized the conduct of legislative bodies" (Higginbotham, *GW and the American Military Tradition*, p. 41) The 16 years that Washington spent in the Virginia House of Burgesses and, later, his two years of service in the Continental Congress greatly broadened the rather narrow perspective on events that he had exhibited during the French and Indian War and contributed significantly to his remarkable transformation from a hot-tempered young officer, disdainful of his superiors and of civil authority in general, to a mature man who not only tolerated the criticisms, delays, and inefficiencies involved in legislative decision-making, but was a strong and sincere advocate of that system of government. Washington's greatest weakness in his first war, his handling of civil-military relations, became his greatest strength in his second war.

Washington also became more sensitive to the Anglo-American tradition of civilian control of the military through his careful and comprehensive reading of the numerous pamphlets concerning the political crisis between the colonies and the Mother Country that appeared during the 1760s and 1770s. Along with the arguments that radical Whigs advanced in defense of American rights, Washington came to understand, if not entirely to agree with, their strictures against standing armies as inevitable tools of oppression. Long before the Revolutionary War began, he knew just how difficult it would be to create a military force that effectively could defend American liberties without also endangering them.

As Washington's avid reading of political pamphlets suggests, he was an early and uncompromising advocate of the cause of American freedom. "I think," he wrote his good friend Bryan Fairfax on July 20, 1774, "the Parliament of Great Britain hath no more right to put their hands into my pocket, without my consent, than I have to put my hands in yours for money" (Fitzpatrick, *Writings of GW*, 3:230–234). Five years earlier Washington told his neighbor George Mason "that no man shou'd scruple, or hesitate a moment to use a-ms[sic] in defence of so valuable a blessing [as liberty], on which all the good and evil of life depends," but he promptly added that arms "should be the last resource; the de[r]nier resort" (GW to Mason, April 5, 1769, ibid., 2:500—504). Petitions to the King and Parliament having failed to effect the results that the colonists desired, Washington advocated in 1769 a colonial boycott of British manufactured goods in order to put economic pressure on their "lordly Masters" in the Mother Country (ibid.). Washington and Mason subsequently played leading roles in forming a nonimportation association in Virginia, and on August 5, 1774, the first Virginia convention, of which Washington was a member, elected him a delegate to the First Continental Congress, which that fall agreed on a uniform set of economic sanctions for the 12 colonies represented there.

Washington was elected to the Second Continental Congress by the second Virginia convention on March 25, 1775. Three and a half weeks later fighting began between New England minutemen and British redcoats at Lexington and Concord, and when Washington took his seat in Congress in May, he signaled his readiness to fight for the cause if necessary by putting on a military uniform—probably the dark blue coat with red facings, red waistcoat, and red pants that he had worn as colonel of the Virginia Regiment and in which he appears in the formal portrait that Charles Willson Peale painted of him at Mount Vernon in 1772. Standing six feet, two inches tall in his stocking feet and weighing perhaps 200 pounds, Washington was an imposing figure at the age of 43. He had adopted the fashion of powdering his dark brown hair, which must have begun to gray, and he hid his defective teeth behind firmly closed lips. Not until 1789 did Washington acquire the first of his expensive metal and bone (never wooden) dentures. Nearly everyone felt the gaze of the Virginian's blue-gray eyes, which could be soft and benevolent or hard and commanding, depending on his mood. His friend George Mercer wrote in 1760,

> His features are regular and placid with all the muscles of his face under perfect control, tho flexible and expressive of deep feeling when moved by emotions. In conversation he looks you full in the face, is deliberate, deferential and engaging. His demeanor at all times composed and dignified. His movements and gestures are graceful, his walk majestic, and he is a splendid horseman. (quoted in Freeman, *Washington*, 3:6:)

Recognizing Washington's military expertise, Congress asked him to chair committees on the defense of New York, the procurement of military stores, and the writing of rules and regulations for an army. But when in mid-June Congress agreed to adopt the hastily assembled army of New England militiamen who were besieging the British garrison of Boston and had to name a commander-in-chief for the new Continental Army, it put political considerations ahead of military ones. John Adams's nomination of Washington for the position stirred much debate among the delegates, and several arms had to be twisted outside of the hall to procure Washington's unanimous election as commander-in-chief on June 15, 1775 (see Butterfield, *Adams Diary and Autobiography*,

3:321–323). "We Esteem him well Adapted to please A New England Army and much better Suited to the Temper & Genius of our People than any other Gent not brought up in that Part of the Country," Connecticut delegate Eliphalet Dyer wrote to Jonathan Trumbull, Sr., the next day. "His appointment will tend to keep up the Union & more strongly Cement the Southern with the Northern Colonies, & serve to the removing all jealousies" (Smith, *Letters of Delegates to Congress* 1:495–496).

Washington accepted the proffered command on June 16 with a modesty that contrasted sharply with the brash ambition that had characterized much of his first military career. He told his fellow delegates,

> I feel great distress from a consciousness that my abilities & Military experience may not be equal to the extensive & important Trust: However, as the Congress desire it I will enter upon the momentous duty, & exert every power I Possess In their service & for the Support of the glorious Cause. (Chase, *Papers of GW, Rev. War Ser.*, 1:1–3)

Washington's anxiety was based on a realistic understanding of the dangers and difficulties entailed by a resort to arms, a mature acceptance of his own limitations, and a sincere desire to see the American cause succeed. Also involved, however, was a quite selfish motive—a wish to preserve his hard-won personal reputation. "But lest some unlucky event should happen unfavourable to my reputation," Washington warned the delegates in his brief acceptance speech, "I beg it may be remembered by every Gentn in the room, that I this day declare with the utmost sincerity, I do not think my self equal to the Command I am honoured with " (ibid.). Washington put the matter more bluntly in the letter that he wrote to his brother Jack on June 20:

> This I am sure of, that in the worse event, I shall have the consolation of knowing (if I act to the best of my judgment) that the blame ought to lodge upon the appointers, not the appointed, as it was by no means a thing of my own seeking, or proceeding from any hint of my friends. (ibid., 19–20)

After nearly 20 years, Washington remembered the bitter lesson of Braddock's unexpected defeat, and despite his remarkable growth in maturity since that time and his more restrained and dignified tone, he retained his youthful sensitivity about his reputation deep within his heart.

Most of the delegates were impressed by Washington's selfless patriotism, nonetheless. "There is something charming to me in the conduct of Washington," John Adams wrote to Elbridge Gerry on June 18.

> A gentleman of one of the first fortunes upon the continent, leaving his delicious retirement, his family and friends, sacrificing his ease, and hazarding all in the cause of his country! His views are noble and disinterested. He declared, when he accepted the mighty trust, that he would lay before us an exact account of his expenses, and not accept a shilling for pay. (Taylor, *Papers of John Adams*, 3:25–27)

Washington's refusal of the $500 a month that Congress voted for his pay and expenses apparently benefited him in the long run, because the money that he spent between 1775 and 1783 on his headquarters household, numerous journeys and reconnaissances, express riders, intelligence agents, and other necessities of public service, proved to be enormous, and the runaway inflation that prevailed throughout much of the war further made an expense account preferable to a fixed income. But Washington foresaw little or none of that in June 1775. Far from wishing to profit by his position as commander-in-chief, he earnestly desired to forego any financial rewards, not only to protect his reputation against accusations of greed and self-interest, but also to set a proper example of patriotic virtue, without which, he knew, his appeals to soldiers and civilians for sacrifice and support would carry little weight. There is no evidence that Washington ever padded his expense accounts in the least way or that any responsible contemporary ever accused him of doing so. "In comparison with the heads of state of his own era, or the commanders and chief executives of ours," biographer Marcus Cunliffe says, "Washington was recompensed on a most frugal scale" (Foreword to Klapthor and Morrison, *G. Washington: A Figure Upon the Stage*, p. 11).

The president of Congress, John Hancock, signed Washington's commission as commander-in-chief of the Continental Army on June 19, 1775, and four days later the new general set off for Massachusetts to assume command of the troops outside Boston. "I go," he wrote Martha minutes before his departure from

Philadelphia, "fully trusting in that Providence, which has been more bountiful to me than I deserve, & in full confidence of a happy meeting with you sometime in the Fall" (Chase, *Papers of GW, Rev. War Ser.*, 1:27–28). Their next meeting occurred on December 11, 1775, not at Mount Vernon as Washington expected, but at his headquarters in Cambridge, Massachusetts, where Martha journeyed to spend the winter with him. Washington did not see his Virginia home again until he stopped there for a few days on his way to Yorktown more than six years later. "I am now Imbarkd on a tempestuous Ocean from whence, perhaps, no friendly harbour is to be found," Washington wrote his brother-in-law Burwell Bassett on June 19, 1775, with more truth than he may have realized. "I can answer but for three things, a firm belief of the justice of our Cause—close attention in the prosecution of it—and the strictest Integrity" (ibid., 12–14). Neither Congress nor anyone else ever had serious reason to doubt that pledge.

Accompanied by Major General Charles Lee, Washington arrived at Cambridge on July 2 in a heavy rainstorm that forced postponement of the welcoming ceremonies to the next day. Lieutenant Joseph Hodgkins wrote his wife early on the morning of July 3,

> The generals to Day . . . are to take a vew of ye Army & that will be attended with a grate deal of grandor[.] there is at this time one & twenty Drummers & as many feffors a Beting and Playing Round the Prayde. (Wade and Lively, *This Glorious Cause*, p. 171)

Washington undoubtedly appeared at the review in his new Continental uniform—dark blue coat with buff-colored facings and gold epaulets, buff waistcoat and trousers, knee-high black boots, and black hat with a black cockade (see Thacher, *Military Journal*, p. 20). Such, with small variations, was his formal dress throughout the war. Beginning on July 14, 1775, Washington indicated his rank by wearing a light blue ribbon several inches wide draped across his chest between his coat and waistcoat. In June 1780 the ribbon was replaced by three gold stars on each epaulet.

Whatever apprehensions Washington may have felt about the future as he took command of the Continental Army, he had little doubt about his ability to deal with the task immediately at hand—creating a competent, well-disciplined army out of the largely untrained horde of New England volunteers who had been sitting on the hills around Boston for more than two months defying the British garrison commanded by Washington's former friend, General Thomas Gage. Most of the soldiers who composed the nascent Continental Army, the Massachusetts Provincial Congress informed Washington in its welcoming address,

> Have not before seen Service. And altho' naturally brave and of good understanding, yet for want of Experience in military Life, have but little knowledge of divers things most essential to the preservation of Health and even of Life. (Chase, *Papers of GW, Rev. War Ser.*, 1:52–53)

Washington quickly found out for himself what he already suspected: the popular American belief that a virtuous citizenry in arms could offset their lack of discipline and experience with native courage and patriotic zeal had little foundation in reality. "They are by no means such Troops, in any respect, as you are led to believe of them from the Accts which are published," Washington wrote his manager and distant relation, Lund Washington, on August 20, 1775. "I daresay the Men fight very well (if properly Officered) although they are an exceeding dirty & nasty people" (ibid., 334–340).

That conclusion did not particularly disconcert Washington, for he had dealt with similar men during the French and Indian War, albeit on a much smaller scale. During his first days at Cambridge, Washington closely followed his proven formula for military success by instituting efficient administrative procedures and setting high standards of personal conduct. His orders for July 4, 1775, emphasized three things that he deemed "essential" for the new army, things which he was to stress again and again in the months ahead–discipline, cleanliness, and colonial unity. Having been taken into the pay and service of the Continental Army, the officers and men of the army, Washington hoped, would lay aside "all Distinctions of Colonies . . . so that one and the same spirit may animate the whole, and the only Contest be, who shall render . . . the most essential service to the great and common cause." "Exact discipline" and "due Subordination," he warned, would be required of all, "as a Failure in these most essential points must necessarily produce extreme Hazard, Disorder and Confusion; and end in shameful disappointment and disgrace." Washington insisted particularly that the articles of war forbidding "profane cursing, swearing & drunken[n]ess" be strictly enforced and that "all Officers, and Soldiers, not engaged on actual duty," attend divine services "to implore the blessings of heaven upon the means used for our safety and defence." Officers were further admonished "to keep their Men neat and clean—to visit them often at their quarters, and inculcate upon them the necessity of cleanliness, as essential to their health and service" (ibid., 54–58).

Throughout the remainder of the summer and into the fall, Washington diligently tutored both officers and men in their duties, touching upon such diverse subjects as the correct saluting of general officers and the digging of proper camp latrines. Few details escaped his eye, but he knew when to look the other way. The men under his command, Washington understood, were not only inexperienced, but also imbued with what Higginbotham calls "historic militia attitudes" (Higginbotham, *GW and the American Military Tradition*, pp. 48–49). Most considered themselves as citizens who had temporarily put on the garb of soldiers, and accordingly, they remained tenacious of their individual liberties. They could be pushed only so far so fast, even when earnest appeals were made to their patriotism. Washington succeeded in dealing with the citizen soldiers of the Continental Army by exercising the same sort of mild but strict form of discipline that he had used in the Virginia Regiment, acting with patience and perseverance and carefully distinguishing matters of substance from those of ceremonial form. "Require nothing unreasonable of your officers and men," Washington advised Colonel William Woodford on November 10, 1776, "but see that whatever is required be punctually complied with" (Chase, *Papers of GW, Rev. War Ser.*, 2:346–347).

One area of discipline in which Washington refused to compromise was the treatment of civilians. In his orders of July 5, 1775, he strictly enjoined his officers to prevent "all Invasions and Abuse of private property," and he expressed the hope "that every private soldier will detest, and abhor such practices, when he considers, that it is for the preservation of his own Rights, Liberty and Property, and those of his Fellow Countrymen, that he is now called into service" (ibid., 1:62–64). Washington never lost sight of the fact that the war was as much a political contest for the hearts and minds of the American people as it was a military struggle between two armies (see Higginbotham, *GW and the American Military Tradition*, p. 53; Shy, *A People Numerous and Armed*, pp. 218–219). He would not risk alienating the men and women on whose support he and his army ultimately relied, by treating them in a callous manner, as he had seen British troops sometimes do during the previous war and in the years since that war.

Washington tried to minimize conflicts between soldiers and civilians by keeping them apart as much as possible. He routinely confined both officers and men to camp, prohibiting them from loitering in local towns and on local roads without leave from their superiors, and whenever he could, he located camps outside of major population centers. Continental troops were seldom quartered in private homes, but lived, instead, in tents or improvised huts if barracks were not available. When troubles inevitably occurred, Washington depended on his officers to control their men and to maintain good relations with inhabitants. Offenses usually involved property damage, such as the destruction of fences and crops, or pillaging of livestock and other goods, none of which was tolerated by Washington and all of which unfailingly evoked prompt action to correct matters. Washington disliked using even legal impressment to take supplies and equipment from civilians, and on those occasions when he did resort to it, he insisted on strictly following all relevant state and local laws and on issuing proper claim vouchers to affected property owners.

Washington was equally careful to prevent his men from unnecessarily offending community sensibilities, hence, his great emphasis on morality and neat appearance in the ranks. Hearing complaints in late August 1775 that soldiers bathing near the Cambridge River bridge were "running about naked upon the Bridge, whilst Passengers, and even Ladies of the first fashion in the neighborhood," were crossing, Washington immediately halted their flagrant exhibitionism by forbidding bathing at or near that place (Chase, *Papers of GW, Rev. War Ser.*, 1:346–348). The American invasion of Canada that began in September 1775 prompted Washington to caution his Protestant troops to respect the Roman Catholic beliefs of the French-Canadians, and when he learned of plans at Cambridge to observe Guy Fawkes Day on November 5 with "that ridiculous and childish Custom of burning the Effigy of the pope," he was outraged. In his general orders for that date, Washington expressed

> his surprise that there should be Officers and Soldiers, in this army so void of common sense, as not to see the impropriety of such a step at this Juncture; at a Time when we are soliciting . . . the friendship & alliance of the people of Canada. . . . In such Circumstances, to be insulting of their Religion, is so monstrous, as not to be suffered, or excused. (ibid., 1:455–456; 2:300–301)

Washington's heavy reliance on the officer corps to enforce his standards of discipline and conduct mirrored the management style that he had employed in the Virginia Regiment, but he was confounded by the very different breed of officers that he found at Cambridge. Washington wrote to Richard Henry Lee on Aug. 29, 1775,

> It is among the most difficult tasks I ever undertook in my life to induce these people to believe that there is, or can be, danger till the Bayonet is pushed at their Breasts; not that it proceeds from any uncommon prowess, but rather from an unaccountable kind of stupidity in the lower class of these people, which believe me prevails but too generally among the Officers of the Massachusetts part of the Army, who are nearly of the same Kidney with the Privates; and adds not a little to my difficulties; as there is no such thing as getting Officers of this stamp to exert themselves in carrying orders into execution—to curry favour with the men (by whom they were chosen, & on whose Smiles possibly they may think they may again rely) seems to be one of the principal objects of their attention. (ibid., 1:372–376)

The election of officers by the enlisted men, which was a common practice among the New England troops, ran counter to everything Washington believed about what officers ought to be and do. Too much familiarity with one's subordinates, he told William Woodford, led to "a want of that respect, which is necessary to support a proper command" (ibid., 2:346–347). Good discipline and order required officers to keep a certain distance between themselves and the "common herd," a distance that Washington, capitalizing on his natural reserve, cultivated to a high degree of aloofness (Morgan, *Genius of GW*, pp. 6–7, 47). Officers, Washington also thought, should serve as models of correct behavior for their men. He said in his general orders of Aug. 22, 1775,

> When Officers set good Examples, it may be expected that the Men will with zeal and alacrity follow them, but it would be a mere phenomenon in nature, to find a well disciplin'd Soldiery, where Officers are relax'd and tardy in their duty. (Chase, *Papers of GW, Rev. War Ser.*, 1:346–348)

Washington was particularly disappointed to discover soon after arriving at Cambridge that several officers stood accused of cowardice at the Battle of Bunker Hill and some were charged with fraudulently drawing more pay and provisions than their units were allowed. Many others were absent from camp. Washington had the worst offenders tried and cashiered and ordered absentees to report to the army without delay. Officers who decided that they could not serve because of ill health or family problems were discharged with few questions asked. The rest of the officer corps became students in Washington's school of military education. They were instructed by his daily general orders, invited to dine in small groups at his headquarter's table, and given ample opportunities to practice their duties during the relatively quiet months of the army's continued siege of Boston. Every effort was made to instill a professional ethic in them. Lacking the power to select officers that he had exercised as commander of the Virginia Regiment, Washington, nevertheless, used his influence with congressmen and legislators, who held that power, to see that officers were appointed and promoted on the basis of military merit rather than their success in recruiting and winning the votes of soldiers. The practice of electing officers ended when Washington reorganized the officer corps for 1776, and under his tutelage many officers began to develop professional attitudes and abilities.

Washington's program of discipline and training was set back considerably, however, during the last two months of 1775 when it became evident that, contrary to what he had intimated to his wife, the war would not end in the fall and that few of the New England troops, all of whose enlistments expired in December, were willing to remain in the army. Disbanding one army and recruiting another "within musket shot" of the British garrison in Boston proved to be a delicate and dangerous business. Washington spent many anxious days and nights in December and January endeavoring to keep the American lines adequately manned and hoping that the British would not discover and exploit his weak points (GW to John Hancock, Jan. 4 and Feb. 9 1776, ibid., 3:18–21, 274–277). Equally troubling to the commander-in-chief was the fact that the large turnover in the ranks meant that much of the hard work of disciplining and training men to be soldiers would have to be repeated. Washington explained to Joseph Reed on Feb. 1, 1776,

> It takes you two or three Months to bring New men in any tolerable degree acquainted with their duty. It takes a longer time to bring a People of the temper, and genius of these into such a subordinate way of thinking as is necessary for a Soldier—Before this is accomplished, the time approaches for their dismission, and your beginning to make Interest with them for their continuance for another limited period; in the doing of which you are oblig'd to relax in your discipline, in order as it were to curry favour with them, by which means the latter part of your time is employd in undoing what the first was accomplishing and instead of having Men always ready to take advantage of Circumstances you must govern your Movements by the Circumstances of your Inlistment. (ibid., 237–239)

During his first months in command of the Continental Army, Washington carefully avoided voicing any support for long-term enlistments or recruiting bounties because such measures might stir up American fears of standing armies, fears that were especially deep-rooted in New England. The crisis brought on by the recruiting of the new army prompted Washington to break his silence on those subjects, however. In a letter to John Hancock dated February 9, 1776, he tactfully urged Congress to consider creating a permanent army by authorizing bounties of $20, $30, or more for soldiers who would enlist for the duration of the war. Washington wrote,

> Since the first of December, I have been devising every means in my power to secure these Incampments, and though I am sensible that we never have, since that period, been able to act upon the Offensive, and at times not in a condition to defend, yet the cost of Marching home one set of Men—bringing in another—the havock & waste occasioned by the first—the repairs necessary for the Second, with a thousand incidental charges

> and Inconviencies which have arisen, & which it is scarce possible either to recollect or describe, amounts to near as much as the keeping up a respectable body of Troops the whole time—ready for any emergency—would have done. (ibid., 274–277)

As reasonable as Washington's appeals to economy and military efficiency were, Congress was slow to adopt his suggestions, and even after it did approve them, he was never able to obtain as many long-term soldiers as he needed. The Continental Army continued throughout the war to experience periodic manpower crises as well as frequent shortages of provisions and equipment. Washington vented his frustrations in private letters from time to time, bewailing the lack of public spirit and expressing his own discouragement. He confided to Joseph Reed in a letter of January 14, 1776,

> I have often thought how much happier I should have been, if, instead of accepting of a command under such Circumstances I had taken my Musket upon my Shoulder & entered the Ranks, or, if I could have justified the Measure to Posterity, & my own Conscience, had retir'd to the back Country, & livd in a Wig-wam. (ibid., 87–92)

Yet Washington never seriously considered resigning his commission before the war ended, and in hundreds of public letters to officers, Congressmen, governors, legislators, local officials, and private citizens, he maintained a uniformly tactful tone, placating and encouraging them on behalf of the American cause. Whatever irritations Washington may have felt at the slowness and mismanagement that he often encountered in civil officials, he never challenged their authority. He told the Massachusetts general court in April 1776,

> A regard to every provincial institution, where not incompatible with the common Interest, I hold a principle of duty, & of policy, and shall ever form a part of my conduct. (ibid., 4:8–9)

His army, Washington constantly assured his fellow citizens with both words and actions, would defend their liberties, not threaten them, and he would "ever be . . . a faithful Servant of the Public," not a Caesar or Oliver Cromwell (G.W. to John Hancock, April 18, 1776, ibid., 80–81).

Washington also was politically astute enough to avoid getting ahead of public opinion on a major issue such as American independence. Because of his discretion in the matter, it is not certain exactly when Washington became convinced that the colonies ought to sever their ties with Great Britain, but he clearly was prepared to take that step several months before Congress actually did so. When Washington went to Cambridge in June 1775, he apparently shared the general expectation that a display of American willingness and ability to fight for their rights would oblige the British government to back down, but he gave up all hopes of an accommodation four months later, upon learning that the King and ministry intended to take forceful measures to suppress resistance to parliamentary authority. The arrival in early January 1776 of a copy of the King's speech to Parliament, which harshly chided the rebelling colonists, confirmed Washington in his opinion and led him to make a private declaration of independence in his letter to Joseph Reed of February 10, 1776:

> If every Man was of my Mind the Ministers of G.B. should know, in a few Words, upon what Issue the cause should be put. . . . I would tell them, that we had born much— that we had long, & ardently sought for reconciliation upon honourable terms—that it has been denied us—that all our attempts after Peace had provd abortive and had been grossly misrepresented—that we had done every thing that could be expected from the best of Subjects—that the Spirit of Freedom beat too high in us, to Submit to Slavery; & that, if nothing else would satisfie a Tyrant & his diabolical Ministry, we were determined to shake of[f] all Connexions with a State So unjust, & unnatural. This I would tell them, not under Covert, but in Words as clear as the Sun in its Meridian brightness. (ibid., 286–291)

Washington, nevertheless, was willing to let events take their course. He wrote Reed on April 1, 1776,

> My Countrymen, I know, from their form of Government, & steady Attachment heretofore to Royalty, will come reluctantly into the Idea of Independency, but time, & persecution, brings many wonderful things to pass. (ibid., 9–13)

People had to feel an evil before they would act on it, Washington believed, and in any case it would be pointless to proclaim independence without a strong public consensus in favor of it. He told Reed on 15 April,

> I am exceedingly concern'd to hear of the divisions & Parties which prevail with you, and in the Southern Colonies on the Score of Independance &ca—these are the Shelves we have to avoid, or Our Bark will split & tumble to pieces—here lays our great danger, and I almost tremble when I think of this Rock. Nothing but a disunion can hurt our cause—this will Ruin it, if great prudence, temper, and Moderation is not mixed in our Councils, & made the governing principles of the Contending Parties. (ibid., 71–72)

Much of Washington's life after July 4, 1776, was devoted to achieving and maintaining the unity necessary to sustain the independence that Congress declared on that date. The establishment of a free and self-sufficient American nation became a major goal of Washington's life, ranking with and sometimes overshadowing the two goals that he had set for himself as a youth.

For all of Washington's sensitivity to political considerations and his respect for civilian authority, he kept the reins of military command tightly in his own hands, demanding obedience from his subordinates and allowing little outside interference in the basis decisions of troop deployment and strategy. "I will steadily (as far as my judgment will assist me) pursue such measures as I think most conducive to the Interest of the cause," he told an influential Massachusetts legislator in August 1775, "& rest satisfied under any obloquy that shall be thrown conscious of having discharged my duty to the best of my abilities (ibid., 1:349–351). Because the position of Continental commander-in-chief was a new one, its duties and powers were at first vague and ill defined. Washington began the process of definition a few days after reaching Cambridge by writing to John Hancock:

> I feel the Weight, Importance & Vanity of my present Duties too sensibly, not to wish a more immediate & frequent Communication with the Congress. I fear it may often happen in the Course of our present Operations, that I shall need that Assistance & Direction from them which Time & Distance will not allow me to receive. (ibid., 83–97)

It was Washington's polite way of telling Congress that any sort of shared command was totally impracticable and that they would have to trust him to make good military decisions. Washington did keep Congress fully informed of his plans and actions by a regular correspondence, and he consulted the occasional delegates who visited his headquarters about a variety of matters. In May 1776 he journeyed to Philadelphia to discuss the coming campaign with several congressional committees, but the decisions reached during that visit were broad ones that left the details of deployment to Washington's discretion. By the summer of 1776 Washington had become, as Dave Richard Palmer observes, "the country's executive authority for waging war" (Palmer, *Way of the Fox*, p. 62). Although Congress attempted on a few occasions thereafter, primarily during 1777 and 1778, to dabble in strategy, Washington successfully resisted their intrusions for the most part, usually by ignoring them.

Within the army Washington periodically assembled councils of war, consisting of all the general officers at or near his headquarters, to discuss courses of action. Some critics have cited that practice as evidence of weakness and indecisiveness on Washington's part. Nothing could be further from the truth. Councils of war were an established part of military procedure in the British army during the eighteenth century, and Washington had seen both Braddock and Forbes hold them on more than one occasion. Like his British mentors, Washington used councils of war to elicit a wide variety of views and to form a consensus of opinion among his officers. Washington alone decided when to call councils of war, framed the questions to be considered by the members, stipulated whether their answers were to be oral or written, and made the final decisions after hearing or reading what everyone had to say. It was a practical, rational way of reaching decisions that particularly suited Washington's methodical mind and which he used with equal effectiveness in dealing with his cabinet as president.

Washington never pretended to be an innovative strategist, but he understood some fundamental principles of warfare—the necessity of concentrating one's forces, the advantages of mobility and offensive action, and the importance of geographical factors. From the beginning of his tenure as commander-in-chief, Washington had to refuse numerous requests to send Continental detachments to defend coastal communities and other localities from British raids. "The great Advantage the Enemy has of transporting Troops by being Masters of the Sea will enable them to harass us by Diversions of this kind," he explained to James Warren in July 1775, "& Should we be tempted to pursue them upon every Alarm, The Army must either be so weaken'd as to Expose it to Destruction or a great Part of the Coast be still left unprotected" (Chase, *Papers of GW, Rev. War Ser.*, 1:195–196). Local defense, Washington steadfastly maintained, should be provided by the militia, allowing the Continental Army to mobilize maximum strength against the chief threat to all American Patriots—the British army. "Wars were won by destroying or disarming the enemy, not by trying to spare civilians from occupation," Edmund Morgan writes. "And Washington was bent on winning" (Morgan, *Genius of GW*, p. 10).

Washington's overriding desire to achieve victory was nowhere more evident than at the siege of Boston. Although he assumed during his first weeks at Cambridge that he was responsible for merely containing the British garrison within Boston, Washington began seeking as early as September 1775 an effective way to attack the city in order to end the war quickly and avoid the cost and trouble of continuing the siege into the winter months. "The State of Inactivity, in which this Army has lain for some Time," he wrote Hancock on September 21, "by no Means corresponds with my Wishes, by some decisive Stroke to relieve my Country from the heavy Expence, its Subsistence must create" (Chase, *Papers of GW, Rev. War Ser.*, 2:24–30). When Washington heard a short time later that massive British reinforcements would arrive in America sometime in the spring, he became even more determined to strike a decisive below while his enemy was still relatively weak. Delay could only worsen his situation. Shortages of men and ammunition thwarted Washington's plans the following winter to make "a bold & resolute Assault" on Boston across the frozen harbor, and similar deficiencies hampered his freedom of action throughout much of the war. (GW to Hancock, Feb. 18–21, 1776, ibid., 3:335–337). Washington, nevertheless, did not exclude "the spirit of the offensive" from his mind "even when circumstances . . . dictated a defensive war" (Palmer, *Way of the Fox*, p. 143). He never ceased seeking a way to put "the axe to the root . . . and make a radical cure" by destroying his enemy's military power at its source, whether it be the French at Forth Duquesne in 1758 or the British at New York 20 years later (memorandum,

May 1, 1782, Fitzpatrick, *Writings of GW*, 24:194–215).

The overwhelming buildup of British forces during the spring and summer of 1776, which Washington had foreseen but failed to nullify, obliged him to adopt a more cautious defensive stance to preserve the Continental Army, but not before he learned some painful lessons at New York, principally that fortifications and naval obstructions were of little value against the maneuvers of a professional army and navy and that the risks involved in placing his whole army in a position where its retreat might be cut off were unacceptable regardless of political pressures not to yield American soil without a fight. Washington took those lessons to heart, and following his humbling defeat on Long Island, he embraced a new strategy. He wrote Hancock on September 8, 1776,

> History, our own experience, the advice of our ablest Friends in Europe, the fears of the Enemy, and even the Declarations of Congress demonstrate that on our Side the War should be defensive. It has even been called a War of Posts. That we should on all Occasions avoid a general Action, or put anything to the Risque, unless compelled by a necessity, into which we ought never to be drawn. (Fitzpatrick, *Writings of GW*, 6:27–33).

Washington was greatly aided in waging a protracted "War of Posts" by his shrewd appreciation of military geography. From the earliest days of the war, he understood the strategic importance of the corridor that the Hudson River and Lake Champlain formed between Montreal and New York City. Not only was it a natural invasion route to or from either city, but occupation of that corridor by the British would effectively isolate New England from the rest of the colonies. When the British evacuated Boston in March 1776, Washington immediately moved almost his entire army to New York City in a carefully orchestrated march, correctly anticipating that it would be the enemy's next major target, and during the following weeks he sent large detachments to Canada in an effort to secure the other end of the vital corridor. After his impressive victories at Trenton and Princeton, Washington effectively maneuvered the British forces out of New Jersey without further fighting by positioning his army in the hills of northern New Jersey.

In several subsequent campaigns, occupation of that strategic location or a similar one in the Hudson Highlands enabled Washington to protect the Continental Army from destruction by encamping it in rugged, easily defensible terrain, while at the same time such centrally located positions enabled him to move swiftly to intercept British incursions both north and south. "The ability to operate on interior lines—that is, the ability to march on the chord of a circle while the enemy has to travel around the circumference," Palmer says, "was Washington's only counter to British seaborne mobility" before the French alliance made aid from a friendly fleet a possibility (Palmer, *Way of the Fox*, p. 138). Although French naval power opened up new strategic opportunities after 1778 and enabled Washington to win a decisive victory at Yorktown, the reluctance of French admirals to commit themselves to specific land operations meant that he continued to fight a patient, protracted war throughout most of the later years of the Revolution. "War in Theory and the modes of defence are obvious and easy," Washington told John Hancock in May 1777, "but in practice they are more difficulieutenant Unhappily for us, the means in our power, do not always accord with our wishes, or what would be our Interest to pursue" (Fitzpatrick, *Writings of GW*, 8:34–36).

Washington ended his Revolutionary War career in Annapolis on December 23, 1783, much as he had begun it eight and a half years earlier by standing before Congress and giving a short, modest speech:

> Happy in the confirmation of our Independence and Sovereignty, and pleased with the oppertunity afforded the United States of becoming a respectable Nation, I resign with satisfaction the Appointment I accepted with diffidence. A diffidence in my abilities to accomplish so arduous a task, which however was superseded by a confidence in the rectitude of our Cause, the support of the Supreme Power of the Union, and the patronage of Heaven. . . . Having now finished the work assigned me, I retire from the great theatre of Action. (ibid., 27:–284-85)

Contrary to his expectations, Washington was to return to that theater within a few short years to take another part, because he discovered that the United States had not become as respectable a nation as he had hoped. Deeming the confederation government weak and ineffectual, Washington used the enormous prestige that he had gained as commander-in-chief to support efforts to create a new form of national government. As president of the Constitutional Convention which met in Philadelphia in 1787, he fostered the writing of the United States Constitution, which featured a chief executive modeled closely on the role that he had played in the Revolution. It was quite natural for Washington to be the first person to fill that new position. During the eight years (1789–1797) that Washington served as president of the United States, he strove to create a respectable national reputation for the country with the same energy and determination that he had exhibited in earning and protecting his own personal reputation. "We are a young Nation," he had written his brother Jack in 1783, "and have a character to establish. It behooves us therefore to set out right for first impressions will be lasting, indeed are all in all" (GW to John Augustine Washington, June 15, 1783, Fitzpatrick, *Writing of GW*, 27:13). Under Washington's guidance, the new nation not only endured but made a very good first impression, indeed, on the larger world.

George Washington was not an indispensable actor in the great drama of the American Revolution. "It will appear evident to a close Examiner," he wrote to Reverend William Gordon in July 1783, "that there has been a concatenation of causes to produce this Event; which in all probability at no time, or under any Circumstances, will combine again" (ibid., 49–52). No one person can take credit for the widespread, diverse political and social upheaval that occurred in America during Washington's lifetime. Nevertheless, there was nothing foreordained about the Patriots' military victory, and Washington by any account played an especially critical role in achieving it. His very real talents as a military administrator enabled him to create an army competent enough to win the war in the long run, and his equally impressive political skills helped him to minimize the consequences of governmental incompetence and inefficiency while soothing ingrained American fears of standing armies. In the difficult business of devising military strategy, Washington stumbled on occasion but never lost his head. He had an uncommon ability and willingness to learn from his mistakes and seldom made the same ones again. His strategic flexibility allowed him to safeguard the existence of the Continental Army when it was necessary and to attempt to defeat British forces when possible. "In the Revolutionary War," Palmer observes, "there were times crying for victory and others demanding avoidance of defeat. The watchword some days was audacity; on others it was take care. Washington seemed always to know the difference" (Palmer, *Way of the Fox*, p. 200).

Washington's greatest contribution to American victory, however, may have been his simple refusal to quit under any circumstances. He had a clear vision of what he was fighting for and steadfastly resisted any forces that might divert him from accomplishing his purposes. According to Morgan,

> Washington had been fully persuaded that the king of England and the minions surrounding him were conspiring to destroy the liberties of Americans.... He never doubted that the United States must be a republic. And the principles of republican liberty as he saw them dictated that the military must be forever subordinate to the civil power. (Morgan, *Genius of GW*, pp. 12–13)

If the Continental army was, as Higginbotham terms it, "a Washington-shaped army," it can be said with equal truth that the United States was, in its inception at least, a Washington-shaped nation (Higginbotham, *GW and the American Military Tradition*, p. 104).

Philander D. Chase

REFERENCES

W.W. Abbot, "An Uncommon Awareness of Self: The Papers of George Washington," *Prologue, 21* (1989):7-19; ———, et al., *The Papers of George Washington, Colonial Series*, 7 vols. to date (1983–); George Athan Billias, *George Washington's Generals* (1964); L.H. Butterfield, et al., eds., *Diary and Autobiography of John Adams*, 4 vols. (1961); Philander D. Chase, et al., eds., *The Papers of George Washington, Revolutionary War Series*, 4 vols. to date (1985–); John E. Ferling, *The First of Men: A Life of George Washington* (1988); John C. Fitzpatrick, ed., *The Writings of George Washington from the Original Manuscript Sources, 1745–1799*, 39 vols. (1931–1944); Paul Leicester Ford, ed., *The Writings of Thomas Jefferson*, 10 vols. (1892–1899); Douglas Southall Freeman, *George Washington*, 7 vols. (1948–1957); Don Higginbotham, *George Washington and the American Military Tradition* (1985); Donald Jackson and Dorothy Twohig, et al., eds., *The Diaries of George Washington*, 6 vols. (1976–1979); Margaret Brown Klapthor and

Howard Alexander Morrison, *G. Washington: A Figure upon the Stage* (1982); Paul K. Longmore, *The Invention of George Washington* (1988); Edward S. Morgan, *The Genius of George Washington* (1960); David Richard Palmer, *The Way of the Fox: American Strategy in the War for America, 1775–1783* (1975); John Shy, *A People Numerous and Armed: Reflections on the Military Struggle for American Independence* (1990); Paul H. Smith, et al., eds., *Letters of Delegates to Congress, 1774–1789*, 16 vols. to date (1976–); Robert J. Taylor, et al., eds., *Papers of John Adams*, 8 vols. to date (1977–); James Thacher, *Military Journal of the American Revolution* (1862); Dorothy Twohig, et al., eds., *The Papers of George Washington, Presidential Series*, 3 vols. to date (1987–); Herbert T. Wade and Robert A. Lively, *This Glorious Cause: The Adventures of Two Company Officers in Washington's Army* (1958); Russell F. Weigley, *The American Way of War: A History of United States Military Strategy and Policy* (1973).

Washington, Martha Dandridge Custis (1731–1802)

First Lady of the United States. Martha Washington was the wife of George Washington, whom she married in 1759 after the death of her first husband, Daniel Parke Custis. She had no direct active involvement in the political and military responsibilities of her second husband, but she provided him with the comfort and affection that defined his private life and strengthened his public resolve. She was deeply committed to her family and domestic pursuits, and she entertained and charmed virtually everyone she met in society.

Martha was born on June 2, 1731, at Chestnut Grove Plantation on the Pamunkey River in New Kent County, Virginia. She was the oldest of eight children. Her father was John Dandridge, the son of an immigrant merchant, and her mother was Frances Jones Dandridge, the granddaughter of the Reverend Rowland Jones, first rector of Bruton Parish Church. Though her family had only modest means, Martha grew up in the world of wealthy Virginia planters. Little is known of her childhood. Her education was limited, with an emphasis on social and domestic accomplishments. She was presented to Governor Sir William at age 15 and entered Williamsburg society.

Here she met Daniel Parke Custis, who was 38 years old. He was the son of Colonel John Custis of Williamsburg, one of the richest men in Virginia. Though Martha was 20 years younger than Daniel, they formed a deep attachment. There are hints that the colonel objected to the marriage of his son to a woman with little wealth, but the marriage took place in 1749. A few months later Colonel Custis died, and Daniel inherited 17,348 acres of land, along with many business enterprises. There was conflict over the estate because of claims of family members living in Antigua, but the newly married couple was able to live a luxurious life on the Custis estate on the Pamunkey. They had four children, two of whom died in early childhood. The surviving children were Martha, known as Patsy, and John Parke, called Jacky.

In July 1757 Daniel died intestate, leaving 26-year-old Martha the wealthiest widow in Virginia. She received her dower rights, which were one-third of the Custis land and slaves, along with 32,000 pounds in cash. She also became guardian of her two minor children and the two-thirds of the estate that they had inherited. During her widowhood she personally administered the Custis property, working with the Custis business agent. She made loans, negotiated mortgages, and exported crops. In the spring of 1758, George Washington began to court her, and a few weeks after, they were betrothed. Their marriage took place on January 6, 1759, probably on the Custis plantation.

Little is known of the intimacy of the marriage between George and Martha, largely because Martha burned their letters to each other shortly after George's death. Only two of his letters to her and one of hers to him have survived. Other evidence supports the view that theirs was an agreeable and loving marriage. They spoke affectionately about each other to family and friends, expressed sorrow when forced to be apart, and took great pains to be together whenever possible. Martha referred to her husband as "Papa" and he called her "Patsy." He wore a painted miniature of her around his neck, and he was never unfaithful to her. One of the sorrows of their married life was that they had no children of their own, but this never seemed to interfere with the loving relationship that they established.

The early years of her marriage to George were quite conventional. She spent much of her time performing domestic duties, though she always spent an hour after breakfast in prayer or reading devotional literature. She was a prodigious needlewoman, making many of the clothes that were worn by the family and slaves at Mount Vernon. She was proud of her ability to cure meat and of the soap she made with rose and mint water. She got great pleasure from the many visitors that come to Mount Vernon, about 2,000 between 1768 and 1775. She complained of the house being dull when there was no company. She traveled herself, visiting family and going to Williamsburg with George when the House of Burgesses was in session. Her health was good, though she did have a serious bout of measles in 1760. She was interested in fashion and wore high-quality clothing in a plain style, which suited her short, plump figure.

George ordered most of her clothing from London, as Martha had handed over all financial dealings and all aspects of estate management to him when they married. The task of handling her estate and the inheritance of her children was quite complex. His responsibilities also included guardianship of Patsy and Jacky, and he acted as their father, treating Martha's children as if they were his own. George and Martha were particularly indulgent of the fragile Patsy, who died at the age of 12, probably from epilepsy. George oversaw the rearing and education of Jacky, while Martha spoiled him outrageously, especially after the death of her daughter. Patsy's death depressed Martha so much that she was not able to attend her son's wedding nearly a year later.

The quiet, rural, domestic life that Martha loved ended with the beginning of the American Revolution. George's appointment as commander-in-chief began a series of long separations and caused Martha great anxiety for his safety. It is assumed that Martha shared George's commitment to American independence, but little is known of her political opinions. She never talked about politics, and her letters only vaguely refer to political events, with an occasional mention of her support for "the cause." Her awareness of political life is evident in her ability to anticipate George's reaction to events, but she did not express her own views on these matters, even to her grandchildren. Her discretion was complete, and her lack of public political statements was one of the reasons that she never made an enemy. She was gracious and warm to everyone, making friends throughout her life. Even her husband's most critical political enemies, like Albert Gallatin, found her to be "a very good-natured and amiable woman." Abigail Adams

wrote that Martha was one of those unassuming people who create love and esteem. Her greatest gift was her ability to handle human relations, and no man or woman ever wrote of her with enmity. Her interests were family, friends, and household routine. She created a happy home, something that George had longed for since childhood. She let him know that she wanted him by her side, but she never nagged about the military and political commitments that dominated their lives after 1775. Mercy Otis Warren correctly evaluated Martha when she wrote that Martha's gentleness qualified her "to sweeten the cares of the hero and smooth the rugged paths of war."

Martha was at Mount Vernon in 1775 when George joined his troops in Cambridge. Many in Virginia feared that Governor Dunmore would seize Martha in revenge for George's commitment to the American cause, so Martha set out to join George and the army in Massachusetts. This was the first of many trips she made during the war; she joined George every year after his army had set up winter camp. She always went home when military campaigns began because George was afraid for her safety. She also needed to be at Mount Vernon because she had to manage the estate in George's absence. She underwent great hardship on her travels, in part because she was afraid of war and guns, but she never hesitated to join her husband when he indicated that he would like her to be with him. The general submitted her travel expenses of 1,064 pounds to Congress for reimbursement because he said that her visits to him took the place of the time he should have been allotted each year at Mount Vernon.

Martha's presence at the army's winter encampments improved the atmosphere considerably. When she would arrive, social activity increased. Other officers' wives would join their husbands, and there would be dinners, parties, and afternoon teas. The social events were never ostentatious, even when foreign dignitaries were in attendance. Except on the most formal evening occasions, Martha was usually knitting, and she always dressed in plain clothing and served simple foods. She might be called Lady Washington out of respect, but she did not act in an aristocratic manner. She worried about the condition of the ordinary soldiers, often carried soup to them, and gave them socks that she had knitted herself. She underwent discomfort, but she made the sacrifice because the "poor general was so unhappy that it distressed me exceedingly." She believed her support of him was her primary responsibility.

Her greatest sorrow during the war years was the death of her son Jacky from camp fever contracted at the Battle of Yorktown in 1781. Her sorrow was immense, but a week after his death she traveled to Philadelphia with George to celebrate the American victory. The war years were wearying, and she greeted news of peace and George's return to Mount Vernon on December 24, 1783, with great happiness. She anticipated a return to the prewar life she had enjoyed so much.

For five years she once again lived a life full of domestic activity and private contentment. She superintended the household and entertained a continual parade of visitors who came to see the foremost hero of the new United States. Along with the illustrious guests came many common soldiers and officers who had served with the general. War veterans were always introduced to Martha, who was usually sewing when they were brought into her drawing room. Two of her grandchildren came to live with the Washingtons after Jacky Custis died. Martha indulged, even spoiled, Eleanor Parke Custis and George Washington Parke Custis, but she also saw that they had proper education and training. Her grandson was sent away to school even though his absence saddened Martha, and Nellie was made to study the piano for four hours a day. Martha's letters to friends between 1784 and 1789 reveal a woman who was content with her life, looking forward to growing old with her husband, surrounded by their relatives.

Much to Martha's distress, George was elected President in 1789, and she once again had to leave her beloved Mount Vernon. She did not attend the inauguration but made her way to New York shortly after. George sent her some American cloth to make a dress on her journey north to symbolize her patriotism. She was greeted warmly in every town through which she traveled. In Philadelphia she made a public speech, thanking the city for treating her so warmly. It would be over a hundred years before the wife of a President would again speak in public.

At first she was not happy in New York, because she had so little to do. George's secretary, Tobias Lear, ran the household and kept ac-counts. She seldom went out because neither she nor George was sure as to what her role as wife of the President should be. Gradually her social life expanded, and she went to balls, dinners, and the theater. She attended church and charitable functions as George's surrogate. She arranged frequent dinners on Thursday evenings, inviting all congressmen and their wives in turn. On Fridays she held open drawing rooms, patterned after those of Queen Charlotte. On special occasions, such as Christmas, she held open house. She made frequent calls throughout the city, driving a cream-colored carriage that was a gift from the state of Pennsylvania. As her social engagements increased, she bought many clothes and found that she had to have her hair dressed every day. When the capital moved to Philadelphia, the social activities were more numerous and ostentatious. She tried to retain simplicity in her manner and dress, but she was aware that there was criticism of "Washington's Court." Such criticism did not bother her. She enjoyed life in Philadelphia more than she had in New York, because the home she occupied was larger, and she was able to have relatives and friends stay with her.

Throughout her years as wife of the President, she performed domestic, social, and ceremonial duties. She did not play any political role. She supported George's decision to run for a second term, and she was glad when he won. The criticism he endured upset her very much. However, her political discretion remained intact, and her personal views were never expressed. She was glad that George decided to return to Virginia at the end of his second term, and she looked forward to a few years of domestic happiness.

By 1797 her health was no longer good, and George hired a housekeeper to take over household duties for her. She tired easily, had frequent colds, and often was unable to greet visitors personally. George composed her letters for her, and she copied out what he had written. She did continue her needlework and made all of George's stockings. She faced George's death in December 1799 with great calm and fortitude but was unable to attend his funeral. She wrote Abigail Adams that she had suffered grief and anguish of mind when the general died. She retired to an attic room, a common practice for aged widows at this time. She spent many of her last days sewing, but she greeted most of the visitors who arrived at Mount Vernon. She inherited George's estate valued at $600,000 for her lifetime, but she left its management in the hands of her granddaughter's husband.

George's decision in his will to free his slaves at Martha's death created a difficult situation for her. Freeing his slaves was a complicated undertaking because not all of the Mount Vernon slaves were his. About 150 were part of Martha's dower and at her death would become the property of Custis heirs. George's slaves had often intermarried with the dower slaves, thus the decision to free his own slaves would cause strain and upheaval in the slave community. George postponed the inevitable disturbance by delaying manumission until Martha's death. If the instructions in his will had been carried out, Martha would have had to live the rest of her life with slaves anticipating her death because it meant their freedom. This caused her so much concern that she decided to free George's slaves a year after he died. She worried about their future welfare and told Abigail Adams that she wished that something could be done to ensure their well-being after freedom. She freed his slaves even though she did not share his disapproval of slavery. When Martha died, she bequeathed slaves who were her personal property to relatives instead of freeing them. Martha expressed concern about the future of her slaves, and throughout her life she treated the Mount Vernon slaves with compassion and kindness, but she accepted the institution of slavery.

Martha did not outlive her husband for very long. In the spring of 1802 she developed a "severe fever" and died on May 22. She was buried at Mount Vernon beside George in the tomb enclosure that he had planned. The life Martha Washington lived reflected the values of womanhood embedded in eighteenth-century American society. She excelled as a wife and housekeeper; she performed her public duties with grace and discretion; she dedicated herself to the care and love of other people, and she had in turn been loved, admired, and respected.

Allida McKinley

REFERENCES

Mary Wells Ashworth, "Martha Washington," *Notable American Women*, ed. by Edward T. James (1971); Betty Boyd Caroli, *First Ladies* (1987); George Washington Parke Custis, *Recollections and Private Memoirs of Washington* (1861); Douglas Southall Freeman, *George Washington: A Biography*, 7 vols. (1948–1957); Anne Hollingsworth Wharton, *Martha Washington* (1897).

Washington, William Augustine (1752–1810)

Continental Army Officer. The eldest son of Bailey Washington, William Washington was born in Stafford County, Virginia, on February 28, 1752. A distant kinsman of George Washington, William was trained for the ministry but never practiced his profession. When the war came, Washington sided with the rebels.

On February 25, 1776, Washington was appointed captain in the 3rd Virginia Continentals, a regiment that served under General Hugh Mercer. He participated in the New York and Jersey campaigns of 1776. He was wounded at the Battle of Long Island and then was wounded again at the Battle of Trenton. Captain Washington and Lieutenant James Monroe, of Washington's company and a future president, led a charge on two Hessian cannon on King Street in Trenton. Both were wounded. Washington sustained a wound on the hand. The two cannon were captured.

Several days later at the Battle of Princeton in January 1777, Washington was with General Mercer as he was mortally wounded. On January 27, 1777, Washington was promoted major and appointed to the 4th Dragoons, leaving the infantry for the rest of the war.

After Colonel George Baylor's 3rd Dragoons were badly mauled by General Charles Grey at Old Tappan, Major Washington was transferred to the 3rd to restore its spirit and to refill its ranks. On November 20, 1778, Washington was appointed lieutenant colonel of the 3rd Dragoons, replacing Baylor in command.

In November 1779, General Washington sent Lieutenant Colonel William Washington's dragoons to the south to reinforce General Benjamin Lincoln's forces in Charleston. Washington brought with him a composite force of dragoons from the various Continental dragoon regiments. Washington and his dragoons were soon actively embroiled in the vicious mobile fighting that characterized the southern campaigns of the 1780s.

Washington skirmished with Colonel Banastre Tarleton's legion at Lieutenant Governor Thomas Bee's plantation on March 23, 1780, and then got the better of Tarleton three days later at Governor John Rutledge's plantation along the Ashley River. A short time later Washington's men, along with other American units, were beaten at Moncks Corner and again at Lenud's Ferry. At Moncks Corner near the head of the Cooper River, Washington and other officers were forced to flee on foot through swamps to escape the British pursuit.

Washington's survivors were present at the Waxhaws but not fully involved. After the American disaster at the Battle of Camden, Washington joined with General Daniel Morgan's troops. After the Americans had an opportunity to recover and to regroup from their battering at the hands of Cornwallis and Tarleton, they began to harass the British.

Just as General Nathanael Greene arrived to assume command of the southern American army from General Horatio Gates, Morgan sent Lieutenant Colonel Washington on a daring raid. Washington's men struck at Rugeley's Mill, 12 miles north of Camden. Colonel Henry Rugeley, a Loyalist, had fortified his property and manned it with over 100 men. Without enough force to take the site, Washington instead resorted to trickery. He had his men take a pine log and fashion it into what looked like an artillery piece on a carriage.

This "weapon" was brought into view as an officer carried a flag to Rugeley to demand his surrender. Totally taken in by the trick, the Loyalists surrendered to Washington in a bloodless coup. Washington burned the fort, seized supplies, captured 112 men, and gave the Americans their first good news in a long time.

Washington followed up this effort with the Hammond's store raid in Laurens County, South Carolina, of December 27–31, 1780. Washington succeeded in routing 250 Georgia Loyalists. The Loyalists suffered 150 killed and wounded, and an additional 40 were taken prisoner. Washington's dragoons then joined Morgan in time to fight at the Battle of Cowpens on January 17, 1781.

At Cowpens, Tarleton's assault on Morgan's position failed. The charge of Washington's dragoons from behind the American left helped to clinch the American victory. In the melee, Tarleton and Washington came face to face. Washington's 14-year-old bugler saved his leader's life by shooting one British officer in the shoulder who was about to kill Washington. An American sergeant major parried the thrust

of another British officer who lunged at Washington. Tarleton fired a pistol at Washington that creased the American's knee and wounded his horse. Washington had broken his sword fighting against Tarleton but defended himself nonetheless, wounding Tarleton's right hand in the process. Tarleton got away in the chase, but his legion was effectively routed and his total force destroyed. For his bravery and actions at Cowpens, William Washington received a silver medal from Congress.

Following Cowpens, Washington played an active role in screening for General Greene's army as it raced ahead of Cornwallis's pursuit to the River Dan in Virginia. When Greene returned to North Carolina, Washington's men were part of the vanguard.

Washington led his dragoons with distinction at the Battle of Guilford Court House in March 1781. His brave charge at the final American line almost gave Greene a victory over Cornwallis. At Hobkirk's Hill in April 1781, Washington fought well but was delayed in his attack, got sidetracked, and then was overwhelmed with prisoners his men had collected on their sweep in behind the British lines. Busy organizing prisoners, Washington's dragoons never got into the main battle and were unable to help Greene's main force.

At Eutaw Springs on September 8, 1781, Washington had his horse shot from under him and was bayoneted. Unable to escape, he became a British prisoner for the remainder of the war.

In the spring of 1782 Washington married Jane Elliott (Elliot), the daughter of Colonel Charles Elliott of Sandy Hill, South Carolina. A local beauty, she had no difficulty capturing William Washington's attention. When his dragoon regiment needed a battle flag, it was Jane Elliott who had fashioned one from a heavy crimson silk curtain. The battle flag flew first at Cowpens and in every one of Washington's engagements thereafter.

After the war, Washington settled at his wife's family home near Charleston. He did serve in the state legislature but never felt comfortable in public, particularly when addressing crowds. Washington turned down running for governor, but he did accept a commission as a brigadier general on July 19, 1798, and served until June 15, 1800.

William Washington died on March 6, 1810, and was buried at Live Oak, a plantation near Sandy Hill, where the Elliott family cemetery was located.

A plump, round-faced cavalryman, Washington stood six feet tall. He was athletic, energetic, and manly in carriage. A good-natured man, he was pleasant, genial, and friendly. He was not given to working out details but instead relied more on bravery and spirit to accomplish his military ends. Impulsive and daring on the field, he always cared for his men. Yet he was not a particularly strict disciplinarian, sometimes to his own disadvantage in battle. William Washington appears to have been the epitome of the courageous, spirited southern cavalryman.

Paul J. Sanborn

REFERENCES

Appleton's Cyclopedia of American Biography (1887); J.D. Bailey, *Some Heroes of the American Revolution* (1976); *DAB;* Nat and Sam Hilborn, *Battlefield of Freedom* (1970); Henry Lee, *The American Revolution in the South* (1969); Burt Garfield Loescherg, *Washington's Eyes* (1977); John S. Pancake, *This Destructive War* (1985).

Washington's Navy

Upon taking command of the Continental Army outside Boston in July 1775, General George Washington was faced with many problems. Those of how to overcome a shortage of gunpowder and how to contain the British in the city led him to consider a maritime solution to both—the creation of a force of small armed vessels to intercept British supply ships bound for Boston. Some of the ships that might be captured surely would contain powder and other supplies sorely needed by the Continentals, and if enough supply ships could be taken, the British would be unable to support logistically any major thrust outward. They might even decide to abandon their lodgement and evacuate Massachusetts.

Washington had within his army the 21st (Marblehead) Regiment under the command of former trader Colonel John Glover, composed mainly of seamen from the merchant and fishing fleets. Although his orders did not specifically empower Washington to create a navy, the Continental Congress had concluded those instructions issued to him by stating: "You are . . . upon . . . any occasion . . . to use your best circumspection . . . to order and dispose of said Army under your Command as may be most advantageous for obtaining the end for which these forces have been raised." In early August, he set about chartering vessels to be armed, directing that they be officered and manned by the seafarers among his troops. Because this force of ships operated singly for the most part and had no permanent operational structure, the activities of each will be considered in the order in which each entered service.

The schooner *Hannah*, probably the property of Glover, was taken over on August 24, 1775, and armed with four four-pounders and a few swivels. She first sailed as a warship on September 5 under the command of army captain Nicholson Broughton, and two days later the *Hannah* captured the sloop *Unity*, laden with naval stores and provisions. Upon returning to port, the crew mutinied when it was thought their share of the prize money would be less than promised. With a new crew, she sailed again in late September. On October 10, she was forced to run aground by the HMS *Nautilus*. A stout defense by the crew and people on shore finally drove the *Nautilus* off, and the *Hannah* was refloated. She shortly thereafter was dropped from service.

The *Hancock* had been the schooner *Speedwell* prior to her acquisition in October 1775. She was armed with six four-pounders. Her first skipper was a failure, and he was replaced on January 1, 1776, by John Manley, who already had made a name for himself. Under Manley, she took five prizes, and two more under his successor. Late in 1776, she was found unfit for further war service and was returned to her owner early in the following year.

Fitted out at about the same time as the *Hancock* was the *Franklin*, the former fishing schooner *Eliza*, armed with two four-pounders, four two-pounders, and ten swivels. She sailed on her first cruise on October 22, 1775, under John Selman, who proved to be incompetent and who was removed upon its return to port. In May 1776 under the command of James Mugford, the *Franklin* made the second major arms capture by Washington's squadron when she took the armed transport *Hope*, carrying 1,500 barrels of powder and other munitions. She was returned to her owner later in the year.

The *Triton*, a fishing schooner, was chartered and outfitted in October 1775, sailing on October 26 as the *Harrison* under Captain William Coit, a sometime-lawyer. A not particularly seaworthy craft armed with four four-pounders and six swivels, the *Harrison* nonetheless managed to take four prizes by December 1. Crew dissatisfaction kept her in port for several weeks, and in January 1776 she was frozen in harbor at Plymouth, Massachusetts. When freed, she sailed on two ineffectual cruises under a new skipper; then she was returned to her owner.

The schooner *Two Brothers* was chartered in October 1775 and placed in service as the *Lee* under the command of Captain John Manley on October 28, armed with four four-pounders and two two-pounders. The *Lee's* first prize, the sloop *Polly* carrying Spanish milled dollars with which to pay British troops in Boston, was taken on November 27. Shortly thereafter, she took the large brig *Nancy*, which more than met Washington's expectations for military supplies. She contained 2,000 muskets with bayonets, 31 tons of musket balls, 30,000 cannon balls of various sizes, 100,000 musket flints, 11 mortar beds, and a 13-inch mortar. In the next three and a half months, the *Lee* took five more prizes, one of which also had a military cargo. Following the British evacuation of Boston on March 17, hunting continued to be good as enemy ships continued to arrive, unaware of what had transpired. The Continental Army's "navy" continued its activities even as the parent organization relocated to the vicinity of New York City. The *Lee* continued operations until October 28, 1777, taking eight additional prizes in the interim. A few days later, she was returned to her owner. She was the last of Washington's navy in service.

Another October charter was the fishing schooner *Hawk*, soon renamed the *Warren*. She sailed on October 31, 1775, under the command of Captain Winborn Adams, armed with four four-pounders and ten swivels. She took two prizes on her first cruise, including a brig laden with 153 quarter casks of wine. Following repairs and a change in command, the *Warren* began her next cruise on March 25, 1776, after the British had evacuated Boston. It proved fruitless. Blockaded for a time, she got to sea again in June and very nearly met disaster when she attempted to take the heavily armed transport *Unity*. While escaping under heavy fire, a powder supply on *Warren's* quarterdeck exploded, killing three and wounding seven. On her next cruise, the luckless *Warren* encountered His Majesty's Frigate *Liverpool* and soon became a British prize. Taken into the Royal Navy as a tender to the HMS *Milford*, the *Warren* was wrecked near Portsmouth, New Hampshire, around Christmas of 1776.

The schooner *Endeavor* was the largest unit chartered on orders from Washington. Rerigged as a brigantine and armed with six six-pounders, four four-pounders, and ten swivels, she was renamed the *Washington* and placed under the command of Captain Sion Martindale. She first sailed on November 23 and almost immediately found herself the prey of frigate HMS *Tartar*. She managed to get away after nightfall; a day or so later, she took her first prize, a provision-laden sloop. Martindale headed back to sea as soon as he saw his prize safely into port, but an unruly crew caused him to return quickly to port, where their grievances (lack of winter clothing, unwillingness of some enlistees to serve at sea) were attended to and order was restored. Within a day of returning to sea on December 5, the *Washington* ran into the frigate HMS *Fowey*, and after seven warning shots, she surrendered. Taken into Boston, the ship was found unsuitable for service in the Royal Navy and rotted away where she lay.

The schooner *Lynch* was placed in service on February 1, 1776. Armed with two 4-pounders, two 2-pounders, and four swivels, her first captain was John Ayres. She participated in the capture of two British provisions ships serving the British evacuation of Boston, and two more afterward. On three occasions, she narrowly escaped capture by units of the Royal Navy, the last time only by jettisoning all her guns and water. Upon return to port, at the end of September 1776, she was laid up. In February 1777 the *Lynch* was reactivated to carry dispatches to the American commissioners in France. Shortly after beginning the return trip, on May 19, 1777, she was captured by the HMS *Foudroyant*, a ship of the line.

George Washington's navy, for all its misfortunes and malfeasance, probably was more successful than the Continental Navy or any of the state navies in fulfilling its mission. In the captures of the *Nancy* and the *Hope* as well as those of troop transports and provisions ships, the "navy" gained for Washington the hoped-for military stores with which he could prosecute the siege of Boston and gave the British cause for concern about their supply line. It also underscored the general's understanding of the importance and uses of sea power, an understanding that was important in his strategy at Yorktown in 1781.

Tyrone G. Martin

REFERENCES

Donald W. Beattie and J. Richard Collins, *Washington's New England Fleet* (1969); Lieutenant Cmdr. William L. Dike, "The Navy's First 'Lady,'" *United States Naval Institute Proceedings* (June 1974):84–85; William M. Fowler, *Rebels Under Sail* (1976); Dudley W. Knox, *The Naval Genius of George Washington* (1932); Edgar S. Maclay, *History of American Privateers* (1899); Nathan Miller, *Sea of Glory* (1974); Navy Department, *Dictionary of American Naval Fighting Ships*, 9 vols. (1964–), 2,3,4,8.

Waxhaws, South Carolina, Battle of the (May 29, 1780) (Alternate name: Buford's Massacre)

There has been disagreement over the Battle of the Waxhaws since the day it was fought. Many Americans view the incident as a notorious example of a British atrocity. On the other hand, most of those who support the British consider the action an outstanding field success.

Waxhaws occurred on Monday, May 29, 1780, near the settlement of the friendly Waxhaws Indians (who are now considered extinct) in north-central South Carolina close to the North Carolina border. The action lasted less than a half-hour.

Following the fall of Charleston, on May 12, 1780, the rebellion in South Carolina for all practical purposes appeared to be crushed. British military influence spread across the state. There was only one American force of any size left in the area. Colonel Abraham Buford was in command. Buford led a group of approximately 350 infantry of the 3rd Virginia Continentals. These were accompanied by two six-pounders (artillery), several smaller pieces, and a few cavalry under the command of Lieutenant Colonel William Washington. The American cavalry were the survivors of actions at Moncks Corner and Lenud's Ferry. The total American force numbered over 400 men.

Buford and his men arrived at Lenud's Ferry on the Senate River about 40 miles from Charleston when word of the surrender of General Benjamin Lincoln's American garrison reached them. Buford was hastening to support Lincoln. Now it was too late. On the orders of General Isaac Huger, Buford began marching for Hillsborough, North Carolina, before the British could catch him and his troops.

In Charleston General Henry Clinton learned of Buford's position from Loyalist informers. He immediately dispatched General Charles Cornwallis and a force of 2,500 infantry, along with five cannon and Lieutenant Colonel Banastre Tarleton's cavalry after Buford. Cornwallis's goals were to capture the governor of South Carolina, who was with Buford; to destroy Buford's regular line unit of the Continental Army; and to subjugate the interior of South Carolina.

Cornwallis pushed his men. Yet by May 26, the British had only reached Nelson's Ferry on the Santee River near Eutaw Springs. They were not able to make up Buford's 10-day lead. On May 27, Cornwallis sent Tarleton ahead with 170 cavalry, 100 mounted infantry, and a 3-pounder to catch Buford.

By mounting his men double and by overworking his horses, Tarleton covered 60 miles in the heat and humidity over rutted, dusty roads so quickly that his van rode into Camden, South Carolina, on May 28. Learning that Buford was not far ahead, Tarleton rested his men until 2 a.m., May 29, and then rode out to overtake the Americans.

Tarleton, a daring, young, energetic, and gallant cavalry officer, pushed his men over 105 miles within 54 hours to bring Buford to bay. From Camden, Tarleton led his men through swamplands and pine barrens for 12 miles to Clermont, where Colonel Henry Rugeley's house and mill were located.

Yet, in spite of his speed, Tarleton had missed the governor of South Carolina. Governor John Rutledge and his councillors had fled Charleston before the American surrender, and they had joined Buford for protection. Hearing of the rapid British pursuit, Rutledge and his staff departed from Buford's unit at Rugeley's and headed off. Tarleton pressed on after Buford.

Just past Clermont, Tarleton came upon Buford's men in the vicinity of the Waxhaws early in the afternoon of May 29, 1780. Spotting the rear of Buford's column, Tarleton dispatched an officer to Buford with a demand for surrender. The terms offered were essentially the same as those accepted by General Lincoln at Charleston earlier that month. In addition, Tarleton claimed to have 700 men, with Cornwallis and the remainder of the British army close behind.

This was a lie. Tarleton had no such number, and those he did command were strung out over miles, unable to maintain the rapid pace Tarleton kept. Buford, realizing the trick, kept his infantry moving at double time. The American guns and baggage were at the head of the column and moving rapidly to safety. Buford held a conference with his officers. It was decided that there was no honor in surrender, nor would it help to disperse in the face of such a mobile British force. Another alternative was to use the baggage wagons to protect the men for a fight. If Cornwallis was near, though, then all would be lost if that was the choice.

In the end, Buford kept his men moving along the road as fast as possible. Buford told Tarleton: "I reject your proposals, and shall defend myself to the last extremity ." Buford's sole chance was to reach North Carolina, where reinforcements were expected.

As this exchange of proposals went on, Tarleton prepared his men for the attack. He had caught Buford at a crossroads about eight miles from modern Lancaster, South Carolina, in a lightly wooded, mostly flat area. When Buford noted that Tarleton was preparing to charge, the American colonel placed his men in a single line off the road in the woods. Ensign Cruit placed the colors in the center of the American line. The American artillery and baggage kept moving away from the field.

Tarleton decided to hit the American line on its left and center at the same time, while simultaneously crashing in behind the American right. The Americans did not attempt to disrupt the British as they made their preparations to attack. The action opened when the British eliminated the American rear guard. At that point, shortly after 3 P.M., MAjor Cochrane and 60 dragoons charged the American left, supported by fire from 60 dismounted legion infantry.

Captain Corbet and Kinlock led 40 men of the 17th Light Dragoons in a charge on the American center. Tarleton himself and 30 select cavalrymen, along with a few infantry, charged around behind the American right. The strag-

glers, who were still trying to catch up, and the single British cannon took up position on a slight hill in the center of the British line, serving as the reserve.

During the charge, Tarleton claimed he heard Buford's officers give the orders to hold fire until 10 paces. This unfortunate tactic may have worked well against infantry. It turned out, however, to be a serious error for the Americans to use against Tarleton's cavalry. By the time the Americans did fire, it was too late. The solitary volley had no real physical effect on the rushing British. Tarleton's men reached the American line relatively untouched and full élan, already sensing their victory.

The British crashed into the single American line. They easily broke it. Worse, the Americans were caught with their weapons unloaded after discharging their ineffective volley. The British cavalry slashed left and right with their sabers, cutting down the almost defenseless Americans.

A battle frenzy spread across the field when word spread that Tarleton had been killed. Tarleton had led his men in behind the American right and rode straight for an Ensign Cruit with the colors. The American officer was attempting to surrender, raising the white flag, as Tarleton reached him to cut it down. Then Tarleton's horse was hit and Tarleton fell beneath it, pinned.

With Tarleton supposedly dead, the remaining British officers lost control of their men. The British showed no quarter. Bayonets soon joined sabers in doing bloody work on the hapless Americans as the British infantry reached the fight.

Yet Tarleton was not dead. Aides pried off the carcass of the horse, and Tarleton mounted another horse. Meanwhile, Tarleton's men were moving about the field bayoneting the wounded. Even those who might ordinarily have escaped were killed when the British bayoneted those bodies covered by the bodies of others.

In a very short time, the "battle" was over. Buford's unit was destroyed as a fighting force. The British killed 113 American officers and men. They wounded another 150, many of whom were left on the field as too seriously wounded to remove. Some 53 Americans were captured and taken to Camden. The British cavalry also took the American cannon and 26 baggage wagons.

Approximately 100 Americans escaped Tarleton at Waxhaws, including Buford, who successfully rode off with several other mounted Americans. The local farmers came when it was all over and buried most of the American dead in a common grave on the field. The American wounded left behind by the British were taken to the Old Log Waxhaws Presbyterian meetinghouse. There they were nursed by several women, including the mother of future President Andrew Jackson.

Several Americans made amazing recoveries. Ensign Cruit lived to tell of his encounter with Tarleton. Lieutenant Pearson was horribly scarred on the face but survived. Captain John Stokes's story is most vivid and deserves its own retelling. Stokes was savagely mauled by two dragoons as the British charge turned into a melee. The dragoons hacked off his right hand through the metacarpals, took off his left forefinger, and hacked his left arm in eight to ten places from the wrist to shoulder. They finished him off by laying open his head on the top from his brow over the crown. Stokes was not dead, however, and now had to contend with the infantry.

A British soldier ran up to Captain Stokes as he lay seriously wounded on the ground and asked if he wished quarter. His answer was no. The British soldier proceeded to bayonet him through the body and then did it a second time and moved on. A second British soldier approached and asked the same question of Captain Stokes. His answer had not changed. Again a soldier used the bayonet on Stokes, not once but twice.

It is impossible to tell how long this would have gone on. Fortunately, a British sergeant approached, did not ask the question, and saved Captain Stokes from further wounds. In the end, Captain Stokes suffered from 23 individual wounds. He survived to tell the tale and display the scars.

Tarleton suffered 5 dead and 14 wounded. The British horsemen had 31 dead or wounded. After the action, Tarleton returned to Camden, where he was joined by Cornwallis on June 1. The British reigned supreme in South Carolina after Waxhaws and now prepared to move on to North Carolina.

In commentary on the affair at Waxhaws, it is plain that Buford took position on terrain more suitable to cavalry. His infantry was not protected, either by wagons or earthworks. Forming his men into a single battle line, rather than using a square or a multiple-lined, rolling volley formation, was unfortunate for the American infantry. It may have been that Buford and his Continental Line had not had much experience in dealing with cavalry in the past.

Some critics have supported Buford by claiming he had no choice in his selection of the field of action. It is true that Buford could have taken a position at some point earlier along the line of march when defensive terrain might have provided the Americans with a chance. Buford ran until he was run down. It was not necessary to allow Tarleton to do that. Buford did not seize the initiative from his opponent.

Buford did not make use of the artillery in his train. Hindsight, of course, calls for the use of every weapon Buford had at his disposal. In any event, Buford lost everything. However, decisions in battle work out quite differently. Buford evidently did not wish to gamble on losing everything, hoping his men could hold off Tarleton long enough for the baggage and artillery to escape.

American artillery loaded with grape and canister would have had some effect on Tarleton's men. The baggage wagons would have broken up a cavalry charge, even if momentarily. Buford must have known that Tarleton, as a cavalry officer, would rely on that branch of service more than any other. If a cavalry charge can be broken or even delayed, it is often the case that cavalry spirit and élan decline quickly in an engagement.

Tarleton did not have an abundance of infantry in support of his brash cavalry assault at Waxhaws. Nor did he soften his opponent's line with artillery. He took a risk, and it paid off handsomely. At Cowpens in January 1781, the somewhat different risk he took played out the other way. Both instances illustrate the impetuous nature of Tarleton's tactics. Buford never learned to deal with them. Daniel Morgan did.

In the eighteenth century, breaking the enemy line was the primary objective of a field action. Tarleton unleashed his attack outnumbered about two to one, since many of his men were still lagging behind. When the American line waited until the last minute to fire their volley, they neither stopped the charge nor dismayed the attackers. The cavalry hit the Americans with full force. Since the American weapons had been fired but there had been no time to reload, the cavalry had no real need of infantry support immediately. Cavalry sabers did their work without interference. The American line broke easily, and the battle was won for Tarleton. In the melee, it was difficult to maintain civility. The fighting was vicious and intense.

Buford was later court-martialed and exonerated for his actions at Waxhaws. Tarleton became known as "Bloody Ban" in the South, a rallying cry for Americans to use as they joined together to attack the British. "Tarleton's Quarter" became a second, more ominous cry that Americans used on Loyalists in the bitter fighting of the civil war that developed on a wide scale from May 1780 until the war ended three years later. One example of this was the brutality shown at King's Mountain in October 1780.

Tarleton's quarter referred to the British refusal to accept any surrenders after Buford's men had stopped fighting. The British claimed the Americans had tricked them by surrendering and then fighting again when the British guard was down. The Americans were inflamed by this type of bitter warfare, one that had not been common practice in the War of Revolution up to that time.

The British made Tarleton into a hero during a war that had dragged on much too long. They complimented him and his legion for their daring and effectiveness in putting down a rebellion against the King's law and order. Here was a cavalry officer who knew how to fight and take advantage of any weakness shown by the enemy. Some compared his ability in the cavalry with that of General Charles Grey of the infantry. Lord Cornwallis was extremely confident of his talents and used him regularly with effect throughout the southern campaign. Massacre or successful military action, Buford's defeat at the Waxhaws was a great victory for Cornwallis in bringing South Carolina once again under royal rule.

On the battlefield today, there stands a white monument above the common American grave. Not many visit the field, since few even know of the "battle." But those who do travel to the Waxhaws may read an inscription from the writings of British historian Charles Stedman:

> At this battle the virtue of
> Humanity
> was totally forgotten.

Paul J. Sanborn

REFERENCES

Robert D. Boss, *The Green Dragoon* (1973); Nat and Sam Hilborn, *Battleground of Freedom* (1970); Henry Lee, *The American Revolution in the South* (1969); Benson J. Lossing, *The Pictorial Field Book of the Revolution*, 2 vols. (1851–52), rpr. 1983; George Scheer and Hugh Rankin, *Rebels and Redcoats* (1957); Christopher Ward, *The War of Revolution*, 2 vols. (1952); Russell F. Weigley, *The Partisan War* (1970).

Wayne, Anthony (1745–1796)

Continental Army officer. Born on the family estate at Waynesborough, Chester County, Pennsylvania, Wayne was a rambunctious youngster, although he did well at the Academy in Philadelphia. In 1763 the handsome Wayne became a surveyor. By 1765 he was the agent and soon after the superintendent of a land company in Nova Scotia, but the scheme collapsed in that same year. He returned home to work as a surveyor and to manage his father's business interests. By 1770 Wayne, a vociferous Whig, was active in politics. He served in the Pennsylvania Provincial Convention, on the Chester County Committee of Public Safety, and in the Pennsylvania Assembly (1774–1775). The fiery Patriot read avidly on military science, and he organized a company of militia.

Appointed a colonel January 3, 1776, by his state, Wayne commanded the 4th Battalion. By April 4, his unit was on Long Island preparing for the forthcoming British invasion. Ordered to join General John Sullivan in the Canadian campaign, Wayne led his men to Fort Ticonderoga by late May. In his first task of combat at Trois Rivières on June 8, the Pennsylvanian neatly extricated his regiment from an enemy trap. During the disastrous retreat up the Sorel River, Wayne performed capably in evacuating his troops to the Isle-au-Noix and then to Ticonderoga. When the campaign ended in October, Wayne was posted to Ticonderoga during the winter of 1776–1777. As a result of a near mutiny by militia there, Wayne became an advocate of an army composed of regulars.

Promoted to brigadier general on February 21, 1777, Wayne was posted to Morristown, New Jersey. The Pennsylvania regiments participated in the maneuvering near New Brunswick during June. After a brief stay at Ramapo in July, Wayne's men marched to defend Philadelphia. At the Battle of Brandywine, Wayne's division was at Chadd's Ford. For three hours Wayne fought to repulse Hessian advances over the river as the American left wing deteriorated. In the retreat to Chester, Wayne inspired his men by his bravery.

As the British converged on Philadelphia, Wayne's 1,500 troops attempted to harass the enemy. Assuming that the American presence was undetected, Wayne camped close to the British lines. What became famous as the Paoli Massacre ensued. On September 20–21, in a skillful night attack led by Major General Sir Charles Grey, the British bayonneted Patriot soldiers. With 300 casualties, Wayne was inevitably subject to criticism. An official inquiry by five ranking officers held that Wayne was not guilty of misconduct but that he had erred in tactics. Enraged, the tempestuous Wayne demanded a full court-martial. On November 1, a board of 13 ranking officers declared that Wayne had acted with honor. Yet Paoli remained a stigma on the ambitious soldier's career.

Meanwhile, Wayne participated in Washington's daring attack on Germantown October 3–4. Always the charging warrior, Wayne plunged into battle, but due to several factors, the bold stroke failed. During the confusion complicated by fog and smoke, Wayne's men even fired on American units.

Wayne wintered with his troops at Valley Forge. While his troops suffered severely due to shortages in clothing and provisions, he bitterly criticized Congress for the neglect of the army. Intent on improving drill formation, enforcing discipline, and maintaining hygienic regulations, Wayne became a virtual martinet. One incident there exemplified his adventurous spirit. In February 1778 he led a month-long expedition into New Jersey to forage for livestock, neatly avoiding a near-entrapment by the British while recrossing the Delaware.

The Pennsylvanian next performed meritoriously at the Battle of Monmouth on June 28, 1778. What could have been an American victory ended in defeat. Due to faulty reconnaissance and misunderstandings between Washington and Major General Charles Lee, the assault on the enemy rear as the British marched through New Jersey nearly became a rout. Wayne adroitly maneuvered to defensible positions, thereby providing Washington with time to reform his lines.

Wayne next requested command of the corps of light infantry. He planned meticulously for the storming of Stony Point. In a brilliantly executed night assault on July 15–16, 1779, by 1,300 men armed only with bayonets and, generally, unloaded muskets, Wayne captured nearly the entire garrison on the Hudson Highlands. Stony Point was his personal triumph, for the raid bolstered American morale, and its results demoralized the British.

For the remainder of 1779, Wayne's command was relatively inactive in the stalemated war in the North. His raid on July 20 at Bull's Ferry was a fiasco. Encamped soon after at Tappan, New Jersey, when General Benedict Arnold attempted to surrender West Point, Wayne hurried to Haverstraw with his troops to counter a possible British thrust at the fortress.

During the winter encampment of 1780–1781 at Morristown, where again the men suffered acutely from shortages of provisions, Wayne lobbied in Congress and in the Pennsylvania Assembly for assistance. In the mutiny of the Pennsylvania Line in January 1781 Wayne was the principal mediator in settling the dispute over rations, amnesty, back pay, and terms of discharge.

Ordered to march south on March 7, 1781, to assist the Marquis de Lafayette in Virginia, Wayne refused to move until his men were adequately equipped. By May 26 his troops headed to the Rappahannock River, linking with Lafayette on June 3. As the British army under General Lord Cornwallis withdrew to the coast, Lafayette and Wayne tried to hit the enemy flanks. On July 6 at Green Spring the Americans attacked the British rear guard. Disregarding Lafayette's warning, Wayne impulsively probed at a large force cunningly concealed by Cornwallis. In the American retreat here Wayne was fortunate to escape in the darkness.

After protecting several sites from British raids, Wayne joined Lafayette at Williamsburg in August as Cornwallis retired to Yorktown. By September 28, the American-French army arrived in Virginia and Cornwallis was soon trapped on land and at sea. Recovering from a wound, Wayne saw little action at the siege of Yorktown.

Wayne's next assignment was to assist General Nathanael Greene in the recapture of Charleston and Savannah. Joining the Rhode Islander on January 4, 1782, on the Edisto River, Wayne had an independent command in Georgia. By January 19, he was encamped 14 miles from Savannah, confronted by the wily Brigadier General Sir Alured Clark and 1,000 regulars. Wayne encountered many difficulties in pacifying the area—skirmishing with the British, surpressing Loyalists, and fighting with the Creeks and Choctaws, who nearly overran the American camp on January 24. By May, the campaign floundered, for Wayne's 500 troops were insufficient to take Savannah. After the opponents agreed to an armistice (May 27), the British evacuated Georgia on July 14, 1782.

Though Wayne's performance in the South was not outstanding, he merited praise for grinding down the British defenses at Savannah and for campaigning under arduous circumstances. For his services, the Georgia Assembly awarded Wayne a sum of 4,000 guineas and Richmond, an 847-acre plantation. Though Wayne rejoined Greene on August 15, 1782, near Charleston, he was too ill from fever and gout to assist in dislodging the British, who eventually left South Carolina on December 13, 1782. The war was over, and in October 1793, Wayne was breveted a major general.

Wayne's career in the immediate postwar years was less distinguished. Returning to Pennsylvania he served in the assembly (1784–1786), and he was a member of the American Philosophical Society and the Society of the Cincinnati. As a politician Wayne was active in assisting a reform of the state's constitution, supporting legislation to assist veterans and measures to enfranchise those who had formerly refused to take loyalty oaths to the state. Wayne also aided in the state's revision of the Articles of Confederation, and, as a staunch nationalist, he was a delegate to the Constitutional Convention.

In 1785 Wayne returned to Georgia to oversee his holdings on the Savannah River. Not an astute businessman, he borrowed heavily to increase the productivity of his rice crop, taking loans on his Waynesborough property. Constantly pressed by creditors, Wayne remained in Georgia to avoid legal proceedings against him in Pennsylvania. Not until 1791 when he sold his Richmond plantation was he free of major debts.

Still dabbling in politics, Wayne campaigned unsuccessfully as a senatorial candidate to Congress from Georgia in 1788. Though he was elected as a representative from Georgia in 1791, his campaign manager was charged with corrupt electoral practices. As a result, after serving only a few months, Wayne was expelled from the House of Representatives on March 16, 1792.

Wayne was at the lowest point in his career. Fortunately for him, in April 1792 Washington appointed him to command an expedition into the Ohio country against the Indians. Capably organizing the Legion of the United States, Wayne marched to Fort Washington (Cincinnati) by May 5, 1792. After establishing a chain of forts as he advanced toward the Maumee River, Wayne won a decisive victory at the Battle of Fallen Timbers (August 20, 1794) against the Delaware and Shawnee. After building Fort Wayne he began an inspection of British outposts that had been recently ceded. The crusty soldier died at Presque Isle (Erie, Pennsylvania) on December 15, 1796.

How does one judge this vain warrior who was one of Washington's top field commanders? Wayne was the epitome of the swashbuckling military figure, the fearless leader who glorified in the excitement of war, the reckless soldier who displayed valor under fire and who inspired men in battle. The sobriquet "Mad Anthony" apparently derived from two characteristics. Wayne was known for his invectives and for his temperamental outbursts. Perhaps he was the most famous swearer of all the Continental generals. Likewise, the adjective "Mad" was actually a compliment from his colleagues, who admired the daring and audacity of this romantic hero.

Richard L. Blanco

REFERENCES

Thomas Boyd, *Mad Anthony Wayne* (1929); Clarence M. Burton, "Anthony Wayne and the Battle of Fallen Timber," *Michigan Pioneer and Historical Collection*, 31 (1909):472–489; Henry B. Dawson, *The Assault on Stony Point* (1863); Eldon Jones, "The British Withdrawal From the South, 1781–83," in *The Revolutionary War in the South: Power, Conflict and Leadership: Essays in Honor of John Richard Alden* (1979); Paul David Nelson, *Anthony Wayne, Soldier of the Early Republic* (1981); Samuel W. Pennypacker, *Anthony Wayne* (1908); Henry J. Pleasants, "The Battle of Paoli," *Pennsylvania Magazine of History and Biography*, 72 (1948):44–53; Jonathan Gregory Rossie, *The Politics of Command in the American Revolution* (1975); Charles Janeway Stille, *Major-General Anthony Wayne and the Pennsylvania Line in the Continental Army* (1893); Glen Tucker, *Mad Anthony Wayne and the New Nation: The Story of Washington's Front-Line General* (1973); Harry Emerson Wilder, *Anthony Wayne: Trouble Shooter of the American Revolution* (1944).

Webb, Samuel Blatchley (1753–1807)

Continental Army officer. A native New Englander, Webb participated in pre-Revolutionary political activity and in West Indian trade. He served as secretary to Silas Deane, his stepfather, and as scribe to the Connecticut Committee of Correspondence. After the Battle at Lexington, Webb became commander of the Wethersfield militia company and marched his men to Boston. He first participated in a military engagement at the Battle of Bunker Hill, where he was wounded and cited for bravery. In July 1775 Webb was promoted to the rank of major and appointed to aid Major General Israel Putnam. Within a year, Webb's rank was advanced to lieutenant colonel, and he became secretary to Washington. Webb continued his military activity in New England and was wounded at the Battles of White Plains and Trenton. In January 1777 an additional Continental regiment (Webb's Regiment) was formed, which Webb, recently upgraded to the rank of full colonel, led. In December 1777 Webb was captured at Long Island. He remained a prisoner for three years, being released in 1781. He rejoined his regiment, now the 3rd Connecticut, until June 1783, when it dispersed. Three months later, Webb was named a brigadier general. After the war, he moved to Claverack, New York.

Elizabeth D. Schafer

REFERENCE

Worthington C. Ford, ed., *The Correspondence and Journals of Samuel Blatchley Webb* (1969).

Weedon, George (1734–1793)

Continental Army officer. One of four Virginians (the others—Horatio Gates, John Muhlenberg, and Charles Scott) who held the rank of general early in the war and served until its end, George Weedon was raised in Westmoreland County and Stafford, Virginia. Weedon, through his marriage to Catharine Gordon in 1763, became proprietor of a tavern in Fredericksburg, one of the most popular among the gentry in all of the colony. George Washington and governors of the colony were patrons. Washington, visiting his mother and the Lewises in Fredericksburg, frequently "spent the evening at Weedon's," like others, playing cards and billiards and watching entertainment. Washington put his drinking bill on "club" (account). Weedon helped start subscription horse racing in Fredericksburg and was longtime president of the town's Jockey Club. Weedon became a close friend of Hugh Mercer, a physician and apothecary. After the death of Mercer at the Battle of Princeton, the Weedons raised the Mercer children (Hugh Mercer was the brother-in-law of Weedon's wife). Weedon particularly gave attention to Billy Mercer, whom he had apprenticed as an artist with Charles Willson Peale. The younger Mercer, a deaf-mute, became an accomplished artist in his own right. Weedon had a plantation, Crab Cove, on the Potomac, which never amounted to much; he successfully supplemented his income, however, by operating a slaughterhouse on the tavern grounds.

Portly in physique and congenial, Weedon had a way of reporting his activities very colorfully and often in a risque fashion. His battle accounts are among the most perceptive of any witness. Though few personal letters survive, there are rich collections of his correspondence involving military affairs.

On the eve of the Revolution, Weedon's tavern became a meeting place for Patriot groups, and as J.F.D. Smyth, a lodger at Weedon's tavern in 1774, later reported, Weedon was "very active and zealous in flowing the flames of sedition."

During the French and Indian War, serving in Washington's Virginia Regiment, after the General Edward Braddock's defeat, Weedon held commissions of ensign (September 14, 1755, ranking the last of Washington's 46 officers), lieutenant (July 26, 1757), and at the end of the war (in 1760) captain lieutenant. He saw no important action during the war, through he was probably with the Forbes expedition. He spent much time in garrison duty, particularly at the former French posts in western Pennsylvania.

Weedon entered military service during the Revolution, upon his appointment by the Virginia Convention, January 12, 1776, as lieutenant colonel of the 3rd Virginia Regiment. When Hugh Mercer was made brigadier general in the Continental Army, June 5, 1776, Congress, having taken the Virginia regiments into the Continental Army, elected Weedon colonel of the 3rd Virginia Regiment. Weedon and his regiment arrived at Manhattan, September 11, 1776, just in time to fight at the Battle of Harlem Heights, at which Weedon and his Virginians distinguished themselves; Weedon was bruised in the thigh by a "spent ball," which struck the guard of his sword. At White Plains, Weedon and his regiment were foremost in the action. Weedon had the honor of conducting the Hessians prisoners to Philadelphia. From January 13 to February 28, 1777, Weedon was acting adjutant general of the Continental Army. He was promoted to brigadier general on February 21, 1777.

As brigade commander, Weedon showed determination, but received scant recognition for personal distinction on the battlefield. His brigade (in Greene's division) held fast in a "ploughed field" at the Battle of Brandywine, with hand-to-hand combat, stalling part of Cornwallis's army from entering a pass in the forested hills. At Germantown, along with Greene's division, his brigade arrived late for the action and became involved in the confusion that forced a retreat. His reports on both Brandywine and Germantown are the best firsthand accounts of the battles.

At the end of 1777 Congress reordered the seniority of the Virginia brigadier generals—leaving Weedon last, behind William Woodford (whom he had previously outranked) Muhlenberg, and Scott. Considering this an affront to his honor as an officer, Weedon requested that Congress retire him from the army. Congress, however, tabled Weedon's petition, but Weedon went home anyway. Eventually, August 18, 1778, Congress conditionally granted Weedon's desire: Weedon would have retirement status, but without pay and rations; he could be called back whenever "the inconveniences he now labors under can be removed." Woodford's death in 1780, shortly after the capitulation at Charleston, now more or less cleared the way for Weedon to reenter active service. Congress, however, saw fit that he be assigned to the southern army at the discretion of General Horatio Gates. Though not called upon for active duty in the Carolinas by either Gates or his successor, General Nathanael Greene, Weedon saw substantial duty as brigadier general in command of the Virginia northern military district (above the James River) in raising troops and overseeing supplies of arms and provisions for Continental units and militia engaged against the Brit-

ish invasions of 1781, especially in assisting Lafayette.

At the Battle of Yorktown, Weedon himself took to the field, commanding 1,500 militia, for the purpose of dislodging the British army units at Gloucester, across the York River from Yorktown. Weedon had the responsibility for supplying boats to Washington and for erecting obstructions in the event that Cornwallis attempted to flee across the York and make his way northward. The Duc de Lauzun, commanding the French Legion, was assigned to assist Weedon. An enmity developed between the two men, and Weedon's troops were not available to aid Lauzun in a skirmish against Banastre Tarleton's troops. The haughty Lauzun, unjustly, called Weedon a coward and a "sloth." At the surrender at Gloucester (along with Yorktown), Weedon's militia were not allowed in the ceremony for fear that they would take retribution against Tarleton and his dragoons, who had previously butchered Virginia troops at the Waxhaws.

Weedon, at war's end, leased his tavern and in 1786 moved into his newly constructed house overlooking the Rappahannock in Fredericksburg, the Sentry Box (beautifully preserved and in private ownership today). Long suffering intensely from the gout, Weedon died December 23, 1793.

Weedon had performed ably, if perfunctorily, during the war, and like many of Washington's general officers, he had a down-to-earth quality that appealed to the rank and file; supposedly he was called "Joe Gourd" by his soldiers because of his reputation as a tavernkeeper for dispensing rum punch with a gourd. In the early days at Valley Forge, he was thought by some of his men, however, as being uncaring and hard-hearted. Weedon was a very warm admirer of Greene, and his correspondence to Greene is lively and quite revealing about Weedon.

Harry M. Ward

REFERENCES

Harry M. Ward, *Duty, Honor or Country: General George Weedon and the American Revolution* (1979); George Weedon, *Valley Forge Orderly Book of General George Weedon of the Continental Army under Command of General George Washington, in the Campaign of 1777–8* (1912), rpr. 1971; George H.S. King, "General George Weedon," *William and Mary Quarterly, 20* (1940):237–252; John A. Stevens, "The Allies at Yorktown, with Appendix of Contemporary Letters," *Magazine of American History, 6* (1881):1–53.

Weitzel's Mill, North Carolina, Engagement at (March 6, 1781)

After failing to trap the American general Nathanael Green in the race for the Dan River, Lord Cornwallis had to reappraise the situation. Encamped between Alamance Creek and Stinking Quarter Creek in North Carolina, his British army was short of supplies and fodder. Cornwallis had to decide whether to withdraw to Wilmington or to force Greene to combat. As Cornwallis retired from the Dan, Greene returned to North Carolina, sending advance units to harass the enemy. But until he had an advantage in manpower over the better-trained British army, Greene avoided battle. Awaiting reinforcements, the Americans were concentrated along the north side of Reedy Ford Creek, while other units were scattered farther east along the stream. Some American troops were on the north side of the Alamance, guarding the road from Guilford Court House to Hillsborough. Cornwallis was tempted to attack the Light Division under Colonel Otho Holland Williams in order to force Greene to fight near Weitzel's Ford on the Reedy Fork. Williams's troops were strung out too erratically for a sound defense. In particular, the Virginia militia under Colonel William Campbell was vulnerable to a quick enemy thrust. Cornwallis saw the opportunity and ordered the British Legion under Colonel Banastre Tarleton to strike. The Legion attacked and easily overran Campbell's camp. Now the British could advance to the key junction at Weitzel's Mill. Sensing the danger, Williams withdrew from his camp at High Rock Ford to the ford at Weitzel's Mill. He also sent Henry Lee's legion and William Washington's cavalry to assist Campbell.

Campbell managed to reach Weitzel's Mill, but his men were harassed continually by the British, who advanced in long columns that were deployed quickly for skirmishing. Fortunately for Campbell's men, Williams helped them to move their wagons through the stream, and he covered their retreat with riflemen under Colonel William Preston.

Now Tarleton's troops engaged Preston's men in wooded areas on the road to the mill.

Preston's riflemen resisted fiercely until Tarleton committed more soldiers to the fighting, driving the Americans over the creek at various points. The British followed closely, for a victory seemed feasible. What saved the Americans was that, with the aid of Lee's infantry and some Continentals under Colonel John Eager Howard, the riflemen under Campbell and Preston managed to reform. Hit by a withering fire along the creek, the British line halted briefly. But some British units waded through the water and outflanked the Americans. As the American line began to collapse, Williams ordered a retreat, with Lee protecting the rear. Because Lee's infantry and Washington's cavalry did not panic, Tarleton hesitated to charge. After retiring for three miles, Williams ordered his troops to reform for battle. But the British ended their attack.

Although this skirmish—which cost each side about 30 to 40 men—may seem minor, it had important consequences. While the fighting was underway, Greene moved his main army to the Haw River, planning another retreat to Virginia. For Cornwallis, the opportunity to weaken Greene's force by a quick blow and then to force him to battle had passed. Due to a shortage of men and supplies, Cornwallis decided not to risk a decisive fight that day. Yet within nine days and with virtually the same number of troops, Cornwallis would challenge Greene's reinforced army at the decisive Battle at Guilford Court House.

Richard L. Blanco

REFERENCES

Kenneth R. Haynes, Jr., "The Race to Weitzel's Mill, 6 March, 1781, *Gorget and Sash, 3* (1989):1–11; A.K. Newsome, ed., "A British Orderly Book, 1780–1781," *North Carolina Historical Review, 9* (1932):57–58, 163–186, 273–298, 368–392; Hugh F. Rankin, *The North Carolina Continentals* (1971).

West Indies in the American Revolution

With the entrance of France into the war by April 1778, the West Indies were no longer merely an area to supply the American rebels or the British war machine nor the hunting ground of privateers. Strategic naval warfare now took priority here. If the North American colonies were a string of pearls laid along the coast, then the West Indies were the diamonds of the empires that would fight in the West Indies during the war. As trade items for settling claims at a peace conference they were important. As Captain Charles Middleton, later Lord Barham, would say, "the name of an island returned by a treaty makes a good sound, and will claim something valuable in return."

In 1773 there were 42,000 British settlers in the West Indies, but only 1,060 troops fit for duty, from Jamaica to Barbados. The French outnumbered the British, in both white population as well as troops, and their island possessions were more concentrated. None of the West Indies islands was self-supporting, and they required seasonal convoys to bring supplies. England drew, in 1776, 4,250,000 pounds sterling in trade from the West Indies (compared to 1,500,000 from the East Indies). Thirty percent (5,250,000 pounds) of France's imports and 35 percent of her exports went to the West Indies. Winds were predominately northeasterly, so Jamaica's trade went up the Yucatan Straits onto the Florida Straits, while the Windward Islands trade collected at St. Kitts. British ships could undergo minor refits at English Harbor, Antigua, and at Barbados, but the anchorage at the latter was poor, especially due to hurricanes. So the British were faced with the problem of defending convoys originating and sailing from opposite corners of the West Indies, and facing enemy islands to the windward of them. A windward position lost could take days or weeks to recover.

The French lacked a major repair base and, like the British or the Dutch, had to return to Europe to undergo major refits. The Spanish had a major base at Havana, but it was only for use of their navy. The French would send home many of their key convoys from St. Domingue (modern-day Haiti), from their largest port at St. Nicholas Mole at Cap François in northern St. Domingue. The Spanish would use the port of Havana as the final port of call before returning to Europe. Due to the prevailing winds, both French, Spanish, and British reinforcements would arrive first in the Lesser Antilles There were really two stations in the West Indies—the Windward Station, which was the Lesser Antilles, while the Leeward Station was made up of the larger four islands, along with the Spanish and Gulf coasts.

There was a reluctance on the part of the under-garrisoned islands to send militia or regular troops to help other islands that were under attack. Further, planters hesitated to put up a fierce resistance, as this would threaten their highly flammable sugar plantations and their most valuable commodity, their slaves. The British planters were also reluctant to seize the French and Spanish islands, as this would upset the amount of sugar then available for the British market, thus driving down prices.

Both the French and the Spanish navies were animated by a renaissance of spirit, but both suffered from a defensive attitude as well as pronounced class differences. The French navy had the unique problem of generals transferring and becoming admirals. Her 49-year-old admiral of Toulon, at the start of the war, was the brave but eccentric Vice Admiral Comte d'Estaing, a former general.

France had several possible strategies, which would change and evolve in the course of the war. She could (1) assault Britain in her home waters, (2) launch a major enterprise in India, (3) vigorously prosecute the war in North America, (4) launch a trade war, or (5) attack Britain's possessions in the West Indies. The last strategy would be the arena in which France would make several major efforts and would suffer her worst defeat. The initial French strategy was one of forcing the British to disperse their armed forces. For France (and Britain too), the islands lent themselves to an offensive strategy, as it was hard to hold the islands and easier to take the enemy's.

War in the West Indies opened in September 1778 with a descent on British Dominica by the Marquis de Bouille, the governor of Martinique; the island quickly fell. The stronger British squadron at Barbados was unaware that war had broken out.

The British rear admiral, Sir Samuel Barrington, waited until he was reinforced, both with troops and ships from Admiral Sir Richard Howe's fleet and General Sir Henry Clinton's army at New York. He then attacked St. Lucia in December. St. Lucia easily toppled. In the midst of the attack on the island, d'Estaing arrived from North America with 12 ships of the line (SOL) including two 80-gun SOL. Barrington had seven, of which only one, the largest, was a 74-gun SOL. D'Estaing attacked Barrington in harbor, but was beaten off, and an attempt by land also failed. Frustrated, d'Estaing sailed for Martinique on December 28, leaving the British in possession of a port 30 miles from the French base at Port Royale, Martinique, which would be an excellent observation post for the remainder of the war. D'Estaing would remain at Martinique until spring, exhausting the supplies there and waiting for reinforcements, and more importantly, naval supplies. D'Estaing realized that without additional naval supplies, even a victory would leave his fleet immobilized.

When he moved in 1779, it was to snap up the islands of St. Vincent and Grenada. Vice Admiral John Byron had taken command of the British fleet at this point and had received reinforcements, as had d'Estaing. Both fleets would eventually number 22 SOLs for the British, and 25 SOLs for the French. The vast majority of ships were the smaller 64- and 74-gun SOLs. It was only later that the large three-decked SOLs, usually considered to be worth 11/2 the value of a 74, would appear frequently in the West Indies. It was these reinforcements and the need to protect a British convoy forming at St. Kitts that would result in a French victory. Byron sailed to watch for the main French reinforcement under the dashing Commodore La Motte-Picquet (five SOLs and 45 merchant ships), but had to leave his station to protect the British convoy to Europe. While waiting for La Motte, d'Estaing moved rapidly, easily capturing St. Vincent with a small portion of his fleet on June 16.

While Byron was still involved at St. Kitts, La Motte arrived at Port Royale, on June 27, 1779. By June 30, d'Estaing left Martinique with 25 SOLs, 5,500 troops, and 12 frigates, bound for Barbados, but persistent adverse winds caused him to sail for Grenada. By July 3 Grenada had fallen (159 regular troops and about 300 militia could offer little resistance), along with 30 merchant ships in the harbor, to the assaulting French troops under the personal leadership of d'Estaing, literally leading the land assault, as he would later do at Savannah.

By now the alarm had been raised, and Byron hurried south from St. Kitts with 21 SOLs, but faulty intelligence had led him to believe that fully half the French fleet was still at Port Royale. Byron was sighted by a scouting French frigate as he neared Grenada on the night of July 5. Thus warned, d'Estaing weighed anchor and began heading out of harbor at dawn on July 6, as the British fleet bore down. Byron, after detaching three SOLs to guard his own troop convoy from the numerous French frigates, ordered general chase, as he thought he outnumbered the French, and they were disordered in the light winds as they issued from the harbor. As the British formation stretched out, with the faster sailers rushing ahead and the slower sailers trying to catch up, the winds picked up and the French formed a line of battle to the leeward. The ensuing action saw one British 64 (the *Lion* under Captain Cornwallis) chased off to Jamaica. Three other 64s were badly damaged, in part due to a change of orders from Byron in the course of the approach to battle. But d'Estaing, true to French naval notions of "assuring or preserving a conquest to that, more brilliant perhaps, but actually less real, of taking a few ships," did not force a more decisive action. With Grenada's conquest maintained, he sailed on to Savannah and later home to France, though leaving 13 SOLs of the French squadron at Martinique and St. Domingue through the hurricane season.

This turn of events brought planter influence on the British government to send out 7,000 troops (3,000 destined for Jamaica) as reinforcements and replacements. Additional reinforcements were sent to General Sir Henry Clinton in New York.

Several small actions were fought during the remainder of 1779, in which the British outnumbered the French. After June 19 and the Spanish declaration of war, Vice Admiral Peter Parker, admiral of the Jamaica station, took the Spanish port of Omoa on the Nicaraguan coast and seized a small Spanish treasure fleet present. The Spanish governor Bernardo de Galvez at New Orleans, then Spanish Louisiana, immediately went on the offensive and seized Baton Rouge, then part of British West Florida.

On December 18, Vice Admiral Hyde Parker (Byron handed over his command in August and sailed for home) with five SOLs and one 50-gun ship chased a French convoy into Martinique. Parker seized 10 merchant ships, and forced four ashore. A short action ensued with La Motte's small squadron of three SOLs as La Motte tried to save the convoy, but the outnumbered French returned to port. On December 20 the French lost two frigates and a corvette.

D'Estaing had not achieved any great deed in 1778 or 1779, and the Comte de Vergennes, the French foreign minister, was discouraged by the mobilization of British resources to fight the war. With the failure of the invasion of England in

1779, the 1780 campaign would see the main allied war effort in the West Indies. The new year opened with the French sending a major convoy to Martinique, covered by 17 SOLs under Vice Admiral Comte de Guichen. Loaded with supplies, it also carried 4,400 troops. As it left Brest, Vice Admiral Rodney entered Gibraltar, after his victory over part of the Spanish fleet in the "Moonlight Battle." Another such defeat would possibly knock Spain out of the war.

Guichen arrived first at Martinique with his concentrated fleet, which numbered 22 SOLs. Before he could undertake any major operation, other than a threatening cruise off of St. Lucia, Guichen learned of the arrival of Rodney and returned to port.

Rodney appeared off Port Royale, but Guichen, the most tactically precise French admiral, declined battle. Instead Guichen tried to steal Barbados in a coup de main. On April 13 Guichen proceeded to sea with 22 SOLs and 3,000 troops. But Rodney chased him and, with 20 SOLs and one 50-gun ships fought the Battle of Martinique on April 17. Rodney attempted to fall upon the rear of the French line but failed, either through his officers not understanding his intent or the simple failure of the officers to follow orders. What followed was a classic line-to-line action, though Rodney's flagship actually passed through the French line at one point and was severely damaged by the French. Thus another indecisive action resulted in this, the second great naval action of the war (the first being Ushant in 1779).

Next Guichen, still avoiding tactical risk, anchored off Guadeloupe and then maneuvered to attempt to land and capture St. Lucia. Rodney (21 SOLs) kept Guichen (23 SOLs) from success and, after some maneuvering, caught Guichen on May 15, 1780. The Battle of St. Lucia Channel followed and was equally indecisive. These fleets cruised about until May 19, when yet a third action was fought. In this three-hour action, the second Battle of Martinique, three British ships were damaged, the *Cornwall* later sinking. Rodney had to return to port for repairs, while the French retired to port with provisions running short. It is interesting to note that Rodney would not have been inferior in numbers except for the fact that adverse winds kept a squadron of five SOLs in their English port for three months.

As both fleets retired (to Port Royale, Martinique, for the French, and Carlisle Bay, Barbados, for the British), Rodney was startled to learn that a Spanish fleet was on its way from Cadiz. The vital move in the 1780 campaign was unfolding with the sailing of the next great convoy. Admiral Don Jose Solano's Spanish convoy contained 13 SOLs , 2 frigates, a sloop, 2 smaller warships, 97 merchant ships, and 12,416 troops. These troops were to be used against Jamaica, if the opportunity arose. Coming on the heels of the Spanish losses at the Moonlight Battle off the coast of Spain, it was vital that this convoy get through safely.

Solano's fleet, when it arrived in the West Indies, was to join with Guichen's fleet, and then attack Jamaica. Bound for Martinique, Solano sighted a British frigate as he neared the island and so shifted to Guadeloupe. There he was joined by Guichen on June 9 with 15 SOLs (6 SOLs were left at Port Royale under Governor the Marquis de Bouille, thus threatening St. Lucia or Barbados). Due to an epidemic racing through the fleet, Solano proceeded to Havana for medical aid for his crews. The combined fleet left on the night of July 5, 1780, and Guichen escorted Solano with 24 SOLs as far as Cap Francois. There Guichen met La Motte's small squadron, bringing his fleet to 27 SOLs and 6 frigates. Guichen's fleet then returned to France, departing on August 16, with 18 SOLs and a convoy of 95 merchant ships filled with West Indian produce, leaving the other 9 SOLs under Commodore Baron de Monteil at Cap Francois. Guichen arrived at Cadiz on October 24, sending the merchant ships on to Toulon under convoy of five SOLs.

Rodney had deployed six frigates to search for the French, but they failed to find the allied fleet when it departed Port Royale. The frigates seized a French ship with false orders, which Rodney believed, and thus he did not capitalize on the absence of the French fleet. On July 12 Captain Walsingham finally arrived with reinforcements. Rodney split his fleet into three parts to help gather up merchant ships scattered throughout British possessions in the islands, and they gathered in two convoys at St. Kitts. One convoy departed with two damaged SOLs in August, and the second in October 1780.

With the approach of the hurricane season, Rodney sped north with 10 SOLs to challenge the French fleet at Newport, Rhode Island. His stay was quite short and accomplished little. By December 1780 he was back in the West Indies.

The major project in the Leeward Islands in 1780 was a British plan to attack Nicaragua, to push across to the Pacific, and to disrupt the Spanish Empire. Governor John Dalling of Jamaica led the expedition. Some 1,500 troops and militia sailed from Jamaica in March and advanced up to Lake Nicaragua. But the force of the attack was spent, and the British withdrew to Jamaica. Only 1,350 troops under General Garth arrived as reinforcements against a descent by the allied fleet upon Jamaica. By August 1780, even with reinforcements, the British mustered only 3,554 men fit for duty from St. Lucia to St. Kitts. This figure must be placed in perspective with the 7,000 troops sent out from England that previous spring.

Two small actions were fought in 1780 in the Leeward Station. La Motte, with three SOLs, a 50, and a frigate, was escorting a convoy off Cap Francois in late March. He fought an action on March 20 with three British ships, under Captain Cornwallis. La Motte was wounded in the action. The next morning a British SOL and two more frigates came up and chased off the French.

Cornwallis's fleet had an action with four SOLs, a 50-gun ship, and a frigate against Commodore Chevalier de Ternay's squadron and convoy on June 20, 1780. Cornwallis had seen a Jamaica convoy as far as Bermuda and was returning to Jamaica when Ternay was sighted. The convoy of 30 ships held General Rochambeau's 6,000 troops bound for Rhode Island, and it was guarded by seven SOLs and two frigates. Ternay simply chased the British off and did not attempt action. He was concerned for the safety of his ships in case he encountered a British fleet at Rhode Island.

The final event of the year was a great hurricane that swept across the West Indies in October. It sank 3 British warships, damaged 8 more, and swept a 74-gun ship to England. Ten smaller British ships were also lost.

By 1781 English naval resources were spread thin. With commitments worldwide, Britain found that she lacked seamen, soldiers, and merchant ships. Her limits to naval expansion had been reached, and another enemy beset her. The entry of the Dutch into the war hurt Britain's war planning.

When the war with the United Provinces broke out, a message was rushed out to Rodney in the West Indies. He immediately moved against the richest island in the West Indies—St. Eustatius. While Port Royale had been a major port for rebel trade until France entered the war, St. Eustatius, a small Dutch-owned island near the Virgin Islands, had developed into a booming port. Leaving six SOLs under Rear Admiral Francis Drake to cover Port Royale with its four French SOLs, Rodney rushed down with the remainder of his fleet and easily captured the island on February 3, 1781. He took goods worth three million pounds and 150 merchant ships. Rodney also learned that a convoy had just left, and he ordered out a detachment. It captured the Dutch *Mars* (60 guns) and 23 merchant ships in the convoy. The British also landed in Surinam.

The Dutch impact on the war in the West Indies was virtually complete as soon as war was declared. With her small obsolescent fleet confined to the North Sea, Holland was further hampered by a concept of defending possessions and trade, instead of maintaining an active fleet at sea conducting offensive operations. For most of the war she maintained two SOLs at Curaçao. Beyond some convoy operations, the enthusiasm for the war on the part of the Patriot Party in the United Provinces was not translated into deeds on the high seas.

The brave, strategically insightful, and careful Vice Admiral Comte de Grasse was 58 years old when he took command of the French fleet of 20 SOLs, 3 frigates, and 2 smaller ships. His flagship was the *Ville de Paris* (110 guns). His first duty was to escort a convoy of 150 ships to the West Indies and North America. After that, de Grasse was to aid Washington and the Comte de Rochambeau in North America, after giving aid requested by his Spanish ally at Havana. De Grasse departed Brest on March 22, 1781.

Rear Admiral Samuel Hood, the most vigorous of Britain's admirals in this war, arrived to reinforce Rodney in January with 8 SOLs, after escorting over 100 merchant ships. He was then deployed off of Port Royale with Drake's squadron, totaling 17 SOLs and 5 frigates. In Port Royale lay Admiral Monteil with nine SOL and six smaller warships. Hood was alerted to move against Curaçao, but Rodney's involvement with the rich prize of St. Eustatius (and the prize money it represented) paralyzed Rodney, and so the Curaçao expedition never left. Ironically, two-thirds of the convoy with the money and goods seized at St. Eustatius would end up being recaptured by the French as it neared England by a copper-bottomed French squadron out of Brest under La Motte.

Before de Grasse's campaign, two events of note took place in the summer in the Leeward Station. Galvez was now ready to move against Pensacola. Galvez received 3,700 men (800 being French), whom, combined with his original 1,400, brought his strength up to 5,100 men, and a part of Solano's Spanish fleet (including four French SOLs) for the siege of Pensacola. He would face Brigadier John Campbell's 1,200 men, who would hold out from mid-March to May 8, when Pensacola fell. Solano, on July 29, dispatched to Spain a treasure fleet from Havana, guarded by four SOLs, which would arrive safely in this autumn high tide of allied fortunes.

On April 28 de Grasse's fleet was seen approaching after a quick crossing of 36 days. He was to the windward of Hood with a superior fleet (20 SOLs and three frigates), but Hood (18 SOLs and five frigates), with all his ships with coppered bottoms, was faster. A long-range cannonade took place on April 29, which caused some damage to several British ships. With the vagaries of the wind, the damage incurred, and Monteil sending four SOLs out to support de Grasse, Hood was forced to retire. The French fleet and convoy had slipped into Port Royale on May 6, 1781. When Rodney learned of this action and the strength of the French fleet, he quit St. Eustatius and joined Hood off Antigua to take in stores.

Bouille and de Grasse immediately took advantage of the absence of the British fleet by sending a major expedition against St. Lucia and a minor one to seize the island of Tobago. Three British frigates arrived at St. Lucia just after the French arrived, and their crews reinforced the small British garrison, which managed to hold onto the island, and Bouille returned to Port Royale.

Bouille and de Grasse next reinforced the original expedition sent to Tobago while Rodney awaited the return of Drake's squadron sent to Tobago. Rodney, now united with Drake's squadron (20 SOLs) sighted the returning French fleet (24 SOLs) near Grenada on June 5, but declined battle. De Grasse returned to Port Royale and then left again on July 5 with 24

SOLs, a 50-gun ship, and 175 merchant ships in convoy bound for Cap Francois.

Rodney, after some delay and debate, decided that his health required him to go home. The 1781 campaign must be placed in the context of Rodney's ill health (he was 63 years of age and suffered from gout). He sailed on August 1 with a convoy of 150 ships and left Hood in command of the fleet with orders to sail to the North American station. De Grasse had arrived at Cap Francois on July 16 and there began unfolding the move to the Chesapeake.

De Grasse had been ordered to guard the merchant convoy to Europe with 10 warships. But instead, he decided to escort the 126-ship convoy with only one 64-gun ship and some armed transports. He took his fleet of 27 SOLs and one 50-gun ship and proceeded to North America to help Commodore Barras and his eight SOLs facing the British rear admiral Graves and his seven SOLs. But to where? New York or Virginia?

De Grasse received dispatches from Washington and Rochambeau when he was at Cap Francois. He was also helped in his decision to go to America by two Spanish officers. Galvez, who now commanded all land forces in the Caribbean, had sent his aide Francisco de Saavedra to confer with de Grasse. Galvez released all the French ships from duty in the West Indies and lent back to de Grasse the French troops at Cap Francois. Saavedra and de Grasse then planned the coming campaign. The scheme called for the French to sail up to the Chesapeake to assist the American army, returning in November for three months of operations. Solano was supposed to send a small Spanish squadron to sea to threaten Jamaica in de Grasse's absence, though this did not occur. Then, in March 1782, de Grasse would concentrate at Cap Francois for a rendezvous with the Spanish fleet and follow it with a descent on Jamaica with 7,000 French troops and additional Spanish troops under Galvez.

De Grasse sailed for America on August 5, after dispatching his plan to Barras and Washington. Next de Grasse personally pledged his estates to help raise money for the American army. The French traders and planters were agreeable to this, if their convoy was escorted by a large part of de Grasse's fleet. De Grasse refused, but the Spanish in Havana helped again, this time with an oversubscribed pledge of 1,200,000 livres (in part due to the wheat shipments sent to Havana by the United States during the course of the war). De Grasse picked up this loan at Matanzas, Cuba, and quickly sailed north, arriving at the Chesapeake on August 30. De Grasse was further aided by capturing all British ships sighted on the way north, except for one frigate, which ran into Yorktown with the approach of the French fleet. Now the Battle of the Chesapeake transpired.

With victory achieved at Yorktown, de Grasse now hurried south to implement the grand design for capturing Jamaica. Further Spanish reinforcements (four SOLs and 6,000 troops) from Europe were on their way to the West Indies. The French were sending their best tactician, Rear Admiral Vaudreuil with troops, supplies, and seven SOLs to Martinique.

But the crest of the allied high tide had been reached and now the ebb had set in. First a British fleet intercepted the French fleet off of Brest, capturing 20 merchant ships (and 5 others on their way to join) from the convoy. Then a great storm greatly damaged Vaudreuil's squadron, so only Vaudreuil with two SOL and part of the convoy reached Martinique.

Meanwhile, a recuperated Vice Admiral Rodney hurried back to the West Indies with additional reinforcements. From the North American station, first Hood left with his squadron to return to the West Indies. Next, Rear Admiral Robert Digby, who had relieved Graves at New York, recognizing that the French had left the North American station, sent all his SOLs to the West Indies.

The year 1782 opened with Hood having 22 SOLs in the West Indies and with 17 more under Rodney in transit. De Grasse had returned to the West Indies with 33 SOLs, having detached five to escort another convoy to France with Cap Francois. Bouille at this time, with three frigates and 1,500 men, easily recaptured St. Eustatius. Northern Surinam was recaptured at this time by a small French squadron.

De Grasse had to wait for the convoy from Europe before proceeding to attack Jamaica. But he was active. His two attempts against Barbados failed due to the wind (several SOLs suffered storm-related damage in the process), but he did move against St. Kitts with 26 SOLs. In January de Grasse landed troops to besiege the British garrison. Hood raced down with 22

SOLs, hoping to surprise the French, but failed. However, in a remarkable feat of seamanship, Hood seized the French anchorage and anchored his inferior fleet there. De Grasse, on January 25 and 26 made two attempts to break Hood's anchored line, but failed.

However, St. Kitts fell. Thus, Hood now found himself anchored off a hostile shore, and de Grasse reinforced with two more SOLs. Cutting his anchors and with no lights showing, he slipped out on February 14, escaping de Grasse.

De Grasse followed up this operation with the capture of Nevis and Montserrat. Rodney, however, had arrived. The critical moment had been reached. Britain, once again, had the superior fleet. If only they could intercept the reinforcing French convoy—a convoy that held stores vital to the French fleet and the French islands. Hood suggested casting a wide net to capture this convoy, but Rodney believed that they only needed to cover the area to the south of Martinique. Rodney was wrong, and the French convoy slipped by to the north and anchored on March 20 at Port Royale.

De Grasse was now ready to proceed to join with the Spanish fleet and attack Jamaica. Then disaster struck. As de Grasse sailed with 33 SOLs for the rendezvous with the Spanish at St. Domingue, he tried to pass through Iles des Saintes (The Saintes), some small islands to the south of Guadeloupe. Rodney was on him quickly with 36 SOLs and even then might have failed in stopping the French fleet, but the captain of the French SOL *Zele* collided twice with French ships, including once with the flagship, the *Ville de Paris*. The result was that de Grasse was forced into battle. Rodney was further aided because his captain had been trained in a new method of firing that allowed them to deliver more broadsides than the French by traversing their guns a greater distance. Finally, a break in the French line occurred, which the British crashed through in two places, thus splitting the French into three portions. The result was that de Grasse and the *Ville de Paris* were captured, along with four other French SOL. Two other French ships would be captured a few days later.

The French fleet had exhausted its ammunition. Until they were resupplied, the French dared not undertake a major operation. The shattered French fleet, covered by Solano's Spanish fleet of 11 SOLs and two frigates, gathered at Cap Francois. Vaudreuil, now in command, sent

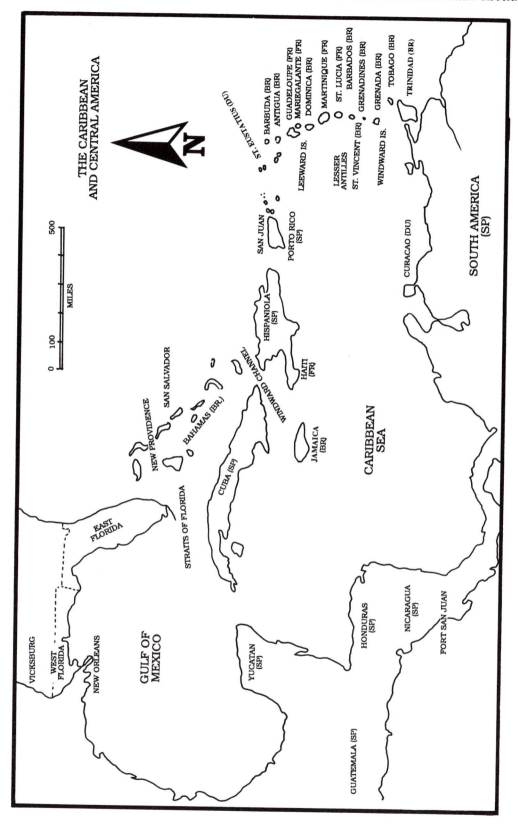

THE CARIBBEAN
AND CENTRAL AMERICA

N

500

100

0

MILES

ST. EUSTATIUS (DU)

BARBUDA (BR)
ANTIGUA (BR)
GUADELOUPE (FR)
MARIEGALANTE (FR)
DOMINICA (BR)
MARTINIQUE (FR)
ST. LUCIA (FR)
BARBADOS (BR)
GRENADINES (BR)
GRENADA (BR)
TOBAGO (BR)
TRINIDAD (BR)

LEEWARD IS.

LESSER
ANTILLES
ST. VINCENT (BR)

WINDWARD IS.

SAN JUAN

PORTO RICO
(SP)

CURACAO (DU)

SOUTH AMERICA
(SP)

HISPANIOLA
(SP)

HAITI
(FR)

WINDWARD CHANNEL

NEW PROVIDENCE
SAN SALVADOR
BAHAMAS (BR.)

JAMAICA
(BR)

CARIBBEAN
SEA

CUBA (SP)

STRAITS OF FLORIDA

EAST
FLORIDA

VICKSBURG
WEST
FLORIDA
NEW ORLEANS

GULF OF
MEXICO

YUCATAN
(SP)

HONDURAS
(SP)

NICARAGUA
(SP)

FORT SAN JUAN

GUATEMALA (SP)

1771

a frigate to Europe with the news. Next, the most damaged SOLs formed with a convoy of 104 merchant ships and were sent off to Europe. Then, the best of the French ships sailed for North America, hoping to repair and take on stores there. Solano returned to Havana, with troops dispersed to the various islands as garrisons. Yet Galvez still managed to use the summer, even after the defeat at The Saintes, to send 2,500 men to seize the Bahama Islands. The Bahamas had been a base for British privateers during the war.

The British followed up the victory with additional news. North's ministry had fallen in March, and Rodney was replaced by Admiral Hugh Pigot, a totally undistinguished officer. Rodney would return to a Britain thankful for his victory.

The British would spend the summer in trying to capture various allied detachments and convoys. But after Pigot's arrival, the war in the West Indies was rapidly coming to an end. By late 1782, both sides were near exhaustion. The French and the Spanish were financially embarrassed and worried that with another defeat such as that at The Saintes, all recent conquests might be lost.

Ironically, with the ending of the war, America resumed her trading practices of old and traded mostly in the West Indies, not with her new allies, but with England.

Jack Greene

REFERENCES

Sir William Laird Clowes, *The Royal Navy: A History from the Earliest Times to the Present*, 7 vols, (1891–1903), *3*, *4*; Jonathan R. Dull, *The French Navy and American Independence, A Study of Arms Diplomacy 1774–1787* (1975); Charles Lee Lewis, *Admiral de Grasse and American Independence* (1945); Piers Mackesy, *The War for America 1775–1783* (1965).

West Jersey Volunteers

This Loyalist unit was also known as the New Jersey Volunteers or Skinner's Brigade. One of the largest and most active of the Loyalist regiments, the West Jersey Volunteers were organized in September 1776 by Brigadier General Cortland Skinner. Robert M. Calhoon estimates that 2,450 men ultimately served in the regiment, and that they came from a pool of 13,000 active New Jersey Loyalists who, with their families, represented 35 percent of the state's population. Thus the Volunteers could count on widespread local support. There were usually three battalions, but a fourth was present at Staten Island in November 1778. Two battalions participated in General Wilhelm von Knyphausen's raid on Springfield, New Jersey, in June 1780. Others were stationed at Paulus Hook, New Jersey, or served in Long Island and the New York City garrison during the last months of the war.

The regiment was plagued by discipline problems and by desertion. Many recruits used the Volunteers as a cover for personal vendettas, and farmers were often coerced into "donating" produce and meat. In some counties Skinner tried to conscript civilians or the local militia. The British retreat from much of New Jersey in 1777 ended this reign of terror, and thereafter the Volunteers operated only in the environs of New York City.

Tom Martin

REFERENCE

Robert McCluer Calhoon, *The Loyalists in Revolutionary America, 1760–1781* (1973).

West Point, New York

Sitting high atop a plain overlooking the beautiful Hudson River, West Point is the oldest continuously active military post in American history. Since 1802, the United States military academy has occupied the site. But West Point's historical importance was realized during the War of Revolution, when it was considered to be the Gibraltar of America and the key to the continent.

During the Colonial period, travel was both an adventure and a physical challenge for any individual under most circumstances. Heavily forested lands, broken by steep hills and mountains, prevented the easy overland movement of trade and commerce. It hindered communications. But more to the point, it severely limited the maneuvering of armies and their lengthy baggage trains. During the eighteenth century, the open highways for commerce and trade, along with military campaigning, were the river systems of North America. And the most important corridor of all by 1775 was the Champlain–Hudson River valley system.

Even at the very beginning of the war, it was clear to the Continental Congress and to the political leaders of New York that the Hudson

River must remain under American control. A delegation was sent to the Hudson River Valley to determine where the fortifications for the river should be built. After careful investigation, the Hudson Highlands were selected as the best region and Martelaer's Rock as the best location for the protection of this crucial passageway, especially if the British succeeded in capturing New York City.

At Martelaer's Rock, an island, the Hudson River curved to the west and then bent back north again at two right angles. The river itself narrows in this turn, with unpredictable winds and a current subject to difficult tides. Sailing ships could not maintain speed as they approached this part of the Hudson. They had to slow and tack carefully. It was a perfect spot to fortify. The ships would be at the mercy of cannon placed along the shores. "Martelaer's Rock" is a corruption of the Dutch "Martelaar's Reik" or Martyr's Reach, obviously named by early Dutch pilots who had experienced the danger of making the shift around the bend of the river.

If the British were able to seize control of the Hudson River, they would possess a natural invasion route into the interior of New York State. There were a number of Dutch, English, Welsh, and other ethnic groups living along the river who remained passively loyal to the Crown. With British control of the river, this Loyalist population would add their strength to that of the royal forces. An open Hudson would permit the British to supply their Iroquois Indian allies, allowing them to attack the valuable Mohawk Valley–Tryon County region of New York State.

In addition, control of the Hudson would allow the British to link up with their forces in Canada through Lake Champlain, providing a British commander any number of points from which he could launch an attack against pockets of rebellion on either side of the waterway. Finally and perhaps most crucial of all, a British capture of the Hudson would practically cut communications and the flow of both supplies and troops from New England south to the rest of the colonies. With a principal supply source for troops, political power, and materials cut off, the British hoped the Revolution would die a natural death in the South. Then with no further revolt in the other colonies, perhaps even the New England radicals would wither on the vine.

The Hudson Highlands begin at Tappan Zee near Tarrytown, New York, and stretch along the Hudson north to the town of Newburgh. The major northeast to southwest land routes of communication and movement crossed the Hudson in the Highlands, from Fishkill to Newburgh in the north and Verplanck's Point to Stony Point at King's Ferry in the south. The Highlands were the highest ground found along the entire corridor from Canada south to New York City. In the middle of the Highlands, along the Hudson River, stood Martelaer's Rock, where construction of the first river defenses began in the fall of 1775.

New York hired a civilian Dutch botanist and cartographer who had English training as a civil engineer, Bernard Romans, to supervise the development and construction of the fortifications on Martelaer's Rock. Romans was not experienced in military engineering, but he was present at Fort Ticonderoga with Benedict Arnold in May 1775 to assist in the repair of the fort. Romans inspected the site and found it suitable, although the opposite bank rose high above the river and dominated the island. This far bank had the name West Point since it was the point of the western shore reaching out into the Hudson as the river twisted its way through the Highlands. A farm occupied the large, flat plain on the top of West Point, and the Highland towered up behind the plain several hundred feed in elevation. Romans never planned to include West Point in his fortification plans.

Civilians were hired to construct the works that Romans laid out on the island. Fort Constitution was to be a grand bastion located on the southwest end of the island, but it was never completed. However, the name stuck and was applied in time to the entire island. The "Constitution" referred to was the English Constitution, from which all English rights flowed. The Americans felt it was these rights that were threatened by the acts of Parliament.

Romans and the New York Commission with oversight over the works had several prolonged arguments over the project. Progress was slow. Funds were short. Materials and labor were either missing or in small quantities. The workers were constantly drunk and undependable. A different commission sent to investigate the situation found the eastward approaches to the island open and undefended. The fort was poorly sited, and dominant West Point was not defended at all. Neither Romans nor New York could handle the military situation properly. In February 1776, Romans was fired from his position.

The Americans then turned to another location along the river at Popolopen Creek, seven miles south of West Point. The work on Constitution Island remained unfinished. The Americans began building Fort Montgomery, named after General Richard Montgomery who died in the storming of Quebec, December 31, 1775. On the south bank of the creek, another work was constructed and named Fort Clinton. In April 1776, Captain Thomas Machin attempted to stretch a chain across the river from Fort Montgomery to the shore by Anthony's Nose. However, the chain broke.

General William Howe captured New York City in 1776 and moved toward the Highlands that summer, which prompted the Americans to increase the speed of their work on the two forts at Popolopen Creek. In October 1777 the British under the command of General Henry Clinton came upriver and, in a brief assault, captured Forts Montgomery and Clinton. Fort Constitution was burned without resistance, and Clinton got as far north as present-day Kingston before stopping. His move was to support General John Burgoyne's force coming south from Canada. Instead of meeting in Albany or along the Hudson, Burgoyne was forced to surrender, and Clinton returned to New York City, having controlled the Hudson Highlands for 20 days. All the American positions he left behind were destroyed.

It was at this point that the American authorities turned to West Point and began to fortify that position as the most suitable in the Highlands. The erection of the fortifications at West Point were not completed without the usual difficulties. Colonel Louis de la Radiere arrived on the scene to plan the West Point defenses. He was European-trained and quite impressed with his own ability, which unfortunately did not match his true competency as an engineer. He also lacked polish as a diplomat. Instead of solving problems, he added to them.

General Alexander McDougall was placed in command at West Point at the end of 1777. By January 1778, work had begun on the new fort under the French engineer's direction. Military troops replaced the unreliable civilians in working on the fortifications. But de la Radiere argued with everyone and made suggestions that worried both the military and political powers concerned with the defense of the Hudson. In March 1778, a 32-year-old French-trained Polish engineer arrived at West Point from service in the north with General Horatio Gates. Sent by Congress to be the chief engineer and to clear up the confusion at West Point, Colonel Thaddeus Koscuiszko was the individual who created the defensive works at West Point. Insubordinate, incompetent, and argumentative, Radiere was soon dismissed from West Point. In a shorter time, Koscuiszko had Fort Arnold on the point almost completed, with work begun on the outer works, including four water batteries named Chain, Lantern, Water, and Knox along the shore. Redoubt Sherburne was dug on the plain to protect Fort Arnold from attacks to the north and from behind.

Koscuiszko was at West Point for 28 months before gaining additional glory in the southern campaign. During that first spring, Thomas Mackin succeeded in stretching an iron chain across the Hudson from the western bank, to the left of Fort Arnold, to Constitution Island. Forged at the Sterling Ironworks by Peter Townsend, 25 miles southwest of the Point, the chain was 1,700 feet in length and had 1,200 links, with each link weighing from 90 to 120 pounds. In total, it was a 60-ton chain attached to logs that floated the chain and kept it at the right depth to stop ships. In front of the chain, downriver, was a log boom that served to slow any ships down before they hit the chain. On April 30, 1778, the chain was finished and in place, thanks to Mackin and Koscuiszko. A ship had to sail upstream against tricky currents with shifting winds and then break through a boom and chain. The Hudson was closed to the British as long as West Point could protect the chain. Even if the ships were to approach the chain, they would be battered by the 60 cannon placed on both shores as they slowed to tack without being able to fire back. West Point was on higher ground than the ships' cannon could reach. Most of the cannon had been captured at Saratoga.

Fort Arnold was constructed on the tip of a 40-acre plain that had been cleared as a farm. After Arnold's treason, the fort's name was changed to Fort Clinton. There were 16 enclosed positions built along with 10 batteries, all formed into three concentric circles around the chain and Fort Arnold to protect both from the possibility of a land attack.

The principal work protecting Fort Arnold from a serious threat was Fort Putnam, constructed by the 5th Massachusetts on the top of 500-foot Crown Hill and named after their colonel, Rufus Putnam. It held 420 soldiers and 14 cannon. It shielded Fort Arnold from the rear and in turn was itself protected by Redoubt #4, which sat on top of the hill overlooking Fort Putnam, Rocky Hill. Three Connecticut regiments constructed forts to guard the southern approach along the western shore of the Hudson. These three forts took the names of the three colonels, Webb, Wyllys, and Meigs. Three redoubts were built atop the hills to the southwest of West Point to provide additional security from British land attack. These redoubts were numbered #1, #2, and #3.

By 1779, West Point reached its fullest development, with land fortifications protecting Fort Arnold, which in turn protected the chain. Across the river, more batteries and Redoubts #5, #6, and #7 were now completed to batter enemy shipping trying to break the chain and to guard against a land attack from the east. Washington took a personal interest in the works at West Point and visited there several times making formal inspection trips, bringing with him General Louis Le Beque Duportail, the army's chief engineer. Duportail contributed suggestions to the plan, especially with regard to Constitution Island, but he could not essentially improve on Koscuiszko's original design. Having had one of "his" engineers (de la Radiere) fail at West Point, Duportail was annoyed that this Polish officer had succeeded where so many had fallen short before. Washington was delighted with Koscuiszko's work.

West Point was a "modern" system of fortifications with mutually supporting strong points constructed around each other, rather than on the traditional eighteenth-century system of one principal strong point holding out against all comers. Koscuiszko had laid out overlapping fields of fire that would make any land attack a costly one.

The British had moved against the Highlands in 1779 and succeeded in capturing Stony Point, a fortification south of West Point. Washington sent General Anthony Wayne to recapture the position in July with the light infantry. In a brilliant move, Wayne captured Stony Point and then destroyed the works. The winter of 1779–1780 was a horrible one—the coldest and most severe of the entire century. The Hudson froze over, and the garrison at West Point almost starved to death. They were also worried over a possible "land" attack coming up the ice of the river, but these worries proved groundless.

West Point became forever identified with the war the following September, in 1780. The commander of West Point had changed from McDougall to Nathanael Greene to Benedict Arnold. Arnold was a twice-wounded hero of Fort Ticonderoga, the march to Quebec, Valcour Island, the Battles of Saratoga, and saving Connecticut from British invasion. On September 21–22, Arnold met with Major John André, Clinton's adjutant general, to arrange the transfer of West Point to British hands for 20,000 pounds sterling. West Point was saved when André was captured on his way back to British lines overland and the papers on the Point were discovered in his shoe. André was tried and hanged as a spy. Arnold escaped to the British before he could compromise West Point.

After the excitement over Arnold's defection had died down, the garrison at West Point settled into a boring but nonetheless important guard along the Hudson. After Yorktown, Washington brought his army to the Highlands and camped them not far from West Point at New Windsor, near the town of Newburgh, where Washington made his headquarters. The American army was there in 1783 when news of the Peace of Paris and the signing of the treaty reached America.

It was appropriate that the American army was in the vicinity of the key to the continent when the War of Revolution ended in 1783 after eight years of bloodshed. West Point was still that vital choke point along a vital corridor of commerce and power that remained in American hands throughout the war except for 20 days. It is appropriate today that the cadets of West Point can take inspiration from the effort and vigilance of their ancestors at West Point, as they walk along Flirtation Walk, passing through the river batteries at the base of Fort Arnold (Clinton) or run up to the top of Crown Hill to visit the reconstructed Fort Putnam or pass by Michie Stadium, realizing that Forts Webb and Wyllys stood nearby. Today at Trophy Point, several links of the original chain still rest not far from where they served their purpose during that long-ago war.

Paul J. Sanborn

REFERENCES

Lincoln Diamant, *Bernard Romans* (1985); James Thomas Flexner, *The Traitor and the Spy* (1975); Miecislaus Haiman, *Koscuiszko in the American Revolution* (1975); Robert M. Hatch, *Major John André* (1986); Richard J. Koke, *Accomplice in Treason* (1973); Dave R. Palmer, *The River and the Rock, the History of Fortress West Point* (1969); Robert B. Roberts, *New York's Forts in the Revolution* (1980).

Westsylvania Statehood Plan

In the spring of 1776 most residents of British North America were preoccupied with the coming political separation from England; however, the frontiermen of the upper Ohio River valley were interested in an additional plan of secession. A vocal faction of citizens residing near Pittsburgh was intent upon creating a new state government.

Since the 1740s Virginia and Pennsylvania had been advancing rival jurisdictional claims for the lands beyond the Allegheny Mountains. Powerful special interest groups in both colonies were especially intent upon controlling the headwaters of the Ohio. Major land speculators, including George Croghan and Alexander McKee, were worried that neither Pennsylvania nor Virginia would recognize the large private grants ceded to them by the various Indian leaders over the last two decades. Accordingly, for some years these would-be land barons had been promoting a scheme with colonial officials in London, which provided that a new trans-Appalachian colony be created and be named Vandalia. Most of the Ohio Valley was to be included in this new entity; however, by 1774 it was quite evident that the Vandalia project would not be approved by the British Parliament.

As a last resort Croghan and his associates swore support to Virginia when the royal governor, Lord Dunmore, promised to sustain their vast landholdings after his government finally imposed undisputed control over that region. In 1774 the colonial legislature in Williamsburg officially incorporated the territory around the headwaters of the Ohio into the newly created West Augusta District; moreover, on November 3, 1774, they further subdivided the district into three new counties of Ohio, Yohogania, and Monongalia. As a means of assuring their rule, the Virginians attempted to secure control over Fort Pitt. Pennsylvania partisans, led by Arthur St. Clair, forcefully opposed these annexation efforts. Throughout the spring of 1775 the populace of Pittsburgh witnessed the attempts by rival sets of officials, from both colonies, to establish sovereignty. But a group of local residents had developed its own solution to the problem.

In June 1776 a mass public meeting convened in Pittsburgh and was chaired by David Rogers, a former burgess in the Virginia General Assembly. The participants at this conclave rejected the existing claims of both Virginia and Pennsylvania. As an alternative they resolved that their region be organized as a new state within the political confederation being created across the mountains in Philadelphia. David Rogers and his allies proposed that the residents of other settlements, such as Redstone, hold similar gatherings to select delegates to a general convention that was to be assembled at a locale south of Pittsburgh known as Beckett's Fort. Participants in that convention were expected to design specific boundaries for the new state, as well as to prepare a provisional government. Also, the conventioneers were to have the authority to elect a delegation that would approach the Continental Congress in order to represent the new state "as the fourteenth link in the American Chain."

However, the proposed Beckett's Fort Convention never officially convened in July 1776 at Fort Pitt. Rogers and various associates publicly refused to swear loyalty oaths to the commonwealth of Virginia. Instead they were framing a petition addressed to Congress that requested immediate recognition of the proposed new state named Westsylvania. By August 1, 1776, it is known that copies of the petition were being circulated in the vicinity of Pittsburgh.

The petitioners stated that the majority of their neighbors were disgusted thoroughly with the longstanding territorial dispute; furthermore, they blamed most of the trouble on the intrigues of key Virginia officials in association with a faction of land speculators led by George Croghan and Alexander McKee. The framers also observed that the capitals of both Virginia and Pennsylvania were nearly 500 miles from Pittsburgh. Obviously, such great distances made it impossible for either state government to be very responsive to the problems confronting the estimated 25,000 families residing beyond the Allegheny Mountains. It was, therefore, a logical solution to establish Westsylvania. The projected boundaries included all lands lying between the Alleghenies and the Ohio River adjoining the Indian boundary of 1768 to a line from the mouth of the Scioto River to the Cumberland Gap. The new state would have possessed lands now lying in Virginia, Pennsylvania, West Virginia, Maryland, and Kentucky.

A delegation, led by Rogers, reached Philadelphia in late October. Although their plan was tentatively supported by Silas Deane, a maverick congressman from Connecticut, the general reaction in Congress was quite negative. Certainly the powerful Pennsylvania and Virginia delegations, led by James Wilson and George Mason, cooperated in aborting the Westsylvania project. Accordingly, they managed to have the petition buried in the congressional committee system. In fact, there is no evidence that this statehood proposal was ever formally discussed on the floor of Congress.

The obvious rejection of the petition seems to have thwarted effectively the statehood movement, because all such agitation had ceased around Pittsburgh by the spring of 1777. Later in the year when George Rogers Clark tried to enlist recruits for his western expedition in Pittsburgh, he was given only lukewarm support, which was confined mostly to Virginia adherents. Within a few years David Rogers and others of the leading Westsylvania advocates had migrated down the Ohio River toward Kentucky. During this period, moreover, Virginia and Pennsylvania negotiators had made great progress in resolving their territorial dispute, which finally ended in May 1783.

Miles S. Richards

REFERENCES

George H. Alden, *New Governments West of the Allegheny Mountains Before 1780* (1899); Solon J. Buck, *The Planting of Civilization in Western Pennsylvania* (1939); Alfred James, *The Ohio Company* (1959); Albert T. Volwiler, *George Croghan and the Western Movement, 1741-1782* (1971).

Whaleboat Warfare

Whaling was a prominent industry in New England, vital to both the colonists and the British. Before the Revolution, the British government offered bounties and regulated the whaling industry, much to the colonists' benefit. However, during the Revolutionary period, English whalers encroached upon traditionally colonial fishing grounds and implemented provisions that hindered American whaling. Many New England whalers sought new fishing areas—near the Falkland Islands and West Africa—due to British capture of vessels and crews. Whalers such as those in Nantucket Island who arranged deals with British officials to continue their whaling practices were viewed as Tories and were harassed by privateers and guerrillas, who often used small whaleboats to reach whaling ships without arousing suspicion.

Tory and British provision and merchant ships were also targets of whaleboat warfare. After the British forces secured New York, they began soliciting American traders to supply them with agricultural products in exchange for European cloth goods. This practice, known as "London Trading," resulted in the British army and navy being well supplied. Traders used small boats to travel to Staten and Long islands and to the British ships to deliver their goods.

Guerrillas off the coasts of New York and New Jersey, disguised as these traders, moved quickly, often unseen, toward the British vessels and initiated whaleboat warfare to retaliate against the British. One example of whaleboat warfare is the incident involving the *Blue Mountain Valley*, a British provision vessel captured off the coast of New Jersey in January 1776. British officers mistook four small boats that sailed toward their craft as fishing vessels. The crews of the guerrilla ships were concealed below deck, surprising the British when they pulled alongside the larger ship and seized it.

Adam Hyler and William Marriner were two of the best known whaleboat warriors. Natives of New Brunswick, New Jersey, the men used small boats, sailing between Egg Harbor and Staten Island, to capture British and Tory ships. The men also forced enemy ships to pay them monetary tributes. Enemy forces destroyed their boats in the summer of 1777, but Hyler and Marriner built new vessels and continued their methodical raids against the enemy, seizing both ships and officers. Marriner was captured on one of the raids and imprisoned on Long Island. After his release he sought his captor, a Major Sherbrook, and incarcerated him. Whaleboat warfare was also used to gather intelligence and distribute false information.

Elizabeth D. Schafer

REFERENCES

James F. Collins, "Whale Boat Warfare on Long Island Sound," *New York History*, 15 (1944):195–201; Joseph L. McDevitt, *The House of Rotch: Massachusetts Whaling Merchants 1734–1828* (1986).

Whipple, Abraham (1733–1819)

Continental Navy officer. Born in Providence, Rhode Island, Whipple went to sea as a youth and became captain of a merchant vessel. During the French and Indian War he was a privateer, and he captured over 20 vessels. Whipple won fame in the Gaspée Affair. A British revenue cutter, which symbolized oppression to New England, ran aground at Gaspée Point, below Providence. On June 9, 1772, Whipple led some 60 men in longboats to the beached ship and burned it, an act widely acclaimed by Patriots.

By June 15, 1775, Whipple was appointed commander of the Rhode Island Navy—two small ships and two row galleys. He was ordered to clear Narragansett Bay of tenders belonging to the British frigate *Rose*. While capturing a tender Whipple fired the first shot at sea in the Revolution by American forces against the British. In late 1775 he was appointed a captain in the Continental Navy and was sent to Philadelphia, where he served under Commodore Esek Hopkins.

On February 17, 1776, Whipple sailed with Hopkins on a successful raid to New Providence, the Bahamas. On the passage home, the squadron encountered the British frigate *Glasgow* on April 6. In a brief encounter the Americans suffered 24 casualties and the enemy vessel escaped. Whipple was blamed for not being more aggressive in the action. He demanded a trial and was acquitted.

Whipple sailed in the *Providence* of 28 guns on March 20, 1778. He forced his way out of the British blockage off Rhode Island and sank a tender. That year he captured many prizes. On June 19, 1779, Whipple departed from Boston along with the ships under his command. In July, off Newfoundland, the squadron captured about 10 enemy vessels heavily laden with cargoes from Jamaica. Early in 1780 Whipple was sent to the relief of Charleston, South Carolina, with four ships. He was captured on May 17 and paroled until the end of the war.

In 1784, as a merchant skipper, Whipple sailed to London, where he displayed the first American flag raised there after the signing of the peace treaty. By 1788 Whipple had moved to Mariette, Ohio, were he farmed. Heavily in debt for expenditures incurred in equipping his vessels during the war, Whipple applied for a pension from Congress in 1811. Thereafter, he lived on half-pay as a captain.

Horace S. Mazet

REFERENCE

Horace C. Mazet, "The Navy's Forgotten Hero," *United States Naval Institute Proceedings*, 63 (1937): 347–354.

Whipple, William (1730–1785)

New Hampshire statesman. Born in Kittery, Massachusetts (now Maine), on January 14, 1730, Whipple went to sea at an early age and achieved command for a merchantman before the age of 21. He prospered from trade with the West Indies and had some involvement in the slave trade. Whipple left the sea in 1759 and established himself as a merchant in Portsmouth, New Hampshire. He was named a delegate to the Continental Congress for 1775, 1776, and 1778, and was one of the three delegates from New Hampshire to sign the Declaration of Independence. In 1777, Whipple was appointed a brigadier general by the New Hampshire Provincial Congress and given command of the 1st New Hampshire Brigade, a unit of the New Hampshire militia. He then led the brigade in the Battles of Stillwater and Saratoga. After the defeat of General John Burgoyne at Saratoga in October 1777, Whipple was one of the officers appointed by General Horatio Gates to discuss the terms of surrender with the British. In 1778, Whipple led New Hampshire troops to support General John Sullivan in an attempt to capture Rhode Island. The plan never matured, and Whipple saw no action. Whipple served in the New Hampshire legislature from 1780 to 1784, as federal tax collector for New Hampshire from 1782 to 1784, and as a judge of the New Hampshire Superior Court from 1782 to 1784. He died on November 28, 1785.

Mark E. Furber

REFERENCES

Jeremy Belknap, *History of New Hampshire*, 3 vols. (1784–1792); Jere Daniell, *Experiment in Republicanism: New Hampshire Politics and the American Revolution, 1741–1794* (1970) Chandler E. Potter,

Military History of New Hampshire from Its Settlement in 1623 to the Rebellion in 1861 (1973); Richard Upton, *Revolutionary New Hampshire* (1971); Charles P. Whittemore, *A General of the Revolution: John Sullivan of New Hampshire* (1961).

White Eyes (?–1778)

Delaware Indian chief. The leading councillor of the Ohio Delaware, White Eyes assumed a pro-American stance from the beginning of the Revolution. On the death of the Delaware chief Netawatwees, White Eyes was named chief of the Delaware nation by the Grand Council in 1774, and the Americans worked to bolster his power. He encouraged Moravian teachings among his people and endeavored to keep the Delawares neutral in the war. He attended the Treaty of Fort Pitt in 1775, and when the Iroquois demanded that the Delaware take up arms for the British, White Eyes formally and dramatically asserted Delaware independence, casting aside the dominance that the Iroquois had claimed for generations.

White Eyes signed the Treaty of Fort Pitt in September 1778, which committed the Delawares to a military alliance with the United States. Despite the controversy surrounding the treaty, he guided General Lachlan McIntosh in his abortive expedition against Detroit that year. When White Eyes failed to return, the Americans reported that he had died of smallpox; in fact, he was murdered by American soldiers. With White Eyes gone, most of the Delawares began to align with the British.

Colin G. Calloway

REFERENCES

Reuben G. Thwaites and Louise P. Kellogg, eds., *The Revolution on the Upper Ohio, 1775–1777* (1908); ———, *Frontier Defense on the Upper Ohio, 1777–1778* (1912); C.A. Weslager, *The Delaware Indians, A History* (1972).

White Plains, New York, Battle of (October 28, 1776)

White Plains was another in a series of British tactical victories during the New York City campaign. General Sir William Howe was unable or unwilling to exploit this success in such a way as to result in the complete destruction of the American army. It was a significant but short engagement with a small number of troops involved in the fighting.

White Plains was named by the Mohican tribe of Indians, who called the land in that part of New York State "Quaroppas" for the many swamps and marches that dotted the grounds, giving off the mists and vapors that regularly developed into a white fog. After being flanked out of Manhattan Island by the British, General Washington brought his American army to White Plains to regroup and to dig in. He reorganized his army into seven divisions. Behind on Manhattan, he left Colonel Robert Magaw in charge of Fort Washington, the last American post on the island.

The eccentric General Charles Lee had returned to join the main American army after his very successful venture in the defense of Charlestown, South Carolina, that summer. He was given a division and ordered to perform the necessary and vital tasks of guarding the rear in the march to White Plains from Manhattan. Six generals—Nathaniel Greene, the bookish military genius; William Heath, a good man for garrison duty; John Sullivan, the New Hampshire lawyer with bad luck in battle; Israel Putnam, now too old to campaign, with his best days behind him; Joseph Spencer, untested in combat; and Benjamin Lincoln, the short, rotund Massachusetts politician—were given command of the other divisions.

Howe could have caught Washington at Throg's Neck, Pell's Point, and New Rochelle, but the Americans slipped the noose each time and made it safely to their new lines north of the main British army. Washington made his headquarters at a Mrs. Miller's house. Lee joined him. In camp, there were approximately 14,000 men. It was one of the largest forces Washington would ever command. By October 22, the Americans had taken position on three hills overlooking the village of White Plains.

Putnam was on the right on Purdy Hill, while General William Heath held the left on Hatfield Hill. Washington commanded the center at the Village. The American line stretched three miles. The American hope was that White Plains would turn into another Breed's Hill for the British. Given the time, the Americans had developed a double line of entrenchments that curved inward at the center with the Bronx River on the right flank and the Mill Pond covering the left. Both

American flanks refused to repel a turning attack. With the hills, grounded flanks, double entrenchment lines, and a large number of troops under some capable officers, Washington had every hope that Howe's attack, if it came, would not turn into an American rout like that at Kip's Bay.

Howe reached New Rochelle on October 21 and stayed there for three days to refit and reorganize. Then he moved to Mamaroneck, three miles away, where he camped four days. Howe had approximately 13,000 men with him at this time, although there were thousands of other British troops in the New York area on duty. Now he was reinforced with General Wilhelm von Knyphausen and the second Hessian division and an additional 3,400 British recruits newly arrived from Europe to swell Howe's ranks. With Knyphausen was Captain Johann Ewald and his jaeger company. Ewald was to keep an extremely valuable diary of his experiences in the war.

On September 28, Howe finally began to make his approach on Washington's position at White Plains. In 10 days, he had moved his army a total of 17 miles. Just as Howe's army came into view of the American lines, Washington realized that his entire line was dominated by Chatterton's Hill, across the Bronx River, on the American right. Two militia regiments were sent over to the hill to dig trenches under the supervision of Rufus Putnam, the army's chief engineer.

Washington opened the battle by sending out General Joseph Spencer with six New England regiments from Lee's division, about 1,500 men, to skirmish with the approaching enemy. Moving across fields from wall to wall, the Americans kept up a running firefight with the British van. The British kept flanking the American skirmish line, forcing it back on the main American line. Finally, Spencer retired off to the American right to Chatterton Hill, and the preliminaries concluded.

Now that it was too late, Washington and his generals realized the value of Chatterton's Hill relative to the American position at White Plains. Worse, the better line of defense could have been chosen at North Castle several miles off. Already, Colonel Johann Rall's men had crossed the Bronx River and attempted to scale Chatterton's Hill. Fortunately for the Americans, the Hessians were forced back by American fire.

Washington sent his aide, Colonel Joseph Reed, to go the half-mile to Chatterton's Hill and take charge of its defense. The hill was actually a ridge, almost a mile long, running in a north-south direction, about 180 feet high. It was cleared and cultivated on the top with rock fences separating the fields. There were heavy woods along the lower slopes of the hill, especially toward the valley of the Bronx River. The Battle of White Plains took place on this hill. The frontal attack Howe ordered on Washington's main line never took place for reasons that remain obscure to this day.

With his aide, Washington sent Colonel John Haslet and his 273 Delawares to the hill, along with General Alexander McDougall's 1,000-man brigade of Maryland, New York, and Connecticut troops. A two-gun battery accompanied this unit, commanded by Captain Alexander Hamilton. McDougall took command upon reaching the hill. Sixteen hundred Americans dug in, with William Smallwood and Haslet in the center, the militia on the far right, and McDougall's brigade on the left, closest to the Bronx River.

The British army now came up in front of the Americans and stood on parade while the officers gathered in a nearby wheatfield to determine the course of British action that day. To the Americans, this view presented a magnificent sight that many men remembered until the day they died. The sky was clear, and the British troops had their weapons polished and shining in the sunlight. It was a lovely fall day. Everything had a sparkle to it that in a small way contributed to the pageantry that often entices one to think of war as something beautiful and exciting.

Once this council concluded, the group of generals broke up and eight regiments and 12 cannon moved toward Chatterton Hill for an attack. The rest of the British and German forces promptly sat down in the fields where they were standing and remained, 10,000 witnesses to the unfolding action to their left on the American right. The British opened with artillery fire that the Americans could not counter. One gun was dragged up, fired two rounds, and was put out of commission. The British ball pounded the hill.

Then the infantry approached the Bronx River, swollen by recent rains. The Hessians refused to cross the river and began building a bridge. General Alexander Leslie, commanding the British troops, learned of a ford farther downstream and led his men through the water there to show up the Hessians and to convince all watching of the bravery and daring of the British Line. The Hessians continued with their bridge, under fire from Smallwood's men and some of the 3rd New York Regiment.

Across the river, Leslie with the 28th and 35th regiments led a bayonet charge up the hill and were repulsed with accurate American fire. The two British regiments fell back on the 5th, 49th, and Hessians coming to their rescue. One reason this assault was stopped was that the company officers of the British line were armed with fusils, or light muskets. Officers leading the charge would fire and then stop to reload. The men followed this example, and the Americans were given the necessary time to reload themselves and pick their targets carefully. Bringing up the rear, the Lossberg regiment crossed a burning field holding their cartridge boxes high so that they would not blow up, and charged up the hill as the first wave fell back. They too were stopped.

With the repulse of this first attempt, the whole British force of eight regiments was brought across the Bronx River in column and marched in line at the base of Chatterton Hill until they were properly positioned. They then faced right to the hill and began their charge. They ran into heavy fire. The British artillery had to stop firing as its own men came into its sights. The Delawares and Marylanders in the center held their own, and the British made little headway on the slope of Chatterton Hill.

It was at this point that Colonel Rall accomplished what the British could not. His regiment had been pushed around to the far right of the American line and faced the two militia regiments. With the Knyphausen regiment and his own, Rall led the Germans on a charge up the hill, which might have been stopped if it had not been for the British dragoons who came riding up the hill behind and through the Germans with their drums and trumpets calling, scaring the militia into a rout. Never having dealt with horsemen of this type before, the militia ranks began to panic, and soon the horsemen were sabering them.

This German and dragoon success uncovered the right flank of Haslett's men. Part of the Delawares ran, but Haslett held with the balance of his men. Pressure on Smallwood's Marylanders

was also telling. Smallwood himself was wounded twice. The Marylanders, Delawares, and New Yorkers of the 3rd Regiment were gradually forced from the hill, fighting the entire way. By 5 P.M. the battle was over.

General McDougall ordered a retreat back to the American lines. The Delawares formed the rear guard and fought sullenly and composedly, holding off any British attempts at valor. Colonel John Glover and his 14th Massachusetts Regiment held the right as McDougall's men rejoined the main American army. Along with Glover's men, the American artillery gave a good showing of themselves and discouraged any further British attacks that day.

The British had captured a hill. They formed and dressed their lines on the top and then did nothing. There was no attempt at pursuit. The British camped where they were. If Howe had attacked in the front as the right on Chatterton's Hill was rolled up, the American army might have ended that day at White Plains. Howe did nothing. The Americans lost anywhere from 150 to 350 casualties. The British lost 28 killed, 126 wounded, while the Germans took 77 casualties.

A second British attack was planned for October 31, but a brutal, drenching 20-hour rainstorm canceled the attack. In any event, Washington used the weather for cover to withdraw to North Castle. The check at White Plains, if it can be called that, and the retreat of Washington, changed Howe's plans. Examination of the American lines at North Castle showed them to be strong and dangerous. The Americans had uprooted cornstalks with the dirt still attached to the roots. These they had placed in piles at entrenchments, and the dirt looked from afar as high redoubts that would be costly to attack.

With his 20,000 men in the field now, Howe moved into the former American lines at White Plains, waited four days there, and then turned west and marched to Dobbs Ferry. From there, Howe and Knyphausen located a promising target, one with a more profitable return. The result led to the fall of Fort Washington, a terrible American disaster in the war.

White Plains was not a victory, but neither was it another American rout or defeat. It was a slow retreat. American morale had been boosted by White Plains. The British had not pursued them. Somehow, the Americans had made a strong effort at Chatterton Hill, and the British, for whatever reason, had decided both to take

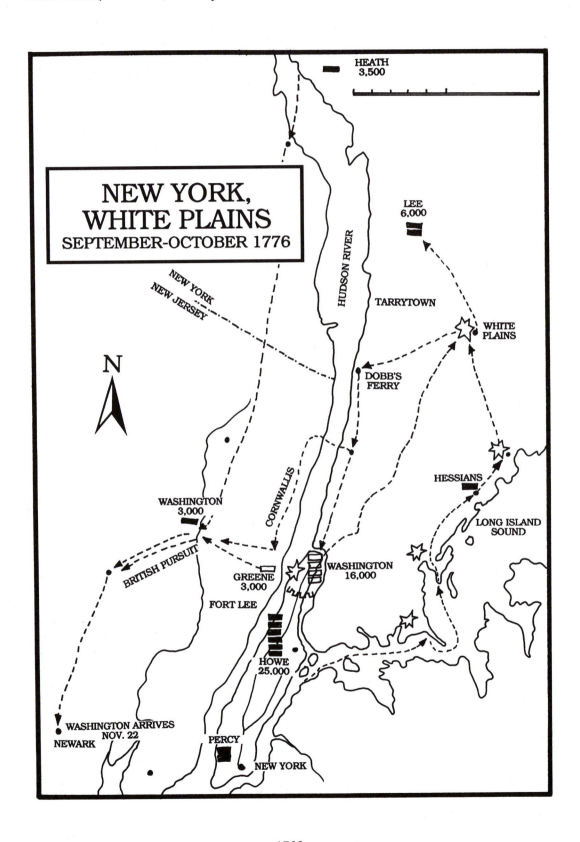

the American defenses at White Plains by frontal attack. Even with Chatterton Hill in British hands, the Americans might still have been able to hold their positions at White Plains.

Howe, commenting later on the war, hinted that there may well have been certain political considerations as well as military ones that stayed his hand at White Plains and other fields during the New York campaign. This may have been true, but it was not something that General Clinton or the German mercenaries wanted to understand. They were there to fight and win, to plunder for reward, and to put down a rebellion. The friction grew between Clinton and Howe. In that British confusion of purpose, the American cause stayed alive for another year. The war went on.

Paul J. Sanborn

REFERENCES

Rodney Atwood, *The Hessians* (1980); George A. Billias, *General John Glover* (1960); T.W. Egly, Jr., *The First New York Regiment* (1981); John Thomas Flexner, *George Washington in the American Revolution* (1968); Thomas Fleming, *1776, Year of Illusion* (1975); Sol Stermber, *The Bicentennial Guide to the American Revolution*, 2 vols. (1974), *1*; Christopher Ward, *The Delaware Continentals* (1941); ———, *The War of the Revolution*, 2 vols. (1952), *1*.

Whitemarsh, Pennsylvania, Engagement at (November 2– December 11, 1777) (Alternate names: Edge Hill, The Camp at Whitemarsh. Whitemarsh is today spelled as one word; however, it was often spelled as two words in colonial times.)

Following the Battle of Germantown, the American army under Washington wandered about the Pennsylvania countryside. Finally on November 2, 1777, Washington led his men to Whitemarsh, where they would subsequently camp for just over a month and fight a series of skirmishes against General William Howe's British army.

Whitemarsh was a strong defensive position, located 13 miles from Philadelphia. Washington was close enough to harass the enemy and stay within supporting reach of the critical river forts, Mifflin and Mercer. The entire line was entrenched along a ridge near North Wales Road

in Whitemarsh Township, Pennsylvania. The American front was protected by a ditched line of abatis. The weather was already turning as the Americans marched into their new camp.

The American position extended over a range of three wooded hills, abreast of each other and connected by ridges. The right hill became known as Militia Hill, since that was where Washington placed the militia. To the east of this hill was the tiny village of Whitemarsh composed of St. Thomas Church (1710) and a few houses. A picket used the church steeple to watch for the British.

To the north of Whitemarsh village was Fort Hill. A strong fortification was placed on its top. This hill rose 200 feet with Sandy Run, a small creek running at its base. The hill lay to the east of the main road to Bethlehem. It was manned by 300 chosen veterans from the whole of Washington's army. The fort was earthen, fortified with logs. There were redoubts at each corner. Fort Hill was the center of the American line.

The third hill was the highest and became known as Camp Hill. It also had Sandy Run at its base. Redoubts were constructed on its top. There was a small hollow between Fort and Camp Hills. (Route 309 and the Pennsylvania Turnpike now run through it.) Camp Hill guarded the church road and the Limekiln Pike. In addition, Washington extended his line to the north beyond Camp Hill to prevent a flanking movement on the part of the enemy.

In front of Camp Hill, about 800 yards removed, was the house of George Emlen, a deceased Philadelphia Quaker wine merchant. His family was living there when Washington arrived to make the Emlen house his headquarters for the Whitemarsh encampment.

There were two main problems with Washington's position at Whitemarsh. There was no easy access to a retreat route connected to main roads. The other problem was that Washington had placed his militia on his flanks. Fortunately, the British could only approach in full view of the Americans, allowing time for the shifting of American troops as necessary.

November's weather turned poor. The rains came, along with the sleet, frost, and biting cold. Desertions increased. Men without clothing and shoes sickened and died. Huts were erected, but they were primitive, barely providing cover. In addition, the troops had been unpaid since the summer. Morale was low, and Washington was hard put to keep an army in the field.

Then, by the middle of November, the Delaware River forts fell, and the supply ships of the British fleet arrived in Philadelphia, bringing with them all the necessities that Howe needed to continue his campaign against Washington. Unable to inspect the forts personally, Washington would ride into Germantown and go to the roof of Cliveden House to observe the river. He often could see the smoke of battle and hear the noise, but he could not tell what was actually happening. The British cleared the river by November 25.

Washington held a series of councils of war to determine whether or not to attack Philadelphia. He was under pressure to do something, especially after Horatio Gates's victory at Saratoga, and the uncovering of the so-called Conway Cabal. Washington's generals were against such a risky move. Washington went to observe the British fortifications in the city to judge for himself. He returned in agreement with his generals.

Washington had also pleaded with Gates to send troops from his northern army. Many delays ensued. Finally the brigades of Enoch Poor, Ebenezer Learned, and John Paterson arrived in camp to swell Washington's ranks by 2,400 men. Meanwhile, Washington kept pressure on the British by testing their lines regularly. This prompted the British to burn some 20 houses within four miles of British lines around the city.

As November ended, Washington had to turn his attention to the selection of winter quarters. Several choices were discussed. Valley Forge was the place eventually chosen. Before leaving Whitemarsh, however, there was some business to attend to. Through the efforts of his spy system, Washington was now aware that Howe meant to strike a blow at the Americans soon. The American army was placed on alert and remained so until December 11, their last day at Whitemarsh. With the Delaware River open, Howe now turned his attention to Washington once more.

Captain Allen McLane of Delaware, one of Washington's most resourceful partisan leaders, and Major John Clark, Jr., chief of Washington's spy system in Philadelphia, were both reporting activity within the British camp. Washington looked for an attack, confident that his lines at Whitemarsh would hold. A British defeat would boost American morale and would help Washington's reputation at the same time.

General Nathanael Greene, Washington's chief tactician, had returned with his division from New Jersey in the vain attempt to save Fort Mercer. Greene was placed in command of the left wing on Camp Hill. General John Sullivan, the New Hampshire lawyer, commanded the right wing on Fort and Militia hills. The Maryland militia under Mordecai Gist was out beyond Greene's flank to screen it. Daniel Morgan's renowned riflemen arrived from Jersey to join Gist. The Pennsylvania militia was posted in front of the American main line with orders to harass and skirmish with the enemy. General Lord Stirling's division and John Glover's brigade formed the reserve.

Washington was sure the British were coming and knew where and how. The story of Lydia Darragh, thought by some to be a myth, rings true and is connected with this action. Little is known of Washington's spy network during the war, since he was so close about its activities. Yet it appeared to have run very effectively, and this is one minor example of it in action. William Darragh was a Quaker teacher and tutor. He married Lydia, and they had at least five children. At the time of the British occupation of Philadelphia, the Darraghs had moved to a house at the corner of Second Street and Little Dock Street. The house had the grand name of Loxley Hall. Lydia was from Dublin, a five-foot-tall, small-boned, dainty woman with blue eyes and well-groomed sandy hair. In December 1777, General Howe's headquarters were directly across the street from the Darragh household.

Often it was the case that the British would rent the upper back room of the Darragh house to hold conferences. Captain John André rented it for the night of December 2 and instructed the Darraghs to go to bed early. The British officers conducted a meeting there that night, which Lydia partially overhead.

Lydia knew that the British were going out of Philadelphia with thousands of men to attack Washington. With Washington's army was Lydia's 22-year-old son Charles. On Thursday, December 4, Lydia left Philadelphia with an empty flour sack to obtain flour at the Frankford Mills. While waiting for the flour, she walked on the west on the Nicetown Road and met an officer she recognized, Lieutenant Colonel Thomas Craig. She told him her story, and he promised Washington would learn of it. He did.

She, or someone like her, evidently kept going along the road to the Rising Sun Tavern, three miles above the city, where she met Elias Boudinot, another of Washington's spymasters. She passed him a needlebook with a message in the last pocket of it that described the British plans. Boudinot related the incident in his journal, and the details matched the Darragh story. Lydia never told her story, but her daughter, Ann, who was living with her mother and was 20 years old at the time, related the story after the war.

General Howe was worried. The Americans were receiving reinforcements from the north. The river forts had fallen, and Washington might very well have attacked if he stayed so close to the city of Whitemarsh. Howe was also getting frustrated with the constant harassment of the American patrols. With Cornwallis and his division back from burning Fort Mercer, Howe decided to move against Washington. His hope was that Washington would leave Whitemarsh and fight in the open at some disadvantage.

General Alexander Leslie was left in the city with 3,000 troops; Howe took 12,000 men north to Whitemarsh to tangle with the Americans. The British left Philadelphia at midnight on a cold and very dark night, December 5, and marched in two columns. Cornwallis led the van and General Wilhelm von Knyphausen directed the main column. Cornwallis took the Germantown Road and immediately skirmished with Americans all the way to Chestnut Hill. Several houses were looted and burned by the British along the line of march. Knyphausen had a more peaceful experience using the ridge or Manatawny Road and joined Cornwallis just beyond Chestnut Hill.

At 3 A.M., the alarm guns in the American camp went off, and the camp fires were set blazing in double the number needed, in order to confuse the British. The baggage and wagons, along with the camp followers, were sent to the rear. The Americans stood to their lines. It was an excessively cold night. The American outpickets such as Captain McLane's men had done well in striking at the British along the line of march, keeping them under continual pressure.

Washington ordered General William Irvine to lead his 600 Pennsylvania militia from Militia Hill on the American right to feel out the British line. The militia and the British light infantry collided in the hollow between the two ridges upon which both armies were now located. Heavy fighting developed for about 20 minutes until General William Irvine had his horse shot from under him as he jumped a fence. The fall injured Irvine's head, and he was shot at the same time, the ball taking off two of the fingers of his left hand. He was captured, and his men broke off the action, retreating back to their original lines. General Israel Potter and his unit of Pennsylvania militia also skirmished with the British. This desultory fighting continued off and on all day.

General Knyphausen and Howe had reached St. Thomas Church with their men, and the two generals studied the American positions from the church steeple. Howe realized that a frontal attack would be too costly. Regular line troops were too valuable to throw away in senseless charges against an entrenched enemy. He felt the American left was the weak link, and it was there he would strike. Meanwhile, the Americans shifted troops from left to right to meet the British threat in the Militia Hill area.

During the afternoon of December 5, the British moved south on the Bethlehem Pike and camped for the night. Nothing of note took place the next day, Saturday, December 6. Howe was waiting for a supply train to come up from Philadelphia to feed and service his army. The more Howe saw, the surer he was that he could march his men to Jenkin's Town before the Americans could react. Their flank could be turned.

Leaving his campfires burning the night of December 6–7, at 1 A.M., his men left their camp near Chestnut Hill and began marching back toward Germantown. There, they turned left on the Abington Road (now Washington Lane) and moved on Jenkin's Town, about two and a half miles from the American left. At dawn on Sunday, December 7, the British arrived at their destination, having burned and looted their way there.

General Charles Grey, commanding the British rear guard, turned left at Church Road and approached the American center to divert them until General Howe was in position to strike. Grey commanded the Queen's Rangers, the light infantry, the 3rd Brigade, and a few other units. In the course of the day's action, both Grey and Howe would assume a position on a ridge that ran parallel to the American line and was about the same height, called Edge Hill. Howe was at Abington, and Grey was closer to the village of Whitemarsh, to Howe's left.

Leading the march was General Cornwallis's van that reached Abington Presbyterian Church at 8 A.M. that Sunday. As Cornwallis formed his men, General Knyphausen brought his troops up on Cornwallis's left and formed them. These two divisions faced the American left under General Greene. (General Gray was across from the American center, commanded by General Sullivan.) The two sides looked at each other across the valley that ran between the two ridges. The provision train that Howe was waiting for caught up with the British at Jenkin's Town, and the soldiers were resupplied. From 8 A.M. until 12 noon, Howe and his men did nothing.

Making the initial move, Washington sent out roughly 1,000 men to feel out Howe's position. Including Morgan's and Gist's men, these units came into contact with Grey's men approaching the American lines by the use of Church Road. Grey had been told to wait until he heard the gunfire from Howe's assault and then attack. He waited past noon and beyond. But Grey's patience was always short, and he moved when the noise of battle never developed. Grey would precipitate the battle.

Grey had the jaegers in the center, the guards on the right, and the rangers on the left. The two sides collided in the woods along Church Road, and the fighting was fierce for a time until the British succeeded in flanking the Americans on both flanks and forced them back. The American troops retreated in good order to their main line. Daniel Morgan lost a horse, shot from under him in the hot action. Grey then fell back.

Two important Americans got caught in the confusion of one of the numerous skirmishes that Sunday afternoon. Joseph Reed had his horse shot from under him. General John Cadwalader jumped off his horse, refusing to leave Reed behind, and prepared to fight to the end as the hated Hessians closed in on the two in a clearing in the woods. Just then, Allen McLane and his horse charged and dispersed the Germans so that Reed and Cadwalader could escape.

Grey bivouacked on or near Edge Hill for the rest of the afternoon, still holding off parties of Americans sniping at him from the woods. In time, General William Erskine with two regiments of Hessians appeared on Grey's right to connect him with Howe's main body.

The Americans enjoyed the advantage of interior lines at Whitemarsh and used them to move troops from the right to meet the threat on the left. Every move the British attempted clearly could be observed by the Americans, who responded accordingly.

Neither Howe nor his generals, Cornwallis and Knyphausen, could detect a break in the American lines, nor a weakness to be exploited. He wanted to flank Washington but was afraid to expose his own flank in marching around the Americans in plain sight of their position. Howe also could not afford to leave Grey's force behind without support. The Americans could fall upon it and destroy it and then turn on him. What worked at Brandywine and Long Island for Howe would not work here.

Morgan's 175 riflemen, Gist's Maryland militia, and Samuel Webb's 2nd Connecticut Continentals were in constant contact all day along the British lines from Grey to Howe. The various skirmishes that took place that Sunday came to be known as the Battle of Edge Hill. It was confused fighting of hit and run, deploy and advance, fall back and reform, in heavy woods with the smoke of battle obscuring the field and troop movements. Firefights broke out along the lines as both sides probed for openings. No openings were found, however.

At no time did any major unit of either army leave its respective ridge. No general action developed. The fighting, intense at times, was left to the light troops and forward elements of both armies. For a time, Morgan and his men dug in on the top of Edge Hill, maintaining their position for a time to keep the British from using it to their advantage. Later they were pushed off it. So it went.

Under these circumstances, neither commander wanted to fight a general action. Washington refused to leave his strong position, and Howe could not lure Washington off the ridge. It ended as a draw that day, but Washington believed that the British would attack him in the morning. The Americans slept on their weapons, formed at 5 A.M., and the morning passed without incident.

Howe found himself in a dilemma. He dared not attack frontally. The cost of this was too excessive, and the Americans could easily escape to the rear if the tide turned against them. His only choice was a wide flanking movement with too many dangers to make it a reasonable risk.

Howe had come to fight. Seeing that it would be difficult to do so, he chose the third alternative and turned his men toward Philadelphia.

On Monday afternoon, December 8, his men began their march back to the city along Old York Road. Grey fell in behind, and the entire column made its way to the city, pillaging, burning, and looting along the way. By 9 P.M., the entire British army was back safe and sound in Philadelphia. That is not to say that it was an easy march. The Americans harassed the rear guard of light infantry and jaegers the whole way.

After four days in the trenches, the Americans stood down. Generally they felt sorry the British had not tried an attack. But that was past. They were still naked, cold, and hungry. Washington issued rum to his men as well as some food that was available, and everyone slept well that night in the American camp. Howe had lost 112 men in the expedition. The American losses were under 100 casualties. Some civilians claim the British lost over 350 men. Once again, there is no way of telling the exact figures.

Shortly after sunrise on December 11, the American army left its camp at Whitemarsh and marched toward Valley Forge, where they would arrive on December 19 to begin their travail of winter cantonment. Washington had brought his army back toward Philadelphia and offered battle. Howe had come out and was unable to accept the American offer. Granted, Washington was fighting a defensive action. But it was incumbent upon the British to put down the rebellion, and to them belonged the offensive. Howe refused the risk.

In three days, Cornwallis would sally forth from the city to lead more expeditions such as the great hay raid and the march that led to the battle of the Black Horse Tavern. The Americans would go to form an army at Valley Forge. Even with a ragtag and bobtail army, Washington had done quite well. In time, he would do much better.

Paul J. Sanborn

REFERENCES

Don Higginbotham, *Daniel Morgan* (1961); John W. Jackson, *Whitemarsh 1777, Impregnable Stronghold* (1984); John F. Reed, *Campaign to Valley Forge* (1965); Ray Thompson, *Washington at Whitemarsh* (1974); Christopher Ward, *The War of the Revolution,* 2 vols. (1952), 2.

Wickes, Lambert (1742–1777)

Continental Navy officer. A native of Kent City, Maryland, Wickes learned seamanship on a pilot boat in the Delaware River. By 1769 he captained a merchant vessel. As skipper of the *Neptune* in 1774 Wickes caught the attention of American Patriots by his refusal to carry a cargo of tea from London.

Commissioned in the navy in April 1776, Wickes sailed on July 3 in the *Reprisal* carrying William Bingham, congressional agent for Martinque, to his post. Wickes captured several prizes en route. On July 27 he encountered the HMS *Shark* off St. Pierre. The *Reprisal* escaped from this encounter—the first gun duel fought in foreign waters by a United States naval vessel.

In October 1776 Wickes took Benjamin Franklin to France in the *Reprisal,* seizing two ships on the passage. Ordered to prey on British shipping in European waters, Wickes departed from St. Lazaire in January 1777. The *Reprisal* was the first United States naval vessel in the area. Returning to L'Orient with several prizes captured in the English Channel, Wickes caused a storm of controversy. Lord Stormont, the British ambassador to France, protested at the breach of French neutrality. Nevertheless, with the connivance of some French officials, Wickes continued to scour the Channel, and he took four more prizes. When he returned to L'Orient, Wickes was again the target of Stormont's complaints. Thought to be technically violating French neutrality, Wilkes claimed the right to repair the leaky *Reprisal,* and the French gave him time to heave and to caulk his vessel.

Using some French crewmen, Wickes took the *Reprisal* and two other American vessels into the Irish Sea on May 28, 1777. The squadron captured somewhere between 18 and 25 vessels and caused a panic in the British merchant marine. Wickes sank some of these ships, released a few, and made prizes of the rest. His major aim—to capture the Irish linen fleet—was aborted due to heavy seas. While heading back to France on June 27, the *Reprisal* was chased by the *Burford,* a 74-gun man-of-war. Wickes managed to escape by jettisoning his guns, and he reached St. Malo. Though the French were delighted with his success, Wickes was a diplomatic embarrassment, and he was ordered to leave. Departing on September 14, Wickes headed home. Off Newfoundland in a storm on October 1, 1777, Wickes and almost the entire crew perished at sea.

Richard L. Blanco

REFERENCES

Helen Augur, *The Secret War of Independence* (1955); William Bell Clark, *Lambert Wickes: Sea Raider and Diplomat* (1932).

Wilkes, John (1725–1797)

English politician. The flamboyant son of a prosperous London distiller, Wilkes was one of the eighteenth century's most colorful figures. He acquired a reputation as a rake early in life and was also known for his charm and quick wit. (Once, it was said, his erstwhile friend Lord Sandwich asked him whether he would die on the gallows or from the pox. Wilkes was quoted as responding, "That depends, my lord, whether I embrace your principles or your mistress.") Opportunistic, Wilkes took an amused and cynical view of the world.

Wilkes entered politics during the Seven Years' War when he was elected to Parliament with the help of Lord Temple, brother-in-law of William Pitt the elder. It was in the bitter journalistic wars of the early 1760s, however, that Wilkes made his mark when the famous 45th number of his anti-administration *North Briton* virtually accused George III of lying to Parliament about the peace settlement. He was arrested for seditious libel, though on a general warrant (i.e., one that did not specify him by name). Initially released by virtue of his parliamentary privilege, Wilkes challenged the use of general warrants as an unconstitutional threat to the liberty of the subject. This action did much to make him a hero and symbol of liberty, first in the eyes of the shopkeepers and tradesmen of London and later in the eyes of many colonial Americans. Eventually the use of general warrants was outlawed. By this time, however, Wilkes had become the object of further government persecution. In the fall of 1763, Parliament resolved that a member's privilege did not extend to cases of seditious libel. Moreover, Wilkes was charged as author of the "Essay on Woman," an obscene parody of Alexander Pope's "Essay on Man." (He was more likely its printer.) Discredited, about to be prosecuted, and wounded in a duel, Wilkes fled to France. He

was convicted *in absentia* and declared to be an outlaw.

Bored and running up debts in exile, Wilkes returned to England in 1768 to face his legal problems. His outlawry was reversed on a technicality, but appeals against his other convictions were denied, and Wilkes was sentenced to 22 months of relatively comfortable imprisonment. He had, in the meantime, plunged back into politics, seeking a seat in Parliament. Unsuccessful in an election in the city of London, he topped the poll in the surrounding county of Middlesex. In 1769, the House of Commons expelled him and ordered a new election. Wilkes stood for the seat a second time and was reelected. Once again the Commons expelled him, resolving in addition that Wilkes was incapable of election. Twice more the sequence of events was repeated before the Commons finally declared Wilkes's opponent elected.

The Middlesex elections generated a large-scale reaction that shook the government and crossed the Atlantic. A well-organized Wilkite movement arose, organizing petitions and clashing with civil authorities. The government, however, ignored the protests and rode out the storm. In America, the events of 1768–1770 confirmed Wilkes's standing as a champion of liberty and made him a hero to American Whigs. The South Carolina Assembly voted money to support his cause, provoking a major disagreement with the governor. Other colonies sent tokens of support (Virginia tobacco, Maryland hams, etc.). Wilkes's treatment confirmed the growing fears of some Americans that the British government meant to crush liberty at home as well as in the colonies. If England's most conspicuous defender of the liberties of the subject could be imprisoned and if an apparently corrupt House of Commons could baldly disregard the rights of the electors of Middlesex, then it seemed credible that threats to American liberty lay behind the Mother Country's colonial policy. Wilkes, for his part, had become friends with Arthur Lee and other Americans in London and had begun openly to take the colonists' side in disputes over the Townshend Duties.

Though out of Parliament, Wilkes was not out of politics. He emerged from prison a major figure in London politics and served terms as sheriff (1771–1772) and lord mayor (1774–1775). In these capacities, Wilkes played a prominent role in opening the debates of both houses of Parliament to newspaper coverage. In the election of 1774 Wilkes again stood for Middlesex and was easily elected. This time the government quietly allowed him to take his seat.

Wilkes's return to Parliament provided him with a platform from which he could oppose the North administration's colonial policy and the resultant war, which he labeled "unjust, felonious, and murderous." Wilkes aided the American cause in other ways, sometimes bordering on the treasonable. He continued his association with Arthur Lee, by now a covert correspondent of the Continental Congress. He also established a relationship with Pierre-Augustin Caron de Beaumarchais that during 1775 and 1776 became a means of transmitting funds to the American cause from British supporters. Though the government suspected Wilkes's involvement in such illegal activities, it did not attempt to arrest him, perhaps out of a desire to avoid another round of popular unrest.

Like many other British opponents of the war, Wilkes was perplexed (though not surprised) by the American decision for independence. Though one of the first to defend the Declaration of Independence in Parliament, he continued for several years to hope that the war could be ended on terms that would leave a link between Britain and America.

Wilkes's influence on pro-American sentiment, especially in London, was significant, but it was not unlimited. For one thing, Wilkes never put aside his personal interests, and some of these cost him popularity in the war years. He aggressively sought and in 1779 finally achieved election to the lucrative office of city chamberlain. He also devoted much of his effort in Parliament to expunging the earlier resolution of his incapacity, finally succeeding in 1782. Wilkes also continued to back other causes such as parliamentary reform and expanded religious toleration. While the former overlapped to some degree with opposition to the American war, the latter was more divisive. There remained a streak of anti-Catholicism among pro-Americans in Britain. When Wilkes took an active role in suppressing the anti-Catholic Gordon riots in 1780 (mounting in the process a spirited defense of the Bank of England), it brought him into conflict, at times quite literally, with some of his former supporters and cost him their support.

By the early 1780s, Wilkes's popularity and influence were declining and his politics were moderating. He supported Shelburne's preliminary treaty of peace in 1783 and later became reconciled to the King (to whom he is supposed to have confessed that he himself had never been a Wilkite). By the end of the war, Wilkes had ceased to be a major political figure in Britain.

Historians will probably always debate the depth of Wilkes's devotion to the causes with which he became associated. Despite his cynicism, he had a major impact on the era of the American Revolution. The Mother Country's foremost symbol of liberty in danger, his career did much to validate the fears about British intentions that undergirded resistance in America. Once the war began, Wilkes remained a champion of the American cause, retaining his popularity across the Atlantic even as it declined at home.

William C. Lowe

REFERENCES

Colin Bonwick, *English Radicals and the American Revolution* (1977); Ian R. Christie, *Wilkes, Wyvill, and Reform: The Parliamentary Reform Movement in British Politics, 1760–1785* (1962); Worthington C. Ford, ed., "John Wilkes and Boston," *Proceedings of the Massachusetts Historical Society*, 47 (1913–1914):190–215; Louis Kronenberger, *The Extraordinary Mr. Wilkes* (1974); Jack P. Greene, "Bridge to Revolution: The Wilkes Fund Controversy in South Carolina, 1769–1775," *Journal of Southern History*, 29 (1963):19–52; Pauline C. Maier, "John Wilkes and American Disillusionment with Britain," *William and Mary Quarterly*, 20 (1963):373–395; Raymond Postgate, *That Devil Wilkes* (1929); John Sainsbury, *Disaffected Patriots: London Supporters of Revolutionary America* (1987).

Wilkinson, James (1757–1825)

Continental Army officer. Born in Maryland, Wilkinson grew up on the family plantation. Educated privately, he became a medical apprentice in Philadelphia (1773). Anxious to serve his country, Wilkinson enlisted as a private in the Pennsylvania Rifle Regiment, and he fought at the siege of Boston. He then took part in the invasion of Canada and in the siege of Quebec, becoming a captain. In 1776 Wilkinson was on the staff of General Nathanael Greene, was an aide to General Benedict Arnold, and became a brigade major to General Horatio Gates. He became lieutenant colonel in January 1777 and was deputy adjutant general of the Northern Department from March 1777 to March 1778. During these years Wilkinson saw action at Trenton, Princeton, Fort Ticonderoga, and Saratoga.

It was Wilkinson—while stopping at a tavern in Reading, Pennsylvania, and while carrying Gates's dispatches to Congress about his victory over General John Burgoyne—who leaked information about a conspiracy to displace Washington as commander-in-chief. But Wilkinson's role in this affair is not clear. Due to Gates, Wilkinson was breveted a brigadier general, but due to protests by ranking officers he was not given a field command, but he was appointed secretary to the Board of War. Wilkinson became implicated in the Conway Cabal, and he also lost the confidence of Gates. He resigned from the Board in March 1778. Due to a fortuitous marriage to Anne Biddle of the prominent Philadelphia family, Wilkinson was named clothier general. Serving in this post from July 1779 to March 1789 he resigned over questions of financial irregularities in his accounts.

Wilkinson's postwar career is more notable—and infamous—for his intrigues in national politics. Moving from Pennsylvania he settled in Lexington, Kentucky, where he speculated in land and became active in commerce on the Mississippi. Whatever were his specific aims—whether to lead Kentucky into a succession from the United States, or to establish a buffer state, or to prepare for a conquest of Mexico, or to take the West into Spanish control—Wilkinson's activities were unquestionably treasonable. In any case, however cloudy his motives, he was bribed by Spanish authorities and was successful in persuading them to open the Mississippi to Americans for trade and navigation (1787).

Wilkinson returned to the area in 1791 and served as second in command under General Anthony Wayne in the Northwest Territory during the campaign against the Indians. He was commended for his role at the Battle of Fallen Timbers (1794). While still receiving a secret subsidy from Spain, he was appointed commander-in-chief of the United States Army in 1796. In 1805 Wilkinson was named governor of the Louisiana Territory. Forever the schemer, Wilkinson became involved with Aaron Burr, the vice president, in a plot to separate the west from the United States, to invade Mexico, and

to establish an independent state. But Wilkinson revealed to Congress the extent of the intrigue and thereby deflected (to some degree) his own involvement in the treasonous activity. Though his political opponents voiced suspicions about Wilkinson's duplicity, his role in Burr's scheme is unclear. Wilkinson testified at Burr's trial in 1807. Wilkinson was acquitted in that hearing and at successive investigations in 1809 and in 1811, when he was finally exonerated.

Appointed major general in 1813 during the War of 1812, Wilkinson bungled the campaign to capture Montreal. Again he was subject to an official inquiry, and again he was acquitted (1815) and honorably discharged. Soon after, he published his memoirs. Wilkinson then traveled to New Orleans and then to Mexico, where he died while attempting to win a land grant. While Wilkinson's military ability is debatable and his personal motives in several plots controversial, clearly he was involved in intrigue against the security of the United States.

Richard L. Blanco

REFERENCES

Thomas Perkins Abernathy, *The Burr Conspiracy* (1954); Thomas R. Hay and M.R. Werner, *The Admirable Trumpeter* (1941); James Ripley Jacobs, *Tarnished Warrior* (1938).

Willett, Marinus (1740–1830)

Continental Army officer. Born on July 31, 1740, at Jamaica (Long Island), New York, he was one of the 13 children of Edward and Aletta (Clowes) Willett and a great-grandson of Thomas Willett, who migrated to the Plymouth Colony in 1632. He attended King's College, but in 1758 he was drawn into the French and Indian War. Commissioned as a second lieutenant in Oliver De Lancey's regiment of New York colonials, he participated in Lord James Abercrombie's ill-fated attempt to take Fort Ticonderoga; later, he accompanied John Bradstreet in the capture of Fort Frontenac. On the return from Canada, Willett took ill and spent more than two months recuperating at the newly built American fort in the upper Mohawk Valley, Fort Stanwix—a post that would figure prominently in his future. He worked as a cabinetmaker following the war and married his employer's daughter, Mary Pease, in April 1760. After her death in 1793, he remarried twice, to

Susannah Vardle in 1793 and to Margaret Bancher in 1800.

As trouble between the colonies and England developed, young Willett took an active role in the growing opposition movement in New York City. He joined the Sons of Liberty, helped rescue Isaac Sears from jail, aided in the colonists' assault on the city's arsenal (April 23, 1775), and initiated the "Affair on Broad-Street" (June 6, 1775), in which he and other colonials prevented the British from carrying away five wagonloads of arms and ammunition when they evacuated New York. Commissioned as a captain in Colonel Alexander McDougall's 1st New York Regiment on June 28, 1775, Willett served under General Richard Montgomery on his 1775 invasion of Canada and briefly commanded the captured fort of St. Johns. He became lieutenant colonel of the 3rd New York Regiment when it was raised and commanded Fort Constitution on the Hudson from November 1776 to May 1777, when he was ordered to Fort Stanwix. He and the 3rd's commander, Colonel Peter Gansevoort, found the Mohawk Valley post in disrepair, but they quickly set about renovating Stanwix in anticipation of a British thrust into the region. During the ensuing siege of the fort by British lieutenant colonel Barry St. Leger (August 1777), Willett performed superbly, leading a successful sortie from the fort on August 6 and later slipping through the siege lines and going for help. That October, the Continental Congress presented him an "elegant sword" for his gallant service in turning back St. Leger's expedition.

Willett remained active throughout the war. He served with Washington's army in 1778 and took part in the Battle of Monmouth. The following year he participated in John Sullivan's expedition against the Indians on the Pennsylvania and New York frontiers, after which he rejoined the main army and conducted several successful raids around New York City in the winter of 1779–1780. He was appointed lieutenant colonel commanding the 5th New York Regiment on July 1, 1780, and became colonel of a new regiment in January 1781 when five New York regiments were consolidated into two. Responding to Governor George Clinton's urgent appeal, Willett returned to the Mohawk Valley in the spring of 1781 to take command of all American forces in the region. There he met frequent raids by the British, Tories, and Indi-

ans during the next two years, winning important victories at Sharon (July 10, 1781) and Johnstown (October 25, 1781). He emerged from the Revolution with a well-earned reputation as an outspoken, aggressive, vigilant, and fearless leader.

Elected to the state assembly immediately following the war, he resigned in 1784 to accept a four-year appointment as sheriff of New York City and New York County. In 1790, President Washington sent him as his personal representative to conclude a peace treaty with the Creek Indians. Two years later, Willett was offered a commission as brigadier general in the United States Army but declined because he disagreed with the proposed use of force against western Indians. He again served as sheriff of the city and county of New York from 1792 to 1796, was appointed mayor of the city in 1807, and ran unsuccessfully for lieutenant governor in 1811. As a merchant and owner of substantial property, Willett enjoyed a comfortable postwar life, maintaining contact with many of the leading military figures of the Revolution through the Society of the Cincinnati, which he helped form. He died at his home in Cedar Grove, New York, on August 22, 1830, 53 years to the day after St. Leger's abandonment of the siege of Fort Stanwix. The passing of the 90-year-old Patriot brought forth a great outpouring of public mourning.

Ralph L. Eckert

REFERENCES

Fred J. Cook, *What Manner of Men: Forgotten Heroes of the American Revolution* (1959); Henry B. Dawson, *Battles of the United States . . .* (1858); *DAB*; Daniel E. Wager, *Col. Marinus Willett: Hero of Mohawk Valley* (1891); William M. Willett, *A Narrative of the Military Actions of Colonel Marinus Willett* (1831).

Williams, Otho Holland (1749–1794)

Continental Army officer. A Marylander, Williams worked for the county clerk in Frederick, Maryland, in 1749, and he held a similar post in Baltimore (1767–1774). In 1775 he was a clerk in a firm in Frederick. Williams was appointed a lieutenant in June 1775. He was promoted to captain at the siege of Boston and to the rank of major in June 1776. In November 1776 he was wounded and captured at Fort

Washington, being made a colonel while a prisoner. Exchanged in 15 months, Williams saw action at Monmouth. In April 1780 he was ordered south with General Baron Johann de Kalb. Williams was at Camden under General Horatio Gates. General Nathanael Greene made him adjutant general. Williams won fame in the southern campaign by aiding Daniel Morgan at Cowpens, in covering Greene's retreat to the Dan, and in repulsing a British attempt to trap his men at Weitzel's Mill (March 6, 1781). Williams also fought valiantly at Guilford Court House, Hobkirk's Hill, and Eutaw Springs. Made a brigadier general in May 1782, he retired from the army in June 1783. After the war he returned to Baltimore, where he held several minor federal posts.

Richard L. Blanco

REFERENCES

Kenneth R. Haynes, Jr., "The Race to Weitzel's Mill, 6 March, 1781," *Gorget and Sash, 3* (1989):1–11; Osmond Tiffiny, *A Sketch of the Life and Service of General Otho Holland Williams* (1851); [Otho Holland Williams], "The Second Battle of Camden, South Carolina—account . . . by Gen. Otho Holland Williams," *Potter's American Monthly, 4* (1875):99–104.

Williamson, Andrew (c.1730–1786)

South Carolina militia officer. The truth about the loyalties of Andrew Williamson of South Carolina remains one of the most hotly debated questions of the American Revolution in the South. Certainly, his career is high drama. Was he the great tragic and forgotten hero of the American cause or a crafty traitor deserving the title of the "Arnold of the South?"

As a frontier elite was emerging in colonial South Carolina, few men had such humble beginnings. Williamson is believed to have been born in Scotland around 1730 and to have come to the Carolina backcountry as a child with his father. After being a cattle driver, he rose to prominence during the Cherokee War of the 1760s, as waggoner, quartermaster, and Indian fighter. As a merchant and planter, the illiterate Williamson became one of the wealthiest men in the Ninety Six District.

The Revolution was not welcomed everywhere on the southern frontier. Nowhere was this situation more dangerous for the American

cause than in South Carolina, where Loyalist leaders such as Thomas Fletchall, Joseph Robinson, the Cunninghams, Moses Kirkland, Richard Pearis, and Thomas Brown could command the allegiance of thousands of armed men.

Andrew Williamson proved an invaluable supporter to the rebel efforts, not only because of his personal influence but because of his intelligent leadership. The Loyalist leadership was badly divided and sometimes inept, but few men could have so successfully understood its shortcomings and exploited its weaknesses as did Andrew Williamson. In 1774, he signed an anti-British grand jury presentment, and the following year he was elected to the South Carolina Provincial Congress. On November 19, 1775, his men, although outnumbered by more than three to one, fought the local Loyalists at Ninety Six, in what was the first battle of the American Revolution in the South. Williamson won the day by negotiation, saving his command from destruction and allowing the South Carolina rebels time to reinforce him. While the Loyalists were dispersed the following winter, Williamson and his men arrested the Loyalist leaders in what became the "Snow Campaign" of 1775–1776. Williamson's command fought the elements as much as it fought the Loyalists (unprecedented snowfall was so deep that Williamson and his men could not touch the ground for eight days). They recovered stolen gunpowder and crippled the Loyalist cause in the South so badly that it never really recovered. The friends of the King either submitted or were forced into exile.

Part of the Patriot success in the South was due to a propaganda campaign reporting that the British were arming the Indians for an attack upon the frontier. This fear was intensified when the Cherokees did attack the frontier in the spring of 1776. A coordinated campaign by American militiamen from Virginia to Georgia retaliated by leveling all but one of the Cherokee villages. The most extensive campaign and the most desperate fighting were by Williamson and the several thousand men he led against the Indians on the frontiers of South Carolina and Georgia. Even many of the Loyalists joined Williamson in this campaign or offered their support. The Cherokees and the Creeks would continue to launch British-financed attacks throughout the war, but the specter of the thousands of Cherokees killed in the 1776 campaigns was an obstacle the British could never completely overcome. In many ways, the destruction of the Cherokees as a people can be traced to the fighting in the summer of 1776.

Thanks largely to Williamson, the South Carolina frontier was at peace. Gratitude for his efforts, however, was slow in coming. His troops did not receive so much as a tent from the South Carolina rebel government in Charlestown. For most of his campaigns, Williamson was only a major. He was not promoted to brigadier general until 1778.

However, South Carolina wanted even more from the illiterate former cattle driver. Weak and exposed, Georgia demanded military help from South Carolina. So many South Carolina troops were called out for Georgia's defense that an attempt was even made to merge the two provinces. Williamson was called upon to send more than the frontier's share of soldiers for Georgia. In 1778, he persuaded 1,000 of his men to follow him in the Georgia invasion of British East Florida. The Georgians were so badly prepared that Williamson's men had to share their limited supplies with the Georgia troops. The South Carolinians had hardly returned to their frontier homes when the Creek Indians attacked the northern Georgia frontier. Williamson and his men again rushed to Georgia's aid. They found no Indians but instead were insulted by an uncooperative Georgia militia under Colonel John Dooly and by Georgians charging the South Carolina militiamen inflated prices for supplies.

The following December, Savannah, Georgia's capital, fell to an invasion force of British regulars from New York. By late January, the British army had captured Augusta, on the edge of the South Carolina frontier. Williamson risked the destruction of the militia brigade by blocking the British advance into the South Carolina frontier. At the same time, Williamson's famous subordinate, Colonel Andrew Pickens, led a ragtag collection of South Carolina and Georgia militia in defeating an uprising of Carolina Loyalists at the Battle of Kettle Creek, Georgia, on February 14, 1779. Completely frustrated in their efforts to reach the Carolina Loyalists, the British coincidentally withdrew from Augusta on that same day. Williamson organized a massive roundup of the persons responsible for the Loyalist uprising. Several of these Tories were imprisoned, and at least five were hanged at Ninety Six. Once the Loyalist movement in the South

Carolina backcountry had been a formidable force led by respected frontier leaders. By 1779, Williamson had reduced it to a shell of its former self, to little more than bands of thieves and uninhibited "white savages" that the more respectable frontier classes had been fighting since the Regulator Rebellion of colonial South Carolina. Williamson claimed that the ringleaders of the Kettle Creek Loyalists were actually hanged for capital offenses committed before the war. The British had invaded Georgia with the intention of raising a Loyalist army that would recover the South and possibly turn the tide of the war. Whatever the real merits of this plan, no single man was more responsible from 1775 to 1780 in preventing this "Southern Strategy" from working than Andrew Williamson.

For the next year and a half, Williamson sent raiding parties into Georgia that worked with the remaining Georgia militia to defeat any armed support found there for the King's cause. By the summer of 1779, the only safe haven for loyalism in Georgia and South Carolina was within the narrow lines around British-occupied Savannah and Sunbury in Georgia. In October 1779, after successful campaigns against the Cherokees and Creeks, Williamson brought his brigade to Georgia, where they joined French and American forces in an unsuccessful offensive against British Savannah. Williamson's command had not only protected South Carolina and Georgia from Indian attacks while crushing all organized support for the British cause, they had even participated in offensives in Georgia against the British in 1778 and 1779.

However, Williamson's successes and sacrifices would soon be forgotten. Charlestown surrendered to the British in May 1780, and soon British and Loyalist provincial troops were moving against the frontier. Williamson believed that his militia could again keep the backcountry out of the King's cause. However, when he pleaded with his men for support, they almost all voted to surrender. Williamson did not abandon his men but went with their decision and arranged for their capitulation as prisoners of war on parole. For most of the remainder of the war, he tried to comply with those surrender terms while not materially aiding the British cause. When Georgia partisan Elijah Clarke kidnapped Williamson in August 1780 to persuade him to aid Clarke in an attack on the Loyalist garrison at Augusta, Williamson declined. However, he also chose not to alert British authorities of Clarke's plans. When the Americans eventually recovered the South Carolina frontier, Williamson was in British-held Charlestown, where he risked his life working as a spy for the American general Nathanael Greene. Greene later testified about Williamson's invaluable help in winning the war in the South.

However, by that time, the mystique of the American cause had already been founded. South Carolinians needed some explanation for the fall of Charlestown and for the two years of bloody civil war that followed. Before the war was over, even some of Williamson's former friends, including Andrew Pickens, were trying to believe that treasonous actions by Andrew Williamson were the cause of their misfortunes rather than their own military and political failures. They wanted to believe that Williamson did not defeat the British regulars in Augusta in January and February 1779 because he was a traitor, ignoring the fact that Williamson's ragtag frontiersmen were hopelessly outnumbered and outclassed by the regular British army. When Williamson was "kidnapped" from the Charlestown area by rebels, South Carolina Patriot Colonel Isaac Hayne was executed by the British in their successful rescue of Williamson. For being a prisoner of war on parole and becoming the objective of Hayne's expedition, Williamson was seen by South Carolina rebels as responsible for Hayne's death.

These arguments, even then, drew far more strength from emotion than from logic. Nothing in the official records of the British officers suggests any collusion with Williamson. In the case of Andrew Pickens, accusing Williamson of being a traitor also conveniently drew attention away from Pickens's questionable account of why he, who eventually received Williamson's old command, reneged on his oath of surrender and returned to the American cause.

At the end of the war, as scapegoat or traitor, Williamson was vulnerable. The restored Patriot assembly of South Carolina ordered a portion of Williamson's property seized because he was supposedly a supporter of the King. Despite protests by Greene and many of Williamson's friends and former officers, the property was not returned until 1791. Andrew Williamson died March 22, 1786, having spent the last years of his life defending his actions and reputation against the whisper campaigns of his largely un-

seen enemies. Very likely he was never a traitor to the American cause in any way but fought his bravest and most desperate campaign to keep the terms of the oath he and his men had made in order to keep the peace, after circumstances beyond his control forced his surrender. Ironically, having fought so long and successfully to crush opposition to the American cause, Andrew Williamson was one of the victims of the American Revolutionary mystique.

Robert Scott Davis, Jr.

REFERENCES

Edward J. Cashin, *The King's Ranger: Thomas Brown and the American Revolution on the Southern Frontier* (1989); Robert S. Davis, Jr., "The Loyalist Trials at Ninety Six in 1779," *South Carolina Historical Magazine*, 80 (1979):172–181; R. Michael Jones, *Andrew Williamson 1730–1786: Cow Driver to General*, (1979); "The Trembling Land: Covert Activity in the Georgia Backcountry during the American Revolution," *Proceedings and Papers of the Georgia Association of Historians 1982* (1983):13–29.

Willing, James (? – ?)

American Patriot. Younger brother of Philadelphia merchant Thomas Willing, James moved to the Mississippi River district of British West Florida in 1772. He secured a land grant near Tunica Bend and, in partnership with his friend Oliver Pollock, opened a small store at that location. He also planted indigo and became a moderately successful landowner. He apparently had an abrasive personality and quarreled with other settlers. Willing returned to Philadelphia with the outbreak of the Revolution and became a partisan of the Patriot cause. As early as 1776, he advocated that a rebel military expedition depart from Fort Pitt, float down the Ohio and Mississippi rivers, and conquer West Florida. He secured permission for such a venture, assembled several dozen men, and began a descent of the river system in early 1778. He carried with him a congressional commission for Oliver Pollock, naming the merchant as official agent at New Orleans. Willing reached the British settlements on February 19 and attacked the town of Natelez. It seemed that his primary objective, however, was to settle old scores with British settlers who had been enemies during his earlier residence in the area. In particular, he ravaged the plantation of his nemesis Anthony Hutchins while his men sacked the farms and houses of other residents.

The Willing group confiscated much of the personal property belonging to local settlers, while the expedition showed little interest in more traditional military objectives.

After capturing a British merchant marine vessel up the river from New Orleans, Willing and his men arrived at the Louisiana capital with their burden of plunder. Oliver Pollock interceded with Governor Bernardo de Galvez, who permitted them freedom of the city and the opportunity to sell their booty as spoils of war. Galvez, however, did hold hearings on the raid and, as a result, returned some of the confiscated items to their British owners. Willing decided not to press ahead with any additional attacks on West Florida. Instead, he and his men returned to the United States. In net effect, the Willing expedition down the Mississippi in 1778 was detrimental to the American cause. His capture of Natchez was only temporary, and after his force left the area, the governor of West Florida reinforced the area with additional troops.

Light Townsend Cummins

REFERENCES

John W. Caughey, *Bernardo de Galvez in Louisiana, 1776–1783* (1934); Light T. Cummins, "Oliver Pollock and George Rogers Clark's Service of Supply: A Case Study in Financial Disaster," *Selected Papers from the 1985 and 1986 George Rogers Clark Trans-Appalachian History Conferences* (1988); Robert Y. Haynes, *The Natchez District and the American Revolution* (1976); James A. James, *Oliver Pollock: The Life and Times of an Unknown Patriot* (1937); J. Barton Starr, *Tories, Dons, and Rebels: The American Revolution in West Florida* (1976).

Women Soldiers

A multitude of women went to war during the American Revolution. Although many of the women worked for the army as cooks, laundresses, and nurses, a few actually donned male clothing to serve in the army as soldiers. Some of these women in the military preserved their identities as soldiers until they fell sick or were wounded in battle. When their secret was consequently revealed during medical treatment they were forced to leave the army. Others never had a chance to bear arms, for their sex was discovered soon after enlistment, and the army quickly dismissed them from the service. A few others probably joined, served, and left the army without ever calling attention to themselves or leaving proper records of their existence. The public expressed mixed feelings about these women. Some people found them humorous, others thought them a disgrace, while still others admired them.

Very little is known about the women who served as soldiers. Deborah Sampson was a rarity in that she published her story. The others are only fleetingly mentioned in folk tales, letters, newspaper reports, and pension records. Sampson was born on December 17, 1760, in Plympton, Massachusetts, to a poor family. From the ages of 10 to 18 she served in the family of Deacon Thomas near Middleborough. After that time she tried to further her education and teach school. Then, according to pension applications, she donned male clothing and enlisted in the 4th Massachusetts Regiment in April 1781 as Robert Shurtleff (there are conflicting reports that say she actually enlisted in May 1782). She managed to keep her sex a secret when she was wounded at Tarrytown, but her subterfuge proved more difficult to maintain when she was later stricken with an illness that put her in a hospital. At this point there are again disparities in her story: one account says her sex was discovered at Yorktown when she suffered a "brain fever," after which General George Washington gave her a discharge and some money; another account declares that a doctor in Philadelphia made the discovery, but gallantly kept her secret, when treating Sampson after she fell victim to an epidemic there. The pension applications do not mention any illnesses, but they do state that she was wounded and that she stayed in the army until released from duty in November 1783. The United States Government later awarded her a pension for her services.

After the war Deborah married Benjamin Gannett, a farmer from Sharon, Massachusetts, and raised a family. She died on April 19, 1827, after suffering for years from the wounds she had received during the war. In the lean years between the end of the war and her death, Deborah Sampson Gannett gave talks on her adventures and permitted her story to be published as well. The author, Herman Mann, presented her as a Patriot who admirably performed her duties as a soldier. However, he also let it be known that she had a masculine appearance and a character that, though sweet and pliable, needed refinement. Mann wrote a pointed note to his female readers that although everyone must do the heroine justice, it would not do for them to adopt her example should the occasion arise. In succeeding wars, however, other women did follow Sampson's example and the example of the other female soldiers of the Revolution.

Among the other women soldiers in the War for American Independence was Sally St. Clair, a young Creole. She reportedly masqueraded as a man so that she could follow her love, a rebel sergeant, to war. Victorian Americans claimed that the sergeant did not know of St. Clair's deception until she was killed at the Battle of Savannah.

Another female in uniform is known to historians only by her enlisted alias: Samuel Gay. She purportedly attained the rank of sergeant before the army discovered her sex and dismissed her.

Unlike Gay, Anna Maria Lane left records of her Revolutionary War service and her life following the war in the pension records. Lane's husband, John, enlisted in the Continental Army in 1776. His wife either enlisted at the same time or accompanied him as a camp follower. If she had not done so already, Anna Maria Lane probably joined the army in September 1777, a month after General George Washington bitterly complained about the numerous women who were a hindrance to the army's movements. Whatever the date of her transformation into a soldier, whether she ever officially enlisted or not, Anna Maria Lane fought and was wounded as a soldier in the Battle of Germantown on October 4. Her sex may or may not have been revealed during the treatment for her injury; if someone did disclose her secret, the revelation did not keep her away from the army, for either as soldier or camp follower, Lane remained with her husband for the rest of the war.

After the war John Lane served in the Virginia State Guard and then in the Virginia Public Guard, while his wife first raised their small family and then later volunteered for nursing duties. From 1801 to 1804 Anna Maria Lane received a stipend as a nurse of the Public Guard. Cutbacks in the guard and ill health finally drove the Lanes into an impoverished retirement. They did receive some help from the government when the Virginia General Assembly awarded each of them a pension: John received $40 a year for life; Anna received over double that amount for her courage and actions at Germantown. After

his wife died on June 13, 1810, and her pension ceased, John had a difficult time. He eventually ended up in the Richmond City Poorhouse.

Other women were not able to stay in the army long enough to fight and earn the consideration and compensation accorded Sampson and Lane. A very young woman enlisted in the 1st New Jersey Regiment in November 1778. Her masquerade was of short duration: she enlisted on a Friday evening only to have her secret revealed, first by her behavior and then by physical examination, the next afternoon. She had joined the army because her father would not permit her to marry the young man she favored. The officers who made the discovery were quite diverted by her behavior, her story, and her banishment from camp the next morning. The officer who had enlisted the woman ordered her marched through Elizabethtown, New Jersey, to the beat of the "Whores' March."

In the spring of 1782, Anne Smith enlisted in the Continental Army under the name of Samuel Smith. She never made it through the initial mustering at Springfield, Massachusetts. After many questions and a close examination, the mustering agents discovered the recruit was female. Instead of acquiring a bounty, Smith received a prison term (besides her falsehoods upon enlisting, she was also allegedly a horse thief). During her confinement in the local jail, Smith offered two stories to explain her conduct: sometimes she declared that this had been the "first scrape the devil ever led her into," while at other times she asserted that she previously had served as a soldier for three months without being discovered. The newspaper article that publicized Smith's escapade noted that she so perfectly acted the part of a man that she might have passed inspection "had not the want of a beard and the redundance of some other matters led to a detection."

Women did serve in the military during the war, but they were anomalies: only a tiny minority of American women stepped out of their domestic sphere to don male clothing and join the army. Some of these women kept their sex secret throughout the war and their service secret after it. Others had their secrets revealed and their stories told, but unfortunately the tales were often scanty or undocumented. Enough was written, however, to determine that the women soldiers of the American Revolution ran the gamut of public opinion and reaction: some people lauded them, others loathed them.

Holly A. Mayer

REFERENCES

Herman Mann, *The Female Review: Life of Deborah Sampson* (1866), rpr. 1972; Sandra Gioia Treadway, "Anna Maria Lane: An Uncommon Soldier of the American Revolution," *Virginia Cavalcade* (1988):134–143; Robert Fridlington, "A 'Diversion' in Newark: A Letter from the New Jersey Continental Line, 1778," *New Jersey History*, 105, (1987):75–78; *The Pennsylvania Packet* (newspaper), June 24, 1782.

Woodford, William (1734–1780)

Continental Army officer. William Woodford was born in Caroline County, Virginia, on October 6, 1734, to Major William Woodford, an Englishman who immigrated to Virginia, and Anne Cocke Woodford. Educated as a Virginia gentleman, Woodford served as a provincial officer in Virginia's forces during the French and Indian War.

After the war Woodford returned to the life of the gentleman farmer. For a time he served as justice of the peace for Caroline County. He became an active member of the Fredericksburg Masonic Lodge and was a regular customer at George Weedon's Fredericksburg Tavern. Woodford joined Weedon's Tavern "Club," a jolly group of friends who spent much of their time together talking politics, and playing cards or billiards. On June 26, 1762, Woodford married Mary (Molly) Thornton, George Washington's niece. The Woodfords had two children.

A supporter of the American cause, Woodford became a member of the Caroline County Committee of Correspondence. From July 17 to August 9, 1775, Woodford sat as an alternate for Edmund Pendleton in the Virginia Convention.

Woodford began his military career in the War of the Revolution on August 5, 1775, when the Virginia Convention in Richmond appointed him colonel of the 2nd Virginia Regiment. Patrick Henry was appointed colonel of the 1st Regiment. Before taking command, Woodford wrote Washington for advice on being a proper officer. Washington's return letter was so instructive that Woodford kept it with him as a ready reference.

Not overly experienced in matters of command and somewhat of a dandy who constantly overdressed his part by wearing the richest and most expensive of uniforms, Woodford did not inspire the love and devotion of his men. Methodical in his actions, Woodford impressed some of his associates as being too concerned with reputation at the expense of possible military success.

In spite of these drawbacks, Woodford's first military expedition was a success. He and his regiment stopped the royal governor of Virginia, John Murray, the Earl of Dunmore, from capturing and burning Hampton, Virginia, in October 1775. Ignoring the seniority objections of Patrick Henry, who was certainly no soldier, the Virginia Committee of Safety later sent Woodford to recover Norfolk from Dunmore's control.

On December 9, 1775, Woodford won the Battle of Great Bridge. Great Bridge was 12 miles south of Norfolk on the south branch of the Elizabeth River. Dunmore had his men fortify one end of the bridge to protect Norfolk from the advance of the Americans. The British fortifications were strongly positioned, with bogs and impassable swampland on both sides of a narrow causeway that led up to and past the fort.

Woodford did not attempt to cross the bridge. Instead, he had his men construct a counter fortification on the other side of the bridge. The future chief justice of the United States Supreme Court, John Marshall, and his father, major Thomas Marshall, were a part of Woodford's force. Legend has it that Major Marshall's trusted Black servant was persuaded to defect to the British with a tale of how small the American force guarding the fortification really was.

The ruse worked. Dunmore ordered an assault with his grenadiers and regulars from the 14th Regiment, about 250 men in all, leading the way. Captain Charles Fordyce commanded the van in the attack. The Americans hid in their fort until the British had closed to within 30 yards. The first volley decimated the British front, and a second volley threw the entire column into confusion. Captain Fordyce died, shot 14 times. Woodford's men captured two guns and wounded 16 men. British losses came to over 60 men. The Americans had one man with a slight hand wound. The fighting lasted 25 minutes. In the first major battle in the war since Bunker Hill, Woodford hailed Great Bridge as a victory that set back the Loyalist movement in Virginia for years.

Woodford's men took Norfolk on December 13 as Dunmore's men retreated. Woodford was joined the next day by Colonel Robert Howe and 250 North Carolinians. From his refuge aboard British naval vessels, Dunmore fired on Norfolk, putting it in flames, on January 1, 1776. Woodford's troops contributed to the destruction by looting and burning Loyalist homes. When the flames died down, Norfolk was virtually destroyed.

On February 13, 1776, Woodford was appointed colonel of the 2nd Virginia Continental Regiment, a unit enlisted for one year. This regiment remained in Virginia for local defense during the 1776 campaign. In September 1776, Adam Stephen of Virginia was promoted to brigadier general by the Continental Congress. This was done in spite of Woodford's seniority. In anger, Woodford resigned his colonel's commission but later reclaimed his rank. This rash act effected endless friction later in the war.

On February 21, 1777, the Continental Congress promoted 10 colonels, including Woodford, to the rank of brigadier general in the Continental service. Due to his earlier resignation of his colonel's commission, Woodford was made the least senior of the three new Virginia generals (John Muhlenberg, George Weedon, and Woodford).

Woodford, Virginia's first war hero, had enjoyed seniority over the other two men since the French and Indian War. Now he put country before honor and, at Washington's urging, agreed to serve with both men. Woodford pledged his friendship and cooperation. He was placed in command of the 3rd Virginia Brigade, which included the 34th, 7th, 11th, and 15th regiments of Virginia Line. Woodford's brigade was coupled with General Charles Scott's brigade in Adam Stephen's division.

Woodford arrived at Morristown, New Jersey, to join Washington's army by May 20, 1777. His brigade played a significant role in the Pennsylvania campaign of 1777. As General William Howe's British army invaded Pennsylvania to capture the rebel capital at Philadelphia, the two armies collided at Brandywine Creek on September 11, 1777. Using his typical tactical plan, Howe attempted to flank Washington by marching around the American right. The successful British flanking move disrupted Washington's army and forced a hurried shift to a new defensive line on Birmingham Hill. Woodford's Virginians were among the first to arrive at Birmingham to meet the British advance. Woodford dispatched Marshall's 3rd Virginia to an orchard in the brigade's front. It was there the fighting opened at 3:30 that afternoon as Howe's army moved in to destroy the American army.

Fighting raged back and forth on Birmingham Hill. Woodford's men held on against repeated British attacks, while other American units were broken and sent streaming to the rear. Woodford was able to recall Marshall's men and hold the hill long enough for General John Sullivan, the American right-wing commander, to regroup his broken line and withdraw in some order. Woodford was wounded in the hand just as his men began their own retreat under increased British pressure.

While Woodford was recovering from his wound in Bethlehem, Pennsylvania, Howe captured Philadelphia on September 26. Just over a week later, Washington's army came rushing out of a Saturday morning fog to attack the main British camp at Germantown, about six miles above Philadelphia. Woodford's men were in General Nathanael Greene's wing. Confusion caused by untrustworthy guides, the fog, and incompetence on the part of Major General Adam Stephen led the Virginians to stray from their target, the British rear area in the vicinity of Market Square in Germantown. Instead, under conditions of very poor visibility, the Virginians ran into the rear of Anthony Wayne's Pennsylvanians. Both lines of Americans fired into each other, and the resulting confusion contributed to the eventual American retreat.

When the Americans moved to their winter cantonment at Valley Forge on December 19, 1777, Woodford's men were placed on the western flank of the front or outer line. By this time Woodford had fully recovered from his wound and had rejoined his men. He made his headquarters with the Samuel Richards family near the Great Valley Baptist Church, about two miles from his brigade.

It was at Valley Forge that Woodford was thrown into one of the most severe contests of his military career—the battle of the Virginia generals. When Major General Stephen was dismissed from the service for his actions at Germantown and previous engagements, Woodford actively sought to fill the vacancy as the senior brigadier general in the Virginia Line. Seniority and rank were matters taken quite seriously by officers in the eighteenth century. A man's honor was at stake when an "inferior" officer was jumped over his "superiors" to a higher rank, for whatever reasons. Rather than serve, many officers would resign their commissions and go home. Woodford had already done just this, and now his action came back to haunt him.

Ordinarily, Woodford would have been the senior Virginia brigadier, and Congress would normally have placed him in a vacant major general's position. However, Woodford had been taken on as a brigadier general with the least seniority, behind General John Peter Muhlenberg and General George Weedon. General Charles Scott, another Virginia general, for a time entered the fray but withdrew early in the contest, since his case was admittedly the weakest of all.

The Virginia generals all left Valley Forge on leave, including Woodford, who departed in March 1778. The issue was referred to Congress to be settled. Congress, true to form, passed the decision back to Washington and his council of generals. These men finally met in March at General Lord Stirling's headquarters at Valley Forge to decide the matter. Woodford was recognized as the senior Virginia brigadier general. Muhlenberg and Weedon were considered to have less seniority. Interestingly, Woodford won his case but was never promoted to major general. Nor were Muhlenberg or Weedon ever promoted. It is assumed this was done because none of these generals would agree to serve under the command of any of the others; they all remained at the same grade.

Once the campaign of 1778 opened, Woodford returned to the army to command his brigade at the Battle of Monmouth in June 1778. Part of his brigade accompanied the advance under General Charles Lee, while the remaining regiments came up with Washington and took a position protecting the artillery on Comb's Hill during the later stages of the battle.

Following Monmouth, Woodford served under Washington's command in the Jersies through the campaigns of 1778 and 1779. By this time, the war had stalemated in the north, and the British had turned their interest and energies to the South. When General Henry Clinton left New York City to attack Charleston, South Carolina, Washington dispatched Woodford with the Virginia Line to Charleston

to assist General Benjamin Lincoln in defense of the city.

Washington considered the Virginia Line to have the best troops in the army. Woodford left the cantonment at Morristown, New Jersey, on December 13, 1779, with about 750 men. Their march south was delayed at Philadelphia for a time, due to bad weather. When Woodford arrived at Fredericksburg, the feud over rank with Weedon was touched off once more. Weedon was requested to help raise troops to fill Woodford's ranks, even if he would not serve under Woodford's command. However, General Scott did agree to serve under Woodford and accompanied him to Charleston.

After a reorganization of the Virginia Line at Fredericksburg and a stop at Petersburg, Woodford set out for South Carolina on March 8. His men proceeded to march 500 miles in the next 29 days in the late winter of 1780 to arrive on April 6 at Charleston. However, the Virginians were unable to gain any advantages for the besieged American army. On May 12, 1780, Lincoln surrendered Charleston and 5,000 men to Clinton. Woodford's entire command became British prisoners.

Woodford was taken to New York City. On November 13, 1780, General William Woodford died in the crowded and dirty encampment the British used to hold American prisoners. He was buried on Old Trinity Church Yard, New York City. He was just over 46 years old.

Paul J. Sanborn

REFERENCES

Nell Moore Lee, *Patriot above Profit* (1988); Benson J. Lossing, *The Pictorial Field Book of the American Revolution*, 2 vols. (1851–1852), rpr. 1972; John Reed, *Valley Forge: Crucible of Victory* (1969); John E. Selby, *The Revolution in Virginia* (1988); John R. Sellers, *The Virginia Continental Line* (1978); Samuel S. Smith, *The Battle of Brandywine* (1976); Harry M. Ward, *Charles Scott* (1988); ———, *Duty, Honor or Country* (1979); ———, *Major General Adam Stephen* (1989); Christopher Ward, *The War of Revolution* (1952).

Wooster, David (1710–1777)

Continental Army officer. Born in Stratford, Connecticut, on March 2, 1710, David Wooster graduated from Yale University in 1732 and shortly thereafter married the daughter of Thomas Clap, Yale's president. From 1732 until 1763 Wooster had a successful military career. He saw service as a captain in a Connecticut regiment in the 1754 Louisbourg expedition, and during the French and Indian War he was promoted to brigadier general. In 1763 he retired from active military service and became collector of customs in New Haven, Connecticut.

When the Revolution began, Wooster was 64 years old. He was still an officer in the Connecticut militia, holding the rank of major general, but by this time in his life he was better known to his fellow militia officers (and to some members of Congress) as a good fellow and storyteller than as a vigorous leader of troops. Instead of granting him a commission in the Continental Army commensurate with his militia rank, the Congress appointed him a brigadier general and ordered him to serve under General Philip Schuyler in the American invasion of Canada. Angered by what he regarded as a demotion, Wooster became bitter and quarrelsome, and as the American army moved down the St. Lawrence to assault Quebec, Wooster was left behind in charge of the Montreal garrison.

Wooster's administration of Montreal was repressive, and he alienated the local population. He took hostages to ensure the compliant behavior of Montreal's residents, and when officers of Canadian militia units refused to surrender their commissions (which they considered to be personal property), Wooster had them arrested and imprisoned. When General Richard Montgomery was killed at Quebec on December 31, 1775, Wooster became the senior officer in Canada, but instead of taking command at Quebec, he remained in the comfort of his Montreal winter quarters. Only in late March, when the weather turned warmer, did he leave Montreal for Quebec, where he spent the next month staging parades and expending much of his scarce artillery ammunition in fruitless bombardments of the Quebec fortress. When General John Thomas relieved Wooster of command at Quebec on May 1, Thomas found the American army sadly demoralized and disintegrating from smallpox and desertions.

After being relieved by Thomas, Wooster faced a court-martial on charges of incompetence, but he was acquitted. He then resumed his role as major general in the Connecticut militia and was given command of a division stationed on the Connecticut—New York border. Wooster was mortally wounded at Ridgefield, Connecticut, in April 1777 while his division was defending the town against British attack. He died May 2, 1777, at Danbury, Connecticut.

John Kramer

REFERENCES

James R. Case, *An Account of Tryon's Raid on Danbury in April, 1777, also the Battle of Ridgefield and the Career of General David Wooster* (1927); Henry C. Deming, *An Oration on the Life and Services of General David Wooster* (1854); Joel T. Headley, *Washington and His Generals*, 2 vols. (1847), 2.

Wrightsborough, Georgia, Quaker Settlement

The settlement of Quakers or members of the Society of Friends was encouraged in the Charter of the Colony of Georgia, June 9, 1932. However, few Quakers came to the province in the early years. In 1768, more than 70 families from the area of Orange County, North Carolina, began settling in a special reserve set aside for them by the Georgia colonial government. The reserve and its town were named Wrightsborough, after Georgia's royal governor, Sir James Wright. Although documents at the time describe these families as all being Quakers, minutes of the Wrightsborough monthly meeting and other records of the Quakers themselves reveal that less than one-fifth of the landholders in this reserve were actually Quakers. Joseph Maddock, leader of the Wrightsborough Quakers, had apparently founded this southernmost settlement of the Society of Friends to escape what he felt was "backsliding" among the North Carolina Friends. However, recognizing the need for a military force to protect the antimilitary Quakers of Wrightsborough, he permitted sympathetic non-Quakers to settle in Wrightsborough. Maddock also succeeded in persuading Wright to erect a fort near the Quakers.

The American Revolution was a particularly trying time for the Georgia Friends. Wrightsborough was the closest settlement in Georgia to the Creek and Cherokee frontier, and in 1773–1774 there were bloody clashes nearby between non-Quakers and the Creek Indians. During the Revolution, Maddock and some of the other Wrightsborough residents actively supported the King's cause. Bandits and rebel partisans committed robberies and murders in Wrightsborough. By May 1781 35 people in the area had been reported as having been killed, 11 in their own beds. Among the worst of the raiders was rebel colonel Josiah Dunn, a former Wrightsborough Quaker who was disowned before the war for horse stealing. Twenty of the Quakers were reported to the Wrightsborough monthly meeting for military activities, mainly for fighting back, and 15 were disowned.

Joseph Maddock was arrested and imprisoned for several months by the rebels in 1779 for having aided Colonel John Boyd in the Kettle Creek campaign. In the autumn of 1781, he and some one-fourth of the Quaker families of Wrightsborough were refugees in British-occupied Savannah, Georgia. When the war was over, Maddock and his followers were allowed to return peacefully to their homes, but he was later disowned by the monthly meeting for refusing to account for money he had improperly solicited to help the Quaker refugees.

Wrightsborough's Quakers were adamantly opposed to slavery, even by the standards of American Quakers, and finally left Georgia for Ohio between 1805 and 1809, over the growing slavery controversy. Wrightsborough survived as a village until the 1920s but is today little more than a wooded field in McDuffie County, Georgia. *See also*: Quakers in the American Revolution

Robert Scott Davis, Jr.

REFERENCE

Robert S. Davis, Jr., *Quaker Records in Georgia: Wrightsborough 1772–1793 and Friendsborough 1776–1777* (1984).

Wyoming Valley Massacre (Pennsylvania) (July 3, 1778)

The so-called Wyoming Valley of Pennsylvania, claimed and settled by Connecticut in the 1750s, is a 25-mile stretch of the Susquehanna below the mouth of the Lackawanna and includes modern Wilkes-Barre. During the 20 years after the arrival of the first pioneers there, Connecticut and Pennsylvania argued bitterly over the ownership of the valley. The Iroquois considered it part of their territory as well. The 3,000 settlers in the area were generally loyal to Connecticut and to the American cause by 1774. That year the Connecticut Assembly created the "township of Westmoreland" in the region. During the same period, Loyalists from western New York also moved into the valley. Minor, although frequent, clashes began to occur; some

of the Loyalists were arrested and sent off to prison in Connecticut. Two forts were built, one by the Loyalist Wintermoot family and the other (Fort Jenkins) by the Patriots. The latter also reinforced seven other blockhouses and posts, including "Forty Fort" (named for the original 40 pioneer families). Tension in the valley was high, and the Patriots lost manpower when 164 of their young men went to join the Continental Army in 1775. The Iroquois had not forgotten their old claim on the valley. It was perhaps inevitable that the Loyalists and Indians would attack.

Still, the valley escaped the direct brunt of the war until the summer of 1778. In January, more Loyalists were arrested, and others fled to New York. In June, a large force of Loyalists and Indians under Colonel John Butler left Fort Niagara, with the intent of devastating the New York and Pennsylvania frontiers and rescuing Loyalist families behind enemy lines. In the raid were over 100 Senecas, anxious for revenge due to their losses at Oriskany. Butler's Rangers, the Royal Greens, and several hundred Indians and Rangers made up this army, usually estimated at 1,100. Joseph Brant, later blamed for the savagery of the Wyoming Valley massacre, was not on the march. The Loyalists marched south by way of Seneca Lake to Tioga, an Indian village on the Susquehanna about 50 miles upstream from the Wyoming settlements. There they rested for several days, making a few forays and building boats. Then the force moved along the river, camping on June 27 and 28. Having heard of their approach, two of the Loyalist Wintermoots brought them 14 head of cattle and promised Butler the use of their fort.

The Patriots, in the meantime. had assembled a force under Captain Detrick Hewett at Forty Fort. About 50 in number, these were untrained volunteers, mainly boys and old men. The settlers called on Colonel Zebulon Butler, a regular army officer home on leave, to take command of the valley's defense. Butler urged all able-bodied men to come to Forty Fort, but most, fearing for their families, remained at blockhouses closer to home. About 300 militia answered the call. An American scouting party killed three of the invaders as they approached the valley, justifying John Butler's later claim that the settlers had fired first.

On July 1, Fort Jenkins and Fort Exeter capitulated, and the Loyalists then set up headquarters at Wintermoot's Fort. There was one minor skirmish, between the Valley militia and a band of Indians who had killed some farmworkers. By the next day, Colonel Zebulon Butler had gathered 368 men at Forty Fort and informed John Butler that he would never surrender "to Tories and savages but stand it out to the last and defend it to the last extremity." On July 3 the militia debated whether to search for the marauders or to wait until the enemy attacked. Pleas for help had been sent to Washington's army, then in New Jersey, but the defenders had no way of knowing whether their messengers had got through or whether reinforcements would be sent. The men at Forty Fort also may have known that Brant's Indians were gathering at Unadilla 80 miles away and that the force now threatening them was a large one. The garrison finally decided to take the offensive, mainly in the hope of protecting their farms and crops from depredation. A patrol discovered that the main Loyalist force was at Wintermoot's Fort. Zebulon Butler assembled his men, hoping to make a surprise attack, but shots were exchanged between the scouts and two Indians, alerting the enemy. In any case, Seneca scouts led by Cornplanter had been watching Forty Fort.

Zebulon Butler immediately deployed for battle among a stand of pine trees and heavy underbrush. He commanded the right, and Colonel Nathan Denison commanded the left. Captain Hewett's men were in the center. Marching toward the fort, they opened fire at 200 yards against a line of Loyalists under Colonel John Butler. At the same time Butler burnt Wintermoot's Fort and Fort Jenkins, to dupe the Americans into thinking he was retreating. Brant's Indians were on his right and the Royal Greens in the center, not yet returning fire. Zebulon Butler assumed that the Loyalists were retreating and advanced rapidly. The Loyalists waited until the Americans had fired three volleys and had advanced about 100 yards. Then the Indians and Greens quickly swept forward and outflanked the Patriots, driving them back to the Susquehanna. Many were tomahawked in the water by the Senecas; St. Jean de Crevecoeur wrote that bloated corpses turned up on the riverbanks for weeks afterward. Captain Hewett was killed, along with two other regular officers and 20 militia officers. The troops scattered, and many were hunted down and killed, but Denison managed to lead about 60 back to Forty Fort. Not until late October were the bodies collected and buried in a mass grave. Colonel Zebulon Butler is believed to have panicked and fled to Fort Wyoming (Wilkes-Barre) with some of the regulars.

A few reinforcements reached Forty Fort that night, but Denison surrendered to John Butler on the morning of July 4. The Wyoming settlers agreed to lay down their arms for the duration of the war, to demolish their forts, and to cease harassment of Loyalists and restore their property. But the Wyoming Valley was left undefended, and during the day and evening of July 4 the Indians and some white Loyalists rampaged through the settlements. Colonel John Butler later reported that 8 forts and 1,000 houses had been destroyed, and over a 1,000 cattle captured, along with sheep and pigs. He had lost only "one Indian, two Rangers and eight Indians wounded." Some noncombatants were murdered, and others were pursued through the forests as far as the Delaware and Wind Gaps, but the savage "massacre" later reported throughout the United States was wildly exaggerated. Typical is the legend of "Queen Esther" Montour, part-French wife of an Iroquois chief, who supposedly tortured and murdered more than two dozen captives. Joseph Brant, supposedly responsible for the massacre, was nowhere near the Wyoming Valley that day, though many of his warriors took part. American propagandists made the most of the "massacre," but the legend was perpetuated primarily by a poem, "Gertrude of Wyoming," written by the Scot Thomas Campbell in 1809. Campbell also mentions palm trees and flamingos in the valley. Whatever the truth, Wyoming became a byword for Tory and Indian cruelty.

Butler's forces remained around Wintermoot's until July 8, when they withdrew suddenly. Evidently the Loyalist commander heard rumors that a large contingent of Americans was on the way. He was at Tioga on July 10, where he wrote a report claiming that no noncombatants had been killed, though 227 scalps had been taken. He then set out for Niagara on July 14. In fact, a battalion of Connecticut troops was on the way, but when they heard about the massacre from refugees, they halted. Zebulon Butler was at the same time gathering troops, but this task took several weeks. Thus it was not until early August that Patriot forces again controlled the valley. The 11th Pennsylvania Regiment under Colonel Thomas Hartley guarded the region until the crops were harvested by the survivors. Colonel Denison, breaking his parole, helped reassemble what was left of the local militia. In September, Hartley and Denison led 130 men up the East Branch of the Susquehanna, destroying a few Indian villages. Although the real culprits were long gone, this expedition did recover a great deal of the booty from the July raid.

Tom Martin

REFERENCES

St. Jean de Crevecoeur, *A Journey into Northern Pennsylvania and in the State of New York* (1801); Barbara Graymont, *The Iroquois in the American Revolution* (1972); Isabel Thompson Kelsey, *Joseph Brant 1743–1807: Man of Two Worlds* (1984); Page Smith, *A New Age Now Begins* (1978); Howard Swiggett, *War Out of Niagara: Walter Butler and the Tory Rangers* (1933).

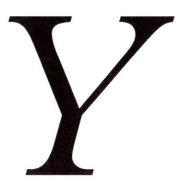

"Yankee Doodle"

Traditional accounts claim that the Revolutionary song "Yankee Doodle" was written in 1758 by Dr. Richard Shuckburgh, an English army officer, to ridicule colonial militia. The British continued this usage during the American Revolution. However, recent research has shown that "Yankee Doodle" is an American folk song reflecting satiric colonial humor and that it originated in the 1740s during King George's War. Although born in England, Shuckburgh, who penned revised lyrics, migrated to the colonies in 1735 and was familiar with American customs.

Stanzas in early versions portray American victories in battles against the French in both King George's War and the French and Indian War. Other versions lampoon social customs such as cornhusking, holidays, and drinking. The Revolutionary versions reveal American provincialism and slang, describing a "country bumpkin's" viewpoint of a colonial military camp. Various lyrics were created to satirize specific groups such as the Sons of Liberty. Edward Bangs is credited for revisions during the Revolution. "Yankee Doodle" emerged as a favorite victory ballad and was played while the British stacked their arms after the Battle of Saratoga. Twelve years later, Paris guards played "Yankee Doodle" after the storming of the Bastille.

Elizabeth D. Schafer

REFERENCES

Sylvia G.L. Dannett, *The Yankee Doodler* (1973); J.A. Leo Lemay, "The American Origins of 'Yankee Doodle,'" *William and Mary Quarterly, 33* (1976):435–465; Frank Moore, *Songs and Ballads of the American Revolution* (1856); Percy A. Scholes, *Oxford Companion to Music*, ed. by John O. Ward (1970); Irwin Silber, ed., *Songs of Independence* (1973).

Yellow Springs Hospital

Before the American Revolution, medical patients were often cared for in the homes of their physicians because hospitals established exclusively for patients were almost nonexistent. When the war began, a variety of buildings and shelters—barns, tents, churches, huts, and private homes—were adapted for use as field hospitals. As a result of these temporary locations, most Revolutionary hospitals tended to be overcrowded and unsanitary, resulting in the deaths of many soldiers, who were more likely to die from improper medical care than in battle.

The Battles of Brandywine and Germantown produced high casualty rates and required the transfer of the wounded to areas on the perimeter of the battlefront. Hospitals were established in Pennsylvania towns, usually in buildings owned by religious orders such as the Moravians and Lutherans. The Valley Forge Medical Department headquarters were located at Yellow Springs, Pennsylvania, to provide care for soldiers encamped at Valley Forge who were chronically ill or whose severe wounds required rehabilitation.

The Yellow Springs Hospital was the only hospital, with the exception of small log cabins built near camps, specifically built to treat and house Continental soldiers. General George Washington ordered the construction of the main building, a three-story hospital named Washington Hall, in 1778.

Located approximately 10 miles west of Valley Forge, Yellow Springs was a well-known health resort with healing natural springs and baths. The hospital was developed on a farm owned by Dr. Samuel Kennedy, who was asked to become a physician there in January 1778. Three barns, already standing, were utilized as hospitals—for surgery and recuperation—in addition to Washington Hall. Kennedy developed a fever while tending the ill and soon died; the army gave his widow $5,000 for use of the property.

Dr. Bodo Otto, director of the medical district, assumed leadership of Yellow Springs Hospital; his three sons assisted him. Yellow Springs, unlike many other Revolutionary hospitals, was able to maintain a clean, healthy atmosphere in which soldiers could recuperate. Chaplain Dr. James Sproat, a frequent visitor, wrote of Yellow Springs: "The Hospitals are well provided for, and the gentlemen take good care of the sick." Sproat often preached to patients and staff who wanted to listen to his inspirational messages.

Neighboring farmers grew food for and distributed clothing and straw (used for bedding) to the patients. They also helped deliver soldiers to assigned hospitals. Yellow Springs could accommodate almost 200 patients at one time. Mortality rates were lower at Yellow Springs than

at other hospitals, mainly due to hygienic conditions.

Several smaller hospitals operated in the area to provide care for less seriously wounded soldiers, and officers at Yellow Springs determined to which of these hospitals each injured soldier was assigned. Efforts to centralize operations resulted in the closing of several of these hospitals. When nearby Lititz Hospital closed in August 1778, the patients were transferred to Yellow Springs.

In the autumn of 1778, an issuing store opened at Yellow Springs Hospital with the purpose of replenishing hospital and regimental medicine chests; Dr. John Brown Cutting oversaw these duties. The commissary depot at Yellow Springs also stockpiled emergency supplies of pharmaceuticals and hospital equipment for neighboring hospitals.

Despite Yellow Spring's role as a storehouse for supplies, its officers continually complained and wrote missives demanding more supplies. The hospital, which treated a substantial number of patients as well as aiding other hospitals, was constantly in need of supplies. Hospital personnel were also dissatisfied. In May 1780 Dr. Otto appealed for economic relief, requesting provisions and money to pay his staff, who threatened to quit because they had not received their full salaries. For the hospital's patients, Dr. Otto sought firewood to provide soothing warmth and straw to cushion their beds. By 1781 Yellow Springs was still in desperate need of crucial supplies and medicines.

In September 1781, as the war front shifted south, a congressional committee and the Board of War decided to close Yellow Springs Hospital, ordering Dr. Otto to send remaining patients to the Bettering House Hospital in Philadelphia, to disperse unused medicine and supplies to functioning hospitals, and to audit his accounts. Dr. Otto moved to Philadelphia, where he performed medical services for several months before being discharged from the Medical Department of the army. Washington Hall burned to the ground in 1902. Yellow Springs, Pennsylvania, is now named Chester Springs.

Elizabeth D. Schafer

REFERENCES

Louis C. Duncan, *Medical Men in the American Revolution* (1931); James E. Gibson, *Dr. Bodo Otto and the Medical Background of the American Revolution*

(1937); Erna Risch, *Quartermaster Support of the Army: A History of the Corps, 1775–1939* (1966); James Tilton, *Economical Observations on Military Hospitals: And the Prevention and Care of Diseases Incident to an Army* (1813); Joseph M. Toner, *Contributions to the Annals of Medical Progress and Medical Education in the United States Before and During the War of Independence* (1874).

Yorktown, Virginia, Campaign (August–October 1781)

This intricate campaign became the decisive American victory in the War of Revolution. Working closely with a French army and two French fleets, Washington and his small Continental Army were able to trap and force the surrender of General Cornwallis's army at Yorktown in Virginia. In a prolonged campaign that depended on so many variables fitting together precisely at the right time in the right way at the right place, historians ever since have tried to explain Yorktown without using phrases such as "as a result of divine providence" or "the miracle of Yorktown."

The story of Yorktown began in May 1780 when two crucial events occurred that would later come together to guarantee American freedom. First, arriving from New York, General Henry Clinton gained the surrender of General Benjamin Lincoln's 4,500-man American army at Charleston, South Carolina. Second, a powerful expeditionary force under the command of General the Comte de Rochambeau set sail from France for America.

Clinton returned to New York, leaving behind General Lord Cornwallis to safeguard British control of the Carolinas and Georgia. When the 10,000 soldiers that he requested arrived from England, Clinton would again go on the offensive. Until then, he stayed in New York. Clinton was a 51-year-old, shy, small, and paunchy man. Quarrelsome, vacillating, and cautious, he served in America for the entire war until 1782. He was dependable but not creative. He played the violin at social gatherings and had an Irish housekeeper as his mistress. He was intelligent and knew the value of sea power and its role in the war. But he became his own worst enemy.

Clinton spoke German, hosted expensive parties, and changed his headquarters frequently among four houses and a farm to avoid being captured. He led simulated fox chases through the streets of New York. Sometimes, however,

he would shut himself off in his room for three or four days at a time. He had difficulty getting along with his peers but was admired by younger officers.

By comparison, where Cornwallis was aggressive and decisive, Clinton was not. Where Clinton wished to conduct a defensive war, Cornwallis did not. Cornwallis was ambitious, aggressive, and capable. A member of the House of Lords, Cornwallis was an American sympathizer who still felt it his duty to fight against the Patriots for the King when asked. He was also brave, confident, and obstinate, especially when dealing with Clinton.

Cornwallis and Clinton mistrusted each other, and both had requested permission to return to England. Cornwallis held a pocket commission that would have allowed him to command in Clinton's place. This tactic insured that no German general would command in North America.

Cornwallis was 42 years old in 1781. Educated at Eton, he was heavyset, tall, and erect; he was respected by both his enemies and his own men. Cornwallis led his army as if it were his family, with him as the father. According to some, he was too lenient and too permissive to be effective, but his men loved him and followed him to the end. He was also vindictive and lacked a sense of humor.

After his defeat of Horatio Gates at Camden in August 1780, Cornwallis was allowed to comunicate directly with Lord Germain in London behind Clinton's back. This developed a triangular relationship that seriously hurt the British cause by destroying any unity of command. Clinton, suspicious and jealous, became more secretive and remained paralyzed behind his New York defenses with his garrison.

Cornwallis proceeded to achieve some success in North Carolina and gain the devotion of Lord Germain who felt he had finally found a general who was willing to take the offensive and gain British goals with the resources at hand. Yet in the final analysis, it was Cornwallis's victories that eventually led him to his final defeat at Yorktown. Each step forward seemed to bring him two steps back in the quest for final victory. But the tenacious Cornwallis would not give up.

An example of his tenacity was the Battle of Guilford Court House (March 1781). Cornwallis and Nathanael Greene fought a fierce battle that resulted in a British victory with 25 percent British casualties. Even though Cornwallis had won, he could not destroy Greene's army and was forced to refit at Wilmington, North Carolina. At that point, Cornwallis felt he had three choices: to return to Charleston by ship, to march back after Greene, who was now attacking British outposts in the Carolinas following his loss at Guilford, or to seize the initiative and invade Virginia.

Cornwallis saw Virginia as the head and heart of the southern American military effort. With Virginia pacified, the Carolinas and Georgia were safe. Clinton had expressly ordered him not to invade Virginia. But Lord George Germain was on Corn-wallis's side. The move of the greatest risk and greatest return was chosen. The British left Wilmington on April 25, 1781, and marched for Virginia. The very same day, Greene was defeated at Hobkirk's Hill, near Camden, South Carolina, by Lord Francis Rawdon. Learning of Rawdon's success, Cornwallis felt vindicated in his decision to go north.

Cornwallis had only 1,435 men fit for duty. It was his goal to join with General William Phillips, General John Burgoyne's old artillery chief, and his large British force, which had been raiding Virginia. Cornwallis arrived in Petersburg on May 20 and found Benedict Arnold in command. General William Phillips had died several days earlier of a fever. The total British force in Virginia now amounted to roughly 7,000 men. With these men, Cornwallis decided to strike into the heart of Virginia. He sent Clinton word, knowing that a full month would pass before a reply could arrive.

Cornwallis unleashed a total war (in eighteenth-century fashion) on Virginia. He no longer tried to bring Loyalists into British service. His sole goal was to take Virginia out of the war. The Americans had sent General Friedrich von Steuben and the Marquis de Lafayette to stop Phillips's and Arnold's raids. As Cornwallis moved out of Petersburg, Lafayette retreated to Ely's Ford on the Rapidan River, where he was joined by General Anthony Wayne and his Pennsylvanians. But this combined force was still too weak to stop Cornwallis. Cornwallis followed the Americans to the North Anna River and then veered off to accomplish his mission.

Allowing his men to plunder and loot, almost at will, Cornwallis confiscated as many horses as he could locate. He mounted over 600 men and had them ride through Virginia terrorizing the people and keeping both Lafayette and the militia out of the British way. Lafayette had to maintain a 20-mile distance between his forces and Cornwallis's at all times or risk the danger of being destroyed. Cornwallis used boats and the river systems to gain entry to the interior of the state and to maneuver rapidly. He freed an estimated 30,000 slaves in the state, many of whom followed behind his army.

His own men loved him, the Americans hated him, and the Virginia politicians were talking of peace with the British. Lafayette was powerless to stop him. The militia would not come out and refused to leave their homes undefended. It was at that point that General Clinton stepped in to save the day for the Americans.

After almost a month of successful raiding, Cornwallis marched his men to Williamsburg, followed carefully by Lafayette's force. There he received a series of contradictory letters from Clinton that ordered Cornwallis to move to the coast, to establish a base, and to send whatever troops he could spare to New York. Clinton felt himself besieged in the city and needed reinforcements.

Cornwallis went to Portsmith and found it unsuitable. Old Point Comfort was also determined inadequate. Meanwhile, Clinton ordered Cornwallis to send his troops to New York, then Philadelphia, then New York, and finally, to keep them in Virginia. Cornwallis was frustrated and had grown weary of fighting against both the enemy and Clinton simultaneously. The stress began to affect his military decisions.

On July 20, Clinton ordered Cornwallis to establish a deep-water port for future British operations in the Chesapeake Bay area. Clinton was sure that the real target of the French and Americans was New York and not Cornwallis. Although he disagreed with Clinton's policy, Cornwallis did move his force to occupy Yorktown and Gloucester Point on the York River in Virginia. In early August, the first troops began to arrive at Yorktown, and by August 22, Cornwallis's full force was present. Clinton gave the move his tacit approval by not voicing any objections.

Cornwallis's force was fortified slowly for a number of reasons. The British navy controlled the Atlantic and the Chesapeake. Cornwallis felt his troops were superior to those of the enemy and did not require extensive protection. If help was needed, it was nearby. In the high heat,

Cornwallis did not wish to fatigue his men needlessly. And it was not yet determined how long the men would stay there. Clinton might change his mind again or winter quarters might be chosen elsewhere. Finally, the Americans under Lafayette had no heavy artillery to properly conduct a siege.

When Rochambeau and his 5,000 men arrived at Newport in July 1780, he found the American cause nearly collapsed. There were no combined successes in which to take pride. The nation was weary of war. Many were more than ready to reach some sort of accommodation with the British. The American currency was worthless, and finances were collapsing. The Americans could raise no credit, obtain no supplies, and had few troops to fill the ranks of their regular line regiments. The South had almost completely fallen to the British, and Virginia was soon to be ravaged. There had already been a huge expenditure of funds, resources, and manpower on the part of France. The troops had mutinied and would again soon. Yet the war continued.

Rochambeau had selected his four regiments with care. The Bourbonnais, Sientonge, and Soisonnais were composed primarily of Frenchmen. The Royal-Deux-Ponts Regiment was a German regiment. In addition to these four line regiments, the Duc de Lauzun's legion came, along with the artillery. This French force arrived in Newport on May 2, 1780. Each regiment selected its best 500 men for each of two battalions sent to America, 1,000 men per regiment. The French expeditionary force was made up of men who tended to be in their mid-20s, serving their first eight-year enlistment term. Most of them had never fought. Almost 33 percent of the total force was Swiss and German. They came from the cities and farms alike, and especially from the provinces of Alsace and Lorraine.

Their uniforms were white except for the celestial blue coats with yellow facings of the Royal-Deux-Ponts. They each carried a 60-pound load and an excellent Charleville musket, model 1777. (One of the best of its type, the Charleville model was later copied by the United States.) The French fought in three ranks, with the third rank passing their loaded muskets to the front with the first two ranks firing. They wore their hair long, tied in the back with a ribbon, and had a long curl hanging down in front of each ear.

They were well-drilled and disciplined.

Upon entering the army, many soldiers took a nom de guerre so that names such as "Ladykiller," "Skipalong," "Ready-to-Drink" and "No Quarter" appeared on the muster rolls. They fought a war that was formally conducted according to rules commonly accepted throughout Europe. Many of the officers were of the nobility. The officers brought their servants, sometimes in great numbers. The generals and staff officers often brought along family as well. Rochambeau had his son and a nephew in the force. The second in command, the Baron de Viomenil, had his brother, a son, a cousin, a son-in-law, and two nephews with him. The army was complete with 100 doctors, pharmacists, dentists, an executioner, and two corporals expert in the administration of the lash.

In May 1781, Rochambeau received word that a French fleet would soon sail for the West Indies with orders to cooperate with the French army in America. Rochambeau called for a conference with Washington. They met at Wethersfield, Connecticut, in late May 1781. Rochambeau was a calm, deliberate man who fit in well with Washington. Both men were aloof, gracious, and never familiar. Rochambeau was 55 years old, six years older than Washington. The French commander was short and stocky, walked with a slight limp, and had 38 years of military service. Washington was frank, dignified, tall, and graying. He was polite yet reserved. Rochambeau made it clear from the start that the French role in the war was that of the auxiliary, subordinate to the orders of the American commander. The two generals worked closely together throughout the Yorktown campaign.

In the conference, Washington suggested New York as the primary allied target. Rochambeau suggested the southern theater also be considered. Rochambeau knew that the British could be struck only in two places, New York and the Chesapeake. He doubted an allied move on New York could be successful. He did not yet know what Phillips and Arnold's force in Virginia would do. From May 20 to 23, during the Wethersfield Conference, Cornwallis was just arriving in Petersburg to join Arnold's men.

Since Clinton's force in New York had been thinned by detachments to other British posts, Washington was fixated on destroying British control in that city. He felt it would deal a deathblow to the English in North America. Washington considered a southern mission as secondary. He had fears that the southern climate would decimate both armies with sickness. It was agreed that the French and American armies would join for combined operations in the New York area while they waited for news from de Grasse.

Rochambeau returned to Newport and wrote Admiral Comte de Grasse about the American situation and the need for his 26 ships of the line in the Chesapeake. The distress of Virginia was described in particular. Rochambeau also asked that de Grasse borrow Saint-Simon's troops from San Domingo. Hard currency was also needed. Rochambeau placed this letter and other dispatches aboard the frigate *Concorde* and sent it to the West Indies. Rochambeau also reached an an understanding with Admiral de Barras, commander of the French fleet in Newport, for cooperation in future operations with the Americans and de Grasse.

De Grasse left Brest on March 26, 1781, and sailed for the West Indies, arriving in late April. Coming to Cap Francois, he ran into the *Concorde* with Rochambeau's dispatches, on July 26. Upon reading these letters, de Grasse decided to sail for the Chesapeake and sent the *Concorde* back to Rochambeau with that news. De Grasse would leave the West Indies August 14 and was available only until the middle of October when he had to return to his former station. De Grasse was afraid of New York harbor and felt the Chesapeake might offer more advantages for the allied cause.

Meanwhile, word arrived from Lafayette that Cornwallis had arrived in Virginia. More bad news came. On June 3, General Clinton had intercepted Washington's dispatches to Congress describing the results of the Wethersfield Conference. Now his nightmares would come true. From that time on, Clinton believed that the allied goal was New York. He became more determined to hold out. After all, if he left the city, the rebels could burn it to the ground behind him. Clinton was also shocked to learn that Cornwallis had left the Carolinas and was in Virginia.

Washington was embarrassed about the capture of the dispatches. There is every reason to believe they were genuine and not falsified to deceive Clinton. In any event, Clinton believed what he read.

The French left Newport on June 10 with approximately 3,500 effectives. They made an impressive sight as they marched. The French custom was to march at dawn and halt at noon, covering an average of 10 to 15 miles a day. They covered 220 miles in 11 days. Their woolen uniforms made the heat unbearable, and therefore they never marched past midday.

As the French neared the Americans, General Benjamin Lincoln with 800 men probed from Peekskill to King's Bridge and tested the British defenses on northern Manhattan Island. Riding out ahead of the French column, Lauzun's Legion was to have cooperated with Lincoln, but the British were alerted and the mission was canceled. The French army arrived at Philipsburg near White Plains on July 6, 1781, to join with the Americans, the same day that Lafayette and Cornwallis fought at Green Spring in Virginia.

In the next few weeks, several reconnaissances-in-force were performed by Washington and Rochambeau to identify possible approaches to New York. These moves did two things. They convinced Clinton of a coming attack against his base, a plan that both Washington and Rochambeau were coming to view as impractical. Without a fleet and more strength, formal siege operations were out of the question.

The second effect was that Clinton ignored Germain's orders to march through the Jersies, to take Philadelphia, and to move into Maryland to link up with Cornwallis and subjugate the southern colonies. Instead he sent Cornwallis to the coast at the moment of his success in Virginia and ordered that troops be returned to New York. Clinton was frozen in place, upsetting Germain's grand design of victory by his lethargy.

On the allied side, the two commanders wisely kept both armies apart. The French army camped, marched, and fought on the American left, since the Americans were the "principals" in this war. The Americans occupied the position of honor on the right to the very end. Each day's sign and countersign were determined by the Americans. It was thought best not to mix the two armies, lest traditional animosities and lack of a common language lead to unnecessary problems.

In their few encounters with the Americans, however, the French found that the Americans marched well enough, did the manual of arms badly, had some good men but many children along with old men in their ranks. Many soldiers were sickly and frail. They had no uniforms to speak of but were dressed in rags and unmatched clothing. Many had no shoes. The Americans carried a light load of 40 pounds and used whatever weapons they could obtain. The French were especially surprised by the bitterness, even hatred, that poisoned the relations between the British and Americans. The French valued a professional air with coolness and less emotion in battle. A revealing difference between the French and American armies was seen in fording a stream. The Americans plowed right through the water. The French stopped, removed their shoes and stockings and crossed, stopping on the other side to replace the footwear.

During that summer, thousands of men in and around New York waited in place for something to happen to break the stalemate. The spell broke on August 14. The message arrived from de Grasse, and within 60 days, Cornwallis and his entire force were captured. A great allied victory was achieved. Rochambeau had felt all along more could be achieved in the South than in New York. When General Le Beque Duportail, the engineer in charge, submitted his report on July 26 that Manhattan could only be attacked by 20,000 men at its center so that the allies would face the enemy on two fronts, Washington himself began favoring the South.

The electrifying news that de Grasse was coming to the Chesapeake Bay with 29 ships of the line and 3,000 fresh troops under Saint-Simon spurred the allies into action. De Grasse also promised money, some of which was donated by the citizens of Havana, Cuba. He would remain until mid-October and then return to the West Indies. It was a great gamble, perhaps the most difficult one taken by an allied officer during the war. De Grasse would bring his entire fleet, leaving the West Indies totally open to British attack.

Washington prevailed upon the northern troops of his army to march to the South. General William Heath was left behind in the Hudson Highlands with 3,000 men to watch the inert Clinton. Washington took 2,500 men, and Rochambeau had 4,000. On August 19, a total force of some 8,800 men began their march of 450 miles for Virginia. Lafayette had sent word that Cornwallis was digging in at Yorktown. To that place the allies would march and join with de Grasse to begin the siege.

The allied armies crossed the Hudson at King's Ferry and moved along the Jersey coast to Chatham to fool Clinton. This campaign was the first and only substantial combined allied offensive of the war. It was also the first and almost only time during the war that the Americans would have temporary control of the nearby sea and not be bound by land.

Clinton depended on Admiral George Rodney in the West Indies to control de Grasse's fleet. Rodney was involved in the capture of the Dutch Island of St. Eustatius and left de Grasse to Admiral Samuel Hood. Hood was an effective admiral, but he and Rodney both failed to allow for the gamble that de Grasse was willing to take by sailing the entire French fleet north into the Chesapeake. In addition, Rodney in his old age of 62 years suffered from the gout and prostate troubles that sent him back to England. Rodney left for home August 1 totally preoccupied with his health and wealth. Hood went after de Grasse with 14 ships of the line.

Rodney should not be seen as a complete fool, however, since the next year, he returned to the West Indies and defeated de Grasse in the Battle of the Saintes, capturing de Grasse and his flagship, the *Ville de Paris*. This naval victory allowed the British public and Parliament to accept gracefully the peace treaty that ended the war.

Rodney knew what de Grasse had in mind and sent the *Swallow* to warn Clinton. The *Swallow* was captured by the Americans. Clinton also had a new admiral to deal with in New York. Admiral Samuel Graves had arrived July 4 to replace the ancient Admiral Marriott Arbuthnot as fleet commander. Graves turned out to be a slight improvement over his predecessor.

De Grasse took the dangerous Bahama Channels, where no French fleet had gone before, to hide from the English. Along the way, de Grasse captured the *Sandwich* (40 guns) with Lord Francis Rawdon, Cornwallis's southern commander, on board. The French arrived in the Chesapeake to find it empty and immediately began landing Saint-Simon's three regiments.

Hood, following Rodney's advice, sailed north to the Chesapeake by the direct route and arrived ahead of de Grasse to find the bay empty. Hood sailed onto New York with his 14 ships of the line, arriving August 28. Graves, who took overall command, decided to sally forth from New York back to the Chesapeake in search of the French. Graves added six ships of the line to

Hood's 14. However, some of the British ships were in poor condition.

On September 5, the British found the French fleet in the bay. With the wind advantage and a golden opportunity to destroy the French fleet as it came out of the bay one ship at a time, Graves graciously allowed the French free passage and then proceeded to fight an inclusive, poorly directed action with de Grasse.

The Battle of the Capes on September 5, 1781, was the pivotal point in the Yorktown campaign. Graves, without losing a ship or the battle, fought de Grasse and then returned to New York to refit, thus losing the war for England. Cornwallis's fate was sealed when Graves disappeared on September 14. The French fleet resumed its position in Chesapeake Bay.

Admiral Hood was livid over Graves's conduct. To add to the damage, Admiral de Barras had slipped out of Newport, while de Grasse sailed north. During the Battle of the Capes, Barras sailed into the Chesapeake untouched with the heavy artillery and more reinforcements for the French army. Now the French had 36 ships of the line against Cornwallis.

Meanwhile, Washington and Rochambeau had their men marching through the Jerseys on the way to Virginia. Ovens were built and supply depots were established to fool Clinton into thinking the allies would attack Staten Island. Fake campfires were lit, boats were collected, and false intelligence was allowed to fall into British hands. All this diverted Clinton's attention from Virginia. Although he later claimed he was not fooled, Clinton did not see fit to warn Cornwallis that the combined armies were headed his way until September 2. By that time, Washington was in Philadelphia, and Clinton was toying with plans to invade Rhode Island.

Both armies marched through the American capital city on their way south. The French made a grand impression with their drill and uniforms. Then the march continued south, with the French now averaging 18 miles a day by moving at night to avoid the heat of the day.

Washington knew on August 17 that the American army had to be paid at least a month's salary in hard currency on their march south, lest they not continue and mutiny instead. Washington wrote to Robert Morris, the American Superintendent of Finance, who was unable to come up with the money. To save the day, Rochambeau lent Morris $20,000, which

amounted to half the money in the French war chest. This currency was then paid to the American line at Head of Elk, Maryland.

At Head of Elk, some of the men were placed on boats and sailed to the staging area in Virginia. Others had to march overland to Baltimore where Admiral de Barras's boats picked them up. Some had to march the entire way. On September 5, Rochambeau and his staff left Philadelphia and took a boat ride down the Delaware River to see the forts of 1777. When they were approaching the dock at Chester, they saw a man jumping up and down in great excitement waving his hat with one hand and a white handkerchief with the other. It turned out to be Washington, who had finally received word that de Grasse was in the Chesapeake. They had Cornwallis trapped at Yorktown. Rochambeau and Washington hugged each other warmly on the dock. They then made their way south. Washington moved so quickly that no one but two aides could keep up with him. He rode 60 miles in one day to reach Mount Vernon, which he saw for the first time in six years.

Rochambeau was Washington's guest at Mount Vernon from September 9 through 12. On September 14, Washington and Rochambeau rode into Williamsburg to receive a warm greeting from Lafayette. The generals found Saint-Simon's force there and inspected his three regiments, the Agenois, the Gatenois, and the Touraine. Washington made his headquarters at the Wythe house, while Rochambeau housed himself and his staff at the Widow Randolph's.

Constant worries beset Washington trying to coordinate the operation. De Grasse had disappeared into the Atlantic on September 5 and had not returned until September 14. De Barras arrived September 10. De Barras's transports were sent north to bring the infantry down from Baltimore, and they finally arrived between September 25 and 27 on James Town Island. De Barras had brought vital supplies for the siege and also the siege artillery. Would Cornwallis try to break out? Where was the British fleet? Could this plan really succeed?

The allies had massed 16,000 men and two naval squadrons in the Chesapeake against Cornwallis's southern army. It was a true tour de force but a logistical nightmare with shortages of boats, carts, oxen, and horses. It was then that Cornwallis could have cut his way out. Between September 17 and 26, he had the chance to break out past Lafayette and Saint-Simon. His scouts had located the best way, by a frontal attack on Williamsburg and then a move west. But on September 14, a letter from General Clinton reached Cornwallis assuring him he had nothing to worry about and that help would be on the way. Cornwallis sat back and lost his last chance, however slim it may have been, to escape by land. Now it was up to Clinton.

Washington, Rochambeau, Henry Knox, du Portail and the Chevalier de Chastellux went by sea on September 17 to meet with de Grasse on his ship the *Ville de Paris*, the largest battleship afloat at the time. The French fleet was anchored in Lynnhaven Bay at the mouth of the Chesapeake. Upon encountering Washington for the first time, de Grasse embraced him fully and called him "My dear small general." The two tall men made quite a sight on the deck, with Washington at six feet, three inches and de Grasse his equal in height.

The army officers persuaded de Grasse to wait until the end of October before leaving for the West Indies. They also obtained material help from him for conducting the siege and had the chance to discuss the upcoming operation in detail, meshing naval and army concerns into a working plan. De Grasse offered 1,800 men from the fleet to the army if they wished to take the town with an assault rather than conduct a siege. The offer was turned down. It took three days for Washington and the others to fight the winds back upriver. They returned to Williamsburg on September 22.

Yorktown had been established by the Virginia Assembly in 1691 on a 35–foot marl bluff overlooking the York River. At Yorktown, the York River shrank to a half-mile in width with Gloucester Point on the other shore. There were 300 houses and approximately 2,500 inhabitants in the bi-level town when the British arrived. Yorktown was a tobacco port with docks on the beach and the major houses and businesses on the bluff. It was already in decline when the war arrived.

In and around Yorktown, Cornwallis had the brigade of guards under General Charles O'Hara (500 men), the 23rd, 33rd, and 71st regiments (670 men). Banastre Tarleton's legion, some light infantry companies, the North Carolina Volunteers under Lieutenant Colonel Hamilton, and the German von Bose Regiment under Major O'Reilly were present. In addition, Cornwallis

commanded the 17th, 43rd, 76th, and 80th regiments (1,600 men) and the Queens's Rangers (248 men). There were two Ansbach regiments (950 men), a Hessian regiment, and Captain Johann Ewald's jaegers (550 men). There were also 200 artillerymen and 800 marines along with other supernumeraries such as the pioneers and naval detachments. Including naval personnel on the British ships at anchor, Cornwallis had almost 9,700 men under his command.

When the siege began, Cornwallis had built a fortified position that included Gloucester Point with 4 redoubts and 19 guns in 3 batteries. At Yorktown, there was an inner line with strong redoubts, some fraise work and abatis protecting the trenches, and 65 guns in 14 batteries. On the outer lines, there were three main redoubts with a redan that commanded the main roads into Yorktown. These outer works were protected with strong abatis and cleared fields of fire. The outer lines also included the fusilier redoubt on the far right and Redoubts #9 and #10 on the left. The outer works dominated ground locally known as Pigeon Quarter.

The French numbered 9,500 men. The Americans had 3,500 regular line and 2,000 militia. The French fleet contained well over 20,000 men. It was a small affair according to European standards. Rochambeau was entering into his 15th siege. A siege was an art form that approached the exactitude of a science. The principles of siege warfare had been developed by Vauban and were meticulously followed ever since by the French and other European armies. As a side note, Vauban's grandnephew was present at the Yorktown siege as a French aide.

The siege became a matter of mathematics. The constant was de Grasse's departure date of November 1. How much earth could be moved and how fast? How many guns were available? How many troops would participate in the siege? The answers to these questions would determine the answer to whether the siege would be a success.

It was soon determined that there would be no time for a starvation siege. Cornwallis must be forced to surrender. The ratio of troops favored the allies two to one. The guns favored the allies. There were 4,000 picks and shovels along with whatever Washington could gather from Virginia. The soil was sandy and loose. That was good. Digging could proceed quickly and easily. But it was also bad, since the sandy soil did not pack well. That meant gabions, fascines, and *saucissons* had to be made by the troops. Fascines, bundles of sticks, could be made at two per hour per soldier. *Saucissons*, or sandbags, could be sewn together at 30 feet per day. Gabions, baskets filled with dirt, could be made only one per day per soldier. These objects would strengthen the works and afford protection for the troops.

Cornwallis then did the allies a big favor by evacuating his outer works on September 30 without a contest. That meant that only two parallels of trenches would have to be dug instead of three. That would definitely save time. Cornwallis had received Clinton's promise that 5,000 men were coming to his rescue by October 5. Cornwallis wished to save the lives of his men and reduce the area of defense, since he had too few men to cover such a large area. With this final development, the trench engineers reported to Washington that the siege would be successful before November 1.

On September 28, 1781, the allied armies left Williamsburg for Yorktown, some 12 miles off. This was the first step in a formal siege—the grand approach. Although the march began at 5 A.M., the heat was high, and some 800 Frenchmen dropped out of the march along the way. The British did not harass the allies in their march, and the allies soon arrived before the British lines. The French moved off to the left and the Americans to the right, as was suitable to the role the French were playing in this drama

September 29 was spent in skirmishing, and then on September 30, Lieutenant Cornwallis abandoned his outer works as already noted above. That day, Tarleton sent out a patrol under Lieutenant Cameron to harass any enemy found in the works, and they ran into a party of Americans under the command of Lieutenant Colonel Alexander Scammell, commander of a unit of American light infantry. In the fray Scammell surrendered and, according to some witnesses, was wounded in the side afterward. He was taken into British lines and later released on parole by Cornwallis. Taken to Williamsburg, he died October 6. His death was mourned by many, particularly in the light infantry, where he had served with honor, and in Washington's staff, where he had been adjutant general.

Cornwallis had at least 2,000 of his men sick with the numbers growing each day. His troops were crowded into a small space along the river.

His cavalry horses had no forage. His ships were trapped, unable to move. Washington and Rochambeau waited for the artillery to move up from the beach before opening the siege lines. The guns were up by October 6, but rain that night postponed the digging.

On the night of October 7, the second stage of the siege began with the opening of the trench. Since the approach to the British right was swampy and broken by Yorktown Creek, it was decided to concentrate the approaches on the British left or American side of the lines. The two parallels were dug there. Artillery positions and some French troops were positioned to cover the British right, however, to guard against a British escape by that route and to harass the British shipping in the river below.

The first parallel was started in perfect silence. Washington took a few ceremonial digs at the dirt with a pick, and then the sappers and troops moved in to continue the work. Fifteen hundred men dug while 3,000 stood guard over them in the dark. The work kept up day and night without a break. The work parties were rotated regularly. A 2,000–yard line was constructed of trenches, redoubts, and gun emplacements. Rapid progress was made with little interference from British fire. Lookouts were posted to call the shots, providing some warning for falling British shells.

The first parallel included the British outer works that Cornwallis had given up without a fight. This move had surprised both Washington and Rochambeau. Such a gift was not the sign of a determined commander who would fight to the death.

Sergeant Joseph Plumb Martin, now a sapper with the American army, wrote of a British bulldog who charged out of the British lines each time a gun would fire and chased the ball toward the American lines. Several Americans wished to send a message back with the dog but were afraid of it due to its large size.

When the trenches in the first parallel were completed, the troops marched in to take possession in another formal siege ceremony. Lafayette's light infantry was the first American unit to occupy the trenches, and it entered with flags flying and music playing. The flag was placed on the parapet. The infantry had followed the covered way and took no loss in coming into the front lines. Colonel Alexander Hamilton ordered his light infantry to mount the parapet, face the enemy, and go through the manual of arms. The British, perhaps stunned at this action, stopped firing their artillery until the light infantry completed their drill. No loss of life occurred in this act of questionable wisdom.

On October 9, the first guns were in place. At 3 P.M. the French fired on the fusiliers' redoubt on the right, and Washington fired off the first American shot on the left. The French also fired off hot shot at the British ships in the York River and eventually hit and burned a frigate, the *Charon*, to the waterline. Soon more heavy guns were firing at the British relentlessly.

Then the second parallel was opened with zigzag trenches running from the first to the second lines to protect the men advancing to dig. During the night, parties of both armies met in the no-man's land between the lines to skirmish, but otherwise, only the constant booming of the guns continued hour after hour. The digging and firing never ceased.

Von Steuben's division, with General Anthony Wayne's Pennsylvanians, opened the second parallel for the Americans. During their tour of duty, lasting 24 hours, it so happened that von Steuben and Wayne, limping from a thigh wound, were caught by a falling British shell. As the fuse fizzled, von Steuben jumped for cover with Wayne right on top of him. After the shell burst, von Steuben rose, dusted himself off, and complimented Wayne on his quick action in covering his general's retreat.

On September 10 the grand French battery opened up on Cornwallis with 14 guns. By the next day, 52 guns were emplaced and firing on the British. On Friday, October 12, "Secretary" Thomas Nelson, the uncle of Governor Thomas Nelson of Virginia, came from British lines under a flag from Cornwallis. He told the Americans that their fire was having great effect on the enemy. Cornwallis had been forced from his headquarters and was working out of a cave down by the river. By this time, the allied lines reached to within 350 yards of the British inner lines.

Progress was made in other areas of the siege as well. Admiral de Grasse complained about the sickness of his crews, the difficulty of getting provisions and firewood for his ships, and problems with the army always asking for more materials. These matters were smoothed over. De Grasse was also persuaded to stay in the bay and not sally forth into the Atlantic to fight the British, who might have arrived at any time. De Grasse was worried over Admiral Robert Digby's arrival in New York, but Digby brought only three ships.

On Gloucester Point, General de Choisy was placed in command of allied forces—Weedon's Virginia militia, Lauzun's legion, and the North Carolina volunteers. The British had 1,000 men on the point opposing the allied 2,600. On October 3, Tarleton and his men went out of lines foraging and were caught by Lauzun's cavalry. A fight broke out, and the British were forced back into their lines, never to venture out again during the siege.

By October 14, the second parallel had reached a point where the two British works known as Redoubts #9 and #10 stood in the way of its completion. Washington determined that they had to be taken. The French grenadiers and light infantry, 400 strong, took Redoubt #9 while the American light infantry under Colonel Alexander Hamilton, also 400 men, seized Redoubt #10.

Both points were attacked simultaneously at 8 P.M. on the signal of six cannon firing from the French lines in a special cadence. At square-shaped Redoubt #10, the Americans quickly overpowered Major James Campbell of the 71st and his 70 men by jumping over the fraise work and abatis. The Americans lost 9 killed and 31 wounded. They used just the bayonet. It took 10 minutes and gained them 17 prisoners and 8 enemy dead. The rest ran for their lives.

Lieutenant Colonel Johnson of the 17th put up a stronger fight in star-shaped Redoubt #9. This was mainly due to the French insistence on proper form. They waited for the sappers to cut through the obstacles before advancing on the 150 British and Germans in Redoubt #9. The French lost 15 killed and 77 wounded. They captured 73 prisoners and killed 18 in return. Many others were wounded. The forlorn hopes of both parties survived the attacks. Jean-Joseph Gimat, John Laurens, and Major Fish of New York assisted Hamilton in his work.

Lafayette, in the emotion of the moment, offered his fellow Frenchmen assistance if they needed it in getting into their redoubt, since there seemed to be some holdup in their assault. The next day, Lafayette was visited by the leader of the French assault and informed his humor was not appreciated in the least. Of course, the French should never have stated that these two points could only be taken by the able French line.

Washington was gravely concerned for the welfare of his men and stood on the parapet to watch the attack on the two redoubts. When Colonel Cobb, concerned that Washington not be killed, inquired for his safety, Washington replied "Colonel Cobb, if you are afraid, you have the liberty to step back." Wherever the action was, Washington was there throughout the war. This siege, the last great event, was no exception.

In spite of heavy rains that night, sappers and miners immediately went into both redoubts and converted them into parts of the second parallel while other troops guarded against a British counterattack. It never came. Cornwallis conducted a surprisingly passive defense throughout the Yorktown campaign that perhaps signified his disgust and discouragement over Clinton's policies or, perhaps, his complete faith in Clinton and Graves to come to his rescue. Shortly, two howitzers were firing from each redoubt.

By daylight on October 15, it was clear that Clinton could never reach Cornwallis in time to free him. The American cannon could now enfilade the British lines. More and more British cannon fell silent, out of rounds or destroyed. American surgeon James Thacher related in his journal how he more than once saw fragments of mangled bodies and limbs of British soldiers thrown into the air by the bursting of the American shells. The second parallel was now completed.

On the morning of October 16, before dawn, Cornwallis sent 350 light infantry under Lieutenant Colonel Robert Abercrombie to assault the allied lines where the French and American armies joined. The British spiked six of the cannon with their bayonets and killed some French, causing some confusion in the lines before being pushed back, with the loss of 8 killed and 12 captured. Within a few hours, the cannon were firing once more, and the damage, for the most part, was undone. This was Cornwallis's *baroud d'honneur*, the gesture a warrior makes before laying down his arms and another part of the formal siege warfare.

During October 16, Colonel Hamilton and General Knox were in Redoubt #10 debating the wisdom of having a soldier on the parapet calling the shots. Hamilton thought it cowardly

and Knox felt it saved lives. If a shell was coming, the men could take cover. Just as the discussion warmed up, the cry for a shell was heard. Two landed in the redoubt. Knox went for the blinds—hogsheads or pipes filled with dirt for protection. Hamilton went right with him and got behind Knox for additional cushioning. Knox threw him off, but he climbed right back. The shells exploded. No one was hurt. As the 280–pound Knox dusted himself off, he turned to Hamilton and said, "Now what do you think about crying out 'shell' and don't use me for a breastwork again!"

The night, October 16, Cornwallis assembled all the boats he could muster and tried to ferry his troops across the York River to Gloucester Point. From there, the British might fight their way clear and march north. The first wave made it safely across, but a windstorm came up as the second wave embarked, and the mission had to be canceled. The first-wave troops were brought back to town after the storm died down. It was Cornwallis's last trick, stopped by an act of nature.

At 10 A.M. the next morning, October 17, a drummer boy appeared on the British works and beat the parley. An officer appeared and was taken into the allied lines blindfolded. Cornwallis asked for a 24–hour truce to discuss surrender. Washington gave him two hours. Cornwallis agreed and wrote out suggested surrender terms. Washington agreed to most and changed a few. On October 18, two allied commissioners, Colonel John Laurens and Viscount de Noailles, Lafayette's brother-in-law, met at the Moore house with two British commissioners, Colonel Thomas Dundas and Major Alexander Ross, to work out the terms. Article 3 caused the greatest difficulty. It required the British to march out to surrender without the full honors of war. It was a harsh term according to the British. But Washington insisted on it, as it was what Clinton afforded Lincoln in the Charleston surrender in May 1780. Finally, after midnight, the British and allies completed the terms. Article 3 remained unchanged.

The French wondered about this condition of surrender. They were willing to grant Cornwallis the full honors of war. Yet Cornwallis did not conduct a heroic defense at Yorktown. His walls had not been breached. One was supposed to wait until the breach had been made, surrender, and then march out through the breach. So, in the end, the French came to understand the harsh terms.

October 19 was a clear, cool autumn day. The country people and visitors from near and far came to witness the great event. The Americans and French sent in parties at noon to take over parts of the British works. Then at 2 P.M., the British marched out of their lines, mainly in new uniforms and with some possibly under the influence of alcohol. They paraded through a long line of well-dressed French troops on the left and the American Continentals on the right, with the American militia in the rear rank. Their colors were cased, and the bands played tunes that no one there at the time seemed to remember. Perhaps they played "When the King Enjoys His Own Again." The British marched somewhat out of step, while the Germans, with their usual precision, put on a splendid display of precision marching.

The surrender articles had been signed in the trenches, and now the final act began. General Charles O'Hara of the guards led the British line. The British turned their eyes to the French as if it were they who had defeated them. Lafayette, seeing this, had the American bands strike up "Yankee Doodle," and the British suddenly snapped right to look upon the ragged and dirty American army that had also beaten them, with a mixture of rage, dismay, and disgust.

O'Hara tried to go to Rochambeau, but he was guided to Washington, who in turn presented him to General Lincoln. Since Cornwallis pleaded illness and had sent his second in command, the American second in command would receive O'Hara's sword, which was immediately returned to him. The British soldiers were marched to a field, where they lay down their arms. Some threw them down hard to try to destroy them. General Lincoln stopped that action. Some British were in tears while the Americans enjoyed the entire ceremony and showed it. This was the Continental Army's greatest day.

De Grasse was sick from asthma and sent de Barras instead. Never a good horseman, de Barras watched the surrender with keen interest and joy. However, his horse decided to vent in the middle of the ceremony and sank down to perform the call of nature. At this, de Barras cried out, "Good Heavens, I believe my horse is sinking" to the amusement of those around him.

The British suffered 156 killed, 326 wounded,

and 70 missing. They surrendered 7,247 men and 840 seamen. Forty sailors were also killed or wounded. The Americans lost 20 killed and 56 wounded. The French suffered 52 killed and 134 wounded.

Cornwallis was permitted to send the *Bonetta* to New York uninspected by the allies. Some 250 Loyalists made their escape on the ship. Cornwallis would leave Virginia for New York on November 4. De Grasse left for the West Indies the same day. Tench Tilghman, Washing-ton's faithful aide, was sent with the news to Congress. The British and Germans were sent off into the interior of Virginia in captivity. The French wintered in Virginia while Washington marched most of his regular army north to take his station once again outside of New York.

Clinton and Graves had finally put together a relief force that arrived at the Chesapeake on October 27. They soon found they were too late and sailed back to New York on October 29. Clinton could have done little to help Cornwallis, but Graves with his sea power was the one who could have. His slow, methodical measures insured an allied victory. With Rodney or Hood in command, events might have turned out differently.

No one knew it at the time, but for all practical purposes, the last battle of the War of Revolution had been fought. De Grasse dictated where and when it was fought. Rochambeau, his army, and his engineers had made it possible. Washington was the leader who pulled them all together. Rochambeau called it a miracle. Perhaps it was.

After the surrender of Yorktown and as Virginians poured in to reclaim property that had been confiscated by the British, an interesting incident occurred. Tarleton was riding down the main street with other officers when he was stopped by a Mr. Day, steward for Sir Peyton Skipwith of Prestwould Plantation. Armed with a gum stick, Day demanded the return of his master's horse. General O'Hara told Tarleton he had better do it. Tarleton meekly got off the horse, and Day led the horse off, having the last laugh over the terror of the South.

Several weeks later, on Sunday, November 25, Lord North , the British prime minister, received word that Cornwallis had surrendered. As if shot in the chest, he staggered and cried out, "O God! It's over!" So it was.

Paul J. Sanborn

REFERENCES

Raoul Camus, *Military Music of the American Revolution* (1976); Baron Ludwig von Closen, *The Revolutionary Journal of Baron von Closen* trans. and ed. by Evelyn Acomb (1958); Adrienne M. Combs, *The Siege of Yorktown* (1976); Henry S. Commager and Richard B. Morris, *The Spirit of Seventy-Six* (1967); Joseph P. Cullen, *October 19, 1781—Victory at Yorktown* (1976); William R. Cummins and Hugh Rankin, *The Fate of a Nation* (1975); Burke Davis, *The Campaign That Won America* (1970); Captain Johan Ewald, *Diary of the American War*, trans. and ed. by Joseph P. Tustin (1979); James Thomas Flexner, *George Washington in the American Revolution* (1968); Gary Friddell, *Miracle of Yorktown* (1981); Louis Gottschalk, *Lafayette in America*, 3 vols. (1942), *3*; Alan Kemp, *Yorktown* (1976); Lee Kennett, *The French Forces in America, 1780–1783* (1977); Henry P. Johnston, *The Yorktown Campaign and Surrender of Cornwallis* (1881); Count de Rochambeau, *Memoirs of the Marshall Count de Rochambeau* (1971); George Scheer and Hugh Rankin, *Rebels and Redcoats* (1957); James Thacher, *Military Journal of the American Revolution* (1827 rpr. 1969); Tench Tilghman, *Memoir of Lt. Col. Tench Tilghman* (1971); Franklin and Mary Wickwire, *Cornwallis: The American Adventure* (1970); Arnold Whitridge, *Rochambeau* (1965); William B. Willcox, *Portrait of a General: Henry Clinton* (1964).

Zane, Elizabeth
(c. 1766–c. 1831)

American heroine. Probably born in 1766 in western Virginia, Elizabeth Zane, known as Betty, lived near Wheeler, a settlement on the Ohio River founded by her brother Colonel Ebenezer Zane. Her grandfather, a follower of William Penn, immigrated to New Jersey about 1677. The Zanes were of Danish descent. When Betty's father William married a non-Quaker, he was encouraged by the local meeting to move to Virginia. Elizabeth was described as being fair-haired and athletic. She attended school in Philadelphia while living with relatives.

Her brother built a fort at Wheeling that was named in honor of Patrick Henry. On September 11, 1782, approximately 250 Indians and 40 British soldiers attacked Fort Henry. Colonel Zane remained in his house, 60 yards outside the fort. After a six-hour battle, the fort's defenders realized their powder supply was low. Although several men volunteered to get the necessary ammunition, Betty insisted that she run to Colonel Zane's house because the men could not be spared. The Indians stared at her, shooting only when she was out of range. She safely returned to the fort, and as a result, the refugees survived.

Historians question the authenticity of legends concerning Betty's heroic feat. Popular western novelist Zane Grey was named for his heroic ancestor. He wrote a fictional account of her life, which he claimed he researched from Colonel Zane's diary.

Betty Zane married twice and had seven children. Like her birth date, Zane's death date is questionable. She probably died in 1831. She was buried in Martin's Ferry, Ohio, and a statue on her grave, a portrait in the Wheeling State House, and a World War II Liberty ship named the *Betty Zane* honor her heroism.

Elizabeth D. Schafer

REFERENCES

Adelaide M. Cole, "Did Betty Zane Save Fort Henry?" *DAR Magazine, 114* (1980):672–675; *DAB*; Elizabeth F. Ellet, *The Women of the American Revolution*, 2 vols. (1969), 2; Zane Grey, *Betty Zane* (1933); Norris F. Schneider and G.M. Farley, *Betty Zane: Heroine of Fort Henry* (1969).

Zubly, John Joachim
(1724–1781)

Loyalist. One of the most important but most forgotten of the pamphleteers of the American cause was the minister of the Independent Presbyterian Church of Savannah, Georgia, the Reverend Dr. John Joachim Zubly. Born on St. Gall, Switzerland, on August 27, 1724, and ordained by the German Church of London in 1744, he arrived in Georgia in 1745. He accepted his post in Savannah in 1758.

During the Stamp Act crisis and various local conflicts in pre-Revolutionary War Georgia, Zubly published his sermons upholding the public's rights against royal authorities. Among his many readers were Benjamin Franklin and John Adams. In 1775, Zubly was elected to the Georgia Provincial Congress and the Second Continental Congress in Philadelphia.

However, the Reverend Zubly could not bring himself either to support the Revolution or independence and returned to Georgia after only a few weeks in Philadelphia. He found himself back in British-controlled Georgia after the fall of Savannah in December 1778. His last years were spent in ill health as a "Loyalist" in the conflict he was responsible for starting but which he could not in good conscience support. He died in Savannah on July 23, 1781.

Robert Scott Davis, Jr.

REFERENCE

Roger A. Martin, "John J. Zubly: Preacher, Planter, and Politicians," Ph.D. dissertation, University of Georgia (1976).

Zweibruecken Regiment
(Royal-Deux-Ponts Regiment)

Colonel Trevor N. Dupuy once noted that the roster of the Royal-Deux-Ponts Regiment contained "an amazing number of Germanic names." There was a very good reason why this was so. Although it was fighting under the French flag, it was a German regiment. The French carried it on the rolls as the "Regiment Royal Deux-Ponts, un Regiment d'Infanterie Allemande" (a German regiment of infantry). Its officers and men, however, knew their unit as the "Zweibruecken Regiment."

This confusion of names stems from the fact that "Deux-Ponts" and "Zweibruecken" mean the same thing in French and German that is, "Two Bridges." The German town of Zweibruecken, in today's Rhineland-Palatinate, is the former capital of the Duchy of the same name. The area has passed back and forth between France and Germany for centuries and was even owned by Sweden for a brief time in the early eighteenth century. In 1731 it passed back into German hands under the rule of the Birkenfeld-Bischweiler line of the ruling house of Bavaria.

Duke Christian IV of Zweibruecken also had close ties with France. Under an agreement with Louis XV, his Zweibruecken Regiment had served in the French army since the unit was first raised in 1757. This was a fairly common practice of the time, and in the late eighteenth century there were many foreign regiments under the French flag. The title "Royal" was the standard prefix used exclusively for these foreign regiments.

The selection of the 1,200-man Deux-Ponts Regiment for Rochambeau's expeditionary corps was no accident. He specifically asked for it, noting it was "as strong in its composition as any French regiment and in the best condition." The French government initially had considered drawing up to one-third of the corps from its German regiments on the rationale that they easily could be kept up to strength by recruiting deserters from Britain's German regiments in America. Even Rochambeau's French regiments had a high proportion of German-speaking troops from Alsace and Lorraine. Both flank companies (grenadier and chasseur) of most French regiments of the time were almost all recruited from German-speaking areas. The French Saintonge Regiment also had a complete German battalion from Trier, but it was still officially a French regiment. The Duc de Lauzun's legion, Rochambeau's cavalry corps, was made largely of Germans, Poles, and Irishmen, and officially considered a "German Regiment." It, however, had actually been raised in France in 1778 as the "Voluntaires Etrangeres de la Marine," like a forerunner of the French Foreign Legion.

In any event, the Royal-Deux-Ponts was the only German regiment in the expeditionary corps raised on German soil. It fought under the French flag, but it also carried its own unique flag of the Duchy of Zweibruecken. While Rochambeau's other six regiments wore the standard white uniform of the French infantry, the Zweibruecken soldiers wore the deep celestial blue coats that marked the French army's German infantry. Citron-yellow collars and facings were the unique distinctions of the Royal-Deux-Ponts.

When it received its marching orders for America, the regiment was under the command of the Duke's oldest son, Christian. The Duke's younger son, Guillaume (William), was the lieutenant colonel of the regiment. On April 4, 1780, the Zweibruecken troops boarded their ships with the rest of the expeditionary force at Brest, but sea conditions prevented sailing until May 2. The 48-vessel convoy eventually took 71 days to make the crossing, experiencing a few minor encounters with British warships en route. They landed at Newport, Rhode Island, on July 11, 1780, but nearly one-third of the entire army was sick with scurvy from the crossing.

For almost a year, Rochambeau's troops languished in defensive positions around Providence and Newport, waiting for a British attack from the sea that never came. In May 1781, Washington and Rochambeau met in Connecticut to work out campaign plans for the coming year. The French force finally started moving on June 19 toward New York. For most of the next three months, the Royal-Deux-Ponts was brigaded with the Bourbonnois Regiment. French and American forces joined above New York City on July 5, and 10 days later the Zweibruecken troops played a minor supporting role in the skirmish at Tarrytown. Up to that point, however, most of the French commanders, even the senior commanders, did not know whether their ultimate objective was to be New York or Virginia.

On August 24, the Brigade Bourbonnois crossed the Hudson River on order and turned toward Virginia. Continuing south, they marched through Philadelphia on September 3 and passed-in-review before the Continental Congress. They made the final two-day leg of their journey by ship down the Chesapeake Bay and took up positions in front of Yorktown on September 28.

During the initial stages of the siege operations, the Royal-Deux-Ponts spent roughly every third day digging in the trenches. When the second siege parallel was started on October 11, it quickly became obvious that the key to the entire operation was two strong redoubts on the British left, which would prevent the completion of the second parallel and stall the siege. They had to be eliminated.

The French and Americans mounted a coordinated attack on the night of October 14. The Americans took Redoubt #10 on the extreme British left; the French took Redoubt #9, to its immediate right. Baron de Viomesnil commanded the three-echelon French column. For the assault echelon he selected the elite grenadier and chasseur (light infantry) companies of the Deux-Ponts and Gatinais regiments. He assigned command of this all-German, 400-man lead element to Count Guillaume des Deux-Ponts.

Redoubt #9 was manned by the Bose Regiment, which produced the irony of German fighting German in this key phase of the final decisive battle for American independence. When the attack signal was fired, des Deux-Ponts and his men stormed forward with axes and ladders in the lead. They took fairly heavy casualties before they gained the top of the parapet, but once there, they were able to fire down on the defenders. Des Deux-Ponts gave the order to fix bayonets and was about to lead his troops down into the redoubt when the defenders surrendered. Moments afterward, Guillaume des Deux-Ponts was painfully wounded in the face by a blast of gravel from a ricocheting cannonball.

Des Deux-Ponts's assault lasted only seven minutes. His force of 400 suffered 77 killed, the single largest allied loss of the entire battle. But the American attack under Colonel Alexander Hamilton also succeeded, and the fate of the British garrison was sealed. The Battle of Yorktown was effectively over.

After the battle, the Royal-Deux-Ponts went into winter quarters in Williamsburg and Jamestown, where many of the troops died from wounds and disease. The regiment marched back to New England the following spring and eventually boarded ships for the French West Indies. It finally returned to France in 1783 and then made the long march from Brest back home to the Palatinate.

During the French Revolution, Zweibruecken's Duke Karl August II let the proprietorship of the regiment slip away from him. Recruiting in the Palatinate was suspended in 1790. In January 1791 the French Revolutionary Assembly eliminated regimental designations and assigned numbers instead. The Royal-Deux-Ponts became the 99th Infantry Regiment of the Line and was forced into standard French uniforms. Most of the German officers in the French army resigned, even the ones with family ties to France. Many later entered Bavarian service.

In 1816 the Zweibruecken Regiment was very briefly resurrected as the short-lived 22nd Bavarian Infantry Regiment. Today, however, the French army's 99th Infantry Regiment holds the primary claim to direct lineage from the Royal-Deux-Ponts. Its regimental flag still bears the red lion arms of the West German city of Zweibruecken.

David T. Zabecki

REFERENCES

Ludwig von Closen, *The Revolutionary Journal of Baron Ludwig von Closen 1780–1783* (1958); Count William des Deux-Ponts, *My Campaigns in America* (1868); Rudolf Karl Tross, *The Zweybruecken or Royal Deux-Ponts Regiment and Yorktown* (1978).

Glossary

Abaft: In the navy, going in the direction of the stern.

Abatis (Abattis): In fortifications, a defensive obstacle composed of sharpened tree trunks and branches closely placed in line and pointed toward the enemy. Usually fixed in front of more substantial defensive works to slow an enemy advance. A military entanglement to make attacks more difficult. The term comes from the French "to beat down."

Abeam: In the navy, being at right angles to the keel or center line of the ship.

Abreast: In the military and common usage, side by side.

Accouterment (Accoutrement): In the army, equipment other than weapons or clothes carried by a soldier to sustain life such as a canteen, haversack, or cartridge box, among other things.

Acting rank: In the military, a temporary rank assigned to an officer who is responsible for duties normally assigned to higher-ranking officers.

Action: In the military, an engagement between two armies or ships, or between any smaller bodies of troops. Also used to designate some memorable act done by individuals or small groups against the enemy.

Ad hoc: In the military, a provisional unit formed for a specific purpose or time period; formed on the spot.

Adjutant: In the army, an officer who serves as the administrative assistant to the commanding officer of a military unit. Usually the duties of this officer include the correspondence, issuing of orders, and administration of the unit. He also is an assistant to the adjutant general.

Adjutant general: In the army, this officer aids and assists the commanding general in his duties as a staff officer. The adjutant general keeps the roll of officers present, conveys orders to all units, is responsible for all posts and outposts, assists in ordering the men for battle, and performs other staff functions for the commander.

Advanced guard: In the military, a unit sent ahead of the main force to insure against ambush, remove obstacles, repair roads and bridges, seize significant geographic features, and cover the deployment of the army.

Advancement: In the military, the goal of all honorable and active officers, which is to gain promotion or preferment in the service through influence or meritorious acts.

Affaire d'honneur: In the military, a victory in which the winning side demonstrates great skill and bravery but fails to gain a significant strategic advantage. From the French for an "affair of honor."

Afterguard: In the navy, the party of men stationed on the rear decks to work the aftersails.

Agent: In the army, the individual in each regiment appointed by the colonel commanding to take care of all money belonging to the officers and men.

Aide-de-camp: In the army, an officer appointed to attend to the needs of a general officer. Usually ranks as a captain and receives extra pay for the satisfactory performance of his duties, which are to carry dispatches and do the bidding of the general in battle.

Alarm: In the military, a sudden warning based upon a report of possible enemy action that causes the men to ready their weapons for an attack. Also, an alert signaled by the discharge of a gun or the beating of the drums in the event of an enemy attack.

Alarmpost: In the field, a position appointed by the quartermaster for each regiment to march to in the case of an alarm.

Amain: In the navy, to signal surrender by lowering a topsail.

Ambersune: In fortifications, another term for embrasure.

Ambuscade: In the army, a body of men in a concealed post poised to fall upon an unsuspecting enemy force.

Ambush: In the army, a place of concealment for troops to surprise the enemy.

American Legion: In the war, the body of Loyalist Americans raised by Benedict Arnold for British service after his attempted betrayal of West Point in 1780.

Amidships: In the navy, being in the middle of a ship.

Amnesty: In the military, an act by which two parties promise to forget and forgive animosities.

Amuse: In the military, to distract the attention of the enemy or to mislead him so that primary maneuvers may go undiscovered. Also, to divert the enemy.

Animate: In the military, the efforts of the officers or others to raise the fighting spirit of the men by the force of their speech.

Annals: In the military, the type of historical record in which events are listed in chronological order.

Annoy: In the military, sending out skirmishers to frustrate the enemy, to disrupt his deployment, and generally to cause the opponent grief before a battle or general action takes place.

Aperto prelio: In military writings, a Latin phrase for "in open battle."

Approaches: In the field, all the defensive works that are constructed which lead toward the place of the enemy. This includes the first, second, and third parallels, trenches, saps, redoubts, and galleries, among other things.

Apron: In the navy, a thin, flattened piece of lead used to cover the vent of a cannon to keep the powder charges dry. Called so because it is held in place by two pieces of cord.

Armistice: In the military, a temporary truce or a cessation of fighting for a very short period of time, in order, for example, to parley or to remove wounded from the battlefield.

Armory: In the military, a warehouse or storage area in which weapons, equipment, and military habiliments are kept for ready use.

Armourer: In the military, the person responsible for keeping the weapons in service and for providing for their repair and storage.

Army of observation: In the army, a force employed to watch and observe the movements of the enemy. Also used by a besieging force to prevent a relief force of the enemy from raising the siege from the other direction.

Articles: In the military, breeches, coats, waistcoats, and other articles worn by the soldiers.

Articles of war: In the military, those known rules and regulations for the better organization and governance of the army.

Artificers: In the army, those individuals whose specialties are in the making of the necessary articles used by the army to campaign. This includes smiths, carpenters, ropemakers, gunsmiths, and other such talented persons.

Artillery: In the army, that branch of men who contribute to its success through the proper use of the great guns, fieldpieces, mortars, howitzers, and other such weapons.

Artillery park: In the army, that place appointed by the generals to encamp the artillery train, troops, ammunition, and stores.

Avenue: In fortifications, any kind of opening or inlet into a fort, bastion, or outwork.

Bad bargain: In the British army, slang term for one of His Majesty's soldiers who is often considered useless in civilian life. Also applied, within the army, to a malingerer.

Baggage: In the military, the clothes, tents, provisions, and other belongings of an army. Also used as a derogatory term for women and children traveling with the army.

Balderdash: In the military, adulterated wine issued at times to the soldiers, especially by sutlers, who mixed water in with the wine to raise profits by cheating the men. A debased alcoholic drink of inferior quality.

Ball: In the military, the projectile discharged from most muskets, rifles, pistols, artillery pieces, and other such weapons against the enemy. Today referred to usually as the bullet. Generally of spherical shape and of varied size (caliber).

Banquette: In fortifications, a step on the inside of the parapet for troops to stand upon when firing.

Barbette: In fortifications, a raised platform enabling guns to fire over the parapet, rather than through an opening in the wall of the fortification.

Barbican: In fortifications, a watchtower erected on the wall from which to see the enemy at great distances.

Barge: In the navy, a ship's boat used to ferry flag officers.

Barracks: In the military, a building erected to lodge officers and men in garrison.

Barrel fever: In the military, the adverse physical effects following heavy drinking. A hangover.

Barricade: In fortifications, an obstruction composed of trees, branches, carts, wagons, and so forth used to stop the approach of an enemy.

Bar shot: In the artillery, a standard-sized ball shot split in half and connected by a short bar. Used primarily against the rigging of a ship in the navy and against tightly formed bodies of attacking troops in the field.

Bastion: In fortifications, a projection from the main wall of the fort that permits defenders to sweep fire along the face of the main wall in order to keep the enemy from breeching or climbing it.

Bateau: In the military, a flat-bottomed boat with tapered ends, made of wood, and propelled by oars, sails, or poles. Heavy and sturdy, these boats were often used to carry heavy loads on rivers and inland waterways.

Bat horse: In the army, a horse that carried the baggage of an officer. "Bat" comes from the French for "pack-saddle."

Batman: In the British army, an officer's servant.

Battalion: In the army, a body of infantry composed of companies, with a strength on the average of 500 to 800 men. The term is often used interchangeably with regiment. In the British army, some regiments were composed of two battalions, such as the 71st.

Battery: In the artillery, any tactical emplacement of artillery. Sometimes the term "brigade of artillery" was also used. Since the late 1800s, the term "battery" has been used to identify any company-sized artillery unit. Prior to that time, they were referred to as artillery companies.

Battle: In the military, a general action between the greater forces of two opposing armies.

Battle array: In the military, also known as the line of battle, it is the drawing up of the army's units in line for an engagement/battle. The first line, supported by artillery, is followed by the rear line 300 paces behind. The reserve comes farther back, 600 paces removed.

Bawmen: In the British army, these individuals were responsible for the care and well-being of the baggage horses.

Bayonet: In the army, a triangular-shaped, pointed spear with a hollow handle that fits around the muzzle of a musket. It was the primary infantry weapon of the professional armies of the period, used to lead the assault to break an enemy line after the discharge of the musketry.

Beacon: In the military, a signal, usually erected on long, high poles with buckets of pitch run to the top, which are ignited to give the alarm in the event of necessity. During the daytime smoking combustibles are used to the same effect.

Belay: In the navy, to cease hauling on a line.

Belts: In the military, those leather or cloth straps, either across the shoulder or around the waist, usually shaded to match the waistcoat, that hold a soldier's accouterments, such as the bayonet, canteen, and cartridge box.

Berm: In fortifications, the ledge at the top of the inner face of the ditch.

Bicorn: In the military, a hat that is cocked twice instead of three times (tricorn).

Bilious fever: In medicine, the disease that today is called typhoid fever. Characterized by the flux and a red rash on the trunk.

Billet: In the army, the quartering of soldiers in houses of any town or village.

Bishop: A mixture of wine and water into which is placed a roasted orange.

Blinds: In fortifications, hogsheads or pipes filled with sand for men to use for protection in the midst of a siege. If enough blinds are assembled, they can replace a bombproof structure.

Blister (to): In medicine, the raising of blisters on the surface of the body to draw excess fluids from the internal portions of the body. Blistering was used in order to restore a harmonious balance of fluids in the patient, causing health to reassert itself.

Bloody back: A slang term for a British soldier, making reference to his red coat.

Boatswain (bosun): In the navy, the warrant officer or petty officer in charge of boats, rigging, and ground tackle aboard ship. Same as swein-keeper.

Bombardier: A specialist title given to artillerymen who were experts in preparing ammunition and in the discharge of mortars. These individuals were awarded higher pay than a gunner.

Boom: In the military, an obstruction that closes a river or other type of water passageway to enemy traffic. Usually it is composed of linked chain supported by wooden beams.

Boose (Bouse): Any alcoholic drink.

Bootlegger: In the navy, smugglers who hid forbidden goods in their large sea boots to avoid detection by customs agents.

Boots: In the military, the youngest officer in the mess whose duties included stirring the fire, snuffing out the candles at day's end, and ringing the dinner bell.

Bore: In the military, the cavity of the barrel of any type of firearm or gun.

Bounty: In the military, granting men money, land, or other inducements to join the army and perform their proper duty.

Breach: In fortifications, to create a gap or opening, in the works of any fortified place.

Breastwork: In fortifications, a defensive work usually in the field and hastily erected to a height usually breast-high.

Breech: In the military, the end or rear of a firearm or gun near the vent.

Brevet: In the army, an honorary temporary rank awarded for meritorious conduct. For example, a captain might be breveted to the rank of major for bravery in the face of the enemy. His actual rank is captain, but he is treated as if he were a major. A British custom adopted by the Americans.

Brig: In the navy, a two-masted square-rigged ship deriving its name from "brigantine," pirates in the Mediterranean Sea.

Brigade: In the army, a tactical unit composed of 3 or more regiments or battalions in the infantry, 8 to 12 squadrons in the cavalry, or 8 to 10 cannon in the artillery.

Brigade major: In the army, the officer appointed to assist the brigadier in the management of the brigade. Usually the most experienced captain in the brigade was chosen.

Brigadier: In the military, the lowest grade of general officer, usually in command of a brigade but sometimes in command of a division. Ranks above the colonel. In the British army, this was a wartime rank only and not that of a general officer, fitting in between the colonel and lieutenant colonel. This British officer commanded a brigade of several regiments.

Bring to bear: In gunnery, particularly in the navy, pointing the ordnance directly at the target assigned to be hit.

British Establishment: In the British army, those troops stationed in the British Isles (except Ireland), subject to and paid for by the British Parliament. It included forces in America.

Broadside: In the navy, this implies the full discharge of all the artillery or guns on one side of a warship at the enemy.

Brother Jonathan: In the war, a term used by the British who delighted in epitomizing American rusticity by calling colonials this name. When the British evacuated Breed's Hill in 1775, a sign was left behind reading "Welcome, Brother Jonathan." The term was highly offensive to Americans. It appears to have been a religious slur against the New England custom of giving children Old Testament names, Jonathan being a somewhat more pretentious name than John.

Brunswicker: In the army, the troops from the Brunswick area of the Germanies who were hired by George III to help put down the American revolt. Oftentimes, the Americans did not differentiate between different German mercenary groups and called them all Hessians after the largest contingent.

Buckskin: Used not only to describe a type of cloth made from deer hide but also a country bumpkin, a person not used to the ways of gentility and culture, since many of this sort wore clothing made of such material.

Bully boys: In the navy, sailors were often called this after the bully beef contained in their rations.

Caboose: In the navy, the name used for the ship's galley, or place where food was prepared.

Cadence: In the military, the regimented and uniform method of marching in step with drum and fifes beating the time. The usual step of 60 to the minute is a slower one than that used today.

Cadet: In the army, a young gentleman serving with pay until a vacancy opens for promotion to a commissioned officer rank.

Caisson: In the artillery, a two-wheeled wagon holding extra supplies of ammunition and artillery supplies for the guns of a battery.

Caliber: In the military, the measured diameter of the bore in a firearm or artillery tube.

Calibogus: In the American army, a mixture of rum and spruce beer sometimes issued to the troops.

Calliper: In the artillery, an instrument used by gunners to measure diameters of shot, shells, and cylinders for the guns.

Caltrops: In the military, pieces of iron with four points all arranged so that any three rest on the ground and one point sticks up. These are scattered on the ground to break up cavalry attacks.

Campaign: In the army, the period of time when the army is in the field during wartime to move against the enemy to achieve objectives.

Camp color man: In the army, usually one man per company who assisted the regimental quartermaster in the duty detail of preparing a new campsite. These men were also often expected to perform some of the more odious tasks about camp. The camp colors were small pennants frequently marked with the regimental number and of the regimental colors that outlined the camp site for the soldiers' use.

Camp fever: In the military, any epidemic fever occurring in the camps that sadly afflicted many men. Today, it is thought this disease was typhus or a related illness.

Camp follower: In the military, usually women who followed the army providing nursing, laundry, housekeeping, and cooking duties along with guarding the men's possessions while they engaged in battle. They received half of the regular ration if they were attached officially to a particular soldier in a regiment. Usually called "Mollies" as a generic name in the American army.

Camphor: In medicine, a substance used as a rubefacient in a topical salve in order to apply external irritation to counter internal irritation, thus restoring a healthful balance of fluids in the patient.

Canister (case shot): In the artillery, a can filled with small objects, such as musket balls, that scatter when discharged from a gun. This was the load of choice against massed infantry and cavalry in the field.

Canteen: In the military, a container made of tin, wood, or some other suitable substance that contained the beverage issued to the men each day.

Cantonment: In the army, another term for the winter campgrounds of an army where they remain until the spring campaigns begin.

Capitulation: In fortifications, when the besieged garrison surrenders under agreed to conditions to the attacking force.

Captain: In the army, the highest grade of officer in command of a company of infantry, artillery battery, or squadron of cavalry. In the navy, the captain commands a major vessel of war, although any ship's commander, holding the rank or a lesser one, is addressed as captain.

Captain lieutenant: In the army, the junior captain in any regiment who commands the colonel's company and stands between the lieutenant and captain in rank.

Carbine: In the military, these are small firelocks used by the cavalry and certain noncommissioned officers.

Carcass: In the artillery, a special incendiary round consisting of hollow iron shot filled with pitch or other intensely burning materials. Flames escaped from vent holes in the shot, burning for approximately ten minutes. This load was particularly good for setting fires on ships or in besieged posts.

Career: In the military, this term originally referred to a race course and was then applied to a running charge made with great spirit by infantry or cavalry.

Cartel: In the military, this term comes from the Italian for card and refers to a written agreement between two warring sides to exchange prisoners. It was originally a written challenge to a duel.

Cartouche: In the military, the older spelling of cartridge, coming from the Italian for a scroll of paper. This was one round of ammunition containing a measured charge of powder, one ball or several buckshot, and contained in a roll or scroll of paper.

Cartridge: In the army, the paper casing holding the powder and ball with the paper itself as the wadding, used as ammunition in the discharge of firearms.

Cartridge box: In the army, that accouterment that hangs on or from a leather belt and holds the cartridges for the soldier's use in battle. Usually this box is covered with a leather flap to protect the cartridges from getting wet in rain.

Caruel: In medicine, caraway seeds used quite effectively as a carminative to relieve the discomfort of flatulence.

Casemate: In fortifications, a bombproof structure for the protection and quartering of troops.

Castramentation: In the army, the art of measuring out the form of a camp on the ground in the normal order of battle so that the troops may turn out in line in quick time. Usually the camp faced that of the enemy or his supposed approach.

Casualty: In the military, that number of men in any unit killed, wounded, or missing in any action. The ratio of wounded to killed in the Revolution was approximately three/four to one.

Cat: In the military, the short name for the cat-o'-nine tails, a nine-corded whip with knots placed on each cord. Used to inflict punishment on soldiers or sailors found guilty of a break in military discipline.

Cataplasm: In medicine, a poultice composed of various medicinals to relieve pain, reduce swelling, or increase the discharge of pus.

Catarrh: In medicine, a disease of a runny nose, sore throat, headache, cough, and chills with fever. Often called a cold.

Cathartic: In medicine, a type of medical potion of varying compounds used to reassert a harmonious balance of bodily fluids by purging excess fluids from the body through the stimulation of the bowels to empty.

Catholicon: In medicine, a remedy that cures just about any imbalance of fluids that causes a sense of disease in any person. Taken from the Latin word "catholicus" meaning universal.

Cautery: In medicine, a hot iron used to cauterize tissue, especially after an amputation.

Cavalry: In the military, those soldiers who fight on horseback rather than on foot.

Chain shot: In the artillery, a standard-sized ball split in half with the halves connected by a chain. This load was especially effective against a ship's rigging and tightly packed masses of troops.

Chamade: In the army, the signal for the parley.

Chandeliers: In fortifications, these are wooden frames filled with various stout materials that are used to erect field breastworks when rocky or frozen ground discourages the usual digging. Prefabricated, they were used by the Americans in the siege of Boston.

Charge: In the military, the amount of powder used to load a firearm or gun for proper discharge.

Chasseurs: In the army, light infantry from the French and German armies were given this title. The term comes from the French and means "to chase."

Chevalier: In the French army, a title given to an individual awarded the Order of St. Louis by the King.

Chevaux-de-frise: In the army, plural for cheval-de-frise. The term comes from Friesland, where obstacles such as these were erected to stop Spanish cavalry attacking a force without horses. The chevaux-de-frise are long beams of wood with pointed stakes crossed and tied to the center beam at several points along each beam. These were used to stop cavalry charges, placed in rivers as obstacles to prevent passage of enemy ships, and served also as road blocks. Often used as a part of field fortifications.

Chirurgeon: In medicine, the older spelling of surgeon with the pronunciation being roughly the same for both.

Cincinnati: In the American army, the society of former Continental officers who banded together for mutual support and fraternity as the war came to a close.

Cipher: In the British army, the initials of the King imprinted on various items such as buttons, plates, drums, and so forth.

Citadel: In fortifications, a fort with four or more bastions raised on advantageous ground.

Claymore: In the army, a great two-handed sword of the Highlanders with both edges sharpened.

Clever: In the military, performing a task with a high degree of spirit and skill.

Closed quarters: In the navy, "closed quarters" or special deck houses where the crew of a ship could take refuge if the enemy successfully boarded and controlled the main deck.

Clubbed: In the military, a sign of surrender used by troops who no longer wished to resist or fight. The musket was inverted or held upside down so as to render them harmless to the enemy.

Clyster: In medicine, any medical infusion inserted rectally into the body, or an enema.

Coatee: In the military, a short, close-fitting coat, often worn by the light infantry and dragoons.

Cock: In the military, the hammer of the lock of the musket in which the flint is held fast, poised to strike the frizzen to create the sparks to ignite the priming powder.

Cockade: In the military, a ribbon designating one's faction, worn on the front of the hat.

Cohoes: A waterfall in the course of a river.

Cohorn: In the artillery, a small, light mortar.

Colonel: In the army, the highest-ranking field officer, who commands a regiment of foot, horse, dragoons, or artillery.

Colors: In the military, these are large silk flags carried on half-pikes by ensigns or flown on ships. They are sacred and honorable symbols of the unit or ship and are carefully guarded at all times. In surrender, the colors are supposed to be turned over to the enemy.

Column: In the army, troops marching in long, deep files, usually four soldiers abreast.

Commissary: In the army, the official who is appointed to inspect stores, provisions, and weapons of the soldiers to insure that they are well armed and clothed.

Commission: In the military, an official certificate from a legal body such as the King or Congress granting an individual the power to exercise command at a particular level within the army or navy. In some armies, such as the British, this commission was purchased from the holder by another.

Communition wives: In the military, the current mistresses kept by officers, particularly those who followed the army on campaign.

Company: In the army, the basic unit of the regiment. Varying in size, it usually had between 30 and 50 men under the command of a captain. The ensign and lieutenant assisted the captain in command of the company. There were eight companies in an American regiment, and eight battalion and two elite companies (grenadiers and light infantry) in the British regiment. Ordinarily a British company would be about 80 to 100 men in strength.

Continental Army: In the American army, that portion of the regular line in the pay and service of the Continental Congress.

Contingent man: In the military, another name for warrant man, that is, fictitious men whose pay was to be used for regimental needs. An example of budgetary padding.

Conversion: In the army, the movement of the battalion (regiment) to turn its front to where its flank was, when that particular flank is threatened by the enemy.

Convoy: In the military, a detachment of one's force to guard any train or supply, money, ammunition, provision, or stores on their way from one's base to reinforce one's army or fleet.

Cornet: In the army, the lowest commissioned officer of the cavalry, equal to the ensign in the infantry, who carried the colors and positioned himself in the center front of the troop of either horse or dragoons.

Corporal: In the army, the lowest rank of the noncommissioned officer who led a squad in a company of infantry.

Corps: In the military, a specially designated body of men, apart from the main portion of the army, that acts as a unit on special missions. The "corps" is not a major division of the army as the term would be used in the American Civil War (1861–1865).

Council of war: In the military, an assembly of principal officers of the army or fleet to arrange future moves or provide advice for the commanding officer.

Counterirritant: In medicine, a medicinal used to produce irritation that counters any bad or harmful irritations that cause disease in a patient. This term could also apply to a medical treatment such as cupping or blistering to provide the necessary counterirritant.

Countermarch: In the army, to reverse the direction of the unit in motion so as to retrace its steps in the opposite direction.

Counterscarp: In fortifications, the exterior slope of a ditch.

Countersign: In the military, the password given to all the men in the army and used in response to the challenge of the parole, which is given out only to the officers.

Coup de main: In the military, a sudden and vigorous assault against an enemy strongpoint, fortification, or position that successfully achieves its objective. This type of action is taken before the preliminaries of a formal siege are begun. Thus, in a coup de main, the enemy's main walls or fortifications are still intact and have not as yet been breached by artillery fire. The term comes from the French for "a stoke of the hand."

Coureur de bois: A French phrase for "runner of the woods" and used for unlicensed French fur traders and hunters. Some of this class served with the British against the Americans in the war.

Courier: In the military, a messenger sent from one unit to another carrying dispatches or messages, usually under the direction of the adjutant.

Court-martial: In the military, a court procedure to determine guilt and set punishment for all individuals in the military charged with certain offenses.

Covered way: In fortifications, a flat space above the exterior slope of the ditch, usually with its own banquette and wall ending in the glacis sloping away toward the field. The traverse is the embankment protecting troops on the covered way from sweeping fire from the enemy.

Cowboys: In the war, marauders who operated in the neutral grounds surrounding New York City from 1778 to 1783. They terrorized the civilians there and were generally of Tory persuasion.

Cravat: A cloth worn about the neck on the outside of the shirt collar. The stock replaced the cravat in the army.

Crow's feet: In the army, another name for caltrops.

Cuirassiers: In the army, a term applied to the heavy cavalry in the German service.

Cupping: In medicine, a process of applying a porcelain cup filled with burning alcohol to the skin to raise blood or other fluids to the surface of the skin for removal. This excess fluid, once removed, would permit the balance of fluids to be restored in an afflicted person.

Curtain: In fortifications, the part of the main wall of the fort that joins two bastions.

CXIII: In the American army, George Washington ordered this mark placed upon all public property in order to reduce theft. It stood for Continental and the 13 colonies. Later, in 1776, the "CXIII" was changed to "U.S."

Dagger: In the military, a short sword with a blade approximately 12 inches long.

Defeat in detail: In the military, a result of poor display or tactics by a general in that the placement of his troops permitted the enemy to mass upon and defeat the parts of his total force one at a time in succession during battle before the other parts could come to their aid.

Defilade: In the military, a person or thing protected from enemy fire by a natural or man-made barrier is said to be covered or "in defilade."

Defile: In the army, a straight, narrow passageway, called so because troops must maintain a small front, or march in single file, as they move through. This circumstance places these advanced troops at a disadvantage, since it is easy to harass or stop them.

Degradation: In the military, to deprive an officer of his original commission and the power of his former rank for certain offenses unbecoming an officer.

Demi-bastion: In fortifications, a bastion with only one face and one flank.

Demi-lune: In fortifications, a crescent- or half-moon-shaped gorged (raised) outwork placed before and in front of the main wall of a fortified position. Its purpose is to slow up and fragment an attack before the enemy can gain the momentum to break through the main wall. The demi-lune also serves to block direct enemy artillery fire, preventing breaches from developing in the main wall. If an enemy attack does succeed in passing the demi-lune, soldiers atop the demi-lune can fire into the rear of the enemy's troops as they attempt to assault the main wall. Also called "ravelins," which served the same end, but were V-shaped.

Depot: In the military, a place of safety beyond the reach of the enemy where troops may assemble and stores of military import may be kept.

Depth of a battalion: In the army, battalions usually fought either two or three lines deep. The Americans generally used two lines while the British varied between two and three, depending upon the battalion and the point of time in the war.

Deranging: In the military, whenever the situation changed significantly (for example, at the end of a war) and the army contracted in numbers, there would be a surplus of officers. More senior officers would then ease out less senior officers from postings until those officers least senior were left without any duty positions at all. "Deranging" is the term for this process of moving and transferring officers from their present position to another according to seniority.

Deserter: In the military, any individual under military discipline who abandons the service by leaving his unit or station without permission. In the face of the enemy, the punishment for this action is death.

Detachment: In the military, an uncertain number of men drawn from several units to perform a special mission as ordered by the commanding officer. In the navy, "on detached service" means the same except that certain ships are sent off from the main fleet to perform a mission.

Devil's books: In society, playing cards, which provided great amusement to the troops in times of leisure but were often disposed of when battle approached, since they were considered tools of Satan.

Discharge: In the military, to dismiss an individual from his military responsibilities at the end of his term of service or at his own request. This term also applies to the firing off of the weaponry as in "the colonel ordered his men to discharge their pieces."

Dismounted cannon: In the artillery, when the carriage of a tube or any other part of the cannon is damaged such that the gun is unfit for service.

Display: In the military, to deploy the men for battle.

Disposition: In the army, the order in which the officer in command of a unit places his men for the most advantageous positions in order strongly to receive an attack or be able effectively to deliver one.

Ditch: In fortifications, a large, deep trench that surrounds a fort.

Diversion: In the military, to draw the enemy's attention by attacking in a place away from the spot where one's major attack will fall.

Dormant commission: In the military, a commission that remains inactive until certain circumstances come into play.

Doxy: In colonial society, a she-beggar, wench, whore, mistress, or prostitute.

Dragoon: In the army, a soldier who fights on horseback but who is also trained to fight on foot as infantry, depending on the situation.

Dress the line: In the army, this command instructs the men to form a straight and even line, with each man directly beside his neighbor, close enough to touch elbows with the men on either side.

Drum major: In the army, the lead drummer who teaches the other drummers the proper calls upon the drum. Also, usually a large, powerful man who is often called upon to carry out punishment by the lash to any soldiers in the battalion.

Drums: In the army, a vital musical instrument through which the orders of the day and those during battle are transmitted to the men. The following are the typical drum calls and their meanings:

- The Alarm—instructs the troops to be aware of a surprise enemy attack on the camp.
- The Assembly—instructs the troops to assemble on the colors.
- The Call to Arms—instructs the troops to take up their arms and prepare for battle.
- The General—instructs the troops to prepare to march.
- The March—instructs the troops to begin their march.
- The Retreat—instructs the troops to withdraw from their positions in battle or in camp, marking the end of the day at sunset for the troops.
- The Reveille—marks the first call of the day and awakens the soldiers to their duty.
- The Tattoo—instructs the troops to retire to their quarters for the night and for the sutlers to close the tap of the liquor barrel. Usually beat at 9 P.M. in the summer and at 8 P.M. in the winter.

Duffle: A coarse, woolen type of cloth used to make some accouterments and uniforms in the military.

Effectives: In the military, the actual number of private soldiers and corporals available to perform active duty or carry a musket on any given day.

Eight bells: In the navy, a ship's bell is struck each time a 30-minute hourglass is turned during a four-hour shift. Thus, eight bells signaled the end of the four-hour shift or watch.

Elevation: In the artillery, the angle between the long axis of a cannon tube and the ground. The higher the elevation, the greater the firing range, up to 45 degrees, at which point the relationship reverses.

Elixir: In medicine, any liquid with more than one component to it, usually but not always including the addition of alcohol.

Embrasure: In fortifications, an aperture or slot for an artillery piece in the parapet, with the sides of the opening slanted to the outside to increase the angle of cannon fire. (The parapet is the top part of the rampart, which is itself in effect the wall of the fortification.)

Emetic: In medicine, a medicinal potion of varying compounds used to induce vomiting in order to evacuate excess fluids out of the body.

Eminence: In the military, the high or rising ground that overlooks and commands the surrounding lower terrain. Military commanders usually attempt to control this ground and use it to their advantage against their opponents.

Encamp: In the army, the erecting of camp on a selected site.

Encounter: In the military, a battle between two persons only. Figuratively used to describe battles, attacks, or larger actions involving armies, detachments, or units.

Enfilade: In the military, enemy fire that sweeps a line of men or an entrenched position from one end to another. In the navy, the equivalent term is to rake. In order to enfilade an opponent, it is necessary to maneuver one's unit into a flanking position, or have the advantage of watching an opponent march directly across one's front, thus exposing their flank to the fire.

Engagement: In the army, a particular or general battle between armies or their detachments. In the navy, an encounter between fleets or their detached ships.

Engineer: In the military, an officer appointed to build, repair, inspect, and improve the works of any fortified place to withstand the attacks of the enemy. This officer is also partially responsible for the development of tactics and strategy against an enemy position in relation to the construction of a fortification.

Ensign: In the army, the lowest-ranking commissioned officer of the infantry, who carried the colors, or "ensign," of the battalion into battle.

Enterprise: In the military, an undertaking attended with some hazard and danger that is performed by select troops known for their courage and ability in battle.

Envelopment: In the military, a flanking attack in which the enemy succeeds in gaining the side or rear of one's line. A double envelopment is when both flanks are either attacked or turned.

Epaule: In fortifications, denotes the shoulder of a bastion or the place where its face and flank meet.

Epaulement: In fortifications, denotes the breastworks constructed to cover the troops in front and sometimes in the flank of a post or any other defended position.

Epaulette: In the military, decorations worn by officers on their shoulders to designate rank. In the American army, silver braid marked infantry and cavalry, while gold braid marked the artillery.

Eprouvette: In the military, a device used for testing the strength of gunpowder.

Equipage: In the military, all kinds of equipment used by the army such as tools, kitchen utensils, saddle horses, baggage wagons, and bat horses.

Escarp: In fortifications, the outward slope of the rampart, usually steep and difficult to mount.

Escort: In the military, another term for convoy.

Esplanade: In fortifications, the sloping of the parapet of the covered way toward the field. It is the same as the glacis of the counterscarp.

Evolution: In the army, the motions made by any body of troops when they are ordered to change their form and disposition.

Exchange: In the military, the process of trading prisoners with the enemy based on exchanging captured personnel of equal rank or working out a deal satisfactory to both sides for the exchange so that valued individuals captured by the enemy can be returned to active duty rather than be kept in prison.

Exercise: In the military, all of those motions and actions together with the whole management of arms an individual must render for service in combat.

Expanding bar shot: In the artillery, a standard-sized ball shot split in half and connected by a slip-joint bar that expands to greater length when the load is discharged. As with standard bar shot and chain shot, it found its greatest use against ships' riggings, and closely massed bodies of infantry.

Expedition: In the military, a quick, secret movement to attack the enemy under the general direction of a preconceived plan. A coup de main is an example. This term implies risk, hazard, and is usually a critical operation.

Fabian: In the military, a delaying action used to hold up the progress of the enemy until more favorable conditions exist to achieve a victory. The word comes from the Roman general Quintus Fabius Maximus who practiced such delaying tactics during Hannibal's invasion of Italy.

Face: In the army, to command the troops to turn in a certain way to present their front in another direction.

Face of a bastion: In fortifications, the two sides reaching from the flank to the salient angles, which are the weakest and easiest turned portions of the bastion and are the first portions approached by the enemy in an assault.

Facings: In the military, the lapels, cuffs, collar, and turnbacks of the coat's skirts are covered or "faced" with a different color than the coat itself.

Faggot: A bundle of branches and sticks good for starting fires (kindling). In the military, men hired to muster by officers whose companies are not complete, so that the officers in question may cheat the paymaster by receiving pay for men who are listed but not actually a part of the unit.

Falling sickness: In medicine, the term used to describe epilepsy.

Family: In the military, the group of officers and assistants, servants, and other individuals who form a general officer's "family" or staff during a campaign.

Farmer George: A nickname for King George III, deriving from his intense interest in agricultural matters.

Fascines: In fortifications, these are faggots, stocks, and brush bound tightly together and used to provide protection for troops on either side of a siege.

Fathom: In the navy, a measurement of depth, about six feet, from the Anglo-Saxon term "faehom," which was the reach of a grown man's arms spread out from tip to tip. In fortifications, a measure of six feet.

Fencing: In the military, an art of swordsmanship that no gentleman, officer or not, is ignorant of. Fencing is practiced with foils.

Fetter: In society, a chain used for the feet to detain prisoners or captives. Also called a shackle.

Feu de joie: In the army, a French term for "fire of joy" in which the men in line discharge their muskets one at a time in quick succession up and down the line. It is a running fire that proceeds from right to left in the front rank and from left to right in the rear rank.

Field: In the army, that place where a battle takes place. Also used to describe an army on campaign. It is said to be in the field or it has taken the field.

Field day: In the military, a day set aside for military exercise.

Field officers: In the army, those officers who properly command the regiment, such as the colonel, lieutenant colonel, and major.

Fife major: In the military, a man who performs the same duties as the drum major. He is the lead fifer and serves to instruct the other fifers in their calls.

Fighting instructions: In the navy, these are the orders of a flag officer to each ship's captain in the squadron or fleet, providing each with guidance and direction in engaging the enemy in an upcoming sea battle.

File: In the army, any number of men drawn up in a direct line behind each other. A rank is the term for when the men stand beside each other. Rank and file covers all the private soldiers in the unit.

File leader: In the army, the first soldier in the front of any file.

File off: In the army, to wheel off from marching in a wide column presenting a wide front to marching in length by files, usually two abreast.

Fire: In the military, the discharge of all sorts of weaponry against the enemy.

Firearms: In the military, all kinds of weapons that are charged or loaded with gunpowder and ball and that are discharged by the explosion of the powder in the charge.

Fire cake: In the American army, a mixture of flour and water baked into thin cakes on hot stones in the cooking fires. Often the only rations available to American troops, particularly early in the war.

Firelocks: In the military, these shoulder weapons used flint and steel to ignite the priming that in turn exploded off the charge of gunpowder in the bore. These weapons, such as the muskets used in all forces of the time, replaced the earlier matchlock weapons.

Fire ship: In the navy, usually an older, worthless vessel set afire and sent toward the ships of the enemy in hope of burning them to their keels. Also a slang term for a woman with venereal disease.

Fireworker: In the artillery, until 1777, the junior lieutenant in an artillery company, responsible for supervising the preparation of ammunition.

Five Nations: The five Indian nations—the Mohawk, the Seneca, the Onondaga, the Oneida, and the Cayuga tribes—that formed the Iroquois league in what is today New York State. The Tuscarora, a tribe displaced from the South, joined the league in 1722, which then became known as the Six Nations.

Flag officer: In the navy, an officer with the rank of commodore or above (admiral) who commands a squadron or fleet and is permitted the honor aboard his flagship of flying his own flag, the color and shape of which designates his rank.

Flank: In the military, the side of a unit, or either end of its line. To turn an enemy's flank means to get in around and behind the enemy so as to be able to fire down his entire line and cause him to retreat.

Flank companies: In the military, the elite companies of light infantry that formed in each British battalion and took their place on either flank of the unit.

Flash in the pan: In the military, when the priming charge ignites but the flame does not penetrate the vent to ignite the main charge in the bore. The phrase is now used idiomatically for a sudden, brilliant effort that fails.

Fleam: In medicine, a device used to slice open a blood vessel in order to let excess blood leave the body. Some fleams were multibladed for differing depths of penetration, depending on the amount of blood to be drawn.

Fleche: In fortifications, a field fort of two faces, usually raised in the earth to cover the redoubts of advanced posts of a camp.

Flint: In the military, the special napped stone carried in the cock of the firearm that causes the spark when struck against the steel frizzen to ignite priming gunpowder.

Flip: A drink of beer and brandy with sugar added.

Flummery: In society, oatmeal and water boiled to a jelly. Also a term for meaningless flattery.

Flux: In medicine, almost any discharge of blood, fluids, or purged matter, especially from the bowels, a condition that constantly plagued all armies of the time.

Flying army: In the army, a strong, mobile force of horse and foot troops, commanded by a general officer, and in constant motion to cover its numerous bases and keep the enemy in a constant state of alarm. The flying camp is the ground on which such a body of men encamps.

Fogey: In the military, a slang term for an invalid soldier who is unable through an injury or sickness to serve in the line.

Fomentation: In medicine, the treatment of bodily distress or discomfort with the external application of warm fluidic solutions, baths, or compresses often containing medicinal herbs.

Foot: In the army, all bodies of men that serve in the infantry and move by foot to accomplish their duties.

Forage: In the military, all hay, straw, oats, and other victuals used to feed the horses and other livestock of the army. Also, a term meaning to search for food or provisions.

Forecastle: In the navy, the forward main deck of a ship where the sailors' quarters were located.

Forlorn hope: In the army, the men detached from several regiments to make the first attack in the battle. In a siege, these men make the initial approach to breach the fort's walls. If successful, they receive an ample reward for their efforts, providing they survive. The term is now used idiomatically for an undertaking with little chance of success.

Fort: In fortifications, a small fortified place, covered on all sides with a ditch, rampart, and parapet. Also called a station.

Fosse: In fortifications, a ditch in front of the main works of the fort.

Fraise: In fortifications, a line of sharpened stakes driven into the face of a rampart to break up a charge over the wall of the fort.

Friction: In medicine, the act of stimulating the skin by rubbing. Oftentimes a medicinal compound is used in the process. Extremely effective on the wrists and as a counteractive to the vapors.

Frigate: In the navy, a fast, three-masted vessel of more than twenty guns used by the admiral of the fleet for scouting and communications missions.

Frock: In the military, a loose hunting shirt, usually made of linen, worn over one's other clothes to provide them with protection while performing difficult tasks such as hunting. This garment was a readily available substitute for the uniform coat in the American army. Its appearance on the field put fear into the hearts of the British who thought everyone who wore such a shirt was an expert marksman.

Frog: In the military, an attachment to the waist belt to support a sword, bayonet, or some other weapon.

Front: In the military, the advanced, or front, line of a battalion. Also, the direction in which the men are facing.

Furlough: In the military, to place a unit on leave, subject to recall, but off government pay and supply.

Furniture: In the military, the metal mounts on a firearm.

Fusee (fugee): In the military, another name for a fusil. This is a lightweight musket carried by officers and light troops.

Gabion: In fortifications, a woven basket filled with dirt and/or stones and placed in position to offer protection in the midst of a siege to artillery or other troops.

Gaiter: In the military, cloth or canvas coverings that protect the lower portion of the leg and stocking from the rigors of the campaign. The gaiters come in long or short styles.

Gallery: In fortifications, an underground passage connecting the inner and outer works of a fort for the protection of the defenders.

Galley: In the navy, a small ship with two triangular sails and oars rigged for war. In the war, they were used in a number of places, such as on Lake Champlain and in the Delaware River campaign of 1777.

Gambling: In the military, a popular diversion, especially for the officers, in which their attention was given to various games of chance and over which large sums of money were often wagered. These games included faro, casino, cribbage, whist, and others.

Gantlope (gauntlet): In the military, a punishment in which the criminal runs between two ranks of men, receiving lashes from each man. The men normally used their ramrods in this.

Glacis: In fortifications, the anterior slope of a fort.

Goloshes (galoshes): In the military, large leather clogs worn by invalids over their regular shoes to protect their already delicate health.

Gorget: In the military, a small, crescent-shaped piece of metal, usually brass, worn by officers around their necks as a sign of their rank. Historically, it is a portion of armor that a knight wore to protect his neck and throat in battle.

Grapeshot: In the artillery, a cluster of small iron balls tied to a spindle and platform, designed to produce a scatter effect farther from the muzzle of the tube than canister. The wooden platform forms the base of this load. A wooden spindle rises up from the platform and the balls are tied to the spindle to keep them in place during loading.

Grasshopper: In the artillery, a British fieldpiece mounted on a special light carriage. Very mobile, it could be broken down and carried by pack animals over difficult terrain. "Grasshopper" was the nickname of the piece, since it tended to hop across fields as it was pulled on its carriage. The term was forbidden for use in official correspondence.

Grenadier: In the military, an elite company of tall, powerful men, originally designated to hurl grenades into enemy works, but in the Revolution, they were chosen to perform the most dangerous missions, requiring bravery, courage, and experience. Each British regiment had one company of grenadiers. The Americans normally did not form such troops. The grenadiers wore wings on the shoulders of their uniforms and high furry caps with brass front plates on their heads.

Grog: In the navy, a mixture of rum and water first introduced into the British navy by Admiral Edward Vernon (of Mount Vernon fame) in the 1740s to cut down on drunken behavior caused by a full issue of rum. So called because Vernon was nicknamed "Old Grog" for the grogram cloak he wore.

Guard: In the military, that portion of one's force regularly detailed to protect the outer limits of one's camp from enemy surprise. The main guard was the group from which all other guard details were drawn. In addition, on the march or going into battle, the army would make use of the van, or advanced guard, in the front and the rear guard in the rear to prevent an ambush.

Guards: In the European armies, specially designated units responsible for protecting the King's or ruler's person. Usually elite battalions with high esprit.

Guides: In the military, country people familiar with the surrounding territory who were questioned by the army for intelligence and direction.

Guidon: In the military, a standard used to maintain order and to rally the soldiers during battle.

Gun: In the artillery, a long cannon, usually firing a nonexploding projectile at a high velocity and flat trajectory. Also, a generic term for any piece of artillery.

Gundalow: In the navy, a flat-bottomed boat pointed at both ends. Usually rigged with two square sails on a single mast. Used in the Battle of Valcour Island in 1776.

Gunner: In the artillery, a specialist title given to the artilleryman with the responsibility for loading and aiming the piece. A gunner was awarded higher pay than a matross.

Gun salutes: In the military, a gun discharge honoring a soldier or sailor for meritorious service. Gun salutes are always an odd number for luck and are discharged at five-second intervals. The number of guns discharged indicates the rank or position of the person being saluted.

Hackle: In the military, a small feather or plume worn in the hat for decoration, which provided uniformity for identification within the unit.

Halberd: In the military, a combination of spear and ax on a long pole. Carried by sergeants as a sign of their rank. The halberd provided some protection in battle and assisted them while drilling the troops. The weapon fell out of use during the war and was sometimes replaced with a fusil.

Halliards (halyard): In the navy, lines used to hoist sails and flags. Comes from the order "haul yards."

Handspike: In the artillery, a short pole inserted into the end of a cannon's trail to give the gun crews leverage in turning and aiming the piece.

Hanger: In the military, a short, heavy cutting sword with a slightly curved blade. An infantry weapon, it is usually carried by noncommissioned officers.

Hard money: Coin or specie rather than any paper currency or notes.

Hartshorn: In medicine, a product produced by boiling a stag's (hart) horn. It can bring relief to any number of physical ailments through internal consumption or external application as an ingredient of a friction.

Hasty pudding: Oatmeal and milk or water boiled to a moderate thickness and eaten if possible with sugar and butter.

Hatchet: In the military, a weapon in the form of a small, light ax used to make fascines or gabions or carried by the soldiers into battle as their third weapon in addition to the bayonet and musket.

Hatman: In the army, a soldier of one of the battalion companies of a regiment, so called because they wore some sort of hat (bicorn, tricorn, etc.). The flank companies wore either helmets or caps in the light infantry or miters or bearskins in the grenadiers.

Haversack: In the military, a bag of grey, coarse linen used to carry provisions and personal items on the march by the soldiers. It took its name from the bag that oats were once carried in to feed horses.

Hawser: In the navy, any heavy line, five inches or more in circumference, used to tow or moor a ship.

Hessians: In the war, mercenary troops from the principality of Hesse in the Germanies that served with the British army in the War of Revolution from 1776 until 1783. Americans generally referred to all German troops as Hessians, although troops from other German states such as Brunswick, Waldeck, Ansbach-Bayreuth, and Anhalt-Zerbst also took part.

Highlanders: In the British army, those battalions raised primarily with recruits from the highlands of Scotland, such as the three battalions of Simon Fraser's 71st Highlanders.

Hominy: A type of grain meal made from coarsely ground parched corn, which is then boiled for food.

Hornpipe: In the navy, a dance and music made to the accompaniment of a hornpipe, a wind instrument.

Hornwork: In fortifications, an outwork that consists of a pair of demi-bastions joined by a curtain or a wall. Often a hornwork is created as an advanced strongpoint to fortify rising ground situated along a main line of fortification.

Hot shot: In the artillery, solid shot heated in ovens to a red-hot state before firing to produce an incendiary effect. As with the carcass, this load was used against wooden ships and besieged garrisons to set off fires.

Howitzer: In the artillery, a short cannon capable of firing any type of ammunition at varying angles of trajectory.

Humor: In medicine, there are four identified cardinal humors (fluids) of the body—blood, phlegm, choler (yellow bile), and melancholy (black bile)—which must be in balance to maintain health. When one fluid predominates in the body, then it determines one's health and mood. When one abounds at the expense of others, then the excess must be removed to restore health.

Hussy: A woman, particularly one of low morals and given too freely to frolicking.

Huzza: In the military, the national cheer of the British, and later the Americans, when general approval from the soldiers was to be voiced. Three huzzas signaled the troops to cheer thrice.

Illumination: In society, a celebratory custom of lighting candles in all windows and illuminating a town, village, or city at night to allow the people to parade about in light.

Independent company: In the army, a company-sized unit not incorporated into a regular line regiment.

Interior lines: In the military, one side has the advantage of having their troops centered so that the troops can shift to cover threatened points along the entire line without being exposed to enemy attack while moving. This is the tactical aspect of this concept. Strategically, an army has interior lines if it can move as a unit laterally from one position to another faster than the enemy.

Invalids: In the military, those individuals whose wounds or sickness excuse them from active duty. They generally served in the safer forts on garrison duty or in the hospitals.

Investing: In the military, sending detachments of infantry and horse to block all avenues of approach to an enemy position or fort, preventing relief from arriving.

Irish Establishment: In the British army, those troops stationed in Ireland and paid for by the Irish Parliament. These troops were not ethnically Irish, since the Test Act of 1673 officially barred Catholics and Presbyterians from army service. These troops were used as a strategic reserve. Most of the British troops that went to fight the War of Revolution shipped out from Ireland.

Irregulars: In the military, troops not counted as a part of the regular order of battle for a particular army. Irregular troops were not a part of the regular establishment or regular line units. Mainly recruited in the loosely controlled partisan units from the militia or available civilian manpower, these men usually harassed the enemy, raided settlements, and created terror among their enemies. Irregular units were used by both sides during the war and were particularly evident in the southern campaigns and in the "no-man's war" outside New York City after 1776.

Jacket: In the military, a short waistcoat or vest with sleeves. Often worn by light infantry, cavalry, or dragoons.

Jack nastyface: In the navy, a slang term for the common sailor. Also called a "Jack-tar."

Jade: In society, a mean or poor quality horse.

Jakes: In society, the privy or "john."

Jalap: In medicine, the powdered root of a plant of the morning-glory family that is commonly found in the vicinity of Jalapa, Mexico. This medicinal is an excellent purgative.

Jeans: A twilled cotton cloth of durable fabric useful for fatigue duties and the rigors of campaigning.

Jersies: New Jersey was at the time of the Revolution only recently considered a unified colony (state). It had been divided into West and East Jersey, hence the name Jersies often seen in colonial print.

Jesuit: In the war, a term applied to Loyalists as being cunning, deceitful, and designing.

Jesuit's bark: In medicine, another name for quinine, extracted cinchona or Peruvian bark, a drug which was particularly effective against the bad air disease or swamp fever (malaria).

Keel haul: In the navy, a punishment in which the victim was tied to a line and dragged under the water on the right side of a ship, hauled along the barnacle-encrusted bottom, and hoisted on deck on the port side. The victim was either drowned or cut to pieces since this was virtually a death sentence. Mutiny or other serious crimes were answered by this drawing of the prisoner under the ship's keel.

Kennel: In society, another name for the sewer or canal that ran down the center of a street to carry off waste. The word comes from Middle English "canel" with the same meaning.

Kid: In the navy, a shallow wooden vessel used to carry food from the galley (kitchen) to the mess table. Took its name from the young boys whose duties were to assist the ship's cook and to serve the food in these containers.

Kill Devil: In society, West Indian rum that was particularly potent in its effect on the sensibilities of any normal man.

Kit: In the military, the whole of a soldier's necessaries contained in his knapsack.

Kleiner krieg: In the military, the German phrase for *la petite guerre* (the little war).

Knapsack: In the military, a rough leather pouch, square in form and worn on the backs of the infantry, within which they carried their necessaries.

Knot: In the navy, one nautical mile, or 6,076.10 feet. It also denotes speed as 30 knots, which means a ship covers that distance in an hour's time. Comes from the number of knots counted on a knotted rope let out from the stern of a ship to determine a ship's speed in a certain time period.

Laboratory: In the military, a place for the manufacture of weapons and ammunition.

Lace: In the military, a flat braid used to trim the lapels, cuffs, button holes, and other parts of the military uniform.

Lapels: In the military, the turned-back upper part of a coat or waistcoat that is worn buttoned back in the summer and buttoned over in the winter.

La petite guerre: In the military, small-scale partisan warfare of outposts, convoys, and ambushes, performed outside the operations of the main army. From the French for "little war."

Larboard: In the navy, the left side of the ship. It derives from "loading side" or port side of the ship so that the starboard or steering oar was protected from the dock.

League: In the navy, generally a sea measurement roughly equal to three English land miles.

Legion: In the military, a unit composed of both infantry and cavalry in battalion size generally used for partisan warfare and ranging on the flanks of the army to protect against surprise.

Letters of marque: In the navy, papers from one's government permitting a ship to capture enemy vessels in the time of war.

Levy: In the military, a new recruit conscripted into the army as part of a requirement that districts and counties send a specified number of men to serve on active duty for a stated period of time.

Lieutenant: In the military, a company grade officer who assists the captain in command of the company, troop, or battery. In the navy, these are assistant officers to the captain of a ship.

Life Guard: In the American army, that detachment of specially selected infantry whose primary function was the protection of General George Washington's life.

Light-bob: In the military, a slang term for a light infantry soldier.

Light horse: In the military, lightly armed and equipped cavalry designed for active field service, fast movement, and scouting assignments.

Light infantry: In the army, an elite company of the best trained, quickest, most veteran men drawn from all the other companies in the regiment to perform the most dangerous duties. Usually all companies of light infantry from all the army's regiments are brigaded in the light corps. These troops were referred to as light infantry because they carried a lighter load than regular line infantry. One of the light infantry's strengths was its mobility, which was facilitated by carrying this lighter load.

Limber: In the artillery, a two-wheeled vehicle designed to fit under the trail of a field carriage, converting the gun or howitzer from a two-wheel to a four-wheel load for transportation.

Line: In the military, the infantry units went into battle formed into a line of battle. The units thus took their names as line units, e.g., the Continental Line or the Pennsylvania Line or the 3rd New York Line Regiment.

Line of communication: In the military, the vital supply route along which supplies, reinforcements, messages, and ammunition flow to the army campaigning in the field.

Linsey-woolsey: A coarse cloth made by mixing linen or cotton and wool. A homemade type of cloth used to fashion such articles as hunting shirts, shirts, stockings, etc.

Linstock: In the artillery, the device for holding the slow match to fire off the artillery pieces.

Lock: In the military, this is that part of the musket that holds the flint that strikes the frizzen (steel) to produce the spark that ignites the priming powder in the pan.

London trade: In the war, the trade that the British maintained with the countryside outside of New York City, mainly for foodstuffs and forage.

Long land service musket: In the British army, the standard infantry weapon of the French and Indian (Seven Years') War. It weighed 14 pounds, had a barrel of 46 inches, and was 0.75 caliber.

Loyalist: In the war, the term preferred by those American colonials who remained loyal to the King and Parliament.

Lunette: In fortifications, works made on both sides of the ravelin to afford it protection.

Lush: Strong beer. To lush meant to drink. Also known as "Sir John Barleycorn."

Macaroni: Taken from the Macaroni Club in London, itself named after the pasta from Italy, this term described an individual much given to the newest styles in dress and affectations. A fop.

Magazine: A storehouse. In the military, usually used to store weapons and gunpowder.

Major: In the military, the lowest grade field officer, who exercises the regiment in its drill and directs the regiment in battle from horseback, taking direct orders from the colonel.

Malaria: In medicine, also called intermitting fever, it was caused by the excessive inhalation of night air. This "bad air" disease caused chills and fever. It was treated with the Jesuit's bark. *See also* Swamp fever.

Malingerer: In the military, any individual who seeks to evade one's duty on the excuse of sickness.

Mantelet: In fortifications, a movable shelter to protect troops attacking a fortified position of the enemy's.

Manual exercise: In the British army, the term for the long, detailed sequence of actions by which a soldier loaded and fired his musket and performed ceremonial actions.

Marauder: In the military, soldiers who without orders go into local houses or villages to plunder and destroy private property.

March: In the army, the principal manner of moving troops from one position to another in an orderly and disciplined fashion.

Marine: In the navy, a soldier specially placed on ships of the line at the rate of one per gun to protect the officers from the crew, maintain order in the ship, and serve as sharpshooters in the rigging when battle is joined.

Marquee: In the military, a large officer's field tent. Washington used three of these whenever on campaign.

Martial law: In the military, this is the law of war that replaces civil authority when in effect. It is arbitrary in that it seeks to maintain order often in a situation where order is most difficult to ensure. In order to accomplish this, martial law encompasses unlimited powers.

Master at arms: In the navy, that officer appointed to teach the crew of ships of war the proper exercise of small arms.

Match: In the artillery, a rope tightly twisted and prepared to retain fire for the use of the artillery in the discharge of their guns.

Mate: In the navy, from the French "matelot" for sailor. Used to denote a friend and also an assistant to a specialist in a particular duty, such as a gunner's mate.

Matross: In the artillery, a private soldier responsible for the semiskilled tasks in firing a cannon.

Medicine chest: In the military, that chest in which the surgical instruments are kept along with those medicines thought appropriate to treat the afflictions of the men.

Meeting engagements: In the military, this type of action takes place when the two sides run into each other on the line of march and a battle begins with both sides throwing in more troops as they arrive on the field.

Merlon: In fortifications, the fort wall or battlement on the top of a wall located between two openings, or embrasures, in the wall.

Mess: In the military, a small group of men who band together to share and cook their rations.

Military chest: In the military, that container holding the money available to the army's commander for use in paying the troops, purchasing supplies, and so forth.

Militia: In the military, those individuals who are at heart civilians but who possess a basic understanding of the exercises of the military such that they may assemble when called up with short notice and for short terms to defend their districts from attack.

Mine: In fortifications, to dig under the works of the enemy besieged to disrupt the strength of their fortifications by the use of explosives within the mine. The enemy may reply to this tactic by the use of the countermine in which they attempt to locate the initial mine and close it off.

Mortars: In the artillery, short cannon of large bore, made of brass or iron, that usually fire hollow shells filled with powder at high arcs to fall into the works of the enemy and explode.

Muster: In the military, to review the troops under arms. At this time, uniforms and weapons are inspected, and the unit is exercised so as to perfect its military skills.

Muzzle: In the weaponry, the opening at the extreme end of the weapon out of which the projectile flies when discharged. This term applies to both artillery and other types of smaller firearms used by the infantry and cavalry.

Nankin: A cotton cloth, lightly colored and durable. Usually used for overalls.

Neutral ground: In the war, the territory surrounding the main British garrison in New York City including much of Westchester County. Neither army controlled this ground.

North River: This is another name for the Hudson River, which flows by New York City and forms a major waterway into the interior of New York State.

On command: In the military, so called when a unit of men is on detached duty.

On the lines: In the military, towns, posts, forts, and other outposts are referred to as "on the lines" when they form a line protecting the main army in winter cantonment.

Opening of the trenches: In fortifications, this is the first breaking of ground by the besiegers in their process of besieging a fort or position held by the enemy.

Order of Battle: In the army, the development of military units in preparation for a battle. In the navy, this term applies to the arrangement of ships of the line as a fleet prepares for battle.

Orderly book: In the military, the company book used by sergeants to write down both the general and regimental orders for the benefit of the officers who may then read them.

Ordnance: In the military, the term that applies to all forms of artillery.

Osnaburg: A German linen and also heavy canvas cloth used for fatigue clothing and the making of sacking of all varieties.

Outliers: In the South, Whigs in the Carolinas who left their homes to avoid taking an oath of loyalty to the King and began living beyond the limits of the law.

Outposts: In the military, a detachment posted beyond the grand guard and the limits of the campgrounds to provide early warning of an enemy approach or from which to conduct harassment attacks on an opponent.

Outworks: In fortifications, ravelins, demi-lunes, hornworks, lunettes, and other types of defense structures that cover the main works of a position.

Overalls: In the military, long-legged trousers meant to be worn over clothing to provide protection during fatigue or field duty.

Over the Mountain Men: In the South, men who lived beyond the Blue Ridge Mountains, generally Whigs, who earned their greatest glory in winning the Battle of King's Mountain in 1780. Also called backwater men.

Packet: In the military, the mail ship bringing orders and dispatches along with personal items to the army, usually designated by the month of its arrival in port.

Palaver: In the military, idle talk meant for flattery that has little value in itself but is geared to influence another's behavior.

Palisades: In fortifications, a kind of wall of stakes made from strong split wood about nine feet high and fixed three feet in the ground in rows about six inches apart. Used to guard a post against a surprise attack. When tied in with the defenses of a fort, it stands three feet from and parallel to the parapet of the glacis.

Parade: In the military, the place where troops assembled to mount guard, drill, or for any other purpose.

Parallels: In fortifications, during a siege, these are trenches dug parallel to those of the besieged. From the first parallel, the attackers dig additional parallels, each one closer to the enemy's works. From the final parallel, an attack may be mounted or an artillery bombardment made to breach the enemy's lines.

Parapet: In fortifications, this is part of the rampart of a work, 18 to 20 feet broad and raised 6 to 7 feet above the rest of the rampart to cover the defending troops.

Park: In the military, a designated place for the army's artillery and related stores.

Parley: In the military, signal given by either side with a drum or trumpet when some matter of mutual concern is to be discussed, such as a surrender or truce for the burial of the dead.

Parole: In the military, a promise given by prisoners of war not to fight until exchanged for an opponent of equal rank. This also means the word given out every day in the orders by the commanding general so that enemies can be distinguished from friends by their knowledge of the password.

Partisan: In the military, light troops or dragoons who serve beyond the normal control of the regular army to harass and harm the enemy whenever and wherever possible.

Party: In the military, a small number of men detached to accomplish a particular mission or perform any kind of duty.

Patch box: In the military, a small compartment made in the stock of a rifle in which the greased patches were contained. *See also* Patched ball.

Patched ball: In the military, a greased patch of cloth wrapped a rifled ball so that a tight fit was achieved in the bore with the rifling so that pressure would build to give the ball force upon discharge and the ball itself would spin to give it better accuracy.

Patrol: In the military, rounds made by the different camp guards in the night to observe the condition of the camp, outposts, sentries, and so forth. Six to twelve men under a sergeant perform this duty every hour from tattoo to reveille.

Pavilion: In the military, the name for a full tent, usually used by high-ranking officers.

Perch: A unit of measure equal to ten feet.

Petard: In fortifications, the engine used to burst open the gates of a small fortress.

Physic: In medicine, the art of healing disease by the beneficial use of medicines.

Picket: In the military, an out-guard posted before an army to give notice of the enemy's approach. The picket is the infantry out-guard. A cavalry picket is called a vidette.

Piecemeal: In the military, the tactic of committing one's forces in parts rather than massing them and placing them in battle as a whole. This tactic is common in meeting engagements.

Pieces: In the military, the name given to cannon of all denominations from fieldpieces to garrison and siege pieces.

Pilot: In the navy, a skilled navigator who was responsible for taking a ship in and out of port, or through a difficult passage.

Pioneers: In the military, specially selected troops detailed to clear obstructions placed in the line of march or before a fort, dig trenches, and construct bridges and roads. Usually considered the strongest and most durable men in the army.

Pistol: In the military, the smallest firearm, generally used by officers and cavalry and considered accurate only at short ranges.

Platoon: In the military, a small body of men formed as a unit within each infantry company, usually two per company.

Platoon exercise: In the British army, the term for their firing system. Volley fire was regulated by words of command.

Poltroon: A coward; a craven individual.

Pontoon: In the military, flat-bottomed boats of wood used to form a foundation for the platform of a quickly erected bridge across a waterway or river.

Poop deck: In the navy, the after deck of a ship. Romans used to carry their "pupi," or small images of their gods, in the stern of their ships for luck and this gave the after deck its name.

Post: In the military, any sort of position where a body of men is stationed to resist any enemy attack if so made.

Postern: In fortifications, the sally port or a small door in the flank of the bastion from which the defenders may quickly enter or exit unobserved in the performance of a mission.

Post of honor: In the military, this is considered the most advanced post toward the enemy, or on the right of the two lines of infantry going into battle. It is given to the eldest and best men in the unit. The center of the line is considered the place of least honor or danger and given to the youngest and most inexperienced men.

Pounder: In the artillery, an expression to specify a certain caliber of bore. The piece discharged a ball roughly the weight and size that the bore indicated (e.g., a 16-pounder discharged a 16-pound ball).

Powder magazine: In fortifications, an arched bomb-proof building expressly constructed to hold the garrison's gunpowder supply safe from enemy assaults.

Pretty: In the military, a term to describe a brave, gallant, stout-hearted soldier or officer in action.

Priming: In the military, that small amount of gunpowder ignited first whose explosion in turn traveled a vent to set off the main charge in the bore of the weapon.

Prison ships: In the war, the British used old hulks, especially in New York harbor, to keep captured Americans in confinement. Considered death traps because of their bad conditions.

Privateering: In the navy, the act of fitting out a private ship of war and taking it on a voyage to raid and capture enemy ports and shipping. Usually legally justified by possession of letters of marque.

Provincials: In the war, any troops raised by the British in the colonies to fight for the King were generally called this.

Provisional battalion: In the military, a temporary assembly of companies from different regiments formed into a battalion. Grenadiers and light infantry were formed into provisional battalions for the duration of a campaign.

Provisions: In the military, a term for all manner of food used in the army for the sustenance of both man and beast.

Provost: In the military, the men specially designated to enforce discipline, search out deserters and other criminals, halt pillaging, and execute sentences of the military courts.

Putrid fever: In the military, another name for the disease typhus.

Quarantine: In the military, a medical detention period due to serious illness. The period of detention lasted forty days after the first case was discovered. The word comes from the French word "quarante" for forty.

Quarter: In the military, a soldier is afforded life if he cries "quarter," and it is granted by a superior enemy. If not, then "no quarter" is ensued and the surrendering soldiers are killed by the enemy. To cry for quarter is to ask for mercy in battle. An old custom called so because officers in surrendering often had to pay a quarter of their annual salary to ransom themselves from captivity.

Quartermaster: In the military, the officer who cares for the quarters, clothing, ammunition, and other necessary supplies issued to the men to maintain an army in the field.

Quartermaster general: In the military, the officer who marks the line of march of an army, selects its encampments, and details its foraging parties. Also responsible for the supply and outfitting of the troops for a campaign.

Quoin: In the artillery, a wooden wedge placed between the breech of a cannon and its carriage to adjust its elevation.

Raid: In the military, any military operation or attack that does not intend to hold the enemy's position that is under siege.

Rake: In the navy, to send one's fire down the length of an opponent's ship, clearing the decks and causing great harm to the ship and personnel. This is called enfilade in the army.

Rally: In the military, to restore the spirit and élan of the troops through personal example and leadership so that they reform and once again are able to function as a military unit to hold off the advance of the enemy.

Rampart: In fortifications, an elevation of earth raised along the faces of any work, 10 to 15 feet high, to cover the inner part of the work against the fire of the enemy.

Ramrod (rammer): In the military, long poles, made of wood or metal, to ram the ball and wadding down the bore of an artillery piece or firearm so that the weapon is ready for discharge.

Range: In the military, the effective distance at which the projectile of a weapon can cause injury upon the troops of the enemy.

Rangers: In the military, a variety of light infantry who ranged out over an assigned territory to reconnoiter and distress the enemy whenever possible. Since rangers are a form of light infantry, they generally performed all of the regular duties assigned to the light troops. John Graves Simcoe's Queen's Rangers were probably the most effective and notorious of the ranger units of the war.

Ranks: In the military, men drawn up in a line, standing side by side.

Rations: In the military, the food issued to troops for their consumption, particularly during a campaign and often of dubious quality.

Rattle: In medicine, that disease caused by an excessive congestion of phlegm that settles in the throat. A throat distemper also called the croup.

Ravelin: In fortifications, a work placed before the curtain to cover it and prevent the flank from being discovered sideways. It consists of two faces meeting in an outward angle. Also called a half-moon or demi-lune.

Recoil: In the artillery, the counterforce of the discharge that forces the artillery piece to fly backward as it is dis-

charged. The piece then has to be repositioned to regain its effectiveness of fire.

Reconnoiter: In the military, the detaching of a body of men, rangers, or scouts to discover the actual position, strength, and intentions of the enemy.

Redan: In fortifications, a two-sided field work pointed toward the enemy and open to the rear. Similar to the ravelin or fleche. Usually stands as a part of the field works rather than part of a fort.

Redcoat: In the war, the term was applied to British troops since their regular soldiers generally wore coats in the King's color red with varying colored facings. Other terms related to redcoat but more negative in connotation were lobsterback and bloodyback.

Redoubt: In fortifications, a kind of work placed beyond the glacis, sometimes in front of a bastion or a ravelin. In the field, it is often a strong point in the earthen lines with raised walls, a ditch, and fraise work to protect it. A redoubt was manned by infantry, usually abut 250 or so in number. Artillery was placed on both flanks to protect the redoubt from being turned.

Reduce a place: In fortifications, to oblige an enemy post or fort to surrender to the besiegers by capitulation.

Refuse a flank: In the military, a maneuver by which a unit turns one end of its line or another at right angles to the rest of the line to counter an enemy attempt to flank or get behind one's line.

Regimentals: In the military, that coat of specified design and particular colors that distinguishes one regiment from any other.

Regulations of 1764: In the British army, the standard procedures for drill and movement that governed the actions of the troops on parade, in the field, and in battle.

Relieve guard: In the military, to place fresh men at every guard post every 24 hours.

Relieve sentries: In the military, the relief of each guard in the series of outposts every two hours.

Rendezvous: In the military, a commonly known place appointed by the commander of a unit at which to rally in the event of a retreat or rout in action against the enemy. Also a place to form in the event of an alarm.

Reserve: In the military, those troops a commander holds out of battle to be used when and if the need arises to save a situation or take advantage of an enemy lapse.

Retrenchment: In fortifications, any work raised to cover a post and provide further protection for it against the enemy. Usually a ditch with a parapet.

Revetment: In fortifications, masonry covering the earthen embankments usually of outworks or field fortifications to provide extra strength and protection.

Review: In the military, the drawing out of all or any part of the army paraded in the line of battle to be viewed (inspected) by the King or commanding general.

Ricochet: In the artillery, mortars and howitzers loaded small charges to fire over the parapet so that the shot would roll along the opposite rampart and thus distress the enemy.

Rifle: In the military, a firearm with spiraling lines and grooves, or rifling, inside the barrel, or bore, so that the ball, when discharged, would spin in the air, giving it better accuracy. This weapon was excellent for hunting but took much longer to load than the musket and did not take the bayonet.

Road: In the navy, a place of anchorage for ships.

Rounds: In the military, to check the sentinels and state of the garrison at periodic times during the night by a detachment of the main guard consisting of an officer, sergeant, and six men. Also used as a term for the ammunition fired off at the enemy by the army. Comes from the round shape of the cartridge.

Rout: In the military, a full, uncontrolled retreat of one's forces off the field of battle, precipitated by the actions and courage of the enemy.

Rover: In the navy, a name for buccaneers' dogs, a term that originally gained its name from riggers who roved from shipyard to shipyard plying their trade.

Royal regiments: In the British army, select units with blue facings chosen for their outstanding service, such as the Guards and the Corps of Invalids.

Running fight: In the army, the type of battle or engagement in which one side is pursued by another while the action of the fight is continued.

Ruse: In the military, a cunning strategy or maneuver to deceive the enemy and place him offbalance so that the main effort has more chance of catching the enemy at a disadvantage.

Saber: In the military, a short, broad, heavy-bladed sword, thick at the rear and curved toward the point. Used by the cavalry, since the saber sliced the enemy and was useful from an elevated position.

St. Anthony's fire: In medicine, one of several skin conditions, such as erysipelas or ergotism.

Salient angle: In fortifications, an angle projecting from a fort into the field.

Sally: In fortifications, a sudden, surprise attack by a small group of defenders against their besiegers during a siege.

Sap: In fortifications, this is an underground gallery dug to get under an enemy position or an approach trench to near the enemy under cover.

Sapper: In fortifications, a military engineer trained in the arts of fortification and siege warfare.

Sap roller: In fortifications, a gabion rolled forward in a trench to protect the digging troops in a siege from enemy fire.

Sarsaparilla: In medicine, a brew or ointment of the root of a common tropical American vine in the lily family that was used as a sudorific to sweat out the impurities of syphilis or other nefarious ailments that plagued mankind.

Sash: In the military, badges of distinction with different colors worn by officers to signify various ranks. Worn over the shoulder or around the waist, some were highly decorative and made of expensive silk, while others were of plainer cloth without design.

Saucissons: In fortifications, long, cloth sacks filled with earth to provide protection to either attacking or defending troops in position. Today known as sandbags. Also considered a large fascine.

Schooner: In the navy, a vessel of fore and aft rig with a shallow draft so that it "schoonered," or skipped, across the waters.

Sea chanties: In the navy, songs sung by the sailors as they performed their duties on board ship.

Secondary attack: In the military, a feint to deceive the enemy and force him to commit his men and attention to a place away from the intended main attack. With the reserves, however, a feint can become the main attack if it succeeds beyond what was expected.

Seniority: In the military, the date of one's commission at each rank determined one's ranking within that particular grade. Seniority was taken very seriously by every officer in the eighteenth century and marked the pecking order in any of the armies of the time.

Sentinel: In the military, a private soldier from the guard, posted to stand watch. Such an individual is instructed not to sleep, smoke, or make noise of any kind on duty but watch intently for the approach of any danger to his unit.

Sentry box: In the military, a small shelter, made of wood, in the form of a hut or upright coffin, to house the sentinel in time of cold or harsh weather.

Shell: In the artillery, an exploding projectile, or bomb, usually a hollow iron ball filled with gunpowder and exploded by a fuse. The fuse is lit by the flash of the explosion in the tube during the discharge of the piece.

Ship of the line: In the navy, any warship with 74 guns or more that was expected to fight the main naval actions of the period.

Shirtmen: In the military, the name given by the British to the American riflemen and later the regular line who wore hunting shirts and were feared for their accuracy in shooting.

Short land, new pattern musket: In the British army, the standard infantry weapon of the War of Revolution. It was lighter than the long land musket, had a 42-inch barrel, and was 0.75 caliber.

Shot: Same as round shot, solid shot, and ball shot. In the artillery, a spherical nonexploding iron or stone projectile.

Side boxes: In the artillery, boxes attached to either side of a gun carriage for carrying a small amount of ready ammunition.

Siege: In the military, the act of surrounding and investing a position, developing approaches toward its walls and forcing its capitulation through bombardment, assault, starvation, or trickery.

Skinners: In the war, the opposing party to the cowboys in the neutral ground marauding around New York City between 1778 and 1783. These men were generally of Whig persuasion.

Skirmish: In the military, a disorganized kind of combat or encounter in the presence of two armies between two smaller parties advanced from the whole in order to probe the enemy's lines and determine his strength and weaknesses.

Skull and crossbones: In the navy, an image on a flag flown by pirate ships indicating that their intent was to capture only the cargo of a ship, allowing its crew to go free. If the pirate ship displayed a red flag, then death and destruction was planned.

Sloop of war: In the navy, a single-decked ship with one mast of various riggings and armed with less than 24 guns.

Slouch: A hat with brims that are not cocked but are allowed to fall down, thus keeping the sun and rain from the wearer's face. Also called a slouched hat.

Slow match: In the artillery, a heavy, loosely spun cord, specially treated to burn slowly so that artillery pieces could be fired off time after time without having to relight a match. Also called the match.

Smallclothing: In the military, those parts of the uniform other than the coat, such as waistcoats, vests, breeches, overalls, and trousers.

Smallpox: In medicine, the principal disease of the period. Could be avoided by inoculations, which thus caused a mild case of the pox. This disease is characterized by fever, vomiting, and pustulant eruptions that leave scars or pits if the patient recovers.

Snare: In the military, catgut or rawhide twisted and strung across the bottom of a snare drum to provide added vibrations to the calls.

Snuff: A preparation of powdered tobacco, usually taken by inhaling it up the nose or placing it against the inside of the cheek and gum. Snuff was commonly used by many of the better sort instead of smoking tobacco.

Sorties: In fortifications, parties that sally out to annoy the enemy in a siege.

Spatterdashes: In the military, of varying sizes, these are cloth or canvas coverings that protect the stockings of the men from being ripped and torn in the performance of their duty in the field. Worn over the stockings, they either go to mid-calf or over the knee. They are usually painted black or white.

Specie: Hard money or coin as opposed to any type of paper currency.

Spider: In the military, a long-legged iron frying pan.

Spiking: In the artillery, the act of disabling a cannon by jamming some metal object into the vent.

Spoiling attack: In the military, a raid with the purpose of disrupting an enemy who is clearly massing for an attack.

Sponge: In the artillery, a wooden pole with a cloth or natural sponge on its end that was dipped into a bucket of water and used to cool down the bore of an artillery piece after firing so that the next round would not explode prematurely.

Spontoon: In the military, a half-pike carried by officers that was gradually replaced by fusils. The spontoon was used to parry bayonet thrusts, signal commands, and encourage the men in line. By 1783, it had mostly been abandoned.

Spruce beer: In the military, a standard drink issued to the American soldiers made of fermented spruce needles and yeast, sweetened with added sugar or molasses.

Squadron: In the cavalry, a body of men composed of 3 troops, between approximately 80 and 120 riders.

Squads: In the infantry, the platoon was often divided into squads (groups), two to the platoon and commanded by the corporal.

Squib: In the military, a blank cartridge of gunpowder that produces only a flash. Generally used for practice during military exercises.

Staff officer: In the military, those officers who did not exercise line command but served to expedite the administration of the unit or army for a general officer. The adjutant, quartermaster general, commissary, paymaster, surgeon, chaplain, and inspector general are examples.

Standard: In the military, the banner or flag of a unit.

Starboard: In the navy, the right side of a ship. The Vikings placed their star, or steering oar, on the right side of their ships.

Station: *See* Fort.

Sterling silver: From "easterling silver," referring to the Baltic Sea region, where all trade had to be carried out with silver. No bartering was permitted in that area, only hard currency.

Stock: In the military, the wooden part of the musket or pistol. Also the black silk, velvet, or leather piece worn about the neck in place of a neckcloth.

Stone: In medicine, an affliction that could affect the bladder, kidney, or gall bladder. Hardened matter that forms within those organs to cause great pain. Also refers to the testicles.

Subaltern: In the military, any officer who holds a rank below that of captain, including ensigns, lieutenants, or cornets.

Sutler: In the military, a private businessman who follows the army and provides the soldiers with many of the items they are otherwise unable to obtain on their own.

Swamp fever: In medicine, a fever caused by exposure to the miasmic swamp vapors, usually deadly. Today referred to as malaria.

Swanskin: A thick, twilled flannel cloth with a soft, downy surface, used for fatigue duty clothing.

Sword: In the military, a weapon with a long sharpened blade used by an officer, worn on the left side, and used both in battle to defend himself and to direct troops under fire when commands cannot be heard above the noise of battle.

Tack: In the navy, the process of coming about by shifting from one tack to another by putting down the helm and swinging the ship's head through the wind. When a ship tacks, she spins on her own axis, receiving the wind from one quarter at one moment and then from the opposite quarter the next. This maneuver changes a ship's direction. When ships of a fleet tack in succession, each ship tacks at the point where the ship ahead tacked so that the battle line doubles back on itself; when a fleet tacks together, the entire line of ships tacks simultaneously.

Tactics: In the military, the high art of command by which the troops are maneuvered to one's advantage to defeat the enemy's force on a particular battlefield. Strategy is the art of winning campaigns and sustained military operations through effective maneuver and surprise.

Taffrail: In the navy, the railing at the stern of a vessel.

Tail: In fortifications, the point of a trench where the besiegers first break ground.

Taken aback: In the navy, when a sailing ship momentarily loses headway due to the sails being blown back on the masts by a shift in the wind. For a sailing ship, if this happens, the ship could be dismasted in the force of the shift of wind.

Tampions: In the artillery, lids of wood used to plug up the muzzle in order to keep the inside of the bore dry from rain.

Tartar emetic: In medicine, a substance of antimony potassium tartrate, a white salt used in a potion to cause expectoration, vomiting, and sweating in a patient.

Terreplain: In fortifications, the flat, top part of the rampart in a fort where cannon and troops are placed.

The Thief's Cat: In the military, a cat-o'-nine tails with more than the usual number of knots placed on the tails. Punishment inflicted with this instrument was a bloody burden on any sailor or soldier.

Toast: A small piece of toast that floated on top of hot toddy and mulled wine in a tankard or mug. To drink a toast meant to drink the beverage and toast in honor of some person or cause.

Toddy: A drink of rum, sugar, and nutmeg, often served hot.

Tory: An Anglicized spelling of an Irish word meaning "pursuer" and applied to Irish attacking English settlers in Ireland. It became associated with the supporters of the King and was used in the war to brand enemies of the United States.

Transpire: In the military, when information or vital intelligence leaks out or becomes common knowledge. It does not regularly mean "to come to pass" or "happen."

Trepanning: In medicine, the drilling of a hole in the skull of a patient with a boring instrument to relieve internal pressure and drain the opened cavity of excessive fluids and matter.

Tricorn: A felt hat with its brim tacked or cocked three times to the crown so that the brim folds in a manner to produce three corners.

Troop: In the military, the cavalry equivalent of the infantry company.

Truce: In the military, the suspension of arms to settle articles of peace, bury the dead, or for other mutual concerns.

Trunion: In the artillery, two short cylindrical lugs cast directly onto the cannon tube that permit the tube to be mounted on a carriage.

Unit of command: In the military, having one direct line of command throughout an organization such as an army. When combined forces, such as naval, artillery, cavalry, and artillery, function as a unit, unity of command means that all cooperate as one under one overall leader.

Untoward: Improper, inappropriate speech or actions.

Vacant regiment: In the German army, a regiment in which the colonel after whom the regiment was named no longer commanded the regiment.

Van: In the military, the shortened term for the advanced guard (vanguard) or the front of an army.

Vault: In society and the military, the privy.

Vedette: In the cavalry, a sentry or outpicket posted on horseback rather than on foot.

Vent: In the artillery or army, a narrow passageway into the breech end of a cannon, rifle, or musket through which the main charge is discharged by means of igniting the priming charge.

Ventpick: In the military, the pick clears the vent of the musket or cannon of powder residue so that a clear passage is made for the explosion of the primer.

Victuals: In the military, rations or food issued to the men to sustain their health and well-being.

Vinegar: In medicine, a sour liquid used as an addition to water to help purify it and prevent the scurvy. Also used as a counterirritant.

Volley: The discharge of a number or group of weapons together at the same time, mainly for its effectiveness in battle or in salute of a high officer officially visiting a camp or fort.

Waistcoat: In the military, a garment worn under the coat like a vest and usually without sleeves.

Waldecker: In the war, a soldier from the German principality of Waldeck hired by Great Britain to fight against the rebels in America.

Warrant men: In the army, particularly the British army, these were six fictitious men kept on the regimental rolls so that "their" pay could be used for the benefit of the colonel, his agent, or any widows of deceased men in the unit. One use was to replace the cost of the weapons and uniforms of deserters.

Watch coat: In the military, a great coat given to every fourth man to be worn during the winter months by the individual of the group on guard duty.

Weather gauge: In the navy, sailing ships having the advantage of the wind so that the ships could steer directly for an opponent while the latter would have to tack against the wind.

Whigs: This term came from one of a number of Scottish insurgent groups who fought against the King in the Scottish rebellion. The term applied to the loyal opposition in Parliament and later was applied to those who supported the cause of the United States.

Whist: A popular card game played by both nobility and commoners that is a forerunner of the modern game of bridge.

Wings: In the military, crescent-shaped pieces of cloth worn on the shoulders of the elite companies or select troops such as the grenadiers, light infantry, or musicians.

Wolf holes: A common way of trapping wolves by digging round holes, two to three feet in diameter and deep enough to keep the wolf from jumping out until someone could kill the animal. In the military, this idea was taken and used in fortifications. Similar holes were dug in front of forts and sharpened stakes placed in the bottom so that careless soldiers would fall into these traps and be injured. In both cases, the openings of these holes were often disguised.

Yankees: A term of uncertain origin, perhaps developed by the Dutch to describe the English (John Bull-Jon) who lived in the Connecticut River valley, who were moving in on the Dutch in New Amsterdam and were fond of cheese (kase). "John Cheese," or "Yankees," properly include only those inhabitants of Massachusetts, Connecticut, Rhode Island, and New Hampshire.

Year of the Hangman: In the military, this was the year 1777. The three sevens reminded people of three gallows. Those who dared participate in a rebellion such as the one the United States was waging against England and who were caught and tried were hanged. Some predicted this year (1777) would be a bad omen for the American cause.

Zig zag: In fortifications, trenches were dug in angled lines resembling connected "V/S" so that no enemy force could fire down the length of a trench and disable the occupying troops.

Paul J. Sanborn

Index

This index includes major listings only.